DATE DUE

| | |
|---|---|
| 5/12/12 ILL | |
| | |
| | |
| | |
| | |
| | |
| | |
| | |
| | |
| | |
| | |
| | |
| | |
| | |
| | |
| | |
| | |

DEMCO, INC. 38-2931

# KANDINSKY
# DRAWINGS

Catalogue Raisonné | Volume Two | Sketchbooks

# KANDINSKY DRAWINGS

Catalogue Raisonné | Volume Two | Sketchbooks

Vivian Endicott Barnett

Städtische Galerie im Lenbachhaus Munich
with the support of the Société Kandinsky Paris

Philip Wilson Publishers
Verlag C.H. Beck

First published in 2007 by
Philip Wilson Publishers
109 Drysdale Street
The Timber Yard
London N1 6ND

Distributed by I. B. Tauris & Co. Ltd, 6 Salem Road, London W2 4BU

Distributed in the USA and Canada by Palgrave Macmillan, a division of
St. Martin's Press, New York, NY 10010



Layout by Norman Turpin

Color origination by Articolor, Verona, Italy

Printed and bound in

ISBN 0 85667 636 5
EAN 9780856676369

*For Claude Pompidou*

# *Contents*

*Kandinsky in his Munich apartment, 24 June 1911. Photograph by Gabriele Münter*

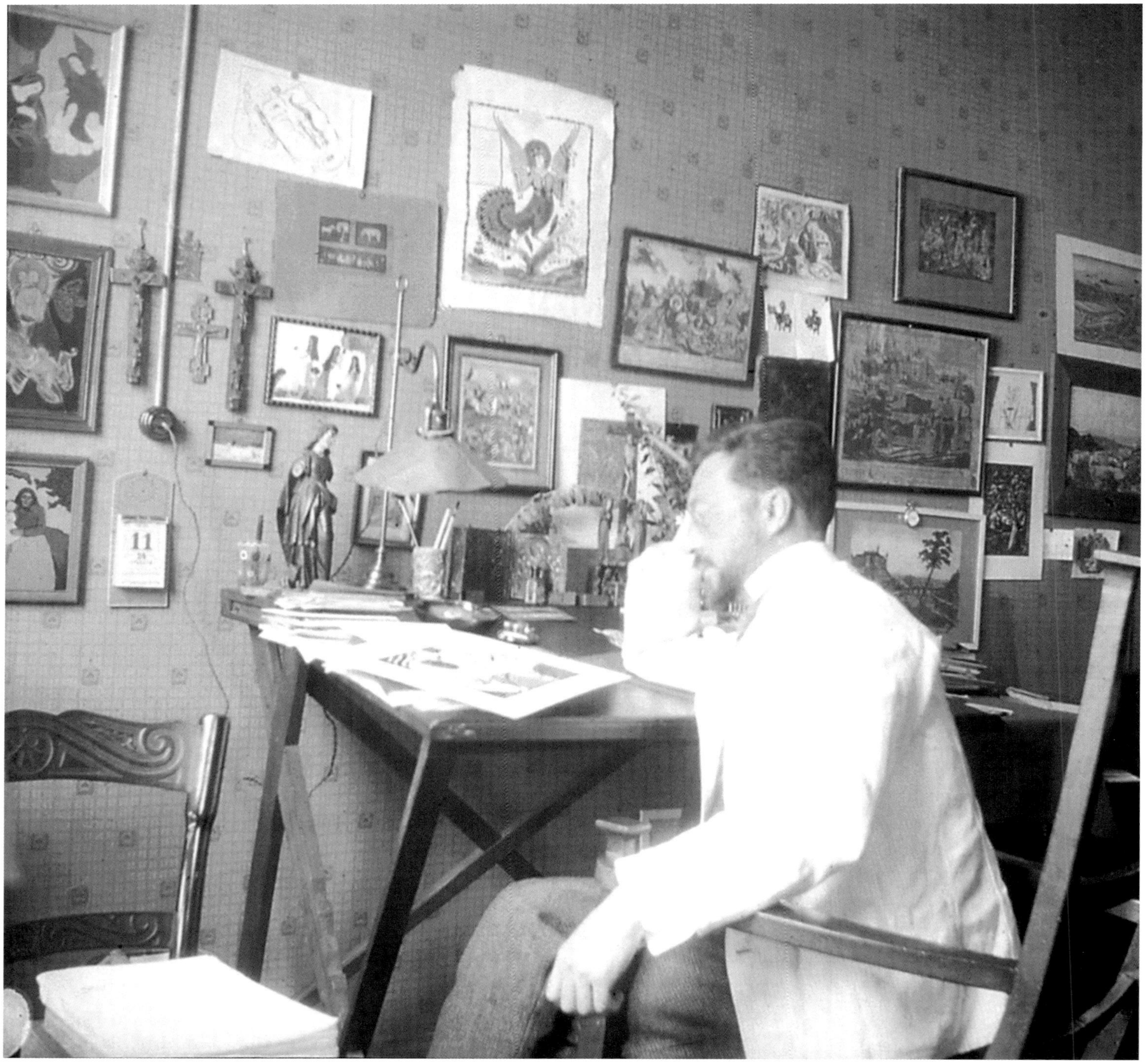

# *Preface*

The last volume of the Kandinsky catalogue raisonné consists of drawings in the thirty-eight sketchbooks that have remained intact. It can be considered the companion to Volume One of *Kandinsky Drawings: Catalogue Raisonné* (2006), which contains numerous pages that originally came from sketchbooks but have been taken apart and dispersed in addition to more than one thousand individual drawings. The intention of the present volume of the catalogue raisonné is not to publish facsimiles of the sketchbooks but to document and illustrate the pages on which Kandinsky made sketches, drawings and watercolors. Since Kandinsky worked in several sketchbooks simultaneously and since he evidently used a sketchbook over a period of years, it is impossible to follow a strictly chronological order. The thirty-eight sketchbooks have been numbered and arranged according to an approximate chronological framework. Within each sketchbook the sequence of pages follows the order of numbered sheets from front to back: it does not place the drawings in a chronological sequence.

The largest number of sketchbooks belongs to the Städtische Galerie im Lenbachhaus in Munich, followed by those in the collection of the Musée National d'Art Moderne at the Centre Georges Pompidou in Paris. The systems of pagination differ between the two institutions: however, the numbers assigned to *pages* by the Lenbachhaus and the numbers assigned to the *sheets* by the Musée National d'Art Moderne have not been changed in the present catalogue.

Kandinsky's companion, the German artist Gabriele Münter (1877–1962), safeguarded his art from the onset of World War I in 1914 until 1957, when she made her magnanimous donation to the Städtische Galerie im Lenbachhaus. Hans Konrad Roethel, director of the museum at that time, played an influential role in Münter's decision; later, the curator Erika Hanfstaengl published selected pages from Kandinsky's sketchbooks in the Lenbachhaus.

The artist's widow, Nina Kandinsky, bequeathed the works of art and art-related material from his estate to the Musée National d'Art Moderne after her death in 1980. Madame Claude Pompidou together with the late Karl Flinker and Pontus Hulten were instrumental in making the Centre Georges Pompidou the largest repository of Kandinsky's art and archives, and in founding the Société Kandinsky to promote and safeguard his work.

*Kandinsky Drawings: Catalogue Raisonné* has been prepared with the support and under the auspices of the Société Kandinsky. I am most grateful to the members of the Société for their encouragement and long-term commitment to this ongoing project. I would like to express my gratitude to the President of the Société, Claude Pompidou, for her sympathetic understanding, to the Vice-Presidents, Thomas Messer and the late Pontus Hulten, and to the Treasurer, Christian Derouet, for their essential support. In recent years I have discussed numerous aspects of the present volume with the Catalogue Raisonné Committee, and I have appreciated the advice of Christian Derouet, Fabrice Hergott, Thomas Messer and Armin Zweite.

Helmut Friedel, the director of the Städtische Galerie im Lenbachhaus in Munich, generously offered to take on the catalogue raisonné project. I would like to thank him and his staff at the Lenbachhaus who have assisted with my work: in particular, Susanne Böller, Annegret Hoberg, Ernst Jank, Kurt Laube, Daniel Oggenfuss and Lore Thürheimer. In addition, the administrator of the Gabriele Münter- und Johannes Eichner- Stiftung, Ilse Holzinger, has been eager to answer numerous questions and to decipher handwriting. She has made Kandinsky's letters as well as Münter's sketchbooks and photographs available to me. Isabelle Jansen assisted me with the database established by the Société Kandinsky of the photographs in the Münter-Eichner Stiftung, and she has shared her knowledge of Münter's art with me.

It has been a pleasure to work in the Cabinet d'Art Graphique and in the Bibliothèque Kandinsky at the Musée National d'Art Moderne. I would like to thank the museum's director, Alfred Pacquement, the curator of drawings, Agnes de La Beaumelle, and Didier Schulmann, director of the Bibliothèque Kandinsky. Macha Daniel and Gilles Pezzana kindly made the sketchbooks available for me to examine on several visits. Anne-Marie Zucchelli and Christine Jullien located documents for me to study, and Brigitte Vincens gave me access to the database of the artist's photographs. Over many years, Christiane Rojouan has assisted me in countless ways.

In preparing the volume on the sketchbooks, I have turned to many friends and colleagues for their expertise: Natasha Kurchanova provided invaluable assistance, Boris Chichlo generously permitted me to read his essay on the 'Vologda Diary', Thomas Guimond and Courtney Barroll reviewed my entries on anatomy, and Dirk H. Breiding enthusiastically provided information about arms and armor. Nadia Podzemskaia had done research on Kandinsky's copies of book illustrations – especially in Sketchbook 6 – and identified some of his sources. Tamara Olivari of the Biblioteca Internazionale in Rapallo helped with my research in Liguria, and Franco Ragazzi later answered specific questions. Cristina Ashjian made available her extensive knowledge of Kandinsky's trip to Tunisia, Sonja Bay helped identify sites in the Netherlands, and Georgia Illetschko responded to queries about specific places in Austria as well as Kandinsky's drawings in general. Eileen M. Kane and Natasha Kurchanova undertook the difficult task of deciphering, transliterating and translating Kandinsky's Cyrillic script. Clara M. Oberle worked on transcribing Kandinsky's notes in German, and Ilse Holzinger reviewed the illegible words. I am most grateful to all the people who have helped me complete the present volume.

Susanne Böller contacted the owners of all works illustrated in the catalogue raisonné, including the appendices, to request permission to reproduce the works. We would like to thank the museums and photographers who waived their fees, and especially Jean-Marc Gutton, general director of ADAGP, and Eva Neuroth of VG Bild-Kunst for their essential support of the Kandinsky catalogue raisonné. Vladana Jonquet at the Réunion des Musées-Nationaux in Paris and Sylvia Hoffmann at the Bildarchiv Preußischer Kulturbesitz in Berlin have been most helpful.

I began to do research on the sketchbooks while a fellow at the Institute for Advanced Study in Princeton New Jersey. My research has been done primarily in New York at the Frick Art Reference Library, the Thomas J. Watson Library of the Metropolitan Museum of Art, the Museum of Modern Art Library and the New York Public Library. In addition, I have benefited from the resources of the Princeton University Libraries, the Bayerische Staatsbibliothek in Munich and the Bibliothèque Kandinsky at the Centre Georges Pompidou in Paris.

Finally, it has been a great pleasure to work with Anne Jackson, Norman Turpin, Krystyna Mayer and Philip Wilson in London, and with Stefanie Hölscher at C.H. Beck in Munich.

Vivian Endicott Barnett
*New York, September* 2006

# *Personal Perspectives: Kandinsky's Sketchbooks, 1889–1943*

*by Vivian Endicott Barnett*

Kandinsky did not intend for his sketchbooks to be published and, had he suspected such an eventuality, he might have torn out a few more pages or edited them. He was exceptionally self-aware as an artist and attentive to the reception of his art. He understood the influence of critics – having written reviews of exhibitions himself – and he was eager to know how his paintings, watercolors and drawings were presented and to which collections they belonged. The sketchbooks, however, present an unedited and essentially unknown aspect of his life and work. They were never exhibited during the artist's lifetime. The sketchbooks from 1897 to 1914 were preserved by Gabriele Münter, his companion from 1903 until 1916. Nina Kandinsky, the artist's wife from 1917 until his death in 1944, saved virtually everything related to art that was in his possession. Because of the two women's dedication, Kandinsky's sketchbooks were kept and became part of his artistic legacy. The drawings in them have never been seen before in their entirety, and the notations written next to the sketches have never been published.

The sketchbooks offer behind the scenes perspectives: studies for pictures, random jottings, images copied from books and quick sketches of subjects that captured his attention while travelling. Most of the sketchbooks are small in size; many were carried on journeys. In fact, the first sketchbook is actually a diary or calendar that Kandinsky took with him on an expedition northeast of Moscow to the remote Vologda Region and as far east as the Ural Mountains in June–July 1889. At that time, he had not formally studied art, and his research was focused on economic, ethnographic and legal questions in relation to his studies at the University of Moscow.[1] His sketches record places, buildings, clothing and artifacts: they present Kandinsky before he had decided to become an artist.

It was only at the end of 1896 that Kandinsky (accompanied by his first wife Anja Shemiakina) moved to Munich in order to study painting at the private art academy of Anton Azbè (1862–1905). There he studied anatomy and, as he later wrote in 'Rückblicke' (Reminiscences), drew the 'two or three models [who] sat for heads or posed nude' [Zwei bis drei Modelle 'saßen Kopf' oder 'standen Akt'].[2] They are probably depicted in Sketchbooks 3, 4 and 5. Sketchbook 3 also contains drawings copied from *Anatomie für Künstler: Kurzgefasstes Lehrbuch der Anatomie, Mechanik, Mimik und Proportionslehre des Menschlichen Körpers* by August Froriep.[3] Sketchbook 2 consists mainly of explanatory notes in Russian with small anatomical diagrams. Kandinsky may have begun to use it first and then worked in other sketchbooks, before making notes on the last pages of Sketchbook 2 in the spring of 1900. Likewise, while a student from 1897 to 1900, he made many anatomical drawings with annotations in Russian, Latin and German in Sketchbook 3, but put it aside for a decade until returning to it and adding studies for prints and paintings on three pages.

After studying at Azbè's school in 1897–1898, Kandinsky took an anatomy course with Siegfried Mollier (1866–1954), a professor of medicine at the university in Munich who taught classes for artists. Subsequently, he studied drawing at the Kunstakademie (Art Academy) with Franz Stuck (1863–1928). Thus, it is extremely difficult – if not impossible – to know which anatomical studies and drawings from the model were executed in which class. It is, however, clear that Kandinsky made anatomical drawings in sketchbooks over a period of years, and that the dates of Sketchbooks 2, 3, 4, 5, 6 and 7 overlap to a certain degree. In general, Kandinsky's anatomy studies seem rather awkward and perfunctory: they lack articulation, fluidity and energy. Certainly, they cannot be compared with the anatomical drawings of Leonardo da Vinci or Michelangelo Buonarotti.

Sketchbooks 6 and 9 contain numerous copies of illustrations of armor and costumes that can be found in German, French and English books which Kandinsky had access to in Munich. Kandinsky's notes – including lists of books – provide clues and make it possible to identify many of his sources. Although his paintings of medieval scenes date from 1901–1904, Kandinsky's interest in arms and armor goes back to his time in Azbè's school. Azbè took a photograph of Kandinsky posing with a sword in one hand and a cigar in the other in Azbè's atelier, where a reproduction of a Holbein drawing is visible on the wall (fig.1).[4] The same sword appears in a photograph of Kandinsky with fellow students Dmitri Kardovsky and Nikolai Zeddler at Azbè's school,[5] of a man wearing armor seated before a curtain[6] and a man in different armor standing on a balcony (fig.2). The standing man is, in fact, Azbè, who was known for his small size as well as his great generosity. Azbè admired the work of Hans Holbein the Younger and Hans von Marées, and he apparently had armor and other costumes.[7] The sword, however, remained in Kandinsky's possession.[8]

In 1900 Kandinsky began to study with Franz Stuck, who was considered 'Germany's foremost draftsman' [der erste Zeichner Deutschlands]. He recalled that 'Stuck opposed my "extravagant" use of color, even in the first studies I made at the Academy, and advised me to paint initially in black and white, so as to study form by itself.

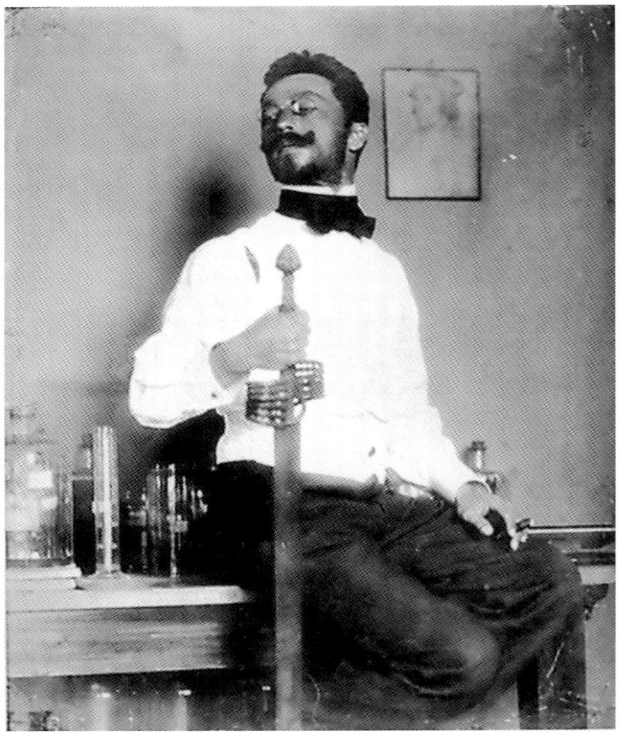

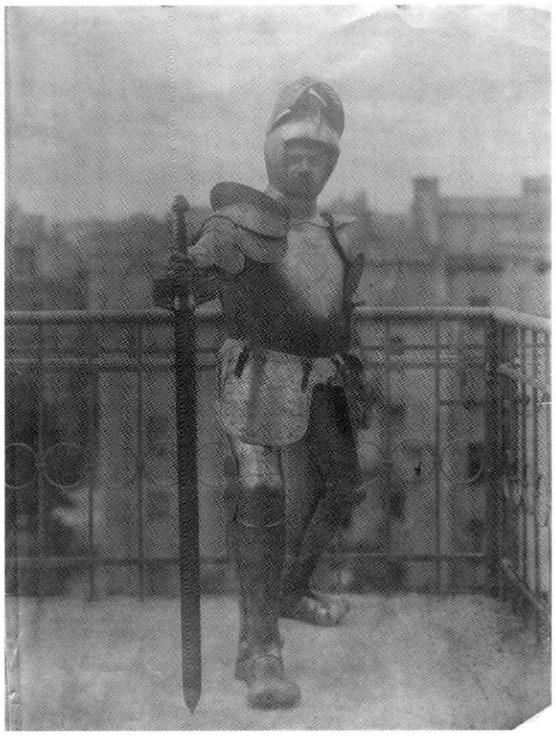

1. *Kandinsky posing with a sword in Anton Azbè's atelier, c.1898. Photograph by Azbè (Münter-Eichner Stiftung)*

2. *Anton Azbè in armor in Munich, c.1898. (Fonds Kandinsky, Paris)*

3. *Kandinsky with his students in Kochel, 1902. (Münter-Eichner Stiftung)*

4. *Kandinsky sketching in Kallmünz, 1903. Photograph by Gabriele Münter (Münter-Eichner Stiftung)*

... I wanted to study only drawing with him, since I had observed at once that he possessed little sensitivity to color, and submitted entirely to his advice.' [Stuck stellte sich schon bei meiner ersten Arbeit auf der Akademie energisch gegen meine 'Extravaganzen' in der Farbe und riet mir, erst schwarz-weiß zu malen, um nur die Form zu studieren. ... Ich wollte bei ihm nur die Zeichnung lernen, da ich sofort bemerkte, daß er wenig farbenempfindlich ist, und fügte mich völlig seinen Ratschlägen.][9]

Already in November 1900 Kandinsky wrote to Kardovsky: 'This summer the conditions were right and so I decided to discuss with several people my long cherished plan, namely to found a new association in Munich with permanent exhibition of works from all areas of art.' [Diesen Sommer fand ich passende Bedingungen und beschloß deshalb, meinen lange gehegten Plan mit verschiedenen Personen zu besprechen, nämlich in München einen neuen Verein zu gründen mit einer ständigen Ausstellung von Werken sämtlicher Kunstbereiche.][10] Soon after finishing his studies, in the spring of 1901, Kandinsky was one of the founders of the Künstlervereinigung 'Phalanx', and that summer he was elected president of the artists' association.

In addition, during the winter of 1901–1902, Kandinsky established the 'Phalanx' school in Munich, where he taught painting. It was in his role as a teacher that Kandinsky became acquainted with Gabriele Münter, who was enrolled in his still-life class and then in his evening class with a model.[11] The following summer, from June to August 1902, he took his students to Kochel, a village to the south of Munich, to paint outdoors from nature. Münter, who is standing next to Kandinsky in a photograph (fig.3), was the only student with a bicycle. They explored the Bavarian countryside together and made many landscape drawings. He began to add color notations to the pencil sketches done from nature, and developed a few of the studies into oil paintings. The drawings in Sketchbook 8 reveal a spontaneity of line, a richness of light and shadow and an awareness of nature. Sketches of trees, branches with blossoms and fruit, clouds and boats on the water emerge as favorite motifs that he would continue to favor.

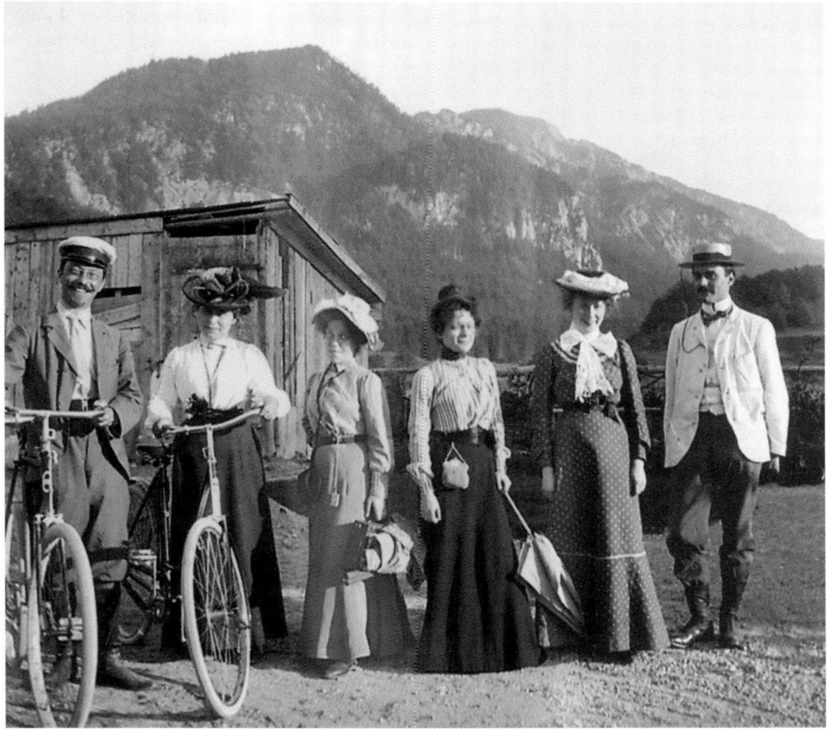

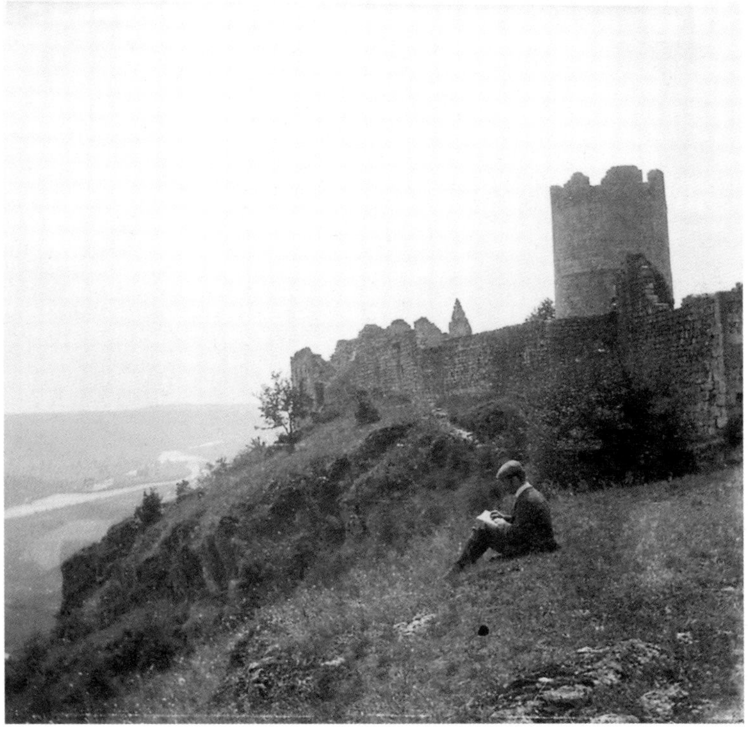

From June to August 1903 Kandinsky took six of his students from the 'Phalanx' school to Kallmünz, a picturesque medieval town in the Upper Palatinate (Oberpfalz). During the previous year his friendship with Münter had grown into love and, in August 1903, he bought engagement rings and promised to marry her in spite of the fact that he was still married to Anja Shemiakina.[12] He painted ladies in medieval dress and knights in armor on horseback.[13] Although Kandinsky copied figures from book illustrations and carefully noted the century and country of the costumes, he rarely incorporated them into his paintings. Through his attention to detail and precise documentation, he created convincingly fanciful medieval scenes. During the summer of 1903 he began to make woodcuts as well as designs for decorative arts – embroidery, handbags, jewelry and pottery: for example, Sketchbooks 9 and 12 contain embroidery designs. Kandinsky had already made studies for furniture in Sketchbooks 5 and 7.[14]

In Kallmünz Kandinsky and Münter continued to work from nature: he probably used Sketchbooks 10, 11, 12 and 13 simultaneously rather than sequentially. There is a drawing of Münter sketching outdoors on page 31 of Sketchbook 12. Münter photographed Kandinsky sketching near the castle above the town (fig.4). While they travelled, not only Münter but probably also Kandinsky took photographs, which can sometimes be related to his paintings and drawings. It must not be forgotten that Kandinsky had made photographs during a stay in Akhtyrka in 1901, and later he based tempera paintings on photographs he had taken in Venice in 1903.[15] A photograph looking down on Kallmünz resembles drawings in Sketchbooks 10 and 11, and raises the possibility that one or both of the sketches might have been done from the photograph (see p.97). Since the sketches done in mid-August in Nabburg are found in Sketchbook 13, it is placed last among the Kallmünz sketchbooks.

Although Kandinsky and Münter worked near each other, they rarely shared the same sketchbook and often selected different images and views to sketch. There are, however, exceptions. In a sketchbook that Münter used in 1903–1904,[16] there are three drawings apparently by Kandinsky (see cat. nos.1237–1239 in the Addendum on pp.319-320). The sketch on page 3, which Kandinsky inscribed in Cyrillic 'Rothenburg 7 November', is remarkably similar to one that Münter made in another sketchbook.[17] The date coincides with a short trip that they took in November 1903 to Rothenburg ob der Tauber.[18] In the same sketchbook belonging to Münter, there is a landscape drawing (cat. no.1238) by Kandinsky and a study with his monogram in a triangle (cat. no.1239) which he made in the Netherlands the following year.

In 1904 Kandinsky and Münter began to travel for extended periods of time so that they could live together. Sketchbooks became an essential part of their trips and a way of recording what they saw. Kandinsky sketched landscapes and buildings, remembering people in distinctive clothes and poses and writing lists of train schedules, hotels, names and addresses. When Kandinsky and Münter travelled in the Netherlands for four weeks in May–June 1904, he made studies and notes in Sketchbooks 15 and 16. They reveal his interest in architectural details, canals, boats and figures in costume, some of which reappear in his paintings. His annotations record specific colors and details. In December 1904 they travelled via Strasbourg, Lyons and Marseilles to Tunisia, where they stayed for almost four months.

By identifying the motifs in the sketchbooks that Kandinsky took with him on trips, it is possible to date them with accuracy. When Münter sketched the same figure or view, she often added the date and place. It is, of course, much easier to recognize the different landscapes of the Netherlands and Tunisia than to distinguish between trees in Bavaria or those in Tyrol. In some cases, sketchbooks can be dated on the basis of internal evidence: for example, Sketchbook 14 can be placed with certainty in 1904 because of the many references and lists it contains. Therefore, the few pages with designs for rings and decorative arts must have been done the same year.

When Kandinsky and Münter travelled in Tunisia, they worked side by side and sketched the same motifs more often than on other trips. There are also numerous photographs that document the places they visited. The costumes, houses, trees and landscapes, as well as the colors and light, were totally different from what they had experienced in Europe. Not surprisingly, Kandinsky and Münter responded more to the picturesque and exotic than they would have in Amsterdam or Rapallo. By comparing Kandinsky and Münter's sketchbooks, and by studying Münter's pocket calendars, it is possible to reconstruct their itinerary and consequently the order of Kandinsky's sketchbooks. Sketchbook 17 shows the streets of Tunis and excursions to Maxula-Rades and El-Ariana nearby, while Sketchbook 18 contains drawings of Sousse and Kairouan, where they travelled in March before return-

5. *Gabriele Münter, Kandinsky sketching in Rapallo, 1906. Städtische Galerie im Lenbachhaus, Munich*

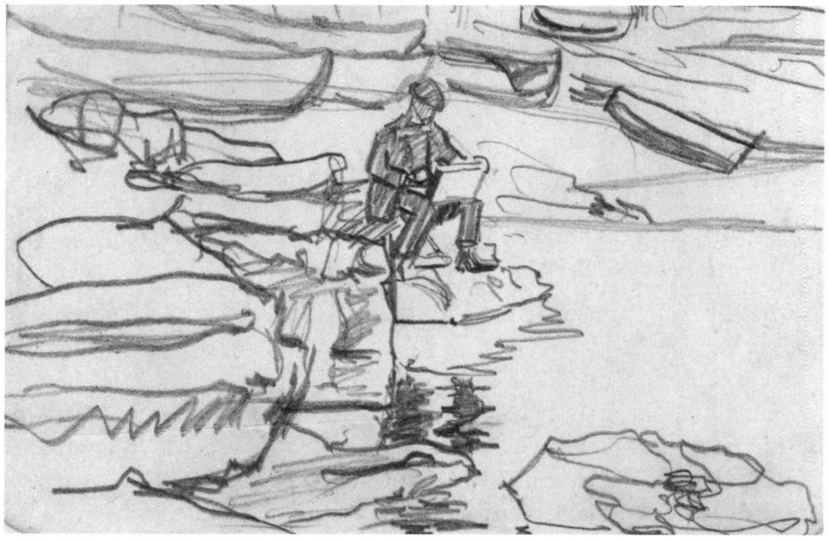

6. *(opposite) The dining room of the 'Russians' House' in Murnau, c.1912. Photograph by Gabriele Münter (Münter-Eichner Stiftung)*

ing to Tunis. Sketchbook 19 presents Belvedere Park and the Arab Cemetery in Tunis juxtaposed with snow-covered mountains and Austrian villages that Kandinsky sketched on the way back to Germany. Thus, Sketchbooks 17–19 can be placed in a sequence and dated with accuracy.

In contrast, Sketchbook 20 was used over a period of time. Toward the back of the sketchbook there are drawings done on Christmas 1905 in Sestri Levante on the Italian Riviera. The majority of sketches were done in Paris in 1906–1907, and it is possible that the first few pages may date from 1903. Sketchbooks 21 and 22 contain drawings of Rapallo, where Kandinsky and Münter lived from January to April 1906. Many of the motifs – harbor scenes, villas, churches and landscapes – are still recognizable and can be identified. Kandinsky and Münter went hiking in the nearby hills and sketched the rocks and harbor (fig.5) near where they rented an apartment. They left Rapallo at the end of April and travelled via Basel to Paris, where they lived for a year.

From May 1906 until June 1907 in Paris, Kandinsky worked in Sketchbooks 20 and 23, although he had probably purchased them and even begun to draw in them earlier. In Sketchbook 23 he made many sketches of his cat Waske and, on the last page, there is also a drawing by Münter.[19] Kandinsky copied illustrations from books noting dates and captions in French, and made studies for paintings that he was working on, such as *Reitendes Paar* and *Das bunte Leben*. He also sketched people relaxing in the park with their children. However, the sketchbooks do not record the exhibitions he saw in Paris or the people whom he met: they continue themes familiar from his earlier sketchbooks.

Kandinsky's travels with Münter in Europe and their restless search for a place to live continued well into 1908. Sketchbooks 24, 25 and 26 often refer to apartments for rent and list travel agencies and addresses in Austria, Italy and England. They also record more intangible aspects of nature – clouds, a thunderstorm near Bad Reichenhall, Lana after the rain – than the earlier sketches of Kallmünz, Tunis and Rapallo. By the summer of 1908, Kandinsky and Münter were looking for a place to settle down and paint, whether in Tyrol or the Salzkammergut in Austria, or near Munich in Germany.

After four years of travelling, Kandinsky and Münter returned to Munich in June 1908 and, in August, stayed for the first time in Murnau, a market town on the Staffelsee to the south. Kandinsky knew the surrounding countryside and nearby villages such as Kochel.

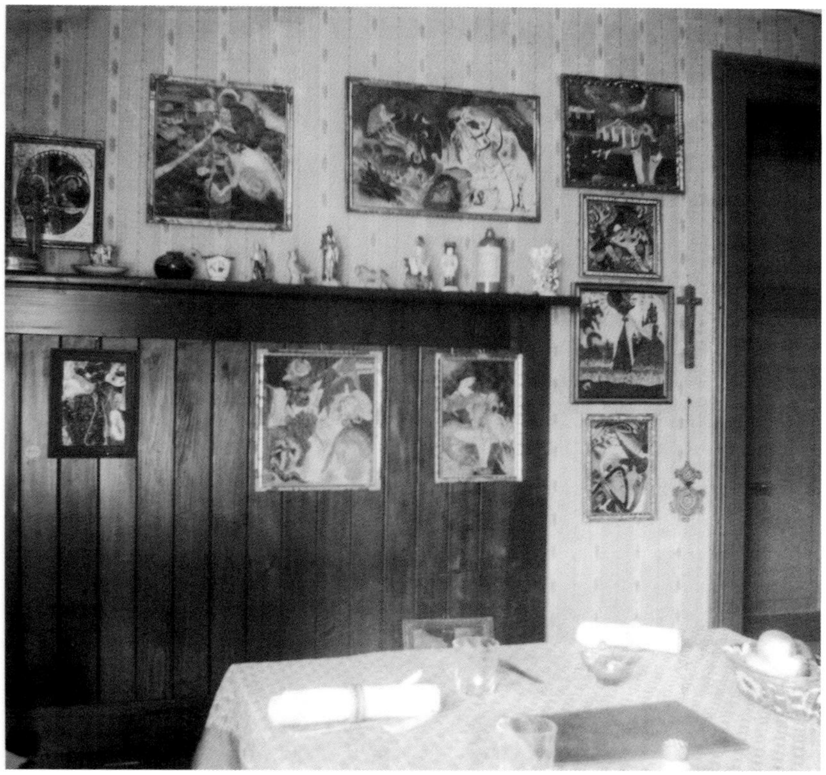

He did not need to record the landscape in his sketchbooks and, as he began to paint from nature, he sketched directly on cardboard with oil paint. Not surprisingly, the characteristics of the sketchbooks change. Sketchbook 26 – which is very small in size – contains studies for Kandinsky's prints and painted wood sculptures as well as the earliest manuscript for his theater composition 'Schwarz und Weiss' (Black and White) of 1908–1909. Sketchbook 27 includes the names of artists and notes about the *Neue Künstlervereinigung München* (New Artists' Association of Munich), analytical drawings of pictures he painted in 1909–1910, sketches of furniture and a floor plan of the house Münter bought in Murnau in 1909.

From 1909 to 1914 Kandinsky and Münter divided their time between Ainmillerstrasse in Munich and the house in Murnau (fig.6). There was space for Kandinsky to work on woodcuts, wood sculptures and furniture, and to paint large canvases as well as 'Hinterglasbilder' (glass paintings). Kandinsky resumed his activities in organizing

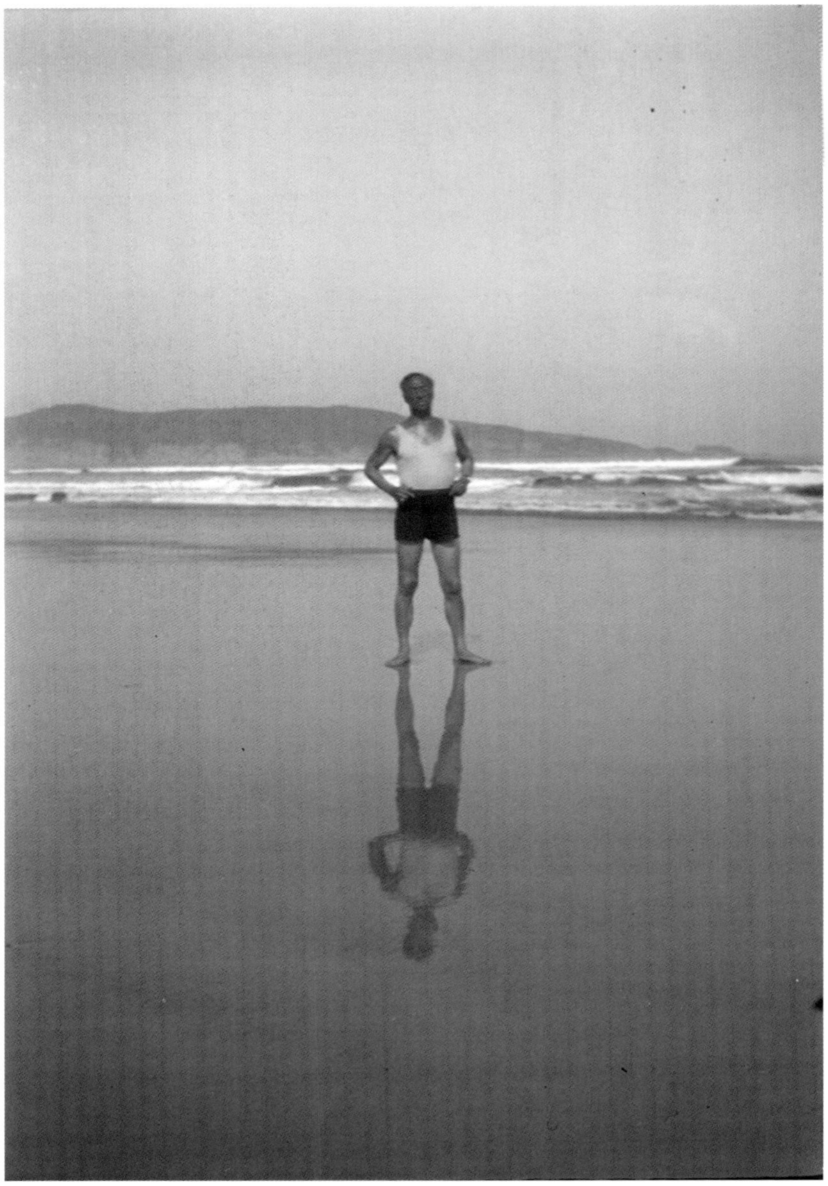

7. *Kandinsky on the beach at Hendaye, 1929. Photograph by Nina Kandinsky (Fonds Kandinsky)*

artists' associations, worked with Thomas von Hartmann on theater projects, and was involved in writing *Über das Geistige in der Kunst* and editing *Der Blaue Reiter* almanac with Franz Marc. The years of travelling, staying in hotels and rented rooms, had ended. Kandinsky drew noticeably less in sketchbooks and more on separate sheets of paper. Many of the individual drawings have larger dimensions: many were executed with India ink and signed, and some were mounted by the artist as if he intended to exhibit them. Certain pages in Sketchbook 27 have a direct relationship to his increasingly abstract art – and so do the sheets from a sketchpad on which he drew from 1909 until 1912.[20] In Sketchbook 28 he made three drawings related to paintings from 1910–1912. There are pages from a sketchbook that is no longer intact in which he executed watercolors and drawings in late 1913–1914.[21] Sketchbook 29 contains landscape studies done in Höllentalklamm near Garmisch in June 1914. Shortly thereafter, on 1 August, the war began, and Kandinsky, a Russian citizen and thus an enemy alien, had to leave Germany immediately.

During World War I Kandinsky lived primarily in Moscow, with the exception of a three-month trip to Stockholm to see Münter. He did not paint in oil during 1915, and from 1915 through 1917 he created a large number of works on paper. Not surprisingly, he relied on sketchbooks again. Kandinsky wrote the date 'November 1915' on Sketchbook 30, he purchased Sketchbook 31 in Stockholm in early 1916, he acquired another sketchbook in Moscow that spring[22] and he inscribed 'autumn 1916' in Sketchbook 32. After making abstract ink drawings on the first nine pages of Sketchbook 32, he probably put it aside until the summer of 1917, when he resumed sketching representational pencil drawings, working in inverse direction from the back of the sketchbook. Kandinsky had followed the practice of using sketchbooks from both the front and back earlier with Sketchbooks 2, 20 and 28.

No sketchbooks have been preserved from 1922, when Kandinsky returned to Germany and began to teach at the Bauhaus, until about 1927. The absence of sketchbooks from this six- to seven-year period is puzzling. It seems doubtful that they might have been lost or destroyed, since the artist and his wife Nina kept correspondence, manuscripts, minor sketches and ephemera. A more likely explanation is that Kandinsky made his small pencil sketches on separate pieces of paper: the many tentative sketches on the backs of invitations, envelopes and scraps of paper – included in the first volume of the catalogue raisonné of drawings – support this hypothesis. Moreover, the numerous studies for the illustrations in his book *Punkt und Linie zu Fläche* (Point and Line to Plane) are found on individual sheets of paper and not in sketchbooks.[23] By the 1920s Kandinsky's research was focused on geometry and line rather than on landscapes and objects. His pedagogical interest coincided with his teaching at the Bauhaus, first in Weimar and then in Dessau. Color remained central to his art: he still made color notations on individual pencil drawings and in the single sketchbook dating from the 1920s. Sketchbook 33 relates primarily to works created in 1929, but it probably spans the years from 1927 to 1930 and includes numerous studies for unidentified and probably unexecuted works.

Vasily and Nina Kandinsky went on vacation every summer and often stayed on the beach – from Binz on the Ostsee to Juan-les-Pins on the Mediterranean or Hendaye-Plage on the Atlantic coast (fig.7). However, he did not take a sketchbook with him to draw the boats, rocks or shore.[24] Nina Kandinsky recalled that her husband had said: 'There were fantastic, indescribably beautiful colors in the sky and especially in the water, he raved, almost never a calm moment, and often one saw pure white, emerald green and deep violet in the ocean at the same moment. ...I had no desire to paint seascapes, but I absorbed the impressions avidly.'['Es gab phantastische unbeschreiblich schöne Farben im Himmel und besonders im Wasser,' schwärmte er, 'fast keine Minute blieb ruhig, und oft sah man in demselben Augenblick reines Weiß, Smaragdgrün, Tiefviolett auf dem Ozean. ...Ich bekam keine Lust, Marinen zu malen, sog aber die Eindrücke gierig ein.'][25] A few pages from a notebook refer briefly to color and light in places he visited on holiday in 1931 and 1932, but do not depict them.[26] When Kandinsky went to Egypt, Turkey and Greece in 1931, he did not sketch the pyramids, the Blue Mosque in Istanbul or the temples in Baalbek and Athens, although he found them awe inspiring.[27]

The Kandinskys left Germany at the end of 1933 and moved to Paris, where they found an apartment in Neuilly-sur-Seine overlooking the river and trees and only a few minutes from the Bois de Boulogne. Kandinsky described the view from the studio in his apartment and the light of Paris in many letters, but he did not sketch his new surroundings. As he related to Alfred Barr, the director of the Museum of Modern Art in New York: 'When I moved to Paris, I was so deeply moved by the light and by the nature there that I did not want to look at any unfamiliar pictures and, for almost two months, I could not paint. ...Paris with its wonderful (intense soft) light had relaxed my palette – there were other colors, other entirely new forms,

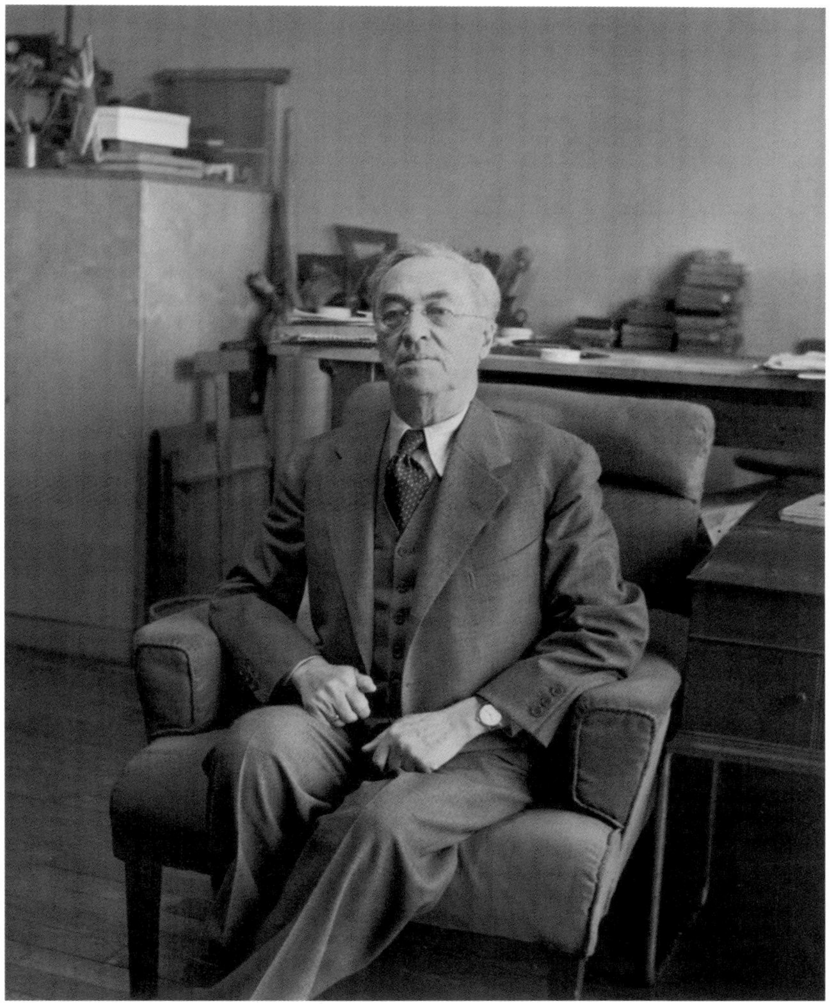

8. *Kandinsky in the studio of his Paris apartment, c.1938–1939. Photograph by Herta Moselsio (Roethel-Benjamin Archive, Guggenheim Museum)*

and some that I had used years earlier. Naturally I did all this unconsciously.' [Als ich nach Paris übersiedelte, war ich vom hiesigen Licht und der hiesigen Natur so erschüttert, dass ich mir keine fremden Bilder ansehen wollte und fast zwei Monate selbst nicht malen konnte. ...Paris mit seinem wunderbaren (stark-weichem) Licht hat meine 'Palette' gelockert– es kamen andre Farben, andre Formen ganz neu, manche habe ich verwendet, die ich mal vor Jahren verwendete. Natürlich das alles unbewusst.][28] From the beginning he made color notes in Russian on his drawings.[29]

In Paris Kandinsky used Sketchbooks 35, 36, 37 and 38 as well as two sketchpads[30] to develop overall compositions and specific motifs for watercolors, gouaches and canvases that he painted in 1935–1943. In spite of the economic and political conditions in Europe, he continued to focus on his creative work, to be inspired from within and to find peace in his studio at home (fig.8). As he wrote to the Swiss collector Hermann Rupf in December 1938: 'I sense that the "Paris air" is favorable to me. In spite of my "abstraction", I depend to some extent upon my "surroundings". What is in this atmosphere is a mystery to me. Of all the various large cities that I know, I feel myself deeply rooted only in Moscow and in Paris.' [Ich spüre ja selbst, dass die 'Pariser Luft' für mich günstig ist. Trotz meiner 'Abstraction' hänge ich doch gewissermassen von der 'Umgebung' ab. Worin diese 'Luft' zu sehen ist, ist mir rätselhaft. Von den verschiedenen Grosstädten, die ich kenne, fühle ich mich organisch verwachsen nur mit Moskau und mit Paris.][31]

In Paris during World War II, Kandinsky made thirty-nine India ink drawings dated 1941 in a sketchbook he purchased at Sennelier. Since the sketchbook is no longer intact and the drawings belong to many different collections, they are included in the first volume of the catalogue raisonné.[32] They appear to be finished drawings – most are signed and dated – and not tentative sketches like his sketchbook pages in general and the drawings dating from 1902–1908 in particular.

Undoubtedly, pages were taken out of Sketchbooks 30, 32, 33, 36, 37 and 38. There is still a drawing signed and dated 1943 in Sketchbook 38, thereby suggesting that it had been intended for sale since others had already been detached.[33] Moreover, the color annotations and certain details were added in pencil so that they could easily be erased. During the Paris years the best drawings were removed from sketchbooks for possible exhibition and sale, whereas during his formative years Kandinsky probably deleted the pages with which he was dissatisfied.

In 1889 as well as in 1897–1907, Kandinsky used his sketchbooks to research, record and observe his surroundings. At the beginning he drew objects: focusing on trees, boats, buildings and clouds. As he moved in the direction of abstraction and sought to free himself from the object, Kandinsky made analytical drawings of the compositions of his pictures and tended to write more than he drew in his sketchbooks. From 1908 to 1910 there are sketchbook pages where there appears to be no connection between what he sketched and the notes he jotted down. Kandinsky's sketchbooks turned inward, as did his paintings, so as to reflect his private perception of the world. Within his mind he possessed nature: he did not need to capture it in sketches.

Years later, after Kandinsky settled in Paris in 1934, he created a new pictorial world and filled his sketchbooks with precise, fanciful forms. Although most of his sketches were executed in black on white, the light and color of Paris permeated his vision. Images developed within his mind and were gradually incorporated into his art. Kandinsky did not describe in words the motifs he sketched in either preparing for known paintings and watercolors, or conceptualizing unknown and probably unexecuted works. Most of his sketches were not meant to be seen. The sketchbooks offer an intimate view of his extraordinary imagination and, until now, they have remained hidden.

NOTES

1. Upon his return to Moscow, Kandinsky published his findings in two papers in 1889. He wrote his dissertation on the legality of laborer's wages, *Le Minimum de salaire et l'encyclique 'Rerum Novarum' par Mgr Sébastien Nicotra* (*Der Mindestlohn und die Enzyklika 'Rerum Novarum' von Mgr. Sébastien Nicotra*), and completed his degree at the University of Moscow in November 1893.
2. Kenneth C. Lindsay and Peter Vergo, eds., *Kandinsky: Complete Writings on Art* (Boston, 1982), p.374 and Hans K. Roethel and Jelena Hahl-Koch, eds., *Die Gesammelten Schriften* (Bern, 1980), p.42. He recalled the models as 'these smelly, apathetic, expressionless, characterless natural phenomena, who were paid fifty to seventy pfennings an hour' [diese übelreichenden, teilnahmslosen, ausdruckslosen, meistenteils charakterlosen, 50 bis 70 Pfennig pro Stunde bezahlten Naturerscheinungen ...].
3. Nadia Podzemskaia has proposed that Kandinsky probably studied the manuals of John Dreper (St. Petersburg, 1868) and Thomas Lanzert (St. Petersburg, 1880) brought with him from Moscow, as well as that of August Froriep (Leipzig, 1890), which he owned. See *Colore, Simbolo, Immagine: Origine della teoria di Kandinsky* (Florence, 2000), pp.32, 210–212.
4. The chalk drawing of Sir Thomas Elyot by Hans Holbein the Younger belongs to the Royal Collection, Windsor Castle. The same drawing and table are found in a photograph of Azbè in costume (see Roethel and Hahl-Koch 1980, fig.5).
5. Jelena Hahl-Koch, *Kandinsky* (Stuttgart, 1993), p.83, ill.88.
6. Podzemskaia 2000, p.116, ill.5.
7. See Roethel and Hahl-Koch 1980, fig.5 for a photograph of Azbè wearing a wig and top hat, and for additional information, see Katarina Ambrozic, 'Die Azbè-Schule 1891–1905' in *Wege zur Moderne und die Azbè-Schule in München* exh. cat. (Wiesbaden, 1988), pp.87–109.
8. Christian Derouet and Jessica Boissel, *Kandinsky: Oeuvres de Vassily Kandinsky (1866–1944). Collections du Musée National d'Art Moderne* (Paris, 1984), p.449. Derouet states that the sword was kept in the corner of Kandinsky's atelier in Neuilly-sur-Seine near his icons.
9. See Lindsay and Vergo, 1982, p.376 and Roethel and Hahl-Koch, 1980, p.44.
10. N.B. Avtonomova, 'Die Briefe Wassily Kandinskys an Dmitrij Kardovskij', in *Wassily Kandinsky: Die erste sowjetische Retrospektive* exh. cat. (Frankfurt, 1989), p.49. The original letter in Russian dated 14 November 1900 is preserved in the Manuscript Department of the State Tretiakov Gallery, Moscow. The English translation comes from Vivian Endicott Barnett, 'Student Years in Munich, 1896–1900', in *Vasily Kandinsky: A Colorful Life. The Collection of the Lenbachhaus* exh. cat. (Munich, 1995), p.35.
11. Johannes Eichner, *Kandinsky und Gabriele Münter: Von Ursprüngen moderner Kunst* (Munich, 1957), pp.37–39.
12. Eichner 1957, p.40. Eichner specifically mentioned that they could only wear their engagement rings when they travelled. Since Eichner was Münter's companion many years later, he related what she remembered.
13. Kandinsky's first gift to Münter was a tempera painting, *Die Nacht (Spazierende Dame)* of 1903, with a medieval theme. See Hans Konrad Roethel, *Kandinsky: Das graphische Werk* (Cologne, 1970), p.12 and Vivian Endicott Barnett, *Kandinsky Watercolours: Catalogue Raisonné, 1900–1921* (London, 1992), no.73.
14. See Sketchbook 5, pp.40, 43, 45, and Sketchbook 7, p.34. It is significant that Stuck also designed furniture.
15. Barnett 1992, nos.117–120.
16. Sketchbook 46/13 was purchased from Jos. Bayerle in Munich.
17. Isabelle Jansen noted that the same motif is depicted in a sketchbook (37/7, p.88) that Münter used mainly in 1904–1905.
18. Eichner 1957, p.204 states that Kandinsky and Münter were in Rothenburg on 5 November 1903.
19. In addition, a drawing by Münter was pasted into the back cover of Sketchbook 28.
20. See Barnett 2006, vol.I, nos. 118–119, 124, 129, 132, 138, 171–175, 177–178, 181–184, 188–191, 232. The sheets have been dispersed and now belong to the Musée National d'Art Moderne in Paris and the Städtische Galerie im Lenbachhaus in Munich.
21. For information on the Haas und Hussel sketchbook, see Barnett nos.327, 334, 339, 346–349, 362, 366 and vol.I, nos.318, 320–324, 326.
22. The sketchbook, which was purchased at Mur and Meriliz in Moscow, has been dispersed: see vol.I, cat. nos.403–409.
23. See vol.I, cat. nos.565–567, 569–572, 574–620, 633–634.
24. An exception is an individual drawing of Cattolica dated 17 August 1930 (vol.I, cat. no.759).
25. Nina Kandinsky, *Kandinsky und ich* (Munich, 1976), p.209. Uta Nitschke-Stumpf kindly assisted in translating the excerpts from German texts.
26. See vol.I, cat. nos.836–839.
27. Nina Kandinsky 1976, pp.206–207.
28. Letter dated 16 July 1936 is preserved in the archives of the Museum of Modern Art, New York. A copy is located in the Bibliothèque Kandinsky at the Musée National d'Art Moderne, Centre Georges Pompidou, Paris.
29. See vol.I, cat. nos.922–923.
30. See Sketchbook 34 and a dispersed sketchpad (vol.I, cat. nos.992–994, 1086).
31. The letter dated 5 December 1938 belongs to the Archiv Rupf in the Kunstmuseum Bern. A copy is located in the Bibliothèque Kandinsky.
32. See vol.I, cat. nos.1122–1160. The sketchbook was dispersed long after the artist's lifetime in 1972.
33. See vol.I, cat. nos.1187–1194.

*Kandinsky in the studio of his Paris apartment, c.1937. Photograph by Boris Lipnitzki*

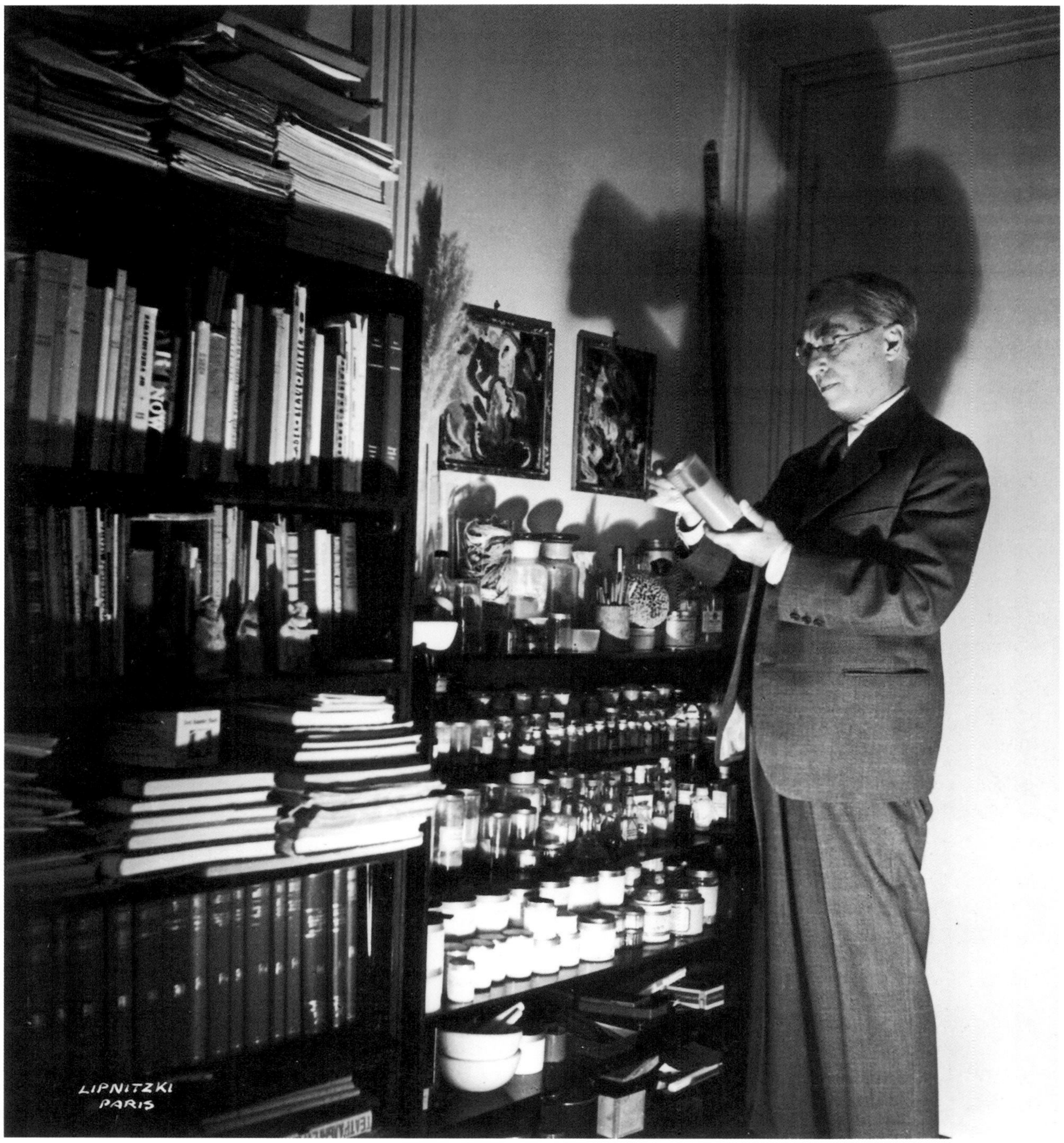

# *Brief Biography*

| | |
|---|---|
| **1866** | Vasily Vasilievich Kandinsky born on 4 December in Moscow |
| **1871–1885** | Lived in Odessa but travelled often to Moscow |
| **1886–1892** | Studied law and economics at University of Moscow |
| **1889** | Travelled to the Vologda region to do ethnographic research; took first trip to Paris |
| **1892** | Married his cousin Anja Shemiakina, from whom he was divorced in 1911 |
| **1896** | Moved to Munich and began to study painting with Anton Azbè |
| **1900–1901** | Continued studies with Franz Stuck and co-founded 'Phalanx' artists association |
| **1902** | Met Gabriele Münter, his student at the 'Phalanx' school |
| **1903** | Made woodcuts for *Stikhi bez slov* (Poems without Words), published in Moscow |
| **1904–1907** | Travelled extensively with Münter in the Netherlands, Tunisia, Italy, Germany and France; lived in Paris for one year from May 1906–June 1907 |
| **1908** | Returned to Munich; spent first of several summers with Münter in Murnau |
| **1909** | Co-founded *Neue Künstlervereinigung München* (New Artists' Association of Munich) and worked on theater compositions |
| **1911** | Worked with Franz Marc on *Der Blaue Reiter* almanac; published *Über das Geistige in der Kunst* (On the Spiritual in Art) at end of year |
| **1912** | *Der Blaue Reiter* almanac published in May; *Klänge* (Sounds) a volume of prose poems and woodcuts completed by end of year |
| **1913** | Publication of 'Rückblicke' (Reminiscences) published in album by Der Sturm |
| **1914** | Left Germany after outbreak of World War I and returned to Russia in December |
| **1915–1916** | Lived in Moscow with the exception of a three-month trip to see Münter in Stockholm |
| **1917** | Married Nina Andreevskaia in Moscow; birth of their son Vsevolod (1917–1920) |
| **1918** | Joined Department of Visual Arts of Narkompros (People's Commissariat for Enlightenment) and taught at Svomas (Free State Art Studios) in Moscow |
| **1919** | Appointed first director of Museum of Painterly Culture, Moscow |
| **1921** | Co-founded Russian Academy of Artistic Sciences; left Russia at end of year for Berlin |
| **1922** | Accepted teaching position at Bauhaus and moved to Weimar; *Kleine Welten* (Small Worlds), portfolio of prints published |
| **1924** | Member of Blue Four artists' group founded by Galka Scheyer |
| **1925** | Moved to Dessau after relocation of Bauhaus |
| **1926** | Published *Punkt und Linie zu Fläche* (Point and Line to Plane) |
| **1928** | Became German citizen |
| **1932** | Moved to Berlin where Bauhaus reopened |
| **1933** | Left Germany after Bauhaus forced to close |
| **1934** | Relocated to Neuilly-sur-Seine outside Paris |
| **1939** | Became French citizen |
| **1942** | Painted last large canvas in July 1942; thereafter small pictures and works on paper |
| **1944** | Worked until summer despite illness; died 13 December in Neuilly-sur-Seine |

# *Explanatory Notes*

**Numbering of sketchbooks**
The sketchbooks have been assigned numbers by the author in order to place them in a generally chronological order. Kandinsky did not number the sketchbooks or the pages in them. For each sketchbook in the catalogue raisonné, the page numbers inscribed or printed on the sheets – to which scholars have referred – have been retained. The numbering of pages is, however, not consistent: the Musée National d'Art Moderne in Paris numbered the sheets and designated the recto and verso of each sheet, whereas the Städtische Galerie im Lenbachhaus assigned a number to each page so that the recto and verso of each sheet have different numbers. Neither Nina Kandinsky nor Gabriele Münter numbered the sketchbook pages.

**Titles**
Kandinsky did not assign titles to the drawings in his sketchbooks. The brief descriptive identification of a sketch is not to be interpreted as a title. In discussing the sketches, references are made to related Kandinsky paintings and watercolors by their original titles.

**Dates**
Kandinsky often used sketchbooks over a period of time, returning to a notebook years later. Inclusive dates for each sketchbook have been determined by the author. Whenever Kandinsky's notes in a sketchbook include dates, they are cited. References are made to related works by Kandinsky or Gabriele Münter when they provide evidence for specific dates.

**Location**
The inventory number or accession number is included in parentheses following the name of the institution and appropriate credit line. Previously sketchbooks have been identified by these numbers.

**History**
The provenance is provided for each sketchbook but not repeated for each page since all sketchbooks are intact.

**Measurements**
Dimensions are given in centimeters followed by inches for each sketchbook. Measurements were taken at the left and bottom edges of the sheet following the orientation of the cover of the sketchbook; height proceeds width. When the orientation of a sketch differs (horizontal rather than vertical), the dimensions are not restated in transposed form.

**Medium**
The medium is described for each drawing. Unless otherwise noted, white or off-white paper is intended.

**Inscriptions**
Inscriptions are transcribed as written; unless otherwise indicated, they are by the artist. Grammatical errors and discrepancies in spelling have not been corrected. Efforts have been made to transcribe annotations adjacent to the sketches, but not every word on a page has been recorded. Sketchbook pages on which there are only notes and no sketches have been omitted. In the few cases where Kandinsky signed or dated sketchbook pages, this fact is noted. The page numbers inscribed by an unknown hand at a later date are not mentioned for each page. The terms 'left' and 'right' refer to the spectator's point of view.

**Exhibitions and References**
The exhibitions and references are as complete as possible: most citations are listed in abbreviated form. The reader will find detailed information in the list of exhibitions (pp.331-371) and the list of abbreviated references (pp.329-330). In some cases where drawings were included in an exhibition catalogue but were not lent or were not on view, the publication is cited as a reference rather than an exhibition.

**Abbreviations**

AM 1981
Inventory numbers of works of art included in the Nina Kandinsky Bequest to the Musée National d'Art Moderne, Centre Georges Pompidou, Paris

Fonds Kandinsky
Kandinsky bequest donated by the artist's widow to the Musée National d'Art Moderne, Centre Georges Pompidou, Paris. Documentation is now located in the Bibliothèque Kandinsky

GMS
Gabriele Münter Stiftung, Städtische Galerie im Lenbachhaus, Munich

Münter-Eichner Stiftung
Gabriele Münter- und Johannes Eichner- Stiftung, Munich, which is located in the Städtische Galerie im Lenbachhaus

| | | |
|---|---|---|
| u.l. upper left | u.c. upper center | u.r. upper right |
| c.l. center left | c. center | c.r. center right |
| l.l. lower left | l.c. lower center | l.r. lower right |
| R recto | | V verso |

cat. no.
Barnett, Vivian Endicott, *Kandinsky Drawings: Catalogue Raisonné. Individual Drawings*, vol.I (London and Munich, 2006)

Barnett
Barnett, Vivian Endicott, *Kandinsky Watercolours: Catalogue Raisonné, 1900–1921*, vol.I (London and Munich, 1992); *1922–1944*, vol.2 (London and Munich, 1994)

Derouet and Boissel
Derouet, Christian and Boissel, Jessica, *Kandinsky. Oeuvres de Vassily Kandinsky (1866–1944): Collections du Musée National d'Art Moderne* (Paris, 1984)

Hanfstaengl
Hanfstaengl, Erika, *Wassily Kandinsky: Zeichnungen und Aquarelle. Katalog der Sammlung der Städtischen Galerie im Lenbachhaus München* (Munich, 1974)

Roethel
Roethel, Hans Konrad, *Kandinsky: Das graphische Werk* (Cologne, 1970)

Roethel and Benjamin
Roethel, Hans K. and Benjamin, Jean K., *Kandinsky: Catalogue Raisonné of the Oil-Paintings, 1900–1915*, vol.I (London and Munich, 1982); *1916–1944*, vol.2 (London and Munich, 1984)

# *Catalogue Raisonné*

SKETCHBOOKS 1–38 AND ADDENDUM

# Sketchbook 1

prepared with the assistance of Natasha Kurchanova

1889

Blue cloth-covered diary with lettering in Cyrillic: 'DEN' ZA DNEM: ZAPISNAIA KNIZHKA I KALENDAR' NA 1889 GOD'. Inside back cover label from A. S/U i K°, Moscow (Tverskaya D[om] Varguina) Contains 503 pages (251 sheets), each 14.3 x 9.3 cm (5⅝ x 3⅝ in), of which pp.211–397 are blank. There are drawings on twenty-two pages. Each page has a printed page number and dual dates in the Julian [and Gregorian] calendars.

LOCATION

Musée National d'Art Moderne, Centre Georges Pompidou, Paris (AM 1981.65.687)

HISTORY

Nina Kandinsky, Paris, until 1980

The page numbers in this diary or calendar have been retained; however, they are not to be interpreted as dates for the sketches. Kandinsky travelled for a month from 14 June to 15 July 1889 in the Vologda Region northeast of the city of the same name. He had arrived in Vologda accompanied by his cousin and future wife, Anja Shemiakina, on 11 June. During his trip Kandinsky made copious notes, but only those on the same pages as his sketches or on the facing pages are transcribed. Dates follow the Western or Gregorian calendar. (Boris P. Chichlo kindly permitted me to read his essay, 'Wassily Kandinskys Erfahrungen in der Ethnographie: Ansichten eines Ethnologen', which will be published in *Wassily Kandinsky. Gesammelte Schriften, 1889-1916: Farbensprache, Kompositionslehre und andere unveröffentlichte Texte).*

**p.48**
16 [28] January 1889
Pencil sketch of decoration for a table
Inscribed u.l. in Cyrillic: 'U.-Kulym / 2 ryby / utka / 3 samovara / Moloko / Khleb / Seno) / itd'; u.r.: 'ryba v 60 k.'; c.: 'sredka stala'; l.r.: 'a- zheltoi / b- sinei / √ - zelenyi / ooo - sinii / c- belyi / oo - sinii / ≈ - zelenyi'

At the upper left Kandinsky inscribed 'Ust' Kulym' followed by a list: '2 fish, duck, 3 samovars, milk, bread, hay etc.' and, at the upper right, he noted: 'fish at 60 k[opeks]'. The drawing on p.65 was also done in Ust' Kulym far to the east of Vologda and was dated 21 June. Above the drawing of the decoration for a table, he wrote: 'the middle became' and then listed the colors corresponding to the letters and symbols in the sketch: 'a- yellow, b- blue, √ - green, ooo - blue, c- white, oo - blue, and ≈ - green.'

Another drawing of a brightly colored table decoration is found on p.50. In *Rückblicke* Kandinsky recalled that during his Vologda trip: 'Ich habe viel skizziert – diese Tische und verschiedene Ornamente' (I made many sketches – these tables and various Ornaments).

**p.49**
Inscribed u.c.: 'Pechal'nyi zvon. Prostoi / Nekrashennyi obychnyi grob / Za grobom medlenno tolpoi / Idet narod. Pred grobom pop… / A solntse zharkoe luchami l'et / teplo. / No ne sogret' emu ostyvshego / kholodnogo chela.'

Kandinsky wrote: 'Sorrowful sound of bells. A plain, unpainted, simple coffin. After the coffin slowly in a crowd, the people march. In front is a priest … And the hot sun pours the warmth with its rays. But it cannot warm up the cooled-off cold brow.'

**p.50**
18 [30] January 1889
Pencil and colored pencil sketches of a belt (above) and decoration for a table (below)
Inscribed u.c. in Cyrillic: 'poias kozhanyi'; c.: 'sistema razvoda list'ev / krashennym iarkimi / tsvetami stolom.'; l.l.: 'a- krasnyi / b- zheltyi / c- sinii / d- zheltyi / e- zelenyi / f- belyi / ╖ - sinii / --- - krasnyi'; l.l.: 's prikreplennymi / kist'iu i / vintom'

1, pp.48-49

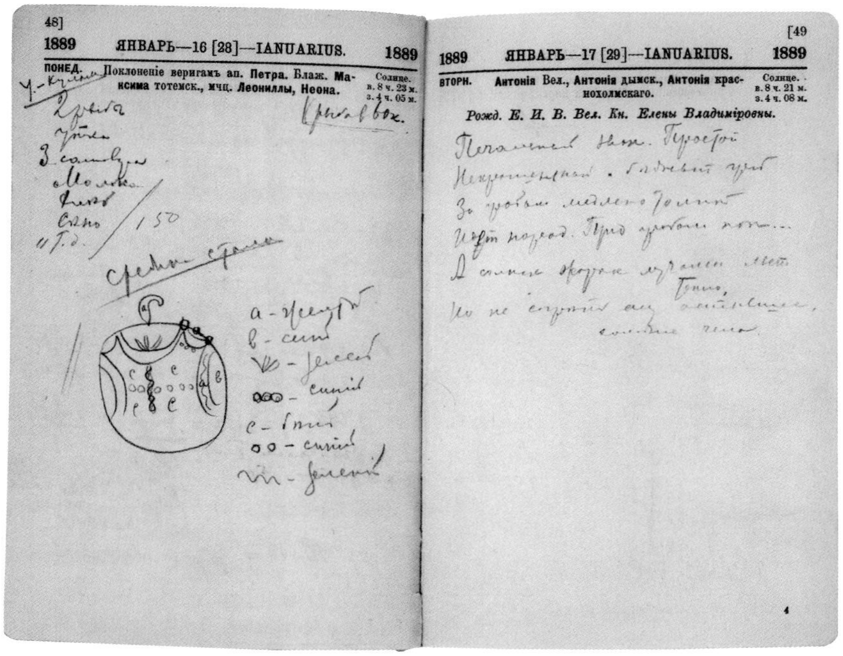


1, pp.50-51

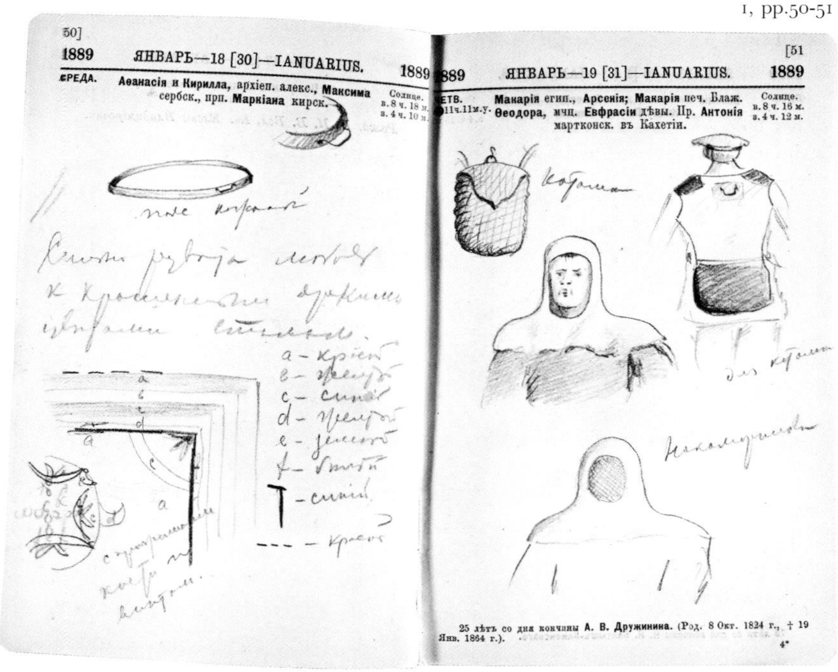

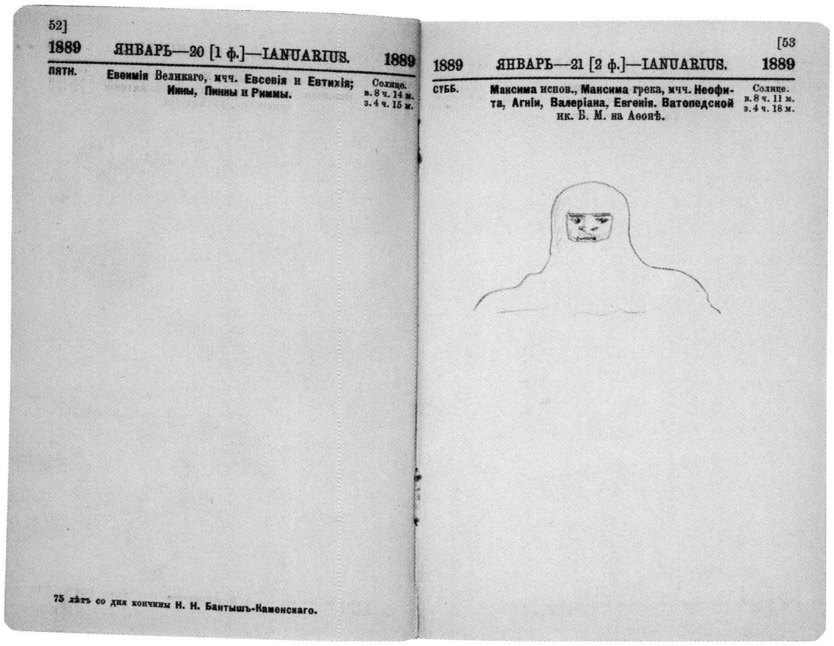


1, pp.52-53

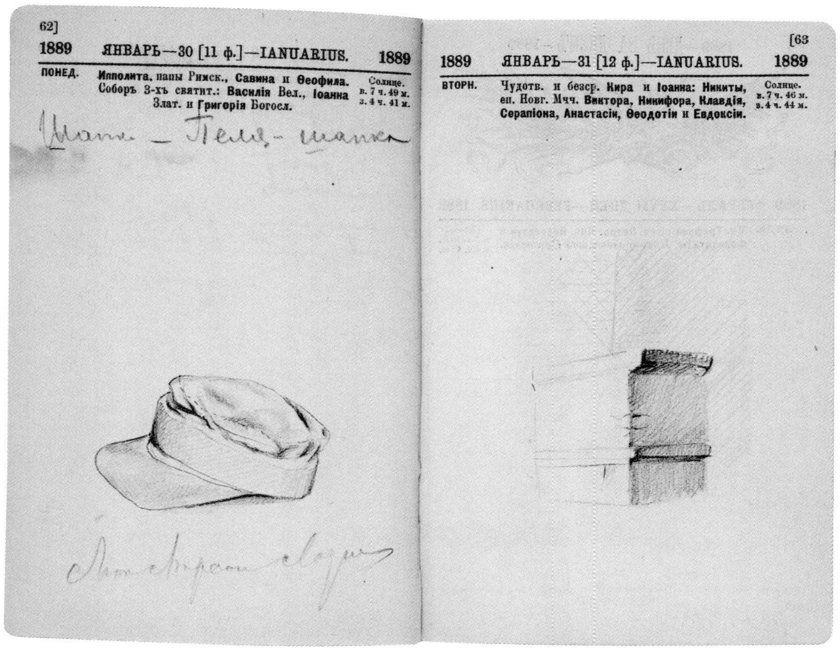


1, pp.62-63

REFERENCES
Roethel and Hahl-Koch 1980, p.38, ill.23
Derouet and Boissel 1984, p.15, ill.
Hahl-Koch 1993, p.36, ill.27
Weiss 1995, pp.16, 17, ill.19
*Kandinsky: Opere dal Centre Georges Pompidou* exh. cat. (Milan, 1997), p.54, ill.

Kandinsky wrote 'leather belt' above and then 'system of unfolding of leaves of a brightly colored table' followed by a list of colors corresponding to the letters in the sketch: 'a- red, b- yellow, c- blue, d- yellow, e- green, f- white, blue --- - red.' At the lower left he noted 'with an attached tassel and a screw.'

**p.51**
19 [31] January 1889
Pencil drawing of a man's clothes and accessories
Inscribed u.l. in Cyrillic: 'kotomka' (sack); c.r.: 'dlia kotomki' (for the sack); l.r.: 'nakamarnik' (net against mosquitoes)

REFERENCES
Derouet and Boissel 1984, p.15, ill.
Weiss 1995, pp.16, 17, ill.19
*Kandinsky: Opere dal Centre Georges Pompidou* exh. cat. (Milan, 1997), p.54, ill.

Kandinsky has shown the man with a hood ('malicha') covering his head with and without mosquito netting. See also p.53 (below).

**p.52** Blank

**p.53**
21 January [2 February] 1889
Pencil drawing of man's head covered with hood

**p.62**
30 January [11 February] 1889
Pencil drawing of cap
Inscribed u.c. in Cyrillic: 'shapka – Pelia- shapka'; l.c.: 'Choc. chapeau-claque'

Kandinsky wrote 'hat – Pelia- hat' in Russian whereas the notes below appear to be in French.

**p.63**
31 January [12 February] 1889
Pencil drawing of architectural detail

**p.64** Blank

**p.65**
2 [14] February 1889
Pencil drawing of landscape
Inscribed l.l. in Cyrillic: 'Ust'-Kulym / 21 Iun' 89'

REFERENCES
Grohmann 1958, pp.20, ill.8, 31
Roethel and Hahl-Koch 1980, ill.19
Hahl-Koch 1993, p.36, ill.25
Sarabianov and Avtonomova 1994, p.107, ill.
Barnett and Friedel 1995, p.34, ill.1
Weiss 1995, pp.17, 19, ill.24

The sketch was made at Ust' Kulym on 21 June 1889.

1, p.65

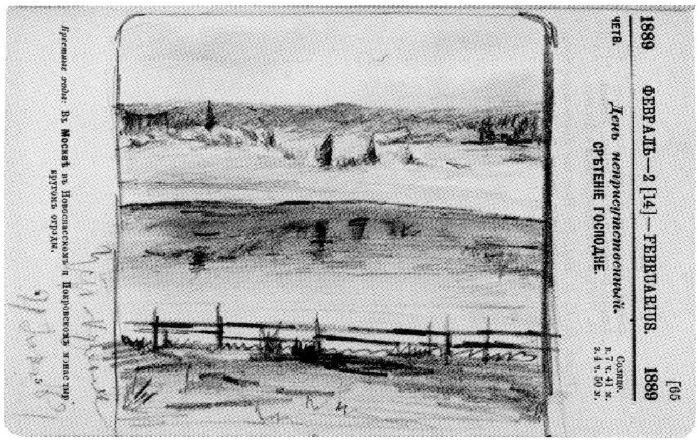

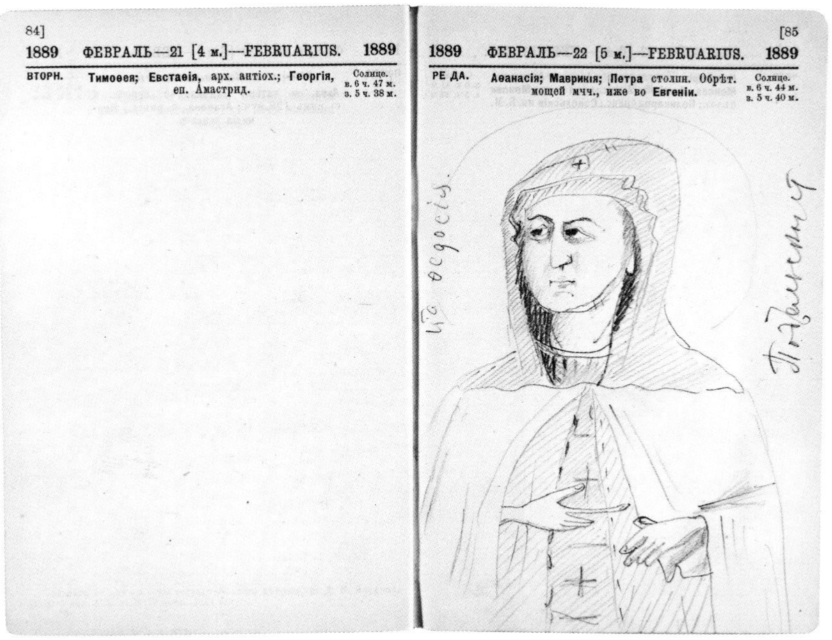


1, pp.84-85

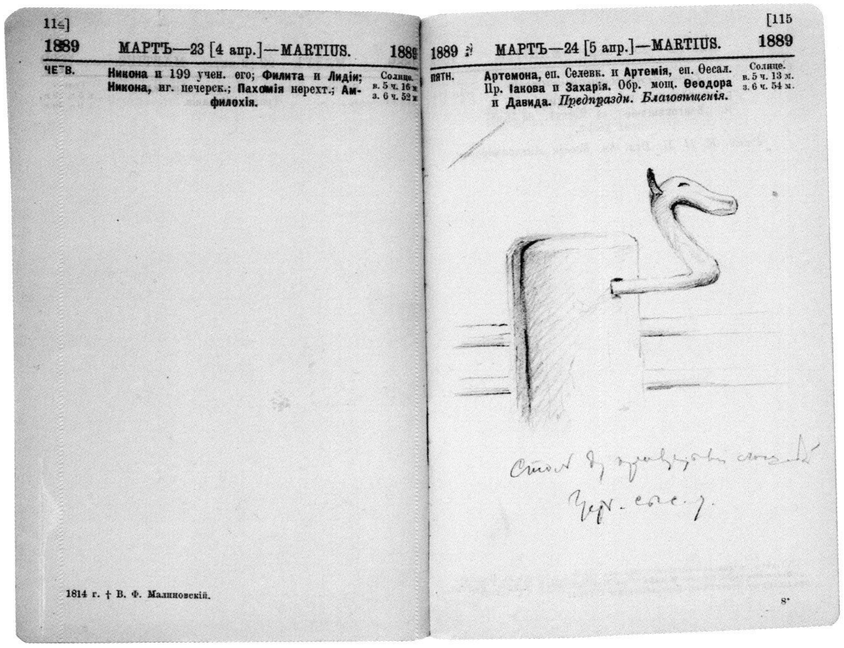


1, pp.114-115

**p.84** Blank

**p.85**
22 February [5 March] 1889
Pencil drawing of St. Theodora
Inscribed c.l. in Cyrillic: 'Sv. Feodosiia'; c.r.: 'Pod'el'skii st'

REFERENCES
Roethel and Hahl-Koch 1980, ill.22
Hahl-Koch 1993, p.36, ill.26
Sarabianov and Avtonomova 1994, p.108, ill.
Weiss 1995, pp.17, 19, ill.23

The drawing depicts St. Theodosia as an icon at Podelskaya station.

**p.114** Blank

**p.115**
24 March [5 April] 1889
Pencil drawing of pole for tying up horses
Inscribed l.c. in Cyrillic: 'stolb dlia priviazyvaniia loshadei / Ust'-Sysolsk'

The drawing depicts a 'pole for tying the horses' at Ust' Sysolsk.

**p.164**
12 [24] May 1889
Pencil drawing of man's clothing
Inscribed l.c. in Cyrillic: 'Malicha / nadevaetsia pod parku / Sever'

Kandinsky explained under the sketch: 'malicha to be put under parka' and added the word 'north'.

**p.165**
13 [25] May 1889
Pencil drawing of parka
Inscribed l.c. in Cyrillic: 'Savira (Parka)'

1, pp.164-165

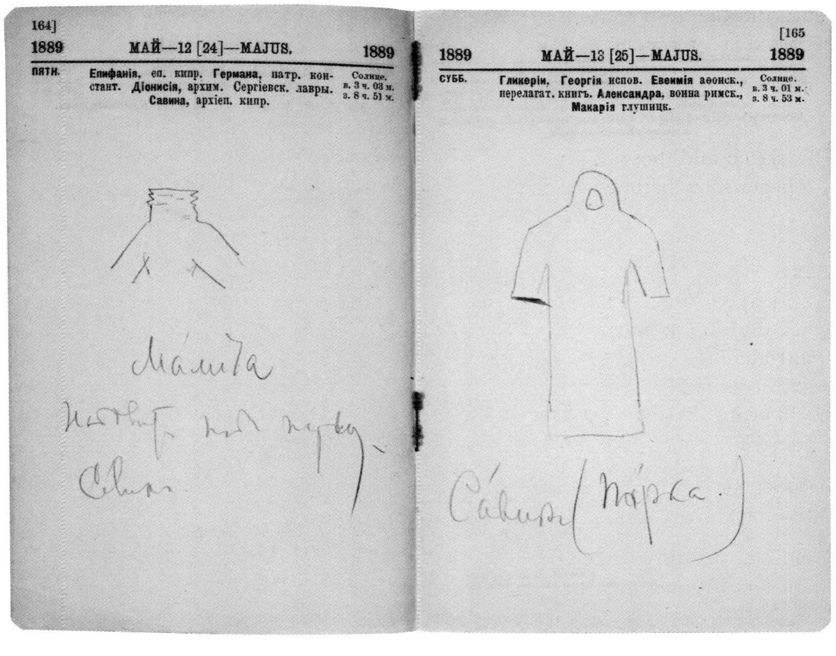

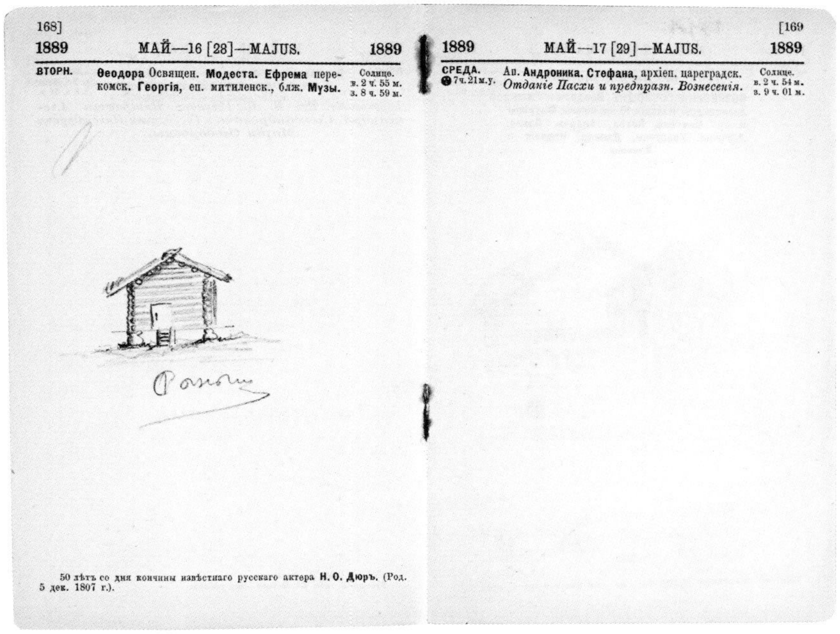


1, pp.168-169

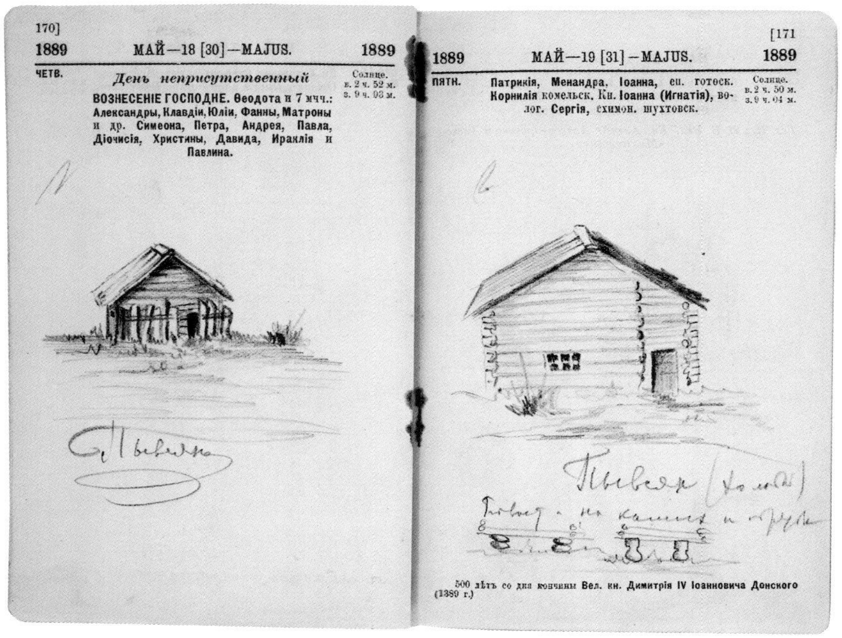


1, pp.170-171

**p.168**
16 [28] May 1889
Pencil drawing of hut
Inscribed c. in Cyrillic: 'Rynysh'

REFERENCES
Weiss 1995, pp.49, 50, ill.47

Weiss illustrated a comparative illustration of a shed for storing grain in Kerchem in Ust' Kulym.

**p.169** Blank

**p.170**
18 [30] May 1889
Pencil drawing of bathhouse
Inscribed l.c. in Cyrillic: 'Pyvsian'

REFERENCES
Weiss 1995, p.233 n.42

This sketch and those on the following two pages show bathhouses.

**p.171**
19 [31] May 1889
Pencil drawing of bathhouse and its foundations
Inscribed l.c. in Cyrillic: 'Pyvsian (kholodnyi) / Byvaet – na kamniakh i obrubiakh'

REFERENCES
Weiss 1995, p.233 n.42

Kandinsky noted: 'Pyvsian (cold) / can be on top of stones and stumps'.

**p.172**
20 May [1 June] 1889
Pencil drawing of bathhouse with dipper and grazing horse
Inscribed c. in Cyrillic: 'Pyvsian (teplyi)'; l.c.: 'kolodets'

REFERENCES
Weiss 1995, pp.17, 18, ill.21, 233 n.42
*Kandinsky: Collections du Centre Georges Pompidou* exh. cat. (Nantes, 1998), p.156, ill.

Kandinsky has shown a bathhouse with steam and noted that it was 'warm'. Below there are sketches of a well, a dipper and a grazing horse.

**p.173**
21 May [2 June] 1889
Pencil sketch of bread
Inscribed above in Cyrillic: 'iasnói, íasnoi ili / iasinyi khleb – pechet[sia] / pirogom iz iachmenia'; and below: 'soloma ne soloma, a / gorit takzhe / govoriat goriachim ego / est' vkusnee M[ozhet] B[yt']!'

REFERENCES
*Kandinsky: Collections du Centre Georges Pompidou* exh. cat. (Nantes, 1998), p.156, ill.

Kandinsky wrote: 'iasnói, iásnoi or iasinyi bread is baked as a pie from barley, straw or not straw, but it burns; also they say that it tastes better when hot. It could be!'

1, pp.172-173

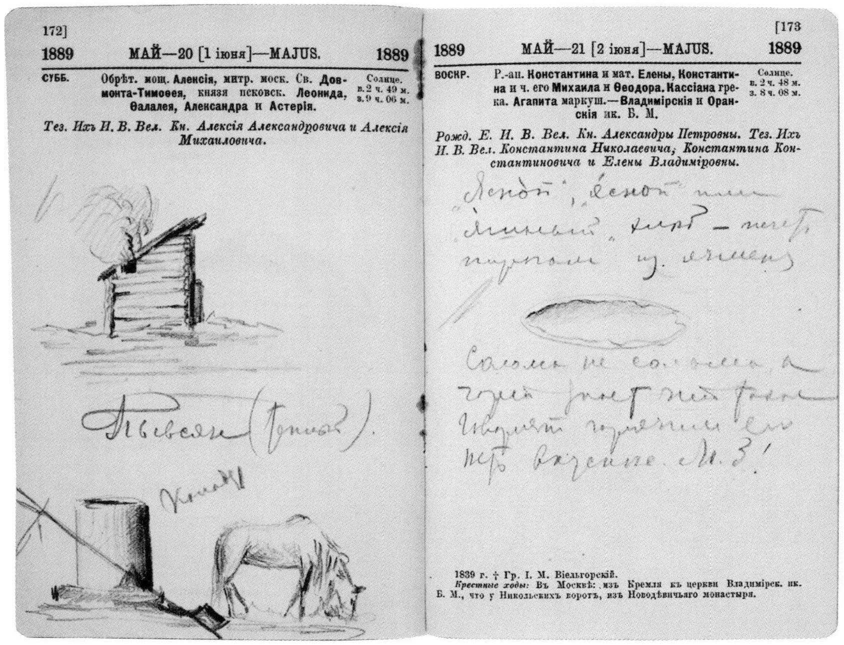

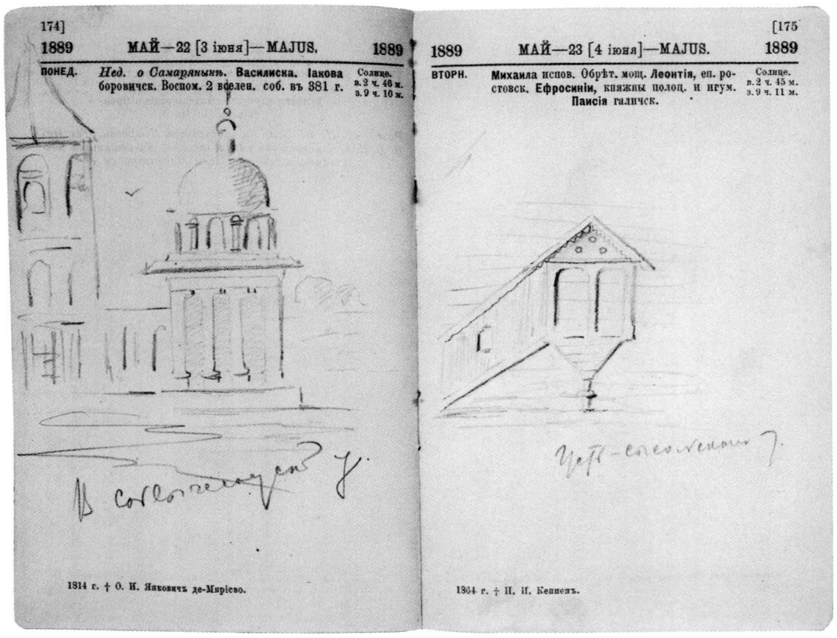


1, pp.174-175

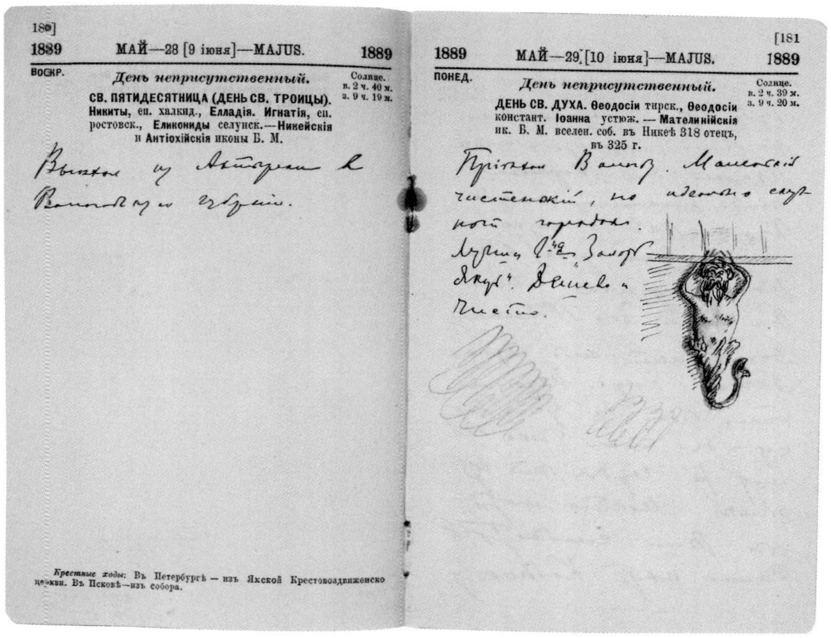


1, pp.180-181

**p.174**
22 May [3 June] 1889
Pencil drawing of building
Inscribed l.c. in Cyrillic: 'V Solvychegodskoi u[ezd]'

REFERENCES
Roethel and Hahl-Koch 1980, ill.20

Kandinsky wrote: 'in Sol'vychegodsk', which is a town north of Velikii Ustiug and far to the east of Vologda.

**p.175**
23 May [4 June] 1889
Pencil drawing of architectural detail
Inscribed l.c. in Cyrillic: 'Ust'-Sysolskogo u[ezd]'

REFERENCES
Roethel and Hahl-Koch 1980, ill.20

Kandinsky referred to 'Ust'-Sysolsk' (now Syktyvkar).

**p.180**
28 May [9 June] 1889
Inscribed u.c. in Cyrillic: 'Vyekhal iz Akhtyrki v / Vologodskuiu guberniiu'

REFERENCES
Podzemskaia 2000, p.144

Kandinsky recorded that he 'left Akhtyrka for the Vologda province' on 9 June. His relatives, the Abrikosovs, had an estate there. His cousin and future wife, Anja Shemiakina, accompanied him to the city of Vologda, where they arrived two days later.

**p.181**
29 May [10 June] 1889
Ink and pencil drawing of a decorative motif in Vologda
Inscribed u.c. in Cyrillic: 'Proekhal Vologdu. Malen'kii / chisten'kii, no ideal'no skuch / nyi gorodok / Luchshaia G[ostini]tsa "Zolotoi / Iakor"'. Deshevo i / chisto.'

REFERENCES
Weiss 1995, pp.12, 13, ill.13

Kandinsky wrote: 'Passed through Vologda. It is a small, clean, but ideally boring little town. The best hotel is the "Golden Anchor." Cheap and clean.'

**p.192**
9 [21] June 1889
Pencil sketches of harrow, plow, chapel and cart
Inscribed u.c. in Cyrillic: 'U Kobeneva nocheval i / obedal. Do 4 ch. peregovorili. / V gorod ia shel s Dmitriem / – shoptarem. Po doroge byvaiut / grabezhi i ia sta / ralsia ne spat' no usnul / dazhe pod livnem. Pro / mokshii nocheval na / vtoroi stantsii. Komary / i ovody!'; l.c.: 'borona' / sokha / chasovnia / telega'

REFERENCES
Roethel and Hahl-Koch 1980, ill.21
Hahl-Koch 1993, p.34, ill.23
Weiss 1995, pp.17, 18, ill.22
*Kandinsky: Collections du Centre Georges Pompidou* exh. cat. (Nantes, 1998), p.19, ill.

The artist identified the sketches as a harrow, plow, chapel and cart below his text, which reads: 'Spent the night and had lunch at Kobenev's. We talked until 4 o'clock. I walked to the city with Dmitrii – a shoemaker. Robberies happen on the road and I tried not to stay with strangers even under pouring rain. Soaked to the

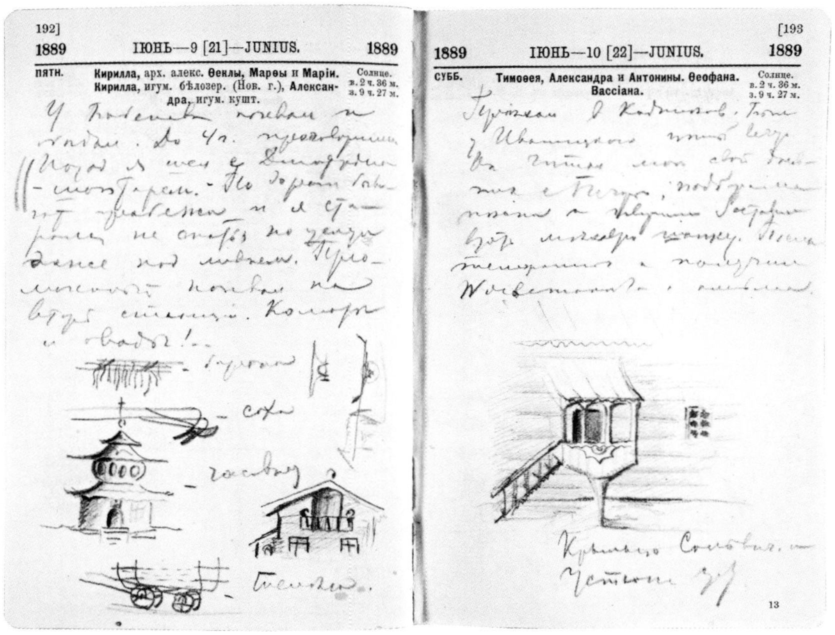


1, pp.192-193

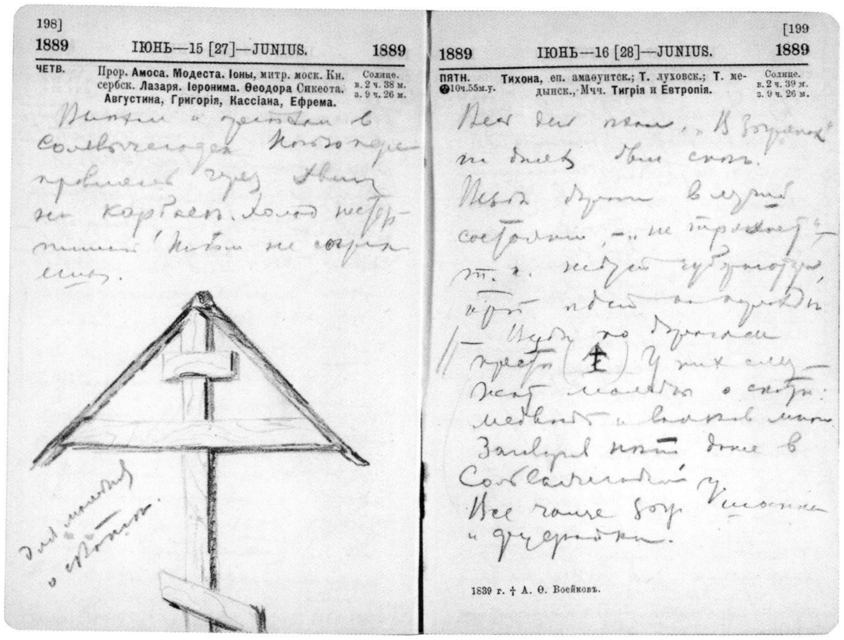


1, pp.198-199

bone, I spent the night at the second station. Mosquitoes and gad-flies!'

Roethel and Hahl-Koch identified the building as a Mongolian chapel.

**p.193**
10 [22] June 1889
Pencil sketch of architectural detail
Inscribed u.c. in Cyrillic: 'Pereekhal v Kadnikov. Byl / u Ivantitskogo tselyi vecher / on chital mne svoi dnev / nik s Pechory. Pogliadeli / ikony i govorili. Zastavili / vziat' mekhovuiu shapku. Poslal / telegrammy i poluchil Wiedermann'a i pis'ma.'; l.c.: 'kryl'tso Sol'vych[egodskogo] i / Ustiuzh[skogo] uezd[ov]'

REFERENCES
Roethel and Hahl-Koch 1980, ill.21
Hahl-Koch 1994, p.34, ill.23
Weiss 1995, pp.17, 18, ill.22
*Kandinsky: Collections du Centre Georges Pompidou* exh. cat. (Nantes 1998), p.19, ill.

Kandinsky wrote: 'Moved to Kadnikov. Spent the entire night at Ivantitskii's. He read to me his Pechora diary. [We] looked at icons and talked. [They] made me take a fur hat. Sent telegrams and received Wiedermann and letters.' Below he has depicted the porch at Sol'vychegodsk, which is in the Velikii Ustiug district.

**p.198**
15 [27] June 1889
Pencil drawing of a cross
Inscribed u.c. in Cyrillic: 'Vyekhal i priekhal v / Sol'vychegodsk. Noch'iu pere / pravlialis' cherez [...] / na korable. Kholod nester / pimyi. Nichem ne sogre / esh'sia.'

REFERENCES
Weiss 1995, p.15, ill.16

Above a sketch of a wooden cross Kandinsky wrote: '[I] departed and arrived at Sol'vychegodsk. At night, we crossed [...] on a boat. It is intolerably cold. Nothing warms one up.' Below he noted: 'for prayers about cattle.'

**p.199**
16 [28] June 1889
Inscribed in Cyrillic: 'Ves' den' ekhal. "V Zorianakh" / na dniakh byl sneg. / Vezde doroga v luchshem / sostoianii – ne "triakhaet"– / t.k. mestnyi gubernator / [...] / Vizhu po dorogam / kresty. U nikh slu- / zhat molebny o skotine: / medvedei i volkov mnogo. / Zagovorov net, dazhe v / Sol'vychegodskom u[ezde]. / Vse chashche dogr[evaius'] shapkoi / i dushegreikoi.'

Kandinsky recorded: 'I was travelling all day. It snowed "in Zoriany" recently. Here the road is in a better condition – "it does not shake you" – because the local governor [...]. I see crosses along the roads. Here [people] pray about cattle: there are many bears and wolves. There are no spells, even in Sol'vychegodsk. More and more often I warm myself up with my hat and my jacket.'

# Sketchbook 2

prepared with the assistance of Natasha Kurchanova and Elena Andreevna Kurchanova

c.1897–1900

Dark grey paper-covered notebook; no label
Contains 120 pages (60 sheets), each 14.6 x 8.6 cm (5¾ x 3⅜ in), of which pp.73–103 are blank
Page numbers inscribed by unknown hand at later date with odd numbers at lower right

Hanfstaengl 1974, p.167

LOCATION
Städtische Galerie im Lenbachhaus, Munich (GMS 346)

HISTORY
Gabriele Münter, Murnau, until 1957

The lower part of the notebook has been stained with oil, which has resulted in stains at the bottom center of the two-page spreads. Since many of the pages contain notes in barely legible Cyrillic and diagrams rather than sketches, a selection has been made and not all of the schematic drawings are illustrated. The first section is primarily in Russian; however, the back of the notebook has notes written in the inverse direction primarily in German with dates in March–April 1900.

**p.1** Pencil diagram of arm muscles flexed
Inscribed u.c. in Cyrillic and German: 'Muskel / Gewehbe (ausser Sehne) [...] / (tochki v pokoe) / Kombinatsii / dvizhenii / Oberschenkelhaut / privodit v dvizhenie srazu 3 kosti / doppelwirkende Muskeln / per (biceps).' and l.c.: 'Podvizhnyi stolb, 34 dvizheniia (7+12+15) / [...] i sviazki pozvonkov. / Sviazki (speredi i szadi vo vsiu dlinu stolba) / [...] socrashcheniia pri peregibakh / (sheia 14:11 cm) / priamo pri izgibakh'

**p.2** Pencil schematic drawing of movement of the spine of four-legged animal (above) and schematic drawing of a thorax inhaling and exhaling (below)

**p.3** Pencil schematic drawing of chest inhaling and exhaling (below)

Above there are notes about the spinal column and the movement of the spine from the neck down to the chest.

2, p.1

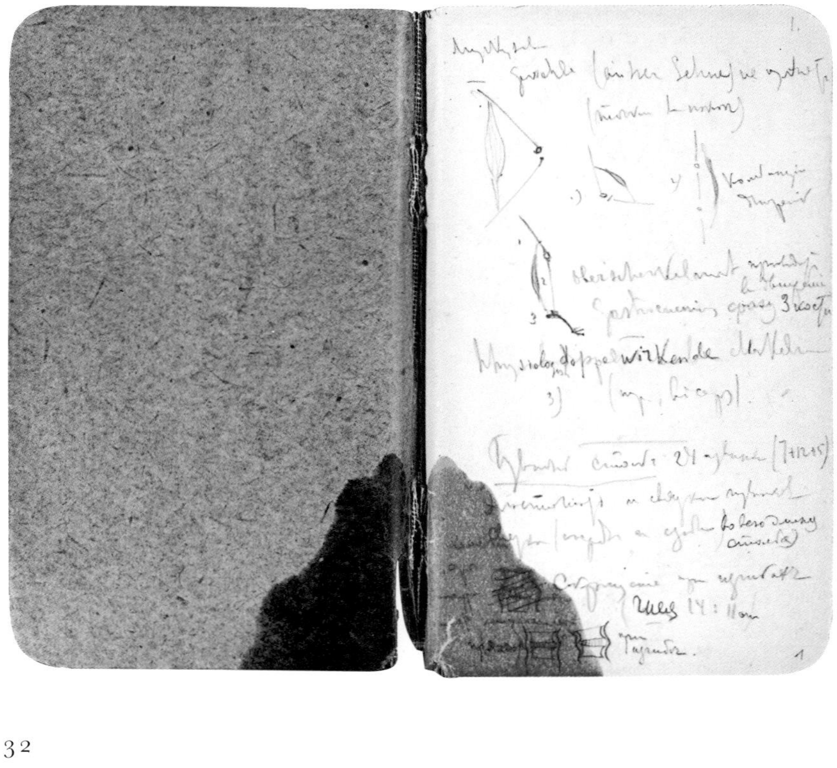

2, pp.2-3

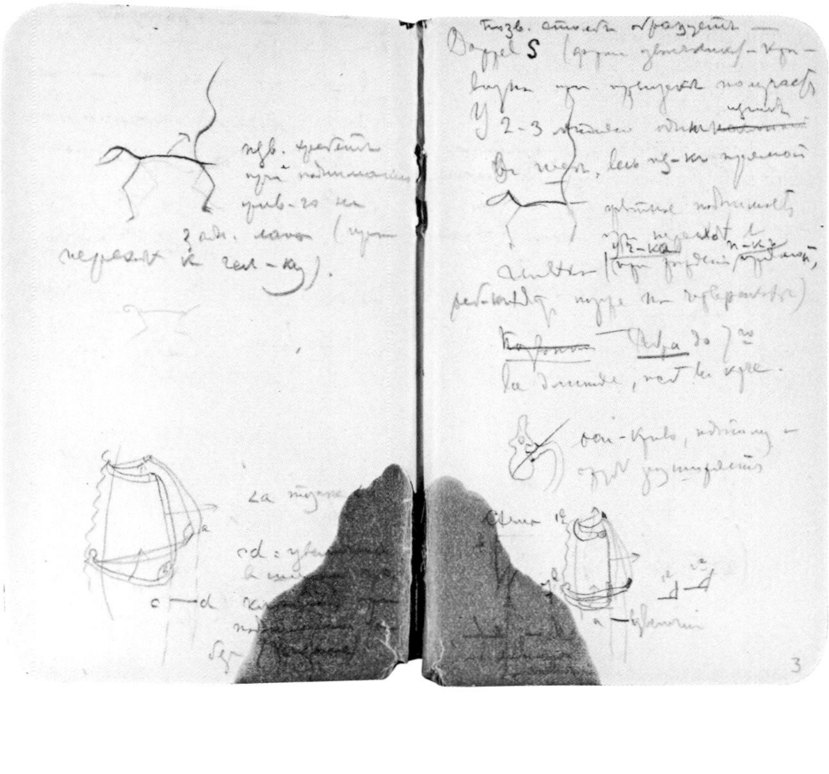

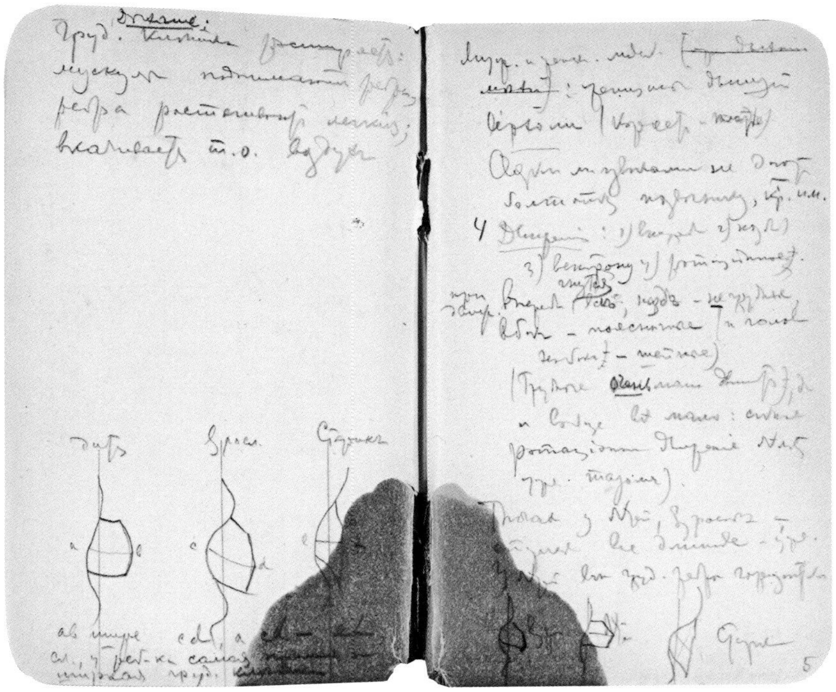

2, pp.4-5

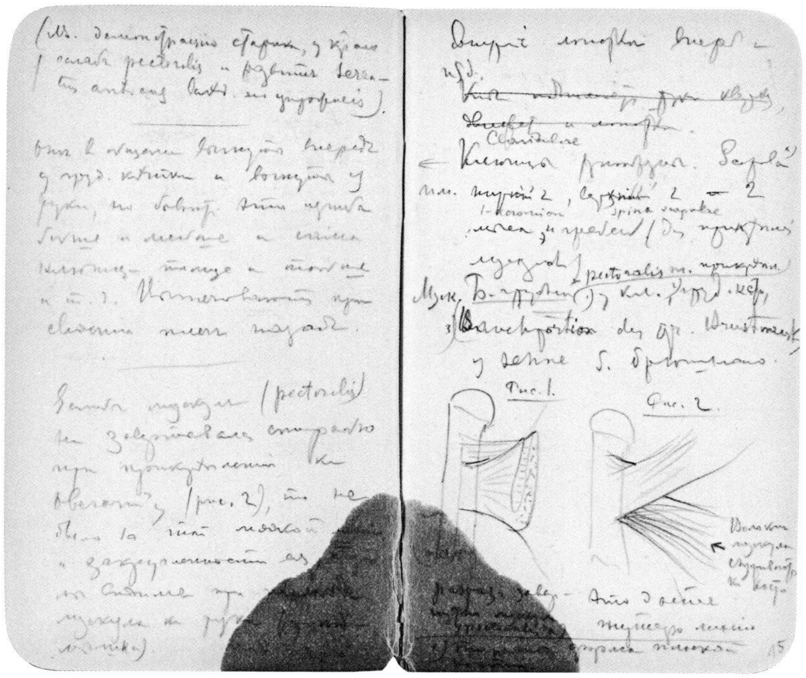

2, pp.14-15

**p.4** Pencil schematic drawings of chest expansion in child, adult and old man

**p.5** Notes about chest expansion and breathing in women
Inscribed u.c. in Cyrillic: 'Muzh[skaia] i zhen[skaia] model'. Zhenshchiny dyshat verkhom (korset i plat'e) … ne daiut boltatat'sia pozvonochniku […]. 4 dvizheniia 1) vpered 2) nazad 3) v storonu 4) rotatsionnoe. Pri dvizhenii vpered gnutsia ([…] nazad – na grudnye, vbok – poiasnichnye, i golova nabok – sheinye.) (Grudnye ochen' malo dvigaiutsia, da i voobshche vse malo: sgib, rotatsionnye dvizheniia […]). Thorax […]

**p.6** Pencil schematic drawing of woman's thorax (not illustrated)

**pp.7–14** Notes in Cyrillic about anatomy

**p.15** Pencil drawing of a cross-section of muscle and the attachment of muscle to bone

**pp.16** Notes in Cyrillic about pectoral muscles

**p.17** Pencil drawing of the ribs and the latissimus dorsi muscles

2, pp.16-17

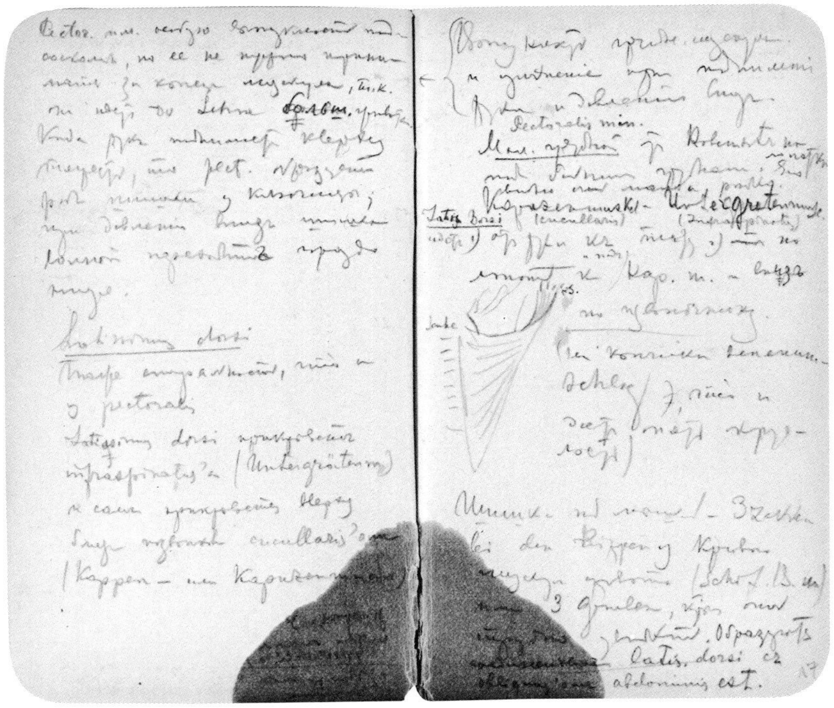

**pp.18–19** Notes in Cyrillic

**p.20** Pencil sketch of the back muscles during movements of the shoulder blades
Inscribed u.l.: '[...] / Rhomb. / lat. dors.'

**p.21** Notes in Cyrillic

**p.22** Pencil drawing of deltoid and latissimus dorsi muscles in arm
Inscribed u.l.: 'delt. / [...] / Kl. hinther'; l.r. in Cyrillic: 'sukhor[ukii] / Musk[ul]'

**p.23** Notes in Cyrillic

**p.24** Pencil drawing of arm and shoulder movement during lifting and lowering
Inscribed u.c. in Cyrillic: 'podnimanie / i opuskanie' and in German: 'Stellungsverenderung / der Schulter- / platte / Lageverenderung / d.S.'

REFERENCES
Hanfstaengl 1974, p.167, ill.

**pp.25–27** Notes in Cyrillic

**p.28** Pencil sketch of upper torso of skeleton with raised arms

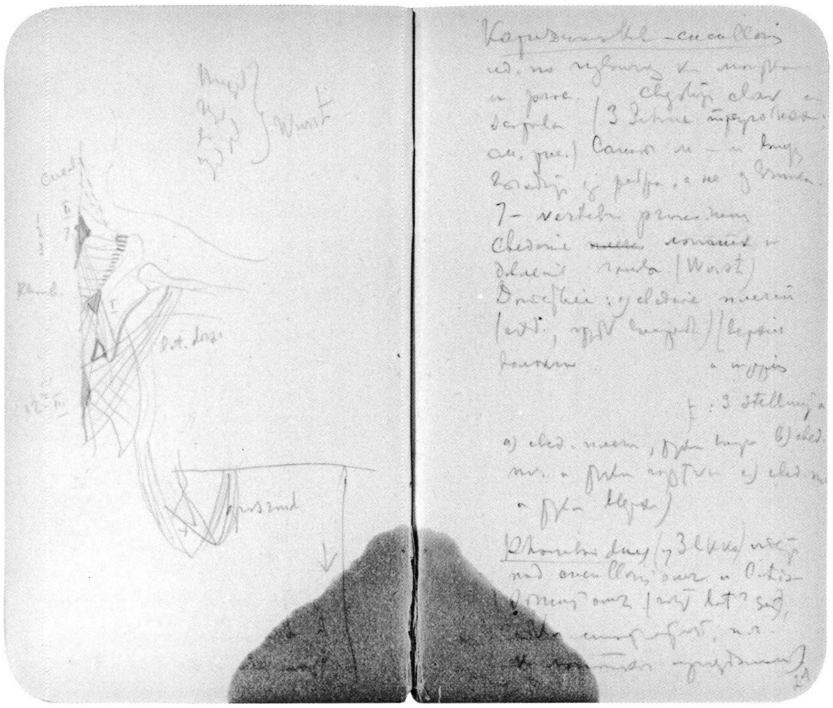

2, pp.20-21

2, pp.22-23

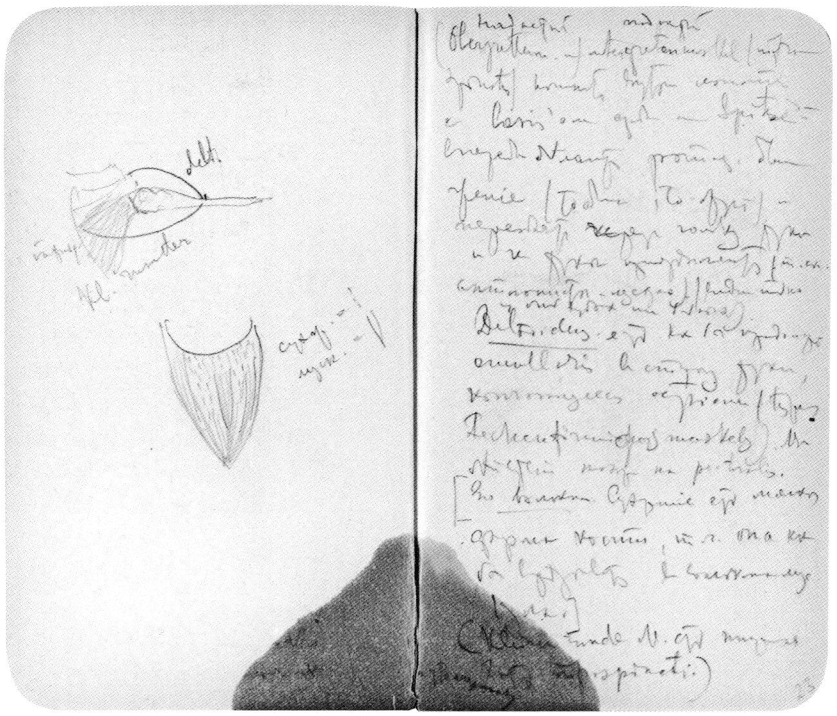

2, pp.24-25

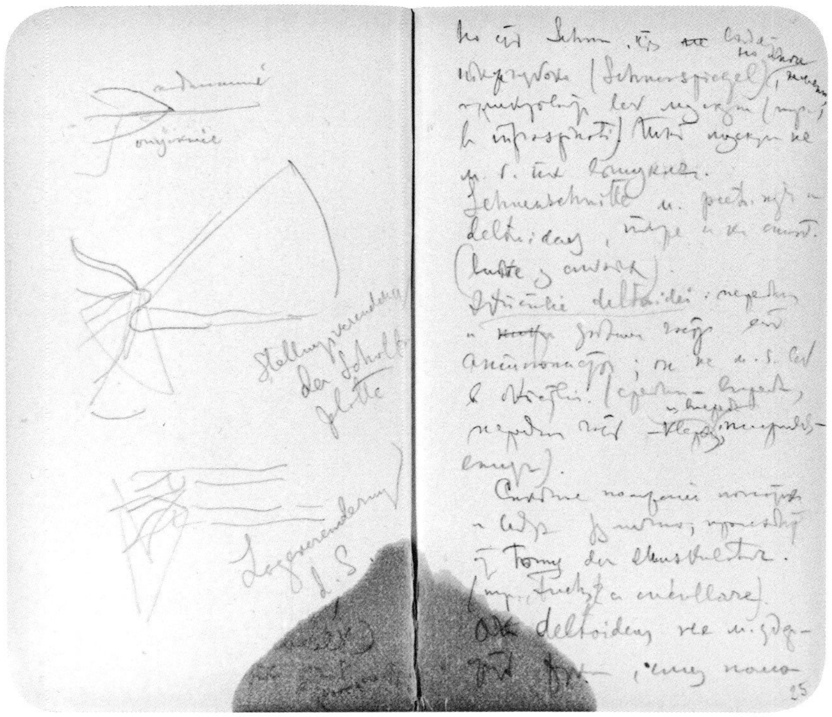

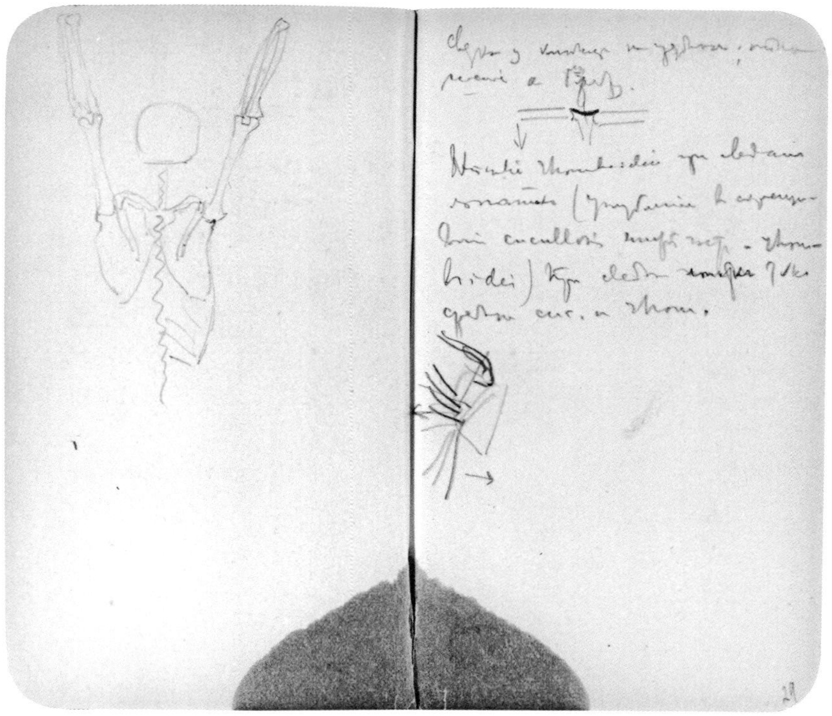

2, pp.28-29

**pp.29–33** Notes in Cyrillic and diagrams

**p.34** Pencil sketch of ribs and scalene muscles
Inscribed c.r.: 'Scalenae / Rippenheber'; l.r. in Cyrillic: 'nerv'

REFERENCES
Podzemskaia 2000, p.32, fig.8

**pp.35–37** Notes in Cyrillic

**p.38** Pencil sketch of arm (not illustrated)
Inscribed c.: 'biceps / triceps'

**pp.39–41** Notes in Cyrillic

**p.42** Pencil sketch of shoulder (above) and articulating joints (below) (not illustrated)

**p.43** Notes in Cyrillic

**p.44** Pencil sketch of movement of hand
Inscribed c.l.: 'Radialseite / Streckerseite'; c.l.: 'Beuger / 1) pronator teres / 2) radial Beuger der Hand'

**p.45** Notes in German about movement of hand

2, pp.34-35

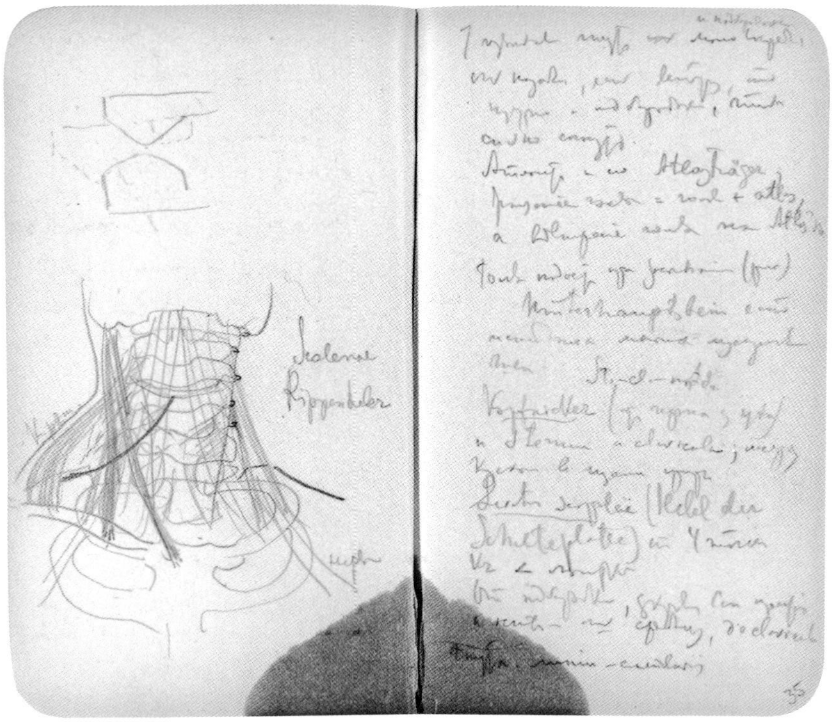

2, pp.44-45

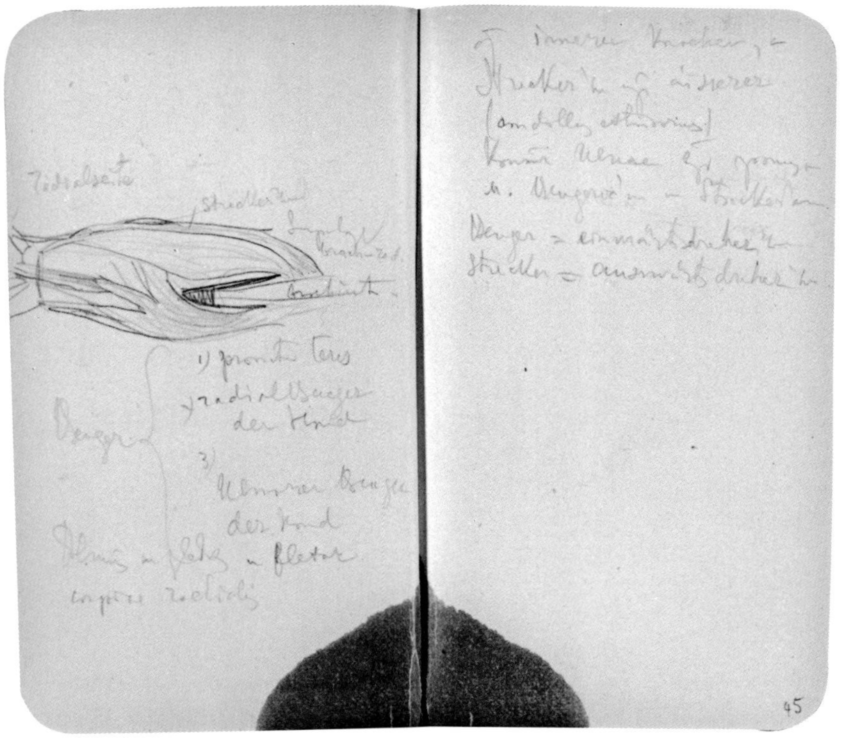

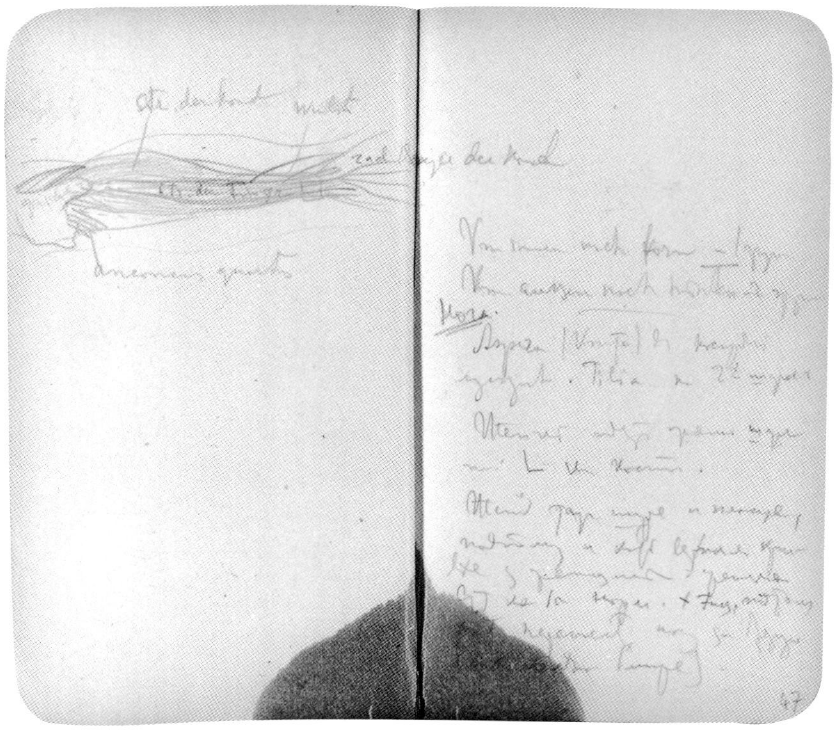

2, pp.46-47

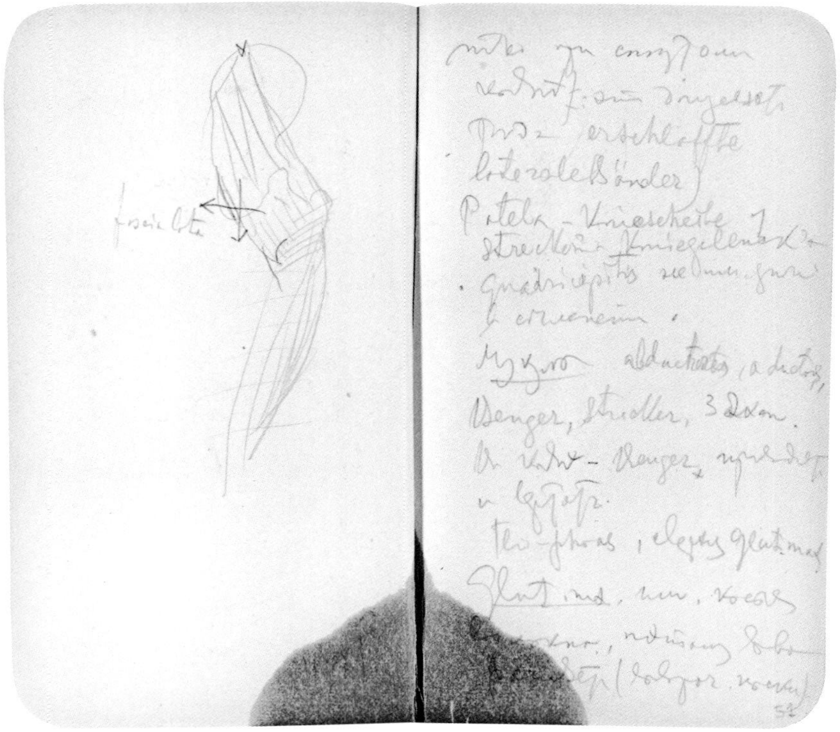

2, pp.50-51

**p.46** Pencil sketch of movement of hand
Inscribed u.c.: 'Str[ecker] der Hand / Wulst / str[ecker] der Finger / rad Beuger der Hand'

**pp.47–49** Notes in Cyrillic and German

**p.50** Pencil sketch of leg
Inscribed: 'fascia lata'

**p.51** Notes in Cyrillic and German

**p.52** Pencil sketches of leg
Inscribed: '(ge)kwätschen / gl. / mx. / glut. med / quadric / aductores ins Schmalbein / sert.'

REFERENCES
Hanfstaengl 1974, p.167, ill.
Barnett and Friedel 1995, no.4, color ill.

**p.53** Notes in Cyrillic and German

**p.54** Pencil sketch of thigh muscles
Inscribed: l.c.: 'aduct.'

**pp.55–57** Notes in Cyrillic and German

**p.58** Pencil sketch of hip and femur (not illustrated)

**pp.59–61** Notes in Cyrillic and German

**p.62** Pencil sketches of ankle (above) and hip and pelvis (below)

**pp.63–71** Notes in Cyrillic and German

**p.72** Pencil sketch of cartilage
Inscribed u.r.: 'Gewebe / Knorp[e]l / Knoch[en] / Kalk [?] in der Knrpl / Band f. Haut / Lamellensystem.'

On the basis of the artist's handwriting and knowledge of German, this sketch was done at a later date than those on the first page of this sketchbook.

**pp.73–103** Blank

**p.105** Blank

**pp.104, 106–118** Notes about binding agents and paint (upside down) listing: 'Leim / Gips / Kaolin / Mohnöl / Honig'

**p.107** Inscribed (upside down): '19 IV 900 / 21 IV 900'

**p.109** Inscribed (upside down): '9 IV 900 / 11 IV 900'

**p.111** Inscribed (upside down): '9 IV 900'

**p.115** Inscribed (upside down): '26 III 900'

**pp.119–120** Diagrammatic drawings of perspective

REFERENCES
Hanfstaengl 1974, p.167
Podzemskaia 2000, p.33

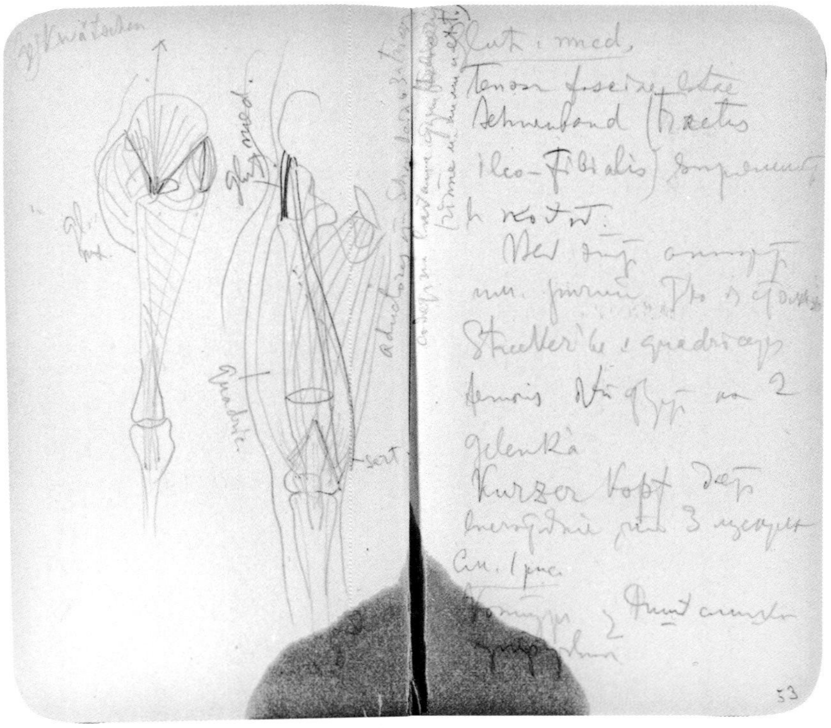

2, pp.52-53

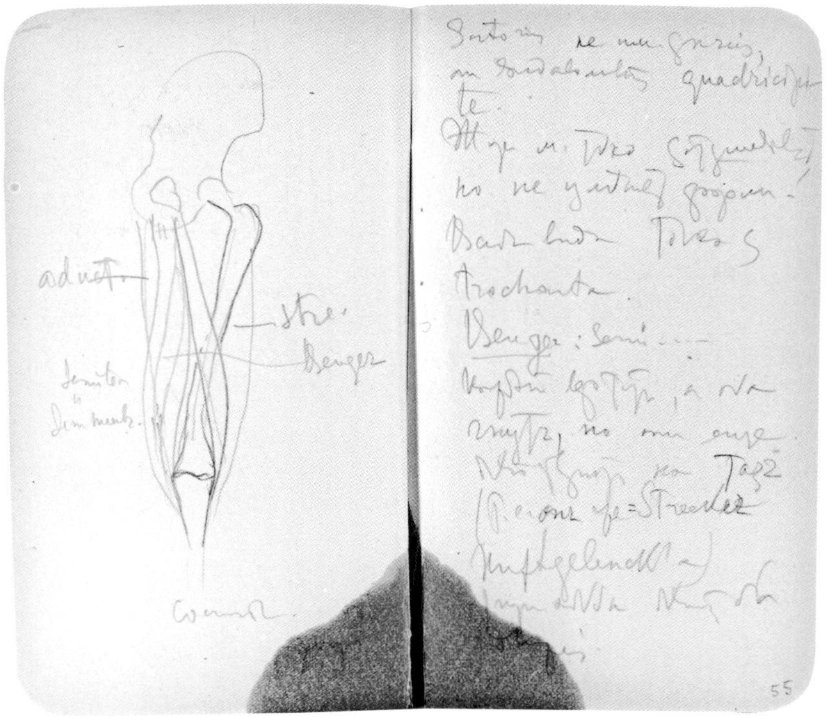

2, pp.54-55

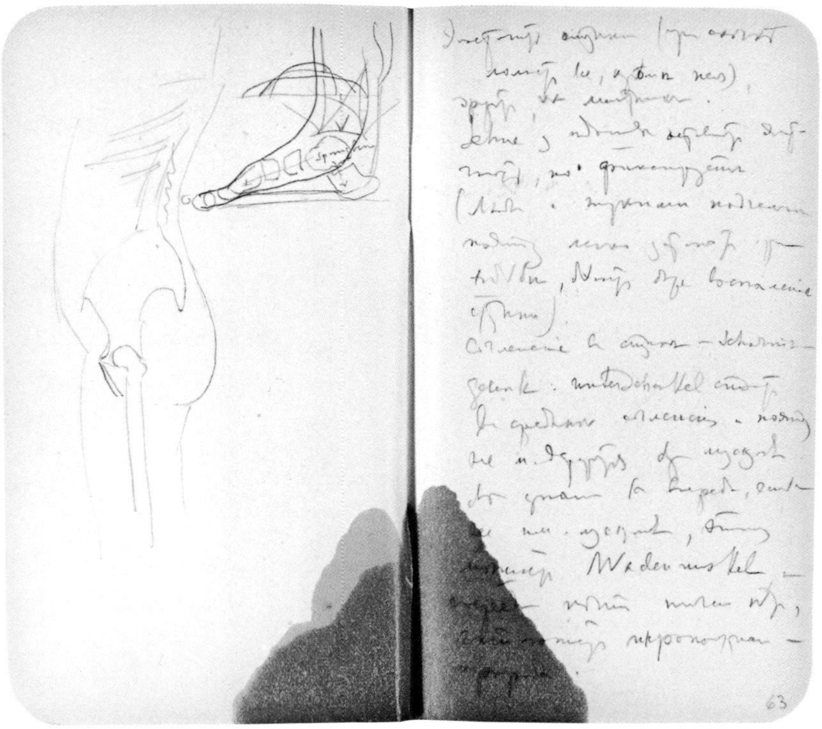

2, pp.62-63

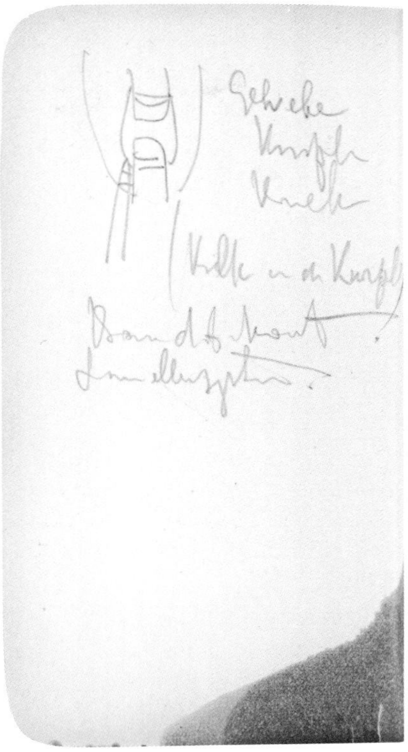

2, p.72

# Sketchbook 3

1897–1900 and 1909–1911

Black cardboard sketchbook with black corners and spine; no label
Contains 54 pages (27 sheets), each 34.5 x 21.5 cm ($13^{5}/_{8}$ x $8^{1}/_{2}$ in), of which pp.36–47 are blank. Several pages have been torn out.
Page numbers inscribed by unknown hand at later date with odd numbers at lower right

Hanfstaengl 1974, pp.163–164

LOCATION
Städtische Galerie im Lenbachhaus, Munich (GMS 344)

HISTORY
Gabriele Münter, Murnau, until 1957

Kandinsky probably used this sketchbook while studying anatomy with Anton Azbè in 1897–1898 and then about 1900 before putting it aside for almost a decade. The first and last pages were done first; pp.48–52 were drawn at a later date.

**p.1** Pencil and red chalk studies of heads (sheet partially torn)
Inscribed u.r.: 'proc. zygomat. / Joch- / bein / Jochbogen / os. zygmaticum / Warzen- / fortsatz / proc. mastoideus / Hinterhauptsdom / Sp. occipitalis / proc. mast.'

**p.2** Red chalk studies of legs (sheet partially torn)

**p.3** Pencil and red chalk studies of heads and seated figures
Inscribed u.l.: 'm. frontalis / orbiabris / oculi / M. lev. con […] / b. propris / 2g min. / 2. major / lev. ang. oris'; c.l.: 'orbiabris / z+zyg. m. + lev. ang. oris / depressor angulae' and extensive annotations in Cyrillic and Latin

EXHIBITIONS
1982 New York, no.79, ill.
1982 Munich, no.8, ill.

REFERENCES
Hanfstaengl 1974, p.163, ill.
Weiss 1979, p.17, ill.2
Barnett and Friedel 1995, no.6, color ill.

Kandinsky may have done these drawings while studying with Anton Azbè in Munich. The seated female figure at the lower left is reminiscent of Azbè's painting *Weiblicher Halbakt* of 1888 (Narodna Galerija, Ljubljana). The posterior view of a head and neck bears a certain resemblance to an illustration in *Anatomie für Künstler: Kurzgefasste Anatomie, Mechanik und Proportionslehre des Menschlichen Körpers* by August Froriep (Leipzig, 1880, fig.8).

(See color plate p.113)

**p.4** Blank

3, p.1

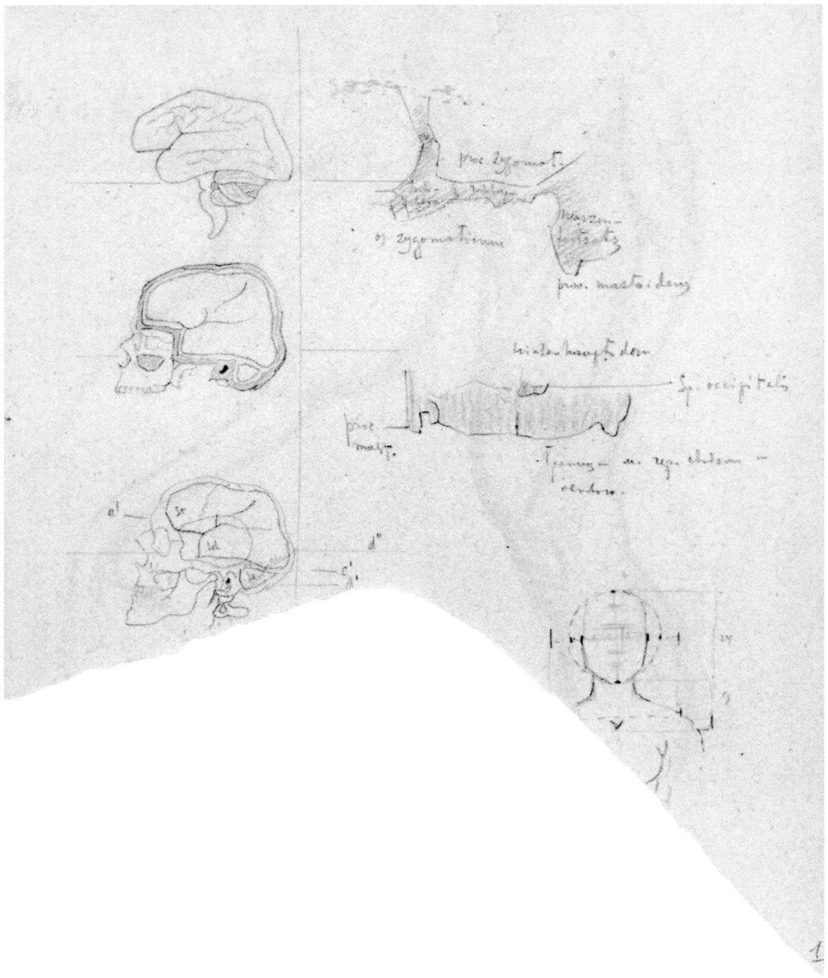

3, p.2

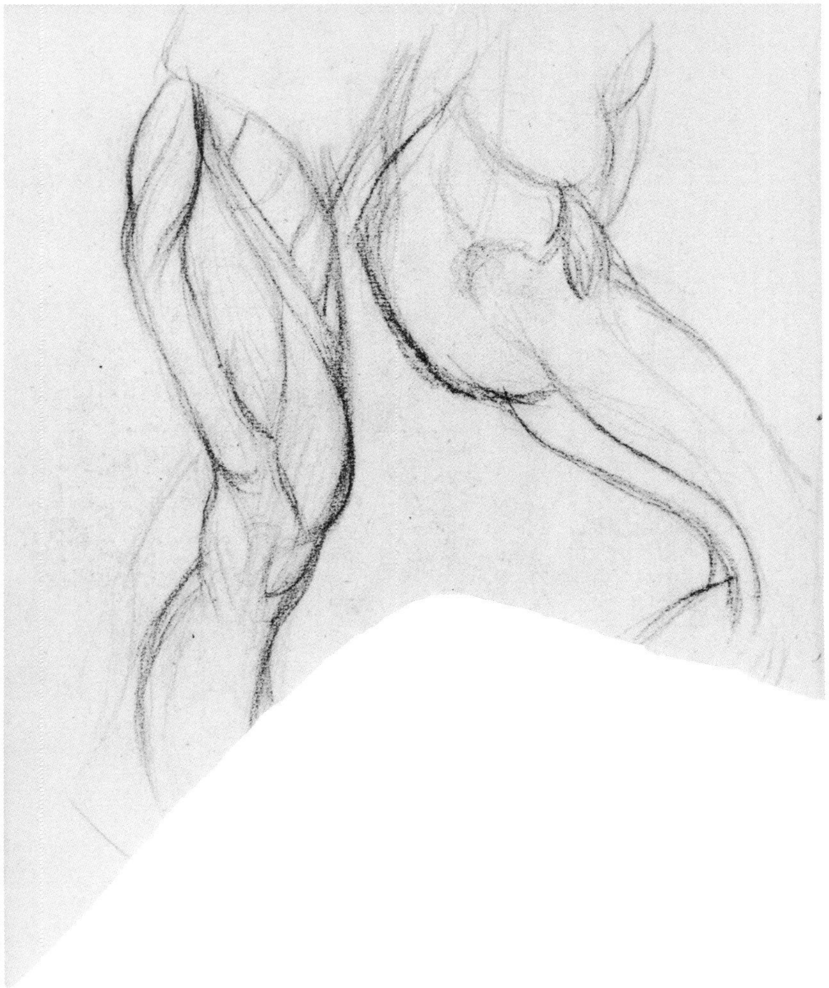

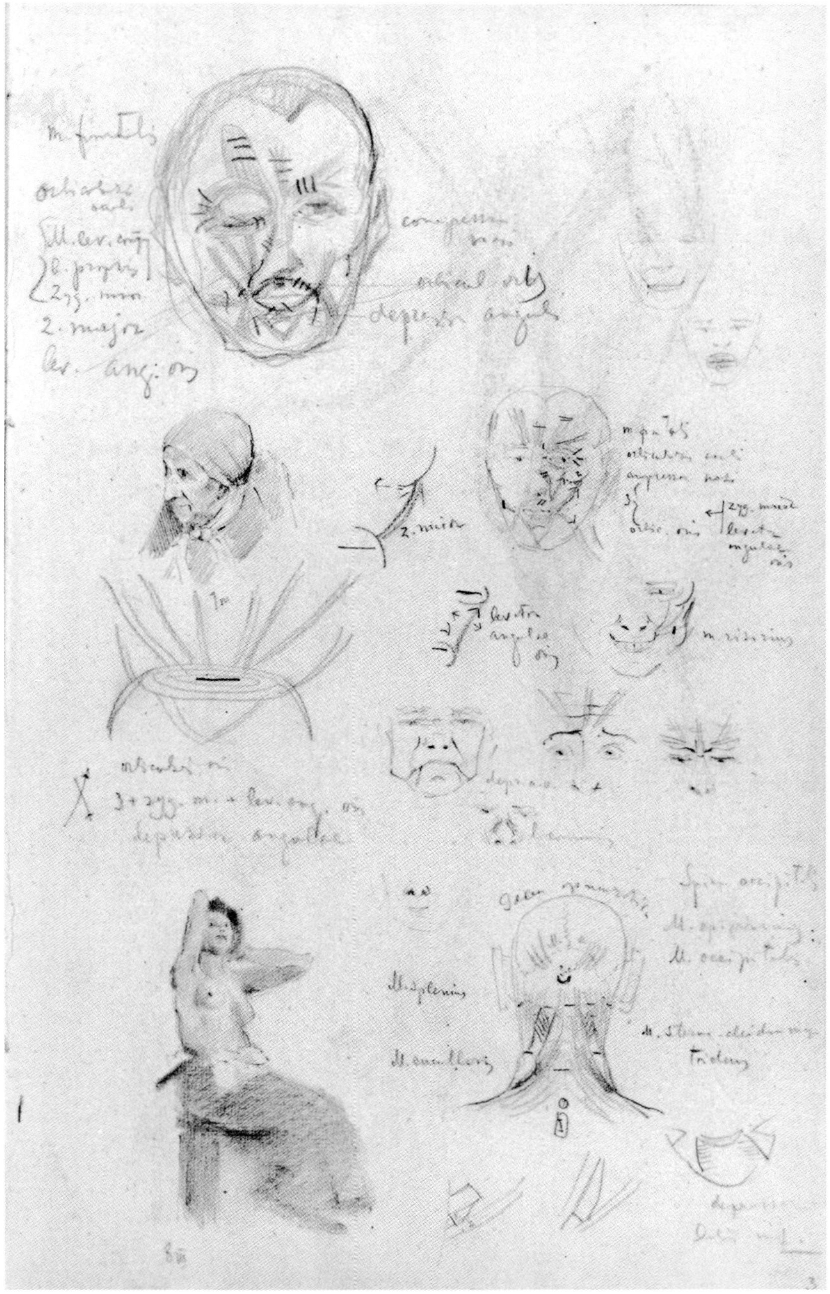

3, p.3

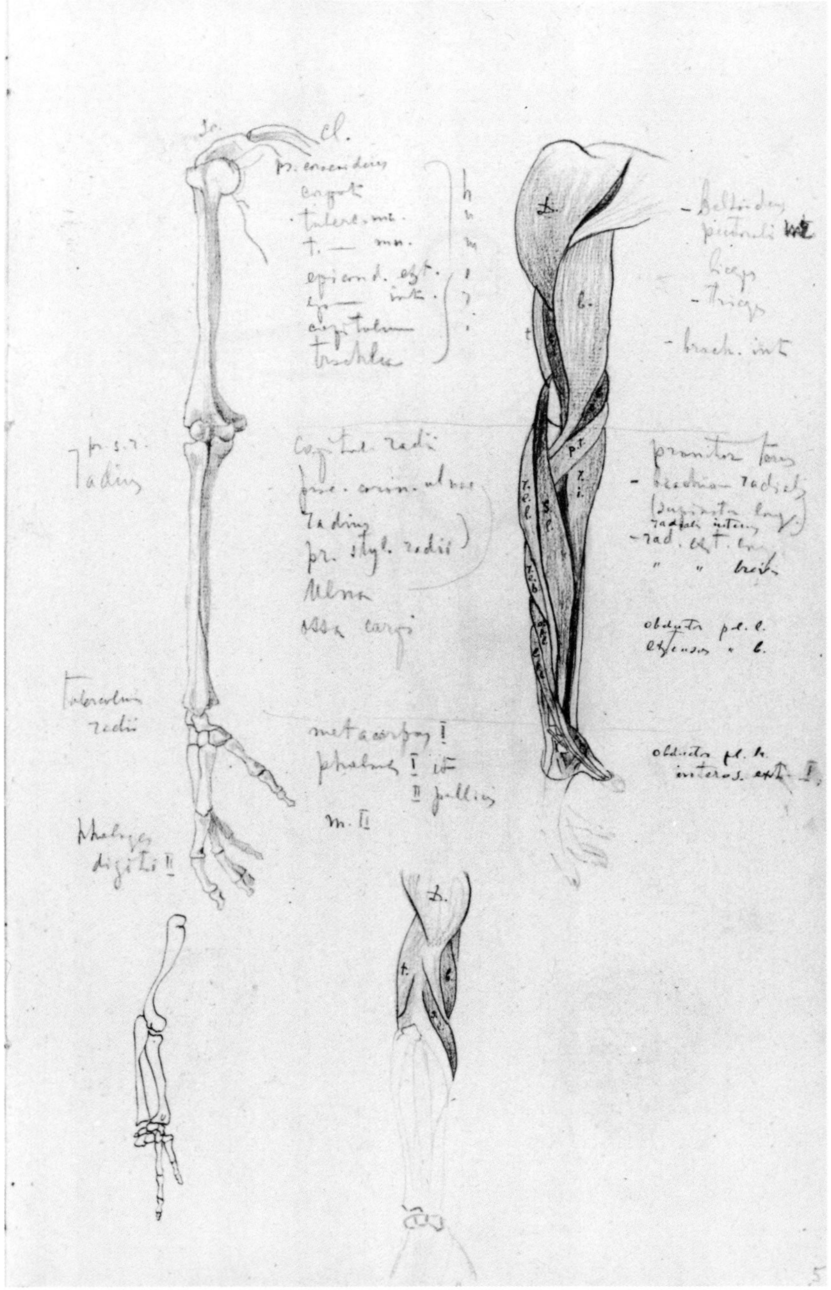

3, p.5

**p.5** Ink, pencil and crayon studies of arms and hands
Inscribed c.l.: 'pr. s.r. / radius / capital. radii / phalanges digitali II'; u.r.: 'Deltoides / pectoralis mr / biceps / triceps / brach int'; c.r.: 'pronator teres / brachio-radialis / (supinator long.) / radialis intern / rad.ext. long. / [rad. ext.] brevis / abductor pd. l. / extensor pd. b.'

REFERENCES
Hanfstaengl 1974, p.164, ill.

The drawing of an arm at the left resembles fig.16 in August Froriep's book *Anatomie für Künstler: Kurzgefasste Anatomie, Mechanik und Proportionslehre des Menschlichen Körpers*, and the drawing of the arm muscles on the right is similar to the adjacent illustration (fig.17) in the same book. Kandinsky owned a copy of Froriep's book, which was published in Leipzig in 1880.

**p.6** Blank

**p.7** Pencil study of man presented in proportion and drawing of head
Inscribed u.c.: 'ronde– 7 1/3'

Kandinsky's drawing shows the ratio of the man's head to his body with one arm extended. It can be related to illustrations in Froriep's book of a man who is 175 cm high and has an arm outstretched (fig.VII) and to a proportional drawing without the figure (fig.IX). However, the detail of a head is not depicted in Froriep's book.

**p.8** Red chalk drawings of legs (lateral views)
Inscribed c.: 'T[ensor] f[asciae] / Gl[uteus] max. / F[ascia] l[ata] / bicep / V[astus] lat[eralis]. / G[astrocnemius]'; l.l.: 'Licht. Ocker- 1/2 - 9 n. / […] L. - […]- 19 n.'

3, p.7

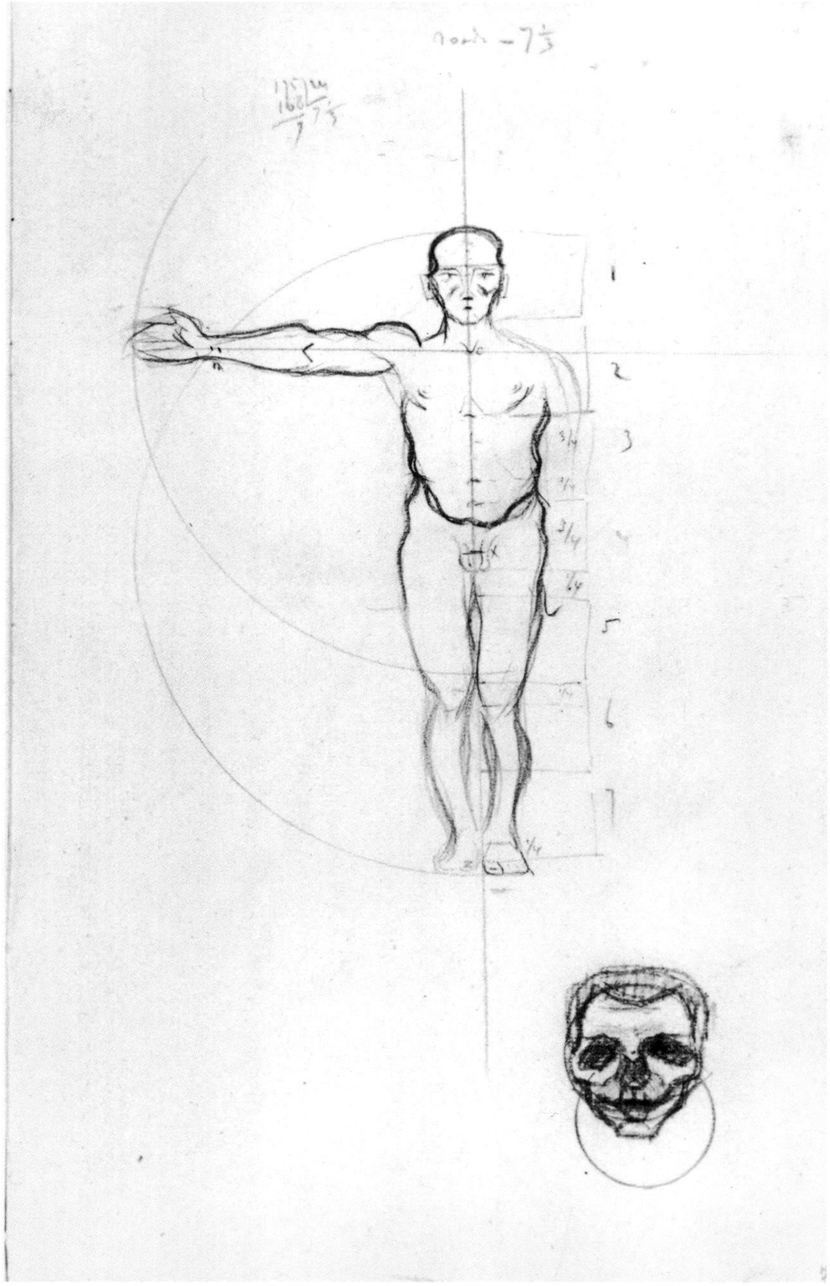

3, p.8

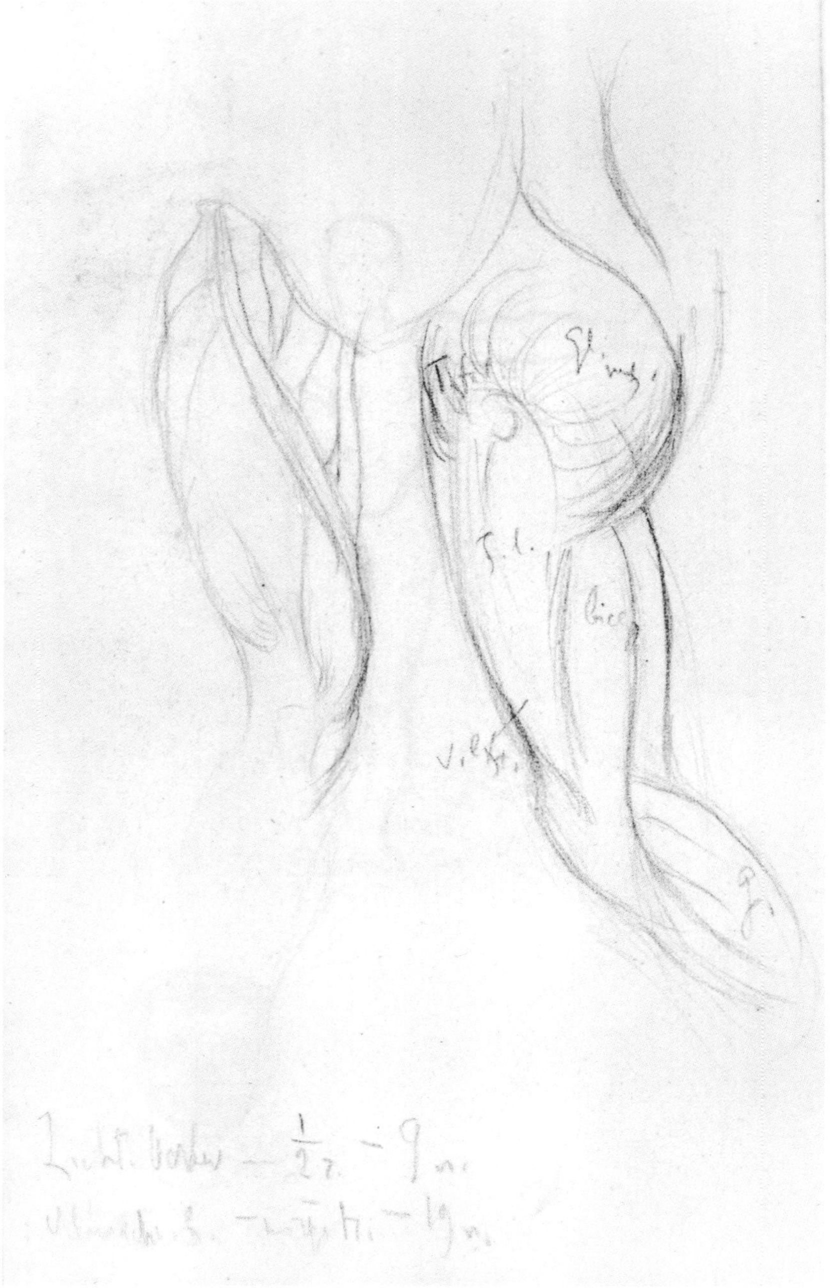

**p.9** Pencil and red chalk drawings of human legs and feet (anterior views)

**p.10** Brown crayon drawing of dog

The sketch brings to mind *Kind und Hund* painted in early 1904 (Roethel and Benjamin no.114) which depicts Kandinsky's dog Daisy. She appears also in earlier pictures: *Winter* of 1901 (Barnett no.42) and *Kochel- Anja mit Daisy*, which Kandinsky painted in the summer of 1902 (Roethel and Benjamin no.57). It is not known when Kandinsky and his first wife Anja acquired the dog.

3, p.9

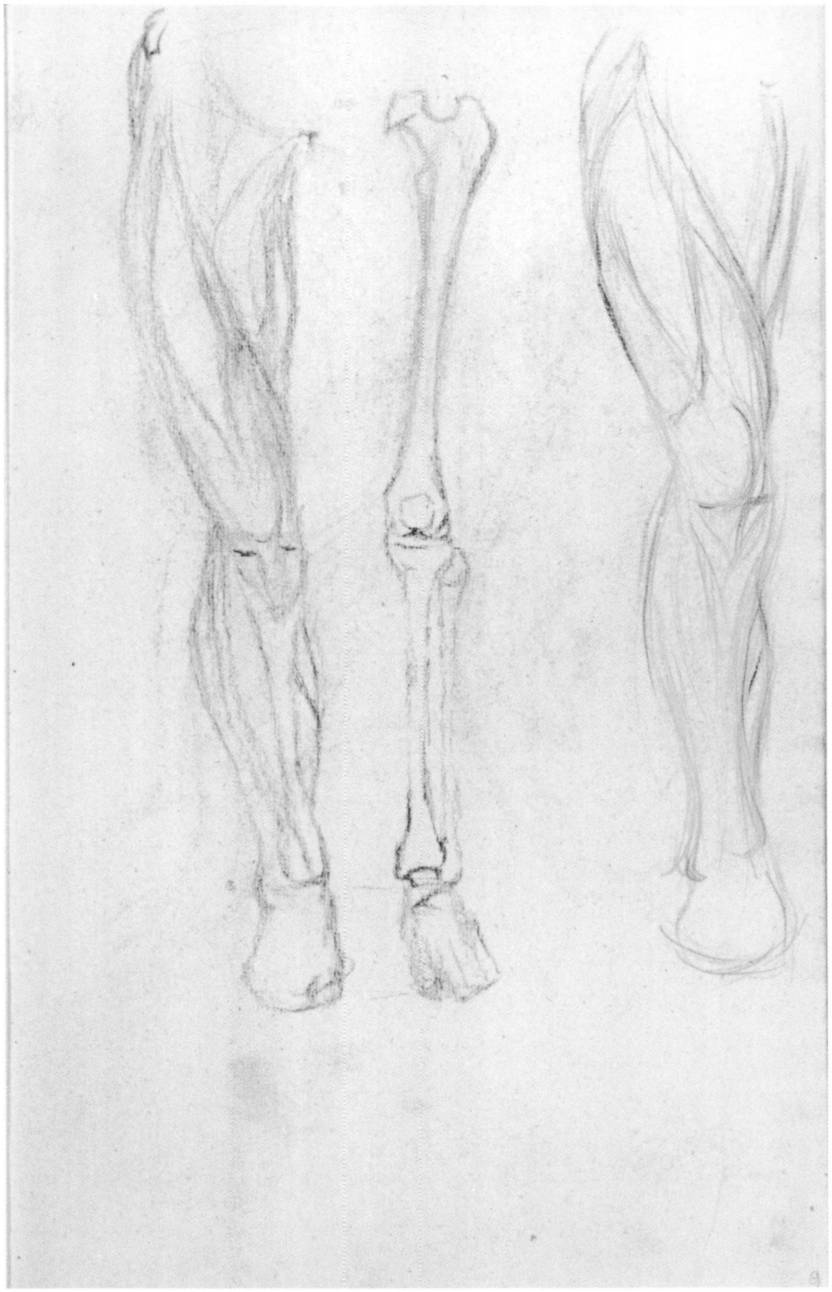

3, p.10

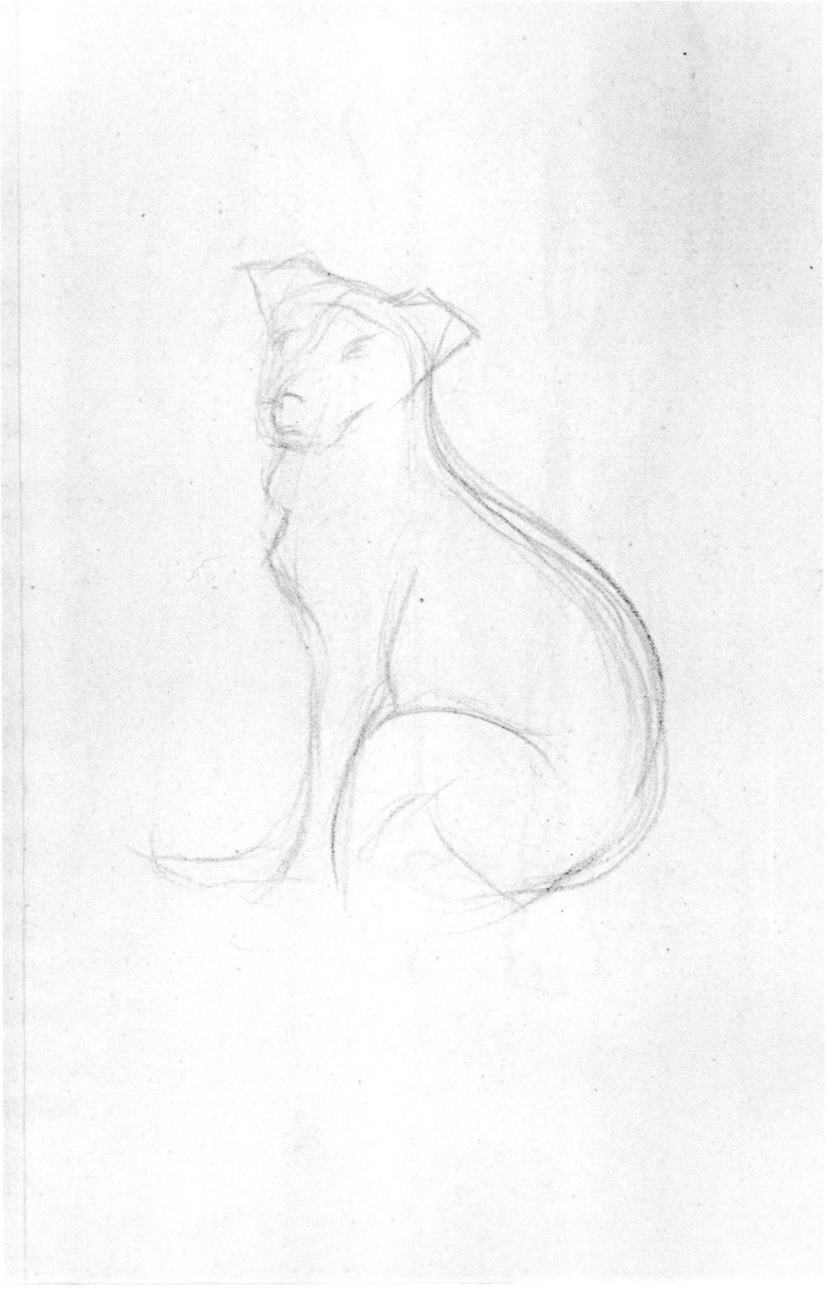

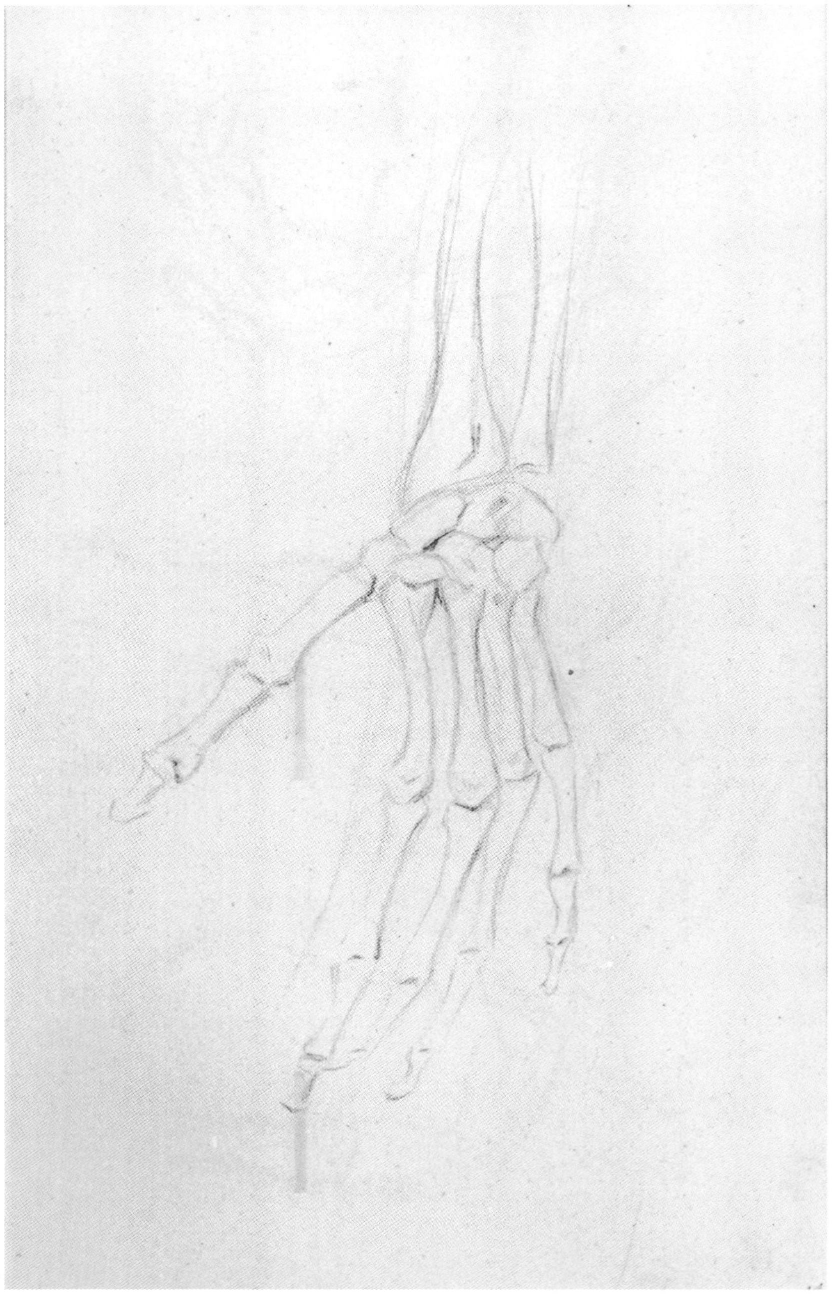

3, p.11

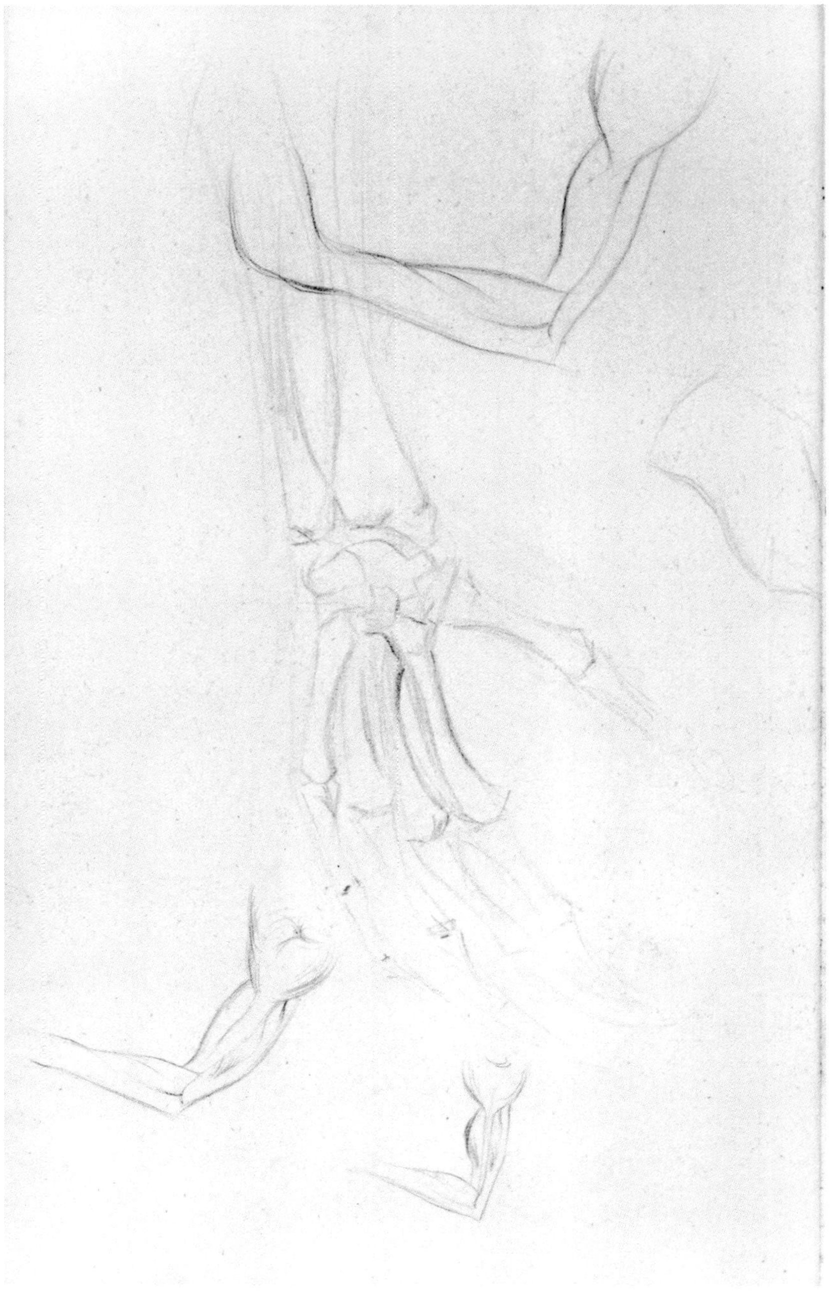

3, p.12

**p.11** Brown crayon drawing of left hand

**p.12** Pencil and crayon drawing of arms and right hand

**p.13** Brown crayon drawings of arms (lateral views)

**p.14** Pencil and crayon drawing of arm (above) and scapula and humerus (below)
Inscribed c.l. in Cyrillic: 'peredniaia poverkhnost / [...] korpus'

Kandinsky wrote 'front surface' next to the anterior view of the scapula and humerus.

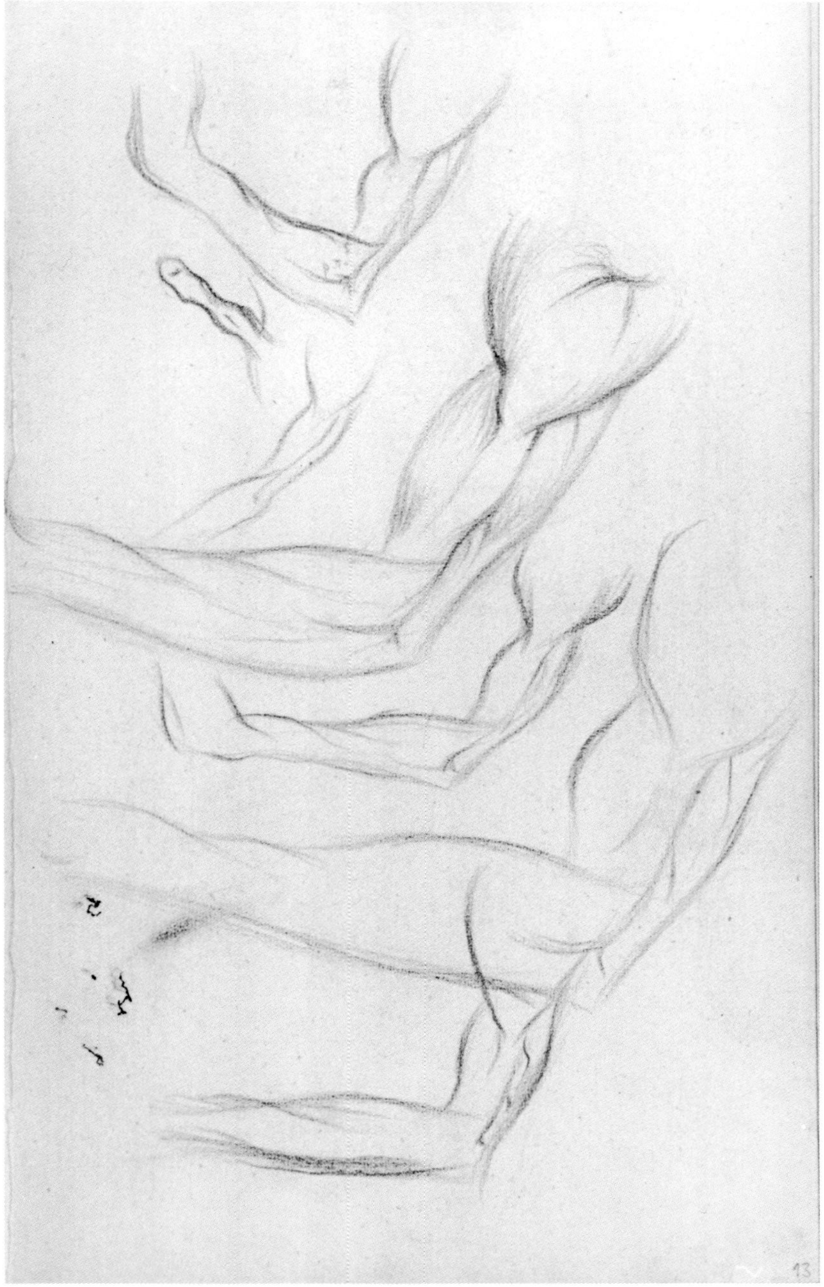

3, p.13

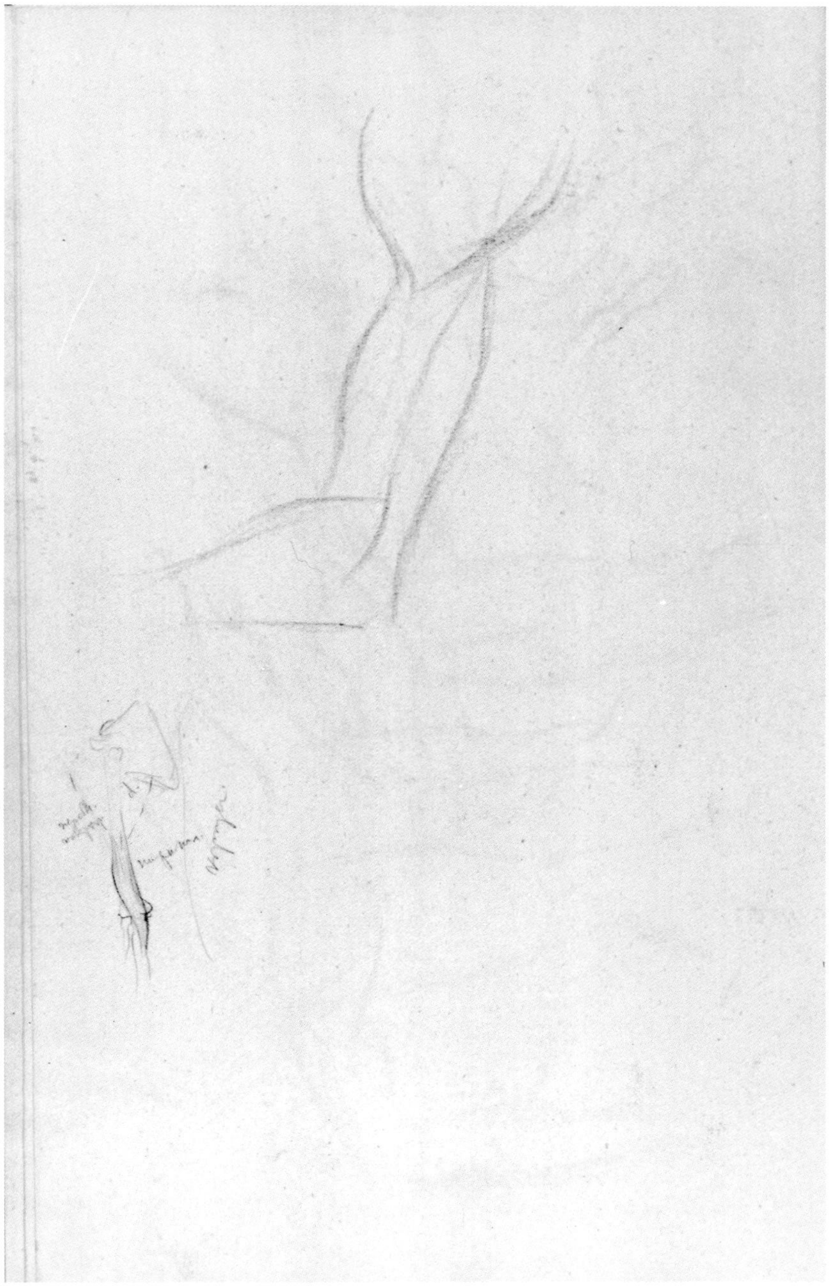

3, p.14

**p.15** Pencil drawing of arms

**p.16** Blank

**p.17** Brown crayon drawing of arm and shoulder

See also pp.19–20 (below)

**p.18** Brown crayon drawing of scapula, shoulder and arm

**p.19** Brown crayon drawing of arm, shoulder and chest (anterior view)

3, p.15

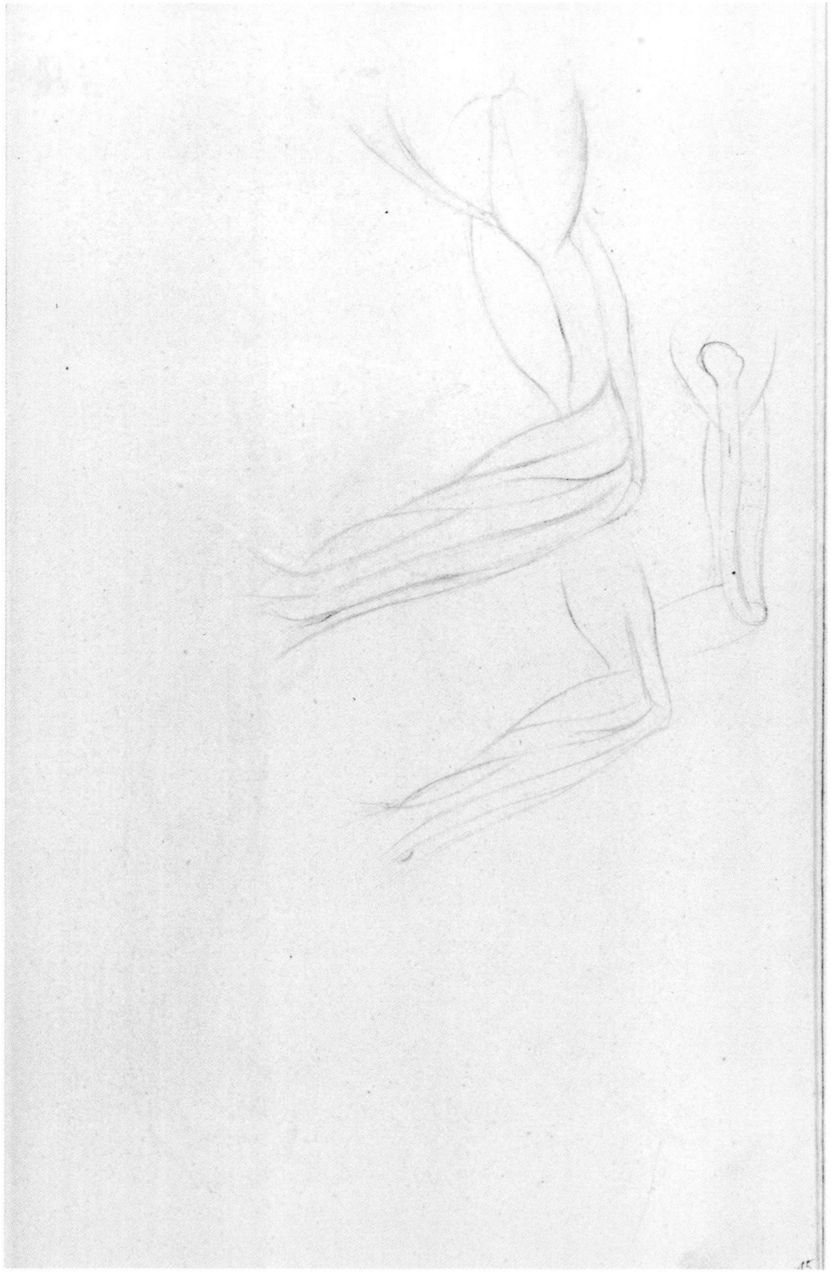

3, p.17

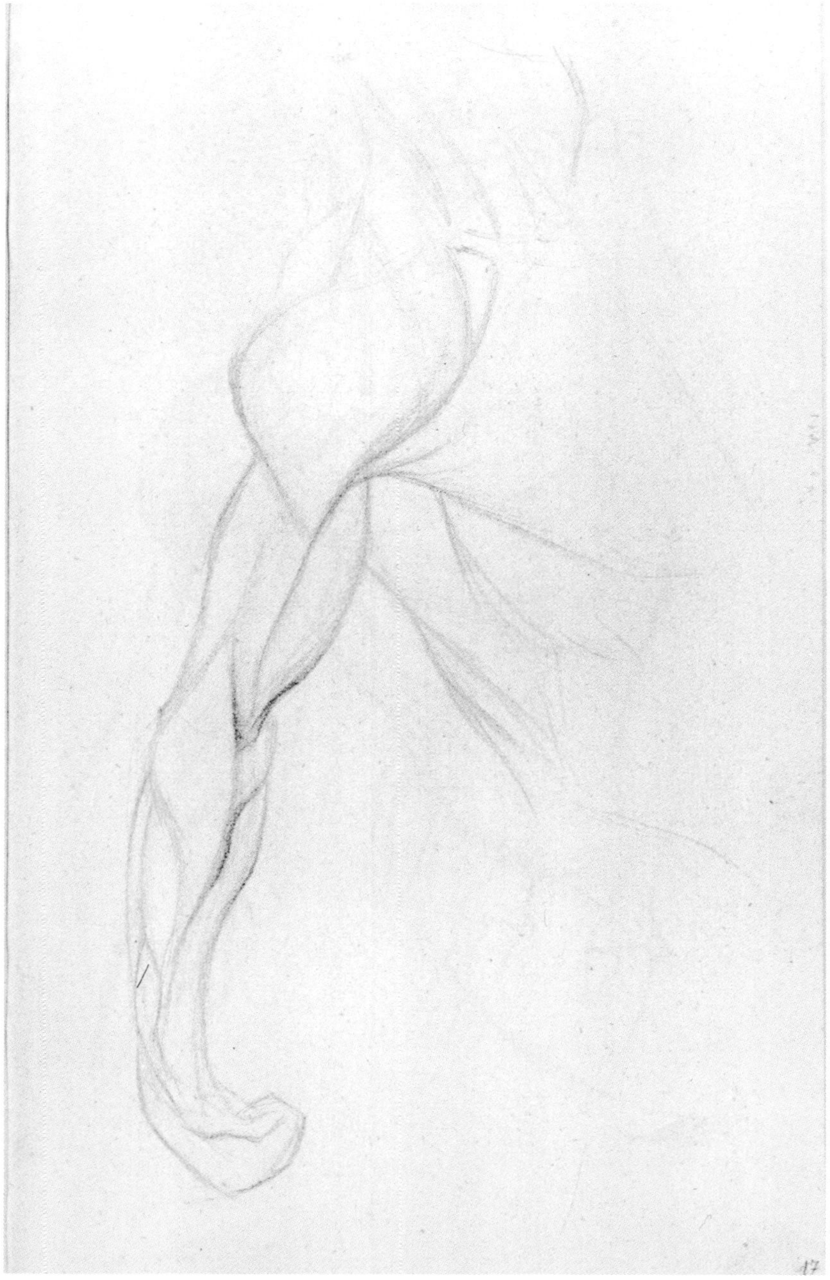

3, p.18

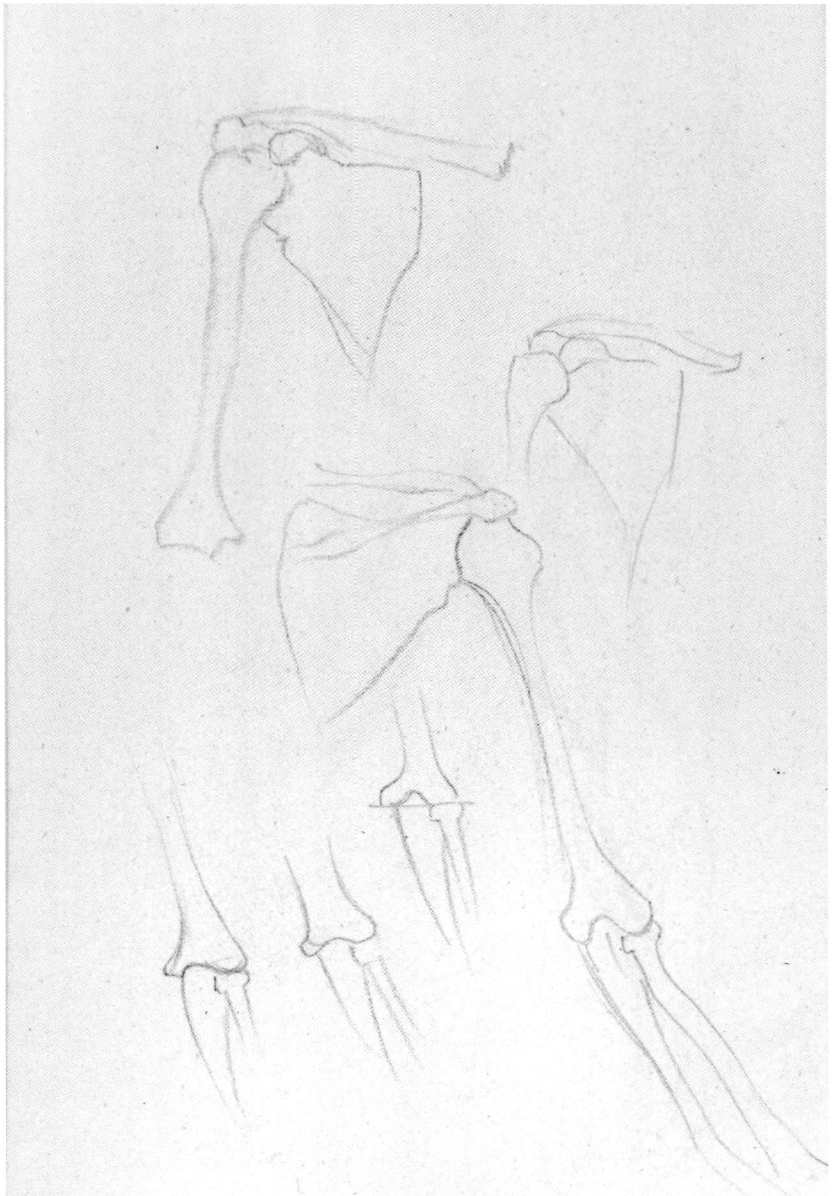

3, p.19

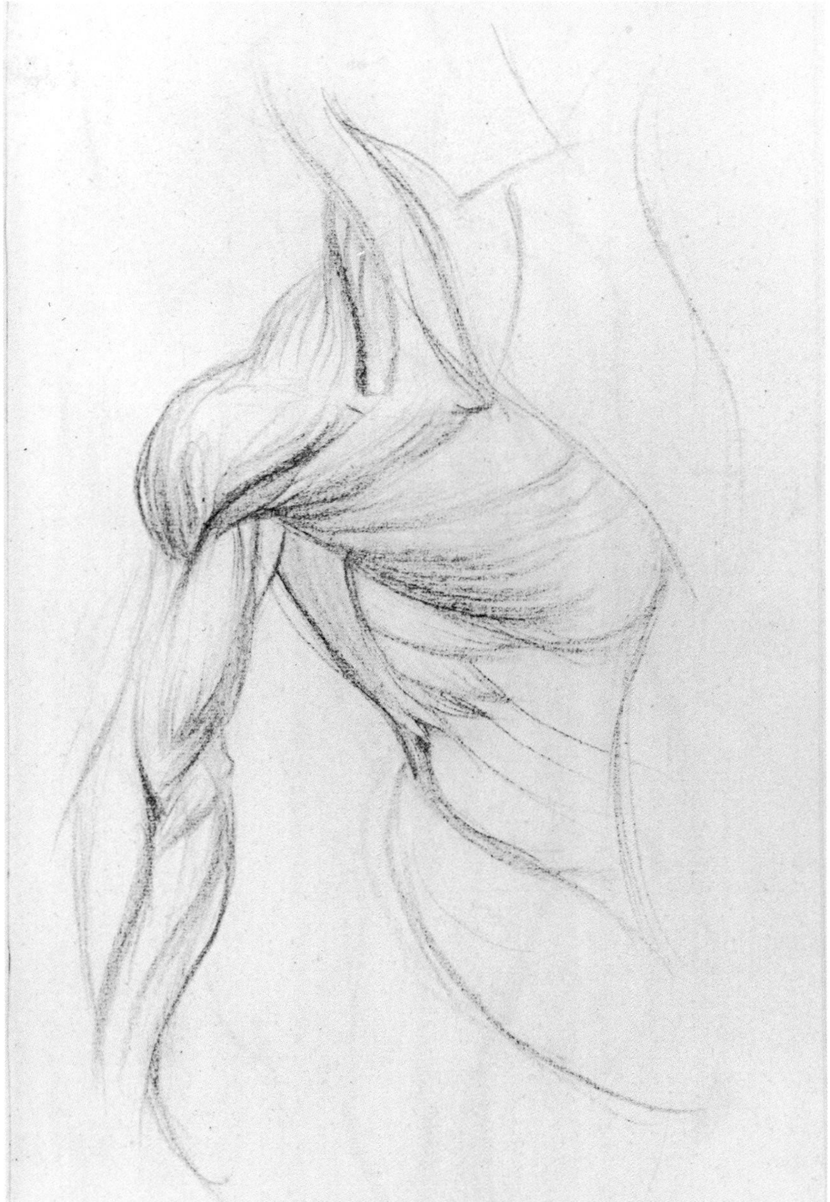

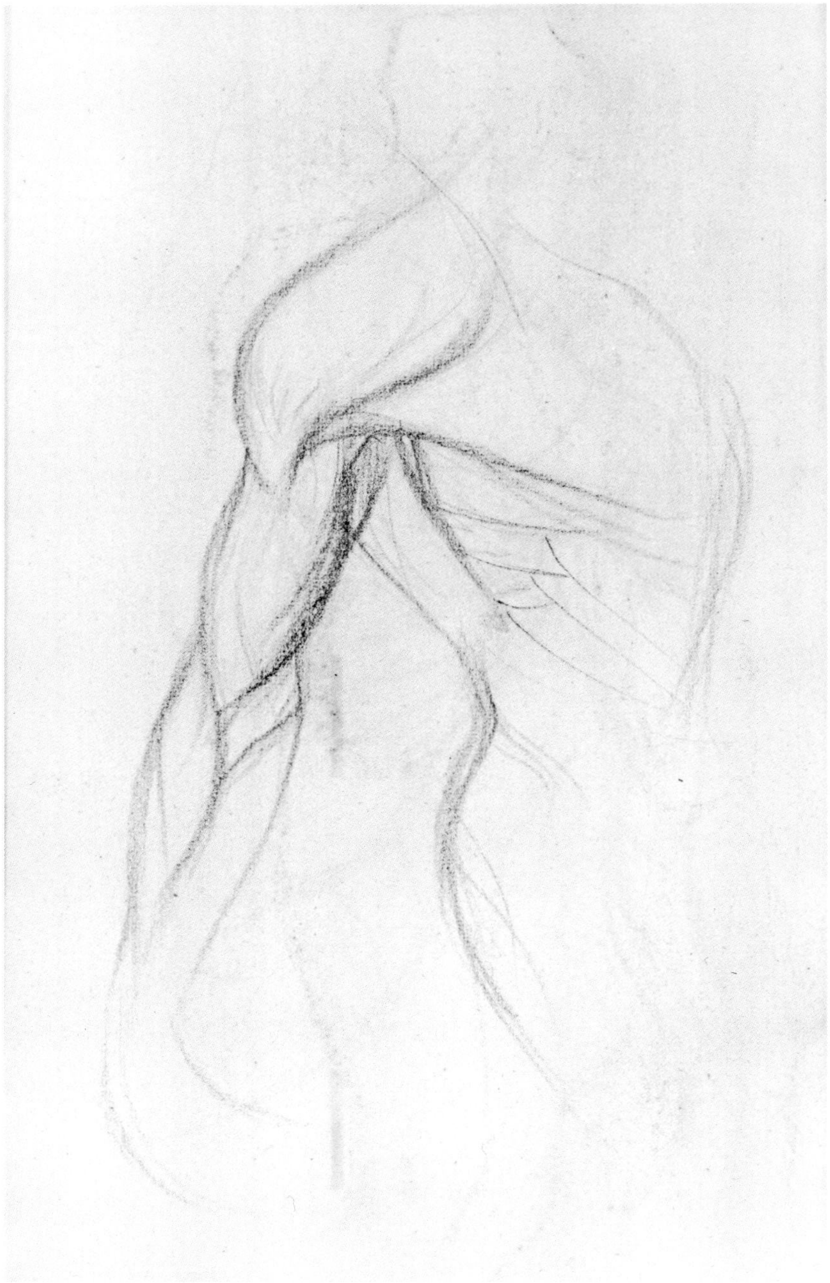

3, p.20

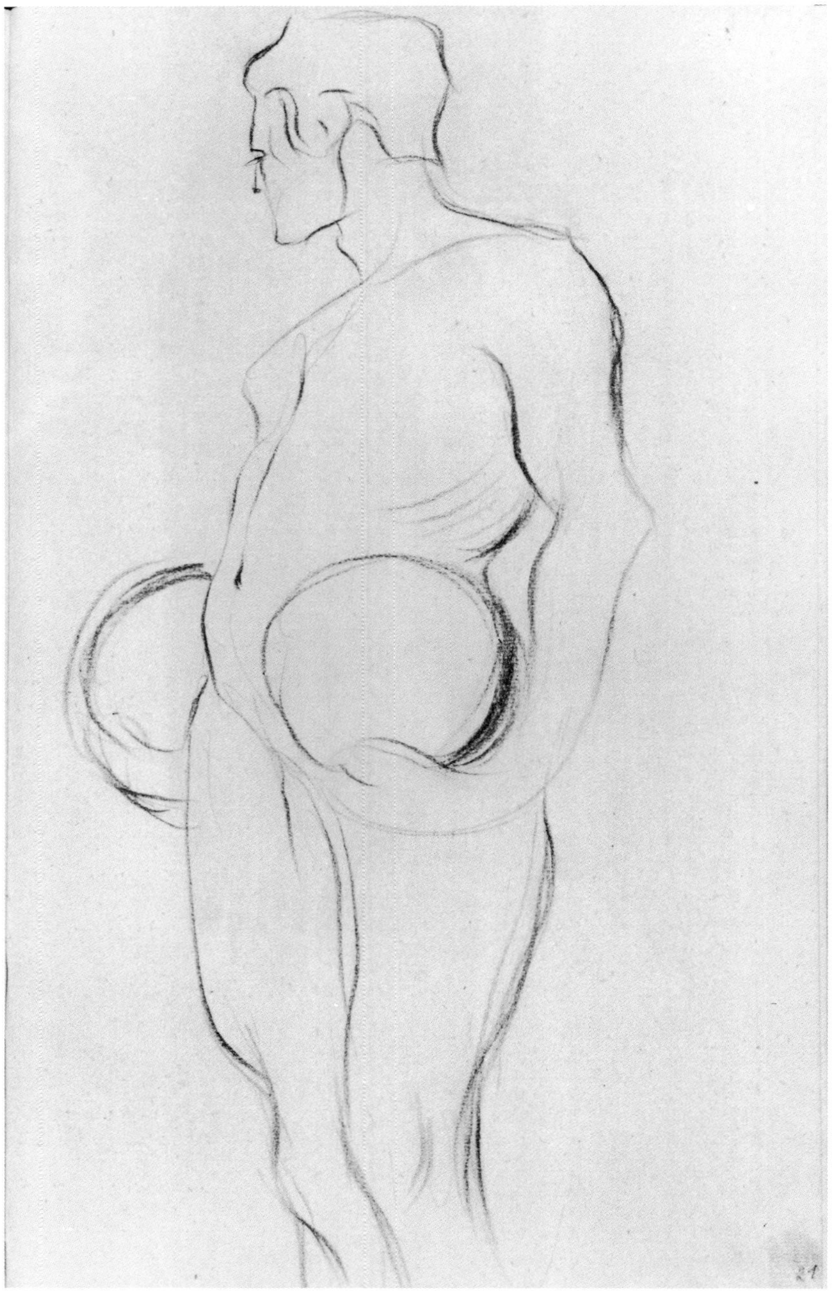

3, p.21

**p.20** Brown crayon drawing of arm, shoulder and chest (anterior view)

**p.21** Red chalk drawing of standing male nude holding balls

Unlike the previous studies, this drawing was probably done from a model.

**p.22** Blank

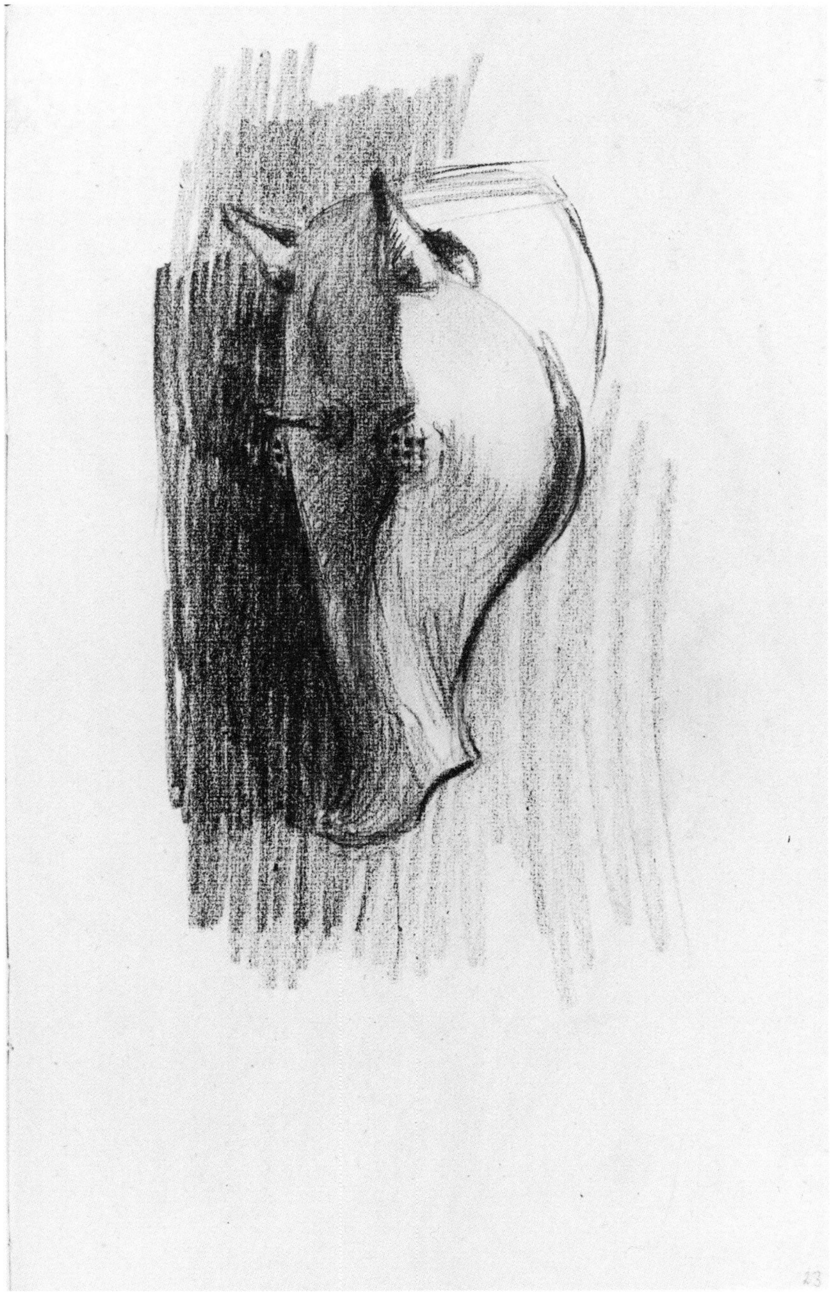

3, p.23

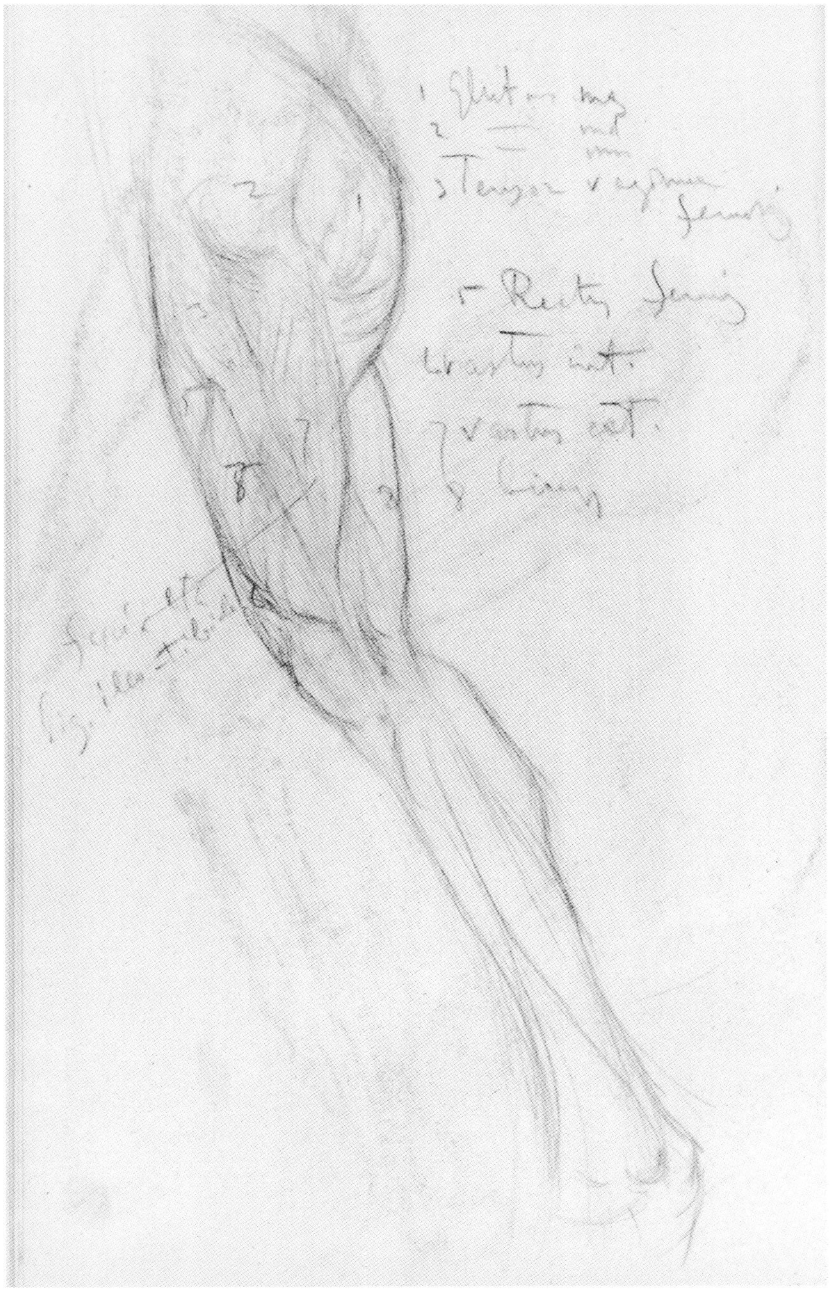

3, p.24

**p.23** Pencil and colored chalk drawing of armor for horse (shaffron)

The drawing appears to be related to those in Sketchbook 6 done after illustrations in *Waffensammlung Kuppelmayr* (Munich, 1895); however, it does not copy a plate in this book. The presence of yellow and red chalk suggests that it might have been done from an object rather than an illustration. The shaffron with coverings to protect the horse's eyes is distinctive (information kindly provided by Dirk Breiding). It is similar to that in a watercolor on the reverse of *Landschaft mit Paar in mittelalterlicher Tracht* of c.1902 (Barnett no.53).

**p.24** Red chalk drawing of leg
Inscribed u.r.: '1 Gluteus max / 2 [Gluteus] med. / [Gluteus] min. / 3 Tensor vag[...] / femoris / 5 Rectus femoris / 6 vastus int. / 7 vastus ext. / 8 biceps'; c.l.: 'fascia l[a]ta / lig. ileo-tibial'

REFERENCES
Hanfstaengl 1974, p.164, ill.

**p.25** Red chalk drawings of lateral views of right leg and of male torso

REFERENCES
Hanfstaengl 1974, p.164, ill.

**p.26** Red chalk drawing of the lower leg and foot and of a man in costume
Inscribed u.r. in Cyrillic and Latin: 'tyl'nyi sgibatel – Tib. ant. / Peron[eus] 3 / podoshva sgibatelia. Gastrocn[emius] / Soleus / Peron[eus] l[ongus]- abductor / et pronator'; l.c.: 'Tib[ialis] post[icus]'

Kandinsky's notes in Russian refer to the rear bending muscle and the base of the bending muscle in the calf of the leg. The figure of a man holding a lance suggests the knight in armor on horseback in Sketchbook 5 (GMS 342, p.36).

(See color plate p.113)

3, p.25

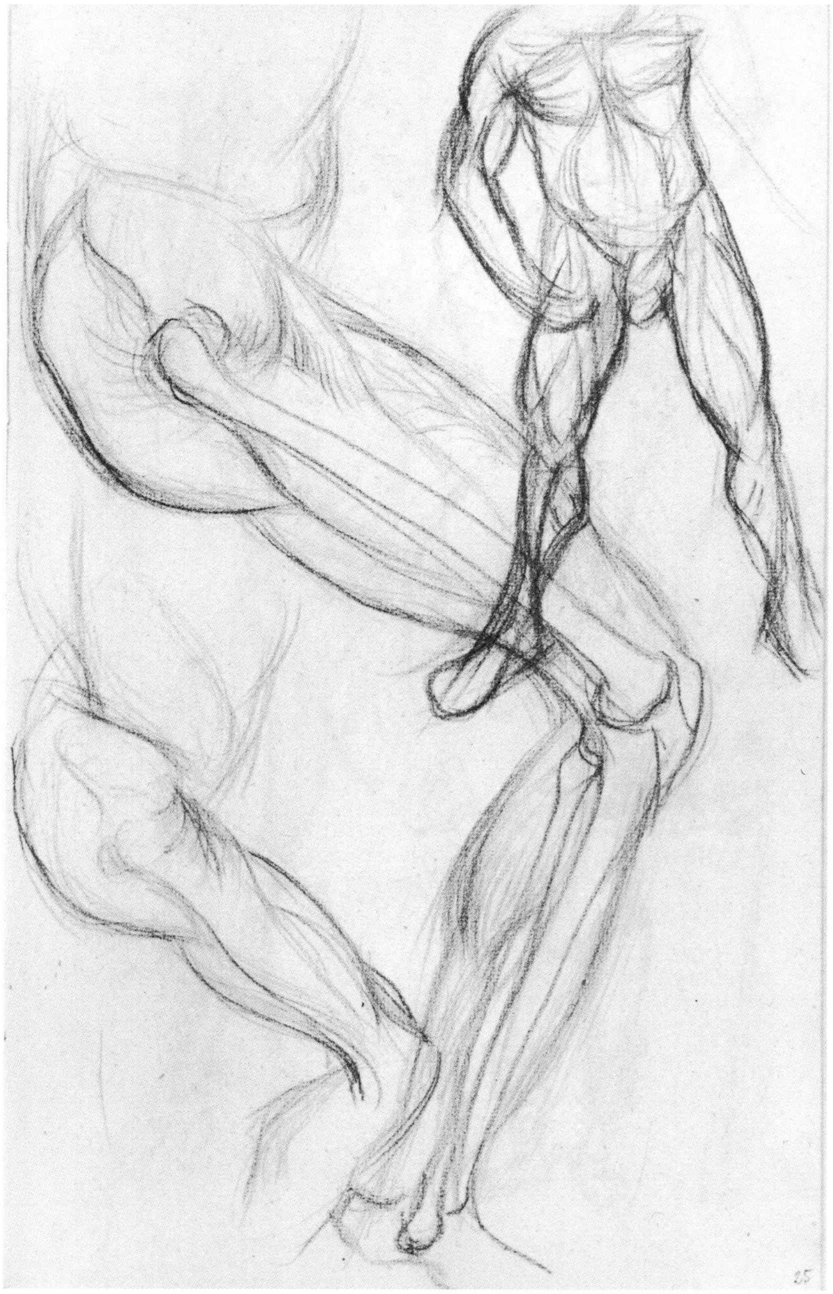

3, p.26

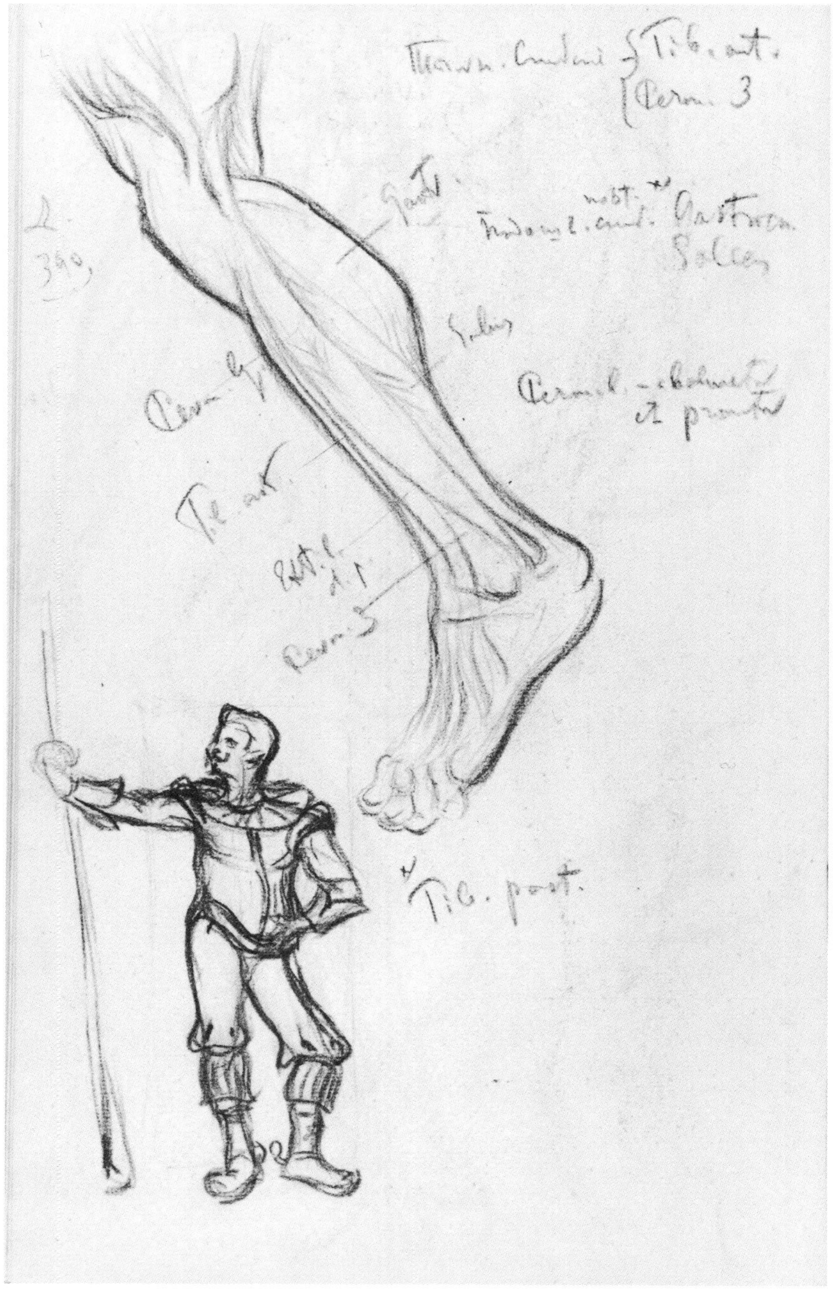

**p.27** Red chalk drawings of leg muscles (anterior view) and bone
Inscribed u.r. in Cyrillic: 'dvusust[avnoe] razgi / banie' and in Latin: 'Quadri-ceps / R[e]ctus f[emoris] / V[astus] int[ernus] / [Vastus] ext[ernus] / Crureus / Pect[ineus] / adduct[o]r G. f. / [adductor] mg. f. / Gracilis / Sart[orius]'

Kandinsky's notes in Latin refer to the muscles in the thigh and those in Russian to a 'double-joint unbending'.

**pp.28–34** Blank

**p.35** Red chalk and pencil study of rider on horseback and walled castle
Inscribed l.r.: '2-2-4 / 3-3-9 / 4-4-16 / 5-5-25 / 6-6-36'

REFERENCES

Hanfstaengl 1974, p.164, ill.
Barnett 1992, p.71
Hahl-Koch 1993, p.85, ill.90
Barnett and Friedel 1995, no.14, color ill.

The motif of a rider and walled castle appears in *Der Komet* (*Nächtlicher Reiter?*) (Barnett no.35), which is dated 1900. The numbers at the lower right indicate a geometric progression.

(See color plate p.113)

**pp.36–47** Blank

3, p.27

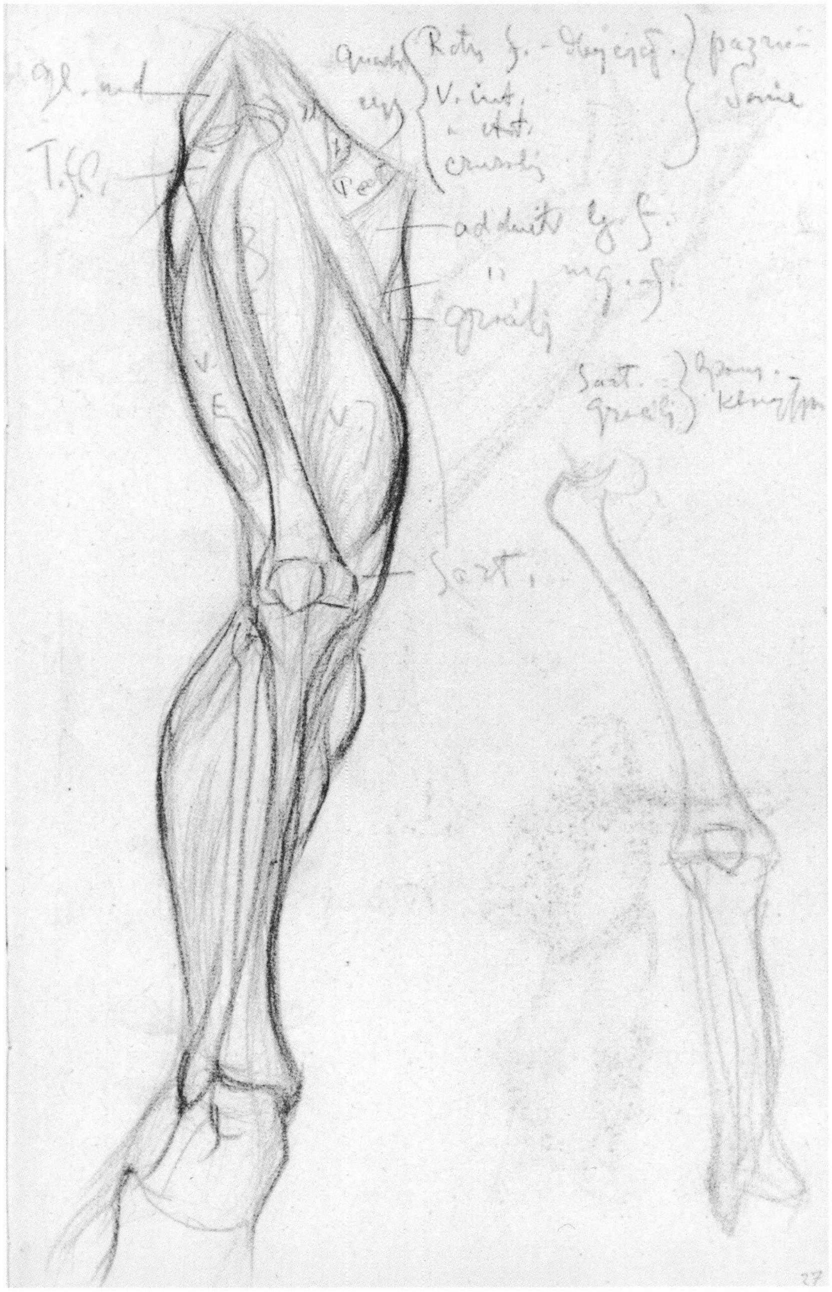

3, p.35

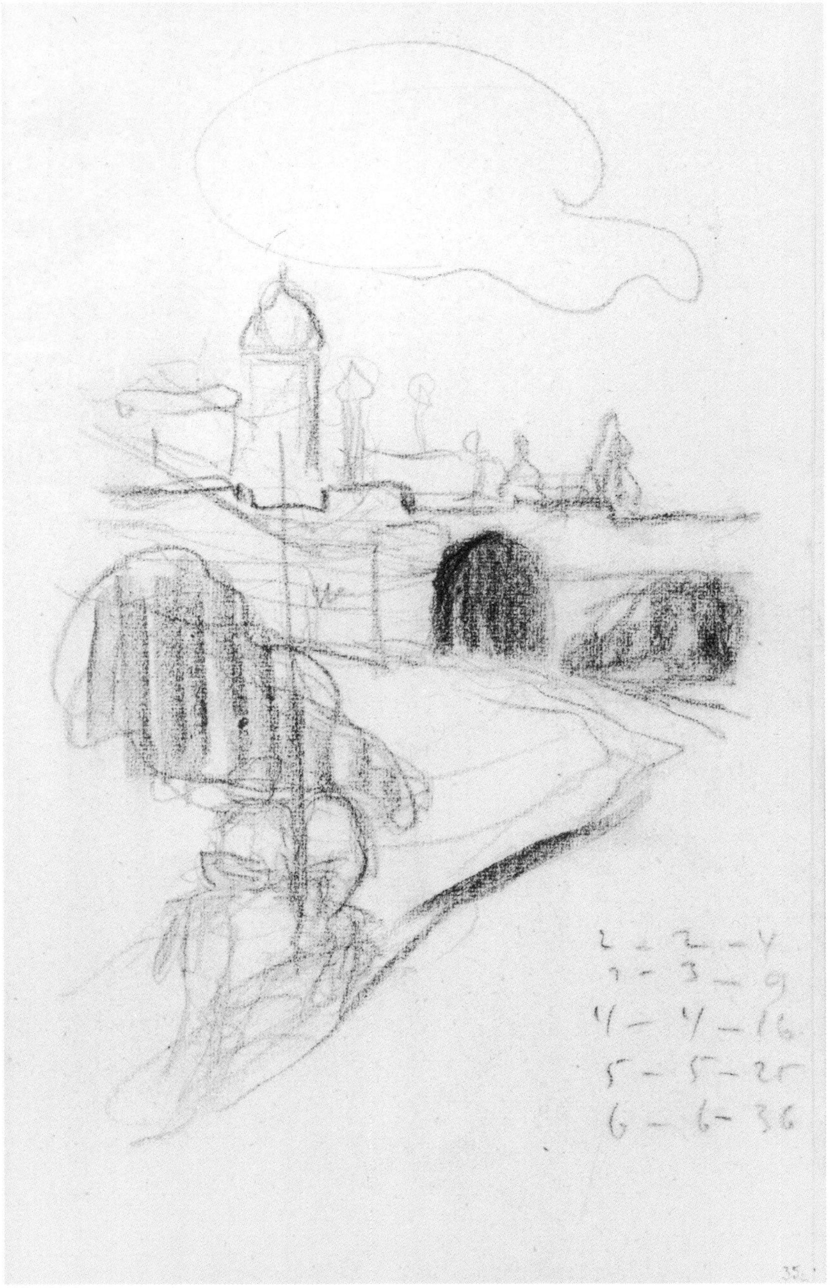

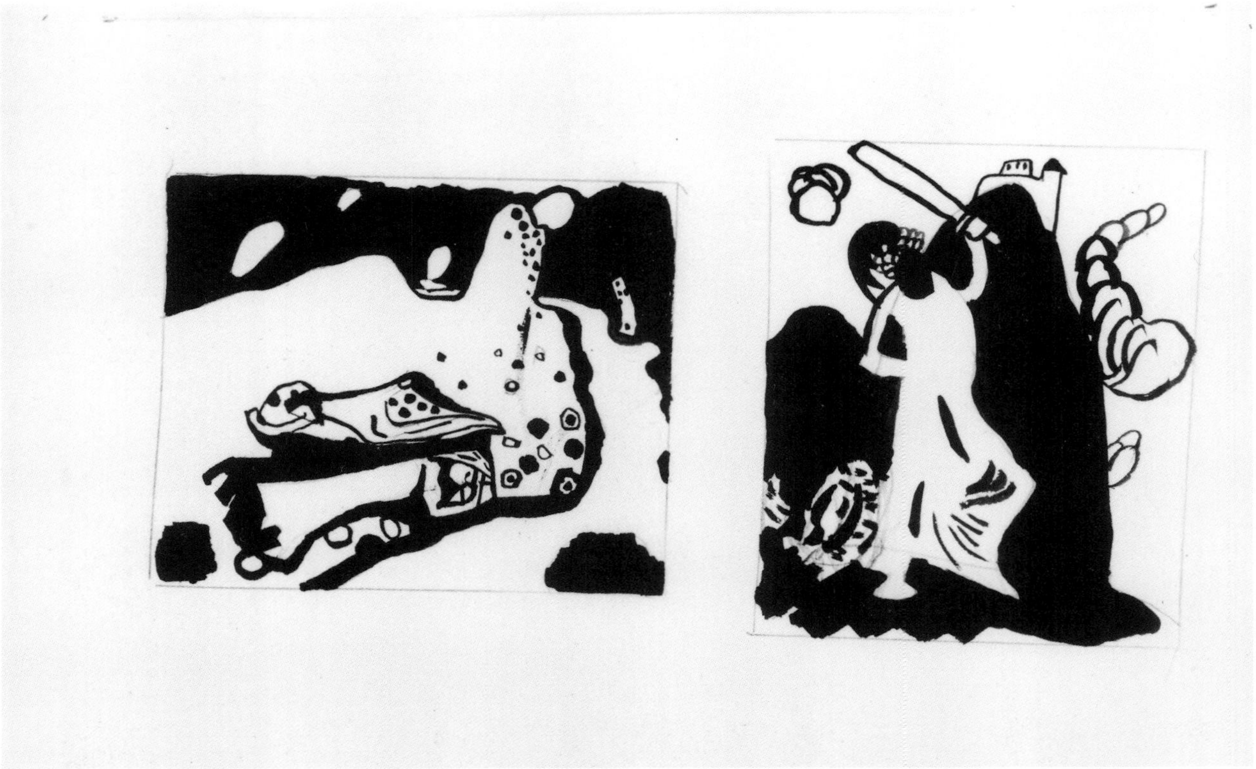

3, p.48

**p.48** India ink and pencil drawings for *Variation nach Improvisation 21, Figur mit Keule* and prints

REFERENCES
Roethel 1970, pp.202, 421, VI, 18, 491, ill.97
Hanfstaengl 1974, p.163

These India ink drawings were done at a much later date than the preceding pages in the sketchbook. Roethel (no.101) related the study on the left to *Variation nach Improvisation 21* of 1911, and considered the drawing on the right to have been done c.1911 for an unexecuted print.

**p.49** Blank

**p.50** Pencil studies of horse and rider and religious scene
Inscribed in image on right: 'Saviour'

REFERENCES
Hanfstaengl 1974, p.164, ill.
Barnett 2006, p.69

The studies are related to a drawing, *Reiter in Landschaft und Reiterstudie* of c.1909 (vol.I, cat. no.114), as well as to paintings of riders and *Improvisation 4* of 1909 (Roethel and Benjamin nos.280–282). The horse also appears in the background of the religious scene, where Kandinsky has identified one of the figures as 'savior': it brings to mind the painting *Gekreuzigter Christus* of 1911 (Roethel and Benjamin no.406).

**p.51** Blank

3, p.50

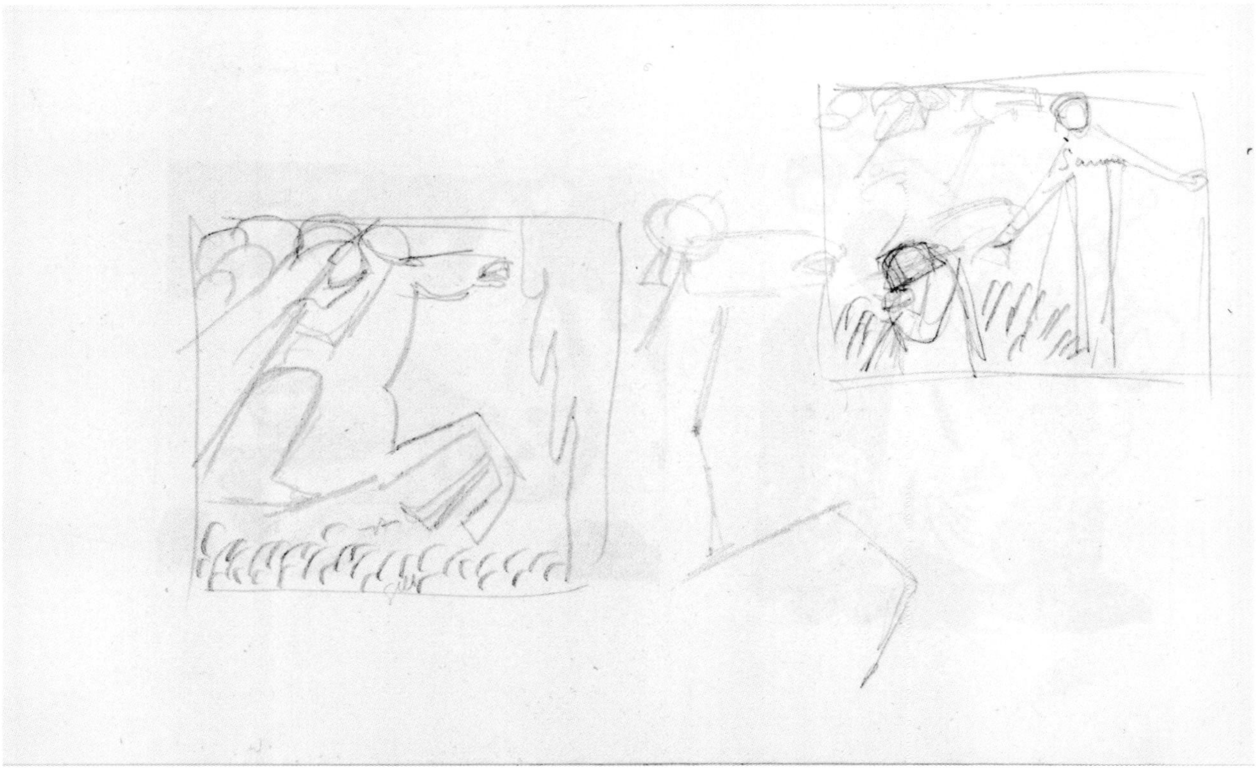

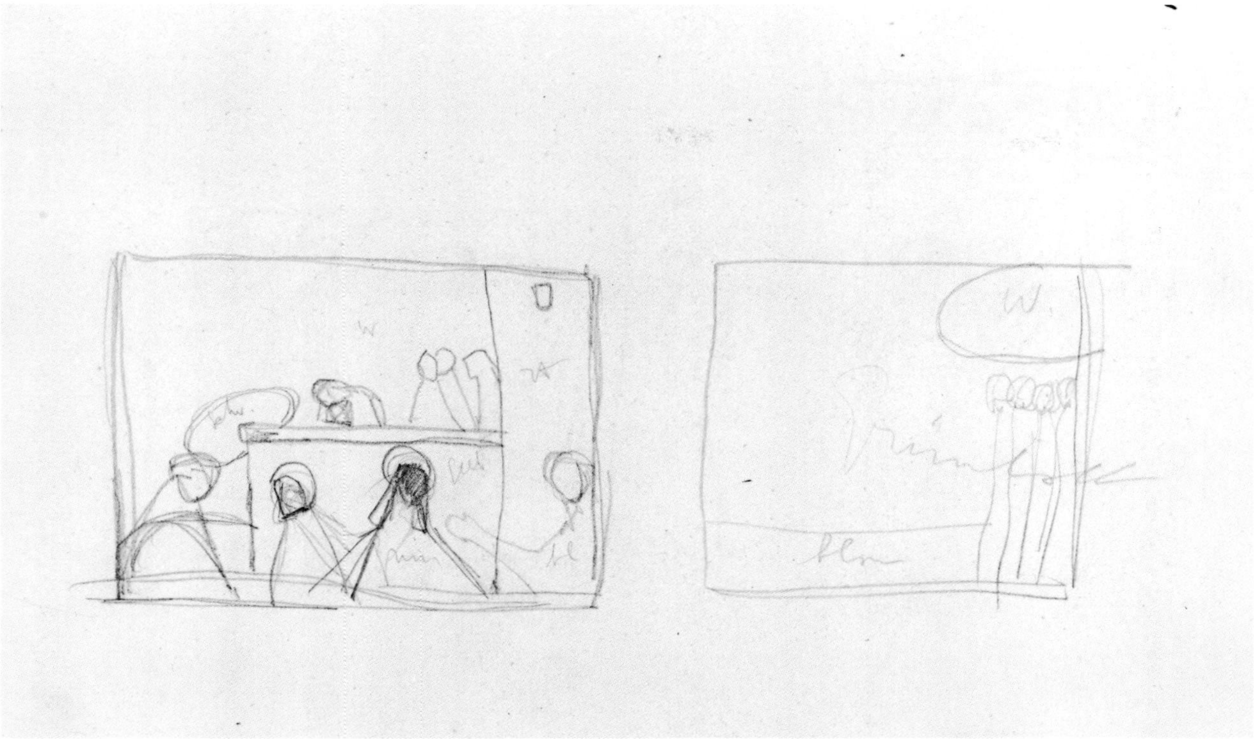

3, p.52

**p.52** Pencil studies related to *Improvisation 19* of 1911 and an unidentified interior scene with figures
Inscribed with color notations c.l.: 'w / rt / Schw. / Gelb / Grün / bl' and c.r.: 'w. / Grünlich / blau'

REFERENCES
Hanfstaengl 1974, pp.163, 164, ill.
Roethel and Benjamin 1982, p.368

The scene on the left was apparently not developed into a painting. Although the figures and the cloud-like shape are similar, Kandinsky's color notes do not correspond to those in his canvas *Improvisation 19* of March 1911 (Roethel and Benjamin no.385).

**p.53** Blank

**p.54** Red chalk and pencil drawing of buildings near Munich

REFERENCES
Hanfstaengl 1974, p.163

The sketch was probably made in Schwabing about 1897–1900: it resembles p.42 of Sketchbook 4 (GMS 348) and is even reminiscent of p.65 in Sketchbook 1 done in June 1889.

(See color plate p.114)

3, p.54

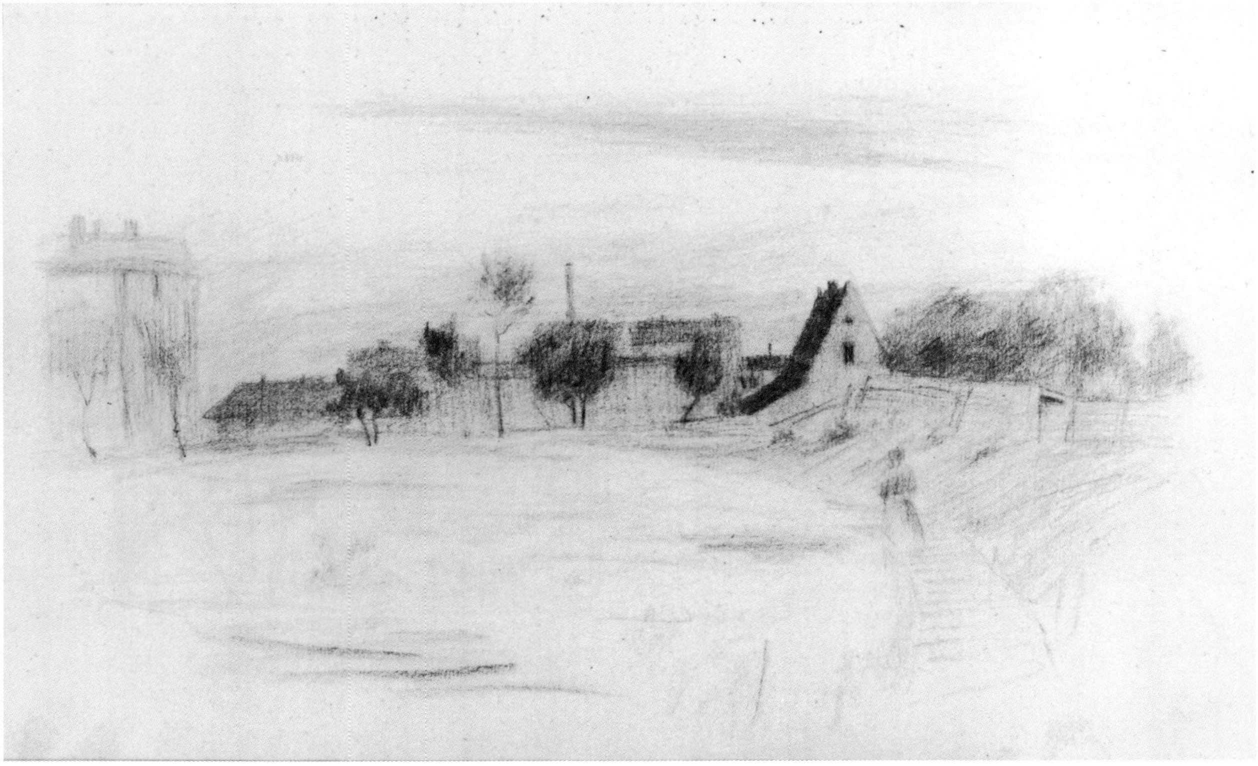

# Sketchbook 4

1897–1902

Grey linen-covered cardboard sketchbook; inside back cover label from Franz Dury, Munich (Amalienstrasse and Theresienstrasse)
Contains 46 pages (23 sheets), each 10.3 x 17.3 cm (4 x 6¾ in), of which pp.31–41 are blank. Several pages were apparently cut out at an early date.
Page numbers inscribed by unknown hand at later date with odd numbers at lower right

Hanfstaengl 1974, p.168

LOCATION
Städtische Galerie im Lenbachhaus, Munich (GMS 348)

HISTORY
Gabriele Münter, Murnau, until 1957

The cover, format and colored pages (green, rose and white) of this sketchbook bear a close resemblance to Sketchbook 5, although the dimensions are different. Erika Hanfstaengl proposed that Kandinsky used them at the same time.

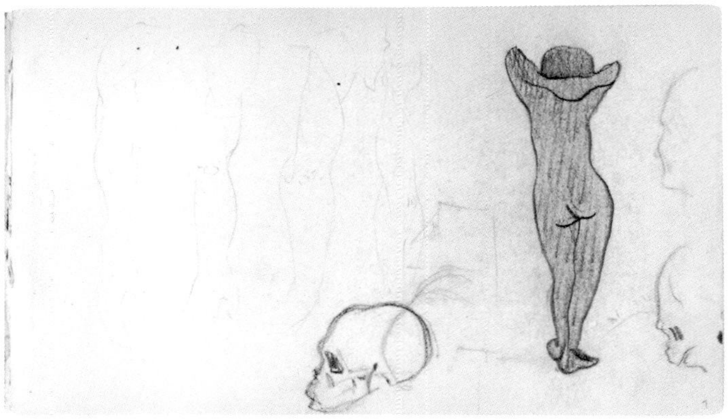

4, p.1

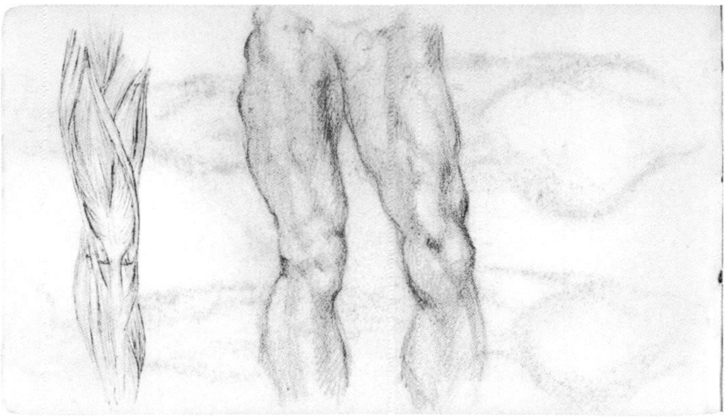

4, p.2

**p.1** Pencil studies of heads, skull, arms and female figure seen from behind

In comparison with the studies on the first page of Sketchbook 3, the skull and female nude are drawn with a greater sense of volume and shadow. Likewise, the anatomical studies in the present sketchbook suggest light and shadow, and several studies are done from life.

**p.2** Pencil studies of legs and ink study of leg at left (anterior view)

REFERENCES
Hanfstaengl 1974, p.168, ill.

**p.3** Pencil studies of legs (posterior views)

**p.4** Pencil studies of elbows
Inscribed l.l. in Cyrillic: 'sboku'; l.r.: 'szadi'

Kandinsky noted 'from the side' and 'from behind'.

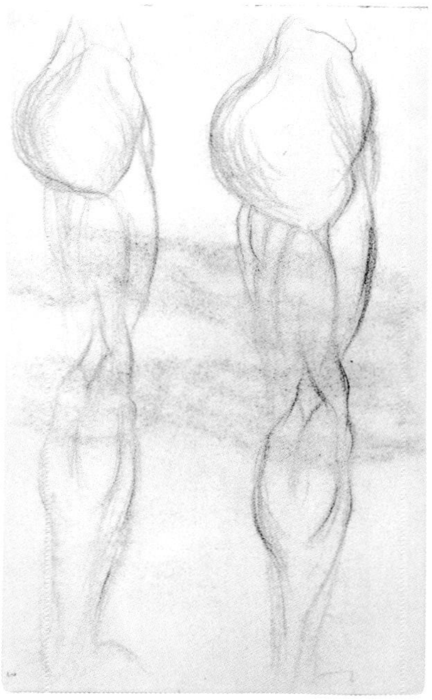

4, p.3

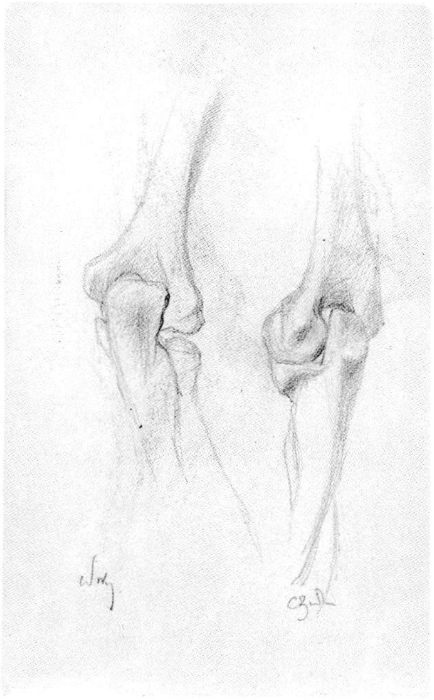

4, p.4

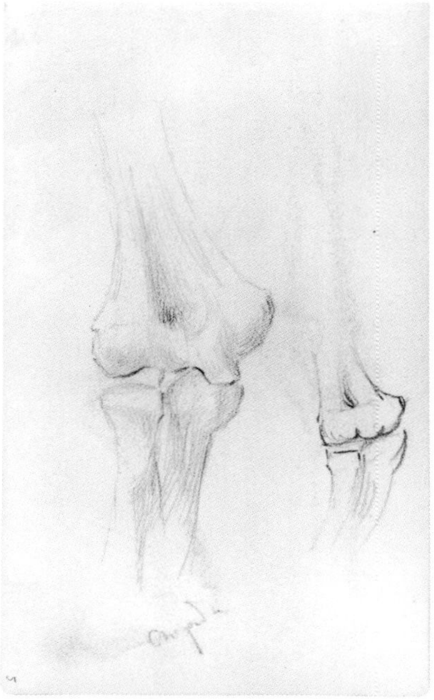

4, p.5

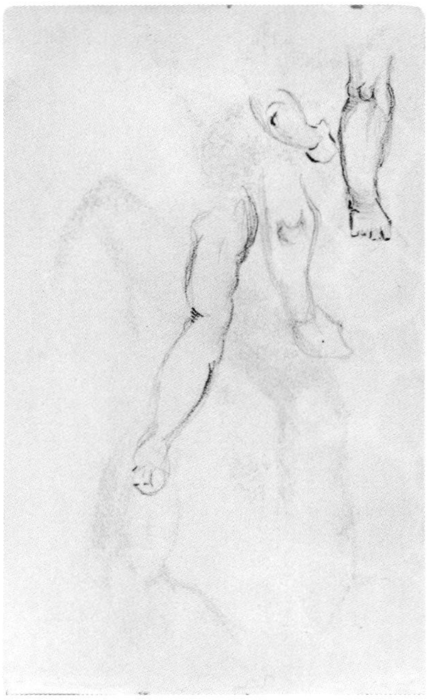

4, p.6

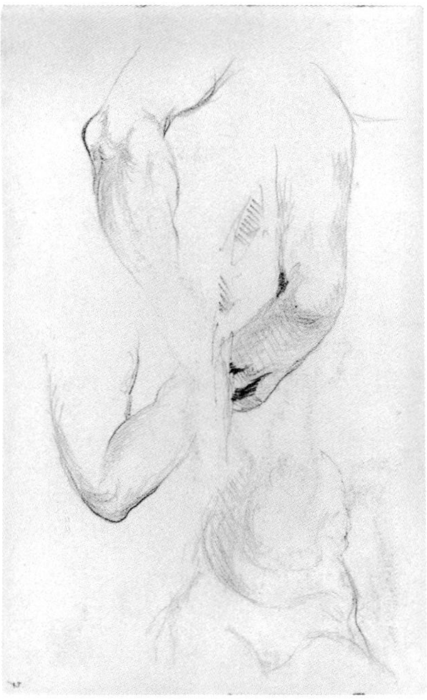

4, p.7

**p.5** Pencil study of elbows
Inscribed l.l. in Cyrillic: 'speredi'

As indicated by the inscription the view is 'from the front'.

**p.6** Pencil studies of arms and hands

**p.7** Pencil studies of arms and female torso

**p.8** Blank

**p.9** Pencil study of nude boy or putto

The suggestion of another figure in the background at the upper right indicates that the study may have been done from a plaster cast in the studio or from an illustration.

**p.10** Pencil study of standing female nude

This study was done from the same model as the sketch on the facing page.

**p.11** Pencil and brown crayon study of standing female nude

4, p.9

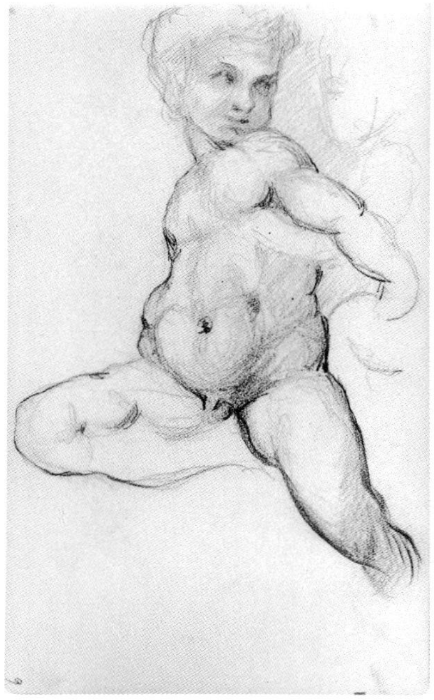

4, p.10

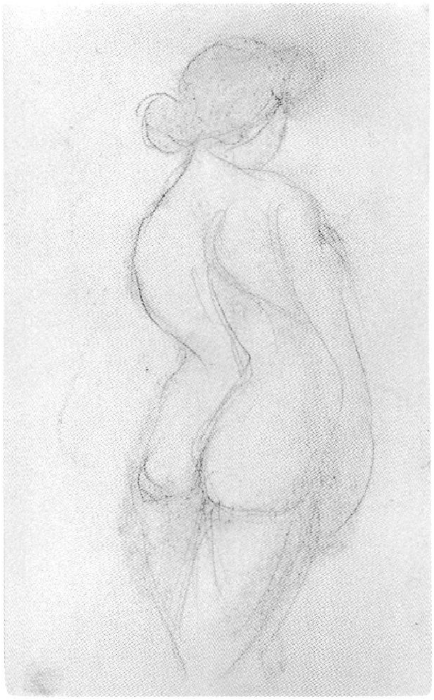

4, p.11

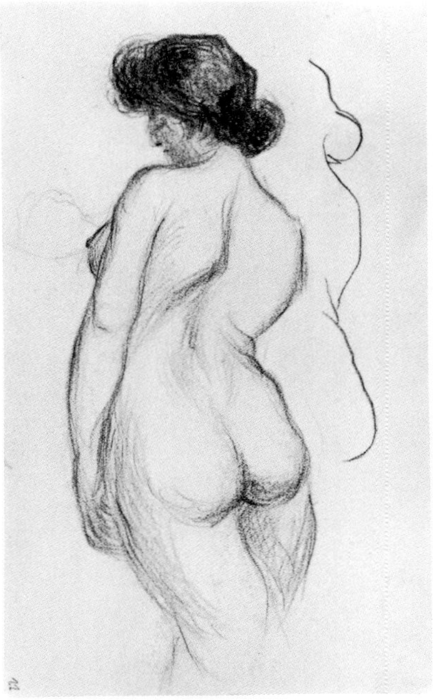

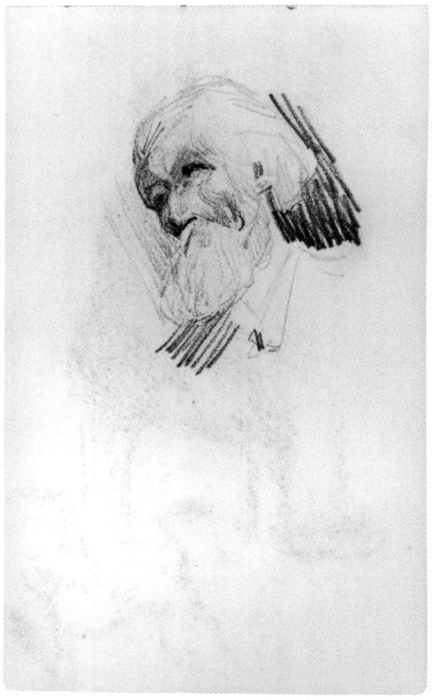

4, p.12

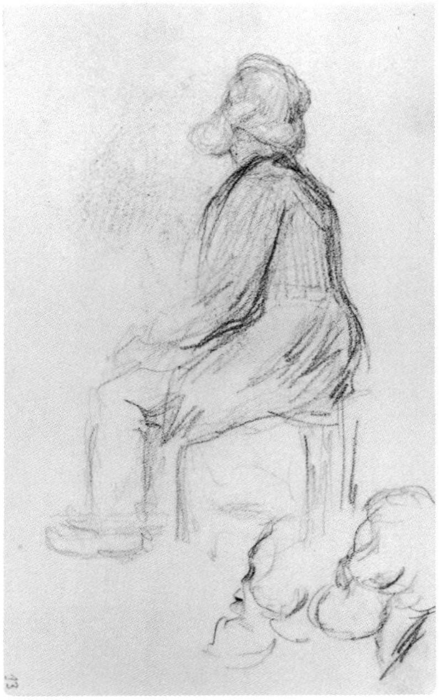

4, p.13

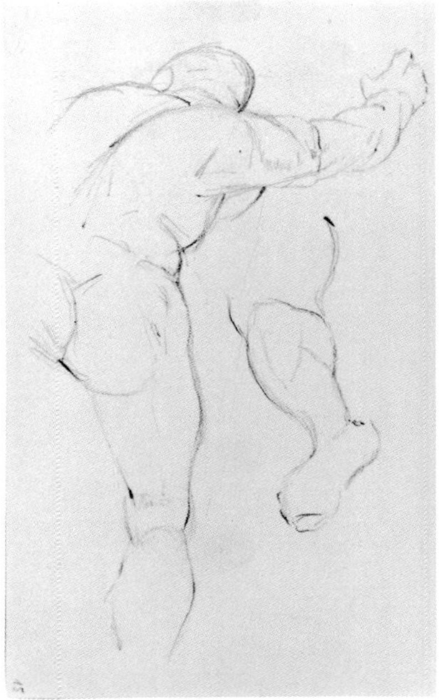

4, p.15

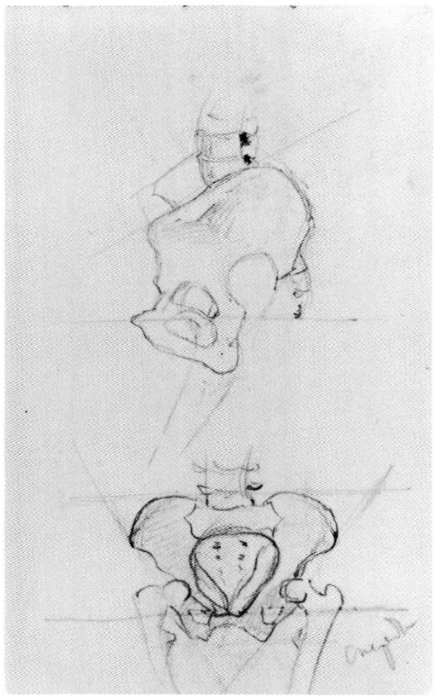

4, p.16

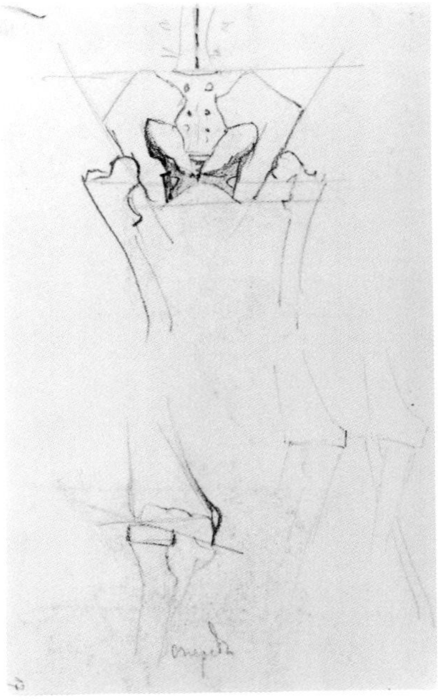

4, p.17

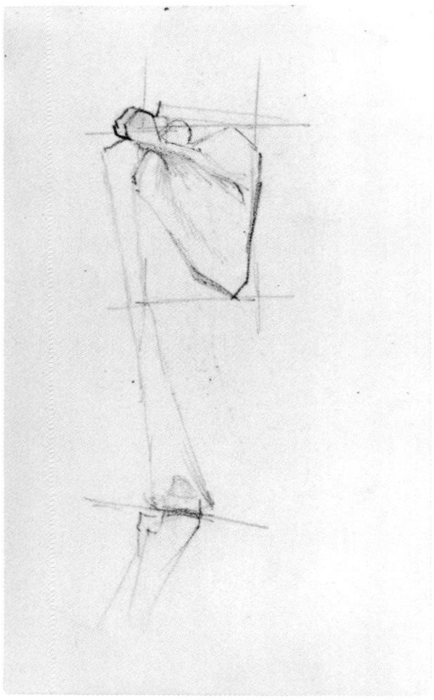

4, p.18

**p.12** Pencil drawing of head of bearded man

REFERENCES
Hanfstaengl 1974, p.168

Hanfstaengl compared the sitter on this and the facing page to the old man shown in Sketchbook 5 (GMS 342 pp.4, 6).

**p.13** Pencil drawing of bearded man and two studies of a head

REFERENCES
Hanfstaengl 1974, p.168

**p.14** Blank

**p.15** Pencil studies of male figure seen from behind

**p.16** Pencil studies of the pelvis with lumbar spine
Inscribed l.r. in Cyrillic: 'speredi'

REFERENCES
Hanfstaengl 1974, p.168, ill.

Kandinsky noted that the drawing below is seen 'from the front'; a lateral view is shown above.

**p.17** Pencil studies of the pelvis and hip with femur (above) and elbow (below)
Inscribed l.c. in Cyrillic: 'speredi'

**p.18** Pencil study of shoulder (scapula) and arm (humerus)

**p.19** Red and black ink, watercolor and pencil studies of arm and elbows on green paper
Inscribed u.l. in Cyrillic: 'Prostoi'; l.l.: 'profil'; l.r.: 'speredi' and u.c. in Latin: 'd[e]lt[oid] / tr[i]c[eps]'; c.r.: 'p[e]ct[oralis] / tr[i]c[eps] / Biceps / Brachialis / Pron[ator]'; c.: 'sup[inator] l[on]g[us]'

REFERENCES
Barnett and Friedel 1995, no.5, color ill.

Kandinsky indicted in Russian that the three views of the elbow are 'simple', 'profile' and 'from the front'. The drawing of the arm is more detailed than the studies found in Sketchbooks 2 and 3.

(See color plate p.114)

**p.20** Pencil study of arm with red ink splatters on green paper
Inscribed u.c.: 'd[e]lt[oid] / tr[i]c[eps] / tr[i]c[eps]'; c.l.: 'S[u]p[ina]t[or] l[ongus]'; c.r.: 'Pron[ator] t[e]r[e]s. / Palmaris l[on]g[u]s. / Sublimus / Ulnaris ant[erior]'

**p.21** Red and black ink, watercolor and pencil study of arm
Inscribed u.c.: 'dlt'; c.l.: 'tricep'; l.l. in Cyrillic: 'szadi'

REFERENCES
Hanfstaengl 1974, p.168, ill.

Kandinsky indicated that the deltoid and tricep muscles are shown 'from behind'.

**p.22** Pencil drawing of left hip, pelvis, torso and shoulder
Inscribed u.r.: 'Rhomb[oid] min[or]'

**p.23** Pencil study of man with beard on rose-tan paper

REFERENCES
Barnett and Friedel 1995, no.7, color ill.

**p.24** Watercolor and pencil drawing of Egyptian motif on rose-tan paper
Inscribed l.r. within image: '43'

REFERENCES
Hanfstaengl 1974, p.168

The number inscribed within the image suggests that the watercolor may be based on an illustration (p.43 or pl.43) although the source has not been identified.

(See color plate p.114)

**p.25** Blank

4, p.19

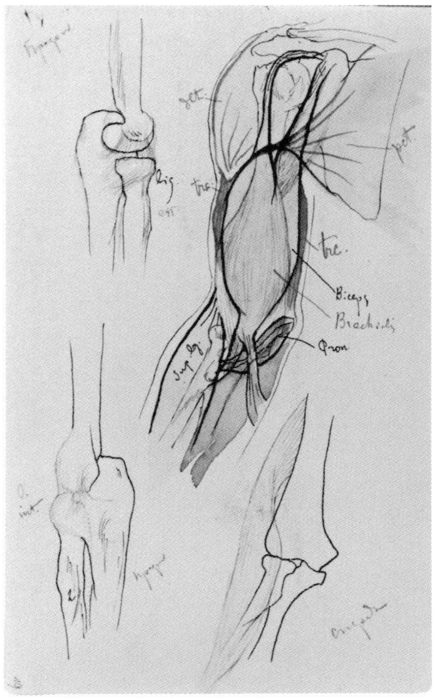

4, p.20

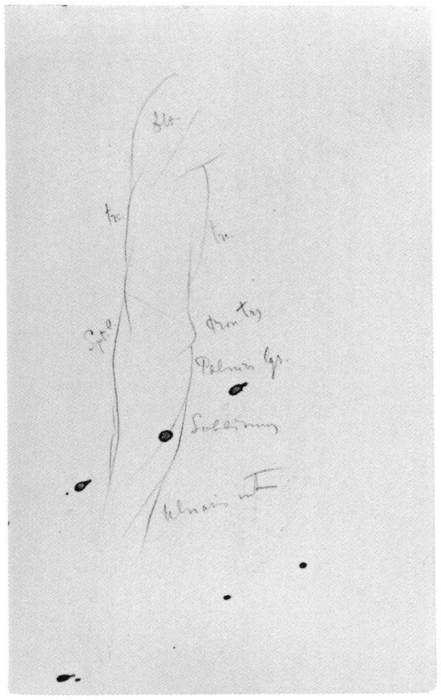

4, p.21

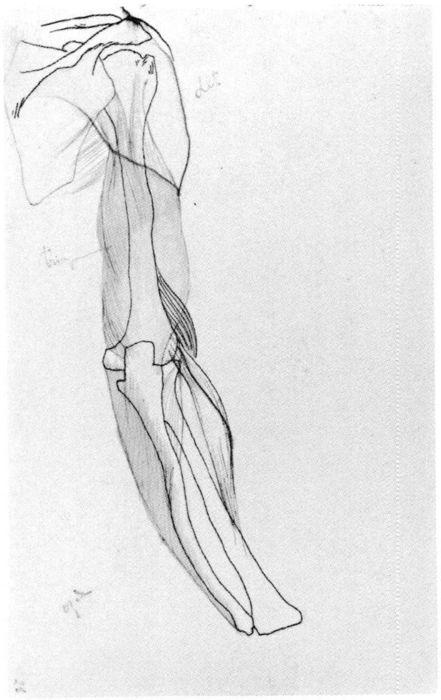

4, p.22

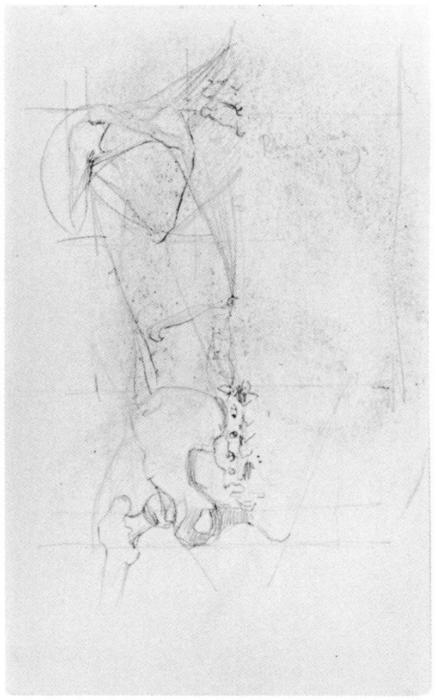

4, p.23

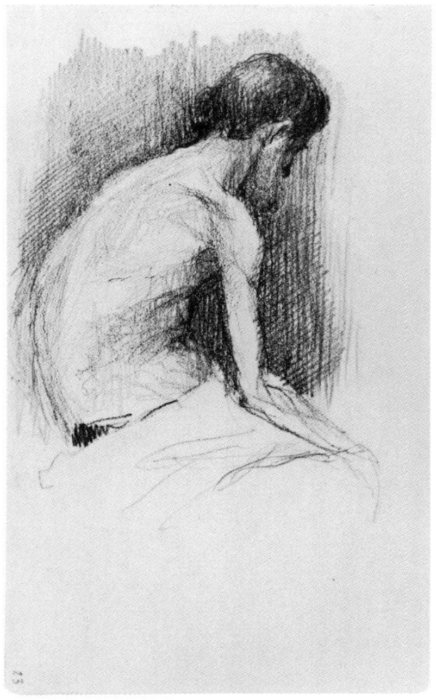

4, p.24

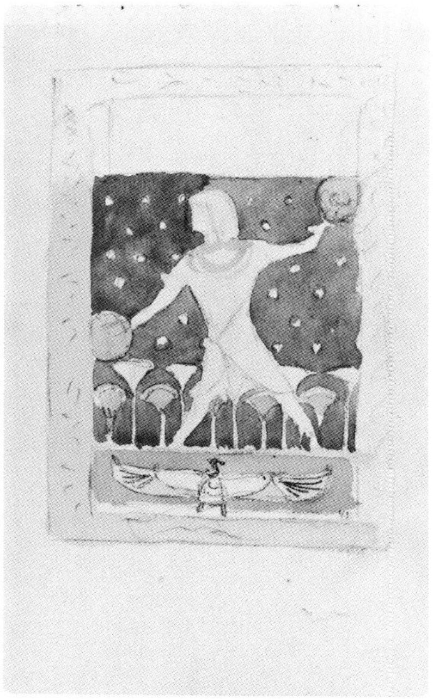

**p.26** Pencil drawing of seated man with beard holding dagger

REFERENCES
Hanfstaengl 1974, p.168

Hanfstaengl questioned whether Kandinsky had made this drawing.

**p.27** Pencil sketch of building with figure at lower left on rose-tan paper

**p.28** Pencil studies of cartilage of nose on rose-tan paper

**p.29** Watercolor and pencil decorative study

REFERENCES
Hanfstaengl 1974, p.168

Hanfstaengl related this study – especially the border – to a colored pencil drawing in Sketchbook 5 (GMS 342, p.31). The format suggests an ex libris or decorative sheet.

**p.30** Pencil and crayon drawing of male and female nudes in landscape

REFERENCES
Hanfstaengl 1974, p.168

Hanfstaengl proposed that the figures might depict Adam and Eve.

**pp.31–41** Blank

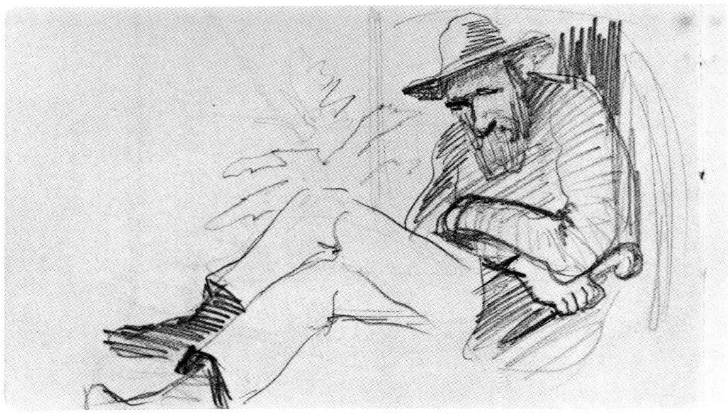

4, p.26

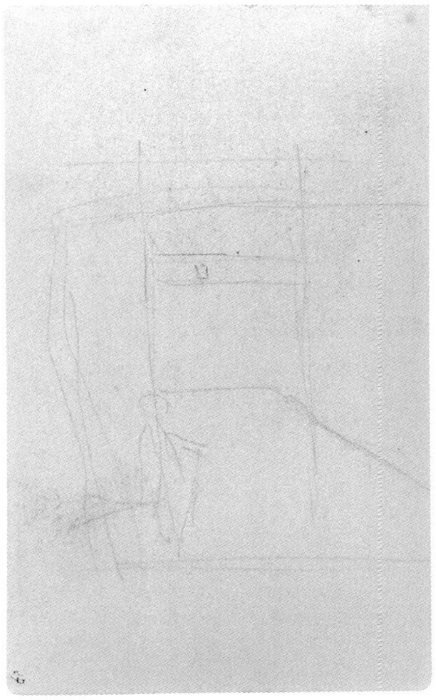

4, p.27

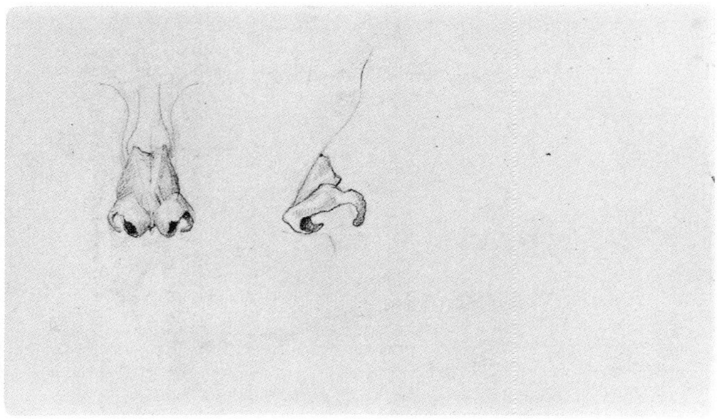

4, p.28

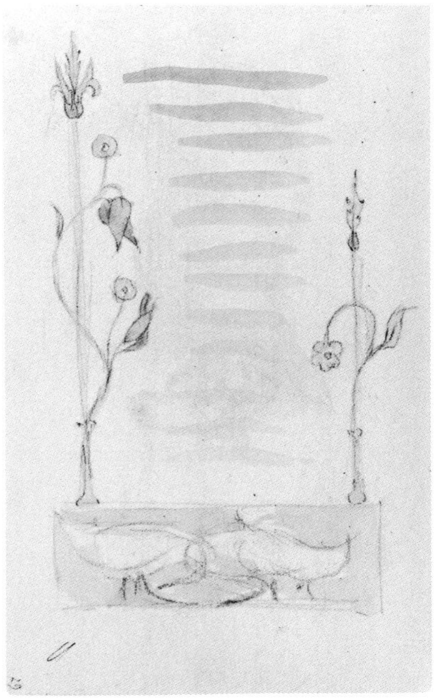

4, p.29

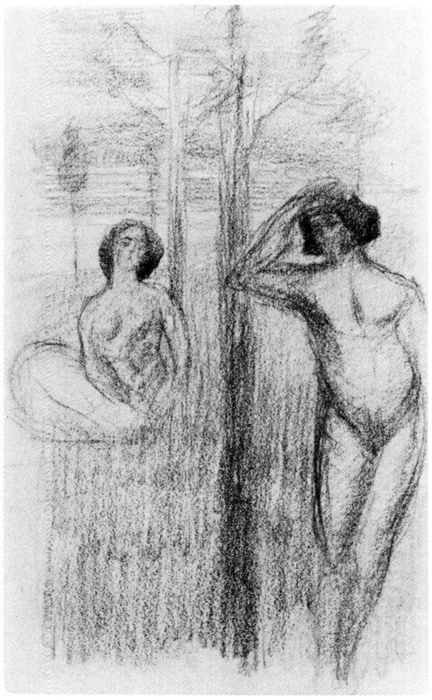

4, p.30

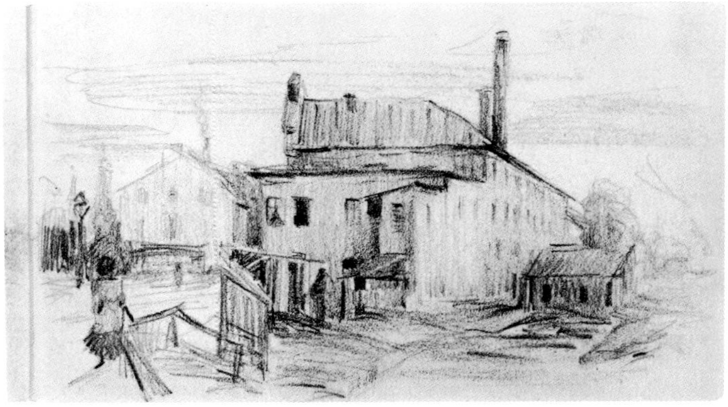

4, p.42

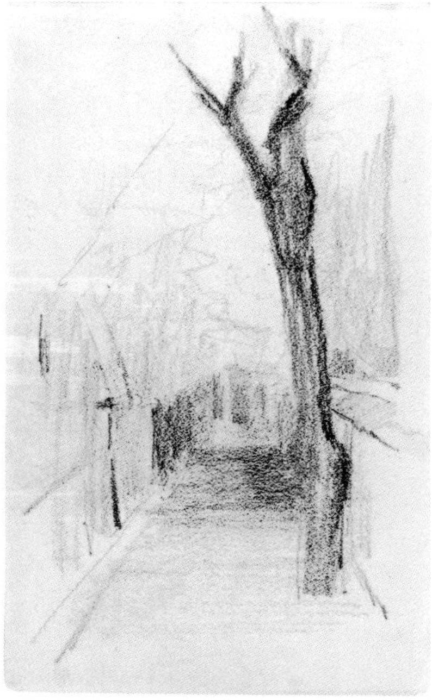

4, p.44

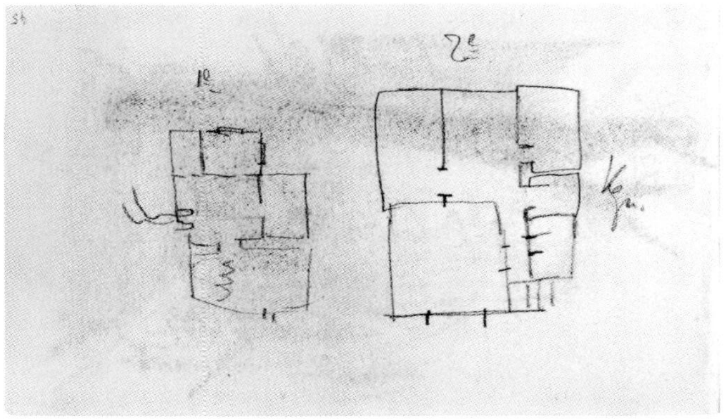

4, p.45

4, p.46

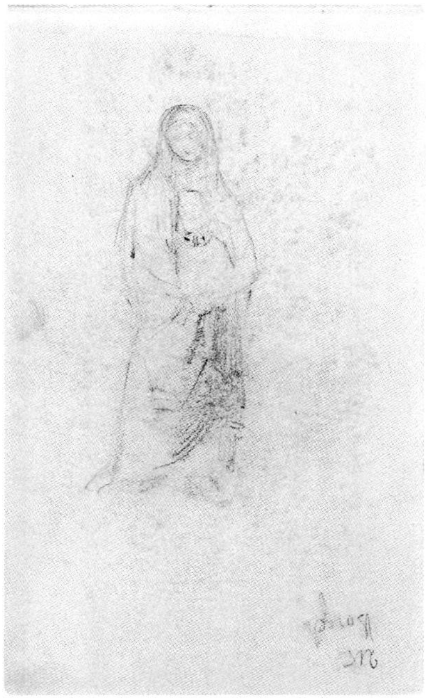

**p.42** Pencil drawing of buildings near Munich

REFERENCES

Hanfstaengl 1974, p.168, ill.
Barnett and Friedel 1995, no.2, color ill.

In comparison with a related study in Sketchbook 3 (GMS 344, p. 54), this drawing displays a greater sense of depth and shadow and also includes a figure of a woman at the lower left.

**p.43** Blank

**p.44** Pencil drawing of street with tree

**p.45** Pencil drawings of floor plans (upside down)
Inscribed above: '1e 2e'; c.r. in Cyrillic: 'Kor.'

Kandinsky noted a corridor adjacent to the floor plan.

**p.46** Pencil drawing of standing female figure (inside back cover)
Inscribed l.r. in Cyrillic (upside down): '215 / Vecher'

There appears to be no connection between the sketch and the inscription ('evening').

# Sketchbook 5

1897–1903

Grey linen-covered cardboard sketchbook; inside back cover label from Franz Dury, Munich (Amalienstrasse and Theresienstrasse)
Contains 52 pages (26 sheets), each 13.4 x 21.5 cm (5¼ x 8½ in)
Page numbers inscribed by unknown hand at later date with odd numbers at lower right

Hanfstaengl 1974, p.162

LOCATION
Städtische Galerie im Lenbachhaus, Munich (GMS 342)

HISTORY
Gabriele Münter, Murnau, until 1957

Erika Hanfstaengl related this sketchbook to Sketchbook 4: she thought that the anatomy studies were dated c.1897–1900 and other sketches were made until c.1902–1903. Both sketchbooks contain sections of different-colored paper, and both were purchased from Franz Dury in Munich. This sketchbook has significantly more studies in watercolor and colored pencil than previous sketchbooks.

**p.1** Brown chalk study of male nude

**p.2** Brown chalk study of seated male nude

REFERENCES
Barnett and Friedel 1995, no.8, color ill.

The manner of modeling with cross-hatching in the figure studies reveals the teaching methods of Anton Azbè with whom Kandinsky studied in Munich.

**p.3** Brown chalk study of standing male nude

REFERENCES
Hanfstaengl 1974, p.162, ill.

**p.4** Pencil study of standing male nude holding pole

REFERENCES
Hanfstaengl 1974, p.162, ill.
Roethel and Hahl-Koch 1980, pp.22, 42, ill.24
Hahl-Koch 1993, p.59, ill.58

According to Hanfstaengl, the study probably depicts the same male model

5, p.1

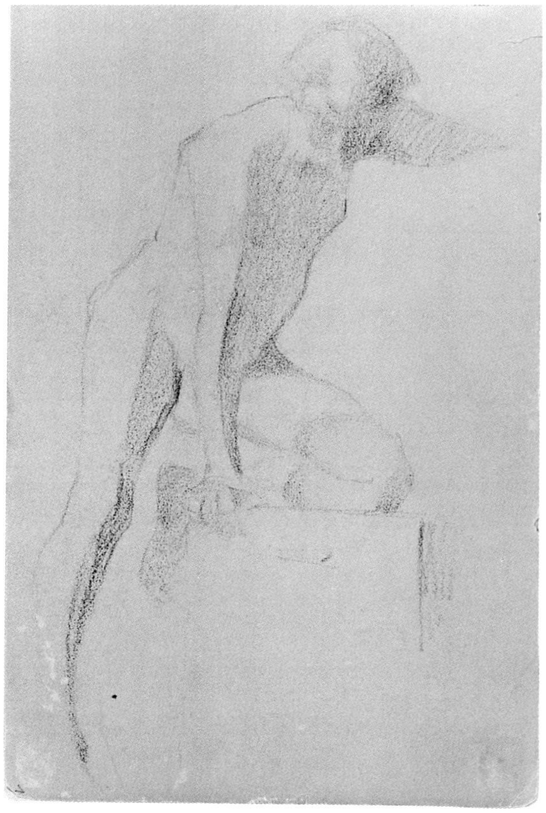

5, p.2

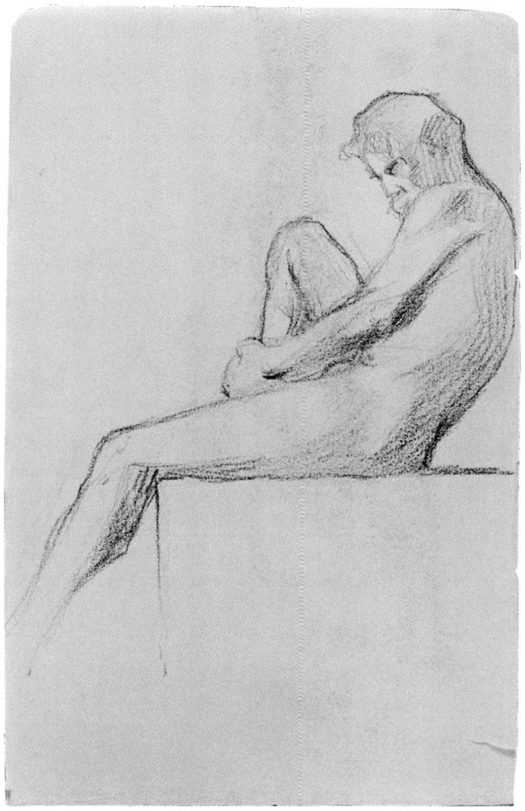

5, p.3

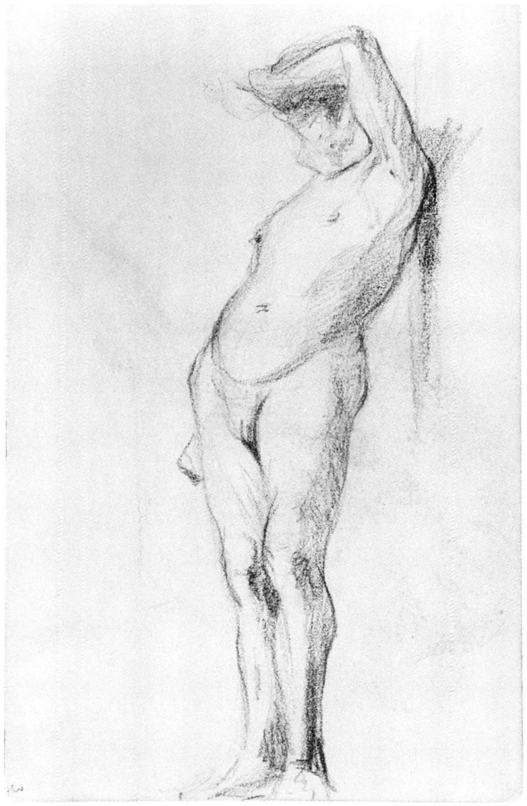

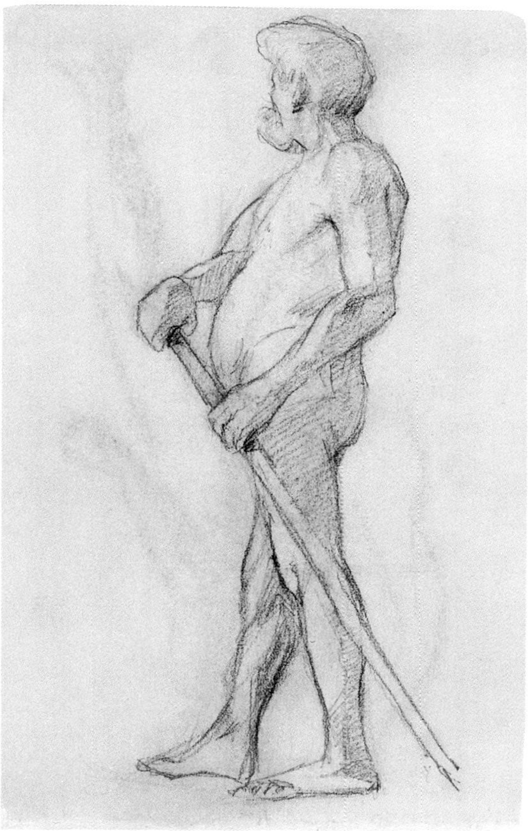

5, p.4

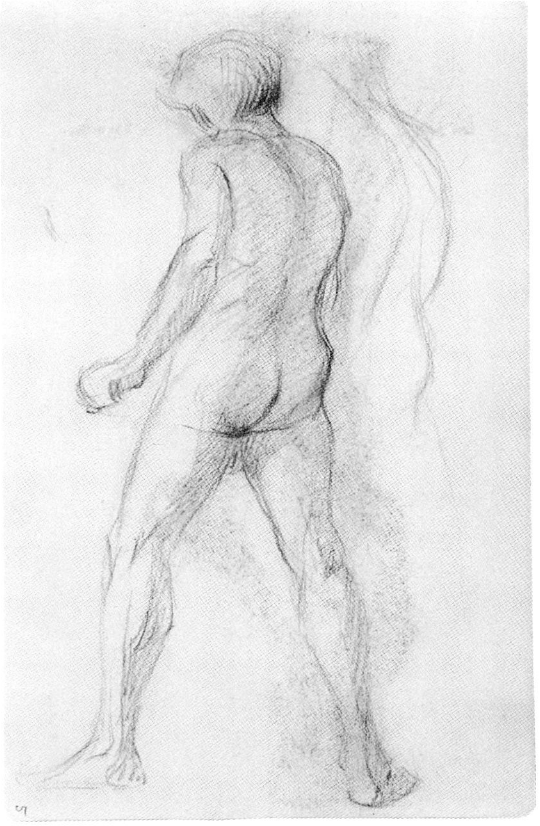

5, p.5

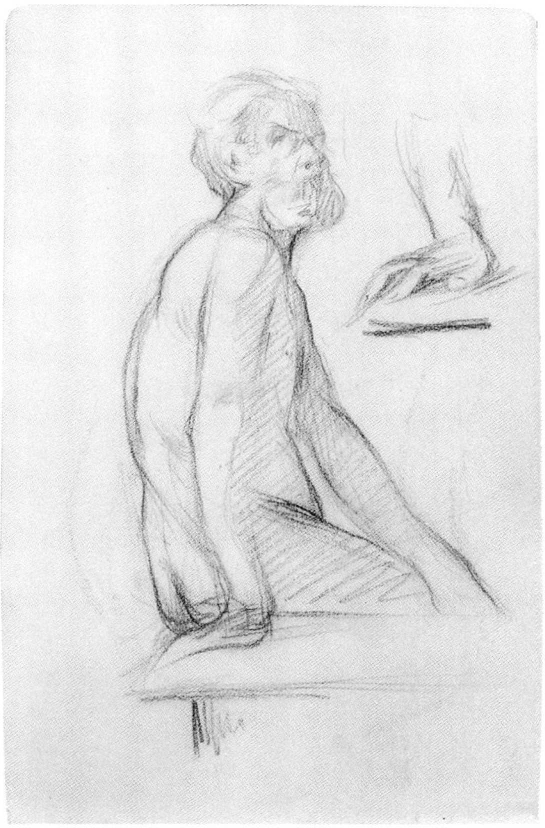

5, p.6

as one shown in Sketchbook 4 (GMS 348 pp.12, 13). Roethel and Hahl-Koch thought that the drawing was made at Azbè's school c.1897.

**p.5** Red chalk studies of male nude

**p.6** Red chalk study of seated male nude and detail of his hand

REFERENCES
Hanfstaengl 1974, p.162, ill.

Hanfstaengl related the drawing to pp.12–13 in Sketchbook 4.

**p.7** Pencil sketch of figure

There is some red chalk transfer from the study on the facing page. The drawing probably shows the same youthful male nude as the one found on the following pages.

**p.8** Pencil drawing of standing male nude

5, p.7

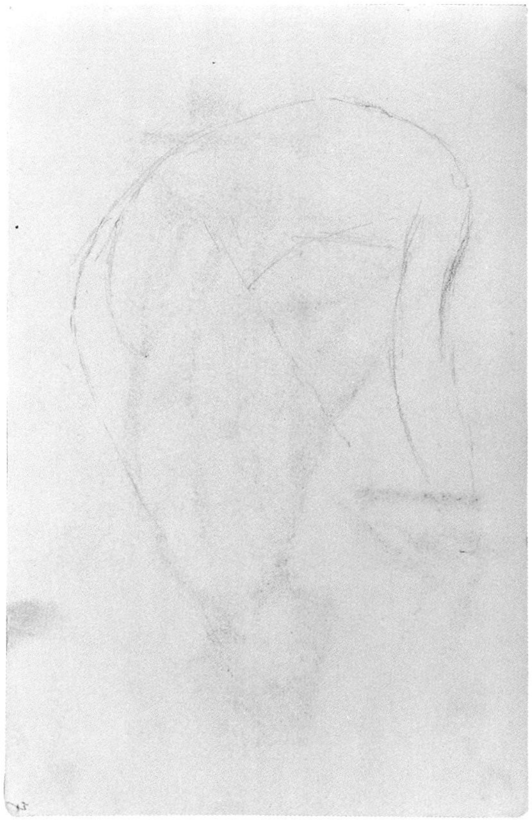

5, p.8

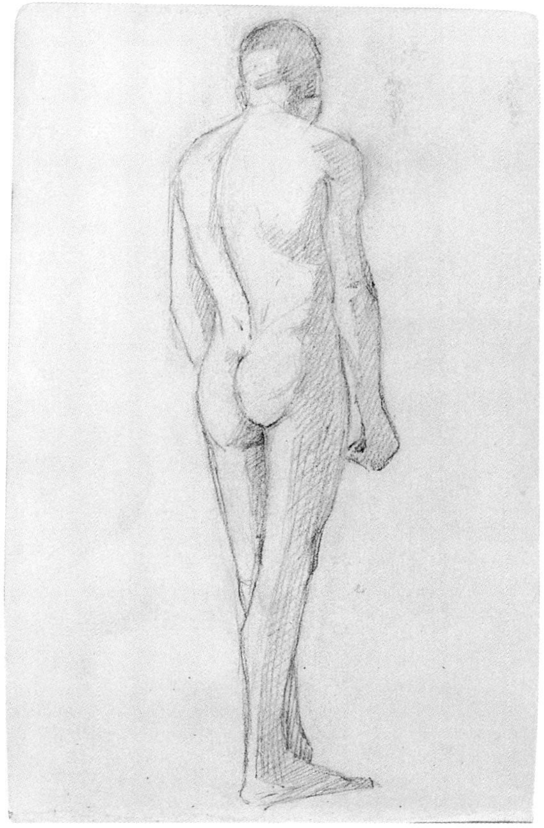

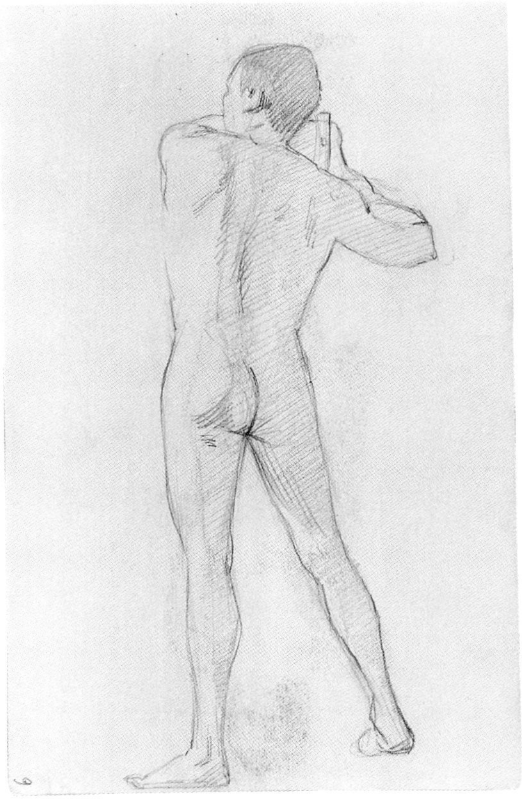

5, p.9

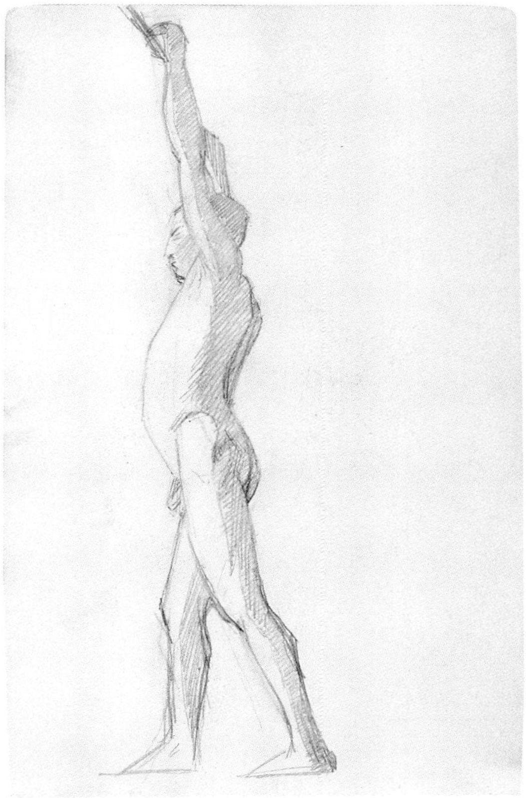

5, p.10

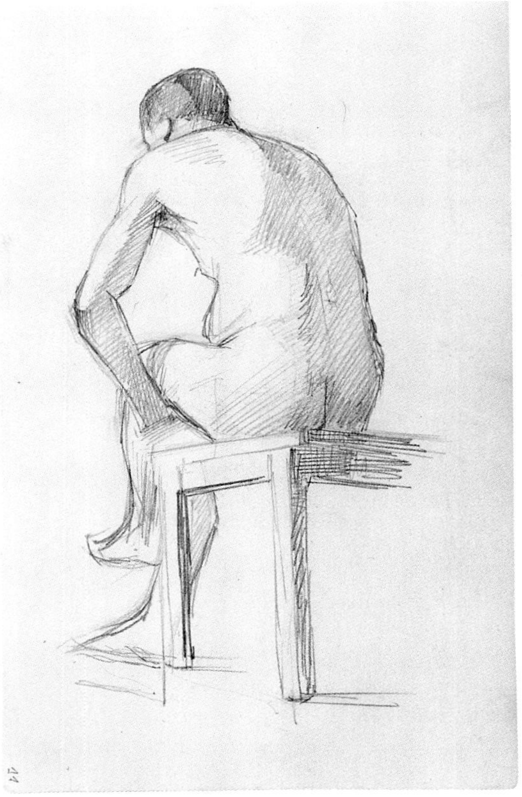

5, p.11

5, p.12

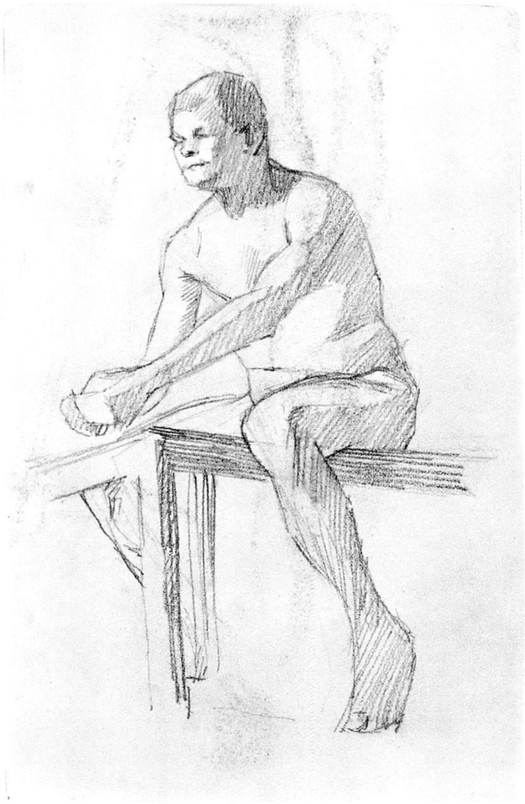

5, p.13

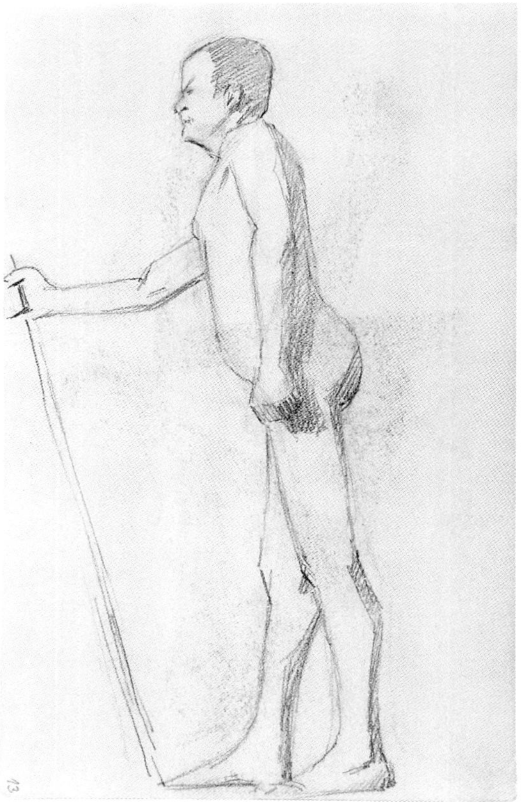

**p.9** Pencil drawing of standing male nude

**p.10** Pencil drawing of standing male nude

**p.11** Pencil drawing of seated male nude

**p.12** Pencil drawing of seated male nude

REFERENCES
Hanfstaengl 1974, p.162, ill.

**p.13** Pencil drawing of male nude standing with pole

**p.14** Pencil drawing of standing female nude

**p.15** Pencil drawing of standing female nude

REFERENCES
Hanfstaengl 1974, p.162, ill.

**p.16** Pencil drawing of standing female nude

REFERENCES
Hanfstaengl 1974, p.162, ill.

**p.17** Pencil study of standing male nude

The figure has been squared up to indicate proportion.

**p.18** Pencil drawing of male nude with arms extended

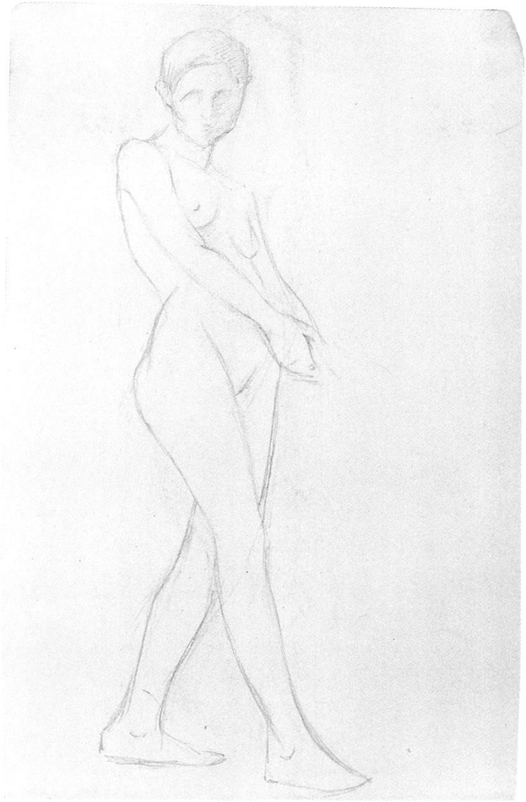

5, p.14

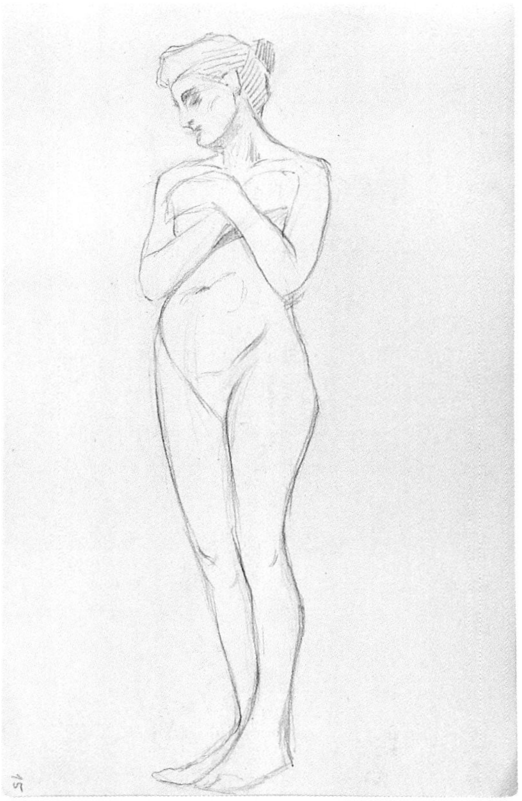

5, p.15

5, p.16

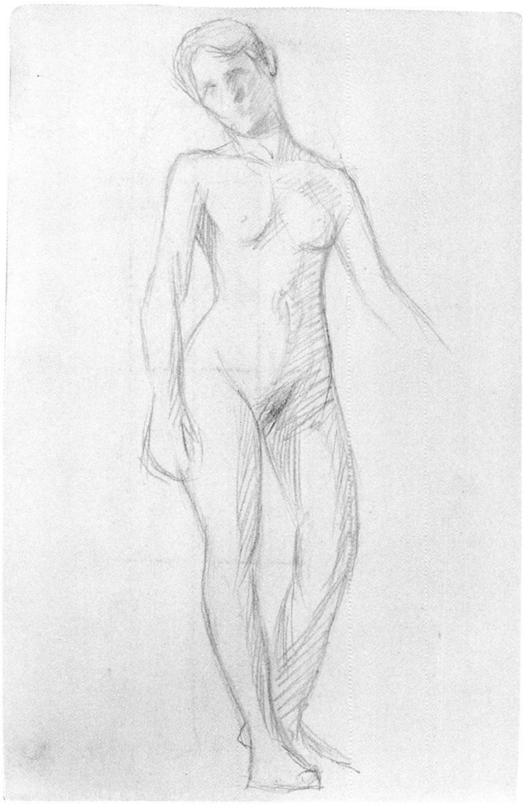

5, p.17

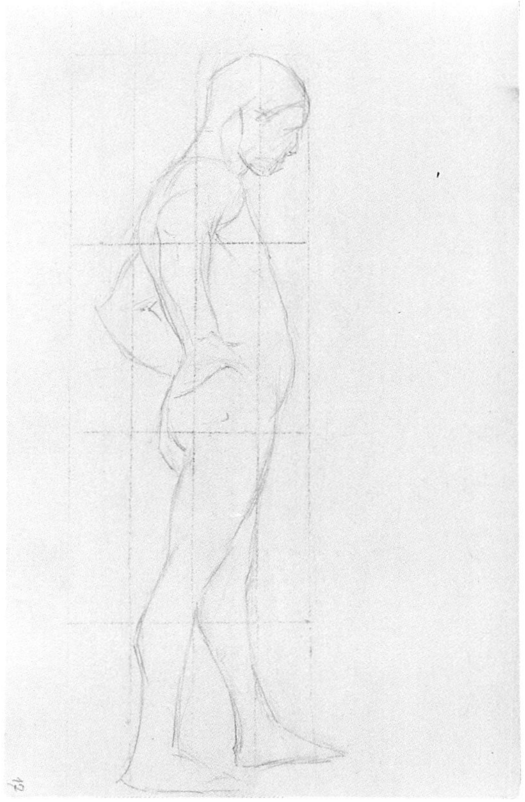

5, p.18

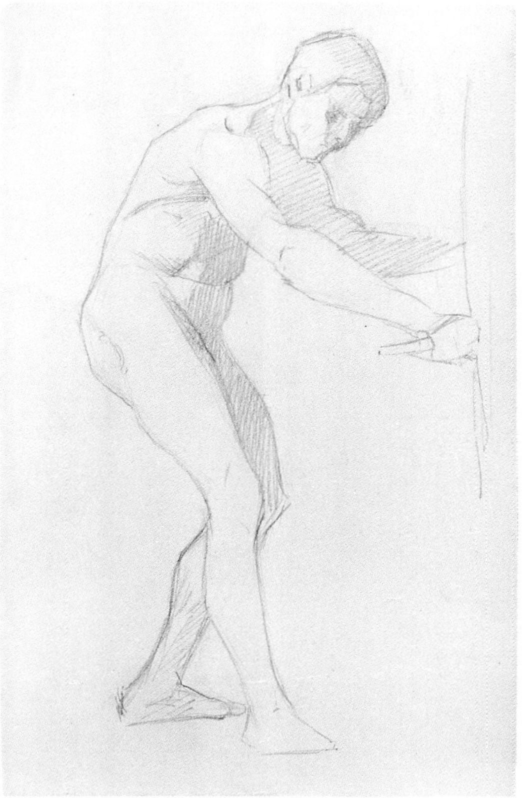

**p.19** Pencil drawing of seated female nude

**p.20** Pencil drawing of standing female nude and detail

**p.21** Pencil drawing of reclining female nude

**p.22** Pencil drawing of standing male nude

**p.23** Pencil drawing of female nude

**p.24** Blank

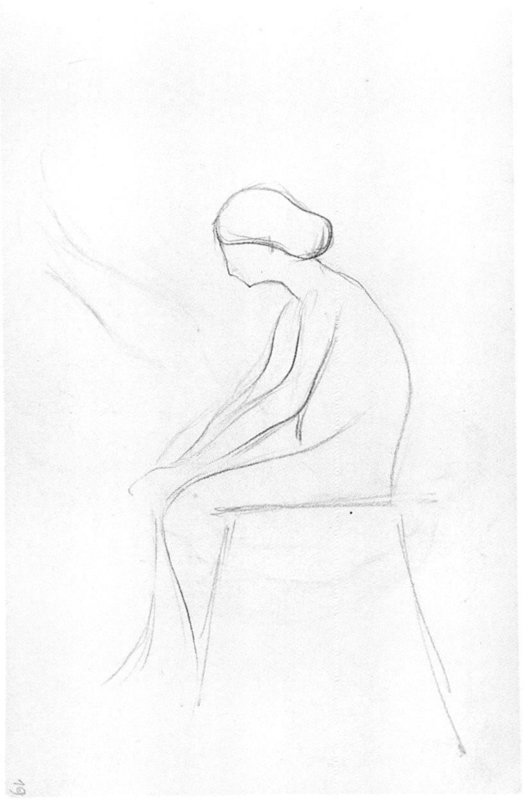

5, p.19

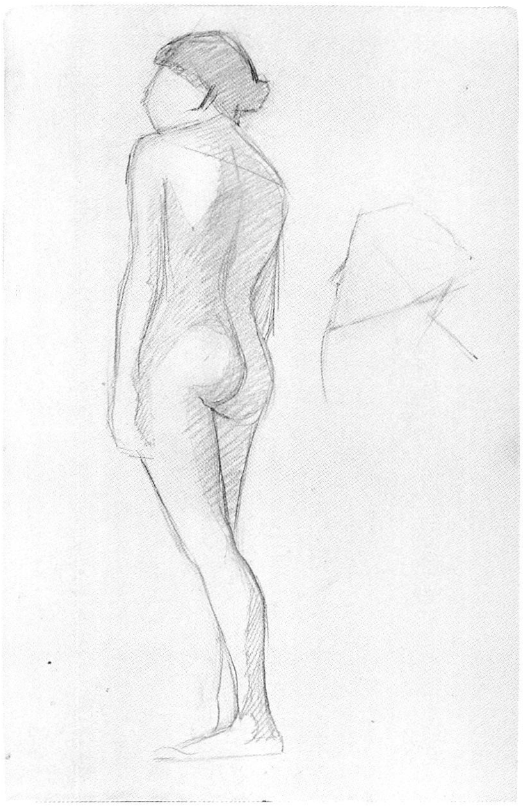

5, p.20

5, p.21

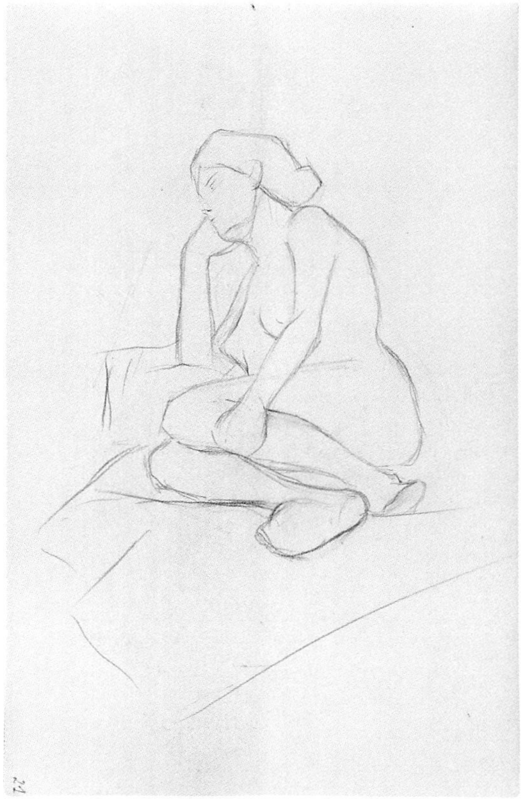

5, p.22

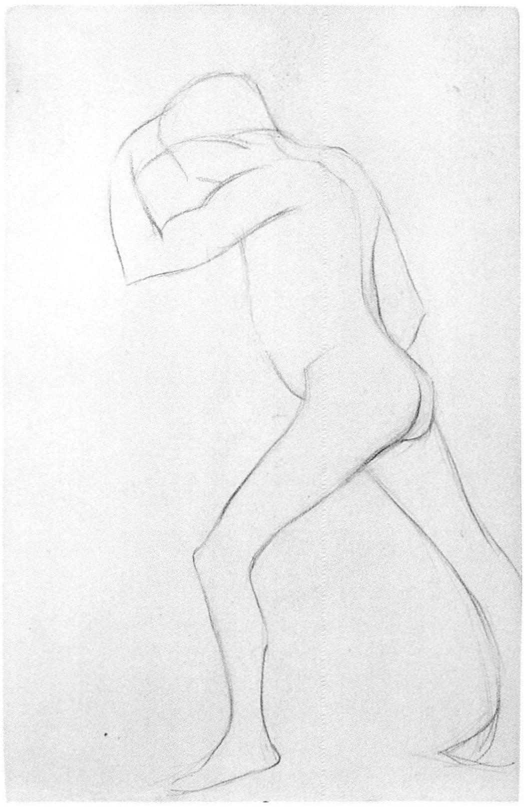

5, p.23

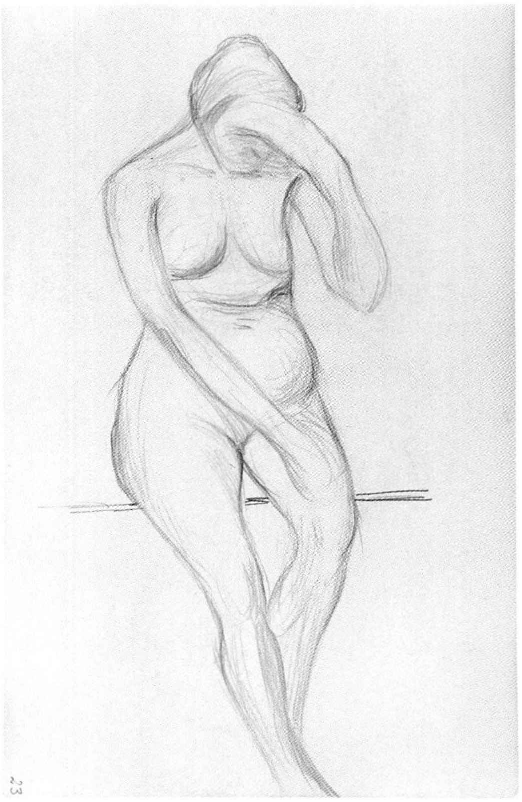

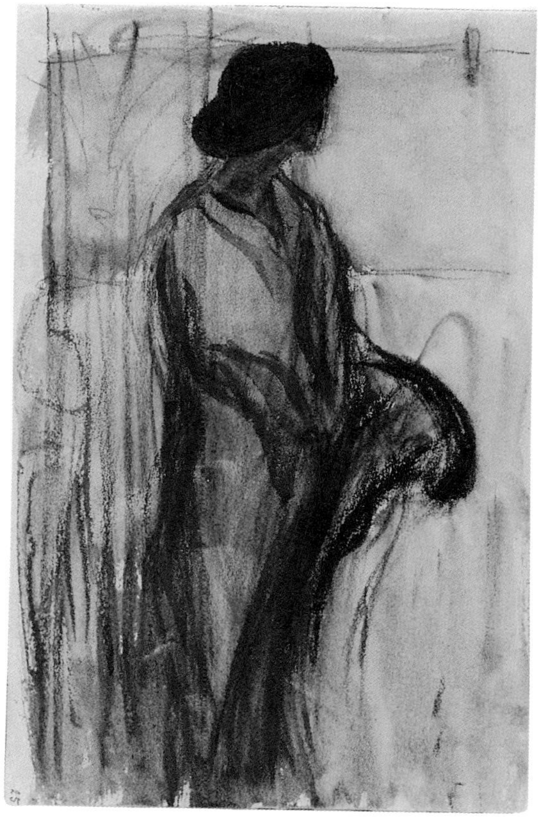

5, p.25

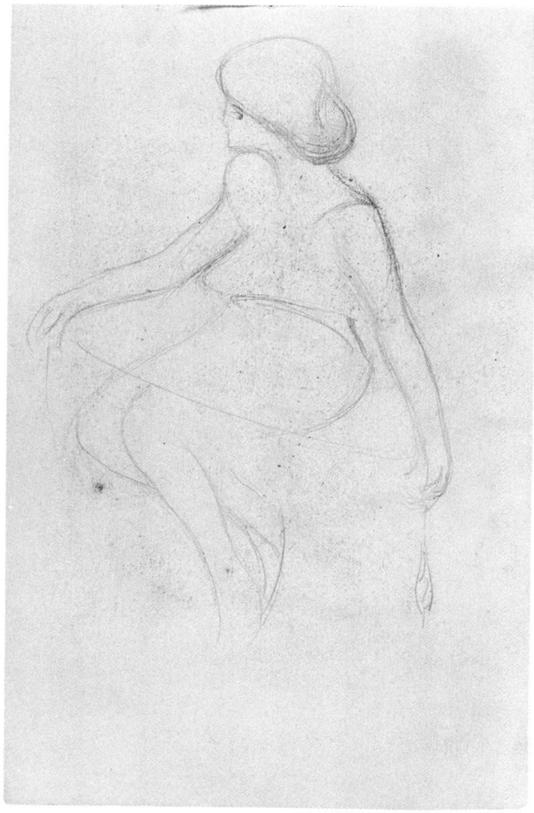

5, p.28

**p.25** Red chalk and wash study of standing female figure

REFERENCES

Barnett and Friedel 1995, no.13, color ill.

(See color plate p.115)

**pp.26–27** Blank

**p.28** Pencil drawing of seated female figure on green paper

The model is probably depicted on p.48 (below).

**p.29** Pencil, colored pencil and crayon drawing of house with garden and pond on green paper

(See color plate p.115)

**p.30** Blank

**p.31** Pencil, colored pencil and crayon drawing of house with garden and pond on tan paper

REFERENCES

Hanfstaengl 1974, p.162, ill.

**p.32** Blank

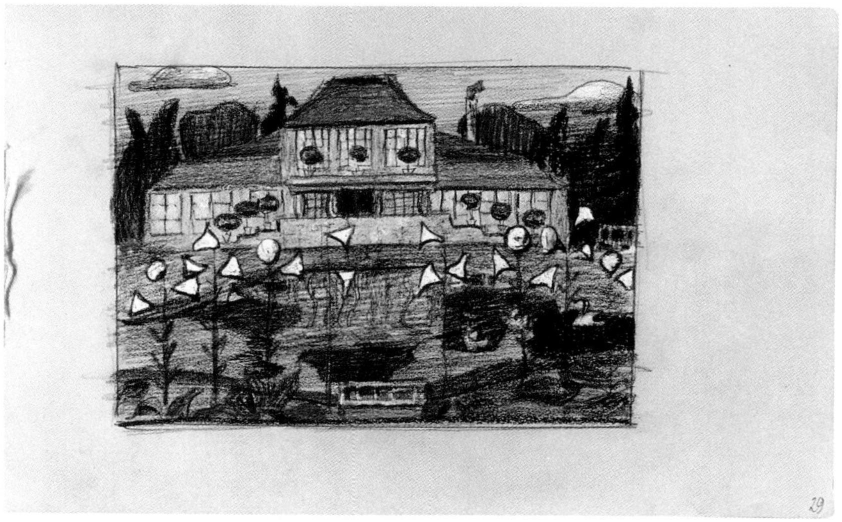

5, p.29

5, p.31

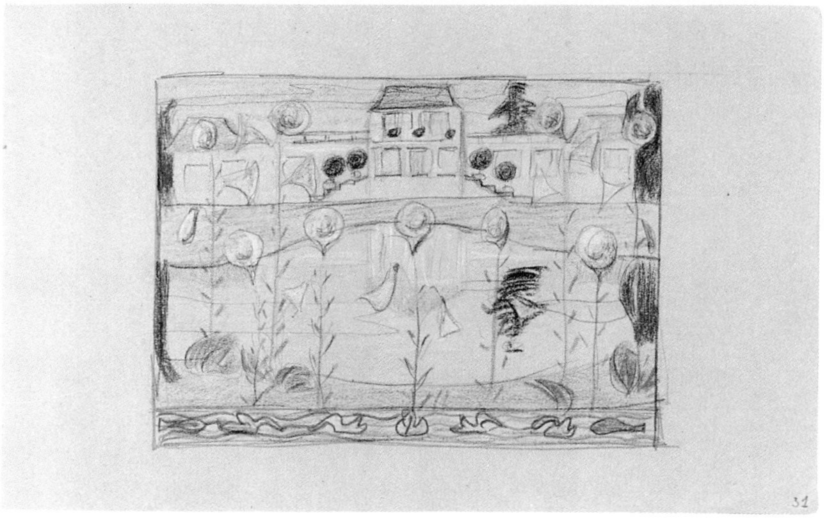

**p.33** Pencil studies of flowers
Inscribed l.c. partially in Cyrillic with color notations: 'cher. Slabo / Krapplack oben / c. zinober roth / kr / zeleno-buromu / (co. Sienoú natur.)'

The color notations refer to weak black, rose red above with vermilion and green-brown.

**pp.34–35** Blank

**p.36** Pencil drawing of knight in armor

REFERENCES
Hanfstaengl 1974, p.162, ill.
Barnett 1992, p.104, ill.a
Barnett and Friedel 1995, no.60, color ill.

The knight in armor can be related to *Weisse Wolke* of 1903 (Barnett no.88) and perhaps to a drawing in Sketchbook 3 (GMS 344, p.26).

**p.37** Pencil drawing of galloping horses with riders

REFERENCES
Hanfstaengl 1974, p.162, ill.

By 1901 the theme of riders and horses had emerged in Kandinsky's art.

**p.38** Blank

**p.39** Colored crayon drawing of woman seated in chair with yellow sun at left

(See color plate p.115)

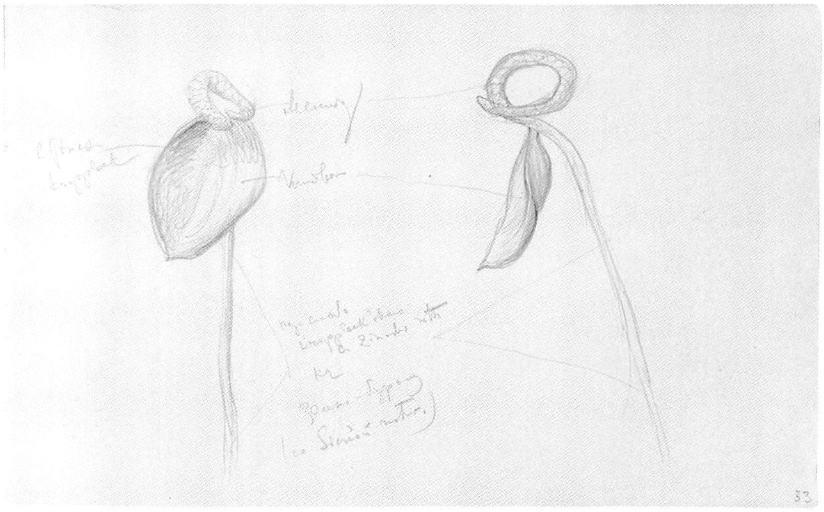

5, p.33

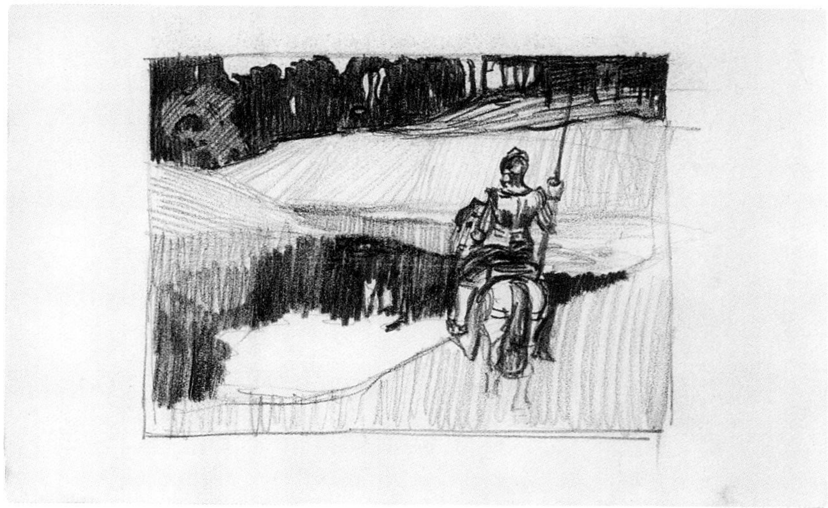

5, p.36

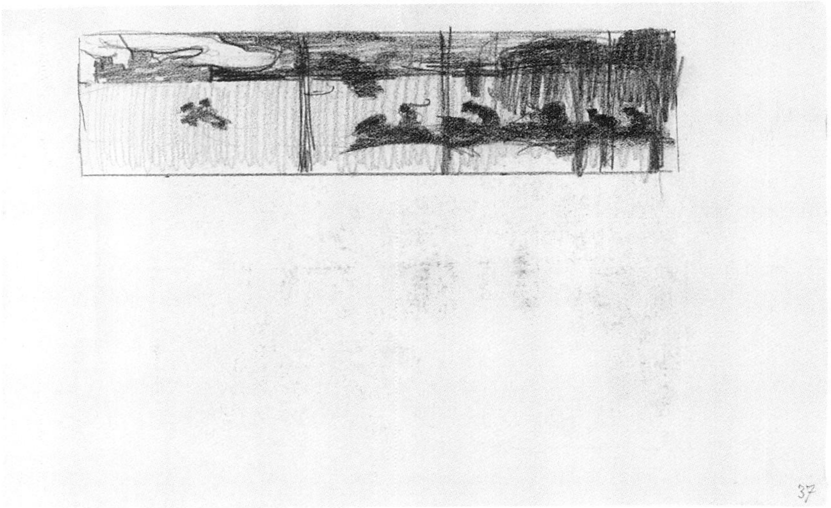

5, p.37

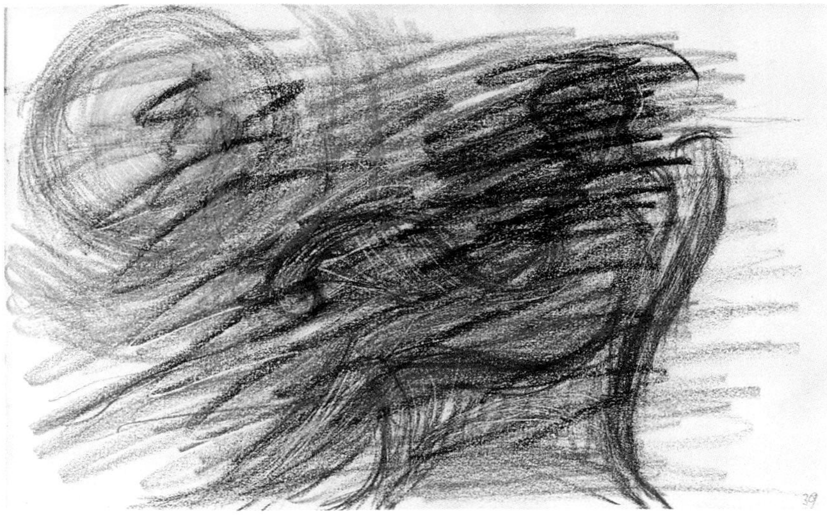

5, p.39

**p.40** Watercolor, metallic paint, colored crayon and pencil designs for furniture
Inscribed u.r. in Cyrillic: 'svetl. m:or. / c. zolotom / spiral / slabee! / sh:toe.'

EXHIBITIONS
1982 New York no.109, ill.
1982 Munich, no.141, ill.

REFERENCES
Weiss 1979, fig.106
Podzemskaia 2000, p.57

There are furniture designs also on pp.43 and 45 (below) and in Sketchbook 7 (GMS 338, p.34), which have been dated c.1902–1903. Weiss dated this sheet 1900–1904.

**p.41** Watercolor and metallic paint study for vase

REFERENCES
Podzemskaia 2000, p.57

(See color plate p.115)

**p.42** Blank

**p.43** Watercolor, metallic paint and pencil drawing of bed

REFERENCES
Barnett and Friedel 1995, no.77, color ill.
Podzemskaia 2000, p.57

(See color plate p.116)

**p.44** Blank

**p.45** Pencil drawings for furniture
Inscribed l.l.: '6 x 14'

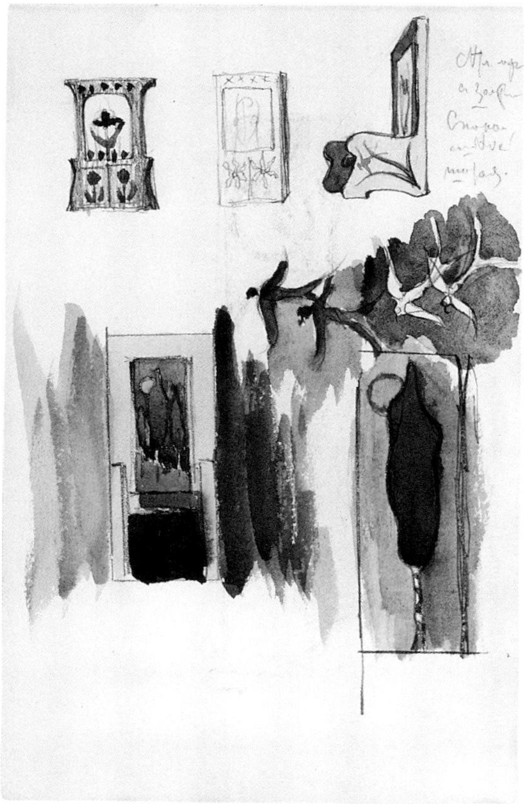

5, p.40

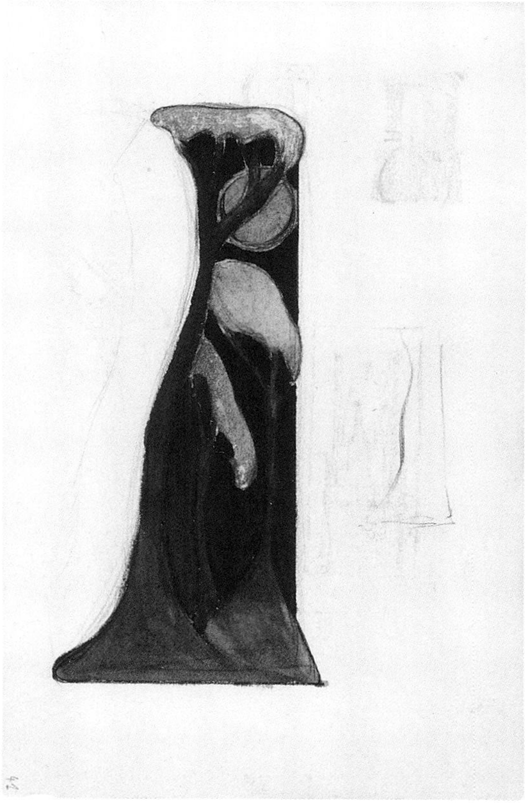

5, p.41

5, p.43

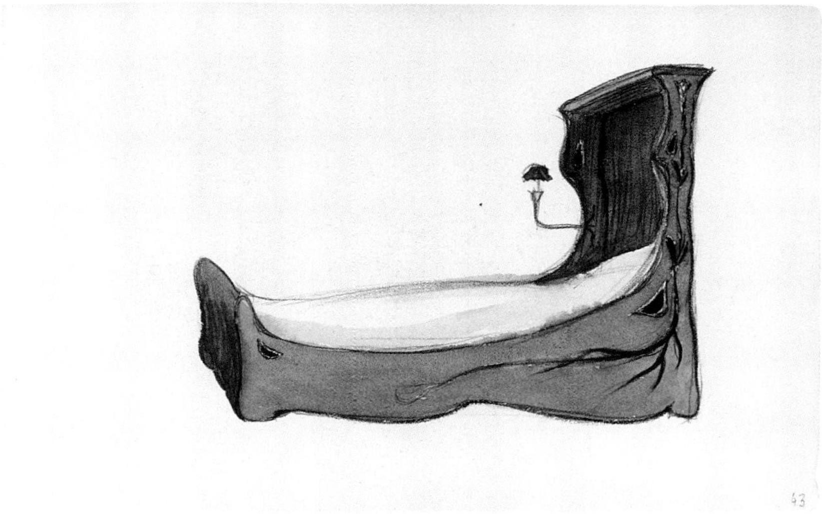

5, p.45

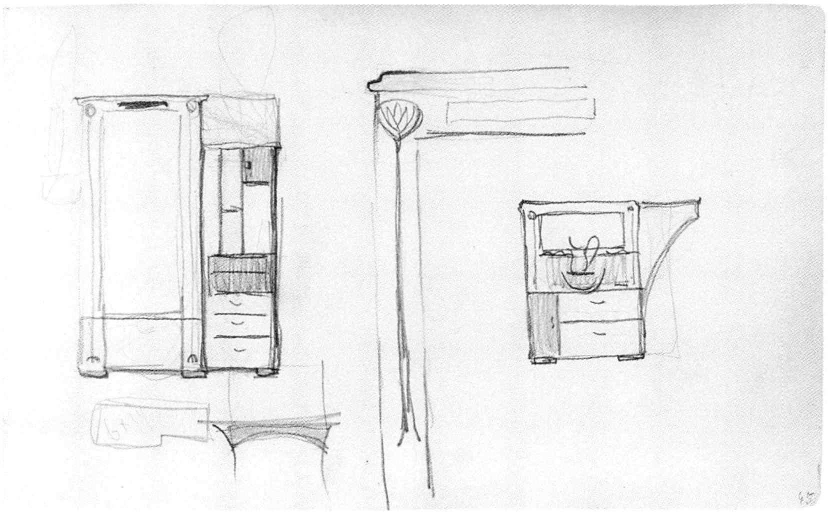

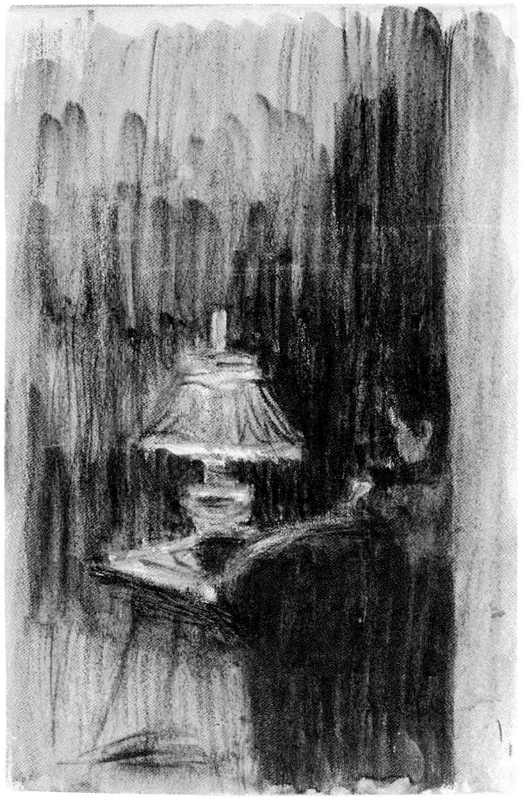

5, p.46

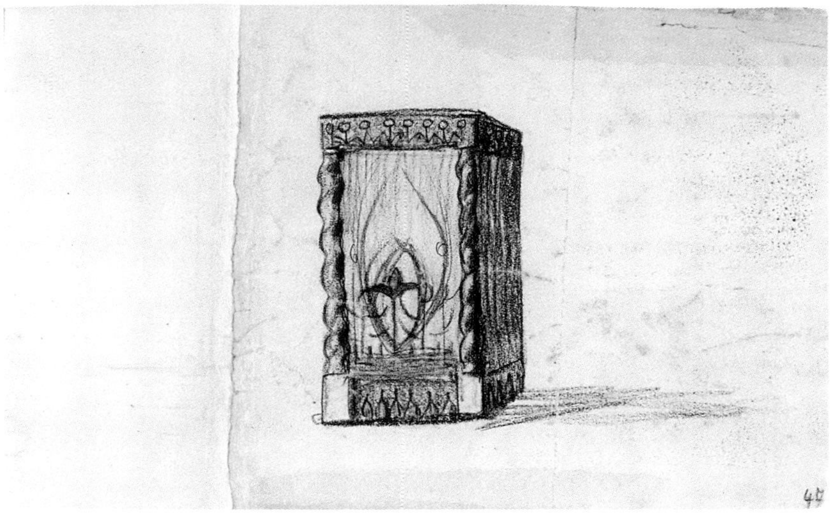

5, p.47

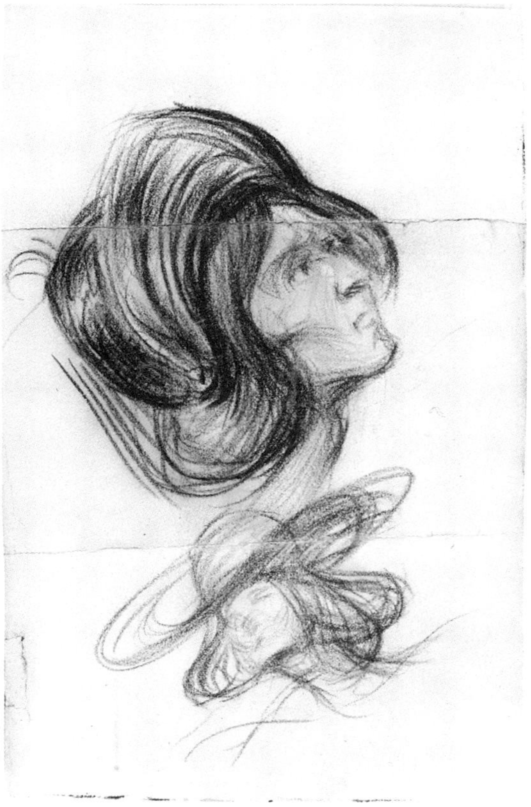

5, p.48

**p.46** Red and brown chalk with wash drawing of figure seated near lamp

(See color plate p.116)

**p.47** Colored pencil and pencil drawing of chest or box

**p.48** Red chalk studies of female head

**p.49** Blank

**p.50** Watercolor, gouache and pencil drawing of boat with red sail and figures in costume

(See color plate p.116)

**p.51** Pencil studies of knight in armor (upside down)
Inscribed u.l. in Cyrillic: '[...] / chugunnyi'

**p.52** Watercolor, gold bronze and pencil studies for locks and keys
Inscribed u.l. in Cyrillic and German: 'Kordov- 25 / Zotov- 25 / Tangrel- 25 / ia- 1.25'; l.r.: 'Beschläge'

EXHIBITIONS
1982 New York, no.149, ill.
1982 Munich, no.171, ill.

REFERENCES
Weiss 1979, p.124, fig.107, ill.
Podzemskaia 2000, p.57

Weiss dated this sheet 1900–1904.

(See color plate p.116)

**[p.53]** Unnumbered sheet added between p.52 and back cover (not illustrated)
India ink and opaque white drawing of saddle on grey paper (10.8 x 19.3 cm)

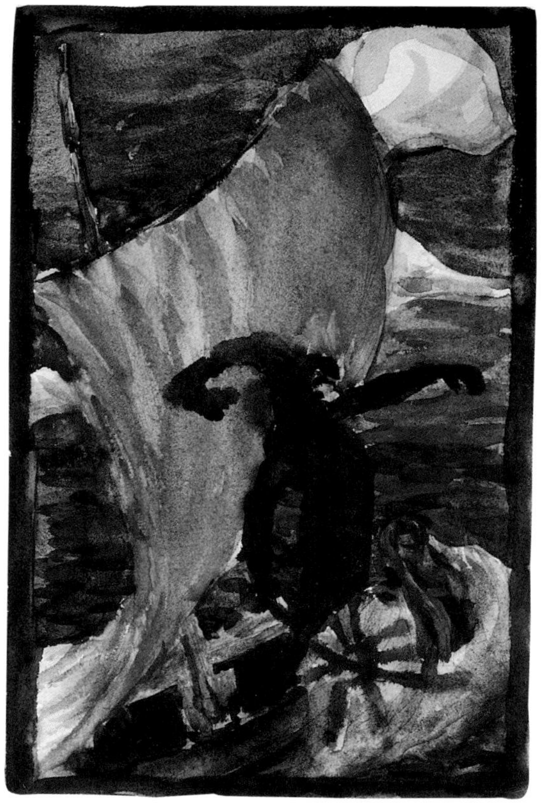

5, p.50

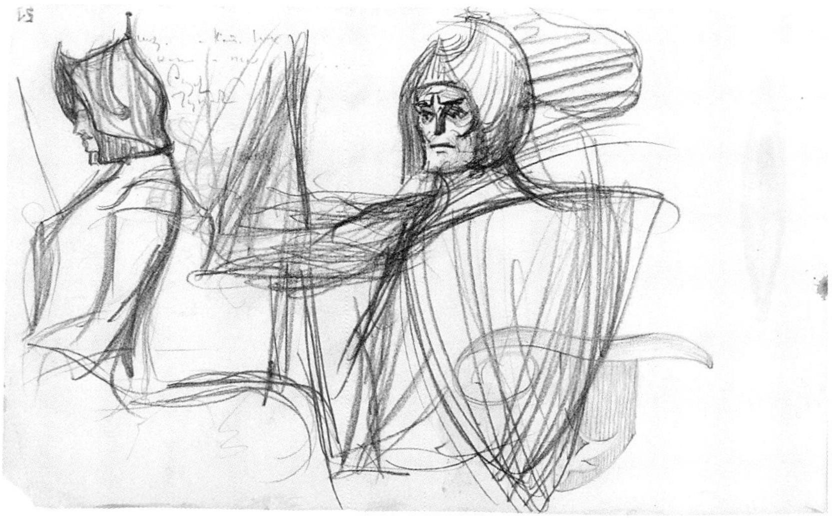

5, p.51

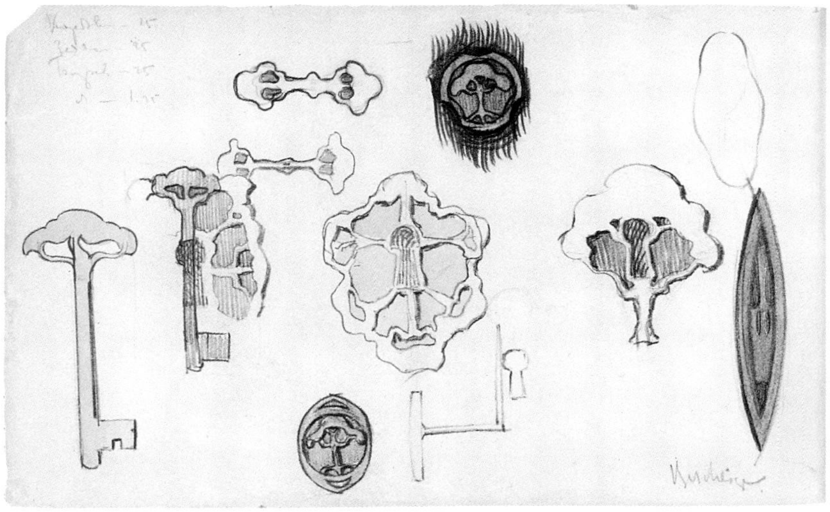

5, p.52

# Sketchbook 6

c.1898–1903

Brown linen-covered cardboard sketchbook with dark brown leather edges; no label
Contains 74 pages (37 sheets), each 9.7 x 16.8 cm (3⅞ x 6⅝ in), of which pp.50–67 are blank
Page numbers inscribed by unknown hand at later date with odd numbers at lower right

Hanfstaengl 1974, p.161

LOCATION
Städtische Galerie im Lenbachhaus, Munich (GMS 341)

HISTORY
Gabriele Münter, Murnau, until 1957

Erika Hanfstaengl proposed that the red chalk drawings on the first and last pages were done earlier than other sheets; she thought that many of the copies dated from about 1900. Nadia Podzemskaia has dated the drawings of armor from book illustrations 1898–1900. Although Kandinsky's paintings of knights in armor date from 1901–1904, his interest in armor goes back to his years of study with Anton Azbè. Kandinsky probably used the sketchbook over a period of years: for example, the costume studies on pp.29–38 in the center were probably done later than the drawings on the first and last pages. The artist's technical skill varies considerably within this sketchbook.

6, p.3

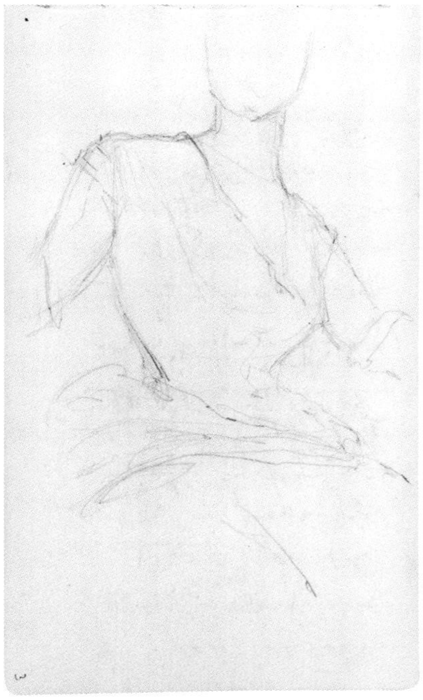

6, p.5

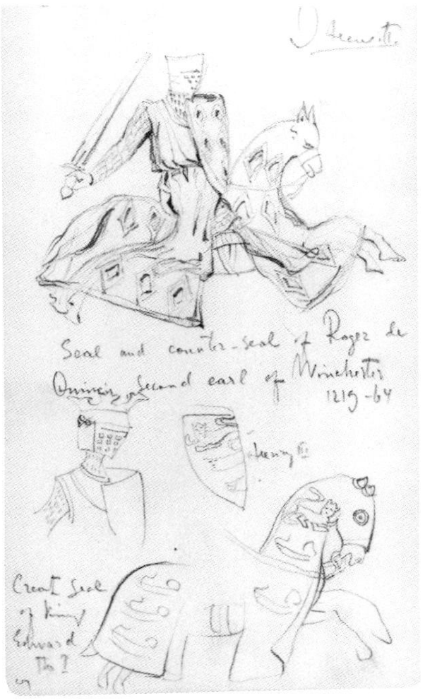

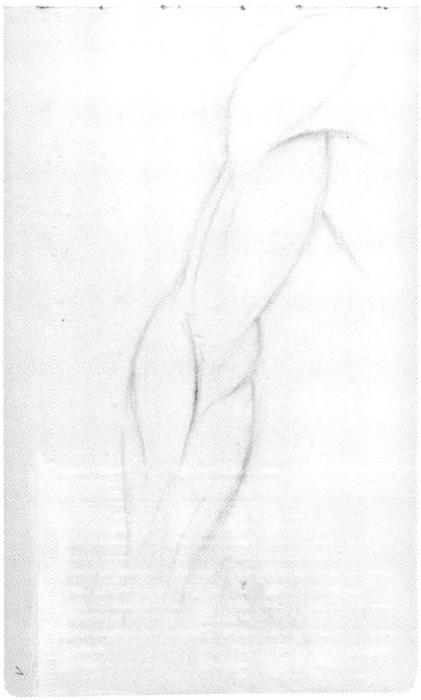

6, p.1

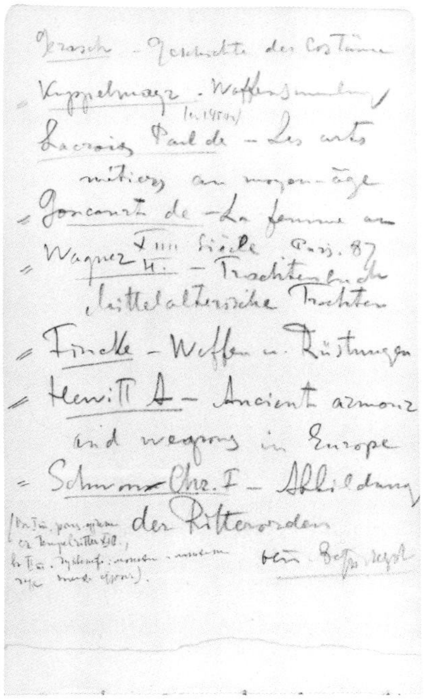

6, p.2

**p.1** Red chalk study of an arm

This study resembles anatomical drawings on pp.15, 16, 19 and 20 in Sketchbook 5 (GMS 344), which can be dated 1897–1900.

**p.2** List of books on costumes and armor: 'Gerasch- Geschichte der Costüme / Kuppelmayr- Waffensammlung / (i 1450 g) / Lacroix Paul de- Les arts / métiers au moyen-âge / Goncourt de- La femme au / XIIII Siècle. Paris 87 / Wagner H.- Trachtenbuch / Mittelalterische Trachten / Fincke- Waffen u. Rüstungen / Hewitt A- Ancient armour / and weapons in Europe / Schwan Chr. F- Abbildung / der Ritterorden'; annotated in Cyrillic: '(v I. t razu. str / s Tempelritter XI v., / v II t. dukhovenstvo: monakhi / i monakhini / [...]'

**p.3** Pencil drawing of seated female figure

**p.4** Blank

**p.5** Pencil drawings after two seals
Inscribed u.r.: 'J. Hewitt.'; c.: 'Seal and counter-seal of Roger de / Quinci, Second earl of Winchester / 1219–64 / Henry III'; l.l.: 'Creat Seal / of King / Edward / The I'

REFERENCES
Barnett and Friedel 1995, no.17, color ill.

Kandinsky copied two illustrations from John Hewitt's book, *Ancient Armour and Weapons in Europe* (London, 1860, vol.I, pp.346, 339): plate LXXXVII with the seal of Roger de Quincy, second earl of Winchester (1219–1264) appears above, and elements from plate LXXXV depicting the Great Seal of King Edward I (1239–1307) appear below. The notes refer to the captions for the illustrations listed at the beginning of volume I. See also p.46 (below).

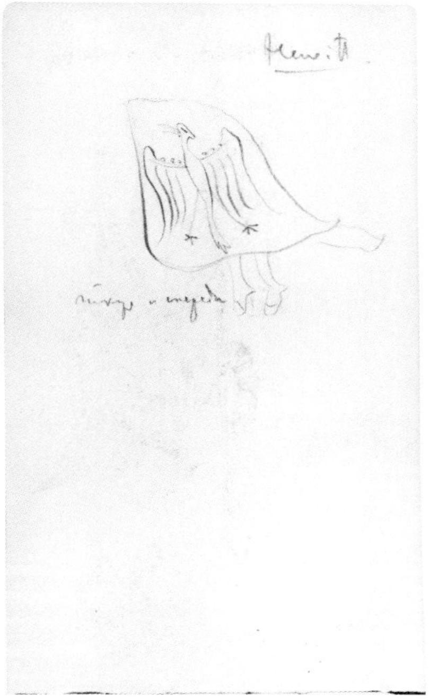


6, p.6

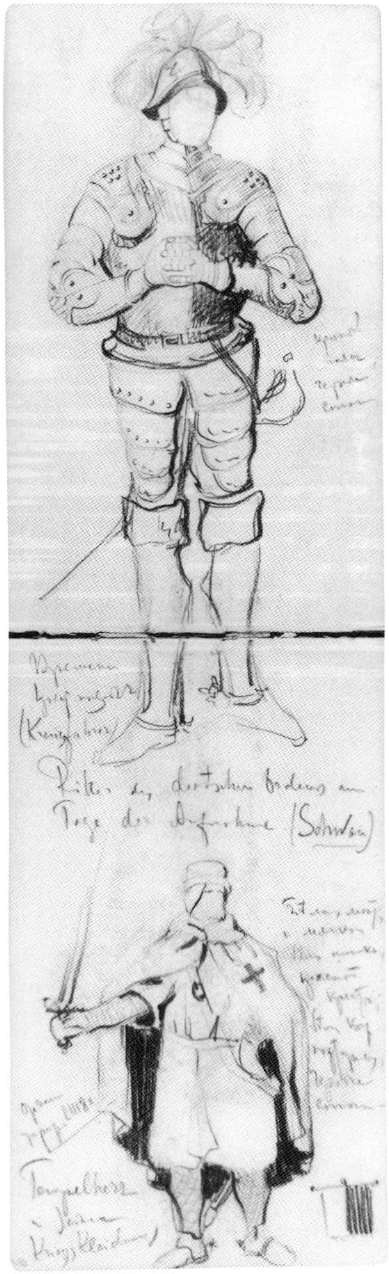

6, pp.8-9

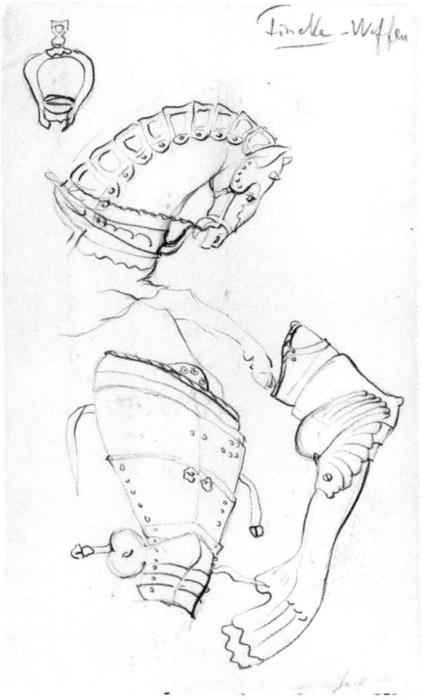


6, p.10

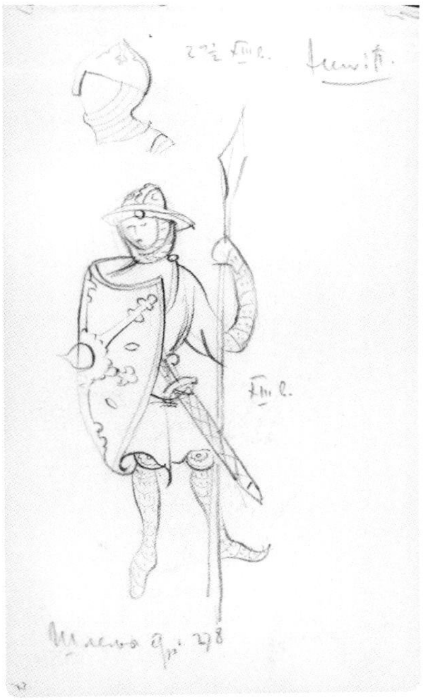


6, p.7

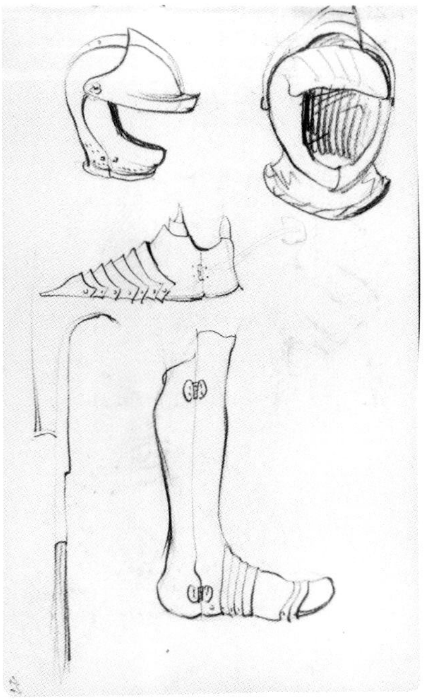

6, p.11

**p.6** Pencil drawing of heraldic emblem for horse
Inscribed u.r.: 'Hewitt.'; c.l. in Cyrillic: '[…] i speredi'

The drawing is based on an illustration on p.195 of Hewitt's book; however, Kandinsky omitted the mounted archer, most of his horse and the sword under the horse's hoofs.

**p.7** Pencil drawing of helmet and knight in armor
Inscribed u.r.: '2½ XIII v. Hewitt.'; c.: 'XIII v.'; l.l. in Cyrillic: 'Shlemy str. 278'

Kandinsky copied the drawing on p.290 in Hewitt's book of a figure from the Painted Chamber at Westminster, which dates from the second half of the thirteenth century. His notes refer to the helmets illustrated on p.278 of *Ancient Armour and Weapons in Europe.*

**pp.8–9** Pencil drawing of knight in armor
Inscribed c.r. in Cyrillic: 'krasnyi / poias, / chernyi / sapogi.'

REFERENCES
Hanfstaengl 1974, p.161, ill.
Podzemskaia 2000, p.124, fig.18

The artist noted 'red belt' and 'black boots' for this study. Podzemskaia has identified the source as plate 13 in Christian Friedrich Schwan's book, *Abbildungen derjenigen Ritter-Orden welche eine eigene Ordenskleidung haben* (Mannheim, 1791).

(See color plate p.117)

**p.9** Pencil and red pencil drawing of templar knight
Inscribed u.l. in Cyrillic: 'Vremeni / Krestonostsev / (Kreuzfahrer) / Ritter des deutschen Ordens am / Tage der Aufnahme (Schwan)'; c.r.: 'Belaia […] / i miagkaia / belaia shapka / krasnyi / krest / belaia […] / chernye / sapogi'; l.l.: 'Orden uchrezh. 1118 g / Tempelherr / in seiner / Kriegskleidung'

REFERENCES
Hanfstaengl 1974, p.161, ill.
Podzemskaia 2000, p.124, figs.18–19

According to Podzemskaia, the source of Kandinsky's drawing is plate 2 in Christian Friedrich Schwan's book (see above), where the caption reads: 'Ein Tempelherr in seiner Kriegskleidung.'

**p.10** Pencil studies of armor
Inscribed u.r.: 'Fincke- Waffen'

Kandinsky copied several elements – armor for an arm, a thigh, a horse's head and a stirrup – from plate IX in Gustav Fincke, *Abbildung und Beschreibung von alten Waffen und Rüstungen, welche in der Sammlung von Llewelyn Meyrick zu Goodrich-Court in Herefordshire ausgestellt sind* (Berlin, 1836).

**p.11** Pencil studies of helmets and armor protecting legs and feet

Kandinsky copied the protective shoe from plate XV, the boot and helmet at the upper right from plate XVII and the helmet at the upper left from plate X of Fincke's book (see above).

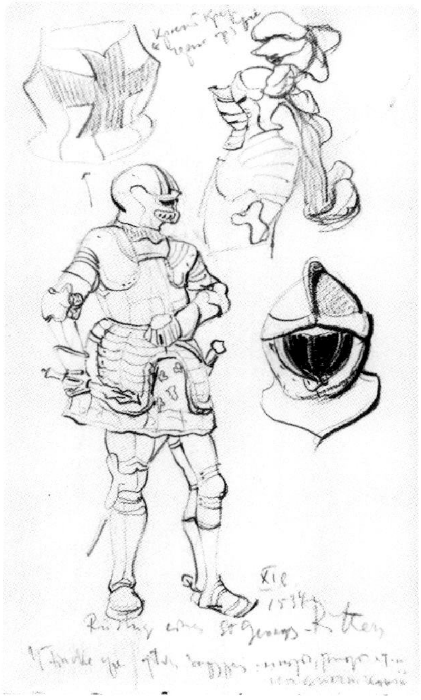

6, p.12

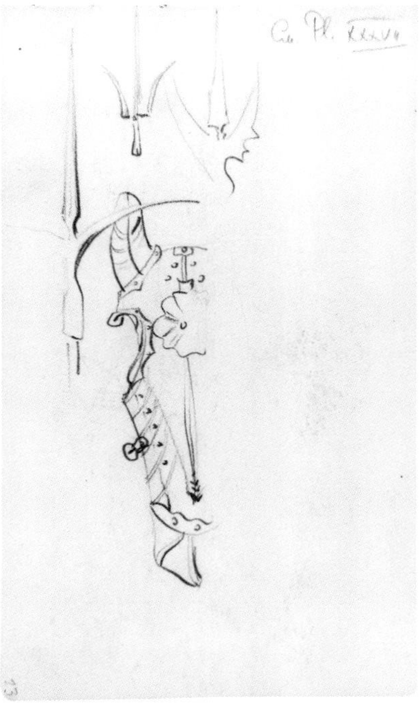

6, p.13

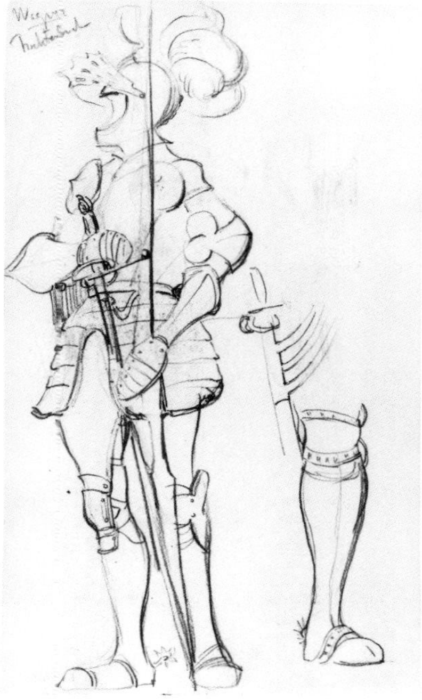

6, p.14

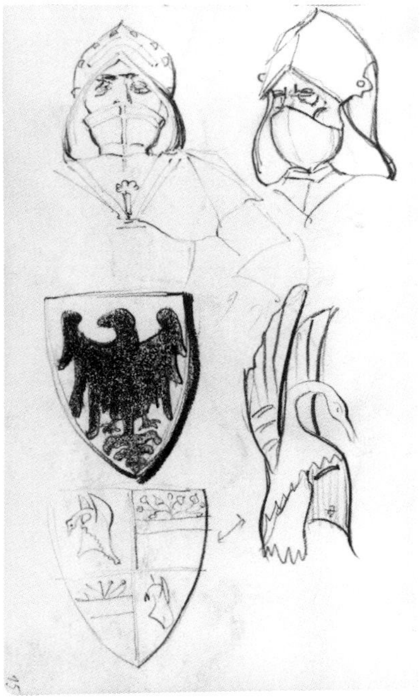

6, p.15

**p.12** Pencil and red pencil drawing of St. George and armor for crusader
Inscribed u.l. in Cyrillic: 'krasnyi krest / chernoe oruzhie'; l.r.: 'XI v. / 1534 g. / Rüstung eines St. Georges-Ritters / i Fincke […] rytsarbi: shpory topory i t.p. / nakonechn. kopii'

REFERENCES
Barnett and Friedel 1995, no.18, color ill.
Podzemskaia 2000, p.124, fig.20

Kandinsky's notes refer to Fincke's book as the source for studies of axes and weapons. The knight in armor and the red cross on the breast plate are found in plate XX, and the helmet comes from plate XXXV in *Abbildung und Beschreibung von alten Waffen und Rüstungen*; the knight in armor with a plumed helmet at the upper right comes from plate XXIX.

**p.13** Pencil drawing of armor
Inscribed u.r. in Cyrillic: 'Sm. Pl. XXXVII'

Kandinsky noted: 'look at pl. XXXVII'; however, the halberds and spears are found in plate LXXXVII and the horse armor appears in plate CXXVIII of Fincke's book.

**p.14** Pencil drawing of knight in armor
Inscribed u.l.: 'Wagner / Trachtenbuch'

REFERENCES
Hanfstaengl 1974, p.161, ill.
Podzemskaia 2000, p.124

As Kandinsky indicated, the source of his drawing is Heinrich Wagner, *Trachtenbuch des Mittel-Alters: Eine Sammlung von Trachten, Waffen, Gerāthen usw. nach Denkmälern* (Munich, 1830, Heft I). The large knight in armor is shown as fig.IV, and the detail of a leg is fig.I in Blatt I of the first issue of the Trachtenbuch.

**p.15** Pencil studies of helmets and shields

REFERENCES
Hanfstaengl 1974, p.161, ill.
Podzemskaia 2000, p.124

According to Dirk Breiding, these studies of helmets and shields are based on well-known effigies. The images were published both in Heinrich Wagner's *Trachtenbuch des Mittel-Alters: Eine Sammlung von Trachten, Waffen, Gerāthen usw. nach Denkmälern* (Munich, 1830, Heft I, Blätter 5, 6 and 7), and in books by J.H. de Alteneck-Hefner. For example, *Trachten des christlichen Mittelalters* [*Costumes du Moyen-âge chrétien d'après des monuments contemporains*] (Frankfurt am Main, 1840–1854, pl.131, 136) illustrates the helmeted heads at the upper left and upper right of this page. The swan (at the lower right) comes from the effigy of Rudolf v. Sachsenhausen, who died in 1370. In one of Münter's sketchbooks used in 1914 (46/44, p.1), Kandinsky wrote: 'Rudolf v. Sachsenhausen †1370'.

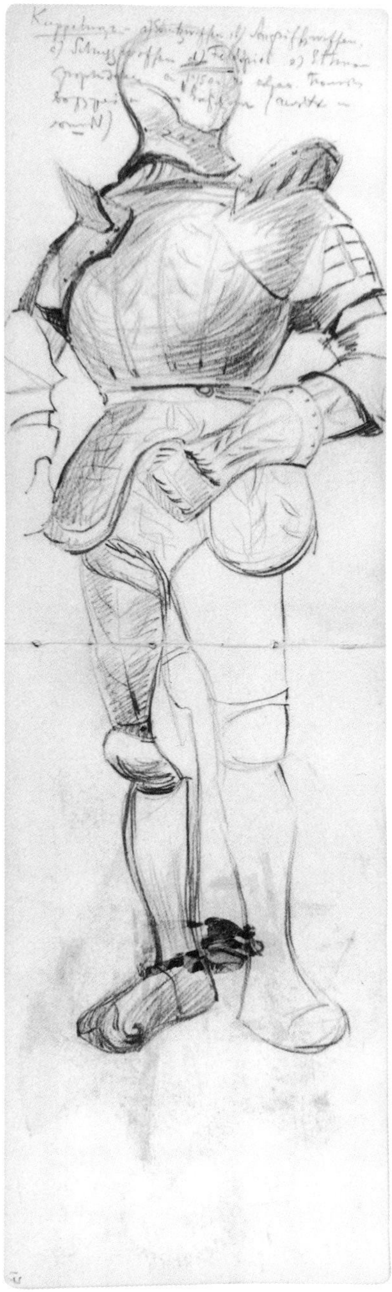

6, pp.16-17

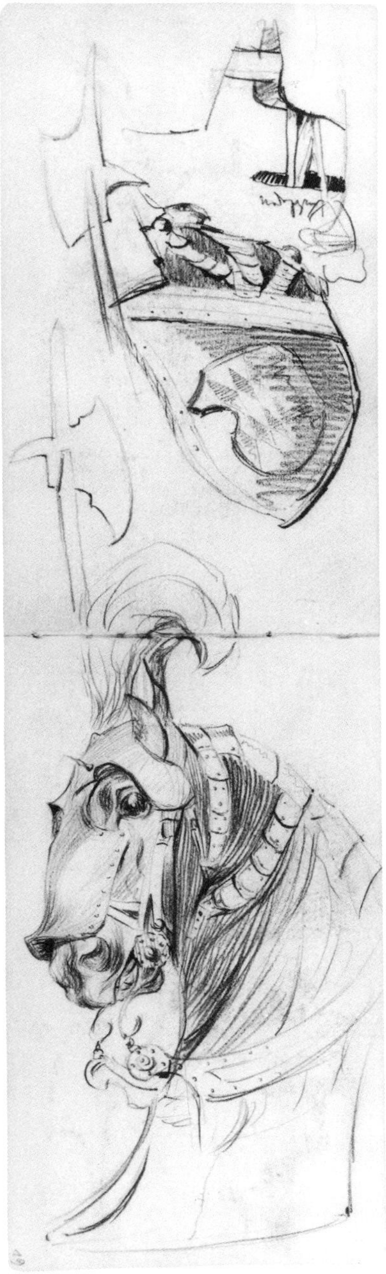

6, pp.18-19

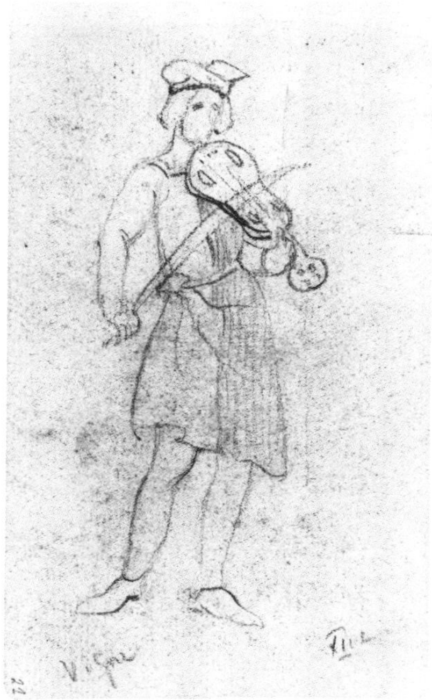

6, p.21

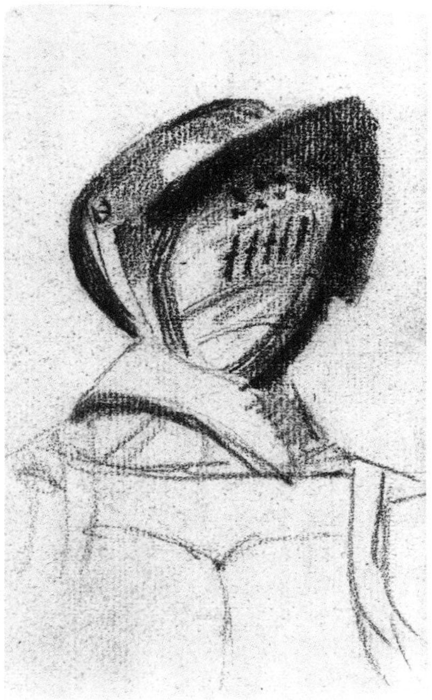

6, p.22

**pp.16–17** Pencil drawing of knight in armor with watercolor study of two small figures between feet (p.17)
Inscribed above (p.16): '<u>Kuppelmayr</u>- a) Schutzwaffen, b) Angriffswaffen, / c) Schutzwaffen d) Feldspiel e) [...] / 1450 g. sobran. polke / voovuzhenii [...]'

REFERENCES
Hanfstaengl 1974, p.161, ill.
Podzemskaia 2000, p.124

Kandinsky copied an illustration from *Waffensammlung Kuppelmayr* (Munich, 1895, pl.III). The armor ('geschlitzter Maximiliansharnisch') dates from 1520–1560. He later added a small watercolor study of a man and woman in modern dress on p.17 near the feet of the armored figure.

(See color plate p.117)

**pp.18–19** Pencil drawings of axes and armor
Inscribed u.r. in Cyrillic (p.18): 'podr[...]'

Kandinsky copied the illustrations of axes from plate II, the saddle and the horse's armor from plate IV of *Waffensammlung Kuppelmayr*. The horse's armor dates to 1550–1600.

**p.20** List of books on costumes and armor: 'Leitner- Waffensammlung des / österr. Kaiserhauses / Louandre- Les arts com- / ptuaires- Histoires du / costume depuis V à XVII S. / Lacroix- Les arts au moyen- / age et à l'epoque / de la renais. Moeurs, usages, / vie militaire et rélig. / XVII s. / XVIII s. / Directoire, consulat, empire / Hefner-Alteneck- Trachten des / christ. Mittelalters / Scheichtgrolle & Sonefelder- / Turnierbuch Herzog Wilhelms / d. IV v. Bayern 1510–45. / Bonnard- Costumes des XIII, XIV / et XV s.'

REFERENCES
Podzemskaia 2000, pp.123, 137

**p.21** Pencil drawing on rose-colored paper of man playing violin
Inscribed l.l.: 'Vigne'; l.r.: 'XII s'

The figure comes from plate 17 in Félix de Vigne, *Vade-Mecum du Peintre: Recueil de Costumes du Moyen-Age* (Ghent, 1835–1840).

**p.22** Pencil drawing of helmet

REFERENCES
Podzemskaia 2000, fig.22

Kandinsky copied a detail of plate VI in *Waffensammlung Kuppelmayr*.

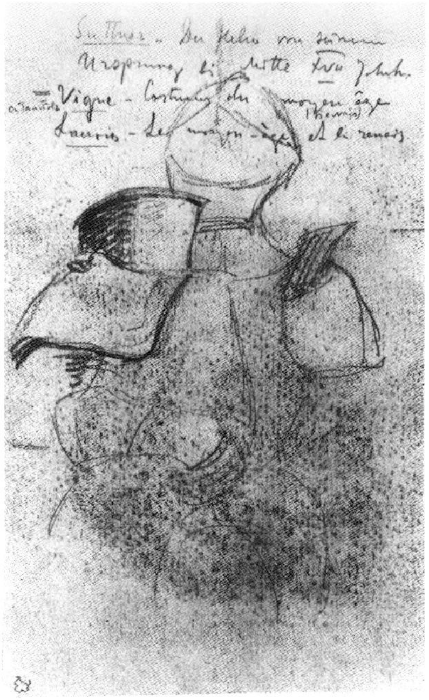

6, p.23

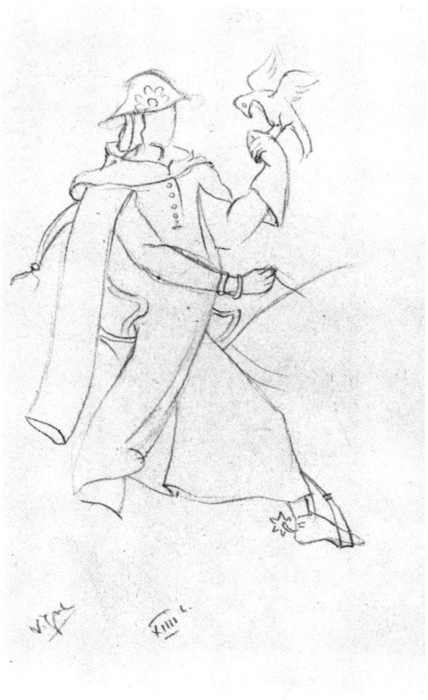

6, p.24

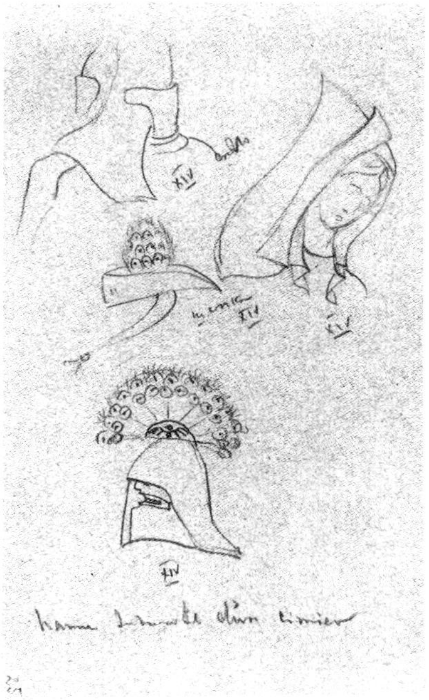

6, p.25

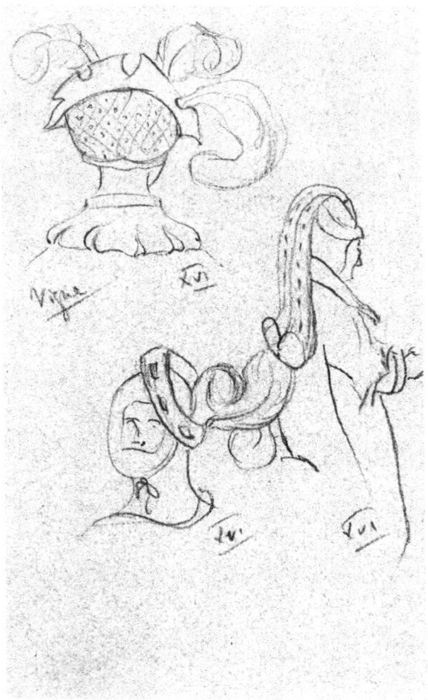

6, p.26

**p.23** Pencil drawing on tan paper of armor
Inscribed above: 'Suttner- Der Helm von seinem / Ursprung bis Mitte XVII Jahrh / Vigne- Costumes du moyen âge / Ch Tannolz / Lacroix- Le moyen-âge et la renais'

In spite of the artist's references to books by Gustav Suttner, Félix de Vigne and Paul Lacroix, the source of the image is plate IX in *Waffensammlung Kuppelmayr*.

**p.24** Pencil drawing on tan paper of knight with falcon
Inscribed l.l.: 'Vigne'; l.c.: 'XIIII v'

Kandinsky copied the figure of a hunter from a thirteenth-century manuscript illustrated in plate 35 of the second volume of Vigne's book, *Vade-Mecum du Peintre: Recueil de Costumes du Moyen-Age*.

**p.25** Pencil drawings on lavender paper of headdresses
Inscribed u.c. in Cyrillic and French: 'XIV […]'; c.: 'shapka / XIV'; l.l.: 'haume surmonté d'un cimier'

The woman's head is based on plate 37, whereas the helmet and crest decorated with peacock feathers come from plate 36 in the second volume of Vigne's book.

**p.26** Pencil drawings on lavender paper of headdresses
Inscribed c.: 'Vigne / XVI'; l.r.: 'XVI / XVI'

REFERENCES
Podzemskaia 2000, p.124, fig.23

The three images of men with sixteenth-century headgear appear in plates 87 and 90 of the second volume of Vigne's book.

**p.27** Pencil drawings on lavender paper of costumes and hats
Inscribed c.l.: 'XVI / XIV'; l.c.: 'XVI'; l.r.: 'XVI'

The woman wearing fourteenth-century headdress (center left) comes from plate 55 in Vigne's book, *Vade-Mecum du Peintre: Recueil de Costumes du Moyen-Age* (vol.II). The plumed hat at the upper left is found in plate 96 and the other three figures come from plate 97 in the same book.

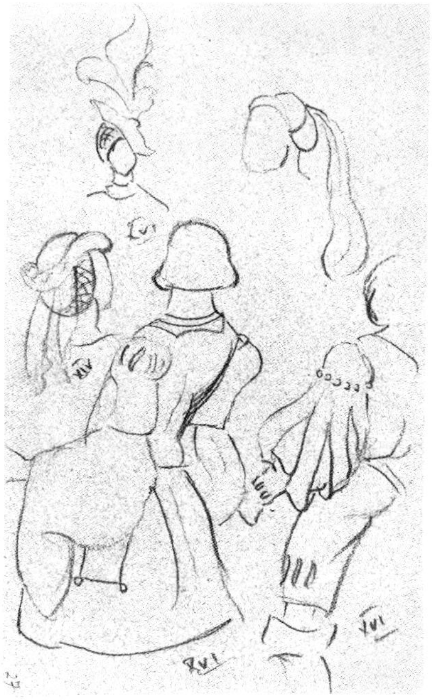

6, p.27

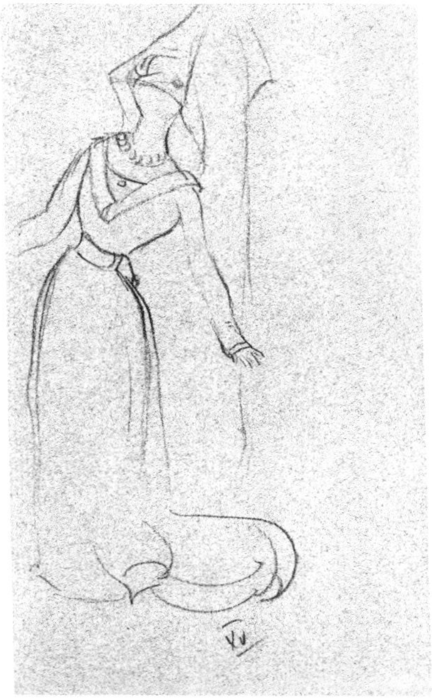

6, p.28

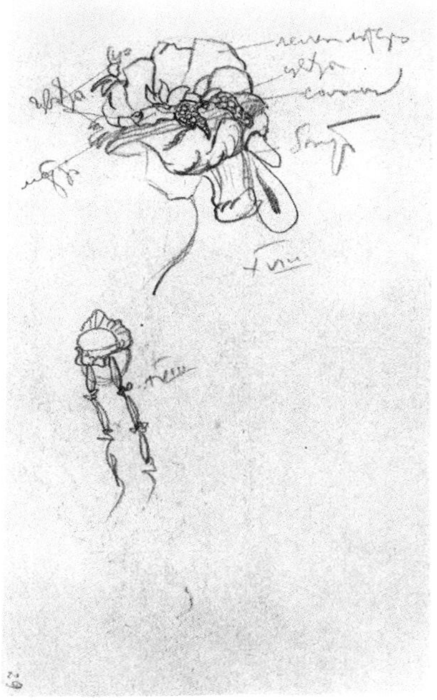

6, p.29

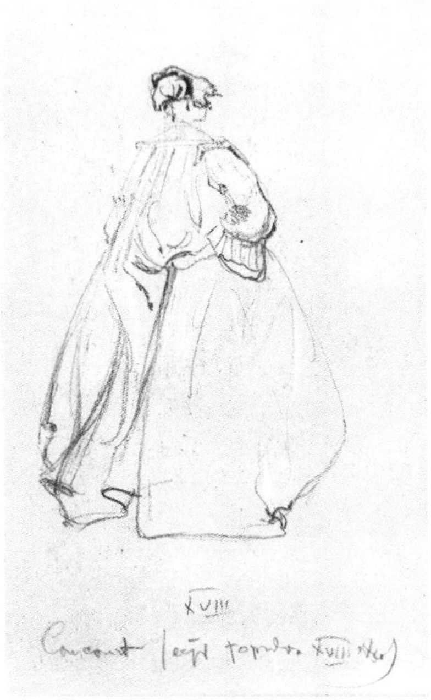

6, p.30

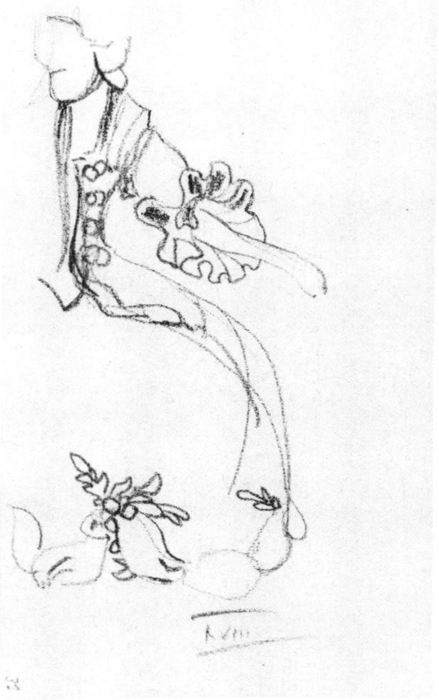

6, p.31

**p.28** Pencil drawing of female figure
Inscribed l.c.: 'XV'

Kandinsky copied the figure of a woman from plate 80 in the second volume of Vigne's book.

**p.29** Pencil drawing on tan paper of flowered hat
Inscribed u.l. in Cyrillic: 'tsvety / […]'; u.r.: 'zelen. tsvet / tsvety / soloma / […]'; c.: 'XVIII / XVIII'

The drawing shows a woman's hair and hat decorated with flowers from a heliogravure by Le Beau, based on a drawing by Le Clerc in Edmond and Jules de Goncourt, *La Femme au dix-huitième siècle* (Paris, 1887) opposite p.256.

**p.30** Colored pencil and pencil drawing on tan paper of standing female figure
Inscribed l.c. in Cyrillic: 'XVIII / Concourt (est' […] XVIII veka)'

As indicated by the artist's notes, the source of the figure is an eighteenth-century heliogravure after a painting by Antoine Watteau found opposite p.246 in Edmond and Jules de Goncourt's book, *La Femme au dix-huitième siècle*.

**p.31** Pencil and crayon drawing of costume
Inscribed l.c.: 'XVIII'

REFERENCES
Hanfstaengl 1974, p.161, ill.

The figure appears in a heliogravure by Voysard after a drawing by Desrais opposite p.262 in the Goncourts' book.

**p.32** Pencil and crayon drawings on rose paper of St. Barbara
Inscribed u.l.: 'Sta Barbara / Pnk'

The studies resemble the painting of St. Barbara on the left panel of the *Sebastiansalter* by Hans Holbein the Elder in the Alte Pinakothek in Munich. Although Kandinsky omitted her attributes and modified her dress, he noted the inscription ('Santa Barbara') found on the frame above the panel.

**pp.33–37** Blank

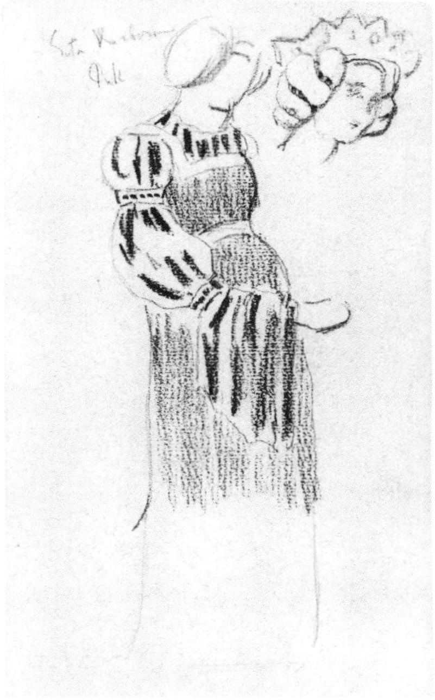

6, p.32

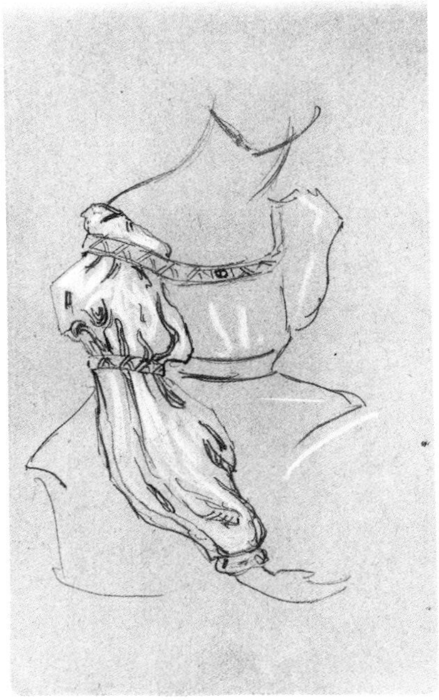

6, p.38

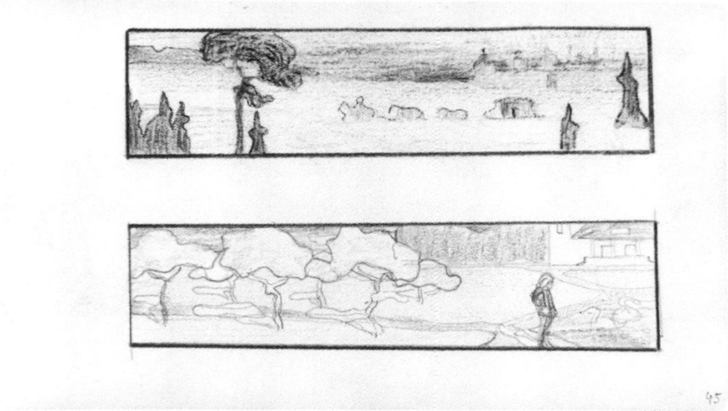

6, p.45

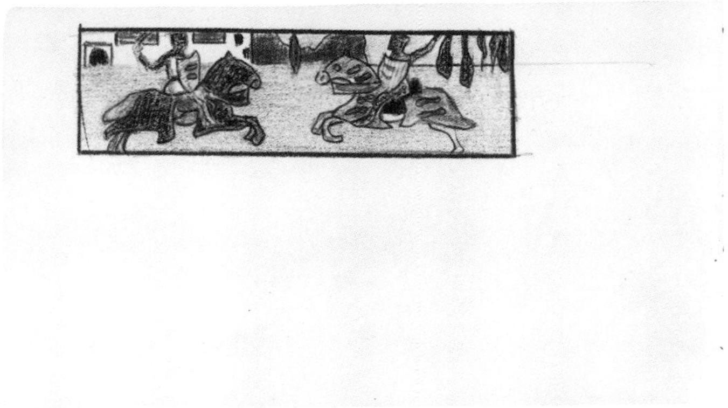

6, p.46

6, p.47

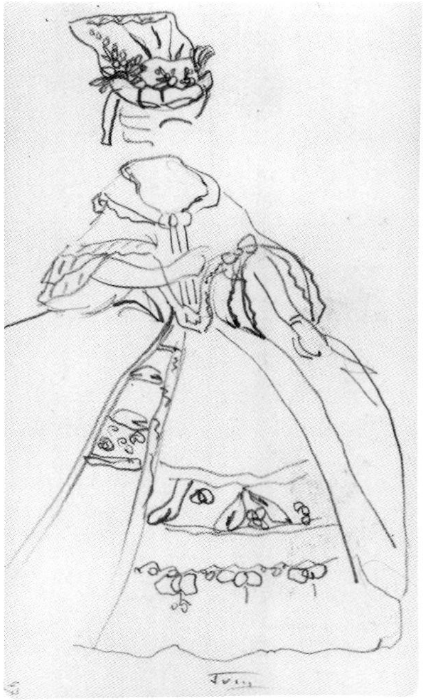

6, p.49

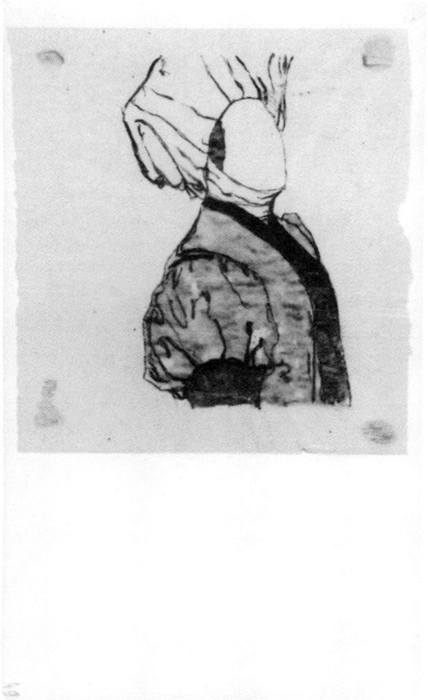

**p.38** Colored pencil and pencil drawing on tan paper of seated female figure

REFERENCES
Hanfstaengl 1974, p.161, ill.

The style of the bodice and sleeve bears a resemblance to the drawing of St. Barbara on p.32 (above); however, the specific source of this drawing has not been identified.

**pp.39–44** Blank

**p.45** Colored pencil and pencil drawing of landscapes with figures

REFERENCES
Hanfstaengl 1974, p.161, ill.
Barnett and Friedel 1995, no.16, color ill.

Hanfstaengl proposed a date of 1902–1903 for these sketches and the following one (p.46).

(See color plate p.118)

**p.46** Colored pencil and pencil drawing of two knights in armor on horseback

REFERENCES
Hanfstaengl 1974, p.161, ill.

The drawing can be related to a tempera painting, *Zweikampf* of 1902 (Barnett no.54), as well as the illustration copied from Hewitt's book (p.5 above).

(See color plate p.118)

**p.47** Pencil drawing of woman's dress and hat
Inscribed l.c.: 'XVIII'

Kandinsky copied the hat and dress in a heliogravure by Voysard after a drawing by Le Clerc opposite p.88 in the Goncourts' book, but he omitted the woman's face.

**p.48** Blank

**p.49** Watercolor, ink and pencil drawing of woman with hat on tracing paper (10 x 9 cm) glued onto sketchbook page

It appears likely that Kandinsky copied this drawing – probably a German portrait – from a book. See p.73 (below).

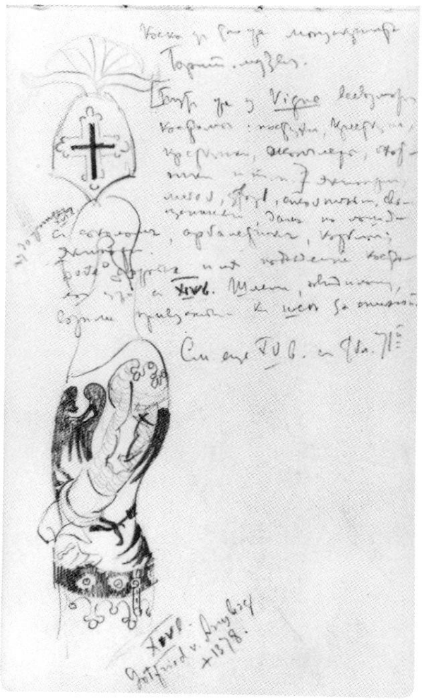

6, p.68

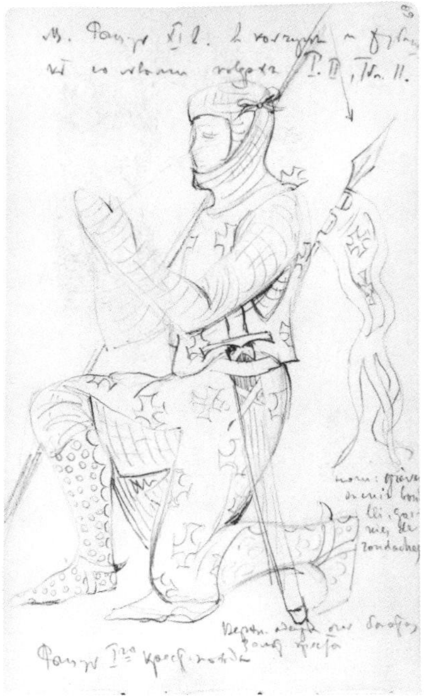

6, p.69

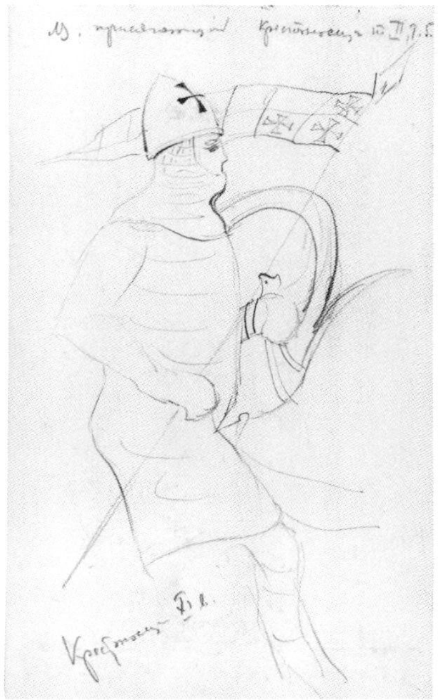

6, p.70

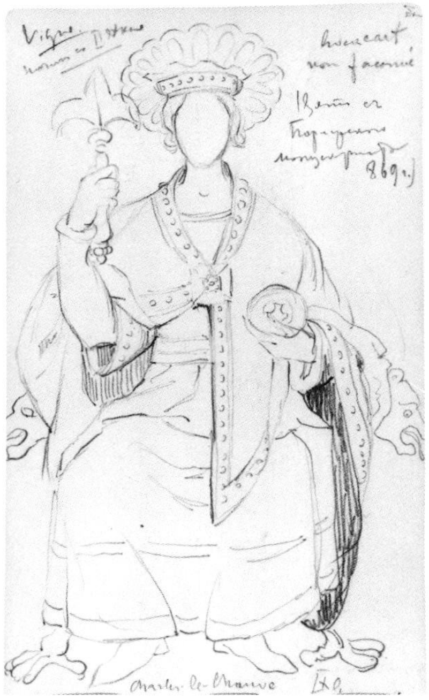

6, p.71

**pp.50–67** Blank

**p.68** Pencil drawing of helmet and knight's tunic
Inscribed u.c. in Cyrillic: '[...] manuskripta / Brit. muzeia / Tut zhe u Vigne vsevozmozhnye / kostiumy post [...], krestki / [...]'; c.: 'Sm. eshche XV v. s. t bl. 71st'; l.l.: 'XIV v / Gotfried v. Arnsberg/†1378.'

Kandinsky copied the figure of Gotfried von Arnsberg from plate 54 and the helmet from plate 20 in the second volume of Vigne's book, *Vade-Mecum du Peintre, ou, Recueil de Costumes du Moyen-Age: pour servir à l'histoire de la Belgique et pays circonvoisins* (Ghent, 1835–1840).

**p.69** Pencil drawing of knight kneeling with sword
Inscribed u.c. in Cyrillic: 'M. rytsar' XI. v. v kol'chuge i rubakhe / [...]s [...] poverkh. t. II, tbl. II.'; l.r.: 'bogi grève / en cuir bouc / lé, gar- / nies de rondaches'; l.c.: 'Verkh. odezhda [...] / bogotoi zolotoi krest / [...] Igo krest. pokhoda'

According to Kandinsky's inscription, the drawing shows a knight from the First Crusade. The source is plate 20 in the second volume of Vigne's book.

**p.70** Pencil drawing of knight in armor with banner
Inscribed u.c. in Cyrillic: 'ts. prisiagaiushchii krestonosets t. II, t. 5'; l.l.: 'Krestonosets XI v.'

According to the inscription, this is a crusader from the eleventh century. Kandinsky copied the figure from plate 7 in Vigne's book, but omitted the horse.

**p.71** Pencil drawing of Charlemagne
Inscribed u.l. in Cyrillic: 'Vigne / nachalo s II veka'; u.r.: '[...] / manuskripta / 869 g.)'; l.c.: 'Charles-le-Chauve IX v.'

Kandinsky copied plate 44 of Vigne's book depicting Charlemagne with a scepter, although his inscription refers to Charles the Bald, who is portrayed in plate 45.

**p.72** Blank

**p.73** List of schedule (M[o]ntag / Dienstag / Don[ne]r[s]t[a]g / Freitag / 9-1) and publications: 'Isselburg-Nürnberger Geschlechter / Mayr-Portraits, meist Augsb[urger] / Patrizian. / Chaponnier- La promenade du / matin / Gabler-Nürnberger Ausrufer / Lafitte- Ein Trauerpferd'

REFERENCES
Podzemskaia 2000, p.127

**p.74** Red chalk drawing of street with figure

REFERENCES
Barnett and Friedel 1995, no.3, color ill.

Like a study in Sketchbook 4 (GMS 348, p.42), this drawing may have been done as early as 1897–1900.

(See color plate p.118)

Inside back cover inscribed: 'Vasensammlung- M[o]nt[ag], Dienstag, D[o]nn[erstag], Sonntag, 9-1 / Kupferstichk[abinet]t'

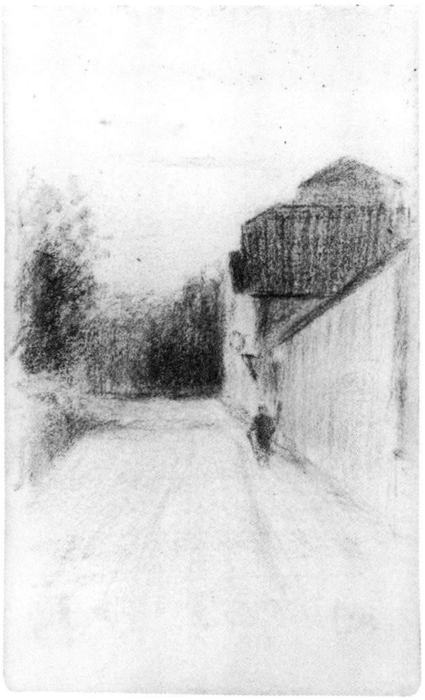

6, p.74

# Sketchbook 7

1900–1903

Grey cloth-covered paper sketchbook; inside front cover label from Franz Dury, Munich (50c Amalienstrasse and 78 Theresienstrasse)
Contains 34 pages (17 sheets), each 17.2 x 25.9 cm (6¾ x 10¼ in), of which several are blank
Page numbers inscribed by unknown hand at later date with odd numbers at lower right

Hanfstaengl 1974, p.159

LOCATION
Städtische Galerie im Lenbachhaus, Munich (GMS 338)

HISTORY
Gabriele Münter, Murnau, until 1957

The anatomical study of a leg and perhaps the studies of a horse at the beginning of the sketchbook were done earlier than the other sheets. The range of dates from 1900 to 1903 proposed by Erika Hanfstaengl seems likely.

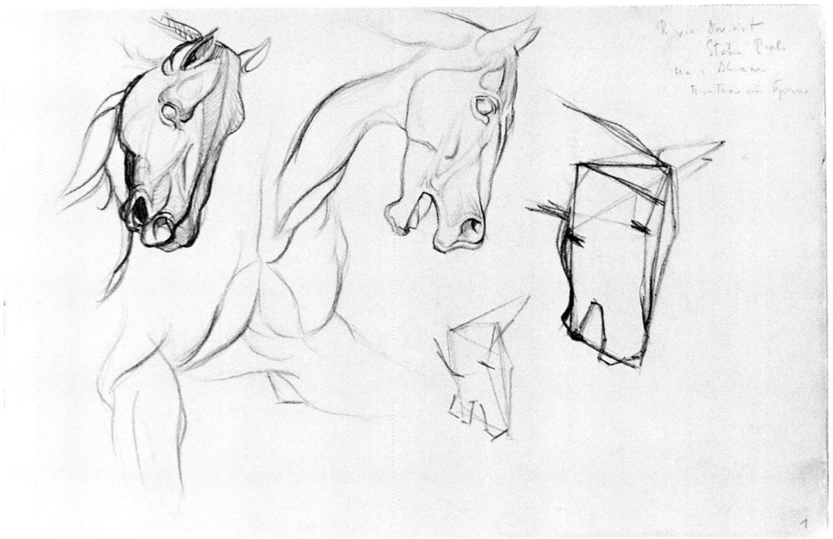

7, p.1

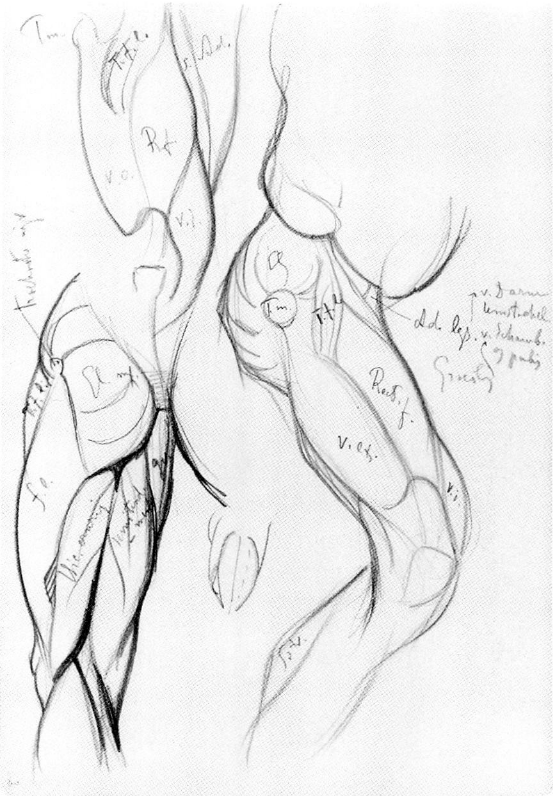

7, p.3

**p.1** Pencil studies of horse
Inscribed u.r.: 'R via Dwinst / Stehe Preli' and in illegible Cyrillic

REFERENCES
Hanfstaengl 1974, p.159, ill.

The horse's head resembles that in *Reisiger Ritter* of 1902–1903 (Roethel and Benjamin no.80). The studies of horses in this sketchbook (see pp.5–6 below) do not resemble the illustrations in the book that Kandinsky knew, *Handbuch der Anatomie der Tiere für Künstler: Band I. Das Pferd* by Wilhelm Ellenberger, Hermann Baum and Hermann Dittrich (Leipzig, 1900).

**p.2** Blank

**p.3** Pencil and red crayon studies of legs
Inscribed c.r.: 'v. Darm / Umstachel / Ad. lgs. v. Schamb. / os pubis / Gracilis' and additional anatomical annotations

REFERENCES
Hanfstaengl 1974, p.159, ill.
Roethel and Hahl-Koch 1980, p.43, ill.26
Hahl-Koch 1993, p.59, ill.57

The studies of legs can be compared to those in Sketchbook 3 (GMS 344, pp.24–27) which Kandinsky used c.1900. Roethel and Hahl-Koch proposed that Kandinsky probably made this study in the anatomy class taught by Siegfried Mollier.

**p.4** Blank

**p.5** Pencil drawing of head and forequarters of horse

See p.1 (above) regarding this and the following page.

**p.6** Pencil drawing of hindquarters of horse

**pp.7–8** Blank

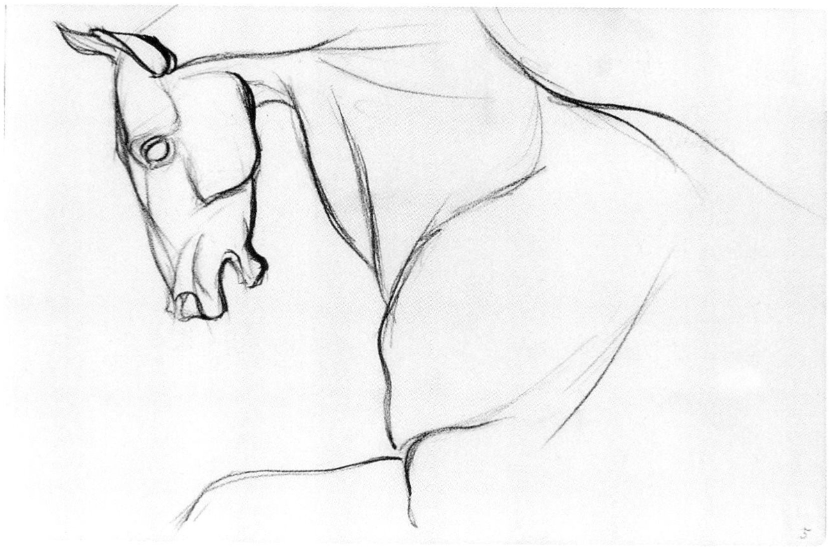

7, p.5

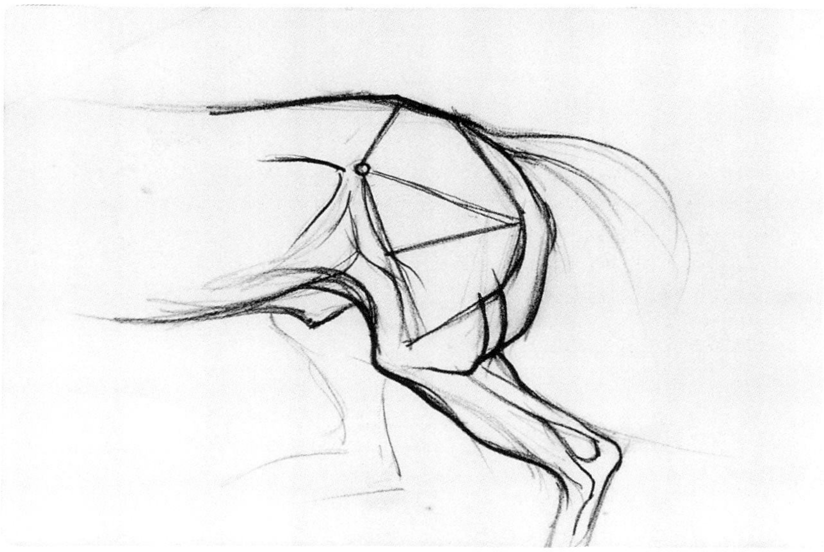

7, p.6

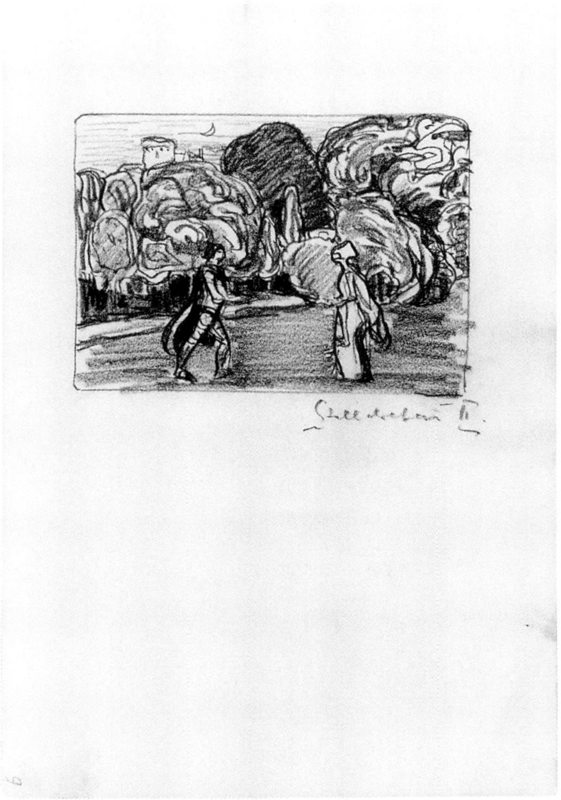


7, p.9

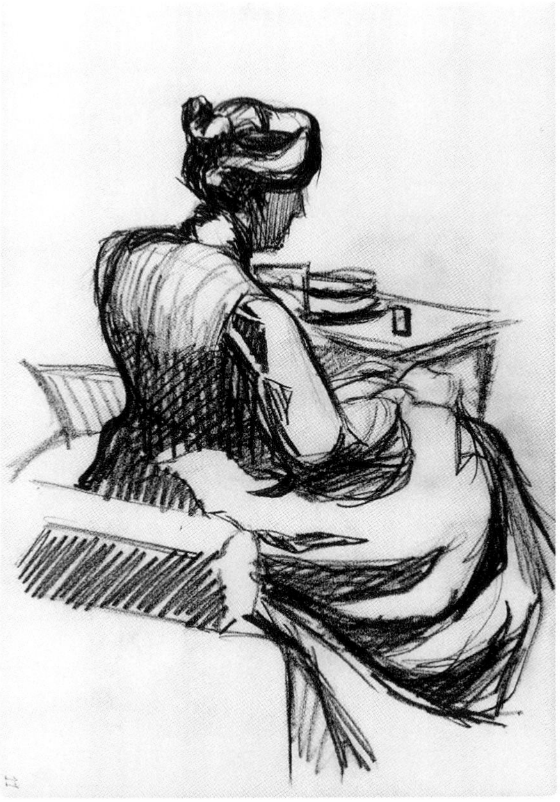

7, p.11

**p.9** Pencil drawing for painting
Inscribed l.r.: 'Stelldichein II.'

REFERENCES
Hanfstaengl 1974, p.159, ill.
Barnett 1992, p.94, ill.a

Kandinsky's inscription relates the sketch to an unknown tempera painting, *Stelldichein II* (Barnett no.72), which dates from early 1903.

**p.10** Blank

**p.11** Pencil drawing of seated woman

REFERENCES
Hanfstaengl 1974, p.159, ill.

This and the following studies (pp.22, 24) portray the same woman and appear to have been sketched in a café or restaurant probably in 1903. See also sketch on calling card added to p.35 (below).

**pp.12–16** Blank

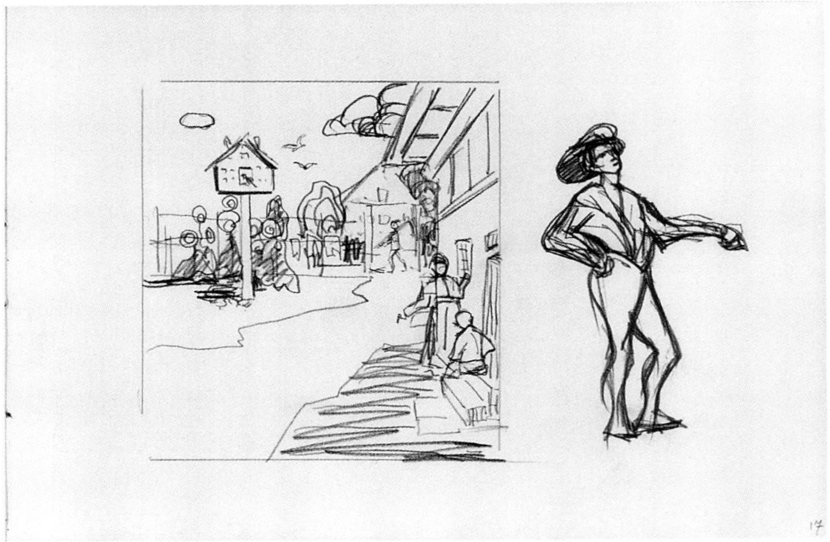

7, p.17

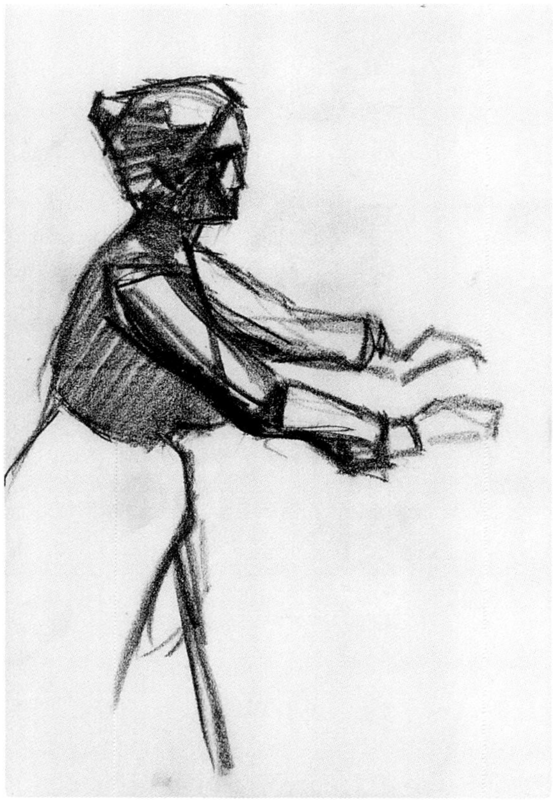

7, p.22

**p.17** Pencil drawing of buildings with garden and dovecote

REFERENCES
Hanfstaengl 1974, p.159, ill.

The study of a street with garden and dovecote may have been done in Bavaria in 1902 or 1903. The sketch of a man suggests figures in medieval dress that Kandinsky included in his paintings c.1903.

**pp.18–21** Blank

**p.22** Pencil drawing of woman

Kandinsky made sketches of the same person on pp.11, 24 of this sketchbook.

**p.23** Blank

**p.24** Pencil drawing of seated woman

REFERENCES
Hanfstaengl 1974, p.159, ill.

**pp.25–31** Blank

**p.32** Pencil studies of sheep and hand

REFERENCES
Hanfstaengl 1974, p.159, ill.
Thürlemann 1985, p.365, ill.2

The study of a hand resembles that in the sketches of a woman on pp.11, 22, 24.

**p.33** Blank

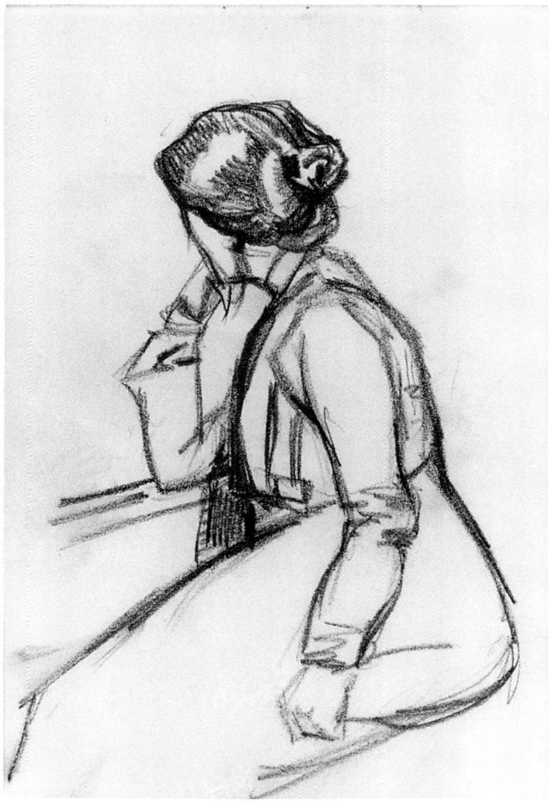

7, p.24

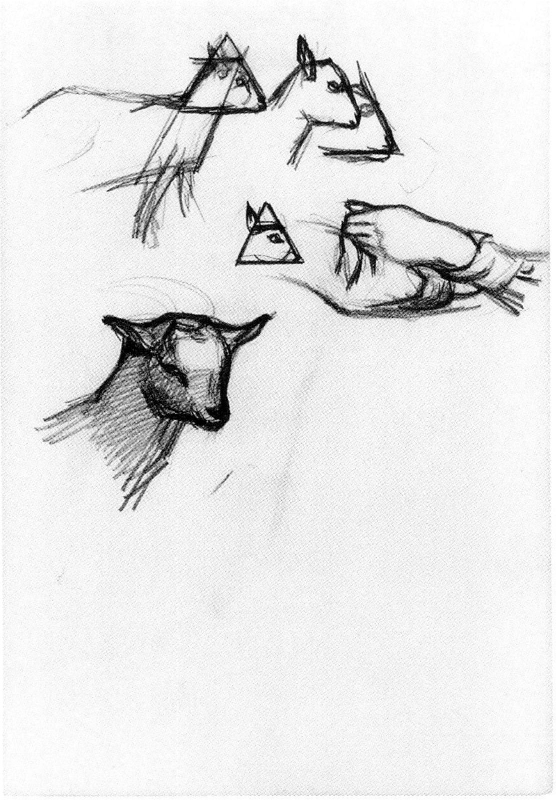

7, p.32

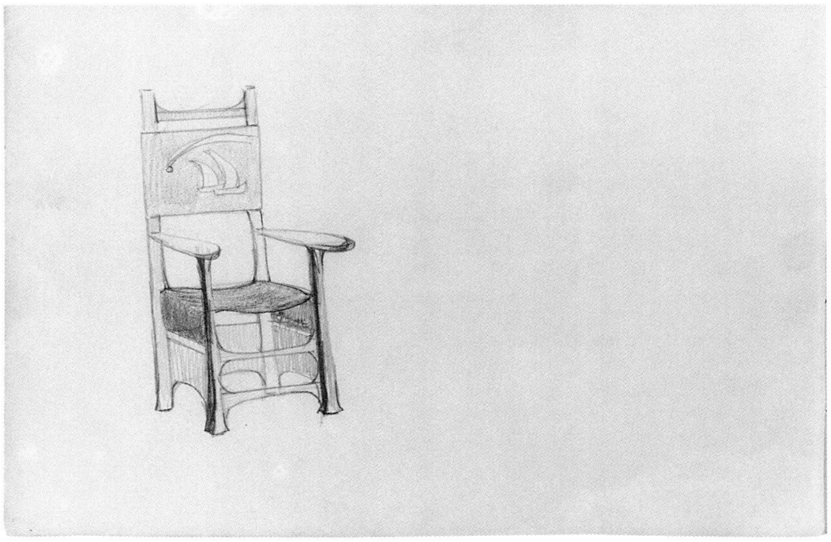

7, p.34

**p.34** Pencil and colored pencil drawing for chair with motif of ships and comet

EXHIBITIONS
1982 New York, no.110, ill.
1982 Munich, no.142, ill.

REFERENCES
Weiss 1979, p.124, fig.105, ill.
Barnett and Friedel 1995, no.78, color ill.
Podzemskaia 2000, p.57

This drawing has been dated c.1902–1903 by Weiss and Barnett. Other furniture designs are found in Sketchbook 5.

(See color plate p.119)

**p.35** Calling card of Wassily Kandinsky, Friedrichstrasse 1, pasted onto torn sheet of sketchbook
Inscribed: 'Tiefviolette See / Heller d. Himmel / Hinten Köpfe in Ton. / Das Licht von oben / Die Schatten viol vorne heller. / Ein Stern / Tischtücher warm / im Schatten kalt / grünlich!'
On reverse: pencil sketch of people sitting in a restaurant or café

The drawing brings to mind that on p.24 of Sketchbook 21 (GMS 333). Kandinsky made a drawing on the reverse of another calling card with the same address, probably in 1905 (see vol.I, cat. no.79). He lived at the Friedrichstrasse address from July 1901 until late September 1904, when he separated from his wife Anja Shemiakina.

**p.36** Blank

**p.37** Newspaper clipping with poem entitled 'Lovis Corinth' citing *Kladderadatsch* has been pasted onto sheet

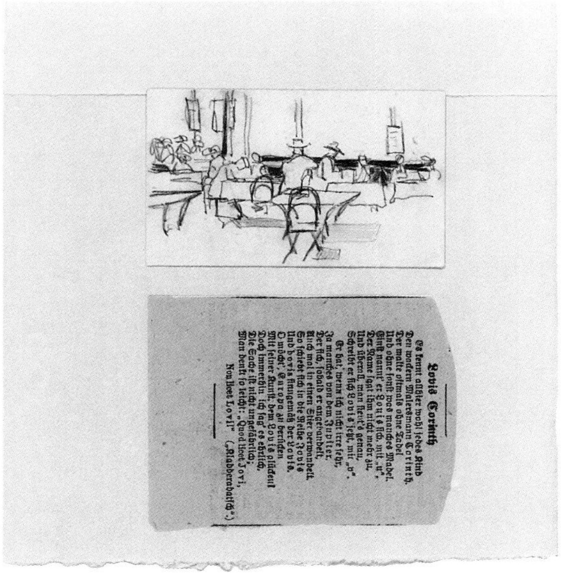


7, pp.35R, 37

# Sketchbook 8

1902

Brown cardboard cover sketchbook with black spine; no label
Contains 40 pages (20 sheets), each 16.9 x 11.1 cm (6⅝ x 4⅜ in), of which pp.37–40 are blank
Page numbers inscribed by unknown hand at later date with odd numbers at lower right

Hanfstaengl 1974, p.160

LOCATION
Städtische Galerie im Lenbachhaus, Munich (GMS 339)

HISTORY
Gabriele Münter, Murnau, until 1957

The sketchbook has the same cover and dimensions as Sketchbook 9. Kandinsky wrote the date 17 August on p.13; he made all the drawings during the summer of 1902 when he went with his students at the 'Phalanx' school to Kochel, a village about 70 kilometers south of Munich.

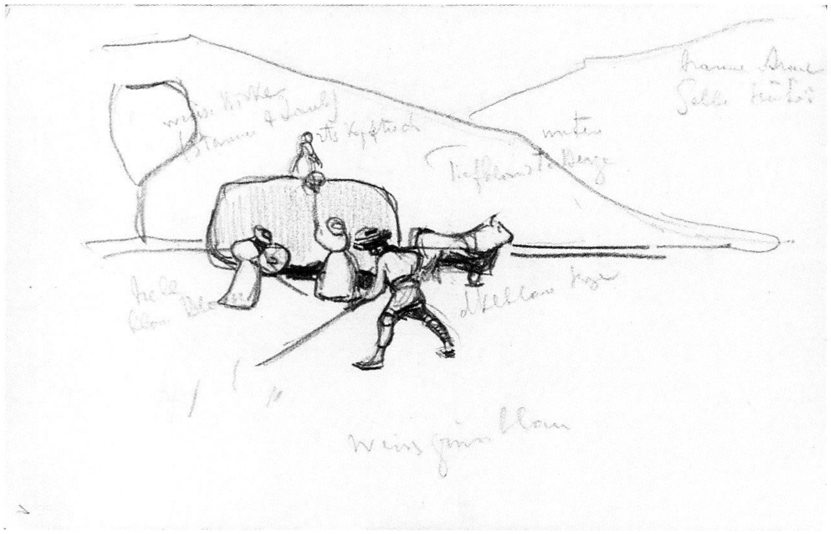

8, p.1

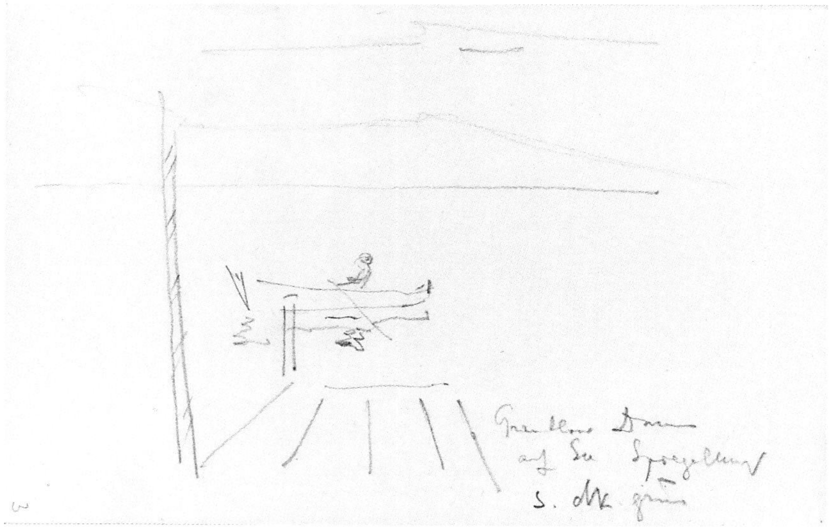

8, p.3

8, p.4

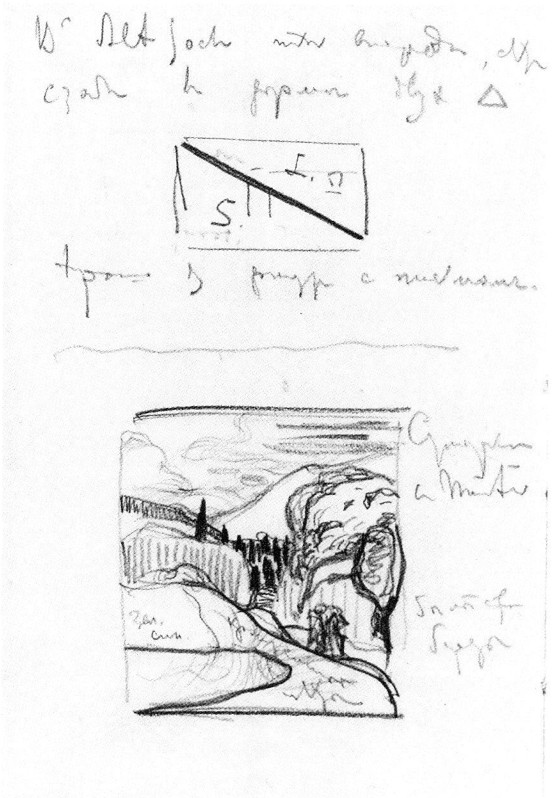

**p.1** Pencil drawing of workers loading hay on wagon

Inscribed u.r.: 'braune Arme / Gelbe Hüte'; u.l.: 'weisse Birke / (Stamm + Laub)'; u.c.: 'rts Kopftuch / unten / Tiefblaueste Berge / dklblaue Hose'; c.l.: 'hell / blaue Blouse'; l.c.: 'weiss grün blau'

**p.2** Inscribed: 'Links war es Tiefblaugrün. Figuren schwarz, / aber Farben s. gut zu sehen und s. Tief.' Kandinsky's notes refer to the drawing on the facing page (p.3).

**p.3** Pencil drawing of rowboat on lake
Inscribed l.r.: 'Graublaue Dame / auf See Spiegelung / s. dk. grün'

REFERENCES
Hanfstaengl 1974, p.160, ill.
Barnett and Friedel 1995, no.40, color ill.
Podzemskaia 2000, p.98

The drawing is a study for *Kochel- See mit Boot* of 1902 (Roethel and Benjamin no.49).

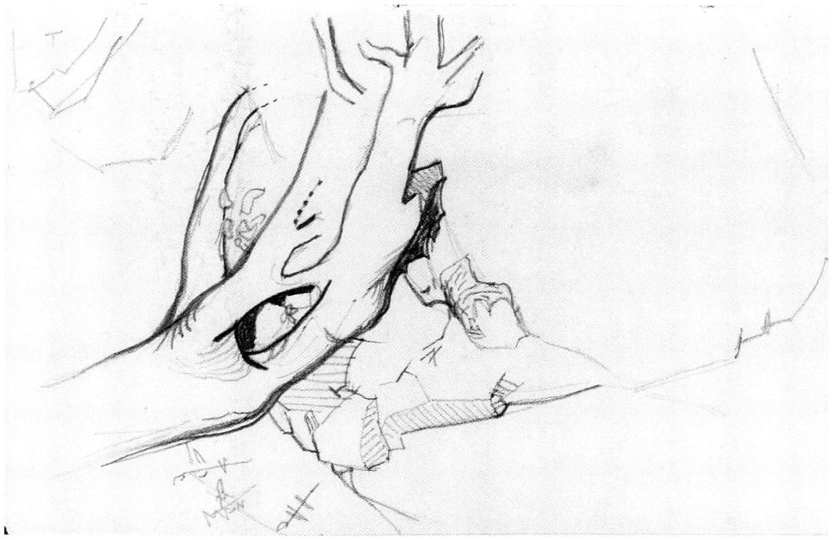

8, p.6

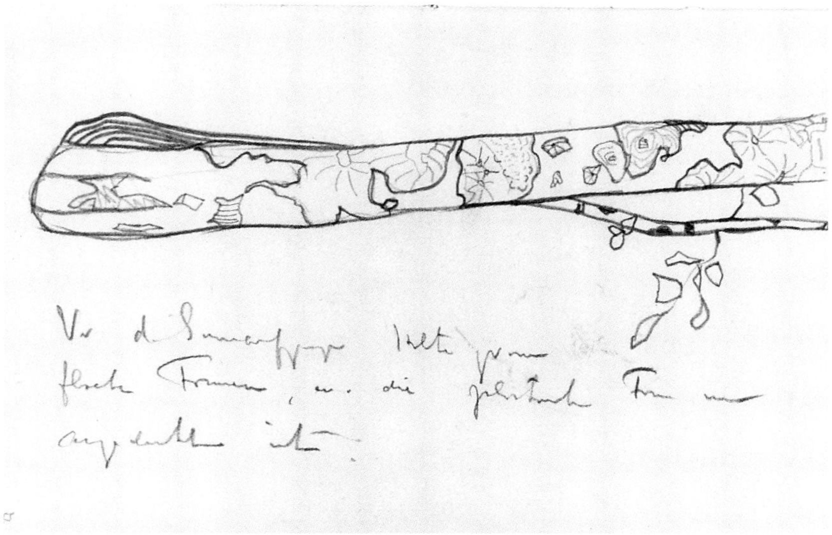

8, p.7

8, p.8

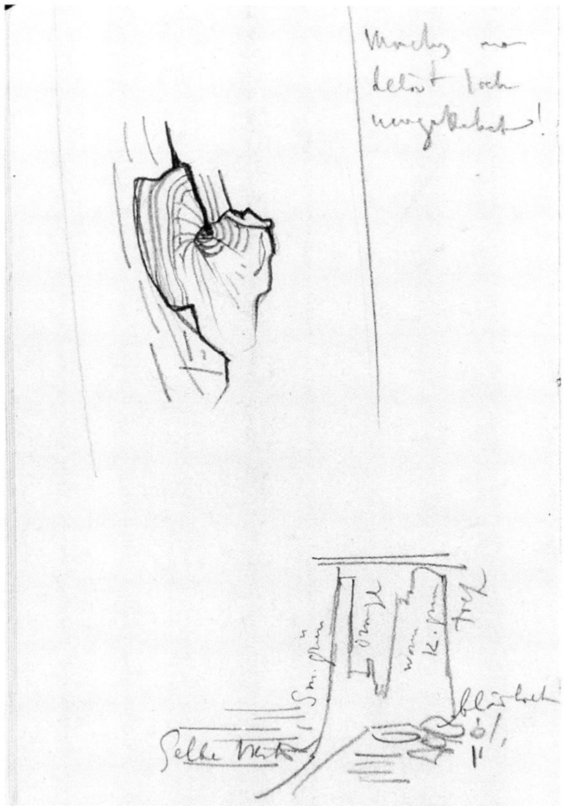

**p.4** Pencil drawing of landscape
Inscribed above: 'B Alt Joch'; in Cyrillic: '[…]vperedi, […] / szadi v forme dvukh' and below: 'Sumerki / s Münter' / belyi stvol / berezy' with color notations in Cyrillic

REFERENCES
Hanfstaengl 1974, p.160

Hanfstaengl suggested that 'Altjoch' refers to the Kesselbergjoch near Kochel, which Kandinsky painted in 1902 (see Roethel and Benjamin nos.56, 58). Kandinsky's notes refer to 'twilight with Münter' and the 'white trunk' of a birch tree.

**p.5** Poem in Cyrillic beginning: 'Molchi, molchi …'

**p.6** Pencil drawing of tree and rocks

**p.7** Pencil drawing of branch with leaves
Inscribed below: 'Vor d. Sonn[en]aufgange kalte grau / flach[e] Formen, wo die plastische Form nur / angedeutet ist.'

**p.8** Pencil sketches
Inscribed u.r.: 'Manches man / […] / umgekehrt!'; l.c.: 'Gelbe Blute'; l.r.: 'bläulich' and with color notations: 'Sm. grün / orange / warm / k. grau / tief'

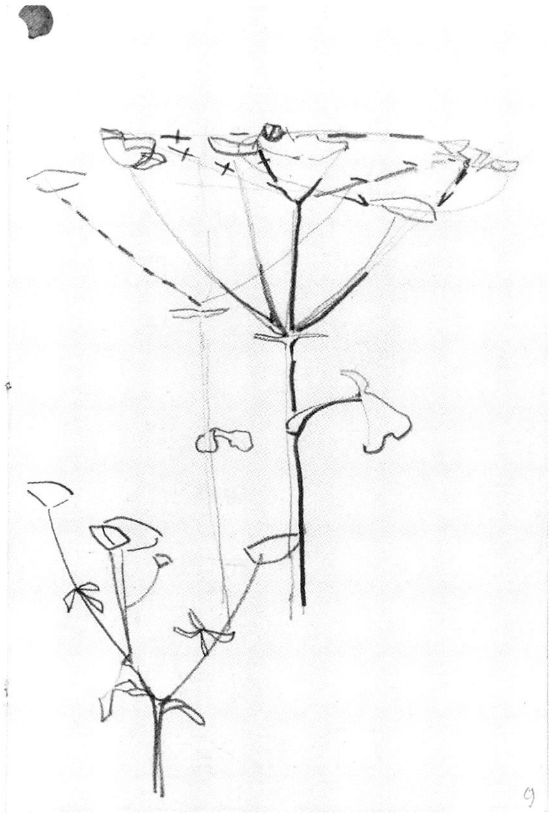

8, p.9

**p.9** Pencil sketch of leaves and blossoms

See also p.21 (below).

**p.10** Pencil sketch of mountains with shadow

The sketch is related to the drawing on the facing page. Similar shading can be found later in Sketchbook 25 (GMS 332, pp.57, 59).

**p.11** Pencil drawing of mountainous landscape

**p.12** Pencil sketch of mountainous landscape
Inscribed c.l.: 'wiese / w-gr. / rth'; c.: 'w / gr. grell / glb Bord / St'

REFERENCES
Hanfstaengl 1974, p.160, ill.
Thürlemann 1985, p.365, ill.3

Hanfstaengl identified the view as the Walchensee as seen from the Jochbergweg.

(See color plate p. 119)

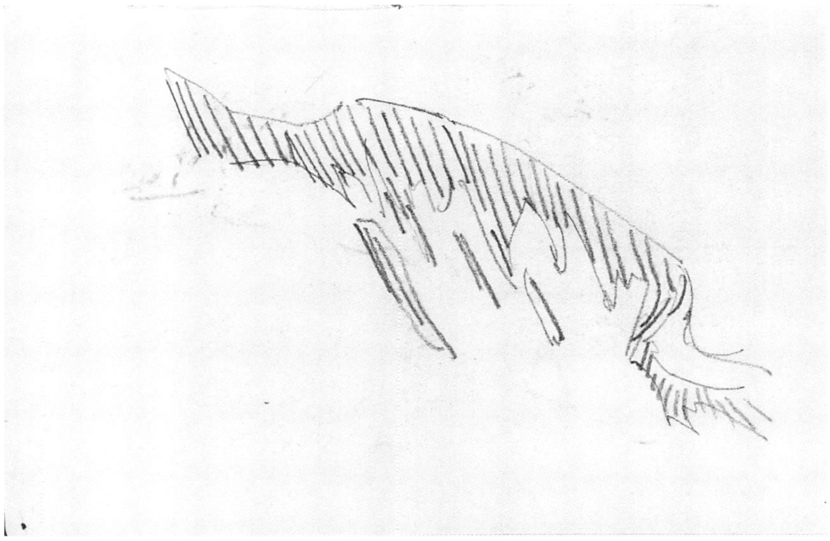

8, p.10

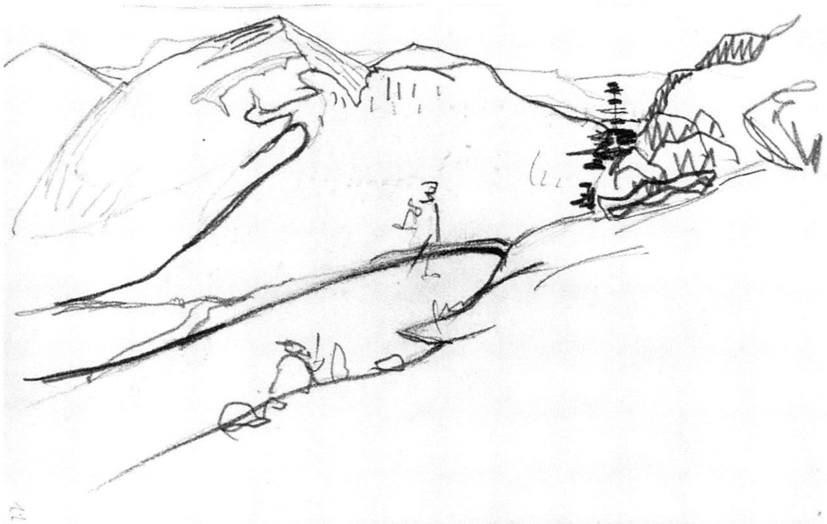

8, p.11

8, p.12

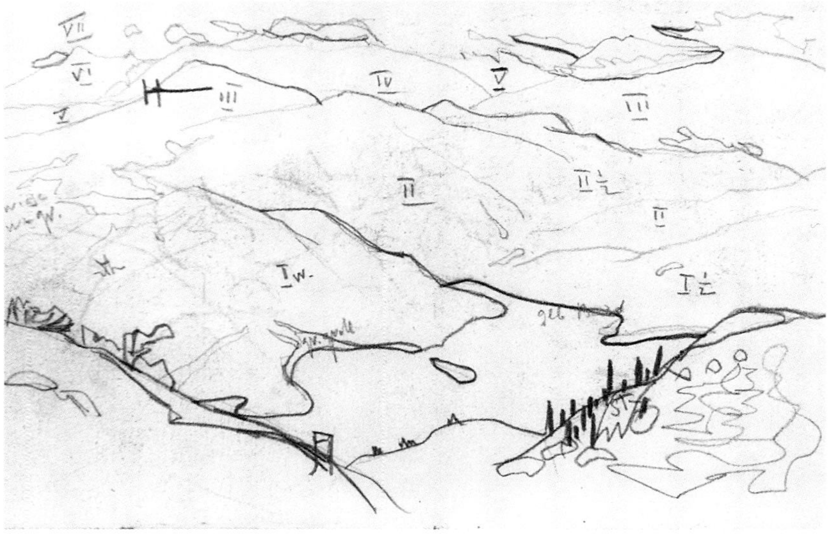

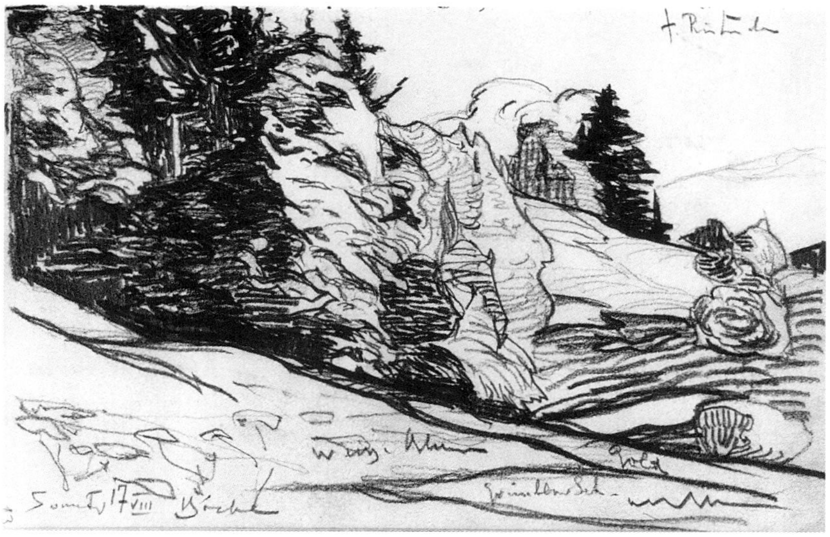

8, p.13

**p.13** Pencil drawing of landscape
Inscribed u.r.: 't. Reitender'; l.l.: 'Sonnt[a]g 17 VIII Koch[e]l'; l.c.: 'weiss. Blumen / grünblaue Sch. / Gold'

REFERENCES

Hanfstaengl 1974, p.160, ill.
Barnett and Friedel 1995, no.49, color ill.
Podzemskaia 2000, p.97

Kandinsky made the drawing in Kochel on Sunday, 17 August 1902, when he took his students there. Gabriele Münter dated one of her sketches 'Kochel 25. VI. 02' (see Munter's sketchbook 46/7, p.58).

(See color plate p. 119)

**p.14** Pencil drawing of landscape

**p.15** Pencil sketch of landscape
Inscribed u.r.: 'Koch[e]l / Cadmiumhäuschen +'

Kandinsky made the drawings on the preceding and following pages near Kochel during the summer of 1902.

**p.16** Pencil drawings of flowers and haystacks

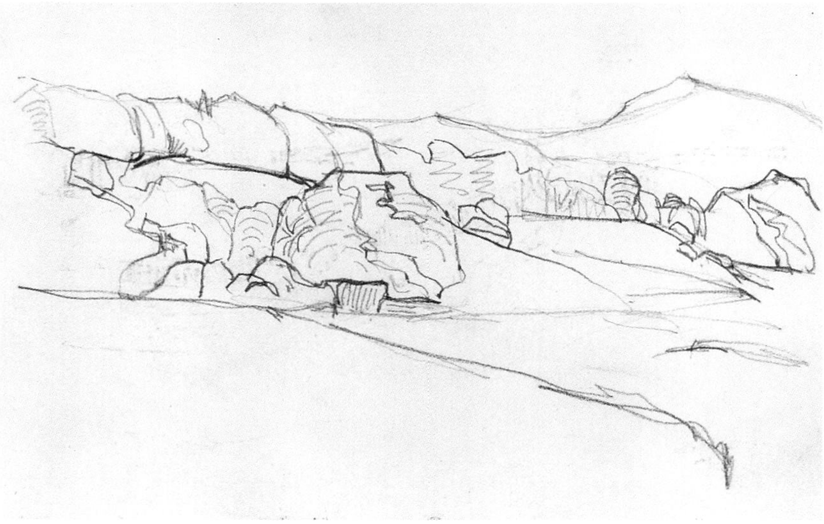

8, p.14

8, p.15

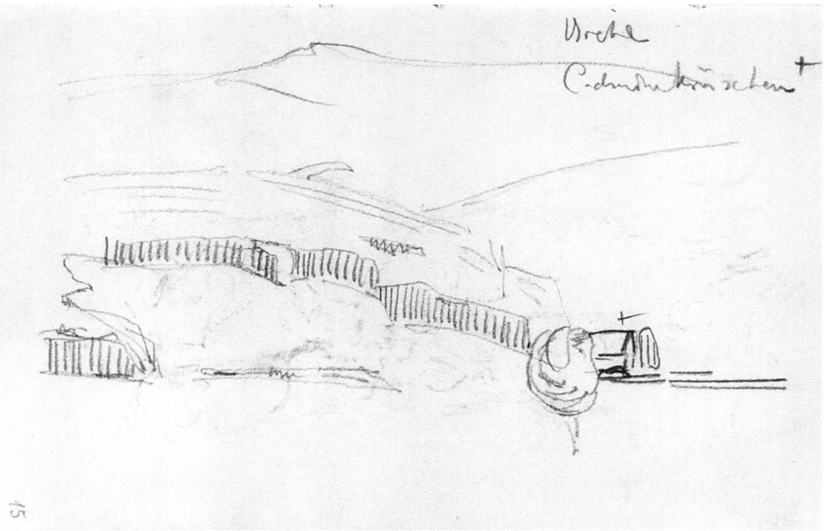

8, p.16

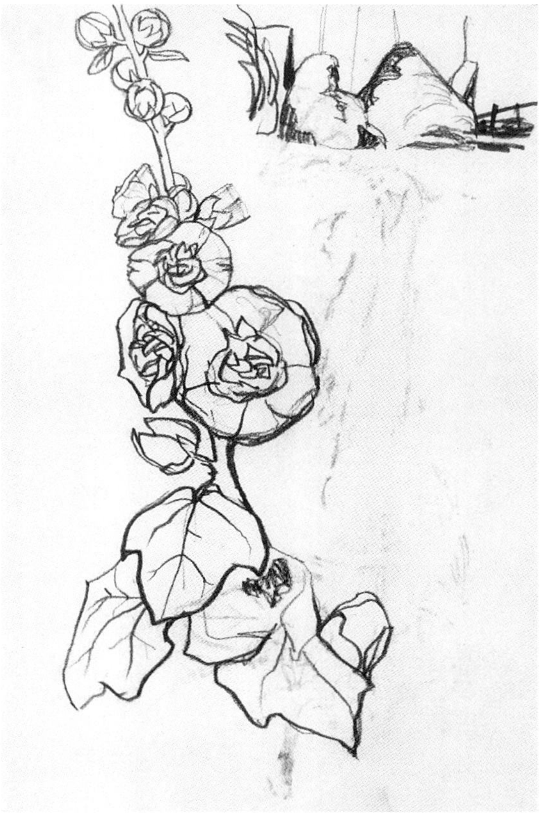

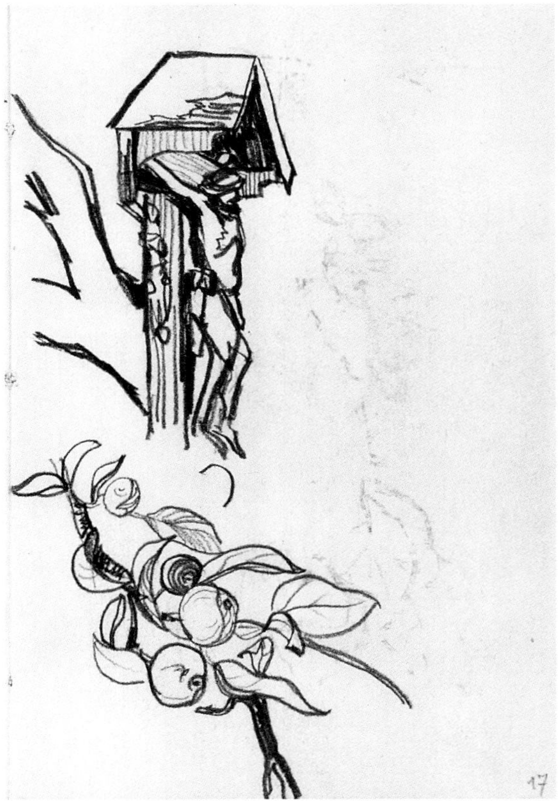

8, p.17

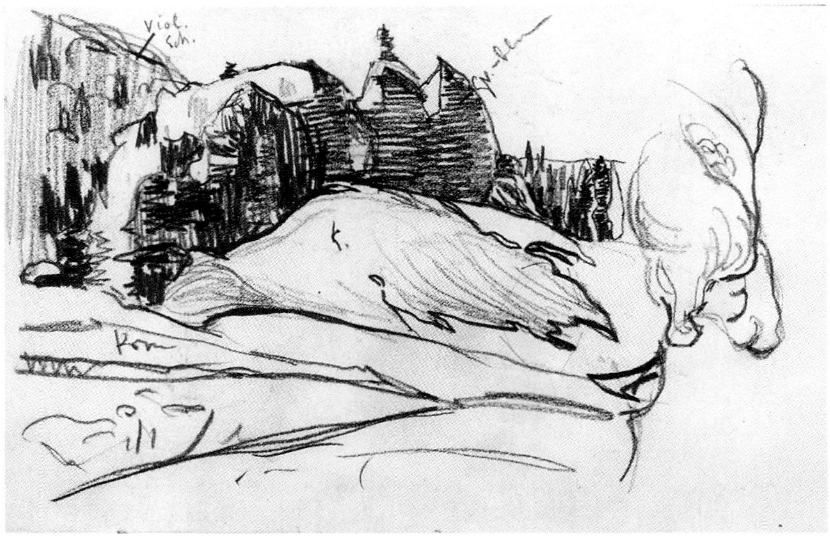

8, p.18

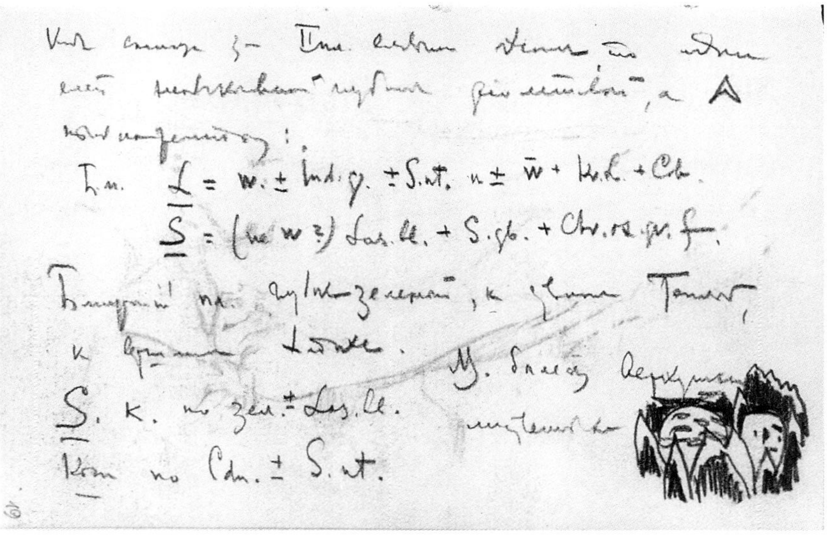

8, p.19

8, p.20

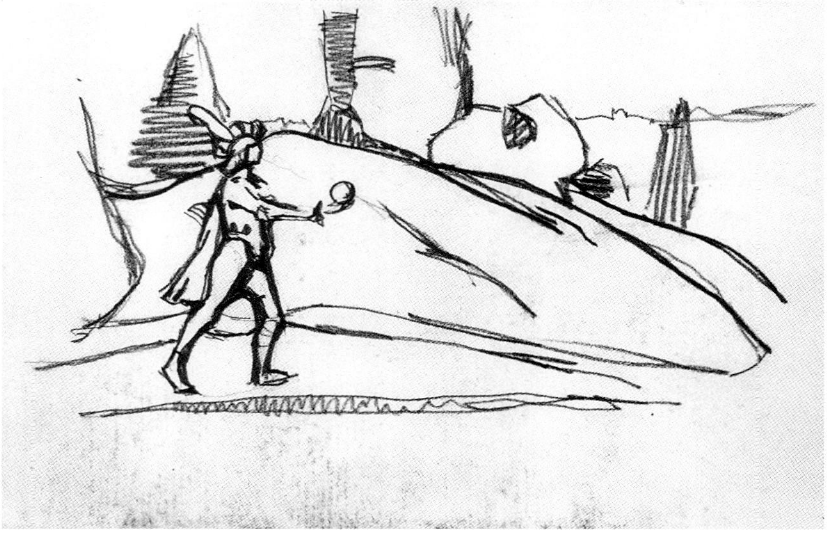

**p.17** Pencil drawings of flowers and shrine with crucifix

**p.18** Pencil drawing of landscape
Inscribed l.l.: 'Korn'; u.c.: 'viol. / sch. / gr.-blau'

**p.19** Pencil sketch of landscape
Inscribed with color notations in Cyrillic and l.l.: '<u>S</u>. K. po zel.+/- / Las.bl. / <u>Korn</u> po Cdm. + S. ut.'

Kandinsky's notes refer to the corn in the landscape on the facing page.

**p.20** Pencil drawing of landscape with man in costume holding a ball

REFERENCES
Hanfstaengl 1974, p.160, ill.

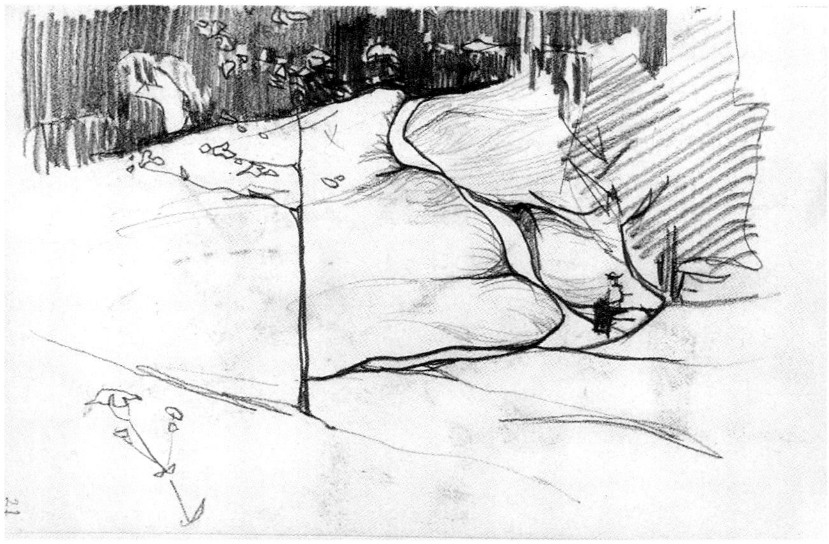

8, p.21

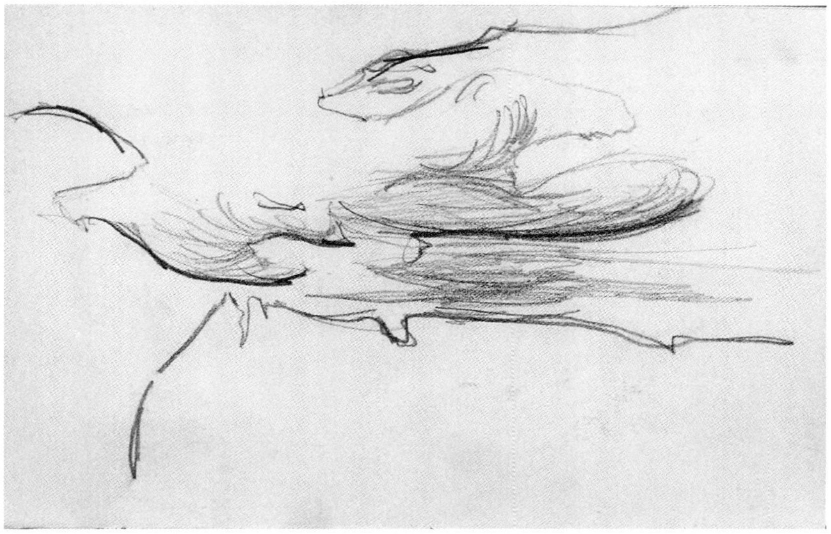

8, p.22

**p.21** Pencil drawing of landscape with seated figure and detail of tree

**p.22** Pencil sketch of clouds

**p.23** Pencil sketches of branch with leaves and tree

**p.24** Pencil drawing of branch with leaves and building with porch

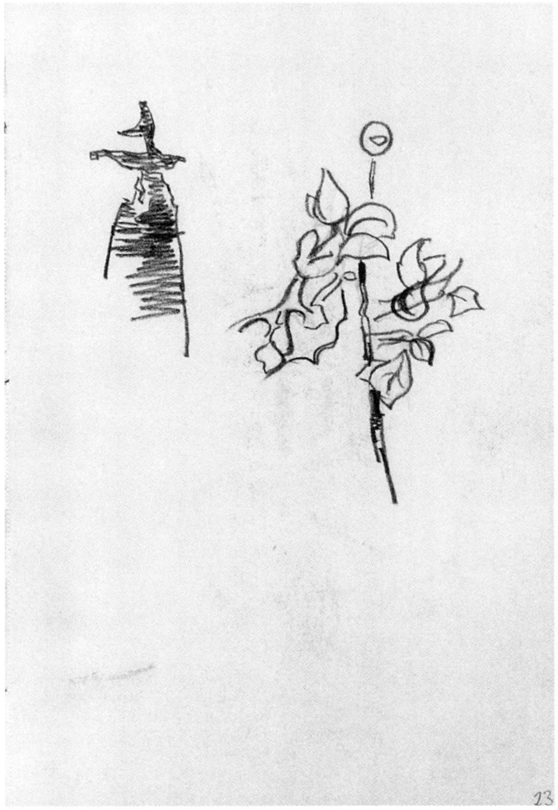

8, p.23

8, p.24

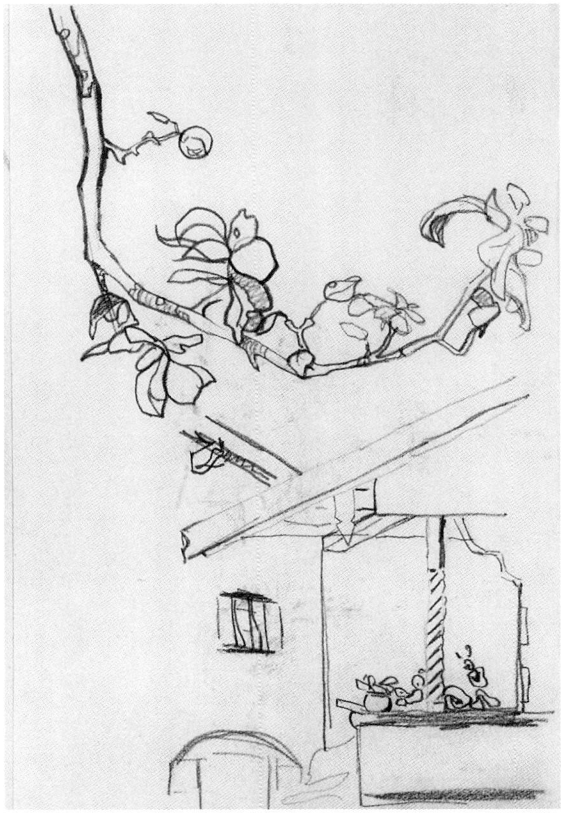

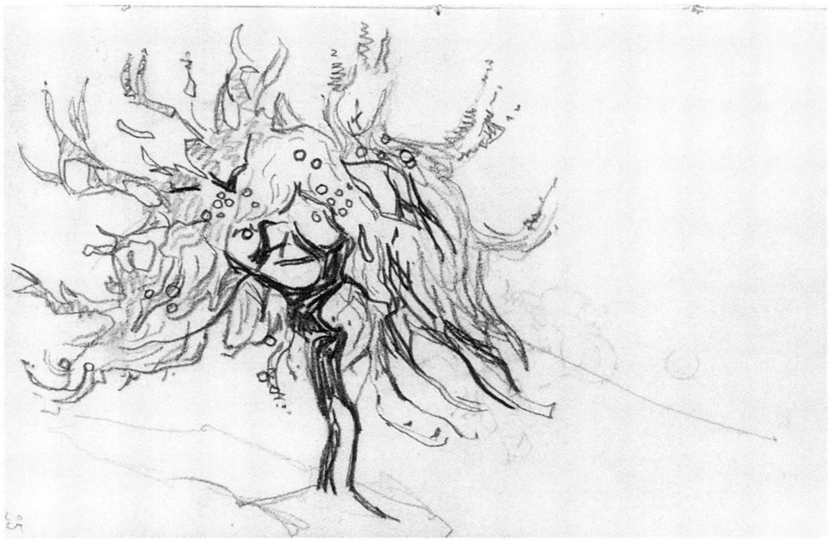

8, p.25

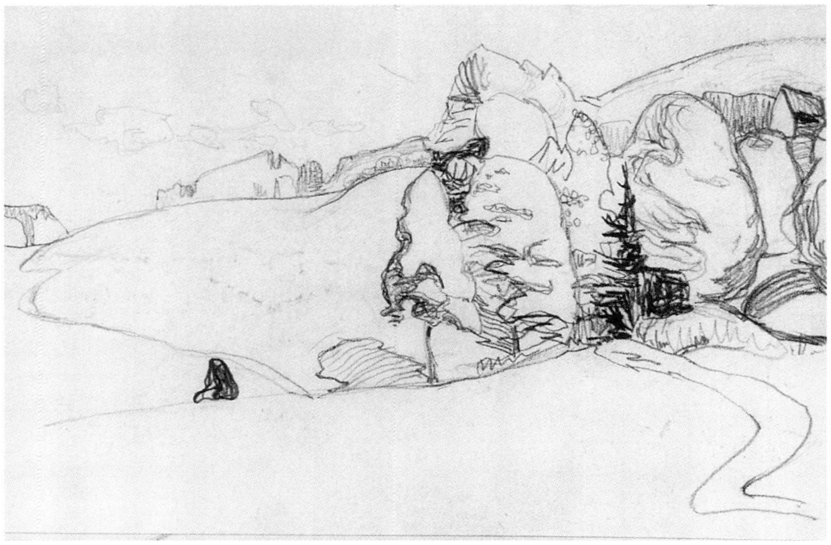

8, p.26

**p.25** Pencil sketch of tree with fruit

REFERENCES
Hanfstaengl 1974, p.160, ill.

Later in 1908 Kandinsky made several paintings of fruit trees in Lana in Tyrol.

**p.26** Pencil drawing of landscape

REFERENCES
Hanfstaengl 1974, p.160, ill.

Kandinsky painted many small landscapes on canvasboard near Kochel during the summer of 1902.

**p.27** Pencil drawing of village

**p.28** Pencil drawing of landscape

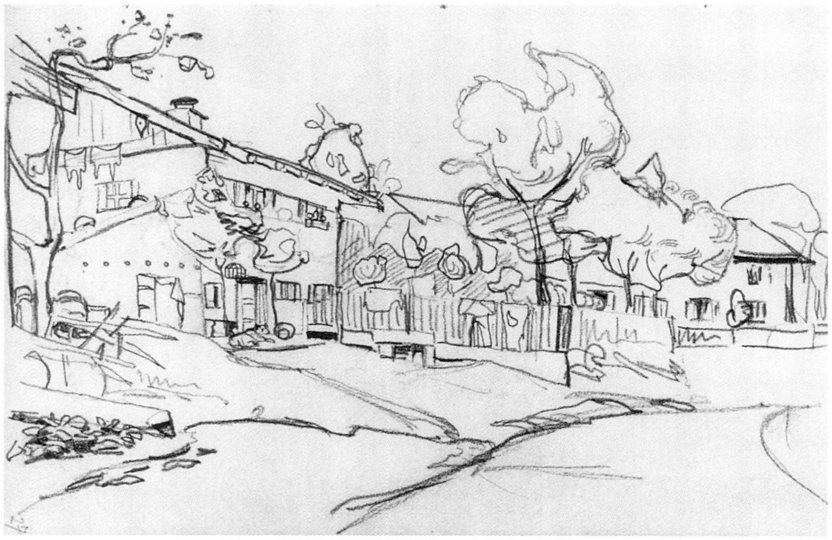

8, p.27

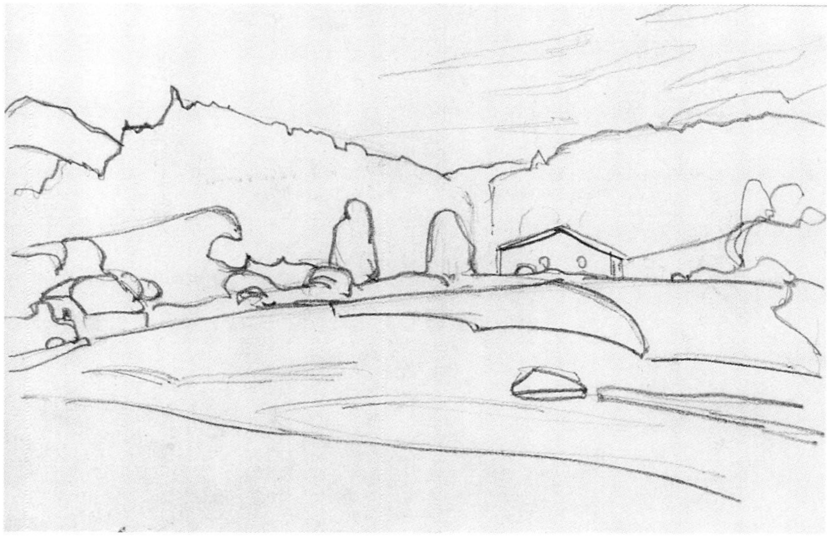

8, p.28

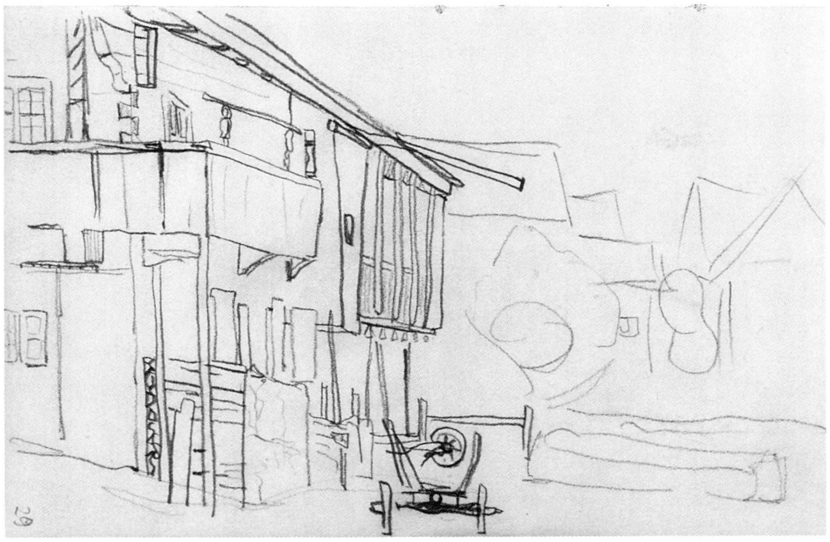

8, p.29

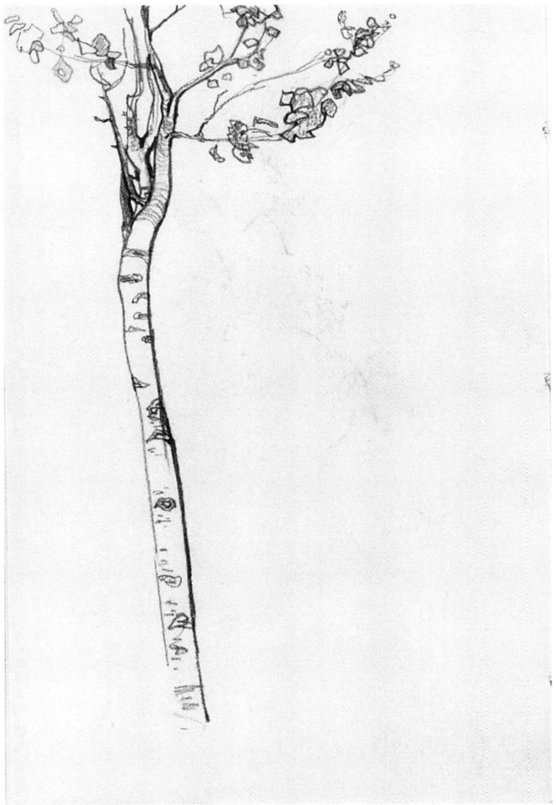

8, p.30

**p.29** Pencil drawing of houses

**p.30** Pencil drawing of birch tree
See also notes on p.4 (above).

**p.31** Pencil drawing of sunflower

**p.32** Pencil drawing of sunflowers

8, p.31

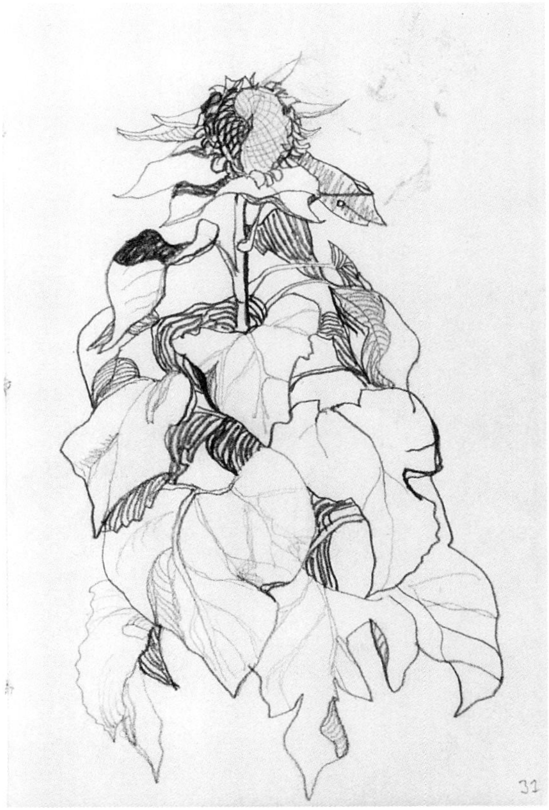

8, p.32

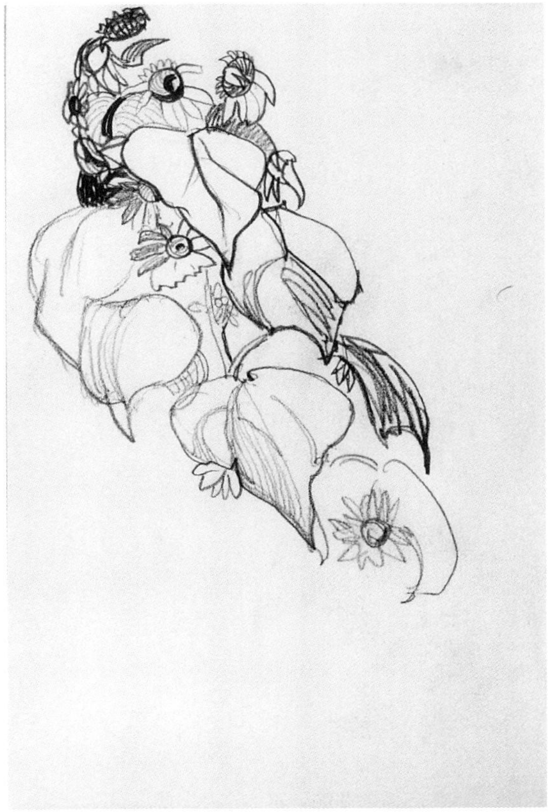

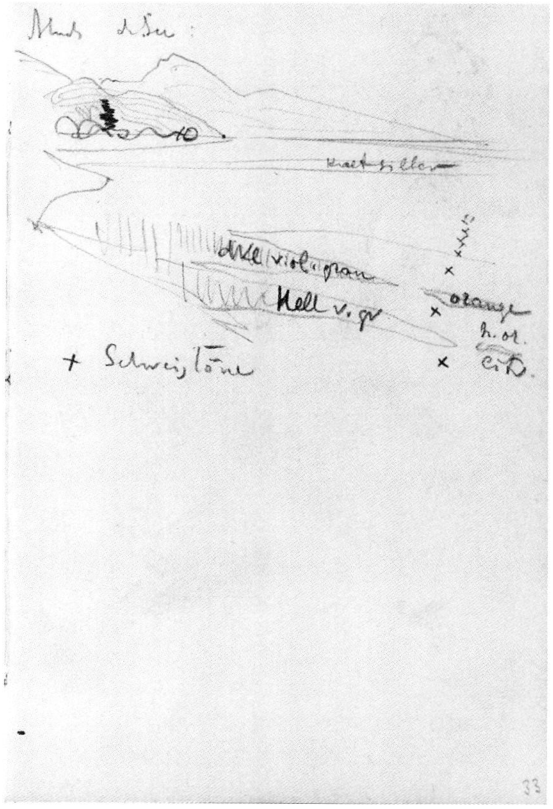

8, p.33

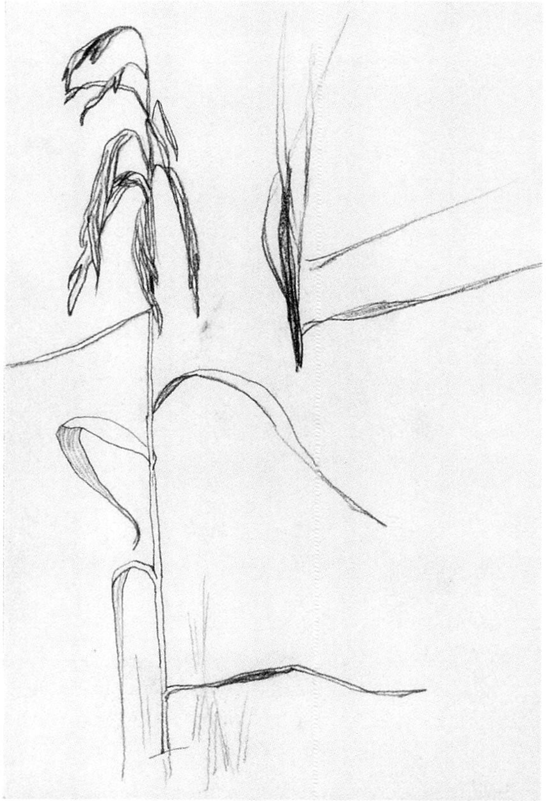

8, p.34

**p.33** Pencil drawing of Kochel See
Inscribed u.l.: 'Abend der See'; c.: 'kalt silber / dkl viol. grau / Hell v. gr'; l.l.: 'x Sch[warz] weis[s] Töne'; l.r.: 'x x x x x / orange / x h. or. / x citr.'

The sketch is related to the drawing on p.3 as well as to the painting *Kochel- See mit Hotel Grauer Bär* of 1902 (Roethel and Benjamin no.69).

**p.34** Pencil sketches of plants

**p.35** Pencil study of branch with leaves and fruit

**p.36** Pencil sketch of landscape
Inscribed u.r.: 'Hellgrünes Gras / grün / ins / gelb'; c.r.: 'viol. und / blau Schatten / Nasse dkl. grüne Steine / viol. grun Wasser'

Kandinsky's notes refer to bright green grass, violet and blue shadows, wet, dark green stones and violet-green water.

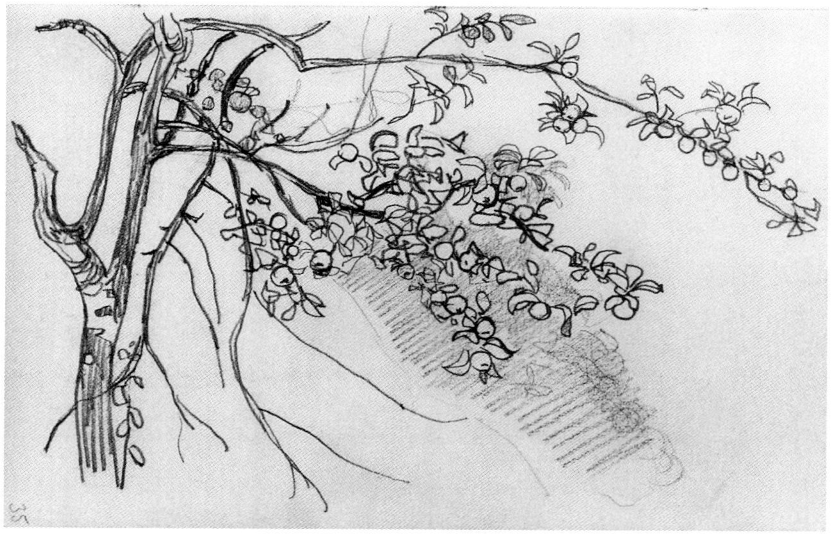

8, p.35

8, p.36

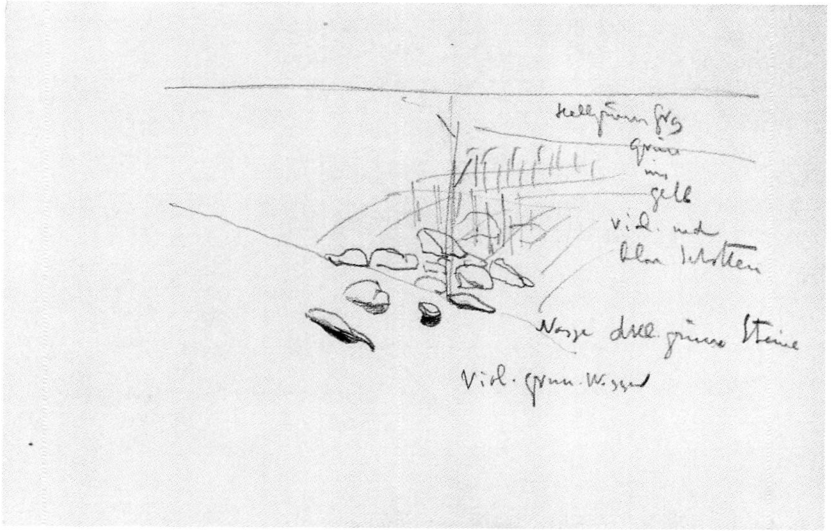

# Sketchbook 9

1902–1904

Brown cardboard sketchbook with black spine; no label
Contains 40 pages (20 sheets), each 16.9 x 11 cm (6⅝ x 4⅜ in), of which pp.12–29 are blank
Page numbers inscribed by unknown hand at later date with odd numbers at lower right

Hanfstaengl p.152

LOCATION
Städtische Galerie im Lenbachhaus, Munich (GMS 330)

HISTORY
Gabriele Münter, Murnau, until 1957

The sketchbook has the same cover and dimensions as Sketchbook 8, which dates from 1902. However, Erika Hanfstaengl dated this sketchbook c.1903–1904. The prevalence of costume studies, knights in armor and illustrations copied from books suggests an earlier date for some of the drawings.

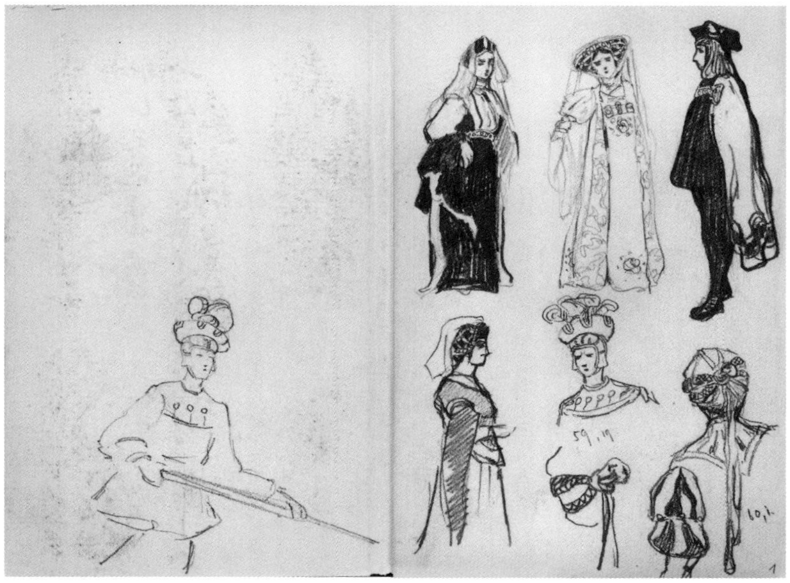

9, pp.0-1

**p.0** (Inside front cover): Pencil sketch of man in costume

The headdress and decoration on the shirt resemble those of the figure shown in the center on the facing page inscribed '59, 19' (see p.1).

**p.1** Pencil studies of costumes
Inscribed c.: '59, 19'; l.r.: '60, 1'

REFERENCES
Hanfstaengl 1974, p.152, ill.
Barnett 1992, p.84
Barnett and Friedel 1995, no.65, color ill.

Kandinsky's annotations refer to plate numbers in Friedrich Hottenroth's book, *Trachten, Haus-, Feld- und Kriegsgeräthschaften der Völker alter und neuer Zeit* (Stuttgart, 1891, vol.II). Plate 59, no.19 depicts a Dutch man from the late-sixteenth to the early-seventeenth century; plate 60, no.1 portrays a similar but not identical figure of a Dutch man from 1480–1580.

**p.2** Pencil study of mercenary
Inscribed l.c.: 'XVI'

Kandinsky made a drawing of two mercenaries on tracing paper (vol.I, cat. no.34), although its source, as well as the sources of other studies in this sketchbook, remain unknown (see p.3 below).

**p.3** Pencil study of mercenary and castle
Inscribed u.r.: 'Norden Wand.'; l.l.: 'Landsknecht XV'

Like the sketch on the facing page, this drawing probably shows a mercenary from the sixteenth (rather than the fifteenth) century, according to information provided by Dirk Breiding. The source of the illustration, which Kandinsky labeled 'north wall' and 'mercenary' in German, has not been identified.

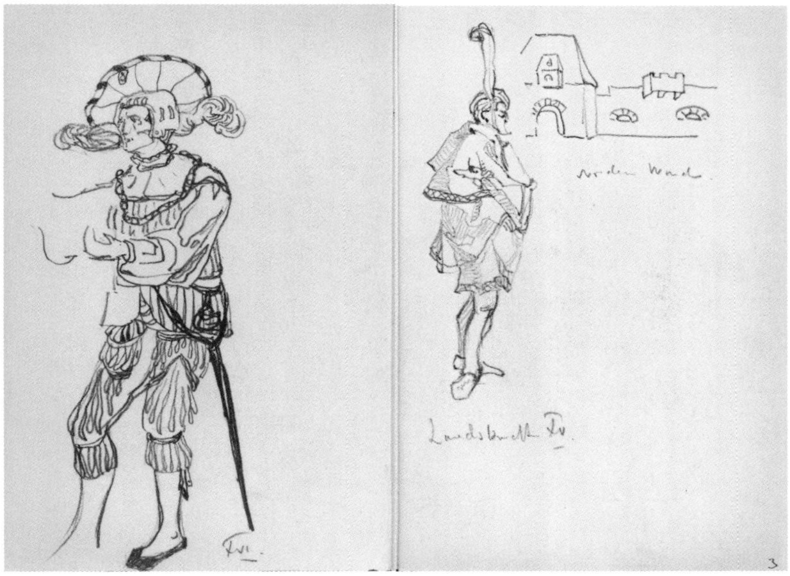

9, pp.2-3

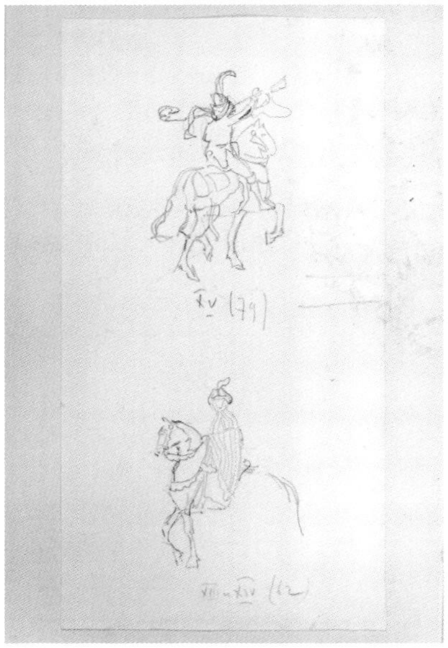

9, p.4

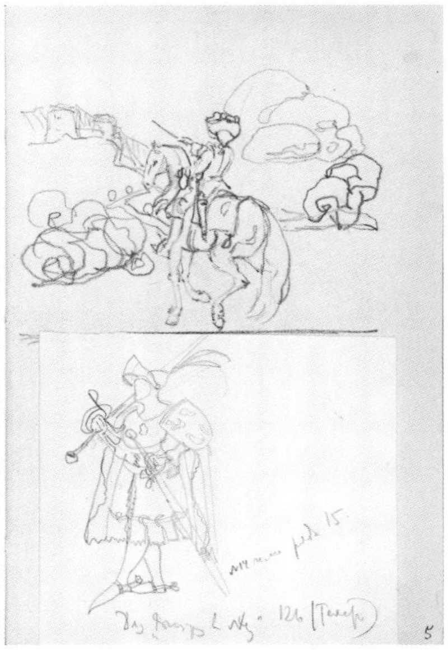

9, p.5

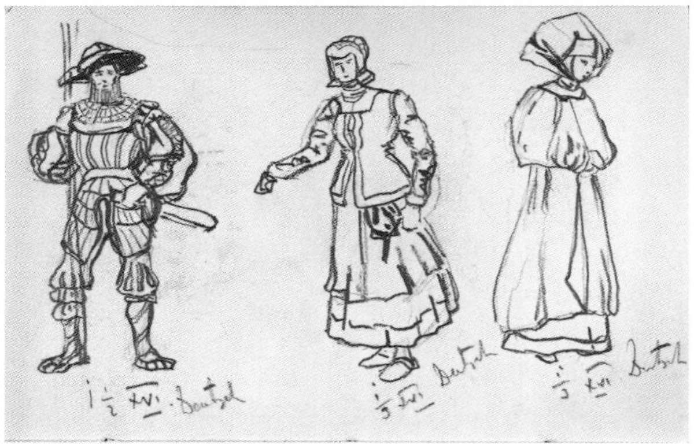

9, p.6

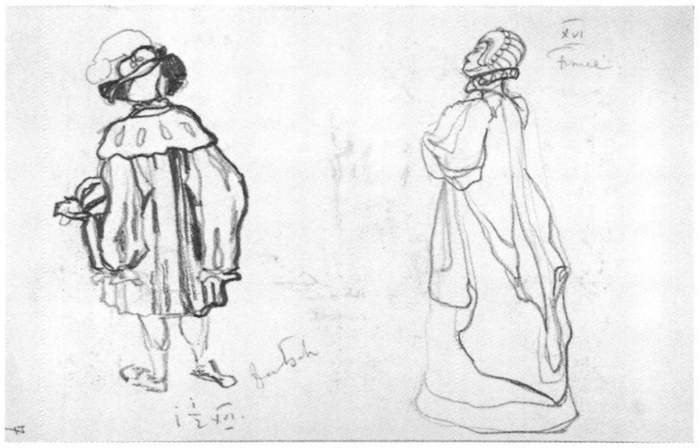

9, p.7

**p.4** Pencil studies of horses and riders on white paper (15.8 x 8.1 cm) pasted on sketchbook sheet
Inscribed c.: 'XV (79)'; l.c.: 'XIII u. XIV (62)'

REFERENCES
Hanfstaengl 1974, p.152, ill.
Weiss 1995, p.224 n.38
Podzemskaia 2000, p.121

Kandinsky copied the knight on horseback (above) from plate 79, no.13 in Hottenroth's book on costumes, and excerpted the figure of a horseman (below) from a group of English knights in plate 62, no.59.

**p.5** Pencil study of rider on horseback in landscape (above) and pencil sketch of knight on white paper (8.4 x 9.1 cm) pasted below on sheet in sketchbook
Inscribed l.r. in Cyrillic: 'N14 ili riadom 15.'; l.c.: 'Dlia rytsania v latakh' 126 (teper')'

REFERENCES
Hanfstaengl 1974, p.152, ill.

The source of the sketch below is fig.30, no.14 on p.126 of volume II of Hottenroth's book. Kandinsky indicated that it was 'for a knight in armor' and noted the number and page. This sketch is done on the same kind of white paper as the studies pasted onto the facing page.

**p.6** Pencil study of costumes
Inscribed l.l.: '1½ XVI Deutsch'; l.c.: '⅓ XVI Deutsch'; l.r.: '⅓ XVI Deutsch'

REFERENCES
Hanfstaengl 1974, p.152, ill.

The three studies of German costumes have been copied from plates 48 and 49 in the second volume of Hottenroth's book, *Trachten, Haus-, Feld- und Kriegsgeräthschaften der Völker alter und neuer Zeit* (Stuttgart, 1891).

**p.7** Pencil studies of costumes
Inscribed l.l.: '1½ XVI Deutsch'; u.r.: 'XVI / France'

The source of the figure on the left is plate 49 of Hottenroth's book (see pp.1, 4, 5, 6 of this sketchbook as well as Barnett no.59).

**p.8** Pencil drawing of Emperor Justinian
Inscribed below: 'Justinian. / Mosaique de St. Vital à Ravenne / (d'après Alinari)'; u.l.: 'Charles Diehl Justinien et la civi- / lisation byzantine au VI Siècle.'; u.r.: descriptive notes in Cyrillic

REFERENCES
Hanfstaengl 1974, p.152, ill.
Podzemskaia 2000, pp.128, 136, fig.25

Kandinsky copied a detail of the mosaic illustrated opposite p.16 in Charles Diehl, *Justinien et la civilisation byzantine au VI siècle* (Paris, 1901) as well as the photo caption. Podzemskaia dated this and the following drawing probably to 1903–1904 or perhaps later.

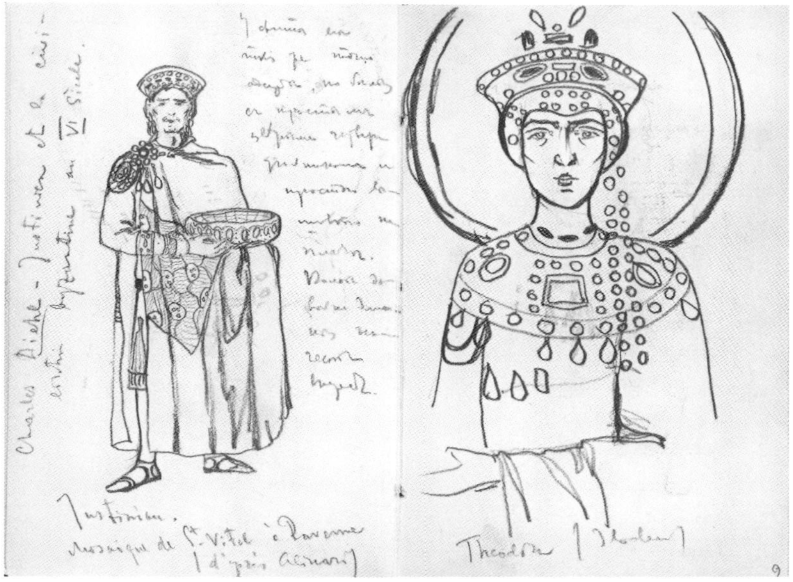

9, pp.8-9

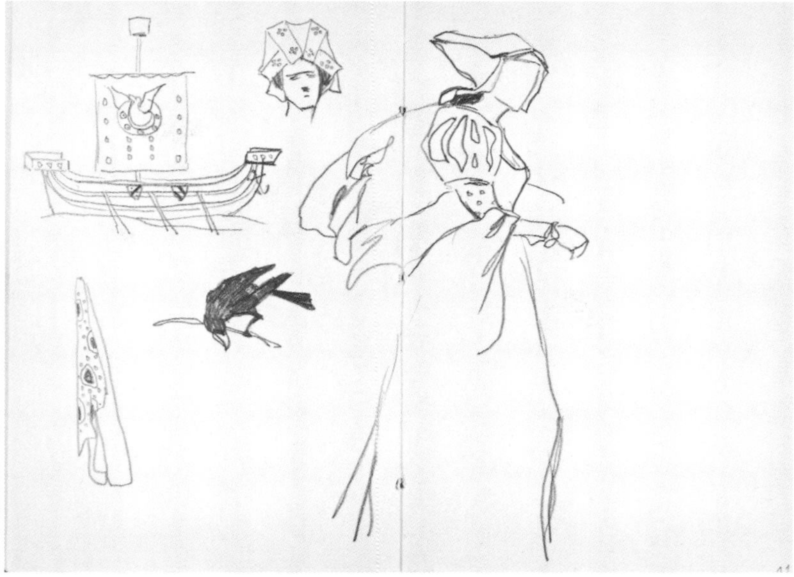

9, pp.10-11

**p.9** Pencil drawing of Empress Theodora
Inscribed below: 'Theodora (Italien)'

REFERENCES
Hanfstaengl 1974, p.152, ill.
Podzemskaia 2000, pp.128, 136

Kandinsky copied the illustration (fig.15) on p.37 in Charles Diehl's book (see p.8 above).

**pp.10–11** Pencil sketches of Viking boat, bird and woman in headdress

REFERENCES
Hanfstaengl 1974, p.152, ill.

The source of the images on this two-page spread has not been identified. However, similar boats appeared in *Flusslandschaft mit Boot und ummauerter Stadt* of 1902 (vol.I, cat. no.26), *Das goldene Segel* of 1903 (Roethel no.8), and the drawing for an ex libris on p.31 (below).

**pp.12–29** Blank

**p.30** India ink drawing of horse and rider

EXHIBITIONS
1982 New York, no.84, ill.
1982 Munich, no.22, ill.

REFERENCES
Hanfstaengl 1974, p.152, ill.
Weiss 1979, p.59, fig.54b
Barnett and Friedel 1995, no.89, color ill.

The horse and rider can be related to the color woodcut *Abschied (Grosse Fassung)* of 1903 (Roethel no.7).

(See color plate p.119)

**p.31** India ink drawing for an ex libris and drawing of horse and rider
Inscribed c.: 'EX LIBRIS'

EXHIBITIONS
1982 Munich, no.27, ill.

REFERENCES
Hanfstaengl 1974, p.152, ill.
Barnett and Friedel 1995, no.87, color ill.

The drawing of horse and rider closely resembles the sketch based on plate 79 of Hottenroth's book drawn on a piece of paper pasted in this sketchbook on p.4. There is no evidence that the ex libris was printed.

(See color plate p.119)

9, pp.30-31

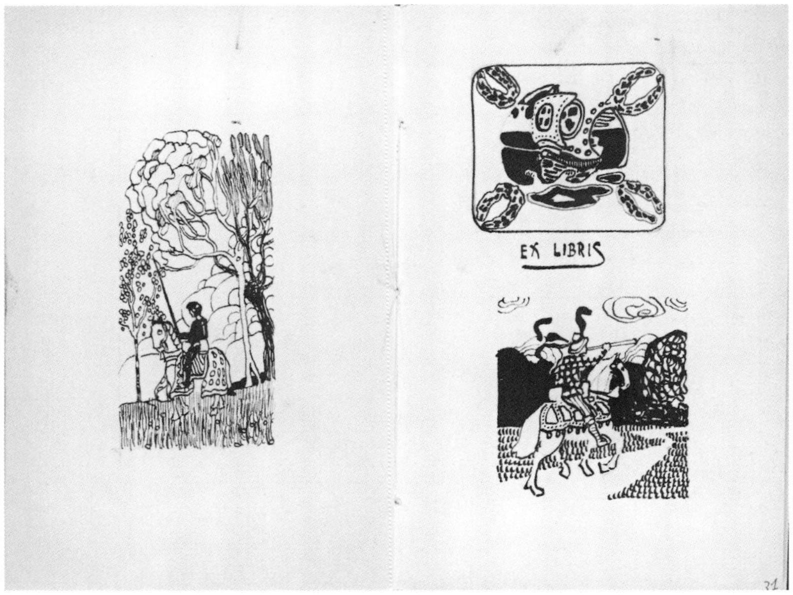

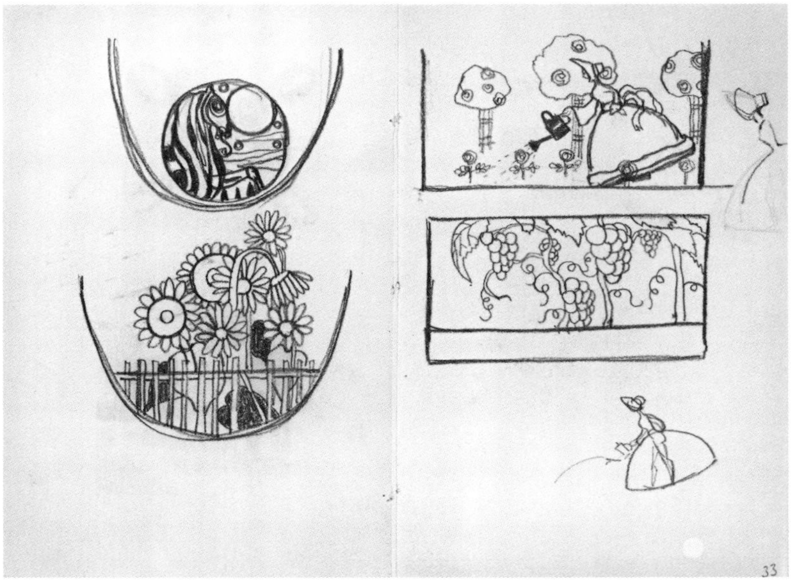

9, pp.32-33

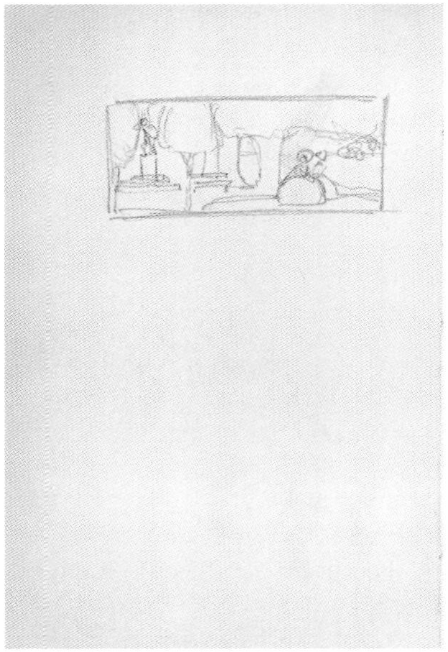

9, p.34

**p.32** Pencil studies for embroidery designs

REFERENCES

Hanfstaengl 1974, p.152, ill.
Barnett 1992, p.144

The drawing of flowers (below) was developed into a gouache *Entwurf mit Sonnenblumen* of c.1904 (Barnett no.146); the circular motif (above) can be related to other drawings of 1903 (see Sketchbook 12, p.45 and vol.I, cat. nos.53–54).

**p.33** Pencil studies for embroidery designs

REFERENCES

Hanfstaengl 1974, p.152
Barnett and Friedel 1995, no.132, color ill.
Barnett 2006, p.49

The figure of a woman wearing a hat can be found in a letter dated 1 June 1903, and in drawings for embroidery designs (vol.I, cat. nos.51, 66). The stylized apple trees appeared in Kandinsky's work during the summer of 1903. These studies are related to a handbag that Gabriele Münter made probably in early 1905 in Tunis.

**p.34** Pencil sketch of two women in a park

The motif of two women sitting on a bench can also be found in drawings of c.1903 (vol.I, cat. nos. 44, 45).

**pp.35–37** Blank

**p.38** Pencil drawing of cat and kittens

Later, when Kandinsky lived near Paris in 1906–1907, he made many sketches of his cat Waske (see Sketchbook 23).

**p.39** Blank

**p.40** Pencil drawing of cat with kittens

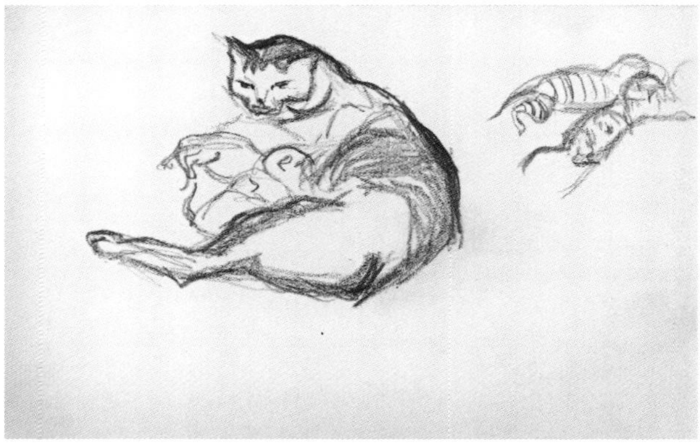

9, p.38

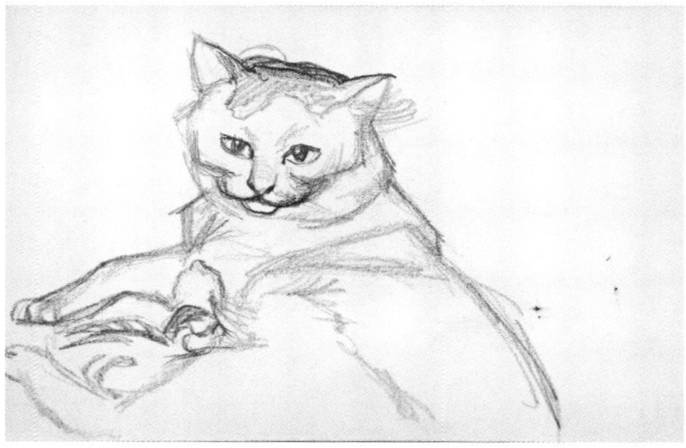

9, p.40

# Sketchbook 10

1903

Tan cardboard sketchbook with black spine; no label
Contains 16 pages (8 sheets), each 27.1 x 17.5 cm (10⅝ x 6⅞ in)
Page numbers inscribed by unknown hand at later date with odd numbers at lower right

Hanfstaengl 1974, p.163

LOCATION
Städtische Galerie im Lenbachhaus, Munich (GMS 343)

HISTORY
Gabriele Münter, Murnau, until 1957

Kandinsky used this sketchbook when he took the students in his painting class at the 'Phalanx' school to Kallmünz from 5 June until 12 August 1903. Kallmünz is a village with a medieval castle dominating the steep hilltop above: it is situated north-west of Regensburg in Oberpfalz (Upper Palatinate), where the Vils and Naab rivers converge.

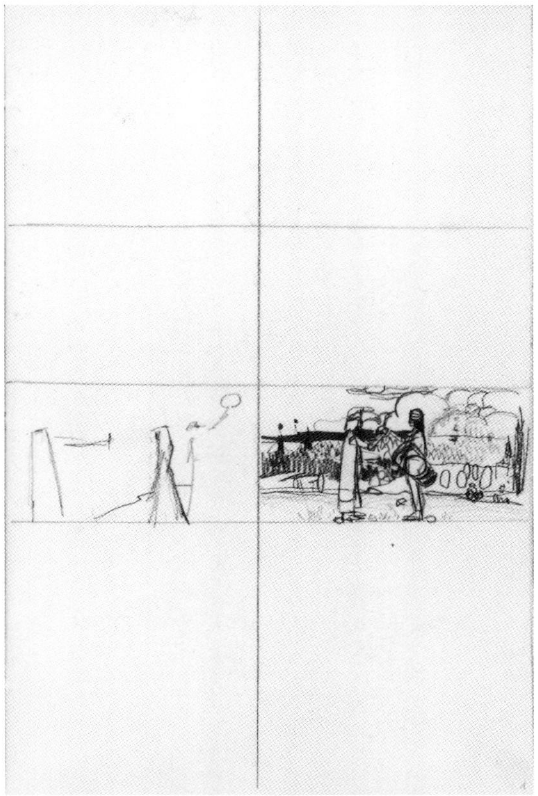

10, p.1

**p.1** Pencil sketches for an unidentified work

REFERENCES
Hanfstaengl 1974, p.163

The sheet has been squared up into eight unequal sections, of which two contain sketches. The image on the right (4.8 x 9.2 cm) shows two male figures within a landscape with towers in the background. Hanfstaengl proposed that the sketch might be related to *Stelldichein*. However, the theme of a tryst focuses on a man and a woman: for example, the drawing for *Stelldichein II* in Sketchbook 7 (GMS 338, p.9) clearly shows a man and a woman. The present sketch shares stylistic similarities with a drawing of a man from 1902 in Sketchbook 8 (GMS 339, p.20), and a later sketch of a man and horse in Sketchbook 23 (GMS 336, p.51).

**p.2** Pencil drawing of thistles (upside down)

**p.3** Pencil drawing of foliage and trees (upside down)

**p.4** Blank

10, p.2

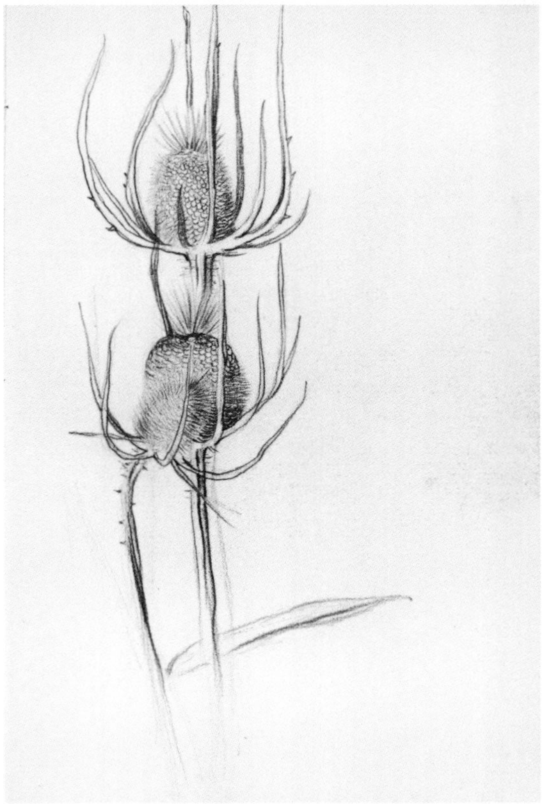

10, p.3

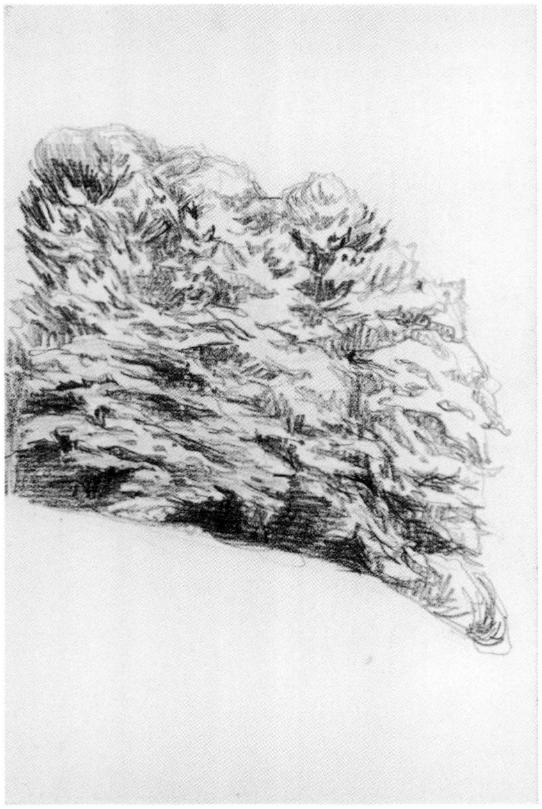

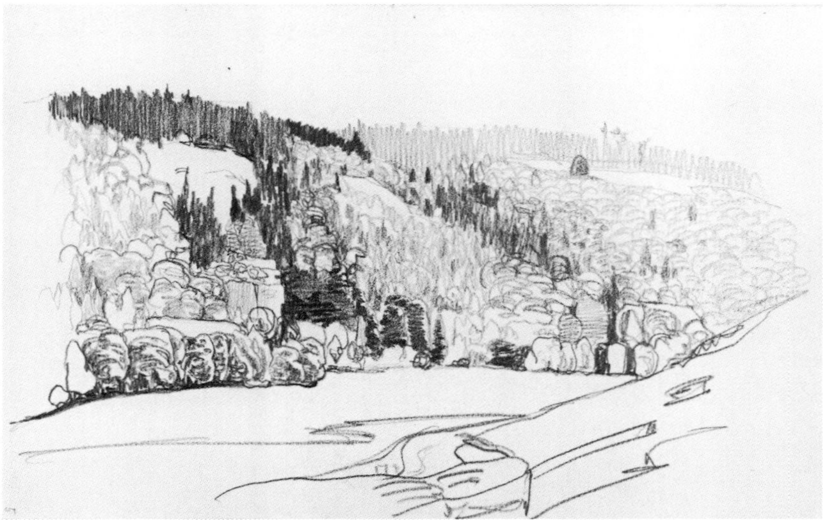

10, p.5

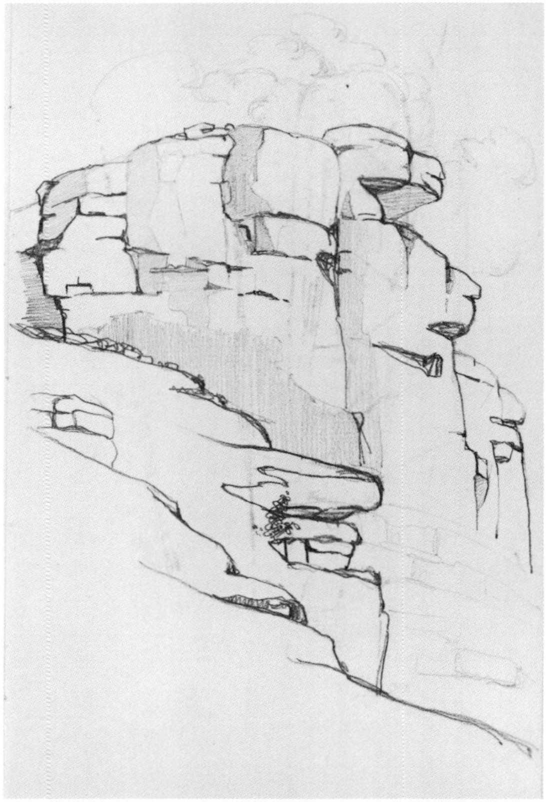

10, p.6

**p.5** Pencil drawing of forest

REFERENCES
Hanfstaengl 1974, p.163, ill.

**p.6** Pencil drawing of rocks (upside down)

Kandinsky also made drawings of rock cliffs in Sketchbook 13 (GMS 329, p.9).

**p.7** Pencil drawing of houses

The sketch resembles those in Sketchbook 12 (GMS 347, pp.9, 37, 40), which Kandinsky also used in Kallmünz during the summer of 1903.

**p.8** Pencil drawing of birch tree and foliage (upside down)

**p.9** Pencil drawing of Kallmünz and small sketch for *Spaziergang (Skizze)* of 1903

REFERENCES
Hanfstaengl 1974, p.163, ill.
Roethel and Benjamin 1982, p.128
Barnett and Friedel 1995, no.106, color ill.

The view of Kallmünz is seen from the castle on the Burgberg. There is a photograph of the same view probably taken by Gabriele Münter (see p.97), and a related drawing in Sketchbook 11 (GMS 337, p.1). The small study at the lower right is for *Spaziergang (Skizze)* of 1903 (Roethel and Benjamin no.107).

10, p.7

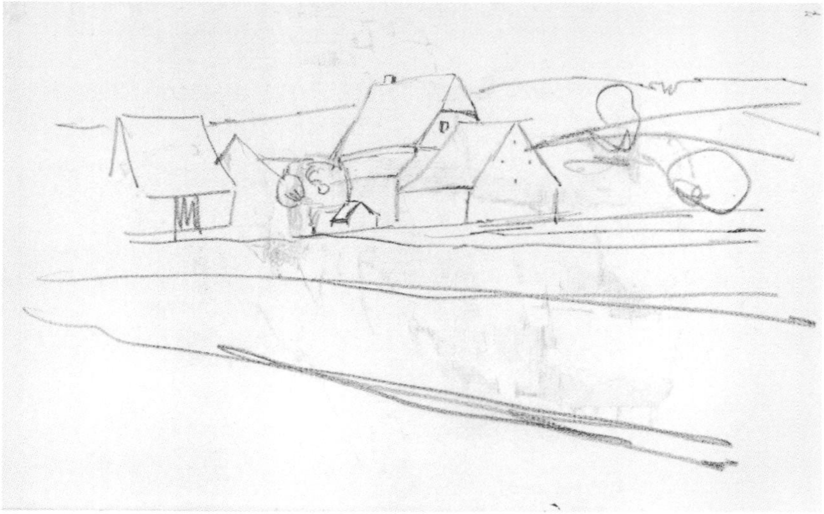

10, p.8

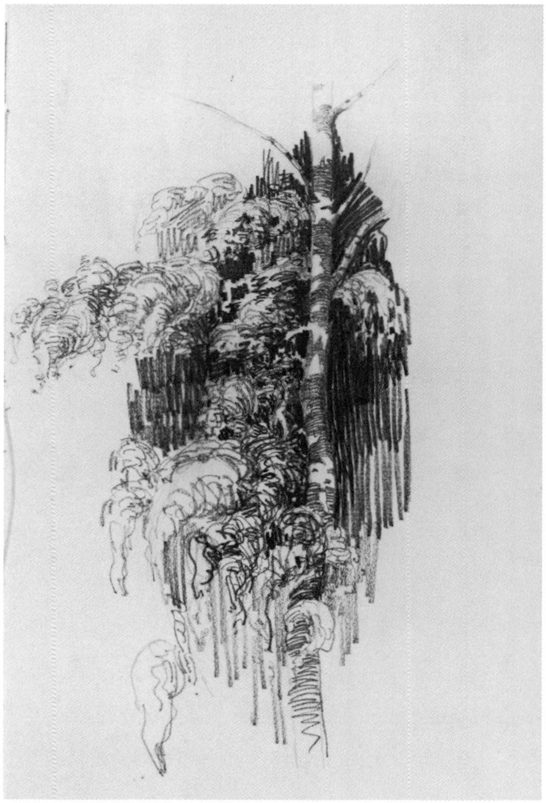

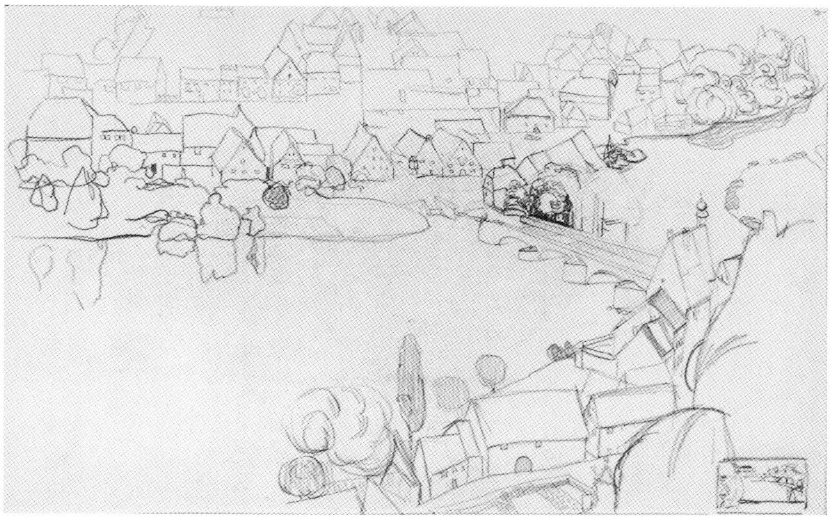

10, p.9

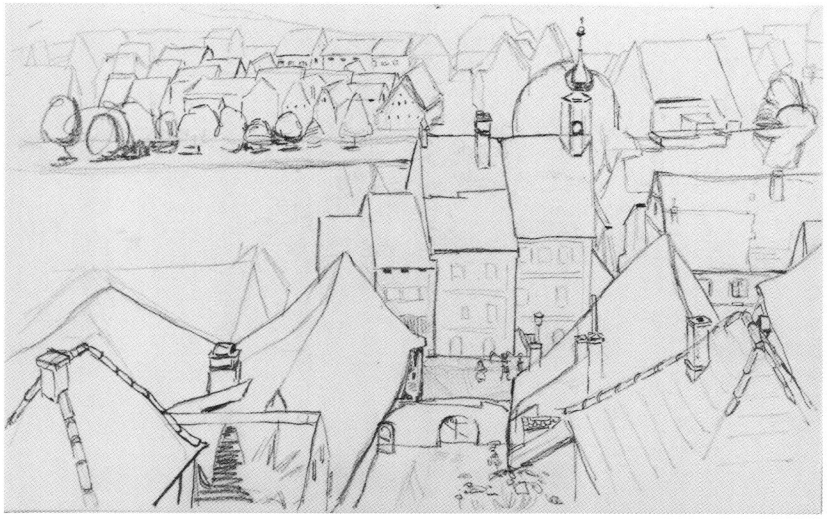

10, p.10

**p.10** Pencil drawing of Kallmünz

REFERENCES
Hanfstaengl 1974, p.163, ill.

See Sketchbook 13 (GMS 329, p.11) for another drawing of the Pfarrkirche in Kallmünz.

**p.11** Pencil drawing of blossoms and leaves

**p.12** Pencil drawing of tree (upside down)

**p.13** Pencil drawing of tree (upside down)

Münter made a remarkably similar sketch in one of her sketchbooks (38/13), which she inscribed 'Kallmünz' and dated 20 June.

10, p.11

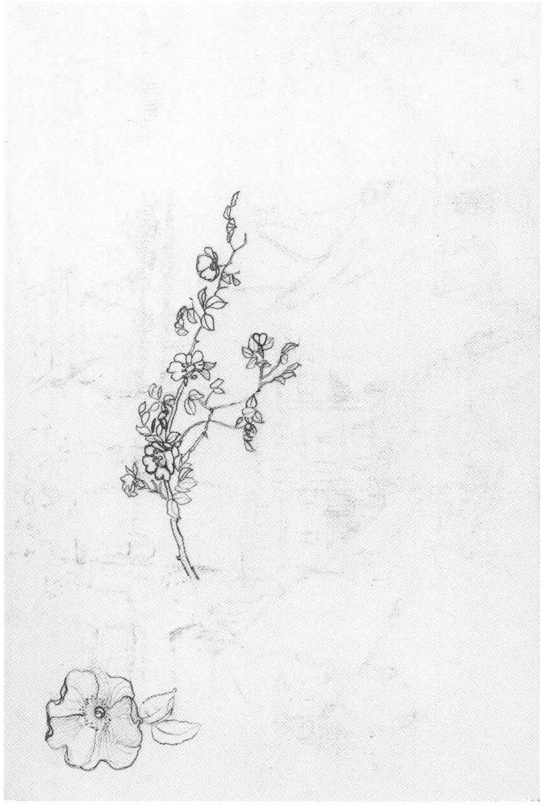

10, p.12

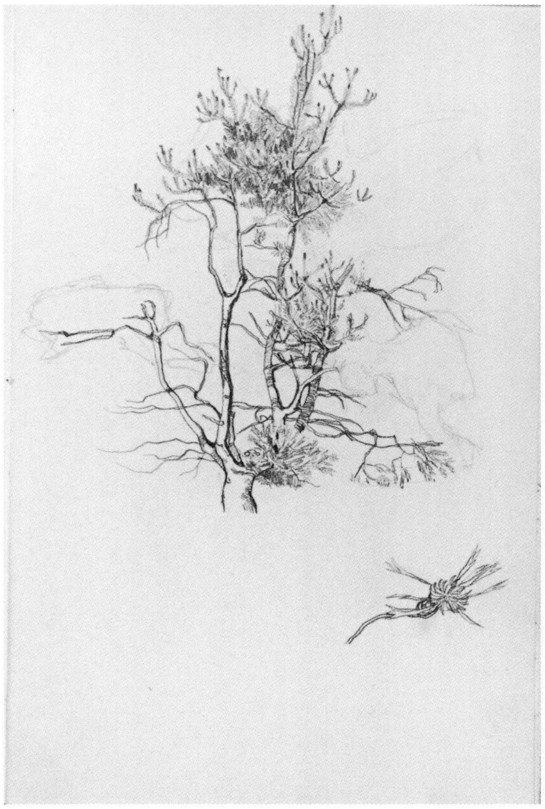

10, p.13

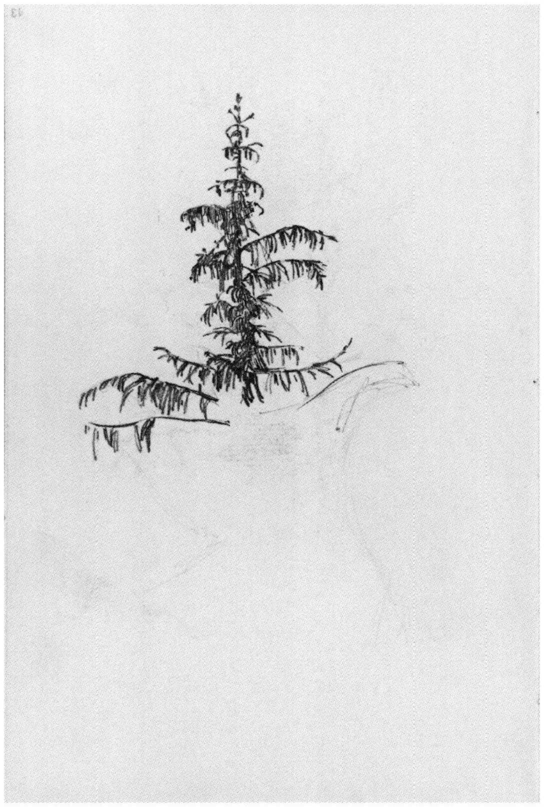

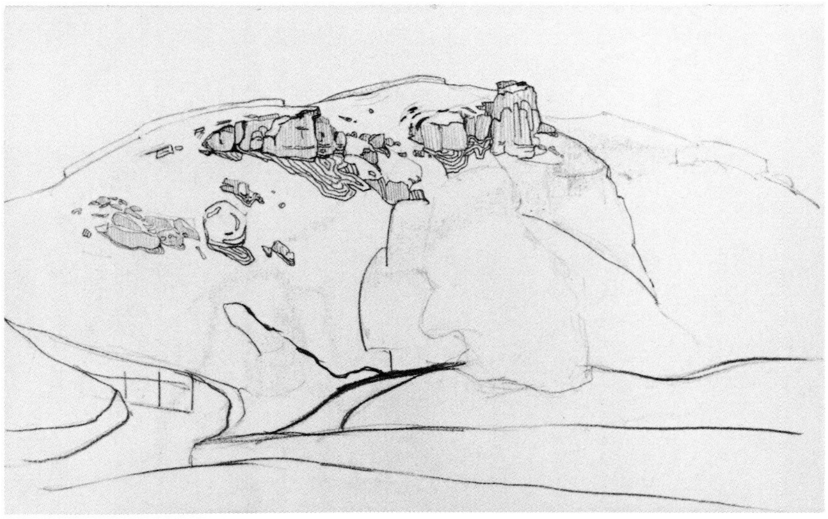

10, p.14

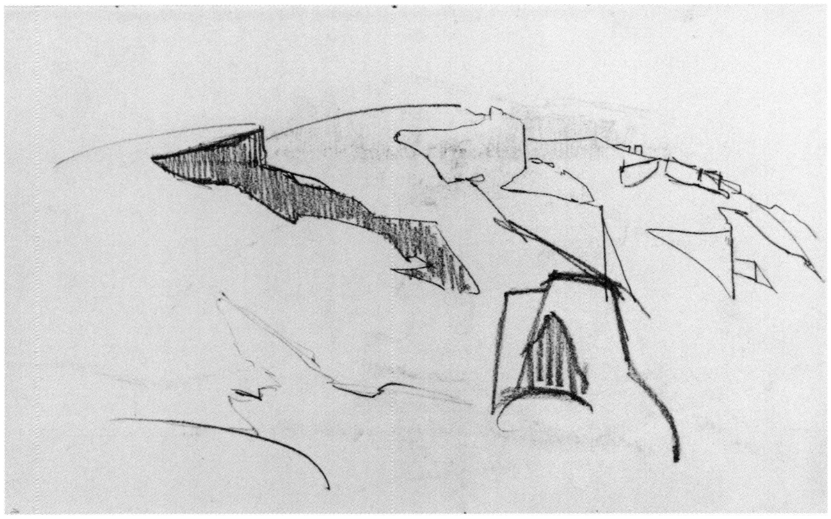

10, p.15

**p.14** Pencil drawing of rocks near Kallmünz in the Upper Palatinate

REFERENCES
Hanfstaengl 1974, p.163, ill.

**p.15** Pencil drawing of rocks near Kallmünz

**p.16** Pencil drawing of couple in medieval dress

REFERENCES
Hanfstaengl 1974, p.164

Hanfstaengl observed that the figures are related to those of a man and woman in *Abschied* of 1903 (Roethel nos.7, 20).

On outside back cover: pencil drawing of kneeling figure

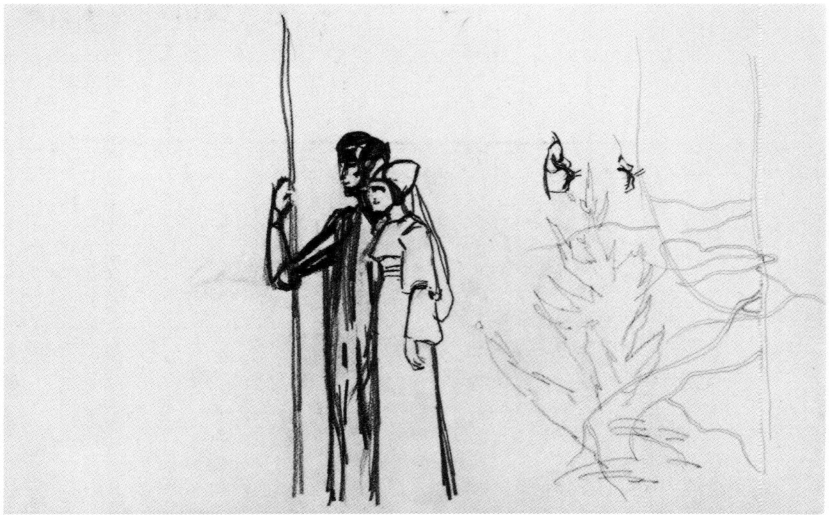

10, p.16

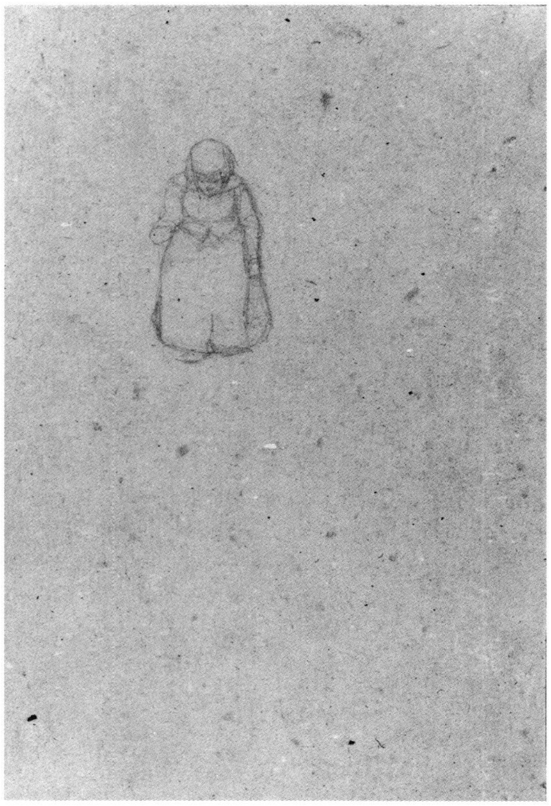

10, back cover

# Sketchbook 11

1903 and 1911

Grey-tan thick cardboard sketchbook; inside front cover stamp from Jos Bayerle, Munich (Akademiestrasse 11). Inscribed on front cover by Johannes Eichner: '1902 ?'
Contains 35 pages (18 sheets) of heavy grey paper, each 19 x 34.5 cm ($17^1/_2$ x $13^5/_8$ in), of which pp.8–35 are blank
Page numbers inscribed by unknown hand at later date with odd numbers at lower right

Hanfstaengl 1974, p.158

LOCATION
Städtische Galerie im Lenbachhaus, Munich (GMS 337)

HISTORY
Gabriele Münter, Murnau, until 1957

All but one of the drawings in this sketchbook clearly relate to the summer of 1903, when Kandinsky and Gabriele Münter stayed in Kallmünz from 5 June until 12 August 1903. The exception is a drawing copied after illustrations in a periodical that Kandinsky obtained in 1911. The date written on the cover by Johannes Eichner is not correct.

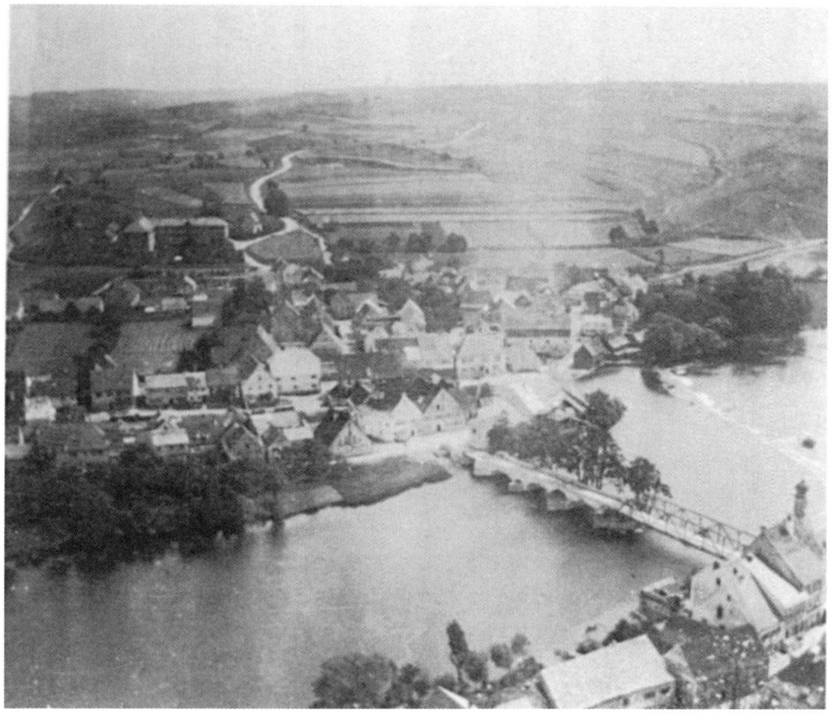

fig.a

**p.1** Pencil and white chalk drawing of Kallmünz as seen from the Burgberg

REFERENCES
Hanfstaengl 1974, p.158, ill.
Barnett and Friedel 1995, no.105, color ill.

The view looking down on Kallmünz is also found in Kandinsky's painting *Kallmünz- Blick auf die Stadt* of 1903 (Roethel and Benjamin no.83), and in a sketch on p.9 of Sketchbook 10 (GMS 343). The angle of the view and the bridge below corresponds to that in a photograph (fig.a) and in the drawing in Sketchbook 10. However, the similar emphasis on white roads and abstracted areas in the photograph probably taken by Münter suggests that this drawing might have been done after the photograph.

(See color plate p.120)

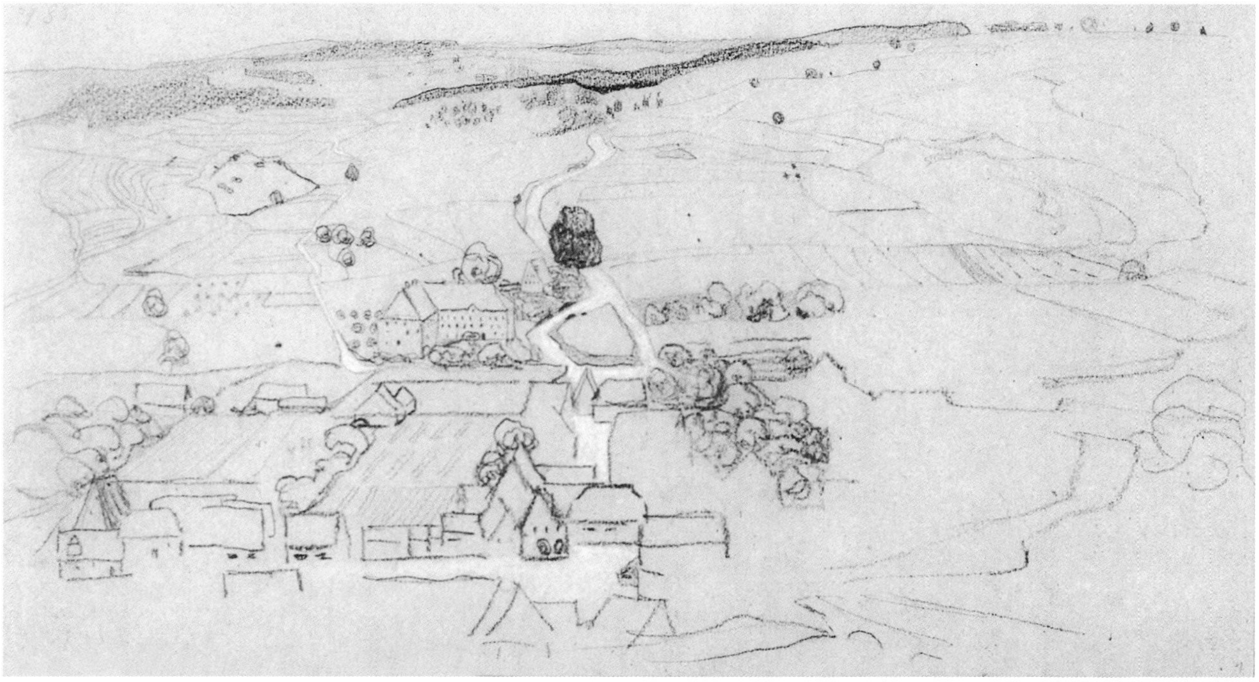

11, p.1

**p.2** Blank

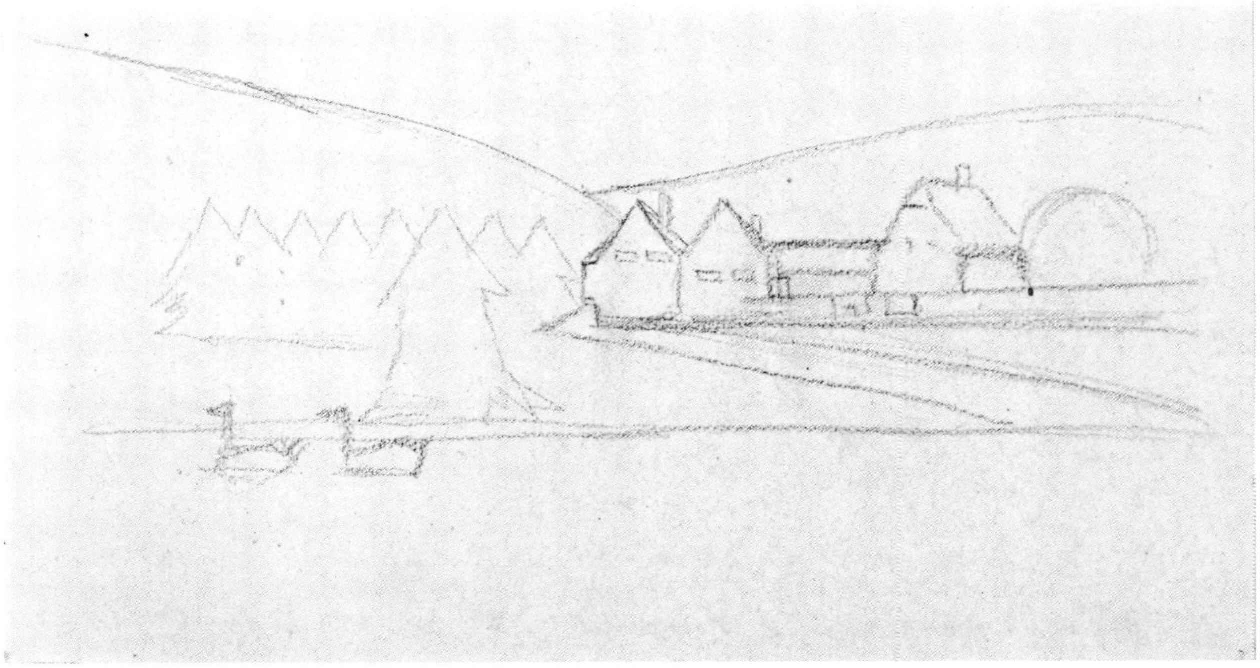

II, p.3

**p.3** Pencil drawing of houses and pond with swans

The drawing is related to those in Sketchbooks 10 and 13, which Kandinsky used in the summer of 1903 (see GMS 343, p.7 and GMS 329, p.41).

**p.4** Blank

**p.5** Pencil drawing of Kallmünz with the Burgberg in the background

**p.6** Blank

II, p.5

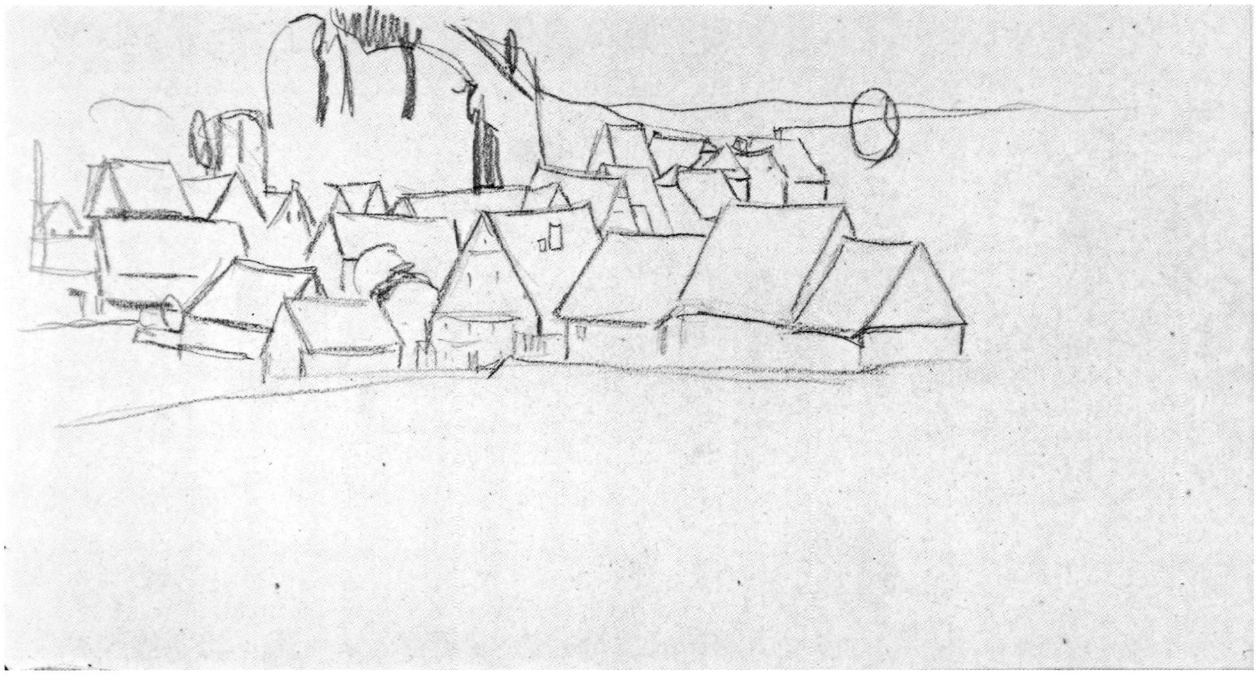

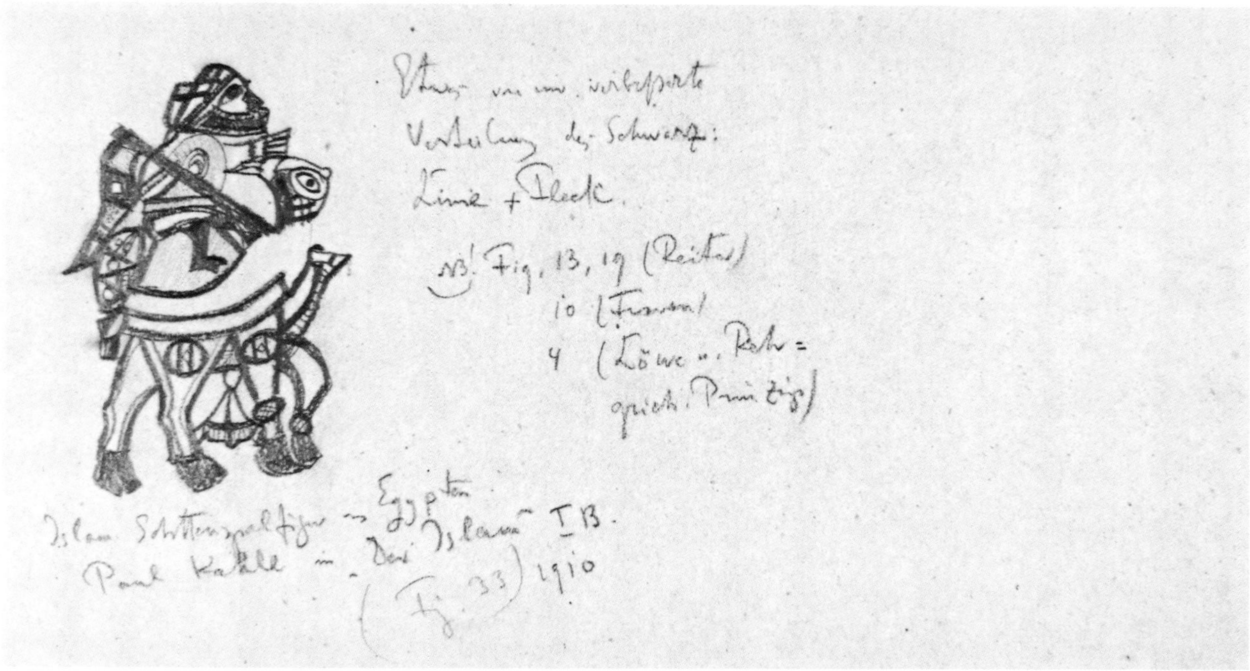

II, p.7

**p.7** Pencil drawing after an illustration in an article by Paul Kahle about Islamic shadow plays
Inscribed c.: 'Etwas von mir verbesserte / Verteilung des Schwarz: / Linie + Fleck. / N3! Fig. 13, 19 (Reiter) / 10 (Frauen) / 4 (Löwe u. Reh= / grieh. Prinzip) / Islam. Schattenspielfigur aus Egypten / Paul Kahle in "Der Islam" I B. / (Fig. 33) 1910'

Kandinsky copied the image from an article, 'Islamische Schattenspielfiguren aus Egypten. Teil 1' by Paul Kahle in *Der Islam* (vol.I [1910], p.292, ills.31, 33). He omitted the middle part (fig.32), and combined fig.31 depicting the rider and fig.33 showing the camel, which appeared in close proximity in Kahle's article. Kandinsky received the issue of *Der Islam* from Paul Marc, brother of Franz Marc, and in April 1911 he wrote to Paul Kahle requesting photographs. (See Katharina Erling, 'Der Almanach *Der Blaue Reiter*' in *Der Blaue Reiter* exh. cat. [Bremen, 2000], p.188). There were nine shadow play figures illustrated in the almanac *Der Blaue Reiter* published in 1912.

REFERENCES

Hanfstaengl 1974, p. 158
Daftari 1991, p.279, ill.143

**pp.8–35** Blank

**p.36** Pencil drawing of houses near Kallmünz and sketch of leaves (facing back cover)

II, p.36

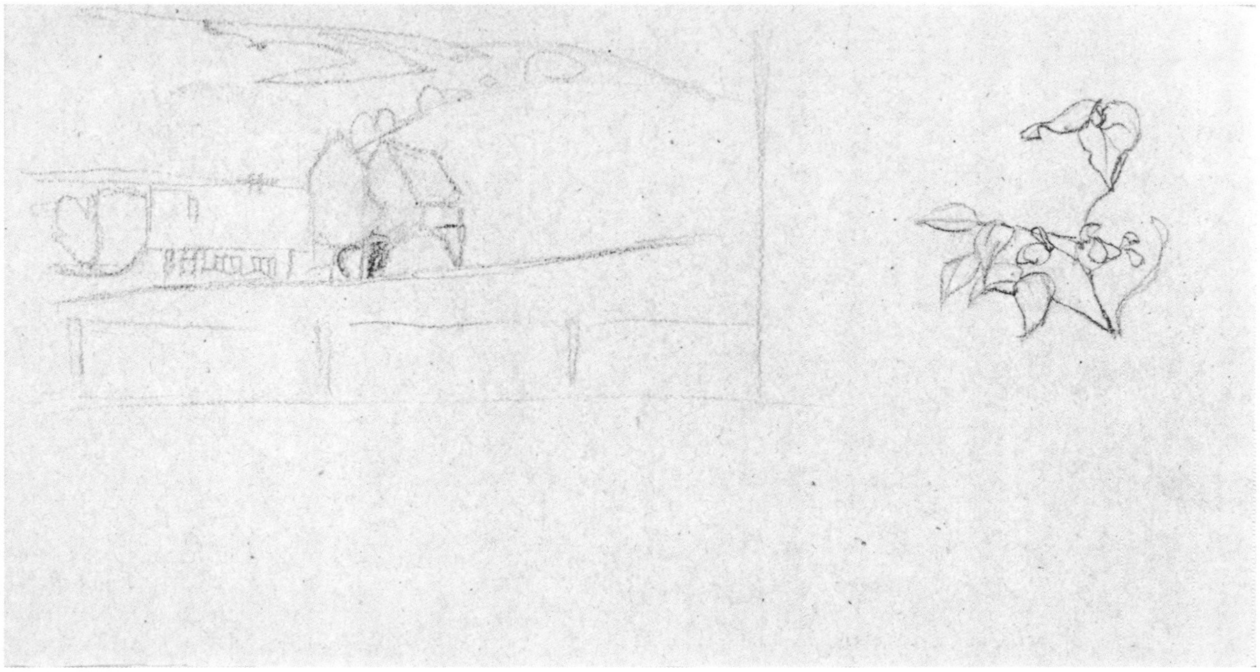

# Sketchbook 12

1903

Dark grey cardboard sketchbook with black spine; inside front cover label from Franz Dury, Munich
Contains 46 pages (23 sheets), each 15.7 x 10 cm (6⅛ x 3⅞ in)
Page numbers inscribed by unknown hand at later date with odd numbers at lower right

Hanfstaengl 1974, pp.167–168

LOCATION
Städtische Galerie im Lenbachhaus, Munich (GMS 347)

HISTORY
Gabriele Münter, Murnau, until 1957

Hanfstaengl dated the sketchbook 1903–1904 because the embroidery designs may have been done after Kandinsky's stay in Kallmünz in the summer of 1903.

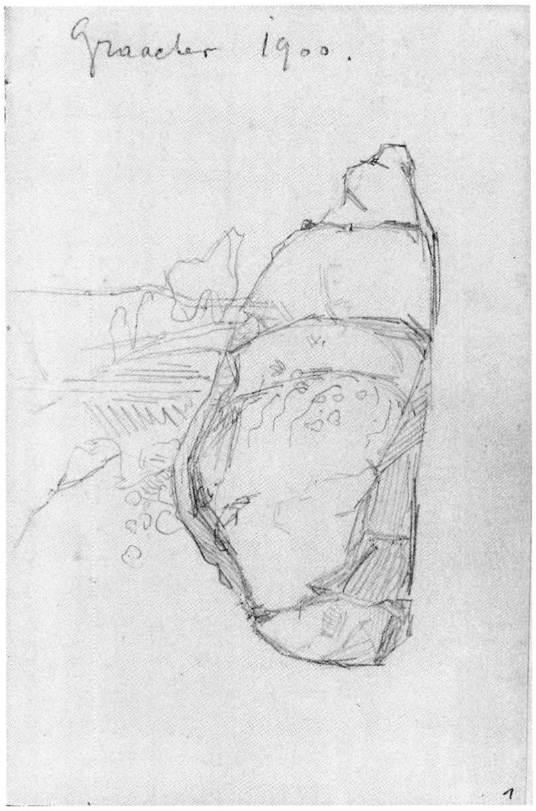


12, p.1

**p.1** Pencil drawing of boulder in rocky landscape
Inscribed u.c.: 'Graacher 1900'

There appears to be no relationship between the year written on the page and the drawing done in Kallmünz in 1903. It is possible that Kandinsky has noted a vintage (Graacher) and the year 1900. The drawing of a boulder in a rocky landscape resembles the sketches on p.41 (below) as well as pp.6, 14 in Sketchbook 10 (GMS 343) and p.9 in Sketchbook 13 (GMS 329).

**p.2** Blank

**p.3** Pencil drawing of landscape

**p.4** Blank

**p.5** Pencil drawing of landscape

**p.6** Blank

**p.7** Pencil drawing of flowers

See also Sketchbook 10 (GMS 343, p.11).

**p.8** Pencil drawing of landscape with bridge reflected in water

**p.9** Pencil drawing of houses in Kallmünz
Inscribed with color notations: 'g. / bl. / w. / wg.'

12, p.3

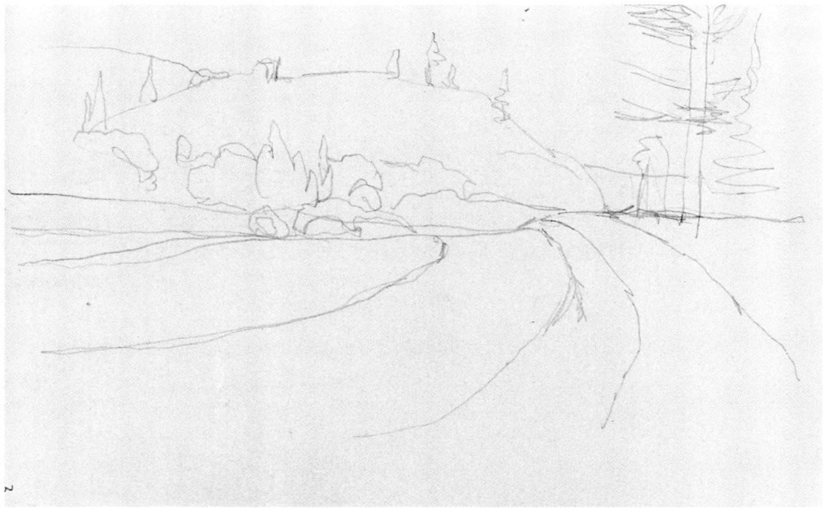

12, p.5

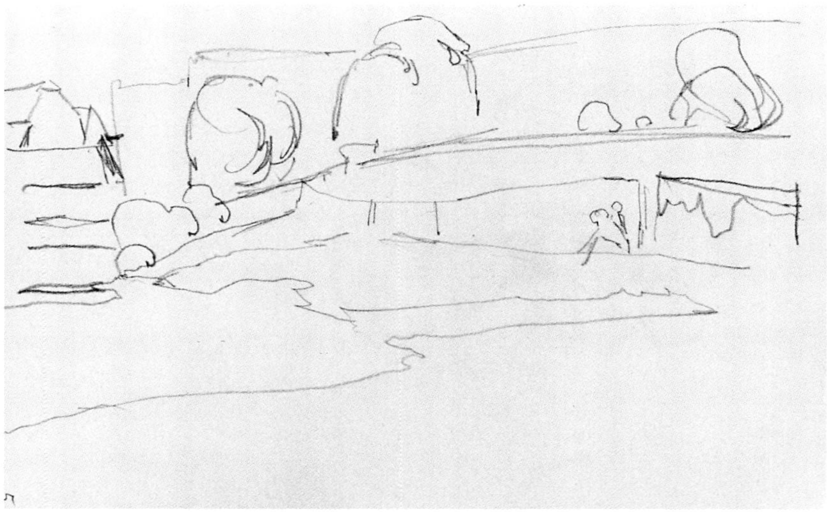

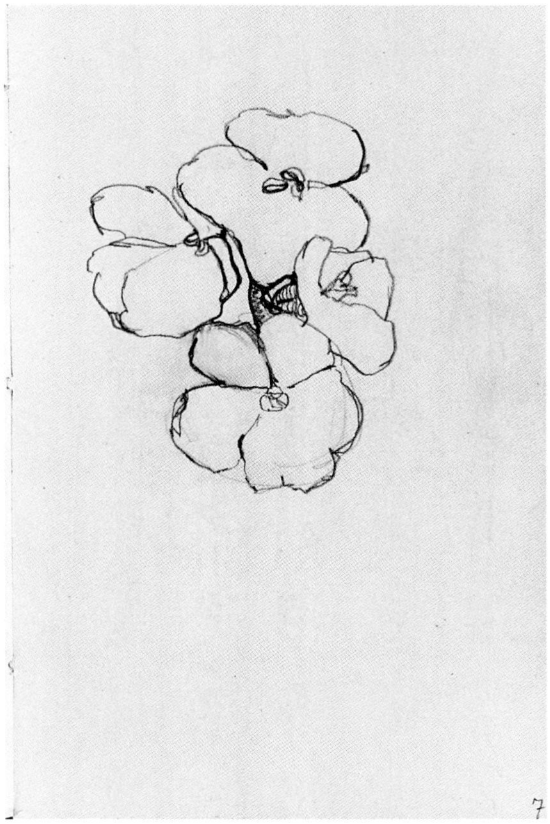


12, p.7

**p.10** Blank

**p.11** Pencil drawing of landscape
Inscribed u.l.: 'Grünglb. Fichten'; u.r.: 'viol. / blaugrün / grün'

**p.12** Blank

**p.13** Pencil drawing of landscape near Kallmünz

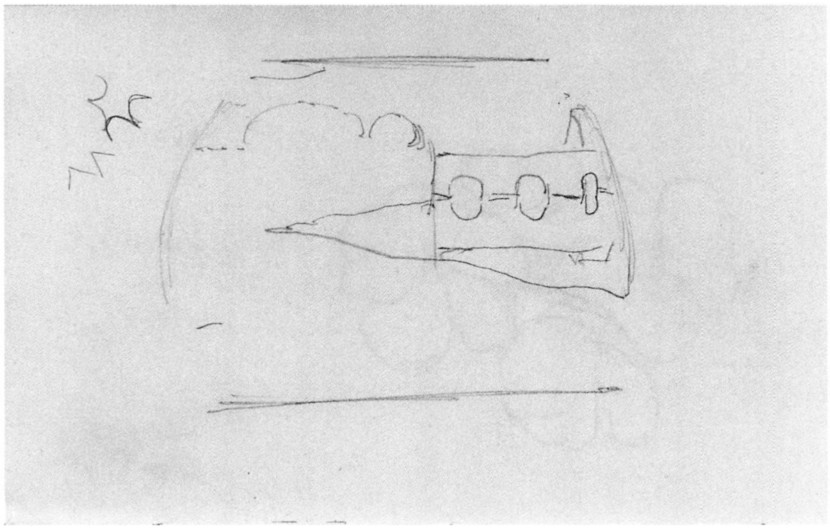

12, p.8

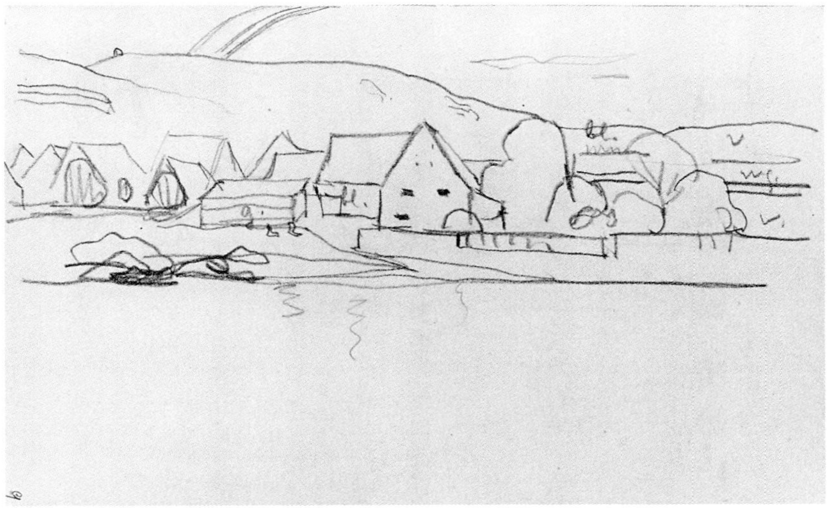

12, p.9

12, p.11

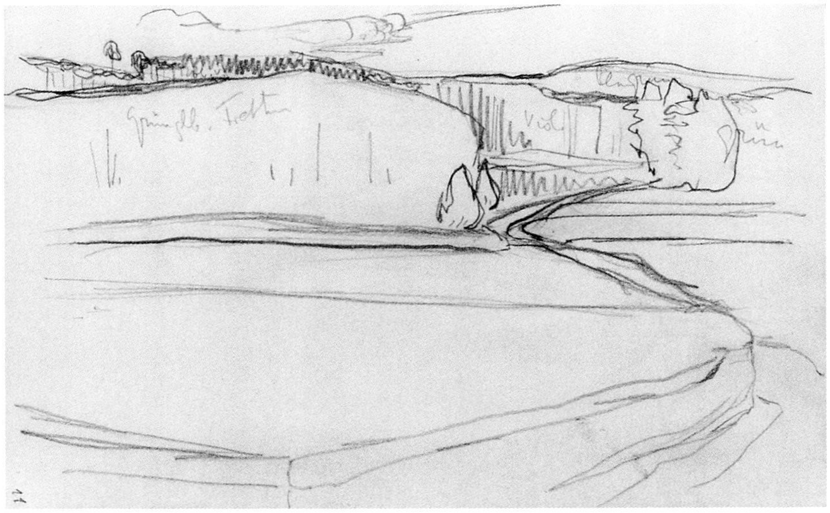

12, p.13

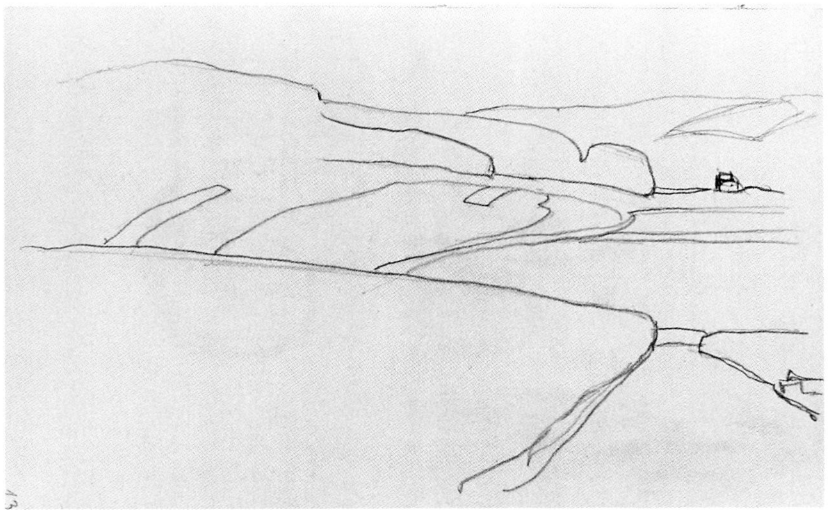

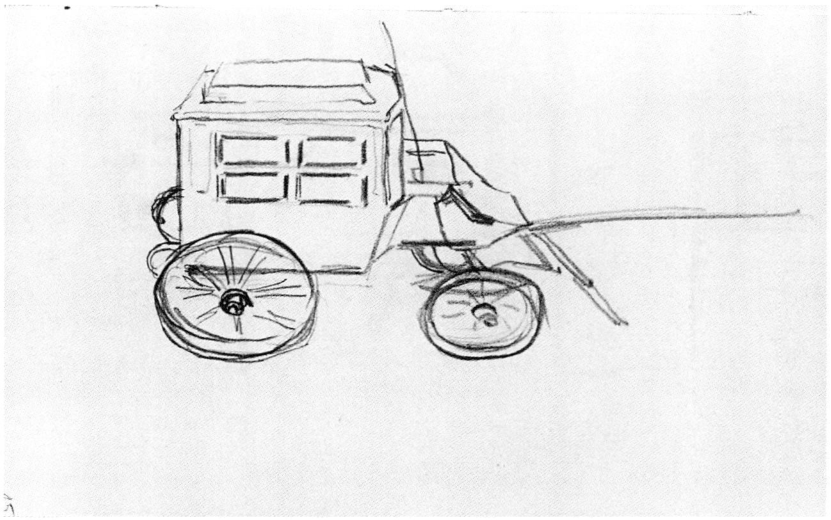

12, p.15

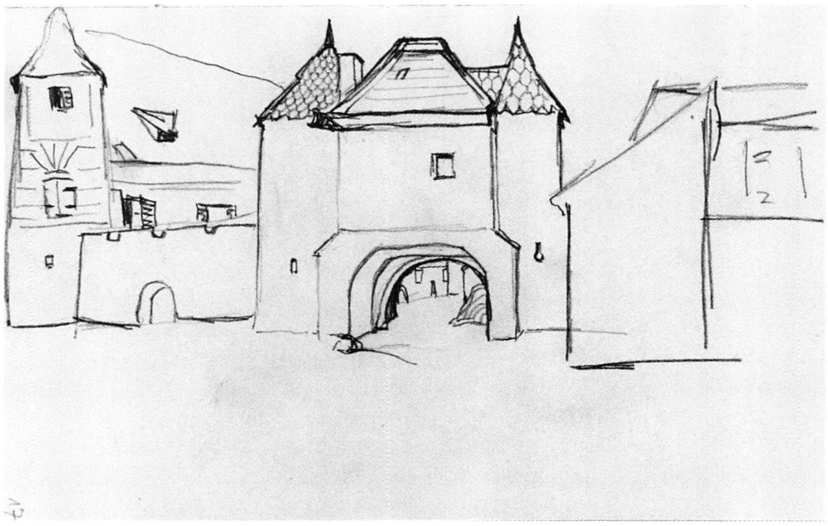

12, p.17

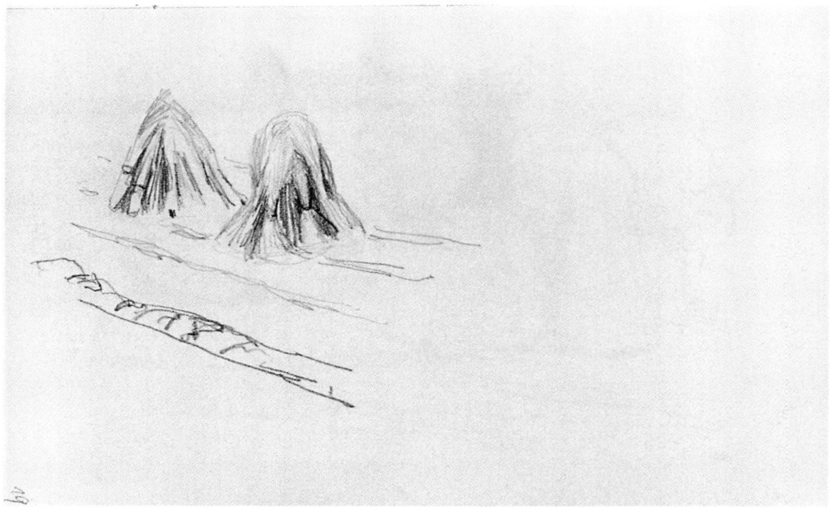

12, p.19

12, p.21

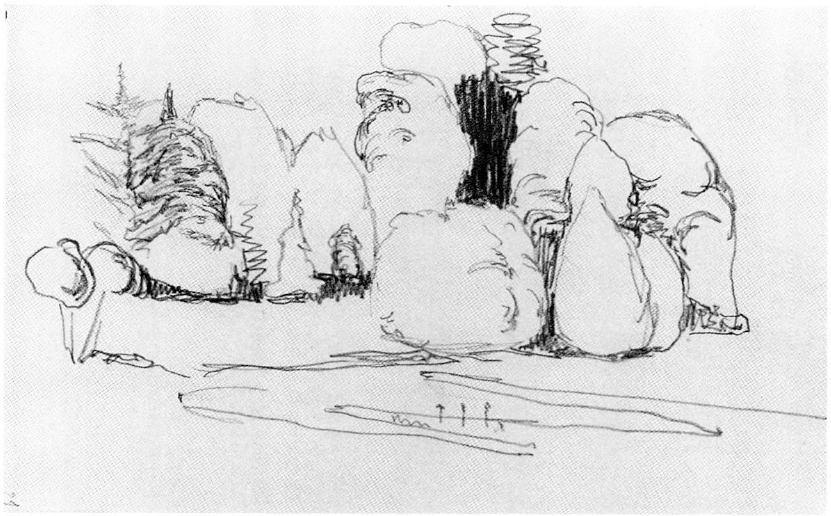

**p.14** Blank

**p.15** Pencil drawing of stagecoach

REFERENCES
Hanfstaengl 1974, p.167, ill.

The motif of a stagecoach appears in *Kallmünz- Gewitterstimmung* of 1904 (Barnett no.18).

**p.16** Blank

**p.17** Pencil drawing of gate

REFERENCES
Hanfstaengl 1974, p.167, ill.

Hanfstaengl identified the site as Burglengenfeld (formerly Altmannsches Schlösschen) in Oberpfalz.

**p.18** Blank

**p.19** Pencil drawing of haystacks in field

**p.20** Blank

**p.21** Pencil drawing of trees in forest

REFERENCES
Hanfstaengl 1974, p.167, ill.

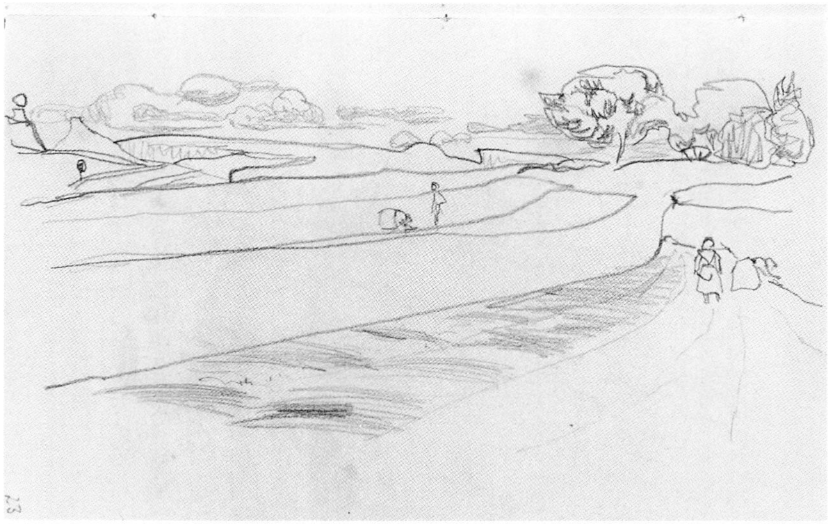

12, p.23

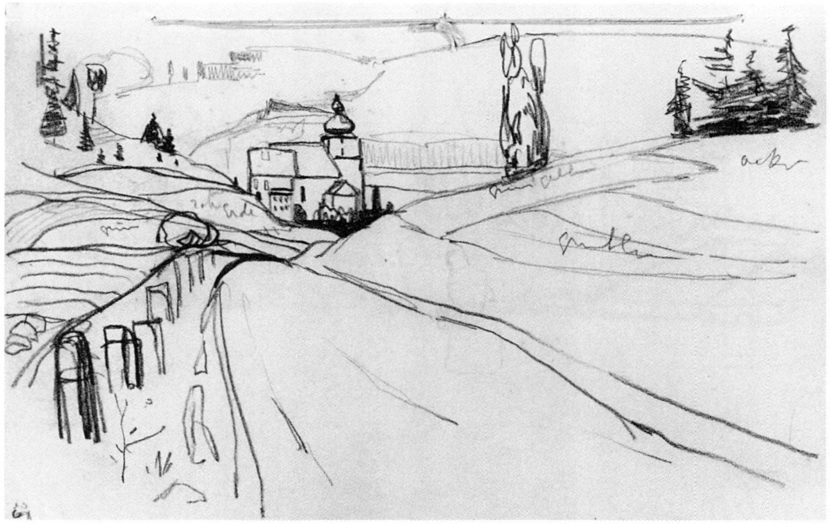

12, p.25

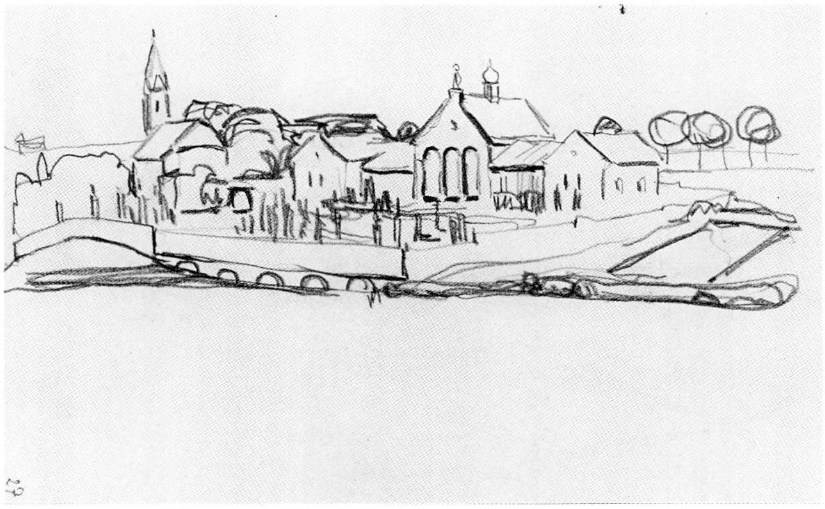

12, p.27

12, p.29

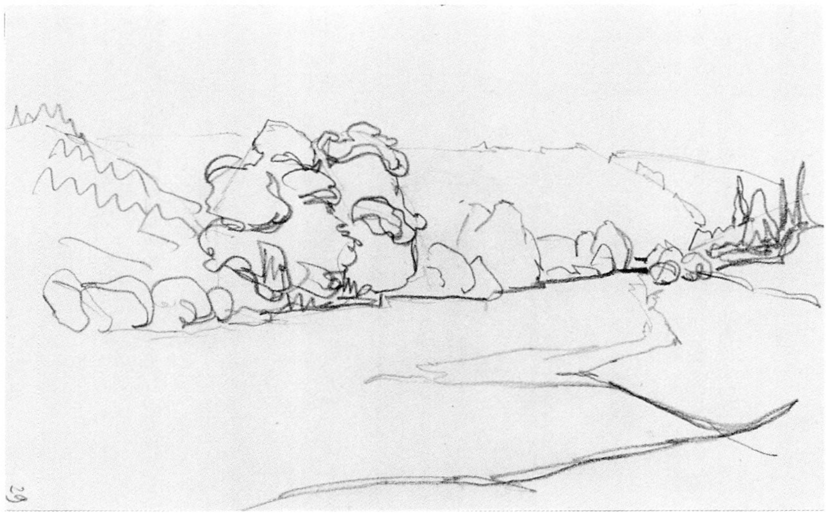

**p.22** Blank

**p.23** Pencil drawing for *Oberpfalz-Landschaft mit gelbem Feld* of 1903

REFERENCES
Hanfstaengl 1974, p.167, ill.
Roethel and Benjamin 1982, p.126
Barnett and Friedel 1995, no.110, color ill.
Barnett 2006, p.48

The drawing is a study for *Oberpfalz-Landschaft mit gelbem Feld* of 1903 (Roethel and Benjamin no.105).

**p.24** Blank

**p.25** Pencil drawing of landscape with church
Inscribed c.l.: 'grün / rote Erde'; u.r.: 'grüngelb / ocker / grnblau'

**p.26** Blank

**p.27** Pencil drawing of village with bridge and churches

**p.28** Blank

**p.29** Pencil drawing of landscape with fields and trees

REFERENCES
Hanfstaengl 1974, p.168, ill.
Barnett 2006, p.48

The drawing resembles *Bergige Landschaft mit Feldern, Bäumen und Häusern* (vol.I, cat. no.48) made during the summer of 1903.

**p.30** Blank

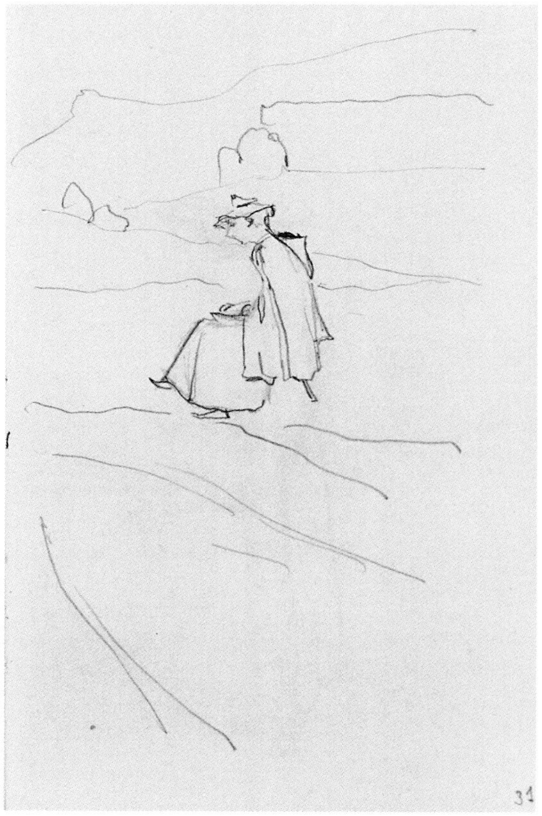

12, p.31

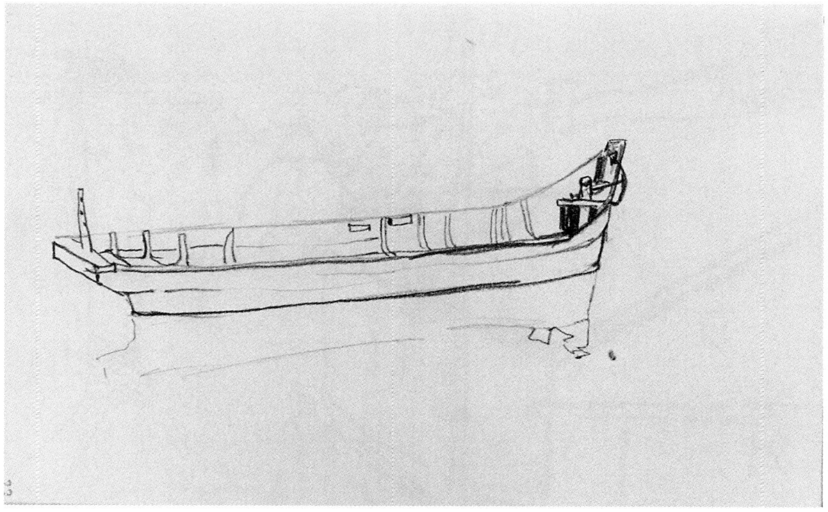

12, p.33

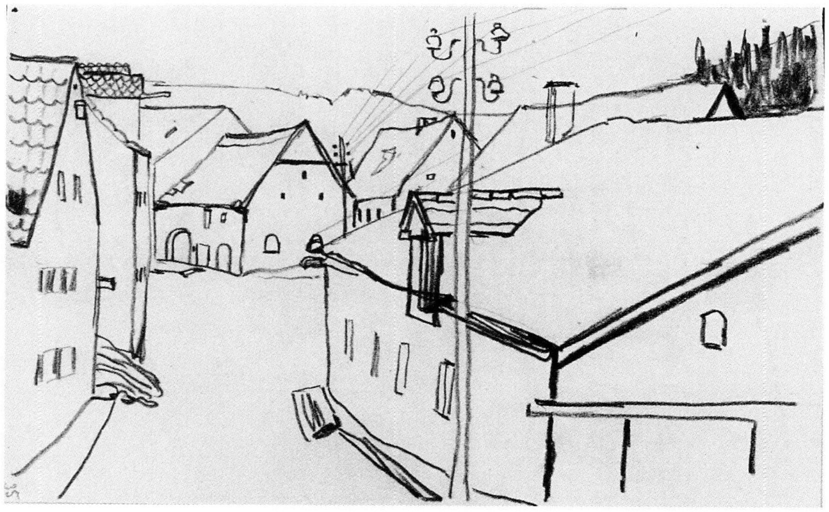

12, p.35

12, p.36

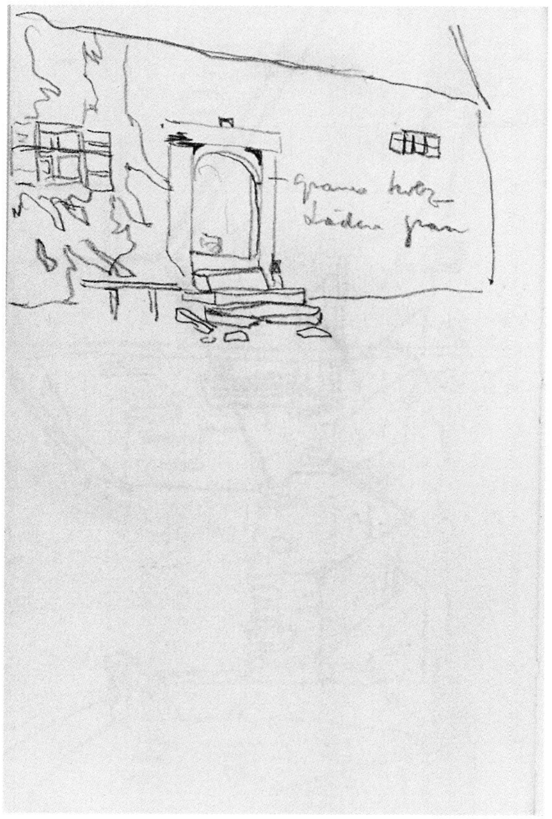

**p.31** Pencil drawing of Gabriele Münter sketching outdoors

REFERENCES
Hanfstaengl 1974, p.167
Poczemskaia 2000, p.92

**p.32** Blank

**p.33** Pencil drawing of boat

**p.34** Blank

**p.35** Pencil drawing of village with houses

**p.36** Pencil drawing of building
Inscribed c.r.: 'graues Holz / Läden grau'

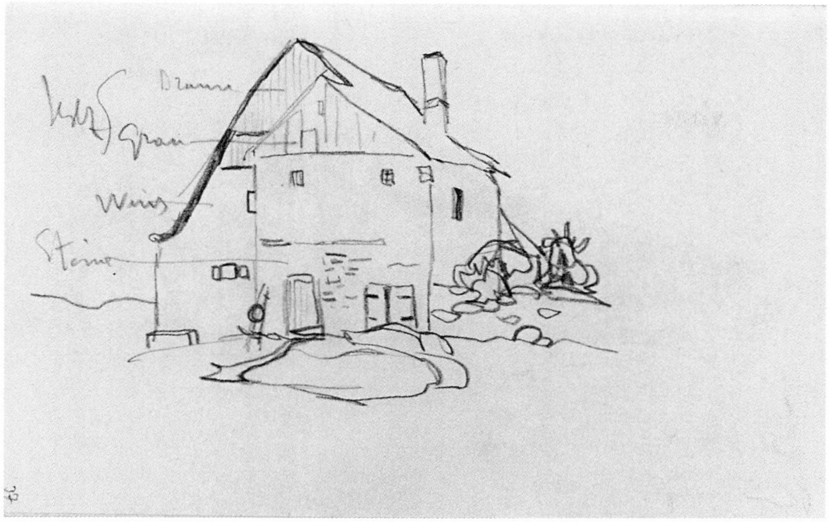

12, p.37

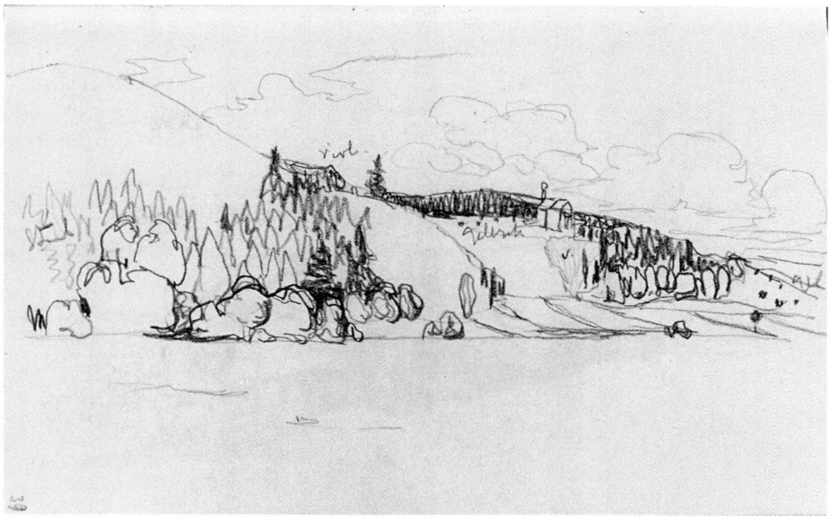

12, p.39

**p.37** Pencil drawing of farmhouse
Inscribed u.l.: 'Holz / Braun / Grau / Weiss / Steine'

**p.38** Blank

**p.39** Pencil drawing of landscape with trees and church
Inscribed with color notations: 'g Laub / viol. / gelbroth / glb'

**p.40** Pencil drawing of village with church
Inscribed l.r.: 'Blm mit rosa / Streifen' and with color notations: 'grau / bl. / rosa / w. / Sienen / gelbe Blumen / weissgrün / gel[bes] Korn'

**p.41** Pencil drawing of rocky landscape with river

REFERENCES
Hanfstaengl 1974, p.168, ill.

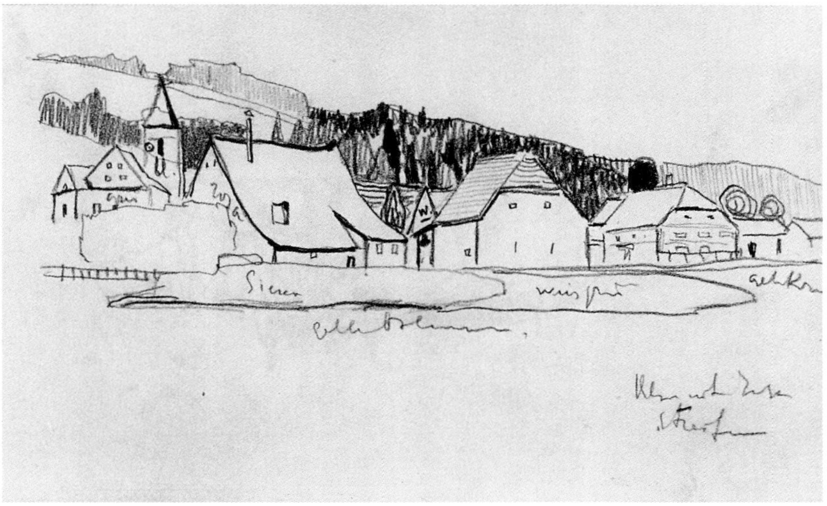

12, p.40

12, p.41

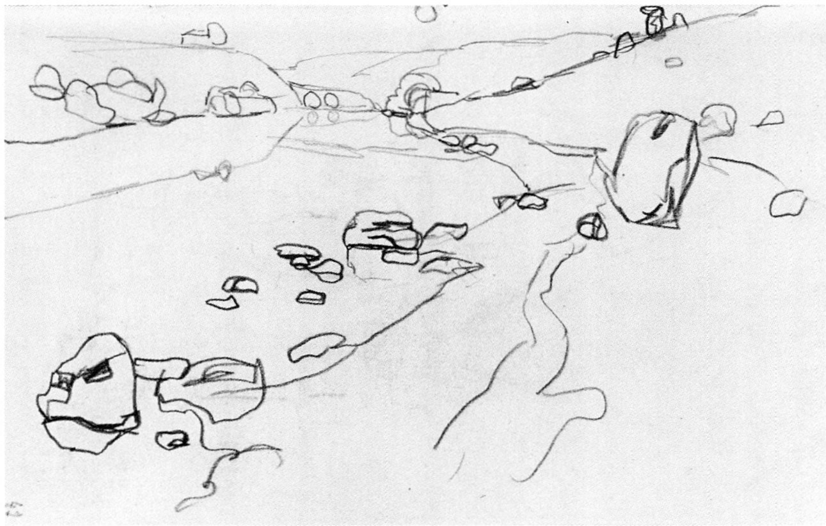

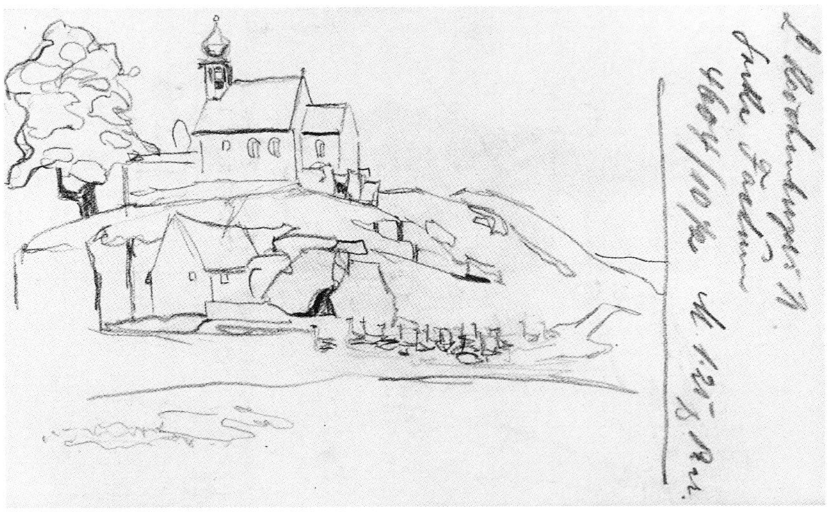

12, p.42

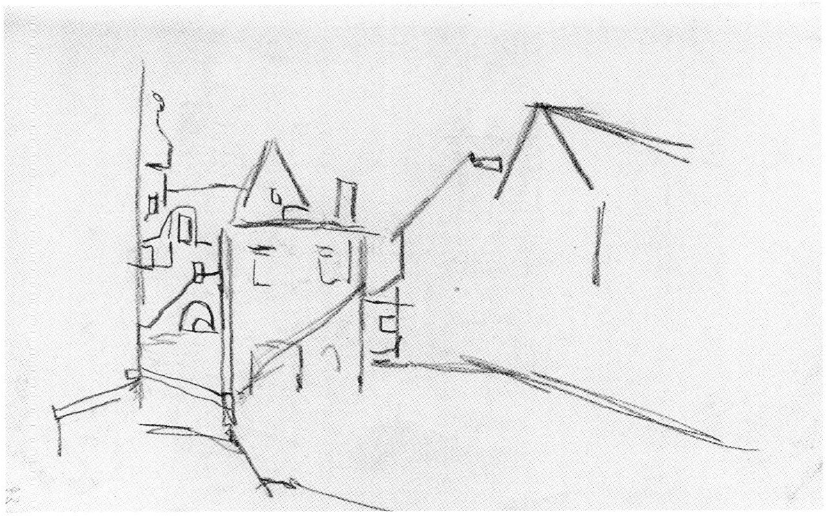

12, p.43

**p.42** Pencil drawing of church and landscape
Inscribed at top (r. edge) by unknown hand: 'L Reichenburger H / Socke Factum / 4604/10½ M.1.25 pro Paar'

REFERENCES
Hanfstaengl 1974, pp.167, 168, ill.

According to Hanfstaengl, the church is in Eich (Burglengenfeld). There is no relationship between the drawing and the note about socks (deciphered by Susanne Böller).

**p.43** Pencil drawing of houses

REFERENCES
Hanfstaengl 1974, pp.167, 168, ill.
Roethel and Benjamin 1982, p.116

Hanfstaengl identified the view as the houses near the Pfarrkirche in Kallmünz, and related it to Münter's color woodcut *Häuser in Kallmünz* of 1903. In fact, it shows the Vilsgasse in Kallmünz, which Münter photographed.

**p.44** List of colors and supplies

**p.45** Pencil drawings for embroideries

EXHIBITIONS
1982 New York, no.238, ill.
1982 Munich, no.283, ill.

REFERENCES
Hanfstaengl 1974, pp.167, 168, ill.
Barnett 1992, pp.144–145
Barnett and Friedel 1995, no.122, color ill.
Podzemskaia 2000, p.92

Kandinsky made several gouache studies for embroideries with stylized trees and abstract loop motifs (Barnett nos.145, 149) c.1903–1904. The sketch for a handbag was apparently not executed. See Sketchbook 14 (GMS 340, p.21) for other studies of circular motifs.

**p.46** Pencil drawings for embroideries (inside back cover)
Inscribed u.l. with shopping list and c.r.: 'Kareth / Lappersdorf [crossed out] / Gopersdf'

REFERENCES
Hanfstaengl 1974, pp.167, 168, ill.
Barnett 1992, p.143
Barnett and Friedel 1995, no.120, color ill.
Podzemskaia 2000, p.92

There is a related gouache study with sun and stylized apple trees for a handbag (Barnett no.144), which Münter inscribed with notes for an embroidery. Kandinsky's notes refer to the towns Kareth and Lappersdorf, north of Regensberg and not far from Kallmünz in the Upper Palatinate. Göppersdorf is a village in Bavaria.

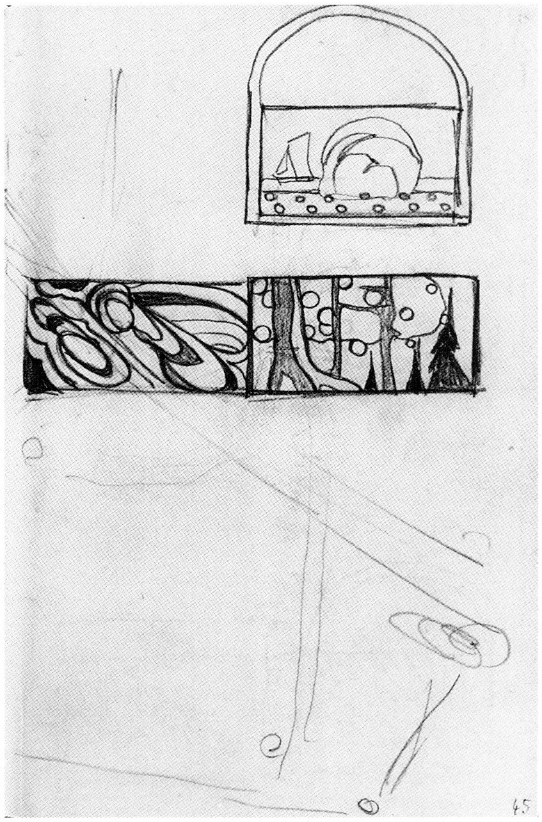

12, p.45

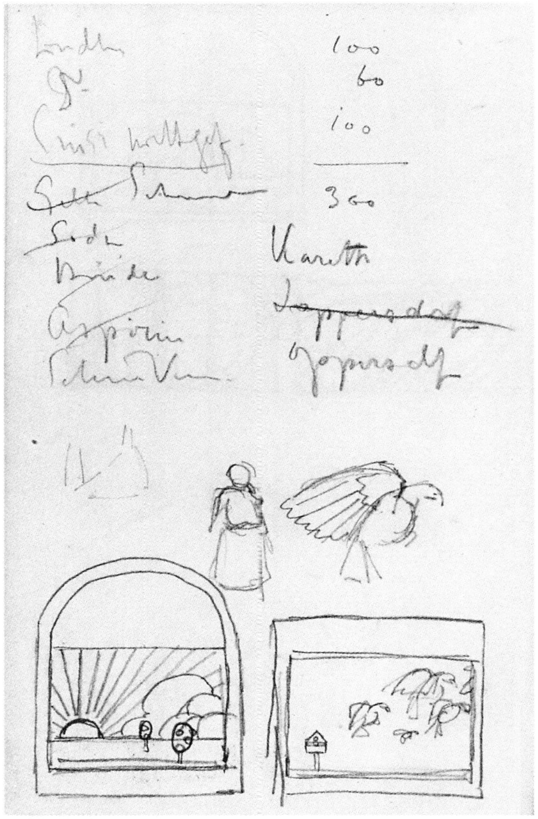

12, p.46

# Sketchbook 13

1903

Grey linen-covered cardboard sketchbook; inside front cover label from Franz Dury, Munich (Ecke Akademie- u. Amalienstrasse 50c and Theresienstrasse 78)
Contains 72 pages (36 sheets), each 17.3 x 10.9 cm (6¾ x 4¼ in), of which pp.44–71 are blank
Page numbers inscribed by unknown hand at later date with odd numbers at lower right

Hanfstaengl 1974, pp.150–151

LOCATION
Städtische Galerie im Lenbachhaus, Munich (GMS 329)

HISTORY
Gabriele Münter, Murnau, until 1957

This sketchbook can be dated to later in the summer of 1903 than the preceding sketchbooks because it includes many drawings of Nabburg, where Kandinsky and Gabriele Münter went about 14–15 August. The linen-covered sketchbook is similar to Sketchbook 15, which Kandinsky used in 1904.

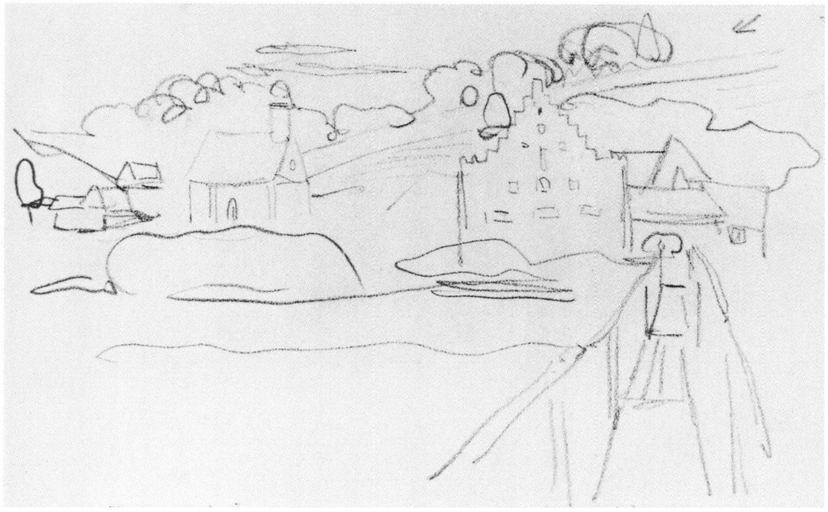

13, p.1

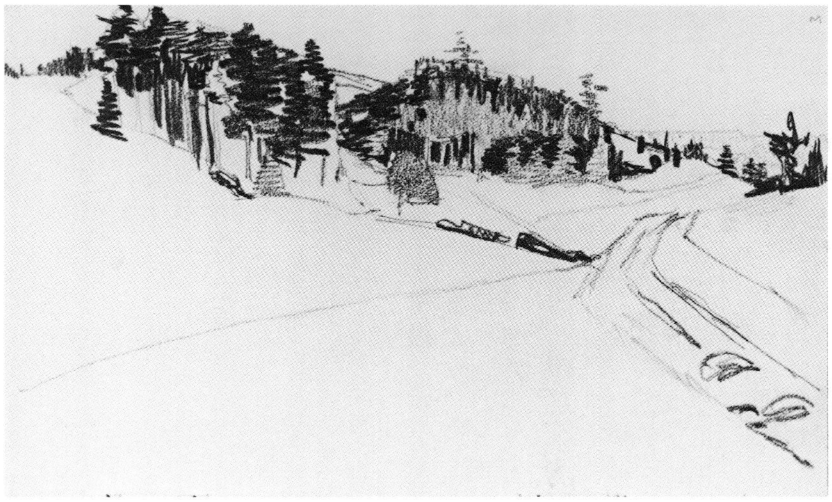

13, p.3

13, p.5

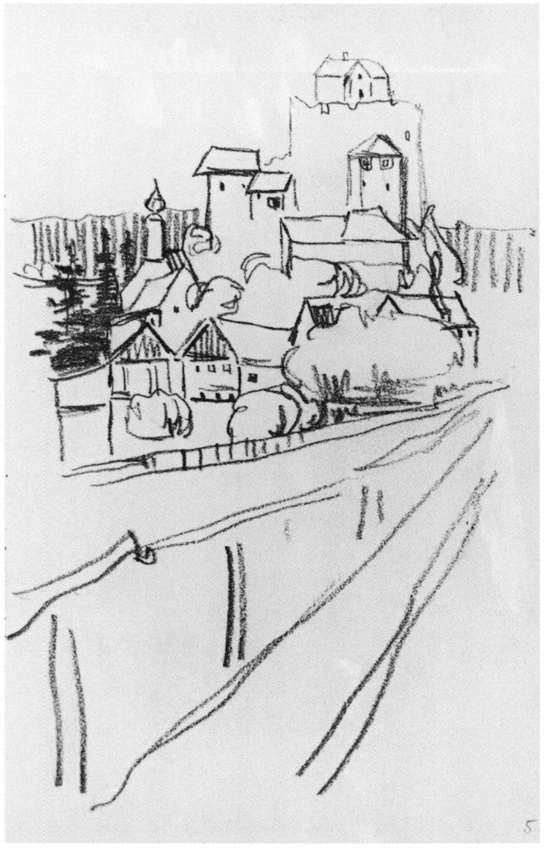

**p.1** Pencil drawing of Kallmünz in Oberpfalz (Upper Palatinate)

The drawing shows the Vilsbrücke as well as the Rathaus and Pfarrkirche in Kallmünz. Kandinsky and Münter spent the summer of 1903 in Kallmünz, a picturesque village north-west of Regensburg.

**p.2** Blank

**p.3** Pencil drawing of landscape with trees and hills

The drawing resembles the sketch on p.7 (below) and another in Sketchbook 10 (GMS 343, p.5).

**p.4** Blank

**p.5** Pencil drawing of Burgberg in Kallmünz

REFERENCES
Hanfstaengl 1974, p.150, ill.
Roethel and Benjamin 1982, p.111

The drawing includes the bridge over the Vils River as well the distinctive mountain dominating the village of Kallmünz.

**p.6** Blank

13, p.7

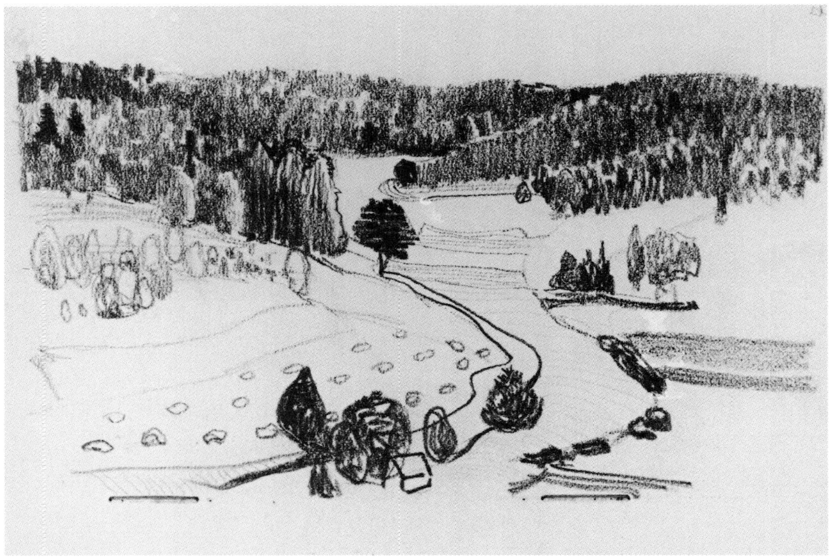

13, p.9

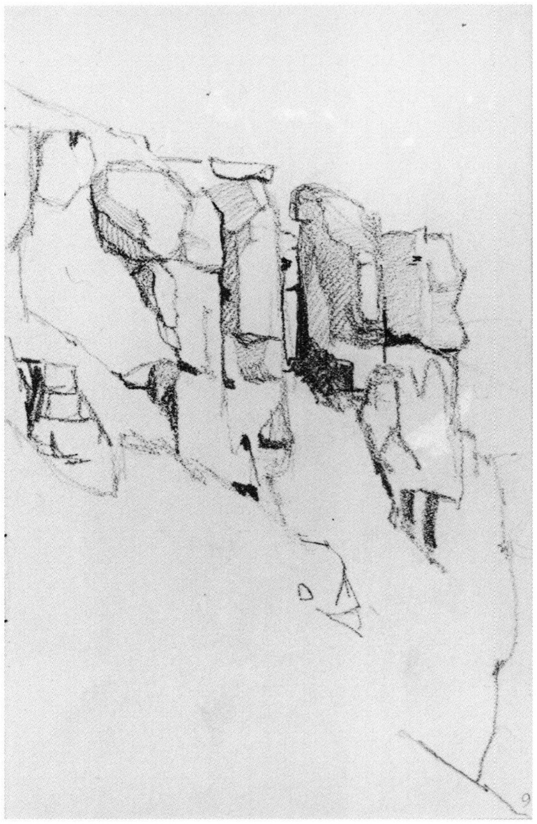

**p.7** Pencil drawing of landscape with forest

REFERENCES
Hanfstaengl 1974, p.150, ill.

**p.8** Blank

**p.9** Pencil drawing of rock cliffs

There is a similar study of cliffs in Sketchbook 10 (GMS 343, p.6).

**p.10** Blank

**p.11** Pencil drawing of Kallmünz from Burgberg

REFERENCES
Hanfstaengl 1974, p.150, ill.

The Pfarrkirche is visible in this view looking down on Kallmünz and in other drawings in Sketchbook 10 (GMS 343, pp.9, 10).

**p.12** Blank

**p.13** Pencil drawing of ruined castle in Kallmünz

REFERENCES
Hanfstaengl 1974, p.150, ill.

**p.14** Blank

13, p.11

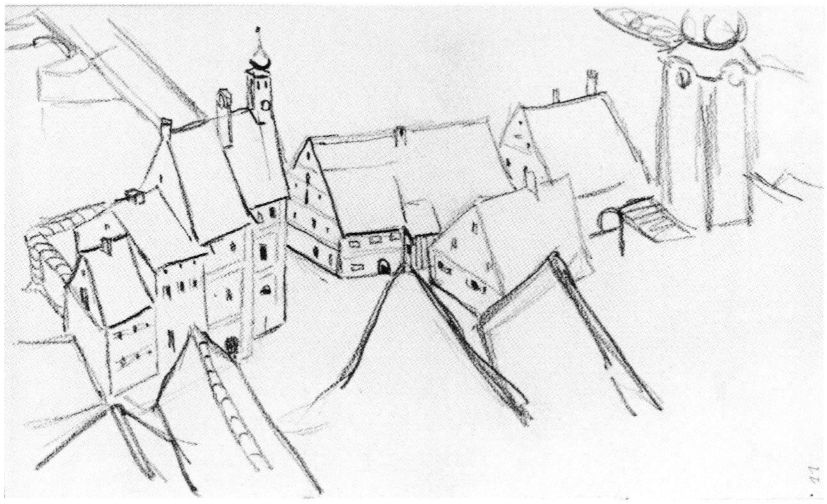

13, p.13

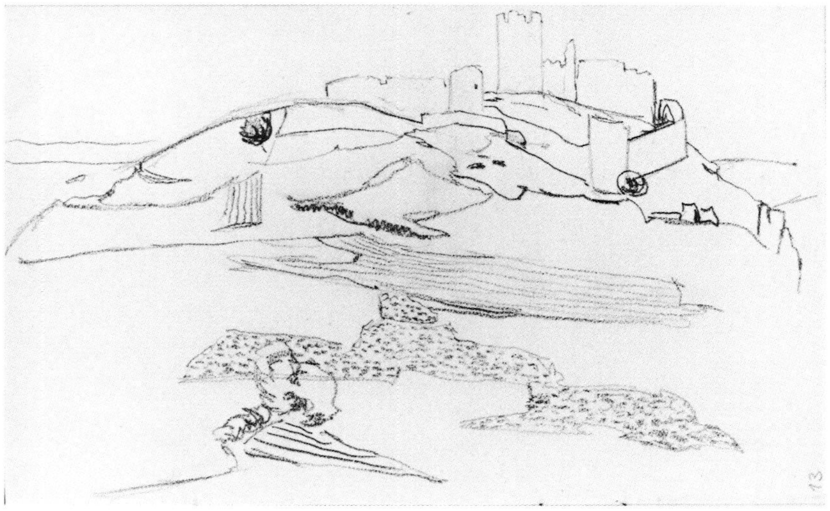

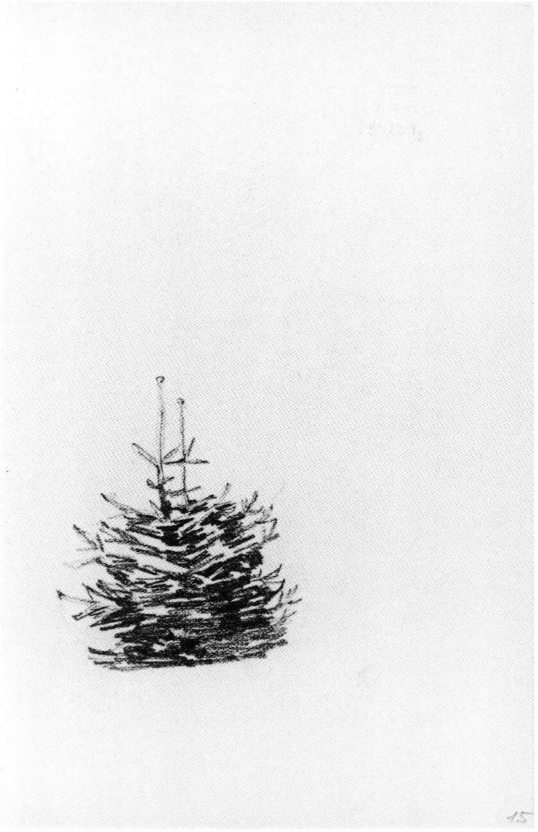

13, p.15

**p.15** Pencil sketch of tree

**p.16** Blank

**p.17** Pencil drawing of the Mähntor in Nabburg

REFERENCES
Hanfstaengl 1974, pp.150, 151, ill.
Barnett 1992, p.107

Kandinsky made this drawing in mid-August in Nabburg, a town north of Kallmünz in the Upper Palatinate; Münter sketched a similar view of the tower, which she inscribed 'Nabburg' (46/12, p.1). Kandinsky included the tower in the background of his tempera painting *Altes Städtchen* of 1903 (Barnett no.92).

**p.18** Blank

**p.19** Pencil drawing of Marktplatz in Nabburg

REFERENCES
Hanfstaengl 1974, p.151, ill.
Barnett 1992, p.102

This drawing is related to *Marktplatz mit spazierendem Paar* of 1903 (Barnett no.84).

**p.20** Blank

13, p.17

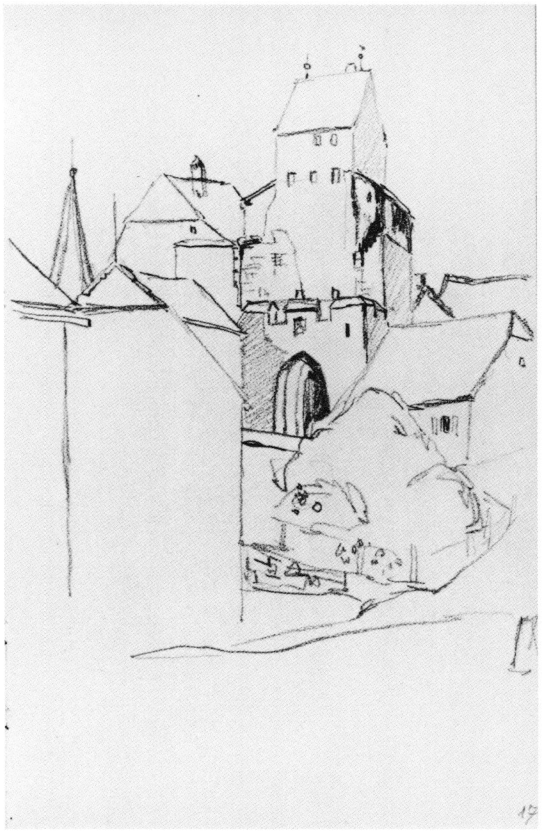

13, p.19

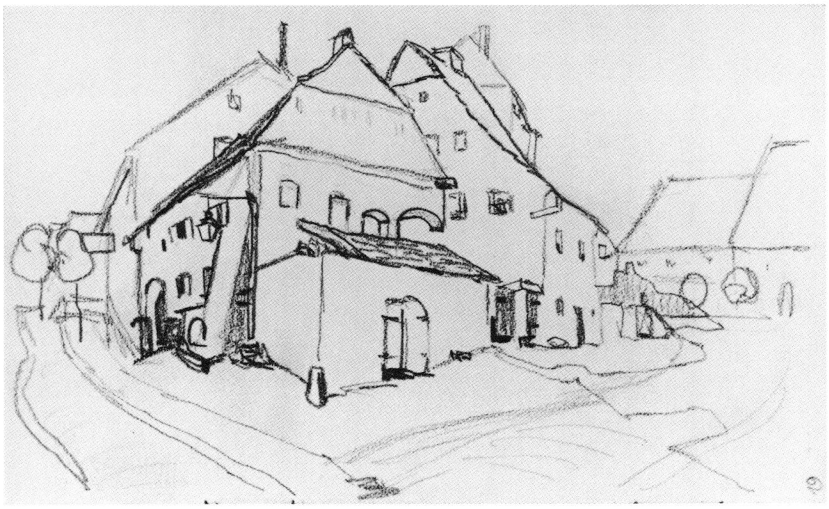

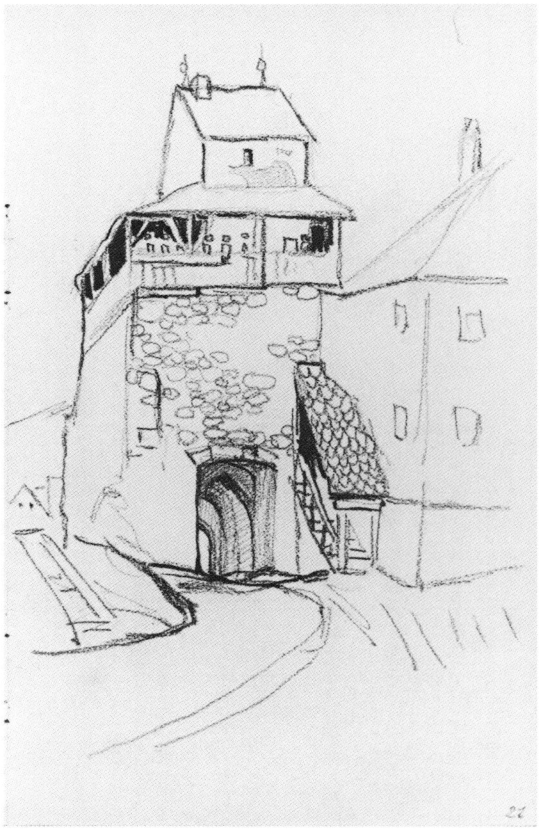

13, p.21

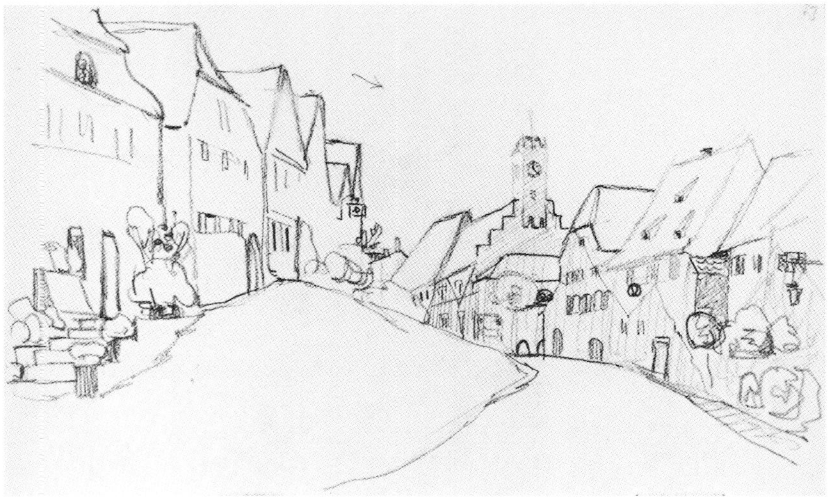

13, p.23

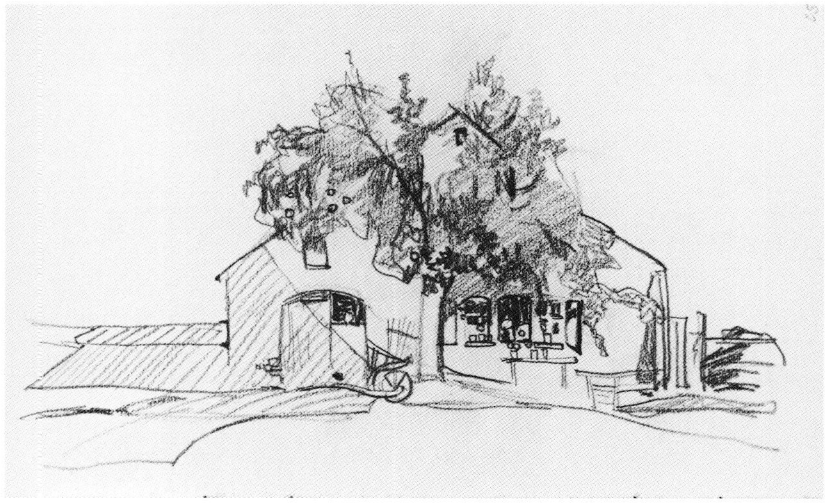

13, p.25

13, p.27

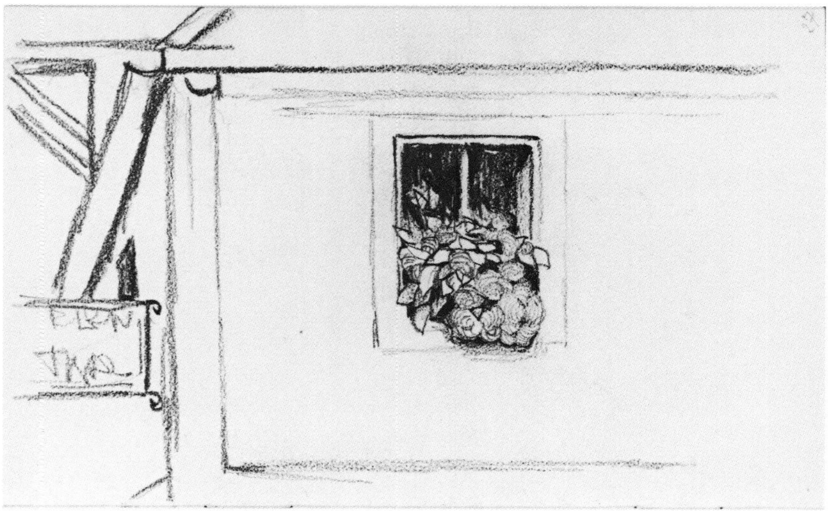

**p.21** Pencil drawing of the Mähntor in Nabburg

REFERENCES
Hanfstaengl 1974, pp.150, 151, ill.
Barnett 1992, p.107
Barnett and Friedel 1995, no.113, color ill.

Like the sketch on p.17 (above), this drawing is related to *Altes Städtchen* of 1903.

**p.22** Blank

**p.23** Pencil drawing of Marktplatz in Nabburg

REFERENCES
Hanfstaengl 1974, p.151, ill.

**p.24** Blank

**p.25** Pencil drawing of farmhouse

REFERENCES
Hanfstaengl 1974, p.151, ill.

**p.26** Blank

**p.27** Pencil drawing of window with flowers

REFERENCES
Hanfstaengl 1974, p.151, ill.

**p.28** Blank

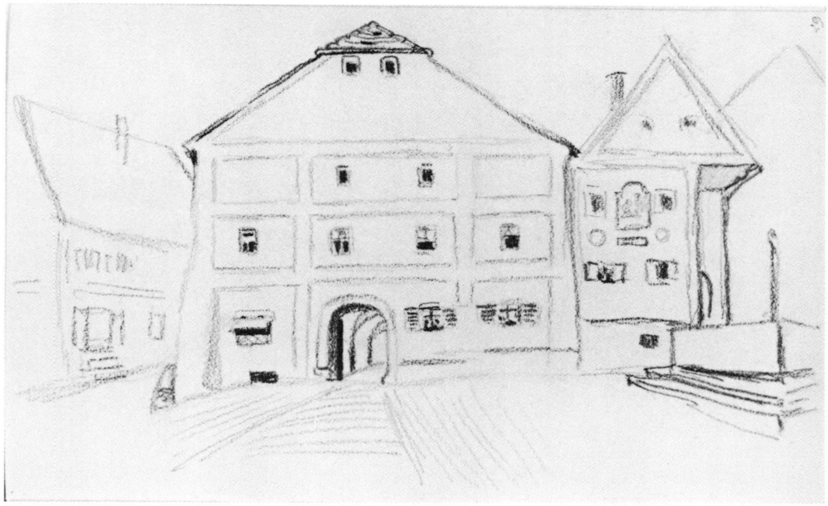

13, p.29

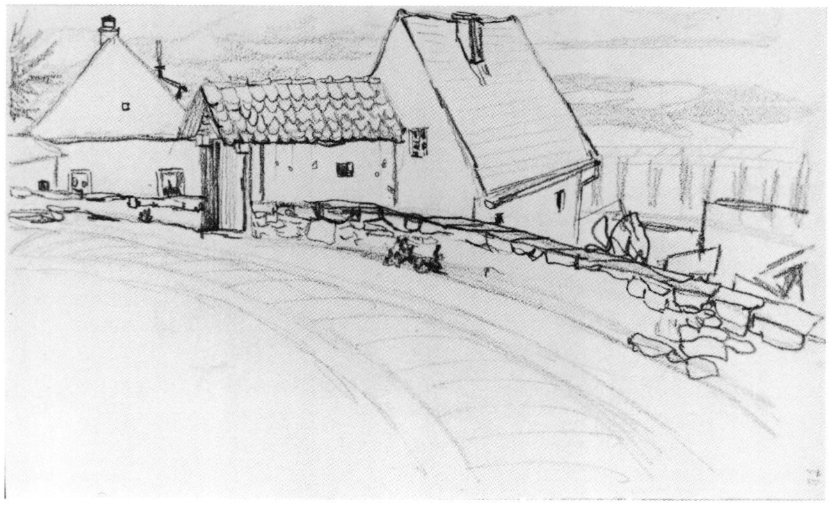

13, p.31

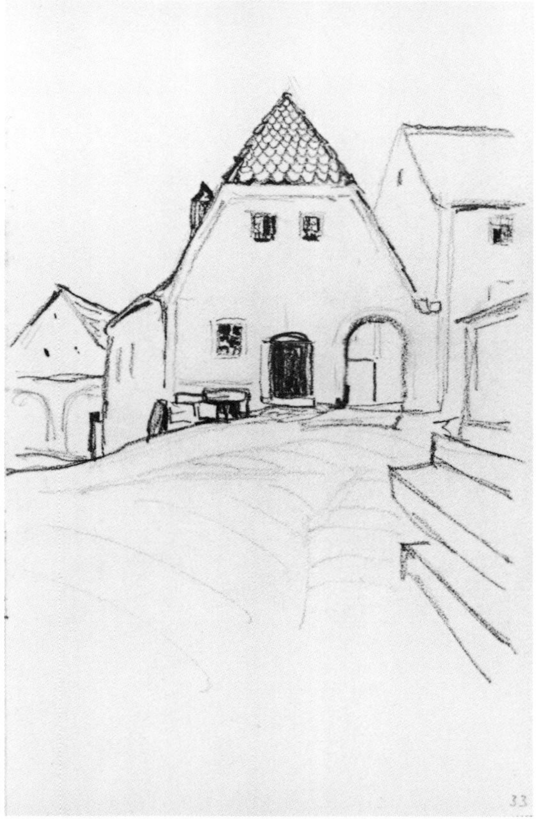

13, p.33

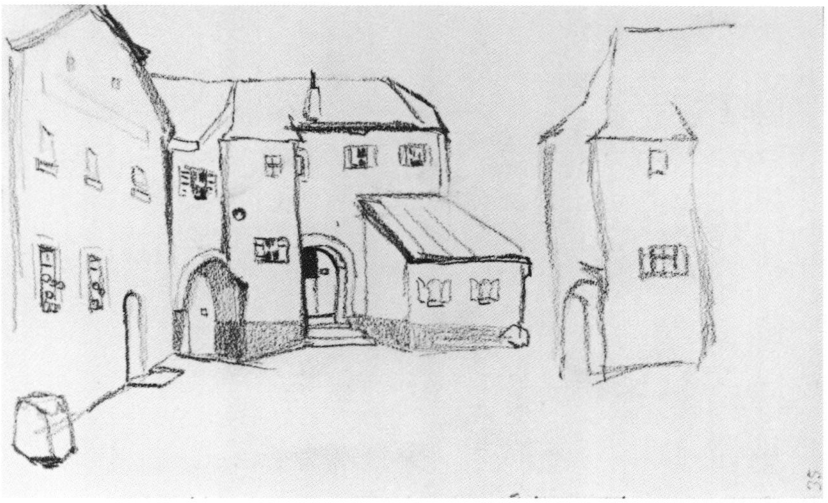

13, p.35

**p.29** Pencil drawing of houses in Nabburg

REFERENCES
Hanfstaengl 1974, p.151, ill.

**p.30** Blank

**p.31** Pencil drawing of houses near Nabburg

**p.32** Blank

**p.33** Pencil drawing of houses in Nabburg

REFERENCES
Hanfstaengl 1974, pp.150, 151, ill.
Barnett and Friedel 1995, no.114, color ill.
Barnett 2006, p.51

This drawing bears a strong resemblance to a study (vol.I, cat. no.57) for the woodcut *Unterhaltung* of 1904 (Roethel no.39).

**p.34** Blank

**p.35** Pencil drawing of houses probably in Nabburg in Oberpfalz

**p.36** Blank

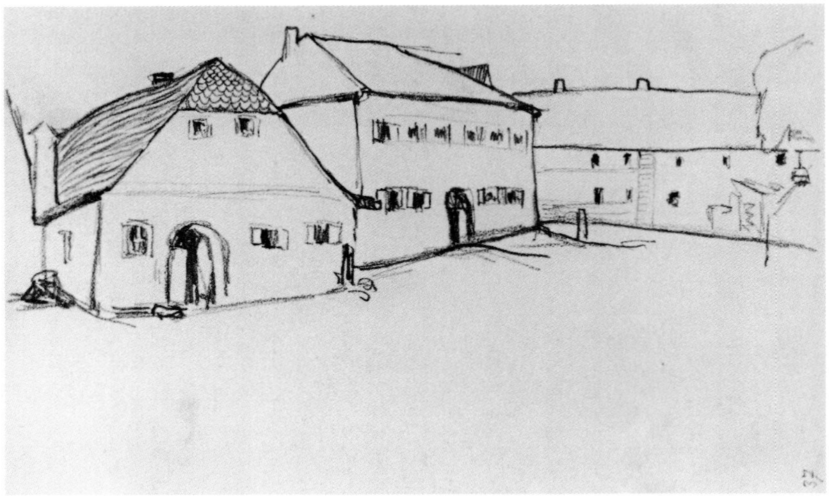

13, p.37

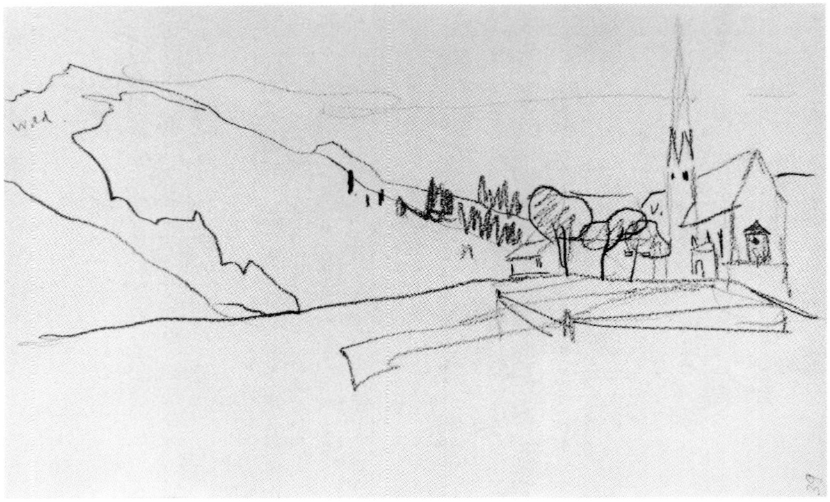

13, p.39

**p.37** Pencil drawing of houses probably in Nabburg

**p.38** Blank

**p.39** Pencil drawing of landscape with church in Oberpfalz
Inscribed u.l.: 'Wald'; c.r.: 'v'

**p.40** Blank

**p.41** Pencil drawing of pond with swan

REFERENCES
Hanfstaengl 1974, pp.150, 151, ill.
Barnett 1992, p.99
Barnett 2006, p.41

Hanfstaengl considered this drawing and the one on p.43 (below) to have been done later. It is, however, clearly related to *Finsterer Abend* of 1903 (Barnett no.78), and also reminiscent of *Skizze für Abend* of 1901 (Roethel and Benjamin no.32). Kandinsky included his own reflection in the foreground.

**p.42** Blank

**p.43** Pencil drawing of women seated at a table

This sketch can be related to coeval drawings (vol.I, cat. nos.44 and 45).

**pp.44–71** blank

**p.72** Pencil sketch of a cup
Inscribed above: 'Landsberg 1½- 2 Stunden'

Landsberg am Lech is a village in Bavaria about 57 kilometers southwest of Munich: thus, the time must have been calculated from Munich rather than Kallmünz.

13, p.41

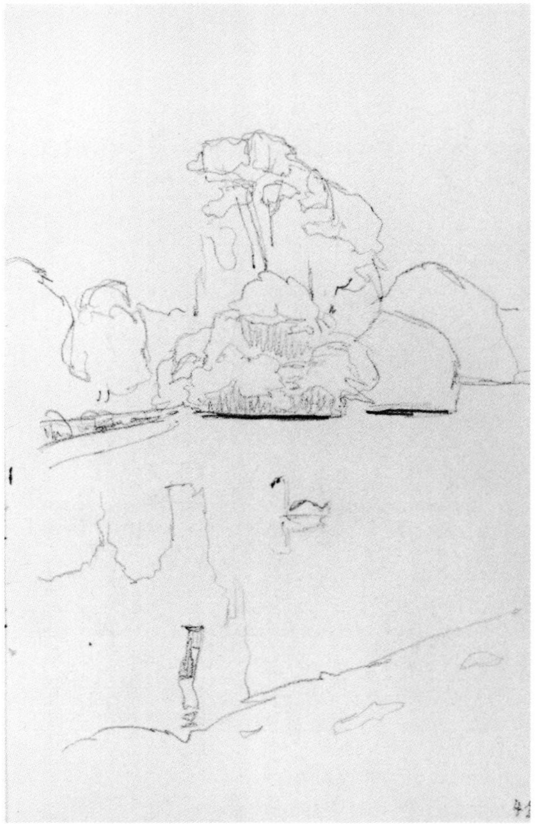

13, p.43

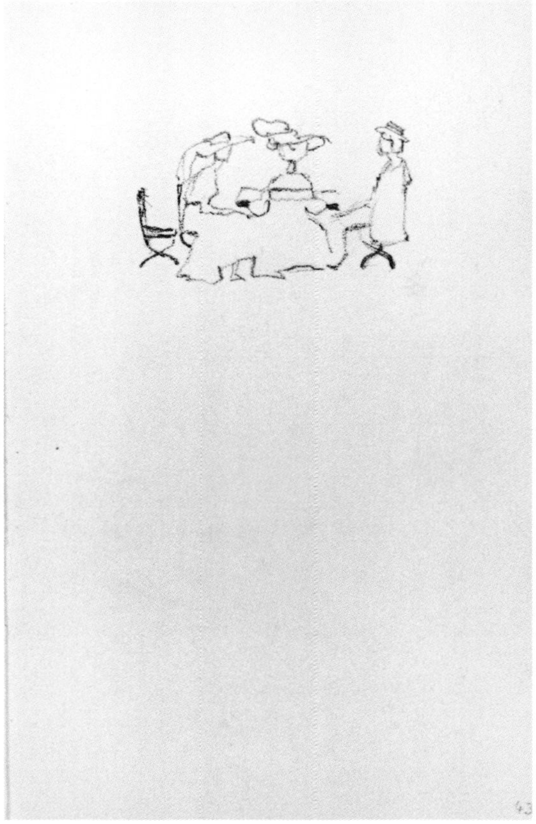

13, p.72

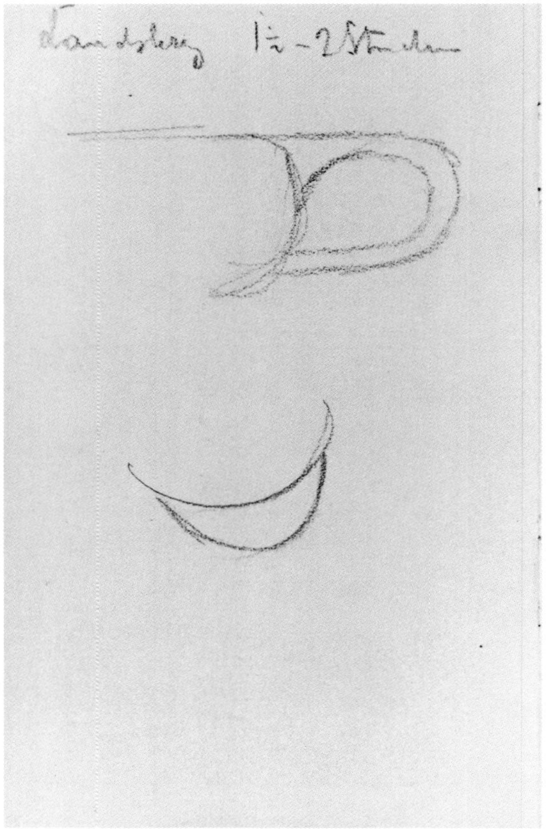

Sketchbook 3
p.3
Studies of heads
and seated figures
1897-1900 (see
page 39)

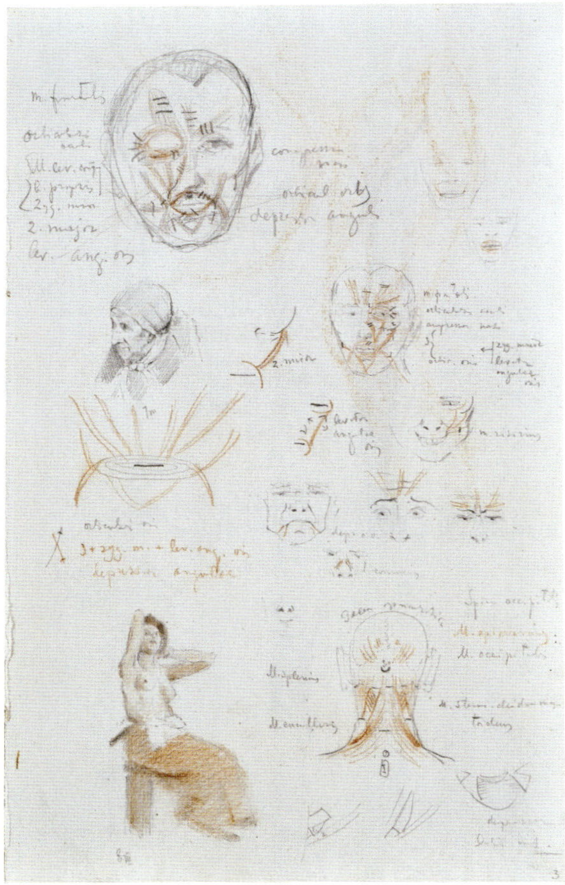

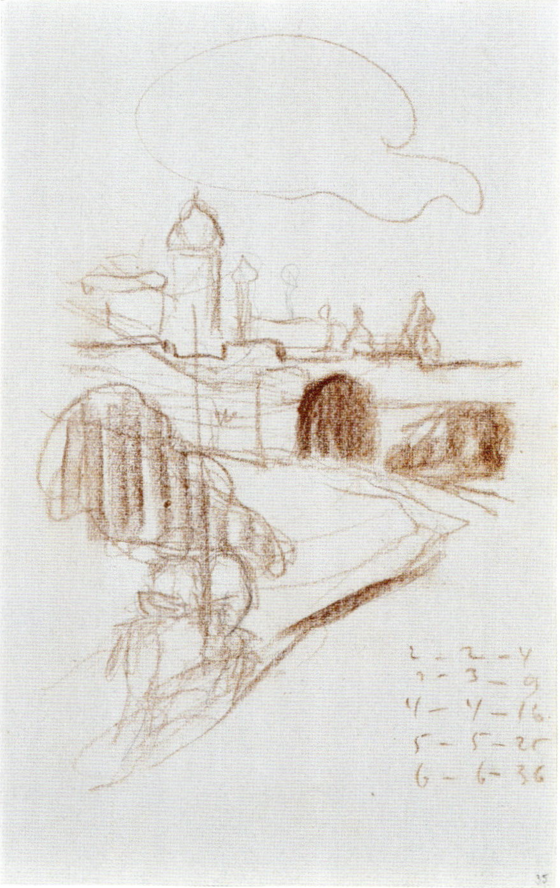

Sketchbook 3
p.35
Study of rider on
horseback and
walled castle
1897-1900
(see page 49)

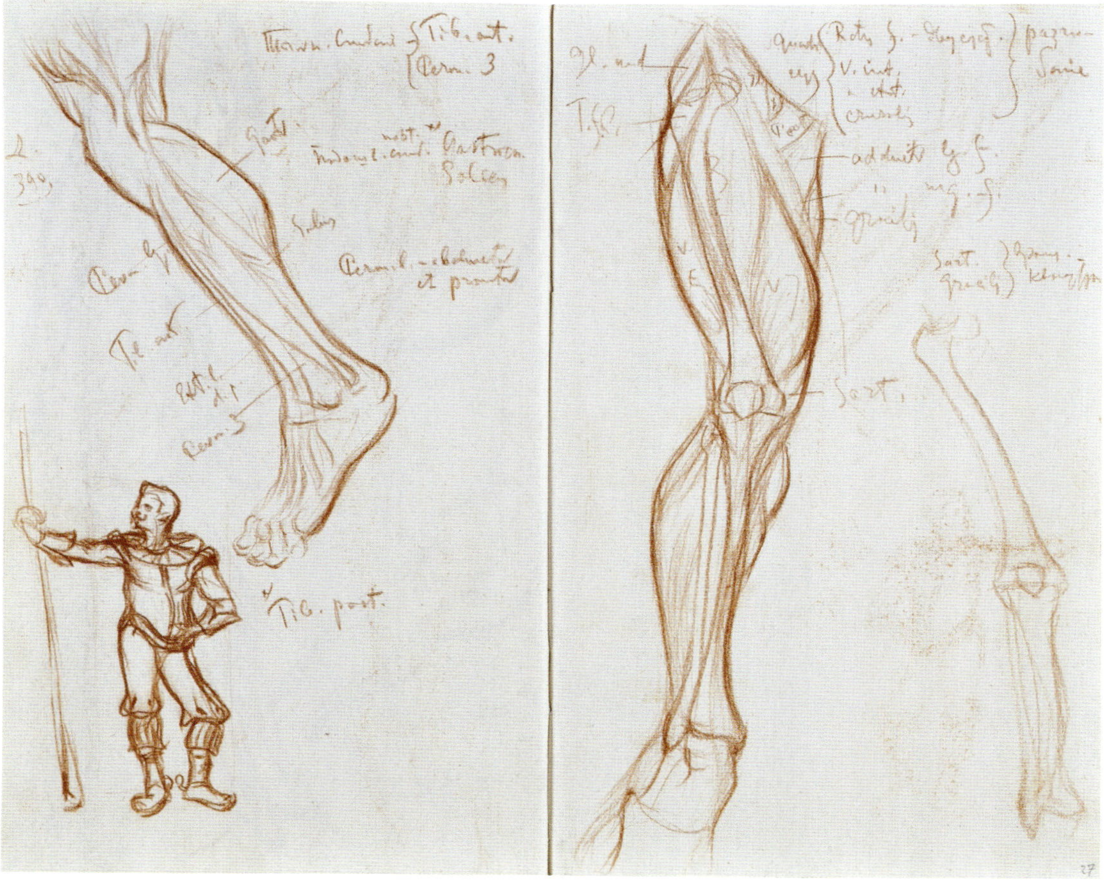

Sketchbook 3
pp.26-27
Drawing of legs and
man in costume
1897-1900
(see pages 48-49)

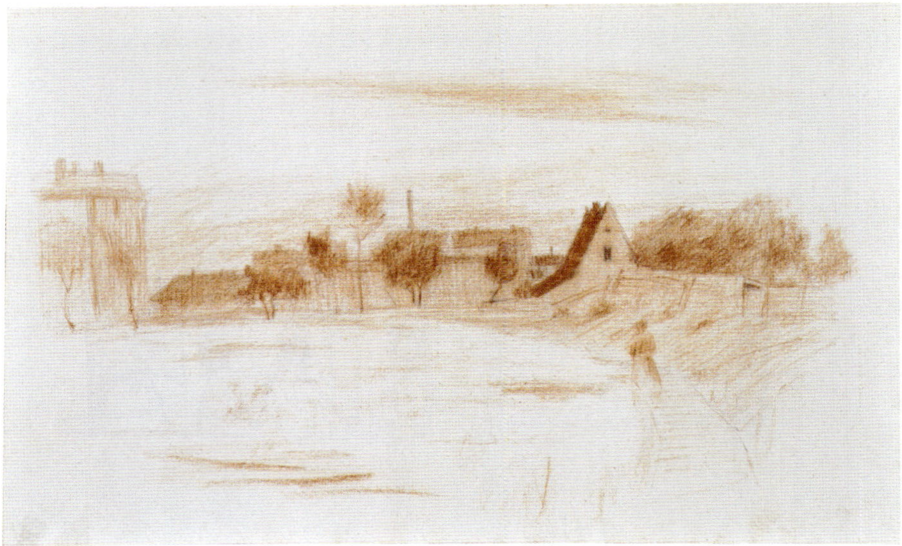

Sketchbook 3
p.54
Drawing of buildings near Munich
1897-1900
(see page 51)

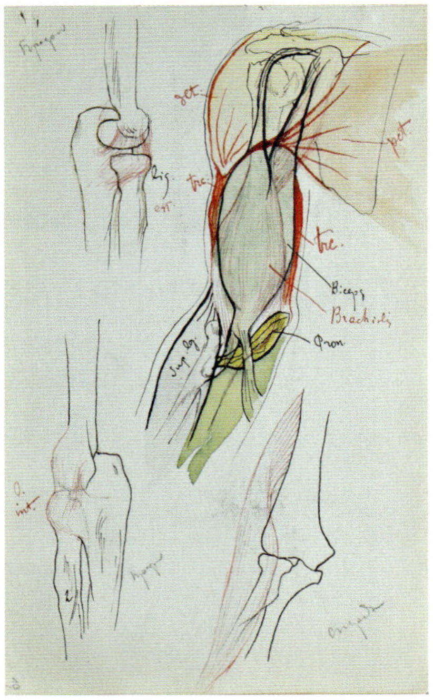

Sketchbook 4
p.19
Studies of arm and elbows.
1897-1900
(see pages 54-55)

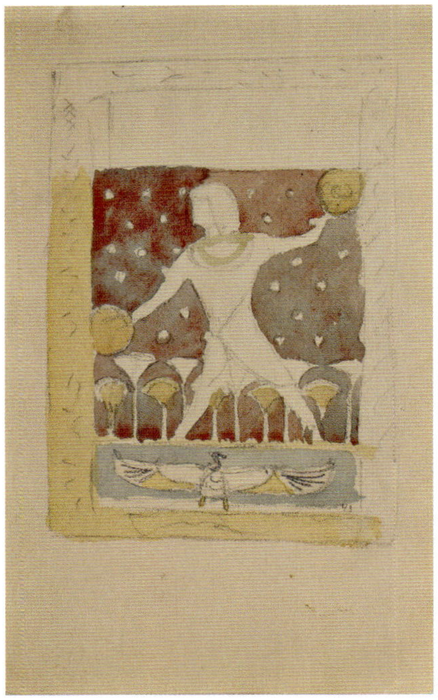

Sketchbook 4
p.24
Drawing of Egyptian motif
1897-1902
(see page 55)

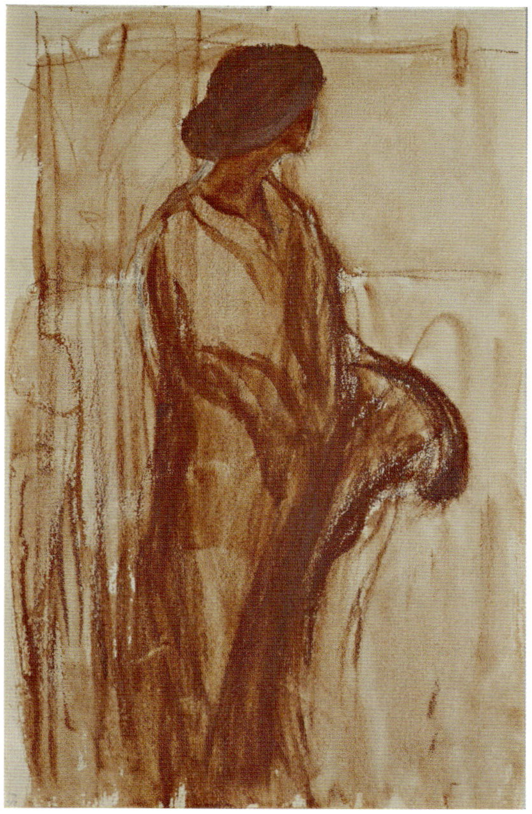

Sketchbook 5
p.25
Study of standing female figure
1897-1903
(see page 63)

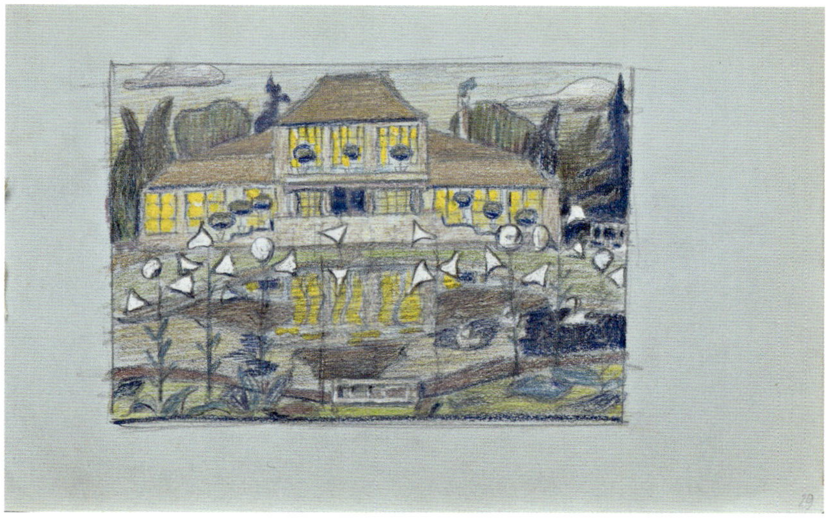

Sketchbook 5
p.29
Drawing of house with garden and pond
c.1900-1903
(see page 63)

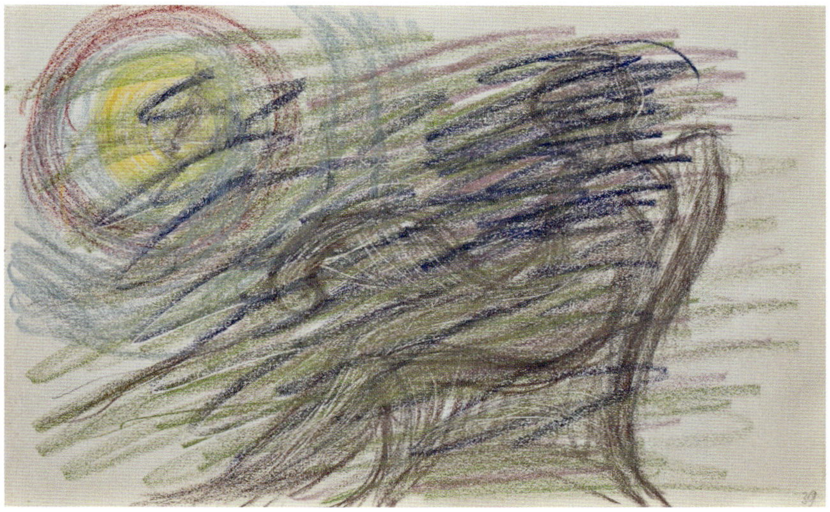

Sketchbook 5
p.39
Drawing of woman seated in chair with yellow sun
c.1900-1903
(see page 64)

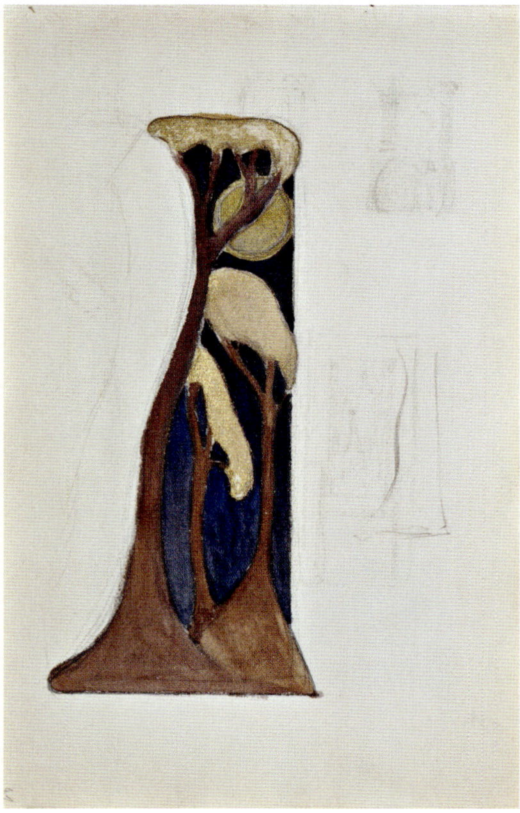

Sketchbook 5
p.41
Study for vase
1900-1903
(see page 65)

Sketchbook 5
p.46
Drawing of figure
seated near lamp
c.1900-1903
(see page 66)

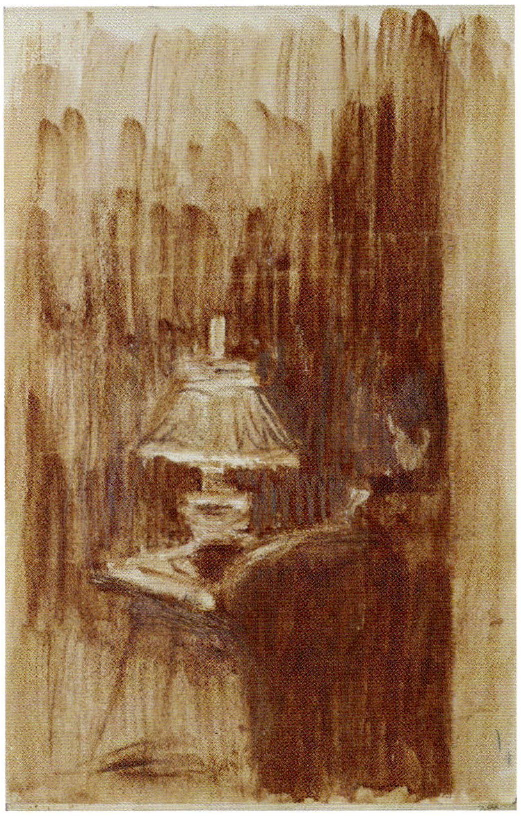

Sketchbook 5
p.43
Watercolor study
of bed
1900-1903
(see page 65)

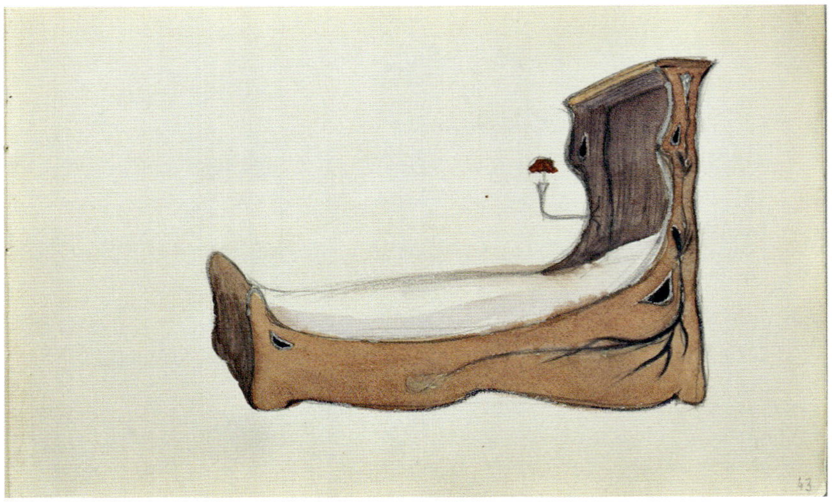

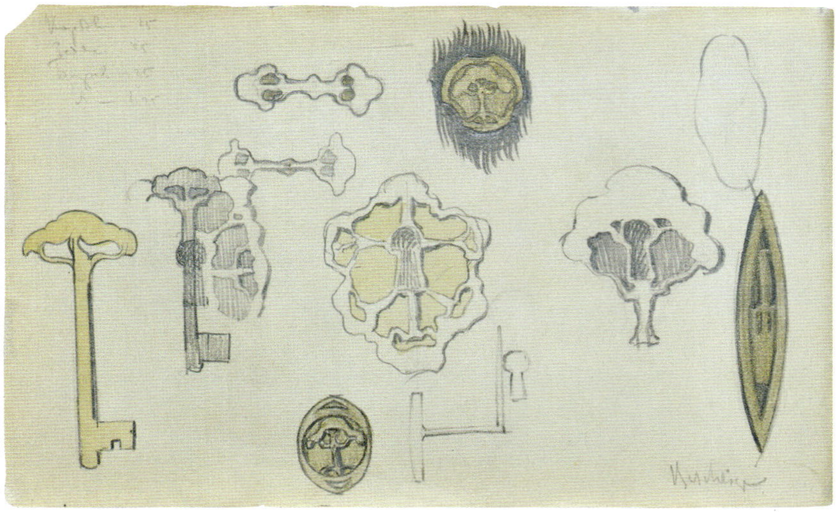

Sketchbook 5
p.52
Studies for locks
and keys
c.1900-1903
(see page 67)

Sketchbook 5
p.50
Watercolor of boat
with red sail and
figures in costume
c.1900-1903
(see page 66)

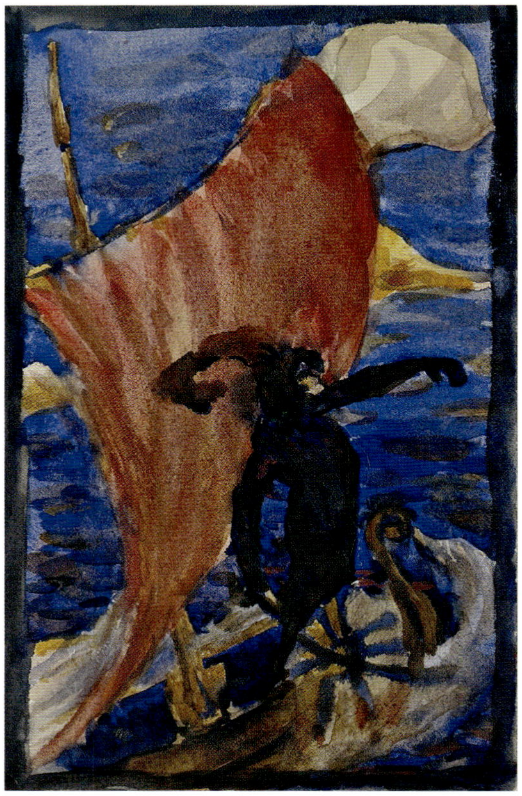

Sketchbook 6
pp.8-9
Drawing of knight in armor
c.1898-1903
(see page 69)

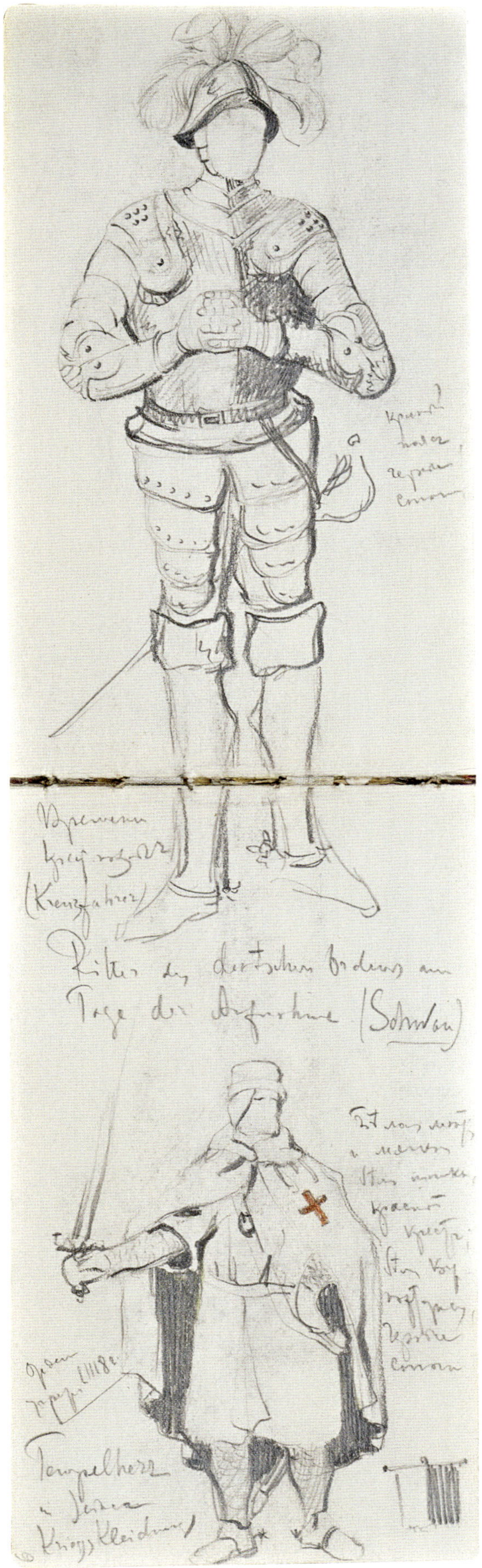

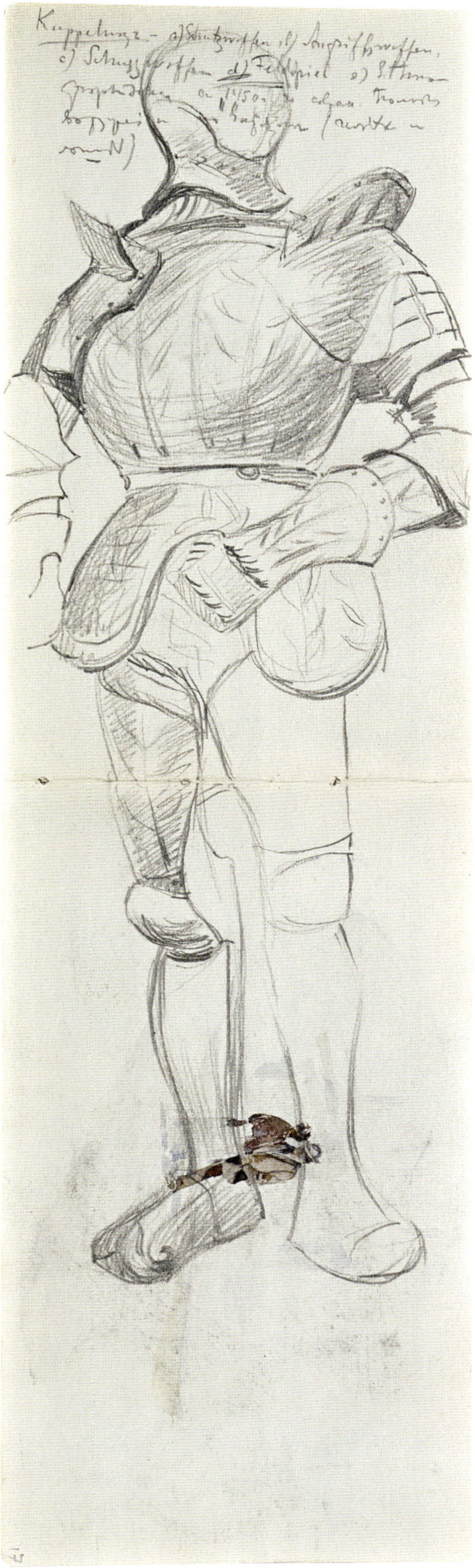

Sketchbook 6
pp.16-17
Drawing of knight in armor with watercolor study of two small figures
c.1898-1903
(see page 71)

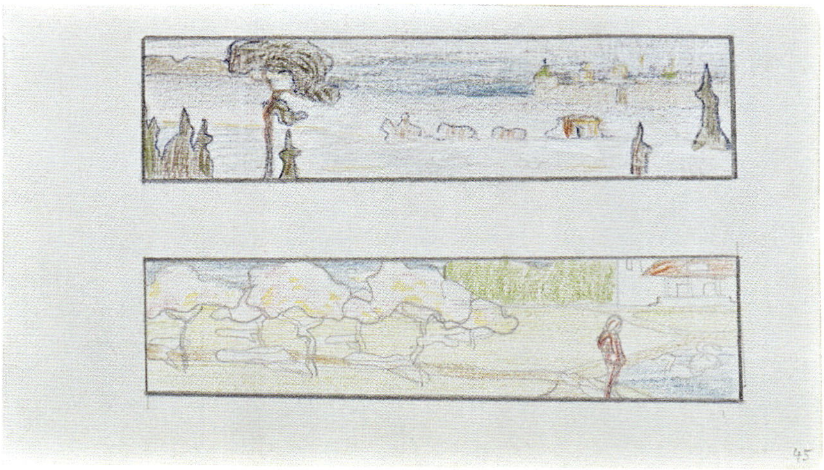

Sketchbook 6
p.45
Drawing of landscapes with figures
c.1898-1903
(see page 74)

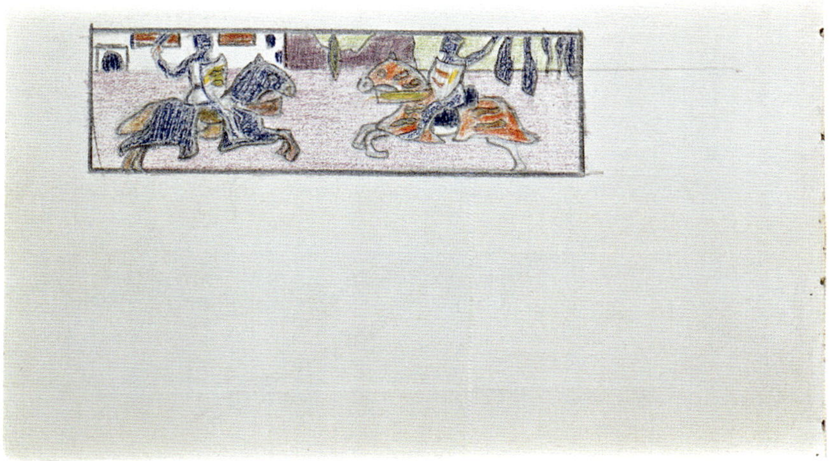

Sketchbook 6
p.46
Drawing of two knights in armor on horseback
c.1898-1903
(see page 74)

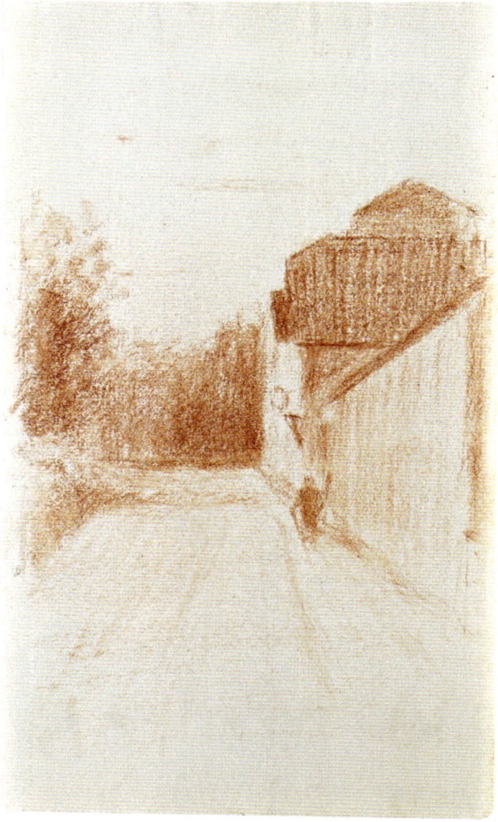

Sketchbook 6
p.74
Drawing of street with figure
1897-1900
(see page 75)

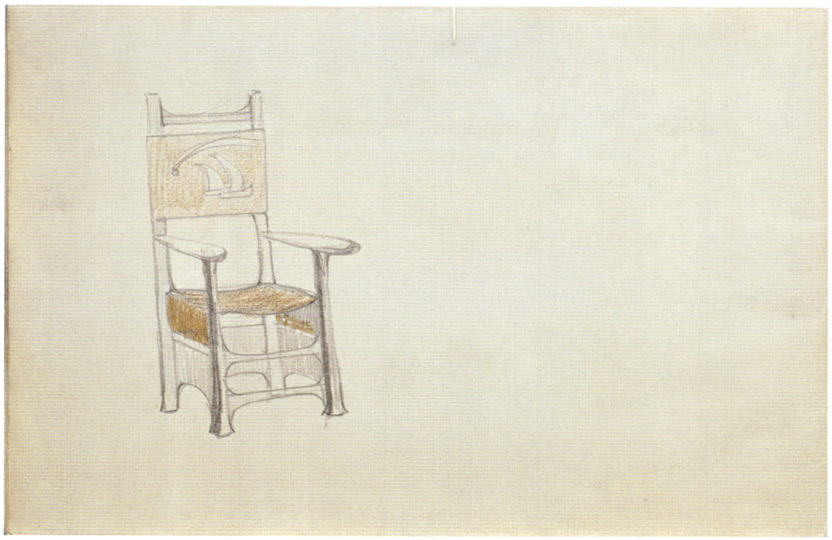

Sketchbook 7
p.34
Drawing for chair
with motif of ships
and comet
c.1902-1903
(see page 79)

Sketchbook 9
p.30
Drawing of horse and
rider
c.1902-1903
(see page 91)

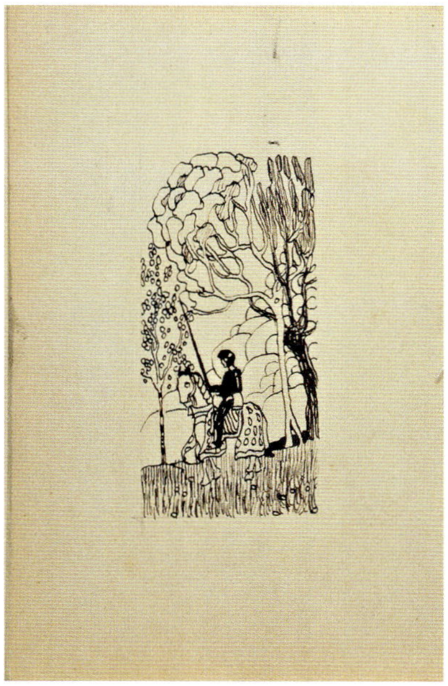

Sketchbook 9
p.31
Drawing of horse and
rider
c.1902-1903
(see page 91)

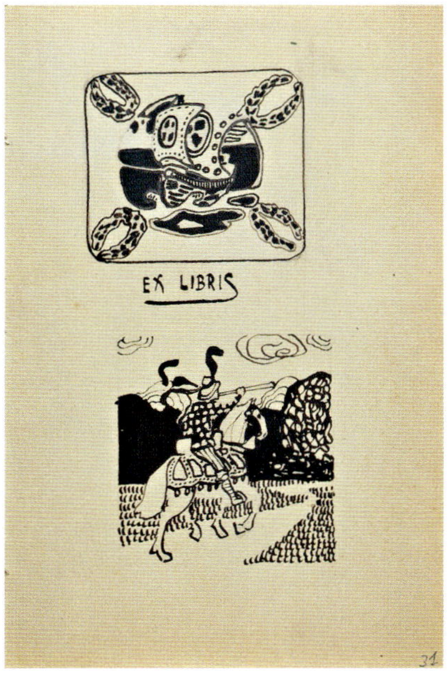


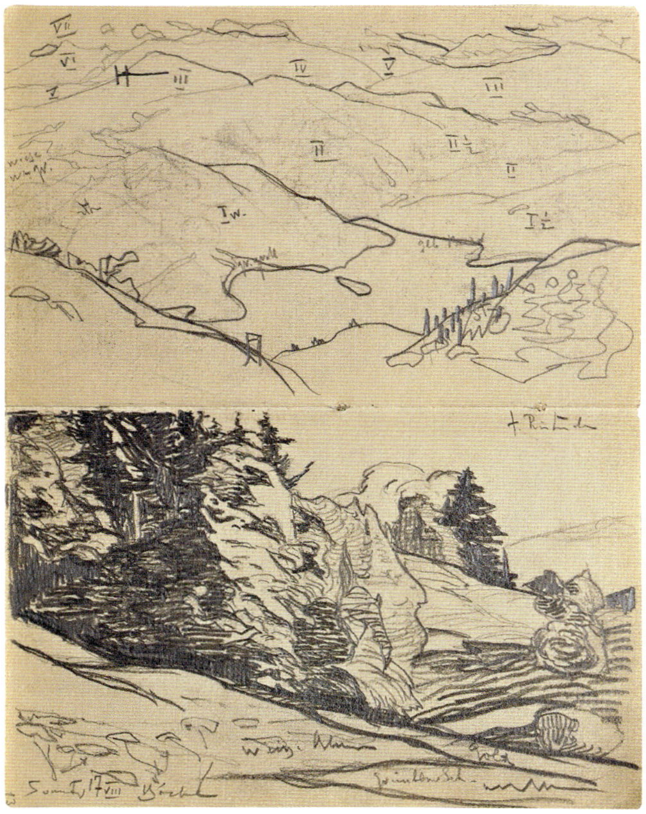

Sketchbook 8
pp.12-13
Pencil drawings
of landscapes
1902
(see pages 82-83)

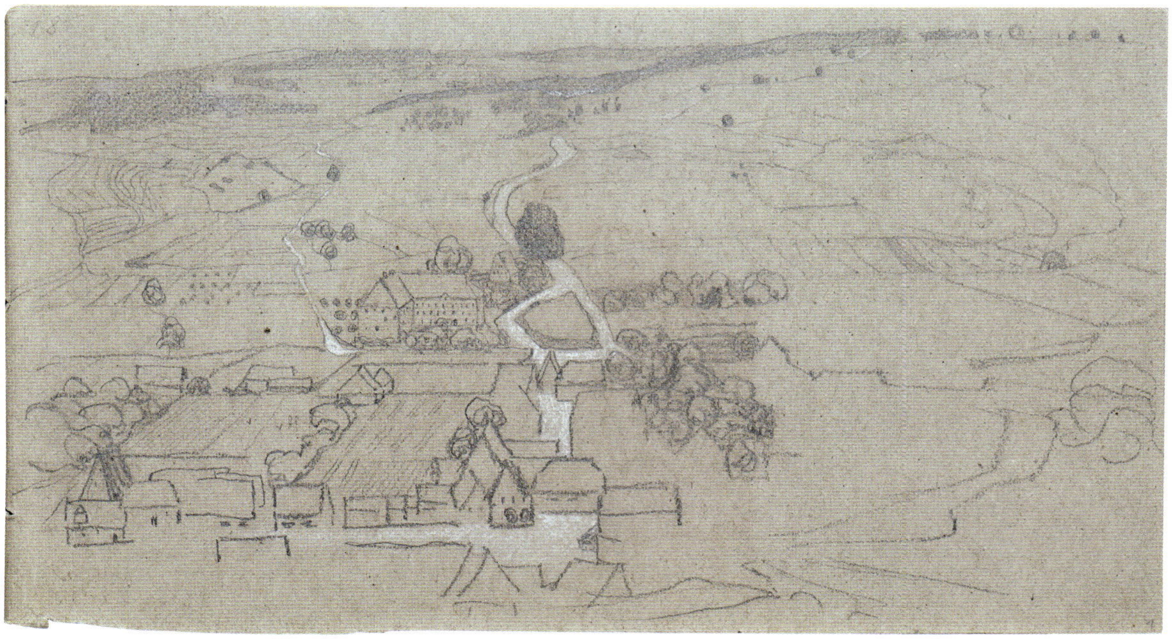

Sketchbook 11
p.1
Drawing of
Kallmünz as seen
from the Burgberg
1903
(see page 97)

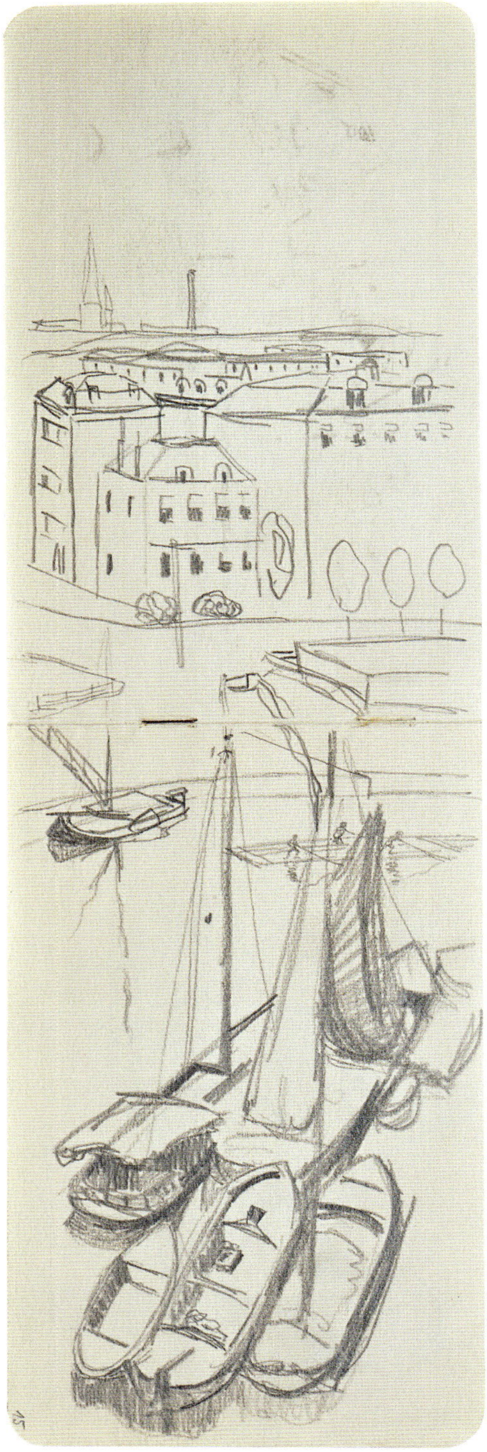

Sketchbook 15
pp.14-15
Sketch of harbor in
Amsterdam with boats
and buildings
1904
(see page 133)

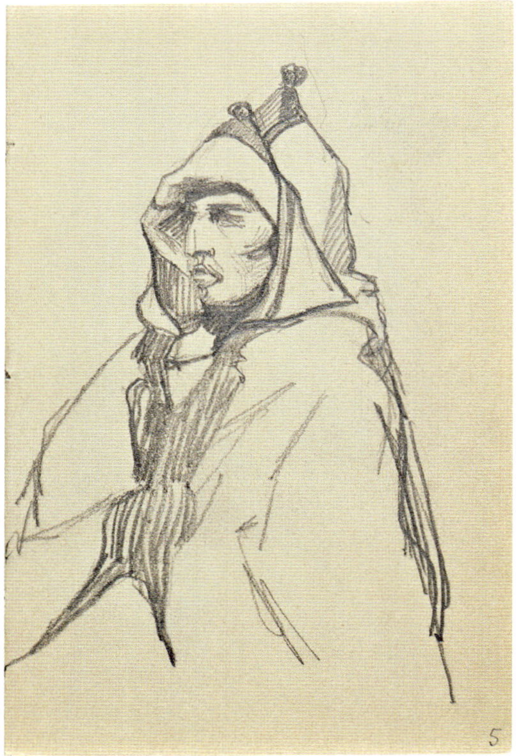


Sketchbook 17
p.5
Sketch of male
figure in Tunisia
1905
(see page 143)

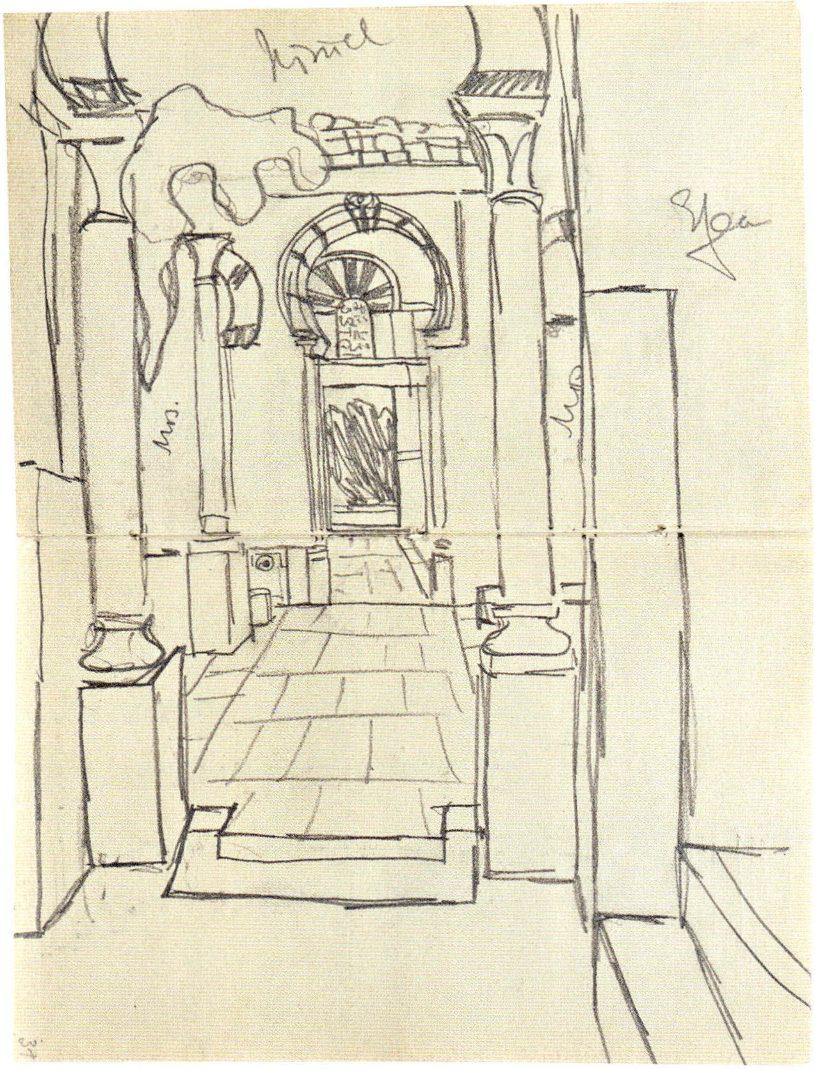

Sketchbook 18
pp.30-31
Drawing of La
Mida in Tunis
1905
(see page 160)

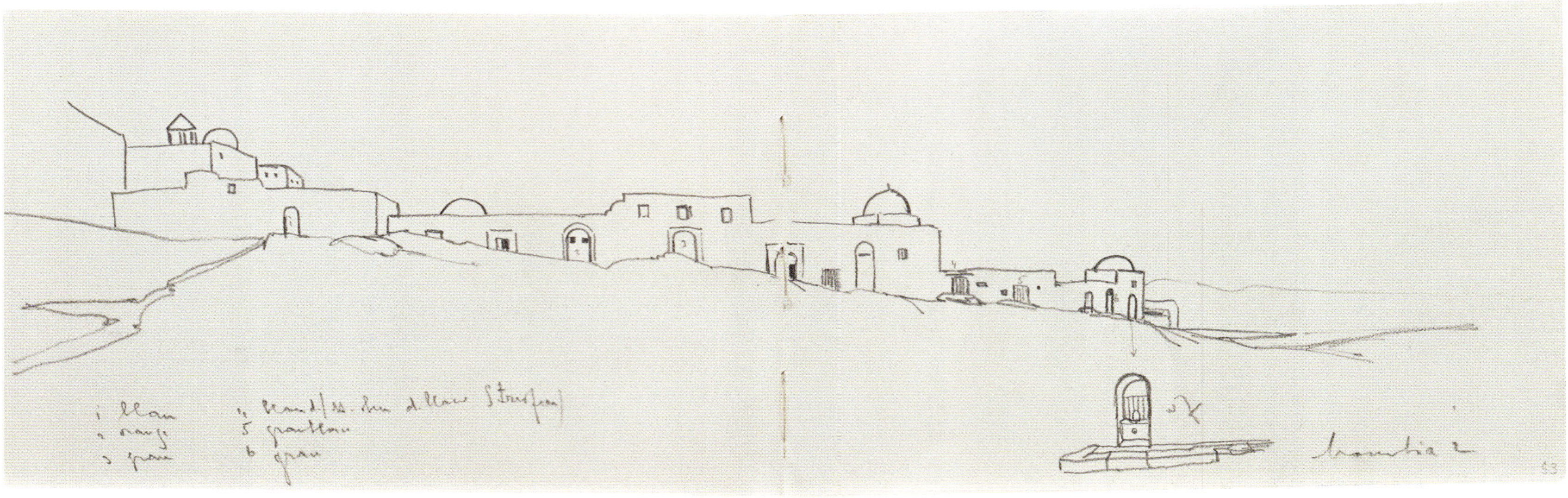

Sketchbook 19
pp.52-53
Sketch of Manouba
with detail
1905
(see page 171)

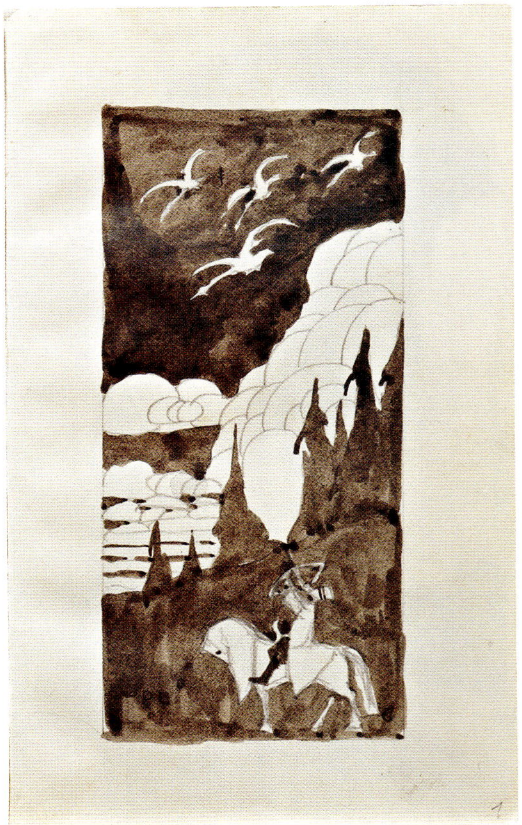

Sketchbook 20
p.1
Drawing for
*Die Jagd*
1903-1907
(see page 176)

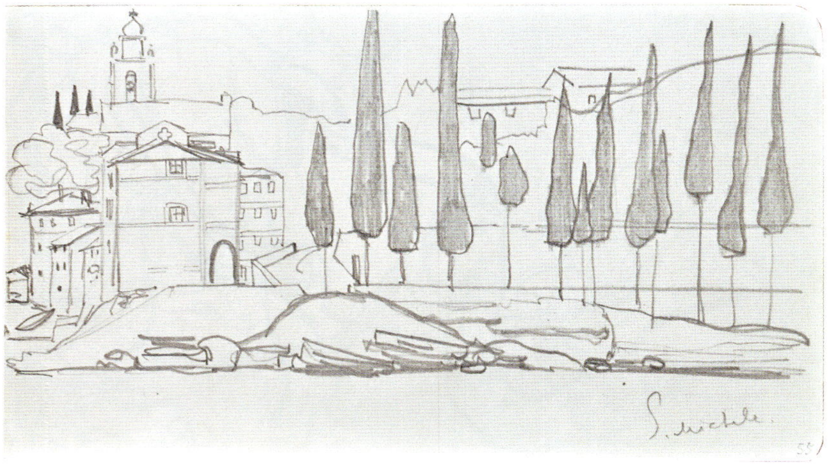

Sketchbook 22
p.55
Sketch of the church
at San Michele di
Pagana
1906
(see page 202)

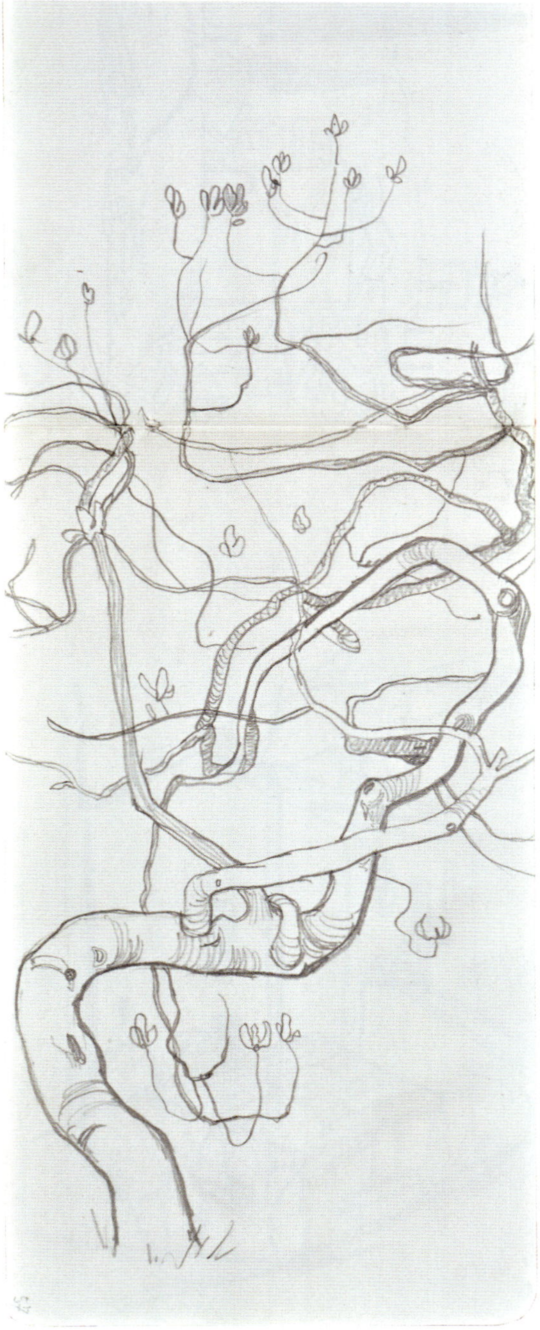

Sketchbook 22
pp.56-57
Sketch of branches
with buds
1906
(see page 202)

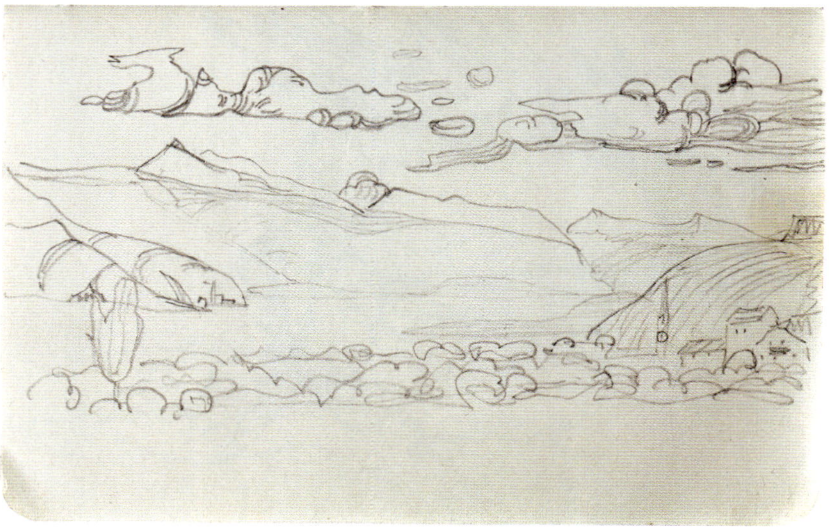

Sketchbook 25
p.60
Sketch of village
and mountains
1908
(see page 223)

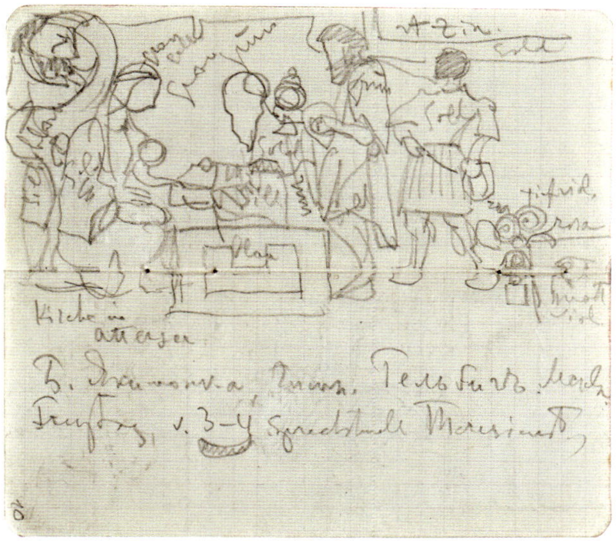

Sketchbook 26
pp.9-10
Sketch of Arrival
of Magi
1908
(see page 226)

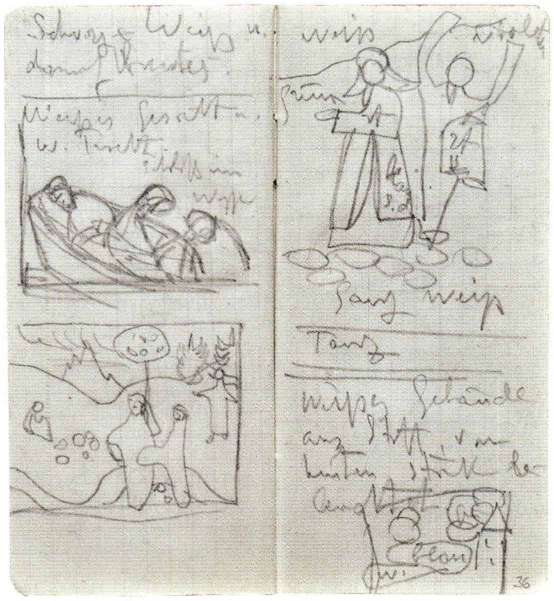

Sketchbook 26
pp.35-36
Studies for stage compositions
c.1908-1909
(see page 228-229)

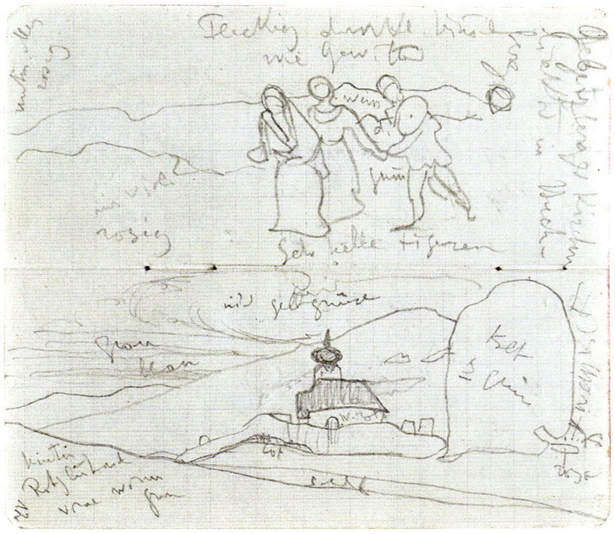

Sketchbook 26
pp.11-12
Sketch of figures in landscape and church
1908
(see page 226)

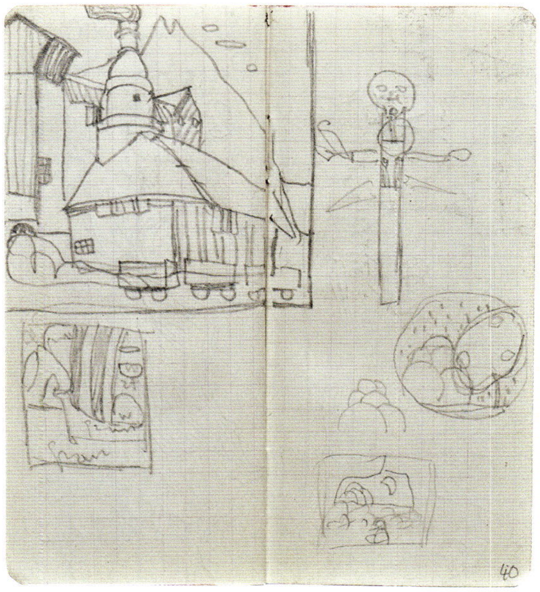

Sketchbook 26
pp.39-40
Studies of building with mountain and stage compositions
c.1908-1909
(see page 229)

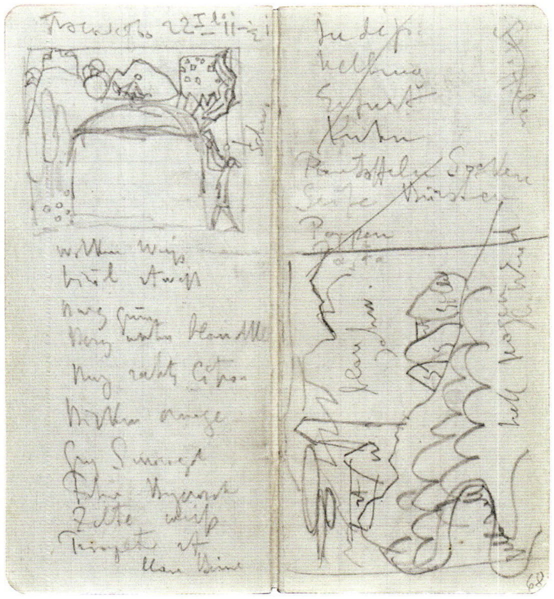

Sketchbook 26
pp.67-68
Sketches of rider in landscape and landscape
c.1908-1909
(see page 232)

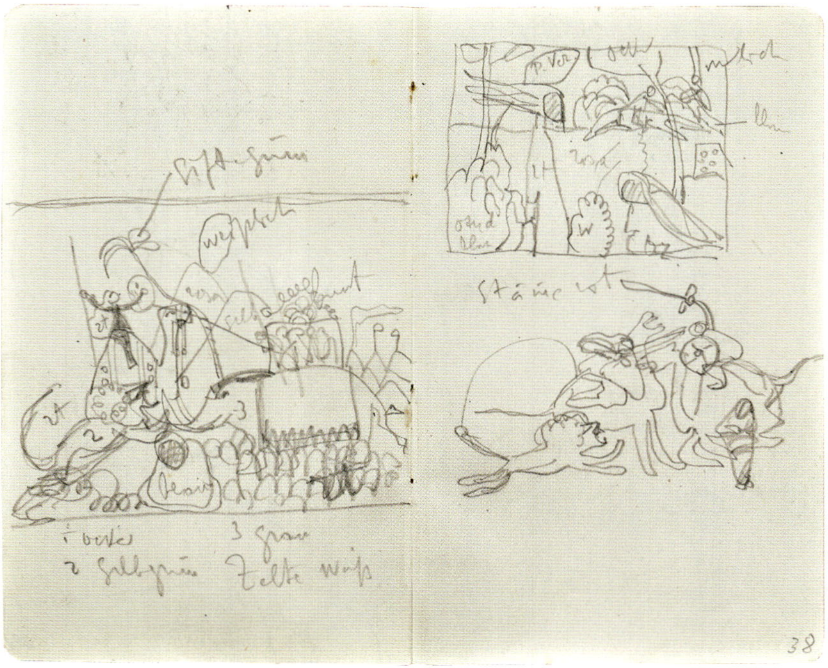

Sketchbook 27
pp.37-38
Studies for *Der Elefant* of 1908 and *Skizze zu 'Improvisation 5'* of 1910
(see page 236)

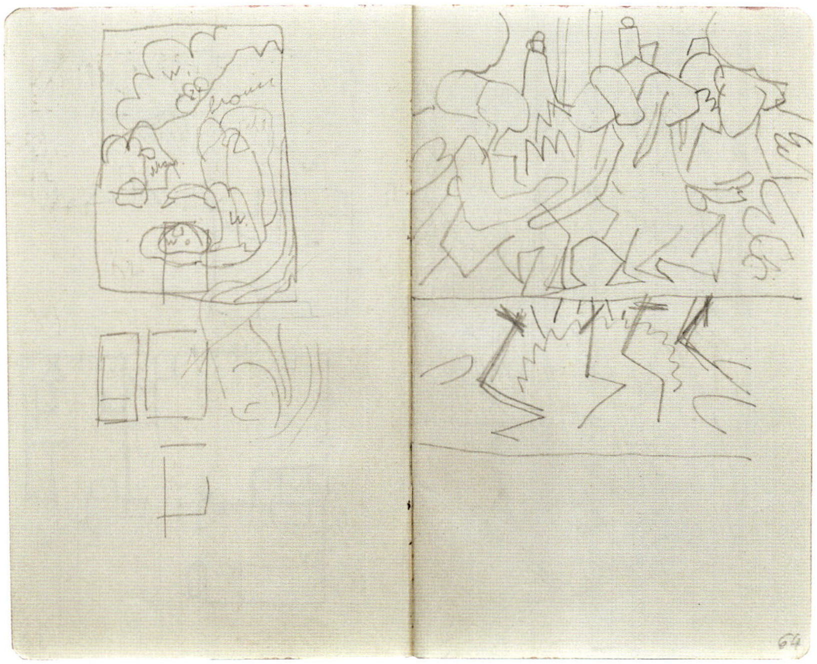

Sketchbook 27
pp.63-64
Studies for an unidentified painting and *Orientalisches* of 1909
(see pages 237-238)

Sketchbook 27
pp.65-66
Studies for *Improvisation 7* of 1910, *Zwei Reiter und liegende Gestalt* of 1909–1910 and *Entwurf zu 'Komposition II'* of c.1910
(see page 238)

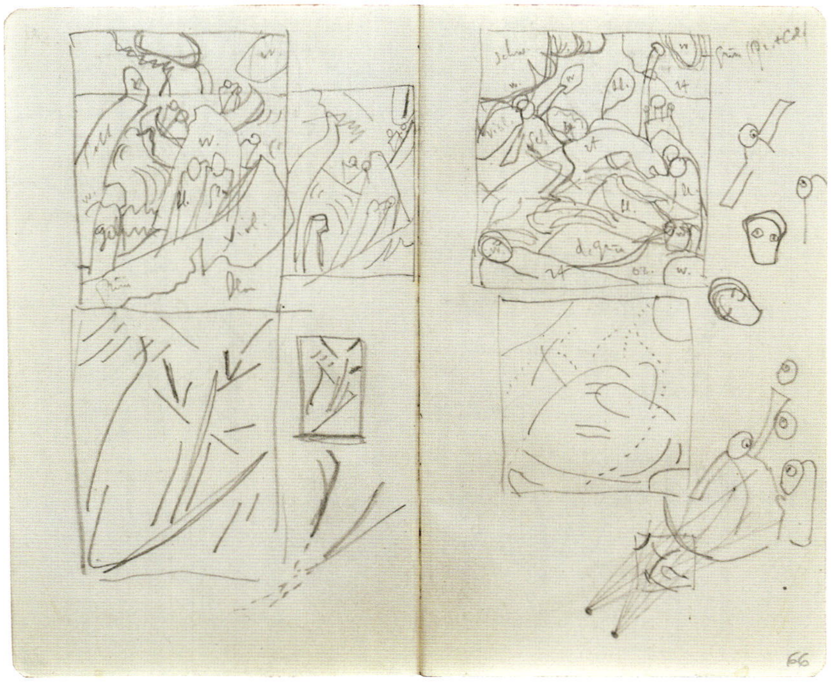

Sketchbook 27
pp.67-68
Studies for unknown works
c.1909-1910
(see pages 238-239)

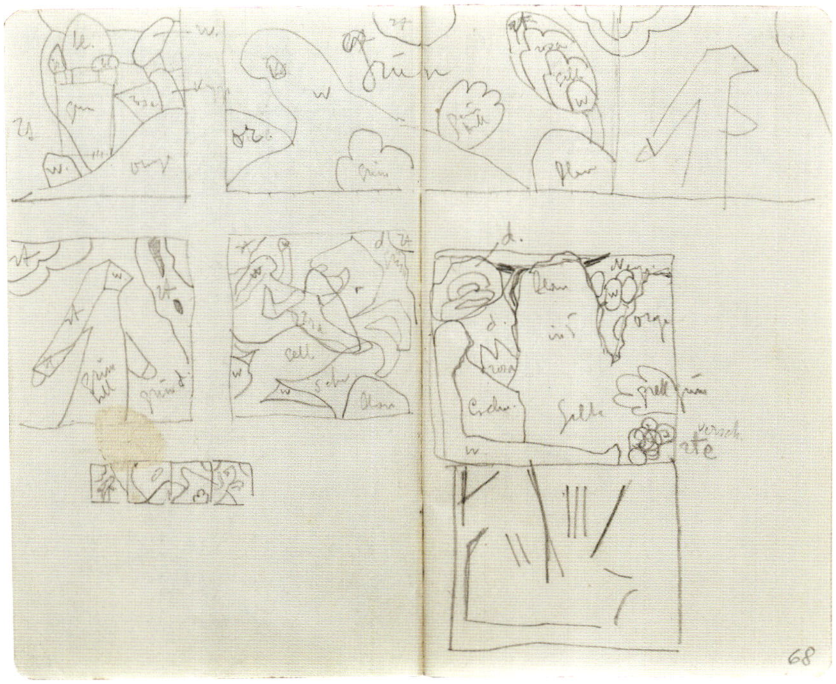

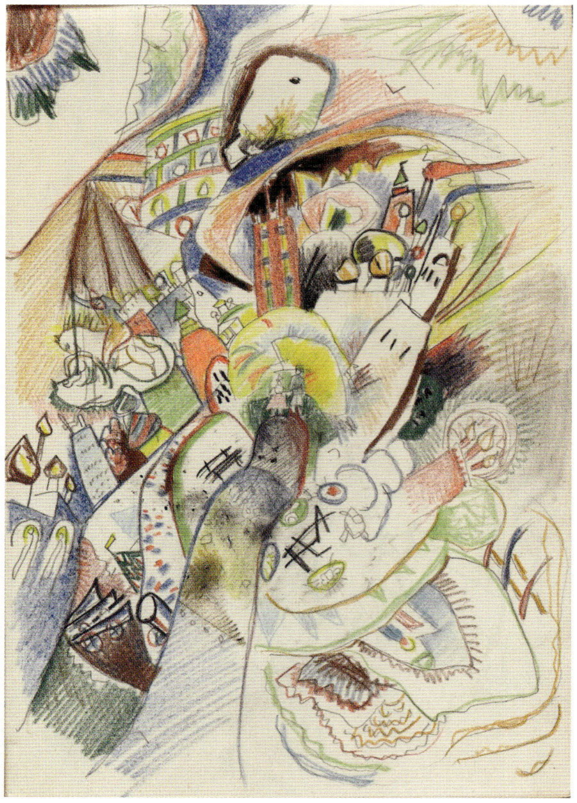

Sketchbook 31
p.5
Study for *Moskau I* of
1915
(see page 268)

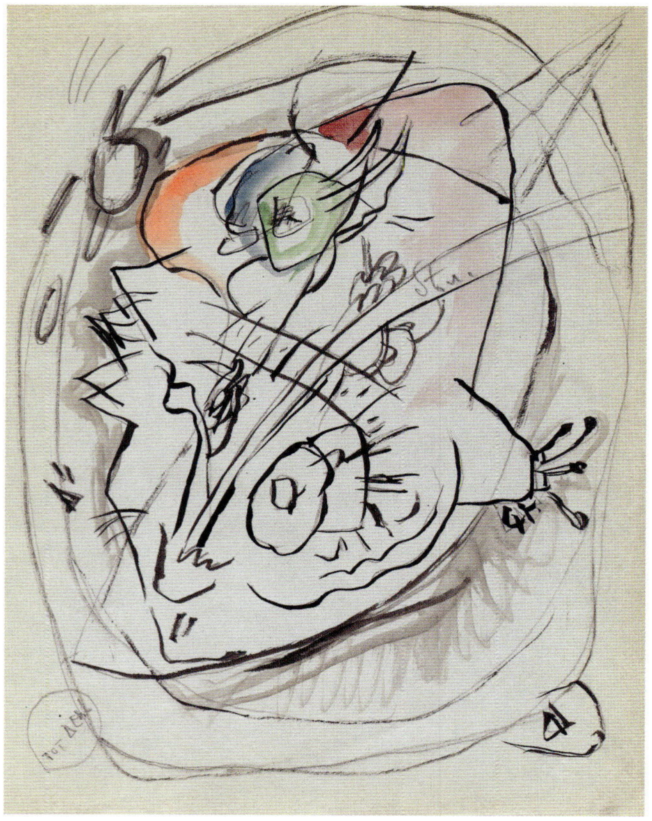

Sketchbook 32
p.8
Untitled drawing
1916-1917
(see page 272)

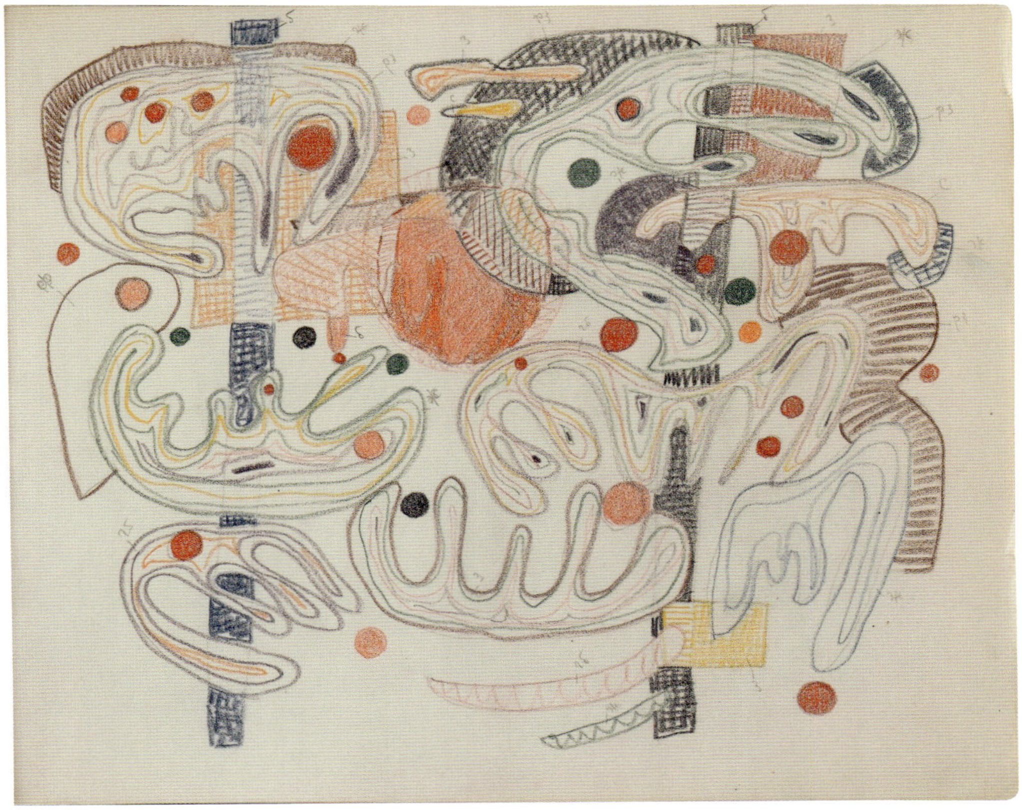

Sketchbook 36
p.2
Study for *Formes capricieuses* of July 1937
(see page 295)

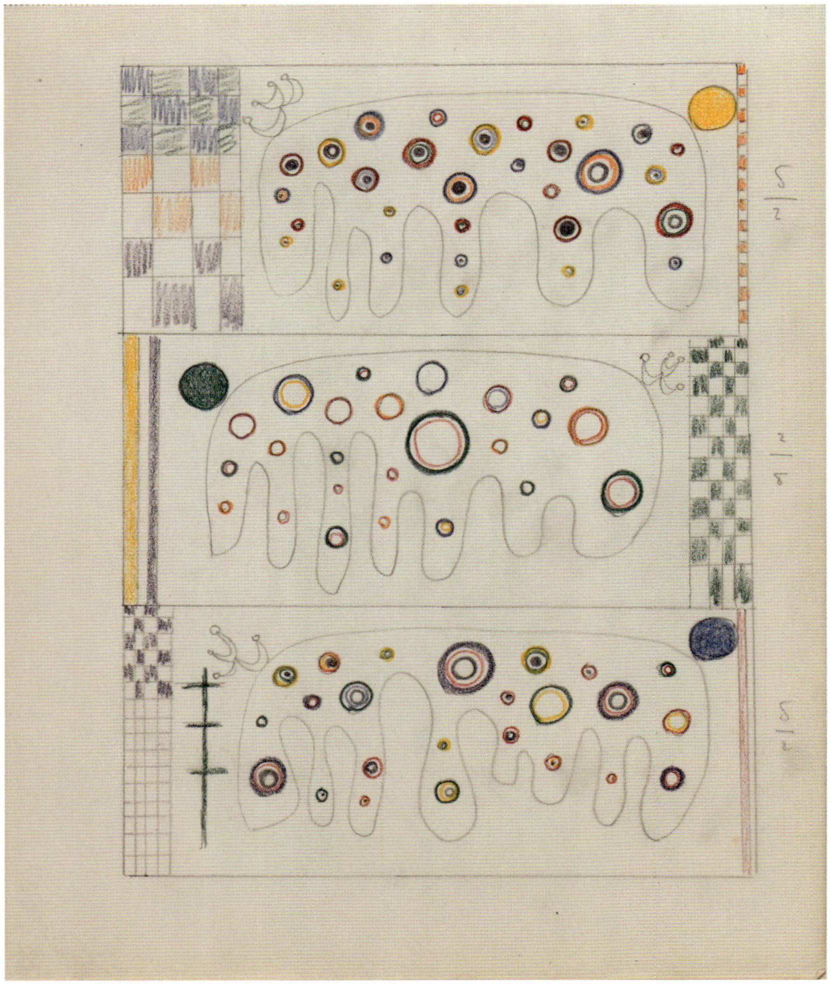

Sketchbook 36
p.18
Study for *Trois* of April 1938
(see page 303)

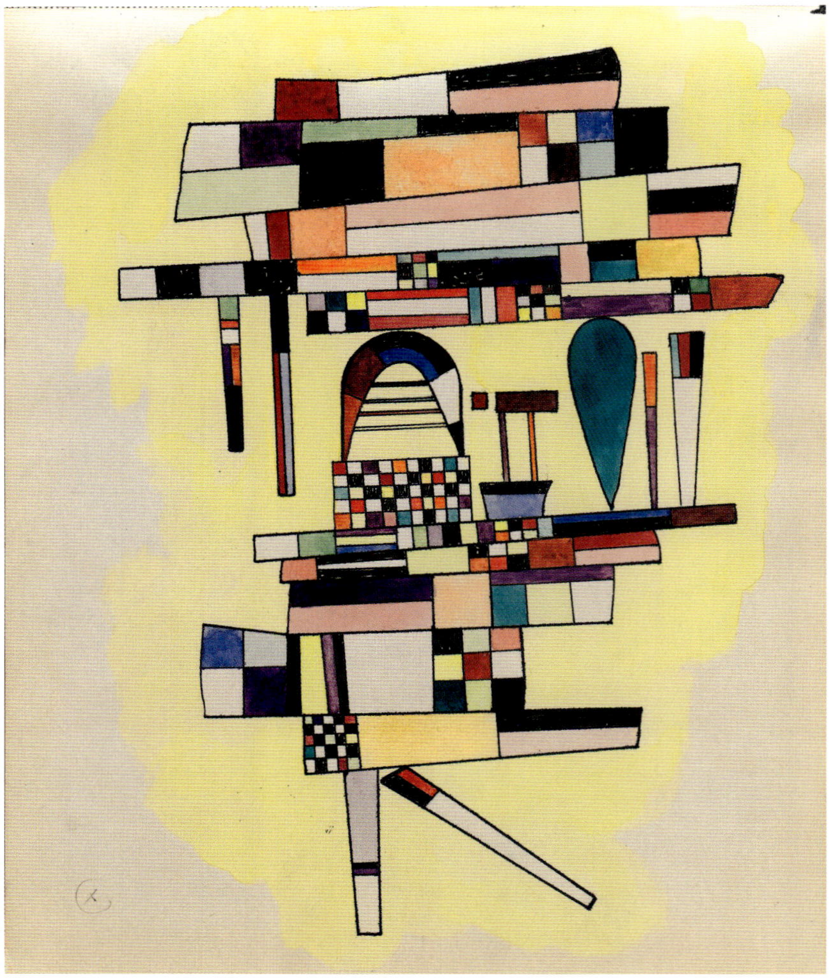

Sketchbook 36
p.21
Study for *La Toile jaune* of
July 1938
(see page 304)

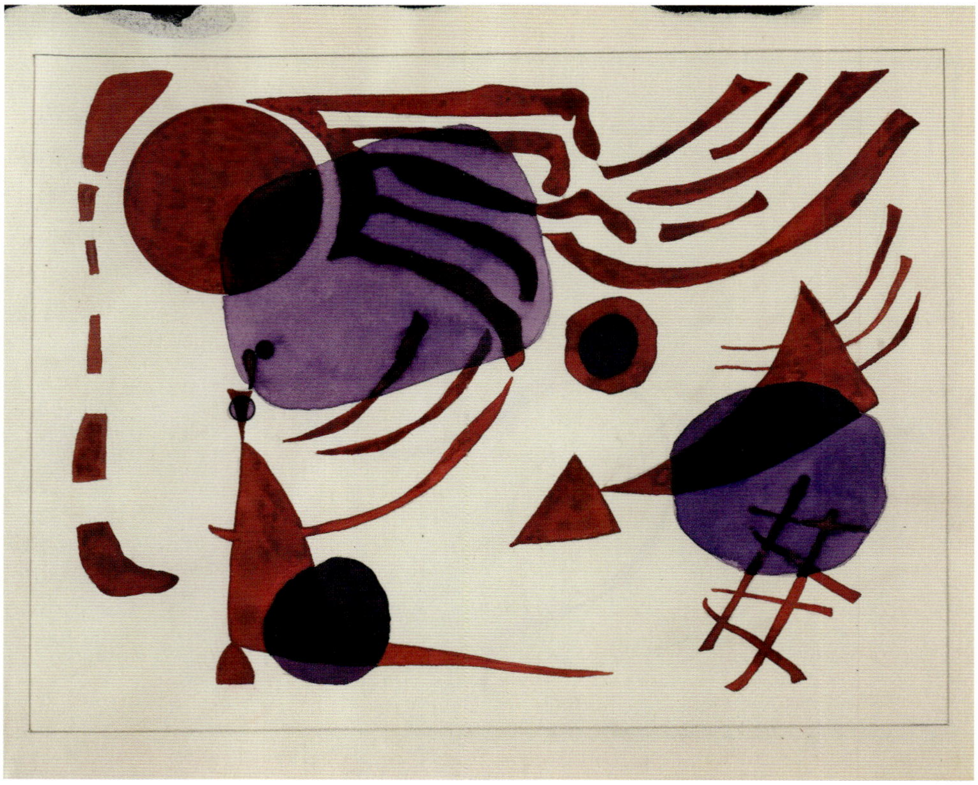

Sketchbook 36
p.24
Untitled watercolor
c.1937-1938
(see page 305)

# Sketchbook 14

1904

Brown linen-covered cardboard notebook; inside front cover stamped '610 Z'
Contains 112 pages (56 sheets) of graph paper, each 16.2 x 10.3 cm (6⅜ x 4 in), of which pp.30–105 are blank
Page numbers inscribed by unknown hand at later date with odd numbers at lower right

Hanfstaengl 1974, p.160

LOCATION
Städtische Galerie im Lenbachhaus, Munich (GMS 340)

HISTORY
Gabriele Münter, Murnau, until 1957

On the basis of the copious notes, this small notebook can be dated to 1904. It contains three sheets with studies for decorative arts.

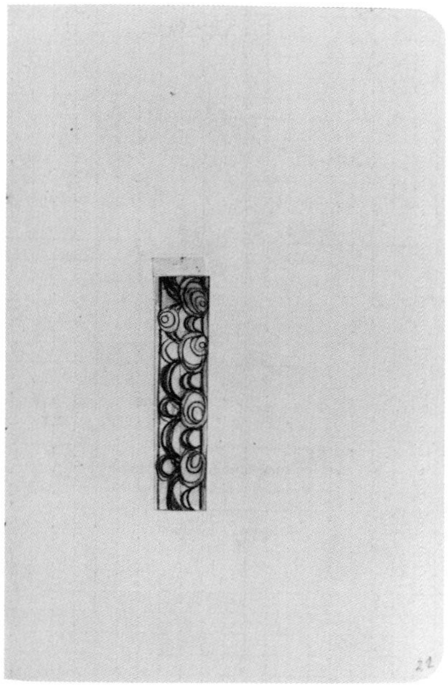

14, p.21

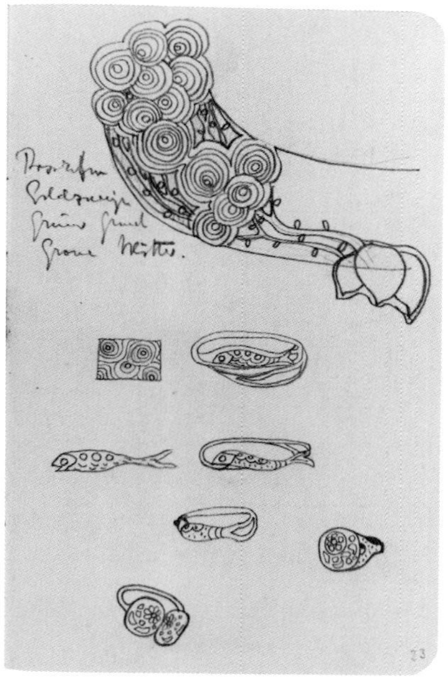

14, p.23

**p.0** (inside front cover) Notes and addresses

**pp.1–13** Notes regarding meetings in early 1904 and plans for exhibitions of the 'Phalanx' Artists Association later in 1904

**pp.14–20** Blank

**p.21** Pencil drawing of decorative design on paper (5.8 x 1.3 cm) taped onto sheet

EXHIBITIONS
1984 New York, no.240, ill.
1984 Munich, no.285, ill.

REFERENCES
Weiss 1979, p.123

Weiss emphasized the influence of Jugendstil design – the curving lines and decorative patterns – on Kandinsky's art in 1902–1904. For similar circular designs, see Sketchbook 12 (GMS 347, p.45) and Sketchbook 21 (GMS 333, p.44).

**p.22** Blank

**p.23** Pencil drawings of designs for rings
Inscribed u.l.: 'Rosareifen / Goldzweige / Grüner Grund / Graue Blätter'

EXHIBITIONS
1982 New York, no.148, ill
1982 Munich, no.170, ill.

REFERENCES
Hanfstaengl 1974, p.160, ill.
Weiss 1979, pp.123, 211 n.51, fig.104
Barnett and Friedel 1995, no.163, color ill.

**p.24** Blank

**p.25** Notes regarding colors

**p.26** Blank

After p.26 Kandinsky pasted notes on a separate sheet (receipt for Gasthof Possenhofen on the Starnberger See) into this notebook.

**p.27** Pencil drawings of designs for rings
Inscribed c.r.: 'vorne / Seite / Smaragd + bl. Email'

REFERENCES
Hanfstaengl 1974, p.160
Weiss 1979, pp.123, 211 n.52

The abstract designs are similar to the studies on p.21 (above) and the ring designs with fish resemble those on p.23.

**p.28** Blank

**p.29** Notes in Cyrillic about thick glue

**pp.30–105** Blank

**p.106** Notes about thin black frames for woodcuts (below)
Inscribed at u.l.: 'Casein 9 Gr / Ammon[ium] con[zen]trat 3 [Gr] / Venez. Terpentin 9 Gr / Canadabalsam 12 gr'; u.r.: 'Wasserbd / Spritzflasche'; c.: 'Schwarze dünne Rahmen f. Holzschnitte.'

**p.107** Notes for mats ('passepartouts') for works on paper

**pp.108–109** Notes about mats and frames for tempera paintings ('colored drawings') done in early 1904

**pp.110–111** Schedule for sending works to exhibitions in Düsseldorf, Dresden, Prague and Berlin in April and May

**pp.112–113** List of canvases, stretchers and frames (for works done in 1904) apparently to be purchased at Dury in Munich

14, p.27

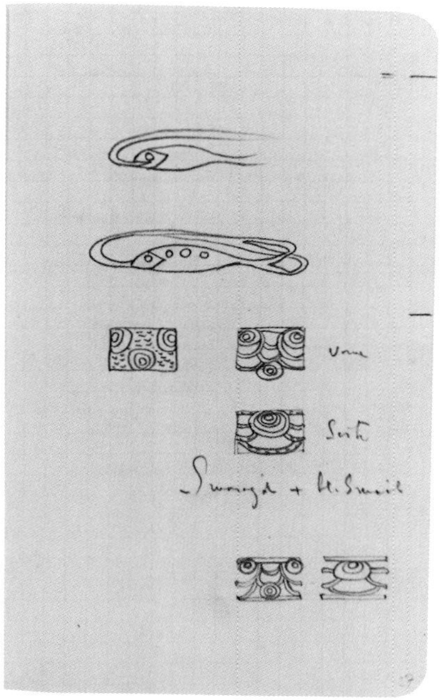

# Sketchbook 15

prepared with the assistance of Sonja Bay

1904

Grey linen-covered cardboard sketchbook; no label
Contains 80 pages (40 sheets), each 11.5 x 17.9 cm ($4\frac{1}{2}$ x 7 in), of which pp.39–80 are blank
Page numbers inscribed by unknown hand at later date with odd numbers at lower right

Hanfstaengl 1974, p.153

LOCATION
Städtische Galerie im Lenbachhaus, Munich (GMS 331)

HISTORY
Gabriele Münter, Murnau, until 1957

The sketchbook resembles Sketchbook 13, which has a label from Franz Dury in Munich and which can be dated to 1903. Erika Hanfstaengl thought the drawings on the first pages of the present sketchbook were done in Kallmünz in 1903, and thus dated it to 1903 and 1904. The majority of the sketches were executed in the Netherlands, when Kandinsky and Gabriele Münter travelled there in late May–June 1904.

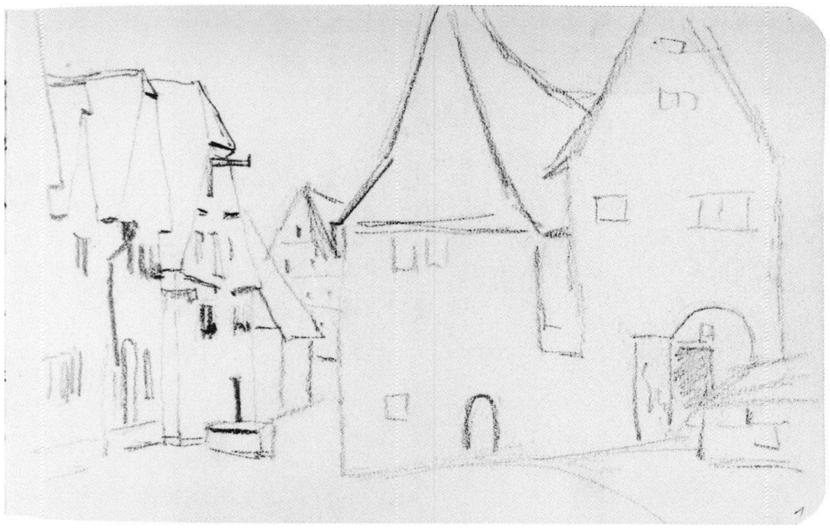

15, p.1

15, p.2

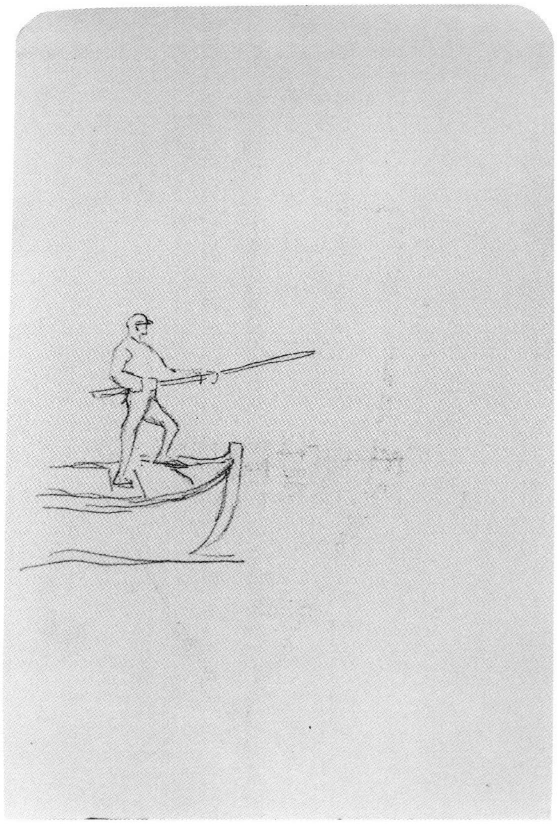

15, p.3

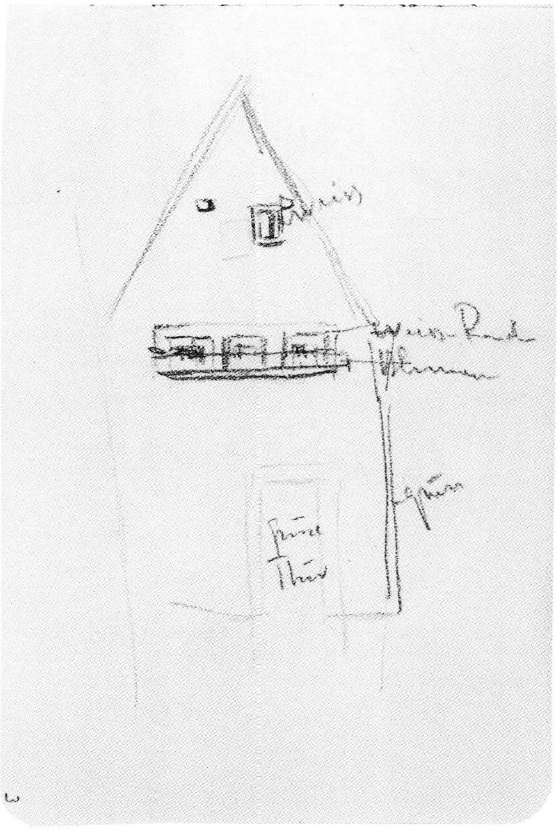

**p.1** Pencil sketch of houses probably done in Germany in 1904

REFERENCES
Hanfstaengl 1974, p.153

The sketch recalls a drawing that Kandinsky made in Rothenburg ob der Tauber on 7 November 1903 (see cat. no.1237 on p.319).

**p.2** Pencil sketch of man standing in boat fishing

Kandinsky probably made this sketch in the Netherlands. He and Münter went to Rotterdam on 23 May and were in Amsterdam in June 1904.

**p.3** Pencil sketch of house probably in the Netherlands

Inscribed with color notations: 'weiss / weiss-Rand / Blumen / grüne / Thür / grün'

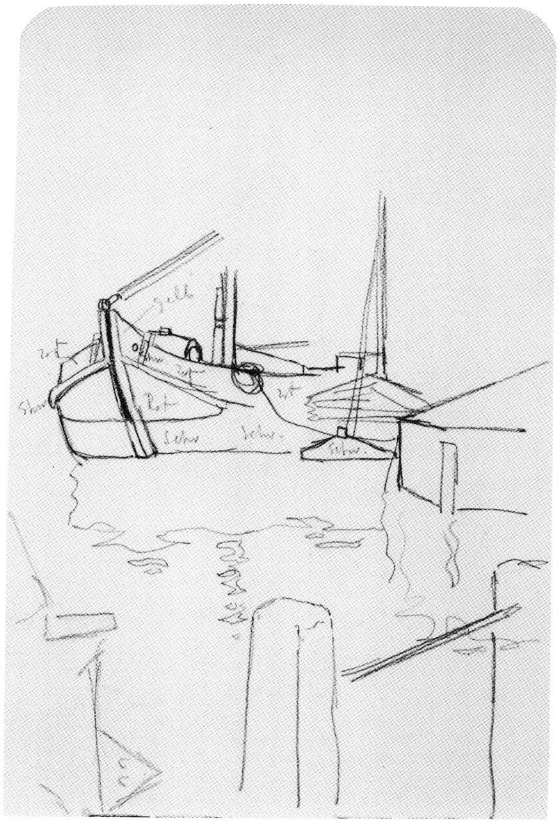


15, p.4

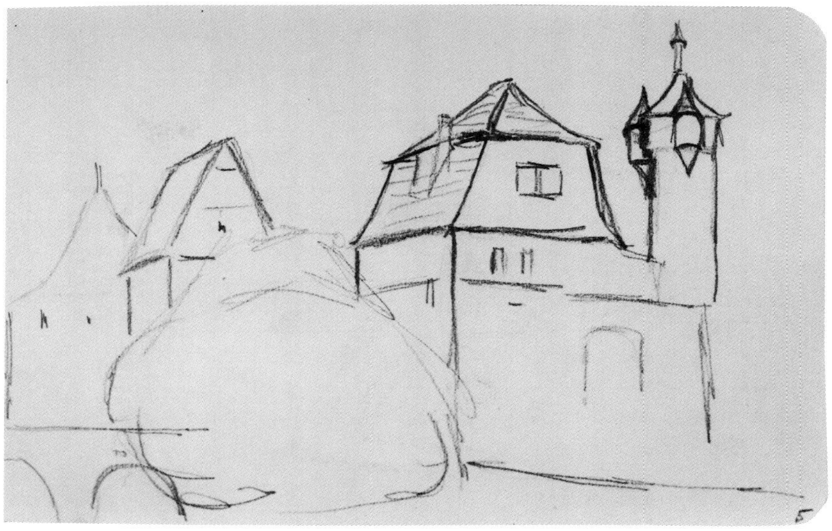

15, p.5

**p.4** Pencil sketch of dock and boats in the Netherlands
Inscribed with numerous color notations: 'rot / gelb / schw'

REFERENCES
Hanfstaengl 1974, p.153
Barnett 1992, p.140

Although Hanfstaengl stated that the first five pages were probably made in Oberpfalz in Germany, this drawing depicting fishing boats or 'botter' is clearly related to works done in the Netherlands (Barnett nos.140, 142).

**p.5** Pencil sketch of medieval houses in the Netherlands

**p.6** Pencil sketch of boats in the Netherlands

**p.7** Pencil sketch of boat in the Netherlands

15, p.6

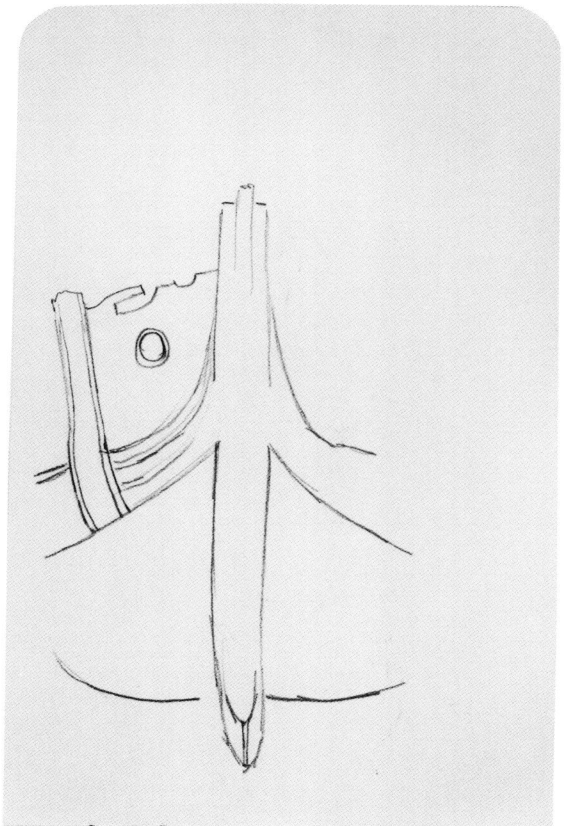

15, p.7

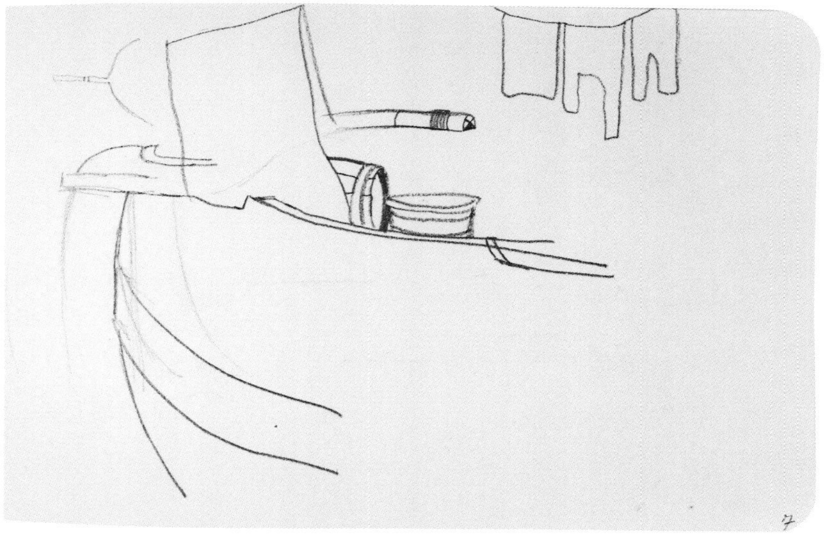

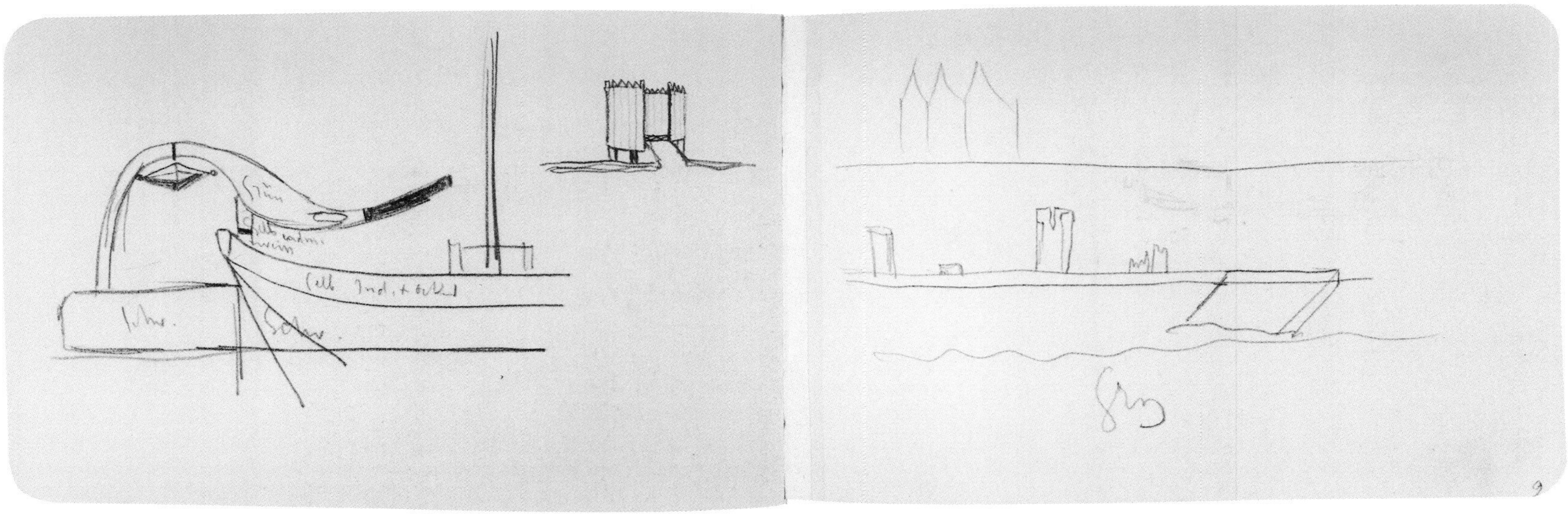

15, pp.8-9

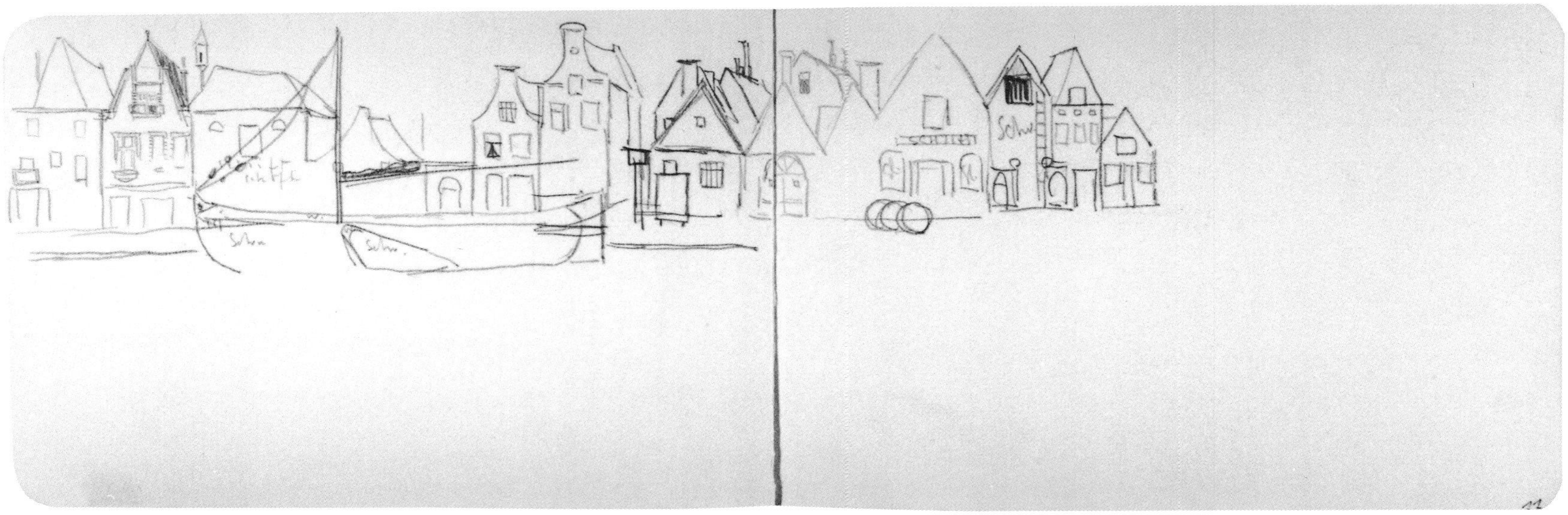

15, pp.10-11

**p.8** Pencil sketch of boat, tiller, dock and fence
Inscribed with color notations: 'grün / gelb cadm. / + weiss / gelb Ind. + Ocker / Schw. / Schw.'

**p.9** Pencil sketch of canal
Inscribed l.c.: 'Grn'

**pp.10–11** Pencil sketch of houses and boats along a large canal in Amsterdam
Inscribed with color notations: 'Schw / w. / Schw.'

The view may show buildings along the Herengracht or Prinsengracht in Amsterdam. Münter took photographs and made similar sketches of houses in Amsterdam dated 12 and 16 June (see 46/13. pp.27, 33, 35).

**p.12** Blank

**p.13** Pencil sketch of medieval house in Amsterdam
Inscribed c.: 'rt'

15, p.13

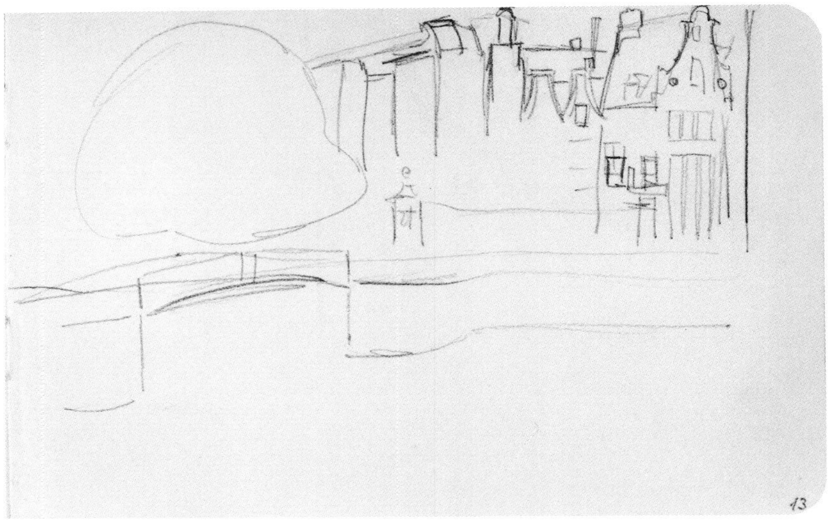

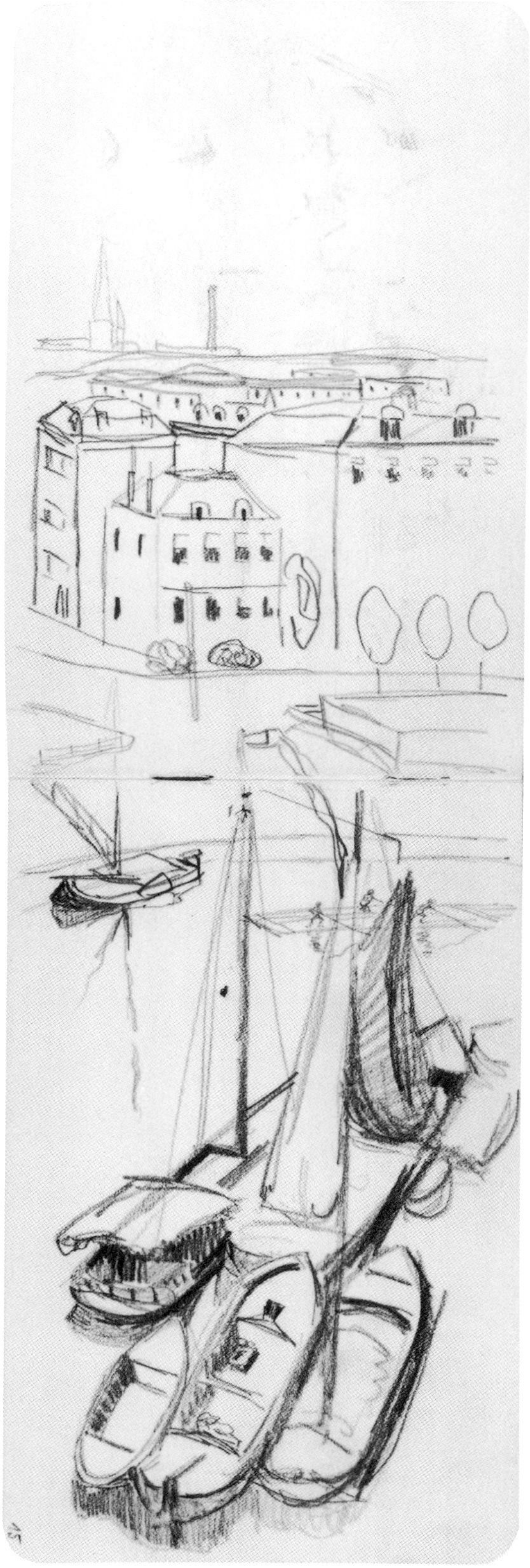

15, pp.14-15

fig.a

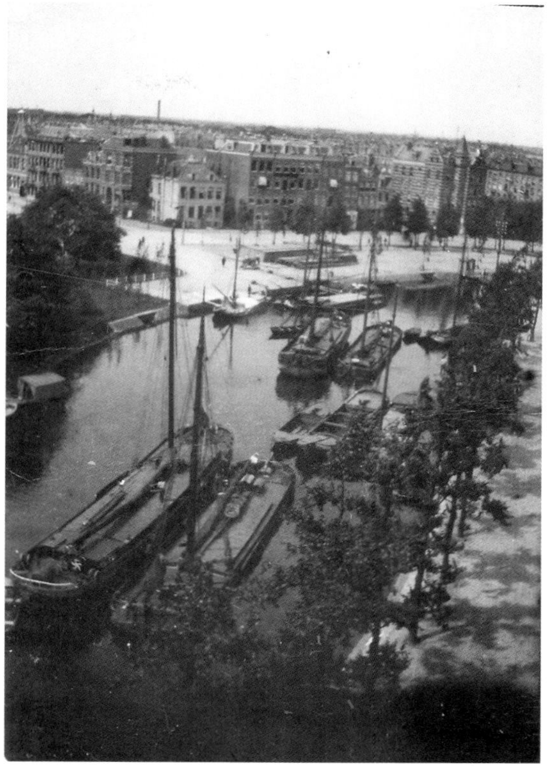

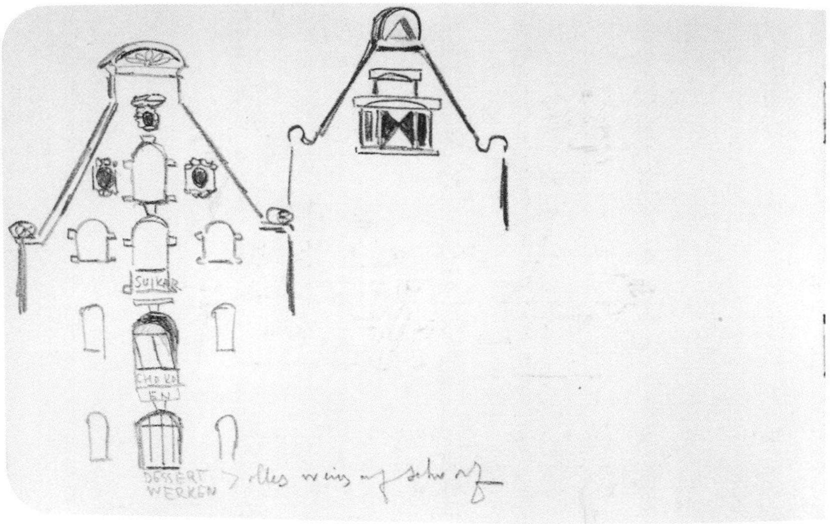


15, p.16

**pp.14–15** Pencil sketch of harbor in Amsterdam with boats and buildings

REFERENCES
Hanfstaengl 1974, p.153, ill.

The view looks down on the harbor in Amsterdam. Münter made a related drawing, which she dated 12 June 1904 in a sketchbook (46/13, p.29), and either she or Kandinsky took a photograph of the view (fig.a).

(See color plate p.120)

**p.16** Pencil sketch of buildings with shops in Amsterdam
Inscribed l.l.: 'SUIKAR / CHOKO / EN / DESSERT / WERKEN / alles weiss auf schwarz'

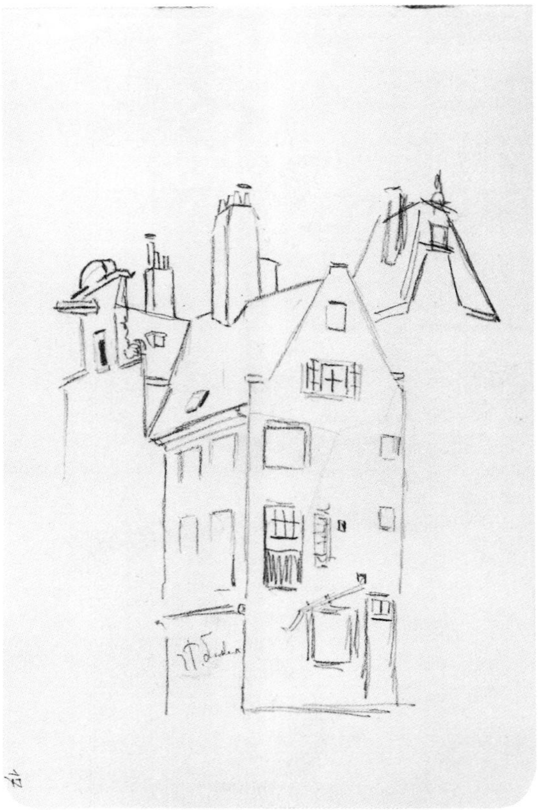

15, p.17

15, pp.20–21

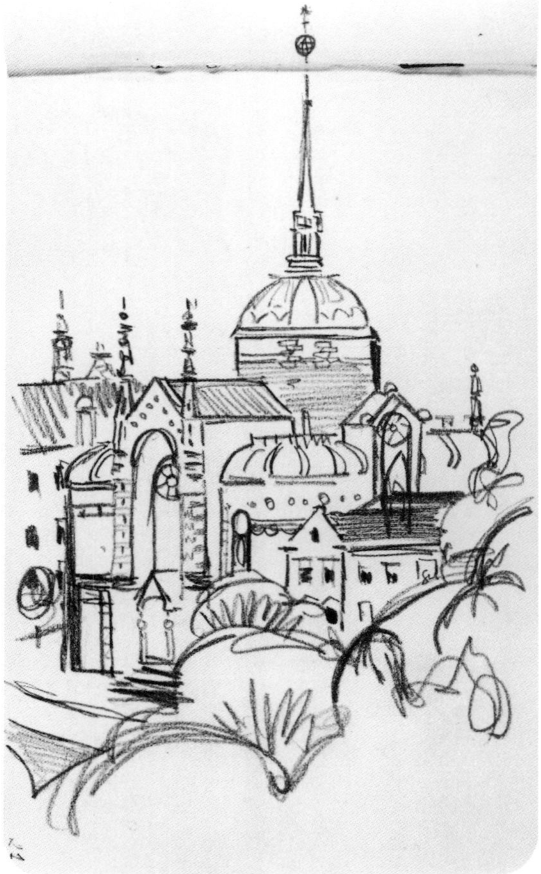

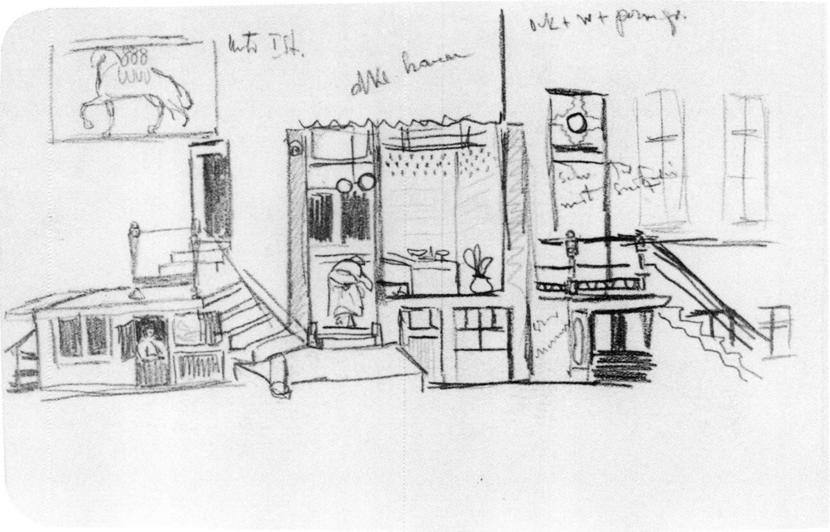

15, p.18

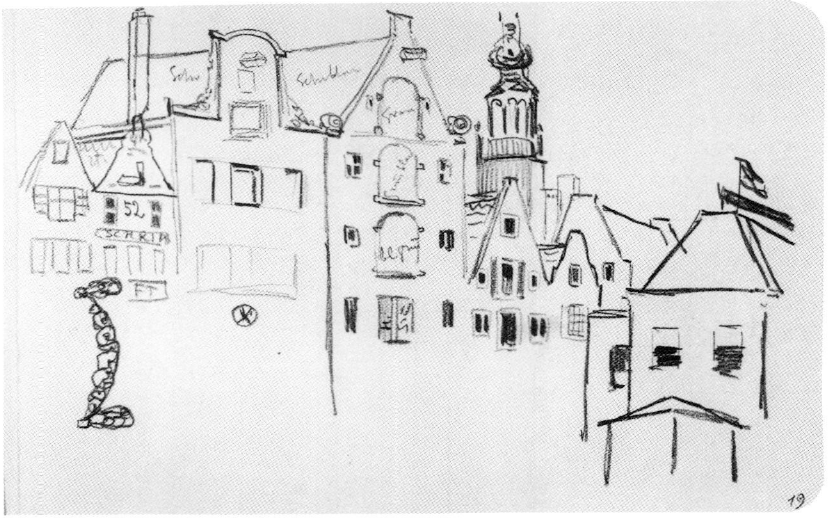

15, p.19

**p.17** Pencil sketch of eighteenth-century house in Amsterdam
Inscribed l.l.: 'rt. Laden'; c.: 'gb Schild'

**p.18** Pencil sketch of buildings with shops in Amsterdam
Inscribed u.l.: 'Unter I St. /dkl braun' and with color notations

REFERENCES
Hanfstaengl 1974, p.153, ill.

According to Sonja Bay, the shops are close to the American Hotel where Kandinsky stayed.

**p.19** Pencil sketch of warehouse and tower in Amsterdam
Inscribed with color notations: 'Schw / Schwblau / grau / grünblau / bl grün'

REFERENCES
Hanfstaengl 1974, p.153, ill.

Sonja Bay identified the tower as the Munttoren, but it also resembles the tower on the Oude Kerk in Amsterdam.

**pp.20–21** Pencil sketch of church

The dome suggests the church of Vrije Gemeente, which was near the Leidseplein in Amsterdam (see *Amsterdam omstreeks 1900* [Amsterdam, 1974], pp.104–105).

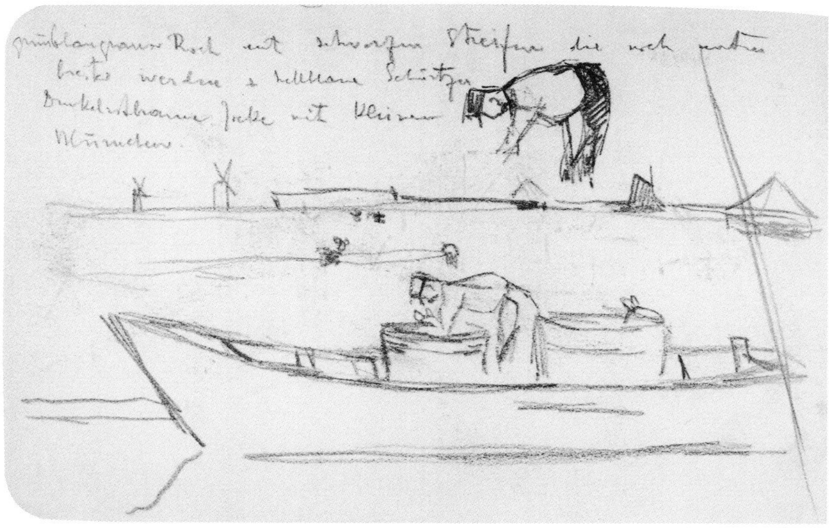

15, p.22

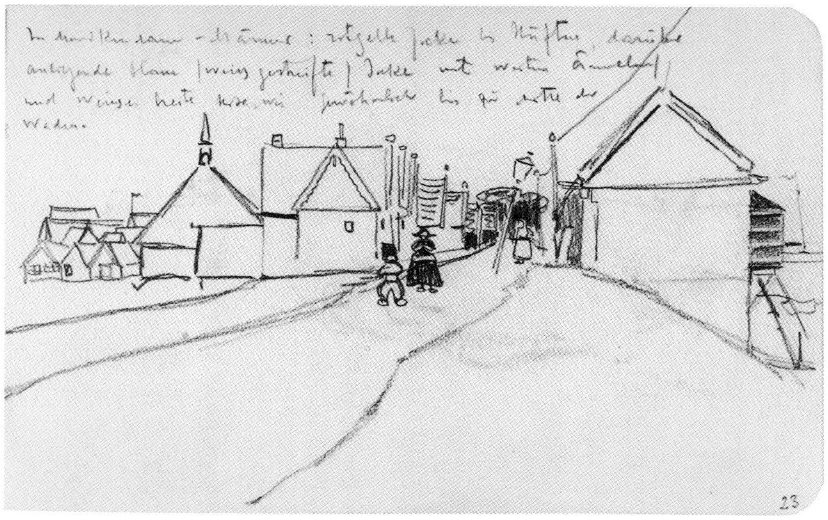

15, p.23

**p.22** Pencil sketches of a man on a boat with windmills in the distance and detail of man
Inscribed above: 'grünblaugrauer Rock mit schwarzen Streifen die nach unten / breiter werden + hellblaue Schürtzen / Dunkelrotbraune Jacke mit kleinen / Blümchen.'

REFERENCES
Hanfstaengl 1974, p.153, ill.

**p.23** Pencil sketch of people and houses
Inscribed above: 'In Monikendam-Männer: rotgelb Jacke bis Hüften, darüber / anliegende blau (weiss gestreifte) Jacke mit weiten Ärmeln / und weisser breite Hose wie gewöhnlich bis zur Mitte der / Waden.'

REFERENCES
Hanfstaengl 1974, p.153, ill.

Kandinsky and Münter went to Monnickendam during their trip to the Netherlands.

**p.24** Pencil sketch of girl knitting

REFERENCES
Barnett 1992, p.135

Münter made a drawing of the girl and boy (p.26) in Volendam on 17 June in her sketchbook (46/13, p.39). Kandinsky's sketch and the studies on pp.25, 27 (below) are related to *Erinnerung an Holland* of July 1904 (Barnett no.128).

**p.25** Pencil sketch of girl knitting

REFERENCES
Barnett 1992, p.135

The girl's cap and clothes are typical of those worn in Volendam and Monnickendam.

15, p.24

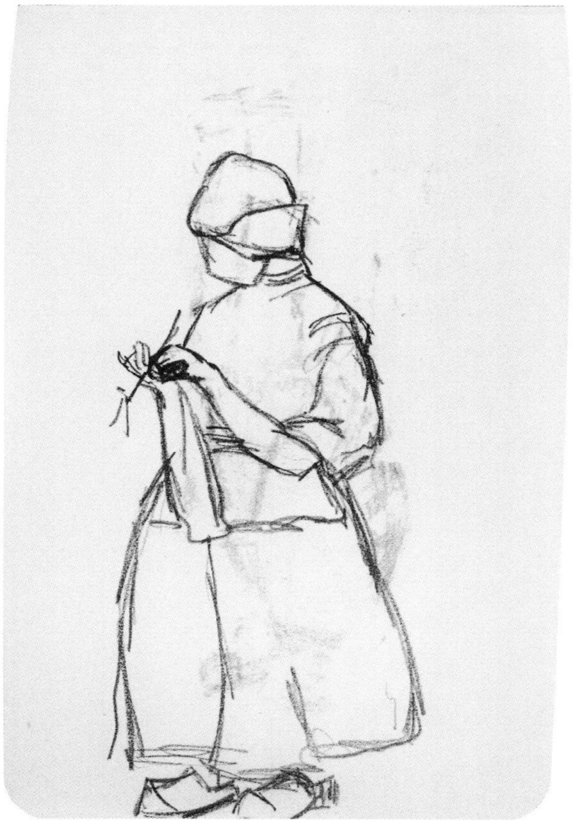

15, p.25

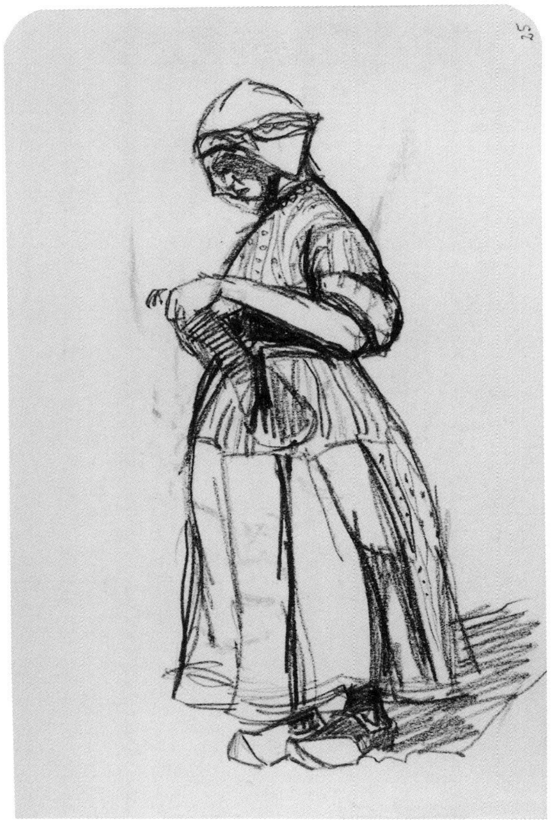

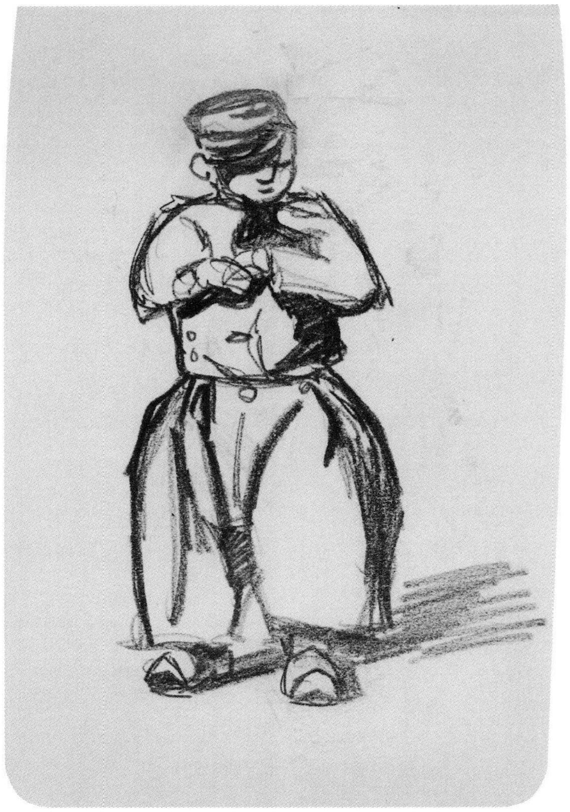

15, p.26

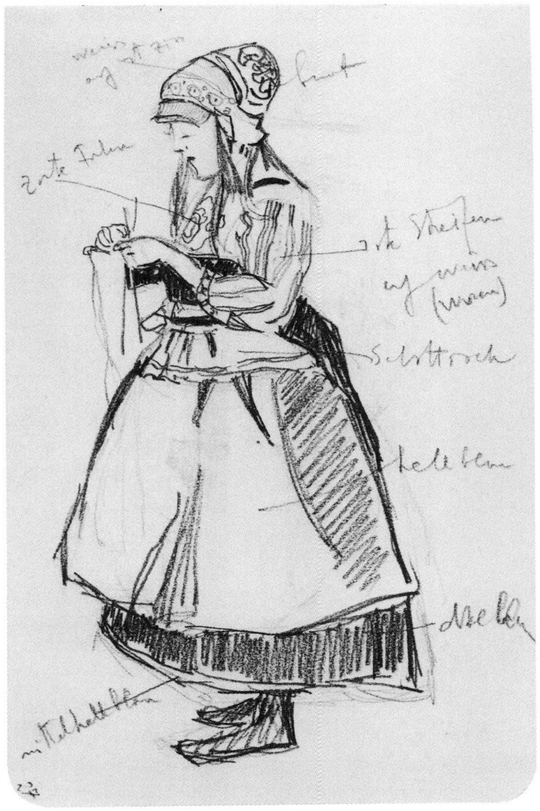

15, p.27

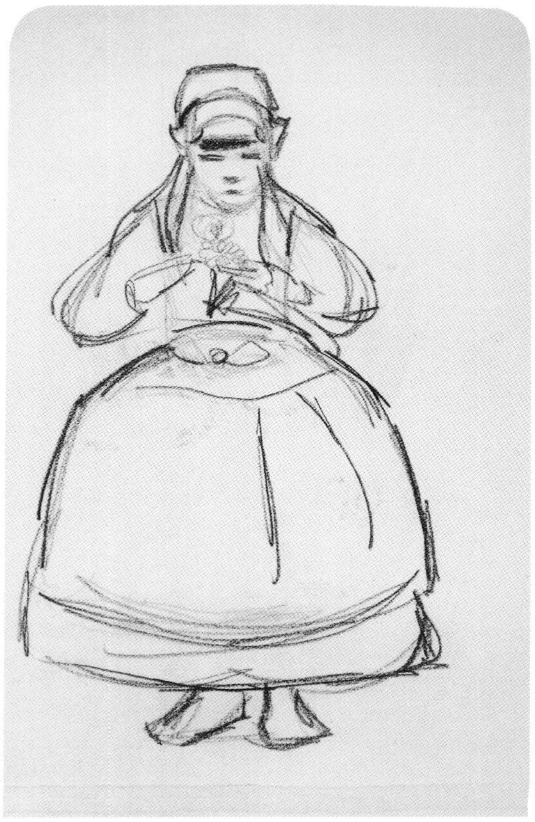

15, p.28

**p.26** Pencil sketch of boy

REFERENCES
Hanfstaengl 1974, p.153, ill.

The sketch can be related to Kandinsky's tempera painting *Die frühe Stunde (Holländisch)* of August 1904 (Barnett no.131). The boy's trousers are characteristic of those worn in Volendam and Monnickendam. Münter made a closely related sketch of the boy in Volendam on 17 June (46/13, p.39) and also took a photograph.

**p.27** Pencil study of girl knitting
Inscribed with color notations: 'weiss / auf rt zin / zarte Farben / bunt / rote Streifen / auf weiss / (warm) / Schottrock / hellblau / mittelhellblau / dkl blau'

REFERENCES
Hanfstaengl 1974, p.153, ill.
Barnett 1992, p.136
Barnett and Friedel 1995, no.146, color ill.

The motif is found in *Erinnerung an Holland, Holländerin* and *Samstag Abend (Holland)* of 1904 (Barnett nos.128, 129, 142). A photograph of a woman with a similar headdress was taken on the island of Marken probably by Münter on 18 June.

**p.28** Pencil sketch of girl

The sketch is related to *Die frühe Stunde (Holländisch)* of August 1904 (Barnett no.131).

**p.29** Pencil sketches of man wearing hat and smoking pipe, buckets and women
Inscribed u.r.: 'Frauen- weisser Rock immer / warm / grüne Schuhe / weisse Schürtzen'

REFERENCES
Hanfstaengl 1974, p.153, ill.

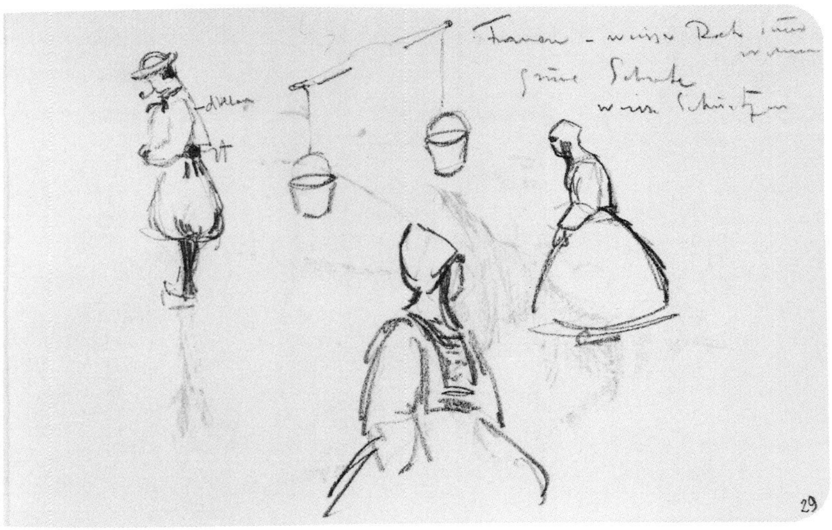

15, p.29

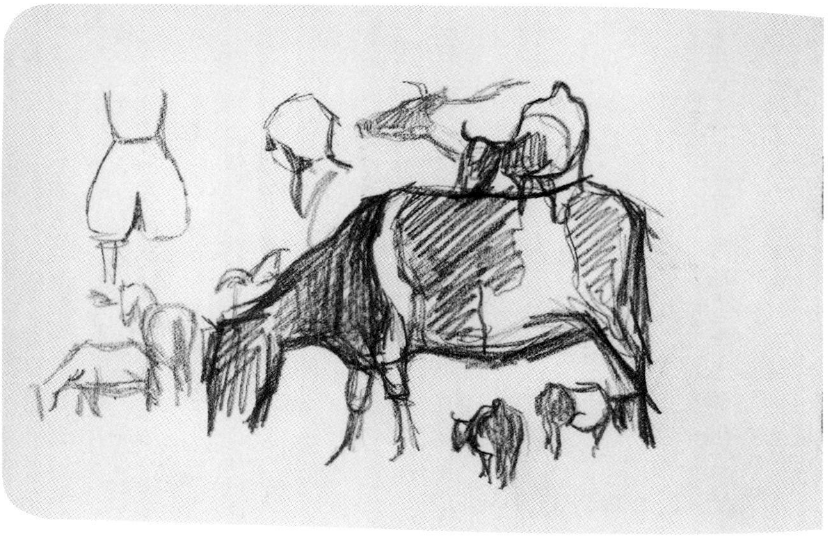

15, p.30

**p.30** Pencil sketches of cows, horses and figures

REFERENCES
Hanfstaengl 1974, p.153, ill.

**p.31** Pencil study of woman with embroidered cap and blouse
Inscribed with color notations: 'weisse Spitzen / gestickt / gewöhnlich / hell-gelb / weiss / Stickerei / x wie unten / blau hell'; l.c.: 'x sehr dkl. blau / od. schwarz'

REFERENCES
Podzemskaia 2000, p.133, fig.27

The embroidered cap and necklace are distinctive of Monnickendam and Volendam.

**p.32** Pencil sketch of horse-drawn cart
Inscribed c.r.: 'Edam'

Kandinsky and Münter went to Edam on 16 June.

**p.33** Pencil drawing of man with hat

REFERENCES
Hanfstaengl 1974, p.153, ill.

15, p.31

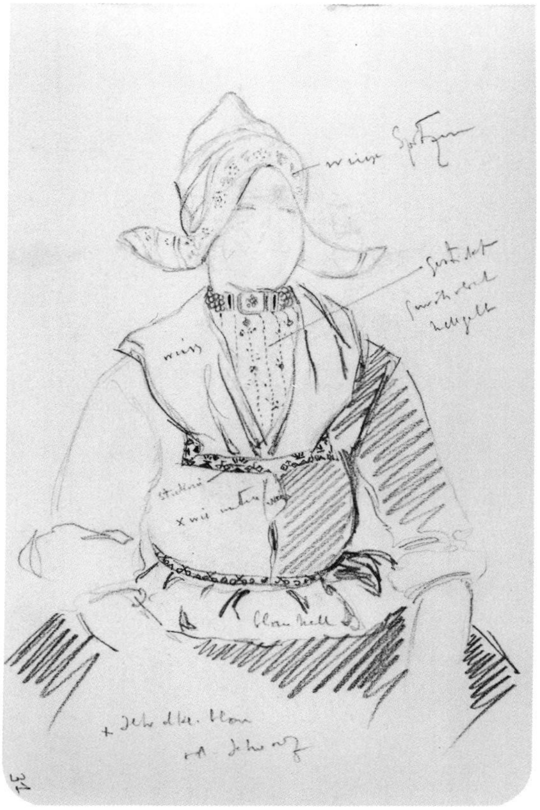

15, p.32

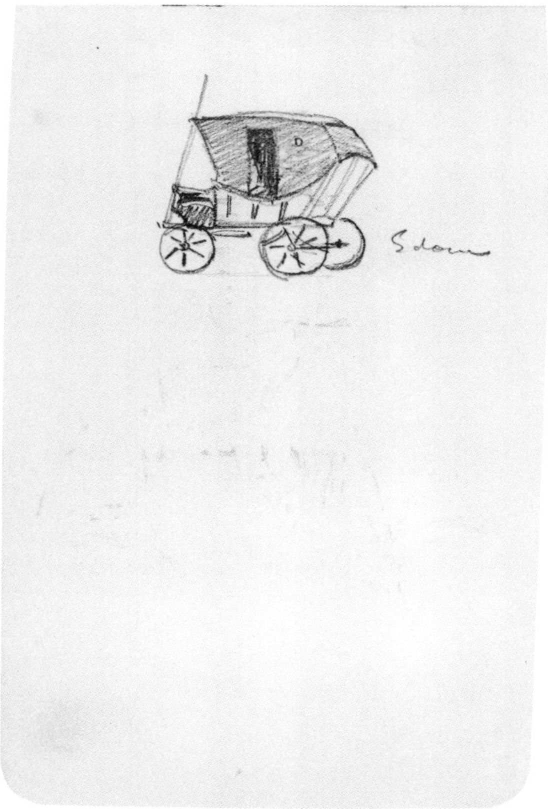

15, p.33

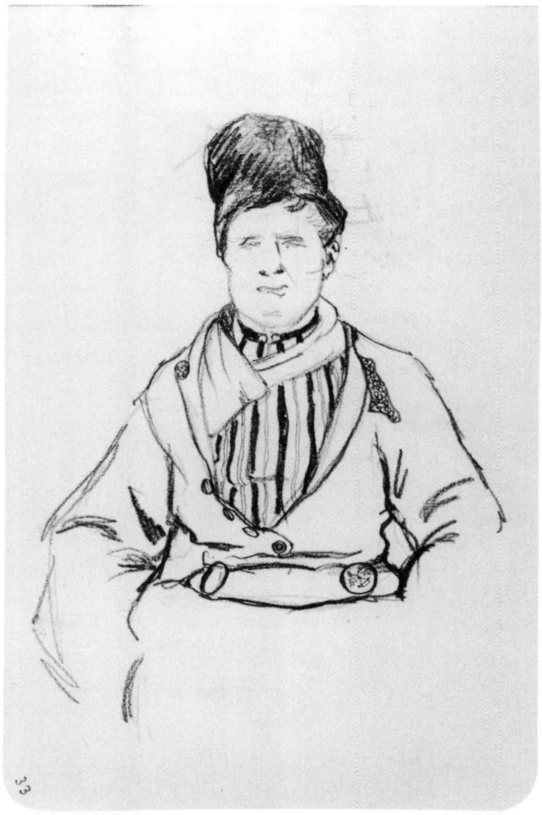

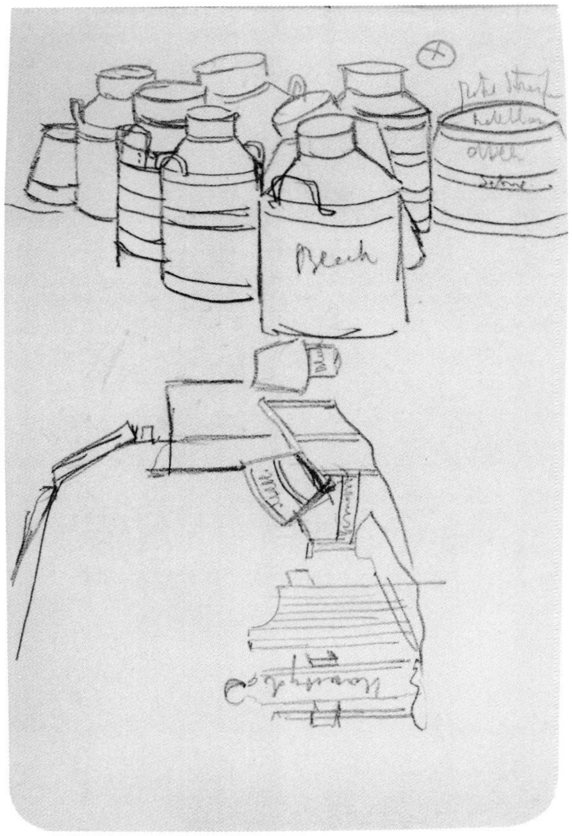

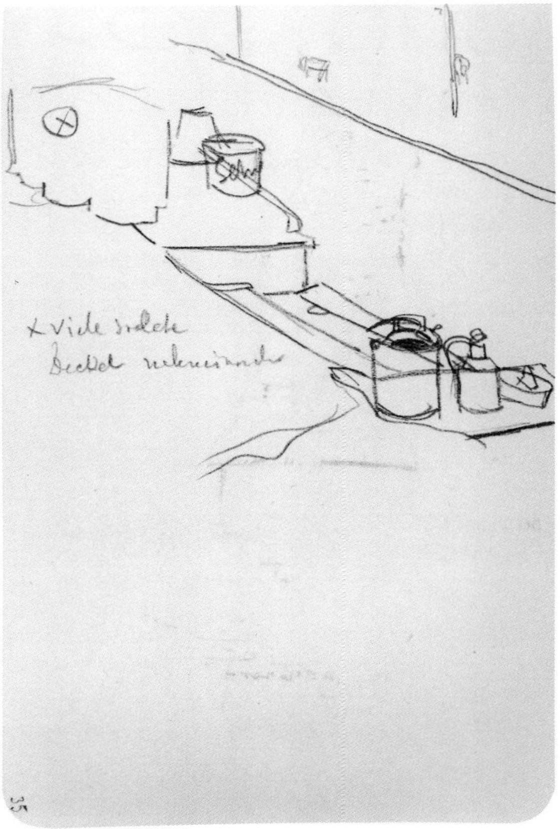

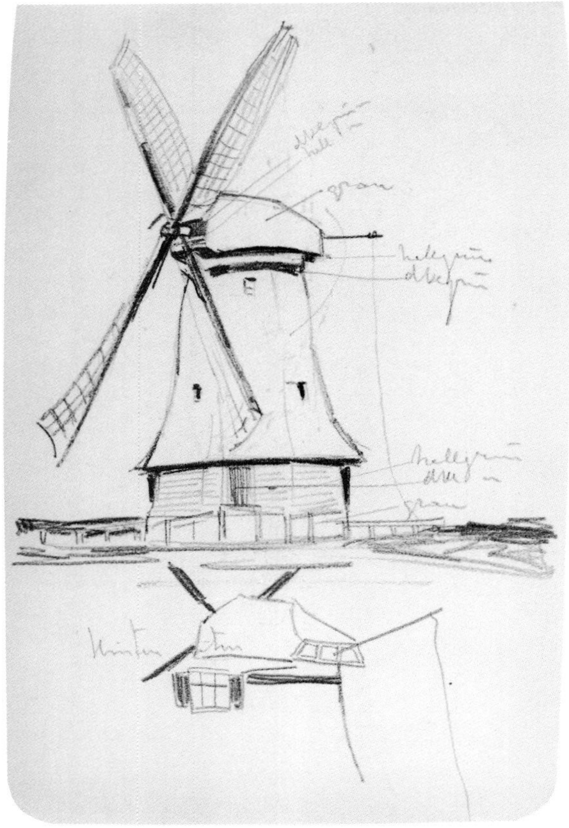

15, p.34

15, p.35

15, p.36

**p.34** Pencil sketches of milk cans
Inscribed u.c.: 'Blech' and with color notations: 'rote Streifen / hellblau / dkbl / schw / blauoxyd'

**p.35** Pencil sketch of buckets and cans
Inscribed l.l.: 'x viele solche / Deckel nebeneinander / Schw'

**p.36** Pencil study of windmill
Inscribed l.l.: 'Hinten unten' and with color notations: 'dklgrün / hell[grün] / grau / hellgrün / dklgrün'

REFERENCES
Barnett and Friedel 1995, no.147, color ill.

Münter made sketches of windmills (see 46/13, pp.25, 55), and Kandinsky included one in his tempera painting *Mühle (Holland)* of 1904 (Barnett no.141).

**p.37** Pencil sketch of houses, tree and figure in the Netherlands

**p.38** Pencil sketch of house in the Netherlands
Inscribed l.l.: 'Zi[e]gel / mit weiss. / Konturen' and with color notations: 'weiss / d grün / rt / w / schw'

**pp.39–80** Blank

Inside back cover inscribed: 'Kwadijk'
Kwadijk is a town in the Netherlands.

15, p.37

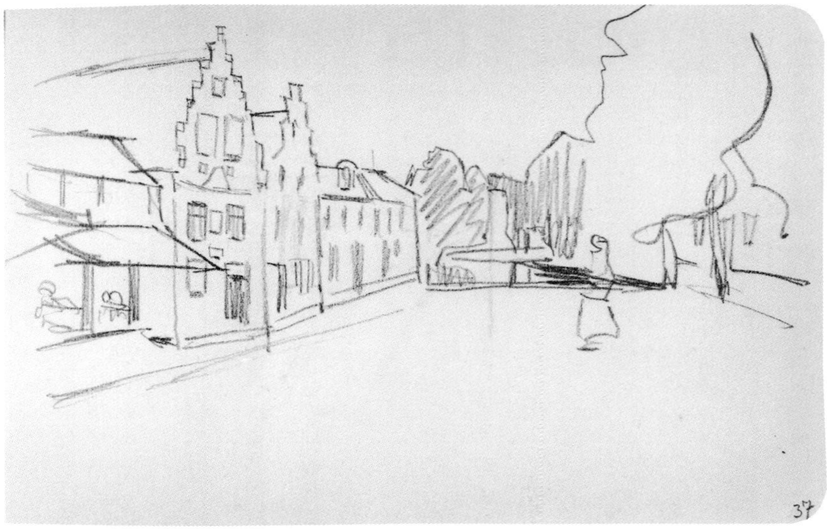

15, p.38

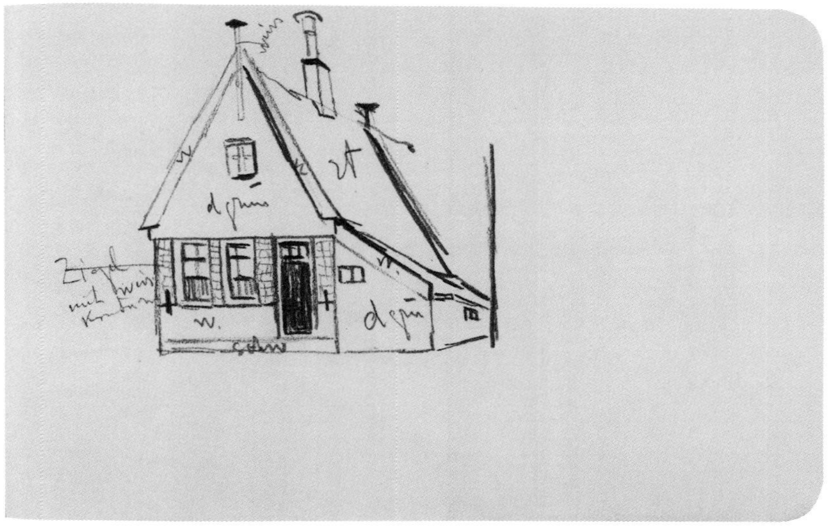

# Sketchbook 16

1904

Red leather notebook; inside front cover sticker from J.C. Konig & Ebhardt, Hannover. Stamped on front cover: 'Merkbuch'
Contains 50 pages (25 sheets), each 11.5 x 7.2 cm (4½ x 2⅞ in)
Page numbers inscribed by unknown hand at later date with odd numbers at lower right

Hanfstaengl 1974, p.156

LOCATION
Städtische Galerie im Lenbachhaus, Munich (GMS 334)

HISTORY
Gabriele Münter, Murnau, until 1957

The first fifteen pages of the notebook contain sketches made in the Netherlands in late May–June 1904, but the following pages of notes refer to Paris, Berlin, Basel, Italy and Tunisia.

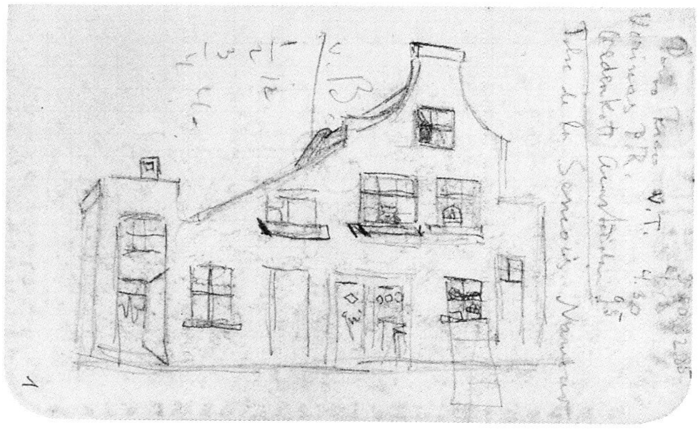

16, p.1

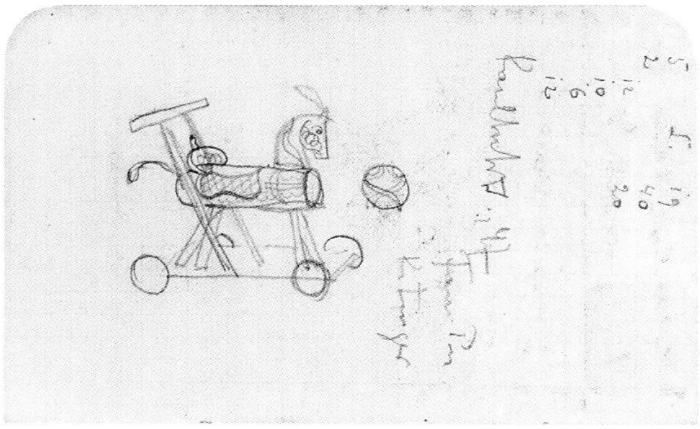

16, p.2

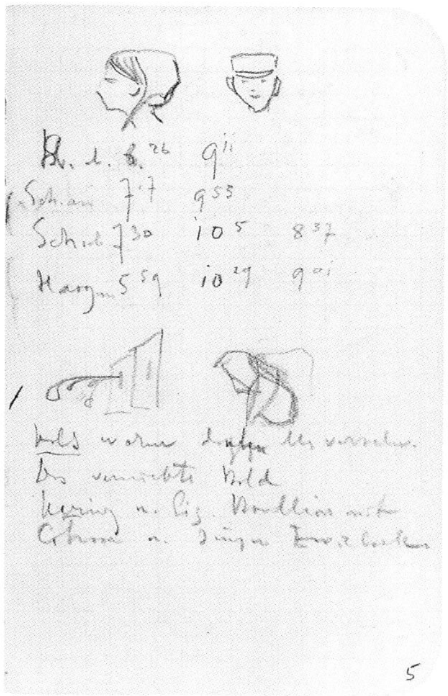

16, p.5

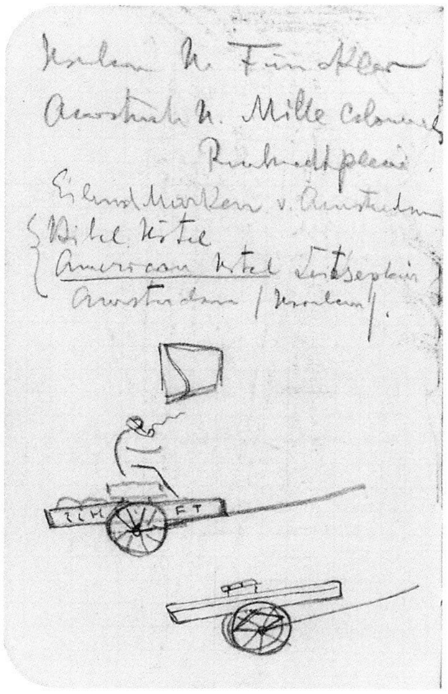

16, p.6

**p.1** Pencil sketch of house
Inscribed at r. edge: 'Porto Rico V.T. / Vorinas P.R. / Credenkott Amsterdam / Tolse de la Se[...] Namour'

**p.2** Pencil sketch of hobby horse
Inscribed at r. edge: 'Kaulbachstr.47 / Fam. Pen. / Kitinger'

REFERENCES
Podzemskaia 2000, p.154

**pp.3–4** Addresses in the Netherlands and Berlin

**p.5** Pencil sketches of heads
Inscribed with train schedule to Scheveningen and The Hague

**p.6** Pencil sketch of cart
Inscribed c.: 'American Hotel / Leitseplein / Amsterdam (Haarlem).'

Kandinsky and Gabriele Münter stayed at this hotel on the Leidseplein in Amsterdam in June 1904.

**p.7** Pencil sketch of landscape in the Netherlands

16, p.7

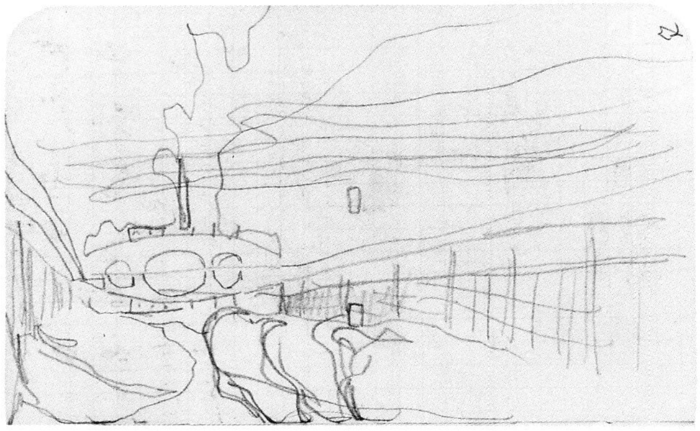

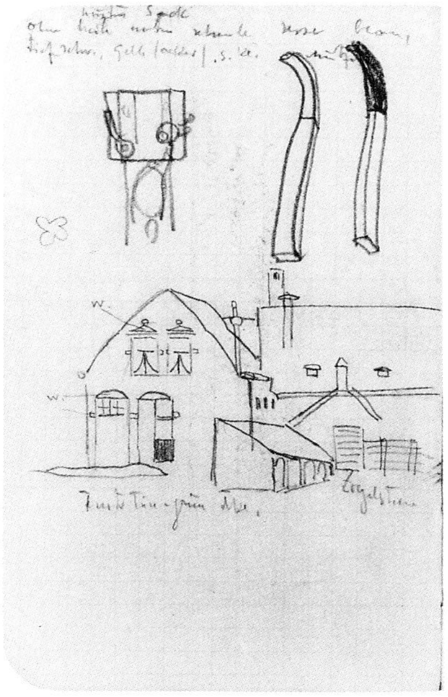

16, p.8

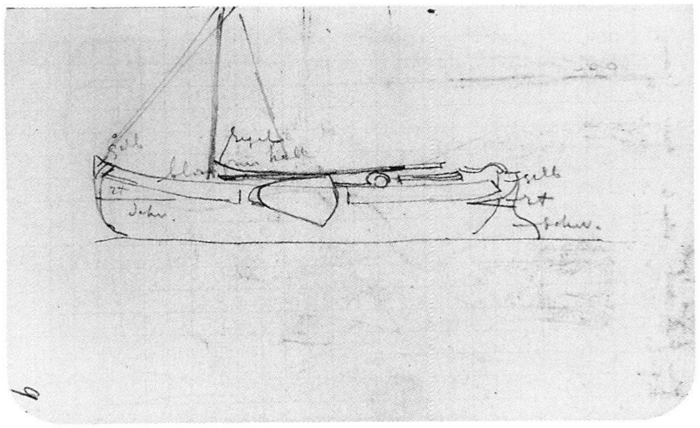

16, p.9

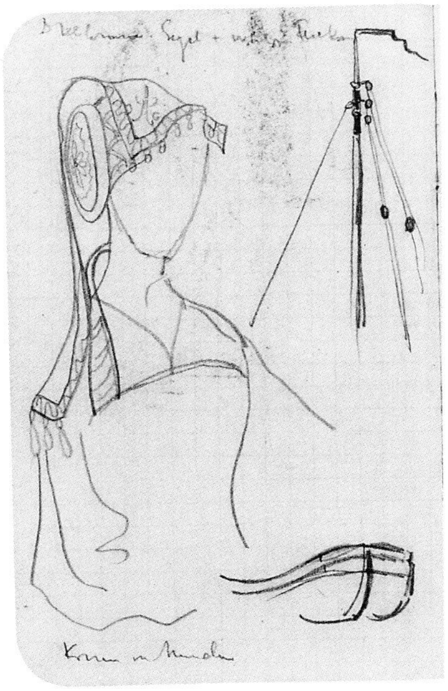

16, p.10

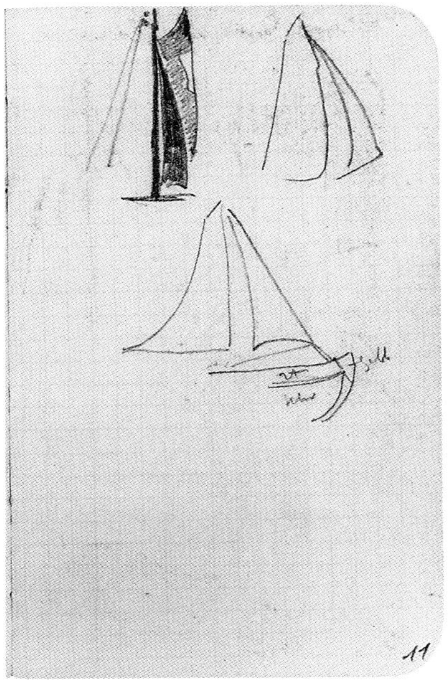

16, p.11

**p.8** Pencil sketch of Dutch farmhouse with architectural details
Inscribed below: 'Fenster Türe- grün dkl. / Ziegelsteine' and with color notations

**p.9** Pencil sketch of sailboat or 'botter'
Inscribed c.l.: 'gelb / Segel' and with color notations: 'blau grün hell / rt / schw.'

REFERENCES
Hanfstaengl 1974, p.156
Barnett 1992, p.140

Kandinsky included the sailboat in *Die Schiffe (Holland)* of 1904 (Barnett no.140).

**p.10** Pencil sketch of woman with embroidered cap and of rigging for sailboat
Inscribed above: 'Dklbraun Segel + weisse Flicken' and below: 'K[...] in Munchn'

**p.11** Pencil sketches of sails and keel
Inscribed with color notations: 'rt / gelb / schw.'

**p.12** Pencil study for *Samstag Abend (Holland)* of 1904

REFERENCES
Hanfstaengl 1974, p.156, ill.
Barnett 1992, p.142

Later Kandinsky developed this sketch into the tempera painting *Samstag Abend (Holland)* of 1904 (Barnett no.142).

**p.13** Train schedule refers to Kwadijk (see inside back cover of Sketchbook 15)

**p.14** Pencil study for *Mühle (Holland)* of 1904
Inscribed c.l.: 'Häuser / t. blau'

REFERENCES
Hanfstaengl 1974, p.156, ill.
Barnett 1992, p.141
Barnett and Friedel 1995, no.148, color ill.
Podzemskaia 2000, p.87

This sketch is a study for *Mühle (Holland)* of 1904 (Barnett no.141).

16, p.12

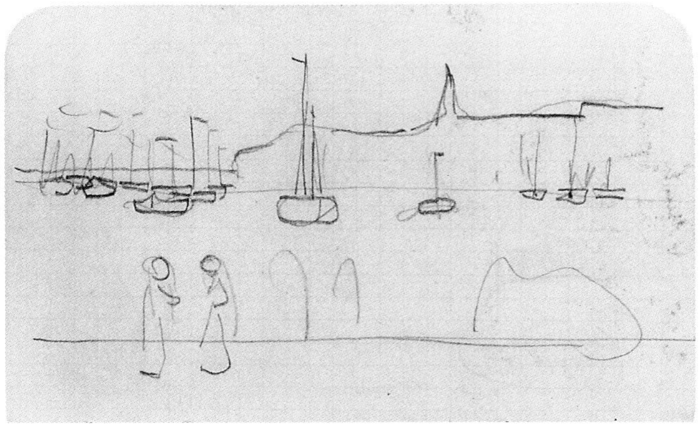

16, p 14

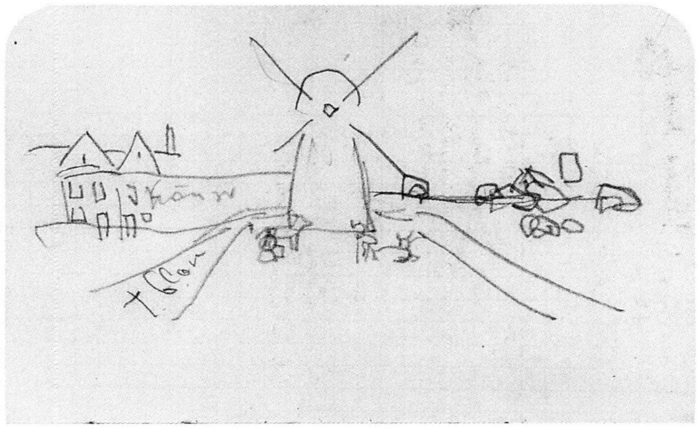

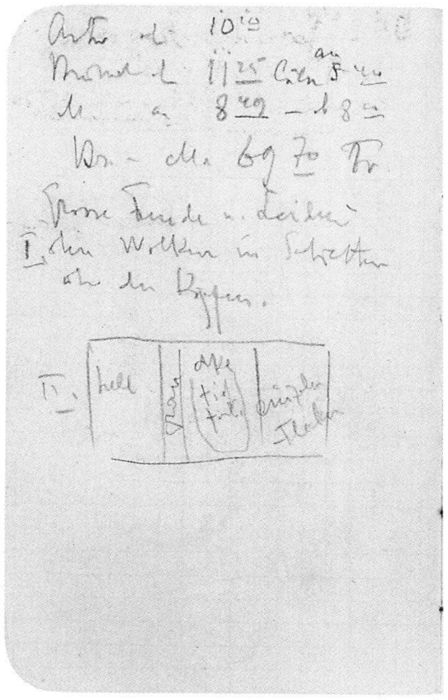

16, p.16

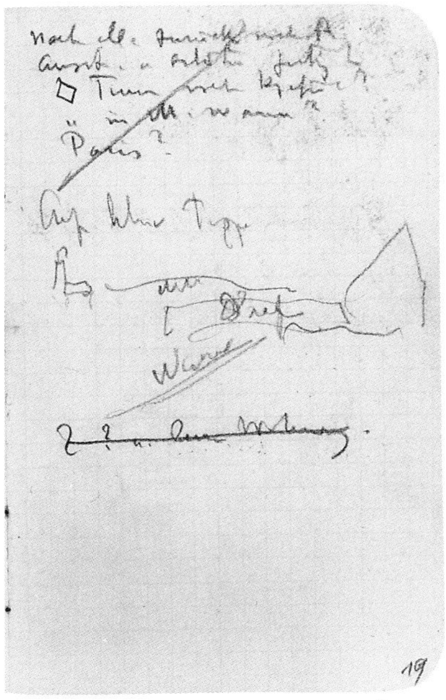

16, p.19

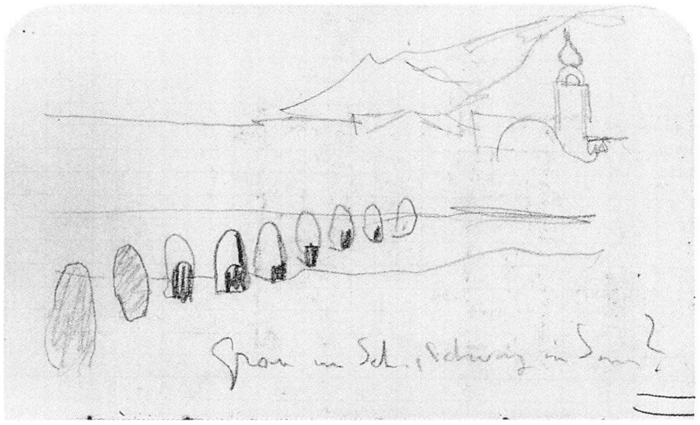

16, p.20

**pp.15** Notes related to the Netherlands

**p.16** Pencil sketch of triptych
Inscribed above with train schedule from Arnheim to Cologne and u.c.: 'Grosse Freude u. Leiden / I. oben Wolken in Schichten / über den Köpfen.'; c.l.: 'II. / hell / grau' c.: 'dkl / tief / Farbe'; c.r.: 'einzelne / Flecken'

**pp.17–18** Notes related to Paris and travel tour of Phalanx exhibitions

**p.19** Pencil sketch of landscape
Inscribed u.c.: 'Nach M. zurück schicken / Ausst. u. Arbeiten fertig? / Turnus nach Krefeld? / [Turnus] in M. wann? / Paris?'; c.: 'Auf kleiner Treppe / dkl / [...] / Warm'

**p.20** Pencil sketch of landscape with mountains and church
Inscribed below: 'Grau in Sch., Schwarz in Sonn[e]?'

REFERENCES
Hanfstaengl 1974, p.156, ill.

**pp.21–25** Notes (in mainly illegible Cyrillic) about Paris and Italy (Florence, Lago di Garda, Bordighera)

**p.26** Notes about *Mercure de France*, Meier Graefe, *Kunst und Künstler*

**pp.27–29** Notes and lists about Paris, Berlin and artists (Max Liebermann)

**p.30** Inscribed above: 'Bab-el-Souïka / Tunisie (Dom + / Mrktpltz). / Le soir à Ch[...]t / Simonson' and below: 'Hintergrund bläulich / damit Brust im Tor / Kleid rosa auf weiss / Bühnen beleuc[h]t[un]g vorne Di- / rigent u. Publikum schwarz / auch Man[n] schwarz oben / mit grün Hdwekh. Dk. / grüne im Hintergrund / Bäume.'

**p.31** Pencil sketch of woman on stage described on facing page (p.30).

REFERENCES
Hanfstaengl 1974, p.156, ill.

**pp.32–33** Blank

**p.34** Pencil sketch (not illustrated)

**pp.35–37** Lists of clothes and notes about Paris

**pp.38–41** Blank

**p.42** Pencil sketch of flower (not illustrated)

**pp.44–50** Lists of packing boxes and notes about Basel (Hotel Krafft), Geneva (Hotel National) and Paris

Inside back cover inscribed above: '20-25 Berlin / 26-29 Köln / 1-8 Nijmegen'; below: 'R. d'Assas et rue Barra / Hotel Pension Lu- / xembg'

16, pp.30-31

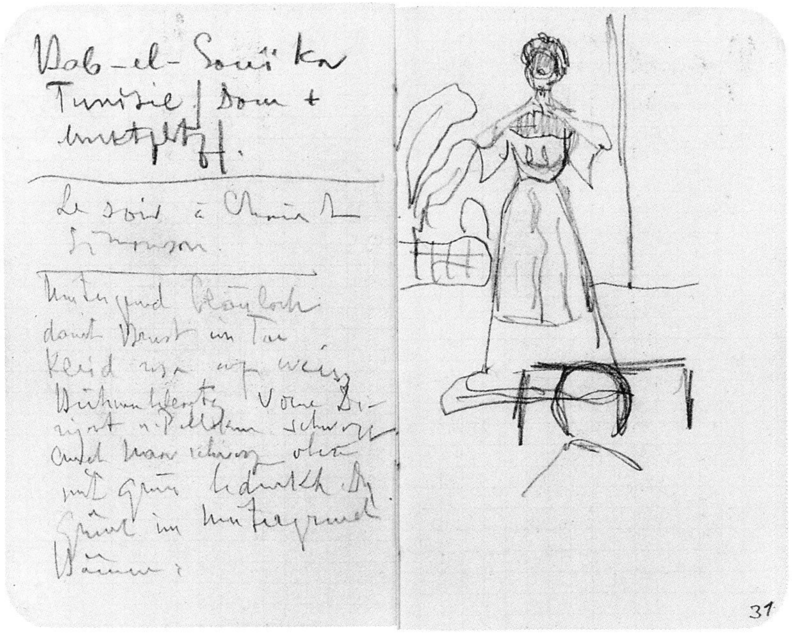

# Sketchbook 17

prepared with the assistance of Cristina Ashjian

1904–1905

Grey cardboard sketchbook with black spine; inside front cover label from Franz Dury, Munich
Contains 40 pages (20 sheets), each 16.6 x 11 cm (6½ x 4⅜ in)
Page numbers inscribed by unknown hand at later date with odd numbers at lower right

Hanfstaengl 1974, p.145

LOCATION
Städtische Galerie im Lenbachhaus, Munich (GMS 326)

HISTORY
Gabriele Münter, Murnau, until 1957

Kandinsky and Gabriele Münter arrived in Tunisia on Christmas Day 1904 and stayed there until 5 April 1905. The sketchbook resembles Sketchbook 18, which Kandinsky also purchased at Dury and took with him to Tunisia.

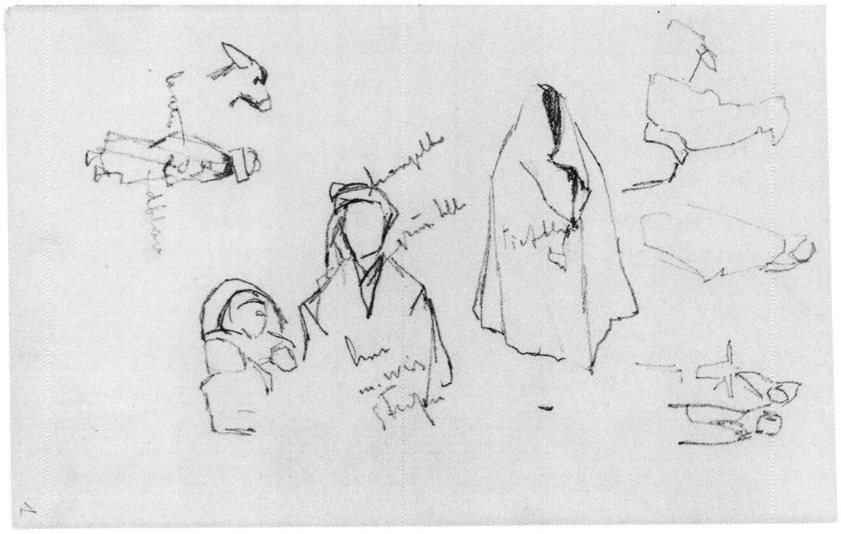

17, p.1

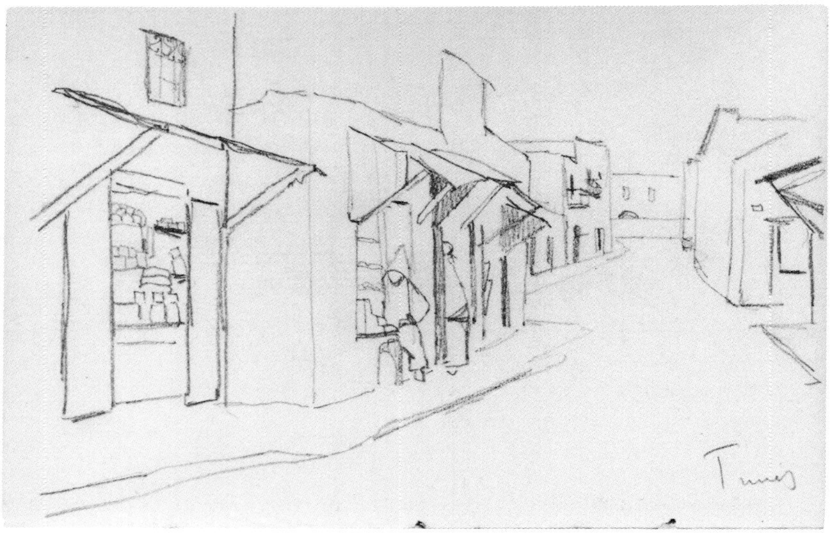


17, p.2

17, p.3

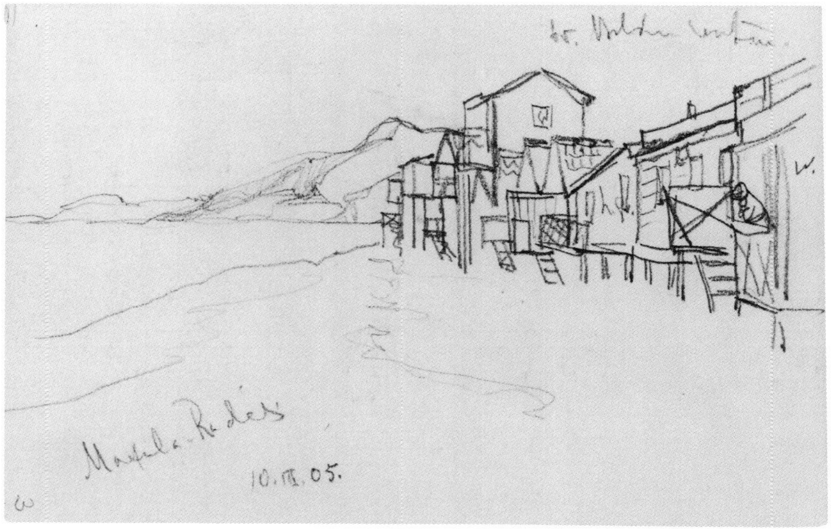

**p.1** Pencil sketches of figures in costume
Inscribed c.: 'braungelb / grün h[e]ll / bra[u]n / m. weis. / Streifen / tiefblau'; l. edge: 'braun / d. blau'

**p.2** Pencil sketch of street with shops
Inscribed l.r.: 'Tunis'

REFERENCES
Hanfstaengl 1974, p.145, ill.
Ashjian 2001, p.73, fig.82

Münter made a similar sketch, which she dated 30 December 1904 (37/7, p.33). According to Cristina Ashjian, the street is probably rue Bab el-Khadra in the medina or old city of Tunis.

**p.3** Pencil sketch of houses on beach
Inscribed l.l.: 'Maxula-Rades'; u.r.: 'br. Balken unten'; and dated l.l. by Münter: '10.III.05'

REFERENCES
Hanfstaengl 1974, p.145, ill.
Ashjian 2001, pp.114–115, fig.191

Kandinsky sketched wooden bathhouses on the beach at Maxula-Rades south of Tunis. The drawing was done on 10 March 1905, the same day that Münter made a sketch (46/17, p.1).

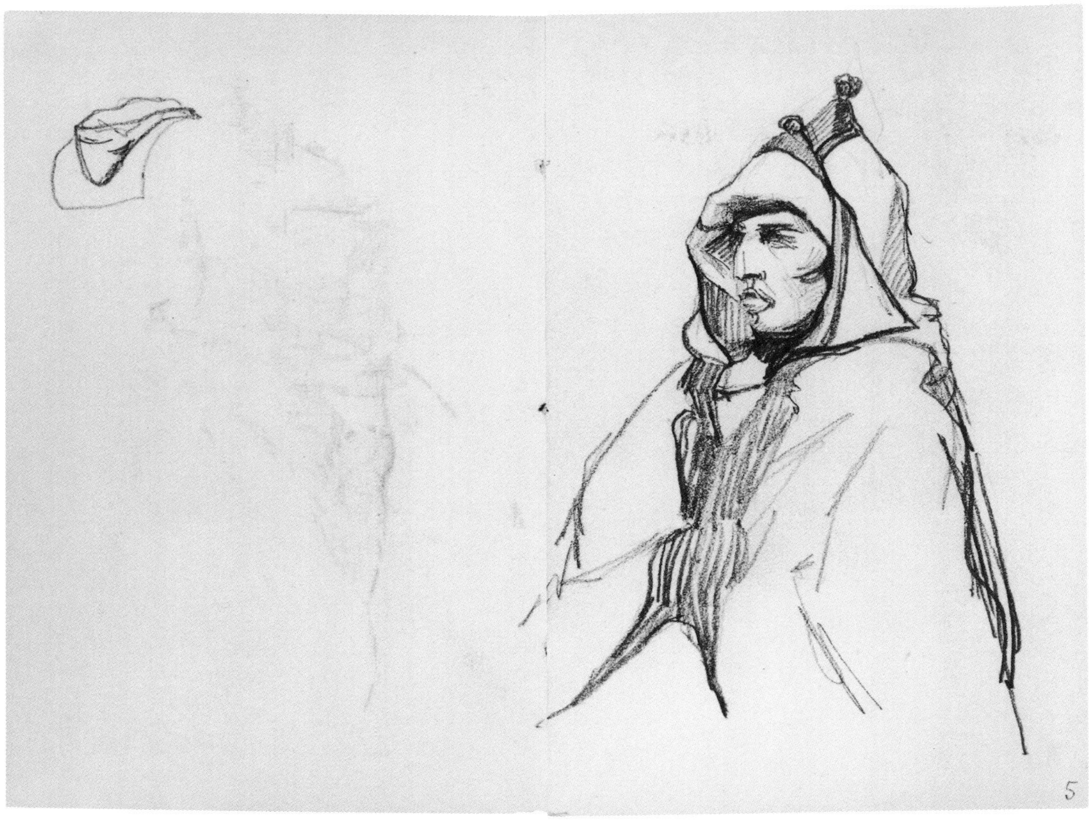

17, pp.4-5

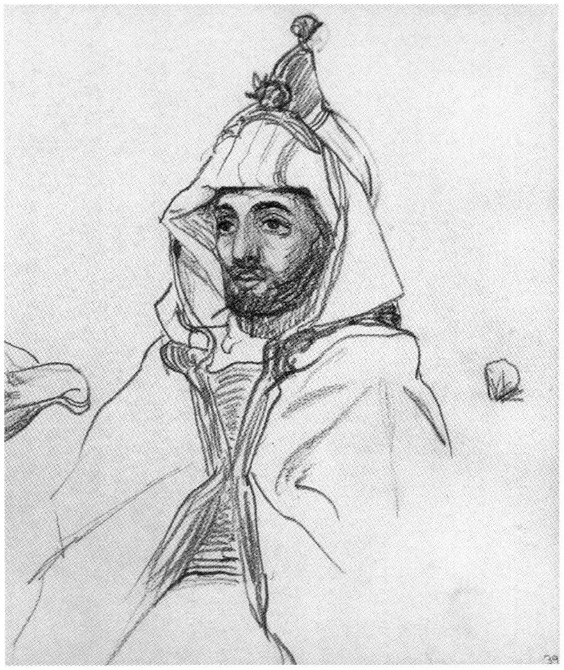

fig.a

**p.4** Pencil sketch of saddle

**p.5** Pencil sketch of male figure

REFERENCES
Barnett and Friedel 1995, no.177, color ill.
Ashjian 2001, p.86, fig.125

The same man is shown in profile on p.7 and in a sketch made by Münter on 2 January 1905 (fig.a; 37/7, p.39). Ashjian has observed that the hooded clothing is that usually worn by agricultural workers in Tunisia.

(See color plate p.121)

17, pp.6-7

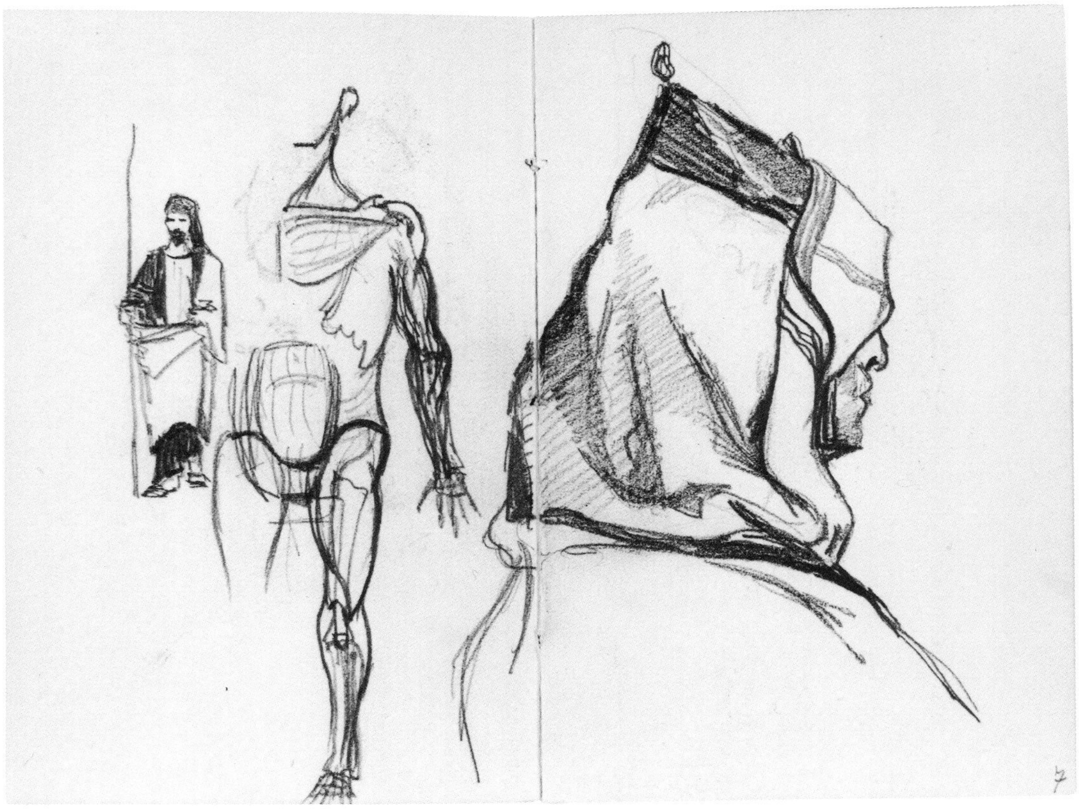

**pp.6–7** Pencil sketches of male figures and nude

REFERENCES
Hanfstaengl 1974, p.145, ill.
Ashjian 2001, p.86, fig.125

The distinctive hood is also found on p.5, where the same man is portrayed.

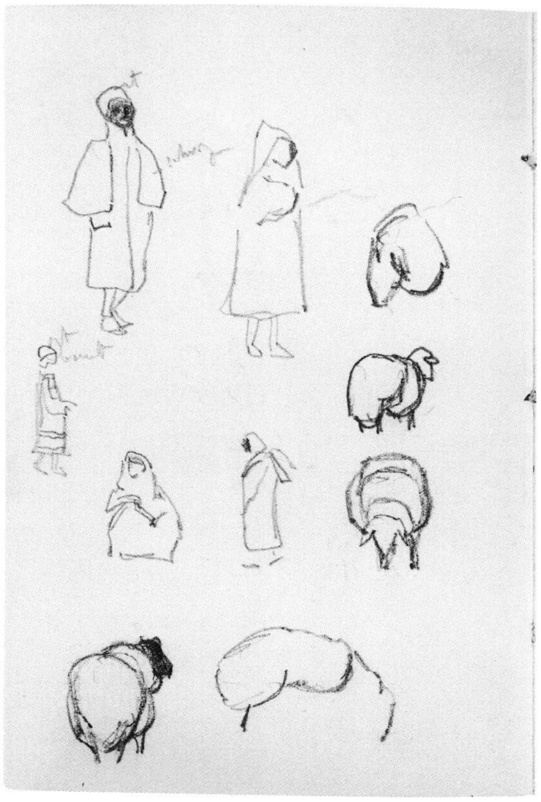

17, p.8

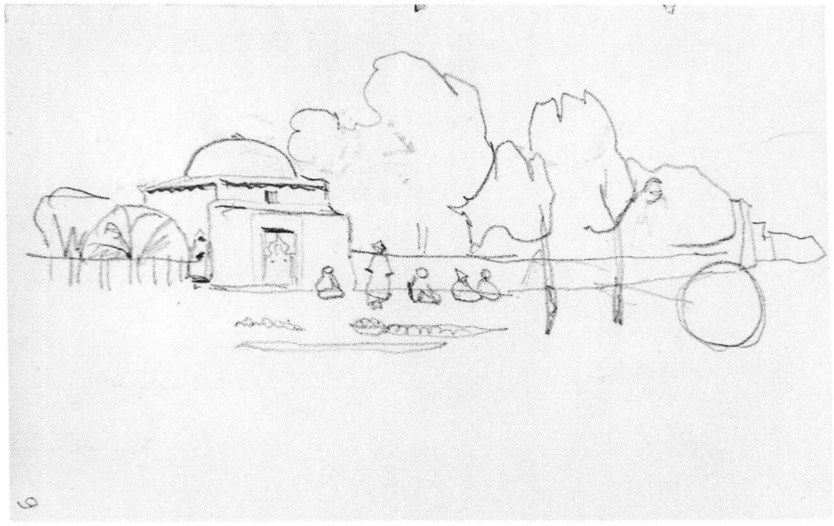

17, p.9

**p.8** Pencil sketches of figures and sheep
Inscribed u.l.: 'rt / schwrz / rt / bunt'

REFERENCES
Barnett 1992, p.163

The sketches are related to *Fest der Schafe* of 1905 (Barnett no.173). The festival observed by Kandinsky in mid-February 1905 was actually the Id al-Adha (feast of sacrifice).

**p.9** Pencil study for *Orangenverkäufer* of 1905

REFERENCES
Hanfstaengl 1974, p.145, ill.
Barnett 1992, p.156
Ashjian 2001, pp.112–113, fig.182

Kandinsky's sketch depicts a marabout or the tomb of a holy man. He developed this study with building, trees and figures selling oranges in his tempera painting *Orangenverkäufer* of 1905 (Barnett no.164). Likewise, Münter did a sketch of the same subject on 3 January 1905 (37/7, p.43), which she later made into a color lithograph entitled *Marabout*.

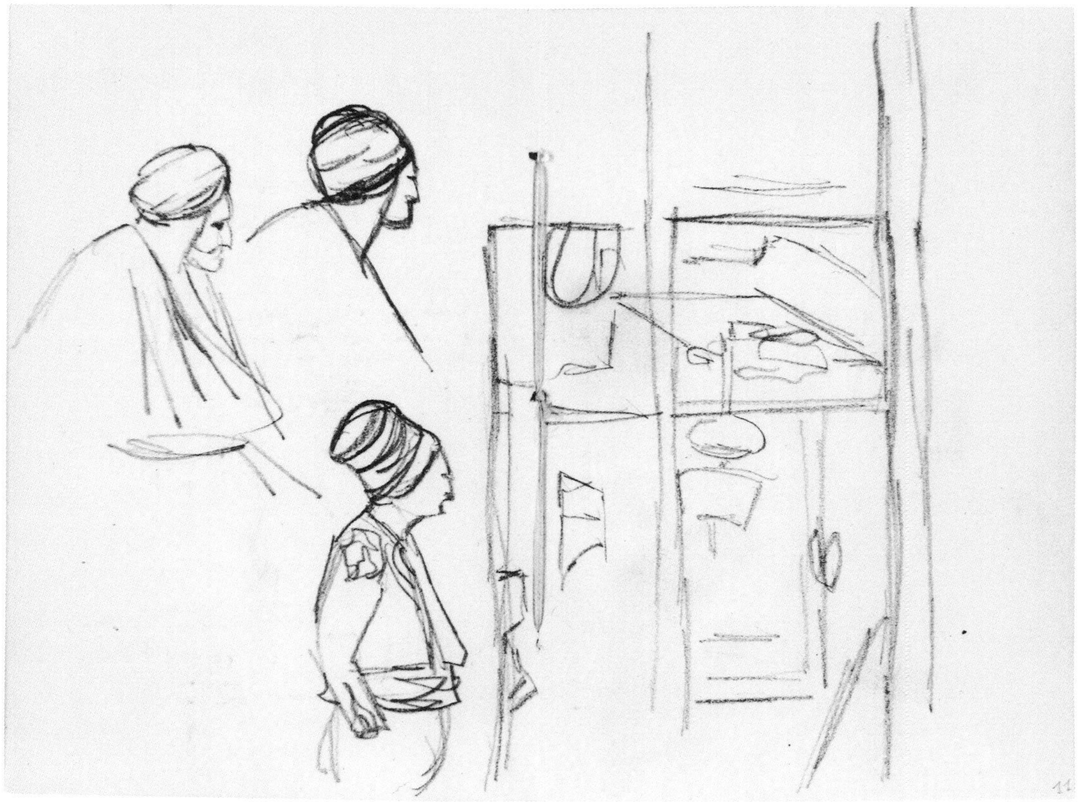

17, pp.10–11

**pp.10–11** Pencil sketches of men wearing turbans and interior scene (upside down)

REFERENCES
Ashjian 2001, pp.83–84, fig.110

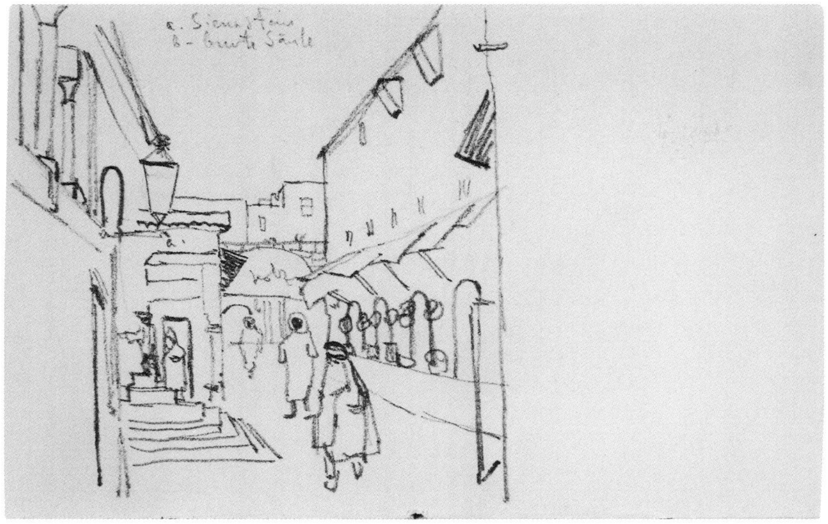

17, p.12

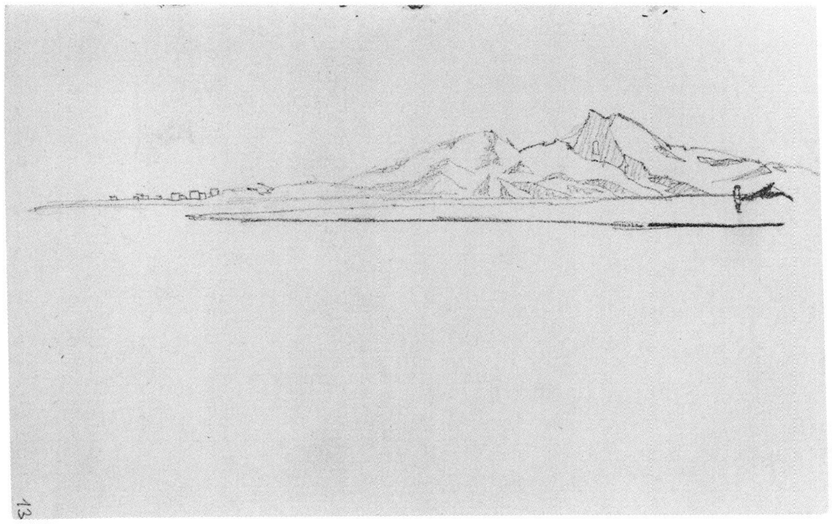

17, p.13

**p.12** Pencil study for *Strasse in Tunis* of 1905
Inscribed u.c.: 'a. Sienastein / b- bunte Säule'; c.: 'Holz'

REFERENCES
Hanfstaengl 1974, p.145, ill.
Barnett 1992, p.161
Ashjian 2001, pp.79–80, fig.97

Kandinsky's tempera painting *Strasse in Tunis* of 1905 (Barnett no.170) is based on this sketch. It depicts the principal entrance to the Zitouna Mosque located in the Souk el-Attarine of Tunis (information kindly provided by Cristina Ashjian).

**p.13** Pencil sketch of landscape with the Bou Cornein mountains

Münter made a sketch of the same mountains (37/7, p.47). Ashjian identified the view and noted that it appears in the background of a painting by Münter, *Landschaft mit blauem Berg* of 1905.

**pp.14–15** Pencil sketch of villas and figures

The figures in the foreground may be related to those in *Arbeitende Neger* of 1905 (Barnett no.174).

17, pp.14-15

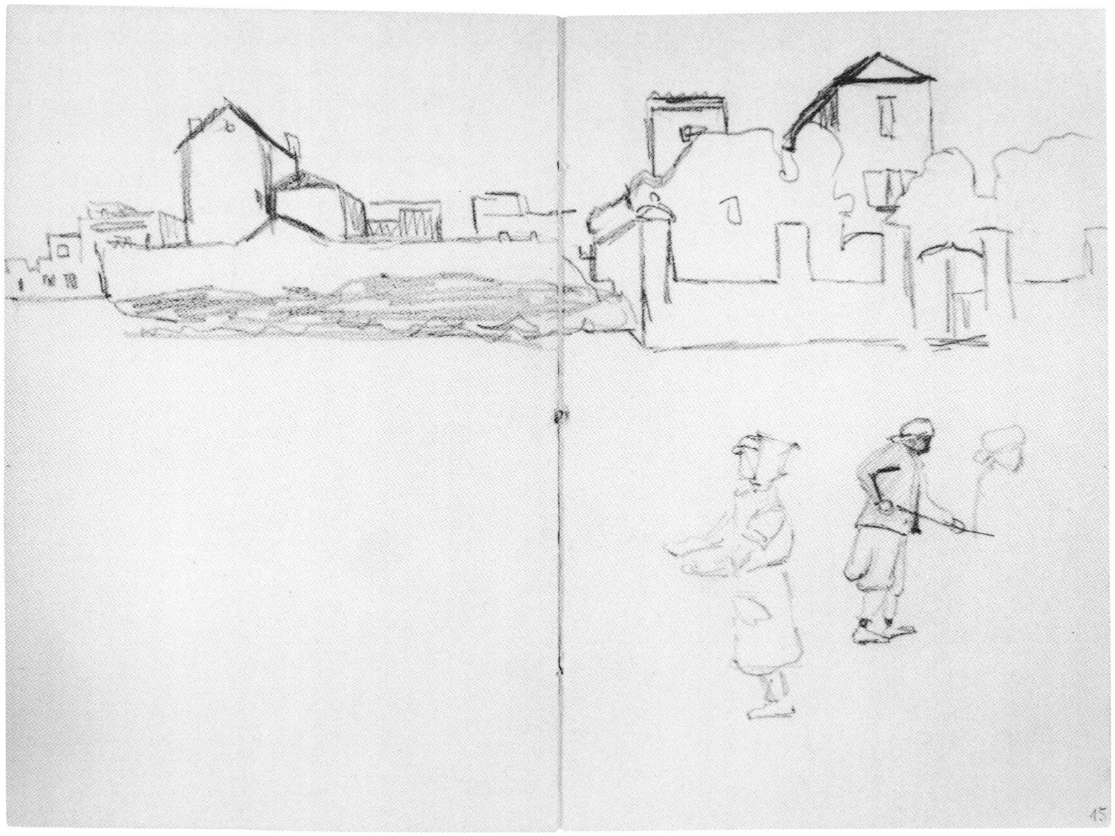

**p.16** Pencil sketch of camels

The camels with their distinctive saddlebags are found in Kandinsky's tempera painting *Platz in Tunis (Kamele)* of 1905 (Barnett no.154).

**p.17** Pencil sketch of camels

There are also photographs taken by Gabriele Münter or Kandinsky of camels outside Tunis.

**p.18** Pencil sketch of street with shops (upside down)

According to Ashjian, the street is one in the Tunis medina, most likely the rue Halfaouine in the Bab Souika quarter.

**p.19** Pencil sketch of turban graves
Inscribed u.l.: '1- rot / 2- grün'

According to Ashjian, turban graves were found in the Sidi Bel-Hassen Cemetery on the outskirts of Tunis as well as at the private mausoleum in the city known as the Tourbet el-Bey. Münter made a sketch of the same grave (46/16, p.18). See also p.26 (below).

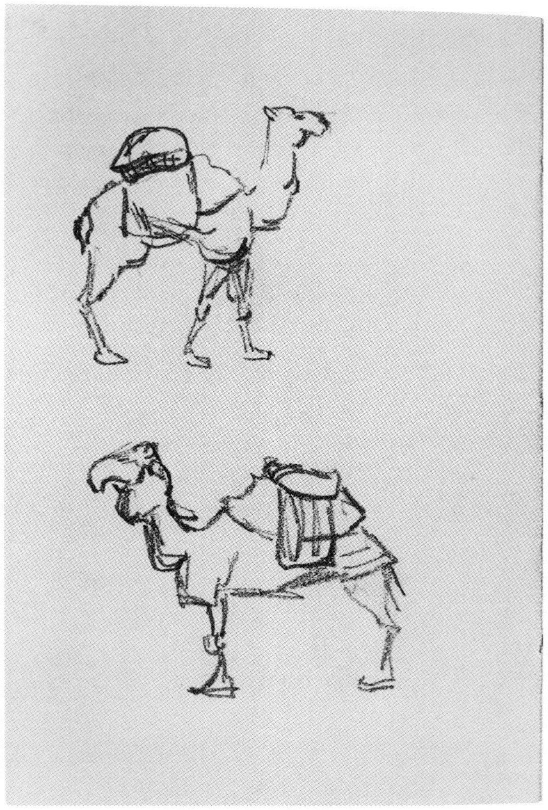

17, p.16

17, p.17

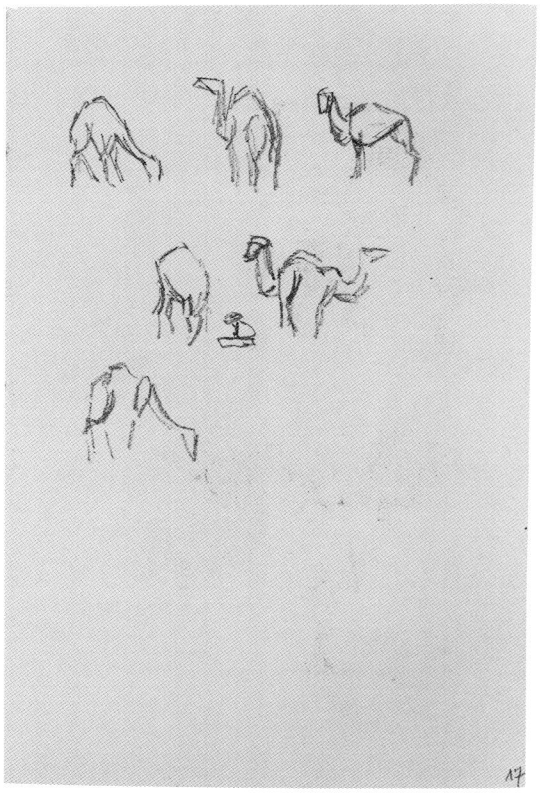


17, pp.18-19

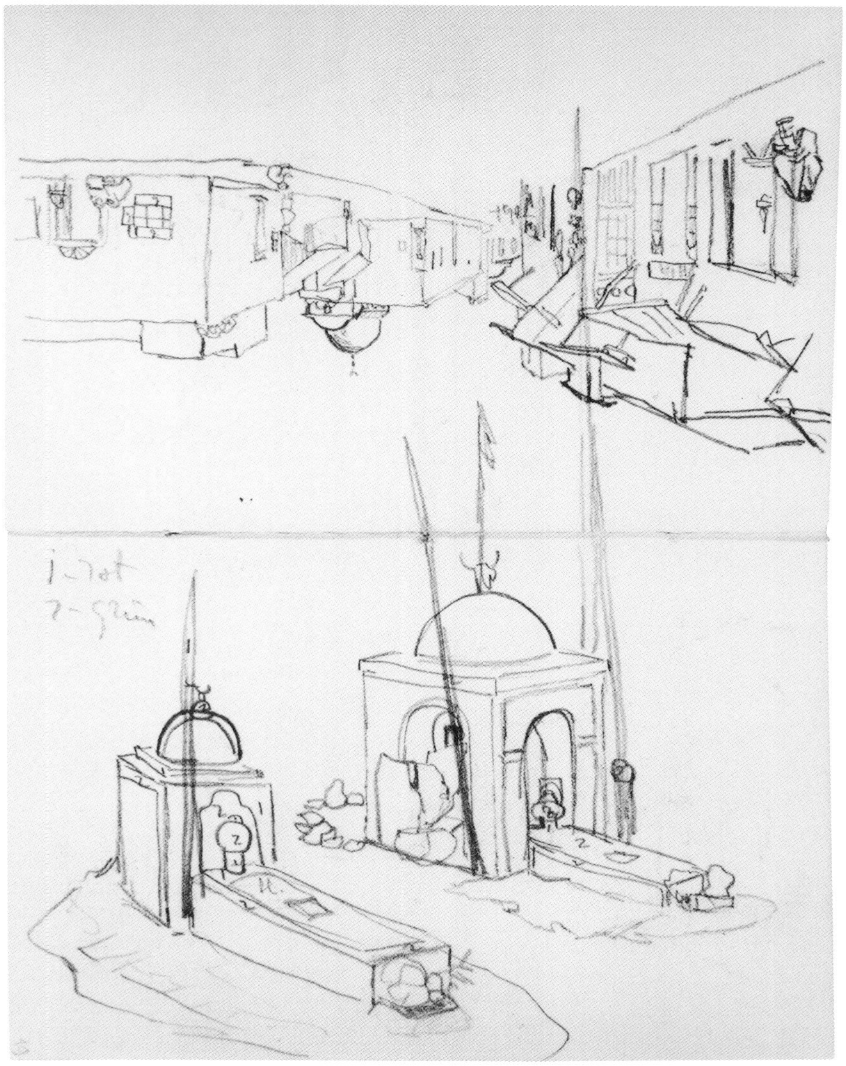

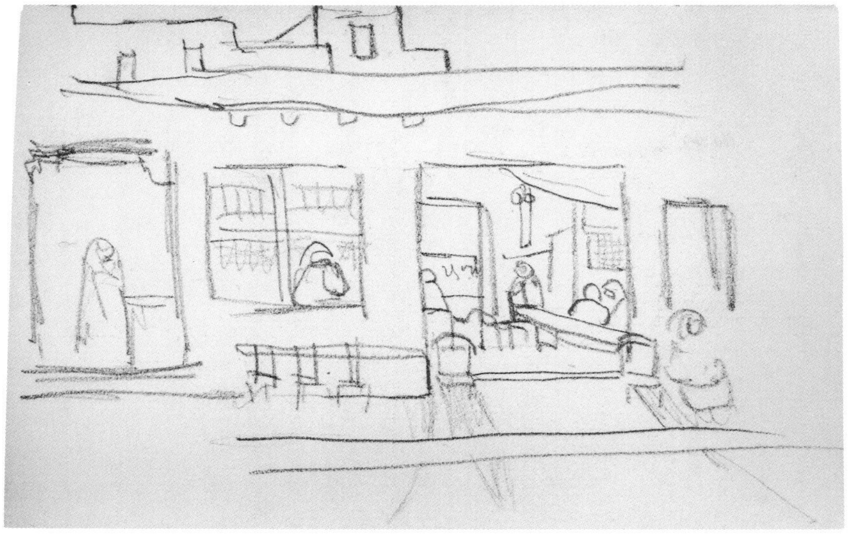

17, p.20

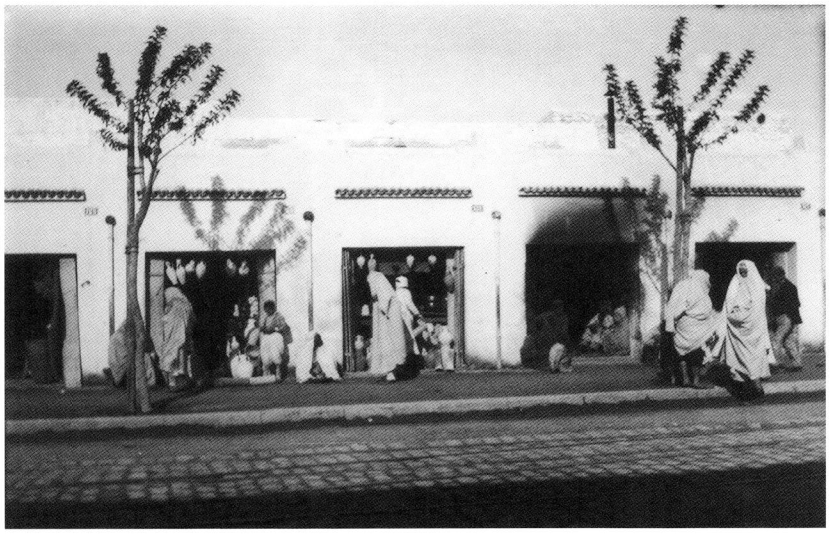

fig.b

**p.20** Pencil study for *Café (Abend)* of 1905
Inscribed c.: 'rs w.'

REFERENCES
Hanfstaengl 1974, p.145, ill.
Barnett 1992, p.156
Ashjian 2001, p.84, fig.116

The sketch is preparatory to *Café (Abend)* of 1905 (Barnett no.165). There are several photographs taken by Münter or Kandinsky of cafés in Tunis (fig.b).

**p.21** Pencil sketch of landscape with villas
Inscribed l.l.: 'Sidi-Bou-Saïd' and with color notations: 'hellbl. / blau / grün-rt / s.grün / gelbrosa Erde / K / grün matt'

REFERENCES
Barnett and Friedel 1995, no.169, color ill.
Ashjian 2001, p.109, fig.173

As indicated by the artist's inscription, the drawing was made in Sidi-Bou-Said, the seaside town north of Tunis.

**p.22** Pencil sketch of place el-Halfaouine

REFERENCES
Ashjian 2001, pp.88, 99, fig.136

According to Ashjian, temporary tents and structures were erected in the place el-Halfaouine (seen here with the Halfaouine Mosque in the background) for the Id al-Adha celebration in Tunis. Kandinsky's tempera painting *Fest der Schafe* of 1905 (Barnett no.173) depicted the festival, which took place in mid-February 1905.

17, p.21

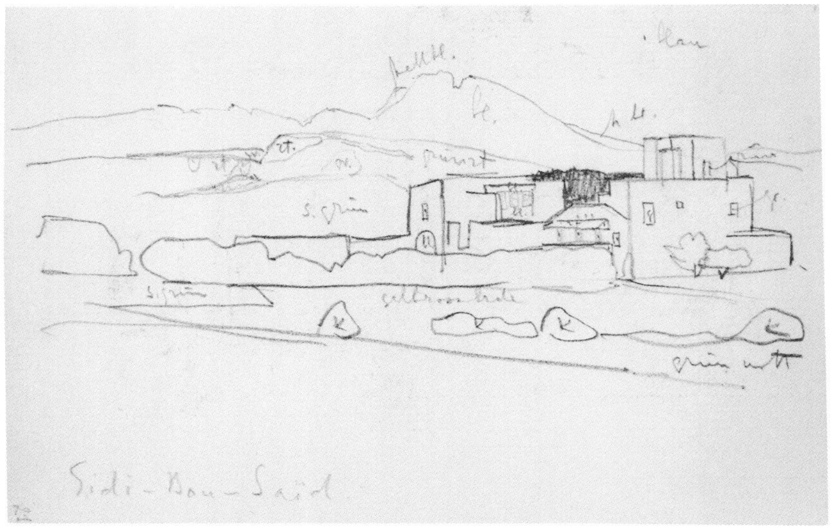

17, p.22

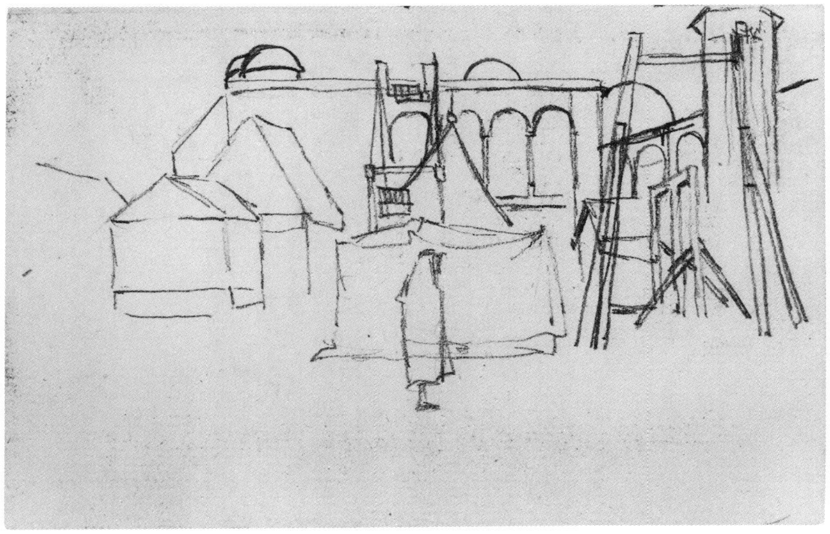

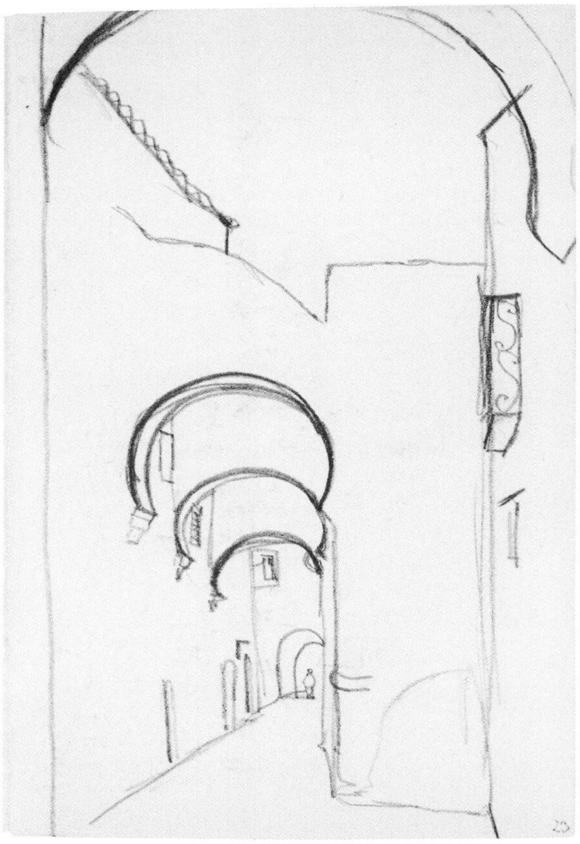

17, p.23

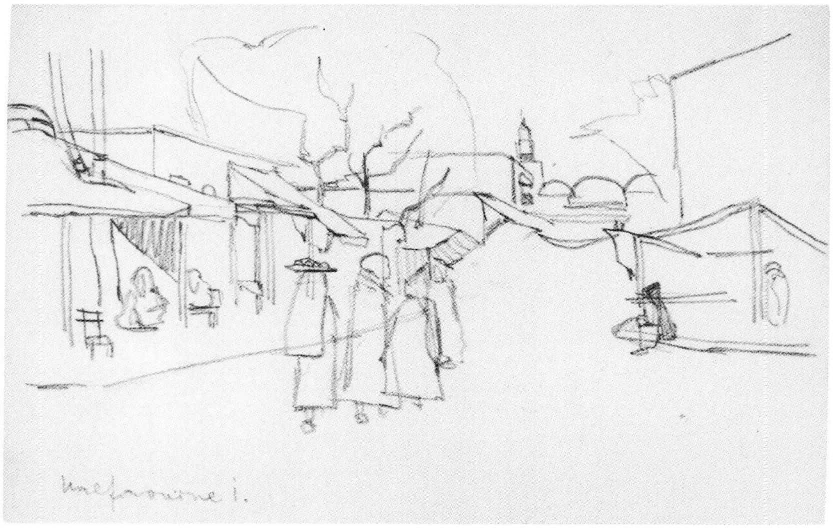

17, p.24

17, p.25

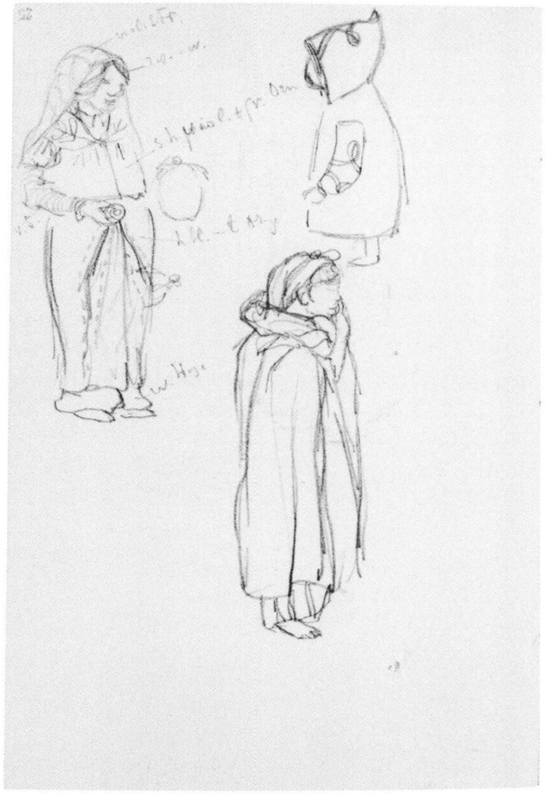

**p.23** Pencil sketch of street with buildings

**p.24** Pencil sketch of shops and figures
Inscribed l.l.: 'Halfaouine 1.'

REFERENCES
Ashjian 2001, p.73, fig.83

The rue Halfaouine is a busy thoroughfare in the northern Bab Souika quarter of Tunis, connecting the place el-Halfaouine and place Bab Souika to the south.

**p.25** Pencil sketch of figures
Inscribed with color notations: 'viol. Str[eifen] / ros + w. / s.h. viol. + gr. Orn / h. bl. mit orange / w. Hose'

REFERENCES
Podzemskaia 2000, p.135, ill.30
Ashjian 2001, p.92, fig.153

Ashjian observed that the woman on the left wears a distinctive Jewish costume and suggested that Kandinsky made the sketches in the village of El-Ariana, which was known to European visitors specifically for its Sunday promenade of colorful costumes.

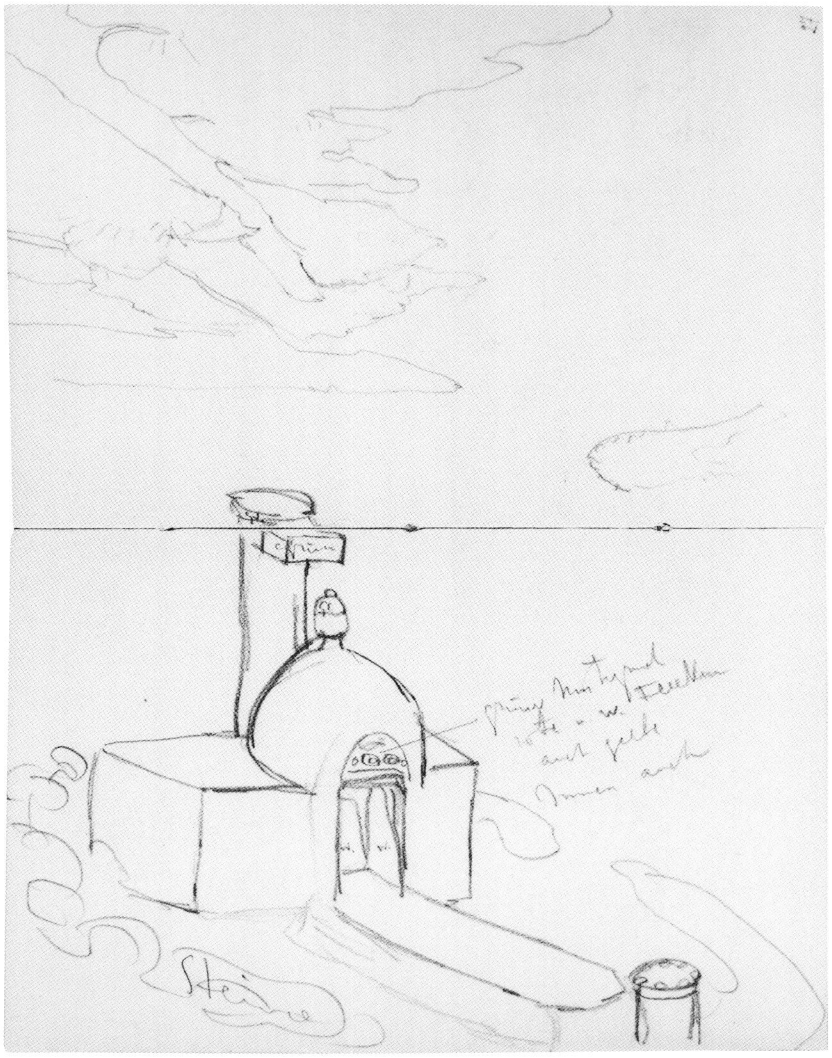

17, pp.26-27

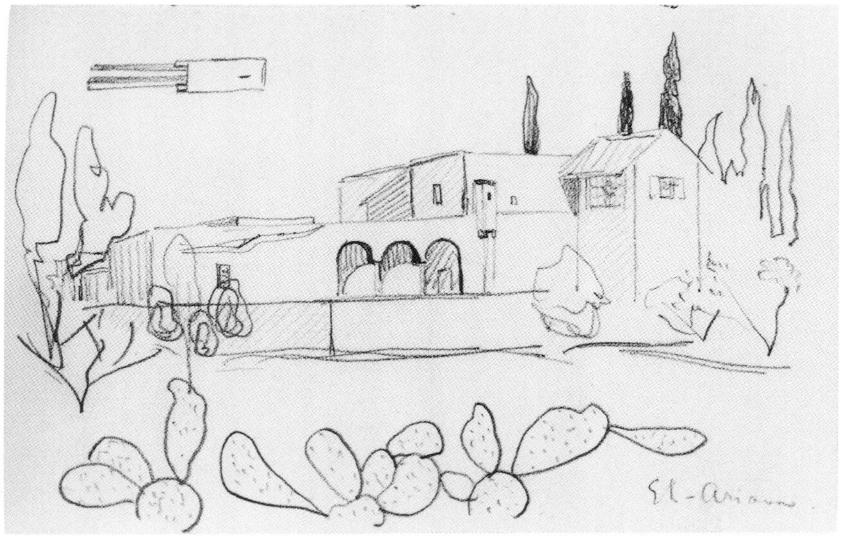


17, p.28

17, p.29

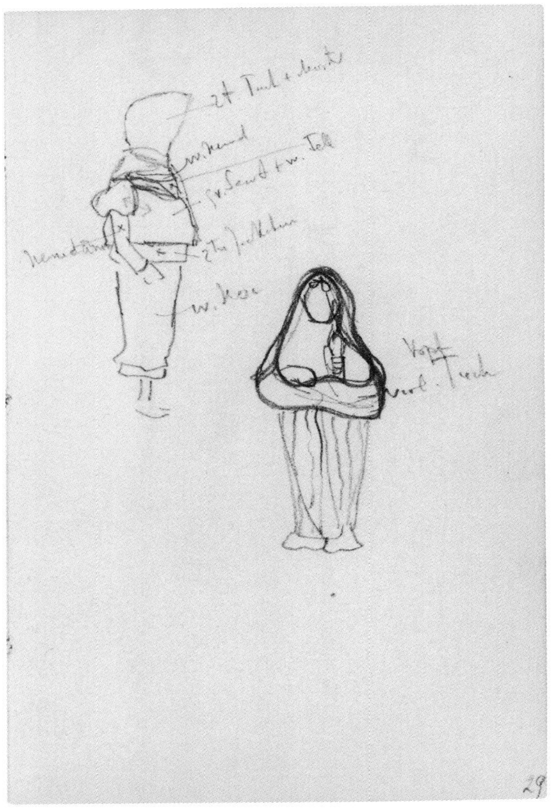

**p.26** Pencil sketch of turban grave
Inscribed u.c.: 'rt. / grün'; c.: 'grüner Hintergrund / rote u. w. Flecken / auch gelbe / Innen auch'; l.l.: 'Steine'

According to Ashjian, the red and green colors and the script indicate that this turban grave marks the burial place of a holy man.

**p.27** Pencil sketch of landscape

**p.28** Pencil sketch of villa
Inscribed l.r.: 'El-Ariana'

REFERENCES
Barnett and Friedel 1995, no.170, color ill.
Ashjian 2001, p.92, fig.155

Münter made a similar sketch of a villa with a cactus in the foreground (46/16, p.51) and wrote on the facing page 'El Ariana 9. III. 05.' El-Ariana was a popular excursion to the north of Tunis.

**p.29** Pencil sketches of figures
Inscribed u.c.: 'rt. Tuch + Muster / w. Hemd / gr. Samt + w. Fell'; c.l.: 'Hemdärmel'; c.: 'rtes Jackchen / w. Hose'; l.r.: 'Kopf / viol. Tuch'

REFERENCES
Ashjian 2001, pp.92–93, fig.154

These sketches of clothes worn by Jewish women may also have been done in El-Ariana.

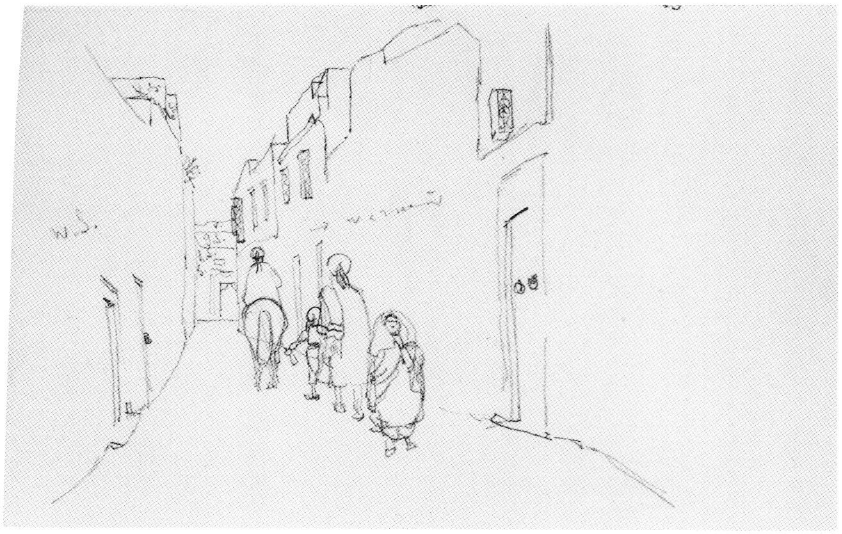

17, p.30

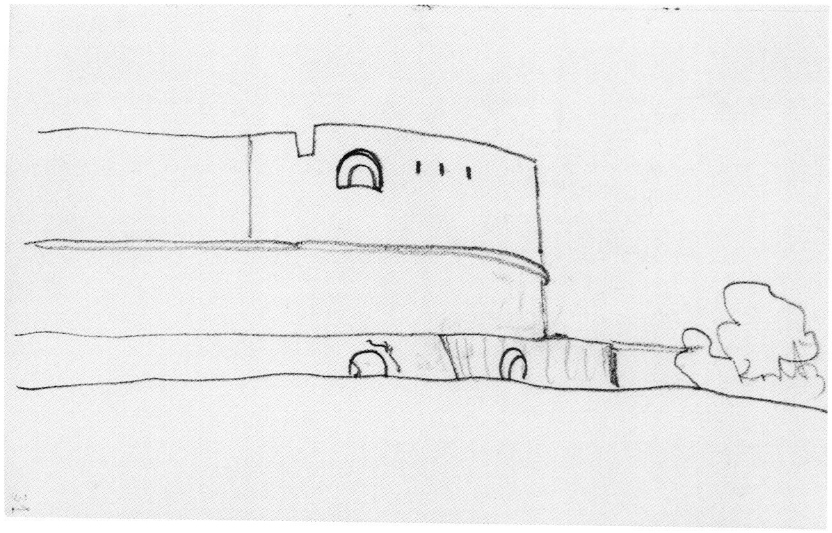

17, p.31

**p.30** Pencil sketch of street with figures
Inscribed c.l.: 'w. S.'; c.: 'g.s. / b.s. / S.', c.r.: 'warmer'

This study was probably done in the medina in Tunis.

**p.31** Pencil sketch of kasbah
Inscribed l.r.: 'Kont'

Ashjian thought that the building on this page and the verso (p.32) was the coastal kasbah in Hammamet.

**p.32** Pencil sketch of kasbah

See above (p.31) and Münter's sketch dated 21 March 1905 (46/17, p.25).

**p.33** Pencil sketch of landscape near Hammamet
Inscribed below: 'bei Hammamet nach Sonnenuntergang.' and with color notations: 'wie Rauch finster schwarz / grün wie schwarz / grünlich las. / orange / T. blau viol.'

Hammamet is a seaside village where Kandinsky probably spent the night on the way from Tunis to Sousse. He sketched the view over the gulf of Hammamet after sunset.

17, p.32

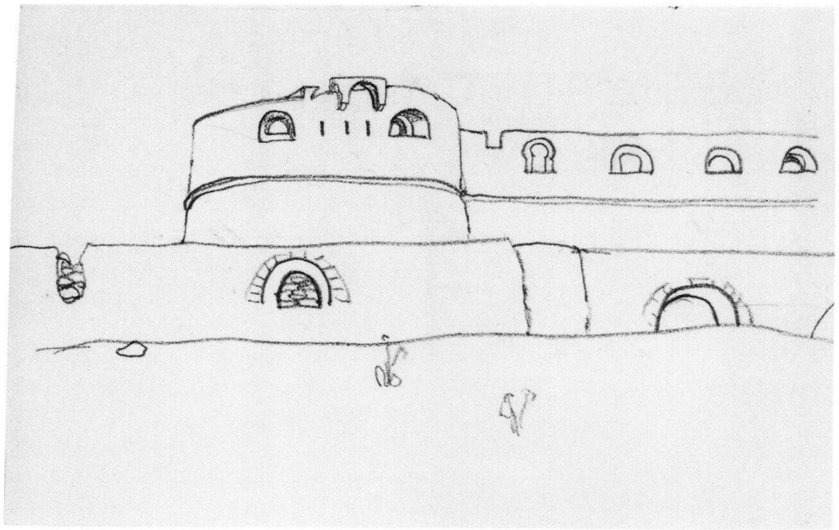

17, p.33

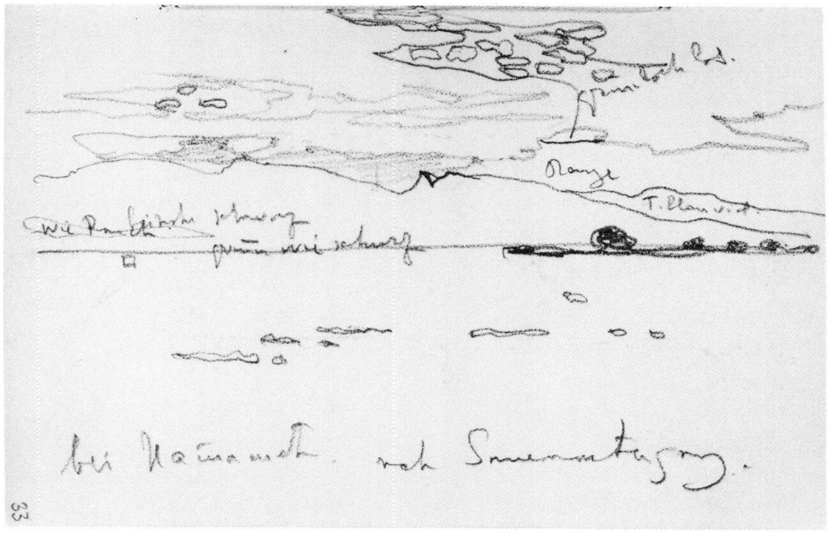

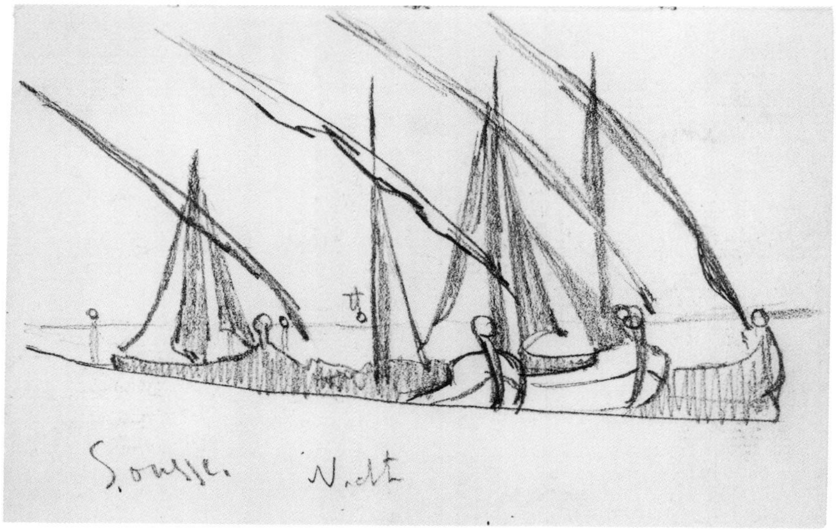


17, p.34

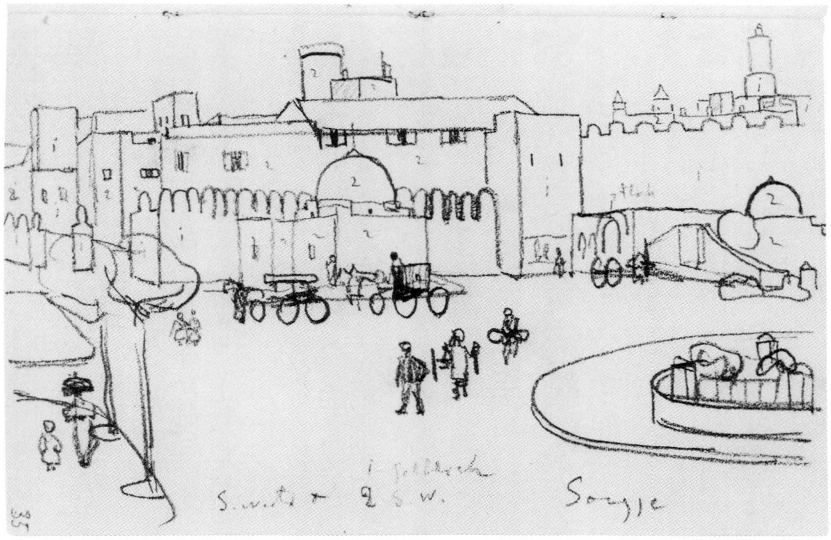

17, p.35

**p.34** Pencil sketch of boats at night in Sousse
Inscribed l.l.: 'Sousse. Nacht'

Kandinsky and Münter were in Sousse on 16 March on their trip to Kairouan, and they stayed there again on their return from 19 to 21 March. Kandinsky made numerous drawings in Sousse, including studies of fishing boats in Sketchbook 18; Münter made similar sketches of boats (see 37/7, pp.64, 66, 71).

**p.35** Pencil study for *Arabische Stadt* of 1905
Inscribed l.r.: 'Sousse'; l.l.: 'S. roter +'; l.c.: '1 gelblich / 2 s.w.'

REFERENCES
Hanfstaengl 1974, p.145, ill.
Barnett 1992, p.173
Ashjian 2001, pp.120–121, fig.208

Kandinsky depicts the place Pichon in Sousse, which is located between the medina and the French colonial quarter. The round tower adjacent to the Great Mosque is visible in the center, and to the right are the turret and exterior walls of the Ribat or fortified monastery (information kindly provided by Cristina Ashjian). Kandinsky based his tempera painting *Arabische Stadt* of 1905 (Barnett no.184) on this study.

**p.36** Pencil sketch of harbor in Sousse
Inscribed l.l.: 'Sousse.'

REFERENCES
Hanfstaengl 1974, p.145, ill.
Ashjian 2001, p.117, fig.195

According to Ashjian, this view of Sousse was done from the northern quay of the new French harbor. It shows the fortified walls of the city, the round turret of the Ribat to the right and the Tour de Khalef of the kasbah to the left.

**p.37** Pencil sketch of man and camel in Sousse
Inscribed l.l.: 'Sousse'; u.c.: 'Meer'

REFERENCES
Hanfstaengl 1974, p.145, ill.
Ashjian 2001, p.117, fig.196

Kandinsky made numerous sketches of the port in Sousse with boats, figures and animals.

17, p.36

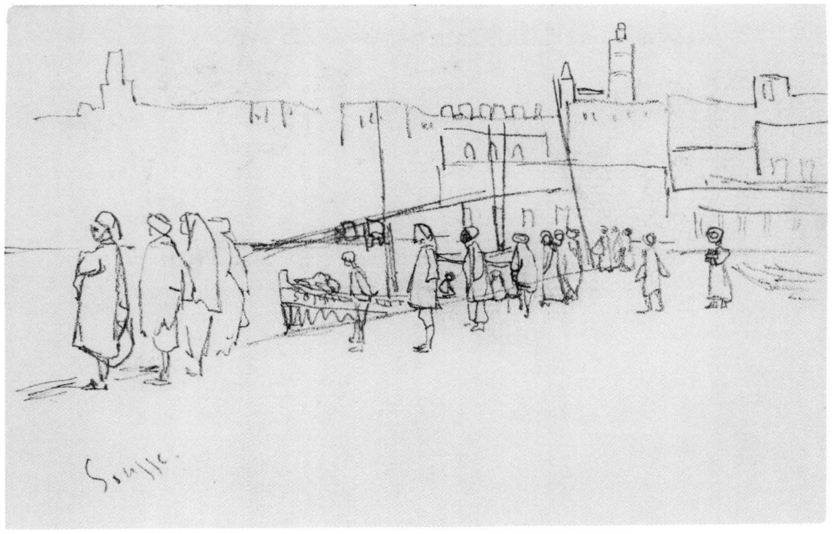

17, p.37

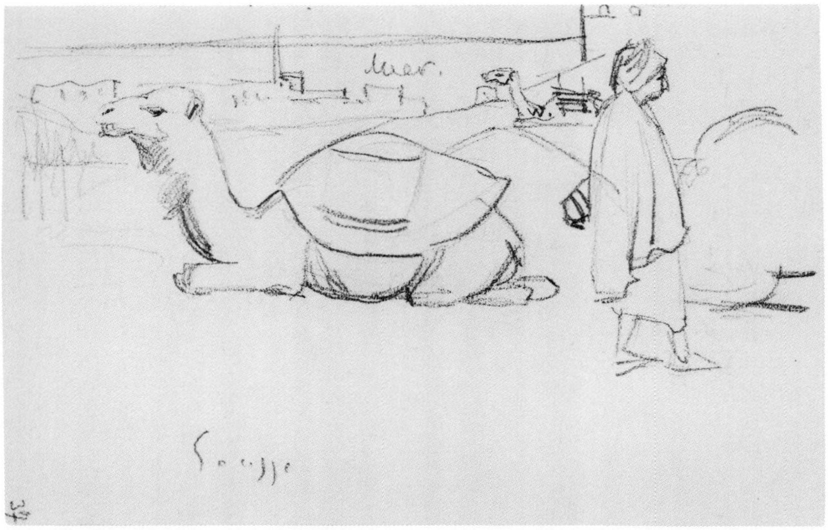

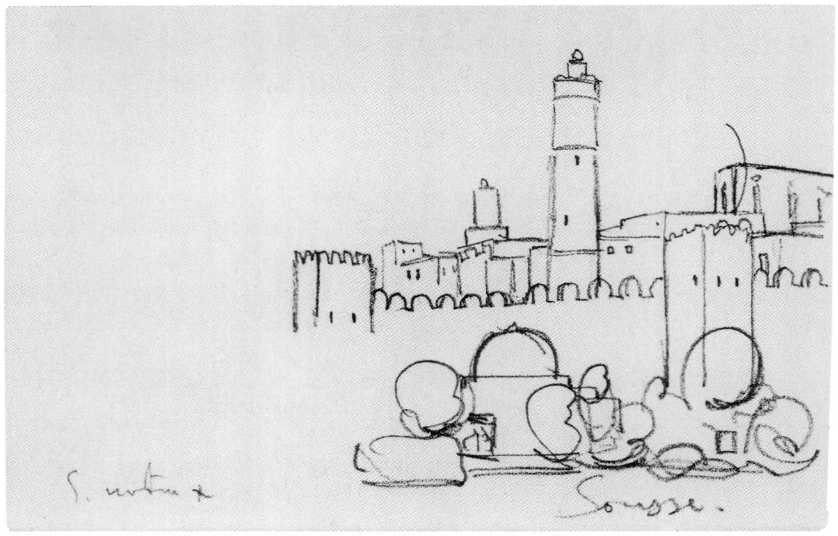

17, p.38

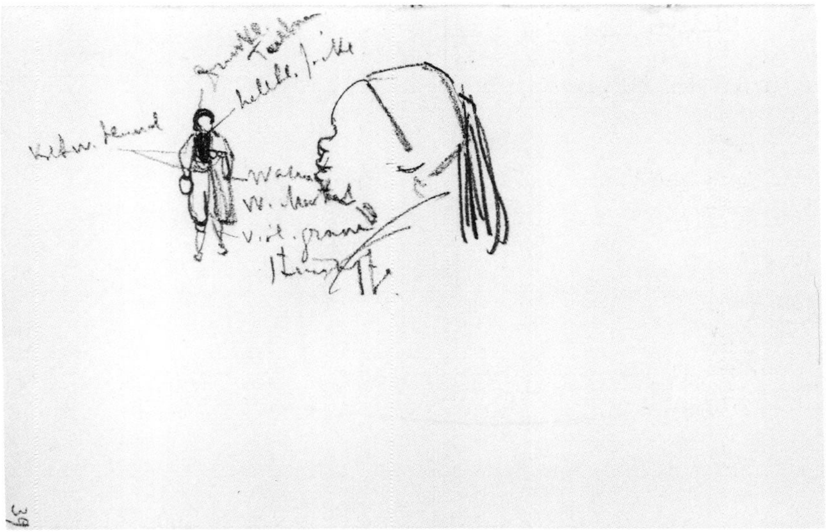

17, p.39

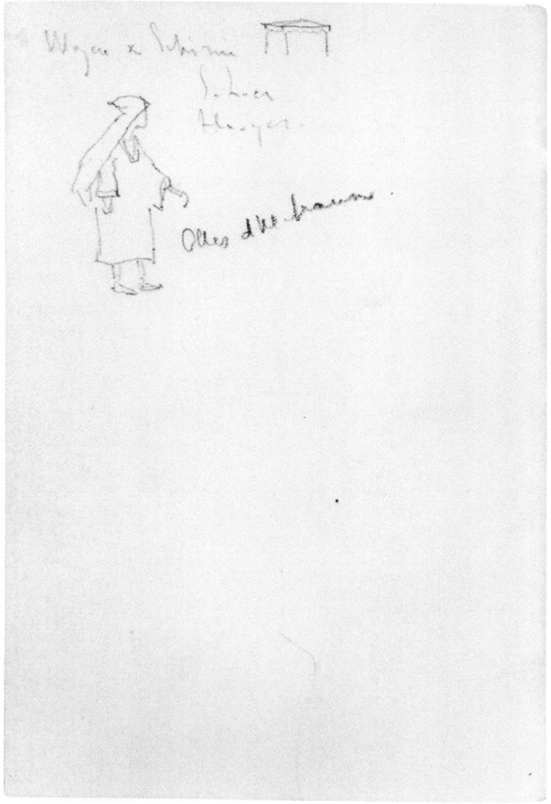

17, p.40

**p.38** Pencil sketch of fortified monastery
Inscribed l.l.: 'S. unten x'; l.r.: 'Sousse'

According to Ashjian, Kandinsky's sketch describes the Ribat complex in Sousse as seen from the place Pichon (see also p.35 above).

**p.39** Pencil sketches of head in profile and male figure
Inscribed u.c.: 'Dunkl. / Turban / hellbr. Jacke'; l.c.: 'Kalt w. Hemd'; c.: 'warm / w. Mantel / viol. graue / Strümpfe'

REFERENCES
Ashjian 2001, p.100, fig.165

The figure and notes may refer to the facing page. According to Ashjian, the man whose head is seen in profile wears a 'chechia' cap (see also p.8 above).

**p.40** Pencil sketch of figure
Inscribed 'Wagen + Schirm / Schwer / Hänger / Alles dkl braun'

The figure wears a dark brown cloak characteristic of rural costume, and the sketch above shows a wagon cover or canopy (observation made by Cristina Ashjian).

# Sketchbook 18

prepared with the assistance of Cristina Ashjian

1905

Dark grey cardboard sketchbook with black spine; inside front cover label from Franz Dury, Munich (Amalienstrasse Ecke Akademie-strasse)
Contains 40 pages (20 sheets), each 16.5 x 11.3 cm (6½ x 4½ in), of which pp.37–40 are blank
Page numbers inscribed by unknown hand at later date with odd numbers at lower right

Hanfstaengl 1974, pp.141–142

LOCATION
Städtische Galerie im Lenbachhaus, Munich (GMS 324)

HISTORY
Gabriele Münter, Murnau, until 1957

The sketchbook is similar to the previous one – Sketchbook 17 – which was also purchased at Dury in Munich. Erika Hanfstaengl had dated the sketchbook 1904–1905, but the sketches were made in Sousse and Kairouan, where Kandinsky and Gabriele Münter went in March 1905, and after their return to Tunis.

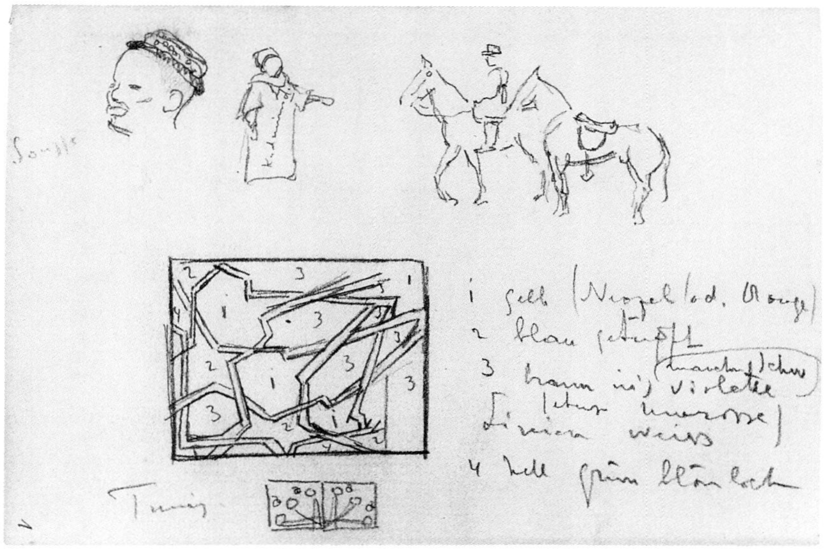

18, p.1

**p.1** Pencil sketches of figures, horses and tile
Inscribed u.l.: 'Sousse'; l.l.: 'Tunis'; l.r.: '1 gelb (Neapel / od. orange) / 2 blau getupft / 3 braun in's violette / manchmal Schw / Schw Umrisse) / Linien weiss / 4 hell grün bläulich'

REFERENCES
Hanfstaengl 1974, p.141, ill.
Ashjian 2001, p.53, fig.42

As indicated by the artist's notes, the sketches of figures and horses were made in Sousse, whereas the drawing with detailed notes about the colors in a geometric tile was done in Tunis. Cristina Ashjian has observed that the tile pattern ('polygones étoiles') was admired by Europeans, and has pointed out that the schematic diagram below shows how this tile (one of four) would integrate into a larger panel. See also Sketchbook 19, p.4. In addition, Münter made a similar drawing of a tile (37/7, p.74).

**p.2** Blank

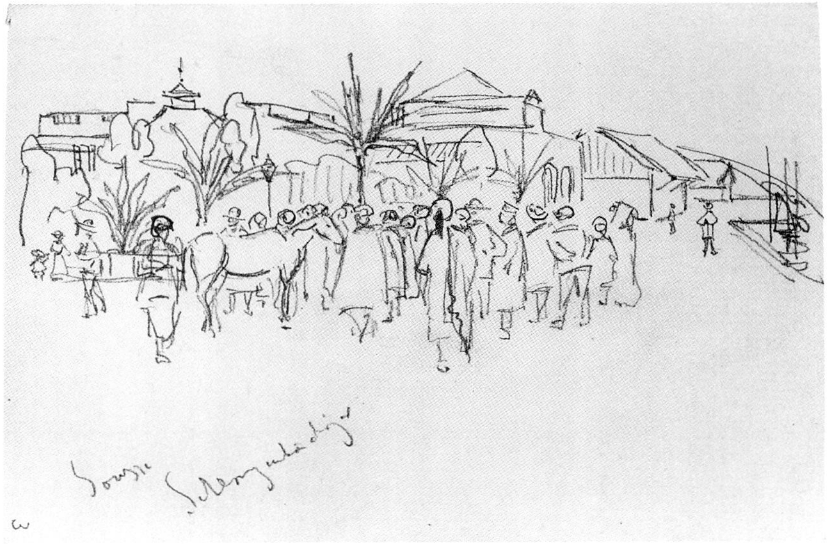

18, p.3

**p.3** Pencil sketch related to *Schlangenbändiger* of 1905
Inscribed l.l.: 'Sousse / Schlangenbändiger'

REFERENCES
Hanfstaengl 1974, p.141, ill.
Barnett and Friedel 1995, no.176, color ill.
Ashjian 2001, pp.117–119, fig.202

Kandinsky sketched a group of people watching a snake charmer in the port of Sousse. He changed the composition in his tempera painting *Schlangenbändiger* of 1905 (Barnett no.163).

18, p.4

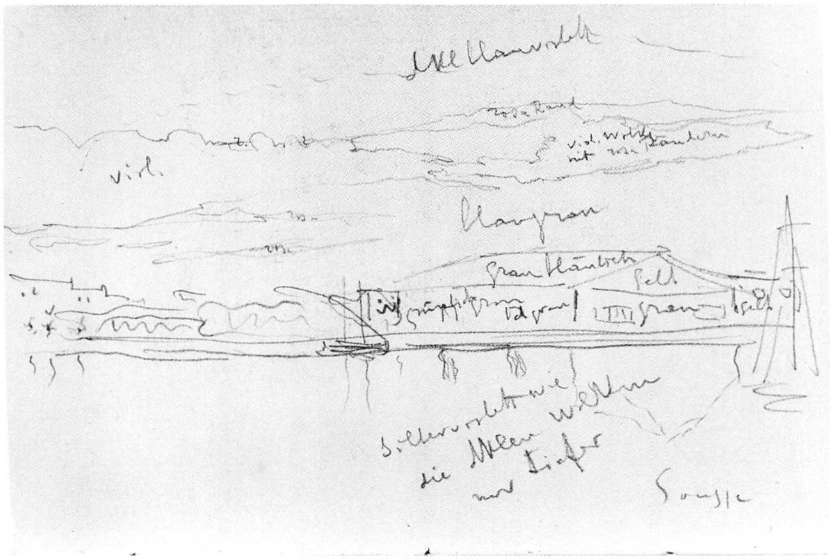

**p.4** Pencil sketch of harbor in Sousse
Inscribed l.r.: 'Sousse'; u.l.: 'viol.'; u.c.: 'dkl blauviolett / rosa Rand / viol. Wolke / mit rosa Rändern / blaugrau / grau bläulich'; l.c.: 'Silberviolett wie / die dklen Wolken / nur tiefer'

REFERENCES
Hanfstaengl 1974, p.141, ill.
Ashjian 2001, p.117

Cristina Ashjian has observed that Kandinsky sketched the port of Sousse from a point of view near the customs building and steamboat dock in the French colonial town.

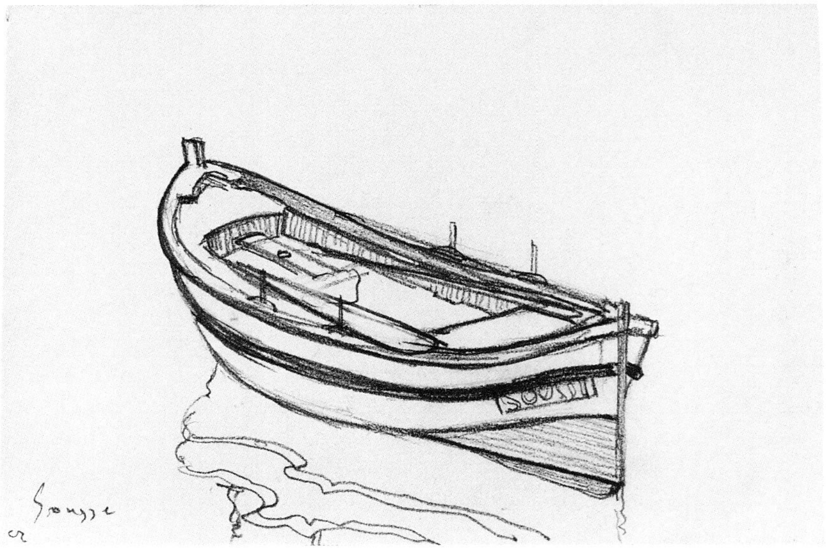

18, p.5

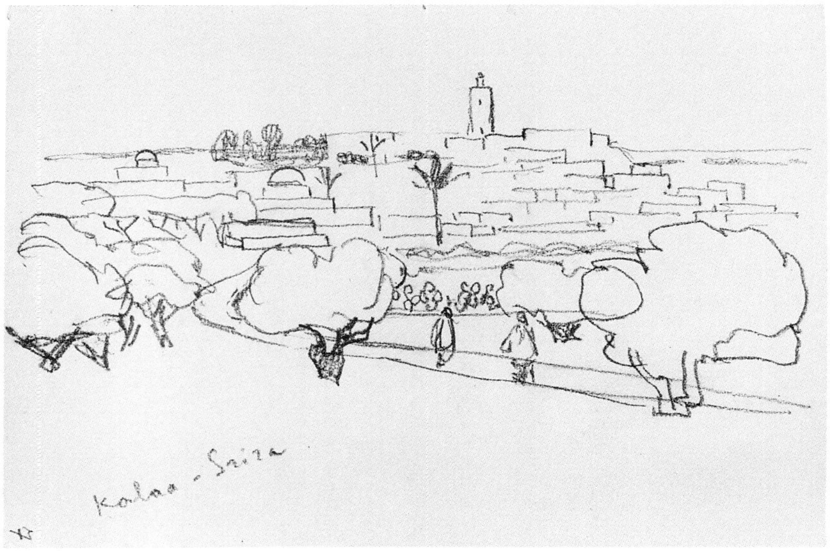

18, p.7

**p.5** Pencil sketch of rowboat
Inscribed l.l.: 'Sousse'

**p.6** Blank

**p.7** Pencil sketch of Kalaa-Srira
Inscribed l.l.: 'Kalaa Srira'

REFERENCES
Hanfstaengl 1974, p.141, ill.
Ashjian 2001, p.122, fig.212

Kandinsky's sketch is similar to one by Münter dated 17 March and also identified as Kalaa-Srira (46/17, p.11).

Ashjian suggested that the sketch was made near the railway station where Kandinsky and Münter would have changed trains on their way to Kairouan.

**p.8** Pencil sketch of male figures
Inscribed l.l.: 'Kairouan'

REFERENCES
Hanfstaengl 1974, p.141, ill.
Ashjian 2001, pp.84, 129, fig.111

Kandinsky and Münter arrived in Kairouan on 17 March and stayed there until 19 March 1905.

**p.9** Pencil sketch of houses
Inscribed l.c.: 'Kairouan'; c.: 'Hof';
l.r.: 'Hof'

In this view of Kairouan as seen from above, Kandinsky noted the courtyards in private houses. Münter made a similar drawing dated 18 March (46/17, p.15).

18, p.8

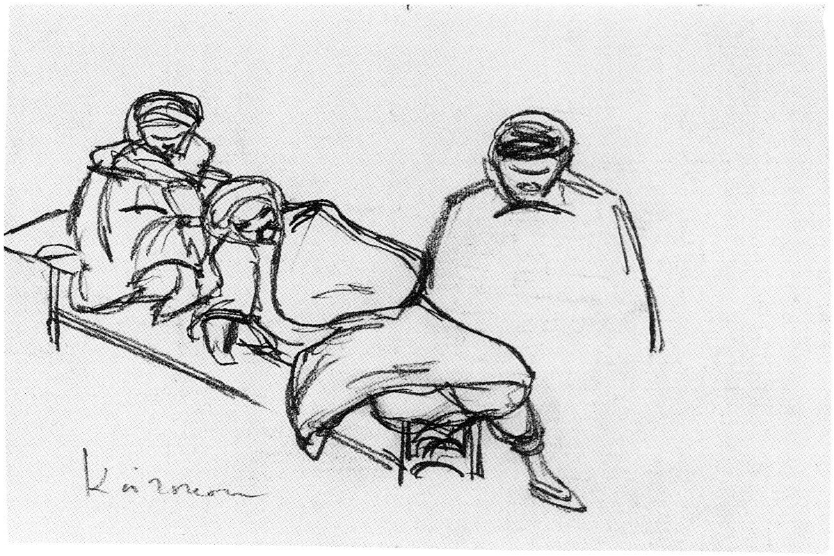

18, p.9

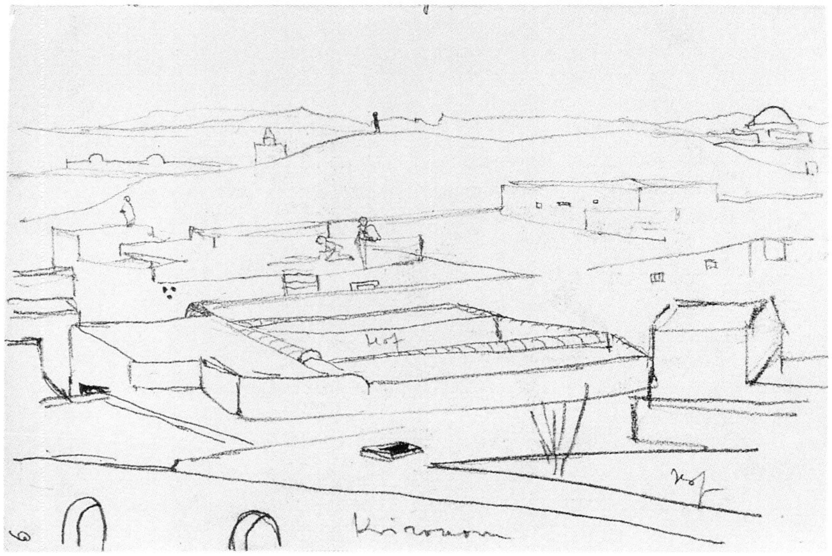

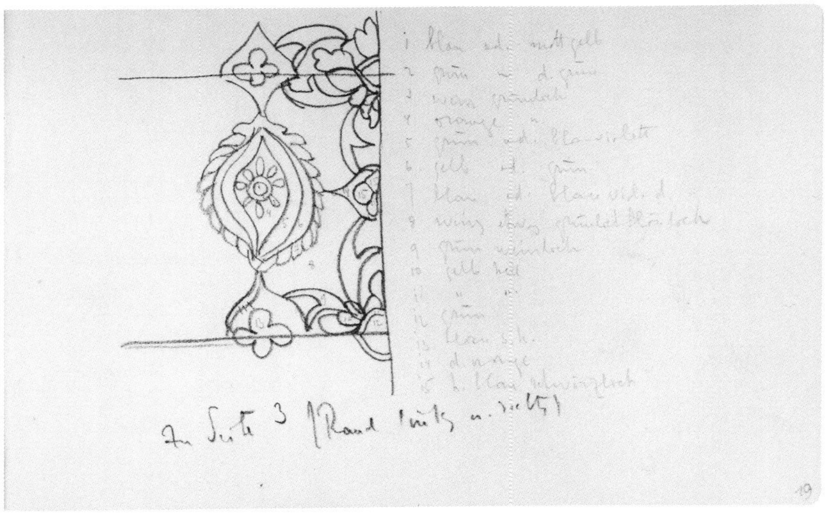

19, p.19

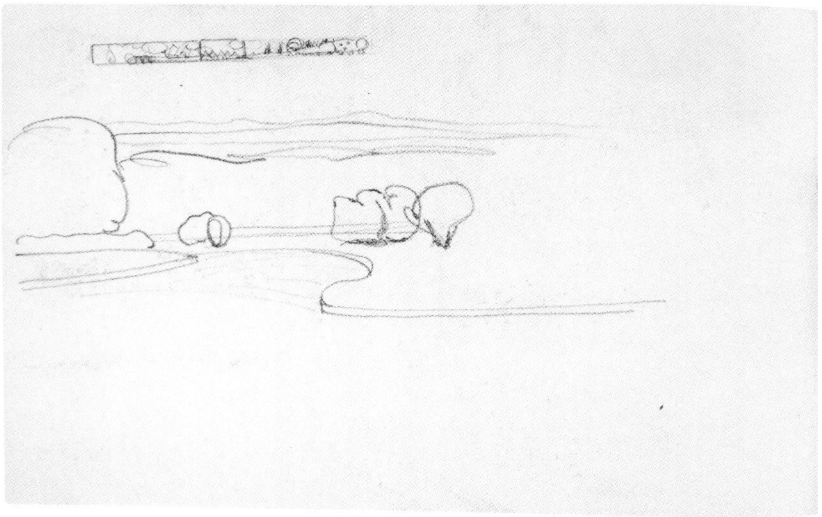

19, p.20

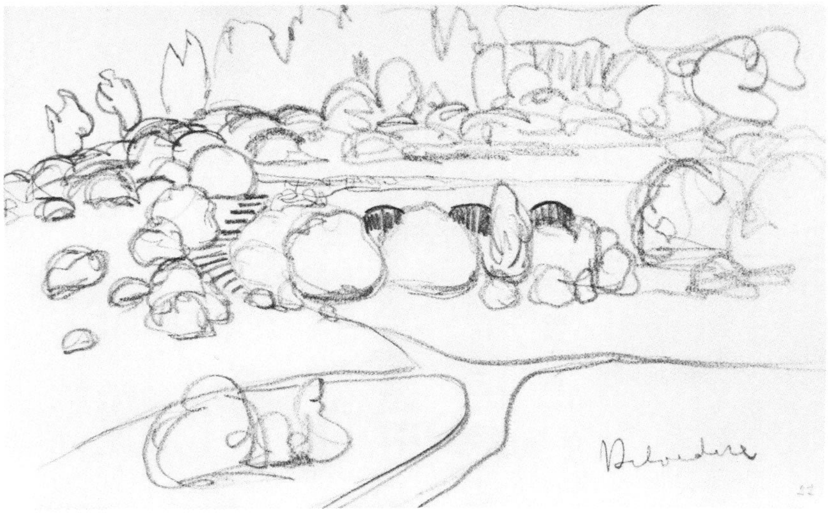


19, p.21

19, p.23

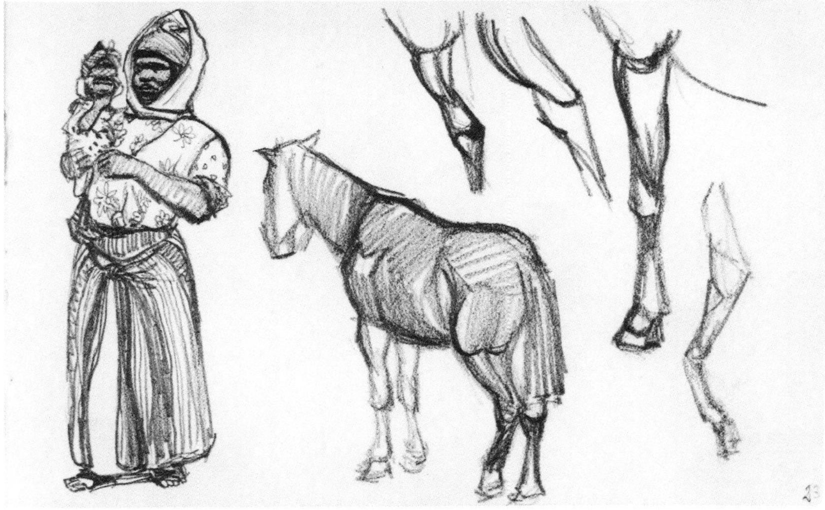

**p.20** Pencil sketches of landscape with trees

Like the drawing on the facing page, these two sketches were done in the Belvedere Park overlooking Tunis and nearby mountains.

**p.21** Pencil sketch of landscape
Inscribed l.r.: 'Belvedere'

REFERENCES
Hanfstaengl 1974, p.143, ill.
Ashjian 2001, p.51, fig.34

Located in the northern part of Tunis, Belvedere Park contained architectural pavilions such as La Mida as well as a casino. This sketch depicts the winding paths and trees with foliage.

**p.22** Blank

**p.23** Pencil sketches of horse and woman holding a child

REFERENCES
Hanfstaengl 1974, p.143, ill.
Podzemskaia 2000, p.135, ill.23
Ashjian 2001, p.86, fig.126

Ashjian has pointed out that the Berber or Bedouin people in Tunisia were often the subject of commercial photographs at the turn of the century.

**p.24** Blank

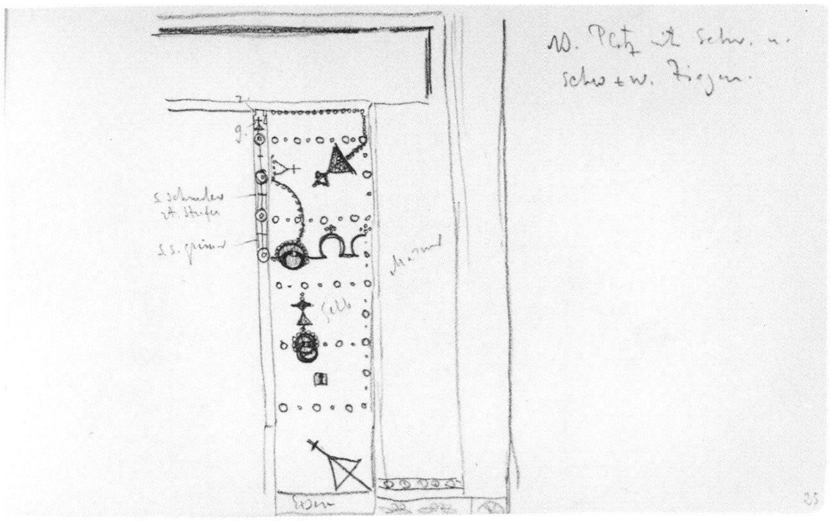

19, p.25

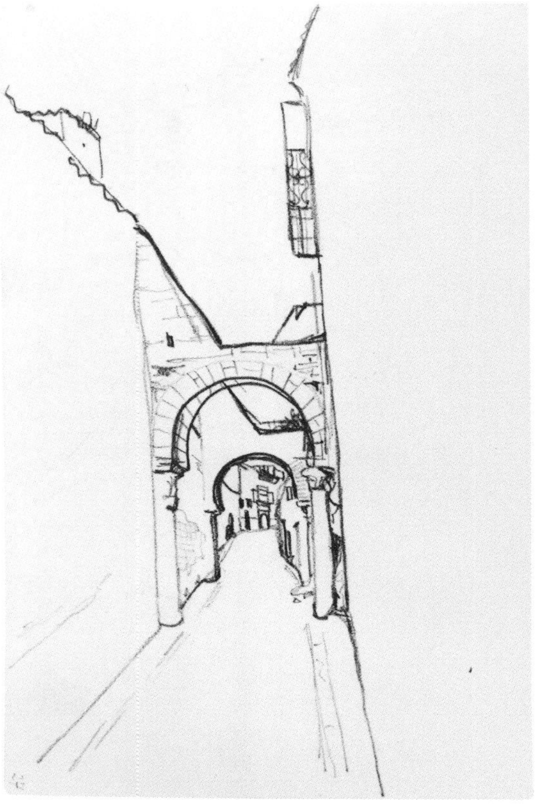

19, p.27

**p.25** Pencil sketch of decoration on door
Inscribed u.r.: 'B. Platz mit schw. u. / schw + w. Ziegen'; c.l.: 's. schmaler / rt. Stufen / s.s. grüner / gelb / Marmor'; l.c.: 'Eisen'

Münter made a similar drawing of a door in a sketchbook (46/17, p.29). Kandinsky indicated the marble surround, iron elements and colorful decoration of this wooden door. See also p.34 (below).

**p.26** Blank

**p.27** Pencil sketch of street

This sketch resembles another view of a street in the medina in Tunis in Sketchbook 17 (GMS 326, p.23).

**p.28** Pencil drawing of marabout
Inscribed l.l.: 'Marabout an der Souk'

Kandinsky sketched the entrance to a marabout or shrine to a holy man located in the souk of the historical medina in Tunis (information kindly provided by Cristina Ashjian).

**p.29** Pencil sketch of marabout
Inscribed u.c.: 'Holz Holz / Balke[n] / Balke[n]'; and with color notations: 'rt / gr / rt / w / gr'

REFERENCES
Daftari 1991, p.260

The sketch presents a detail of the drawing on the facing page with the hanging lamp and wooden doorway at the entrance to a marabout (see p.28 above) with Arabic script.

19, p.29

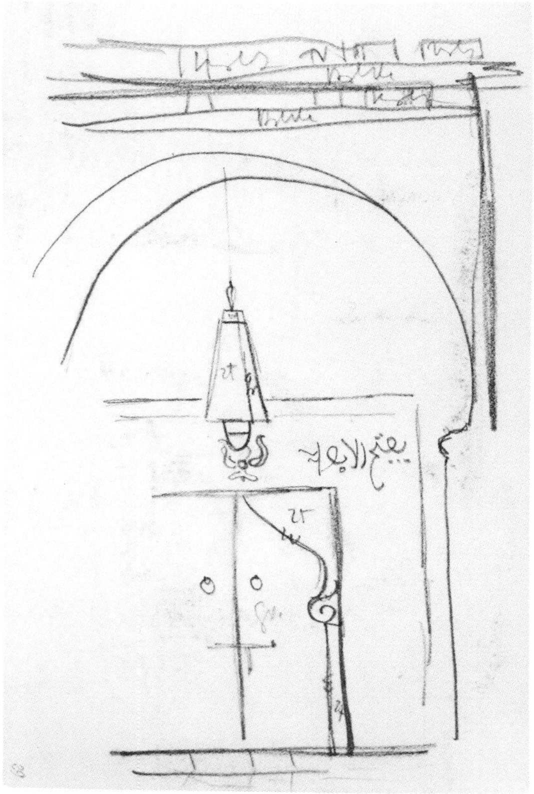

19, p.28

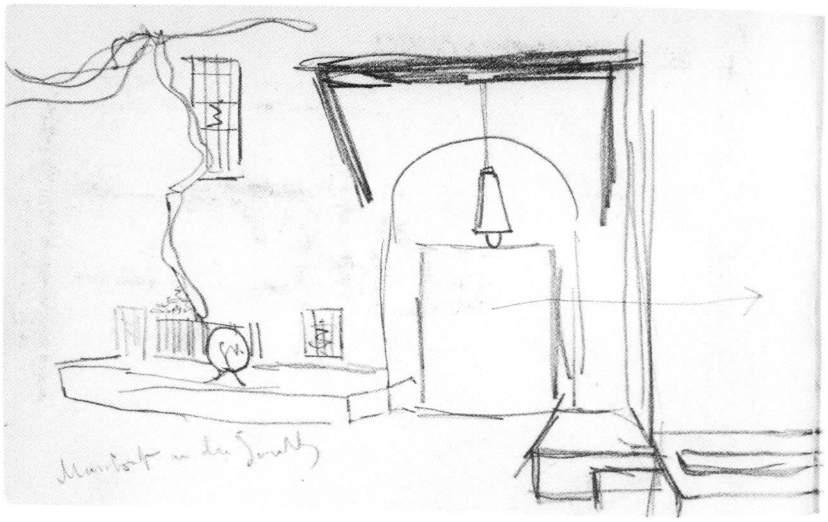

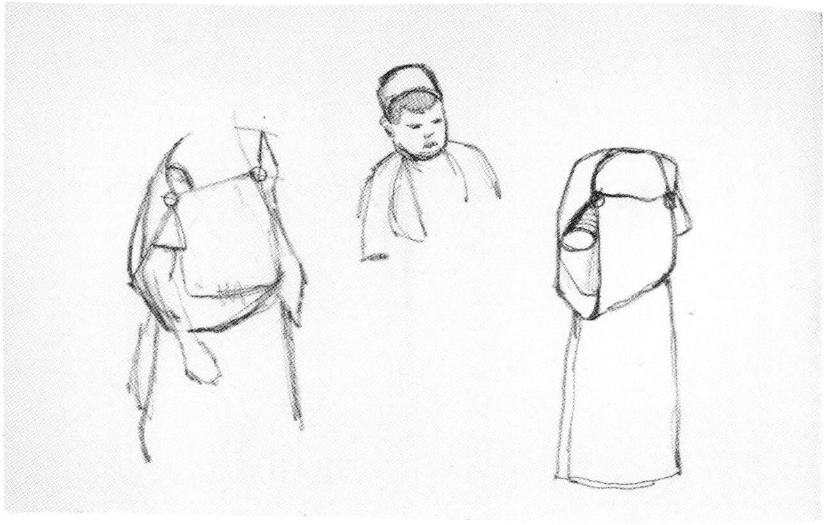

19, p.30

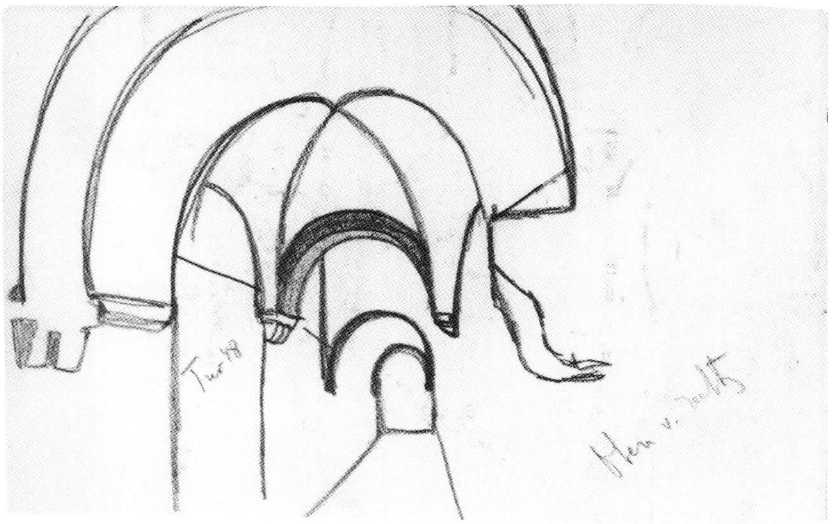

19, p.32

**p.30** Pencil sketch of boy and women's clothes

According to Ashjian, the costume sketches at the left and right show the characteristic tunic worn by Tunisian women.

**p.31** Blank

**p.32** Pencil sketch of street and arches
Inscribed l.l.: 'Tur 48'; l.r.: 'Oben v. rechts'

The view of a street in the medina emphasizes the underside of a vaulted passage and is related to that on the facing page.

**p.33** Pencil sketch of street
Inscribed u.l.: '48 / gelbrt / Gr.'; u.r.: 'L'

Ashjian has observed that Kandinsky made the sketch in the same vaulted passageway as that on p.32 (above) and represented two common styles of doors, the horseshoe shape on the left and the rectangular one on the right. The door on the left is also numbered 48 in the sketch on the facing page.

**p.34** Pencil sketch of boy and decoration on a door

REFERENCES

Hanfstaengl 1974, p.143, ill.
Ashjian 2001, p.77, fig.95

Kandinsky made several drawings of metalwork decorations on wooden doors in the medina in Tunis (see p.25 above) and in Kairouan (see Sketchbook 18, pp.14–15). The sketch of a boy wearing a cap is similar to that on p.30 (above). In addition, Münter sketched the decoration on the doors (46/17, p.29).

19, p.33

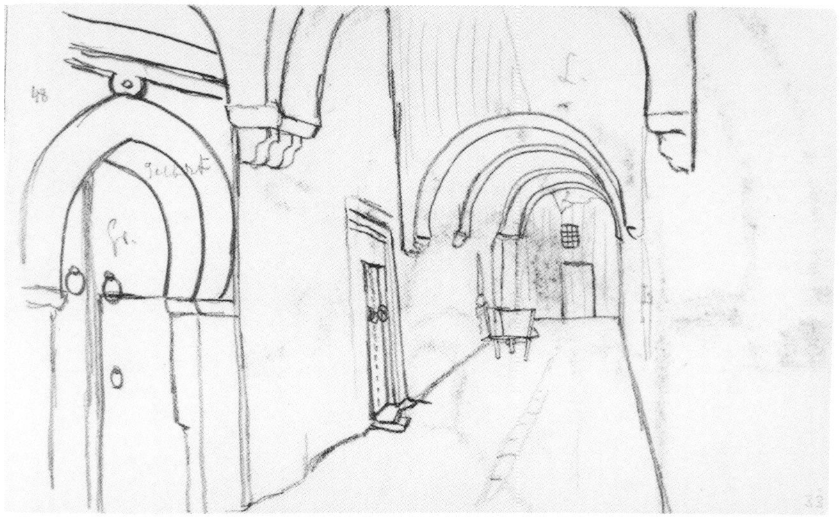

19, p.34

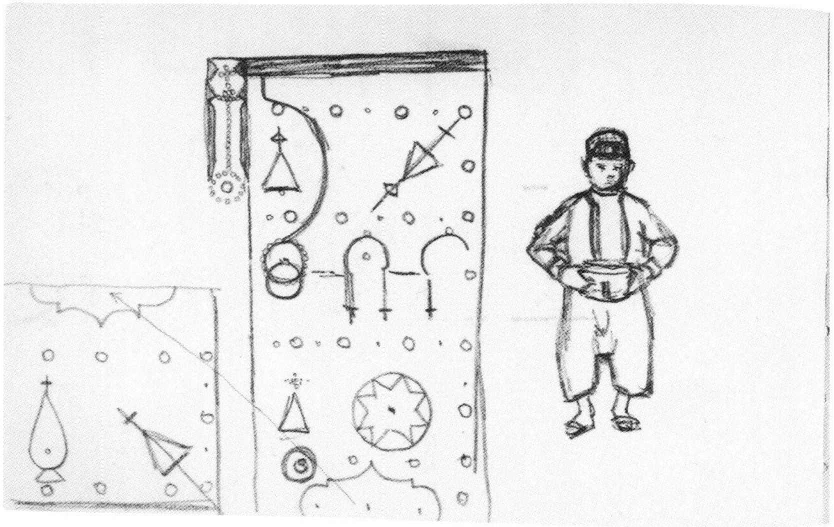

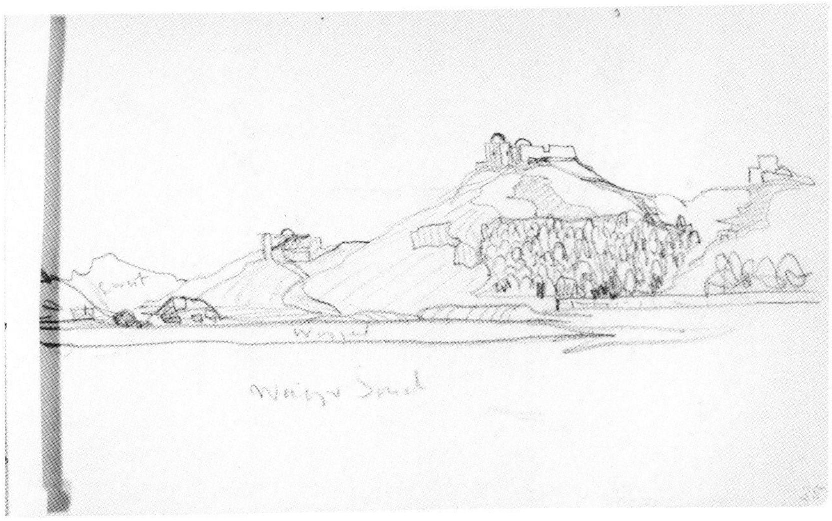

19, p.35

fig.a

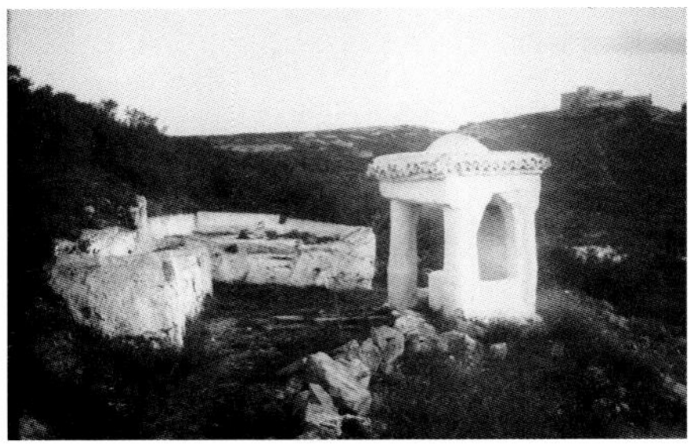

19, p.37

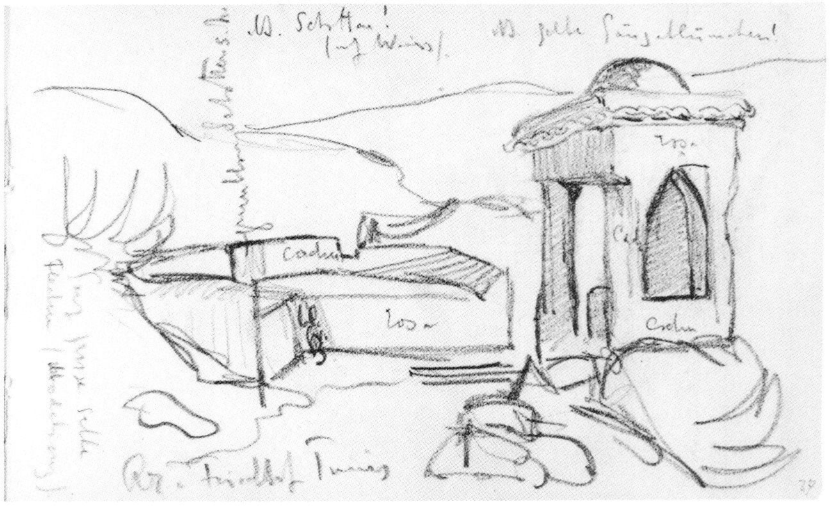

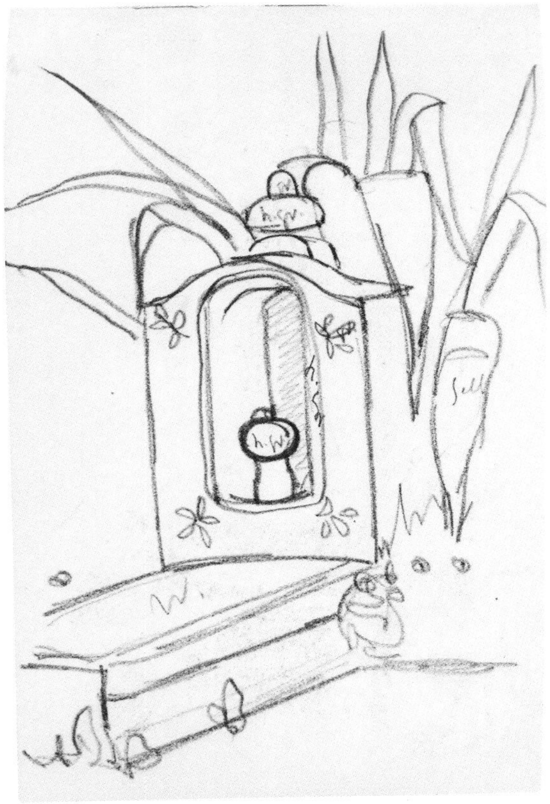

19, p.36

19, p.39

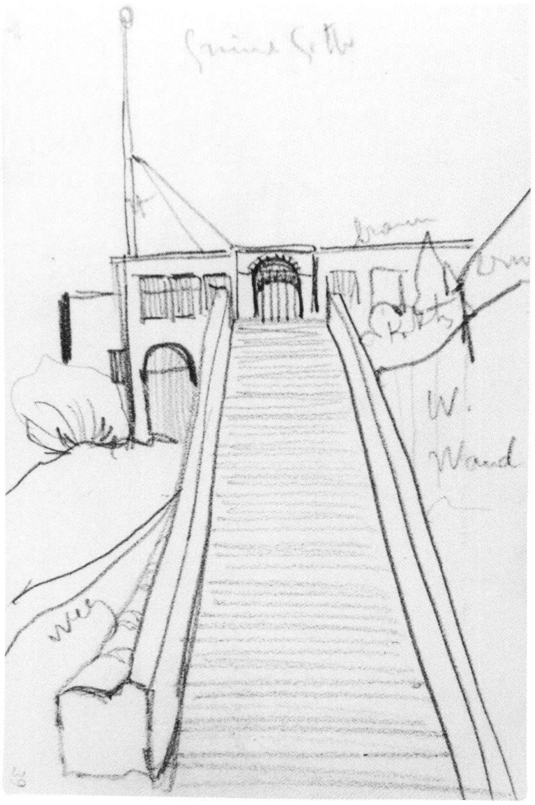

**p.35** Pencil sketch of landscape
Inscribed c.l.: 's. weiss / w.'; l.c.: 'Wasser / weisser Sand'

According to Ashjian, the view is across El-Bahira or the Lake of Tunis toward the inland hills surrounding the city, which had fortifications: it may include the Sidi Bel-Hassen fort.

**p.36** Pencil sketch of turban grave
Inscribed with color notations: 'gr / h. gr. / gelb / w.'

Kandinsky probably made this sketch of a turban grave with a large aloe in the Sidi Bel-Hassen Cemetery located in the southern part of Tunis (information on the cemetery kindly provided by Cristina Ashjian). See p.47 (below).

**p.37** Pencil sketch of Arab Cemetery
Inscribed l.c.: 'Ar. Friedhof Tunis'; u.c.: 'B. Schatten! / (auf weiss). / B. gelbe Gänseblümchen!'; l. edge: 'Ganz grosse gelbe / Flecken (Modelierung)'

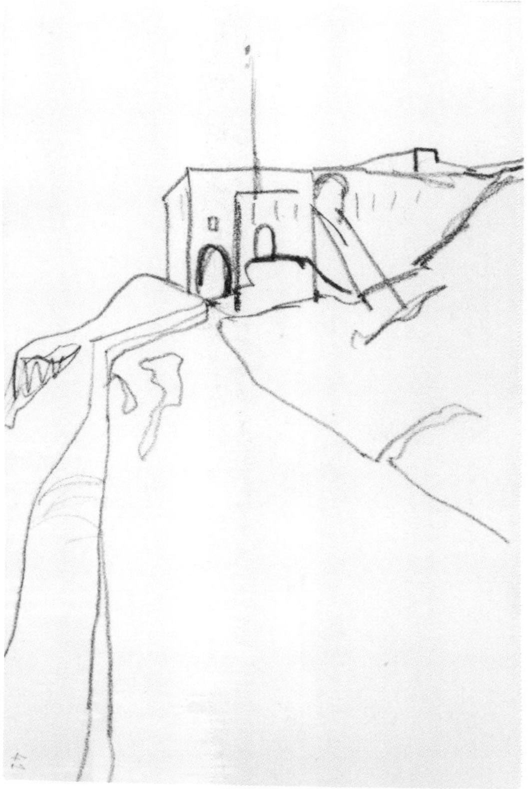

19, p.41

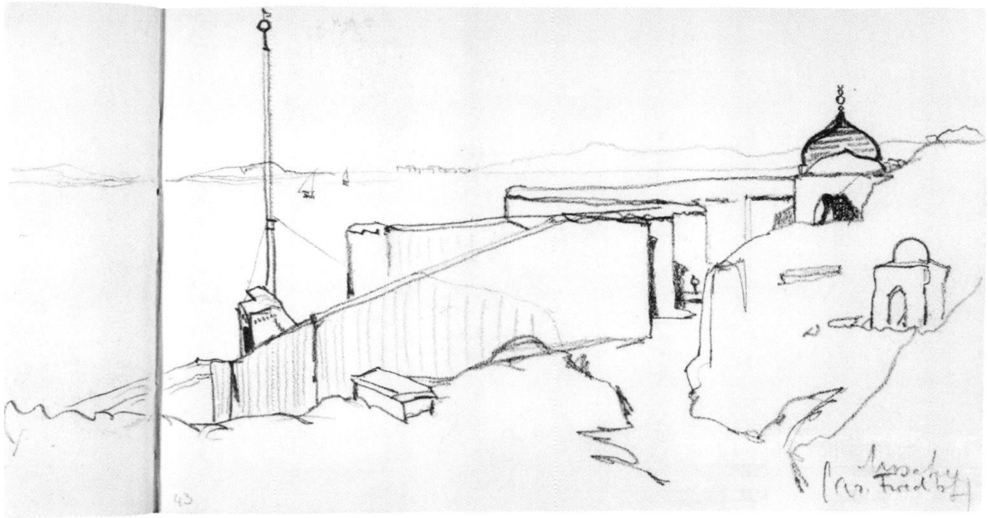

19, pp.42-43

and with color notations: 'cadm. / rosa / bl. / gr. / rs'

The artist's inscription refers to the 'Arab Cemetery', as the Sidi Bel-Hassen Cemetery was known to European visitors to Tunis. Münter or Kandinsky took a photograph of the graves (fig.a; 2586).

**p.38** Blank

**p.39** Pencil sketch of stairs to Arab Cemetery
Inscribed u.c.: 'Grüne Gitter'; l.l.: 'Weg'; c.r.: 'braun / w[a]rm / Kaktus / W. / Wand'

According to Ashjian, this sketch – and those on the following pages – was made in the mosque or Zaouia Sidi Bel-Hassen in the Arab Cemetery in Tunis. This view shows the stairs leading up to the entrance to the mosque (seen from above in the drawing on pp.44–45).

**p.40** Blank

**p.41** Pencil sketch of Arab Cemetery

**pp.42–43** Pencil sketch of mosque in Arab Cemetery
Inscribed l.r.: 'Moschee / (Ar. Friedhof)'

Kandinsky sketched the walls of the Zaouia Sidi Bel-Hassen with a small tomb in the foreground, and mountains, lake and sailboats in the background.

**pp.44–45** Pencil sketch of mosque in Arab Cemetery
Inscribed l.r.: 'Moschee / (Ar. Friedhof)'

This view of the Zaouia Sidi Bel-Hassen is seen from above and presents the layout of the stairs to the entrance, the surrounding walls and the mosque within the complex.

**p.46** Blank

19, pp.44-45

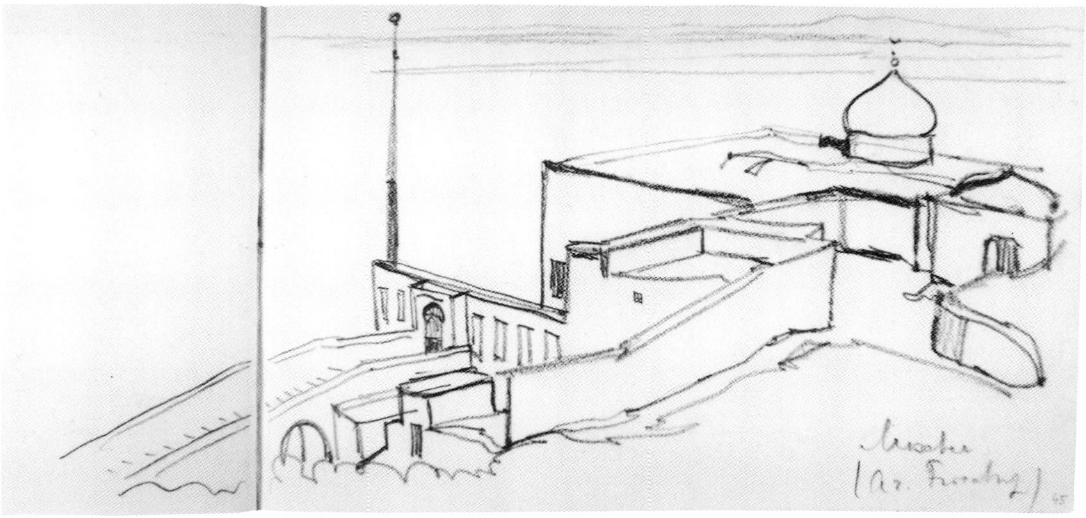

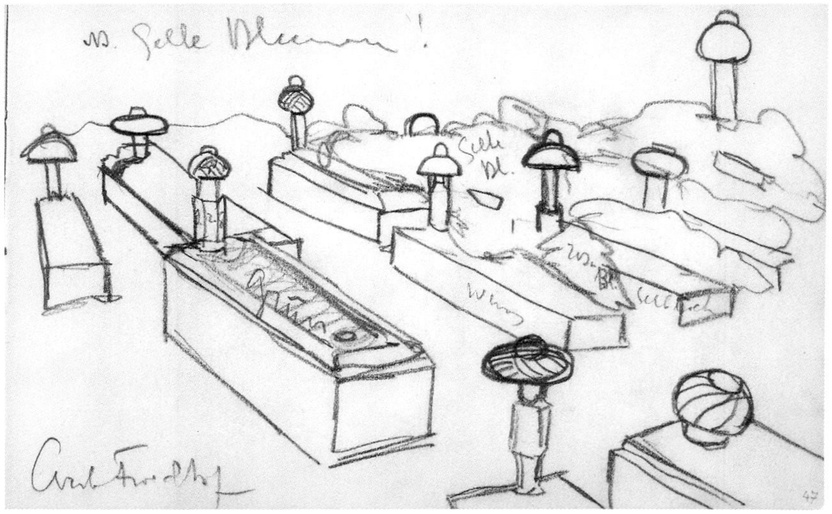

19, p.47

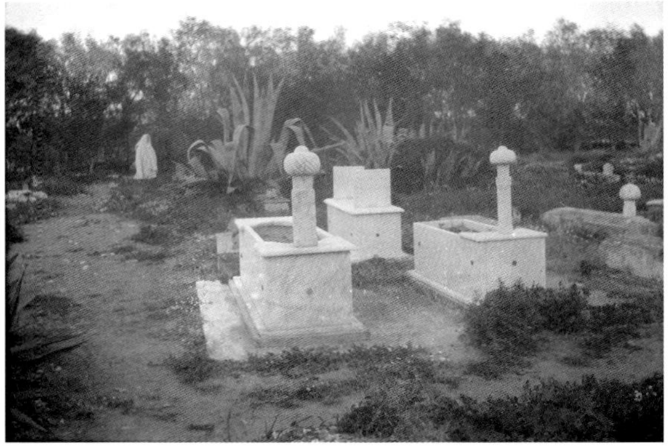

fig.b

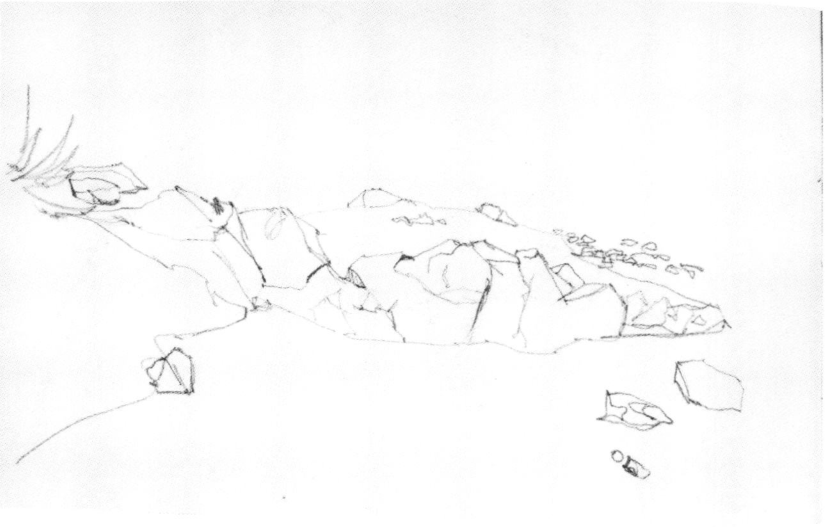

19, p.48

19, p.49

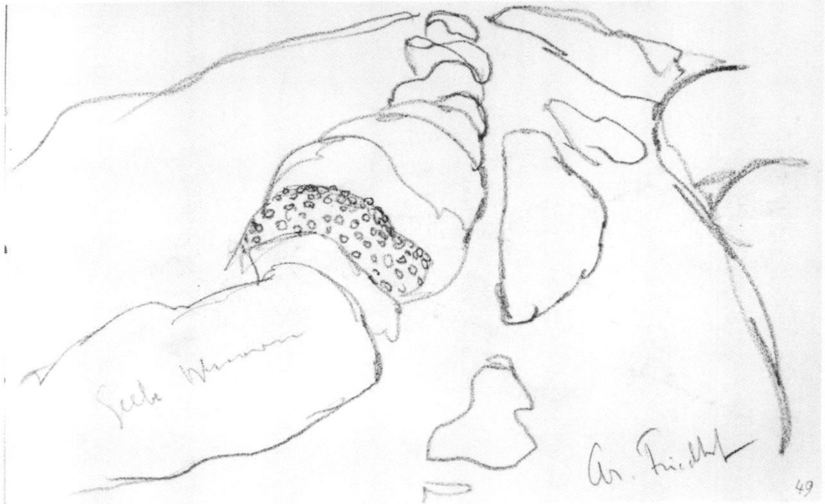

**p.47** Pencil sketch of turban graves in Arab Cemetery
Inscribed l.l.: 'Arab. Friedhof'; u.c.: 'B. gelbe Blumen!' and with color notations: 'grün / weiss / rosa / gelblich'

REFERENCES
Hanfstaengl 1974, p.143, ill.
Roethel and Benjamin 1982, p.269
Ashjian 2001, p.114, fig.190

Kandinsky described the turban carvings and colors of the sarcophagi and also noted the 'yellow flowers' (see p.49 below). Münter or Kandinsky took photographs of the cemetery (see fig.b; 2580). Four years later Kandinsky referred to the Arab Cemetery in his painting *Araber I (Friedhof)* of 1909 (Roethel and Benjamin no.283); however, this drawing is not a study for the painting.

**p.48** Pencil sketch of landscape

Ashjian has suggested that Kandinsky sketched the rocks near the Sidi Bel-Hassen Cemetery.

**p.49** Pencil sketch of Arab Cemetery
Inscribed l.l.: 'Gelbe Blumen'; l.r.: 'Ar. Friedhof'

**pp.50–51** Pencil sketch of Manouba
Inscribed l.l.: 'Manubia 1 (S. weiter!)'

This is the first of four drawings of the Manouba villa complex outside Tunis, which is located about 2 kilometers west of the Bardo palace. The road, entrance and buildings seen at the right on p.51 are repeated at the left on p.52, as indicated by Kandinsky's annotation 'S. weiter!' (see further!).

**pp.52–53** Pencil sketch of Manouba with detail
Inscribed l.l.: '1 blau / 2 orange / 3 grau / 4 blau d. (u. oben d. blaue Streifen) / 5 graublau / 6 grau'; l.r.: 'N7 / Manubia 2'

REFERENCES
Hanfstaengl 1974, p.143, ill.
Ashjian 2001, pp.104–106, fig.169

Kandinsky continued his panoramic view of Manouba and specified the colors for the numbered doorways. In addition, he made a detail study below the doorway at the far right, which he numbered 7, and to which he refers in the drawing on p.57.

(See color plate p.122)

**pp.54–55** Pencil sketch of Manouba

According to Ashjian, the sketch presents a side view of the Manouba villa with the arched entry gate to the complex to the right, and emphasizes the high walls and varied windows.

**p.56** Blank

**p.57** Pencil sketches of Manouba
Inscribed l.l.: 'Manoubia 3.'; l.r.:

19, pp.50-51

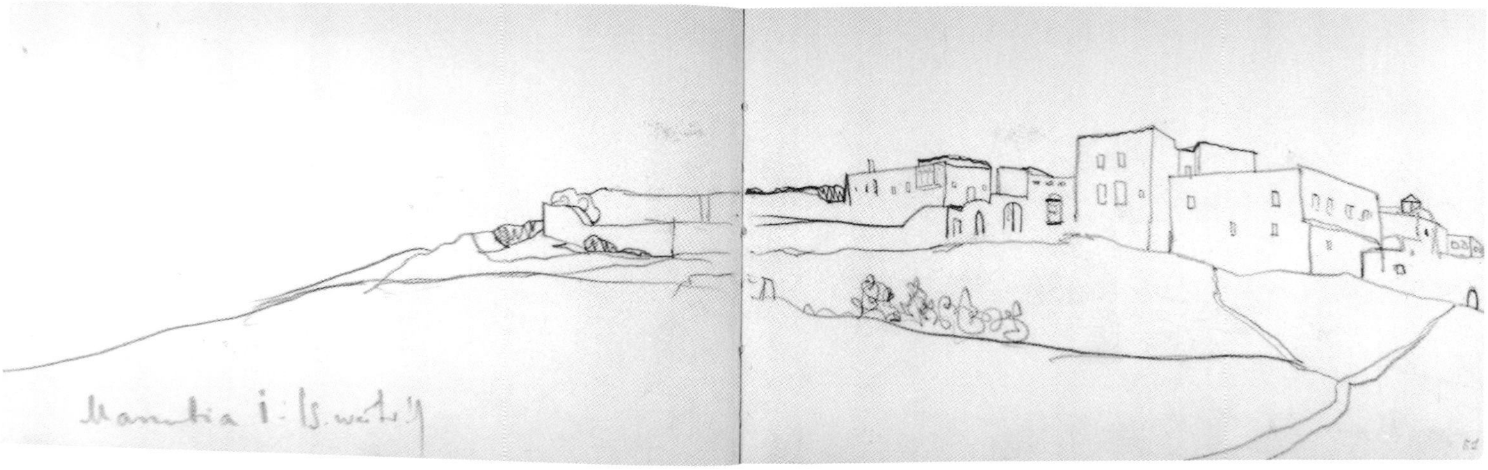

19, pp.52-53

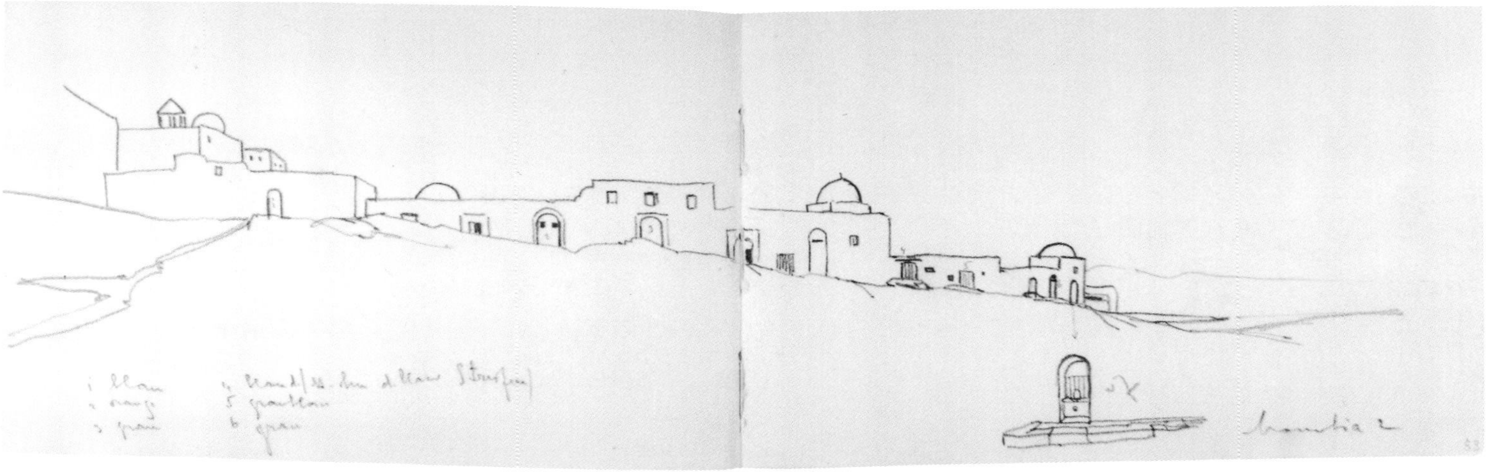


19, p.57

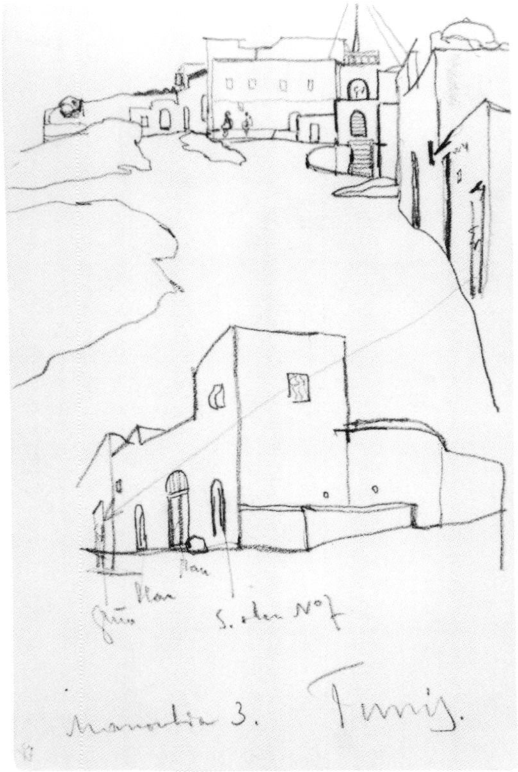


'Tunis'; l.c.: 'grün / blau / grau / S. oben No7'

Kandinsky focused on the doorways and architectural details in the two views of the Manouba villa. An arrow relates the doorway above on the right to that at the lower left. The annotation ('see above No7') refers to p.53, where Kandinsky made a small detailed drawing of a doorway and marked it number 7.

19, pp.54-55

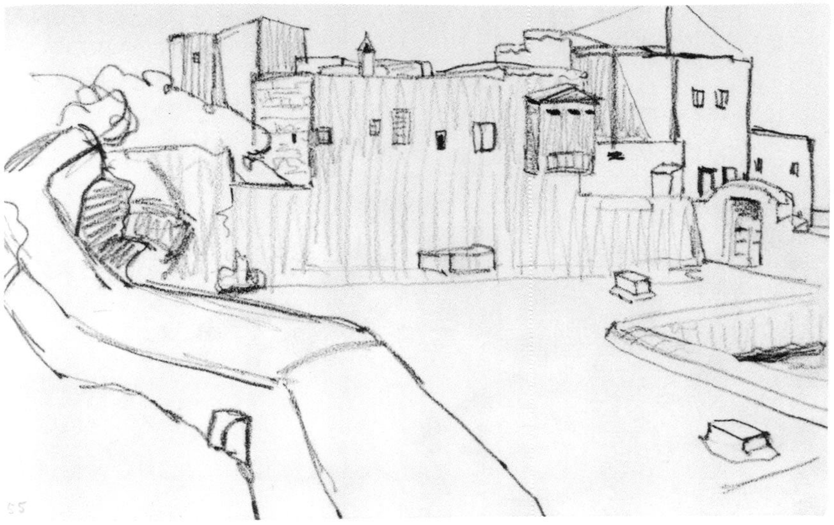

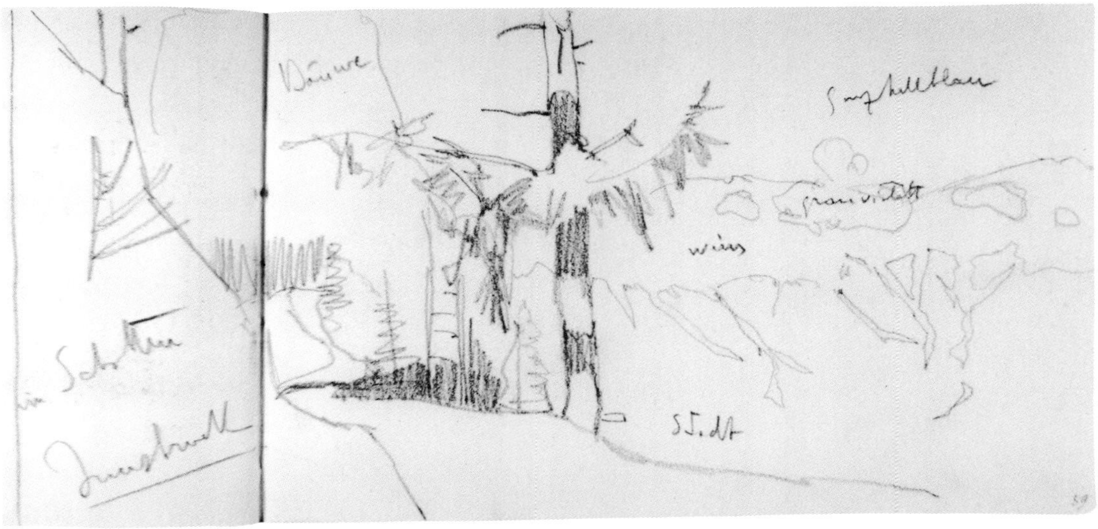

19, pp.58-59

**pp.58–59** Pencil sketch of landscape with trees in Innsbruck
Inscribed l.l.: 'im Schatten / Innsbruck'; u.l.: 'Bäume'; u.r.: 'ganzhellblau'; c.: 'weiss / grauviolett'; l.c.: 'Stadt'

REFERENCES
Hanfstaengl 1974, p.144, ill.

After returning from Tunisia by way of Italy, Kandinsky stayed in Innsbruck from 16 to 20 April and visited the nearby villages of Igls and Hötting.

**p.60** Pencil sketch of landscape
Inscribed l.l.: 'Schneeformen'

Kandinsky made several studies of snow formations in the Austrian alps.

**p.61** Pencil sketch of landscape with clouds
Inscribed l.l.: 'Wolkenschatten'

REFERENCES
Hanfstaengl 1974, p.143, ill.
Barnett and Friedel 1995, no.188, color ill.
Barnett 2006, p.57

There is a related drawing (vol.I, cat. no.76) executed with colored pencils.

**p.62** Pencil sketch of landscape
Inscribed l.l.: 'Sch[n]eeformen' and with color notations: 'w'

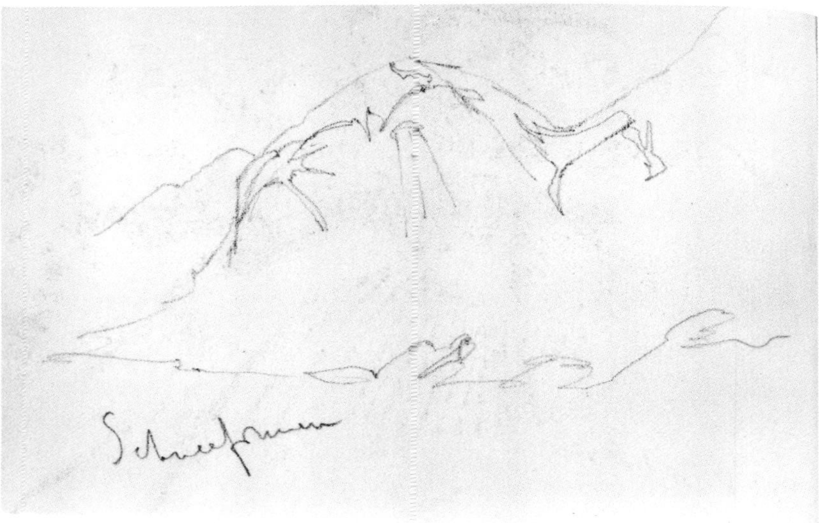

19, p.60

19, p.61

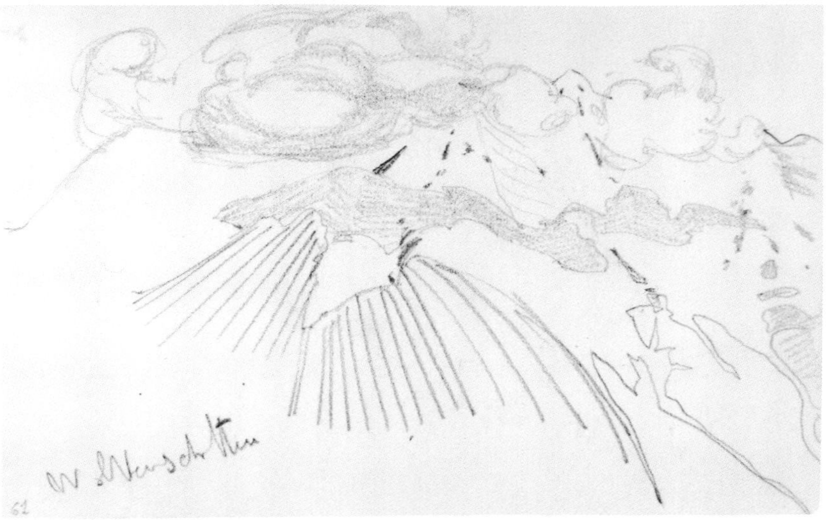

19, p.62

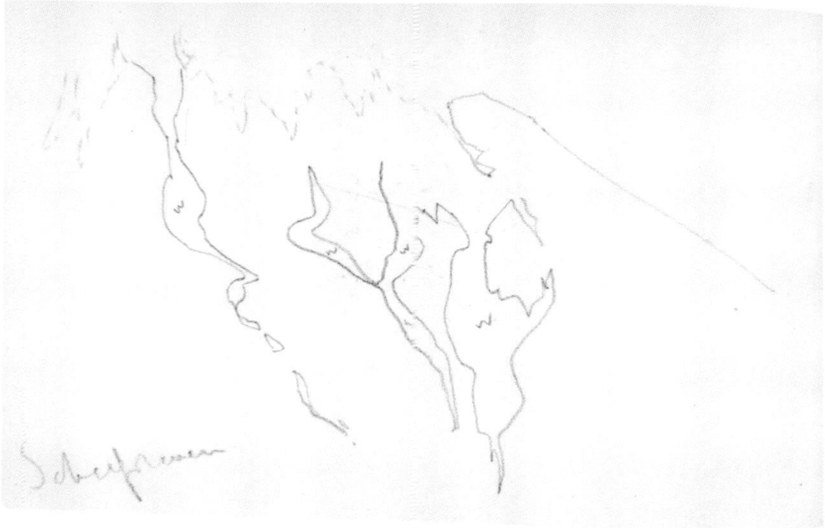

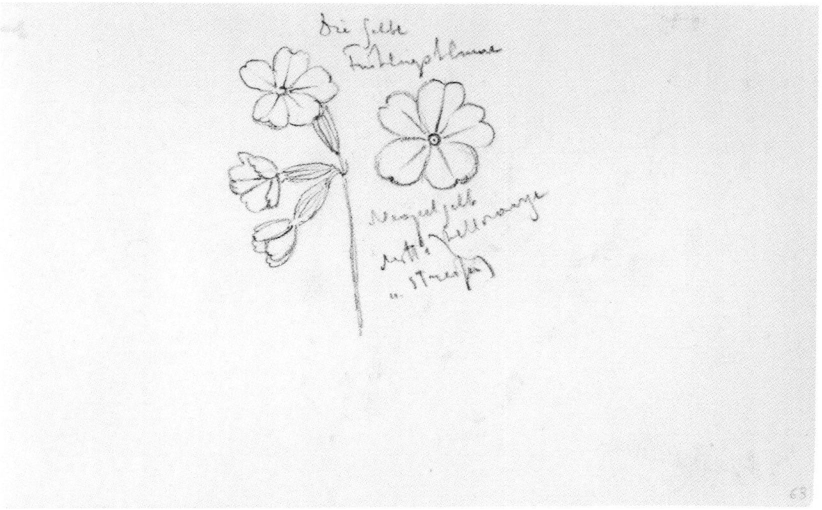

19, p.63

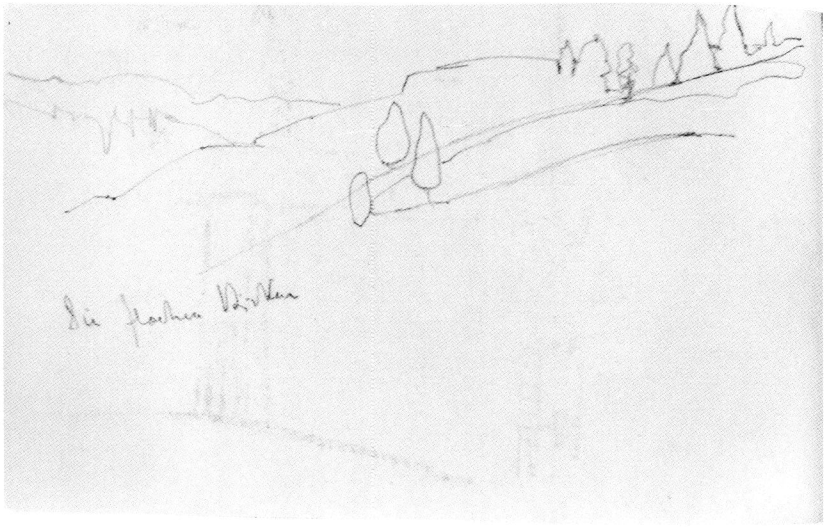

19, p.64

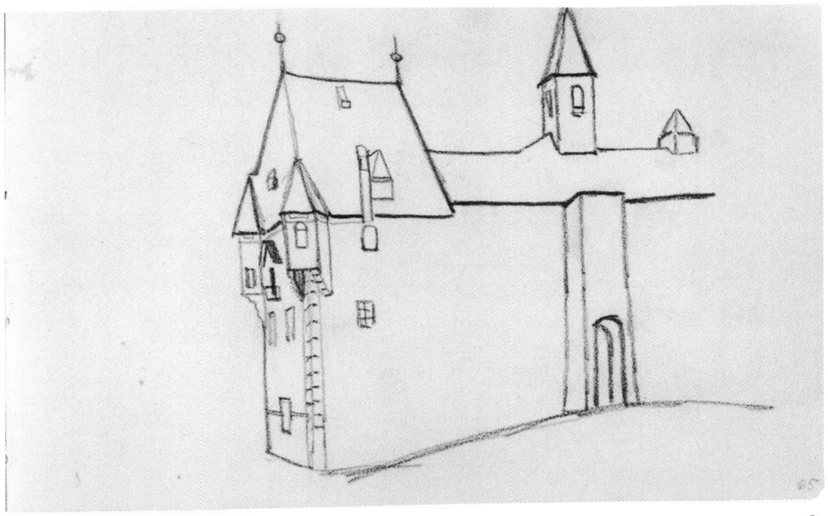

19, p.65

**p.63** Pencil sketch of flowers
Inscribed u.c.: 'Die gelbe / Frühlingsblume'; l.c.: 'Neapelgelb / Matte hellorange / u. Streifen'

Kandinsky probably drew 'the yellow spring flowers' and the birch trees (p.64) in Austria.

**p.64** Pencil sketch of landscape
Inscribed l.l.: 'Die flachen Birken'

**p.65** Pencil sketch of building

Kandinsky probably made this drawing in Tyrol, possibly in Innsbruck.

**p.66–67** Pencil sketch of mountains

REFERENCES
Hanfstaengl 1974, p.144, ill.

19, pp.66-67

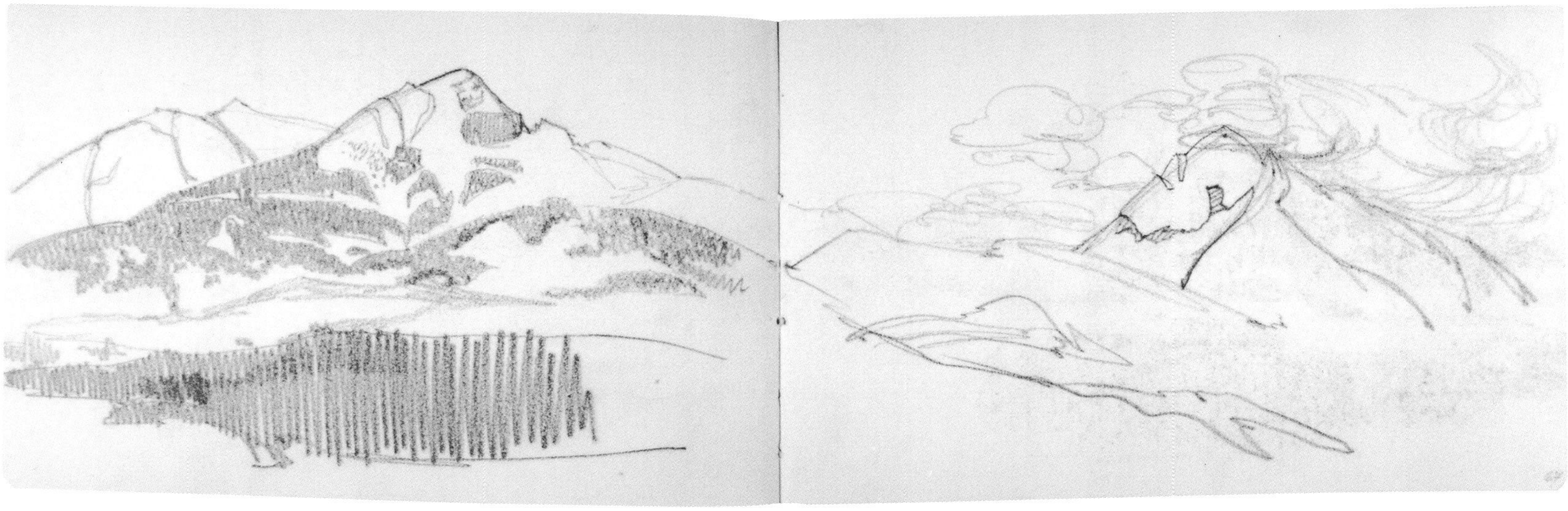

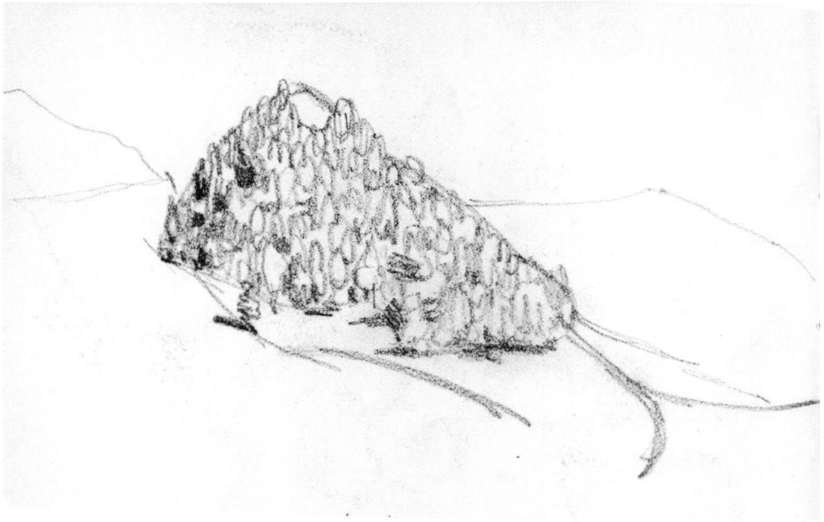

19, p.68

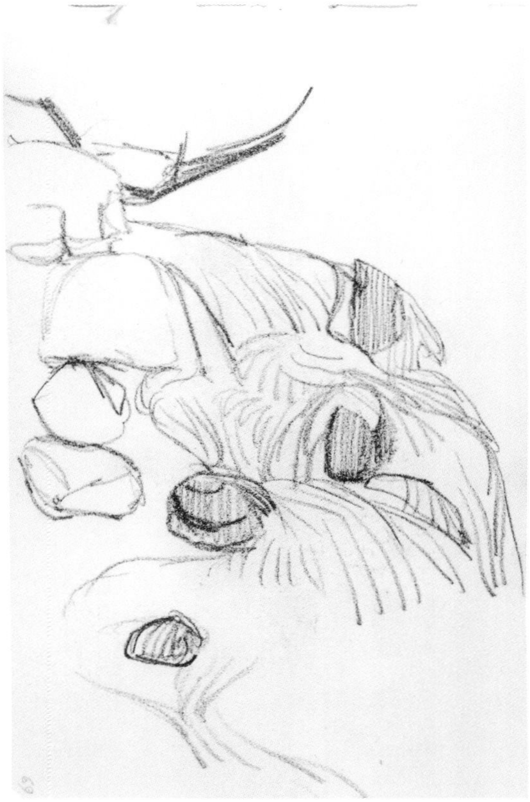

19, p.69

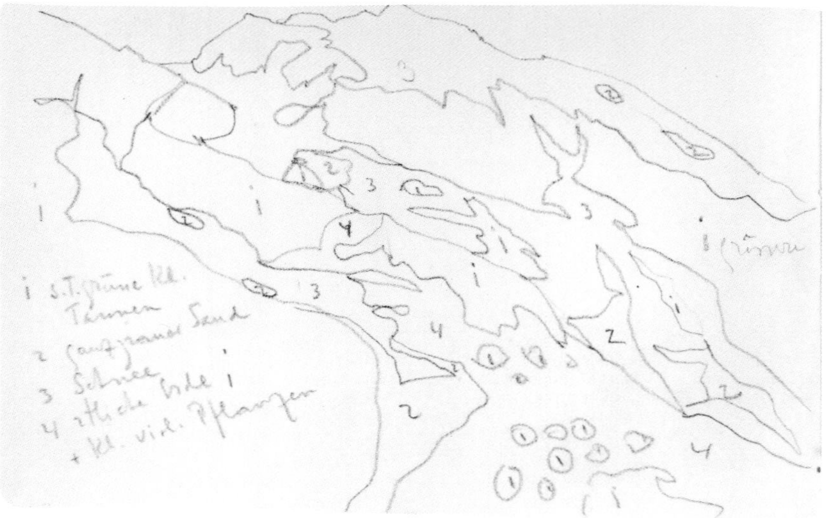

19, p.70

**p.68** Pencil sketch of landscape with woods

**p.69** Pencil sketch of landscape with rocks

**p.70** Pencil sketch of mountainous landscape
Inscribed l.l.: '1 s.t. grüne kl. / Tannen / 2 ganzgrauer Sand / 3 Schnee / 4 rtliche Erde / + kl. viol. Pflanzen'; c.r.: 'grünere'

REFERENCES
Hanfstaengl 1974, p.144, ill.

**pp.71–102** Blank

**p.103** Pencil sketch of walled city

REFERENCES
Hanfstaengl 1974, pp.143–144, ill.

Hanfstaengl interpreted the walled city as a Russian motif and related the sketch to a picture done later in Paris *Morgenstunde* (Barnett no.221). It is, however, reminiscent of the walled city in Sousse and may relate to his trip in Tunisia.

**p.104** Blank

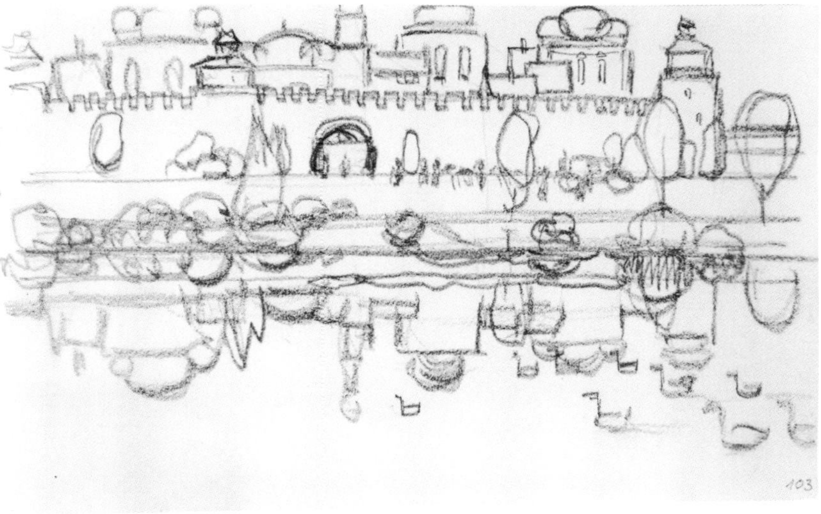

19, p.103

**p.105** Pencil sketch of bridge and houses
Inscribed c.l.: 'Hötting'; u.l.: 'Oben s schw. Berge / Schnee u. Wolken'; u.c.: 's.w. Haus / d. gr. Tannen'

Hötting is a village outside Innsbruck in Austria.

**pp.106–107** Blank

**p.108** Pencil sketch of village with figures and shrine
Inscribed l.l.: 'Hötting'; u.l.: '1- w. / 2- schw / 3- rt od. rs. / 4- gelb'; u.r.: 'Bäume'

REFERENCES
Hanfstaengl 1974, p.144. ill.
Barnett and Friedel 1995, no.184, color ill.

Kandinsky also made a drawing of the old parish church in Hötting (vol.I, cat. no.72).

Inside back cover inscribed:
'Arzler Scharte'
The reference is to a mountain near Innsbruck.

19, p.105

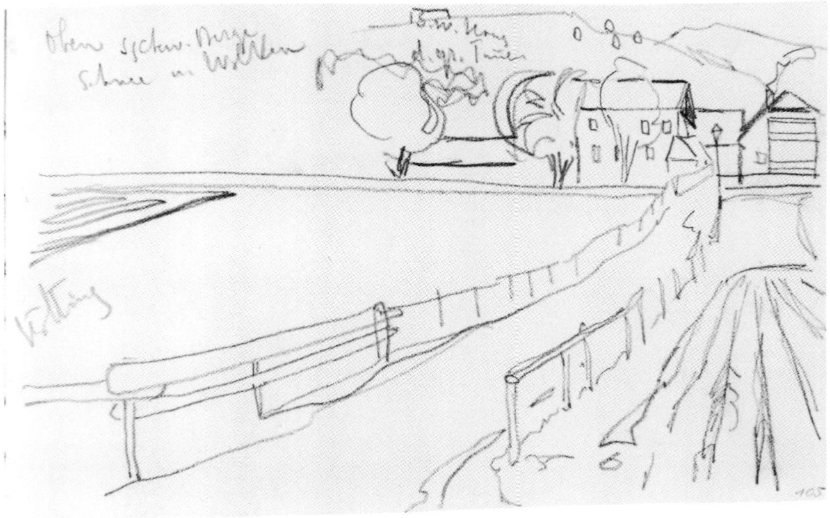

19, p.108

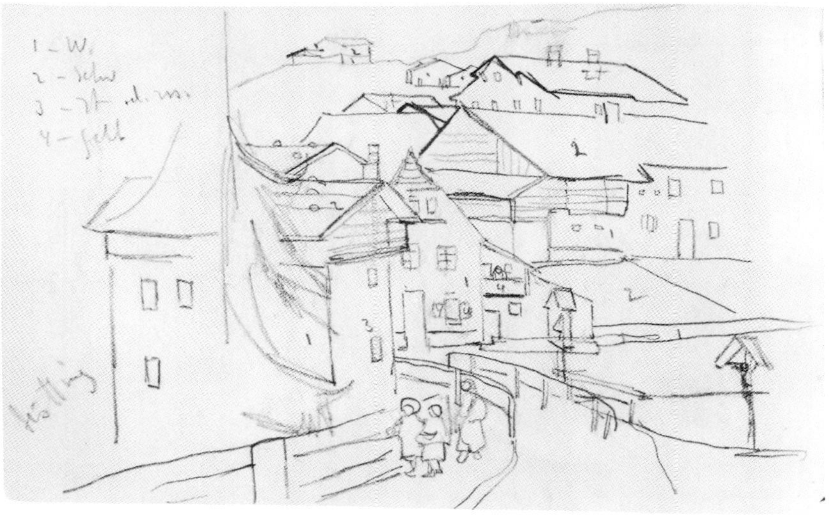

# Sketchbook 20

Probably 1905–1907

Dark grey cardboard sketchbook with black spine; inside back cover stamp from Franz Sauer, Munich (Türkenstrasse 87)
Contains 80 pages (40 sheets), each 15.8 x 10.3 cm (6¼ x 4 in), of which pp.35–49 are blank
Page numbers inscribed at later date with odd numbers at lower right

Hanfstaengl 1974, pp.146–147

LOCATION
Städtische Galerie im Lenbachhaus, Munich (GMS 327)

HISTORY
Gabriele Münter, Murnau, until 1957

The sketchbook has been dated c.1903 and 1905–1907. The last pages contain sketches done in Sestri Levante at the end of 1905, and the first pages have been related to prints of 1903. However, it is plausible that pp.1–4 were done in Paris during Kandinsky's stay there from May 1906 to June 1907. The majority of studies in the sketchbook date from this time.

**p.1** Brown ink and pencil drawing for *Die Jagd*

REFERENCES
Hanfstaengl 1974, p.146
Barnett and Friedel 1995 no.100, color ill.

This drawing has been related to *Die Jagd* of 1903 (Roethel no.23), which was first published in *Gedichte ohne Wörte* in late 1903 or early 1904. It is, however, possible that Kandinsky made this study in Paris in 1907, when the black and white woodcut appeared several times in the French periodical *Les Tendances Nouvelles* and was developed into a color linocut, *Der Jäger* (Roethel no.50).

(See color plate p.122)

**p.2** Pencil sketch for *Dreiköpfiger Drache*

The motif of the three-headed dragon appears in Kandinsky's woodcut in early 1907 (see facing page).

**p.3** Brown ink and pencil drawing for *Dreiköpfiger Drache*

REFERENCES
Hanfstaengl 1974, p.146
Barnett and Friedel 1995, no.102, color ill.

Roethel dated the woodcut *Dreiköpfiger Drache* to 1903 (Roethel no.26), although it was not included in Kandinsky's album *Gedichte ohne Wörte*. It was first published in *Les Tendances Nouvelles* (no.28) early in 1907. Kandinsky changed the serpent's head into a three-headed dragon in the woodcut.

20, p.1

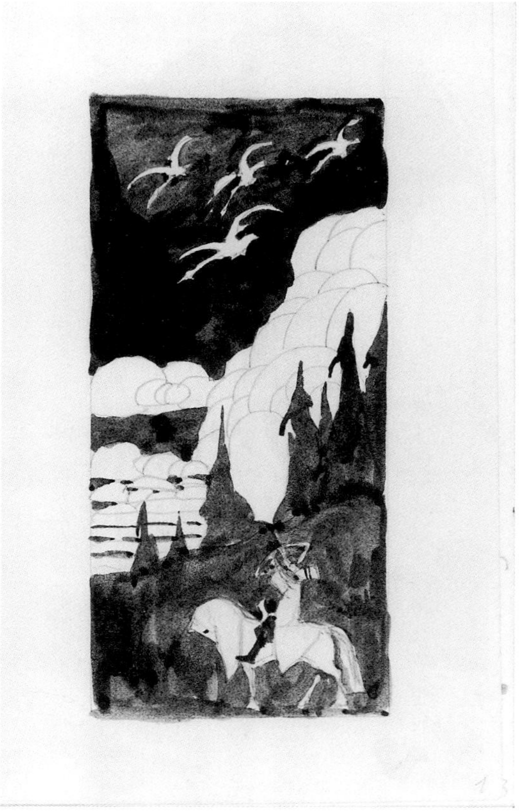

20, pp.2-3

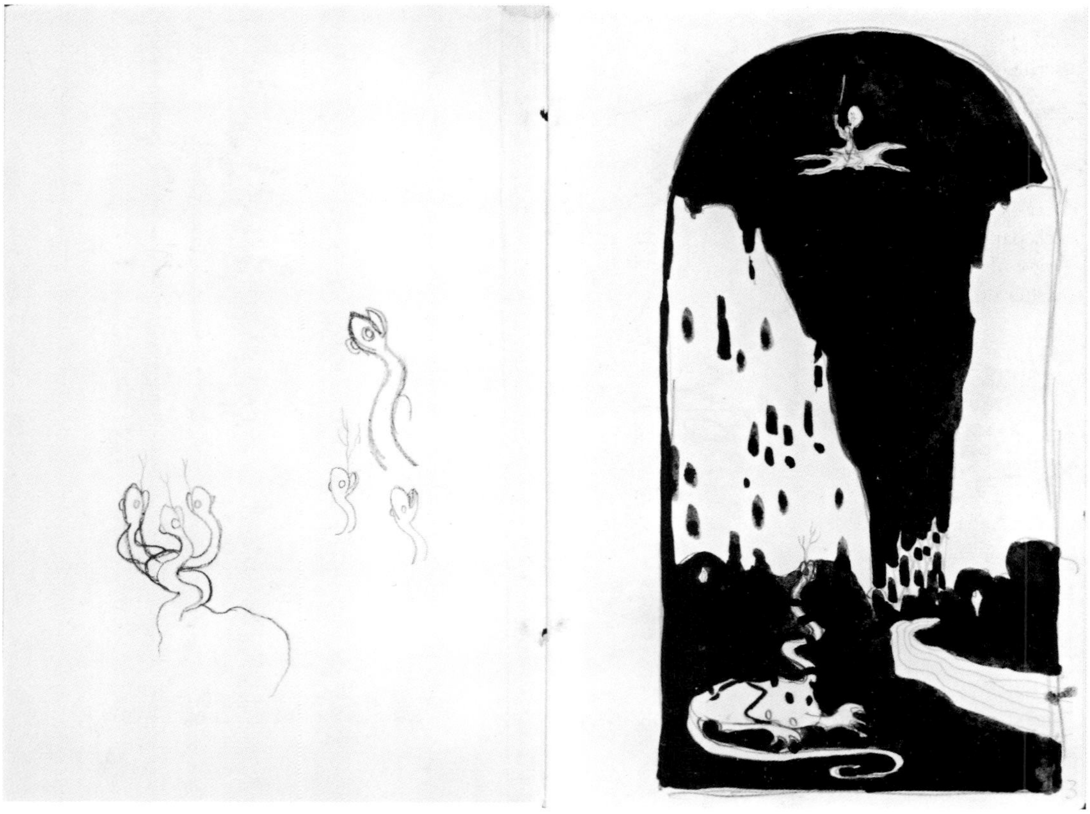

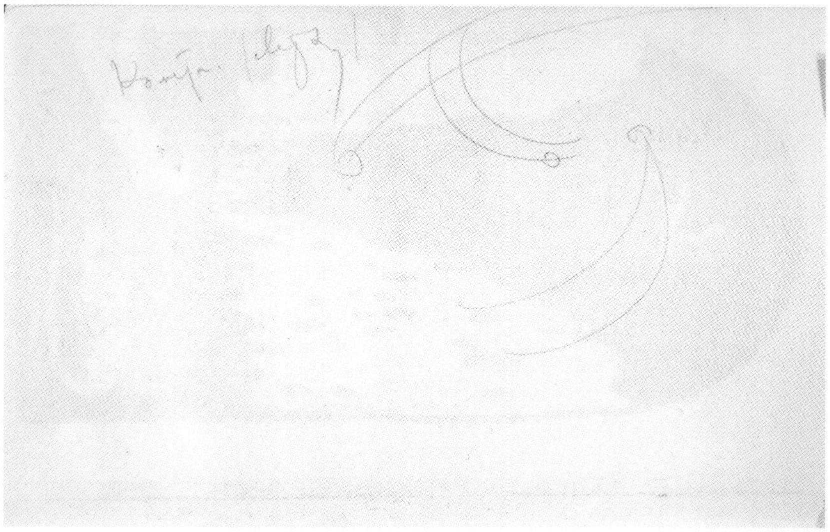

20, p.4

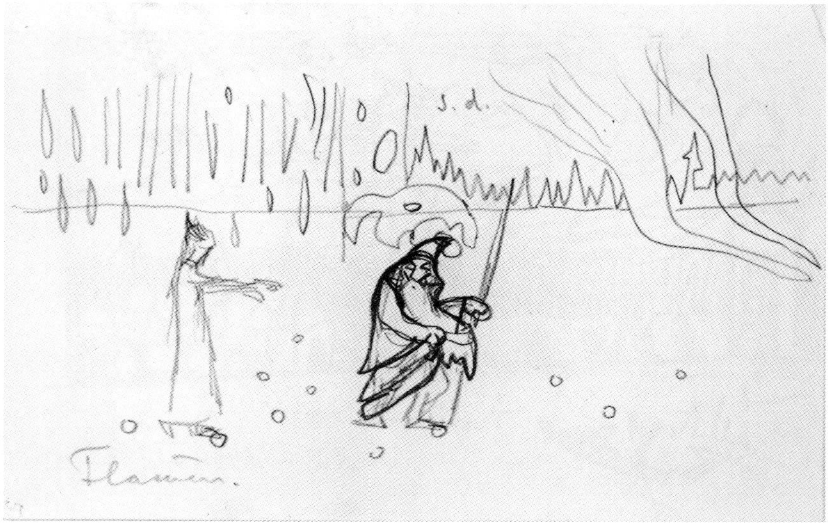


20, p.5

**p.4** Pencil sketches of comets
Inscribed u.l. in Cyrillic: 'Kometa (svet)'

The sketch is inscribed 'comet' and 'light'. The image is reminiscent of Kandinsky's work *Der Komet* of 1900, which may be identified with *Nächtlicher Reiter* (Barnett no.35), and also the decoration on Kandinsky's study for a chair in Sketchbook 7 (GMS 338, p.34).

**p.5** Pencil study for *Flamme* of 1907
Inscribed l.l.: 'Flammen'; u.c.: 's.d.'

REFERENCES
Hanfstaengl 1974, p.146, ill.
Barnett 1992, p.208

There is also a gouache study on black paper for Kandinsky's woodcut *Flamme* of 1907 (Barnett no.238; Roethel no.66).

**p.6** Blank

**p.7** Pencil study for *Glocken* of 1907
Inscribed l.l.: 'Glocken'; l.c.: 'Das Boot'; l.r.: 'stellen braun' and with color notations

REFERENCES
Hanfstaengl 1974, p.146, ill.
Washton Long 1980, pp.43, 167 n.9, ill.12
Zweite 1982, pp.156–157, ill.30
Barnett and Friedel 1995, no.224, color ill.
Barnett 2006, p.62

This sketch is related to an ink drawing, *Glocken* (vol.I, cat. no.92), which is a study for the tempera painting *Sturmglocke* that Kandinsky painted in Paris in 1907 (Barnett no.224).

**p.8** Blank

**p.9** Pencil study for *Morgen* of 1905
Inscribed u.c.: 'Grün giftig'; c.: 'weiss'; l.l.: 'rosa gelb'; l.r.: 'schw. / w. / grau / Morgen'

REFERENCES
Hanfstaengl 1974, p.146, ill.
Barnett 1992, p.181, ill.a

Kandinsky's tempera painting *Morgen* (Barnett no.196), which he first exhibited in the Salon d'Automne in Paris in 1907, is known only from this study.

**p.10** Blank

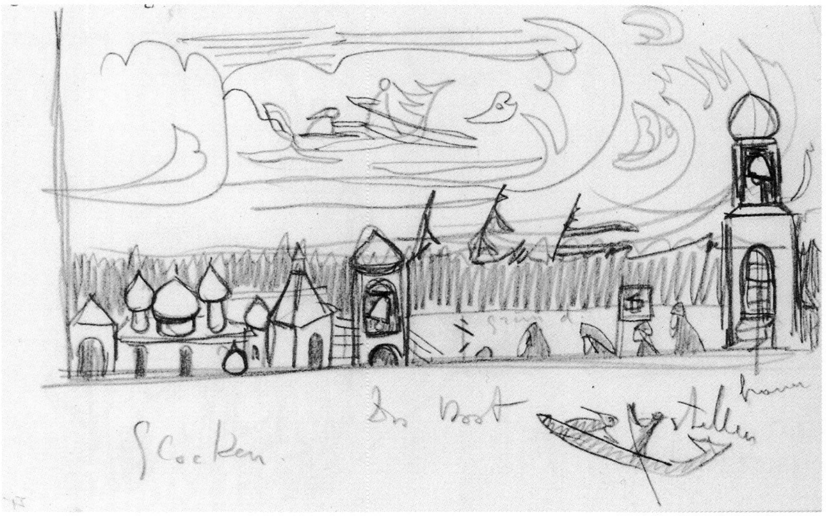


20, p.7

20, p.9

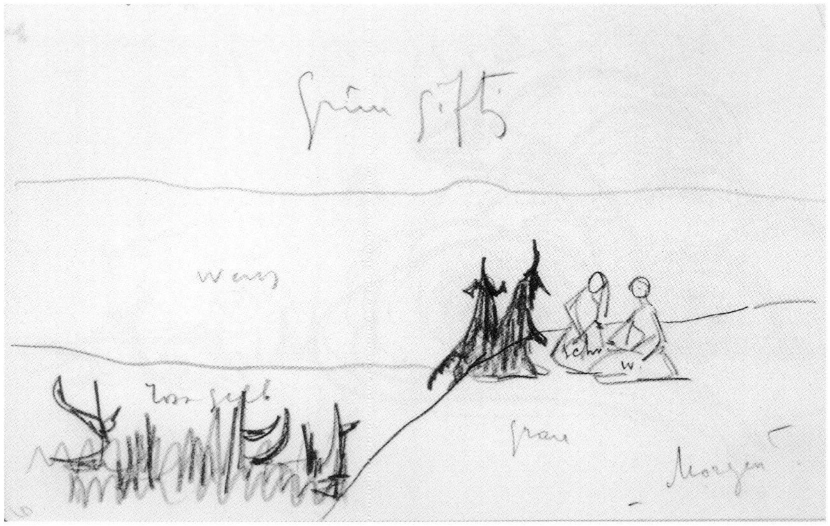

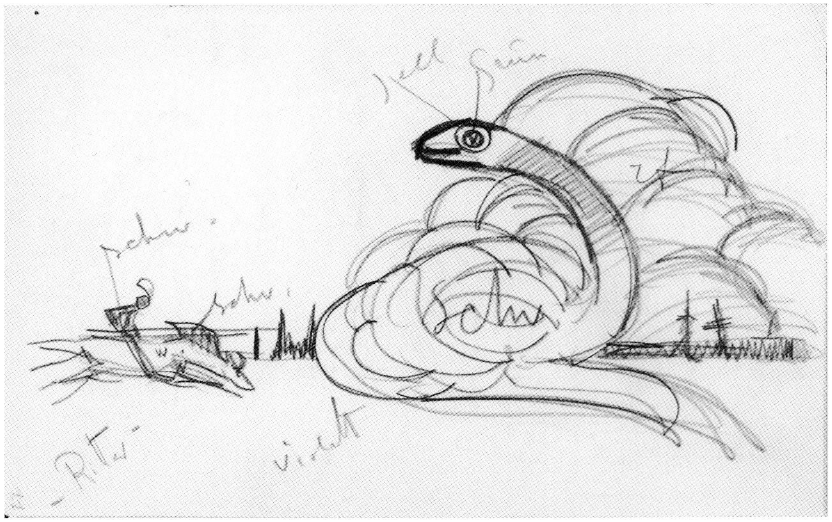

20, p.11

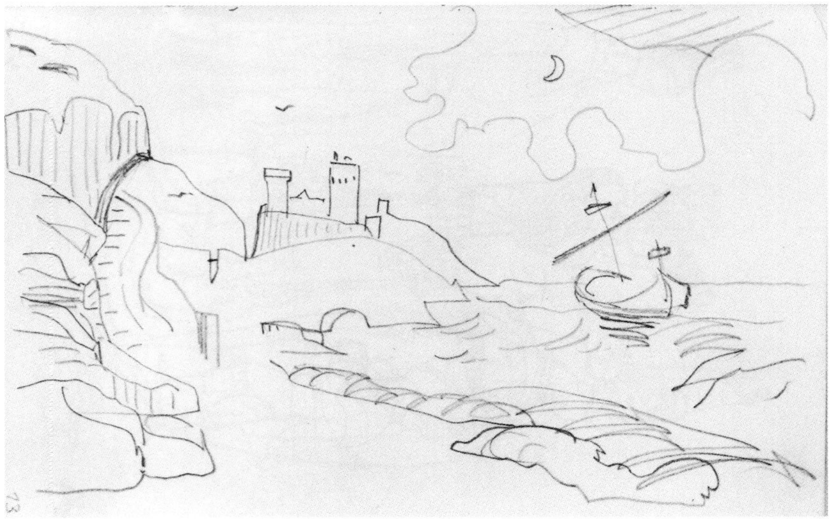

20, p.13

**p.11** Pencil study for *Schlange* of 1907
Inscribed l.l.: 'Ritter'; c.l.: 'schw. / w. / schw. / violett'; c.: 'Schw'; u.c.: 'grell grün / rt'

REFERENCES
Hanfstaengl 1974, p.146, ill.
Weiss 1982, p.78, ill.41
Barnett 1992, p.205
Becks-Malorny 1993, p.20, ill.
Weiss 1995, pp.74, ill.70, 76

Weiss (1995) identified the sketch as St. George battling the dragon and dated it c.1903–1904; however, the sketch is clearly related to Kandinsky's tempera painting *Schlange* of 1907 (Barnett no.229).

**p.12** Blank

**p.13** Pencil drawing of castle and ship

REFERENCES
Hanfstaengl 1974, p.146, ill.
Zweite 1982, p.152, ill.15

Hanfstaengl related the scene to other drawings of ships on stormy seas: for example, a drawing of c.1908 (vol.I, cat. no.103) and a coeval study in Sketchbook 26 (GMS 328, p.18). It seems likely, however, that this night-time seascape with castle and ship was intended for an unknown or unexecuted picture. Although it was probably inspired by the castle in Rapallo, where Kandinsky and Gabriele Münter stayed for several months from late December 1905 until 30 April 1906, it does not depict a specific view of the harbor in Rapallo. The drawing can be related to *Rapallo-Stürmische See* and *Rapallo- Bucht* (Roethel and Benjamin nos.146, 156).

**p.14** Pencil studies of four figures in medieval costume
Inscribed u.c.: 'XIV'

The source (or sources) from which Kandinsky copied these figures and those on pp.16–17, 20–24, 26–27 has not been identified.

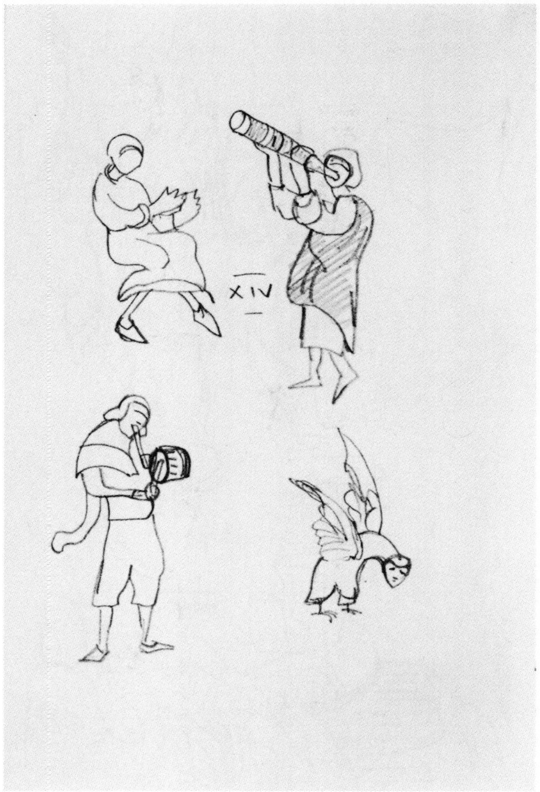


20, p.14

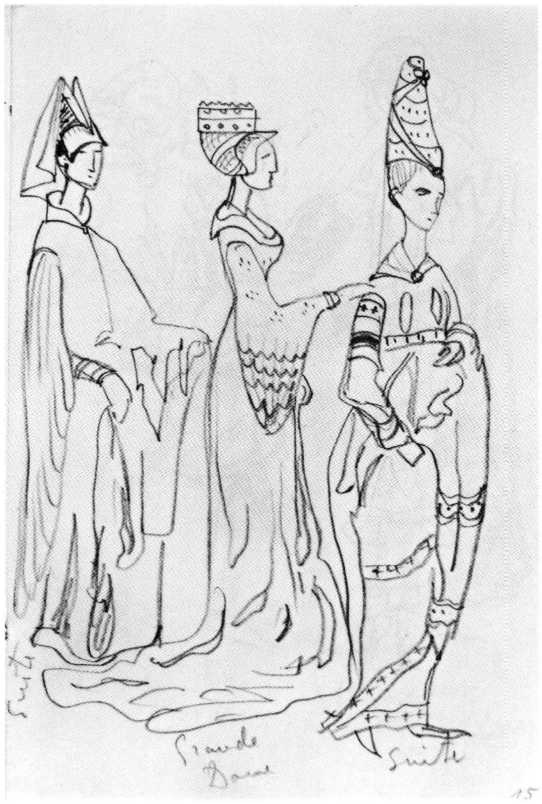


20, p.15

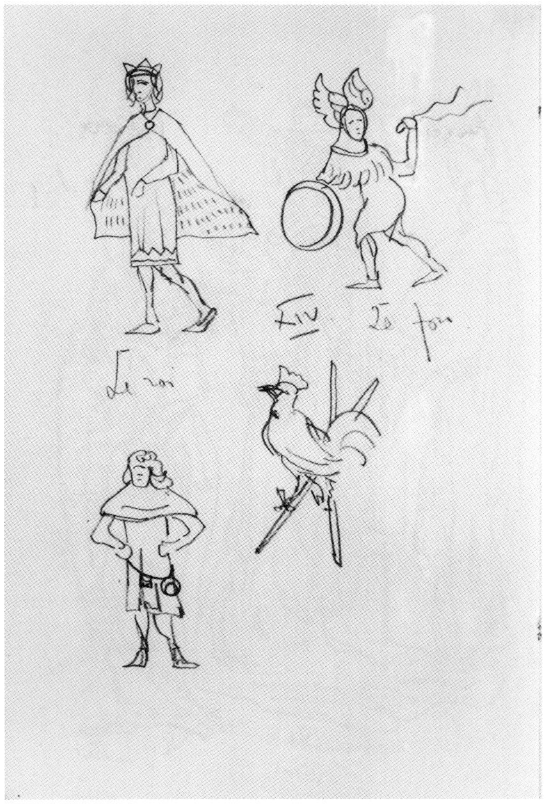


20, p.16

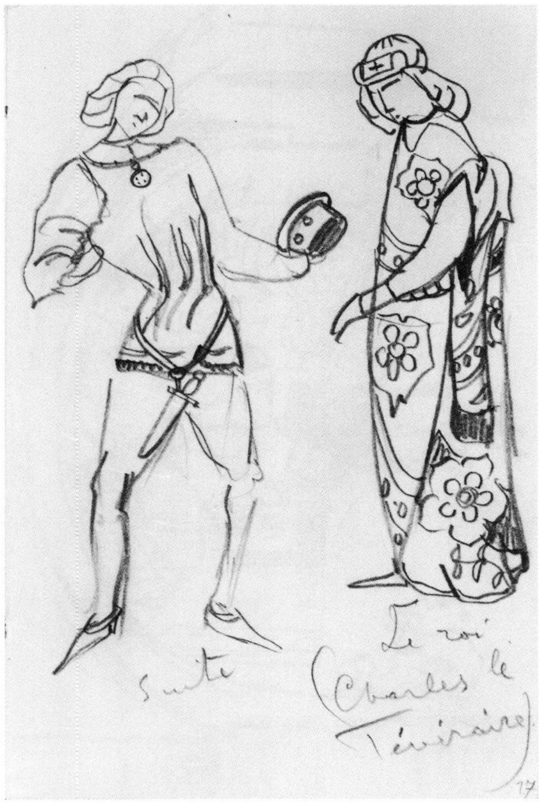


20, p.17

**p.15** Pencil studies of three women in costume
Inscribed l.l.: 'Suite'; l.c.: 'Grande / Dame'; l.r.: 'Suite'

REFERENCES
Podzemskaia 2000, p.128

Kandinsky copied these fifteenth-century figures from J. Quicherat's book *Histoire du costume en France* (Paris, 1877, pp.297, 307), probably when he lived near Paris in 1906–1907. For other drawings copied from Quicherat's book, see vol.I, nos.39–41.

**p.16** Pencil studies of four figures in medieval costume
Inscribed c.l.: 'Le roi'; c.: 'XIV'; c.r.: 'Le fou'

REFERENCES
Podzemskaia 2000, p.128

These studies were probably made when Kandinsky lived near Paris, since the captions are in French and other drawings in this sketchbook were done in France.

**p.17** Pencil studies of two men in medieval costume
Inscribed l.l.: 'Suite'; l.r.: 'Le roi / (Charles le / Téméraire)'

REFERENCES
Hanfstaengl 1974, p.146, ill.

The inscription refers to Charles the Bold (1433–1477), who was the Duke of Burgundy.

**p.18** Blank

**p.19** Pencil sketch of cityscape
Inscribed l.r.: 'Rennes'

REFERENCES
Hanfstaengl 1974, pp.146, 147, ill.
Barnett 1992, p.185
Barnett and Friedel 1995, no.213, color ill.

In late July 1906, Kandinsky took a trip to Brittany, where he may have stopped in Rennes. Smokestacks also appeared in his sketch for *Affiche einer französischen Brauerei* (Barnett no.205) and in Sketchbook 23 (GMS 336, p.97).

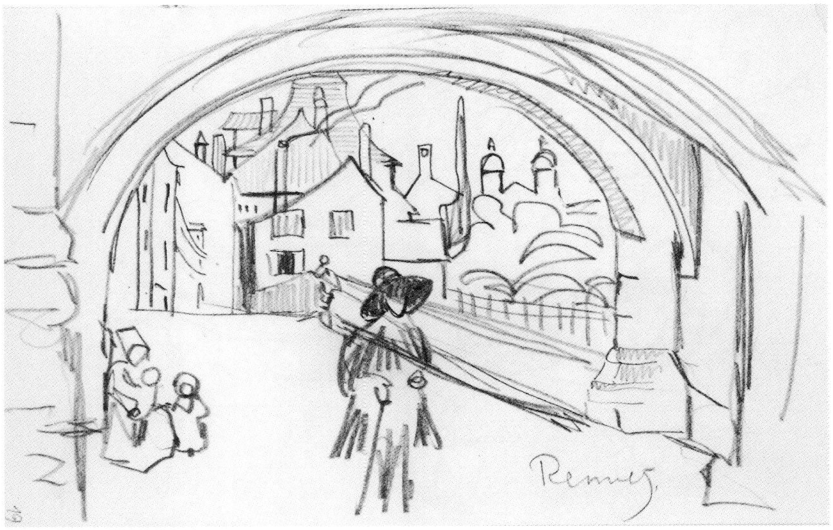


20, p.19

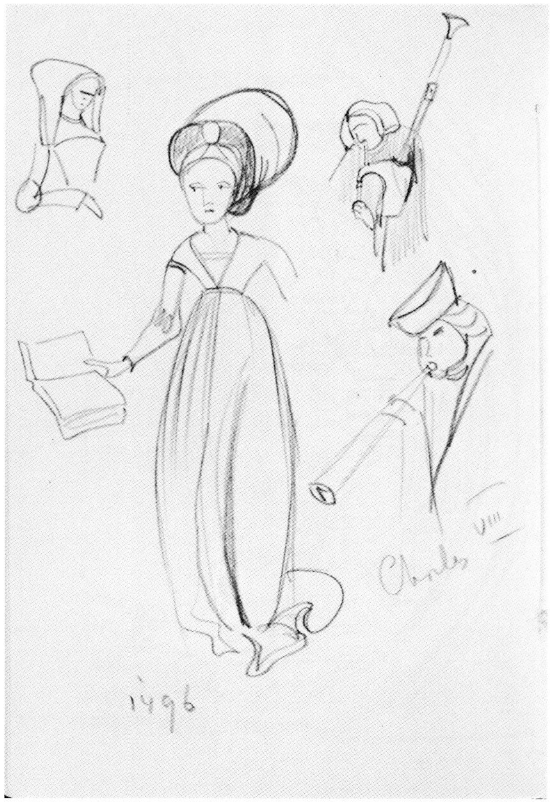


20, p.20

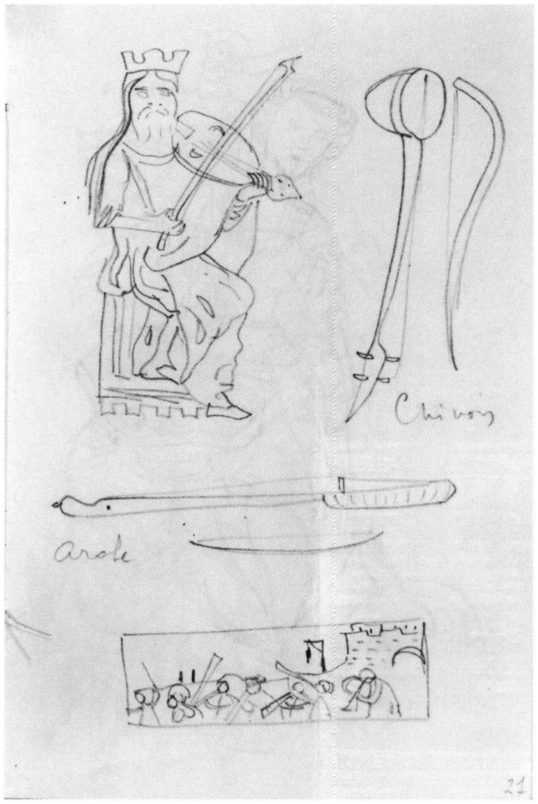


20, p.21

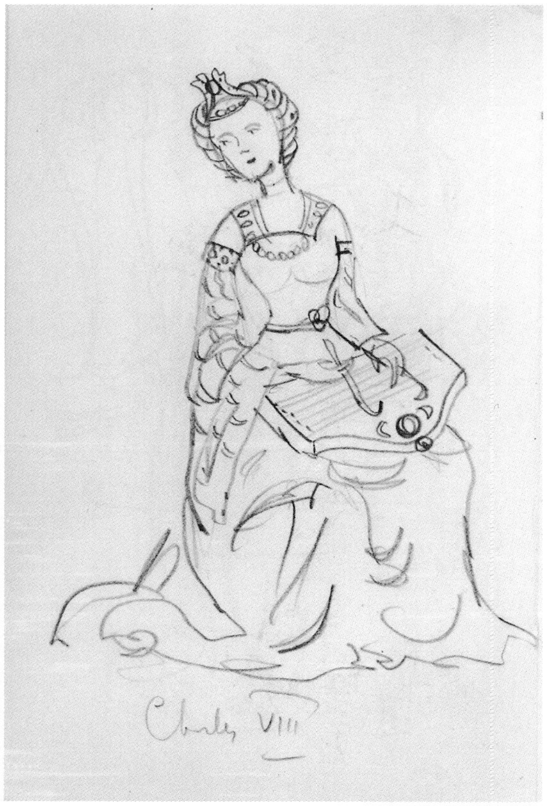


20, p.22

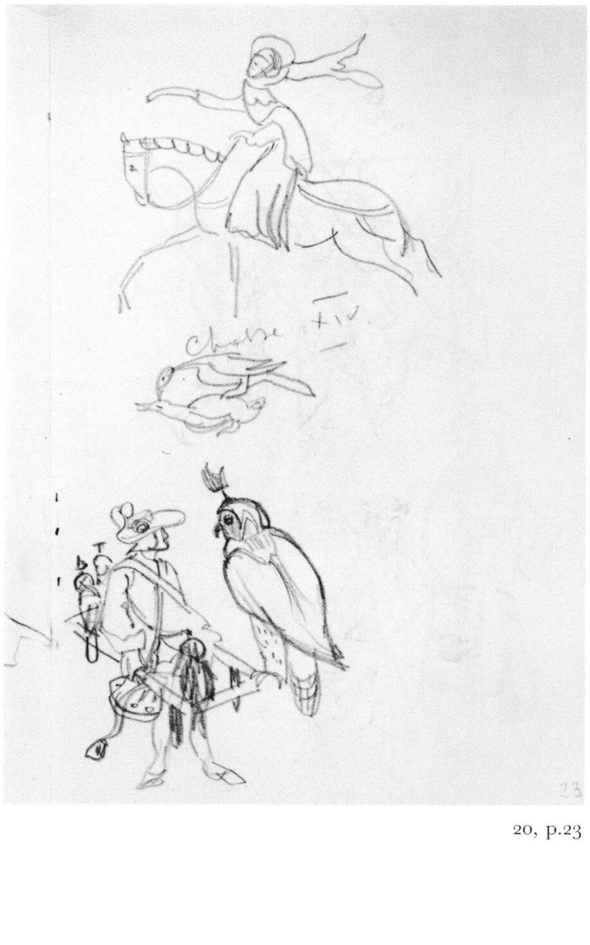

20, p.23

**p.20** Pencil studies of four figures in costume
Inscribed l.l.: '1496'; l.r.: 'Charles VIII'

REFERENCES
Podzemskaia 2000, p.128

Charles VIII (1470–1498) was king of France from 1483 to 1498. It is not known which publication contained the illustrations that Kandinsky copied (see pp.21–24 below)

**p.21** Pencil studies of battle scene (below) and musical instruments (above)
Inscribed c.l.: 'arabe'; c.r.: 'chinois'

REFERENCES
Hanfstaengl 1974, p.147, ill.

The source of these images in a French publication has not been identified.

**p.22** Pencil study of woman in costume
Inscribed l.c.: 'Charles VIII'

Charles VIII was king of France from 1483 to 1498; he married Anne of Brittany in 1491.

**p.23** Pencil sketches of hunting scenes
Inscribed c.: 'Chasse XIV'

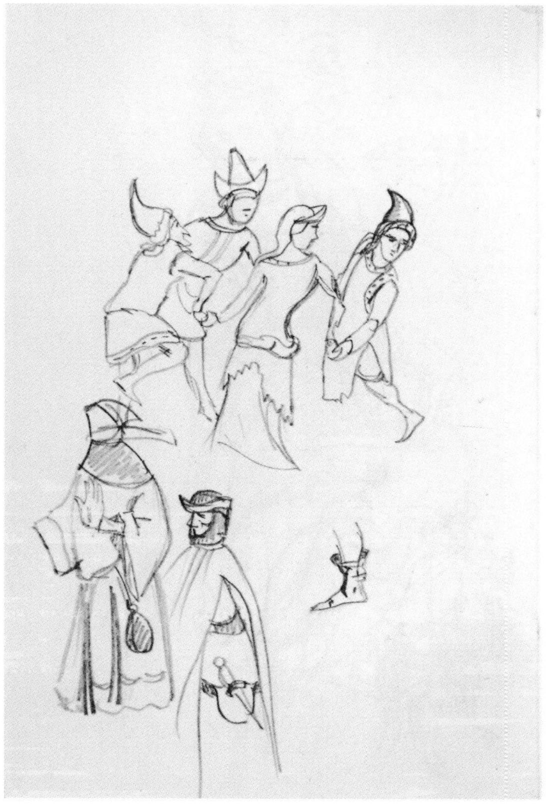

20, p.24

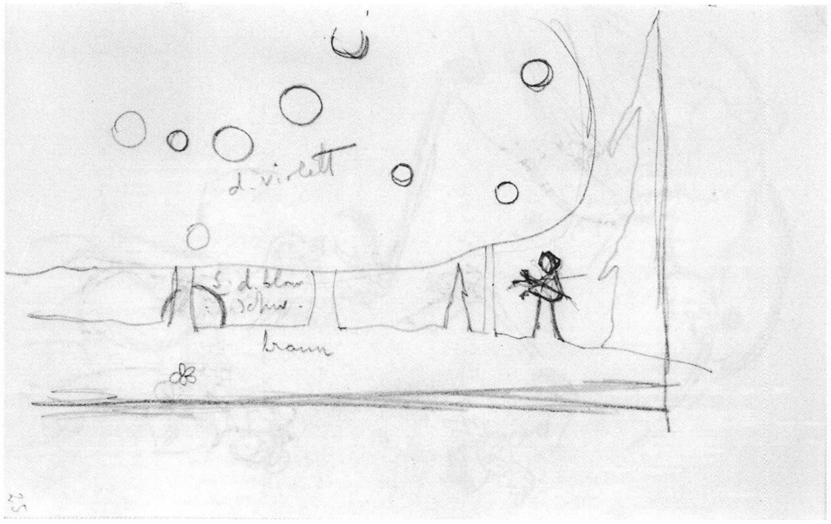


20, p.25

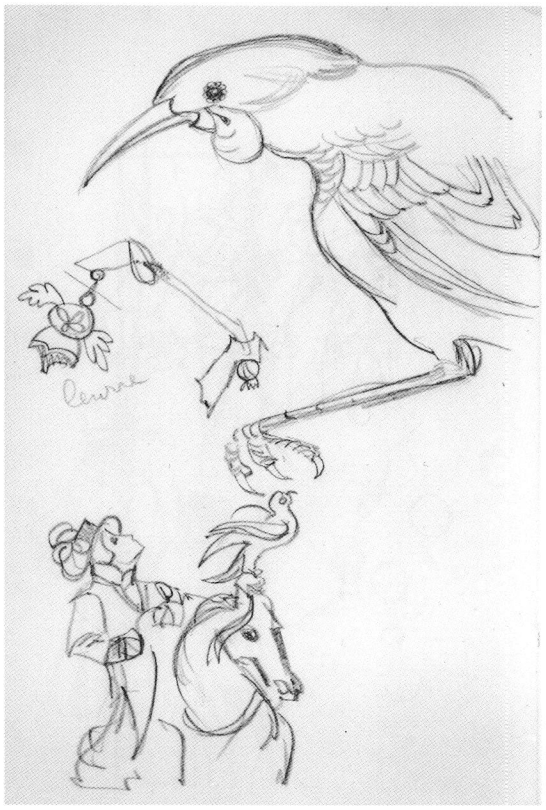


20, p.26

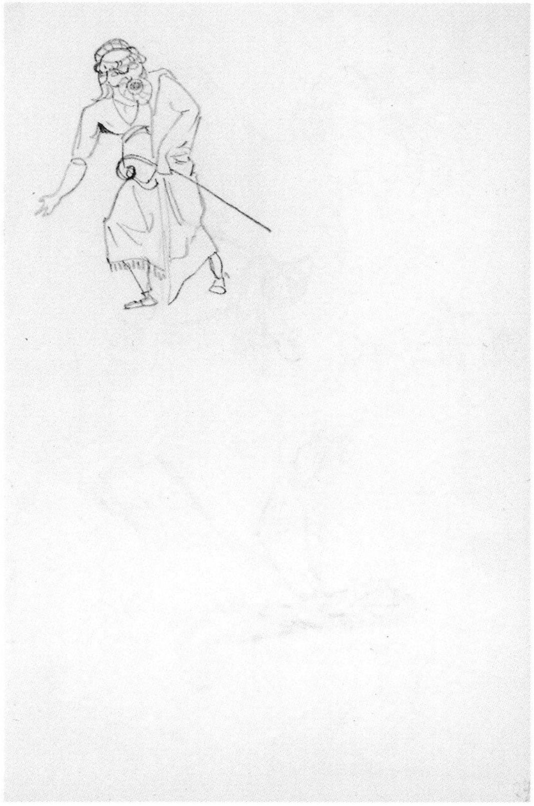

20, p.27

**p.24** Pencil sketches of medieval costumes

**p.25** Pencil study of figures in landscape
Inscribed c.: 'd.violett / s.d. blau / schw. / braun'

REFERENCES
Hanfstaengl 1974, p.147, ill.

This sketch was probably made for an unexecuted work.

**p.26** Pencil sketches of hunting scenes
Inscribed c.l.: 'leurre'

This drawing may come from the same unidentified French source as the sketch on p.23. In addition, it bears a resemblance to those in Sketchbook 23 (GMS 336, pp.95, 96).

**p.27** Pencil sketch of man in Greek costume

Kandinsky copied an unidentified illustration.

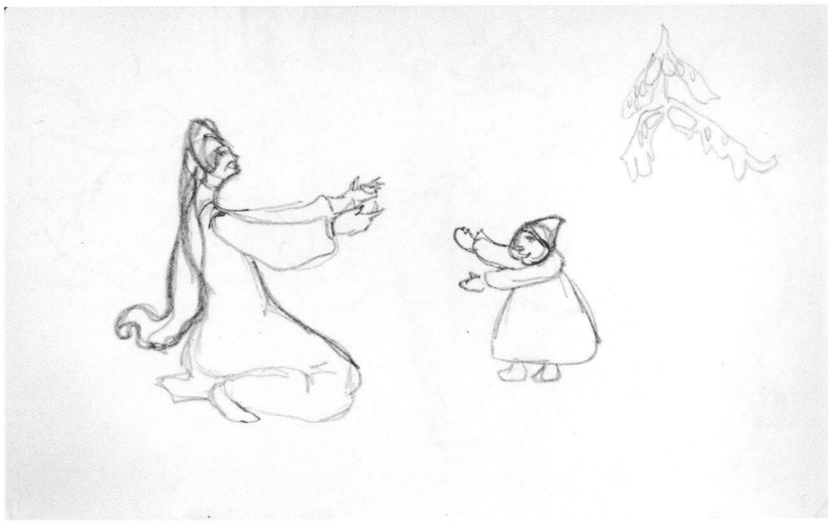

20, p.28

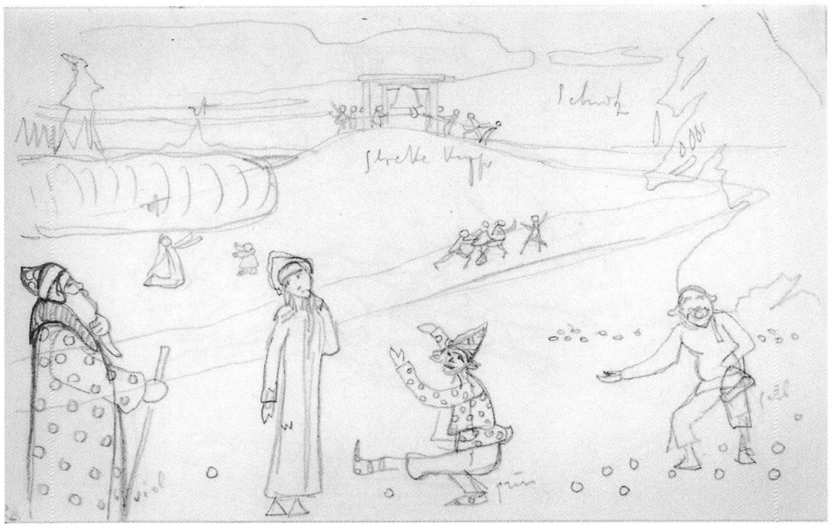

20, p.29

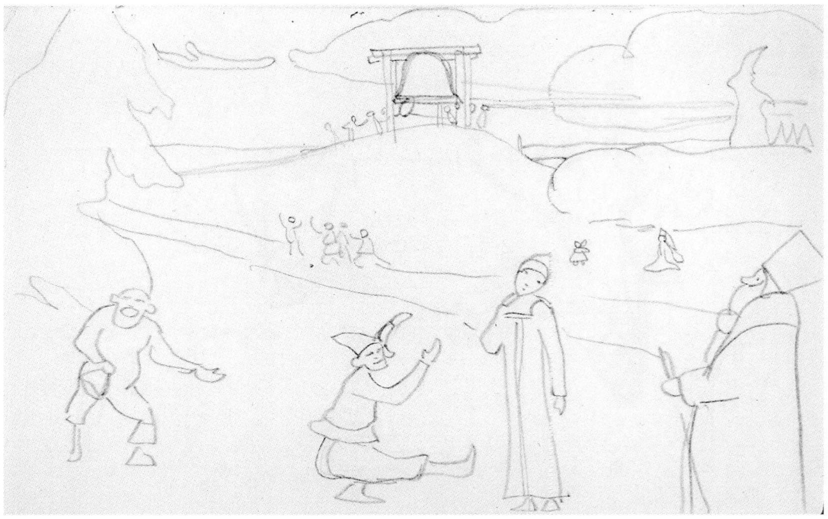

20, p.30

20, p.31

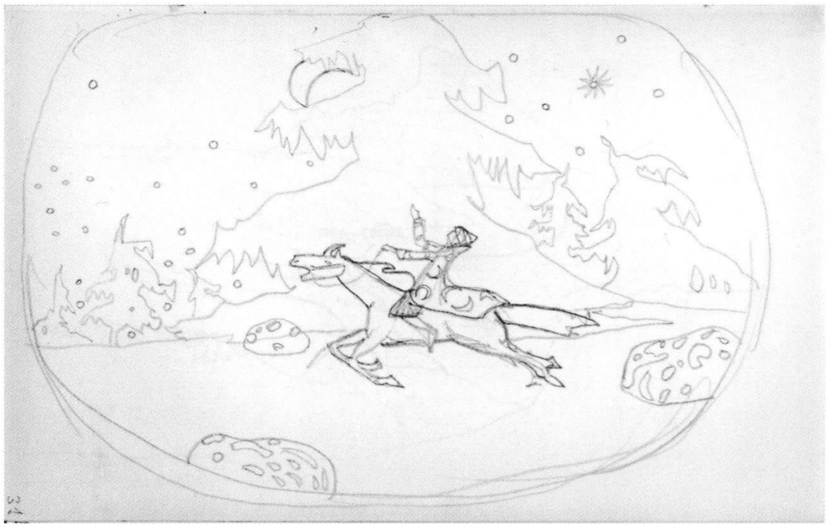

**p.28** Pencil study for *Sturmglocke*

REFERENCES
Hanfstaengl 1974, p.146
Barnett 1992, p.202

The sketch of a woman and small child reappears in the background of the study on the facing page for *Sturmglocke* of 1907 (Barnett no.224).

**p.29** Pencil study for *Sturmglocke*
Inscribed u.l.: 'rt / rt'; u.c.: 'Glocke Kupf[er]'; u.r.: 'Schwtz'; l.l.: 'viol'; l.c.: 'grün'; l.r.: 'gelb'

REFERENCES
Hanfstaengl 1974, p.146
Barnett 1992, p.202

**p.30** Pencil study for *Sturmglocke*

REFERENCES
Barnett 1992, p.202
Podzemskaia 2000, p.130, fig.26

The drawing presents the overall composition for *Sturmglocke*, but seen in reverse.

**p.31** Pencil study of rider on horseback

REFERENCES
Roethel 1970, p.479, ill.48
Hanfstaengl 1974, pp.146, 147, ill.
Barnett 1992, p.219

This sketch is related to *Entwurf für den Farbholzschnitt 'Berge'* of 1908–1909 (Barnett no.248) and a drawing in Sketchbook 26 (GMS 328, p.43).

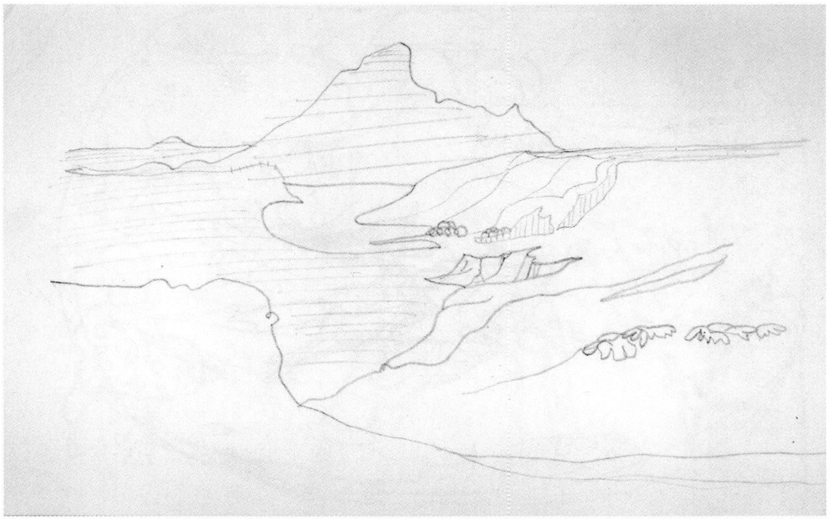

20, p.32

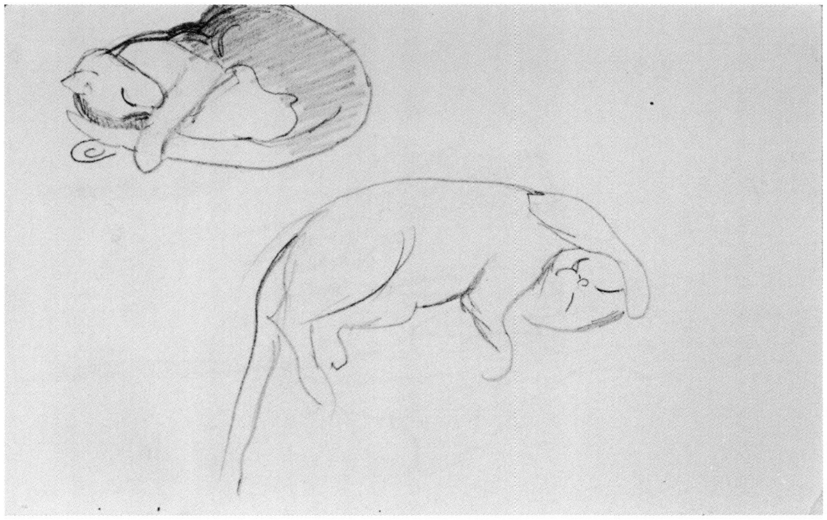

20, p.34

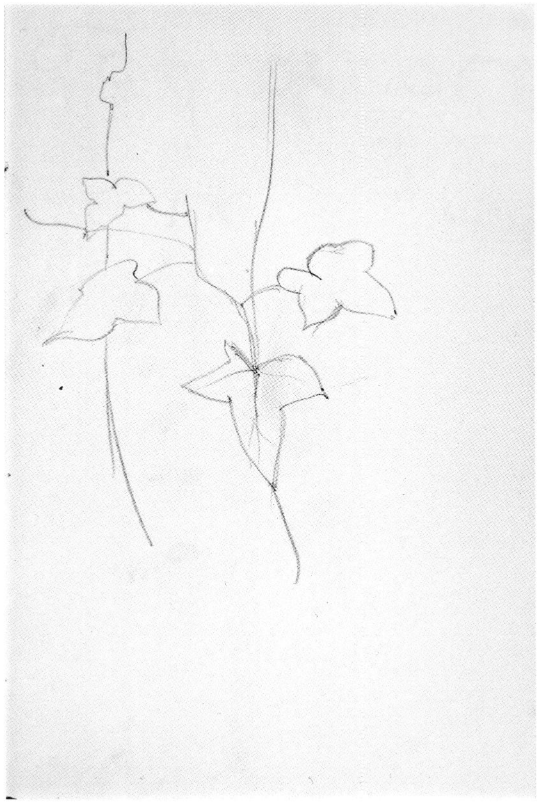

20, p.50

**p.32** Pencil sketch of landscape with hills and lake

The landscape resembles that in Sketchbook 26 (GMS 328, pp.15–16) as well as studies made in Sketchbook 25 in South Tyrol in 1908. However, this drawing may have been done earlier when Kandinsky was in Bad Reichenhall in July 1907.

**p.33** Blank

**p.34** Pencil sketches of cat

When Kandinsky lived in Sèvres near Paris in 1906–1907, he made many drawings of his cat Waske in Sketchbook 23.

**pp.35–49** Blank

**p.50** Pencil study of leaves (upside down)

**p.51** Blank

**p.52** Pencil study of foliage
Inscribed l.c.: 'einzelne Flecken / Alter grosser / artiger Baum.'

20, p.52

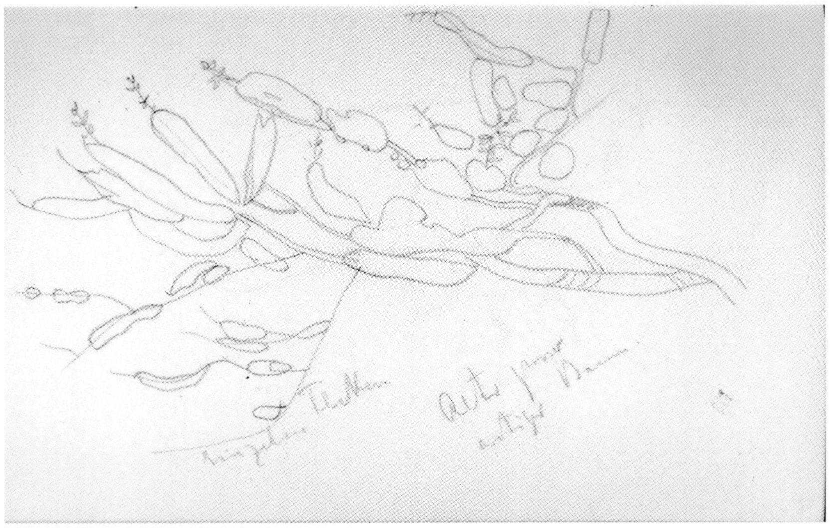

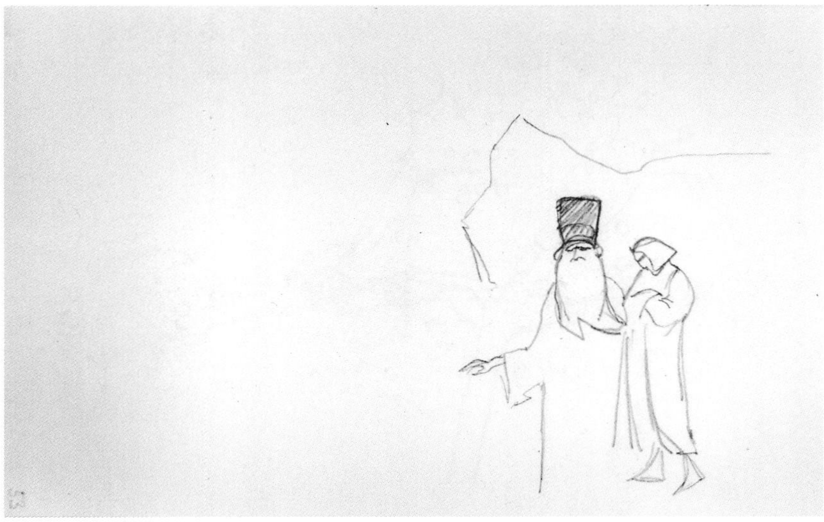

20, p.53

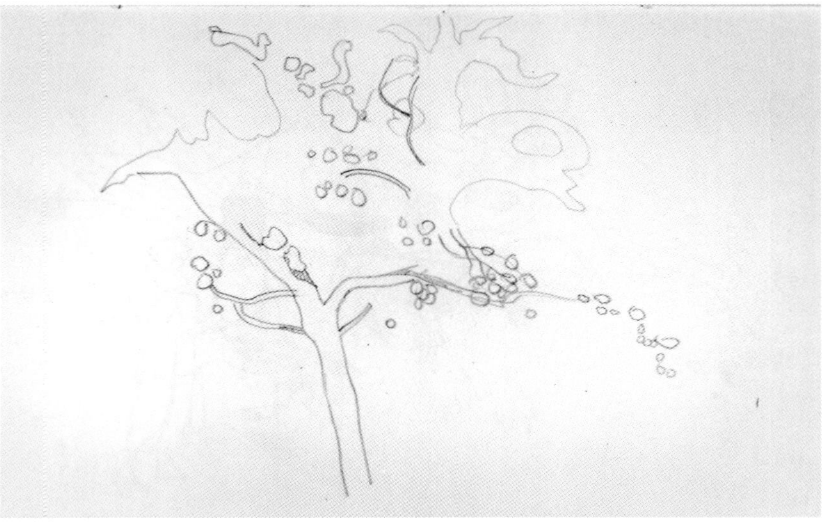

20, p.54

**p.53** Pencil sketch of two men

REFERENCES
Hanfstaengl 1974, p.146

The figures can be related to those in *Das bunte Leben* and *Morgenstunde* of 1907 (Barnett nos.219, 221).

**p.54** Pencil study of tree branches with blossoms

Kandinsky made drawings of tree blossoms in Rapallo in 1906 and paintings such as *Baumblüte in Lana I* (Roethel and Benjamin no.190) in 1908: however, these studies were probably done a year earlier in Paris

**p.55** Pencil study of tree branches with blossoms (upside down)

**p.56** Pencil study of tree branches (upside down)

**p.57** Blank

**p.58** Pencil sketch of cityscape with arch
Inscribed l.l.: 'Bellevue'; c.l.: 's. bl.'

REFERENCES
Barnett 2006, p.63

Kandinsky probably made this sketch of Bellevue in Paris in 1906. It bears a certain resemblance to another drawing (vol.I, cat. no.95).

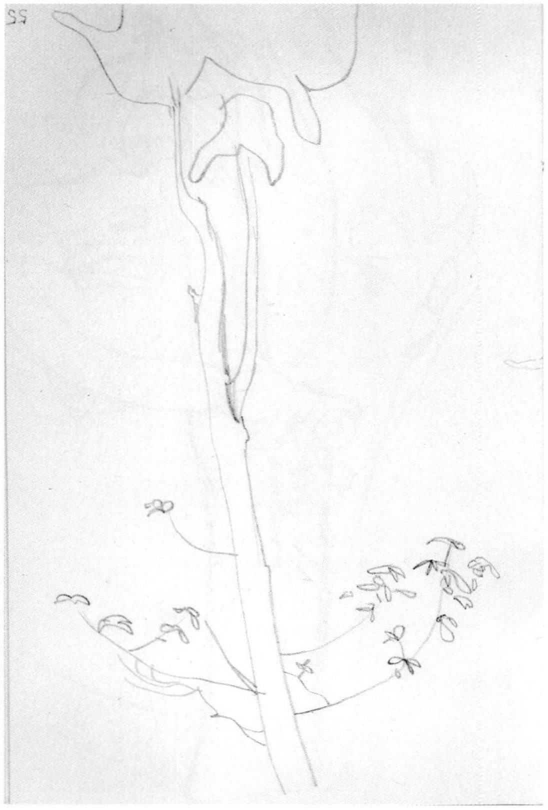

20, p.55

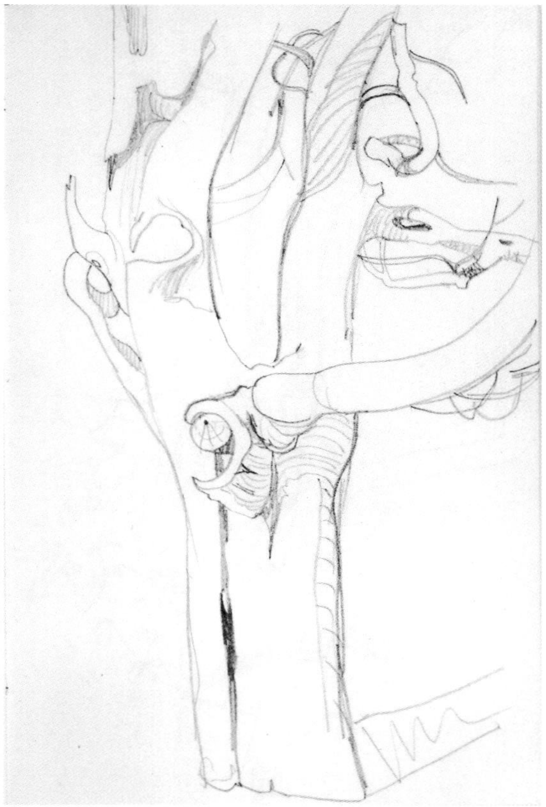

20, p.56

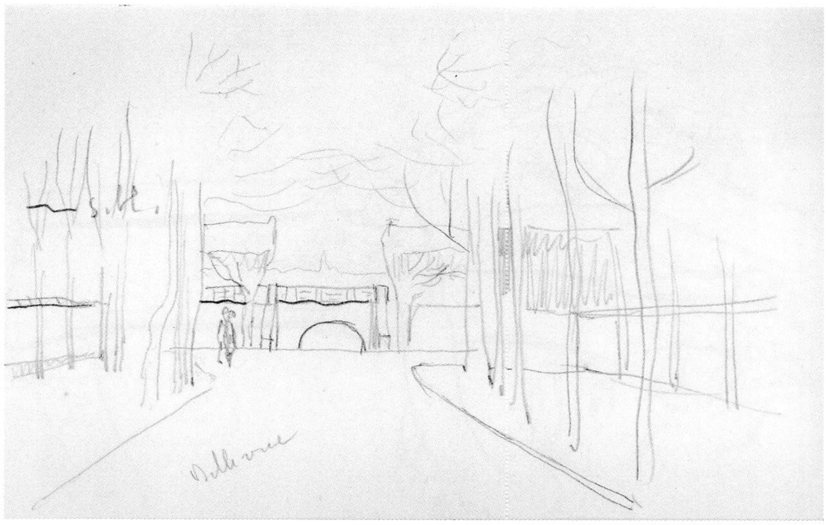

20, p.58

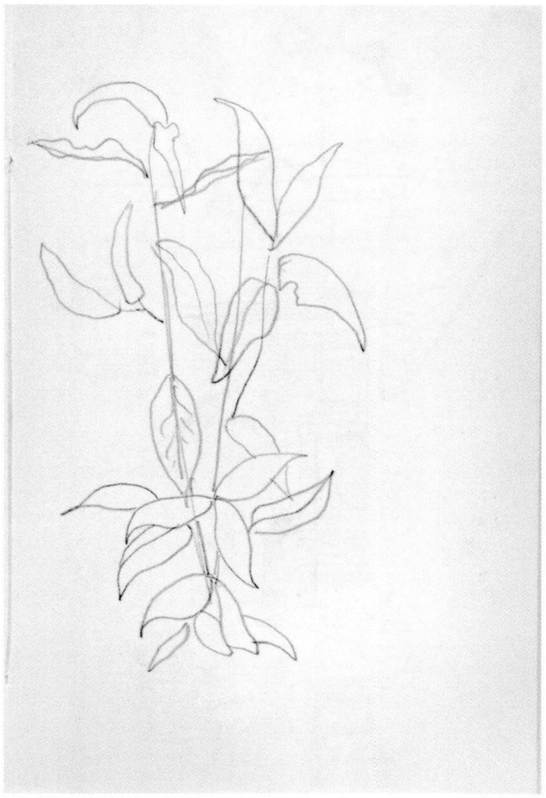

20, p.60

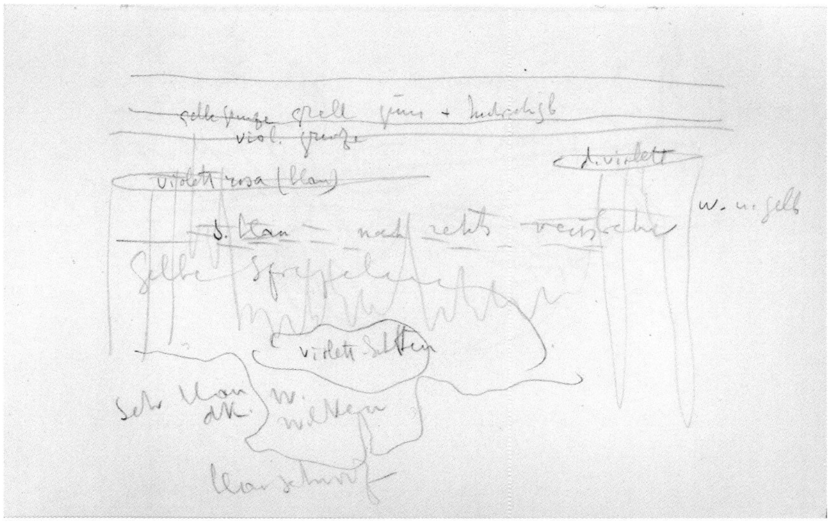

20, p.62

20, p.64

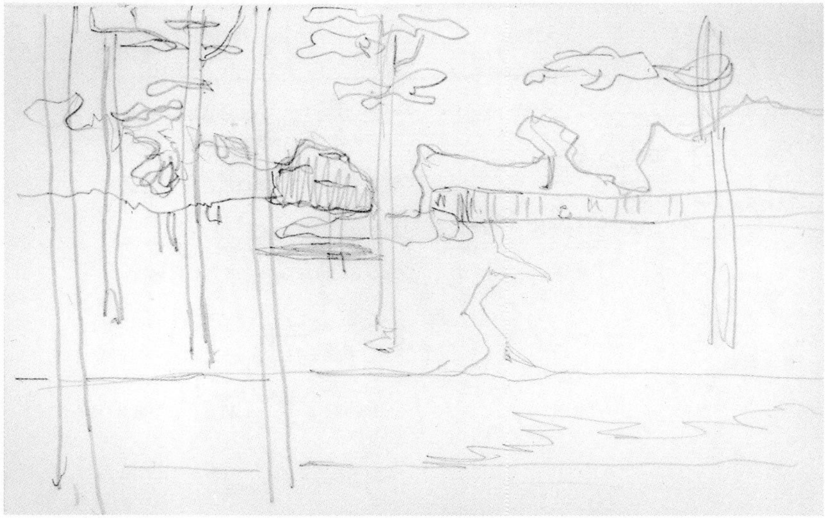

**p.59** Blank

**p.60** Pencil study of plant with leaves (upside down)

**p.61** Blank

**p.62** Pencil study of landscape
Inscribed u.c.: 'gelbe Grenze grell grün+ Indischgb / viol. grenze / violett rosa (blau)'; u.r.: 'd. violett'; c.: 'S. blau nach rechts weiss sehr'; c.r.: 'w. u. gelb'; c.: 'gelbe Spiegelung / violett. Schatten'; l.l.: 'sehr blau / dk. / w. / Wolken / blau schwarz'

This landscape drawing brings to mind studies of clouds that Kandinsky made in Austria in April 1905 (see Sketchbook 19, p.61); however, these sketches may date from late June–July 1907.

**p.63** Blank

**p.64** Pencil sketch of landscape

REFERENCES

Hanfstaengl 1974, p.147, ill.
Barnett 2006, pp.63–64

This landscape drawing may have been done in Paris in 1906–1907 or earlier in Rapallo. See vol.I, cat. nos.96, 98.

**p.65** Blank

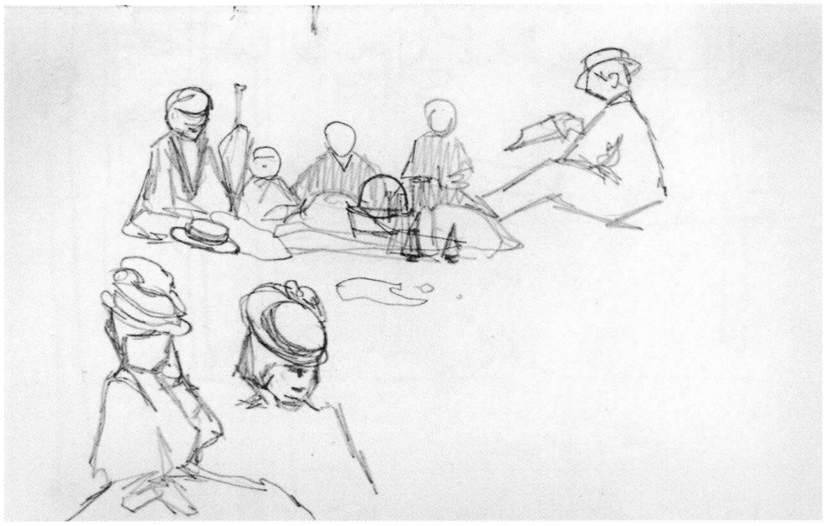

20, p.66

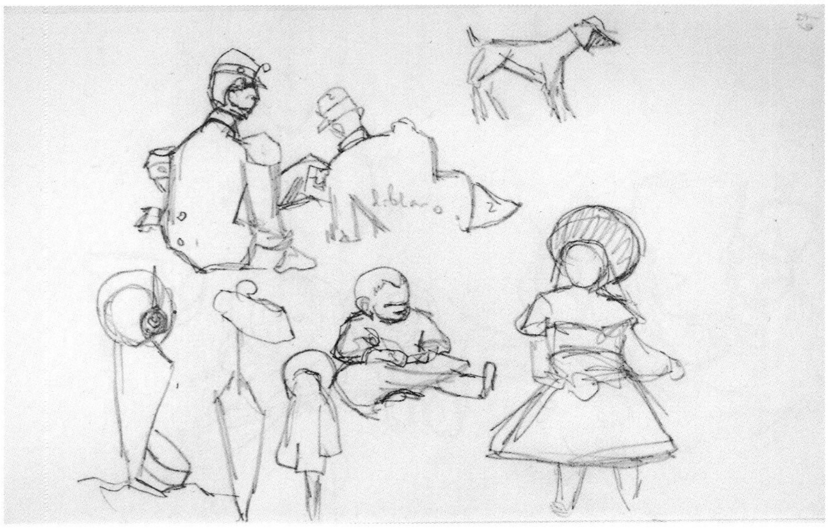

20, p.67

**p.66** Pencil sketch of figures in a park

REFERENCES

Hanfstaengl 1974, p.147, ill.

Kandinsky made these sketches of people in a park in Paris in 1906–1907.

**p.67** Pencil sketch of figures and dog in a park
Inscribed u.c.: 'd. blau / r'

REFERENCES

Hanfstaengl 1974, p.147, ill.

**p.68** Pencil sketch of people with baby carriage in a park

**p.69** Pencil sketch of figures in a park probably in Paris

20, pp.68-69

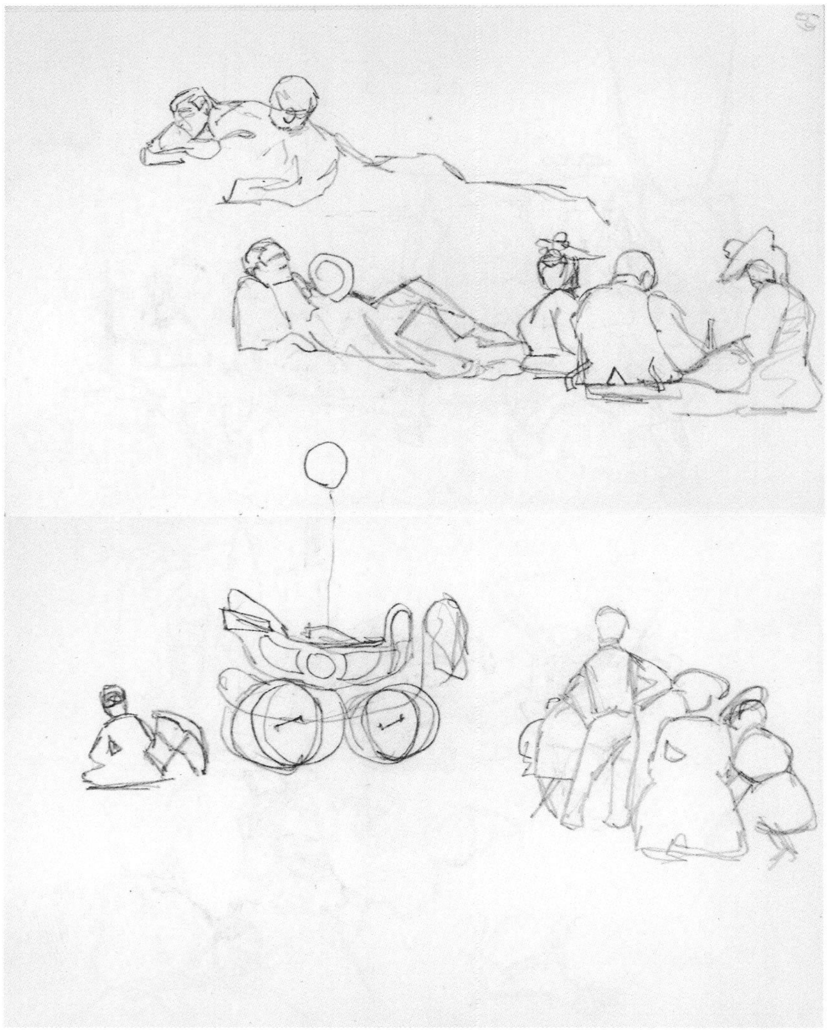

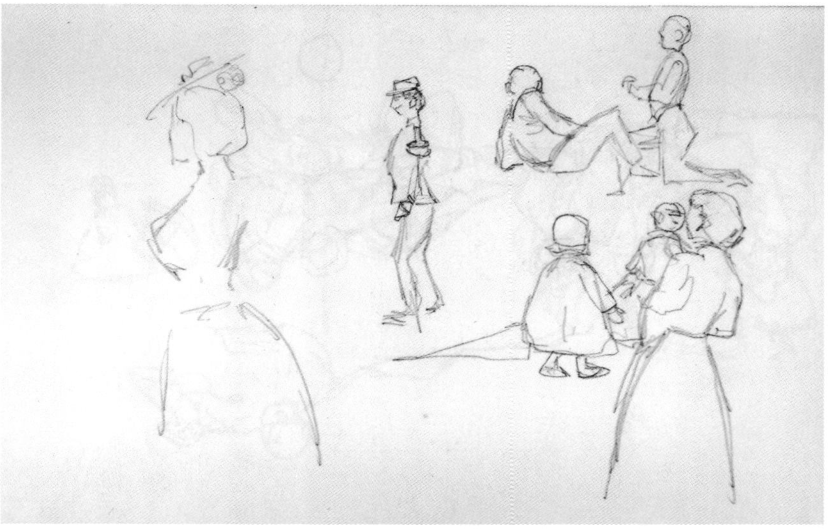

20, p.70

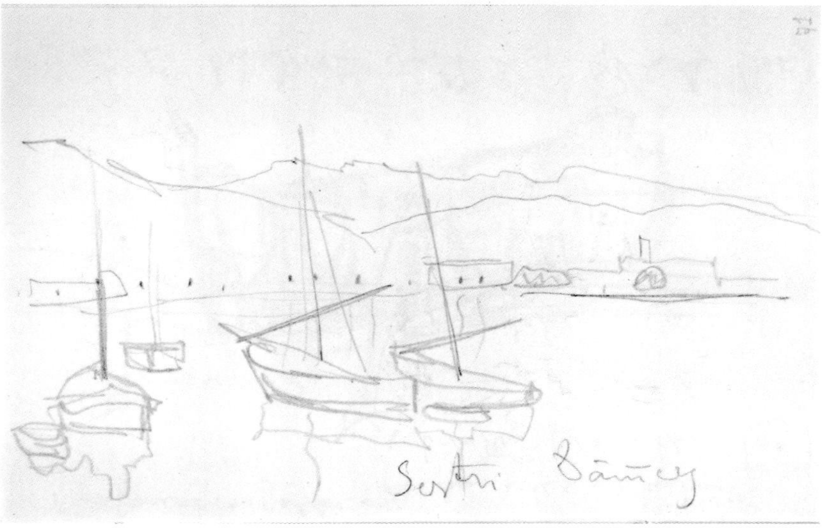

20, p.71

**p.70** Pencil sketches of figures in a park probably in Paris

**p.71** Pencil study for *Italienischer Hafen* of 1906
Inscribed l.r.: 'Sestri Dämmer[un]g'

REFERENCES
Hanfstaengl 1974, p.146
Rudenstine 1976, p.214, ill.a
Roethel and Benjamin 1982, p.155
Barnett 1992, p.186, ill.a

Kandinsky and Münter went to Sestri Levante, south of Rapallo, for Christmas 1905 (see p.76). He noted that this study depicts the harbor in Sestri at dusk, and later he made a tempera painting of the motif (Barnett no.207). Münter sketched the same boats in the harbor, which she annotated 'Nachts Sestri' in her sketchbook (46/15, p.49).

**p.72** Pencil studies of boats for *Waschtag* of January–February 1906
Inscribed u.c.: 'i- canariengelb / B. den hellvioletten Rock / Schatten (derselben Tag)'; c.: 'Schw / Schw / gr / sanftgrün / Zinnober'; l.c.: 'Sestri L. Das Boot für bunten Wäsche (Sonne)'

REFERENCES
Hanfstaengl 1974, p.146

The artist's annotations confirm that the studies of boats were for his tempera painting *Waschtag* of January–February 1906 (Barnett no.201) and that they were done in Sestri Levante.

**p.73** Pencil study of boat in Sestri Levante

Kandinsky made several studies of boats with laundry draped over them to dry when he was in Sestri Levante. There women washed clothes in the Baia delle Favole and dried them on fishing boats. The distinctive boats appear in *Waschtag* (Barnett no.201), as well as in *Rapallo- Boote* (Roethel and Benjamin no.145).

20, p.72

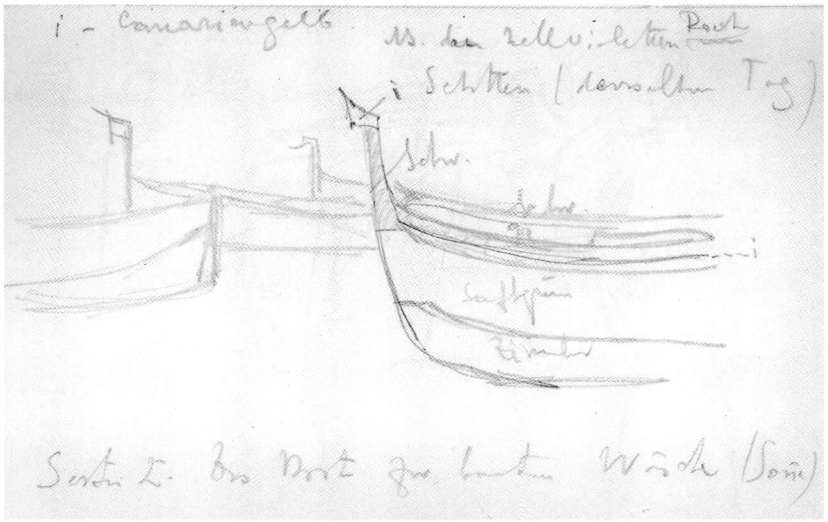

20, p.73

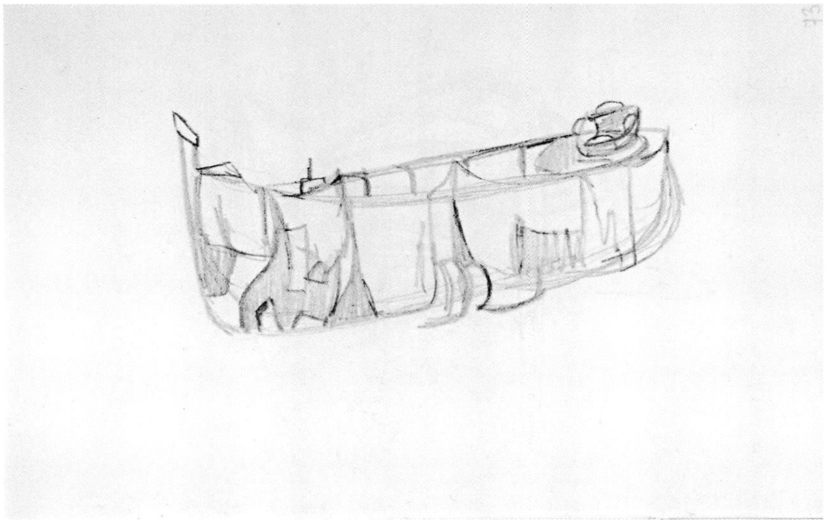

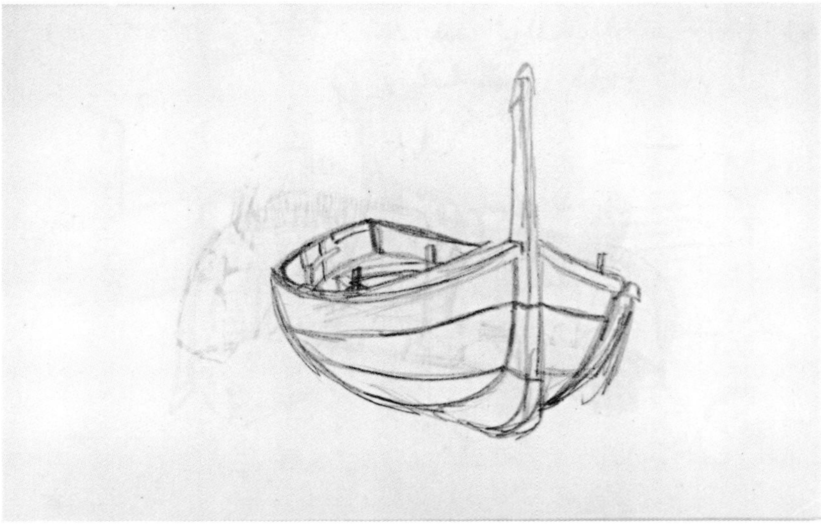

20, p.74

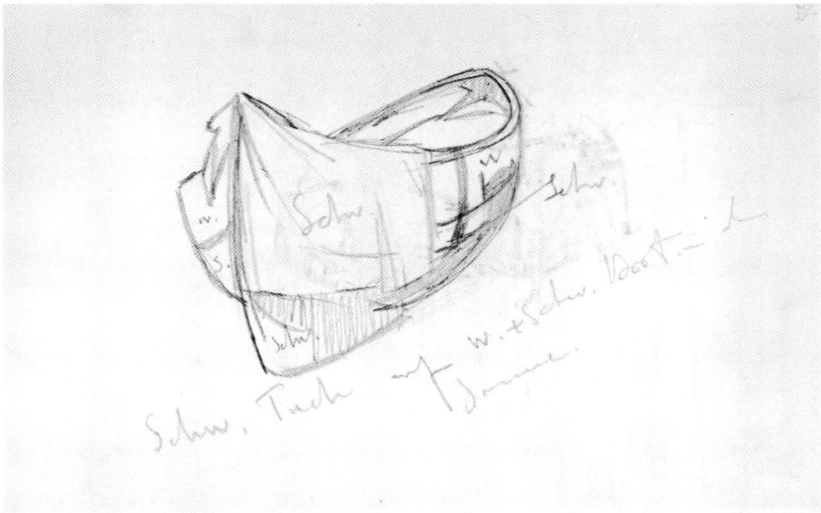

20, p.75

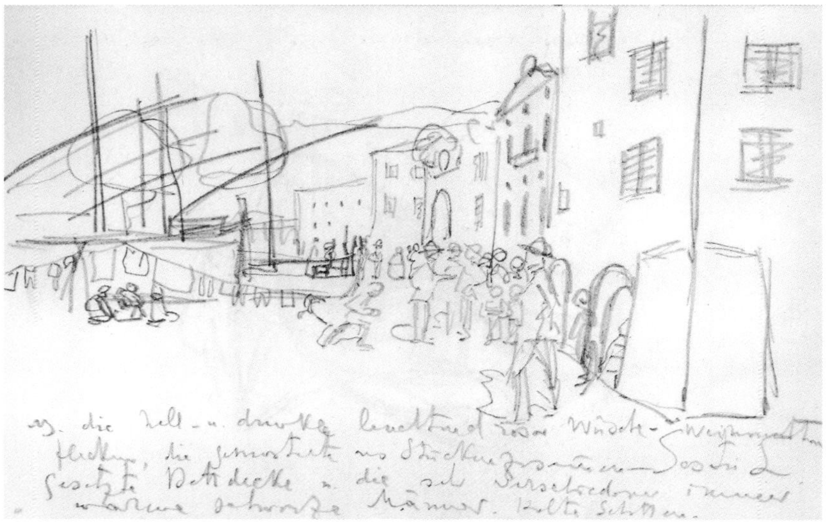

20, p.76

**p.74** Pencil study of boat in Sestri Levante

**p.75** Pencil study of boat in Sestri Levante
Inscribed below: 'Schw. Tuch auf w.+ schw. Boot in der / Sonne.' and with color notations: 'w. / s. / Schw'

fig.a

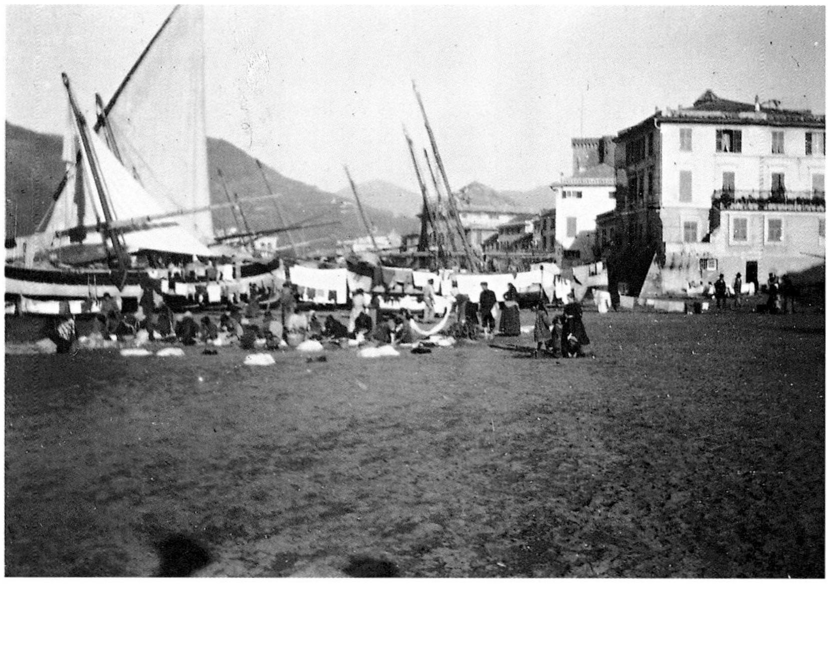

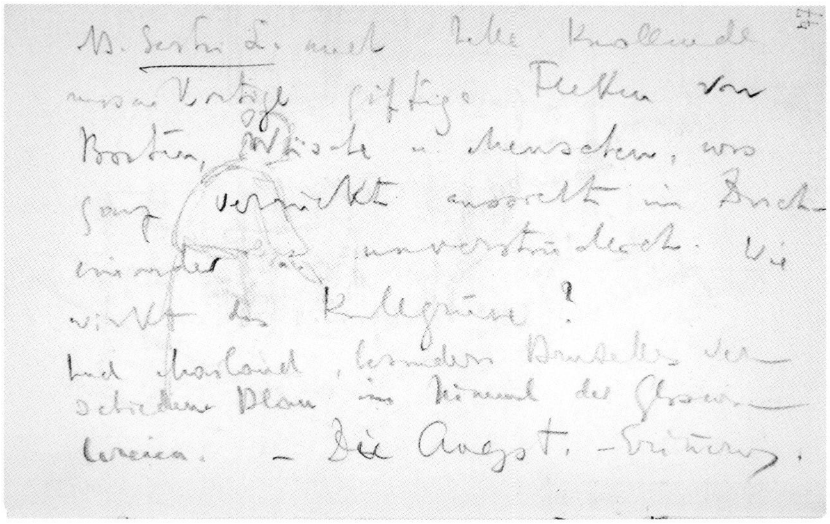

20, p.77

**p.76** Pencil sketch of harbor at Sestri Levante
Inscribed l.r.: 'Weihnachten / Sestri L.'; l.c.: 'B. die hell- u. dunkle leuchtend rosa Wäsche- / flecken, die gemusterte aus Stücken zusammen- / gesetzte Bettdecke u. die sehr verschiedene[n] immer / warme schwarze Männer. Kalte Schatten.' (continued p.77)

REFERENCES
Hanfstaengl 1974, pp.146, 147, ill.
Podzemskaia 2000, p.98

Kandinsky dated this detailed sketch of the harbor at Sestri Levante Christmas Day. However, it seems unlikely that the women were actually doing laundry on Christmas. Gabriele Münter took photographs of the women washing clothes in the Baia delle Favole (fig.a; 2726), and Kandinsky made them the subject of his tempera painting *Waschtag* (see pp.72, 77).

**p.77** Pencil sketch of figure
Inscribed: 'B. <u>Sestri L.</u> auch helle knallende / aussen Kantige giftige Fle[c]ken von / Booten, Wäsche u. Menschen, was / ganz verrückt aussieht im Durch- / einander u. unverständlich. Wie / wirkt das Knallgrüne? / Und Mailand, besonders Bruxelles ver / schiedene Blau im Himmel der Glasur- / linien. – Die Angst. – Erinnerung.'

**p.78** Pencil sketch of farmhouse
Inscribed u.l.: 'Seeshaupt' and throughout: 'a'

Kandinsky may have made this drawing in May 1905, when he went to the Starnberger See near Munich.

**p.79** Pencil sketch of windows
Inscribed u.l.: 'weisses Haus / graues Holz a.'

The sketch is related to that on the facing page, where the grey wood architectural elements are indicated with 'a'.

**p.80** Blue pencil notes related to travel agencies in Paris and hotel in Dieppe (upside down)

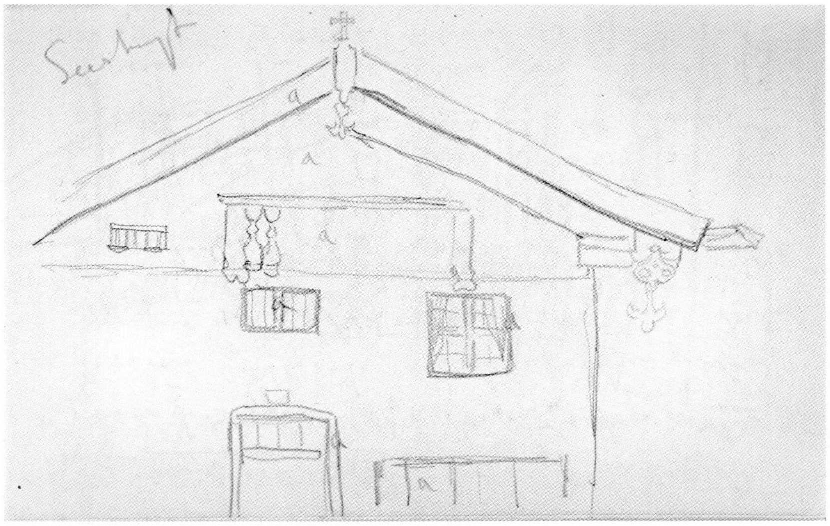

20, p.78

20, p.79

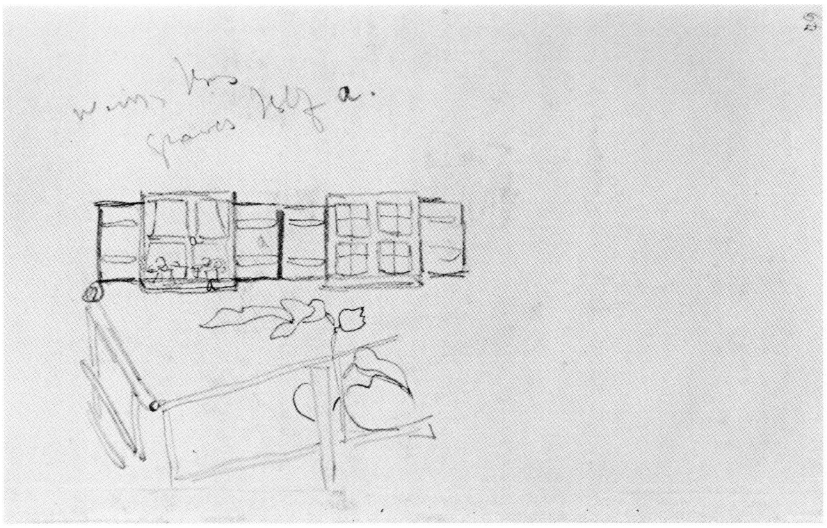

# Sketchbook 21

1905–1906

Green leather notebook with gold-colored, patterned endpapers; no label
Contains 44 pages (22 sheets) of ruled paper, each 13.6 x 7.8 cm (5³⁄₈ x 3¹⁄₈ in)
Page numbers inscribed by unknown hand at later date with odd numbers at lower right

Hanfstaengl 1974, p.155

LOCATION
Städtische Galerie im Lenbachhaus, Munich (GMS 333)

HISTORY
Gabriele Münter, Murnau, until 1957

Kandinsky purchased this notebook well before he and Gabriele Münter travelled to Italy in December 1905. Certainly, he began to make notes and sketches during the summer of 1905 (see pp.22–23, 42). The majority of sketches were, however, done in Italy from January to April 1906.

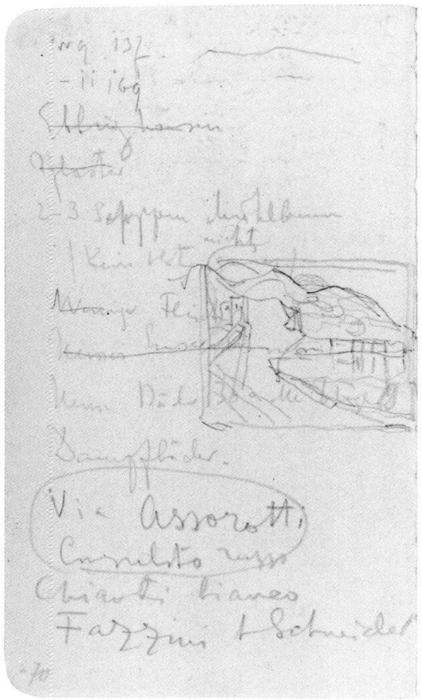

21, p.o

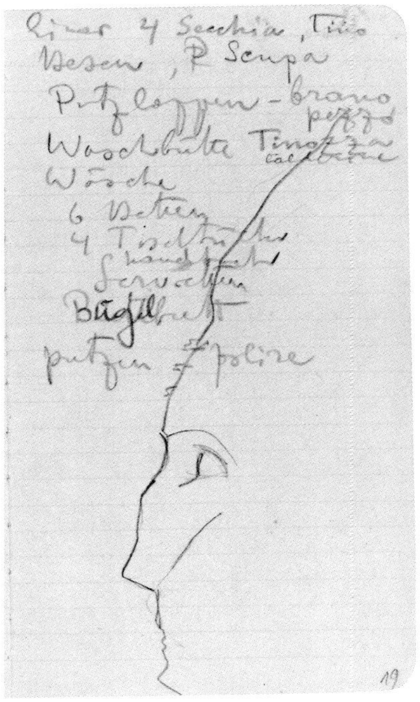

21, p.19

**p.o** (inside front cover) Pencil sketch of landscape, probably Santa Margherita on the Italian Riviera Inscribed below: 'Via Assorotti / Consulato russo / Chianti bianco / Fazzini – Schneider'

Kandinsky circled the reference to the Russian consulate in via Assarotti in Genoa. He and Münter arrived in Genoa on 15 December and stayed briefly in Santa Margherita on 20–21 December, before renting an apartment in Rapallo and travelling to Sestri Levante for Christmas (see Sketchbook 20, p.76).

**pp.1–18** Notes and lists of addresses

**p.6** Inscribed 'Dr. phil. H. Austin Aikins / Prof. zu Cleveland Ohio / 40 Cornell St. / Ver. Staat.

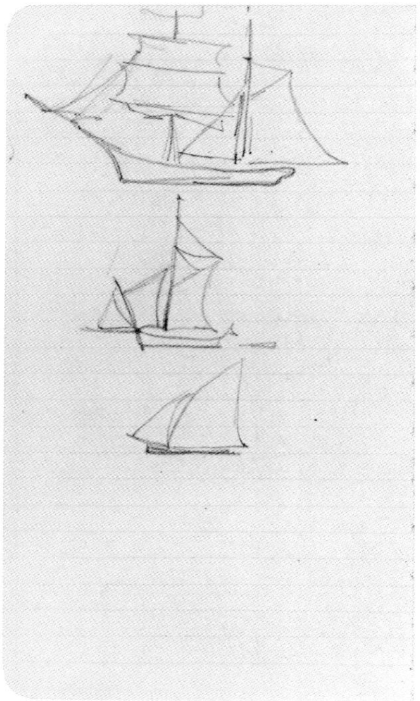

21, p.20

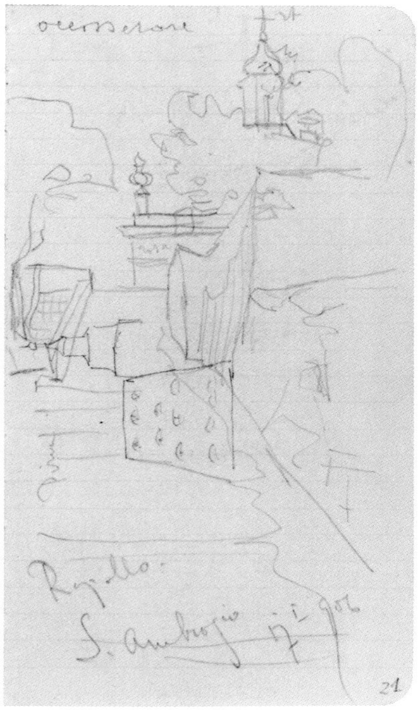

21, p.21

Nordamerika. / Carl Palme- Svalmäs Djursholm / Schweden. / Fanny's Sachen im Zimmer / Friedrichstr. I iv / 1 Kiste / 2 Tische, 2 Stühle / 1 Kommode / 1 Ottomanne / das ganze Bett.' Kandinsky's list of items to pack continued on p.7, where he noted: 'Herzogstr. 79 ii Frau Dengler.' These notes may date from as early as 1904, when Kandinsky separated from his wife Anja Shemiakina and moved out of the apartment on Friedrichstrasse on 30 September. Fanny Dengler was their housekeeper.

**p.11** Notes probably about Phalanx exhibitions: '<u>Hüsgen</u>-1 XII 905 alles / <u>Salzmann</u>- 1 I 06 [crossed out] / 1 X nicht noch 100 / <u>Hornig</u>- noch 2 nicht be- / zahlen alles fällig. Bezahlt Aug- Sept statt / M.200 nur 120 (70 + 50)'
The reference to Wilhelm Hüsgen is dated 1 December 1905.

**p.12** Inscribed: 'Bei Gondrand 28 IX 905 / 1) Koffer Holz m. br. Uberng 27 / 2) [Koffer] gelb W.K. (Tietz) flach / 3) [Koffer gelb] W.K. hoch / 4) Holzkiste / 5) Apparat / 6) Rad'

The date 28 September 1905, the reference to Odessa on p.12 and the train schedule from Vienna to Kiev confirm that Kandinsky made these notes regarding his trip to Odessa from 29 September to 10 November 1905.

**p.16** Notes about places to stay in Santa Margherita

**p.17** Notes about Chiavari and Zoagli near Rapallo

**p.18** Notes about apartments to rent in Rapallo

**p.19** Pencil sketch of head in profile Inscribed above with lists of German words and Italian equivalents and a list of household items

**p.20** Pencil sketches of brigantine and two smaller boats with sails

See p.32 below and a sketch by Münter inscribed Sestri Levante (46/5, p.47).

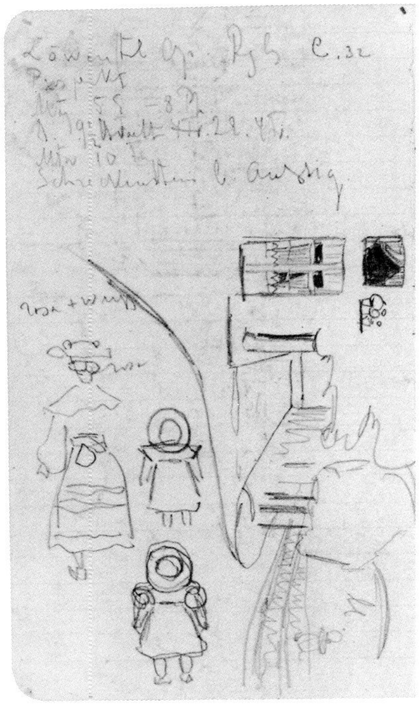

21, p.22

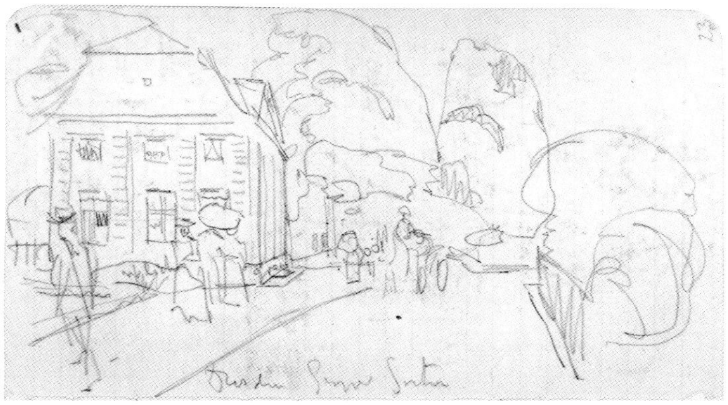

21, p.23

**p.21** Pencil sketches of San Ambrogio outside Rapallo
Inscribed below: 'Rapallo. / S. Ambrogio 17 I 906'

Kandinsky made two sketches – one vertical and another placed horizontally on the sheet – of the church of San Ambrogio in the hills above Rapallo. He dated the sheet 17 January 1906. From 23 December 1905 until 30 April 1906, Kandinsky and Münter rented an apartment at via Montebello 24 in Rapallo, which is near the road and hiking paths to San Ambrogio in Zoagli. Münter made a similar sketch (46/15, p.50) and also took a photograph (2764) of the church and the steps leading up to it.

**p.22** Pencil sketch of children, female figure and garden
Inscribed above: 'Schreckenstein b. Aussig' and color notations above woman: 'rosa + weiss / rosa'

REFERENCES
Hanfstaengl 1974, p.155, ill.

The woman and child bear a close resemblance to the figures at the left of a small sketch, *Personen auf Gartenbänken*, which was probably done in Dresden in the summer of 1905 (vol.I, no.79). Schreckenstein and Aussig are towns to the south of Dresden.

**p.23** Pencil sketch of figures in garden
Inscribed below: 'Dresden Grosser Garten'

REFERENCES
Hanfstaengl 1974, p.155, ill.
Barnett and Friedel 1995, no.192, color ill.

Kandinsky and Münter stayed in Dresden from June until 15 August 1905. He made other drawings of the 'Grosser Garten' (see vol.I, nos.77–78).

**p.24** Pencil sketch of men seated at tables in outdoor café

REFERENCES
Hanfstaengl 1974, p.155, ill.

The drawing resembles one inserted into Sketchbook 7 (GMS 338, p. 35).

**p.25** Pencil sketch of figure and architectural detail
Inscribed c.: 'r. Bl.' and with illegible poem in Cyrillic

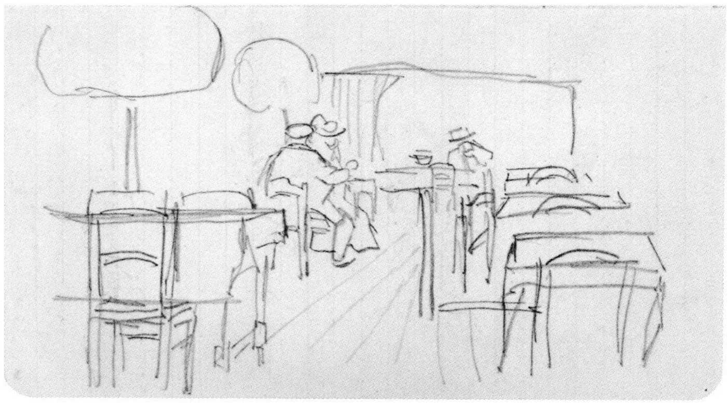

21, p.24

21, p.25

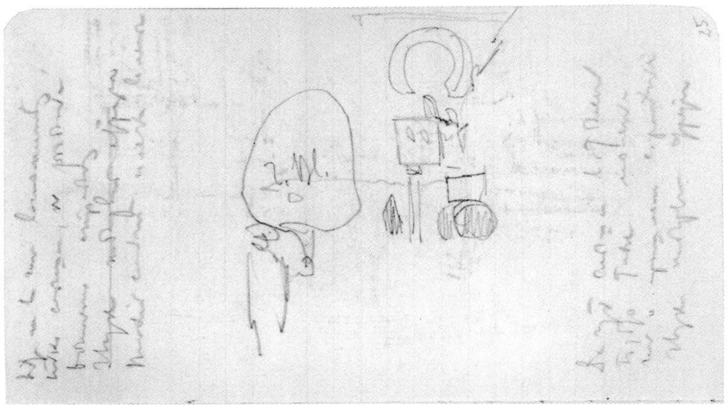

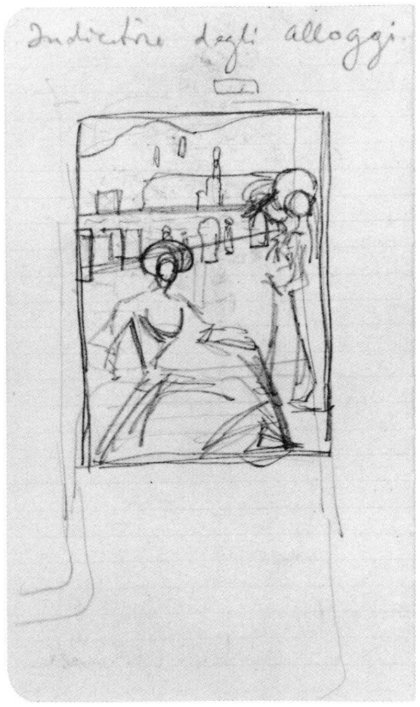

21, p.26

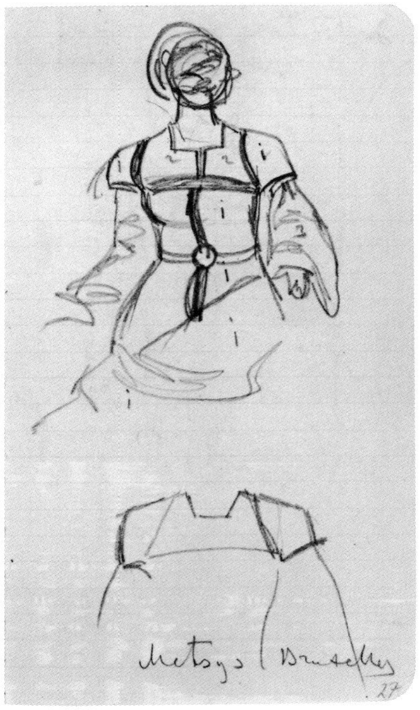

21, p.27

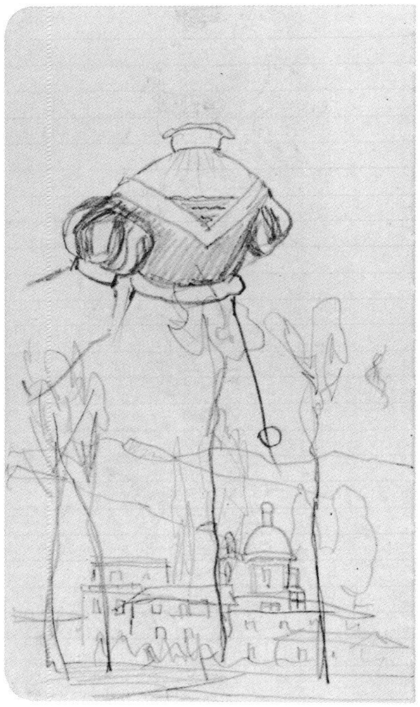

21, p.28

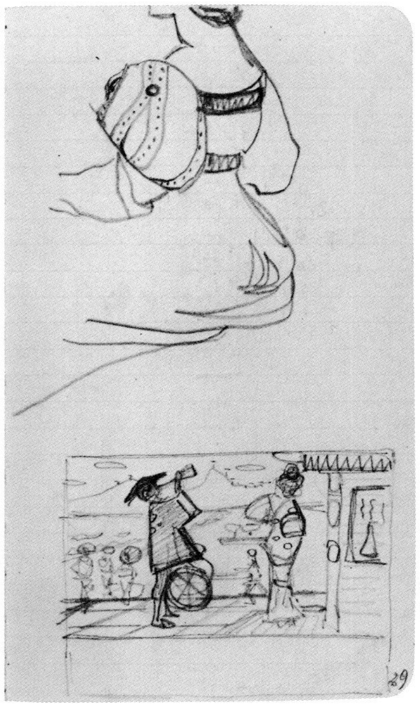

21, p.29

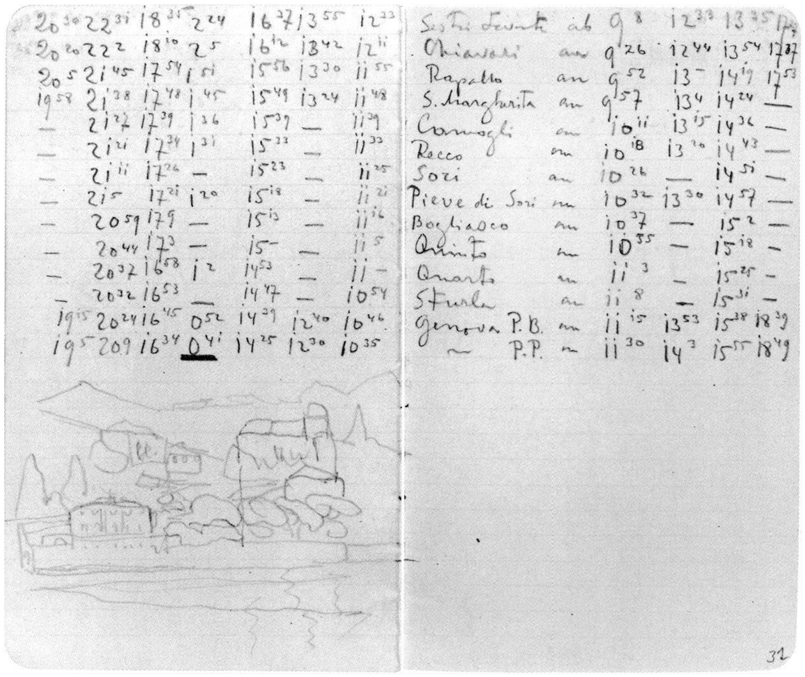

21, pp.30-31

**p.26** Pencil sketch of figures probably in Santa Margherita
Inscribed above: 'Indicative degli alloggi'

REFERENCES
Hanfstaengl 1974, p.155, ill.

The view of the harbor with mountains in the background resembles Santa Margherita more closely than Rapallo.

**p.27** Pencil sketches of female figure and her costume
Inscribed below: 'Metsys Bruxelles'

REFERENCES
Hanfstaengl 1974, p.155, ill.

Kandinsky copied the center panel of the *St. Anne Altarpiece* by Quinten Metsys in the Musées Royaux in Brussels, which was probably known to him from a reproduction.

**p.28** Pencil sketch of costume (above) and landscape (below)

The sketch of a domed building and mountains was probably done on the Italian Riviera.

The dress may come from a book illustration (see preceding and following pages).

**p.29** Pencil sketch of costume (above) and figures in Oriental clothes (below)

REFERENCES
Hanfstaengl 1974, p.155, ill.

The source of the woman in costume has not been identified, but may have been a publication on Flemish or Dutch painting. Likewise, the source of the Japanese (?) illustration below remains unknown.

**pp.30–31** Pencil sketch of Santa Margherita and train schedule

REFERENCES
Hanfstaengl 1974, p.155, ill.

Kandinsky recorded the train schedules from Sestri Levante to Chiavari, Rapallo, Santa Margherita, Camogli, Recco and other towns on the way to Genoa.

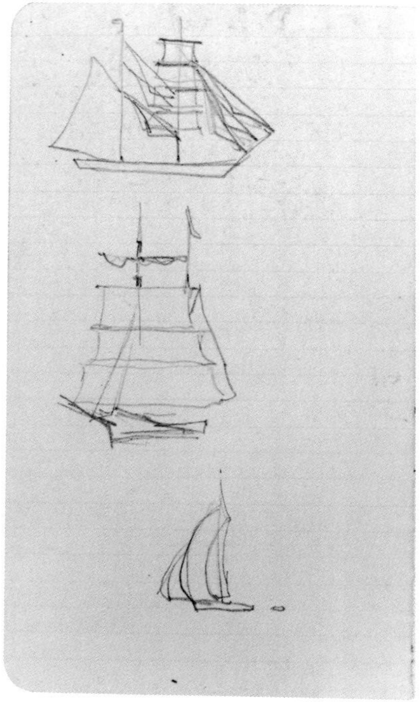

21, p.32

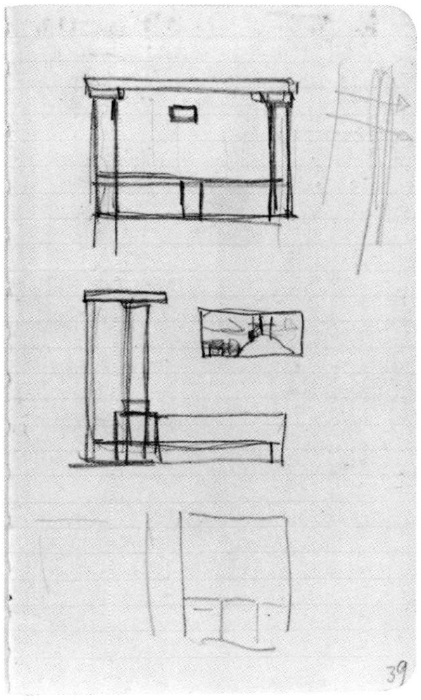

21, p.39

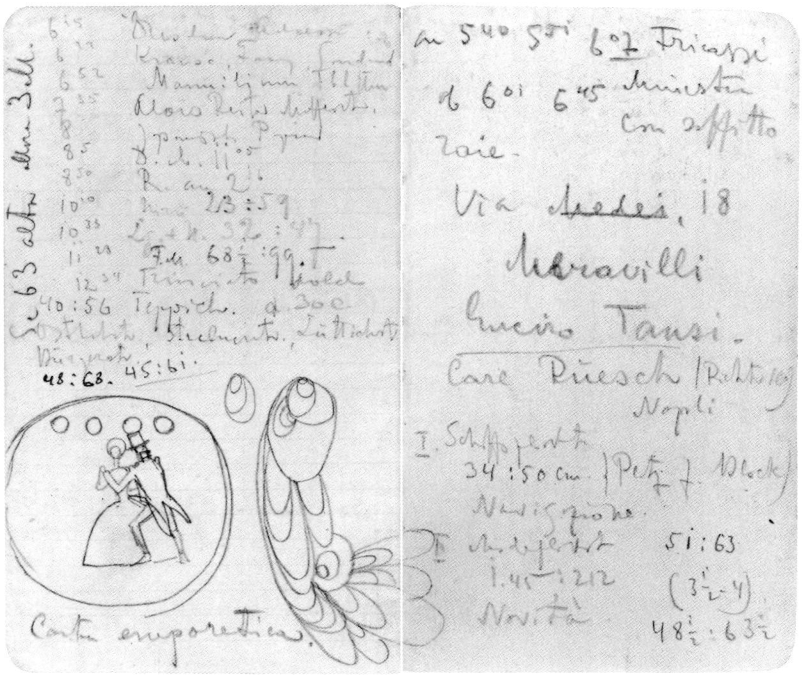


21, pp.44-45

**p.32** Pencil sketches of brigantine, bark and sailboat

**p.33** Addresses in Genoa, Rapallo and Moneglia

**pp.34–35, 37** Münter's draft of a letter about her coat

**pp.36–38** Notes and calculations

**p.39** Pencil sketches of architectural details and picture

The drawings bring to mind earlier studies for furniture in Sketchbooks 5 and 7 (GMS 342, p.45 and GMS 338, p.34), which can be dated to c.1902–1903.

**pp.40–44** Several lists including one of forty works shipped by Gondrand to Dresden (p.40), notes about words for food in German and Italian (p.41) and list of photos and prints sent to Rossi on 13 June 1905 (p.42).

**p.44** Pencil sketches related to *Tanz unter Lampions* and *Entwurf mit Schlingenmuster* of c.1905
Inscribed below: 'Carta emporetica.'

REFERENCES
Hanfstaengl 1974, p.155
Barnett 1992, p.145

The figures of a man and woman dancing under hanging lanterns also appear in a gouache *Tanz unter Lampions* (Barnett no.148). The loop motifs resemble those in *Entwurf mit Schlingenmuster* of c.1905 (Barnett no.149) and Sketchbook 12 (GMS 347, p.45), which Kandinsky used in 1903. Above the sketches he made a list and recorded train schedules from Dresden.

**p.45** (inside back cover)
Inscribed above with notes in Italian and addresses in Italy and below: 'I. Schiffsplakat / 34:50 cm, (Platz f. Block) / Navigazione / II. Modeplakat 51:63 / 1.45:212 ($3^{1}/_{2}$ - 4) / Novità $48^{1}/_{2}$ : $63^{1}/_{2}$'

REFERENCES
Barnett 2006, p.34

Kandinsky's notes refer to *Entwurf für ein Schiffsplakat* (vol.I, no.2).

# Sketchbook 22

1905–1906

Red imitation leather sketchbook with silver-colored lettering: 'Album'; no label
Contains 108 pages (54 sheets), each 10.1 x 17.7 cm (4 x 7 in), of which pp.64–86 and 88–106 are blank
Page numbers inscribed by unknown hand at later date with odd numbers at lower right

Hanfstaengl 1974, pp.138–139

LOCATION
Städtische Galerie im Lenbachhaus, Munich (GMS 322)

HISTORY
Gabriele Münter, Murnau, until 1957

There is no indication where Kandinsky purchased this sketchbook, which he used during his stay on the Ligurian coast in Italy from December 1905 until the end of April 1906.

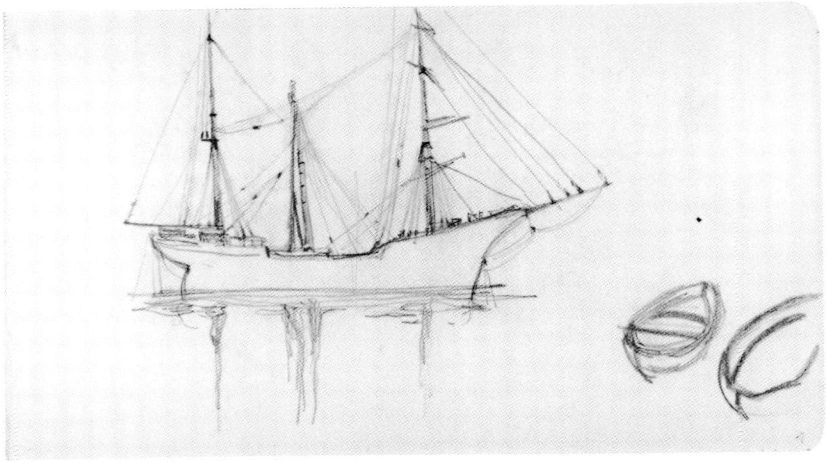

22, p.1

**p.1** Pencil sketches of barkentine and rowboats

The boats resemble those in *Entwurf für ein Schiffsplakat* of 1906 (vol.I, cat.no.2), and other sketches made in Rapallo and Santa Margherita in Liguria in Sketchbooks 20 and 21 (GMS 327, p.71 and GMS 333, pp.20, 32).

The sketch was done in Sestri Levante probably in late December 1905 and is related to *Waschtag*, which Kandinsky painted in January–February 1906 (Barnett no.201). See also Sketchbook 20 (GMS 327, pp.73–76) and a photograph probably by Gabriele Münter (see p.188).

**p.2** Blank

**p.3** Pencil sketch of washerwoman

REFERENCES
Hanfstaengl 1974, pp.138–139, ill.
Barnett 1992, p.183
*Kandinsky, Vrubel', Jawlensky e gli artisti russi a Genova e nelle riviere* exh. cat. (Genoa, 2001), no.137a, color ill.

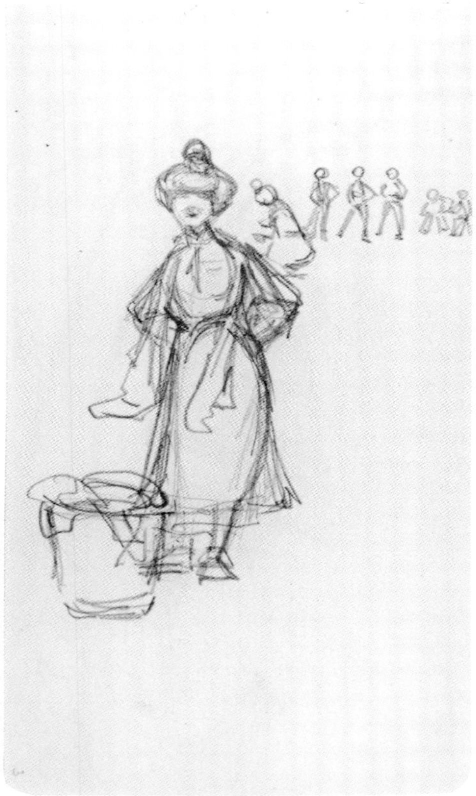

22, p.3

**p.4** Blank

**p.5** Pencil sketch of rowboat

REFERENCES
*Kandinsky, Vrubel', Jawlensky e gli artisti russi a Genova e nelle riviere* exh. cat. (Genoa, 2001), no.137b, color ill.

Kandinsky made the sketches of boats and men fishing on the Ligurian coast between December 1905 and the end of April 1906.

22, p.5

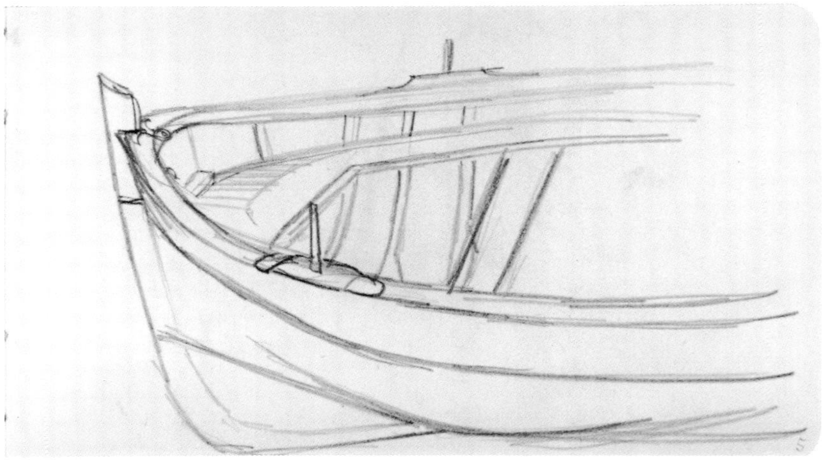

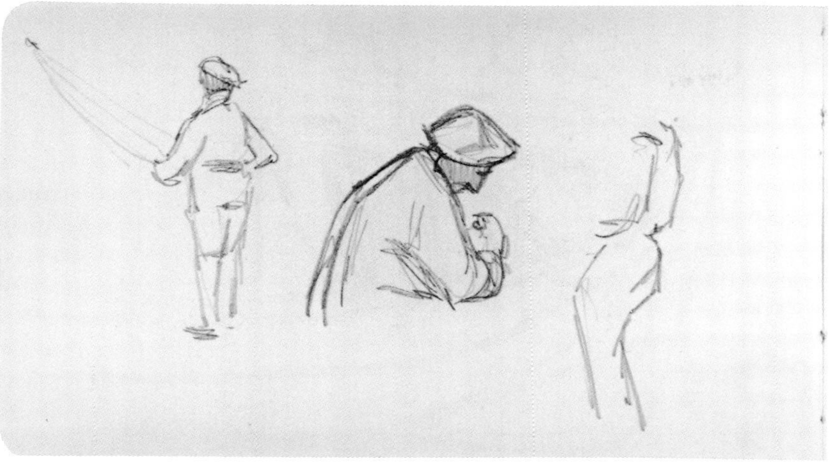

22, p.6

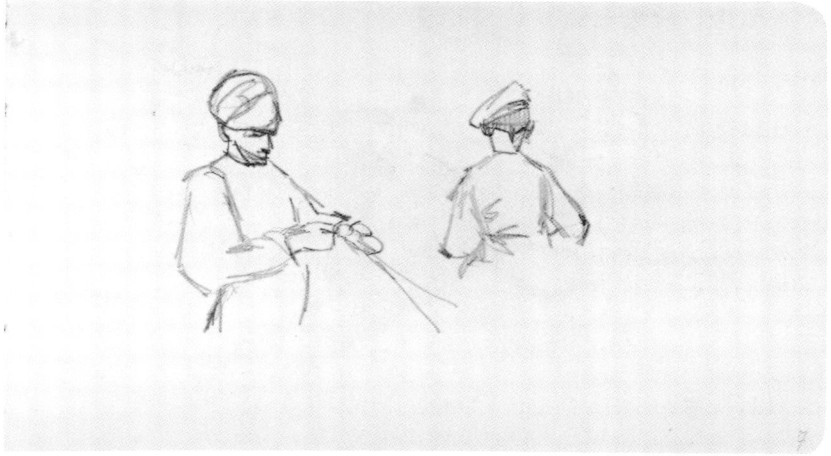

22, p.7

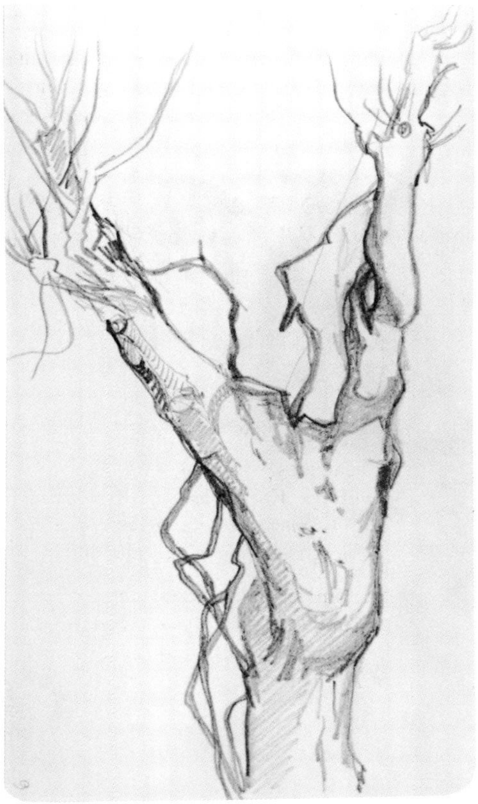

22, p.9

**p.6** Pencil sketch of men fishing

**p.7** Pencil sketch of men fishing

**p.8** Blank

**p.9** Pencil sketch of tree branches

**p.10** Blank

**p.11** Pencil sketch of boat

REFERENCES
*Kandinsky, Vrubel', Jawlensky e gli artisti russi a Genova e nelle riviere* exh. cat. (Genoa, 2001), no.137c, color ill.

**p.12** Blank

**p.13** Pencil sketch of boat
Inscribed with color notations: 'weiss / grün hin u. h rosa sch. vor netz'

REFERENCES
*Kandinsky, Vrubel', Jawlensky e gli artisti russi a Genova e nelle riviere* exh. cat. (Genoa, 2001), no.137d, color ill.

22, p.11

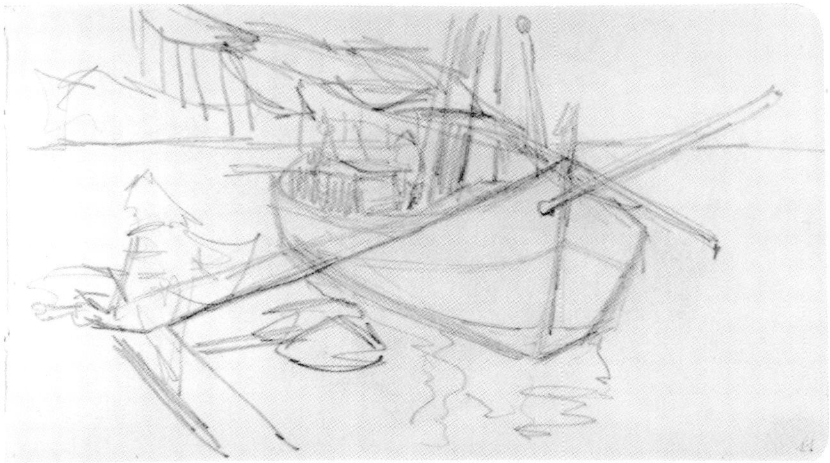

22, p.13

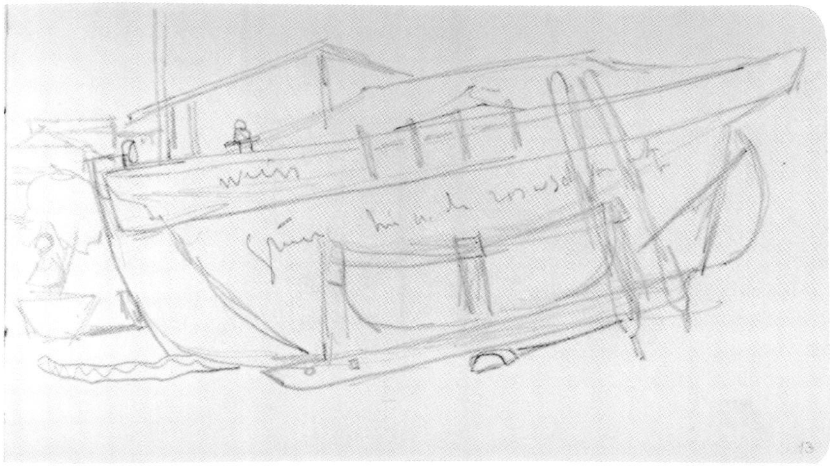

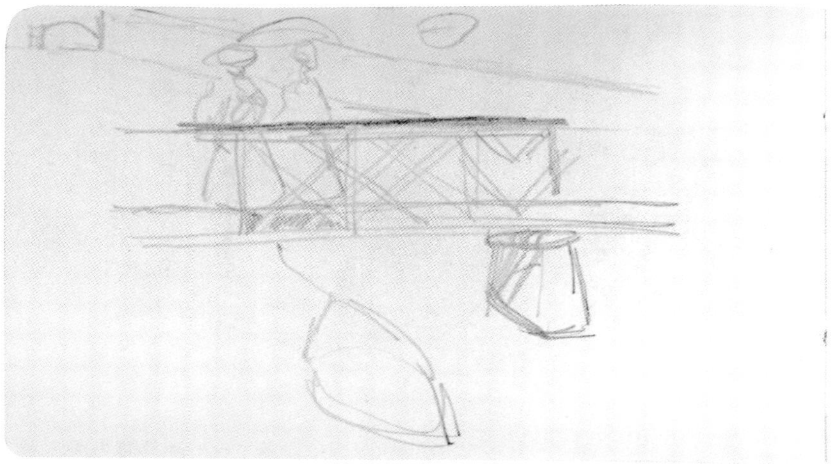

22, p.14

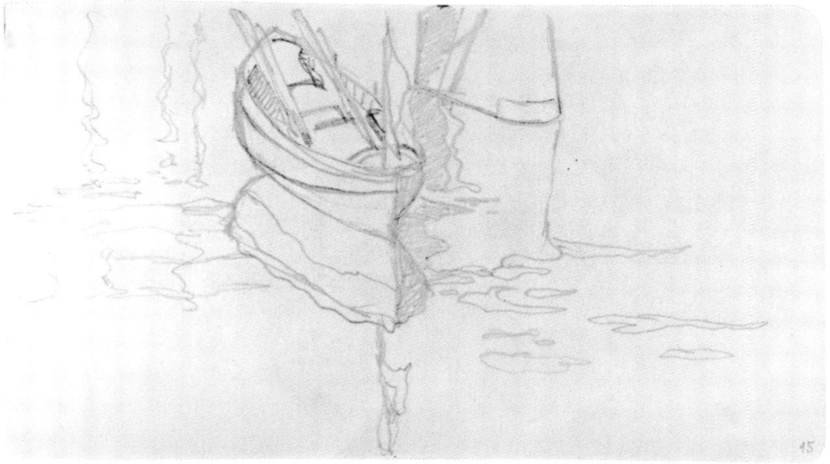

22, p.15

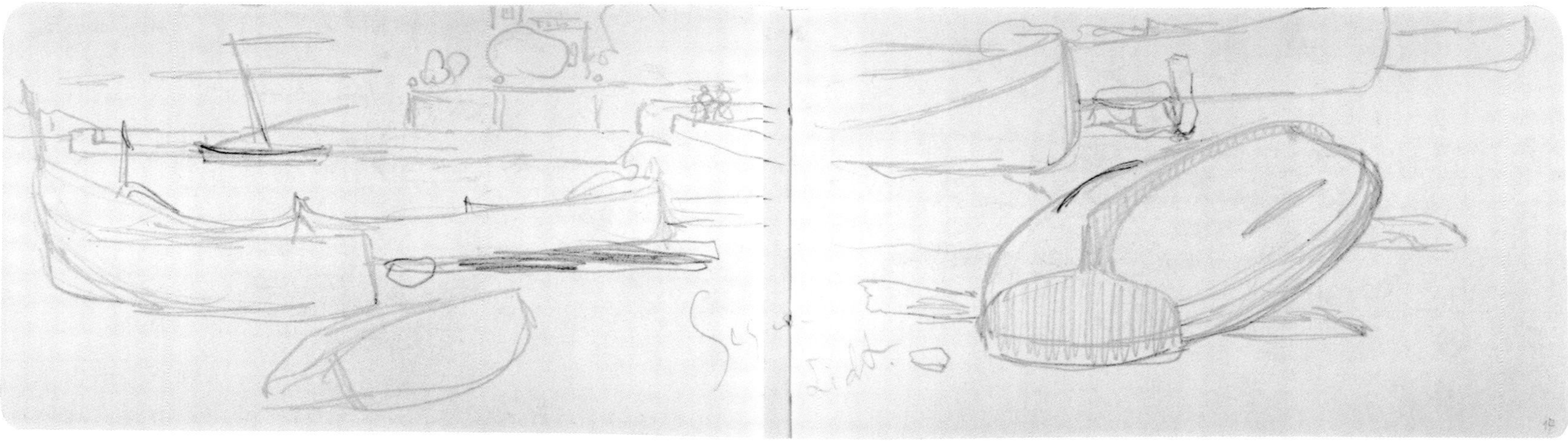

22, pp.16-17

**p.14** Pencil sketch of two women on bridge

The bridge-like gangplank resembles that in *Entwurf für ein Schiffsplakat* (vol.I, cat. no.2).

**p.15** Pencil sketch of rowboat with reflections in water

REFERENCES
Hanfstaengl 1974, p.139, ill.

**p.16** Pencil sketch of boats
Inscribed l.r.: 'Gegen'

REFERENCES
Hanfstaengl 1974, p.139, ill.

Kandinsky made numerous studies of boats when he was in Rapallo and nearby villages on the Ligurian coast. This sheet brings to mind *Rapallo-Boote* of 1905 (Roethel and Benjamin no.145).

**p.17** Pencil sketch of boats
Inscribed l.l.: 'Licht'

REFERENCES
Hanfstaengl 1974, p.139, ill.
*Kandinsky, Vrubel', Jawlensky e gli artisti russi a Genova e nelle riviere* exh. cat. (Genoa, 2001), no.137e, color ill.

This sketch facing p.16 is a continuation of the same view. The artist inscribed 'Gegen Licht' (against the light) across the two pages.

**p.18** Blank

**p.19** Pencil sketch of rowboats

**p.20** Blank

22, p.19

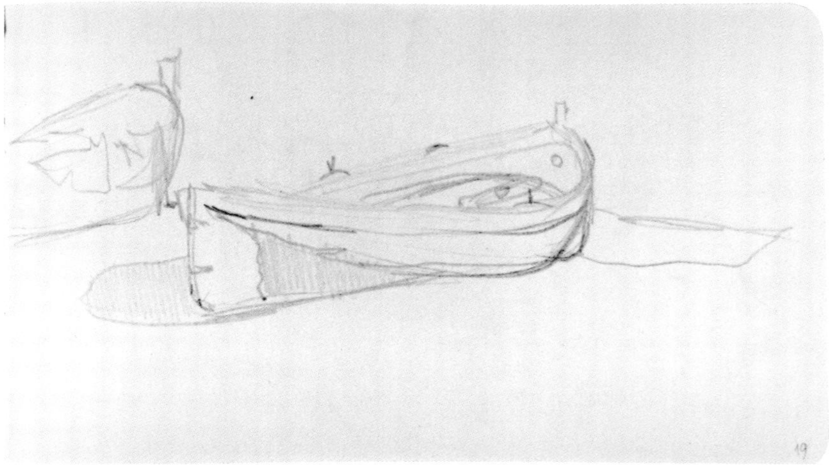

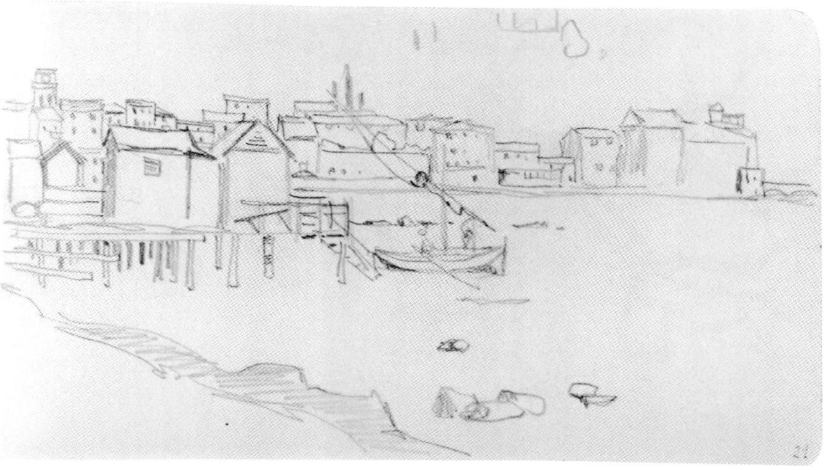

22, p.21

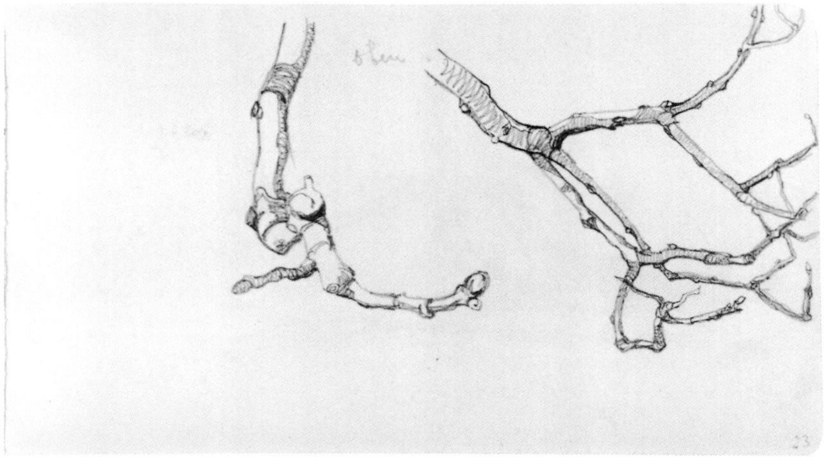

22, p.23

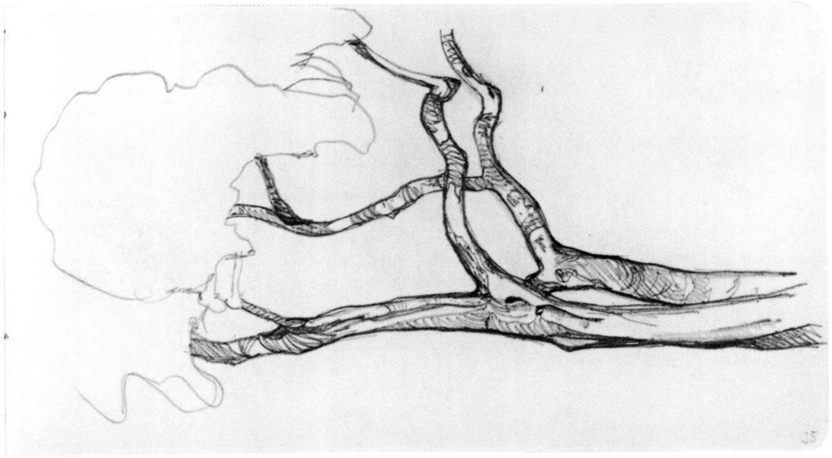

22, p.25

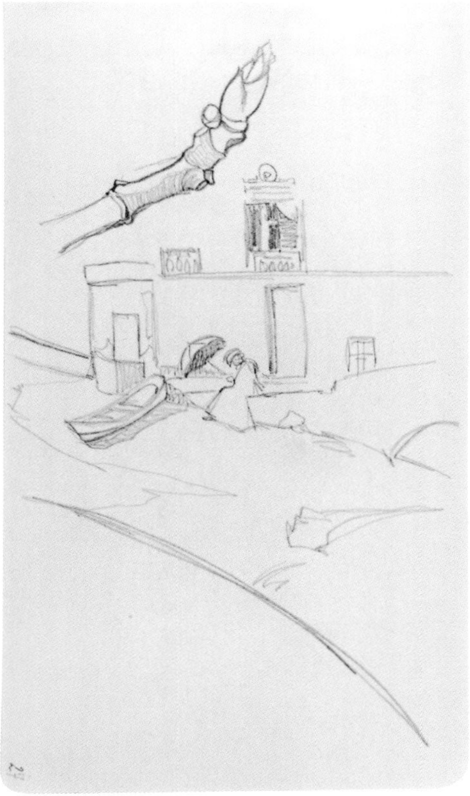

22, p.27

**p.21** Pencil study for *Rapallo- Bagni Luisa* of 1906

REFERENCES

Hanfstaengl 1974, pp.138–139, ill.
Roethel and Benjamin 1982, p.161
Barnett and Friedel 1995, no.200, color ill.
*Kandinsky, Vrubel', Jawlensky e gli artisti russi a Genova e nelle riviere* exh. cat. (Genoa, 2001), no.137f, color ill.

The drawing is a study for *Rapallo-Bagni Luisa* of 1906 (Roethel and Benjamin no.150), depicting baths in the Baia dei Sogni near where Kandinsky and Münter lived. It bears a resemblance to photographs (2740 and 2741) probably taken by Münter in 1906 in Rapallo.

**p.22** Blank

**p.23** Pencil sketch of tree branches
Inscribed u.c.: 'oben'

Münter took photographs (2757 and 2761) of trees in bloom in the spring of 1906.

**p.24** Blank

**p.25** Pencil sketch of tree branch

**p.26** Blank

**p.27** Pencil sketch of Münter sitting under umbrella sketching and detail of branch

REFERENCES

Hanfstaengl 1974, pp.138–139, ill.

Kandinsky made this drawing of Münter seated on a footbridge over a canal near where they stayed in Rapallo; she is holding an umbrella and probably sketching. The buds on the branch indicate that both sketches were done in the spring.

**p.28** Blank

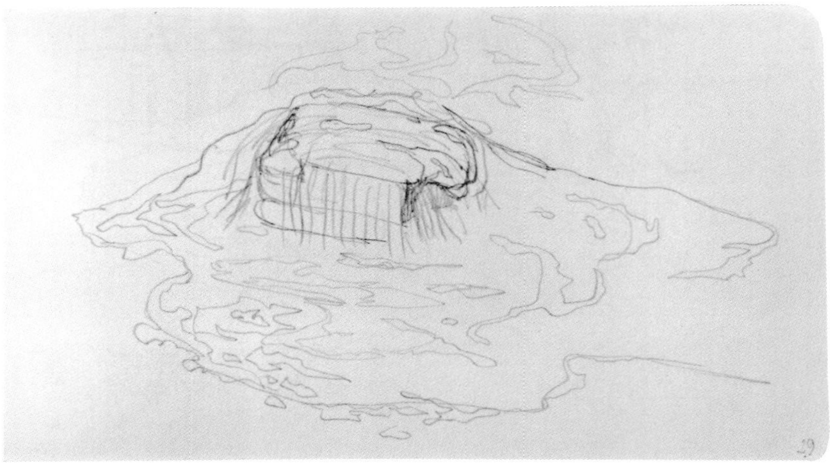

22, p.29

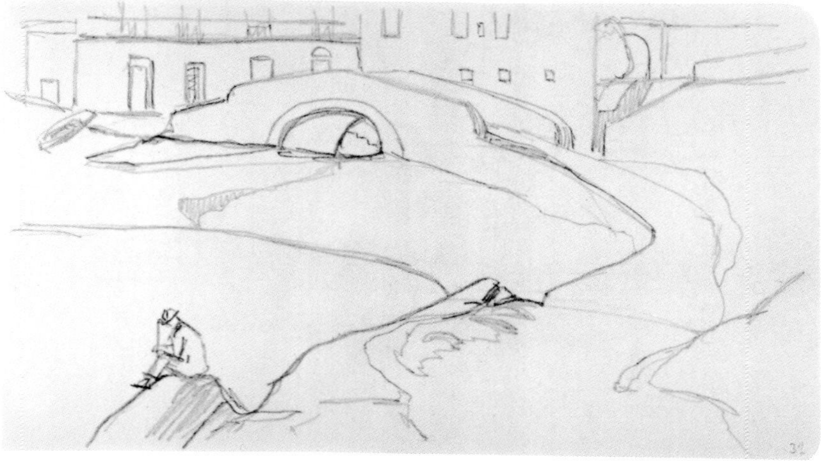

22, p.31

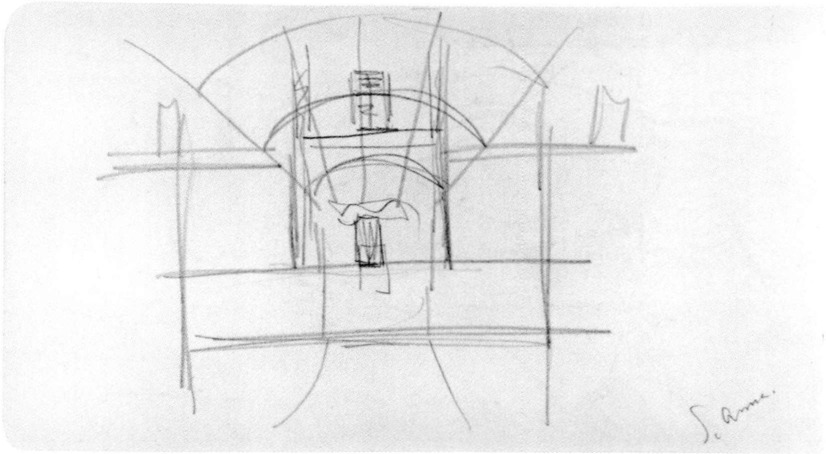


22, p.32

22, p.33

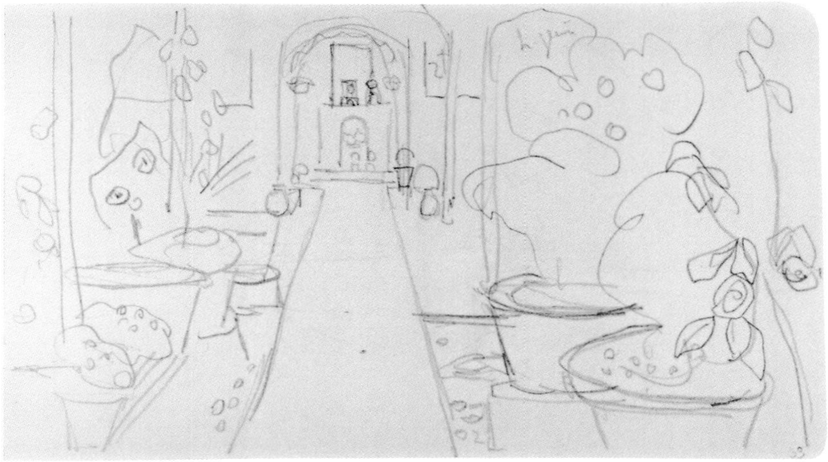

**p.29** Pencil sketch of rocks and water

Similar rocks are found in the harbor along the Lungomare Castello near where Kandinsky lived in Rapallo.

**p.30** Blank

**p.31** Pencil sketch of man sitting on rock

REFERENCES
Hanfstaengl 1974, p.138
*Kandinsky, Vrubel', Jawlensky e gli artisti russi a Genova e nelle riviere* exh. cat. (Genoa, 2001), no.137g, color ill.

Although Hanfstaengl suggested that Münter might have drawn this figure (presumably of Kandinsky), close examination of the pencil lines does not confirm this hypothesis. The man is sitting on a rock – perhaps reading a newspaper – near the same foot-bridge over a canal that is depicted on p.27 and not far from where Kandinsky and Münter lived in Rapallo. In the background, the rail-road bridge is visible.

**p.32** Pencil sketch of church
Inscribed l.r.: 'S. Anna'

REFERENCES
*Kandinsky, Vrubel', Jawlensky e gli artisti russi a Genova e nelle riviere* exh. cat. (Genoa, 2001), no.137h, color ill.

Although the sheet is inscribed 'S. Anna', the architecture bears a striking resemblance to the small church of San Bernardo near San Ambrogio in the hills above Rapallo (see Sketchbook 21, p.21). Münter or Kandinsky took a photograph (2765) of the exterior of this church, which is a considerable distance from the church of Santa Anna.

**p.33** Pencil sketch of garden and entrance to church
Inscribed u.r.: 'rt / h. grün'; l.c.: 'or'

The garden and porch can be identified as the church of San Bernardo outside Rapallo: the motif is also found on the facing page.

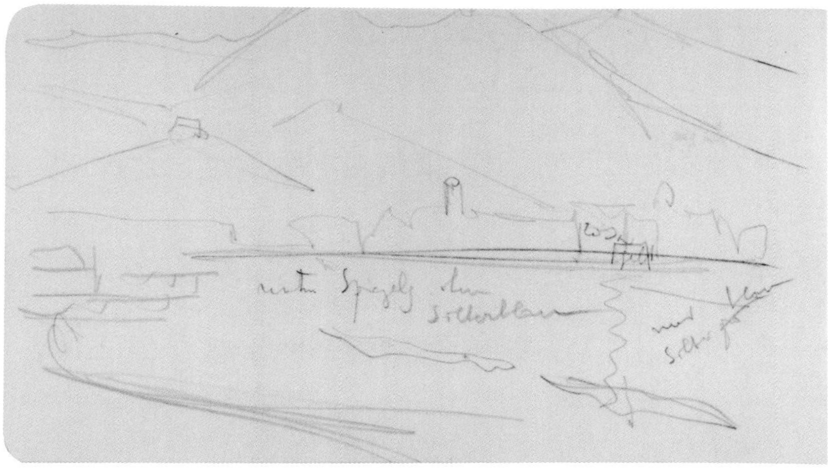

22, p.34

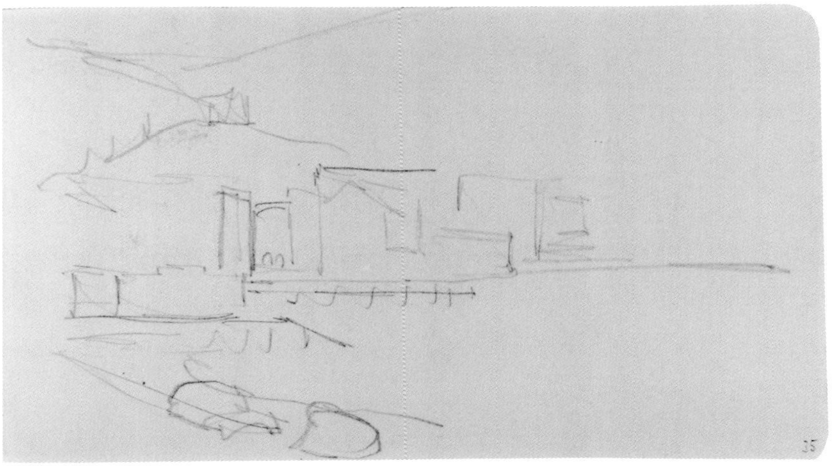

22, p.35

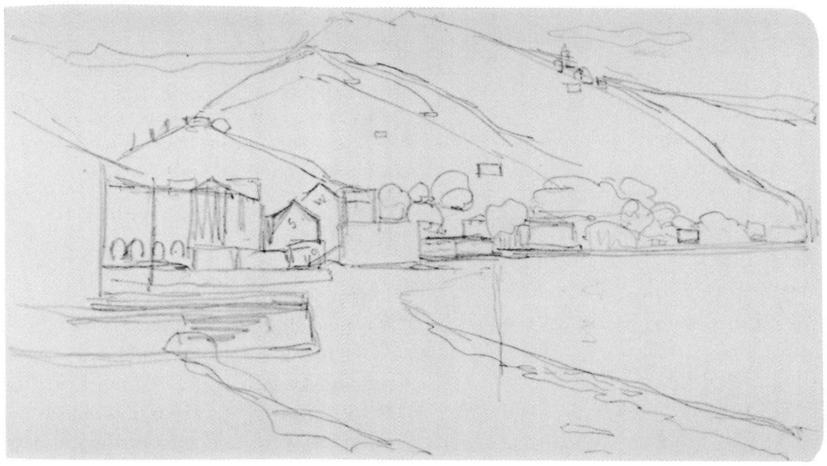

22, p.37

22, p.39

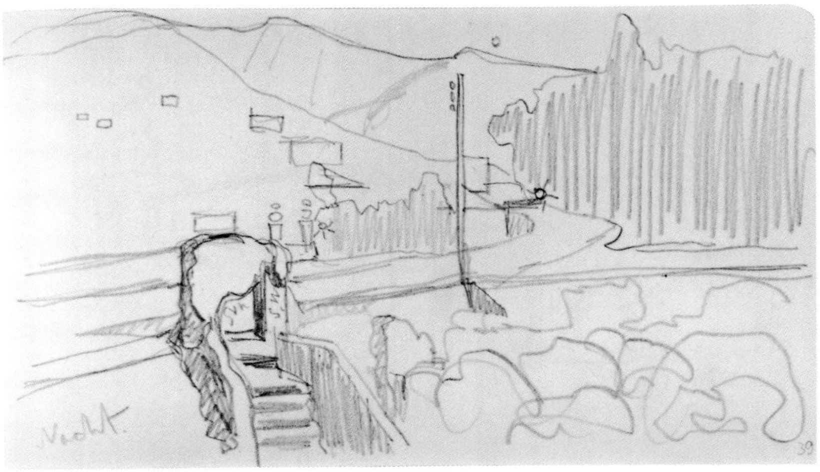


**p.34** Pencil sketch of Rapallo seen from the harbor
Inscribed below: 'unten Spiegel[un]g oben / Silberblau / nur Silberblau'; c.r.: 'rosa / gelb'

REFERENCES
*Kandinsky, Vrubel', Jawlensky e gli artisti russi a Genova e nelle riviere* exh. cat. (Genoa, 2001), no.137i, color ill.

**p.35** Pencil sketch of Rapallo

**p.36** Blank

**p.37** Pencil sketch of Rapallo with the church of San Ambrogio on the distant hillside

REFERENCES
Hanfstaengl 1974, p.139, ill.
*Kandinsky, Vrubel', Jawlensky e gli artisti russi a Genova e nelle riviere* exh. cat. (Genoa, 2001), no.137l, color ill.

The view is similar to that in a photograph (2753) probably taken by Münter.

**p.38** Blank

**p.39** Pencil study for *Rapallo- Blick vom Fenster* of 1906
Inscribed l.l.: 'Nacht.'; c.: 'grn / s. w'

REFERENCES
Hanfstaengl 1974, p.139, ill.
Barnett and Friedel 1995, no.201, color ill.
*Kandinsky, Vrubel', Jawlensky e gli artisti russi a Genova e nelle riviere* exh. cat. (Genoa, 2001), no.137m, color ill.

The drawing is clearly related to *Rapallo- Blick vom Fenster* of early 1906 (Roethel and Benjamin no.160). Kandinsky and Münter lived in the Casa Vallebella at 24 via Montebello, which no longer exists but stood in what is now via Zunino (see Franco Ragazzi, 'Trovato la casa di Kandinsky' in *Il Secolo XIX* (Genoa, 17 November 2001).

**p.40** Blank

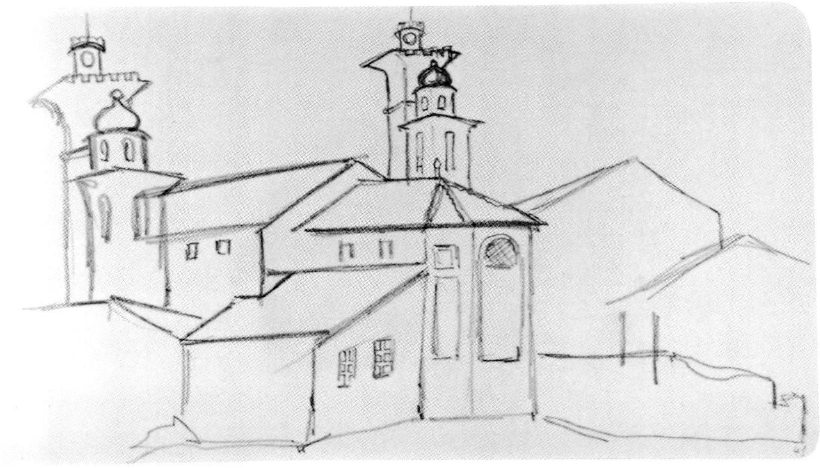

22, p.41

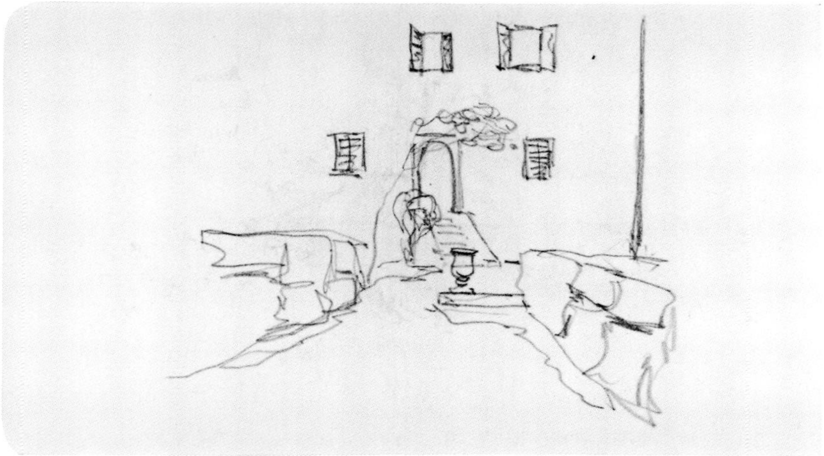

22, p.42

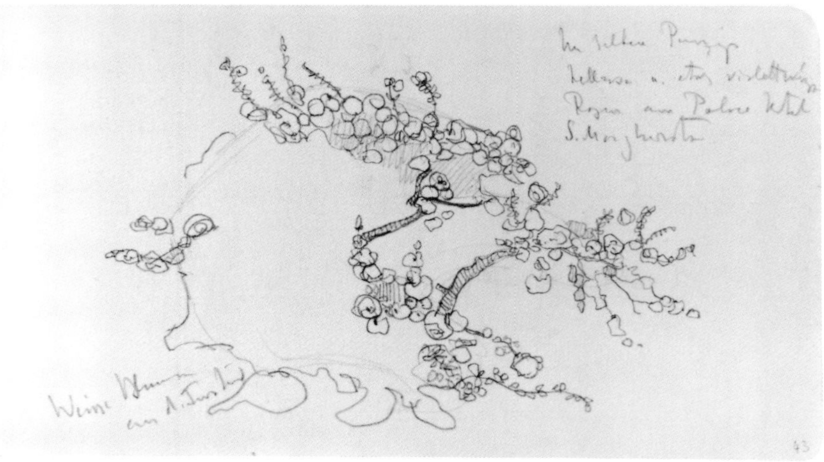

22, p.43

**p.41** Pencil sketches of church and tower

REFERENCES
*Kandinsky, Vrubel', Jawlensky e gli artisti russi a Genova e nelle riviere* exh. cat. (Genoa, 2001), no.137n, color ill.

Kandinsky sketched the Oratorio dei Bianchi and Torre Civica in Rapallo.

**p.42** Pencil sketch of entrance to building

Kandinsky probably made this sketch in Santa Margherita (see facing page).

**p.43** Pencil sketch of flowers at Imperiale Palace Hotel

Inscribed l.l.: 'Weisse Blumen / aus d. Fenster'; u.r.: 'Im selben Prinzip / hellrosa u. etwas violettweiss / Rosen am Palace Hotel / S. Margherita'

REFERENCES
Hanfstaengl 1974, pp.138–139, ill.

As Kandinsky noted, he made this drawing of white blossoms outside the window at the Imperiale Palace Hotel in Santa Margherita. The hotel opened in 1905 after an addition to the original villa was built. Santa Margherita is 3 kilometers from Rapallo.

**p.44** Blank

**p.45** Pencil sketch of mountainous landscape

The sketch probably shows the mountains behind Rapallo.

22, p.45

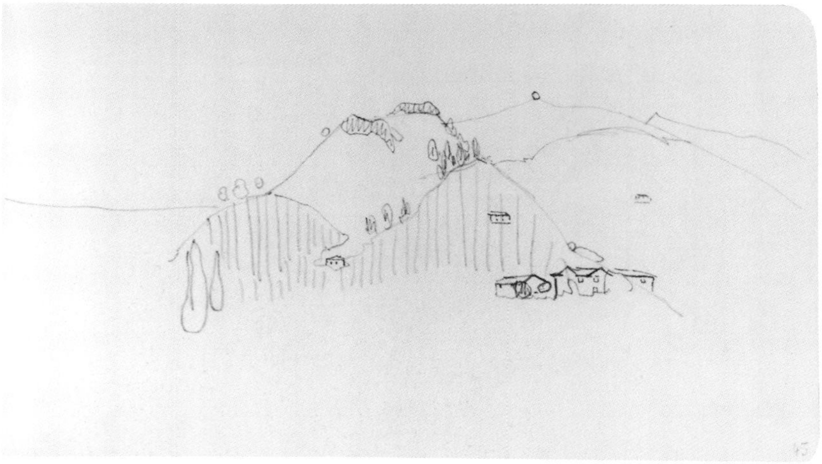

22, p.46

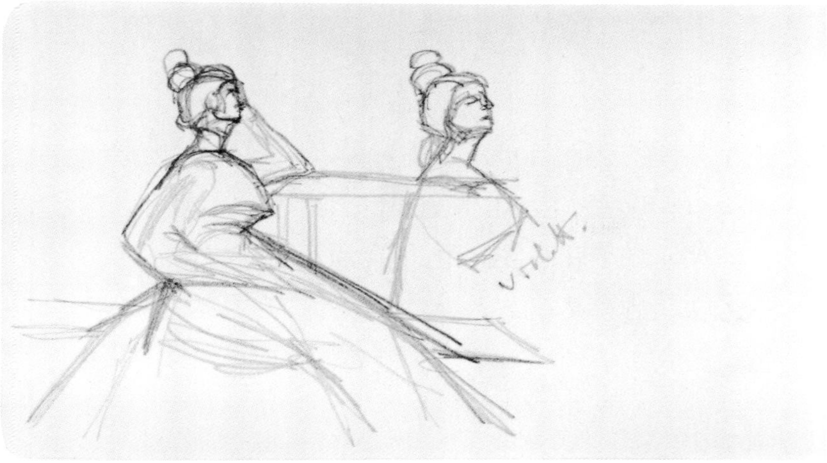

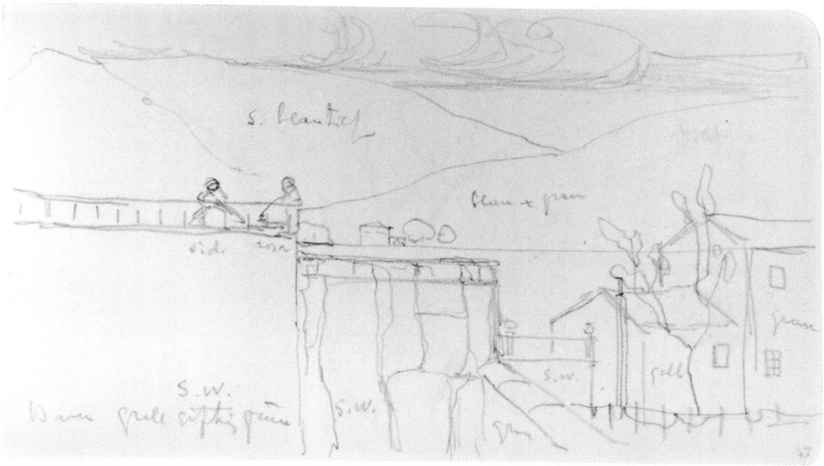

22, p.47

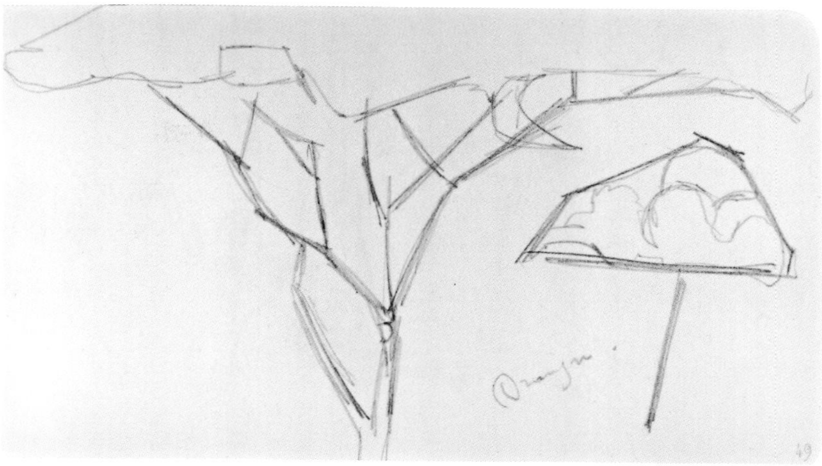

22, p.49

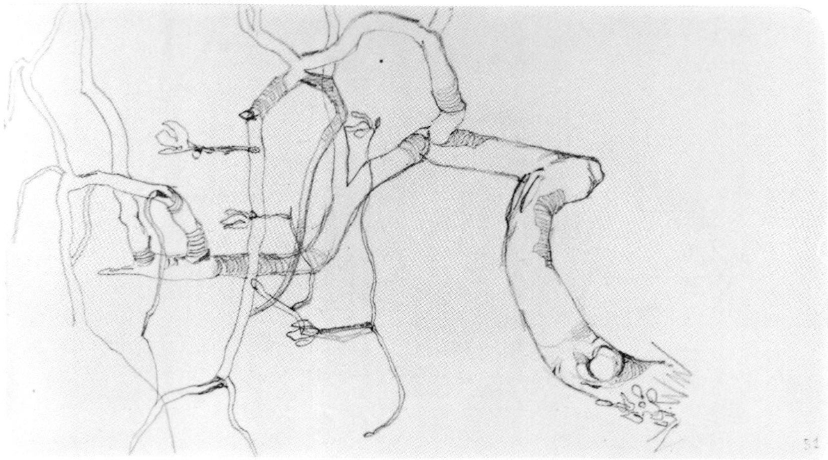

22, p.51

22, p.53

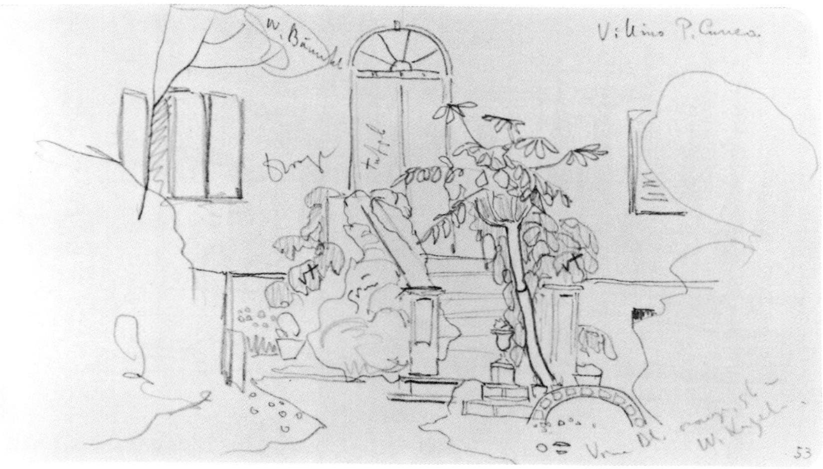

**p.46** Pencil sketches of woman
Inscribed c.r.: 'violett.'

The woman seated on the left with her elbow raised may also be depicted in the sketch on the facing page (p.47).

**p.47** Pencil sketch of landscape
Inscribed u.c. with color notations: 's. blautief'; c.: 'viol. / rosa / blau + grau'; l.l.: 's.w. / Baum grell giftig grün'; l.r.: 's.w. / gelb / grau'

REFERENCES
Hanfstaengl 1974, p.139, ill.

The sketch was probably made in the hills above Rapallo.

**p.48** Blank

**p.49** Pencil sketch of tree branches
Inscribed l.r.: 'Orangen'

**p.50** Blank

**p.51** Pencil sketch of tree branches with buds

The drawing resembles those on pp.23, 25, 56–57 of this sketchbook.

**p.52** Blank

**p.53** Pencil sketch of villa
Inscribed u.r.: 'Villino P. Cuneo.' and u.l. with color notations: 'w. Bäumkl'; c.: 'Orange / tiefgb / vt / grün'; l.r.: 'Vorne Bl. orange, gb u. / w. Kugeln.'

REFERENCES
Hanfstaengl 1974, pp.138–139, ill.
*Kandinsky, Vrubel', Jawlensky e gli artisti russi a Genova e nelle riviere* exh. cat. (Genoa, 2001), no.1370, color ill.

A photograph in the Münter-Eichner Stiftung (fig.a: 2772) shows the entire building. According to information kindly provided by Franco Ragazzi, the Villa Cuneo no longer exists but was located near the Torrente Boate in Rapallo. Curiously, the building bears a resemblance to the Villa Palme on via Cuneo in Santa Margherita, where the garden and entrance are remarkably similar.

fig.a

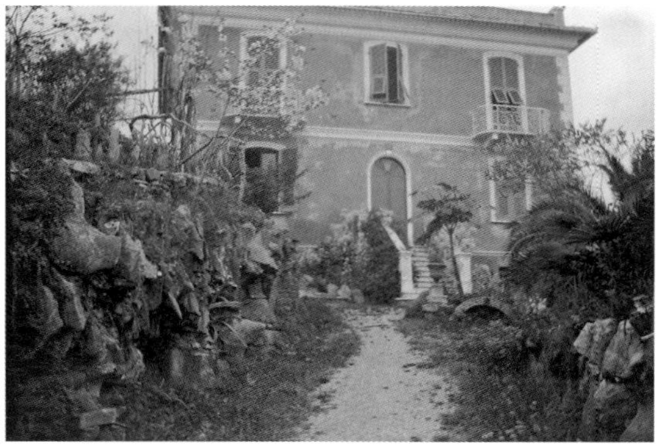

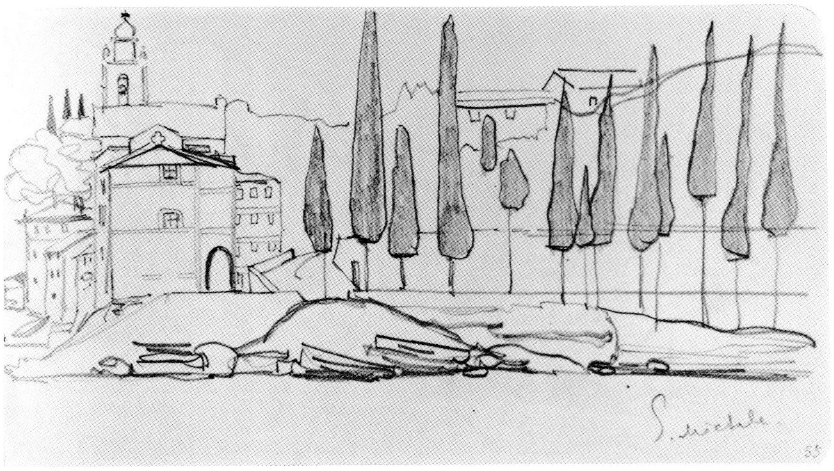

22, p.55

**p.54** Blank

**p.55** Pencil sketch of the church at San Michele di Pagana
Inscribed l.r.: 'S. Michele'

REFERENCES
Hanfstaengl 1974, pp.138–139, ill.
*Kandinsky, Vrubel', Jawlensky e gli artisti russi a Genova e nelle riviere* exh. cat. (Genoa, 2001), no.137p, color ill.

The drawing shows San Michele di Pagana between Santa Margherita and Rapallo as seen from the water. The view was depicted in many postcards from that time.

(See color plate p.122)

**pp.56–57** Pencil sketch of branches with buds

REFERENCES
Hanfstaengl 1974, p.139, ill.
*Kandinsky, Vrubel', Jawlensky e gli artisti russi a Genova e nelle riviere* exh. cat. (Genoa, 2001), no.137q, color ill.

There is a similar photograph (2757) annotated by Münter 'Rapallo / Portofino' in the Münter-Eichner Stiftung (kindly brought to my attention by Isabelle Jansen).

(See color plate p.123)

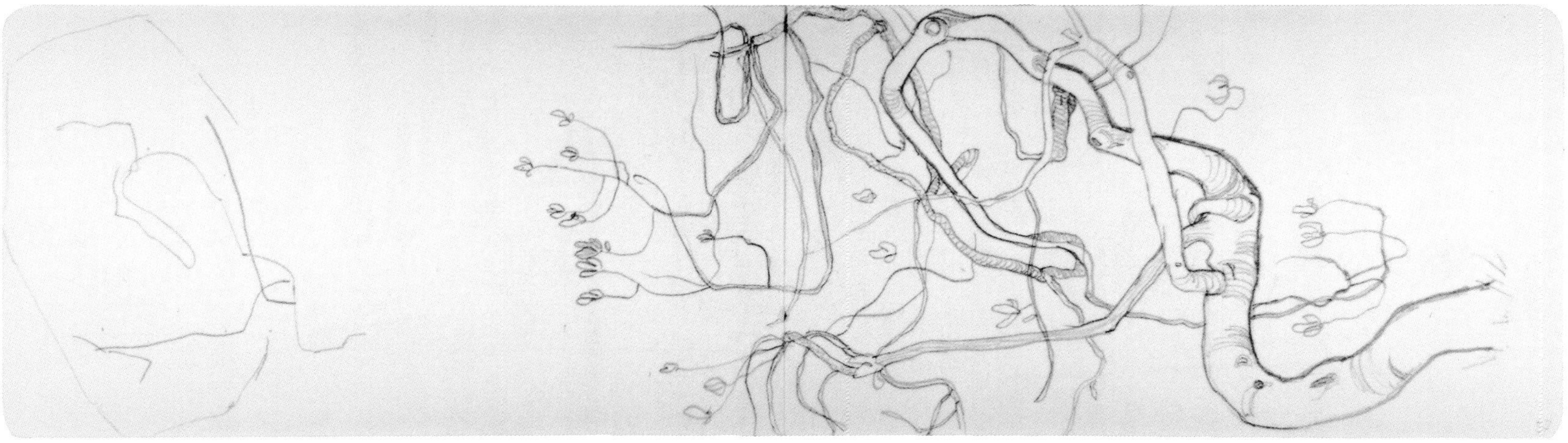

22, pp.56-57

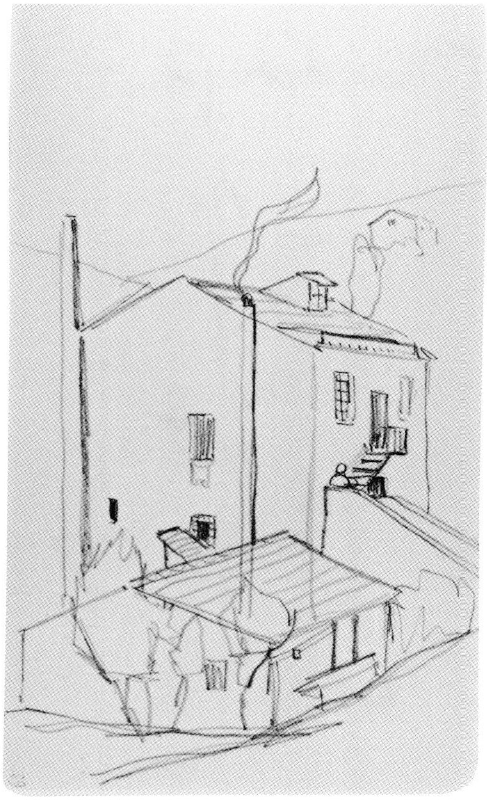

22, p.59

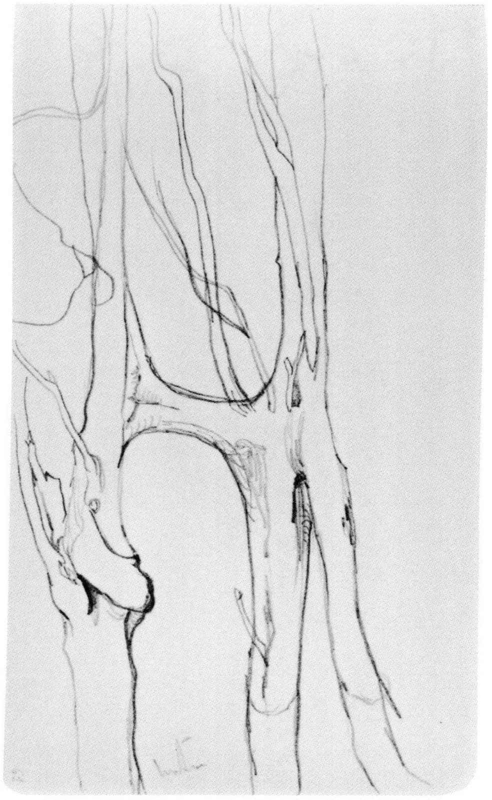

22, p.61

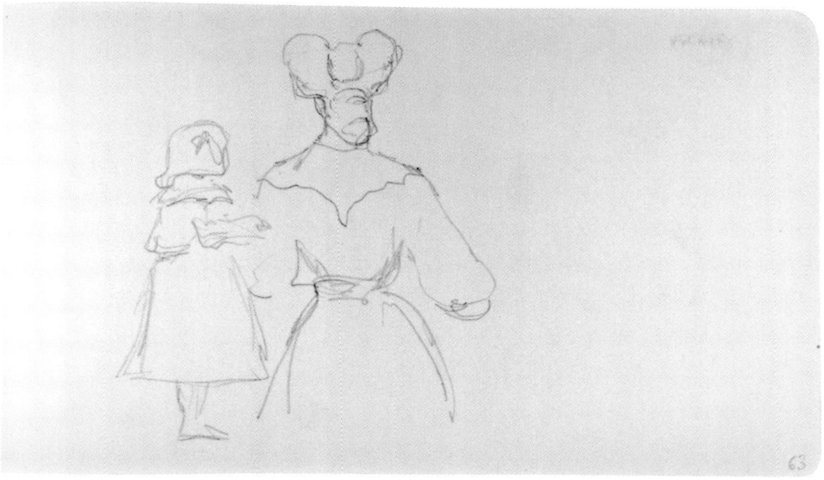

22, p.63

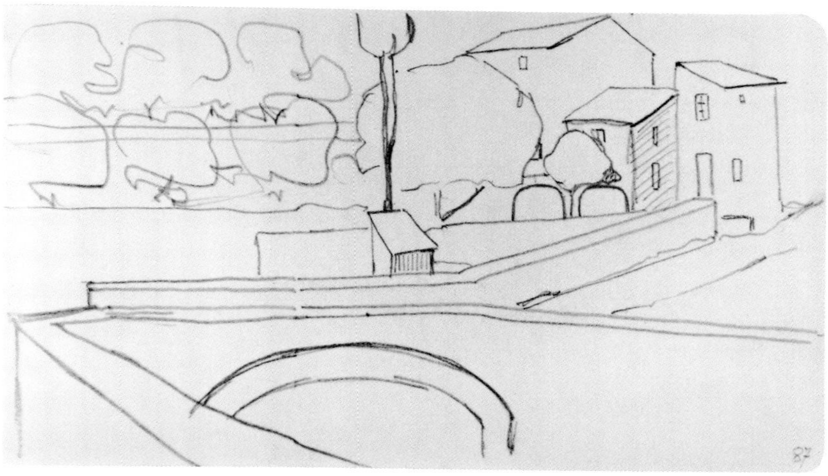

22, p.87

22, p.107

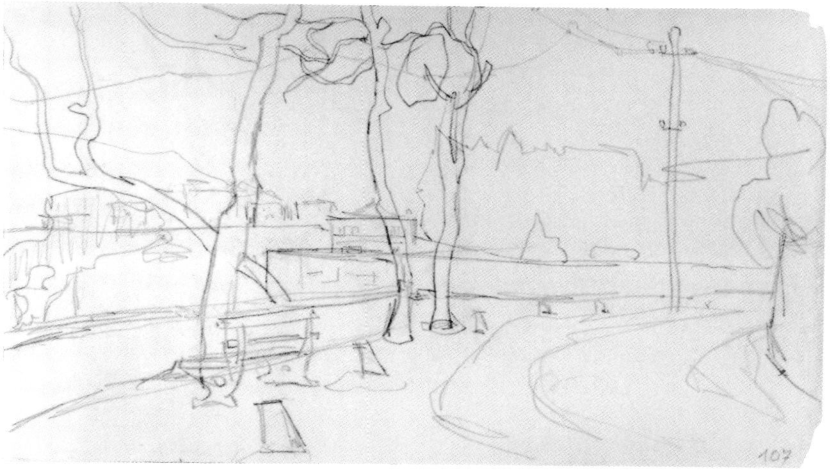

**p.58** Blank

**p.59** Pencil sketch of houses

The buildings resemble those near San Ambrogio in the hills above Rapallo. The house with external staircase suggests photographs taken by Münter or Kandinsky (2766 and 2767).

**p.60** Blank

**p.61** Pencil sketch of tree
Inscribed l.c.: 'unten'

**p.62** Blank

**p.63** Pencil sketch of girl and woman

Münter may have sketched the same woman in a drawing dated 7 March in a sketchbook she used in Rapallo (see 46/24, p.3).

**pp.64–86** Blank

**p.87** Pencil sketch of landscape

REFERENCES
Hanfstaengl 1974, p.139, ill.

The drawing was probably done near Rapallo (see pp.47, 59 above).

**pp.88–106** blank

**p.107** Pencil sketch of landscape with trees, bench, river and buildings

REFERENCES
*Kandinsky, Vrubel', Jawlensky e gli artisti russi a Genova e nelle riviere* exh. cat. (Genoa, 2001), no.137r, color ill.
Barnett 2006, p.60

This sketch has been identified as Rapallo and resembles a drawing made by Münter (see 46/24, pp. 26–27). It can also be compared to a drawing, *Altstadt* (vol.I, cat. no.85), which was probably done in Paris in 1906–1907.

# Sketchbook 23

1906–1907 and probably 1903

Blue cardboard sketchbook with black spine; inside back cover sticker from Sennelier, Paris (quai Voltaire)
Contains 116 pages (58 sheets), each 19.8 x 12.5 cm ($7\frac{3}{4}$ x $4\frac{7}{8}$ in), of which pp.100–113 are blank
Numerous sheets have been removed at the beginning and in the middle of the sketchbook.
Page numbers inscribed by unknown hand at later date with odd numbers at lower right

Hanfstaengl 1974, pp.157–158

LOCATION
Städtische Galerie im Lenbachhaus, Munich (GMS 336)

HISTORY
Gabriele Münter, Murnau, until 1957

This sketchbook bears the label from an art supply store in Paris; however, the first two pages depict scenes of Basel, where Kandinsky and Gabriele Münter stopped on their way to Paris in May 1906. Moreover, other pages can be related to works that Kandinsky executed in 1903. Thus, it appears likely that he acquired the sketchbook by 1903. Most of the drawings, however, were done in 1906–1907.

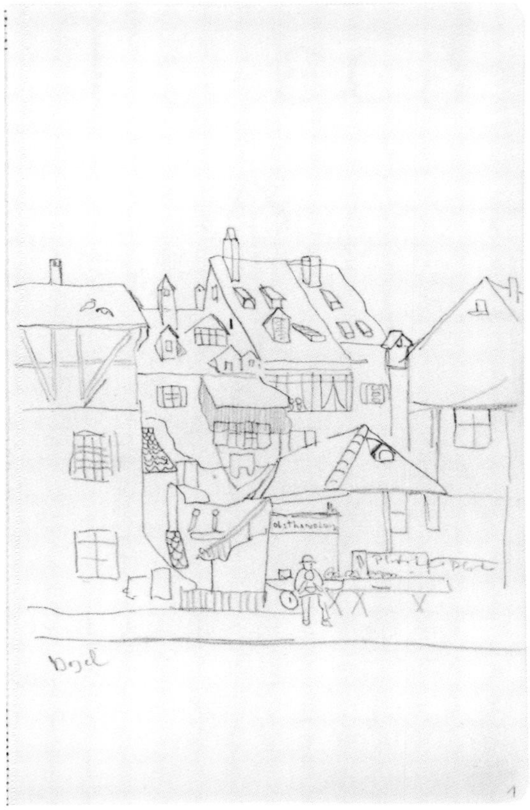

23, p.1

23, p.3

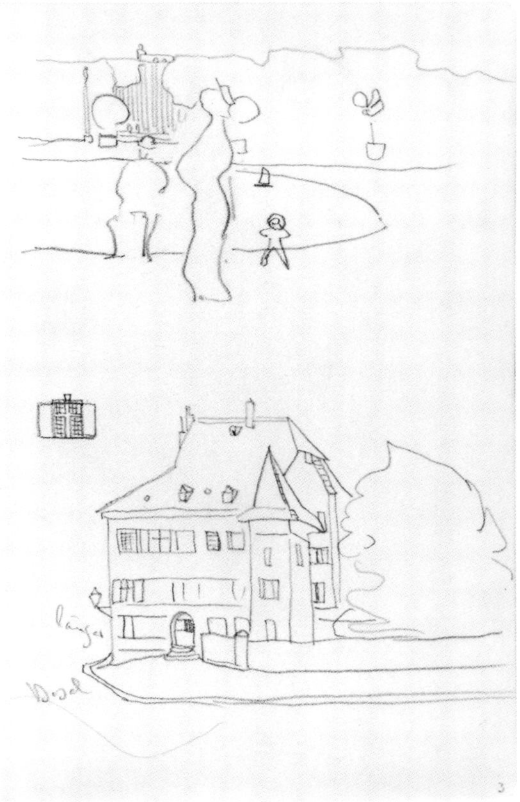

**p.1** Pencil sketch of houses and shops in Basel
Inscribed l.l.: 'Basel' and in image: 'Obsthandlung / Plakat / Plak[ate]'

REFERENCES
Hanfstaengl 1974, p.157
Barnett 1992, p.184
Barnett and Friedel 1995, no.203, color ill.

Kandinsky and Münter stayed in Basel on 20 May 1906; they arrived in Paris on 22 May. Kandinsky's inscriptions identify this sketch and another on p.3 as having been done in Basel, although the sketchbook was apparently purchased in Paris. There is no photograph of this view, which he might have copied later in Paris (kindly confirmed by Ilse Holzinger). The sketch brings to mind a gouache showing shops on the Barfüsserplatz in Basel (Barnett no.204).

**p.2** Blank

**p.3** Pencil sketch of figures in park (above) and of house and window detail (below)
Inscribed l.l.: 'länger / Basel'

REFERENCES
Hanfstaengl 1974, p.157, ill.
Barnett 1992, p.184
Barnett 2006, p.63

The drawing of a park with people is related to other drawings (see vol.I, cat. no.95 and Sketchbook 20 (GMS 327, pp.66–70) done in Paris. Kandinsky visited Basel two days before arriving in Paris on 22 May; he lived in or near Paris until 1 June 1907. Both sketches on this page appear to have been drawn with the same pencil.

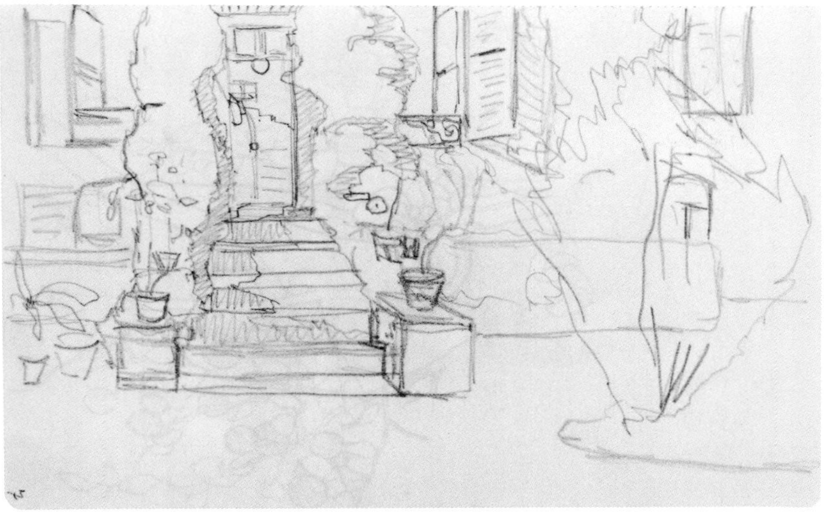

23, p.7

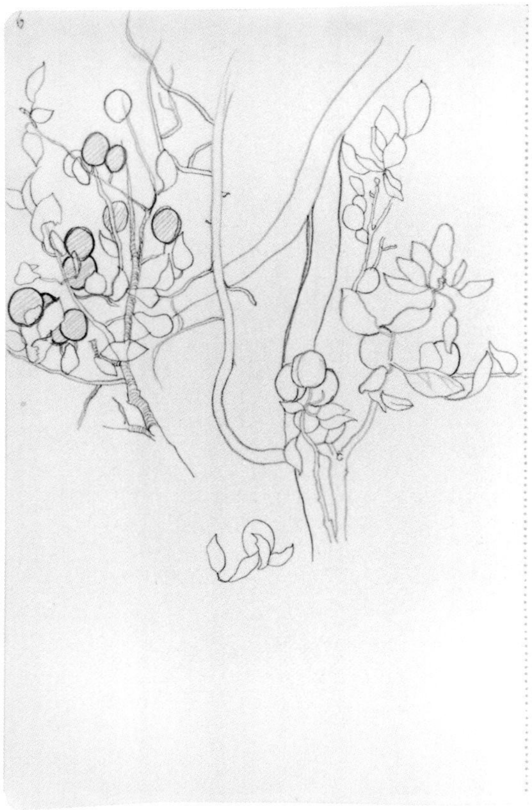

23, p.9

**pp.4–6** Blank

**p.7** Pencil study for *Unterhaltung im Garten* of 1903–1904

REFERENCES
Hanfstaengl 1974, p.157
Barnett 1992, p.114

The windows, doorway, steps and flowerpots recur in a tempera painting *Unterhaltung im Garten* (known only from a photograph in the Münter-Eichner Stiftung), which was probably done in 1903–1904 but may have been painted later (Barnett no.101).

**p.8** Blank

**p.9** Pencil study of foliage and branches (upside down)

REFERENCES
Barnett 1992, p.86
Barnett 2006, p.63

**p.10** Blank

**p.11** Pencil sketches of the artist's cat Waske

Kandinsky made many sketches of his cat Waske in this sketchbook and in Sketchbook 20 when he lived in Sèvres near Paris.

**p.12** Blank

**p.13** Pencil sketch of cat

**p.14** Blank

23, p.11

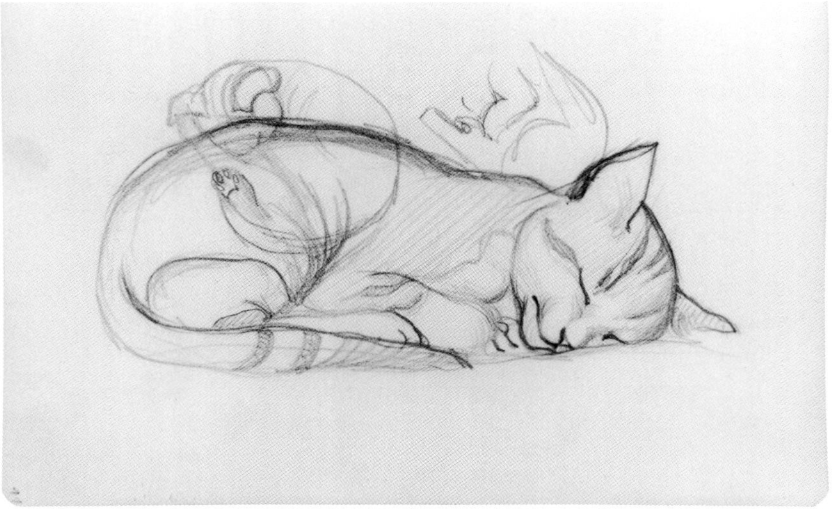

23, p.13

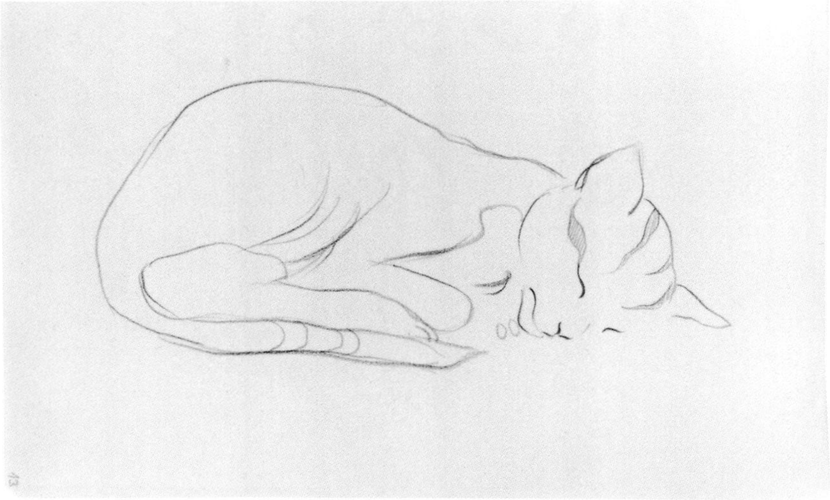

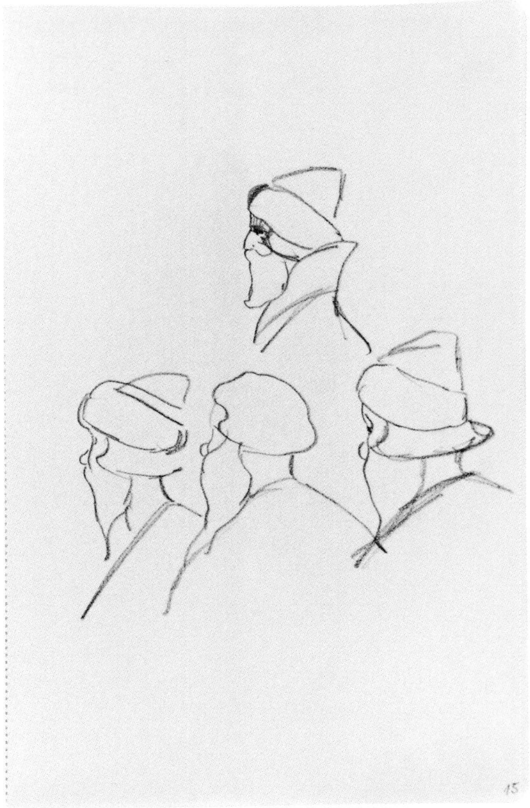

23, p.15

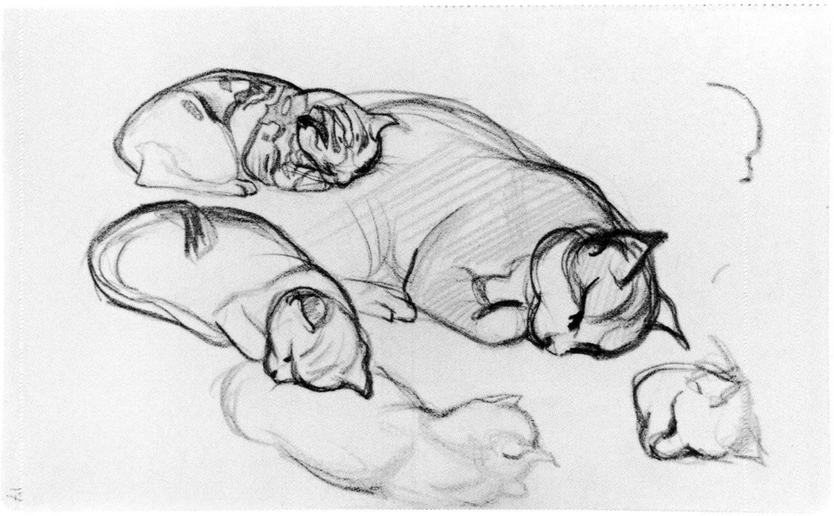

23, p.17

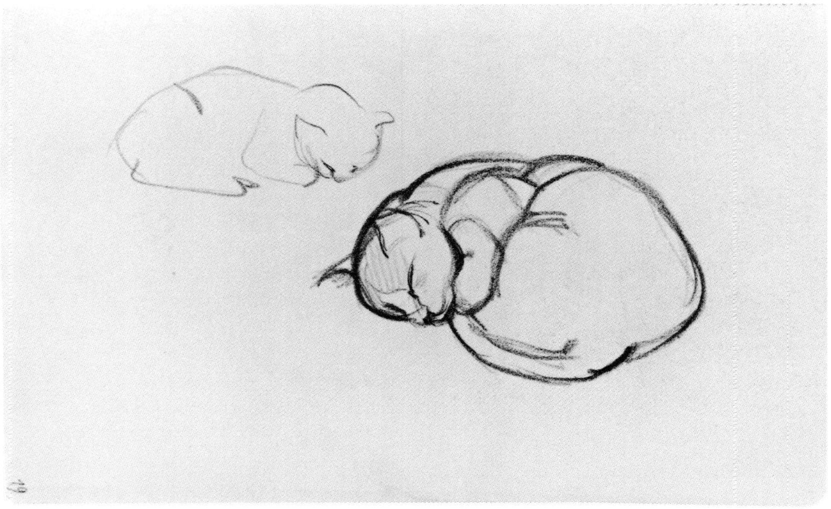

23, p.19

23, p.21

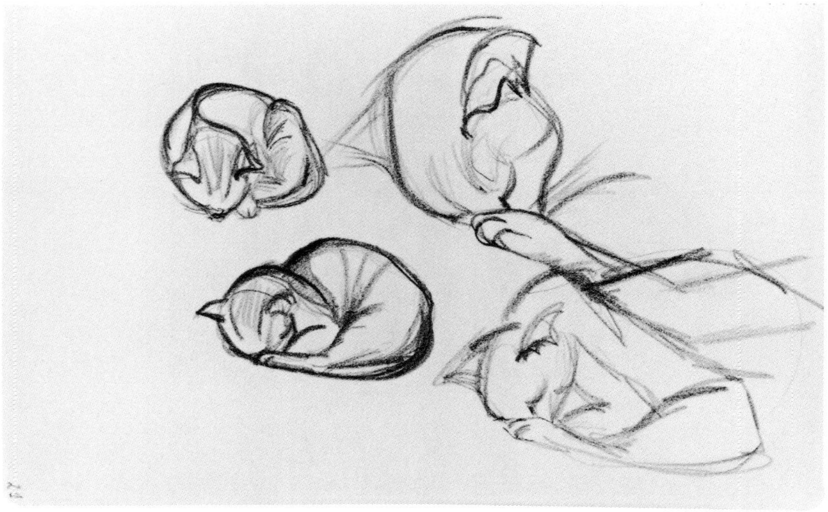

**p.15** Pencil sketches of man with beard wearing cap

REFERENCES
Hanfstaengl 1974, p.157, ill.
Podzemskaia 2000, p.130

The male figure is related to *Der Bär* of January–February 1907 (Barnett no.217) and possibly *Sturmglocke* of 1907 (Barnett no.224).

**p.16** Blank

**p.17** Pencil sketches of cat

REFERENCES
Hanfstaengl 1974, p.157, ill.

**p.18** Blank

**p.19** Pencil sketches of cat

**p.20** Blank

**p.21** Pencil sketches of cat

REFERENCES
Hanfstaengl 1974, p.157, ill.

**p.22** Blank

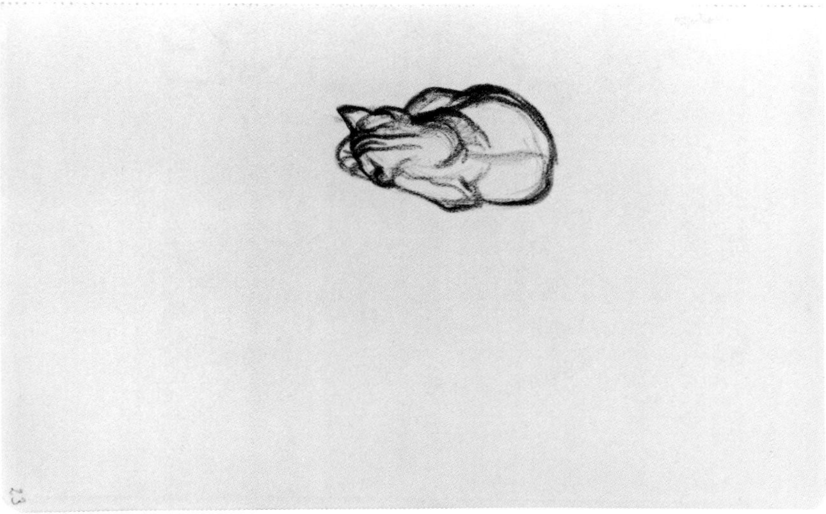

23, p.23

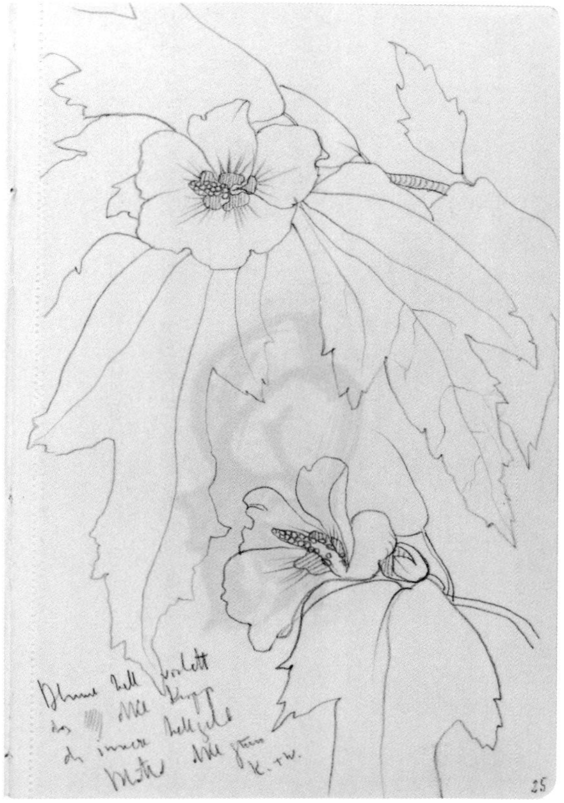

23, p.25

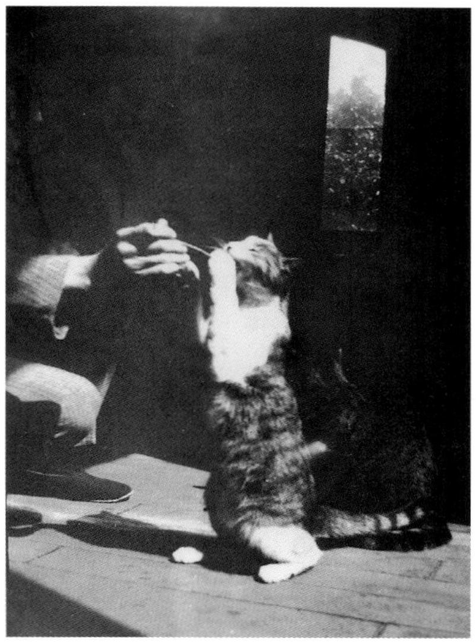

fig.a

**p.23** Pencil sketch of cat

**p.24** Blank

**p.25** Pencil sketch of flowers
Inscribed l.l.: 'Blume hell violett / das//////dkl Krapp / das innere hellgelb / Blatter dkl grün / K + w'

**p.26** Blank

**p.27** Pencil sketch of cats

Münter took this photograph (fig.a) of Kandinsky feeding Waske with another cat in the background: they resemble the cats in this study. For other sketches of cats, see vol.I, cat. nos.93–94 and pp.17–23, 28–41, 53–55, 61–63 and 67 in this sketchbook.

**p.28** Pencil sketch of cat's head

23, p.27

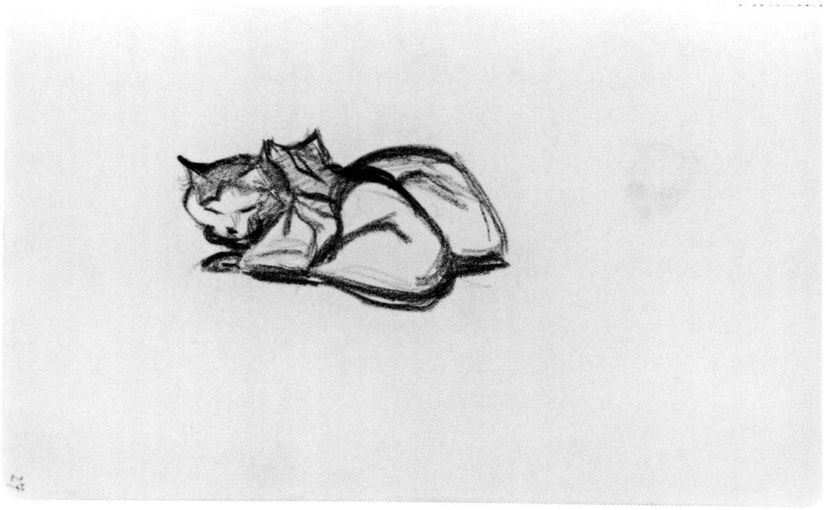

23, p.28

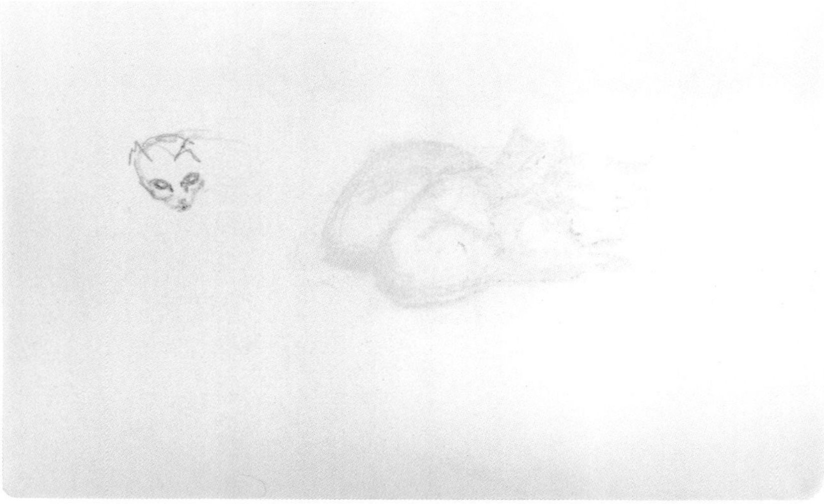

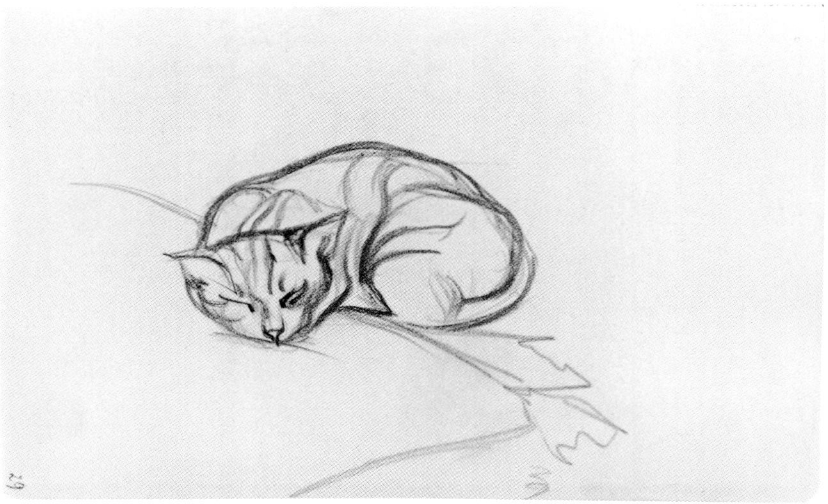

23, p.29

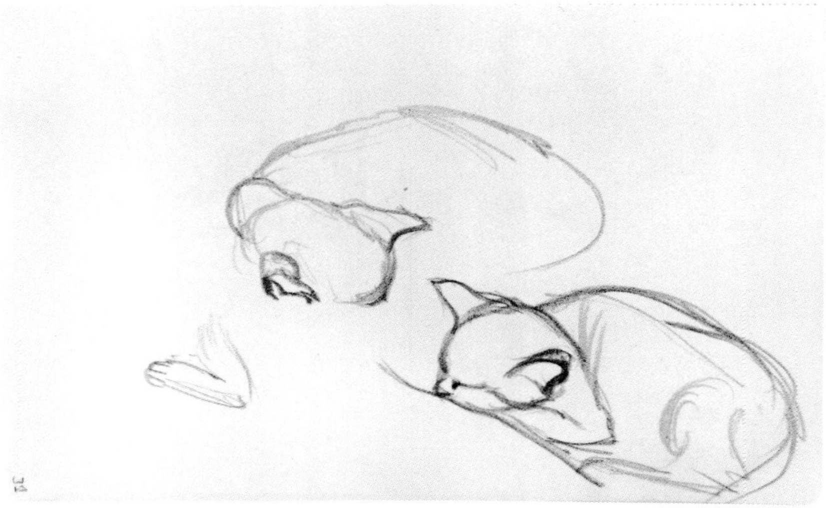

23, p.31

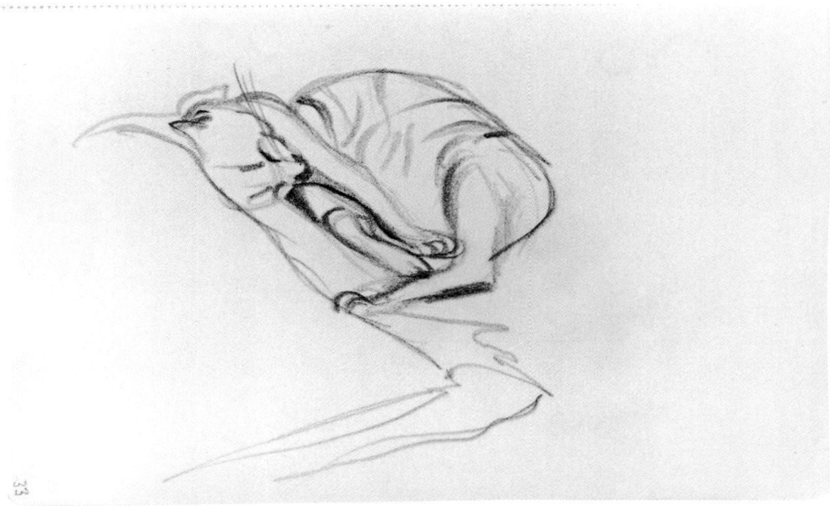

23, p.33

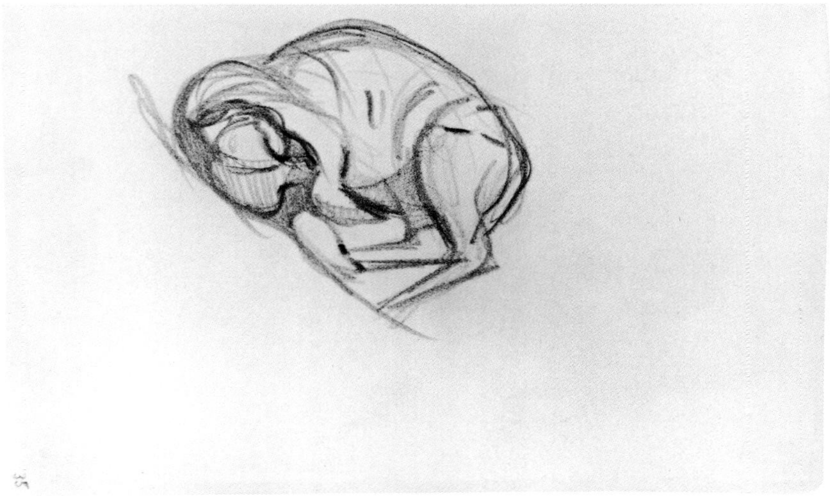

23, p.35

23, p.37

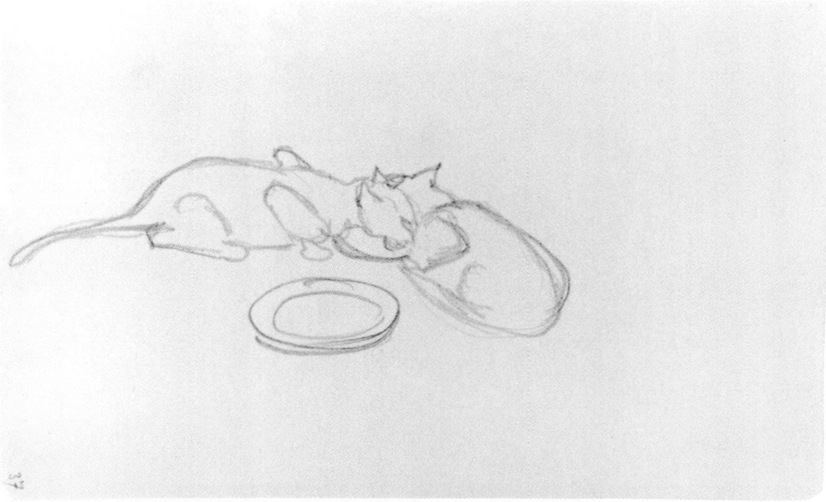

**p.29** Pencil sketch of cat

**p.30** Blank

**p.31** Pencil sketch of cats

**p.32** Blank

**p.33** Pencil sketch of cat

**p.34** Blank

**p.35** Pencil sketch of cat

**p.36** Blank

**p.37** Pencil sketch of cats

**p.38** Blank

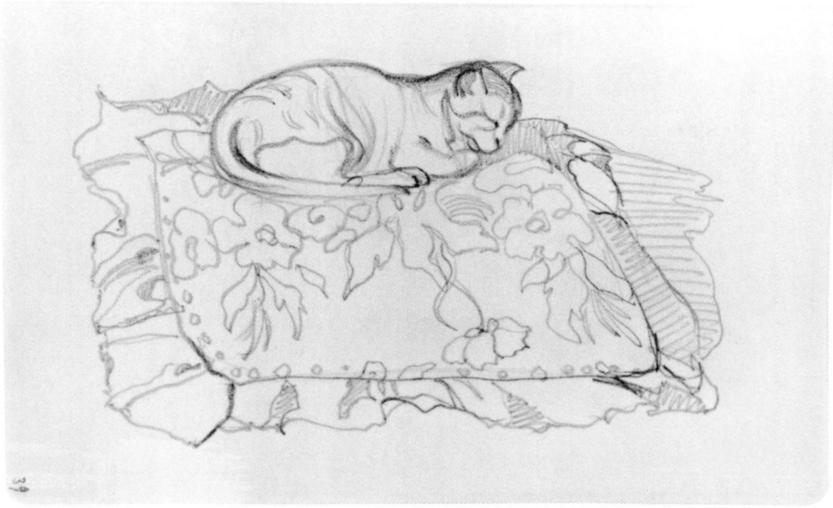

23, p.39

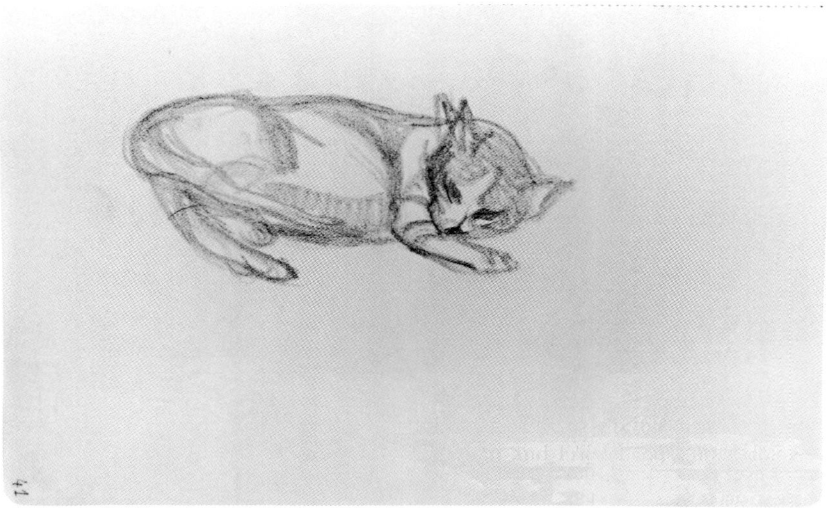

23, p.41

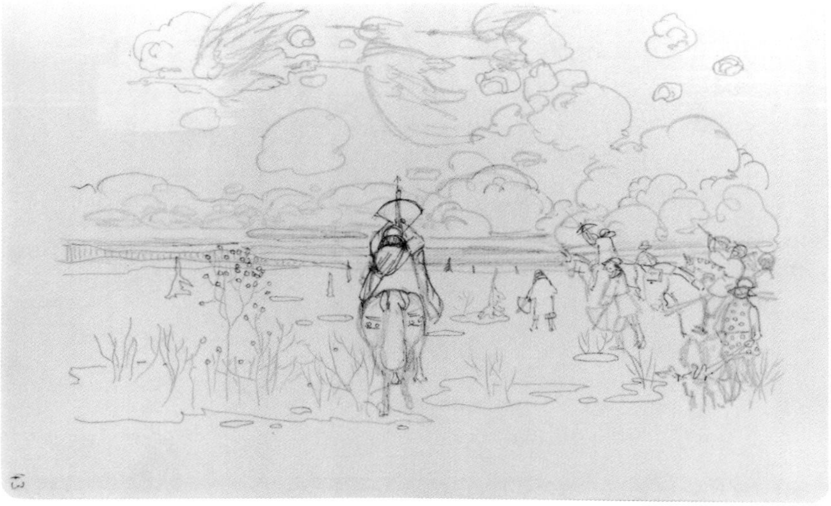

23, p.43

23, p.45

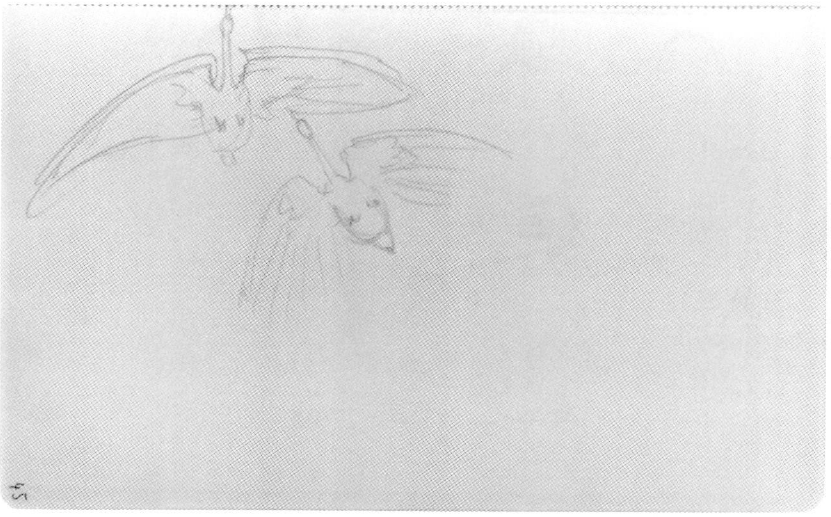

**p.39** Pencil sketch of cat

REFERENCES
Barnett and Friedel 1995, no.235, color ill.

The motif of a cat on a pillow is related to Kandinsky's picture *Gabriele Münter mit einer Katze* of 1907–1908 (Barnett no.236).

**p.40** Blank

**p.41** Pencil sketch of cat

**p.42** Blank

**p.43** Pencil sketch of men on horseback hunting birds with bows and arrows

REFERENCES
Hanfstaengl 1974, p.157, ill.

The sketch seems not to have been developed into a painting or print.

**p.44** Blank

**p.45** Pencil sketch of swans seen from below

The sketch is related to the drawing on p.43.

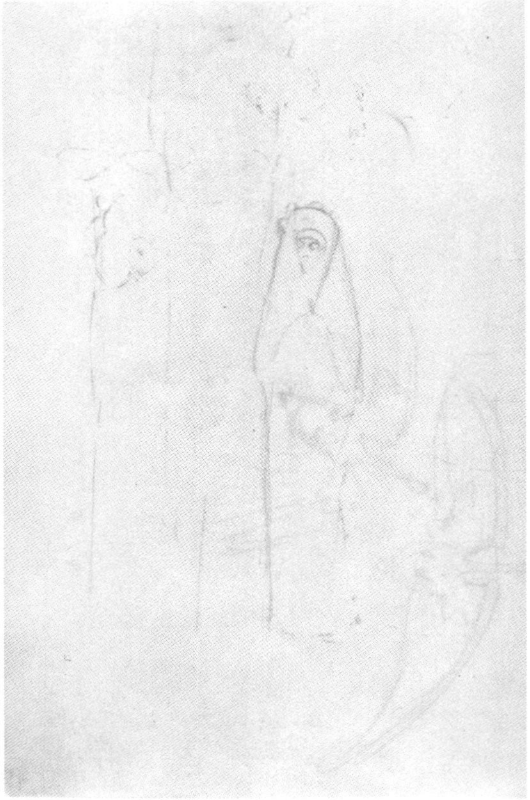

23, p.46

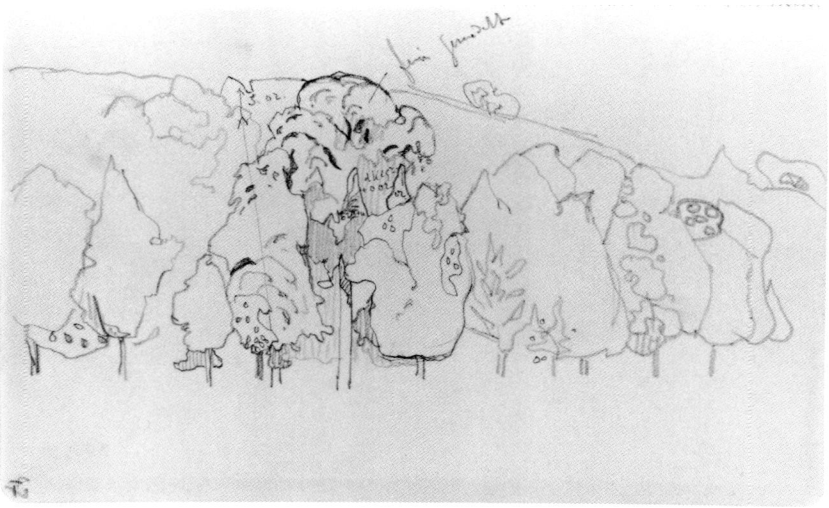

23, p.47

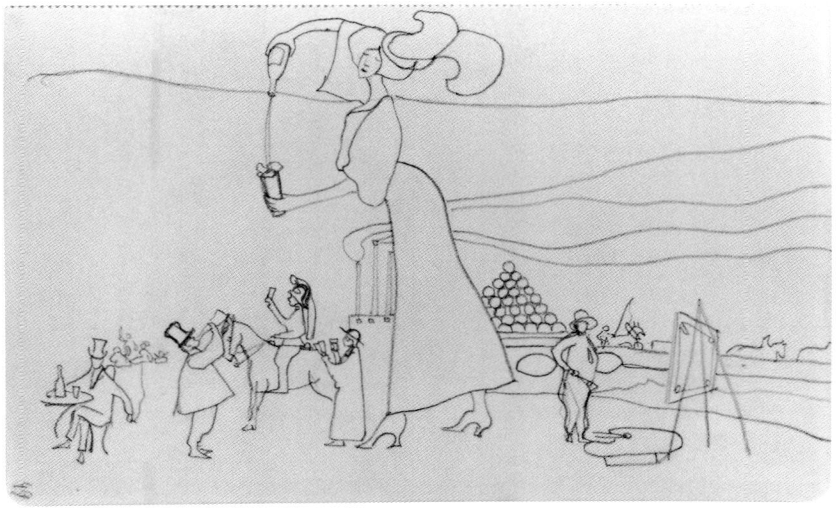

23, p.49

23, p.51

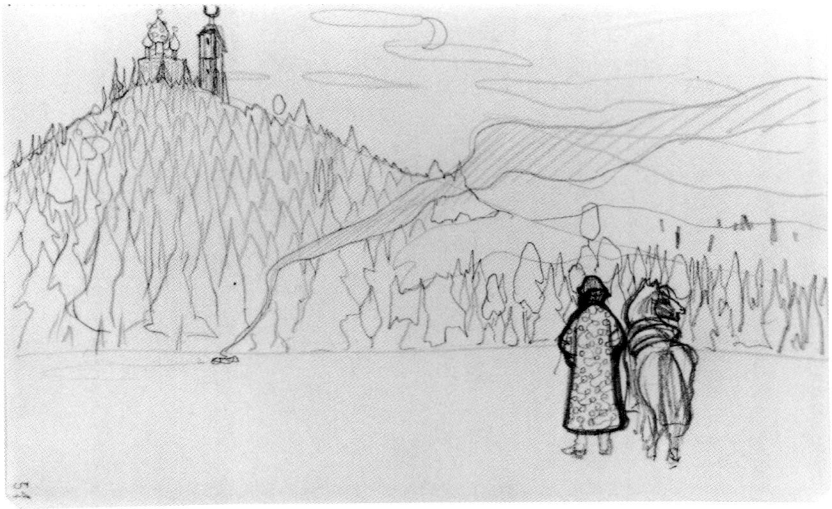

**p.46** Pencil sketch of standing figure

**p.47** Pencil sketch of trees and hill
Inscribed u.c.: 'fein gemischt' and with color notations: 'g. or / dkl gr. / or. / or'

Kandinsky probably made the drawing during autumn 1906 near Paris.

**p.48** Blank

**p.49** Pencil study for poster

REFERENCES
Hanfstaengl 1974, p.157, ill.
Barnett 1992, p.185

Kandinsky made this study for *Affiche einer französischen Brauerei* of 1906–1907 (Barnett no.205) when he lived near Paris.

**p.50** Blank

**p.51** Pencil sketch of horse and Russian rider

REFERENCES
Hanfstaengl 1974, p.157, ill.

This study is related to the hunting scene on p.43 (above) perhaps for an unknown or unexecuted work.

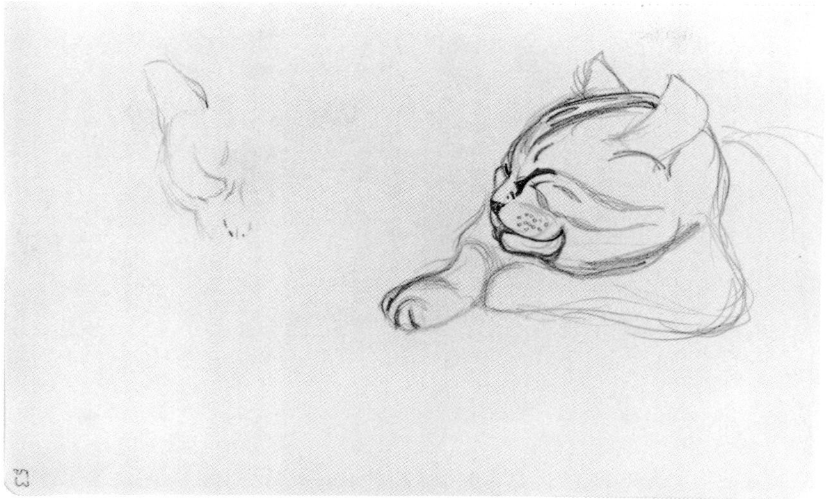

23, p.53

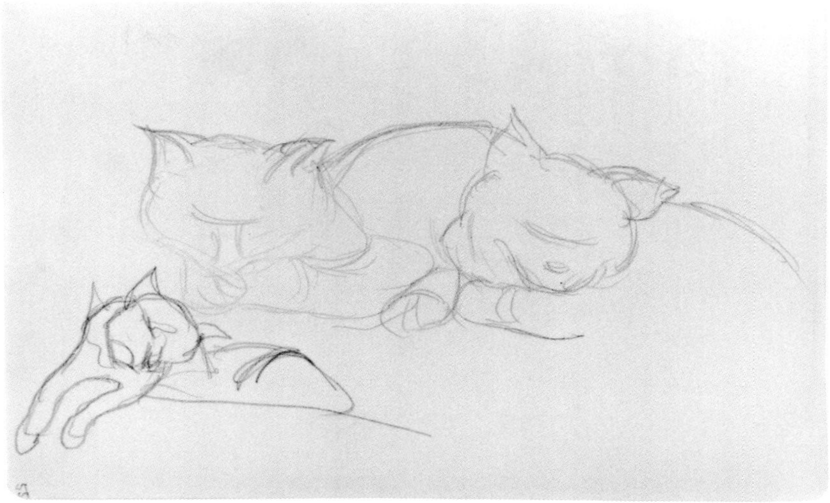

23, p.55

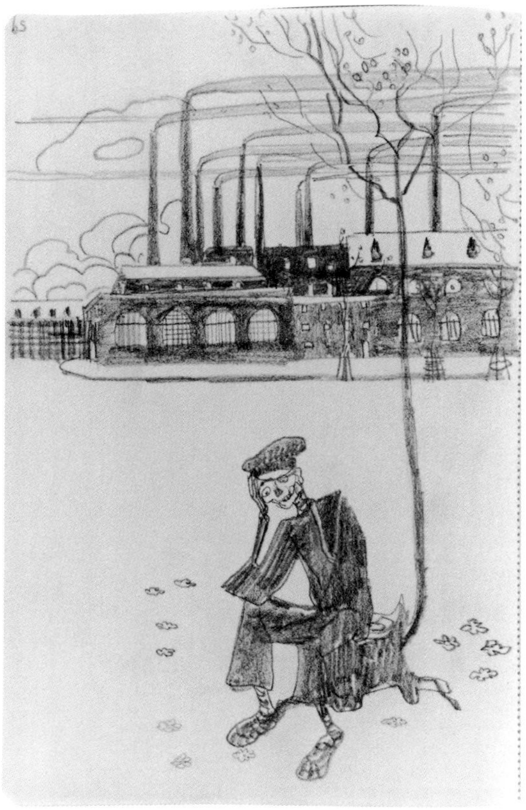

23, p.59

**p.52** Blank

**p.53** Pencil sketches of cat

**p.54** Blank

**p.55** Pencil sketch of cats

**pp.56–58** Blank

**p.59** Pencil sketch of man seated in front of factory (upside down)

REFERENCES
Hanfstaengl 1974, p.157

The smokestacks in the background bring to mind other sketches (p.49 above and p.97 below), p.19 in Sketchbook 20 and *Entwurf für eine Affiche einer französischen Brauerei* of 1906–1907. Hanfstaengl questioned whether the figure was by Kandinsky.

**p.60** Blank

**p.61** Pencil sketch of cats

**p.62** Blank

23, p.61

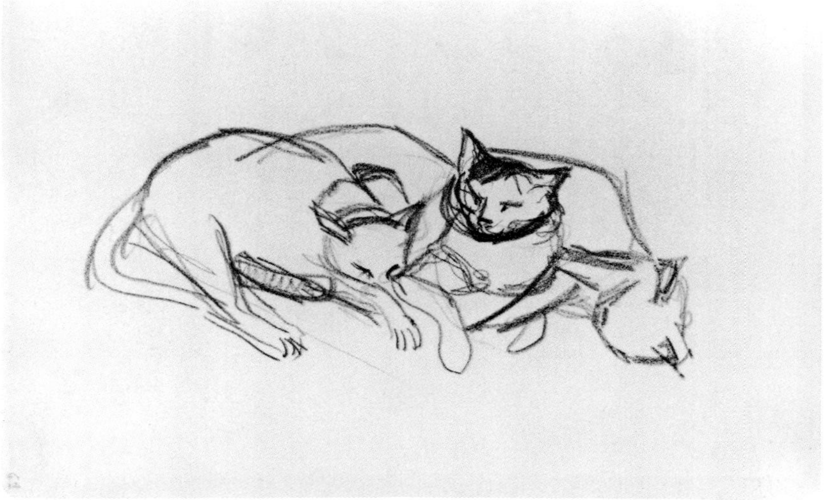

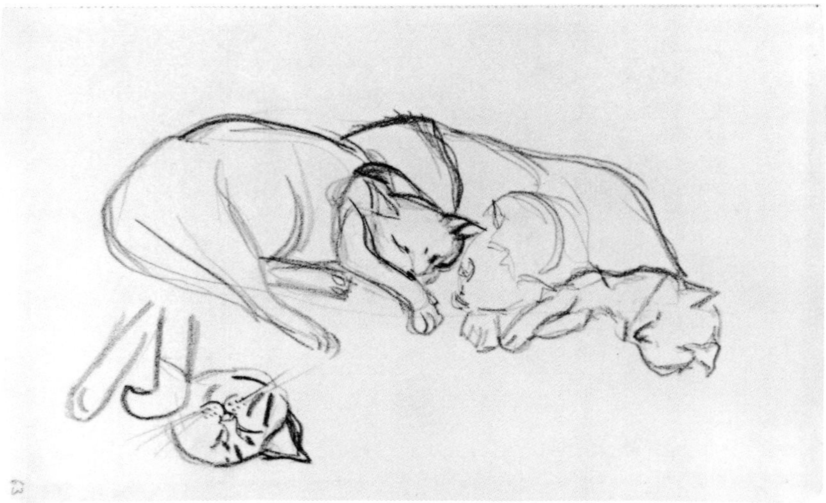

23, p.63

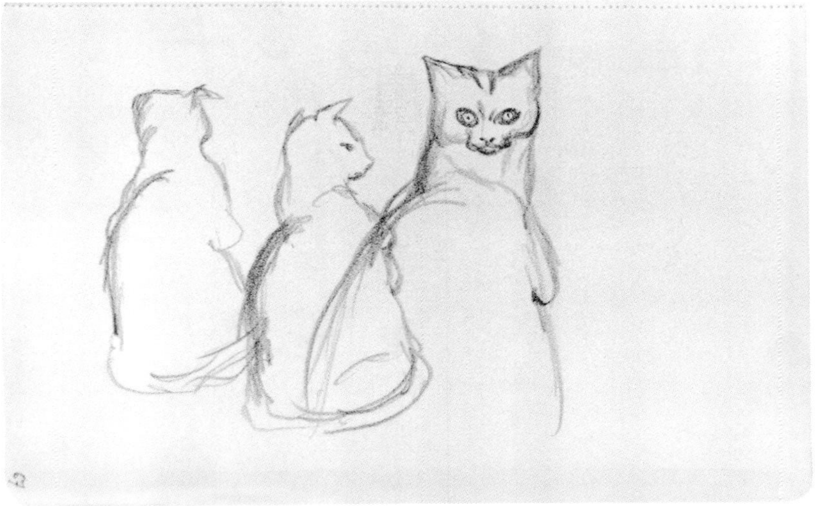

23, p.67

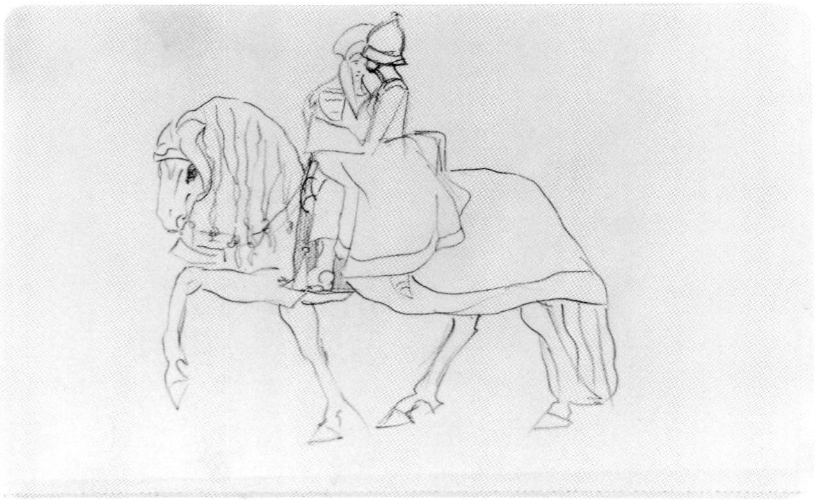

23, p.70

**p.63** Pencil sketch of cats

**pp.64–66** Blank

**p.67** Pencil sketch of cats

REFERENCES
Hanfstaengl 1974, p.157, ill.

**pp.68–69** Blank

**p.70** Pencil study for *Reitendes Paar* of 1907

REFERENCES
Hanfstaengl 1974, pp.157–158, ill.
Roethel and Benjamin 1982, p.186
Barnett 1992, p.192
Hahl-Koch 1993, p.93, ill.102
Barnett and Friedel 1995, no.217, color ill.
Podzemskaia 2000, p.130

This drawing and the studies on the facing page are for *Reitendes Paar* of early 1907 (Roethel and Benjamin no.180).

**p.71** Pencil studies for figures in *Reitendes Paar*

REFERENCES
Podzemskaia 2000, p.130

**p.72** Blank

23, p.71

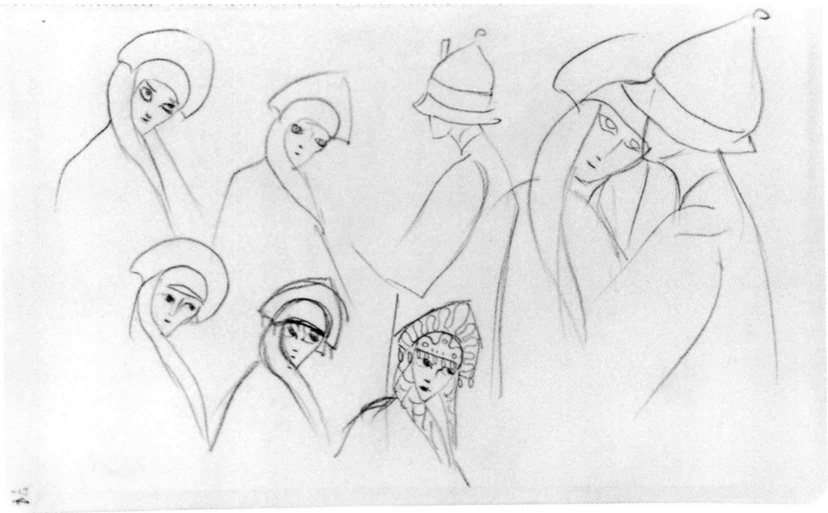

23, p.73

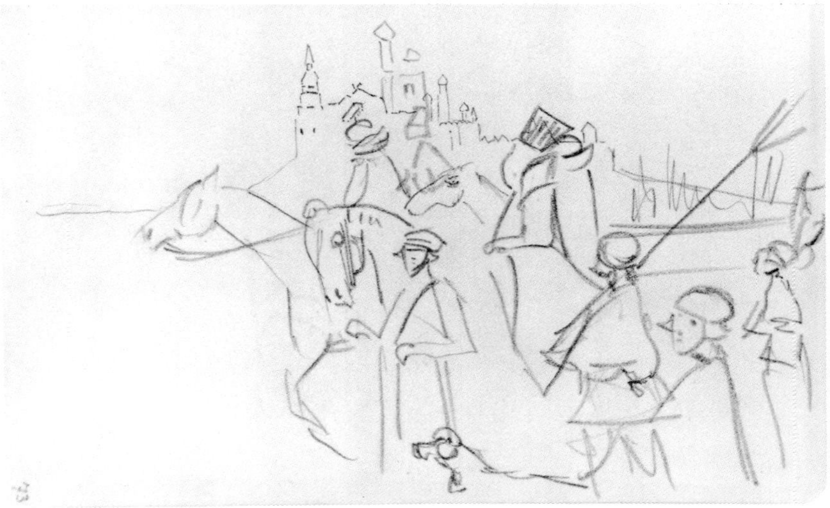

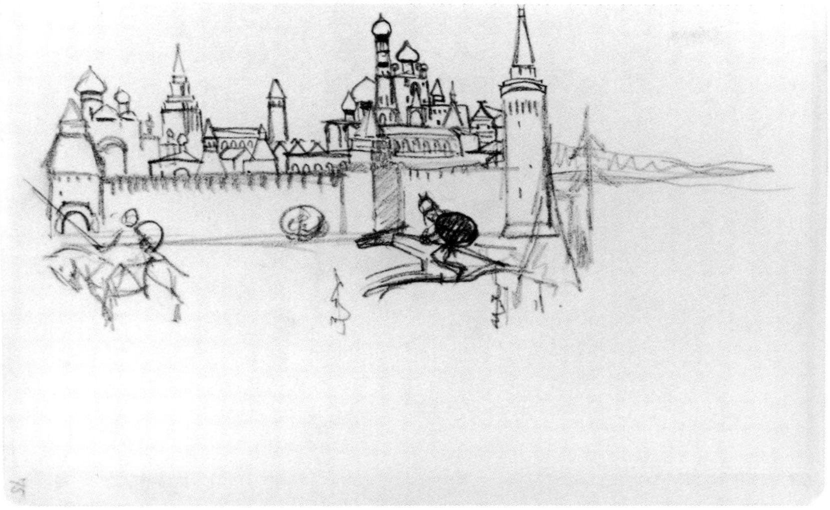

23, p.75

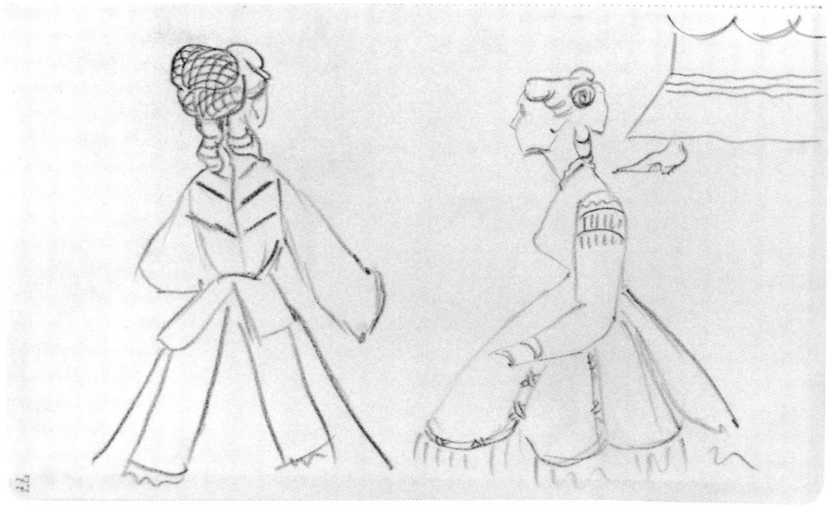

23, p.77

**p.73** Pencil sketch of riders on horseback and kremlin

REFERENCES
Hanfstaengl 1974, pp.157–158, ill.
Weiss 1995, p.39, ill.37

Weiss related this study to the series of paintings on the theme of *Sonntag (Altrussisches)* and dated the sheet to c.1904–1907. However, it bears a resemblance to drawings on pp.43 and 75 of this sketchbook.

**p.74** Blank

**p.75** Pencil study for *Kreuzfahrer* of 1903

REFERENCES
Hanfstaengl 1974, pp.157–158, ill.
Barnett 1992, p.109
Weiss 1995, p. 223 n.22

The study is clearly related to a tempera painting dated 1903, *Kreuzfahrer* (Barnett no.94).

**p.76** Blank

**p.77** Pencil study for *Provinz* of 1906

REFERENCES
Hanfstaengl 1974, p.157
Barnett 1992, p.189

These sketches closely resemble figures in *Provinz* of 1906 (Barnett no.212). See also pp.79, 81, 83 of this sketchbook.

**p.78** Blank

**p.79** Pencil study for *Provinz*

REFERENCES
Hanfstaengl 1974, p.157
Barnett 1992, p.189

**p.80** Blank

**p.81** Pencil study for *Provinz*

REFERENCES
Hanfstaengl 1974, p.157
Barnett 1992, p.189

**p.82** Blank

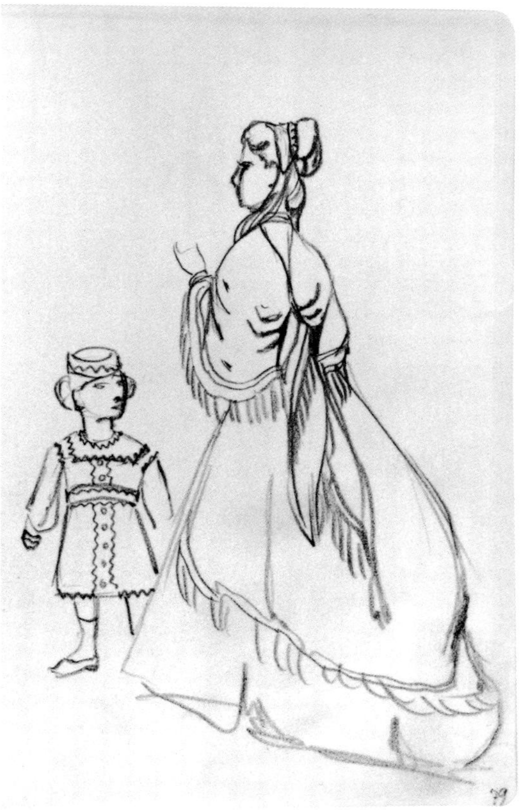

23, p.79

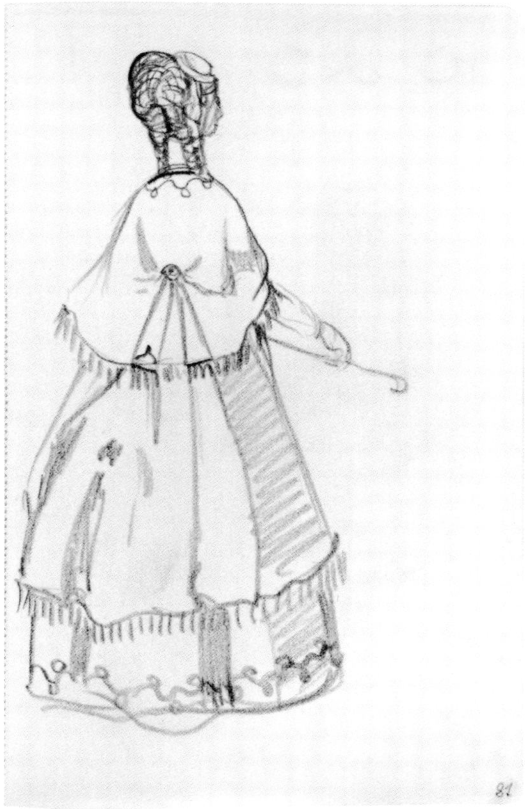

23, p.81

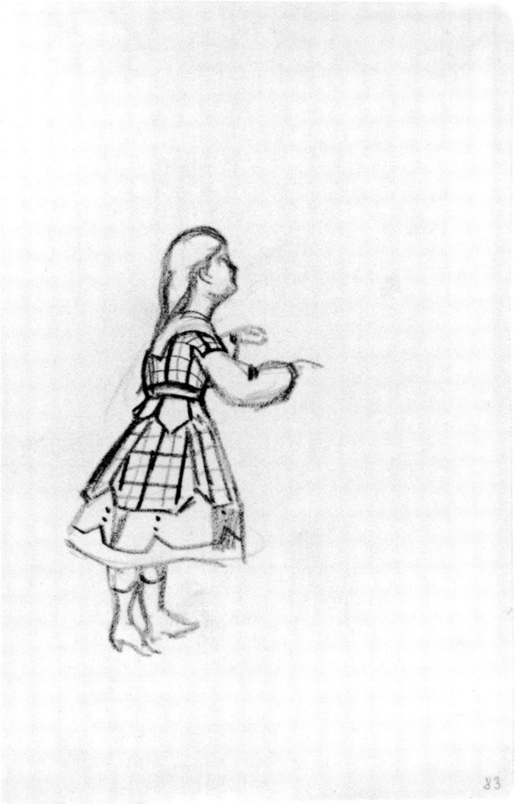

23, p.83

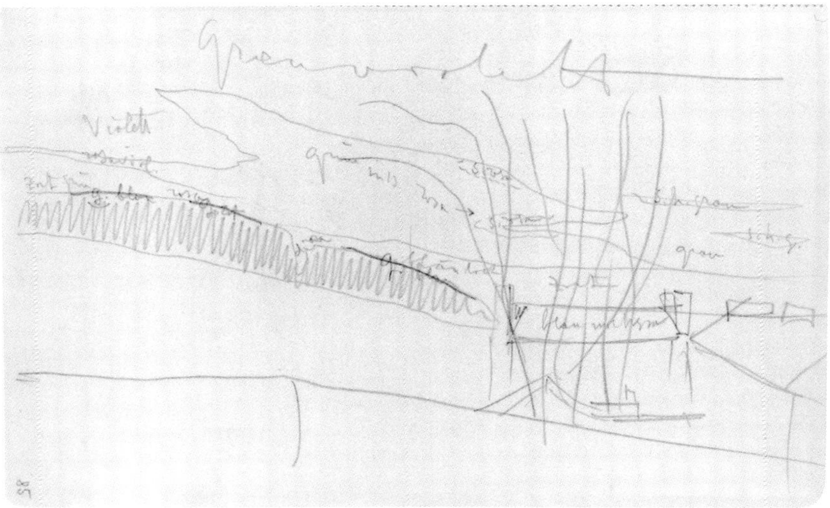

23, p.85

**p.83** Pencil study for *Provinz*

REFERENCES

Hanfstaengl 1974, p.157
Barnett 1992, p.189

**p.84** Blank

**p.85** Pencil sketch of landscape
Inscribed u.c.: 'Grauviolett'; c.l.: 'violett / rosaviol. / zart grün / rosa / G rot'; c.: 'grün in's rosa / rosa / G bläulich zart'; c.r.: 's.h. grau / grau' and with additional color notations

REFERENCES

Hanfstaengl 1974, p.157

Hanfstaengl related this sketch and those on the following pages to Russian themes done in 1905–1907. However, the drawings on pp.85 and 87 appear to have been done from nature, probably during the summer of 1907 in Bad Reichenhall or in Switzerland.

**p.86** Blank

**p.87** Pencil sketch of landscape
Inscribed l.l.: 'Wind'; l.c.: 'kl. weisse harte Wölkchen / nach unten nur in's graublau modelliert.'; c.: 'weisse Streifen / d. rosa / s.h. blau / in's blau u. dkler / in's rosa u. heller / dkl. lila'

REFERENCES

Hanfstaengl 1974, pp.157–158, ill.

Kandinsky drew numerous studies of clouds in Austria in 1905 and probably made these sketches in the summer of 1907.

**p.88** Blank

23, p.87

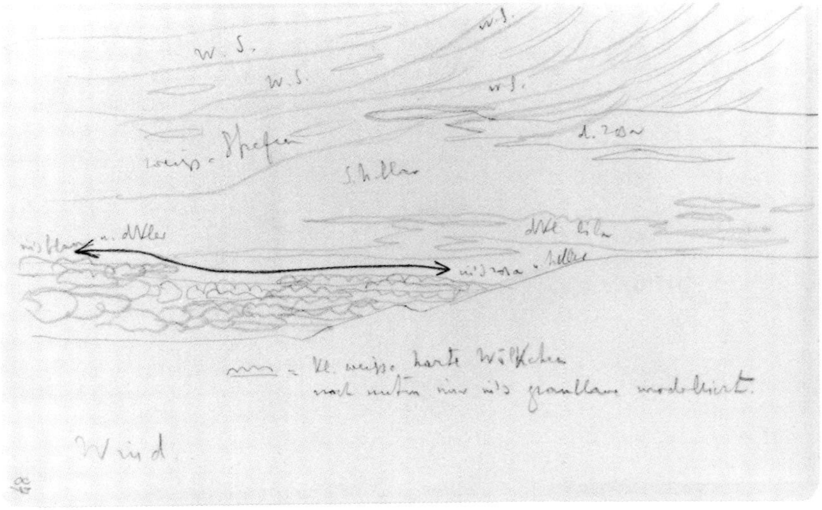

23, p.89

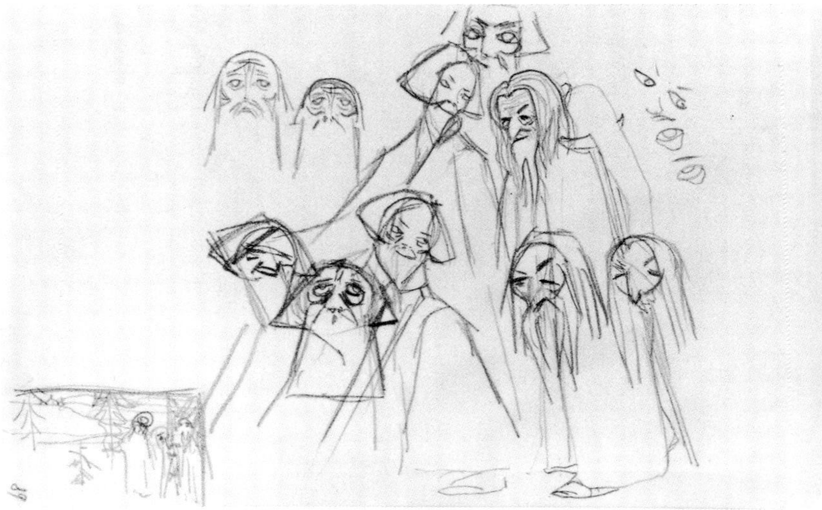

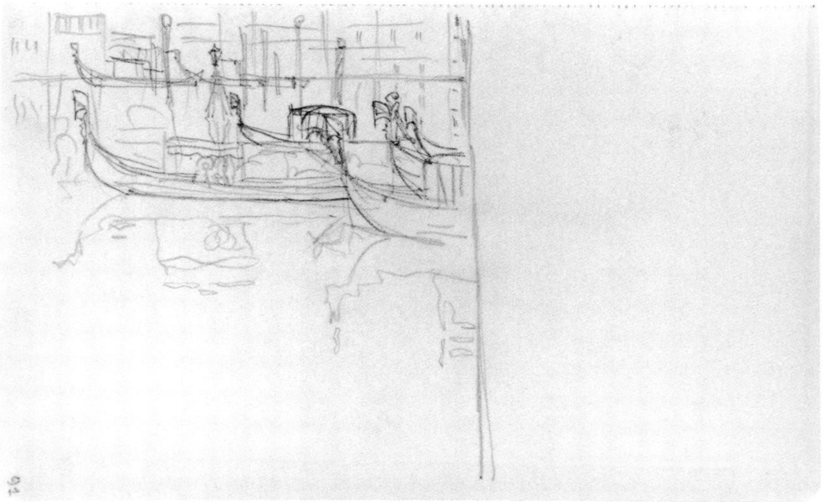

23, p.91

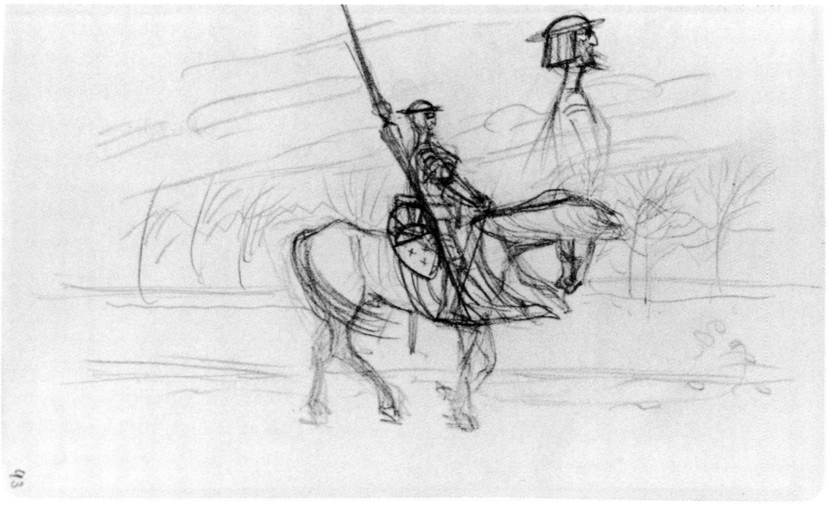

23, p.93

**p.89** Pencil sketches of an old man with beard and small study for a painting l.l. (3 x 5 cm)

REFERENCES
Hanfstaengl 1974, pp.157–158, ill.

The sketches of an old man can be related to *Das bunte Leben, Studie für 'Panik'* and *Panik* of 1907 (Barnett nos.219, 222, 223). However, the small sketch of a religious (?) scene in a landscape cannot be identified with a known work.

**p.90** Blank

**p.91** Pencil study for *Venedig* of 1906

REFERENCES
Hanfstaengl 1974, p.157
Barnett 1992, p.190

According to Kandinsky's Handlist of colored drawings, he executed the tempera painting *Venedig* in Paris in 1906 (Barnett no.213).

**p.92** Blank

**p.93** Pencil study for *Don Quichote* of 1907

REFERENCES
Hanfstaengl 1974, pp.157–158, ill.
Barnett 1992, p.205

Kandinsky made the tempera painting entitled *Don Quichote* in Paris in 1907 (Barnett no.228).

**p.94** Blank

**p.95** Pencil sketches of birds and warrior or hunter

REFERENCES
Podzemskaia 2000, p.130

The bird on the left resembles the extinct *Phorhacos longissimus*; the one in the center, another species of *Phorhacos* and the one on the right, a spectacled cormorant: all three birds were extinct at that time (kindly brought to my attention by Peter DellaVecchia). Although the sources have not been identified, Kandinsky apparently copied illustrations of birds on the following pages (pp.97, 99) and in Sketchbook 20 (GMS 327, pp.23, 26). Podzemskaia, however, thought that the drawings on the following pages (pp.95–99, 114) were done from life.

**p.96** Pencil sketch of armor
Inscribed above: 'Chien de Montargis et le chevalier Macaire / (levrier)'

The reference is to *Le chien de Montargis, ou, La fôret de Bondy*, a three-act melodrama (1814). Macaire, a knight at the court of Charles V, kills one of his companions in the forest of Bondy, an event witnessed by his greyhound ('lévrier').

23, p.95

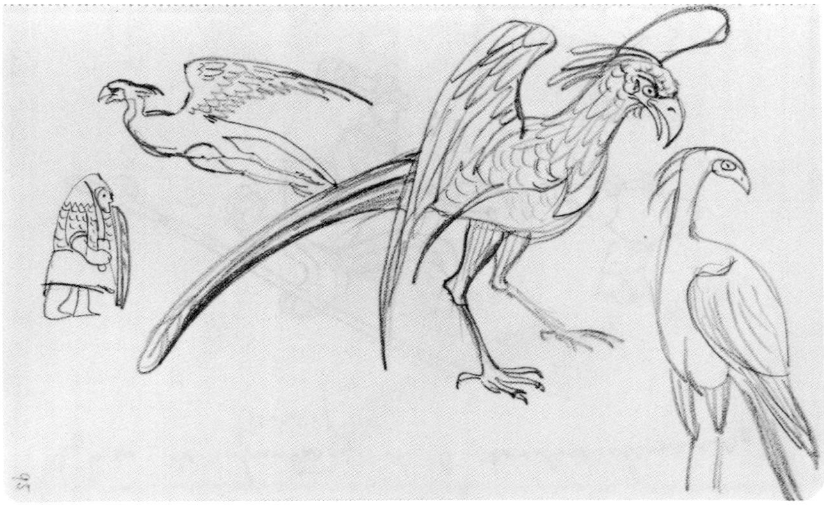

23, p.96

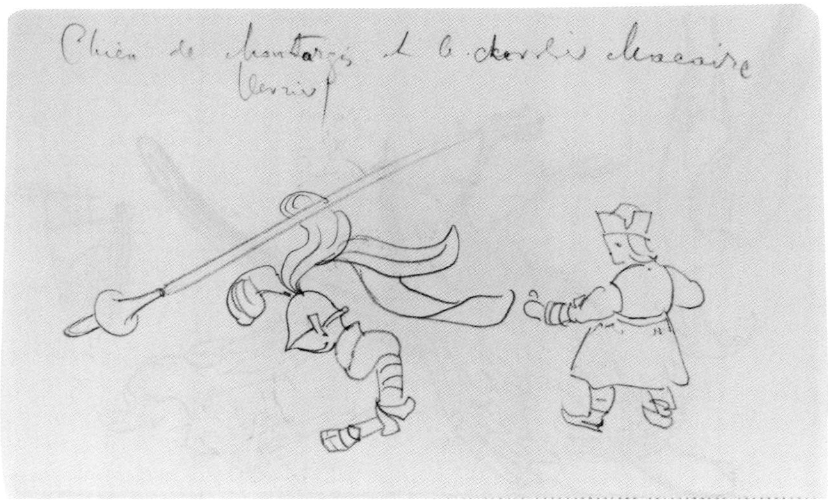

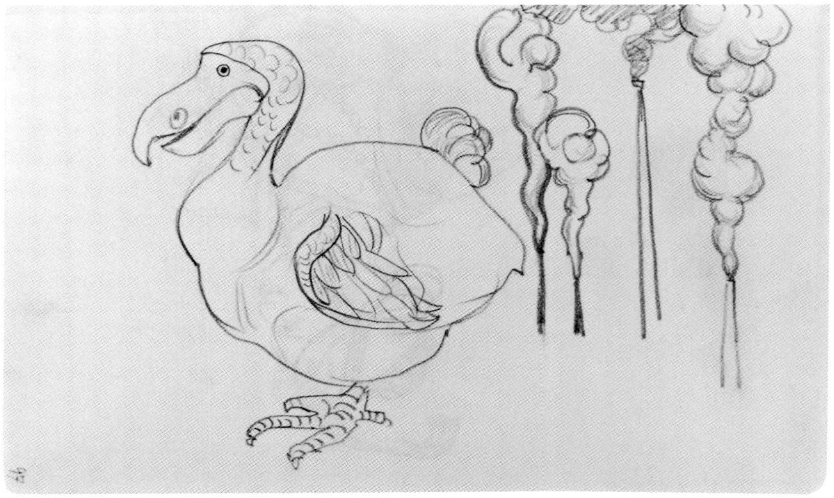

23, p.97

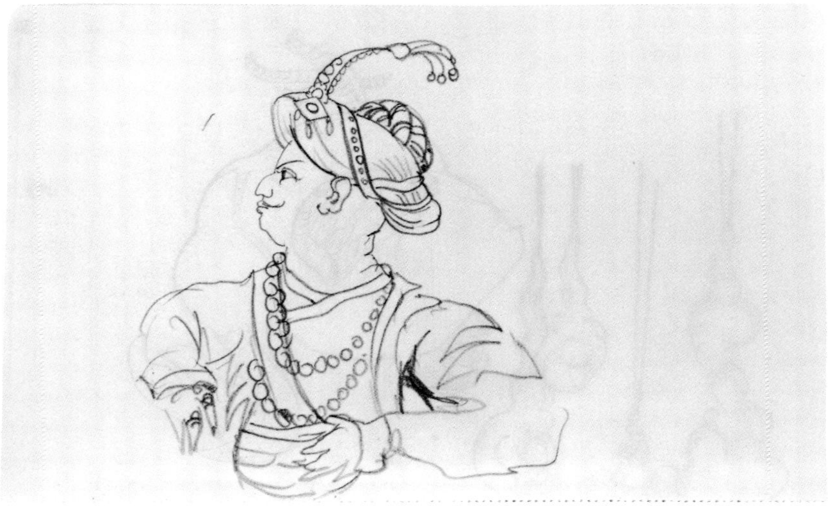

23, p.98

**p.97** Pencil sketch of dodo bird and smokestacks

The image of the dodo closely resembles that in a well-known print by Roland Savery dated 1626. The dodo was already extinct in Kandinsky's time as were certain species of *Phororhacos* and cockatoos (see pp.95, 99). Kandinsky depicted smokestacks in other works done in France in 1906–1907 (see p.59 of this sketchbook, Sketchbook 20, p.19 and Barnett no.205).

**p.98** Pencil sketch of man with turban probably copied from book

REFERENCES
Podzemskaia 2000, p.130

**p.99** Pencil sketch of cockatoo probably copied from book

**pp.100–113** Blank

**p.114** Pencil sketch of a woman probably copied from book (upside down)

REFERENCES
Podzemskaia 2000, p.130

Podzemskaia observed that the woman was in Russian dress and was shown with a jewelry box.

**p.115** Blank

**p.116** India ink and pencil drawing of cats by Gabriele Münter

23, p.99

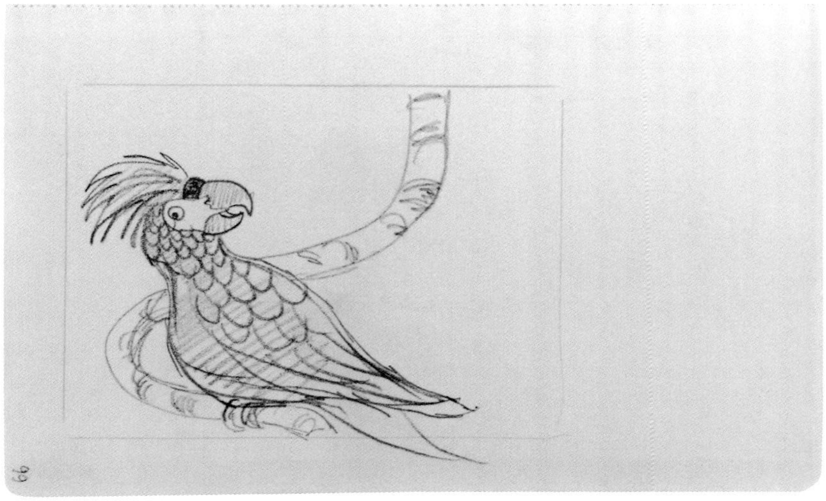

23, p.114

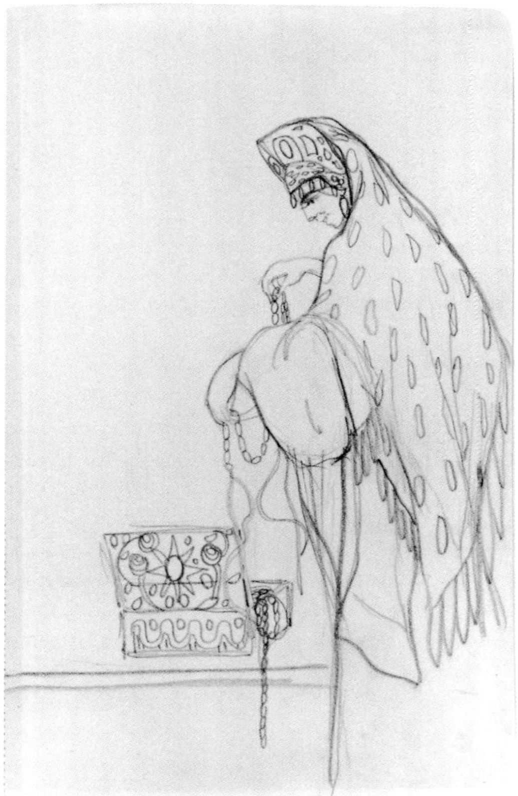

# Sketchbook 24

1907–1908

Dark red leather notebook; with label inside front cover label from A.N. Bogdanoff & Co., St. Petersburg (text in German rather than Russian)
Contains 46 pages (23 sheets of ruled paper), each 12.7 x 7.9 cm (5 x 3⅛ in)
Page numbers inscribed by unknown hand at later date with odd numbers at lower right

Hanfstaengl 1974, p.156

LOCATION
Städtische Galerie im Lenbachhaus, Munich (GMS 335)

HISTORY
Gabriele Münter, Murnau, until 1957

On the basis of the extensive notes contained in this notebook, it can be dated to 1907–1908.

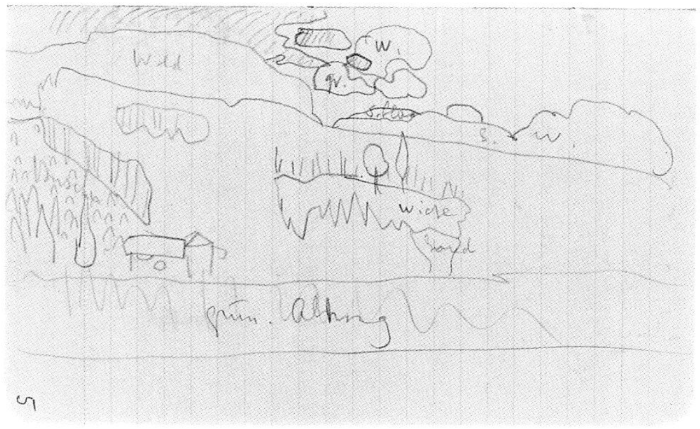

24, p.5

**pp.1–4** Notes regarding Munich, Berlin and Bad Reichenhall (where the artist went for a rest cure from 16 June to 23 July 1907) as well as Salzburg and Salzkammergut in Austria (where Kandinsky and Gabriele Münter travelled in July–August 1908).

**p.5** Pencil sketch of landscape
Inscribed u.l.: 'Wald'; l.l.: 'Busche'; c.: 'Wiese / Sand'; l.c.: 'grün Abh[a]ng' and with color notations

REFERENCES
Hanfstaengl 1974, p.156, ill.

**p.6** Pencil diagram of R[eichenhall], Fronau, Wachte, Ramsau, B[erchtesgaden] and Hallthurm near Bad Reichenhall in eastern Upper Bavaria
Inscribed below: 'Ramsau- Schatten (grosser) vorne / sehr dkl. u. ganz rosa; runde / Lichter darauf auch rosa od. / violett. Weiter hinten die Sonne / (Strasse) sehr weiss ins rosig-violette. / Hinten bunte Häuser im Sch[at]ten / viel heller als der Vordergrund. / Mensch im Sch[a]tten (weiter) auch / hell, flach und leicht con- / turiert. Menschen vorne unter / den Bäumen dunkel aber / sehr flach u. in deutlich[e]n / B. Ton musik … farbiger.'

REFERENCES
Hanfstaengl 1974, p.156

Hanfstaengl related the map to Kandinsky's trip to the Chiemsee and Salzkammergut in July–August 1908.

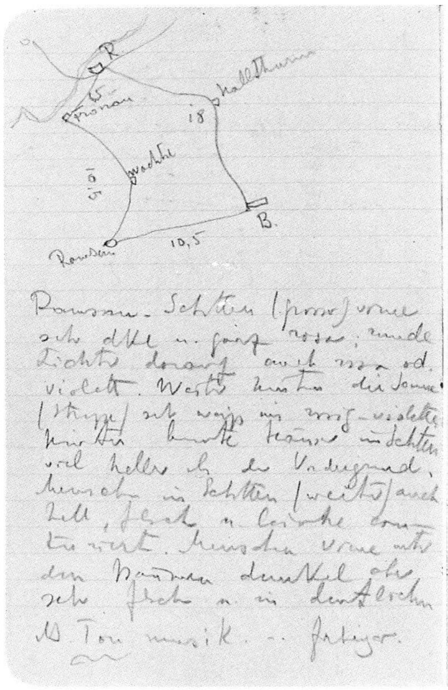

24, p.6

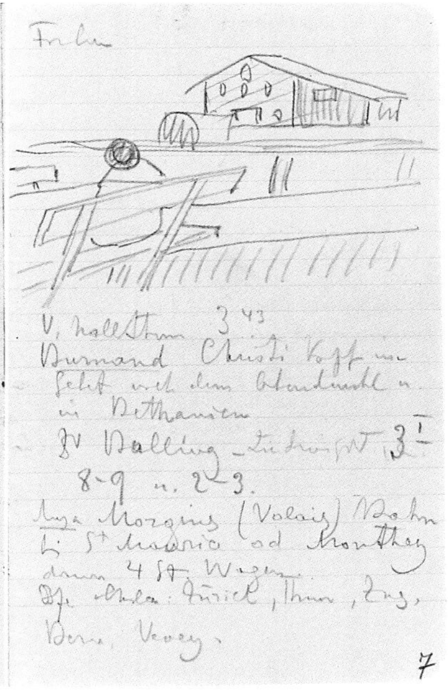

24, p.7

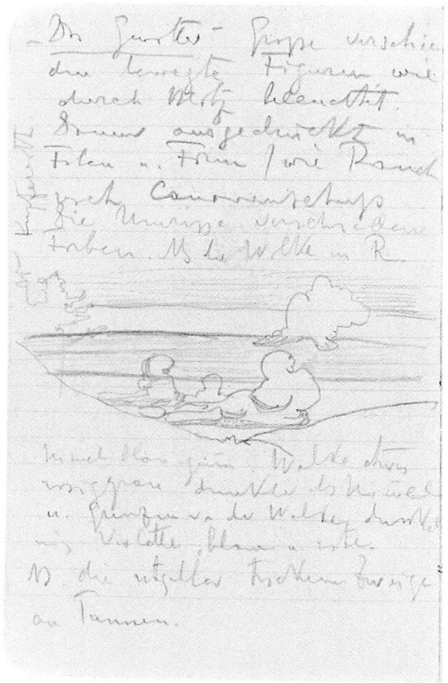

24, p.8

However, he had stayed in Bad Reichenhall from 16 June to 23 July 1907.

**p.7** Pencil drawing of person seated on bench near house
Inscribed u.l.: 'Farben'; l.c.: 'v Hallturm 3:43 / Burnand Christi Kopf im / Gebet nach dem Abendmahl u. / in Bethanien. / Dr. Bulling- Ludwigstr. 3 1/8-9 u. 2-3. / bis an Morgins (Valais) Bahn / bis St. Maurice od. Monthey / dann 4 St. Wagen. / Bfe abholen: Zürich, Thun, Zug, / Bern, Vevey.'

After his stay in Bad Reichenhall, Kandinsky and Münter travelled in Switzerland from 30 July to 19 August 1907.

**p.8** Pencil drawing of clouds
Inscribed above: 'Das Gewitter- Grosse verschie- / den bewegte Figuren wie / durch Blitz beleuchtet. Donner ausgedrückt in / Farben u. Form (wie Rauch / nach Canonenschuss. / Die Umrisse verschiedene / Farben als die Wolke in R.'; below: 'Himel blau-grün. Wolke etwas / rosig grau dunkler als Himmel / u. Grenzen von der Wolke dunkel / ins Violette, blaue u. rote. / B die rotgelben trockenen Zweige / an Tannen'

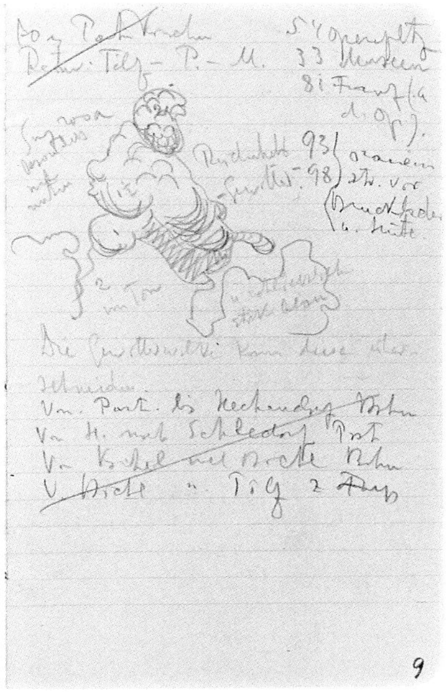

24, p.9

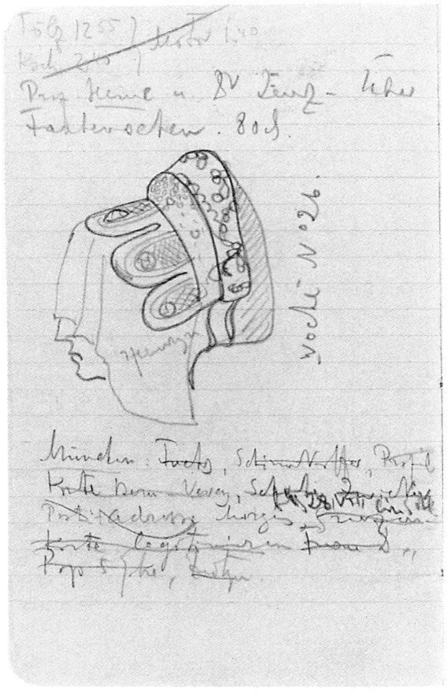

24, p.10

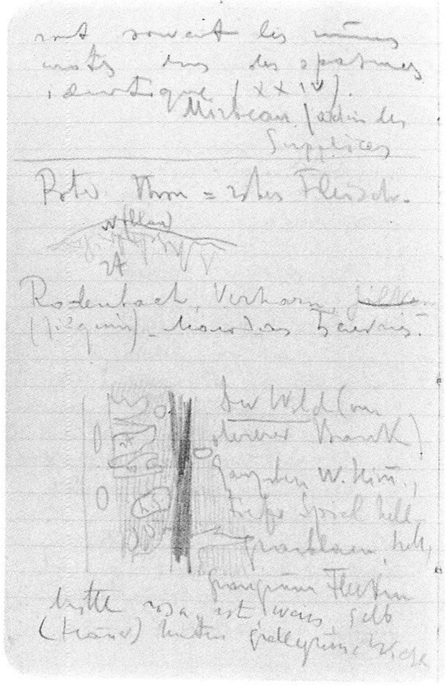

24, p.14

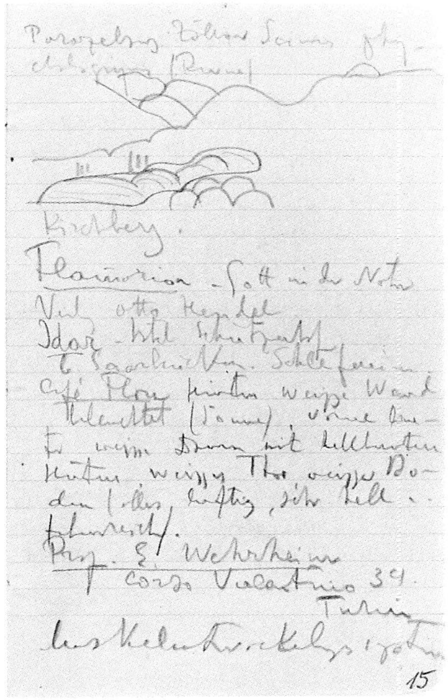

24, p.15

**p.9** Pencil sketch of clouds
Inscribed u.l.: 'Von Partenkirchen / Retour: Tölz- P.- M. [crossed out]'; c.l.: 'Ganz rosa / besonders / nach / unten'; c.r.: 'Reichenhall / Gewitter / u. schliesslich / stark blau'; l.c.: 'Die Gewitterwolke kann diese über- / schneiden. / Von Part. bis Hechendorf Bahn / Von H. nach Schledorf Post / Von Kochel n[a]ch Biehl Bahn / V. Biehl [nch] Tölz z Fuss [crossed out]'

The clouds are related to a thunderstorm in Bad Reichenhall described on the facing page, but the crossed-out notes refer to towns in Bavaria not far from Murnau, where Kandinsky stayed in the summer of 1908.

**p.10** Pencil sketch of woman's headdress
Inscribed above with schedules Tölz-Kochel; u.l.: 'Prof Heine u. Dr Lenz-Über / Farbensehen. 80 pf'; c.r.: 'Woche No26'; and within image in Cyrillic: 'zhemchugi'

Kandinsky wrote 'pearls' on the woman's headdress. The reference above is to *Über Farbensehen, besonders der Kunstmaler* by Leopold Heine and Georg Lenz, which was published in Jena in 1907.

**pp.11–14** Notes in French from Octave Mirbeau, *Jardins des supplices* (Paris, 1907), pp.xxiii–xxiv, 158–159, 200, 256, 258, 291

**p.14** Pencil sketch of forest
Inscribed c.r.: 'Der Wald (an / oberer Bank) / Ganz oben w. Himm. / tiefer Spiel hell- / graublaue, hell / graugrüne Flecken / Mitte rosa, rot, weiss, gelb / (Hauer) hinten grell-grüne Wiese'

**p.15** Pencil sketch of landscape
Inscribed above: 'Parazelsus Zöllner Sci[...] phy / chologus (Revue)'; below: 'Kirchberg / Flammarion-Gott in der Natur / Verlag Otto Hendel / Idar- Hotel Schützenhof / b. Saarbrücken. Schleiferein' and various notes including address for Prof. E. Wehrheim in Turin and reference to 'Muskelentwickelungssystem'

Kirchberg is 10 kilometers east of Kitzbühel in Austria. The reference above is to Paracelsus, the humanist and alchemist, who is buried in Salzburg.

**pp.16–18** Notes about books, hotels and addresses primarily in Switzerland

**p.19** Pencil sketch of cityscape
Inscribed l.l.: 'nach S- Untergang / Berlin' and with color notations: 'rosagelb / grün (etw. blau) / rosagrau / rot blutig'

REFERENCES
Hanfstaengl 1974, p.156, ill.
Barnett and Friedel 1995, no.248, color ill.

24, p.19

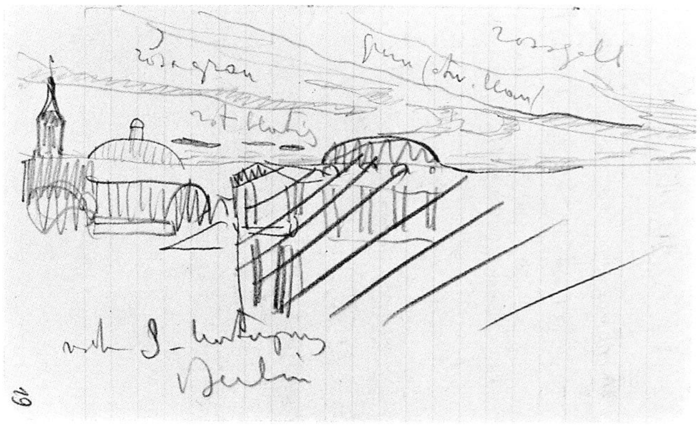

Kandinsky and Münter moved to Berlin in September 1907 and lived there until April 1908.

**pp.20–23** Lists of Berlin names, addresses, prices for apartments and atelier

**p.24** Pencil sketch of woman's head
Inscribed c.: 'x blau / xx grün blau / 2 rtbraun / 3 lila / 4 grüngelb / Licht sehr rosa weiss'; u.c.: 'Erkner / u. Seen / Löckwitz / Blüten /

24, p.24

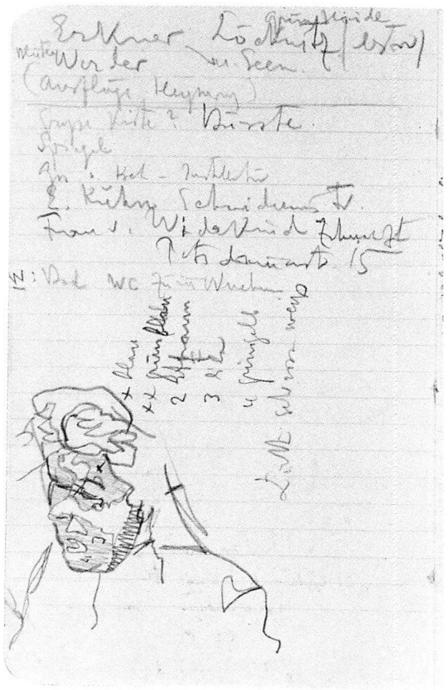

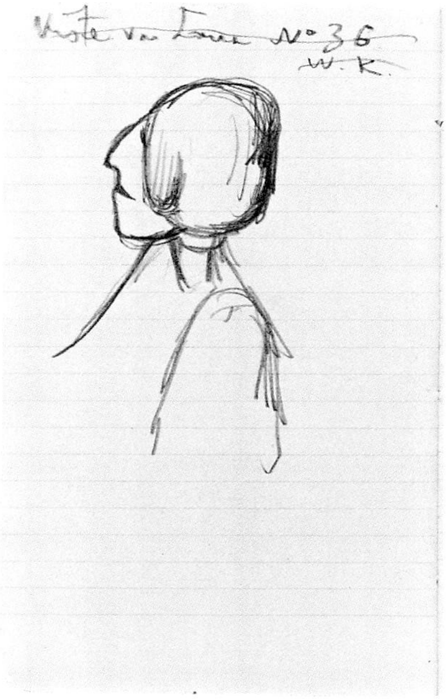

24, p.32

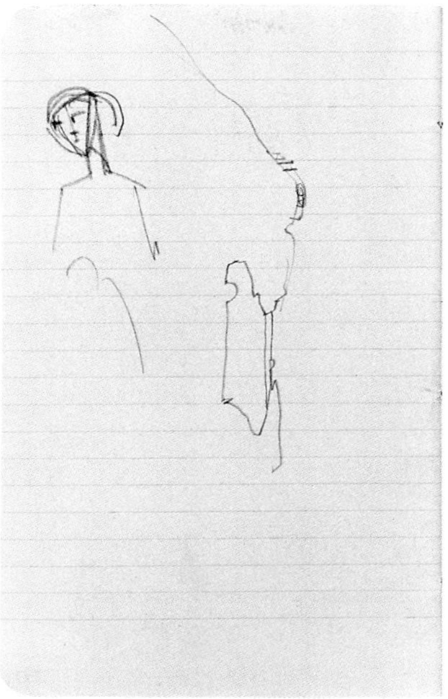

24, p.36

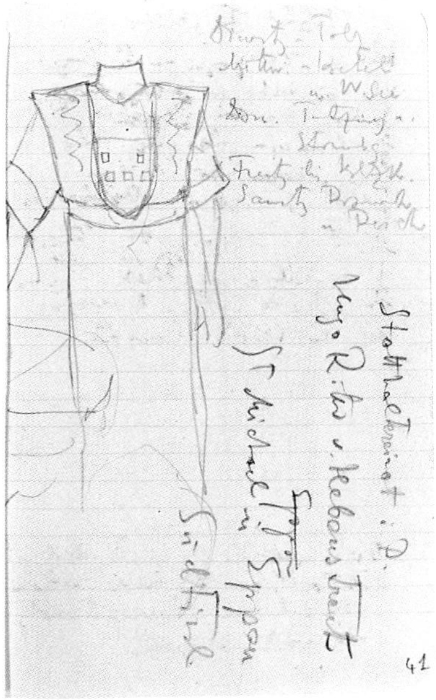

24, p.41

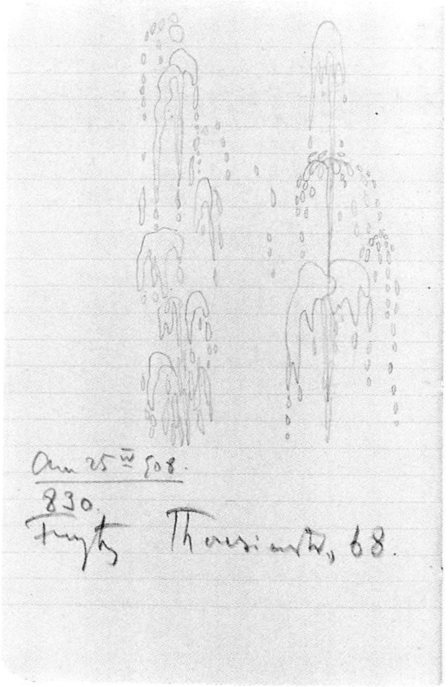

24, p.42

Werder' referring to places near Berlin and 'Frau v. Widekind Zahnarzt / Potsdamerstr. 15'

REFERENCES
Hanfstaengl 1974, p.156

Hanfstaengl observed that the head was related to a work in oil on paper, *Brustbild einer Dame mit Hut* of 1908 or 1909 (GMS 640; 44.3 x 32.5 cm), which cannot be located. On the basis of the inscriptions, the sketch was made in Berlin.

**pp.25–29** Notes referring to schedules, addresses and the Theosophical Society (p.26): 'Theosophische Gesellschaft / (kleine Broschüre I Ziele u. / Aufgaben etc. Selbstverl[a]g des Besant- Zweiges Berlin) / Theosophical Book Co. / 18, Bartlett's Buildings / London, E.C. / The Key to Theosophie by H.T. / Blavatsky 8° 344 p. 7 s. 6 pf'

**pp.30–31** Blank

**p.32** Pencil sketch of woman
Inscribed above: 'Kiste von Lana No36 / W.K. [crossed out]'

Kandinsky and Münter stayed in Lana in South Tyrol from 29 April until late May 1908.

**pp.33–34** Blank

**p.35** Notes in Cyrillic

**p.36** Pencil sketch of woman

The sketch bears a resemblance to the watercolor *Zwei Gestalten vor Hügel mit Baum und weisser Wolke*, which can be dated 1908–1909 (Barnett no.250).

**p.37** Pencil diagram of floor plan

**pp.38–40** Lists of addresses and information about apartments, sketch of floor plan (p.38) and reference to Ainmillerstrasse 36 IV (p.39), where Kandinsky rented the garden house in September 1908.

**p.41** Pencil sketch of woman's dress
Inscribed u.r.: 'Dienst[a]g- Tolz / Mittw[och]- Kochel / u. W[alchen] See / Don[nerstag] Tutzing u. / Starnb[er]g / Freit[a]g bis Holzk[irchen] / Samst[a]g Rosenach / u. Reich'; and l.r. edge: 'Statthaltereinat i. P. / Hugo Ritter v. Hebenstreit. / St Michael in Eppan / Südtirol'

REFERENCES
Hanfstaengl 1974, p.156

The dress is similar to designs in a sketchbook Münter used in 1910 (46/29, pp.20–21). The notes may refer to Kandinsky and Münter's trip to the Staffelsee around 17–20 June 1908 after returning from South Tyrol. The notes at the lower right referring to Eppan appear to have been written at a different time. Münter made sketches there dated 29–30 May 1908 (46/23, pp.53, 55).

**p.42** Pencil sketch of fountains
Inscribed below: 'Am 25 IV 908. / 830 / Freytag Theresienstr. 68'

REFERENCES
Hanfstaengl 1974, p.156

Kandinsky stayed in Berlin until 26 April 1908 and, by 29 April, he and Münter were in Lana in South Tyrol. The reference is undoubtedly to Gustav Freytag (1876–1961), one of the founders of the 'Phalanx' artists' group in Munich in 1901. The drawing of fountains (above) was probably made at a different time and appears not to be related to the notes below.

**p.43** Lists of towns in Switzerland and Germany

Hanfstaengl thought that the list of names of places in Switzerland was related to Kandinsky's trip in August 1907.

**p.44** Lists of items to pack

**p.45** Poem in German

**p.46** Pencil sketches of woman's head
Inscribed u.l.: 'F. 3:28 / B. 7:16 / 106 x 60 / 30'

24, p.46

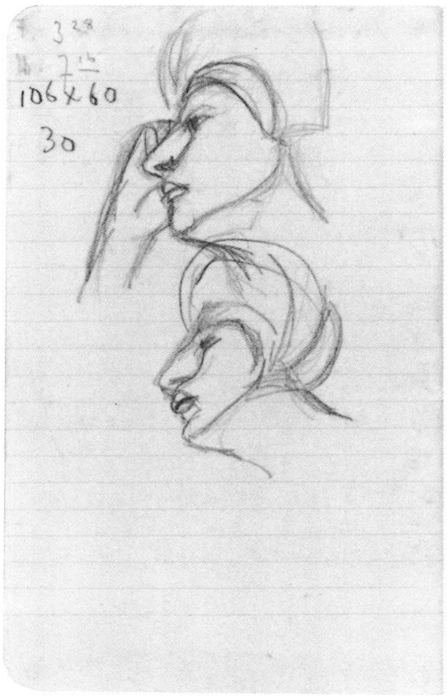

# Sketchbook 25

1908

Maroon and gold-patterned paper notebook; no label
Contains 76 pages (38 sheets), each 10.8 x 7.1 cm (4¼ x 2¾ in), of which pp.18–52 are blank
Page numbers inscribed by unknown hand at later date with odd numbers at lower right

Hanfstaengl 1974, p.154

LOCATION
Städtische Galerie im Lenbachhaus, Munich (GMS 332)

HISTORY
Gabriele Münter, Murnau, until 1957

Although there is no indication of where the notebook was purchased, Kandinsky used it in 1908 primarily in Tyrol.

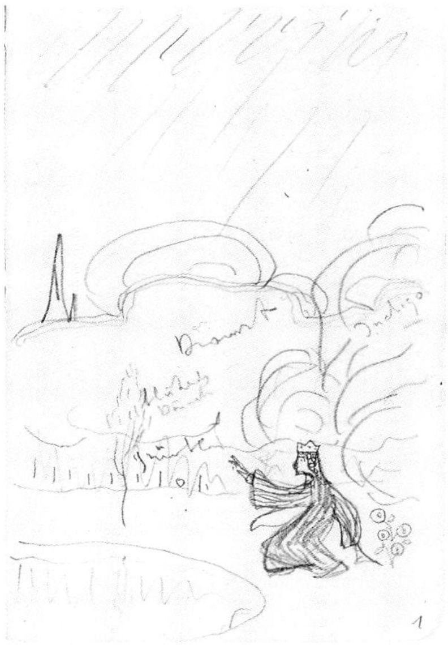

25, p.1

**p.0** (inside front cover) Inscribed: 'Robert Buchtger / Schell. 54 IV'

The reference is probably to the landscape painter Robert Büchtger (1862–1951), who was born in Russia but lived in Munich.

**p.1** Pencil sketch of crouching figure with raised hands in front of flowering bush
Inscribed c.: 'Braunrt / Indigo / blüh[e]nde[n] Busch / grünblau'

REFERENCES
Hanfstaengl 1974, p.154, ill.

Hanfstaengl proposed an earlier date, possibly 1907, for this page. The sketch brings to mind other drawings (vol.I, nos.100–102), and is consistent with the study on p.55 (below).

**p.2** Blank

**p.3** Pencil sketch of Mary Magdalene and saint in front of the Pietà showing the Virgin Mary holding the dead Christ

Kandinsky made several drawings of votive pictures in Tyrol.

**p.4** Blank

**p.5** Pencil sketch of votive painting or sculpture
Inscribed u.c.: 'heller / s. warm / weiss / dunkler'; c.l.: 'Preussisch / auf schwarz / u. grün'; l.l.: 'weisslich / blau'; l.r.: 'rosa'; l.c.: 'gelbgrün'

**p.6** Blank

**p.7** Pencil sketch of two figures kneeling in front of the Pietà
Inscribed l.c.: 'Kapelle in Landeck'; u.l.: 'Indigo'; u.r.: 'in's dunkle'; u.c.: 'rt / grün blau / grün blau / gelb gold'; c.l.: 'brau[n] schw.'; l.l.: 'grün blau / s.d.'; c.r.: 'braun / Schw. / Schw. blau'

REFERENCES
Hanfstaengl 1974, p.154, ill.
Washton Long 1980, p.177 n.14, 179 n.60, pl.83

Kandinsky probably made these sketches in Landeck west of Innsbruck in Tyrol on 4 June 1908 when returning from South Tyrol. The votive picture is not found in the Pfarrkirche in the town, but was probably in a small chapel in the countryside near Landeck. Gabriele Münter sketched similar kneeling figures before a Madonna and Child which she inscribed 'Vor Waldkapelle' and dated 4 June (see 46/23, p.81). There is a related painting inscribed 'Ex Voto' in the Schloss Landeck.

**p.8** Blank

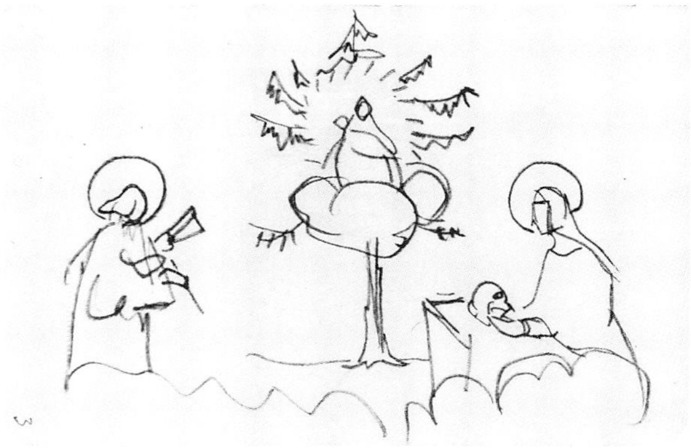

25, p.3

25, p.5

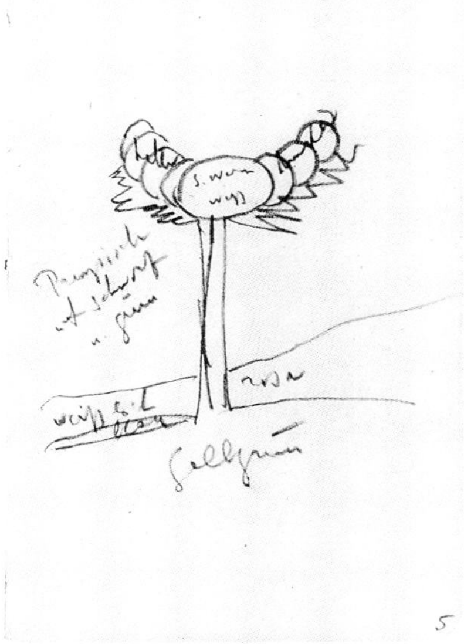

25, p.7

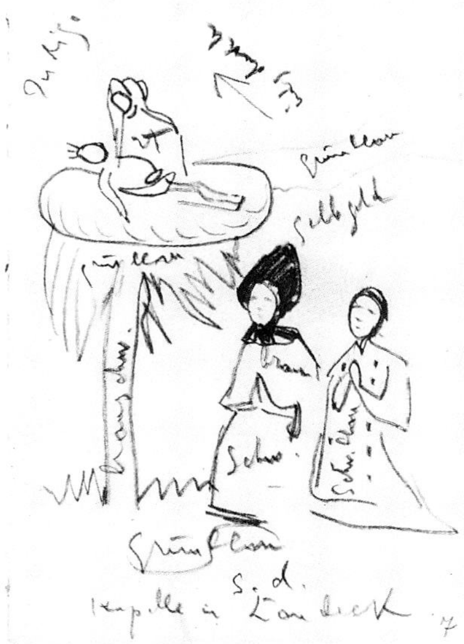

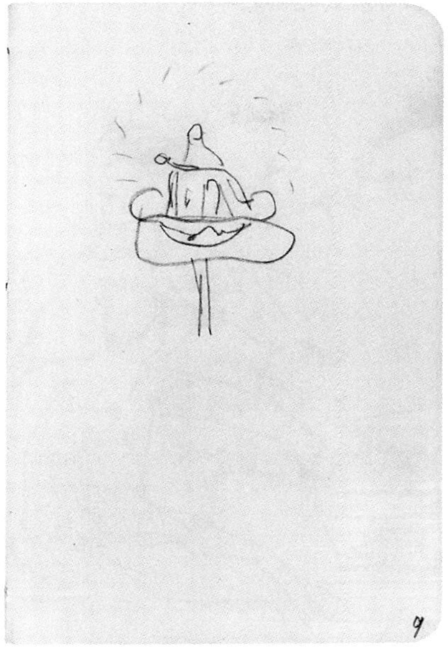

25, p.9

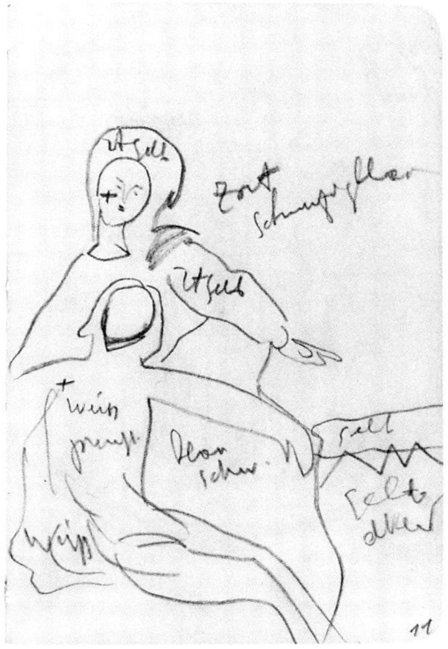

25, p.11

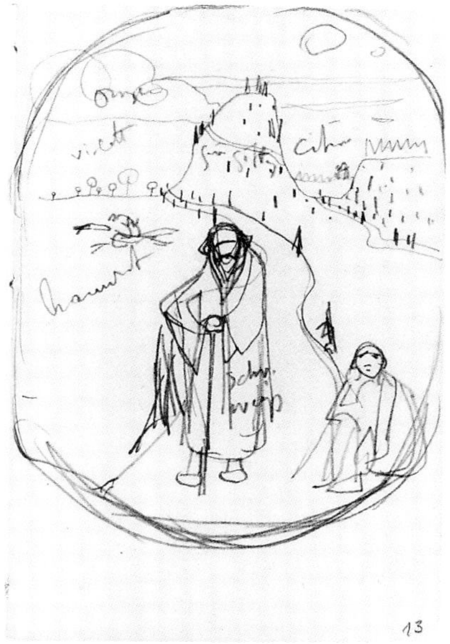

25, p.13

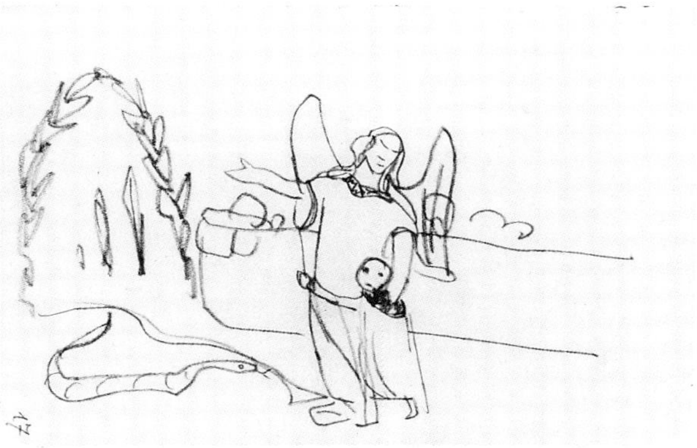

25, p.17

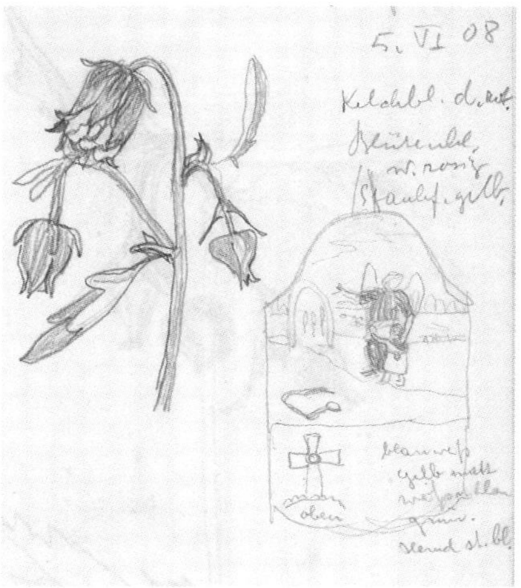


fig.a

**p.9** Pencil sketch related to votive pictures

See p.7 (above)

**p.10** Blank

**p.11** Pencil sketch of votive painting or sculpture of the Pietà
Inscribed u.c.: 'rt gelb / zart / schmutzigblau / rt gelb / weiss / preuss / blau / schw.'; l.l.: 'weiss'; l.r.: 'gelb / gelb dkler'

**p.12** Blank

**p.13** Pencil sketch of figures in landscape with mountain
Inscribed u.l.: 'orange / violett'; u.c.: 'grüngiftig'; u.r.: 'citron'; c.l.: 'braunrot'; l.c.: 'Schw. / weiss'

REFERENCES
Hanfstaengl 1974, p.154, ill.

The oval frame suggests that Kandinsky probably copied a painting.

**pp.14–16** Blank

**p.17** Pencil sketch of angel and boy

The same figures appear in a drawing that Münter made in a sketchbook (46/23, p.87), which she dated 5 June 1908 and inscribed Seefeld (fig.a).

**pp.18–52** Blank

**p.53** Pencil sketch of clouds

25, p.53

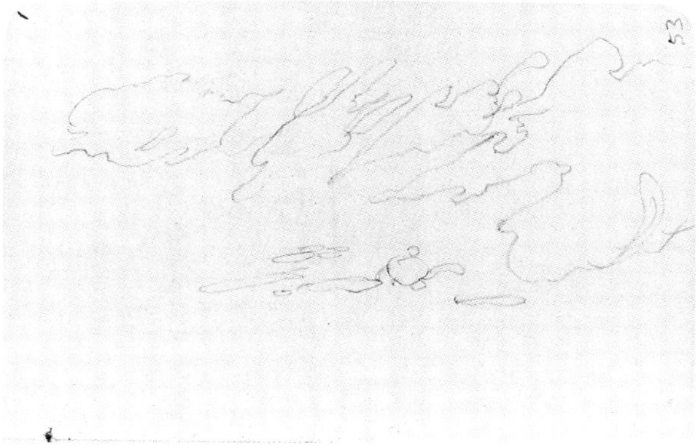

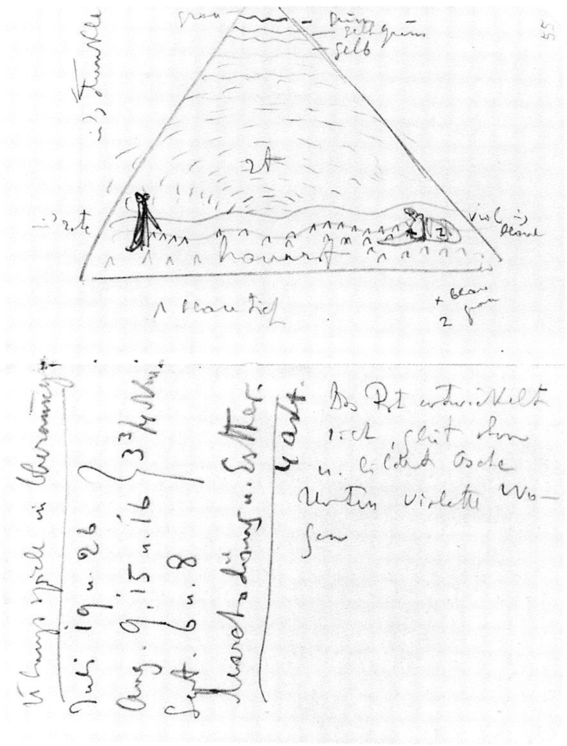

**p.54** Inscribed l. edge: 'Übungsspiele in Oberammergau / Juli 19 u. 26 / Aug. 9, 15 u. 16 / Sept.6 u. 8 / Marchodäus u. Esther. / 4 Akt.' and l.r. edge: 'Das Rot entwickelt / sich, glüht oben / u. bildet Asche / Unten violette Wo- / gen'

Kandinsky was probably referring to performances of Maccabeus and Esther at Oberammergau (information kindly provided by Susanne Böller).

**p.55** Pencil sketch of triangular composition with figures
Inscribed u.c.: 'grau / grün / gelb-grün / gelb'; u.l.: 'in's dunkle'; c.: 'rt / braunrot'; c.l.: 'ins rote'; c.r.: 'viol ins / blaue'; l.c.: 'blautief'; l.r.: 'x blau / z grau'

REFERENCES
Hanfstaengl 1974, p.154, ill.

On the facing page Kandinsky noted that the color red evolved, glowing above and creating ashes, with violet waves below. It is not clear exactly what he is describing.

**p.56** Pencil sketch of clouds

REFERENCES
Hanfstaengl 1974, p.154, ill.

**p.57** Pencil sketch of clouds and mountains

REFERENCES
Hanfstaengl 1974, p.154, ill.

The drawing is similar to that on p.59 (below).

**p.58** Pencil sketch of foliage

**p.59** Pencil sketch of clouds and mountains

REFERENCES
Hanfstaengl 1974, p.154

Hanfstaengl identified the mountain as the Mendel. It is part of the Mendelkamm mountain range between Bozen and Trento in South Tyrol. See also p.72 (below).

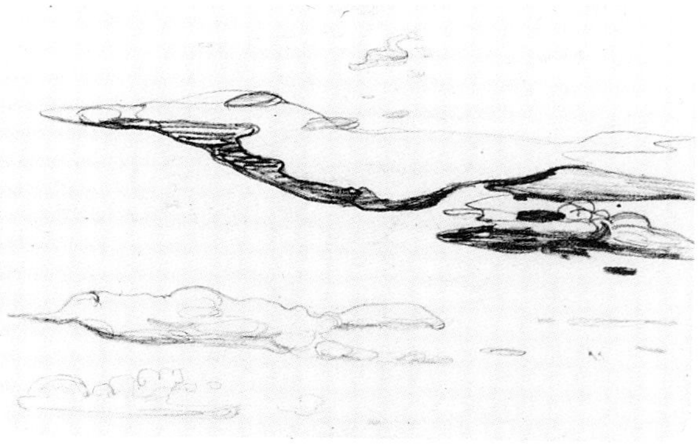

25, p.56

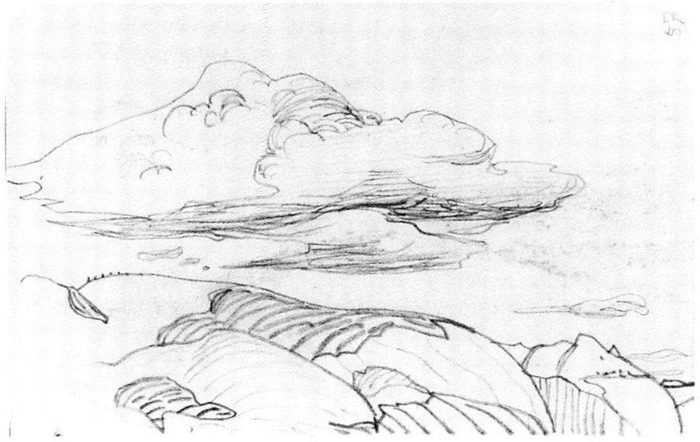

25, p.57

25, p.58

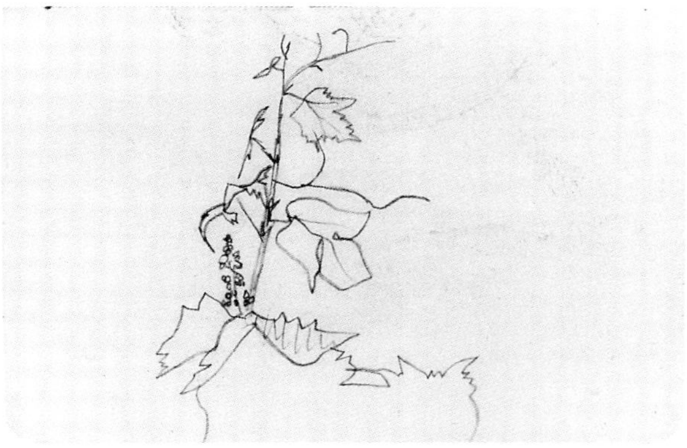

25, p.59

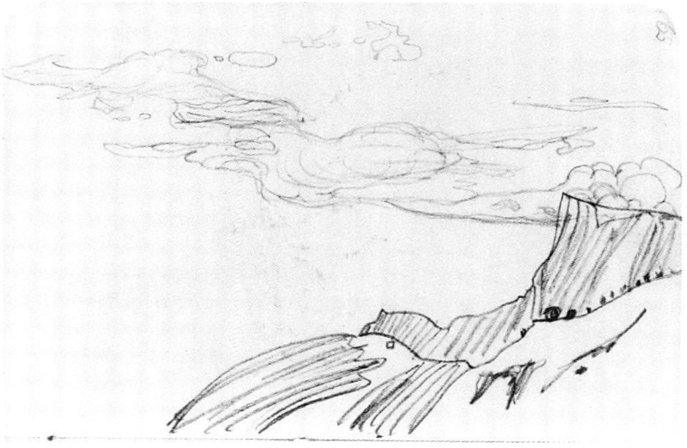

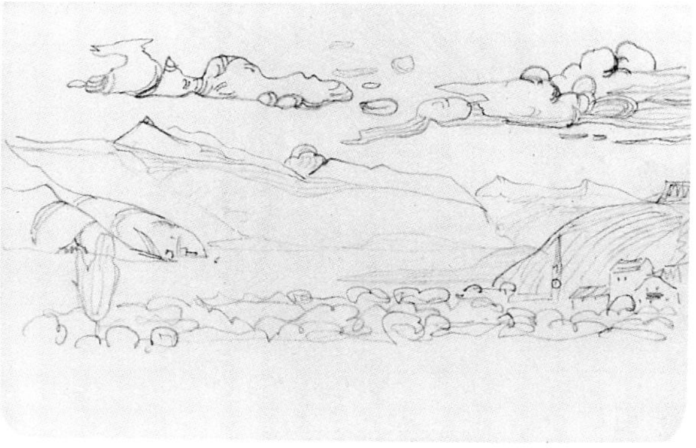

25, p.60

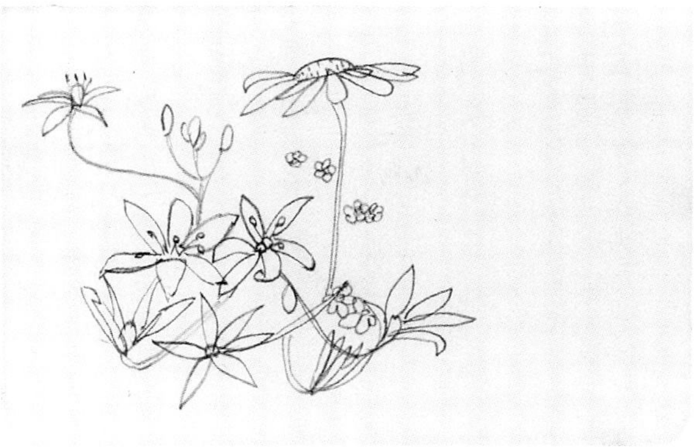

25, p.62

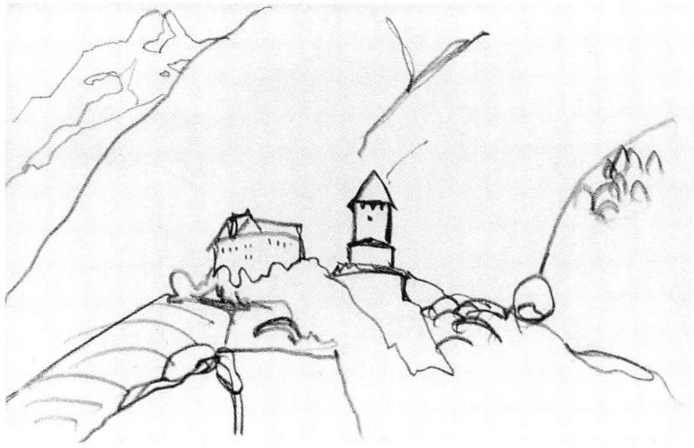

25, p.64

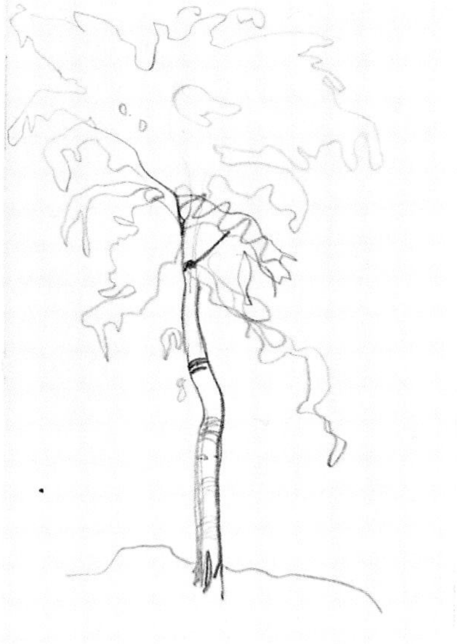

25, p.66

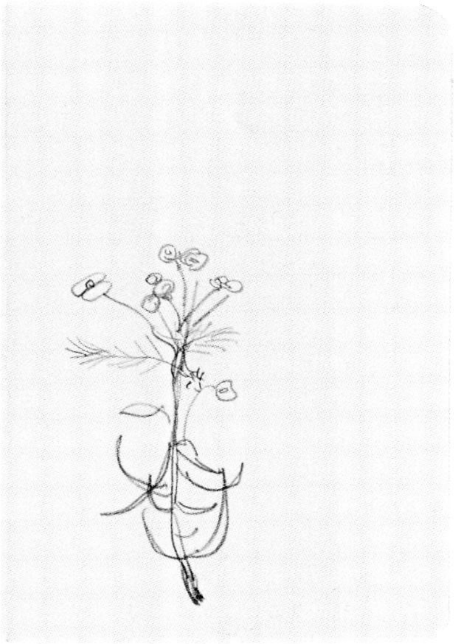

25, p.68

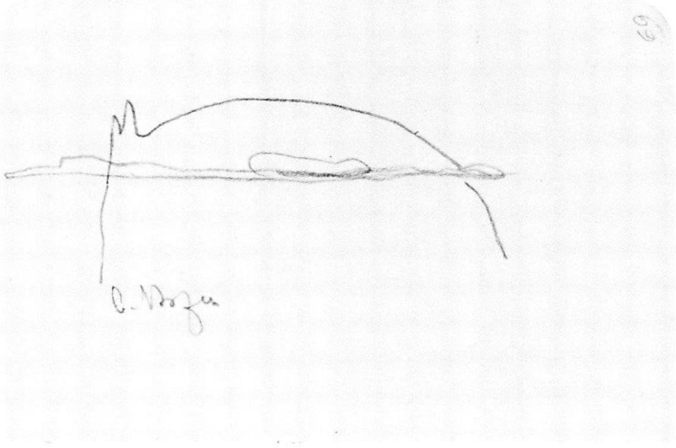

25, p.69

**p.60** Pencil sketch of village and mountains

REFERENCES
Hanfstaengl 1974, p.154, ill.

Kandinsky probably made the drawing in Südtirol.

(See color plate p.123)

**p.61** Blank

**p.62** Pencil sketch of flowers

**p.63** Blank

**p.64** Pencil sketch of mountain landscape with castle

There are many castles and mountains near Lana and Bozen in South Tyrol.

**p.65** Blank

**p.66** Pencil sketch of tree (upside down)

Both Kandinsky and Münter painted blossoming trees in Lana: she made drawings of flowering trees there dated 1 May 1908 (see 46/23, p.11).

**p.67** Blank

**p.68** Pencil sketch of flowers (upside down)

**p.69** Pencil sketch of landscape near Bozen
Inscribed l.l.: 'b. Bozen'

REFERENCES
Hanfstaengl 1974, p.154

Hanfstaengl suggested that the silhouetted mountain was the Schlern in the Sandner-Spitzen, which are part of the Dolomites in South Tyrol.

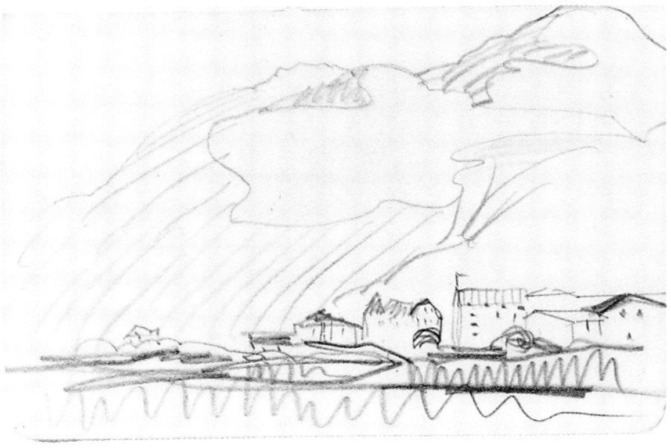

25, p.70

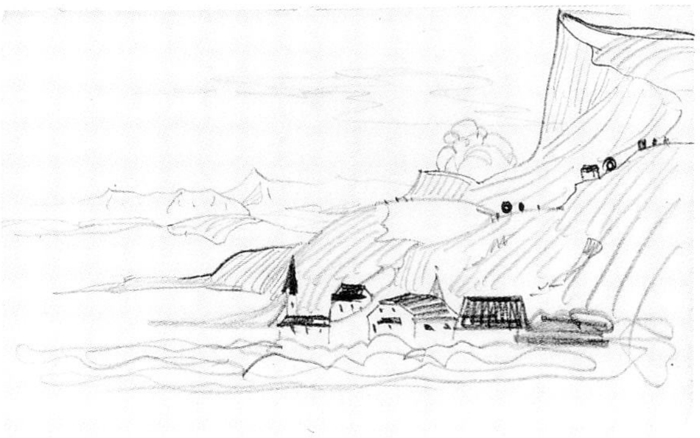

25, p.72

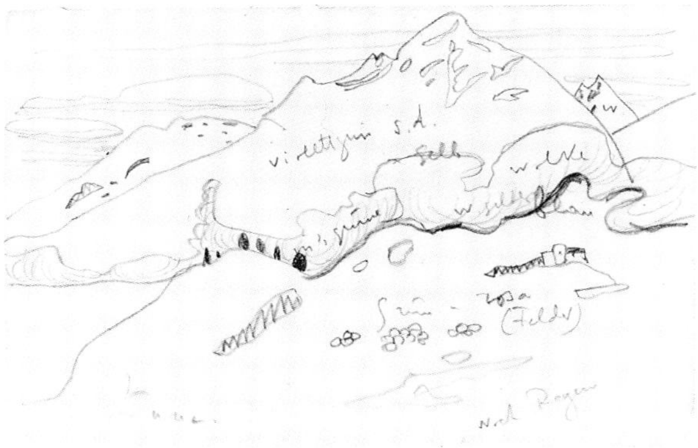

25, p.74

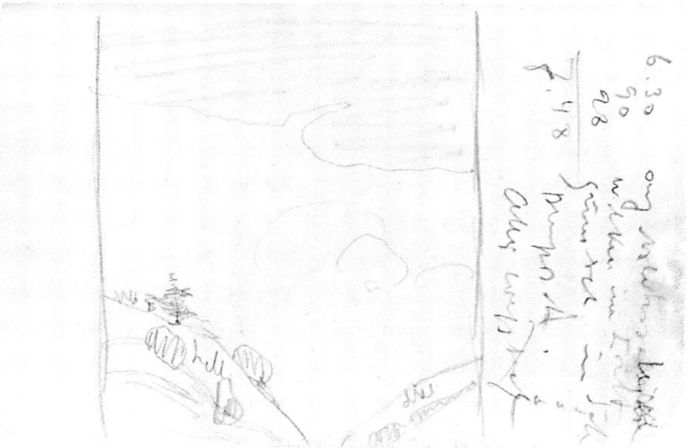

25, p.76

**p.70** Pencil sketch of mountain landscape with village

REFERENCES
Hanfstaengl 1974, p.154, ill.

**p.71** Blank

**p.72** Pencil sketch of mountain landscape with village

REFERENCES
Hanfstaengl 1974, p.154, ill.

Hanfstaengl identified the mountain as the Mendel. See p.59 (above).

**p.73** Blank

**p.74** Pencil sketch of mountain landscape
Inscribed l.l.: 'Lana'; l.r.: 'Nach Regen' and with color notations: 'violettgrün s.d. / gelb / in's grüne / Wolke / w. silber / blau / grün- rosa / (Felder)'

REFERENCES
Hanfstaengl 1974, p.154, ill.
Barnett and Friedel 1995, no.249, color ill.

Kandinsky and Münter stayed in Lana near Meran in South Tyrol for several weeks in May 1908.

**p.75** Blank

**p.76** Pencil sketch of mountain landscape
Inscribed l.l.: 'hell'; l.r.: 'dkl' and at r.edge: 'auf rote rosaliche [?] / Wolken im Licht / grünlich im Sch[atten] / preussisch oben / Alles weisslich.'

Separate sheet (bill for 9,13 in unknown hand) with floor plan has been placed inside the back cover of the notebook
Inscribed on reverse: 'Venzel / Hildensbergerstr. 1 I / Gergen 101 IIr / 1100 / Tapete Preis'

# Sketchbook 26

1908–1909

Black leather notebook with red-patterned endpapers and pencil in leather holder; no label
Contains 90 pages (45 sheets) of graph paper, each 11.7 x 5.3 cm (4⅝ x 2⅛ in)
Page numbers inscribed by unknown hand at later date with even numbers at lower right

Hanfstaengl 1974, pp.148–150

LOCATION
Städtische Galerie im Lenbachhaus, Munich (GMS 328)

HISTORY
Gabriele Münter, Murnau, until 1957

Kandinsky made sketches on a trip to the Salzkammergut in Austria in late July–early August 1908 and continued to draw in this tiny leather notebook in 1909. It contains studies for decorative arts, prints and theater compositions. On p.70 he recorded the date 22 March 1909. There is no indication of where the notebook was purchased.

**pp.1–4** Lists including many addresses in Munich

REFERENCES
Hanfstaengl 1974, p.148

Hanfstaengl noted that Kandinsky wrote on p.4: 'Reinanken- Fische / im Attersee ähnlich wie Renken.' Kandinsky and Gabriele Münter went to the Attersee in the Salzkammergut region of Austria at the end of July 1908.

**p.5** Pencil sketches for five unidentified works with color notations
Inscribed below: 'herunter fliessend / R[o]t und / aufsteigend / Weiss gelb / (Auf Rot / grün / u. blau / (auf weiss / violett) / 1) hier alles blau u. bl. / Gesicht / 2) Der Balkenträger'

REFERENCES
Hanfstaengl 1974, p.148, ill.

**p.6** Pencil sketches of figures and an unidentified work
Inscribed l.r.: 'alles s. d. braun / das dunkleste / violett. / grünblau darauf / tiefleuchtend kaltgrün / u. warmrot (Blut).'

REFERENCES
Hanfstaengl 1974, p.148, ill.

The reclining figures are studies for the painted wood relief *Reiter* of c.1909 (Appendix I, no.4), and perhaps for *Entwurf für den Farbholzschnitt 'Zwei Frauen in Mondlandschaft'* of 1908–1909 (Barnett no.249; Roethel no.100). The crouching figure at the upper right may be related to that on p.20 (below).

**p.7** Pencil sketches probably for furniture and extensive notes

**p.8** Pencil study for *Begegnung* and sketches of three male heads
Inscribed above: 'ins Krapp ← Blau → ins Indigo'; c.: 'grau / gelb / violett / gelb / w.'; below top image: 'Gelb irrdisch grün / 20 x 20 x 46 / 20 x 20 x 50 / Und ein Mädchen / liegt im Walde vorne / dem Rahmen parallel / u. viele Menschen / hinten ein bunten / Durcheinander.'; above heads inscribed in Cyrillic: 'Raz [...] Smol. / Blodl. [...]'

REFERENCES
Hanfstaengl 1974, p.148
Barnett 1992, p.218
Barnett and Friedel 1995, no.323, color ill.

The sketch at the top is preparatory to the painted relief *Begegnung* of c.1909 (Appendix I, no.3) and also resembles *Entwurf zu 'Begegnung' (Gestalten und Kind in Landschaft)* of 1908–1909 (Barnett no.246).

26, pp.5-6

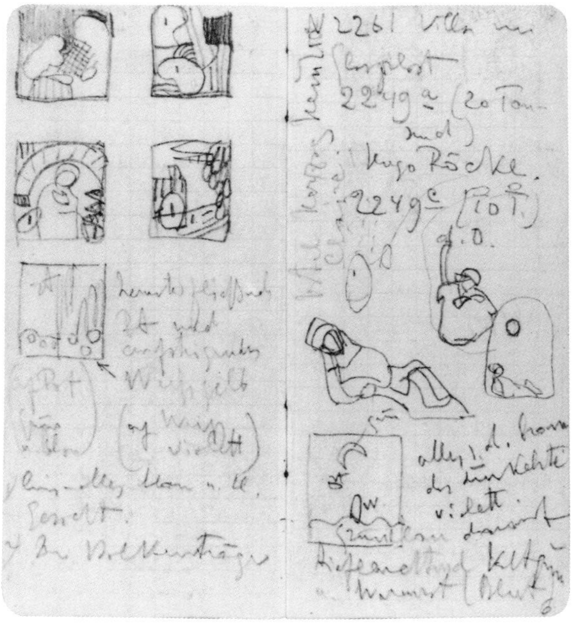

26, pp.7-8

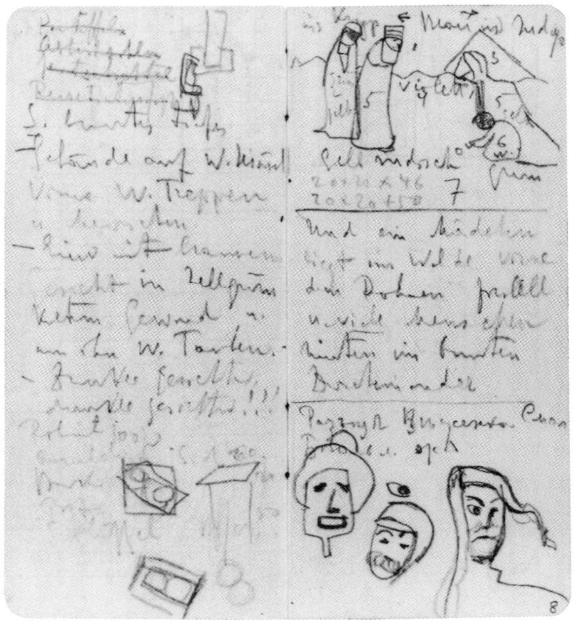

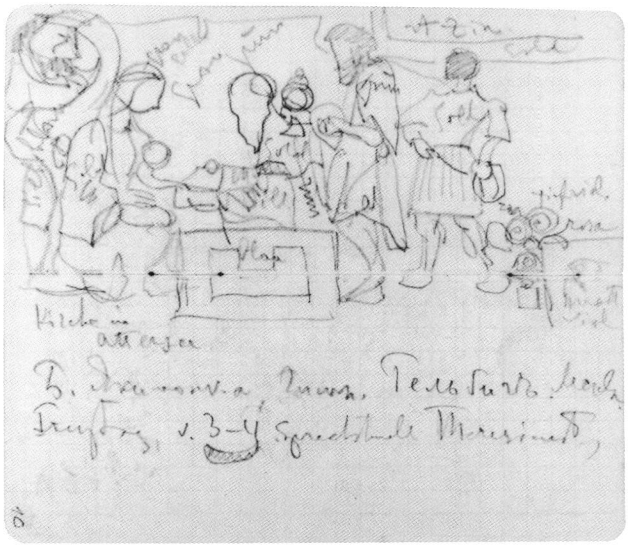

26, pp.9-10

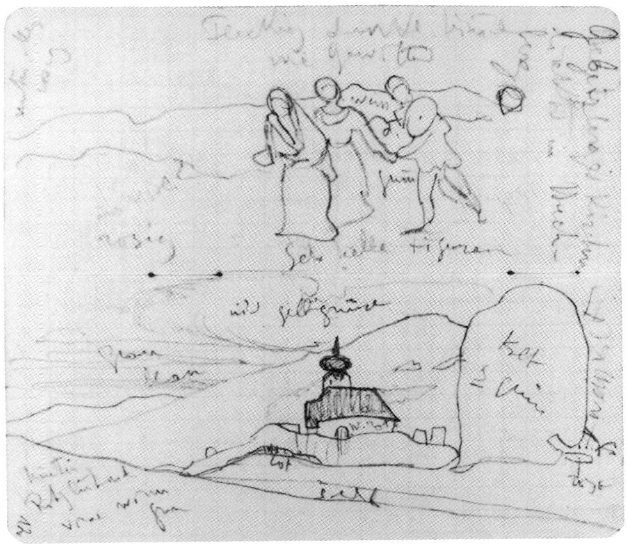

26, pp.11-12

**pp.9–10** Pencil sketch of Arrival of Magi
Inscribed with color notations in image: 'grau / gelb / grau grün / rt zin / gold / silberblau / tiefviol. / rosa' and below (p.10) l.l.: 'Kirche im / Attersee'; l.c. in Cyrillic: 'B. Iakimonka Gmn, Tel'big Moskva' and in German: 'Freytag v. 3-4 Sprechstunde Theresienstr.'

REFERENCES
Hanfstaengl 1974, p.148, ill.

Kandinsky and Münter went to the Attersee around 31 July–1 August 1908, where he made this drawing of the Adoration of the Magi in the Pfarrkirche in Attersee. There appears to be no connection between Kandinsky's notes and the drawing. For another reference to Gustav Freytag, see Sketchbook 24 (GMS 335, p.42).

(See color plate p.123)

**pp.11–12** Pencil sketch of figures in landscape (above) with color notations
Inscribed above image: 'Fleckig dunkle Himmel / wie Gewitter'; at r. edge: 'Gebetzberger Kirchen. / lichter in Buch- / berg'
Pencil sketch of church in landscape (below) with color notations
Inscribed l.l.: 'hinten / Rotglühende / vorne warm / grün'; u.r.: 'kalt / s grün'; r. edge: 'weiss kalt / rosa'

REFERENCES
Hanfstaengl 1974, p.148, ill.

According to Hanfstaengl, the church in Schörfling on the Attersee is probably shown.

(See color plate p.124)

**p.13** Pencil sketch of church and buildings in landscape

**p.14** Pencil sketch of landscape

**p.15** Pencil sketch of mountains

REFERENCES
Hanfstaengl 1974, p.148, ill.

**p.16** Pencil sketch of mountains

REFERENCES
Hanfstaengl 1974, p.148, ill.

Hanfstaengl identified the mountain in the foreground as the Schafberg on the southern end of the Attersee. Münter made a sketch there dated 5 August 1908 (46/20, p.41).

26, pp.13-14

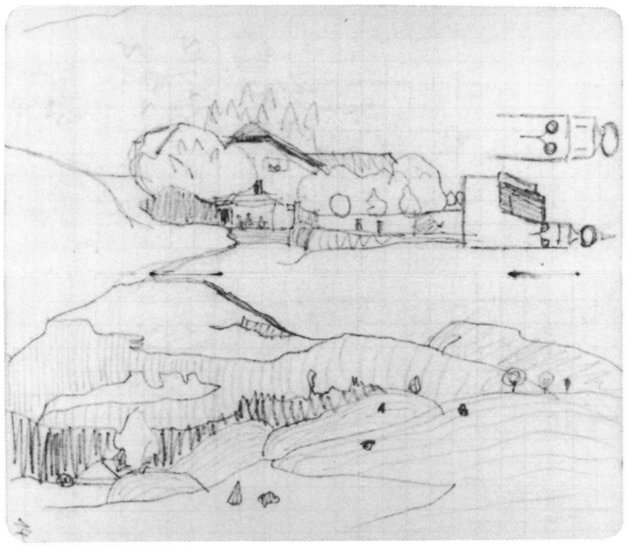

26, pp.15-16

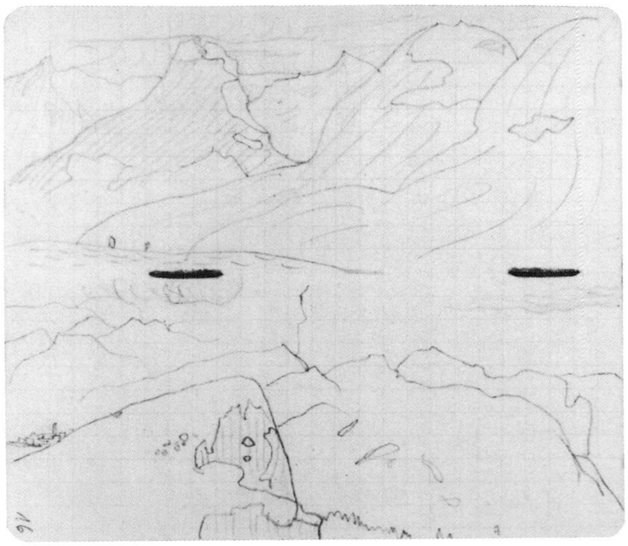

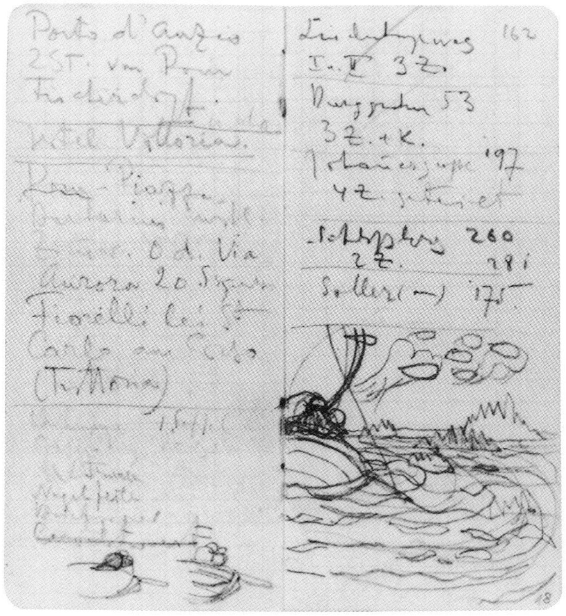

26, pp.17-18

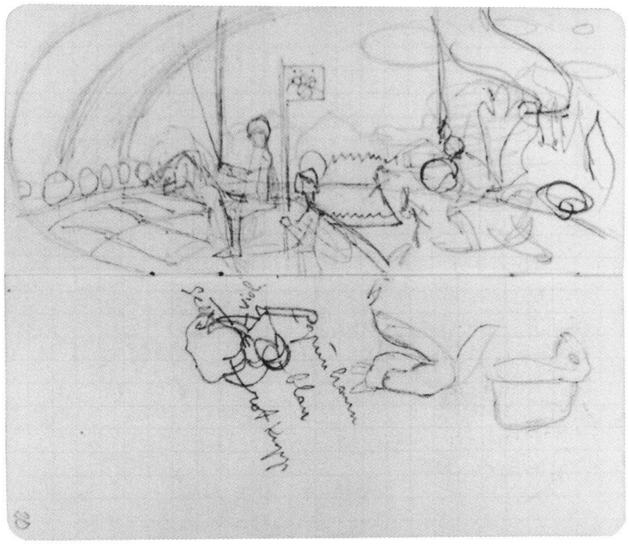

26, pp.19-20

**p.17** Pencil sketches of boat (below) related to p.18; lists of hotels and addresses in Rome and reference to the fishing village Porto d'Anzio (above)

REFERENCES
Hanfstaengl 1974, p.149, ill.

**p.18** Pencil sketch of boat and stormy sea
Inscribed above: 'Lin[...]weg 162 / I u. II 3 Z. / Burggraben 53 / 3 Z. + K. / Johannesgasse 197 / 4 Z. [...] / Schlossberg 260 / 2 Z. 281 / Soller (vorn) 175'

REFERENCES
Hanfstaengl 1974, pp.148, 149, ill.
Barnett 2006, p.66

This sketch is related to those on the facing page, one in Sketchbook 20 (GMS 327, p.13) and a drawing of 1908–1909 (vol.I, cat. no.104). Above Kandinsky made a list of addresses with apartments.

**p.19** Pencil sketch of medieval knights on horseback

REFERENCES
Hanfstaengl 1974, p.149, ill.

**p.20** Pencil sketches of kneeling figure
Inscribed with color notations: 'grünbraun / blau / rot Krpp. / viol. / gelb'

REFERENCES
Hanfstaengl 1974, p.148

Hanfstaengl related the kneeling figure to that on p.6 (above).

**pp.21–22** Sketches of people and horses
Inscribed (p.21) above: 'Pollinger Pasing / Residenzstr.'

**p.22** Pencil sketch of horse and rider
Inscribed above: '32: 43 weiss / 30 Pappen verschieden. / Wien- Goldene Ente. / Warschau- Bristol. / Brüll Hotel / Carl Valenton / Pianos / Herzog Wilhelm / 2.' and with color notations: 'blau / citron'

**p.23** Pencil sketch of figures
Inscribed in image with color notations: 'v. gelb / d blau ins rt /Siena / dkl / v. dkler / rot / blau / Indisch / Graugelb'

REFERENCES
Hanfstaengl 1974, p.149, ill.

It is unclear whether Kandinsky's sketches (pp.23–28) were related to his relief sculptures, or whether he was copying works he saw in Austria.

26, pp.21-22

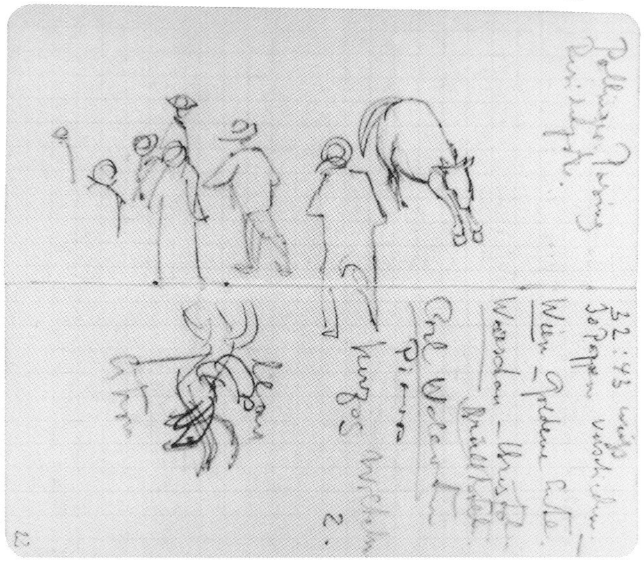

26, pp.23-24

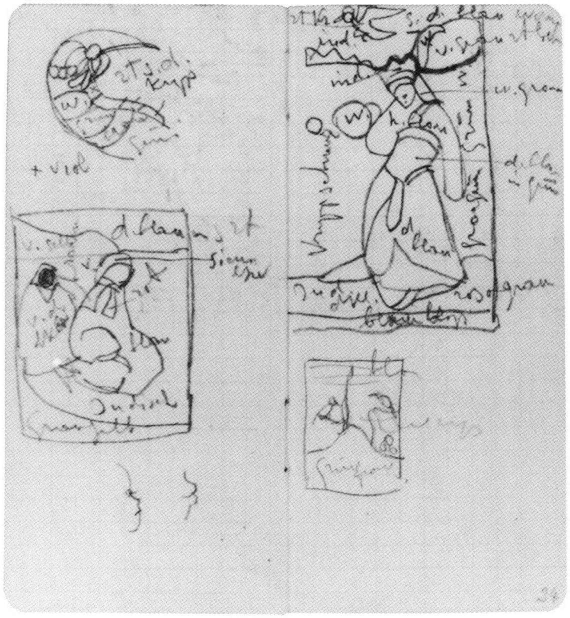

**p.24** Pencil sketch of female saint (above) and sketch of two birds (below)
Inscribed with color notations u.c.: 'rt Kr. / s.d.blau warm / ind. / w. / v. grau rtlich / w. grau / grün / d. blau ins grün / rosagrau'; l.c.: 'blau / weiss / grüngrau'

REFERENCES
Hanfstaengl 1974, pp.148, 149, ill.
Barnett 1992, p.215

The sketch of two birds resembles *Entwurf für Einband oder Titelblatt eines Albums mit Musik und Graphik* of 1908–1909 (Barnett no.243). The sketch of a female figure (above) with extensive color notations has not been identified.

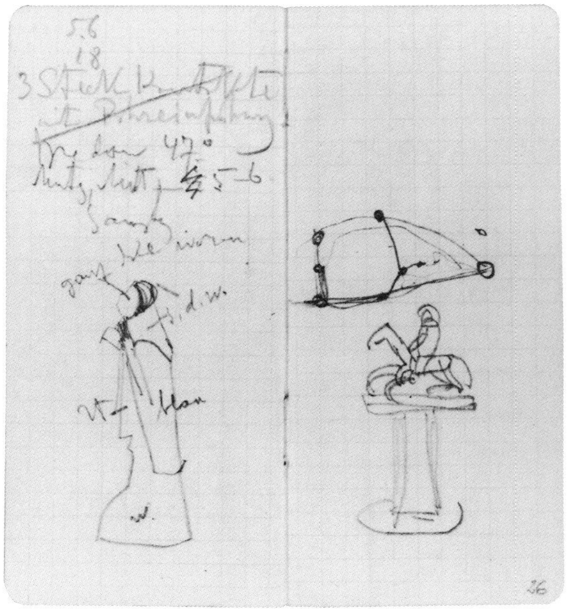

26, pp.25-26

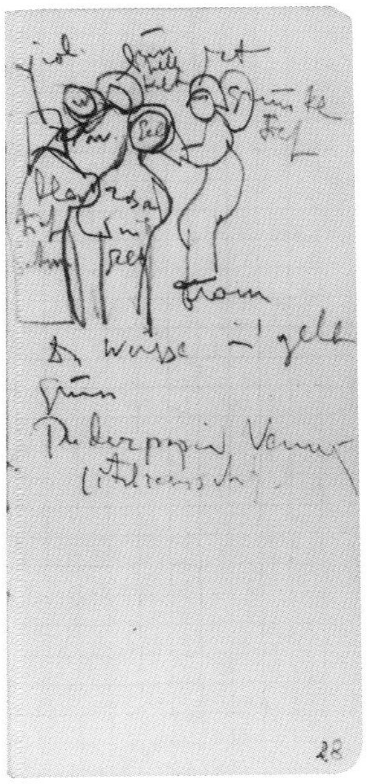

26, p.28

**p.25** Pencil sketch of figure related to sculpture
Inscribed u.c.: '56 / 18 / 3 Steckkontakte / mit Rohreinführung / Drehen 47° / Mntg, Mitt 5-6 / Samstg.' and with color notations in image: 'ganz dkl warm / s. d. w. / rt.- / blau / w'

**p.26** Pencil sketch related to sculpture of horse and rider

**p.27** Notes regarding Just Wolfram: 'Lampe 70% Er- / sparnis / Promenadepl. 7 / Klein / 190 x 32 / 25 u. 27 cm / dunkelbraun Hölzene / Stange 4-5 ob vor / der Seite u. 4 Haken. / 25 u. 27 cm von vorne' and illegible Cyrillic

**p.28** Pencil sketch of figures perhaps related to relief sculpture
Inscribed with color notations and below: 'Das Weisse ins gelb / grün / Puderpapier Venus / (italienisch)'

REFERENCES
Hanfstaengl 1974, p.149, ill.

**p.29** Pencil sketch of figure on cart
Inscribed u.l.: 'Dienstag 3. XI ½ 9' [crossed out]

REFERENCES
Hanfstaengl 1974, p.148

Hanfstaengl observed that 3 November 1908 was a Tuesday.

**p.30** Notes and text
Inscribed below: 'Die Kunst fängt / erst da an, wo die / Nachahmung aufhört. – (O. Wilde / De prof. 78).' The quotation is found on p.78 in Oscar Wilde, *De profundis* (Berlin, 1907).

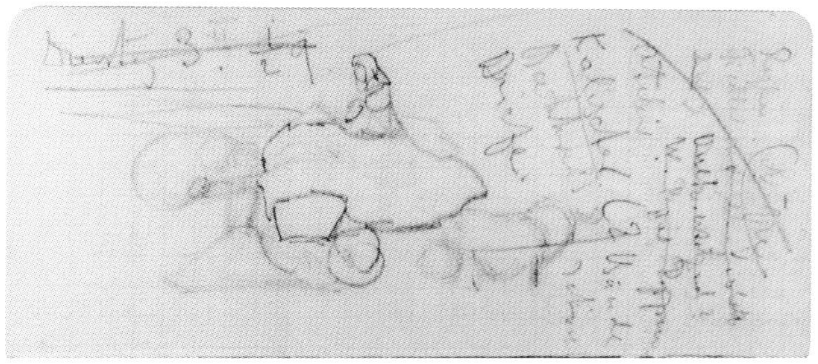

26, p.29

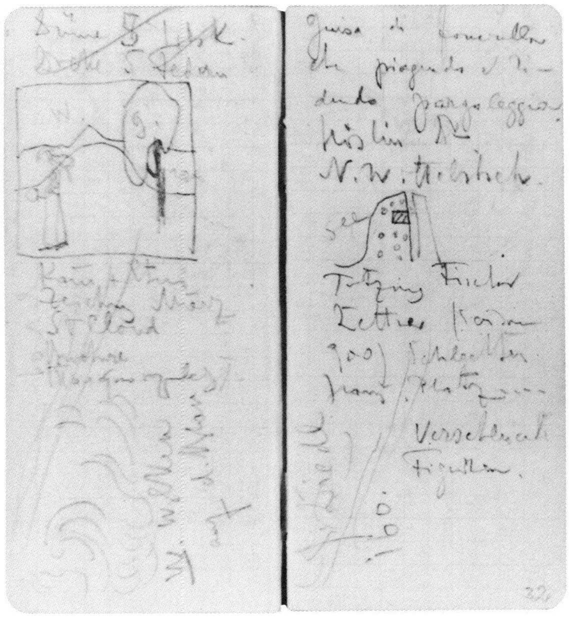

26, pp.31-32

**p.31** Pencil sketch of figure perhaps for print or stage composition
Inscribed above: 'Dünne 5 T[...]K / Dicke 5 Federn'; below: 'Kamm u. Etui / Zeichnung März / St. Cloud / Brochure'; in Cyrillic: 'tolstogo [...]'; l.r.: 'W Wolken / auf d. Blau' and with color notations in image: 'w. / g. / rosa'

REFERENCES
Hanfstaengl 1974, p.149, ill.

On his list below the sketch, Kandinsky's reference to a 'drawing' is probably to his colored drawing or tempera painting *März (Zug mit Dampf)* of 1904 (Barnett no.126).

**p.32** Diagram of Tutzing on the Starnberger See
Inscribed above: 'Guisa di fanciulla / che piagendo e ri- / dendo pargoleggia. / Höslin Dr. / N. Wittelsbach'

Kandinsky went to the Starnberger See in mid-June 1908 and again that autumn.

**p.33** Pencil sketch of figure perhaps for stage composition
Inscribed u.c: 'orange / grün / viol / rosa / citron / viol'; l.c.: 'Hände mit Blume'; r. edge: 'Helio[...]rot'

REFERENCES
Hanfstaengl 1974, p.149, ill.

**p.34** Pencil sketch of landscape
Inscribed l.l.: 'Feuervögel'; l.c.: 'Pflanzenbuch (Ill. in Farben) / Verl. Schreiber in München' and with color notations: 'grün / viol / rt (drauf)'

REFERENCES
Hanfstaengl 1974, p.149, ill.

**p.35** Pencil study for stage composition and print
Inscribed above: 'Schwarz + Weiss u. / darauf Buntes. / Weisses Gesicht u. / w. Tracht / Schloss im / Wasser'

REFERENCES
Ringbom 1970, p.73, pl.3
Roethel 1970 p.252
Hanfstaengl 1974, pp.148, 149, ill.
Barnett and Friedel no.268, color ill.
Barnett 2006, p.121

The study of reclining and seated figures is for 'Schwarz und Weiss' of early 1909, and the sketch below is for

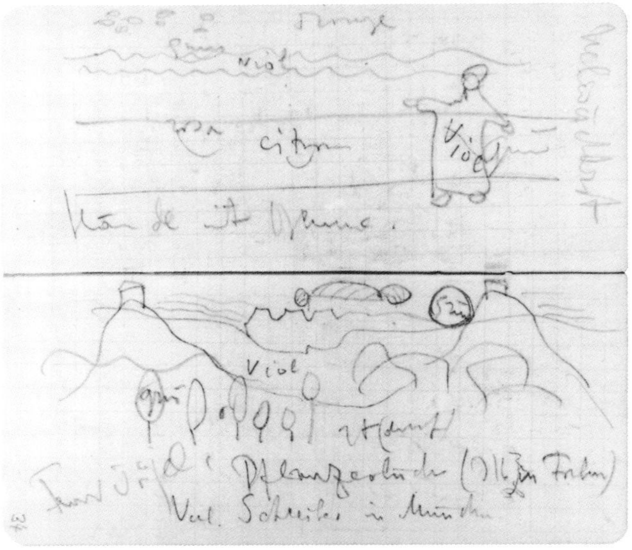

26, pp.33-34

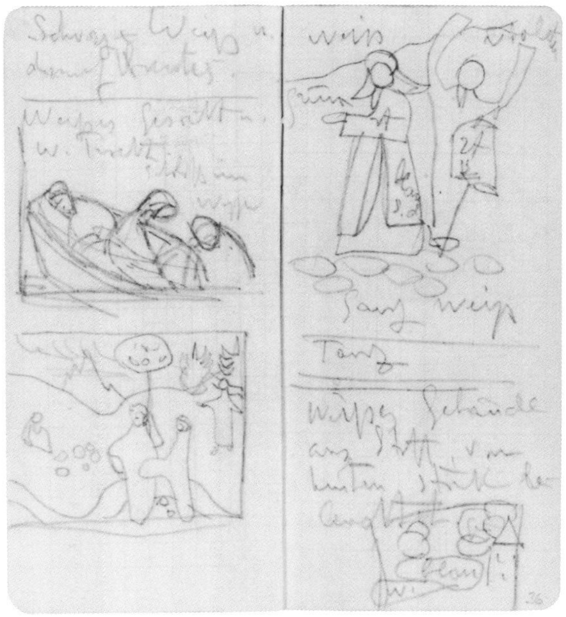

26, pp.35-36

*Apfelbaum* (Roethel no.126), which was included in *Klänge* but may have been executed as early as c.1908. As Ringbom has observed, there are small differences between this early study and the transfer drawing for the print (vol.I, cat. no.246).

(See color plate p.124)

**p.36** Pencil study of figures for 'Schwarz und Weiss'
Inscribed in image (above): 'weiss / violet / grün / rt / rt / blau / s.d.'; c.: 'ganz weiss / Tanz / weisses Gebäude / aus Stoff von / hinten, stark be- / leuchtet' and with color notations (below)

REFERENCES
Hanfstaengl 1974, p.149, ill.

Kandinsky's earliest notes for his theater composition 'Schwarz und Weiss' probably date from late 1908 to early 1909 (see pp.79–81 below).

(See color plate p.124)

**p.37** Pencil sketch of women holding baskets near fruit tree
Inscribed above: 'Kindertennisschläger / 3.50 (70 cm). / Äpfel-Geranium- / lack auf W. la- / siert- Manche / wie Wachs'

**p.38** Pencil sketch of landscape
Inscribed r. edge (below): 'Braun im Licht Viol / mit Preuss' and above: 'London E.C. / Reisebüro Brock / & Co / Queenstr., 90 / 91 / Prosp. ver 50 pf'

The landscape resembles that on p.16 (above).

**pp.39–40** Pencil study of building and mountain (above) and composition with color notations (below)
Inscribed below: 'rt / w. / grün / grau'

REFERENCES
Hanfstaengl 1974, p.149, ill.

(See color plate p.124)

**p.40** Pencil sketches for stage compositions and prints

REFERENCES
Hanfstaengl 1974, pp.148, 149, ill.
Barnett 1992, p.219
Barnett and Friedel 1995, no.267, color ill.
Boissel 1998, p.67, ill.6d
Barnett 2006, p.67

The figure above is related to Kandinsky's stage composition 'Gelbe Klang', and the pencil studies in the center resemble the *Signet der Neuen Künstlervereinigung München* of early 1909 (see vol.I, cat. nos.106, 107). Below, the small pencil study is for *Zwei Frauen in Mondlandschaft* of 1908–1909 (Barnett no.249; Roethel no.100).

(See color plate p.124)

26, pp.37-38

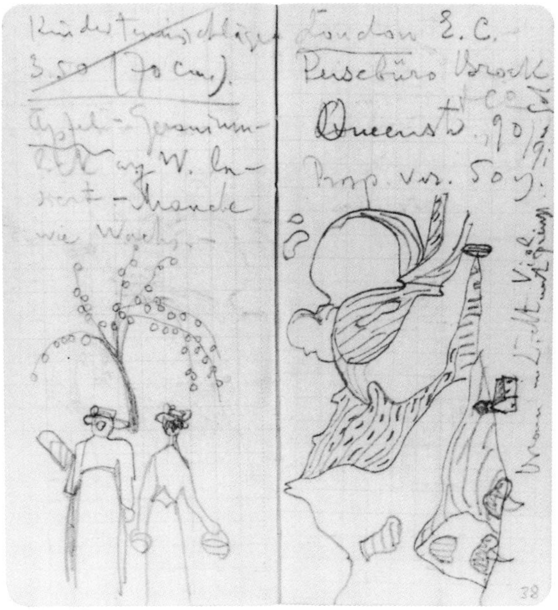

26, pp.39-40

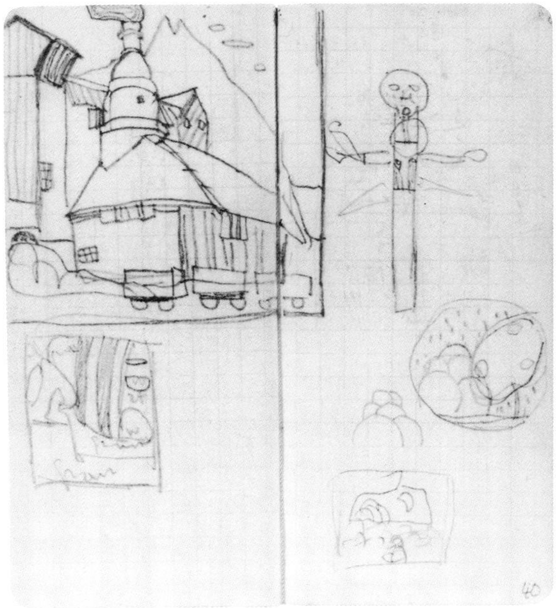

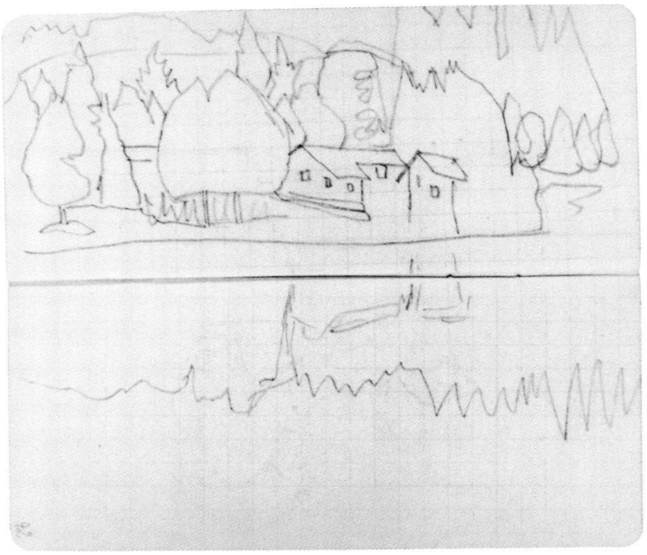

26, pp.41-42

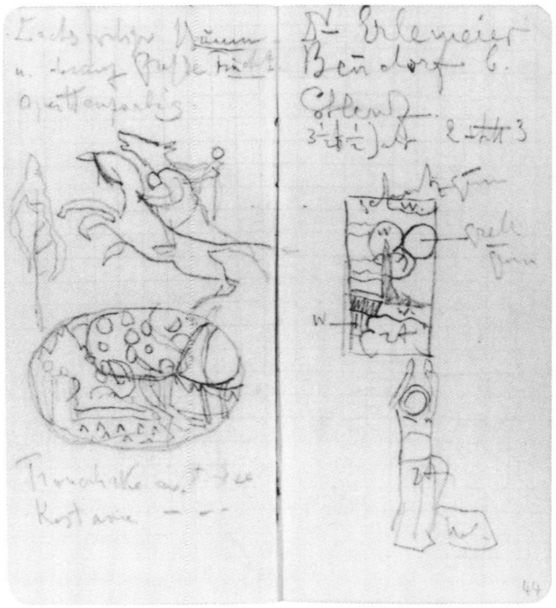

26, pp.43-44

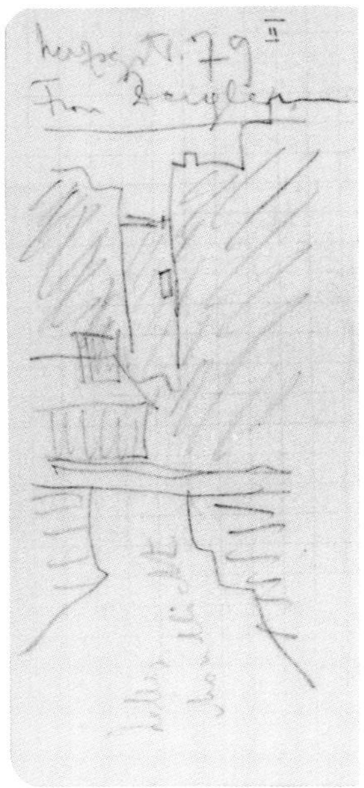

26, p.45

**pp.41–42** Pencil sketch of landscape with building, trees and lake with reflection

**p.43** Pencil studies for prints
Inscribed u.c.: 'Lachsfarbiger Baum / u. darauf grosse Früchte / (quittenfarbig)'; l.c.: 'Trauerlicke an St. See / Kastanie…'

REFERENCES
Hanfstaengl 1974, pp.148, 149, ill.
Barnett 1992, p.219
Barnett and Friedel 1995, no.264, color ill.

The sketches are related to *Entwurf für den Farbholzschnitt 'Berge'* of 1908–1909 (Barnett no.248; Roethel no.122).

**p.44** Pencil studies for prints and stage compositions
Inscribed above: 'Dr Erlemeier / Benndorf b. / Coblenz' and with color notations: 'schwtz-grün / w.w / grell / grün / w. / w / rt / rt / w'

REFERENCES
Hanfstaengl 1974, pp.148, 149, ill.
Barnett 1992, p.218
Barnett and Friedel 1995, no.264, color ill.

The sketches are related to *Leuchtturm* of 1908–1909 (Barnett no.247) and 'Schwarz und Weiss' of early 1909 (see pp.35–36, 79–81).

**p.45** Pencil sketch of nocturnal cityscape
Inscribed above: 'Herzogstr. 79 II / Frau Dengler'; below: 'helles Mondlicht'

Fanny Dengler was Kandinsky's housekeeper (see also Sketchbook 21, p.7, where he noted the same address).

**p.46** List of prints exhibited in Berlin

**p.47** Pencil sketch of landscape
Inscribed with color notations: 'w. / viol. / blau / grün warm tief / Freuss'; at r. edge: '843'

The sketch was probably done in Austria in summer 1908

**pp.48–49** List of names and addresses. At the top of p.48 Kandinsky wrote: 'Kochel No.24 / Hartmann' and below noted Bruckmann Verlag in Nyphenburgerstrasse.

**p.50** Pencil sketch (not illustrated)
Inscribed below in Cyrillic: 'poluchil M 4.75' and in German: '[…]weiss 7 M / Bredaner bis 3 Uhr. / Kr […]'

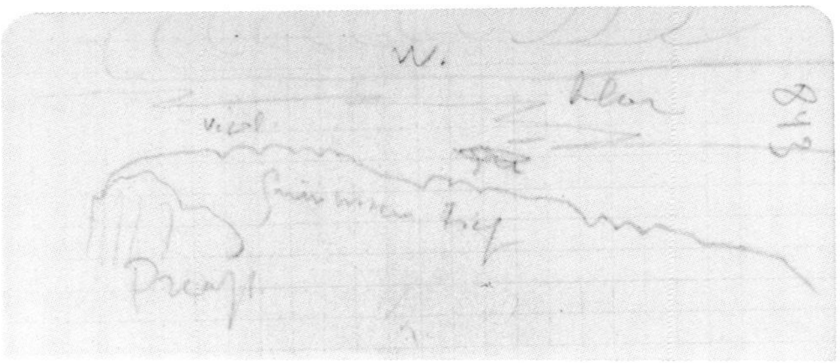

26, p.47

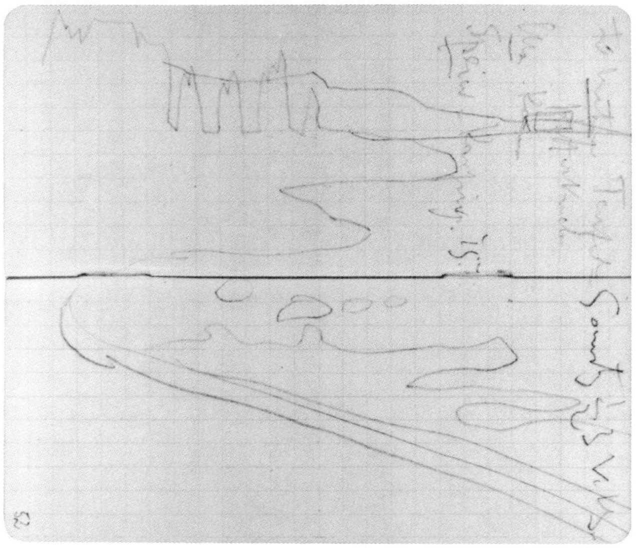

26, pp.51-52

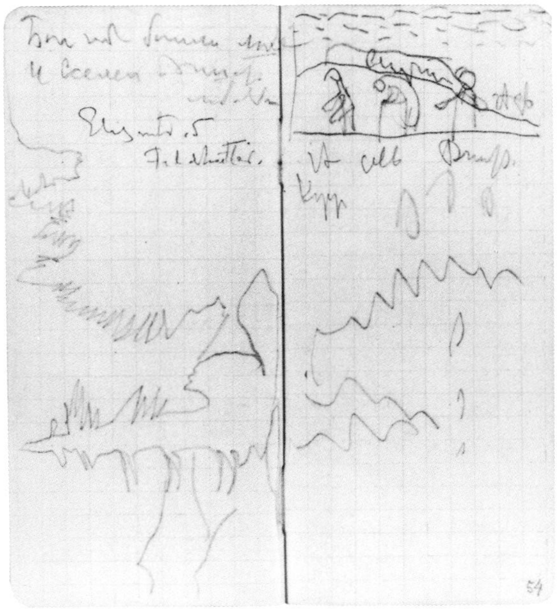

26, pp.53-54

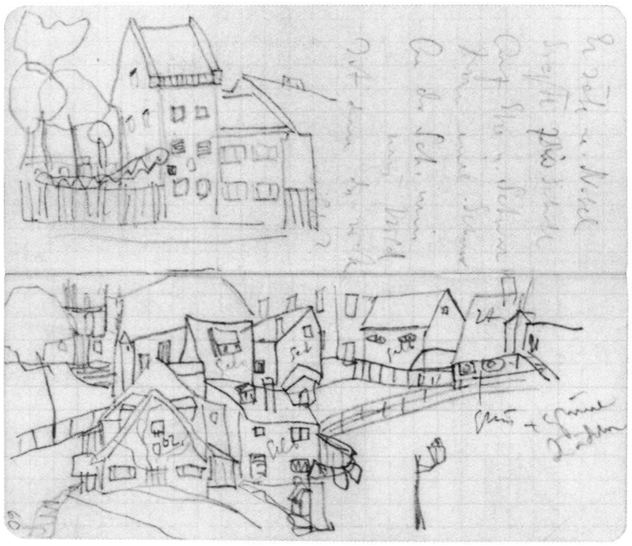

26, pp.59-60

**pp.51–52** Pencil sketch of landscape
Inscribed r. edge: 'Teufel / Herkuchen / Ella- Kamin / Speier-Karfing 15 / Sonntag ½ 3 v. M.'

**pp.53–54** Pencil sketch of trees
Inscribed (above) with illegible notes in Cyrillic and 'Elisenstr. 5 / Feldhütter.'

REFERENCES
Hanfstaengl 1974, p.149, ill.

**p.54** Pencil sketch of figures
Inscribed with color annotations: 'blgrün / rt gb / rt gelb Preuss. / Kr[a]pp'

The sketch can be related to a drawing inscribed 'Flammen' in Sketchbook 20 (GMS 327, p.5), which Kandinsky did in Paris in 1907.

**p.55** Pencil sketch of floor plan
Inscribed above in Cyrillic: '[...] v II k' and below: '2 x Tafelbitter / 2 Päcklinge / 1 pf Thee'

**pp.56–58** Lists of addresses, notes on 'Teilung der Farbfläche' and correspondences between colors and sounds of musical instruments

**p.59** Pencil sketch of houses
Inscribed with poem r. edge (above) that begins: 'Er sähe m. Nebel / Sorgte zur Schule / Auf Str u. Schwarz' and ends with rhyme 'Bild' and 'wild'

**p.60** Pencil sketch of houses
Inscribed l.r.: 'grau + grüne / Laden' and with color notations: 'Sch / gelb / or / gelb'

REFERENCES
Hanfstaengl 1974, p.150, ill.

The sketches bring to mind earlier drawings of an *Altstadt* (see vol.I, cat. nos.82–85).

**pp.61–62** Pencil study for *Ludwigskirche in München* of 1908
Inscribed in image (p.61) with color notations: 'grün / rt / rosig / or / bl / dkler / sch.weiss' and below (p.62): 'Im Schatten Preuss. + Chrm / in den Schatten / Im Licht blaugrün oxyd / in den Schatten'

REFERENCES
Hanfstaengl 1974, pp.148, 150, ill.
Roethel and Benjamin 1982, p.244
Peter Vergo, *The Thyssen-Bornesmisza Collection: Twentieth-century German Painting* (London, 1992), pp.160, ill., 161

Although Kandinsky made slight modifications in the painting, this drawing is clearly a study for his picture of the Ludwigskirche built by Friedrich von Gärtner in Ludwigstrasse in Munich (Roethel and Benjamin no.254).

26, pp.61-62

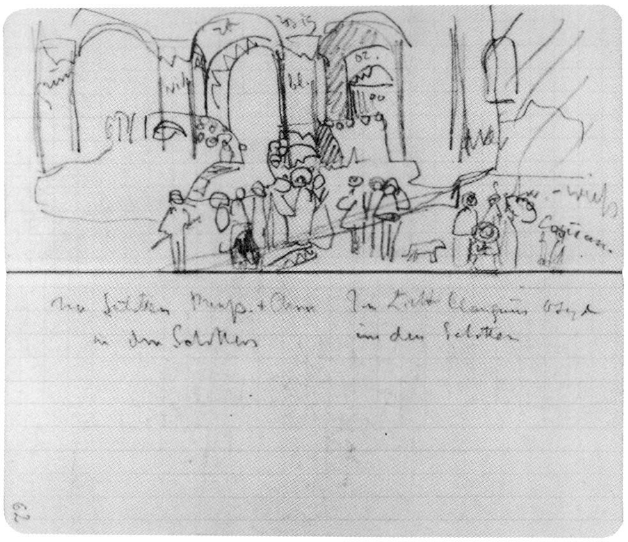

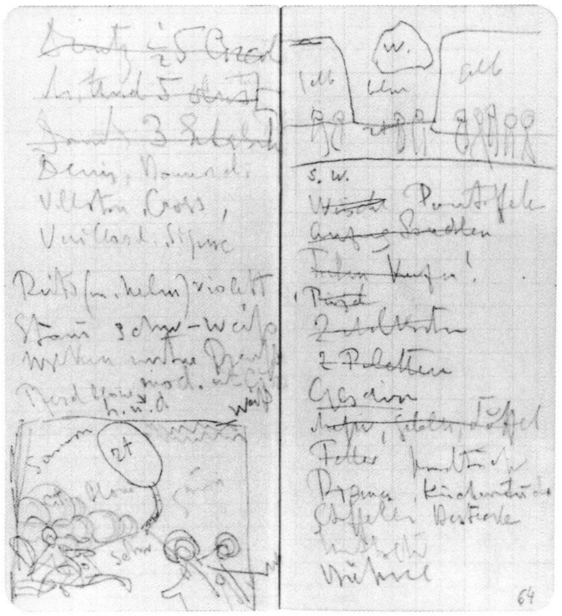

26, pp.63-64

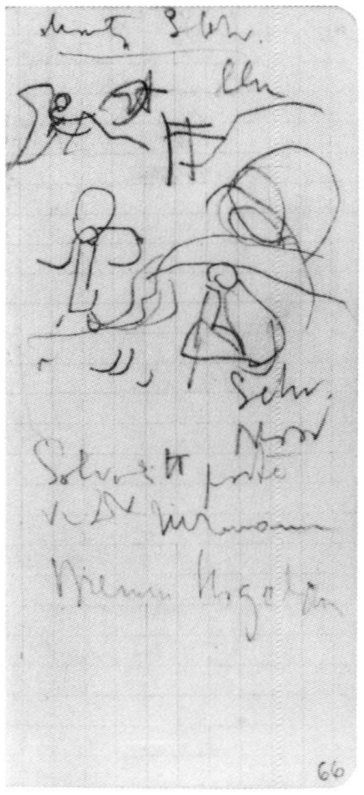

26, p.66

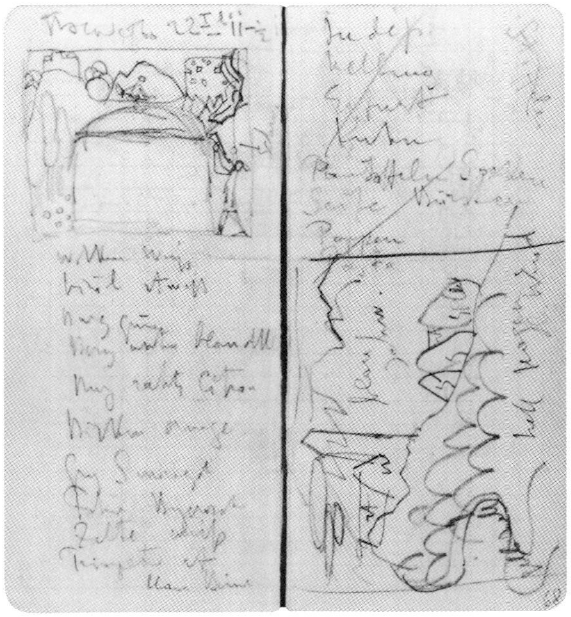

26, pp.67-68

**p.63** Pencil study for relief sculpture
Inscribed above: 'Denis, Bonnard, / Valloton, Cross, / Vuillard, Signac / Reiter (m. Helm) violett / Stamm schw-weiss / Wolken unten Preuss / mod. mit Citron / Pferd blau / h. u. d.' and with color notations in image: 'Saumon / weiss / rt / cit / blau / schw / w'

REFERENCES
Hanfstaengl 1974, p.150, ill.

Kandinsky wrote the names of several Neo-Impressionist artists as well as color notations on this study for *Reiter* of c.1909 (Appendix I, no.4). He probably made the painted wood relief sculptures during the summer of 1909. For a related drawing, see vol.I, cat. no.116.

**p.64** Pencil study for painting
Inscribed in image with color notations: 'gelb / w / blau / gelb / rt'

REFERENCES
Hanfstaengl 1974, pp.148, 150, ill.
Roethel and Benjamin 1982, p.255

Although the colors do not correspond exactly, this study can be related to *Bild mit Kahn* and *Improvisation 2* of 1909 (Roethel and Benjamin nos.268, 274). Below the sketch Kandinsky made lists of things to buy or pack.

**p.65** Pencil diagrammatic sketch
Illegible notes in Cyrillic above
Inscribed: 'Packets u. Bälle / Farben: Victoria Indigo'

**p.66** Pencil sketch of figures
Inscribed below: 'Schw. / Oker / Sch[...] / von Dr. Hermann / Bremen Hagedorn'

REFERENCES
Hanfstaengl 1974, pp.148, 150, ill.

Hanfstaengl related the sketch to the woodcut *Landschaft mit Figuren und Kruzifix* in *Klänge* (Roethel no.134).

**p.67** Pencil sketch of rider in landscape
Inscribed above in Cyrillic: 'Posol'stvo 22 I 11- ½ 1' and below: 'Wolken weiss / Himmel rtweiss / Burg grün / Berg unten blau dkl / Burg rechts citron / Birken orange / Gras Smaragd / Fahne Burgund / Zelte weiss / Trompete rt / blau Beine'

REFERENCES
Hanfstaengl 1974, pp.148, 150, ill.
Roethel and Benjamin 1982, p.247
Barnett and Friedel 1995, no.281, color ill.

The drawing is related to *Landschaft mit Reiter auf Brücke* of 1909 (Roethel and Benjamin no.259). Above Kandinsky noted an appointment or event at the embassy on 22 January from 11 to 12:30 AM.

(See color plate p.124)

**p.68** Pencil sketch of landscape
Inscribed with color notations: 'rt / w. / blau / schw. / hell Hagen / b. Wind' and r. edge (above): 'Indép. / Helbing / Erfurt / Kuhn / Pantoffeln Socken / Seife Bürsten / Pappen / Pasta'

(See color plate p.124)

**p.69** Pencil sketch of woman standing
Inscribed at l. edge: 'Zond fi pao / Gesicht etwas / dunk[l]er'; at r. edge: 'weisser Schweif u. Mähne'

The sketch resembles that on p.19 of Sketchbook 21 (GMS 333).

**p.70** Kandinsky wrote: 'Dienstag 3 Uhr / Frl. Dresler / Tagesordnung 22 III / P. Urquell ½ 9 ab'
The reference is to Emmy Dresler and the *Neue Künstlervereinigung München* in March 1909, and the specific date recorded is 22 March. His notes continue onto p.71.

**p.72** Pencil sketch of landscape
Inscribed u.l.: 'Wind'; l.l.: 'W. Gras mit / b. Blumen'; c.r.: 'blaugrün'

The drawing can be related to that on p.68 (above) and seems to have been done over a schematic sketch in which the words 'Korb' and 'Koffer' are still visible.

**p.73** Inscribed above: 'Bayerstr. 107 / Fr Lehmayer / Herr August Braun'

**p.74** Pencil sketch for *Kuppeln* of 1909
Inscribed with color notations: 'grün / w. / gelb / bl.rot / w.'

REFERENCES
Hanfstaengl 1974, p.148

Kandinsky made this study for *Kuppeln* of 1909 (Roethel and Benjamin no.264) above various notes and a recipe.

**p.75** List of photographs for stage compositions ('Bühnenkompositionen')

**p.76** List of appointments and reference to his dog Daisy

**pp.77–78** Lists of appointments and things to do

**p.78** Small pencil sketch of head
Inscribed: 'tusch / Mann mit weibl. / Gesicht'

Kandinsky made this tiny sketch of a 'man with feminine face' on the page where he noted several appointments and wrote the name of the composer Thomas von Hartmann, with whom he collaborated on stage compositions in 1908–1909.

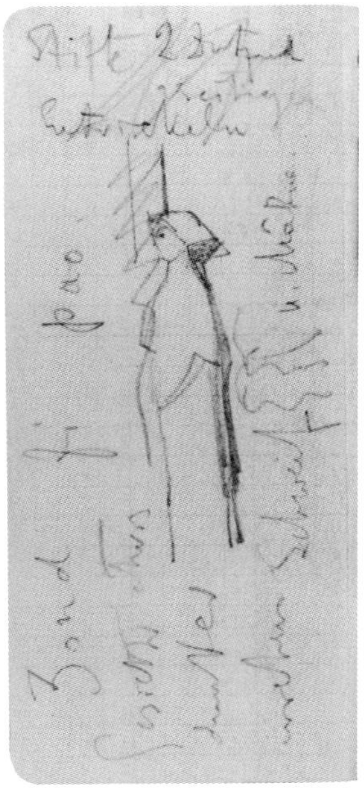

26, p.69

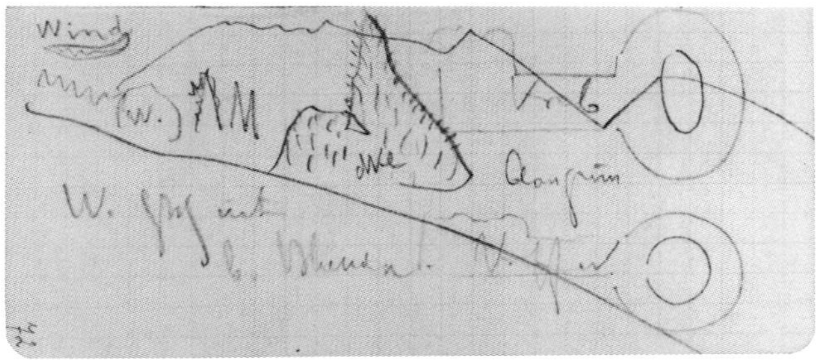

26, p.72

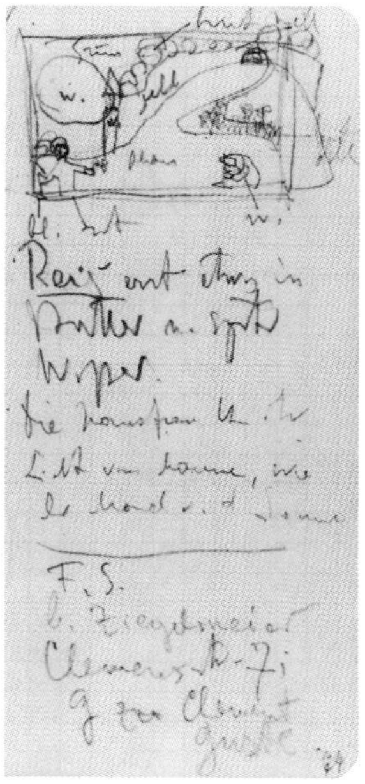

26, p.74

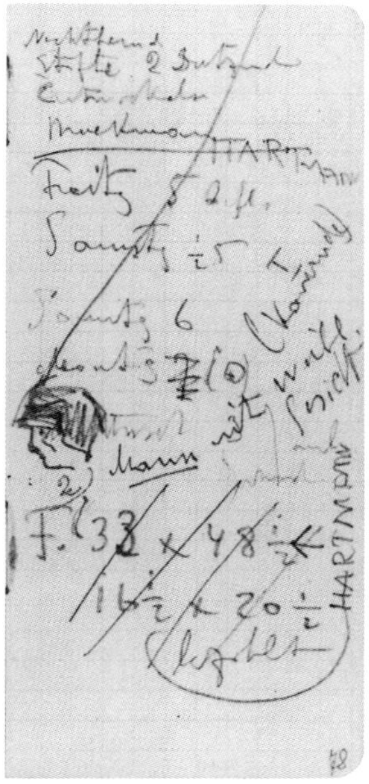

26, p.78

**pp.79–80** Two pencil studies for 'Schwarz und Weiss' (p.79)
Inscribed u.c.: 'I / eine / Bewegung / II Gehen / v. Schwarz / u. Weiss / Gehen viele (rythmisch). / Dann v. l. stehen blei- / ben in gehender Stell[un]g. / Langs[am] umdrehen, / Arme hängen, aus- / breiten. Hinten gehende / Frauen (weiss) v. l. n .r. / Dasselbe im Stehen- / bleiben. (Ein Hornton / s. kurz). Stille, nur / Wolkenbewegung'; continued on p.80: 'Wachsen v. Schwarz. / Einschlafen. / Stimme.'

**p.80** Four pencil sketches, two of which are numbered
Inscribed c.: 'III' / IV Reitern / auf w. Ross / (Äpfel) v. / schw. Reiter / später Wind / in Bäumen. Verschw[inden] / der Wolken. (Hufeisen- / schläge). Menschen / kommen u. setzen / sich im Profil. / Himmel / wird weiss-blau'

REFERENCES
Boissel 1998, pp.98, ill.8a, 100

Boissel identified these sketches and notes as the earliest manuscript for Kandinsky's theater composition 'Schwarz und Weiss', which she dated 1908–1909. The drawing with apples resembles earlier designs for embroideries (see Barnett no.144 and Sketchbook 12, p.46).

**p.81** Pencil sketch related to 'Schwarz und Weiss'
Inscribed c.l.: 'schw.' and below: 'Es wird dunkel. Die / M[enschen] stehen auf. Haben / plötzlich Fakeln w. u. / entfernen sich mit / sonderbaren Bewegungen'

REFERENCES
Boissel 1998, pp.98, ill.8a, 100

See above.

**p.82** Pencil diagrammatic sketch and recipes

**pp.83–85** List for packing and shopping, addresses, train schedules

**p.86** Pencil schematic sketch perhaps of cloud (not illustrated)
Inscribed below: 'Jacques Dalcroze. / Frl. Wörner / Bruderstrasse 5 II'

**pp.87–90** Lists for packing and train schedules (Müggendorf, Fränkische Schweiz)

26, pp.79-80

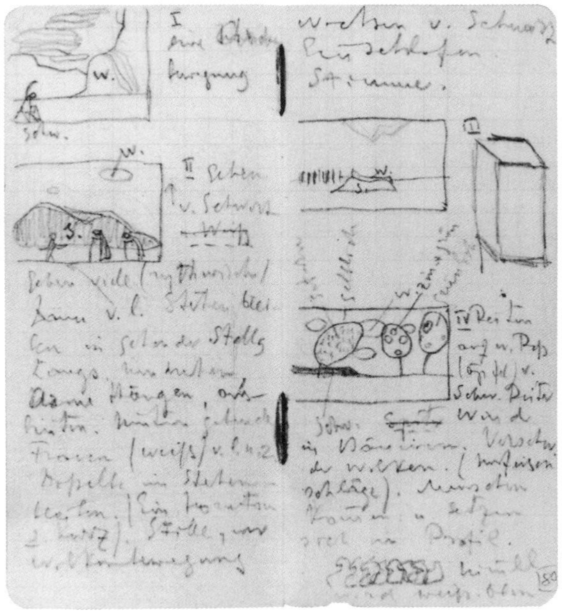

26, p.81

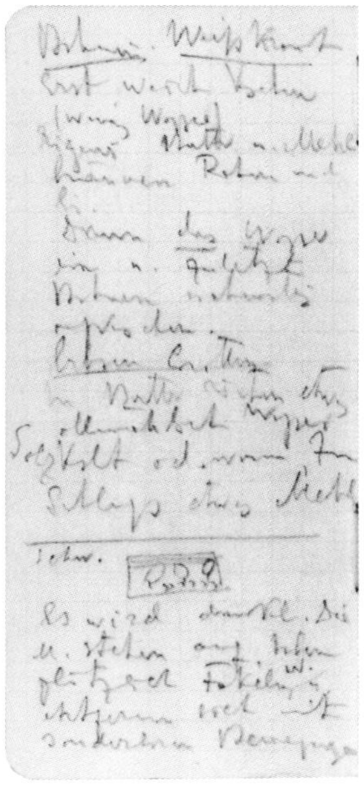

# Sketchbook 27

1908–1910

Black leather notebook; no label
Contains 116 pages (58 sheets) of graph paper, each 13.2 x 8.1 cm (5¼ x 3¼ in)
Page numbers inscribed by unknown hand at later date with even numbers at lower right

Hanfstaengl 1974, pp.165–166

LOCATION
Städtische Galerie im Lenbachhaus, Munich (GMS 345)

HISTORY
Gabriele Münter, Murnau, until 1957

The notebook contains numerous references to dates in 1909. There are, however, drawings for works executed in 1908 as well as 1910: evidence that Kandinsky used the notebook over a period of time rather than only in 1909. Erika Hanfstaengl had assigned it a date of 1909.

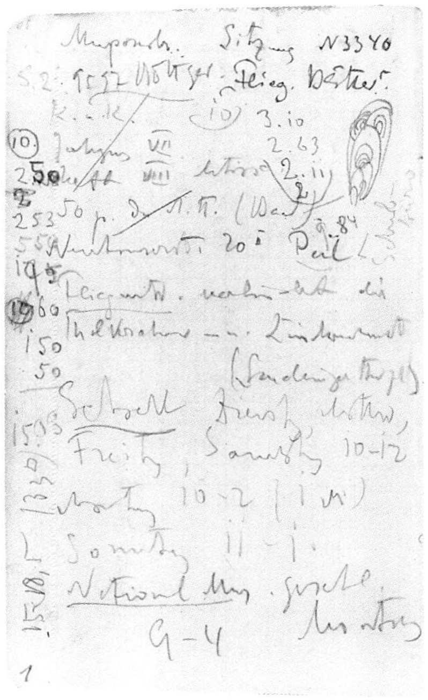

27, p.1

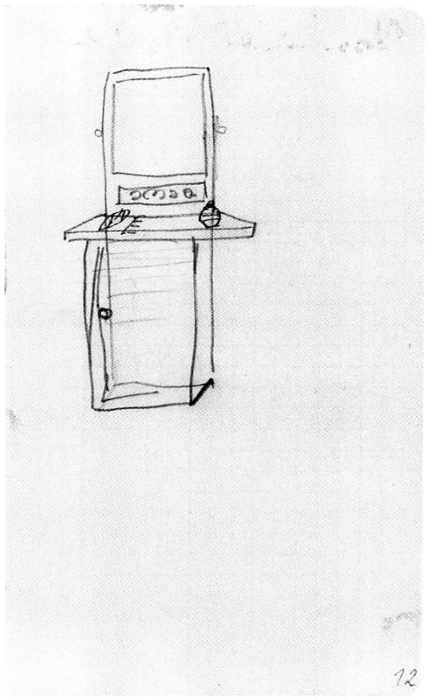

27, p.12

27, p.13

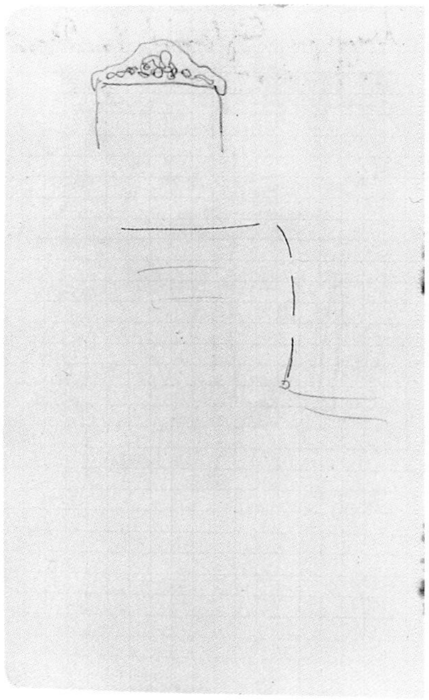

27, p.20

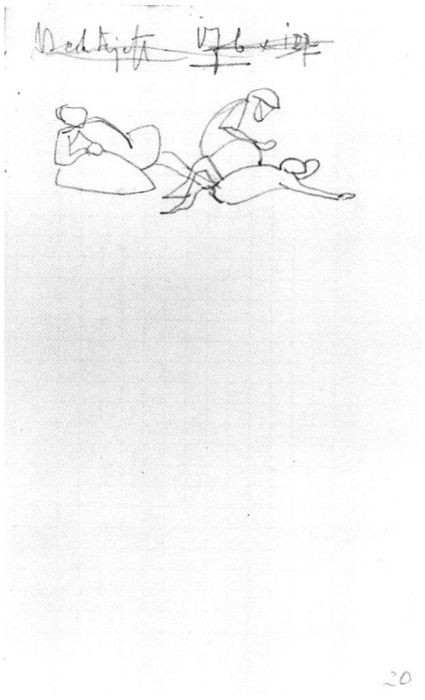

**p.1** Pencil study for decorative design
Inscribed with notes and lists of publications including 'Flieg. Blätter / K. u. K. / Jahrgang VII / Heft VIII / Matisse' and opening hours for Schack-Galerie and National-Museum

The decorative design resembles drawings in Sketchbooks 12 and 21 (GMS 347, p.45 and GMS 333, p.44) as well as the gouache *Entwurf mit Schlingenmuster* (Barnett no.149). *Fliegende Blätter* was a humorous weekly published in Munich. An article by Henri Matisse entitled 'Notizen eines Malers' appeared in the May 1909 issue of *Kunst und Künstler* (VII Jg., Heft VIII, pp.335–347).

**pp.2–4** Notes and lists of things to do and things to pack

**p.5** Notes and small diagrammatic floor plan of two rooms in Murnau
Inscribed u.l.: '3½% bis 17 II 909'; l.l.: 'Zimmer / in Murnau'
The notes apparently refer to rooms for rent and include the date 17 February 1909.

**pp.6–11** Notes and addresses primarily in Munich

**p.12** Pencil drawing of cupboard

REFERENCES
Hanfstaengl 1974, p.165

The sketch brings to mind the *Küchenschrank* (Appendix I, no.12) that Kandinsky painted.

**p.13** Pencil sketch of decoration for furniture

In 1909–1910 Kandinsky painted wood furniture for the house in Murnau that Gabriele Münter purchased in summer 1909.

**p.14** Notes in Cyrillic: 'Martiros Sor'ian ("Zol. Runo") / No 6 1909'
The reference is to the artist Martiros Sar'ian (1880–1972) and the periodical 'Golden Fleece' (kindly brought to my attention by Natasha Kurchanova).

**pp.15–18** Blank

**p.19** Inscribed above: 'Ausstell[un]gen 905 / W 104441'

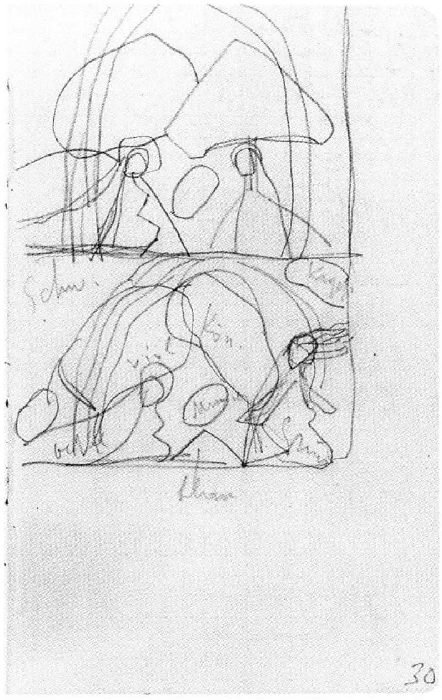

27, p.30

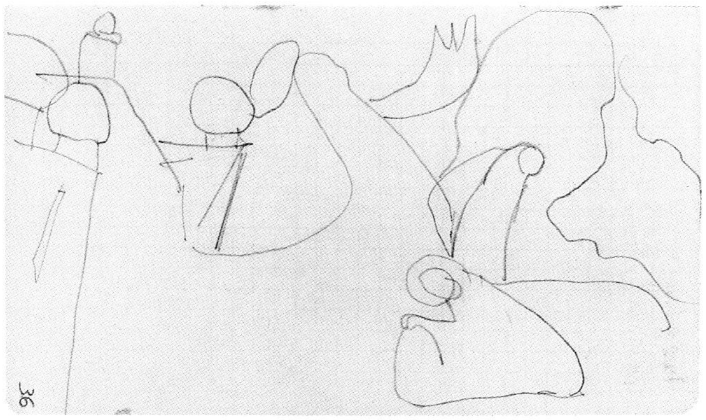

27, p.36

**p.20** Pencil drawing of figures
Inscribed above but crossed out: 'Bechtejeff 176 x 127'

REFERENCES
Hanfstaengl 1974, p.165

The Russian artist Vladimir von Bechtejeff (1898–1971) was a member of the *Neue Künstlervereinigung München*. The figures bear a resemblance to those in Sketchbook 26 (GMS 328, p.6).

**pp.21–25** Notes and lists including references to Giacomo Balla, José Barruecho, Erma Bossi, Maurice Denis, Kees Van Dongen, Othon Friesz, Odilon Redon, Henri Matisse, Félix Vallotton

**pp.26–27** Lists of furniture
Kandinsky wrote on p.26: 'Haus / Bett stellen (in München 3) / vielleicht Art Sofas od. Chaise Longes, / die später in die Ateliers gehen / Nachttische- runde Tischchen, die / auch in At. gehen (dunkel gemalt) / Waschtische- 2 bestellen mit [Wasch] Krönchen / Ständer für Handtücher etc. / Schrank / Esszimmer / Tisch mit Kacheln bestellen / 6-8 Stühle mit Kissen / (oben hängend) bestellen / Sofa wie oben / Tische von München (als Schreib etc.) / Vorhänge englische 260 x 176'

**p.27** Kandinsky listed: 'Stangen (ziehbare) / Küche (Tietz) / Schrank / 2 Tische / Stühle / Geschirr / Teppiche / betten' and at r. edge in Cyrillic: 'Apollon Ochedrednaia khronika k 10 VIII b.'

**p.28** Notes about expenses and an agreement

**p.29** Pencil diagrammatic sketch (not illustrated)
Inscribed u.c.: '35-40 M. / Franz Beyrer / Augustiner 67 I Aufg. M. 6'; c.l.: 'an / 105 / 24 / 93 / 27'

**p.30** Pencil sketches for *Studie für 'Improvisation 10'* of 1910
Inscribed u.l. within lower image: 'Schw.'; u.r.: 'Krapp.'; c.: 'viol / Kön. / Mrm rt'; l.l.: 'Ocker'; l.c.: 'blau'; l.r.: 'Grün'

REFERENCES
Ringbom 1970, pp.77–78, pl.11
Hanfstaengl 1974, p.165, ill.
Washton Long 1980, p.72, pl.30
Roethel and Benjamin 1982, p.316
Barnett 2006, p.82

The image at the bottom is related to an ink drawing on the reverse of *Entwurf für den Holzschnitt 'Reiterweg'* (vol.I, cat. no.148) and *Studie für 'Improvisation 10'* of 1910 (Roethel and Benjamin no.336).

**pp.31–35** Lists of addresses and notes

**pp.33–34** Lists of numbers indicating installation of exhibition

**p.35** Inscribed: 'Herbst 1910 / Alle Räume Thannhausers f[ü]r 6-8 / Wochen / Wieviel Bilder kön[n]en da gehängt werden?'

**p.36** Pencil drawing for *Improvisation auf Mahagoni* of 1910

REFERENCES
Hanfstaengl 1974, p.165
Roethel and Benjamin 1982, p.307

Kandinsky has changed some of the details in his oil painting *Improvisation auf Mahagoni* of 1910 (Roethel and Benjamin no.328).

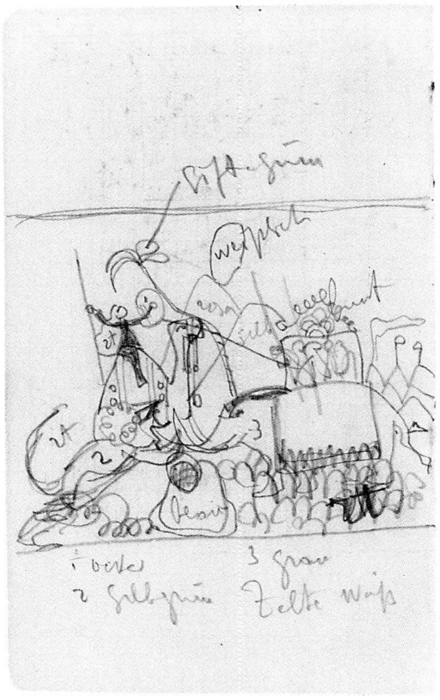

27, p.37

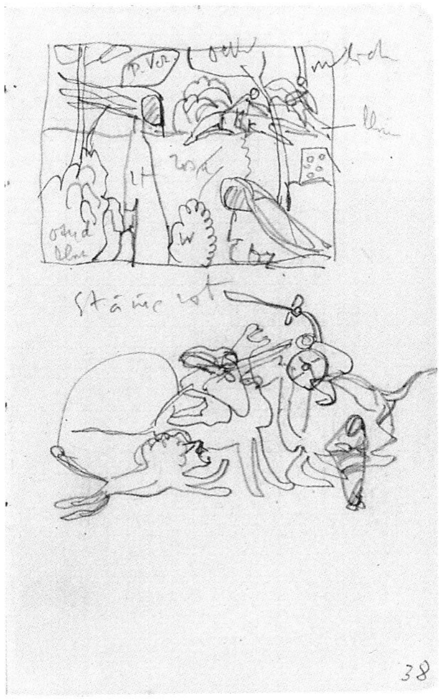

27, p.38

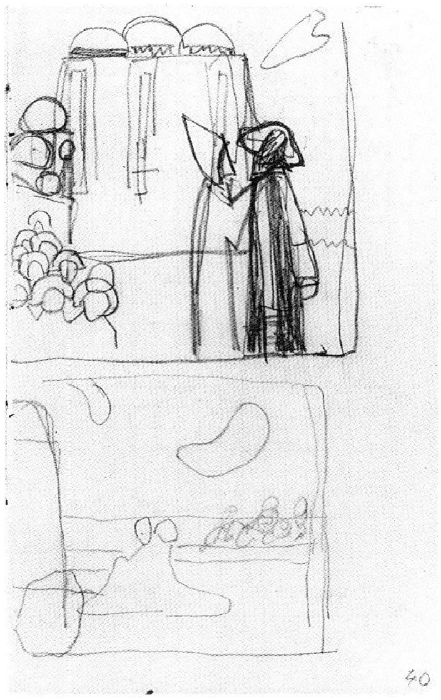

27, p.40

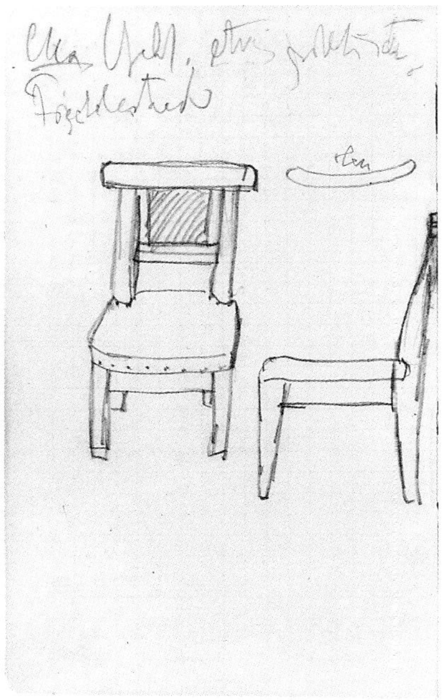

27, p.43

**p.37** Pencil study for *Der Elefant* of 1908
Inscribed above: 'gift-grün'; below: '1 Ocker / 2 Gelbgrün / 3 grau / Zelte weiss' and with color notations in image

REFERENCES
Hanfstaengl 1974, p.165, ill.
Roethel and Benjamin 1982, p.245
Hahl-Koch 1993, p.120, ill.150

This drawing is preparatory to *Der Elefant* of 1908 (Roethel and Benjamin no.256).

(See color plate p.125)

**p.38** Pencil study for *Skizze zu 'Improvisation 5'* of 1910
Inscribed c.: 'Stämme rot' and with color notations in sketch above

REFERENCES
Hanfstaengl 1974, p.165, ill.
Roethel and Benjamin 1982, pp.308, 406
Hahl-Koch 1993, p.161, ill.201

The drawing above is a study for *Skizze zu 'Improvisation 5'* of 1910 (Roethel and Benjamin no.329). The sketch below of a battle between horsemen and a lion appeared later in modified form in *Löwenjagd* of 1911 (Roethel and Benjamin no.418).

(See color plate p.125)

**p.39** Inscribed above: 'Capt. W.A. Collings & Sons / Gamage Buildings, Holborn / London E. C. Box 41'

**p.40** Pencil studies for *Improvisation 1* of 1909 and *Reiter am Strand*

REFERENCES
Ringbom 1970, p.76, pl.8
Roethel 1970, pp.256, 480, ill.51
Hanfstaengl 1974, pp.165, 166, ill.
Roethel and Benjamin 1979, p.80, ill.89
Roethel and Benjamin 1982, p.260, ill.
Barnett and Friedel 1995, no.285, color ill.
Barnett 2006, p.86

The drawing above is a study for Kandinsky's lost painting *Improvisation 1* of 1909 (Roethel and Benjamin no.271), and the one below is related to his ink drawing *Reiter am Strand* of c.1910 (vol.I, cat. no.158).

**p.41** Notes about a torso and the Rondanini Pietà by Michelangelo as well as notes about Greek antiquities, a flea market and shops for antique endpapers ('Vorsatzpapiere') in Rome

**p.42** Blank

**p.43** Pencil studies for chair
Inscribed above: 'Ella Stuhl, etwas gelblich [?] / Fr[...] / oben'

REFERENCES
Hanfstaengl 1974, p.165

Kandinsky's annotation referred to a chair for Gabriele Münter.

**p.44** Pencil diagrammatic sketch
Inscribed above: 'F. 95: 107 etwas zugeben! / 1) heller Gold / dklr [Gold]'

**p.45** Blank

**p.46** Inscribed, not by Kandinsky but probably by Karl Caspar: 'Karl Caspar / 10. Juni- 1. August / Beuron / Hohenzollern / München / Elisabethstr. 38/4'
Karl Caspar (1879–1956) was an artist influenced by the Beuron school who lived in Munich after 1907.

**pp.47–51** Blank

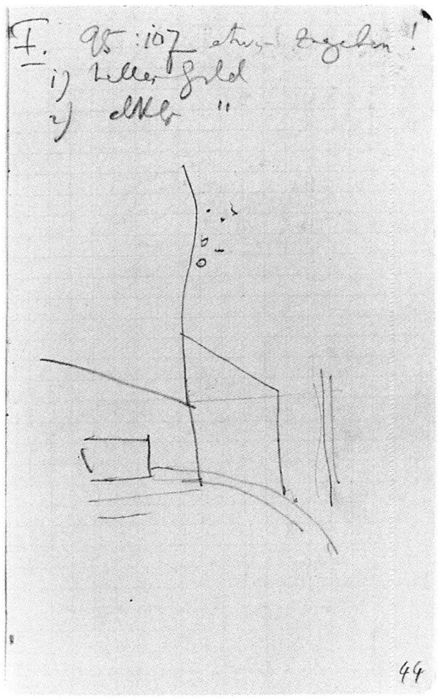

27, p.44

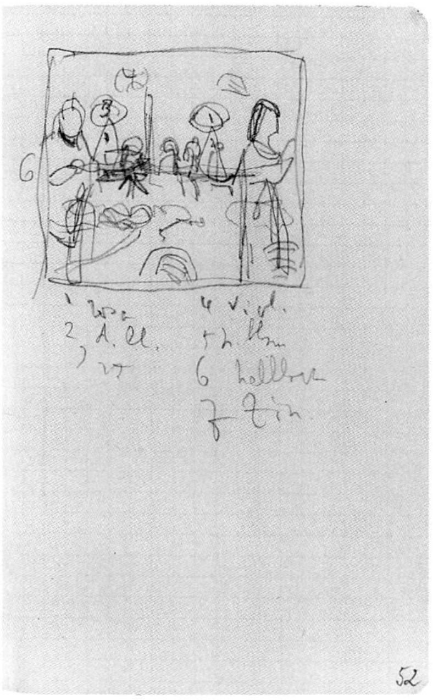

27, p.52

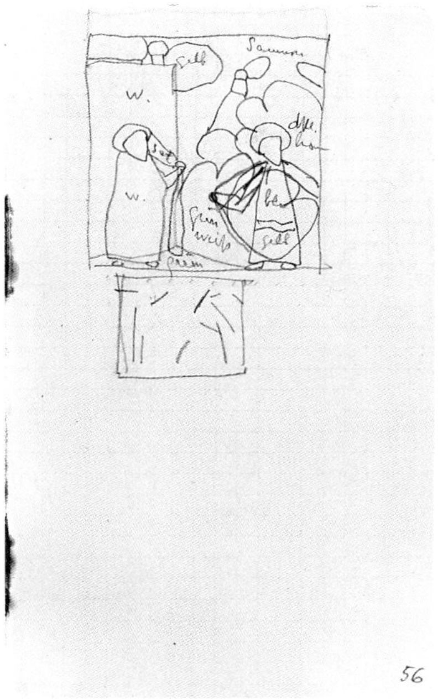

27, p.56

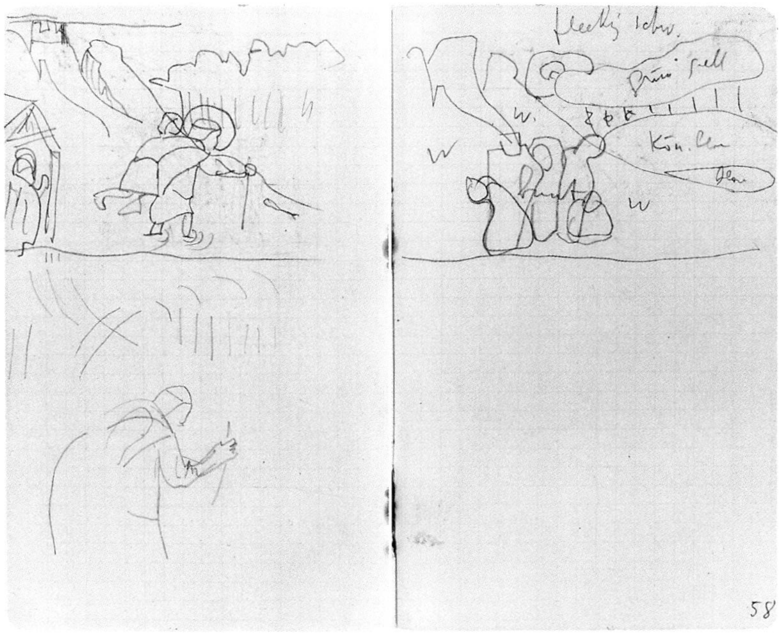

27, pp.57-58

**p.52** Pencil study for an unidentified work
Inscribed below: '1 rosa / 2 d. bl. / 3 rt / 4 viol. / 5 h blau / 6 hellbr[au]n / 7 Zin[nober].'

REFERENCES
Hanfstaengl 1974, p.166, ill.

**pp.53–55** Blank

**p.56** Pencil studies for *Improvisation 6* of 1909
Inscribed with color notations: 'w / gelb / saumon / sat. / dkl / braun / blau / gelb / grün / weiss / grün'

REFERENCES
Hanfstaengl 1974, p.165
Roethel and Benjamin 1982, p.272
Barnett and Friedel 1995, no.302, color ill

The sketch with color notations and the schematic drawing are for *Improvisation 6* of 1909 (Roethel and Benjamin no.287).

**p.57** Pencil studies for an unidentified work

REFERENCES
Hanfstaengl 1974, pp.165, 166, ill.

**p.58** Pencil study for an unidentified work
Inscribed with color notations: 'fleckig schw. / grün grell / w. / rot / w / Kön. blau / blau / bunt / w'

REFERENCES
Hanfstaengl 1974, p.166, ill.

The grouping of figures suggests *Bild mit Kahn* and *Improvisation 2 (Trauermarsch)* of 1909 (Roethel and Benjamin nos.268, 274).

**pp.59–61** Blank

**p.62** Pencil sketches of floor plans for the Murnau house with furniture indicated

**p.63** Pencil study for an unidentified painting
Inscribed with color notations: 'w. / rt / braun / Neap. / gelb / w.'

REFERENCES
Hanfstaengl 1974, p.166, ill.

(See color plate p.125)

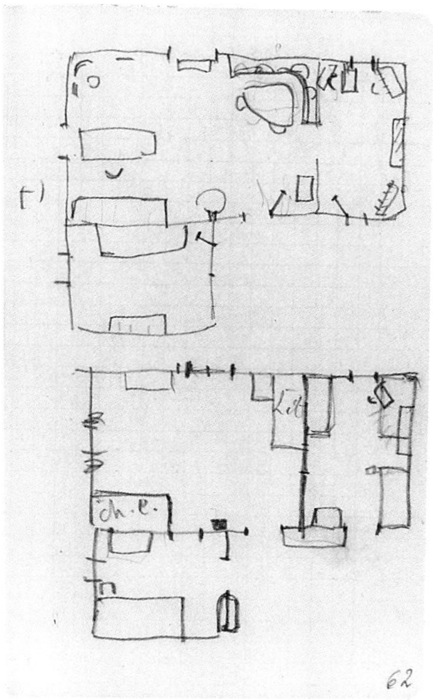

27, p.62

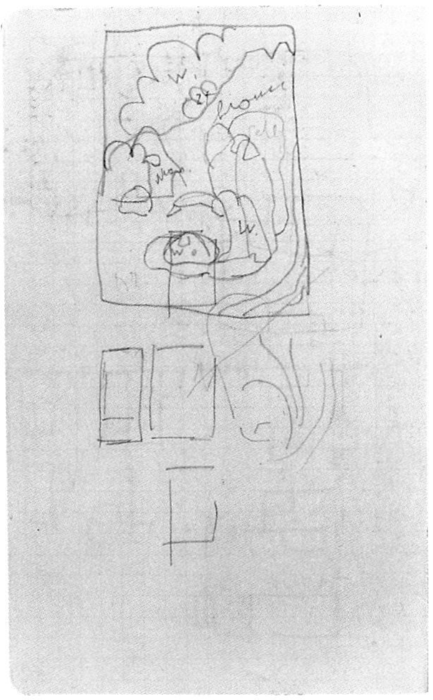

27, p.63

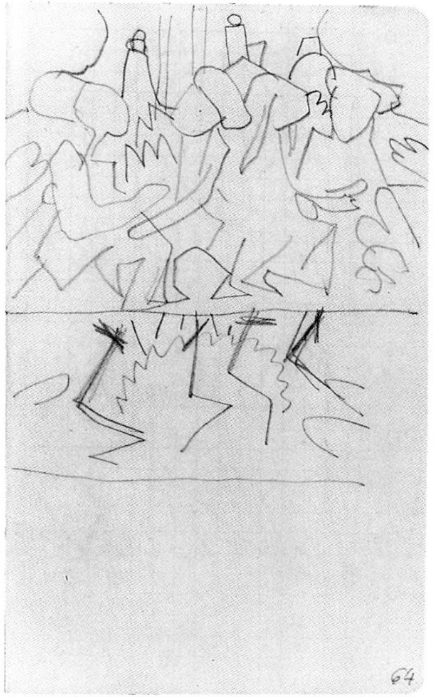

27, p.64

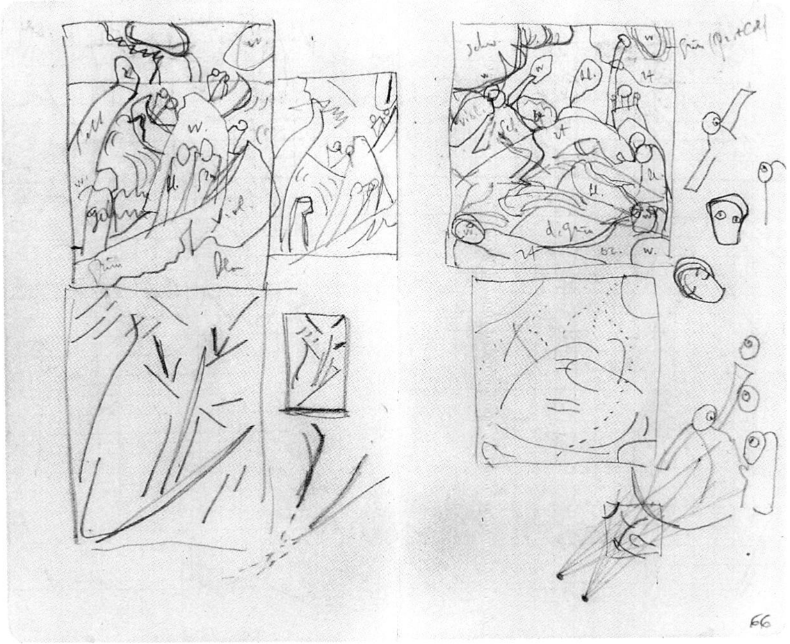

27, pp.65-66

**p.64** Pencil studies for *Orientalisches* of 1909

REFERENCES

Hanfstaengl 1974, p.165
Roethel and Benjamin 1982, p.280
Barnett and Friedel 1995, no.300, color ill.

The studies are preparatory to *Orientalisches* of 1909 (Roethel and Benjamin no.294).

(See color plate p.125)

**p.65** Pencil studies for *Improvisation 7* of 1910
Inscribed u.l. with color notations in image: 'r / w. / gelb / w / bl. / gr[ü]n / viol. / grün / blau'

REFERENCES

Hanfstaengl 1974, pp.165, 166, ill.
Washton Long 1980, pp.73, 178 n.35, pl.31
Roethel and Benjamin 1982, pp.310, 313

The sketch and the schematic drawing are for *Improvisation 7* of 1910 (Roethel and Benjamin no.333).

(See color plate p.125)

**p.66** Pencil studies for *Zwei Reiter und liegende Gestalt* of 1909–1910 and *Entwurf zu 'Komposition II'* of c.1910
Inscribed u.l. in image: 'schw. / w. / viol. / w / '; u.r.: 'w / grün (Pr. + Cd.) / rt'; c.: 'rt / bl.'; l.l.: 'w'; l.r.: 'w.'; l.c.: 'd. grün / rt / or'

REFERENCES

Hanfstaengl 1974, pp.165, 166, ill.
Roethel and Benjamin 1982, pp.305, 314
Barnett 1992, p.223
Barnett and Friedel 1995, no.305, color ill.
Dabrowski 1995, p.64, ill.5
Barnett 2006, p.34

The sketches are related to *Zwei Reiter und liegende Gestalt* of 1909–1910 (vol.I, cat. no.3) and *Entwurf zu 'Komposition II'* of c.1910 (Barnett no.255).

(See color plate p.125)

**p.67** Pencil studies for unknown works
Inscribed with extensive color notations emphasizing red, green, orange with yellow, blue and pink details

REFERENCES

Hanfstaengl 1974, p.166, ill.
Langner 1977, p.141, ill.23

Below the four drawings, a small sketch presents the four pictures together as in a polyptych or stage set.

(See color plate p.125)

27, pp.67-68

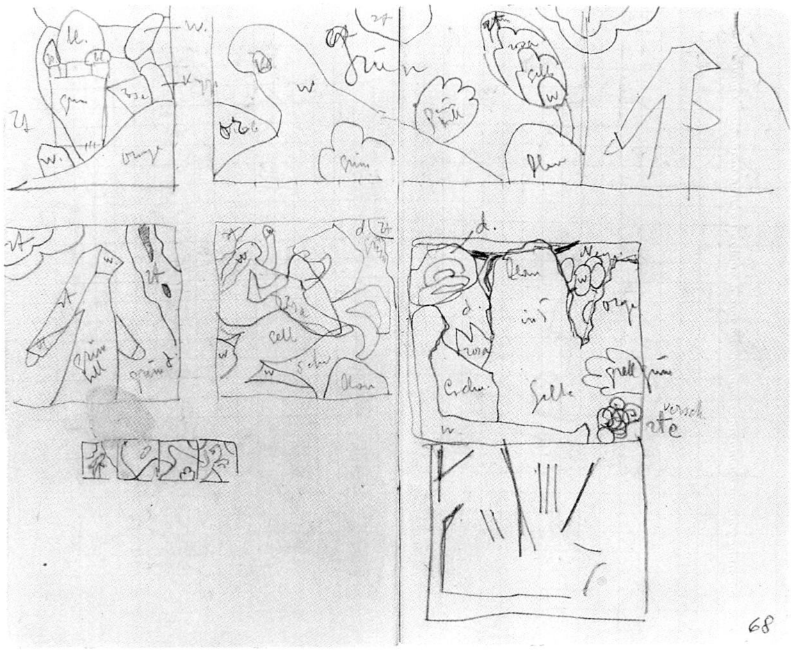

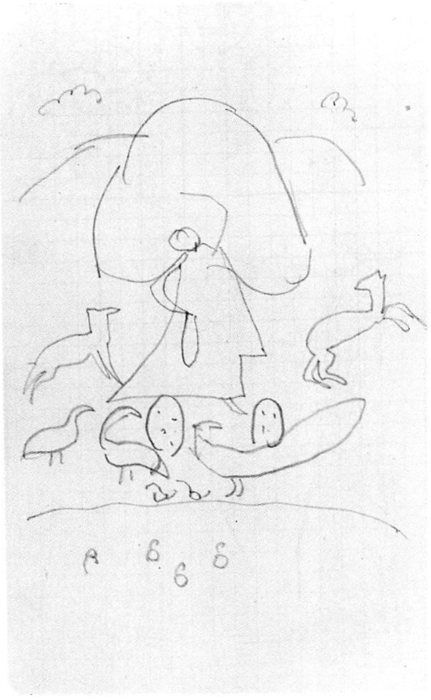

27, p.69

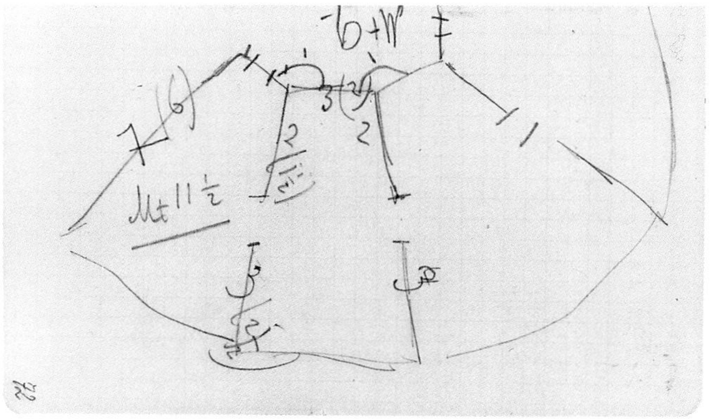

27, p.72

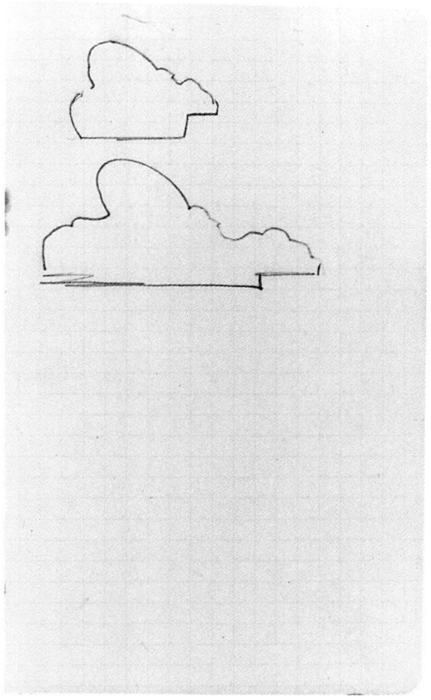

27, p.87

**p.68** Pencil studies for unknown works
Inscribed with color notations throughout

REFERENCES
Hanfstaengl 1974, p.166, ill.
Langner 1977, p.141, ill.23

The study above extends onto p.67: the stylized tree (inscribed with red, pink, yellow and white color notations) at the upper left is part of the sketch on the facing page. The sketch below is for an unknown and probably destroyed work, which is inscribed with color notes: u.l.: 'd / d'; u.r.: 'Neap. w. / orge'; c.: 'blau / ins / Gelbe'; l.l.: 'rosa / Cadm. / w.'; l.r.: 'grell grün / rte' and l.r. by Münter: 'versch[ollen].' The schematic drawing at the bottom repeats this composition.

(See color plate p.125)

**p.69** Pencil sketch of Indian miniature

REFERENCES
Daftari 1991, p.278, fig.141

Fereshteh Daftari identified the source as an eighteenth-century Indian miniature, *Bajadere in stilisierter Landschaft*, which belonged to the Sarre collection. The miniature was lent to the exhibition of Islamic art that opened in May 1910 in Munich. Later that year, probably in December, it was illustrated in *Deutsche Kunst und Dekoration* (vol. XXVII, Nr.4 [1910], p.216).

**p.70** Blank

**p.71** Inscribed: 'I Raum 13 / II [Raum] 11½ / v. Lift'

**p.72** Pencil sketch of floor plan
Inscribed above (upside down): 'M + G'; l.c.: 'Mt 11½'

**pp.73–82** Blank

**p.83** Note about reviews

**pp.84–86** Blank

**p.87** Pencil sketch of cloud-like forms

**pp.88–89** Blank

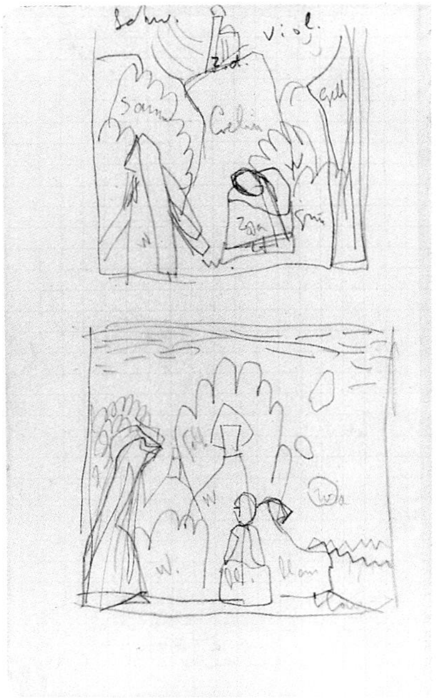

27, p.99

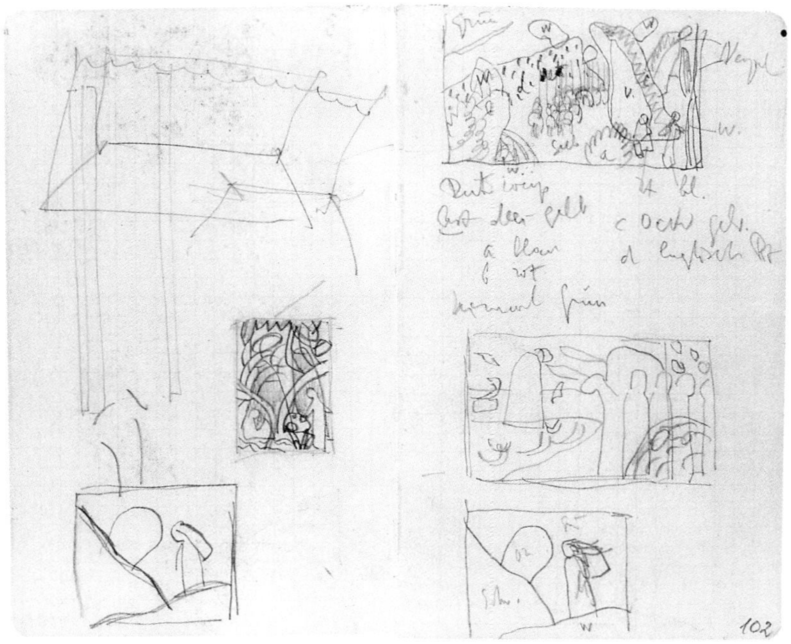

27, pp.101-102

**p.90** Pencil sketch of cloud-like form (not illustrated)

**pp.91–92** Blank

**pp.93–94** Text

**pp.95–98** Blank

**p.99** Pencil study for *Paradies* of 1909 and an unidentified work
Inscribed within top image: 'Schw / r.d. / viol. / saum / Coelin / gelb / w / rosa / rt / grün' and within bottom image: 'gelb / rosa / w / w. / bl. / blau'

REFERENCES
Hanfstaengl 1974, pp.165, 166, ill.
Washton Long 1980, p.101, pl.116
Roethel and Benjamin 1982, p.271

Above Kandinsky made a study for *Paradies* of 1909 (Roethel and Benjamin no.286), and below for a related but probably unexecuted picture.

**p.100** Blank

**p.101** Pencil study related to *Improvisation 10* of 1910 and for an unidentified work

REFERENCES
Hanfstaengl 1974, pp.165, 166, ill.

The sketch at the lower left is related to others on pp.30 and 102 and suggestive of studies preparatory to *Improvisation 10* of 1910: for example, the drawing on the reverse of cat. no.148 and *Studie für Improvisation 10* (Roethel and Benjamin no.336).

**p.102** Pencil study for *Reiterweg* of c.1910
Inscribed below image: 'Reiter weiss / Ast dkl gelb / a blau / b rot / c Ocker gel[b] / d Englisch r[o]t / Himmel grün' and with color notations in upper image: 'Grün / w / w / Neapel / v. / w / gelb / rt / bl.' and inscribed in lower image: u.r.: 'Grün'; c.l.: 'or'; l.l.: 'Schw.'; l.r.: 'w'

REFERENCES
Roethel 1970, pp.222, 478, ill.43
Hanfstaengl 1974, pp.165, 166, ill.
Barnett 2006, p.82

Above Kandinsky made a study for *Reiterweg* of c.1910 (vol.I, cat. no.148). The figures in the sketch in the middle bring to mind those in *Improvisation 19* of 1911 (Roethel and Benjamin no.385), and the drawing below is related to that on the facing page as well as to other studies for *Improvisation 10* of 1910.

**pp.103–113** Blank

**p.114** Pencil sketches of curving shapes (not illustrated)

**pp.115–116** Blank

**p.117** Inscribed in Cyrillic: 'Leva Frenkel'

**p.118** Blank

**pp.119–130** Notes about exhibitions of the *Neue Künstlervereinigung München* and references to the Galerie Brakl, the Moderne Galerie (Thannhauser) and the museum director, Hugo von Tschudi.

**p.119** References to K. Casper 38 IV, Edwin Scharff Herzogstr. 11 III, A. Hertmüller, Segantini

**p.121** Lists publications: 'Dek. Kunst / Hepperin / D.K. u. Dek. / M. Zeitung / M.N.N. / Zukunft / Kunst / M. Post / K.u. Künstler / Allg. Zeitung'

**p.125** Notes continue from those beginning on p.129 and continuing on pp.127–128 referring to: 'V. Brakl 12 X 909 wegen B[rie]f Holst'; 'VI. Brakl 16 X 909 Frankfurt durch Holst'; 'VII Brakl 10 XI 909'

**p.127** Notes: 'II. Düsseldorf durch mich März zwischen 22 XI bei Brakl 5 unten Räume.' and 'Unterrichg mit Brakl am 21 XI 909 in Gegenwart Jawlensky's'

**p.128** Refers to: 'III mit Brakl 24 IX wegen dem Satz in seinem Brief'; 'IV mit Brakl (29 IX bei Than) Dez.- München / Jan.- Leipzig – Chemnitz? / Febr.- Dresden / März Frankf. a.M. / April- Bremen ? / Mitgliedern mitteilen Ende XI bis Ende XII'

**p.129** Inscribed above: 'Tschudi 27 VIII' and below: 'Brakl 28 VIII I.'

**p.130** Inscribed above: 'Joachim v. Bülow (Paris, / deutscher Verein) in / Salon d'Automne. / Brücke Dresden (durch Holst) / Tschudi 30 X 909 / Neues Gebäude für die neue Kunst / Matisse, Picasso' and at r. edge: 'Daisy / Zu 6 X 10.'

1
**Promenade gracieuse (Grosse Fassung)**
Gracious Promenade (Large Version)
c.1904
(see page 321)

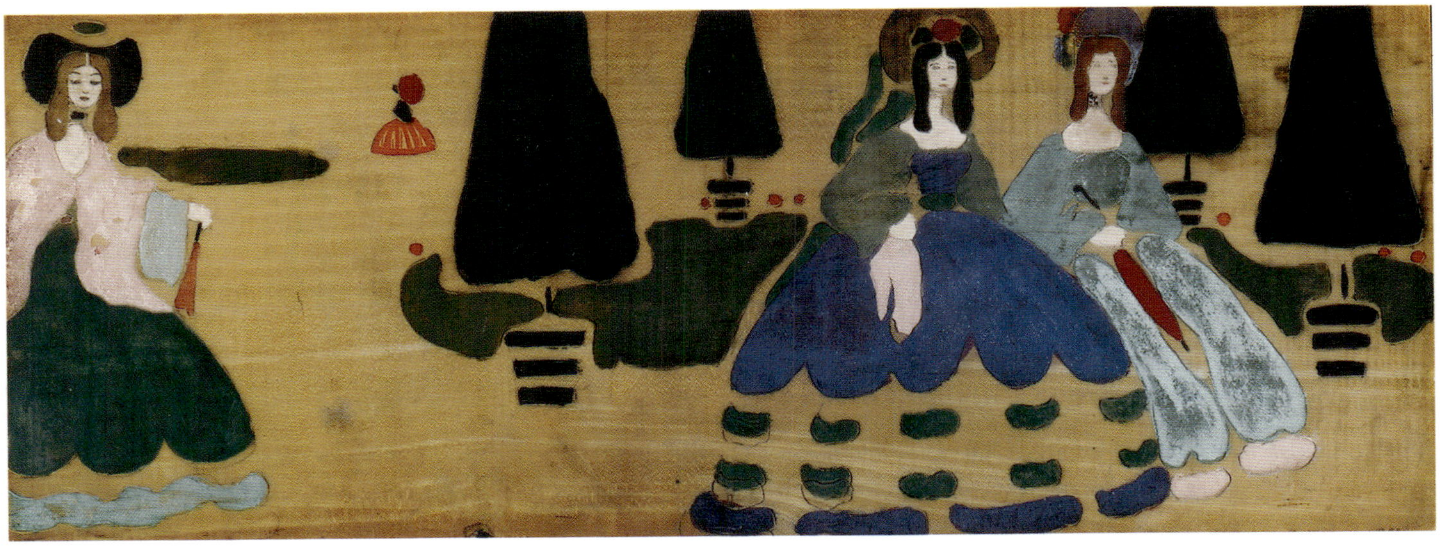

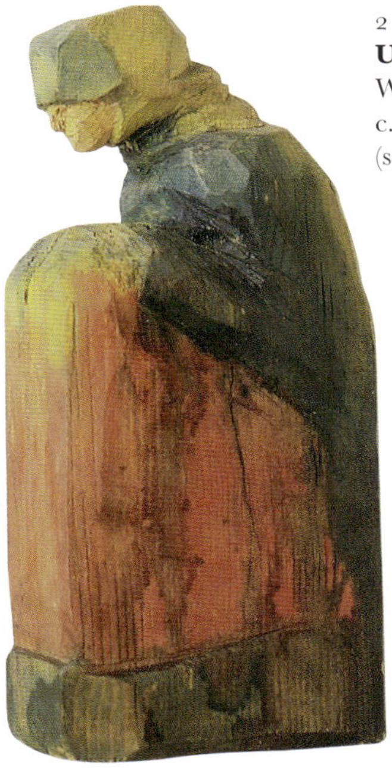

2
**Uhrenständer**
Watch Stand
c.1909
(see page 321)

3
**Begegnung**
Encounter
c.1909
(see page 321)

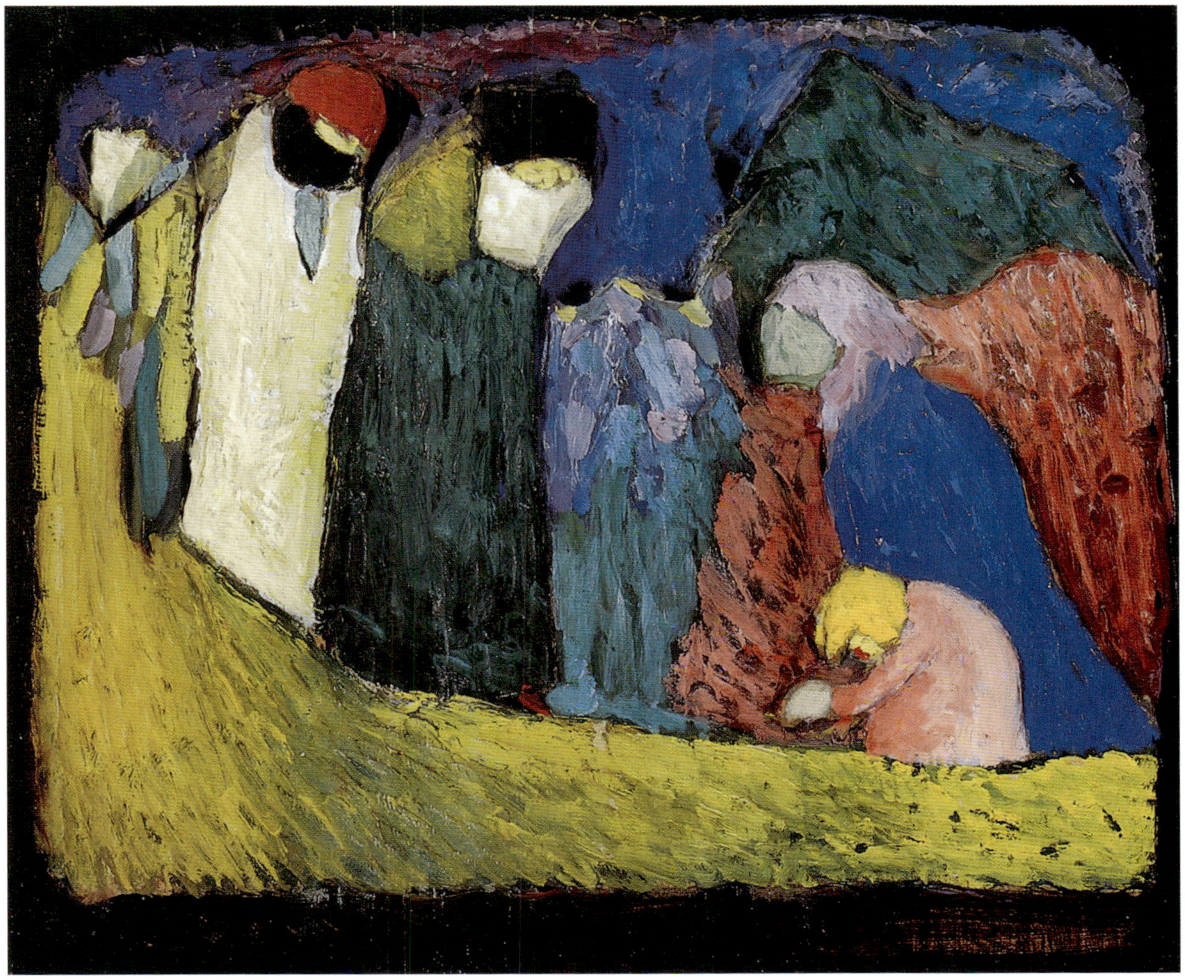

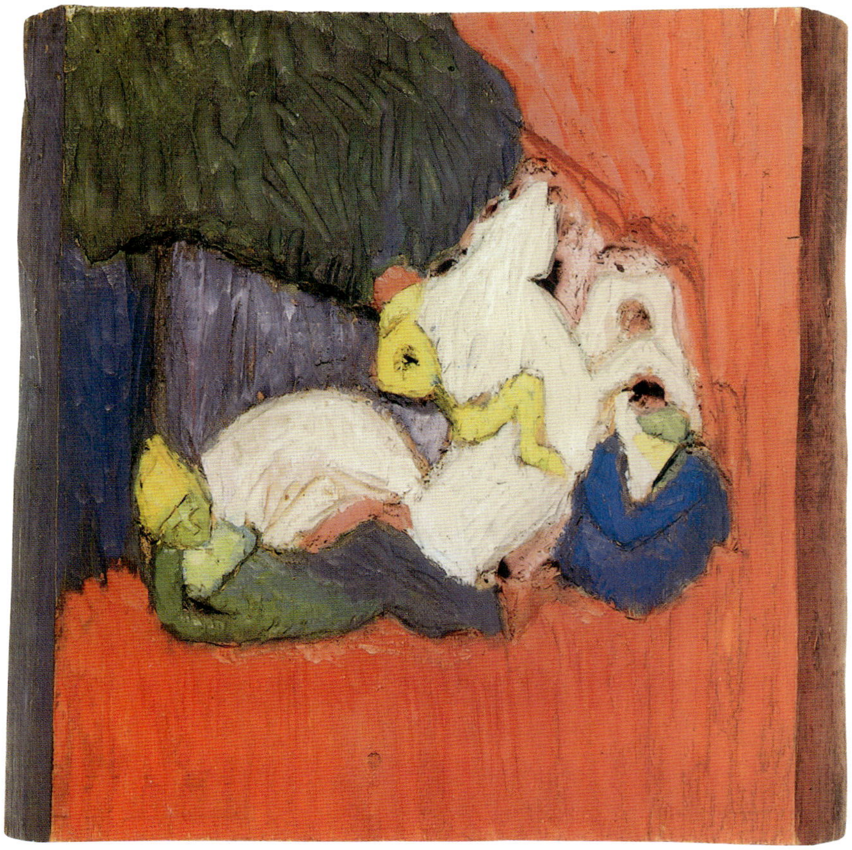

4
**Reiter**
Rider
c.1909
(see page 322)

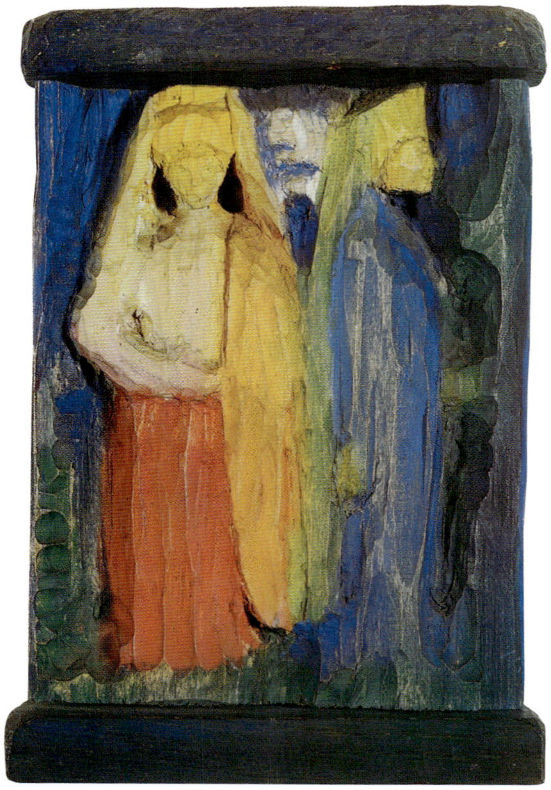

5
**Zwei Figuren**
Two Figures
c.1909
(see page 322)

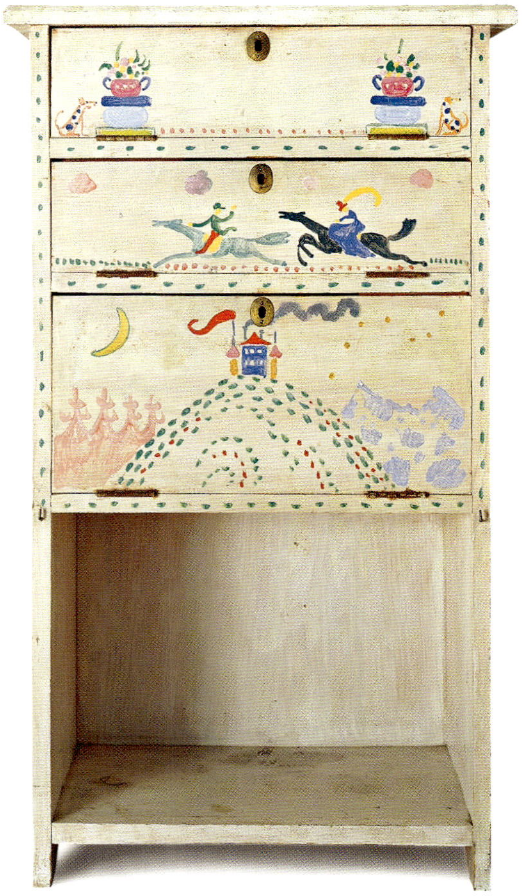

6
**Toilettenschränkchen**
Bedside Table
1909
(see page 322)

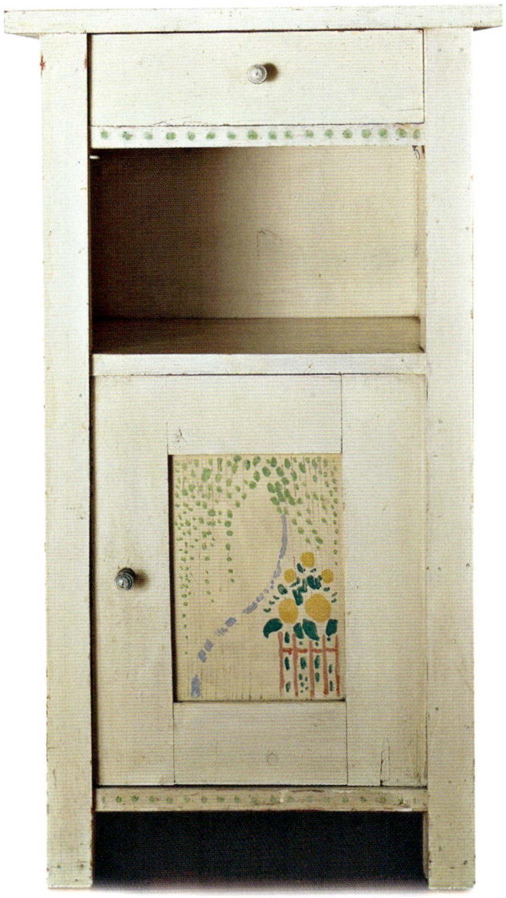

7
**Nachtkästchen**
Night Table
c.1909
(see page 322)

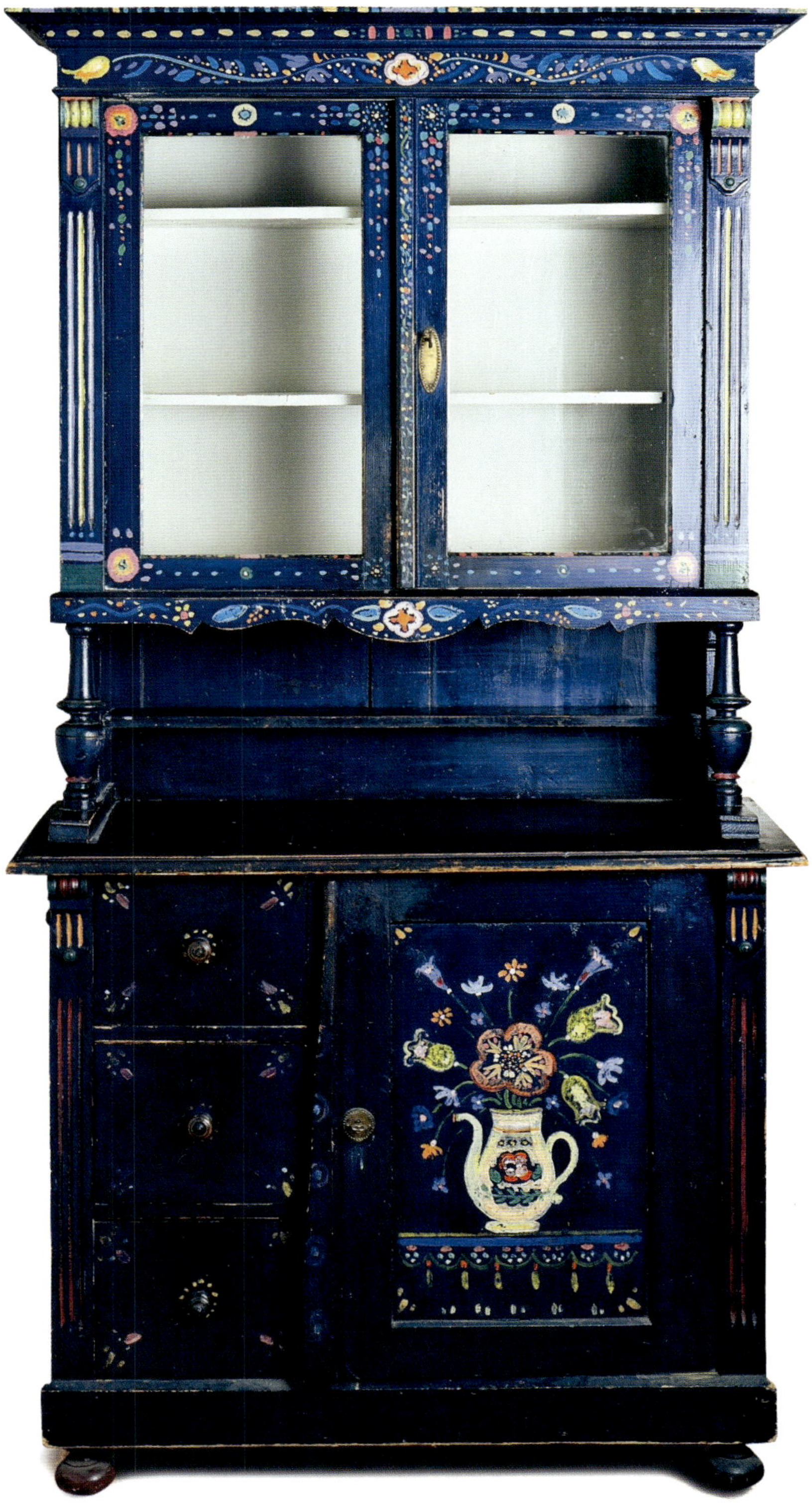

12
**Küchenschrank**
Kitchen Cupboard
c.1910
(see page 323)

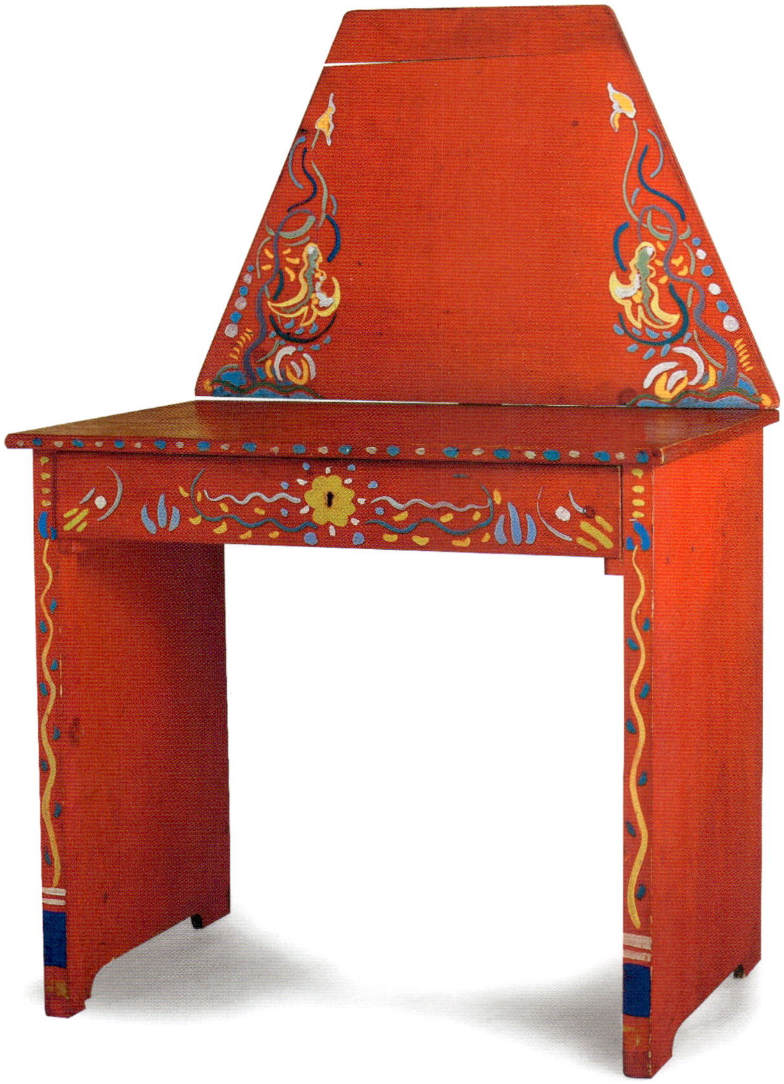

9
**Schreibtisch**
Desk
c.1910
(see page 323)

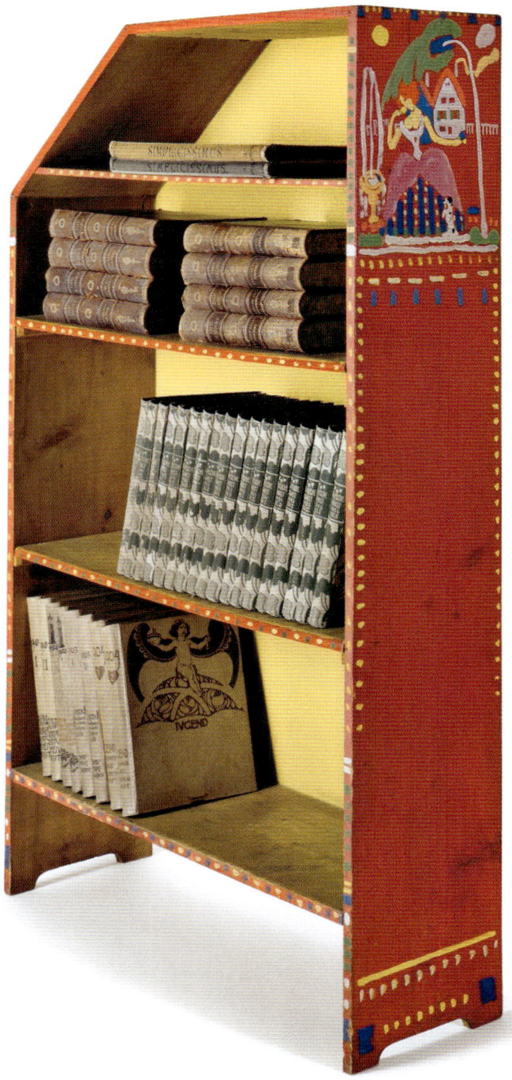

11
**Bücherregal**
Book Shelf
c.1910
(see page 323)

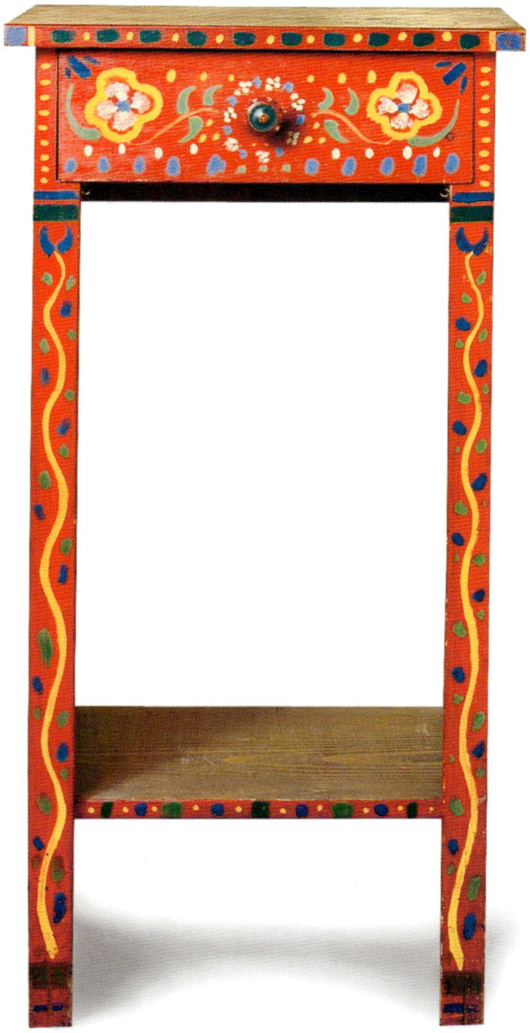

10
**Nachttisch**
Night Table
c.1910
(see page 323)

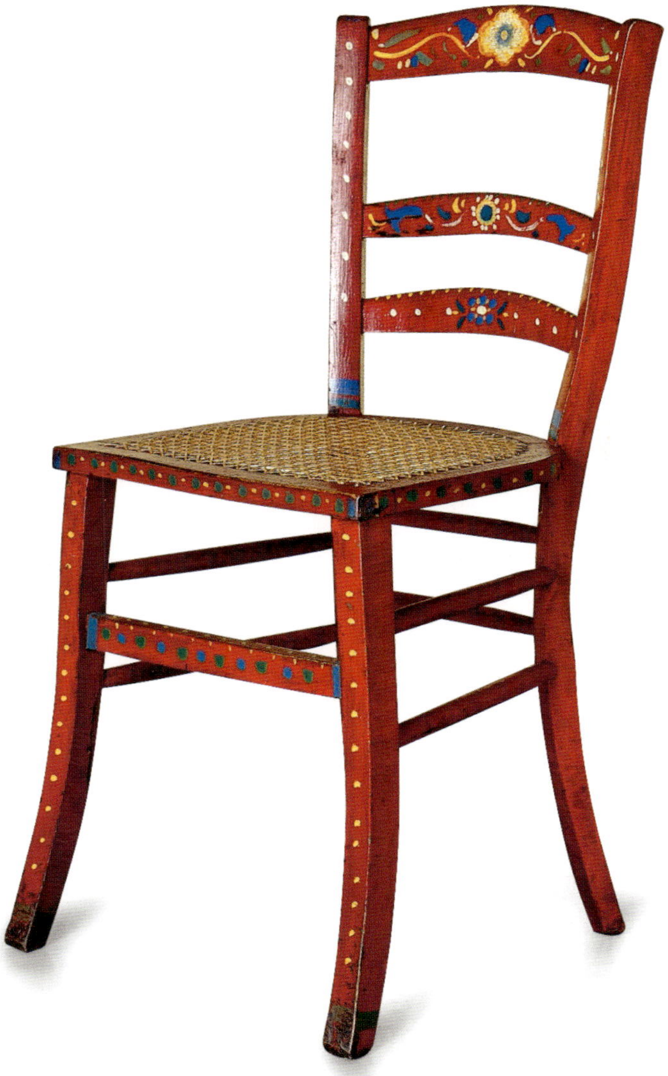

8
**Stuhl**
Chair
c.1910
(see page 322)

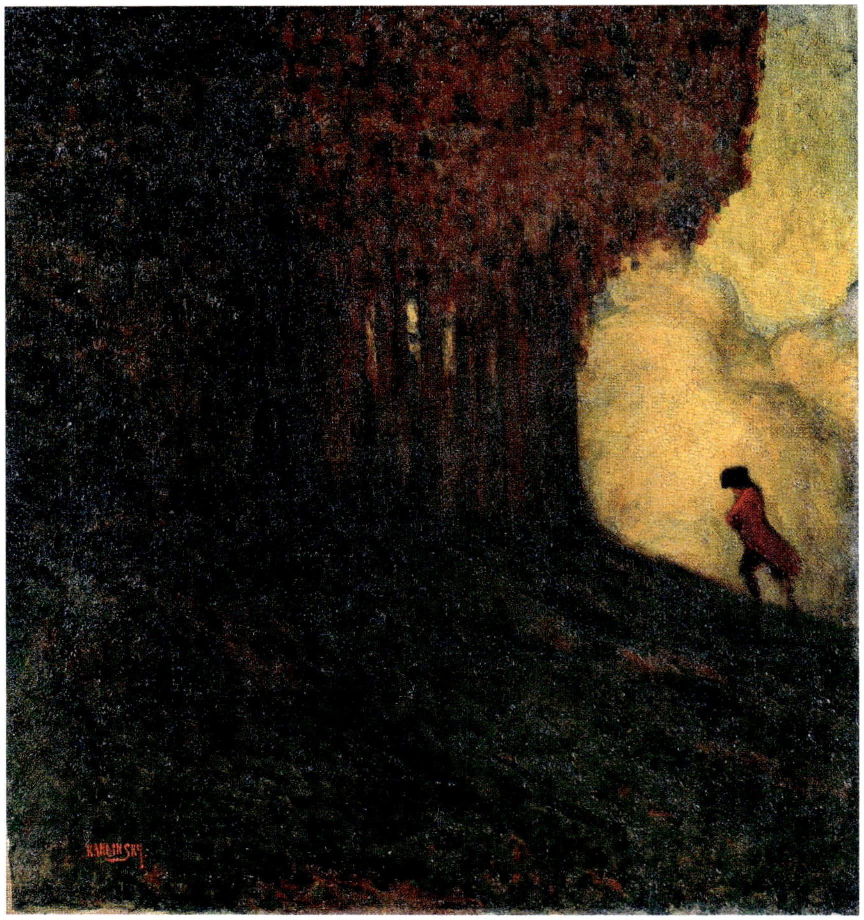

Barnett no.70
**Der rote Dichter**
The Red Poet
January 1903
(see page 325)

Barnett no. 397
**Blaugold**
Blue Gold
1915
(see page 325)

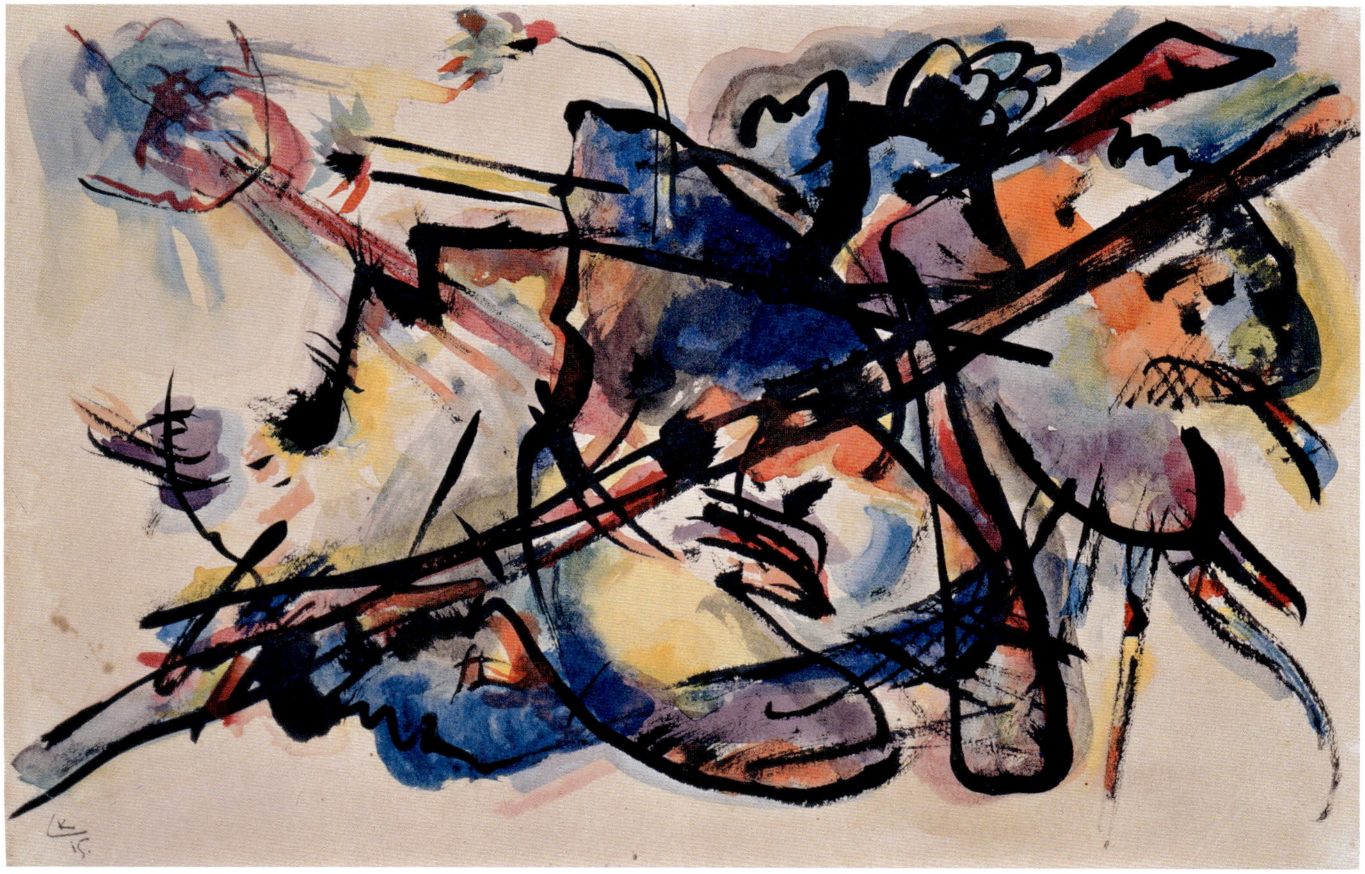

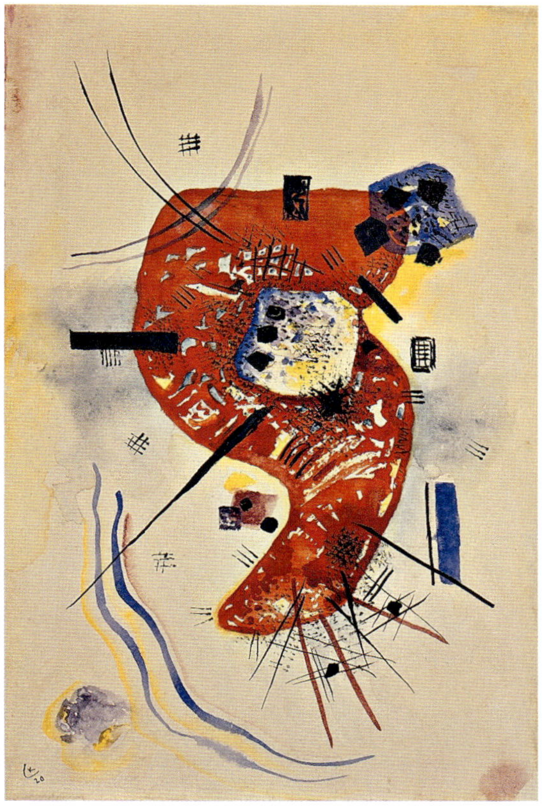

Barnett no.524
**Ohne Titel**
Untitled
1920
(see page 326)

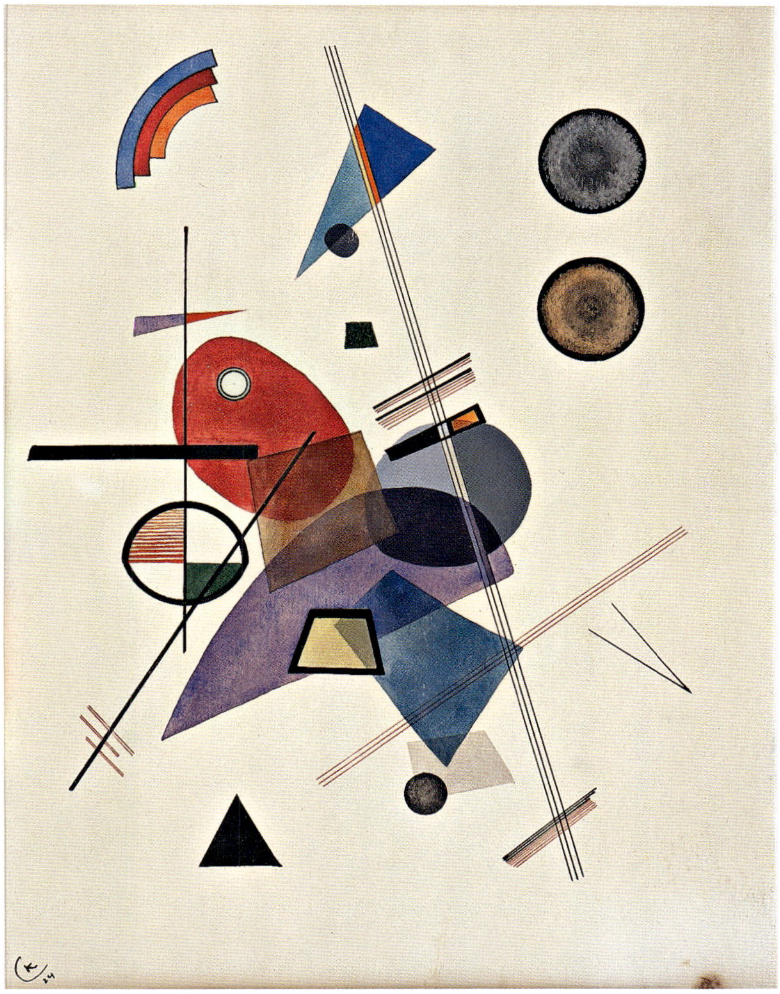

Barnett no.679
**Kühlfarbig**
Cool-Colored
February 1924
(see page 326)

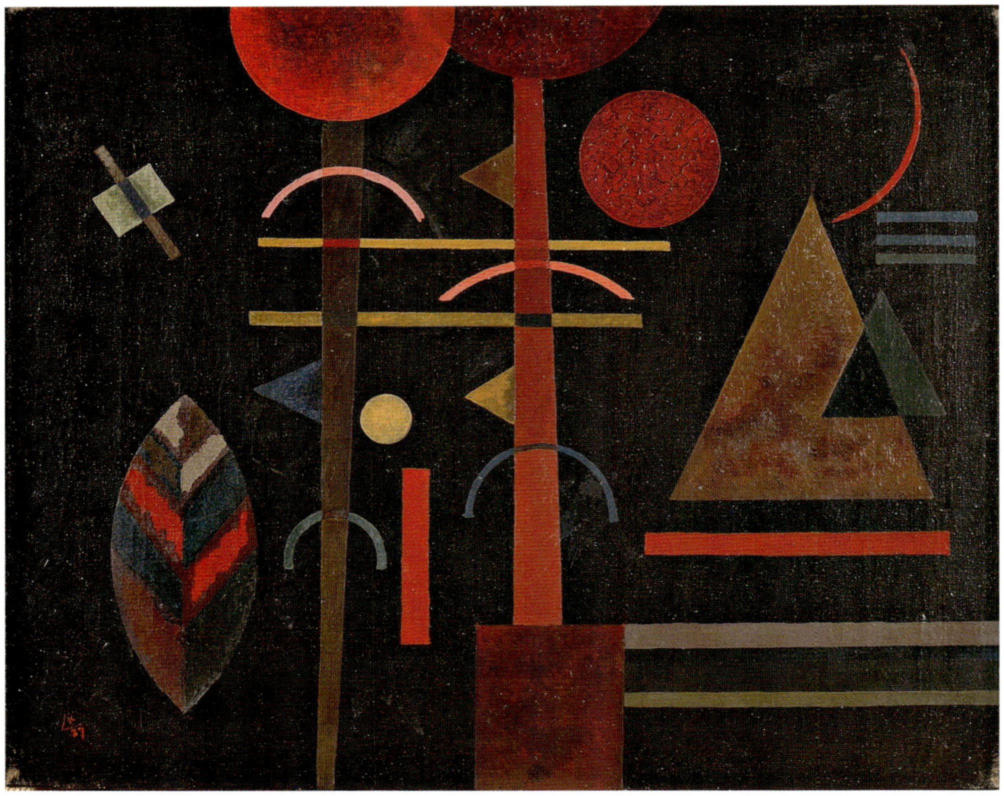


Roethel and Benjamin no.856
**Roter Kreis**
Red Circle
December 1927
(see page 326)

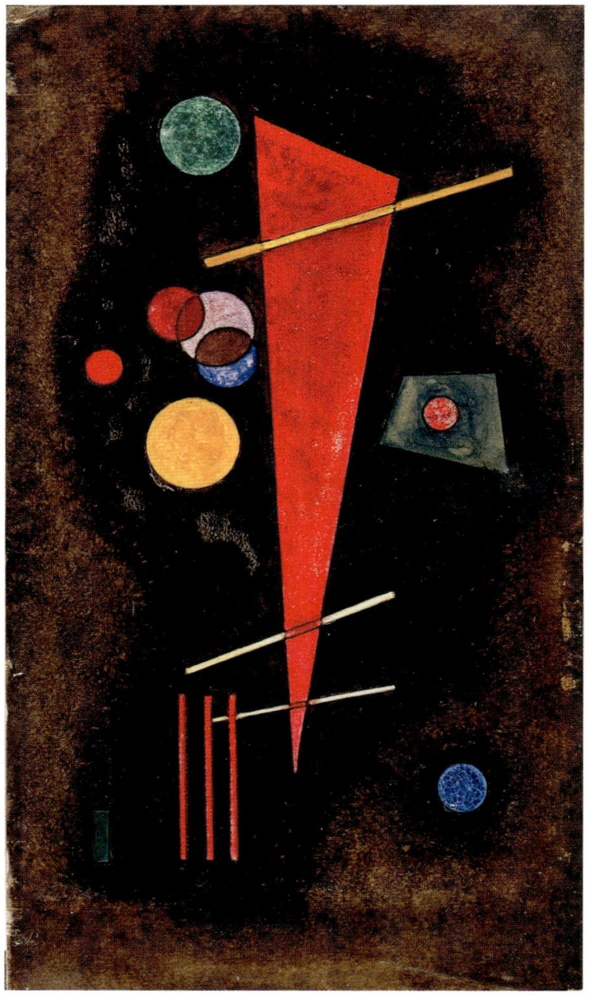

Roethel and Benjamin no.872
**Bestimmend**
Determining
1928
(see page 326)

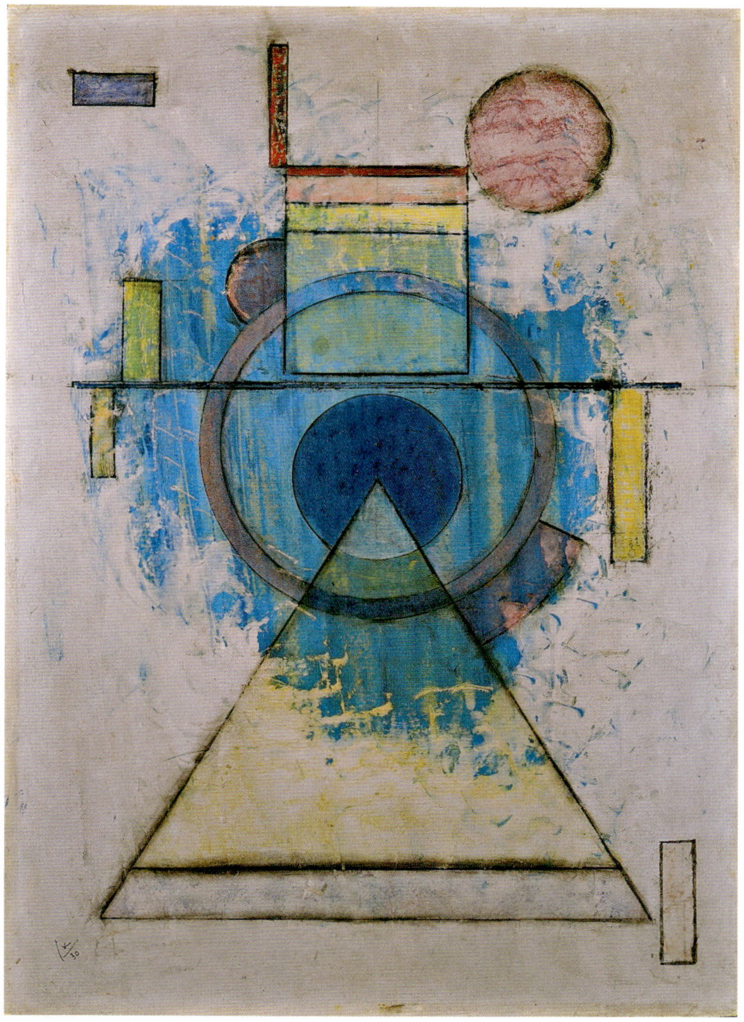

Roethel and
Benjamin no.940
**Zentral**
Central
January 1930
(see page 326)

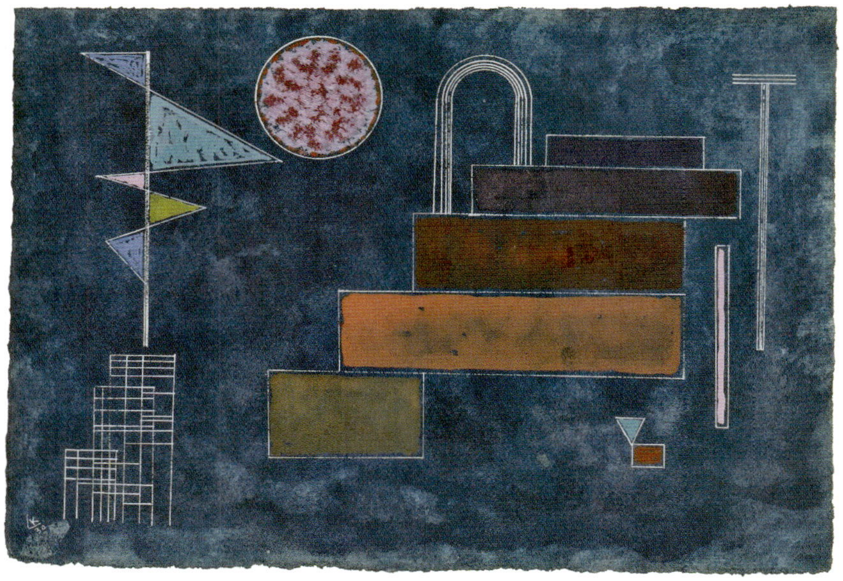

Barnett no.965
**Stufen**
Steps
March 1930
(see page 326)

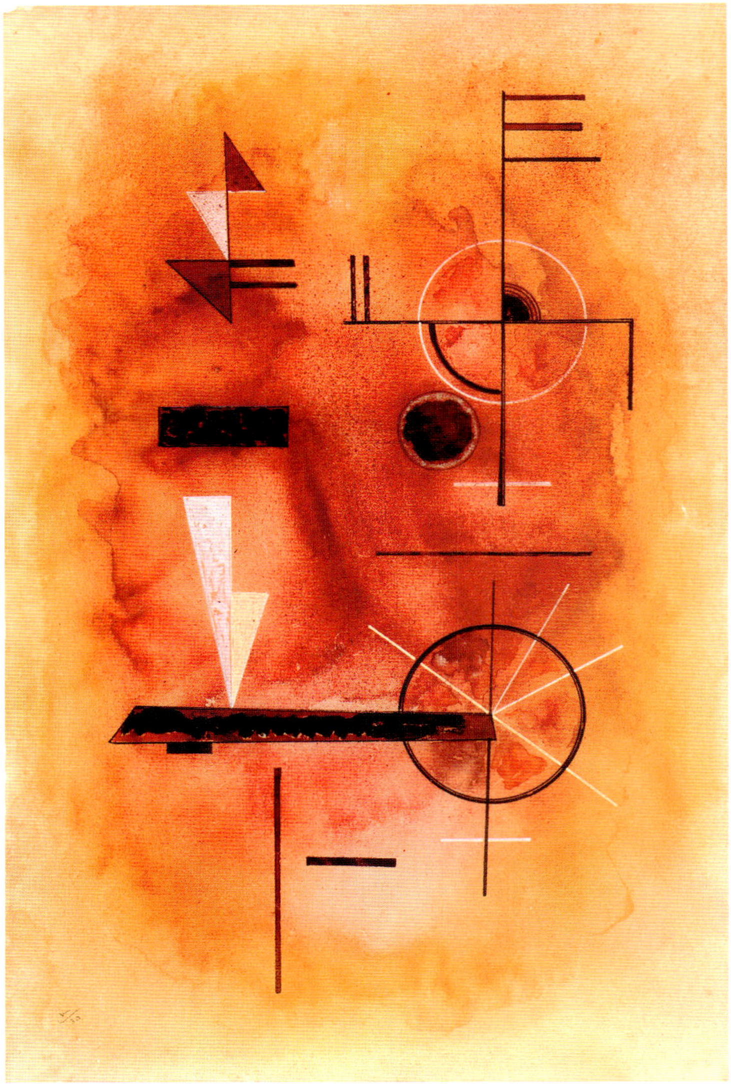

Barnett no.973
**Schimmer**
Shimmer
March 1930
(see page 327)

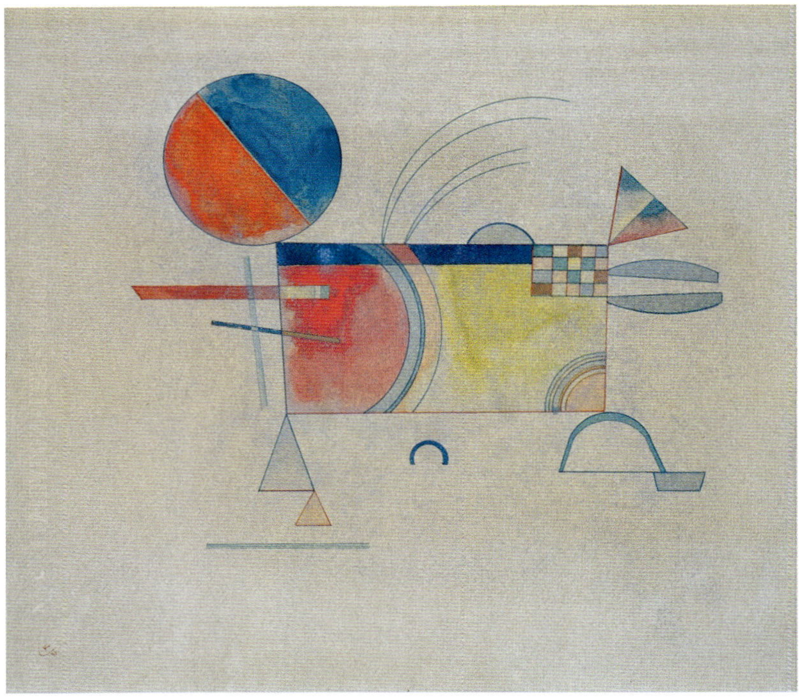

Barnett no.1054
**Geschmücktes Rechteck**
Decorated
Rectangle
July 1931
(see page 327)

Roethel and
Benjamin no.1015
**Zu vier Ecken**
Toward Four
Corners
February 1932
(see page 327)

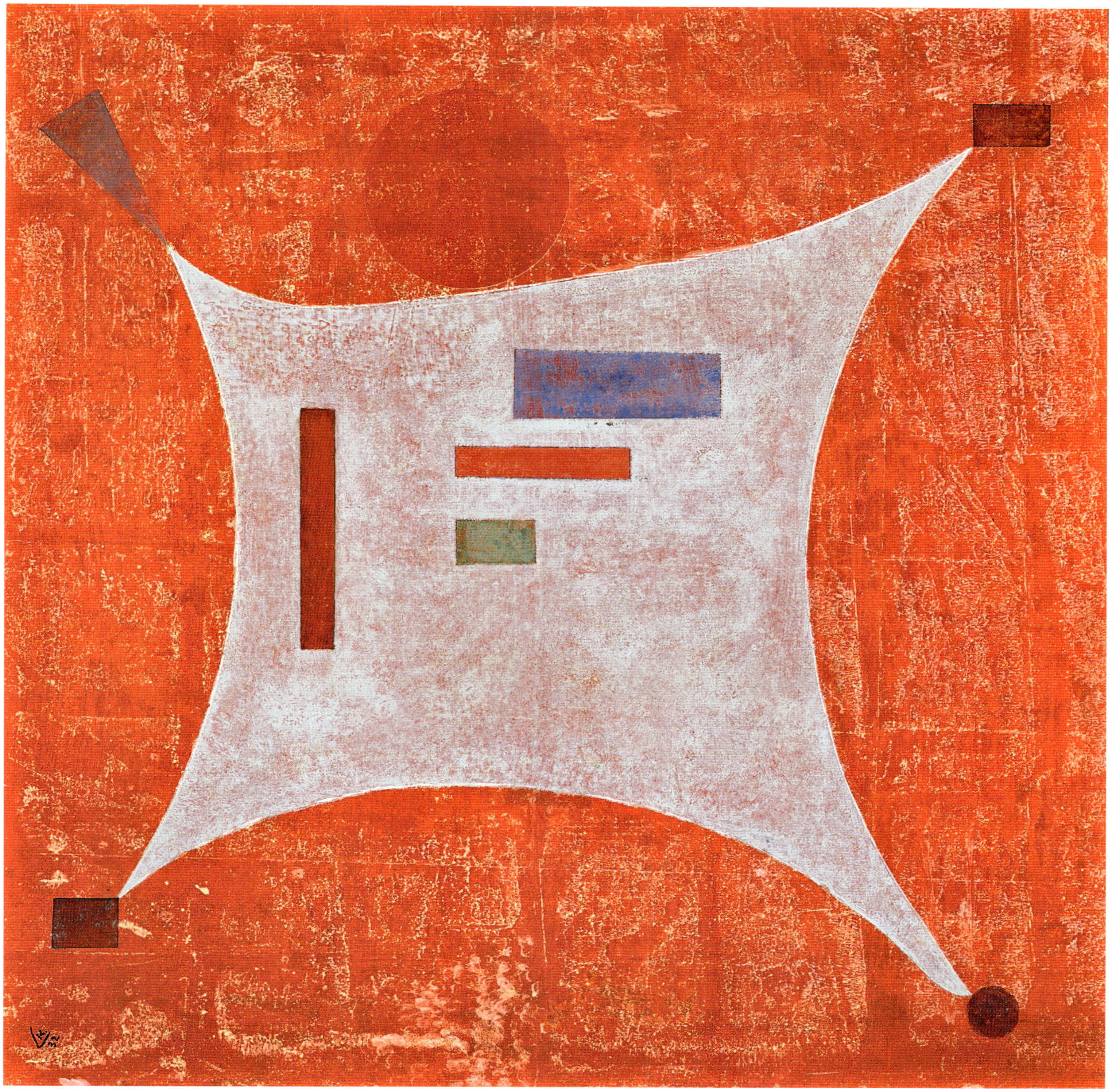

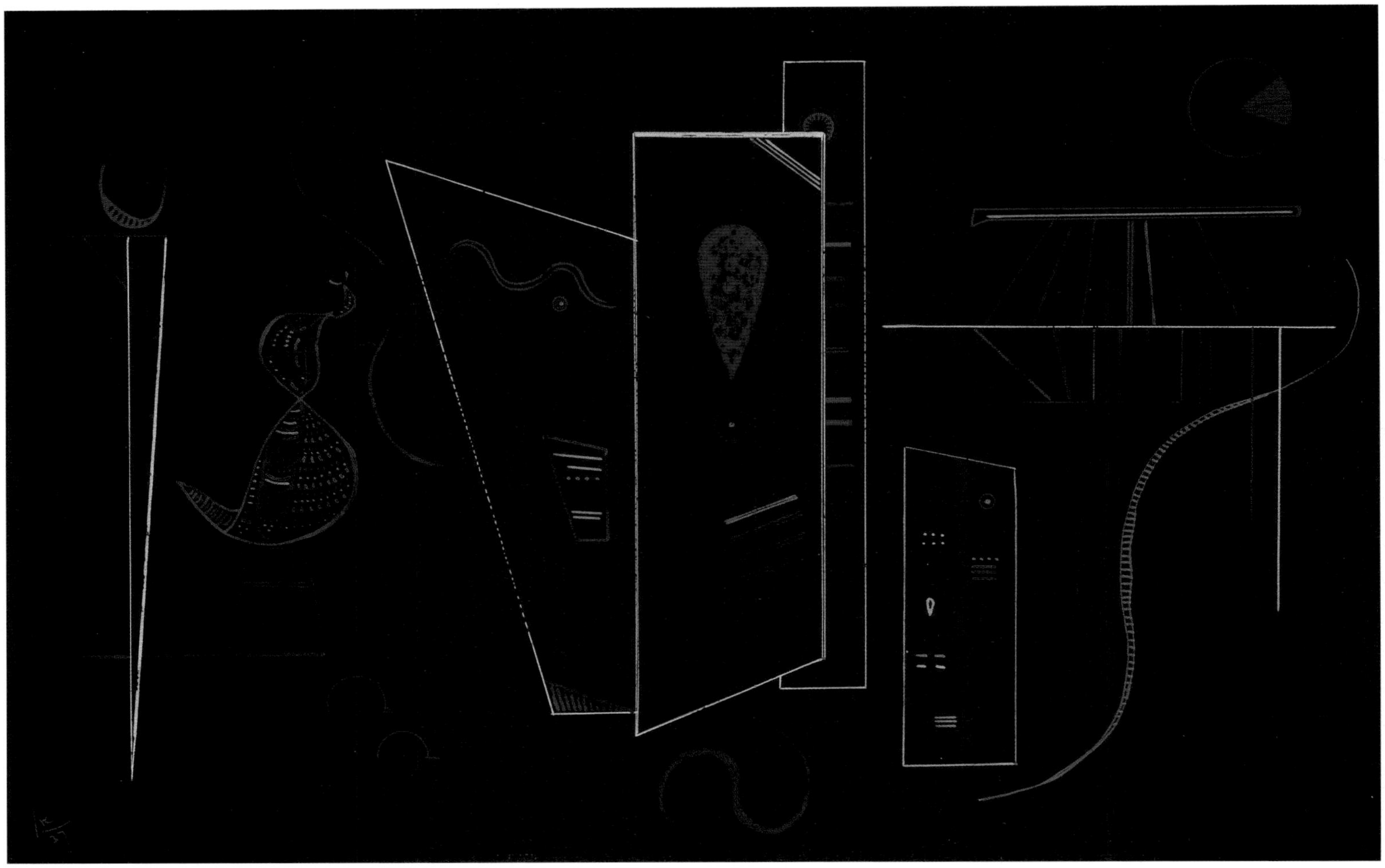

Barnett no.1211
**Oui**
Yes
October 1937
(see page 327)

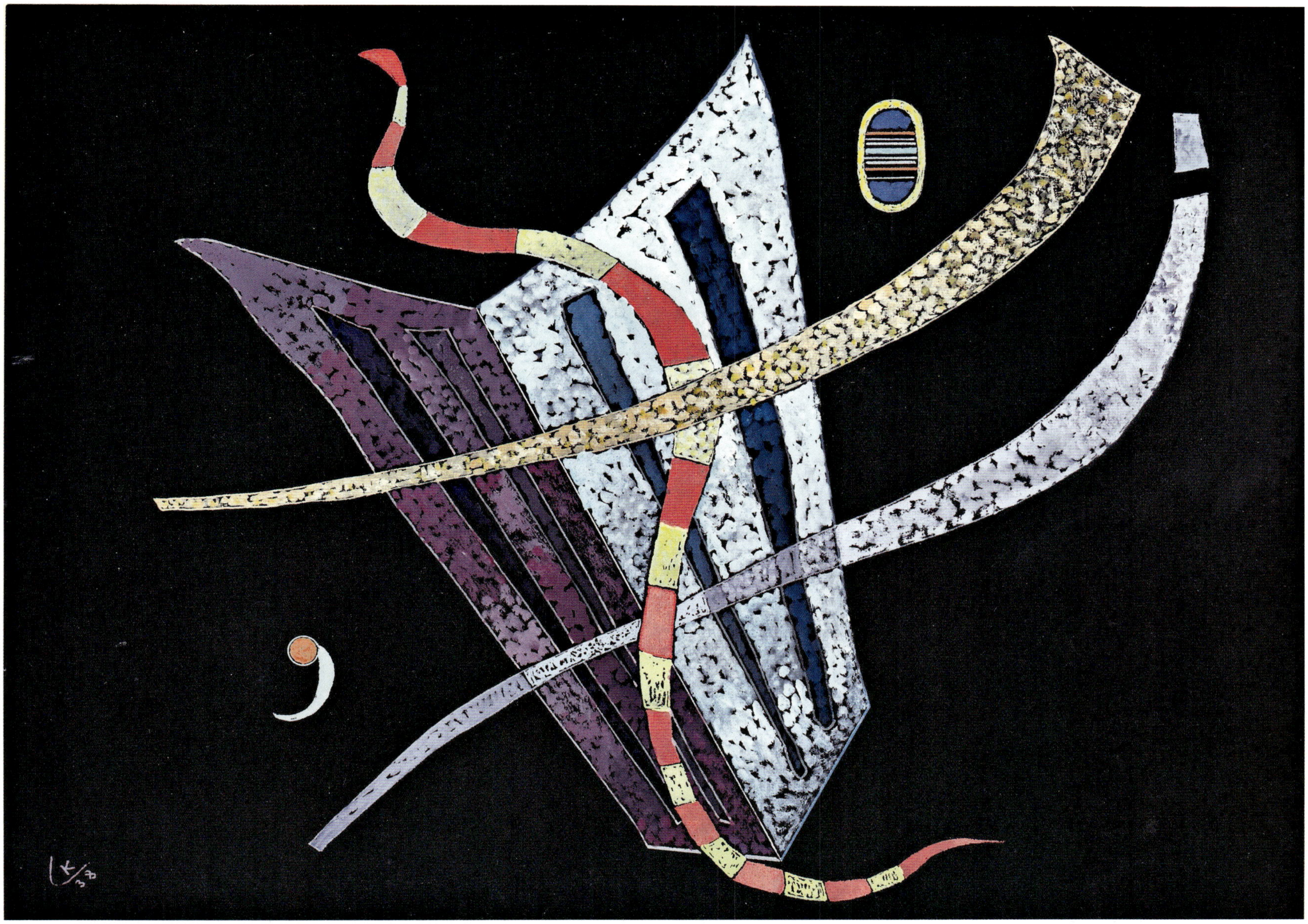

Barnett no.1242
**L'ouverture**
Opening
November 1938
(see page 327)

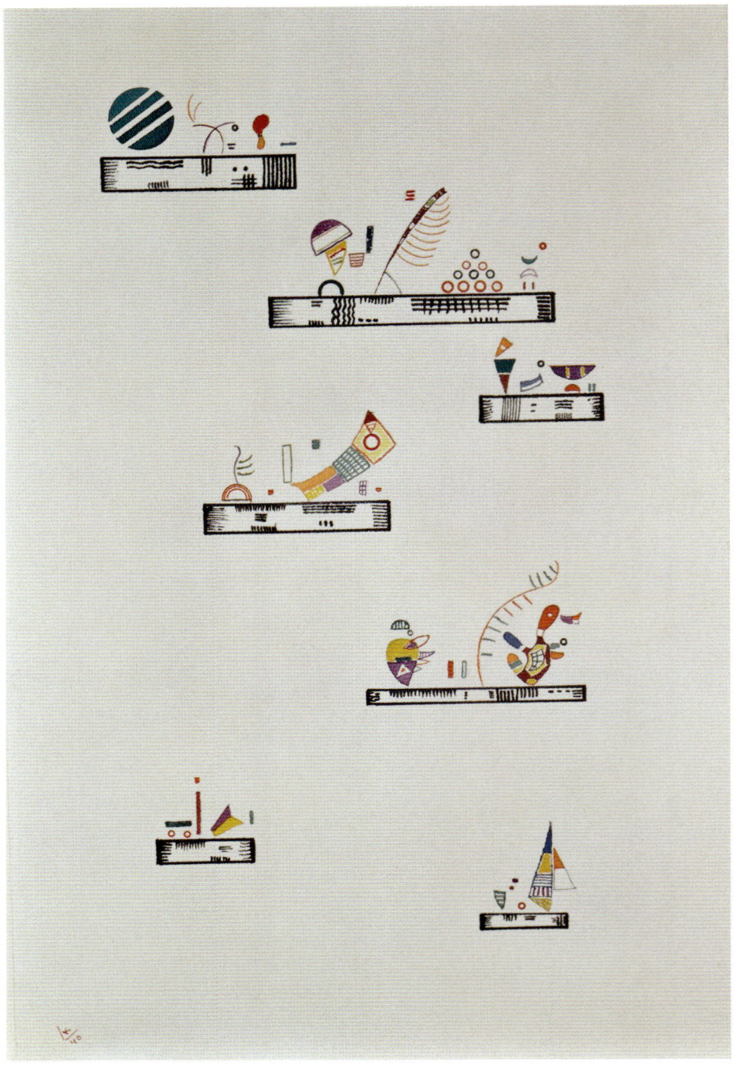

Barnett no.1285
**Sans titre**
Untitled
1940
(see page 328)

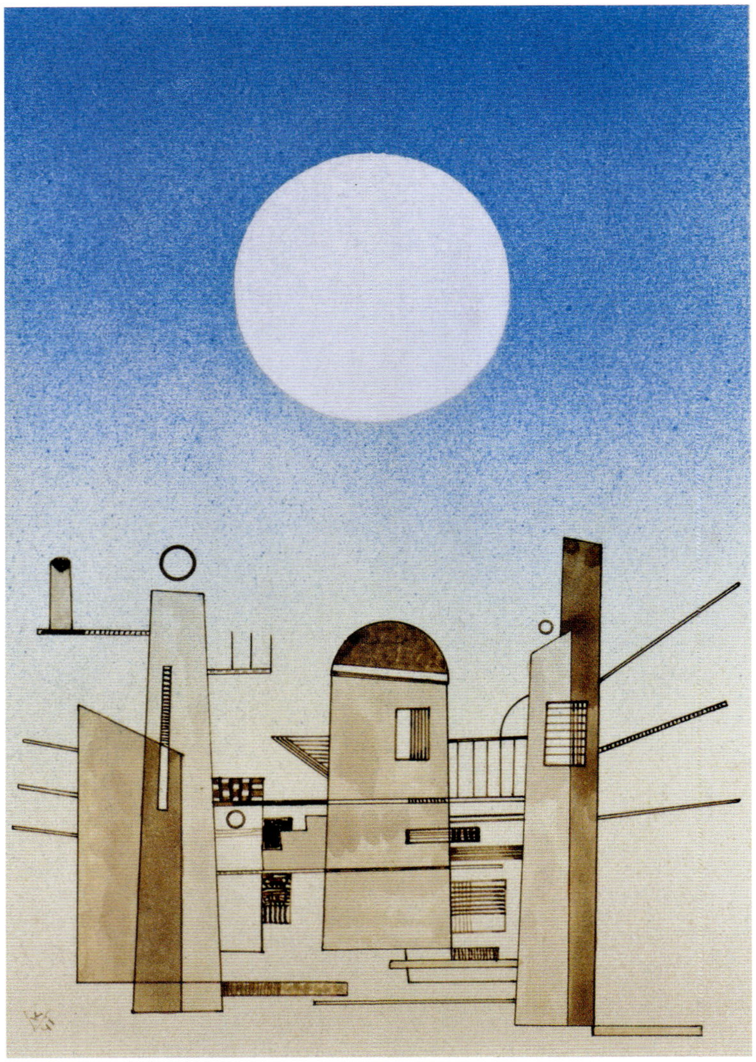

Barnett no.1352
**Sans titre**
Untitled
1941
(see page 328)

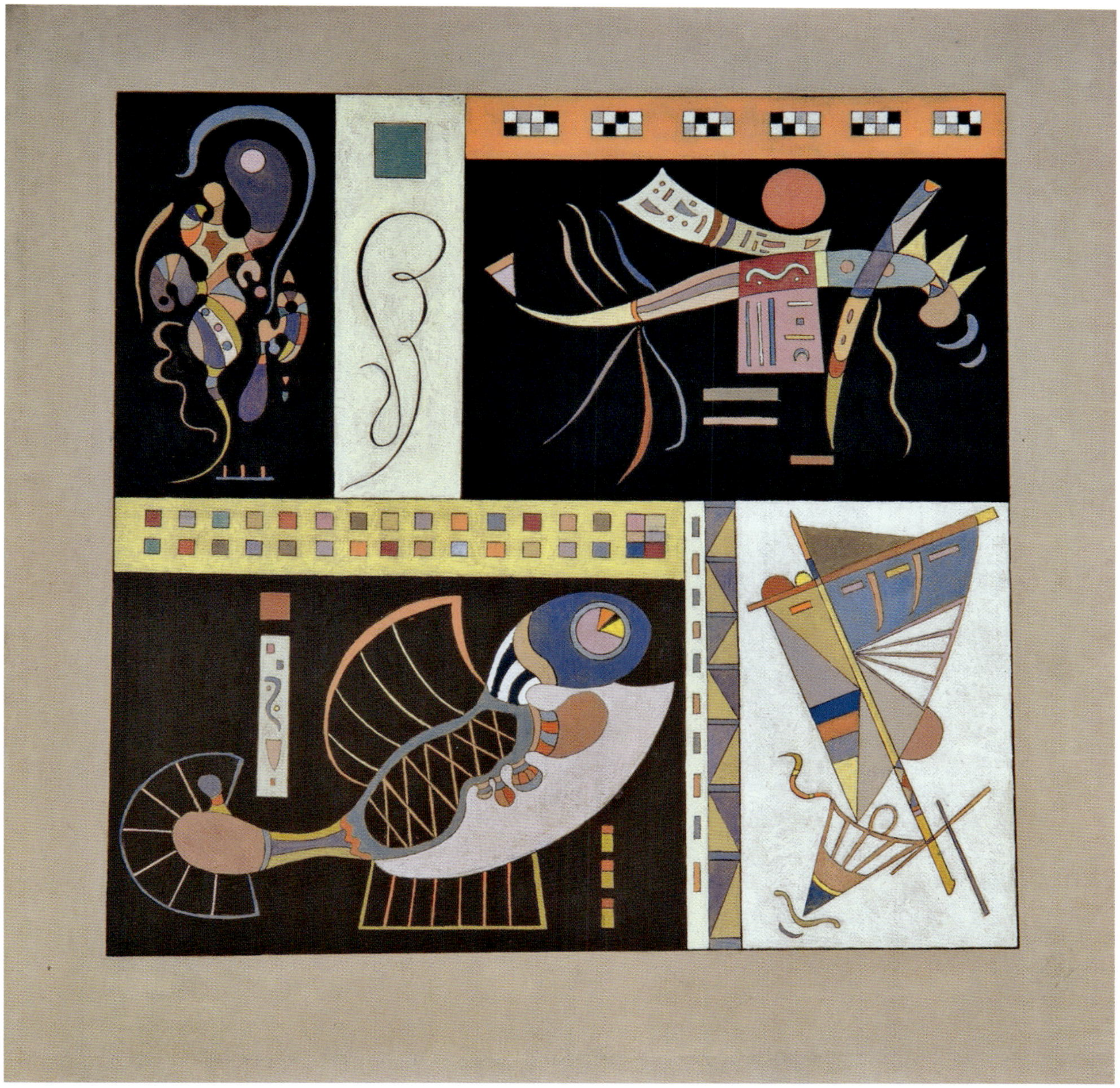

Roethel and
Benjamin no.1137
**Communauté**
Community
November 1942
(see page 328)

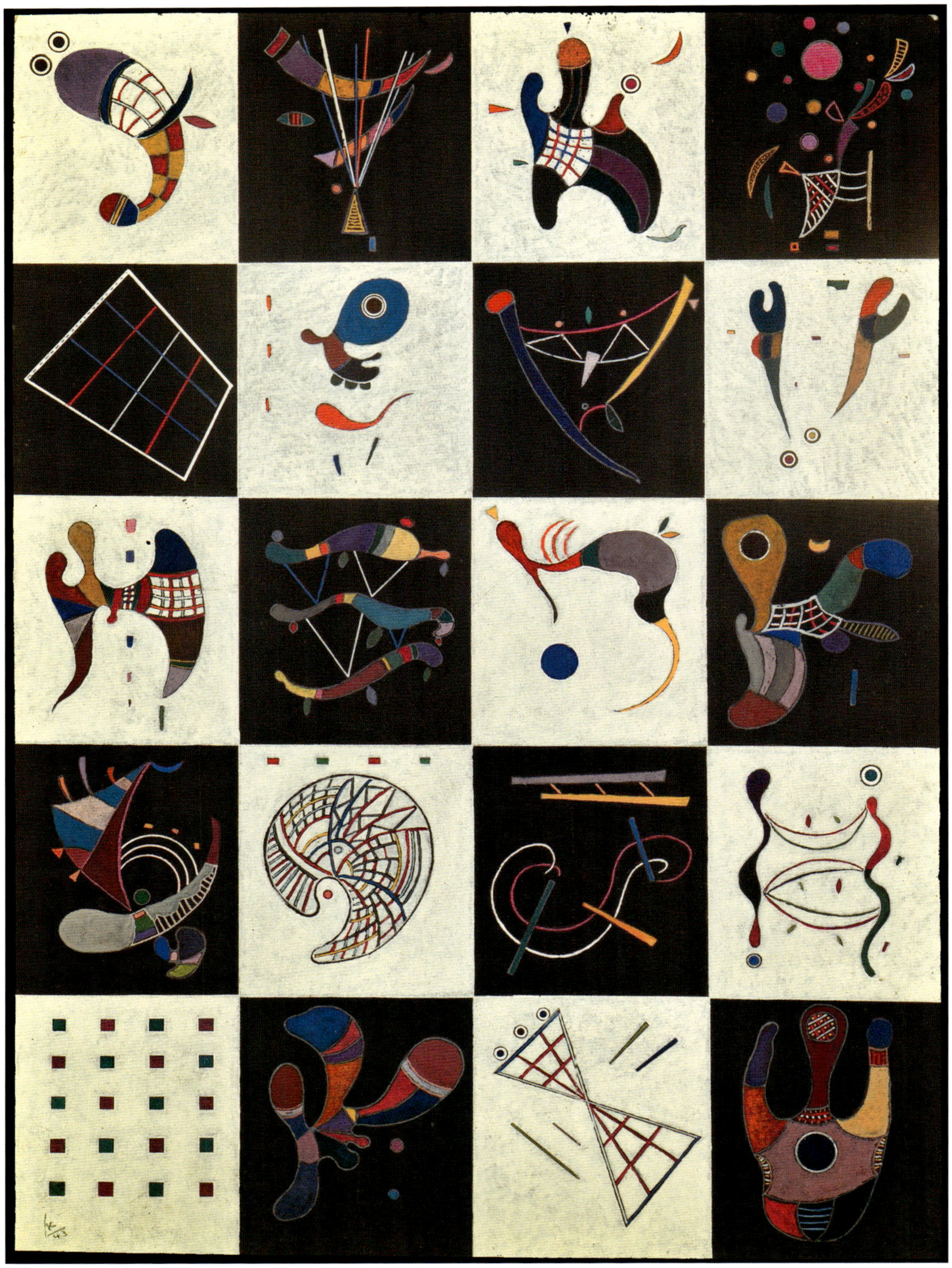

Roethel and
Benjamin no.1162
**4 x 5= 20**
July 1943
(see page 328)

# Sketchbook 28

1910–1912 and probably 1905

Tan cardboard sketchbook with black spine; no label
Contains 48 pages (24 sheets), each 34.5 x 21.8 cm ($13^{5/8}$ x $8^{5/8}$ in), of which pp.5–46 are blank
Page numbers inscribed by unknown hand at later date with odd numbers at lower right

Hanfstaengl 1974, p.169

LOCATION
Städtische Galerie im Lenbachhaus, Munich (GMS 639)

HISTORY
Gabriele Münter, Murnau, until 1957

The sketchbook is considerably larger than most of the ones Kandinsky used from 1897 to 1914 in Munich, although the size is similar to that of Sketchbook 3, in which he made drawings in 1897–1900 and again in 1909–1911. Likewise, Kandinsky appears to have made the studies on p.47 at an earlier date than his three other drawings in this sketchbook. There is a Neumuhle watermark on the heavy tan sheets of paper.

28, p.1

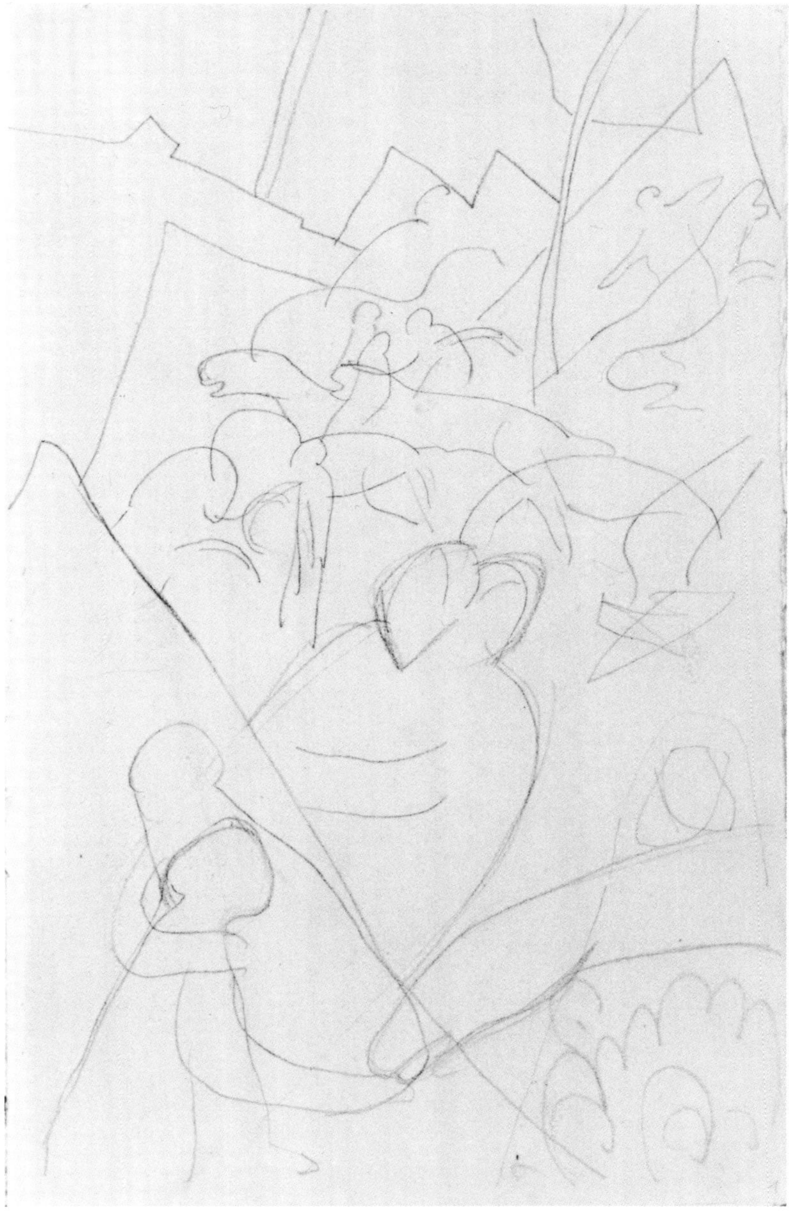

**p.1** Pencil drawing of horses and riders with foreground figures

REFERENCES
Hanfstaengl 1974, p.169, ill.

The drawing is related to *Komposition I* of 1910 (Roethel and Benjamin no.327).

**p.2** Blank

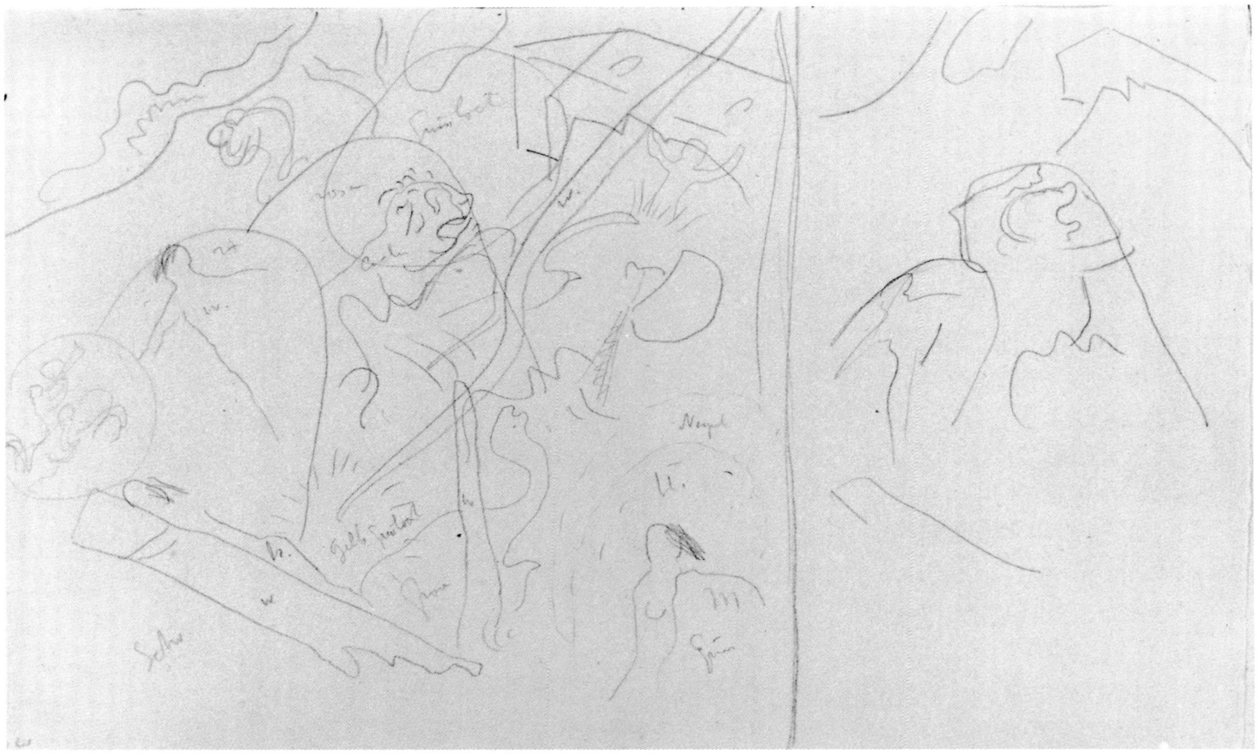

28, p.3

28, p.4

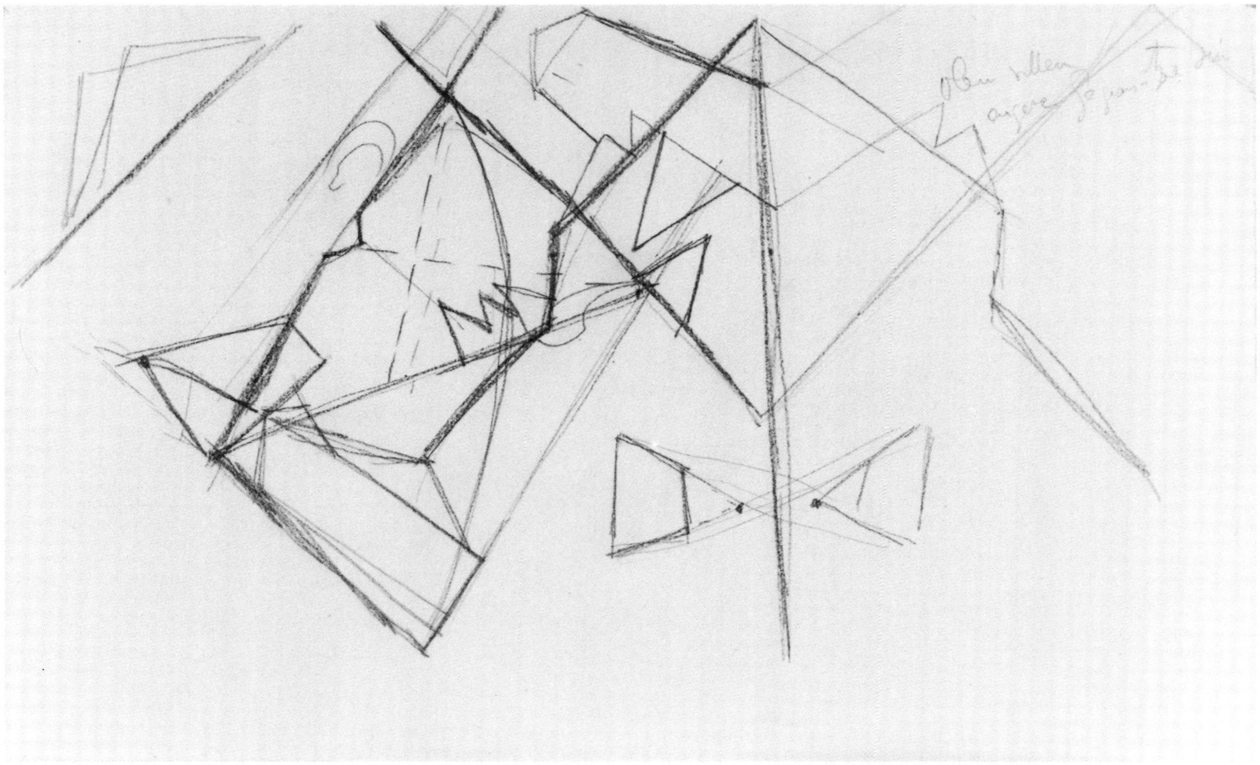

**p.3** Pencil drawing for *Sintflut* of 1912
Inscribed u.c.: 'Grünlich / rosa / cadm. / w.'; c.l.: 'rt / w.'; c.r.: 'Neapel / bl'; l.c.: 'br. / Gelb Grünlich / Grau'; l.l.: 'Sch. / w'; l.r.: 'Grün'

REFERENCES
Ringbom 1970, pp.155–156, fig.57
Hanfstaengl 1974, p.169, ill.
Washton Long 1980, pp.94, 178 n.35, fig.95
Roethel and Benjamin 1982, p.430
Barnett and Friedel 1995, no.465, color ill.
Barnett 2006, p.111

The study is related to *Sintflut I* of 22 March 1912 and a study for it (Roethel and Benjamin nos.433, 440). In addition, Kandinsky made a glass painting on the theme of the deluge in 1911 (Roethel and Benjamin no.425), which was later of crucial importance in the development of *Komposition VI* over the following two years. The motif of the female nude can be found in a drawing (vol.I, cat. no.224) as well as the glass painting; moreover, the images at the right of this sheet resemble those in the glass painting *Sintflut (zu Komposition VI)*.

**p.4** Pencil schematic drawing related to *Sintflut 1*
Inscribed u.r.: 'Oben sollen / engere Gegensätze sein'

REFERENCES
Hanfstaengl 1974, p.169, ill.
Washton Long 1980, p.178 n.26, fig.96
Roethel and Benjamin 1982, p.430

This schematic drawing is also related to *Sintflut I* of 22 March 1912 (see p.3 above).

**pp.5–46** Blank

**p.47** (upside down) Pencil study of Madonna and Child with two angels (6 x 6 cm) and sketches of angel, hands and feet

REFERENCES
Hanfstaengl 1974, p.169
Washton Long 1980 pp.102, 179 n.60, fig.117

Hanfstaengl suggested a date of c.1902, referring to Kandinsky's tempera painting *Drei Kirchenfenster* and *Entwurf für Wandmalerei* of 1905 (Barnett nos.57, 198). The drawing resembles his *Entwurf für Wandmalerei (Madonna)* of September 1905, and suggests Italian paintings in general. The angels standing on orbs bring to mind those in the vaults of the sanctuary in San Vitale, Ravenna (kindly brought to my attention by Lois Drewer).

**p.48** Blank

**p.49** Pencil drawing of mother and child on torn sheet of white paper (22 x 20 cm) pasted onto back cover of sketchbook
Inscribed above by Erika Hanfstaengl: 'Zuliegend: / 4 Blatt Kohlepapier mit / "Zchgen" / 1 Blatt mit Skizze von / Mutter u. Kind'

The drawing was done by Gabriele Münter and originally belonged in one of her sketchbooks (37/12) among several studies of the same woman and young boy.

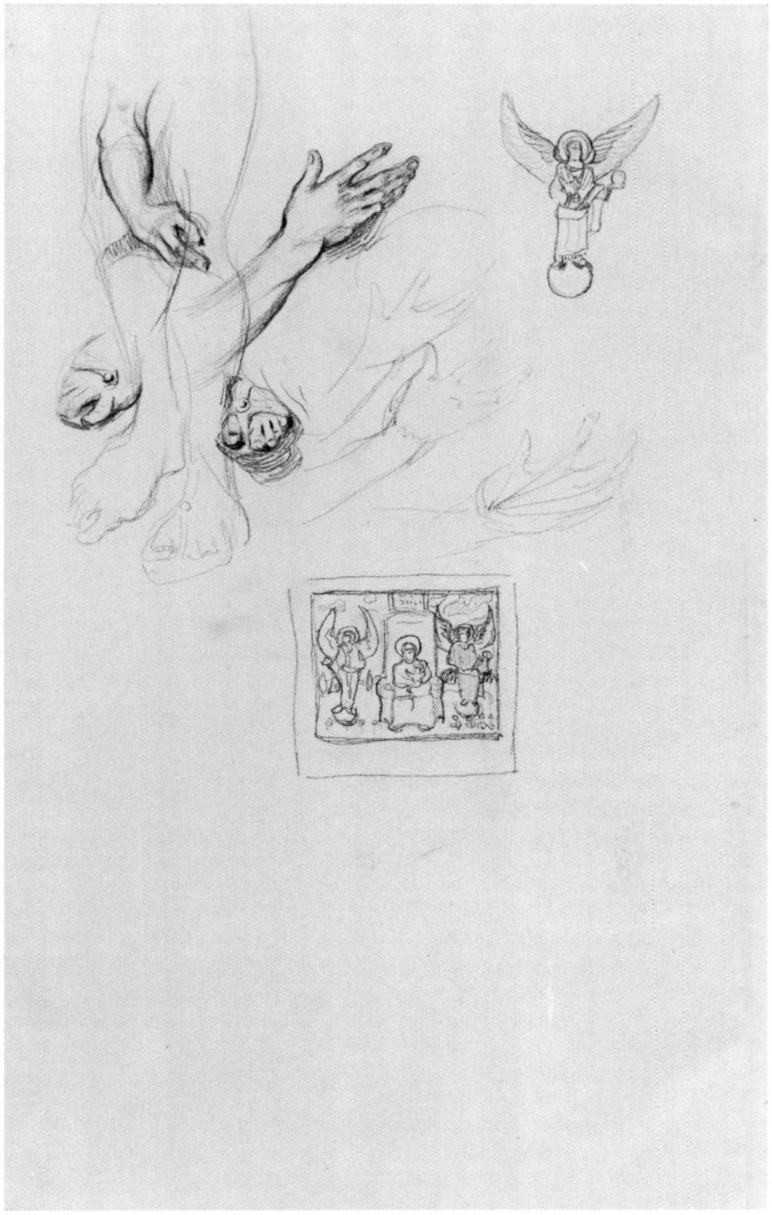

28, p.47

# Sketchbook 29

1913–1914

Faded purple paper notebook; on front cover black-bordered white label
Contains 32 pages (16 sheets), each 20.7 x 16.4 cm (8 1/8 x 6 1/2 in), of which pp.14–32 are blank
Page numbers inscribed at later date with odd numbers at lower right

Hanfstaengl 1974, p.140

LOCATION
Städtische Galerie im Lenbachhaus, Munich (GMS 323)

HISTORY
Gabriele Münter, Murnau, until 1957

It is not known where Kandinsky purchased this notebook, which Erika Hanfstaengl identified as an exercise book ('Schulheft'). Although certain pages bear specific dates in June–July 1914, the other landscape drawings may have been done the previous year. Most of the sketches cannot be considered studies for extant works.

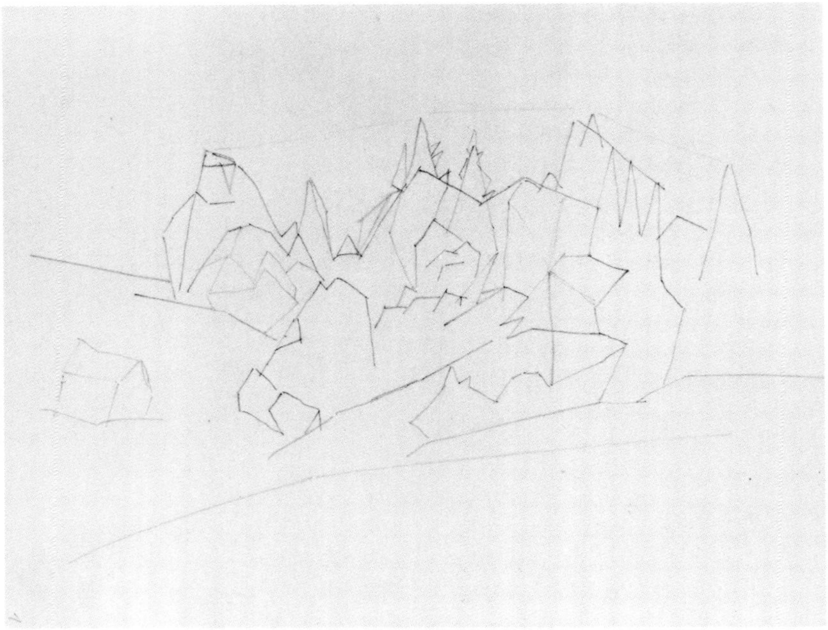

29, p.1

**p.1** Pencil drawing of landscape

REFERENCES
Hanfstaengl 1974, p.140, ill.

Kandinsky probably made the landscape drawings near Murnau. Hanfstaengl suggested that they relate to *Landschaft mit Regen* and *Landschaft mit roten Flecken* I and II of 1913 (Roethel and Benjamin nos.458–460), but they also evoke earlier Murnau landscapes such as *Winter II* of January 1911 (Roethel and Benjamin no.380).

**p.2** Blank

**p.3** Pencil drawing of landscape

REFERENCES
Hanfstaengl 1974, p.140, ill.

The jagged lines and simplified shapes resemble those on pp.1 and 7 of this sketchbook.

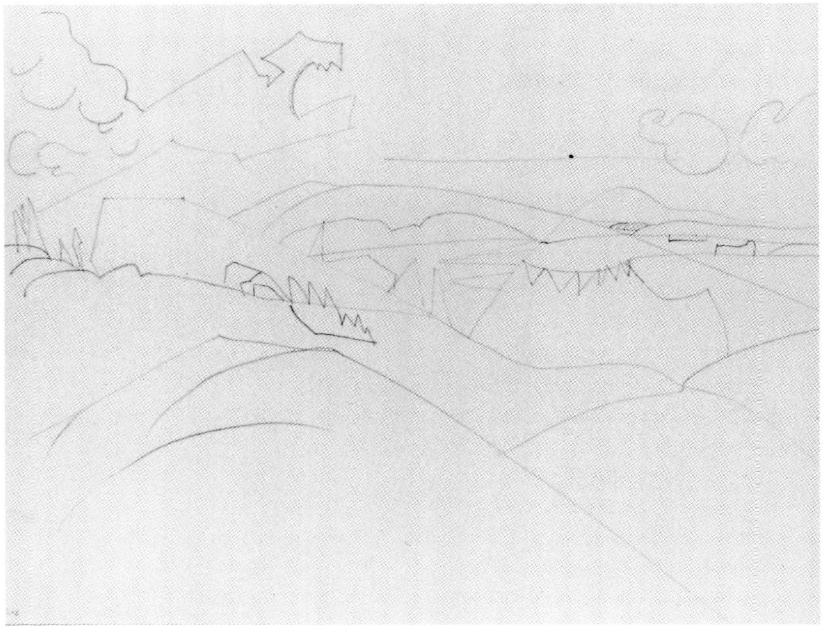

29, p.3

**p.4** Blank

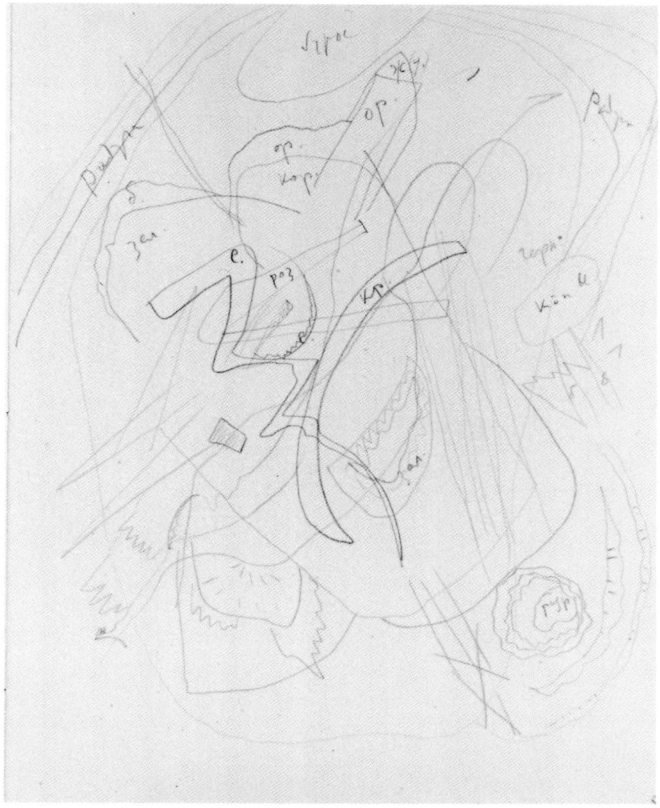

29, p.5

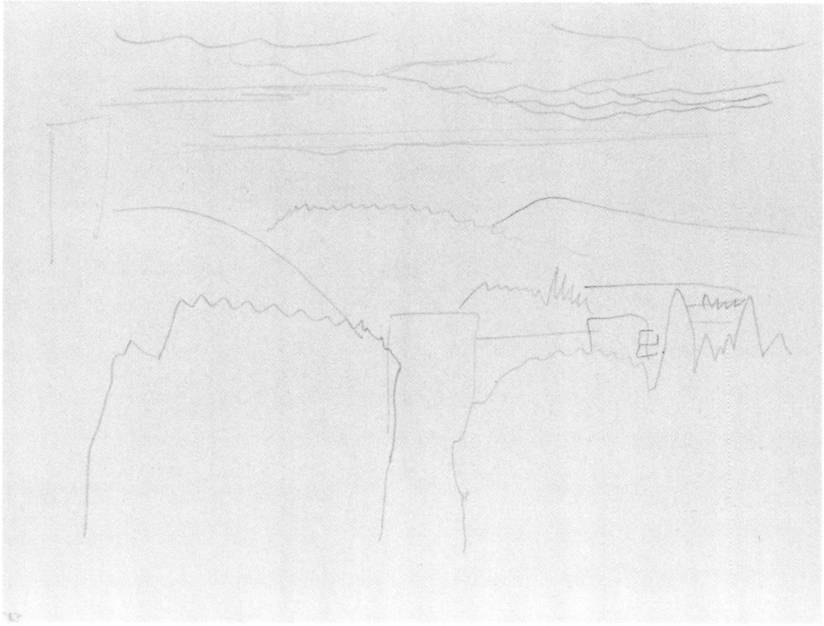

29, p.7

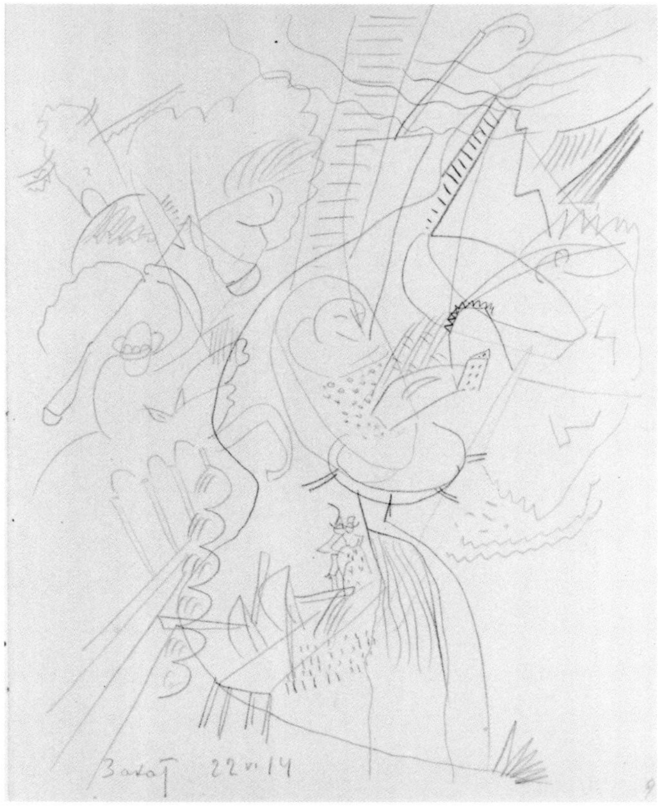

29, p.9

**p.5** Pencil drawing
Inscribed u.l. in Cyrillic: 'raduga'; l.r.: 'razriad'; u.r.: 'raduga'; and with color notations: 'buroe / zh / or / kor. / roz / kr / zel. / chern.'

REFERENCES
Hanfstaengl 1974, p.140, ill.

Kandinsky indicated rainbows at the upper-left and upper-right corners. In 1913–1914 he made studies for presumably unexecuted works with a rainbow, *Entwurf zu 'Mit Wald und Regenbogen'* (vol.I, cat. no.331 and Barnett nos.368–369) and *Mit Regenbogen links* (vol.I, cat. nos.341–343).

**p.6** Blank

**p.7** Pencil drawing of landscape

REFERENCES
Hanfstaengl 1974, p.140, ill.

**p.8** Blank

**p.9** Pencil study for *Improvisation Klamm* of July 1914
Inscribed l.l. in Cyrillic: 'Zakat' and dated '22 VI 14'

REFERENCES
Hans K. Roethel, 'Kandinsky: Improvisation Klamm. Vorstufen einer Deutung' in *Eberhard Hanfstaengl zum 75. Geburtstag* (Munich, 1961), pp.186, 188, ill.7, 191
Hanfstaengl 1974, p.140, ill.
Roethel and Benjamin 1979, p.109, ill.117
Washton Long 1980, pp.128, 185 n.29, fig.180
Roethel and Benjamin 1982, p.508
Hahl-Koch 1993, p.246, ill.291
Hoberg 1994, p.150, ill.78
Barnett and Friedel 1995, no.589, color ill.
Weiss 1995, pp.124, 125 n.24

Kandinsky inscribed this drawing 'sunset'. It is one of several studies for *Improvisation Klamm* (Roethel and Benjamin no.503), which was painted soon after he and Gabriele Münter went to the Höllentalklamm near Garmisch.

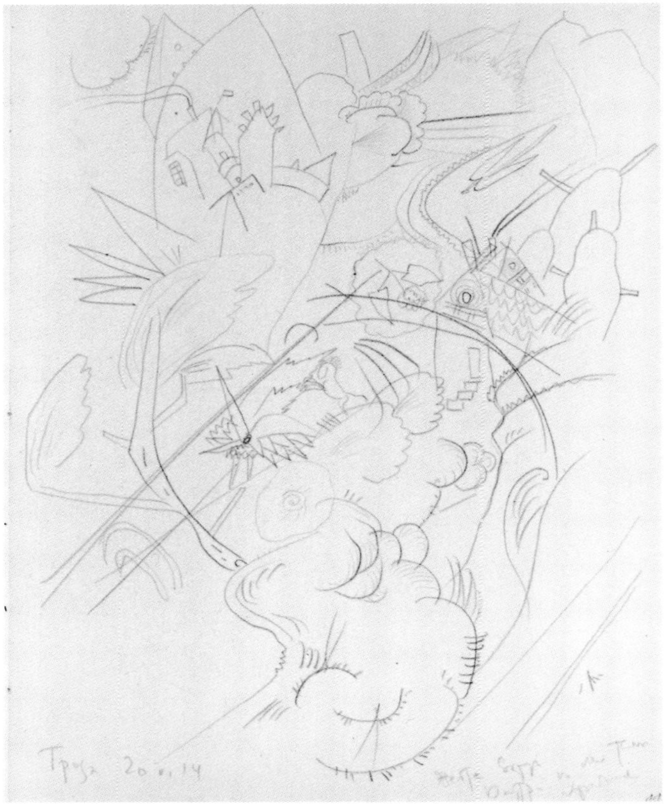

29, p.11

**p.10** Blank

**p.11** Pencil sketch
Inscribed l.l. in Cyrillic: 'Groza' and dated '20 VI 14'; l.r.: 'Zhelta vokrug / vniutri po oblakom temno / […]'

REFERENCES
Hanfstaengl 1974, p.140, ill.
Barnett and Friedel 1995, no.588, color ill.

This drawing is inscribed 'thunderstorm' and dated two days earlier than that on the preceding page. At the lower right Kandinsky noted: 'inside along the clouds dark'.

**p.12** Blank

**p.13** Pencil sketch
Inscribed l.l. in Cyrillic: 'Sumerki' and dated '12 VII 14'; l.r.: 'Sprava beloe / sleva sinee / + zelenoe'

REFERENCES
Hanfstaengl 1974, p.140, ill.
Barnett and Friedel 1995, no.591, color ill.

Kandinsky wrote 'dusk' at the lower left and 'white on the right and blue-green on the left' at the lower right of this drawing dated 12 July 1914.

**pp.14–32** Blank

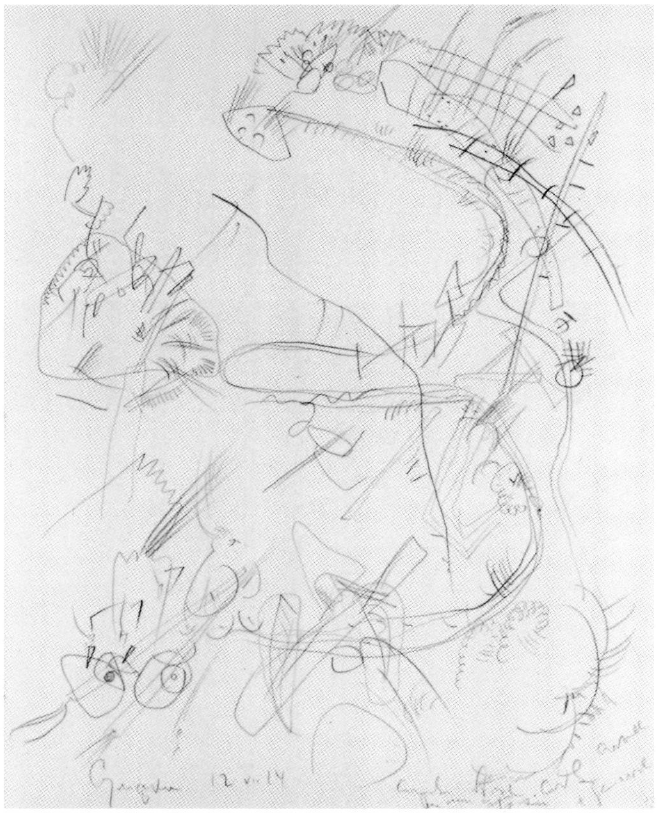

29, p.13

# Sketchbook 30

1915

Pale blue paper sketchbook with three-staple binding; on front cover label from Mur and Meriliz, Moscow, which the artist dated 'XI 15'
Contains 8 sheets, each 25.4 x 34.4 cm (10 x 13½ in), of which some sheets are partially detached from the stapled binding
Pages have not been numbered

Derouet and Boissel 1984, no.184

LOCATION
Musée National d'Art Moderne, Centre Georges Pompidou, Paris (AM 1981.65.672)

HISTORY
Nina Kandinsky, Paris, until 1980

Kandinsky dated the sketchbook November 1915. Other sheets which may have come from this sketchbook include cat. nos.375–378 in Volume I of *Kandinsky Drawings*. There is also another sketchbook with an identical label from Mur and Meriliz that Kandinsky dated spring 1916 (vol.I, cat. nos.403–409).

**p.1** India ink, wash and pencil study

EXHIBITIONS
2001 Strasbourg, p.81, color ill.

REFERENCES
Derouet and Boissel 1984, p.171, ill.
Barnett 1992, p.368
Barnett 2006, pp.190, 192

The drawing is related to another sheet dated 13 November 1915, which was originally part of this sketchbook (vol. I, cat. no.375) as well as a coeval watercolor (Barnett no.420) and a watercolor study for *Trübe* dated 1917 (Barnett no.478). Kandinsky's canvas *Trübe* was painted in September 1917 (Roethel and Benjamin no.615).

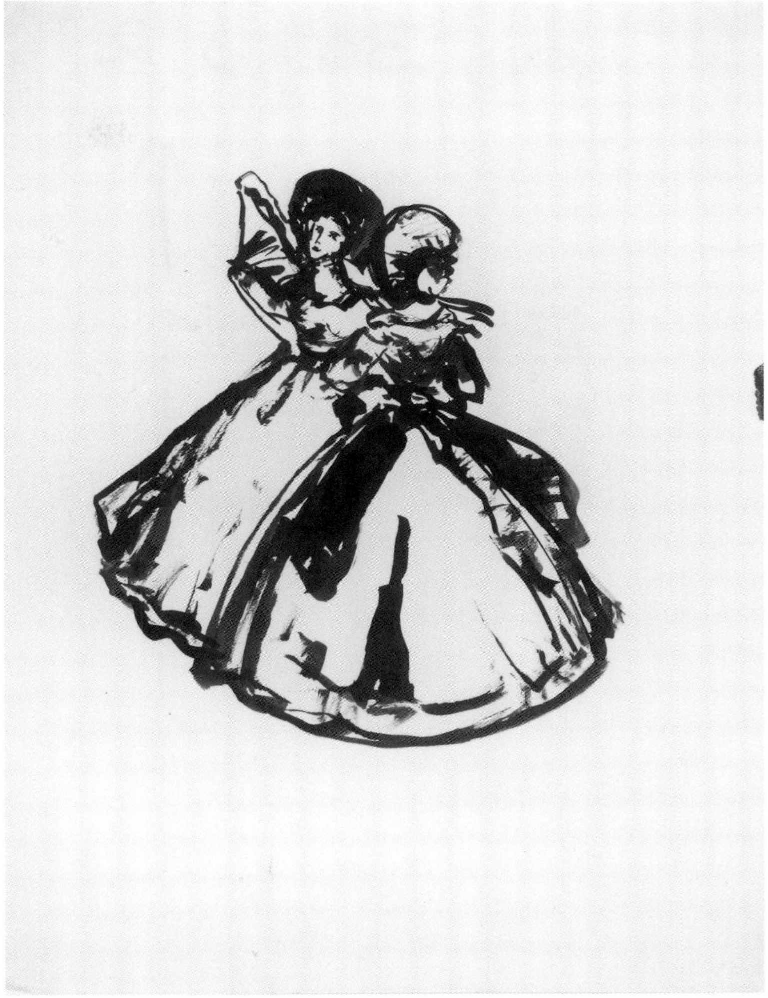

30, p.2

**p.2** India ink drawing of two women holding fans

REFERENCES
Derouet and Boissel 1984, p.170, ill.
Barnett 1992, p.371

The drawing resembles watercolors of women in similar dress of 1915 (Barnett nos.421–422).

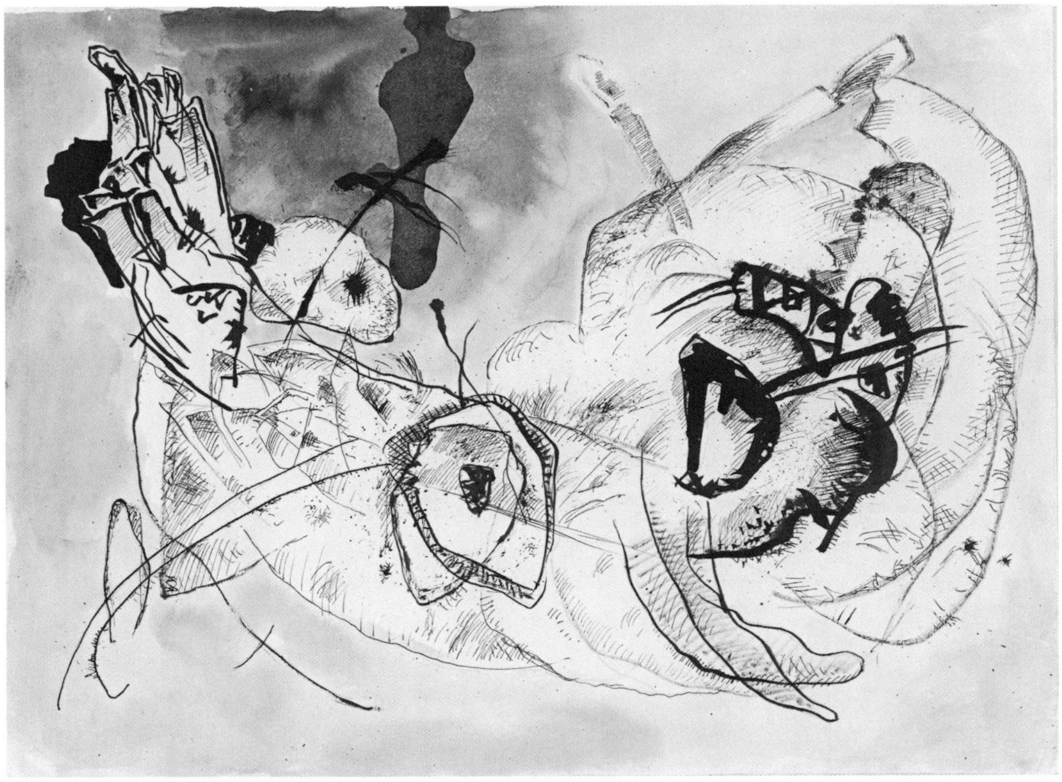

30, p.1

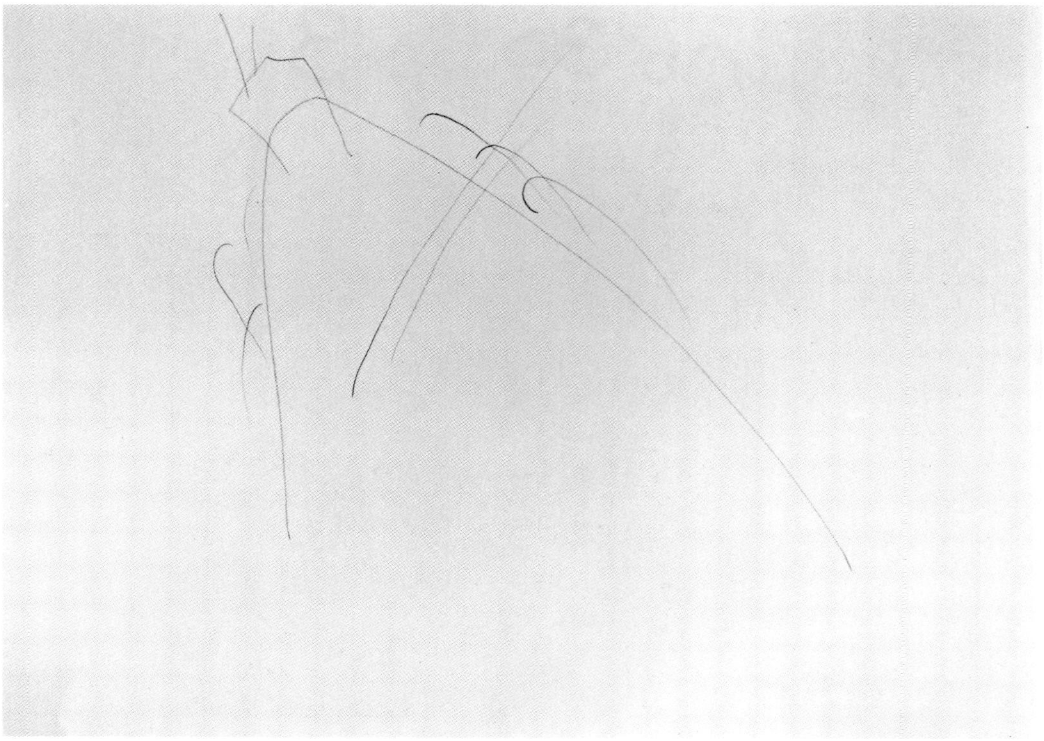

30, p.3

**p.3** Pencil sketch

REFERENCES
Derouet and Boissel 1984, p.170, ill.

**p.4** Pencil sketches

REFERENCES
Derouet and Boissel 1984, p.170, ill.

30, p.4

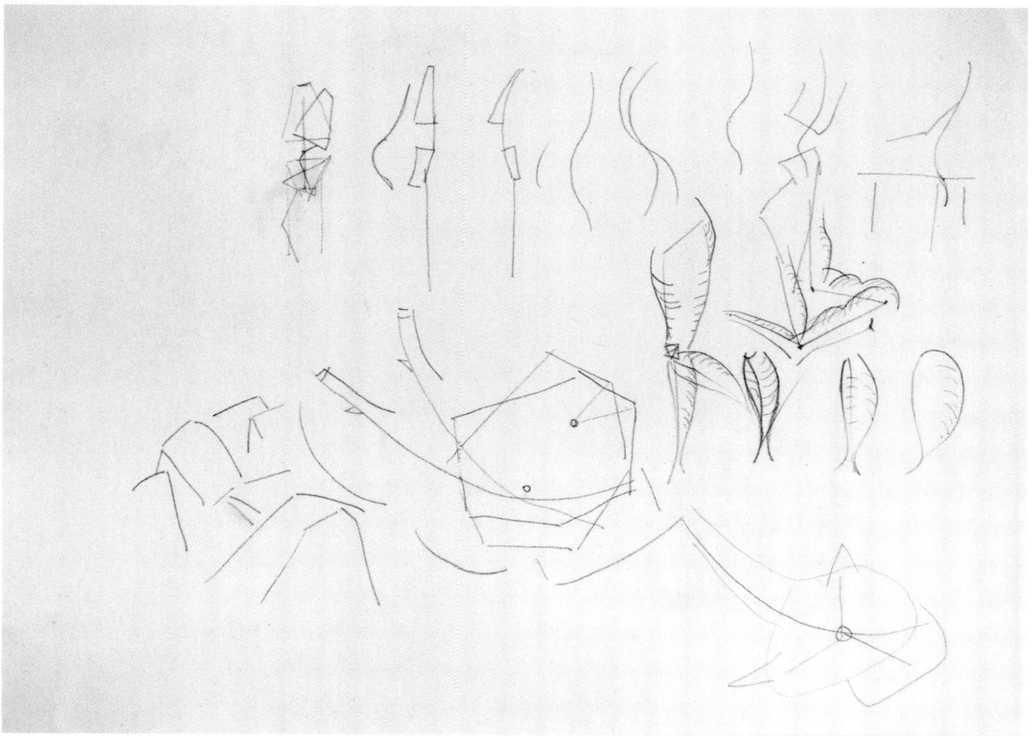

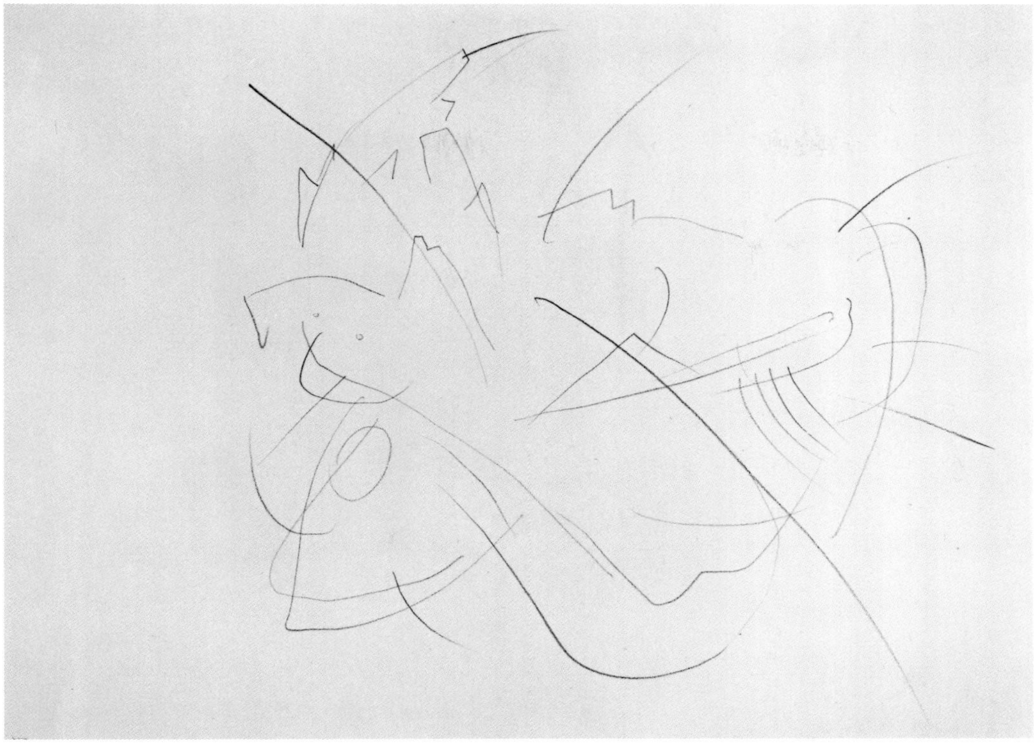

30, p.5

**p.5** Pencil drawing

REFERENCES
Derouet and Boissel 1984, p.170, ill.
Barnett 2006, p.191

The sheet resembles another drawing (vol.I, cat. no.377) which came from this sketchbook.

**p.6** Pencil drawing
Inscribed u.l. in Cyrillic: 'puchok melkik / form kristal'nykh / seroe'; u.c.: 'rozovoe'; u.r.: 'bledno / golubozelenoe'; l.r.: 'krasnoe / sinee / christota / v smutnost'

REFERENCES
Derouet and Boissel 1984, p.170, ill.
Barnett 1992, p.368
Barnett 2006, p.192

The artist's notes refer to dark blue as well as 'purity in murkiness' at the lower right, and a 'cluster of small crystal forms' at the upper left. The drawing shares similarities with the following page and also a sheet that was once part of this sketchbook (vol.I, cat. no.378).

30, p.6

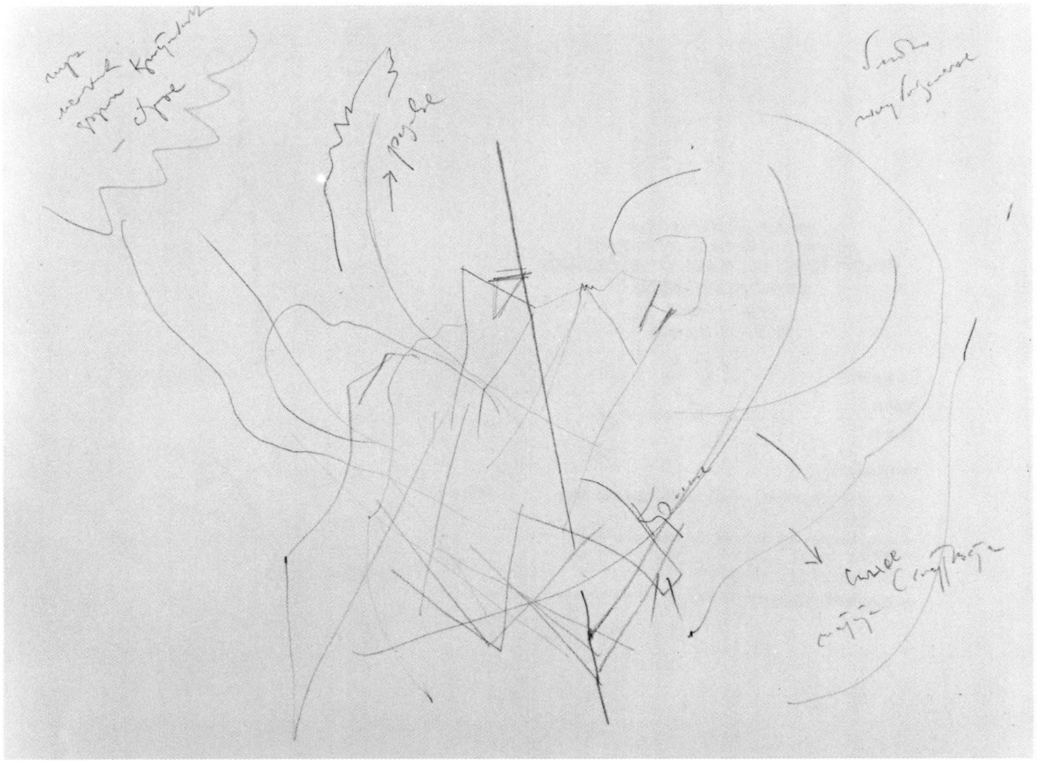

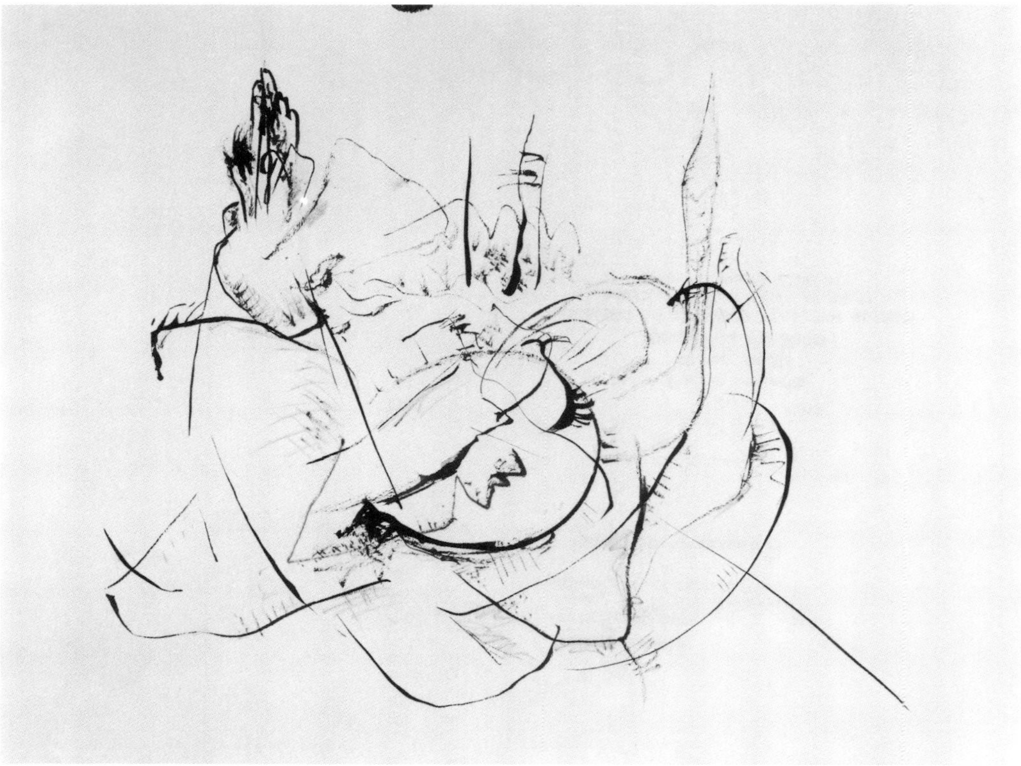

30, p.7

**p.7** India ink drawing

REFERENCES
Derouet and Boissel 1984, pp.170, ill., 171
Barnett 1992, p.368
Barnett 2006, p.192

This study resembles the drawings on pp.1 and 6 (above), and a sheet that originally came from this sketchbook (vol.I, cat. no.378).

**p.8** India ink and pencil drawing
Inscribed l.r. in Cyrillic: 'sgushenie ot / upora vertushki / za nei vse bolee / legkie formy / v konse vrode / shleifa'

REFERENCES
Derouet and Boissel 1984, p.171, ill.
Barnett 2006, pp.191, 210

This drawing can be related to others from 1915–1916 (see vol.I, cat. nos.376, 414). Kandinsky described a 'condensed form' and 'behind it are forms that become lighter and lighter'.

30, p.8

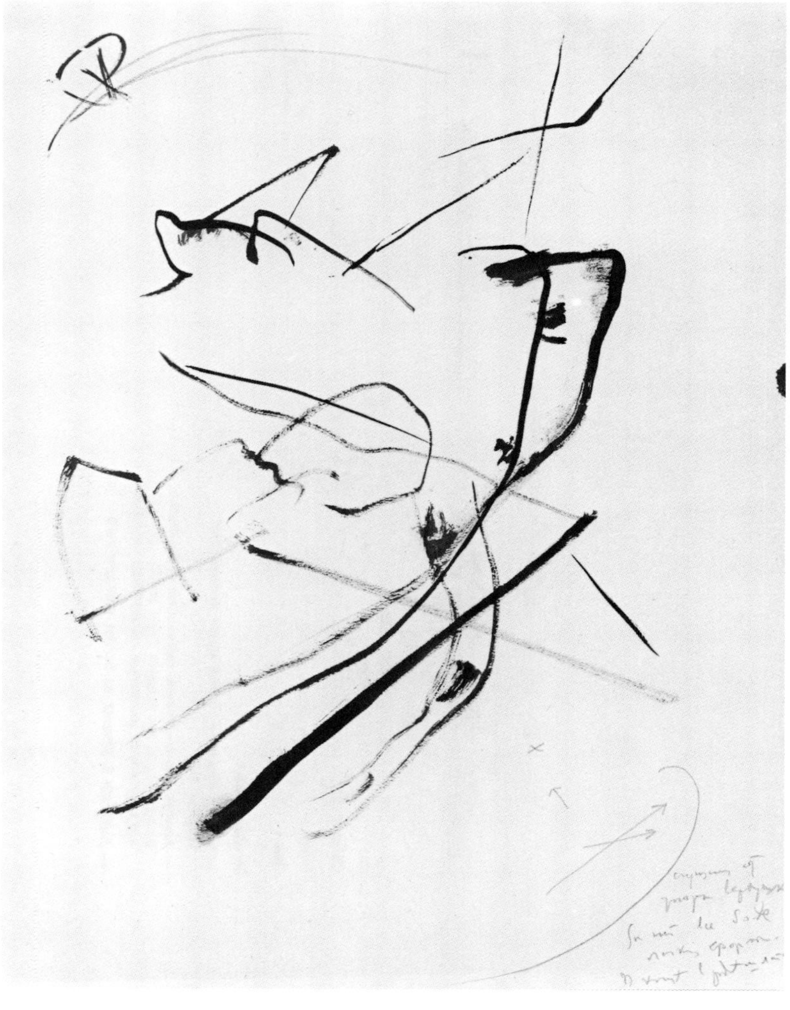

# Sketchbook 31

1916–1917

Brown paper notebook with stapled binding; inside front cover sticker from Wilh. Becker, Stockholm (Kungl. Hopleverantör)
Contains 19 sheets, each 18 x 26.3 cm (7⅛ x 10⅜ in), of which pp.9–19 are blank
Pages have not been numbered

Derouet and Boissel 1984, no.201

LOCATION
Musée National d'Art Moderne, Centre Georges Pompidou, Paris (AM 1981.65.673)

HISTORY
Nina Kandinsky, Paris, until 1980

Kandinsky purchased this notebook when he was in Stockholm at the beginning of 1916; however, he seems to have made sketches in it only after his return to Moscow in March of the same year. He continued to use the notebook the following year.

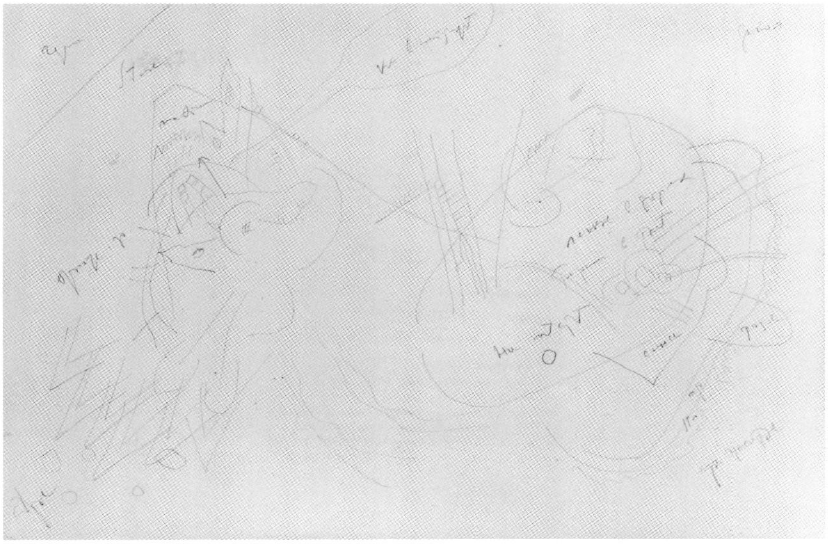

31, p.1

**p.1** Pencil study related to *Trübe* of 1917
Inscribed u.l. in Cyrillic: 'chern. / beloe / [...]'; c.l.: 'oranzh. ze'; l.l.: 'seroe'; u.c.: 'kak v peizazhe'; u.r.: 'fiol'; c.r.: 'legkoe v forme / tiazheloe v ta[...] / na meste / sinee'; l.r.: 'rozovaia / or / bel / gr. zheltaia'

REFERENCES
Derouet and Boissel 1984, pp.183, 188, ill.
Barnett 1992, p.420

The drawing is closely related to a watercolor dated 1917 (Barnett no.478) for the canvas *Trübe* of September 1917 (Roethel and Benjamin no.615). Kandinsky inscribed it with color notations and, at the top, 'like in a landscape'.

**p.2** Pencil study for the triptych for the Abrikosov family
Inscribed above in Cyrillic: 'voda zoloto tela'; u.l.: 'NE TECHET / reka obratno'; u.c. in Greek: 'panta rei'; below l. to r. in Cyrillic: 'na chernom / serebr. doroga / na belom / Reka zolotaia / sinee s krasnym / samoe temnow i glub / krasnaia korova na golub. fone / k zheltomu i sinemu / solutse po zolotu les. / holmy golub. i roz.'; l.l. in Greek: 'panta rei'; l.c. in Cyrillic: 'Ramka serebr. s kryl'iamy' and below color notations in rectangle 'kaima serebrianaia / ramka chernaia'

EXHIBITIONS
1987 Tokyo, no.81, ill.

REFERENCES
Derouet and Boissel 1984, p.183, ill.
*Kandinsky and Sweden* exh. cat. (Malmö, 1989), pp.74, ill.21, 95 n.2
Weiss 1995, p.120 n.9
Barnett 2006, p.212

On 28 April 1916, Kandinsky wrote to Gabriele Münter that he was making studies for the Abrikosov panel ('En même temps je fais des préparatifs pour ce panneau d'Abricosoff ...'). The brother of Kandinsky's first wife Anja had a dacha in Akhtyrka outside Moscow (see also Sketchbook 32). The triptych is known only from this study (Roethel and Benjamin no.604), which describes a silver road, gold river, gold sun, and light blue and pink hills, and specifies a silver border and black frame.

31, p.2

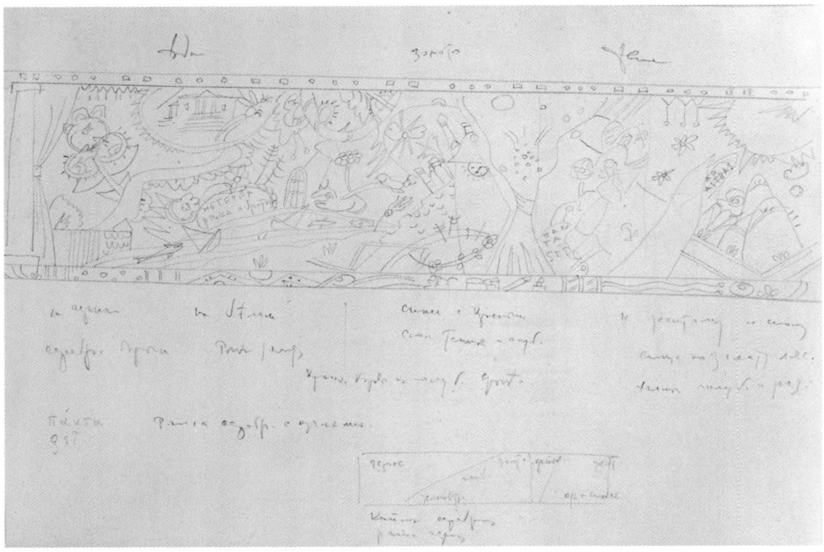

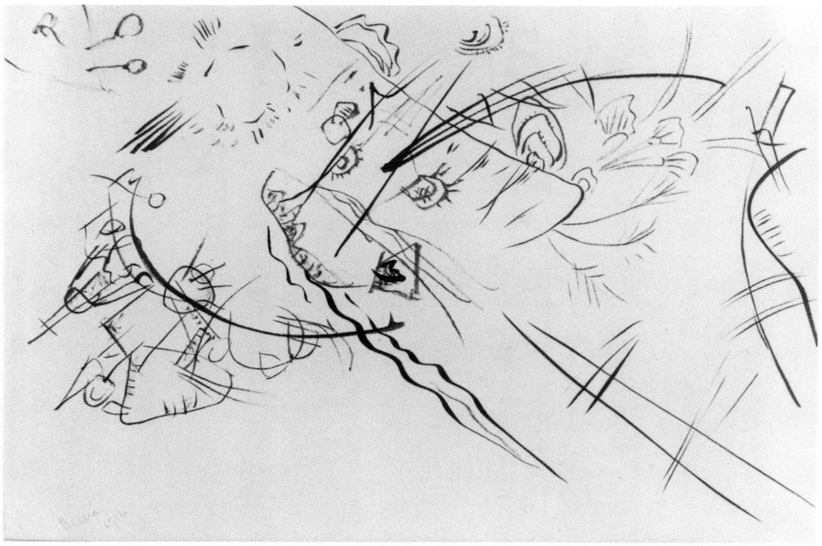

31, p.3

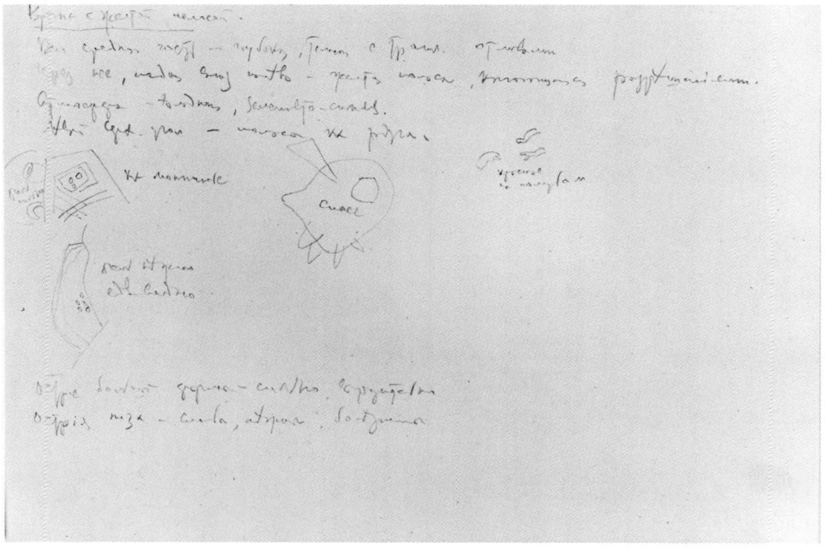

31, p.4

**p.3** India ink and pencil drawing
Inscribed l.l. in Cyrillic: 'Vesna 1916'

REFERENCES
Derouet and Boissel 1984, pp.182, ill., 183

The artist's inscription dates the drawing to 'spring 1916'.

**p.4** Pencil study for 'Painting with a Yellow Stripe'
Inscribed above in Cyrillic: 'Kartina s zheltoi polosoi / Vsia srednaia chast' – glubokaia, temnaia s tragicheskimi otlivami / cherez nee, [...] vniz na levo- zheltaia polosa, konchaiushchaia-sia rasrusheniiamu / Atmosfera-kholodnaia, zelenovato- sinnaia / [...] polosa k raduge'; below l. to r.: 'ochen' / sil'no / k [...] / sinee / krasnoe / na golubom'; c.l.: '[...]'; l.l.: 'ostrye bol'shie formy- silno [...] / ostryia glaza- slabo [...]'

REFERENCES
Derouet and Boissel 1984, pp.182, ill., 183

Derouet and Boissel identified the drawing as a study for *Bild mit orange Rand* (Roethel and Benjamin no.598), which is illustrated in Appendix II on page 325. However, since the inscription clearly refers to a 'yellow stripe' rather than to an orange border, it was probably intended for an unexecuted or unknown painting.

**p.5** Colored pencil and pencil study for *Moskau I* of 1916

EXHIBITIONS
1996 Barcelona, no.14, color ill.
1997 Milan, no.40, color ill.

REFERENCES
Derouet and Boissel 1984, pp.183, 185, color ill.
Shulamith Behr, 'Wassily Kandinsky and Dimitrije Mitrinovic: Pan-Christian Universalism and the Yearbook "Towards the Mankind of the Future through Aryan Europe"', *Oxford Art Journal*, vol.15, no.1 (1992), p.84, ill.4
Weiss 1995, pp.125, 127, ill.120
Daniel 1999, p.90, ill.
Barnett 2006, p.211

This drawing is one of several studies Kandinsky made during the summer of 1916 for the painting *Moskau I* (Roethel and Benjamin no.605). On 4 June 1916 he wrote to Münter: 'Je voudrais faire un grand paysage de Moscou – prendre des éléments partout et réunir dans un tableau – des morceaux faibles et fortes, tout méler ensemble comme le monde est melé des éléments differents. Ça doit être comme un orchestre.' In addition to the sketches on the following pages, there are two individual drawings (vol.I, cat. nos.416, 417).

(See color plate p.126)

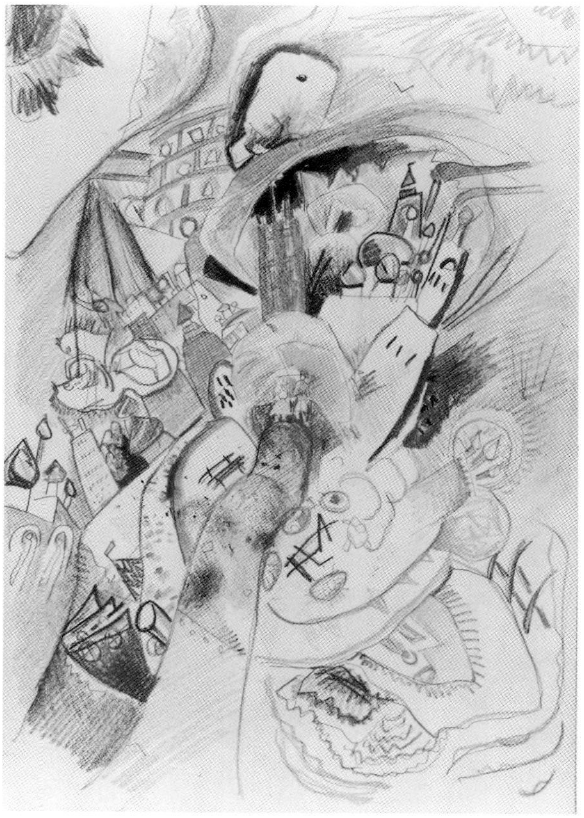

31, p.5

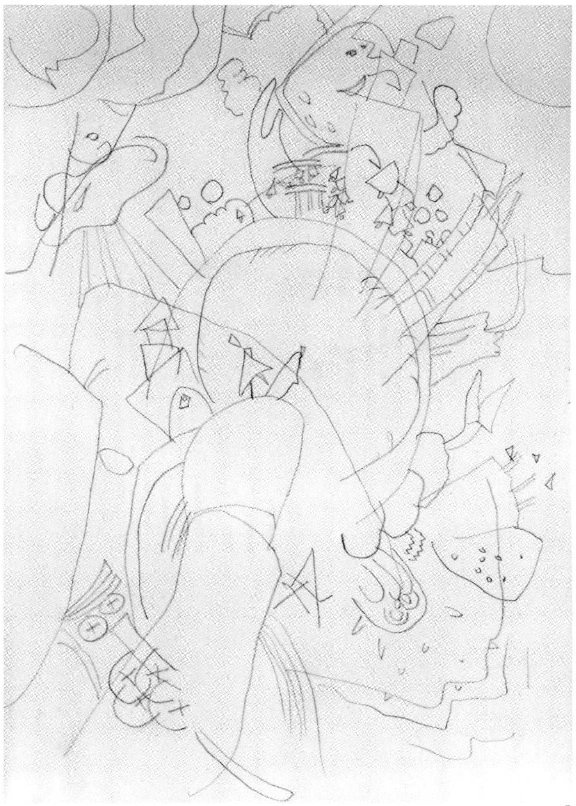

31, p.6

**p.6** Pencil study for a watercolor of June 1917

REFERENCES
Derouet and Boissel 1984, pp.183, 184, ill.
Barnett 2006, p.211

This study is preparatory to an untitled watercolor dated June 1917 (Barnett no.470) related to *Der blaue Bogen (Kamm)* (Roethel and Benjamin no.614) and, more generally, to studies for *Moskau I* of 1916.

**p.7** Pencil drawing
Inscribed u.r. in Cyrillic: 'rad[uga]'; l.r.: '[...] legko / [...]Boga' and with color notations

REFERENCES
Derouet and Boissel 1984, pp.182, ill., 183

Kandinsky mentions a rainbow in this drawing, the study for 'Painting with a Yellow Stripe' (p.4 above) and earlier in Sketchbook 29.

**p.8** India ink drawing

EXHIBITIONS
2001 Strasbourg, p.78, color ill.

REFERENCES
Derouet and Boissel 1984, pp.182, ill., 183
Barnett 2006, p.227

The drawing shares similarities to drawings from 1916–1918 (see vol.I, cat. nos.415, 449).

**pp.9–19** Blank

31, p.7

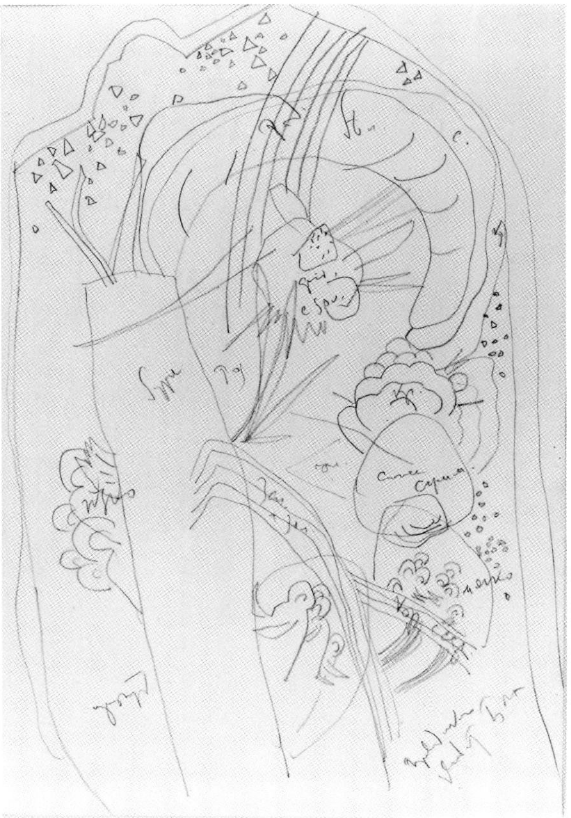

31, p.8

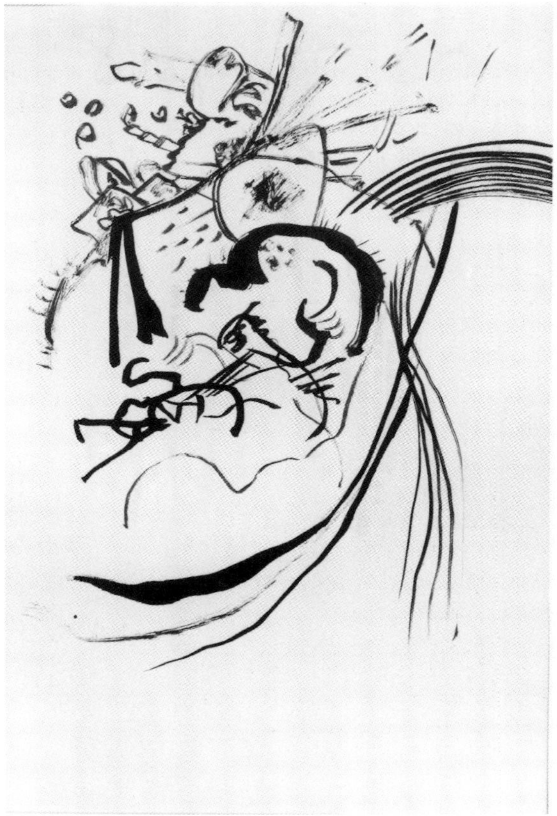

# Sketchbook 32

1916–1917

Blue cardboard sketchbook with black spine; no label. Inside front cover Kandinsky inscribed '1916 osen'.
Contains 17 sheets, each 26.8 x 20.4 cm (10½ x 8 in), with left edge perforated and margin attached to sketchbook. Approximately 35 sheets have been removed.
Page numbers inscribed by unknown hand at later date on margin of sketchbook page

Derouet and Boissel 1984, no.205

LOCATION
Musée National d'Art Moderne, Centre Georges Pompidou, Paris (AM 1981.65.674)

HISTORY
Nina Kandinsky, Paris, until 1980

Kandinsky dated the sketchbook 'autumn 1916', but he continued to use it the following summer, when he and his wife Nina went to Akhtyrka outside Moscow. In the summer of 1917 he made drawings in the inverse direction at the back of the sketchbook. Numerous sheets may have originally belonged to this sketchbook, but have been removed, including cat. nos.420 and 433 in Volume I of *Kandinsky Drawings*.

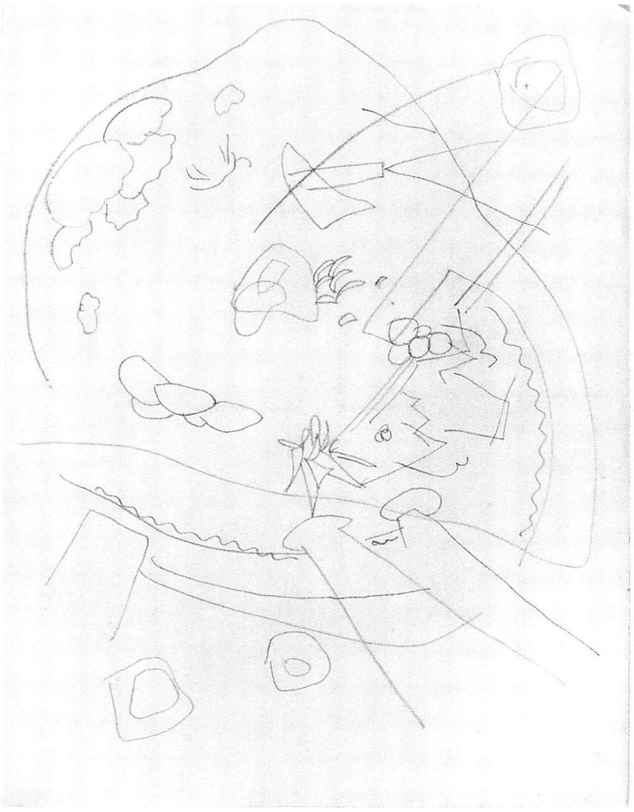

32, p.1

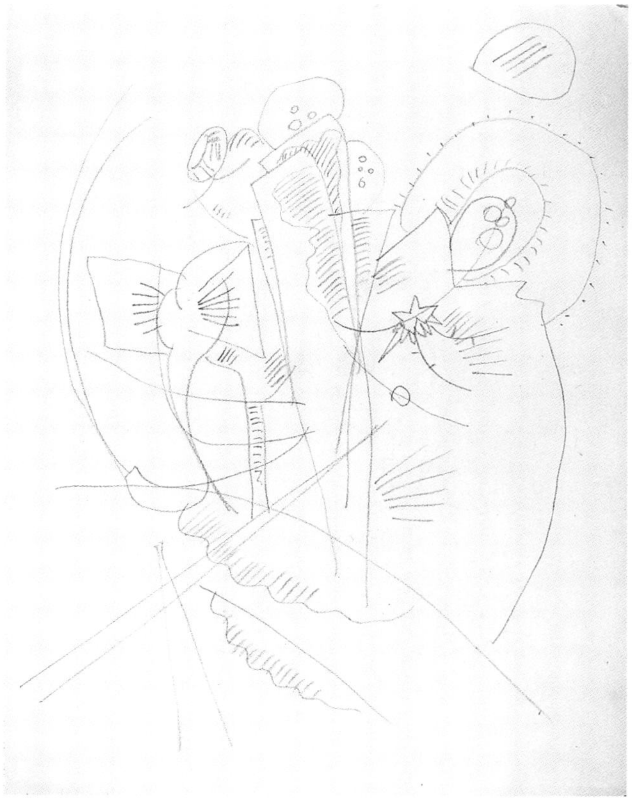

32, p.2

**p.1** Pencil study for a drawing of 1917

REFERENCES
Derouet and Boissel 1984, pp.186, ill., 187
Barnett 2006, p.220

This study is for an India ink drawing dated 1917 (vol.I, cat. no.435)

**p.2** Pencil drawing

REFERENCES
Derouet and Boissel 1984, pp.186, ill., 187

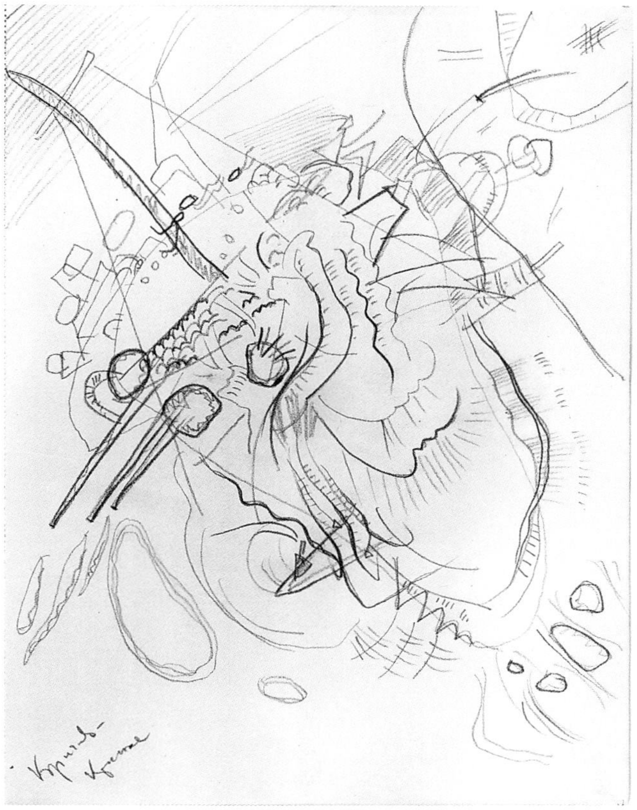

32, p.3

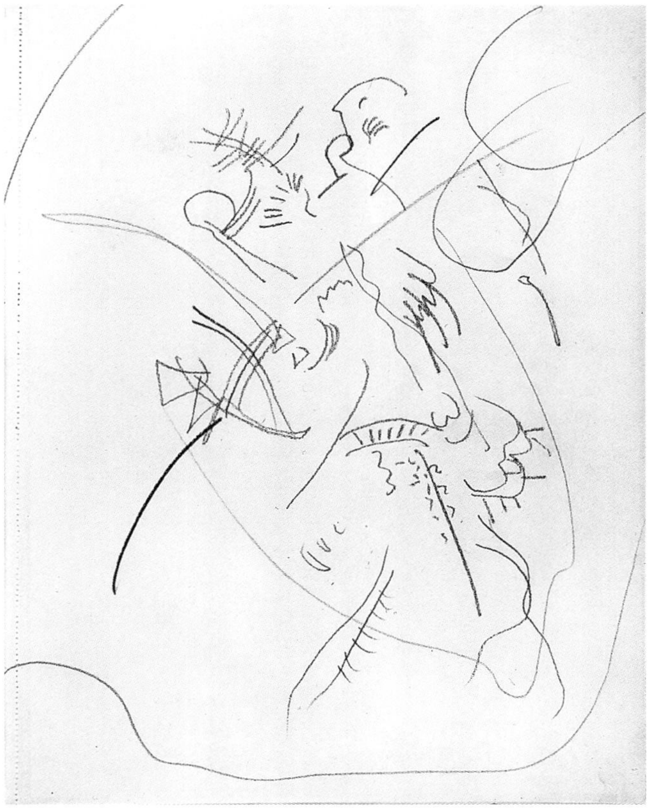

32, p.4

**p.3** Pencil study for a wash drawing of 1916
Inscribed l.l. in Cyrillic: 'Korichivo- / krasnaia'

REFERENCES
Derouet and Boissel 1984, pp.186, ill., 187
Barnett 2006, p.219

This drawing, which is inscribed 'brown-red', resembles an India ink drawing dated 1916, which may have come from the same sketchbook (vol.I, cat. no.433).

**p.4** Pencil study for the watercolor *An eine Stimme* of 1916

REFERENCES
Derouet and Boissel 1984, pp.178, ill., 187

This drawing is one of several studies for the watercolor *An eine Stimme* of September 1916 (Barnett no. 458), including an India ink drawing (vol.I, cat. no.426) and a watercolor dated 1916 (Barnett no.457).

**p.5** Pencil study
Inscribed l.r. in Cyrillic: 'chern. ramka / Sred. rozovaia, [...] golub. / [...] zhelt.[...] seroi' and with color notations

REFERENCES
Derouet and Boissel 1984, pp.186, ill., 187

Kandinsky's notes refer to a 'black border' and 'pink center'.

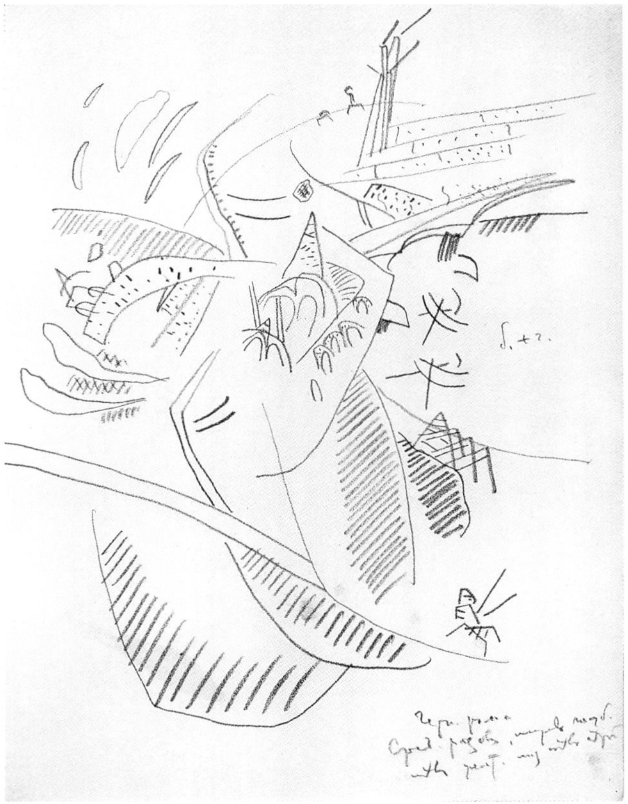

32, p.5

**p.6** Pencil study
Inscribed u.l. in Cyrillic with color notations: 'fiol. / bel.'; l.l.: 'golub. / sv. zel.'; c.r.: 'zhelt. / s […] / kor. / chernaia / och. tem[…]'; l.r.: 'ser. / bel.'

REFERENCES
Derouet and Boissel 1984, pp.186, ill., 187

**p.7** India ink study

REFERENCES
Derouet and Boissel 1984, pp.186, ill., 187

**p.8** India ink, watercolor and pencil drawing (detached)
Inscribed l.l. in Cyrillic: 'TOT DEN'; u.c.: 'bel.'

EXHIBITIONS
2001 Strasbourg, p.92, color ill.

REFERENCES
Derouet and Boissel 1984, pp.186, ill., 187
Barnett 2006, pp.37, 216

Kandinsky wrote 'that day' on this sheet, which can be related to a drawing dated 1916 (vol. I, cat. no.427), a watercolor of 1917 (vol. I, cat. no.13) and the study on the first page of the present sketchbook.

(See color plate p.126)

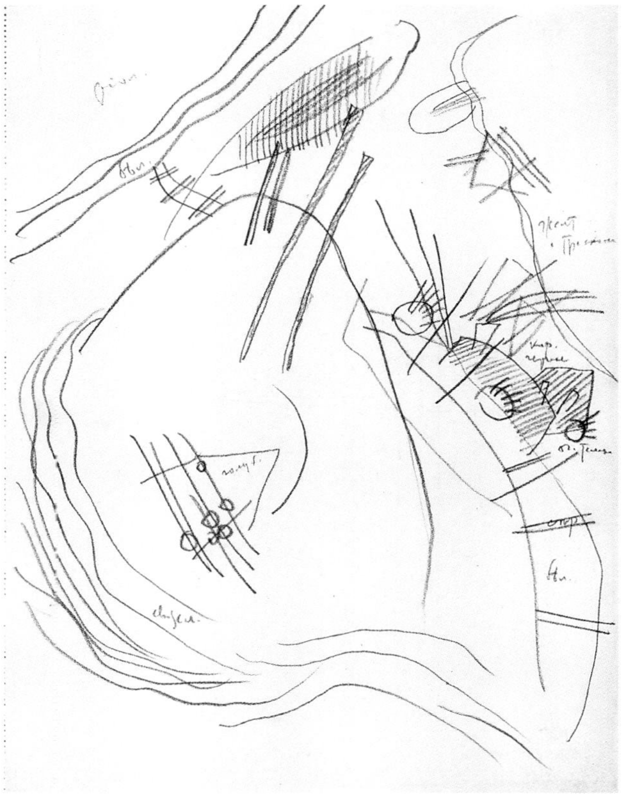

32, p.6

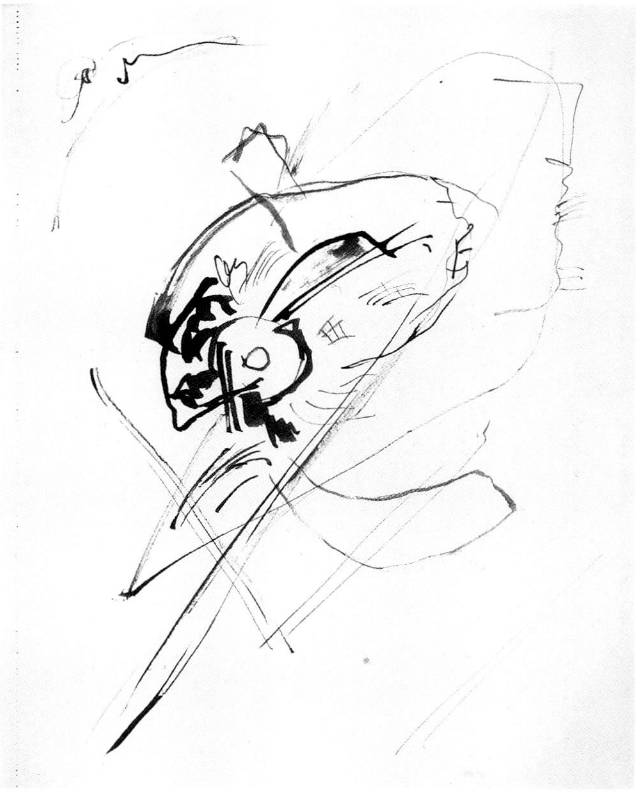

32, p.7

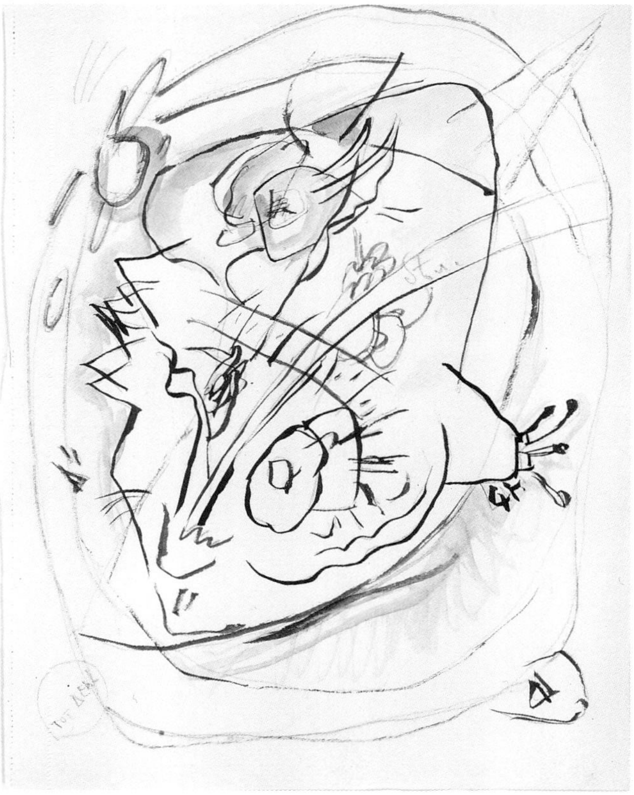

32, p.8

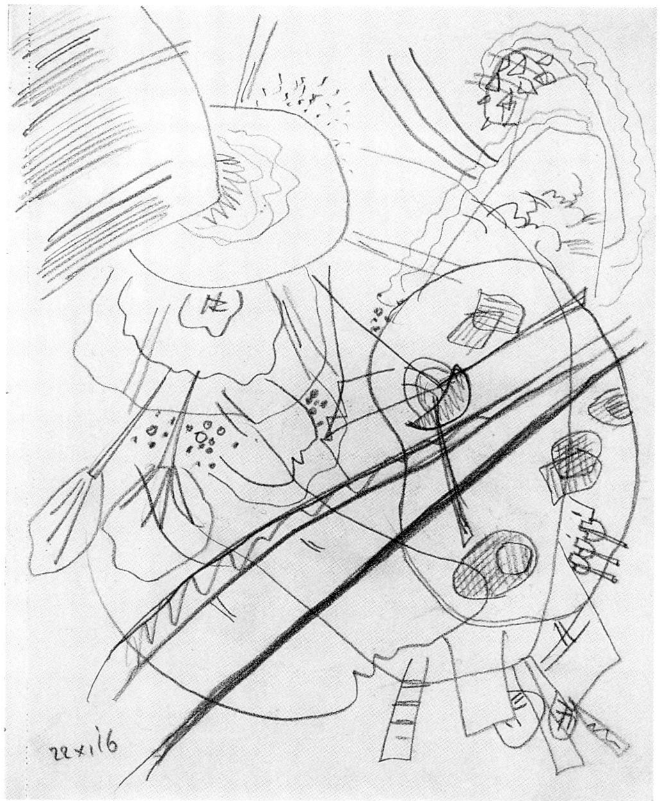


32, p.10

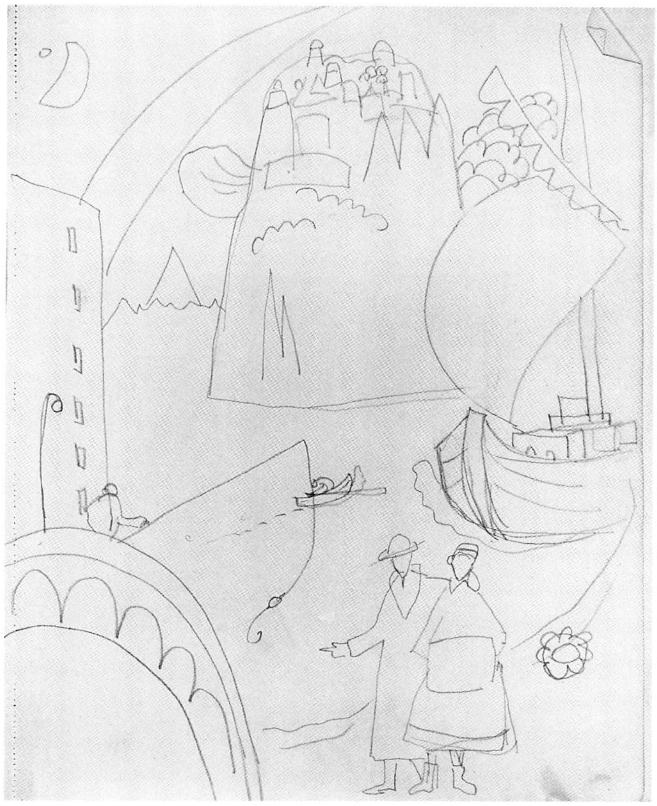

32, p.11

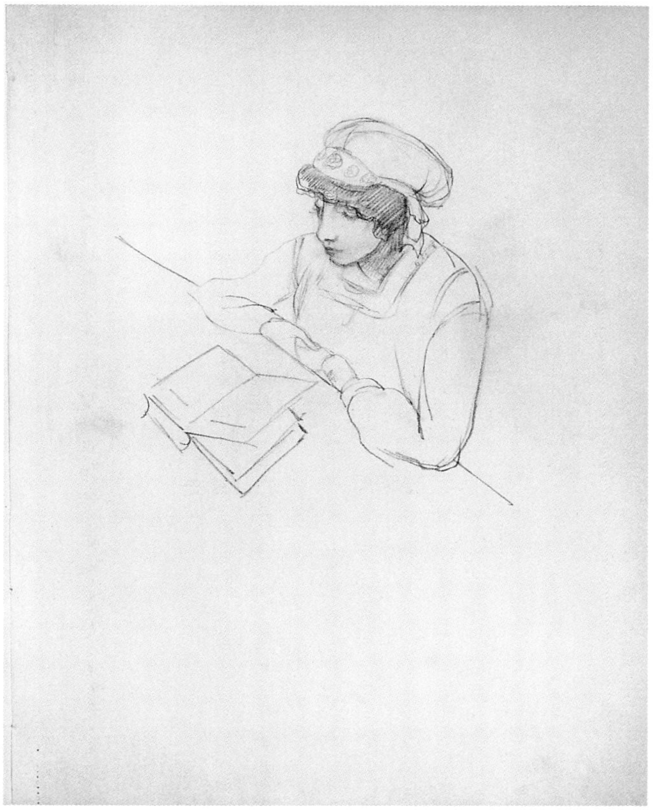

32, p.12v

**p.9** Inscribed l.l.: '28 x' (not illustrated)
Inscribed in Cyrillic on reverse: 'v krasno-zheltom fone / [...] belaia bereza / pravyi niz cherno-beloe / pravyi verkh [...] / levyi verkh na belom fone / polosy [...] cherno-belye / burye i sinie'

REFERENCES
Derouet and Boissel 1984, p.187

Kandinsky wrote the date 28 October on this otherwise blank sheet and, on the reverse, a descriptive text that begins 'on red-green tones'.

**p.10** Pencil drawing dated '22 xi 16'
Inscribed with illegible text in French and Cyrillic on reverse

REFERENCES
Derouet and Boissel 1984, pp.186, ill., 187
Barnett 2006, p.219

This study, which is dated 22 November 1916, resembles other coeval drawings (see vol.I, cat. no.433).

**p.11** Pencil drawing related to *Hafen* of 1916

REFERENCES
Derouet and Boissel 1984, pp.187, 198, ill.
Barnett 2006, p.213

The drawing brings to mind a study for the lost picture *Bild mit Bogenschützen II* of 1916 (vol.I, cat. no.420), which probably came from this sketchbook, as well as the glass painting *Hafen* of 1916 (Roethel and Benjamin no.612).

**p.12** Recto blank
On reverse: pencil drawing of Nina Kandinsky at Akhtyrka

REFERENCES
Derouet and Boissel 1984, pp.187, 197, ill.

During the summer of 1917, the Kandinskys went to Akhtyrka on vacation before the birth of their son Vsevolod in September.

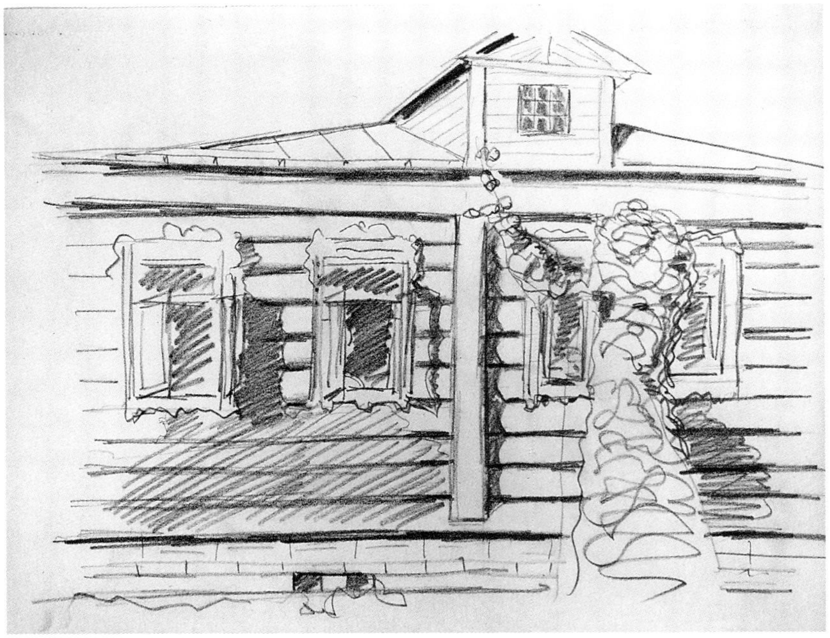

32, p.13v

**p.13** Recto blank
On reverse: pencil drawing of dacha at Akhtyrka

REFERENCES
Derouet and Boissel 1984, pp.187, 196, ill.

The dacha at Akhtyrka outside Moscow also appears in Kandinsky's paintings *Akhtyrka- Nina und Tatjana auf der Veranda* and *Akhtyrka- Vordereingang zur Datscha* (Roethel and Benjamin nos.622, 623).

**p.14** Recto blank
On reverse: pencil drawing of pond, ducks, horse, church and other buildings at Akhtyrka

REFERENCES
Derouet and Boissel 1984, pp.187, 194, ill.

The pond with ducks is depicted in *Landschaft in Akhtyrka mit zwei Damen* of 1917 (Barnett no.472).

**p.15** Recto blank
On reverse: pencil drawing of church and other buildings at Akhtyrka

REFERENCES
Derouet and Boissel 1984, pp.187, 194, ill.

The drawing is clearly related to a watercolor of Akhtyrka (Barnett no.472), and also resembles *Akhtyrka-Landschaft mit roter Kirche* of 1917 (Roethel and Benjamin no.626)

32, p.14v

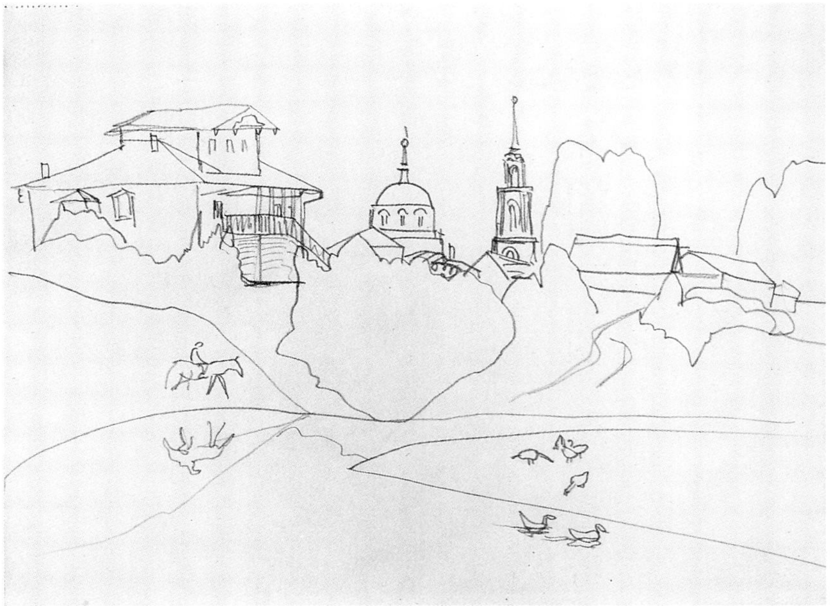

32, p.15v

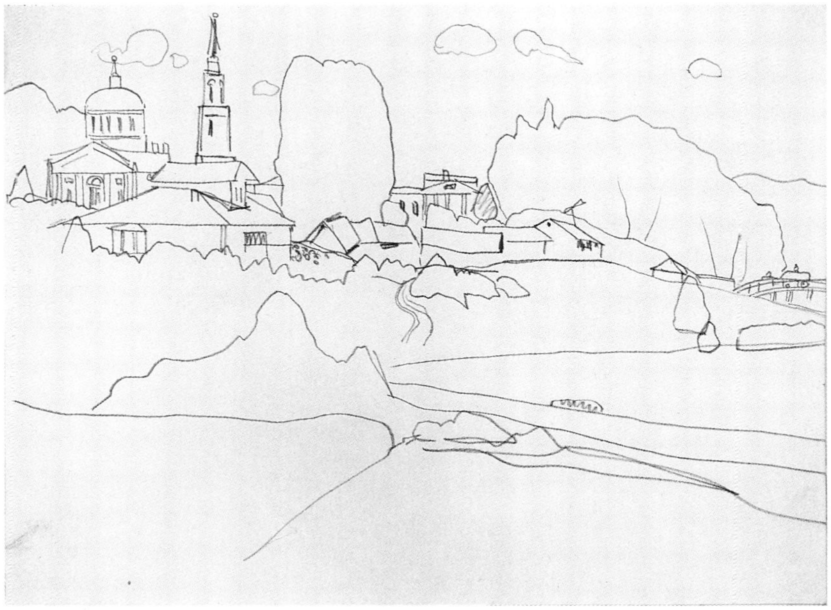

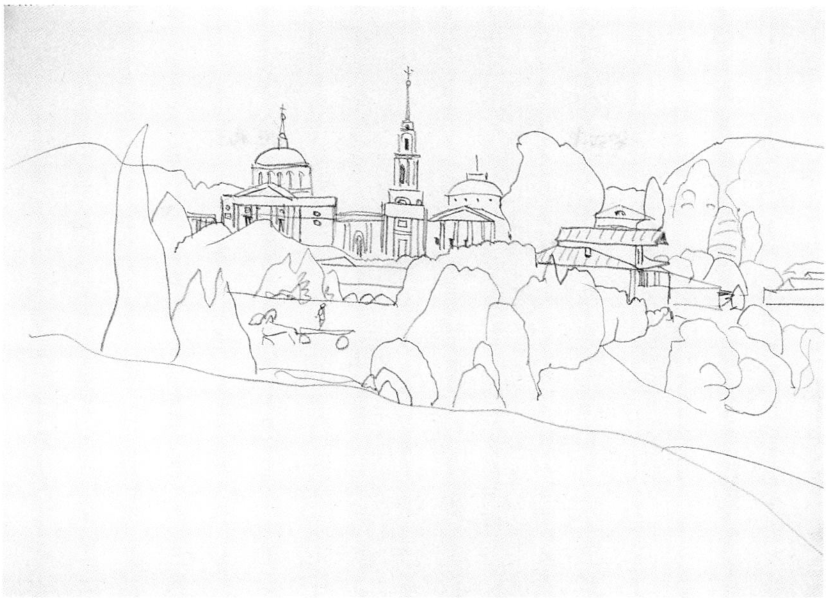

32, p.16v

**p.16** Recto blank
On reverse: pencil drawing of church and other buildings at Akhtyrka

REFERENCES
Derouet and Boissel 1984, pp.187, 192, ill.

**p.17** Recto blank
On reverse: pencil drawing of church and other buildings at Akhtyrka

REFERENCES
Derouet and Boissel 1984, pp.187, 192, ill.

On the last four pages of this sketchbook, Kandinsky has shown in detail the buildings at Akhtyrka, but from a different point of view than the one in the photograph preserved with his papers (fig.a).

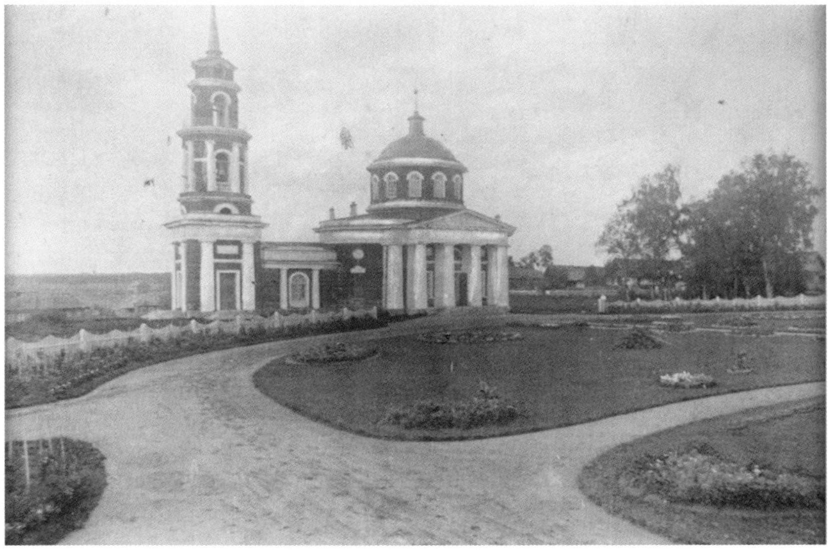

fig.a

32, p.17v

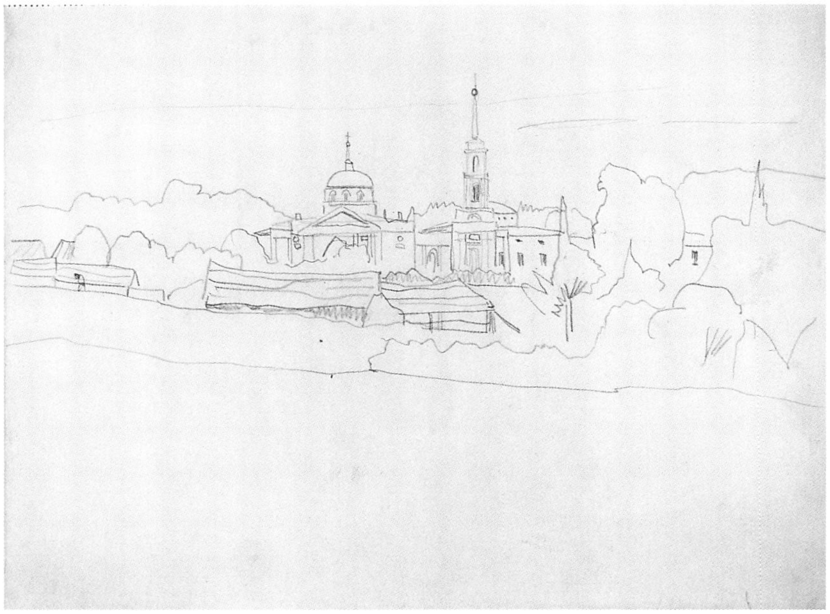

# Sketchbook 33

1927–1930

Blue paper-covered sketchbook with black spine; inside front cover stamp from G. Sennelier, Paris (3 quai Voltaire)
Contains 43 sheets, each 16 x 9.2 cm (6¼ x 3⅝), with left edge perforated and margin attached to sketchbook. Several sheets have been detached.
Page numbers inscribed by unknown hand at later date on margin of sketchbook page

Derouet and Boissel 1984, no.433

LOCATION
Musée National d'Art Moderne, Centre Georges Pompidou, Paris (AM 1981.65.675)

HISTORY
Nina Kandinsky, Paris, until 1980

Christian Derouet and Jessica Boissel dated the sketchbook to 1929. Since there are studies related to works dating from 1927 to 1930, a broader time span is appropriate. It is unclear as to where Kandinsky, who lived in Dessau, purchased the sketchbook, which has a stamp from Sennelier in Paris.

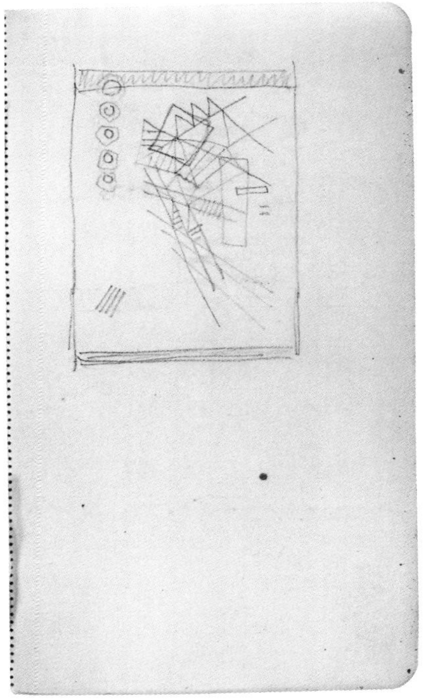

33, p.1

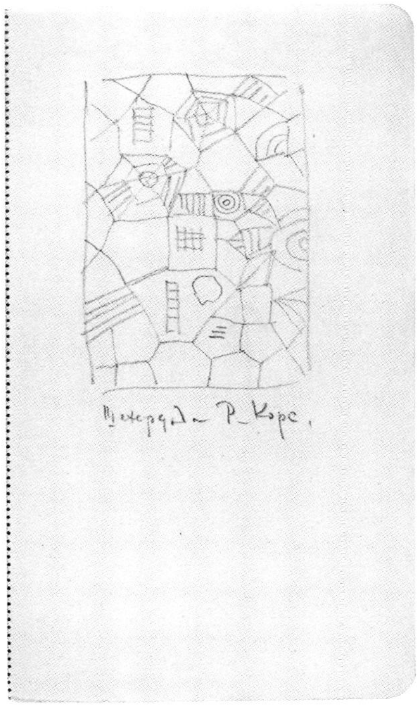

33, p.2

**p.1** Pencil sketch for an unidentified work

REFERENCES
Derouet and Boissel 1984, p.320, ill.

The sketch is reminiscent of *Rosa-Rot* of November 1927 (Barnett no.802).

**p.2** Pencil sketch for an unidentified work
Inscribed l.c. in Cyrillic: 'Shekherezada R-Kors.'

REFERENCES
Derouet and Boissel 1984, p.320, ill.

The inscription refers to the Russian composer Nikolai Rimsky-Korsakov. The drawing is reminiscent of *Einige Flächen* of December 1925 (Barnett no.762).

**p.3** Pencil sketches
Inscribed l.c.: 'gnlich'
On reverse: pencil sketch related to facing page (p.4)

REFERENCES
Derouet and Boissel 1984, p.320, ill. (recto)

The study bears a resemblance to *Leiterform (Auf Flecken)* of February 1929 (Roethel and Benjamin no.893).

**p.4** Pencil sketch
Inscribed l.r.: 'd. R'; l.c.: 'Eng. R-Mitte: Gn oliv. s. d. / schmale V.'

REFERENCES
Derouet and Boissel 1984, p.320, ill.

The sketch can be related to *Bunte Reihe* of July 1928 (Barnett no.890). See p.3.

33, p.3R

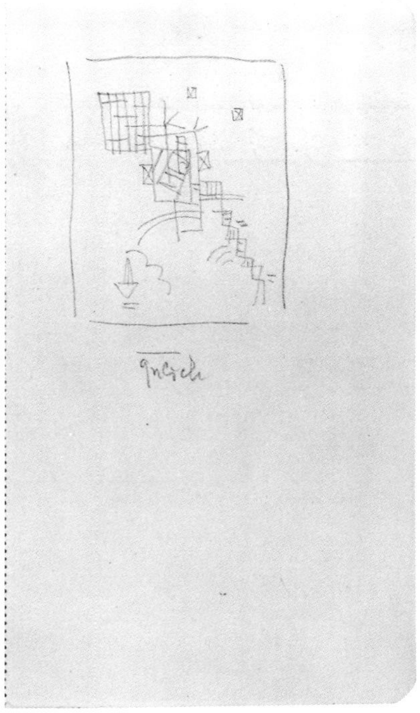

33, p.3V

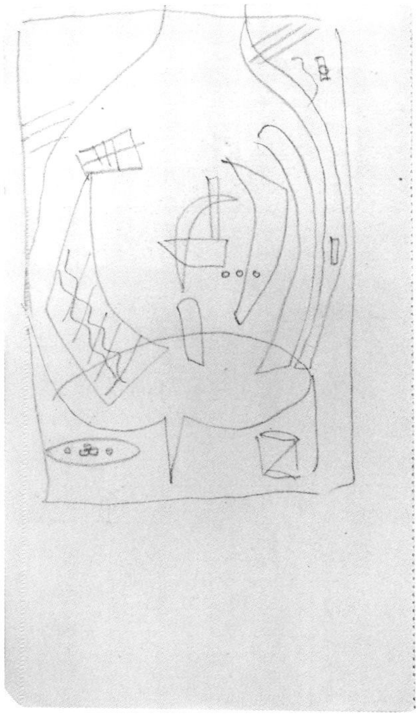

33, p.4

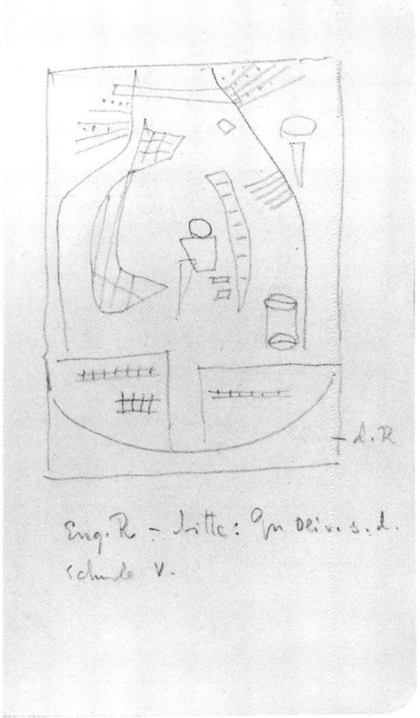

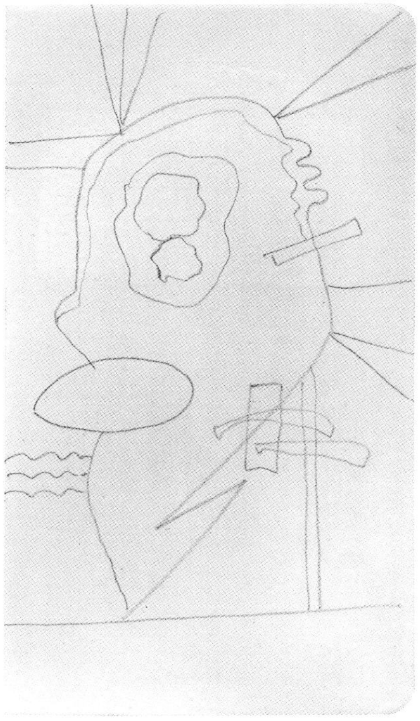
33, p.5

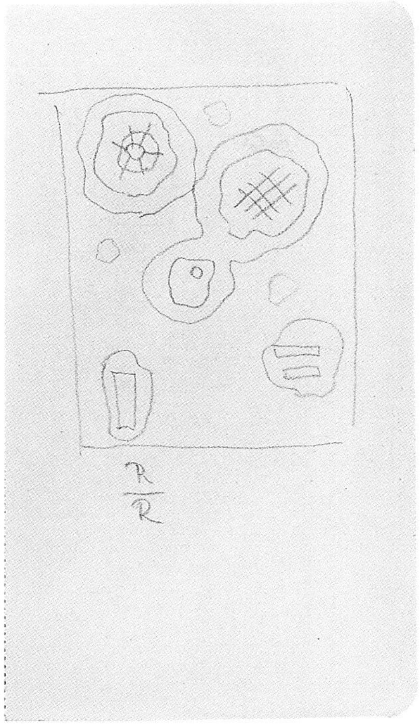

33, p.6

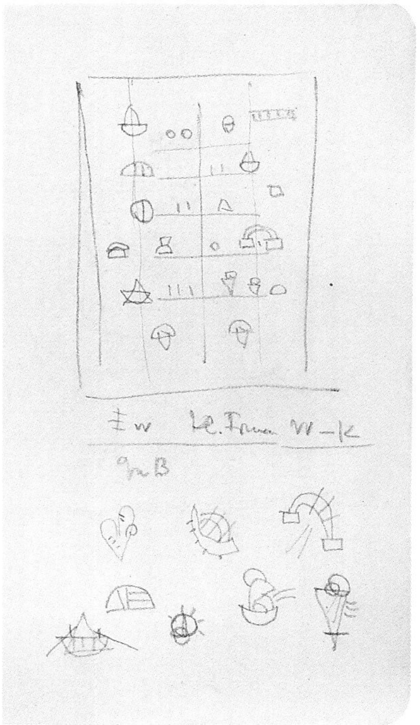
33, p.7

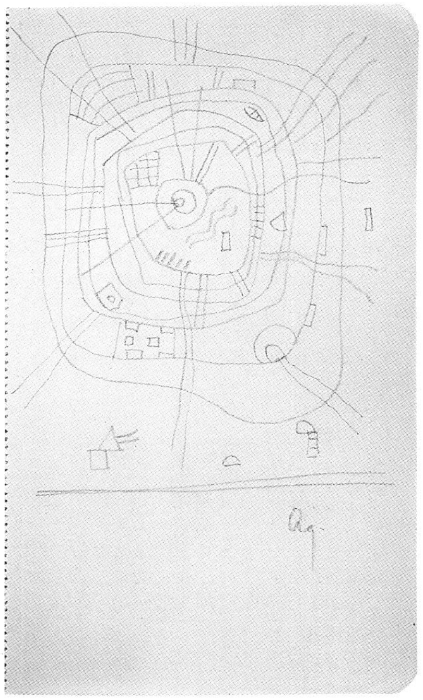

33, p.8

**p.5** Pencil sketch for an unidentified work

REFERENCES
Derouet and Boissel 1984, p.320

**p.6** Pencil sketch for an unidentified work
Inscribed l.l.: 'R / R'

REFERENCES
Derouet and Boissel 1984, p.320

**p.7** Pencil study for *Etagen* of March 1929
Inscribed c.: 'E w Kl. Formen W-K / Gn B'

REFERENCES
Barnett 1983, p.207, ill.a
Derouet and Boissel 1984, pp.320, 322, ill.
Barnett 2006, p.354

The drawing is clearly related to studies (vol.I, cat. nos.704, 705) for *Etagen* of March 1929 (Roethel and Benjamin no.896).

**p.8** Pencil sketch for an unidentified work
Inscribed l.r.: 'Aq.' and on reverse with mathematical calculations

REFERENCES
Derouet and Boissel 1984, p.320, ill.

**p.9** Pencil study for *Ausgleich–Rosa* of January 1933
Inscribed l.l: '9 x 13' and with color notations: 'R / w / G / Gn'

REFERENCES
Derouet and Boissel 1984, pp.320, 342, ill.

This drawing is a study for *Ausgleich–Rosa* of January 1933 (Roethel and Benjamin no.1027).

**p.10** Pencil study for *Schwacher Bogen* of February 1929

REFERENCES
Derouet and Boissel 1984, p.320, ill.

The study clearly resembles *Schwacher Bogen* of February 1929 (Barnett no.926).

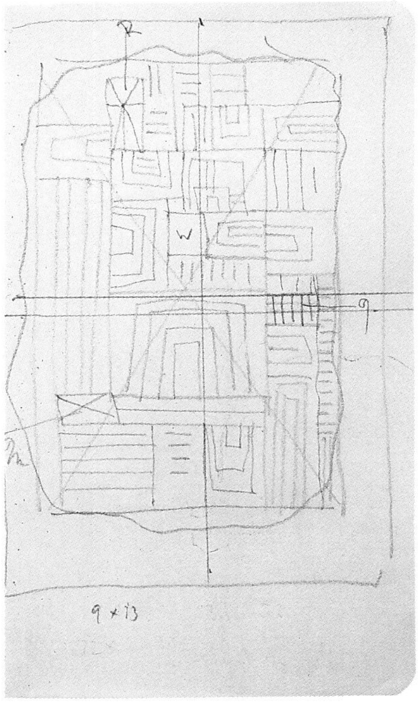

33, p.9

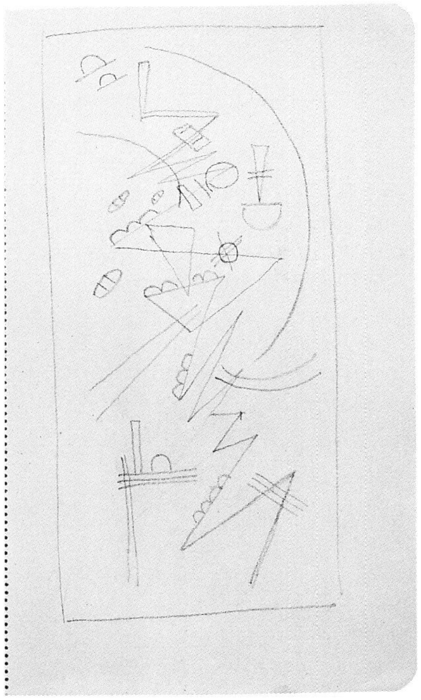
33, p.10

**p.11** Pencil sketch

REFERENCES
Derouet and Boissel 1984, p.320

The sketch can be related to *Um die Ecke* of October 1929 (Barnett no.946) and *Weiss-weiss* and *Winkelschwung* of November 1929 (Roethel and Benjamin nos.916, 917).

**p.12** Pencil study for *Sachte* of March 1929
Inscribed l.l.: 'R-G'; l.c.: 'Sptz (Betrug)'
On reverse: pencil study for *Gespannt* of May 1929
Inscribed on reverse: 'd Gn B Gr / h Gn. / dünner Rahmen S? R?'

REFERENCES
Derouet and Boissel 1984, p.320, ill. (recto)

Kandinsky made a study for *Sachte* of March 1929 (Barnett no.931) on the recto and a sketch related to *Gespannt* of May 1929 (Barnett no.944) on the verso.

**p.13** Pencil study for *Nach rechts* of February 1929

REFERENCES
Derouet and Boissel 1984, p.320

This drawing is for *Nach rechts* of February 1929 (Barnett no.928).

**p.14** Pencil sketch for an unidentified work
Inscribed l.l.: 'unten-oben'; l.r.: '80 x 110'; u.c.: 'S. Kräftig / B mit :.:.: glitzernd'
On reverse: pencil sketch related to *Ein Fleck* of June 1925

REFERENCES
Derouet and Boissel 1984, p.320, ill.

Neither the image nor the dimensions on the recto correspond to the picture titled *Unten-oben* of February 1931 (Roethel and Benjamin no.997), which the artist recorded in his Handlist as having been destroyed. The dimensions correspond to those of *Pfeil zum Kreis* of February 1930 (Roethel and Benjamin no.943), although the motifs do not. The sketch on the verso is clearly related to *Ein Fleck* of June 1925 (Roethel and Benjamin no.760).

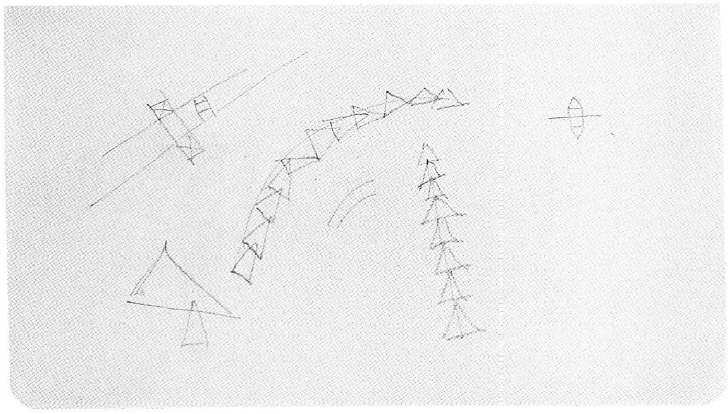
33, p.11

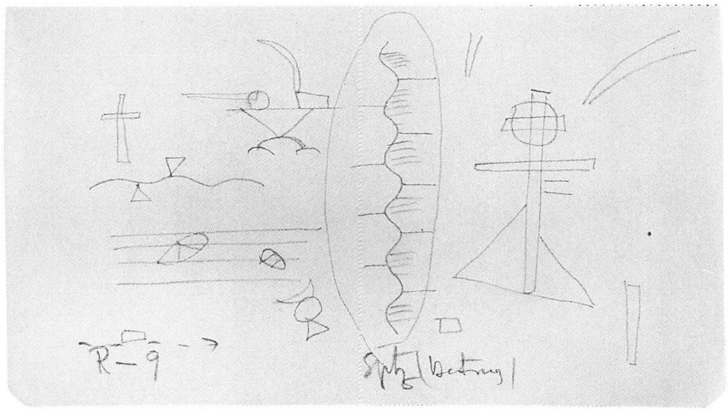
33, p.12R

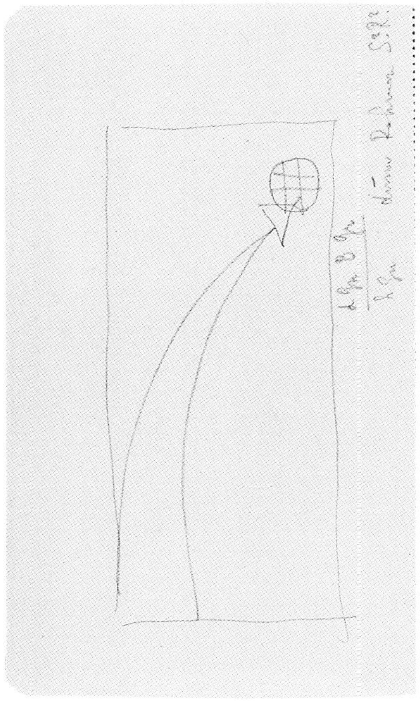
33, p.12V

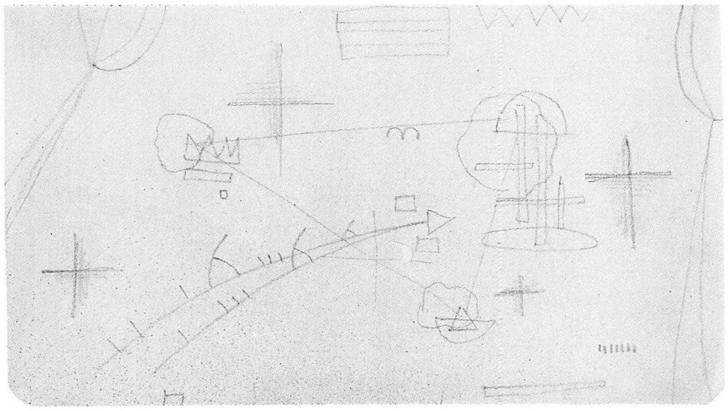
33, p.13

33, p.14V

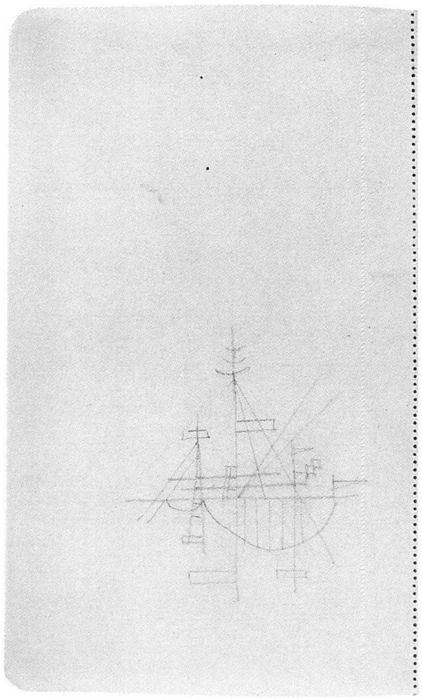

33, p.14R

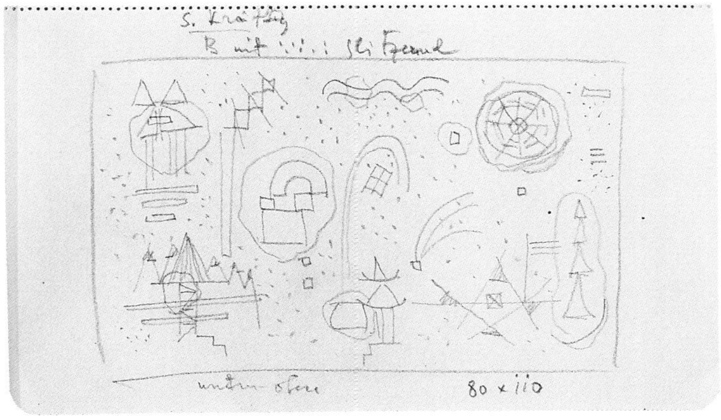

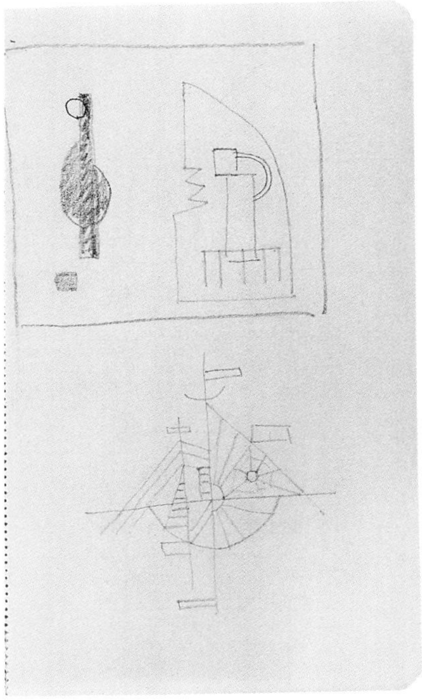

33, p.15R

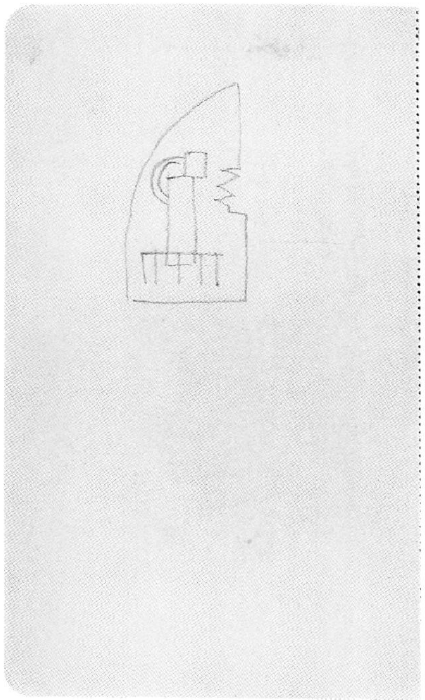

33, p.15V

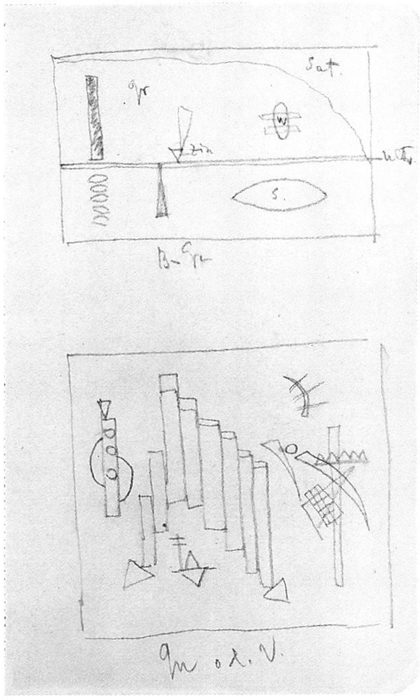

33, p.16R

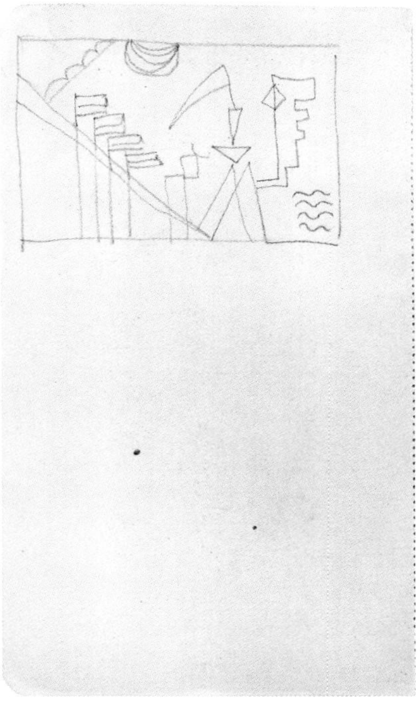

33, p.16V

**p.15** Pencil studies for *Fremd* of March 1929
On reverse: pencil sketch for *Fremd*

REFERENCES
Derouet and Boissel 1984, p.320, ill. (recto)

The sketches on the recto (above) and on the verso are for *Fremd* of March 1929 (Barnett no.929). The other sketch on the recto (below) is related to the study on the facing page for *Ein Fleck* (see p.14v).

**p.16** Pencil studies for *Haltend* of May 1929 (above) and *Herunter* of November 1929 (below)
Inscribed above: 'B-Gn' and with color notations: 'Gr / Sat. / zin / w / Ultr. s'; and below: 'Gn od. V.'
On reverse: pencil study for *Dicht* of April 1929

REFERENCES
Derouet and Boissel 1984, p.320, ill.

There are studies for *Haltend* of May 1929 (Roethel and Benjamin no. 902) on the recto (above) and *Herunter* of November 1929 (Roethel and Benjamin no.920) (below). In addition, there is a sketch for *Dicht* of April 1929 (Roethel and Benjamin no.899) on the verso.

**p.17** Pencil studies for *Leiterform (Auf Flecken)* of February 1929 (above) and pencil sketch related to *Im lockeren Grün* of November 1927 (below)
On reverse: pencil sketch for an unidentified watercolor
Inscribed u.r. on reverse: 'Krapp / nach unten Spritz'; l.r.: 'S / w / Giftgn'; l.c.: 'Gn / B hellst / B h'

REFERENCES
Derouet and Boissel 1984, p.320, ill.

On the recto there are studies for *Leiterform (Auf Flecken)* of February 1929 (Roethel and Benjamin no.893) (above) and *Im lockeren Grün* of November 1927 (Barnett no.797) (below).

33, p.17R

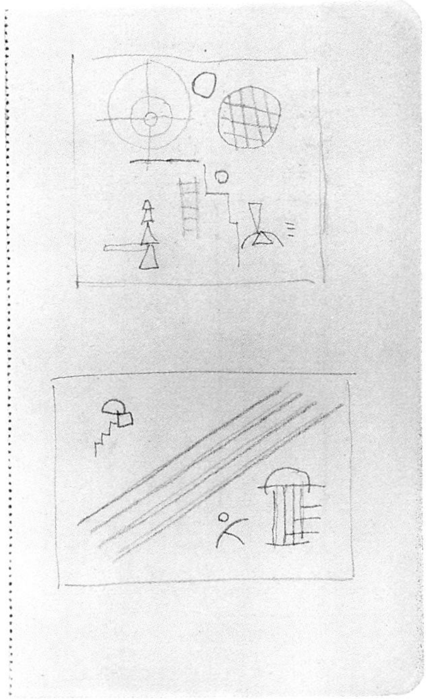

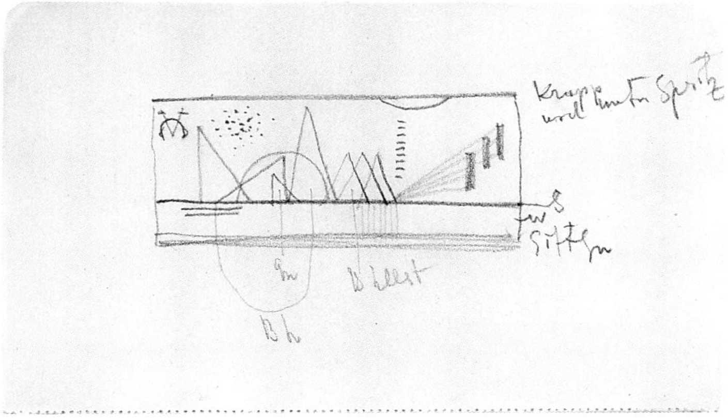

33, p.17V

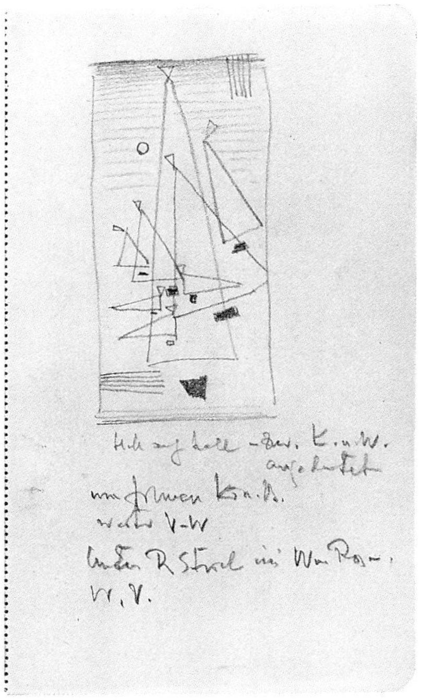

33, p.18

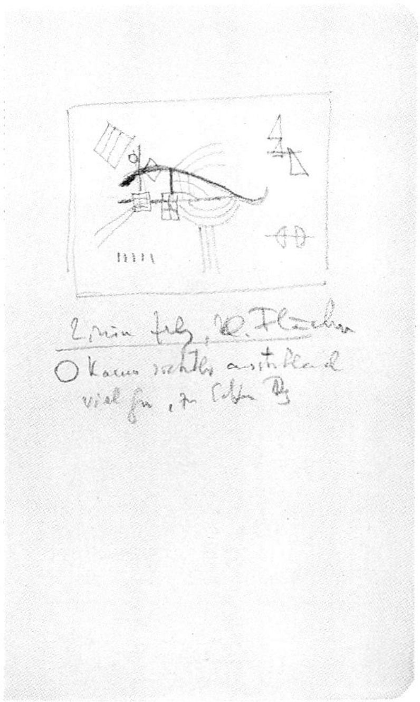

33, p.19R

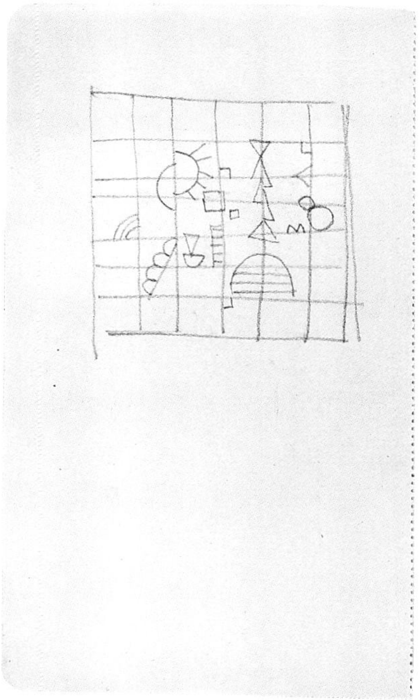

33, p.19V

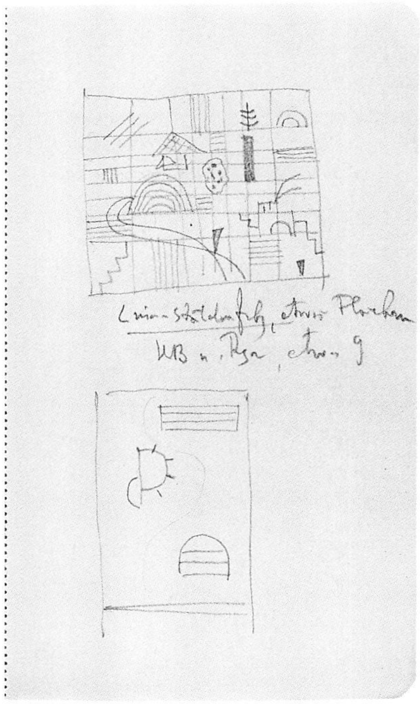

33, p.20

**p.18** Pencil study for *Im freien Blau* of March 1929
Inscribed below: 'Hell auf hell- zur K. u. W. / angedeutet / vorn Formen Kön. B. / weiter V-W / Unten R Strich in's Wm Rosa. / W.V.'

REFERENCES
Derouet and Boissel 1984, p.320, ill.

The sketch is related to *Im freien Blau* of March 1929 (Roethel and Benjamin no.898).

**p.19** Pencil study for *Linie* of April 1929
Inscribed below: 'Linien frbg. Kl. Flächen / O Kaum sichtbr ausstrahlend / viel Gn. zu Ecken Rs.'
On reverse: pencil sketch related to *Variierte Rechtecke* of April 1929

REFERENCES
Derouet and Boissel 1984, p.321, ill. (recto)

The studies are for two watercolors painted in April 1929, *Linie* and *Variierte Rechtecke* (Barnett nos.935, 938).

**p.20** Pencil studies for *Variierte Rechtecke* of April 1929 (above) and *Kurz* of June 1929 (below)
Inscribed c.: 'Linien Stäbchen frbg, etwas Flachen / HB u. Rsa, etwas G'

REFERENCES
Derouet and Boissel 1984, p.321, ill.

There is another study for *Variierte Rechtecke* of April 1929 (see facing page) and a sketch for *Kurz* of June 1929 (Roethel and Benjamin no.906).

**p.21** Pencil study for *Weissgebunden* of March 1929 (above) and pencil sketch related to *Bunte Stäbchen* of 1928 (below)
On reverse: pencil study for *Grün* of June 1929
Inscribed on reverse within image: '1 / 2 / 3 / 4 / 5'; below: 'Akzente / 1 mitte Rsa, / auf h. Gn / Akz / 2 =wie / links / obn. G br / Akz / 3 h B / mitte Gn mit'; l.c.: 'Gn-B fleckig / 4- dkl / 5 h / h / Obn- s.d. / Untr- ins Purpur'

REFERENCES
Derouet and Boissel 1984, p.321, ill.

Kandinsky made sketches related to *Weissgebunden* of March 1929 (Roethel and Benjamin no.895) (above) and *Bunte Stäbchen* of 1928 (Roethel and Benjamin no.877) (below) on the recto, and a study for *Grün* of June 1929 (Roethel and Benjamin no.904) on the verso.

33, p.21R

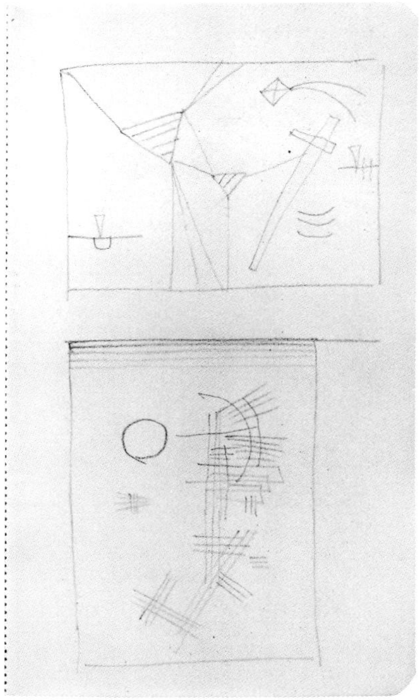

33, p.21V

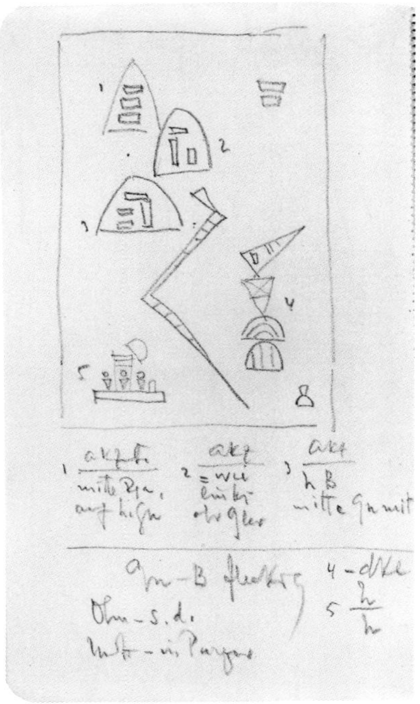

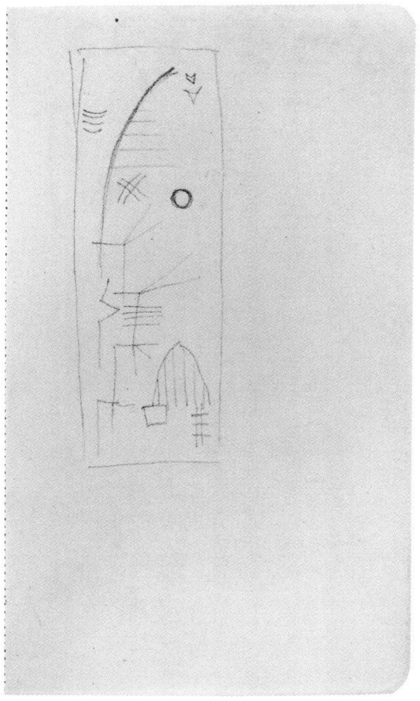

33, p.22R

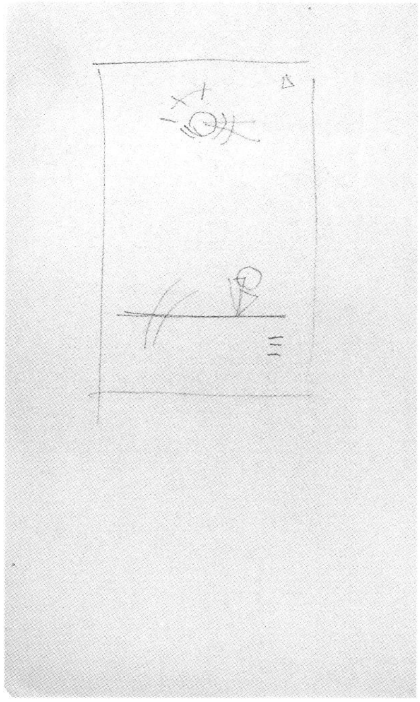

33, p.22V

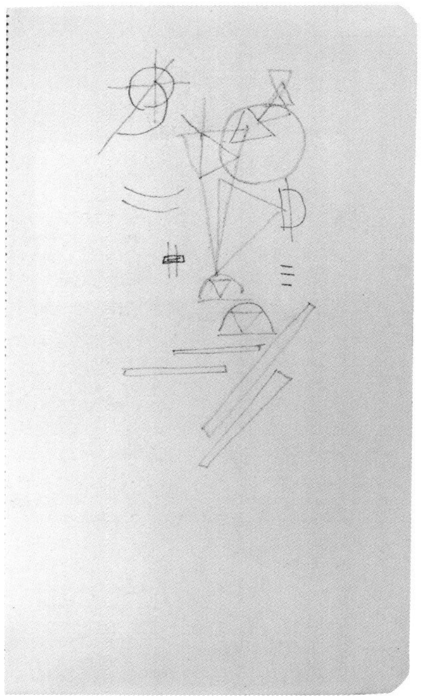

33, p.23R

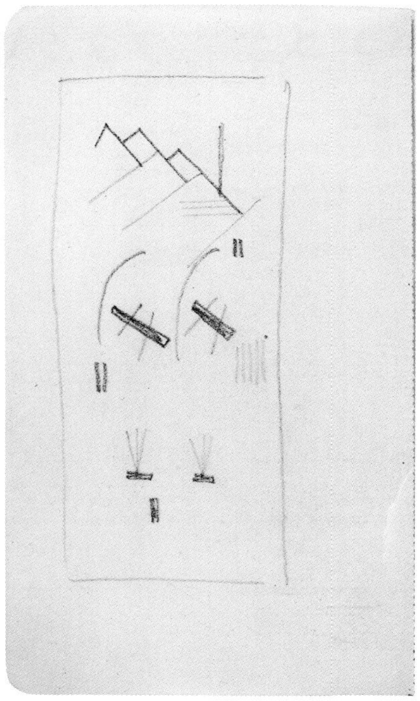

33, p.23V

**p.22** Pencil study for *Steigende Glut* of March 1929
On reverse: pencil study for *Strahlen* of April 1929

REFERENCES
Derouet and Boissel 1984, p.321

There is a study for *Steigende Glut* of March 1929 (Barnett no.930) and, on the reverse, a sketch for *Strahlen* of April 1929 (Barnett no.934).

**p.23** Pencil study for *Schweigsam* of May 1929
On reverse: pencil study for *Und oben!* of May 1929

REFERENCES
Derouet and Boissel 1984, p.321

This drawing is related to *Schweigsam* of May 1929 (Roethel and Benjamin no.900), and the study on the reverse is for *Und oben!* of May 1929 (Barnett no.942).

**p.24** Pencil study for *Aufstieg* of April 1929
On reverse: three arrow shapes (not illustrated) related to unidentified study on facing page

REFERENCES
Derouet and Boissel 1984, p.321, ill. (recto)

The drawing is preparatory to *Aufstieg* of April 1929 (Barnett no.936).

**p.25** Pencil studies for *Tragende Runde* of April 1929 (above) and for an unidentified work (below)
Inscribed l.l.: 'V. Rs. Gh / Zart Gn / Akzente / Gn zu / Formen / gblich'; l.r.: '90 x 90'
On reverse: pencil study related to *Leicht im Schwer* of May 1929

REFERENCES
Barnett 1983, p.208, ill.a (recto)
Derouet and Boissel 1984, p.321, ill. (recto)

Above Kandinsky has made a study for *Tragende Runde* of April 1929 (Barnett no.937) and, on the reverse, a study related to *Leicht im Schwer* of May 1929 (Roethel and Benjamin no.901).

33, p.24

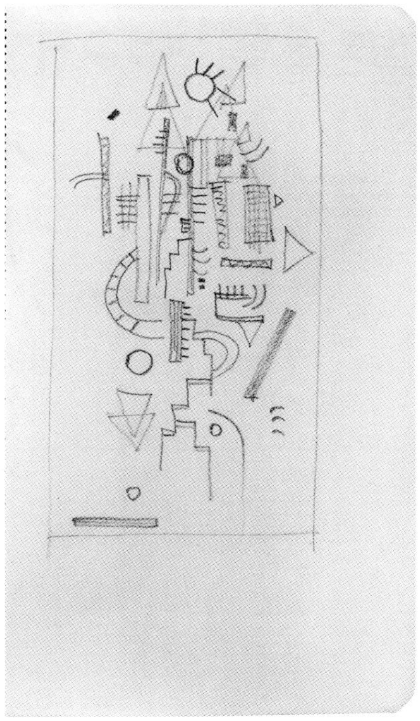

33, p.25R

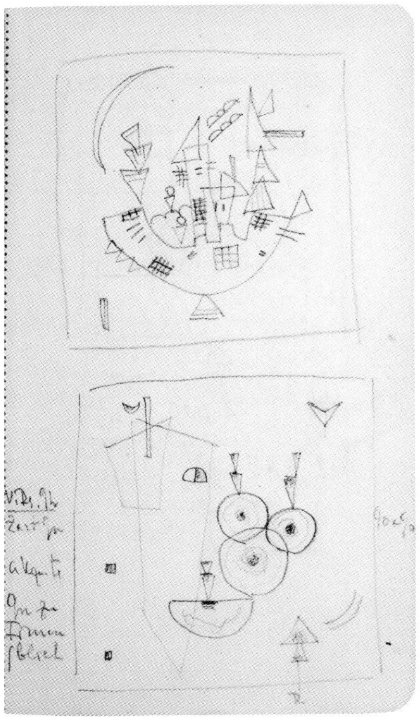

33, p.25V

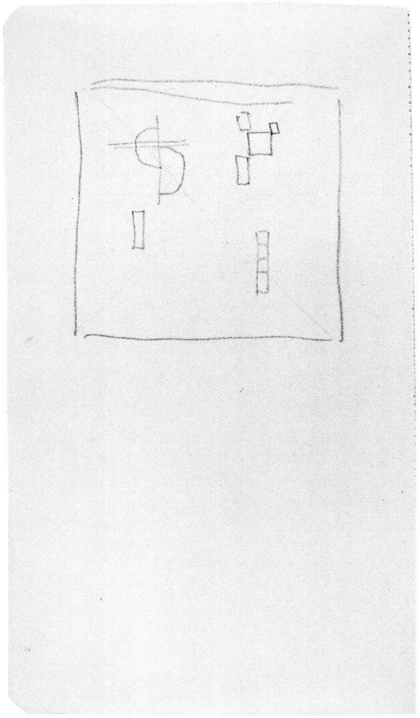

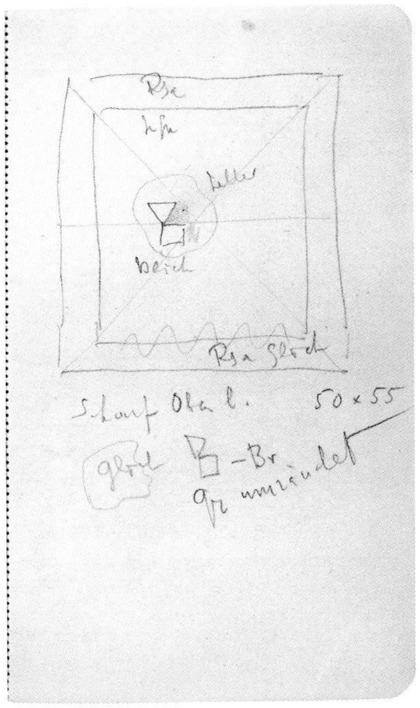

33, p.26R

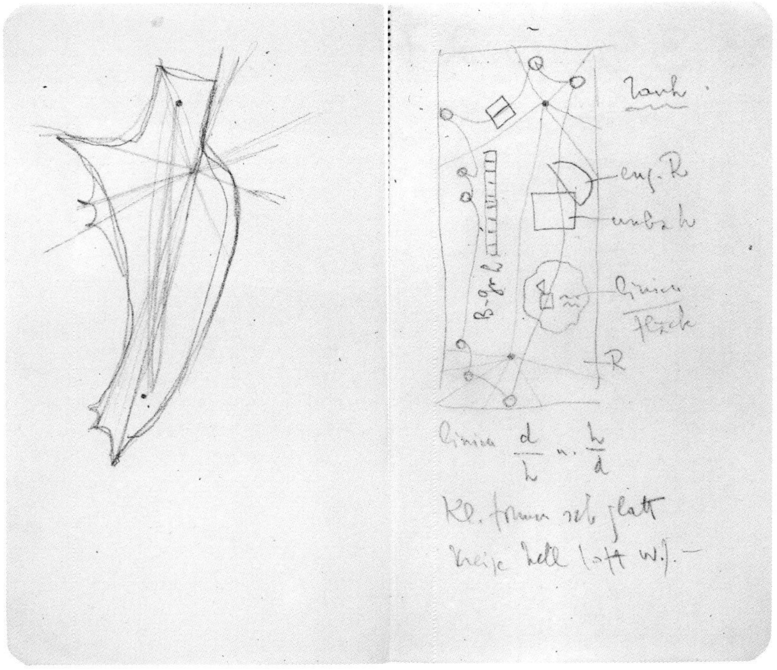

33, pp.26v-27

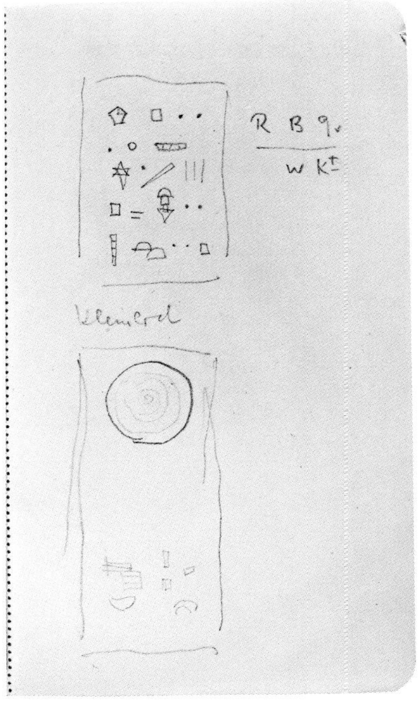

33, p.28

**p.26** Pencil study for *Spitze* of June 1929
Inscribed l.c.: 'Scharf Oben l. 50 x 55 / G lich / Br / Gr umrandet' and with color notations: 'Rsa / h Gn / heller / B lich / Rsa G lich'
On reverse: pencil sketch for *Fixierte Spitzen* of June 1929

REFERENCES
Derouet and Boissel 1984, p.321, ill.

33, p.29

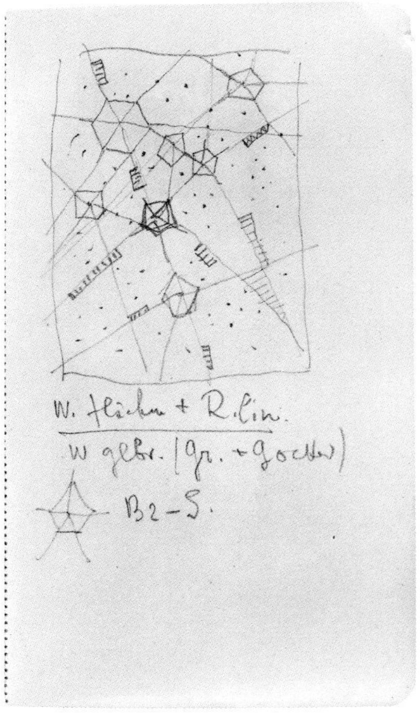

33, p.30

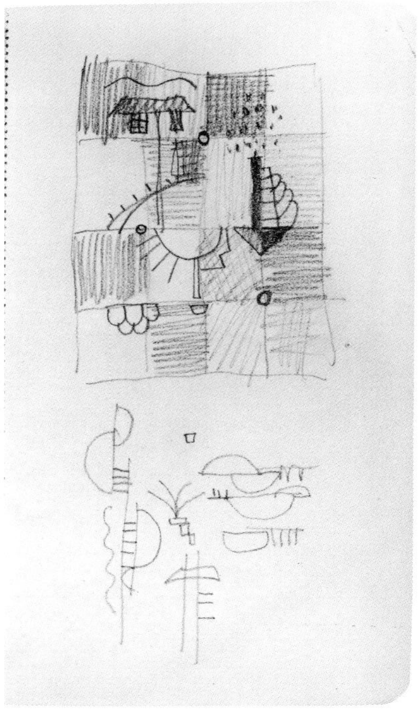

There is a study for *Spitze* of June 1929 (Roethel and Benjamin no.909) on the recto and a sketch for *Fixierte Spitzen* of June 1929 (Roethel and Benjamin no.907) on the verso.

**p.27** Pencil study for *Fixierte Spitzen* of June 1929
Inscribed u.r.: 'rauh. / eng. R / umbr h / linien / Fläche / R'; l.c.: 'Linien d / h u. h / d / Kl. Formen sehr glatt / Kreise hell (oft w.)'

REFERENCES
Derouet and Boissel 1984, p.321, ill.

Like the sketch on the facing page, this drawing is for *Fixierte Spitzen* of June 1929.

**p.28** Pencil study for *Etagen* of March 1929 (above) and pencil sketch (below)
Inscribed u.r.: 'R B Gr / w Kt'; c.: 'Kleinlich'

REFERENCES
Derouet and Boissel 1984, p.321, ill.

The drawing above resembles *Etagen* of March 1929 (Roethel and Benjamin no.896) as well as the study on p.7 (above) and two individual drawings (vol.I, cat. nos.704, 705). The sketch below can be related to *Strahlen* of April 1929 (Barnett no.934) and possibly *Unbiegsam* of December 1929 (Roethel and Benjamin no.927).

**p.29** Pencil sketch related to *Kühle Rede* of May 1929
Inscribed l.c.: 'W. Flächen + R. lin. / w glbr. / (Gr. + G ocker) / Br-S.'

REFERENCES
Derouet and Boissel 1984, p.321, ill.

The sketch can be related to *Kühle Rede* of May 1929 (Barnett no.940) and another study on p.2 in this sketchbook.

**p.30** Pencil studies for *Leicht im Schwer* of May 1929 (below) and an unidentified work (above)

REFERENCES
Derouet and Boissel 1984, p.321, ill.

The study for *Leicht im Schwer* of May 1929 (Roethel and Benjamin no.901) can be related to the sketch on p.25 verso (above).

**p.31** Pencil study for *Grüner Duft* of May 1929

REFERENCES
Derouet and Boissel 1984, pp.319, ill., 321

This drawing is for *Grüner Duft* of May 1929 (Barnett no.941).

**p.32** Pencil sketch for an unidentified work

REFERENCES
Derouet and Boissel 1984, p.321, ill.

**p.33** Pencil sketch for an unidentified work

REFERENCES
Derouet and Boissel 1984, p.321

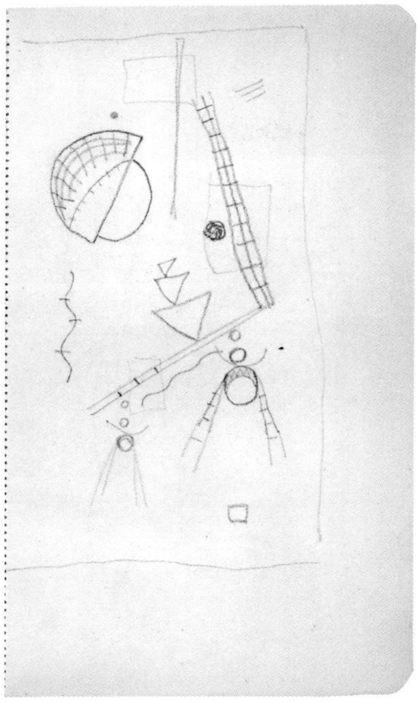

33, p.31

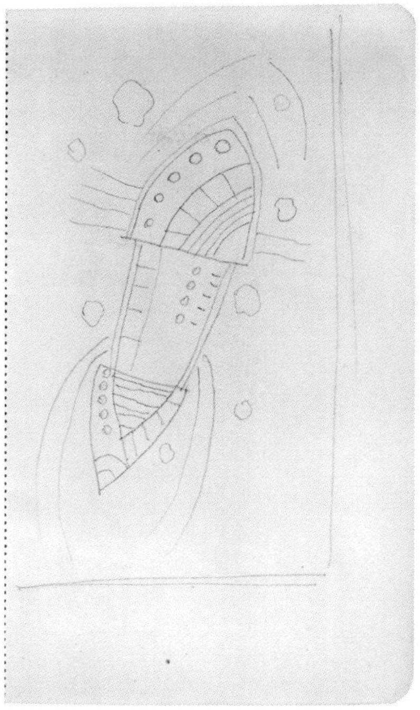

33, p.32

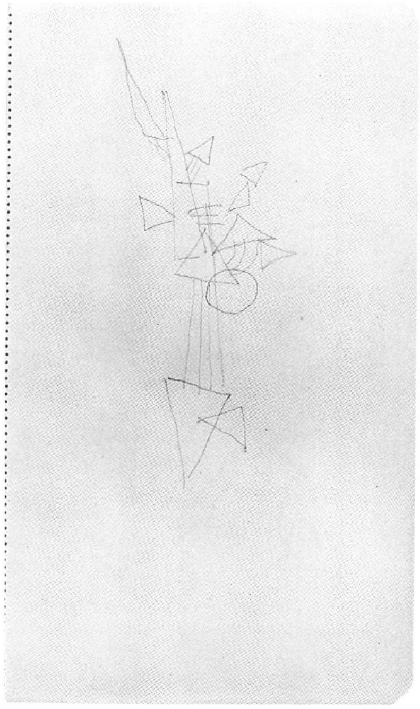

33, p.33

**p.34** Pencil sketch with traces of red sprayed watercolor
On reverse: pencil study for *Fragil* of March 1931 (below) and sketch reminiscent of *Dumpfes Rot* of June 1927 (above)

REFERENCES
Derouet and Boissel 1984, pp.321, 333, ill. (verso)

The sketch on the recto shares similarities with *Bild im Bild* of September 1929 (Roethel and Benjamin no.911). On the verso the sketch (above) is reminiscent of *Dumpfes Rot* of June 1927 (Roethel and Benjamin no.843), and the one below is a study for *Fragil* of March 1931 (Barnett no.1009).

**p.35** Pencil studies for *Kalt* of June 1929 (above) and *Stich in Violett* of December 1929 (below)
Inscribed u.r. with color notations: 'R / w / Dkl' and on reverse: 'Gn dkl'
On reverse: pencil studies for *Kalt* (above) and an unidentified work (below)

REFERENCES
Derouet and Boissel 1984, pp.321, 322, ill.

Kandinsky made studies for *Kalt* of June 1929 (Roethel and Benjamin no.908) at the top of both the recto and verso. In addition, there is a study for *Stich in Violett* of December 1929 (Roethel and Benjamin no.930) on the recto.

33, p.34R

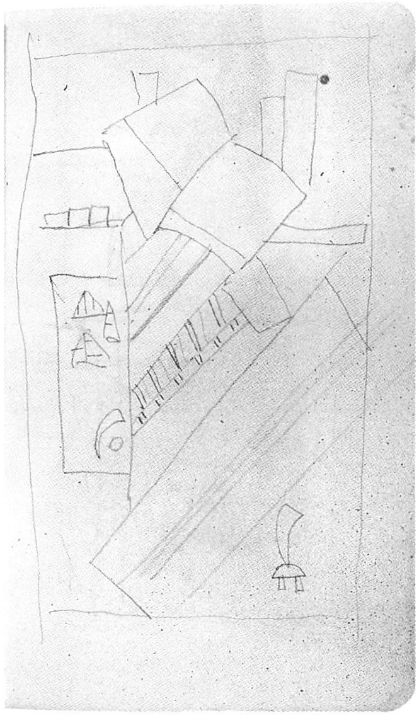

33, pp.34V-35R

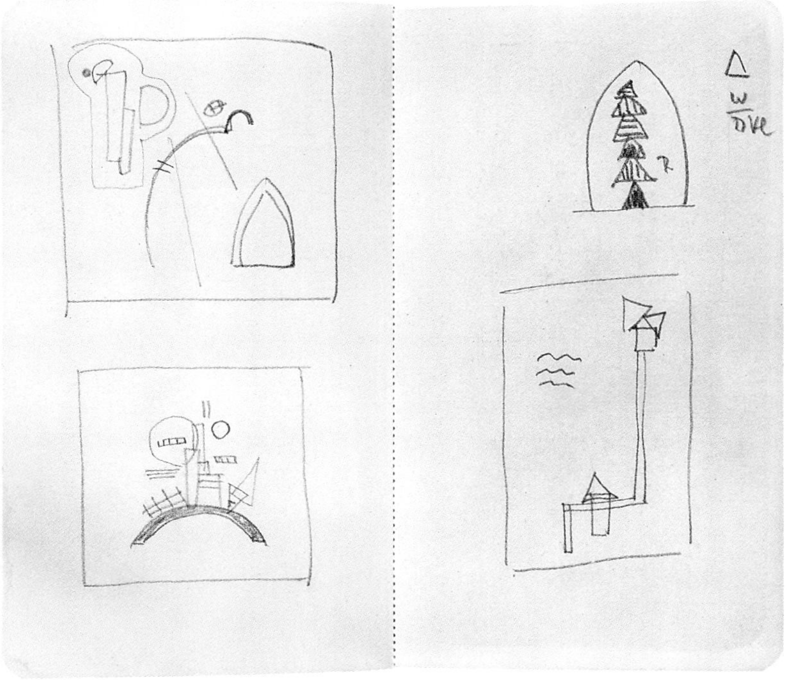

33, p.35V

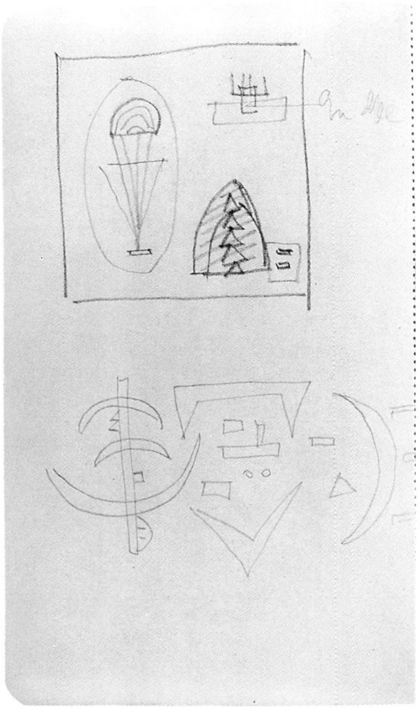

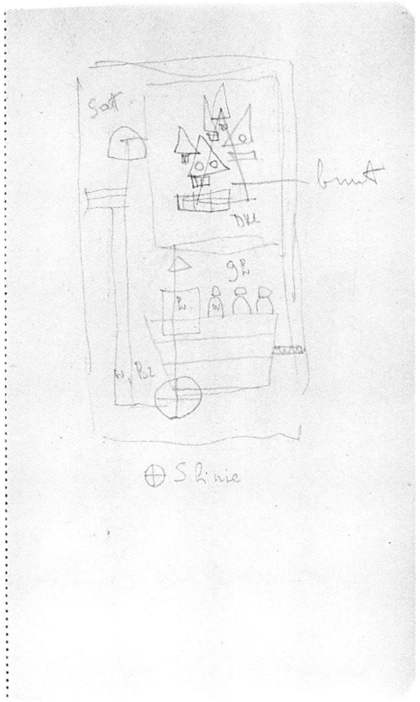

33, p.36r

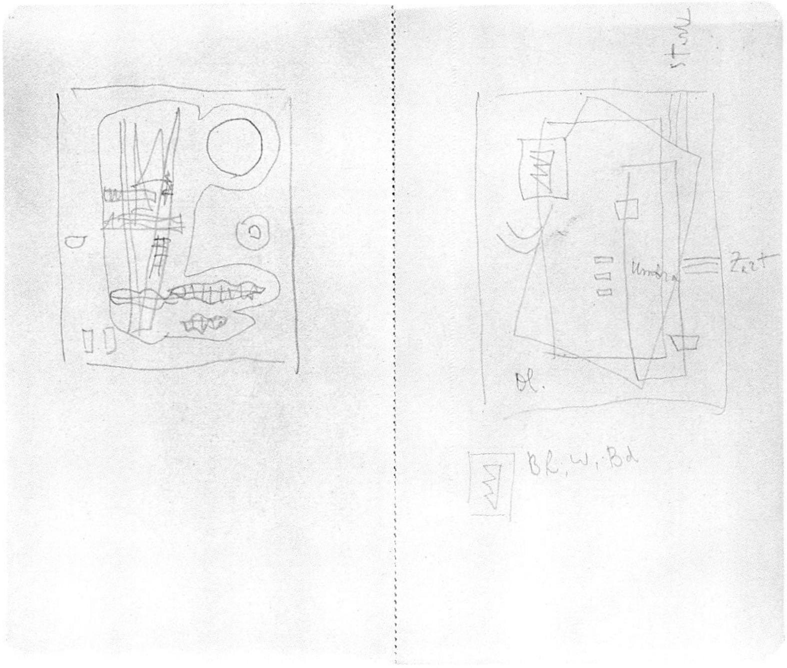

33, pp.36v-37r

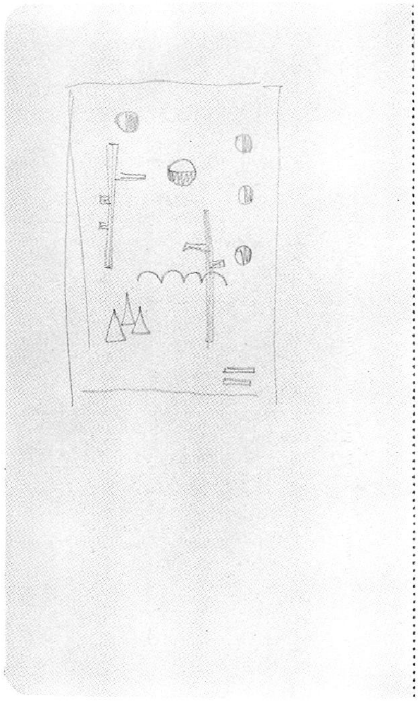

33, p.37v

**p.36** Pencil study for *Bild im Bild* of September 1929
Inscribed l.c.: 'S Linie'; u.l.: 'Sat.'; c.r.: 'bunt / Dkl' and with additional color notations: 'G h / w / Br'
On reverse: pencil sketch for an unidentified work

REFERENCES
Derouet and Boissel 1984, p.321, ill. (recto)

The drawing on the recto is for *Bild im Bild* of September 1929 (Roethel and Benjamin no.911).

**p.37** Pencil sketches
Inscribed u.r.: 'Stark'; c.r.: 'Umbra / Zart'; l.l.: 'Ol.'; l.c.: 'B h. w. Bd'
On reverse: pencil study for *Nahe und weit* of March 1930

REFERENCES
Derouet and Boissel 1984, p.321, ill. (recto)

The sketches on the recto suggest an untitled watercolor of 1930 (Barnett no 1005) and *Schichten* of February 1932 (Roethel and Benjamin no.1014), whereas the drawing on the verso is a study for *Nahe und weit* of March 1930 (Barnett no.971).

**p.38** Pencil study for *Machtlose Fesseln* of September 1929
Inscribed l.c.: 'd B linien H-D Akzente / S h Gn Stumpf' and with color notations: 'Rsa / Citr / Br. / Or.'
On reverse: pencil sketch for an unidentified work
Inscribed l.c. on reverse: 'S- h Gn- dkl Rs / rhytmisch nach O'

REFERENCES
Derouet and Boissel 1984, p.322, ill.

The drawing on the recto is a study for *Machtlose Fesseln* of September 1929 (Barnett no.945).

**p.39** Pencil sketch related to *Weisse Schärfe* of November 1930

REFERENCES
Derouet and Boissel 1984, p.322

The drawing can be related to *Weisse Schärfe* of November 1930 (Roethel and Benjamin no.975) and coeval drawings (vol.I, cat. nos.763, 765).

33, p.38r

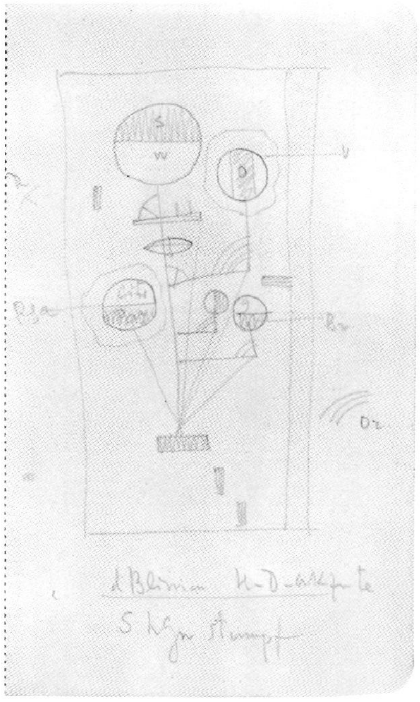

33, pp.38v-39

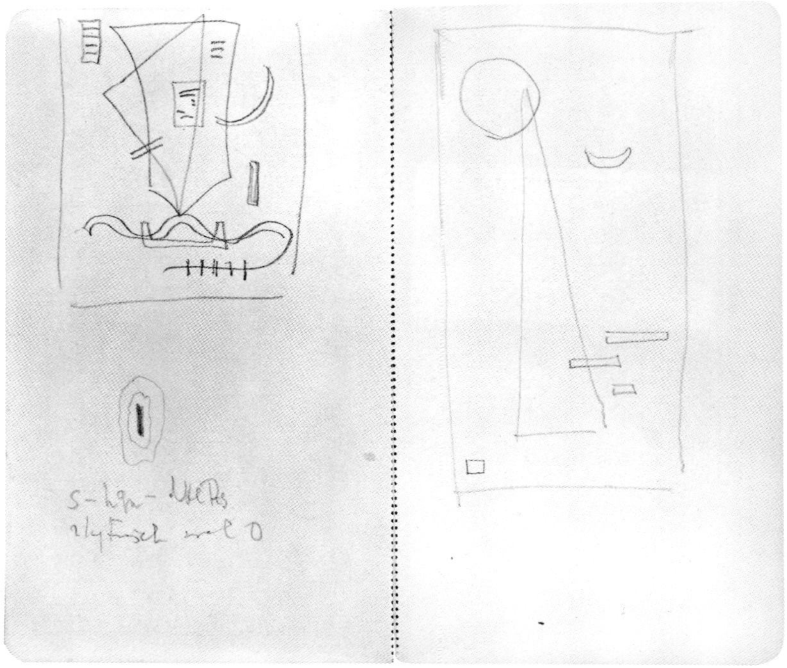

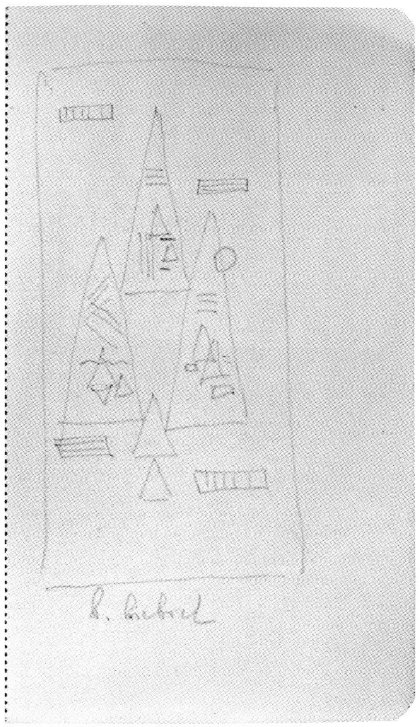

33, p.40r

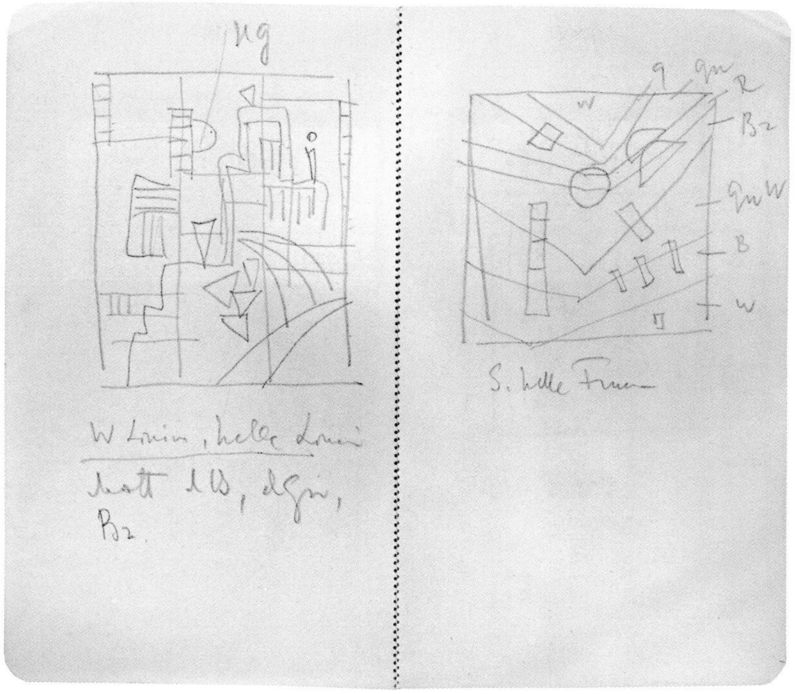

33, pp.40v-41r

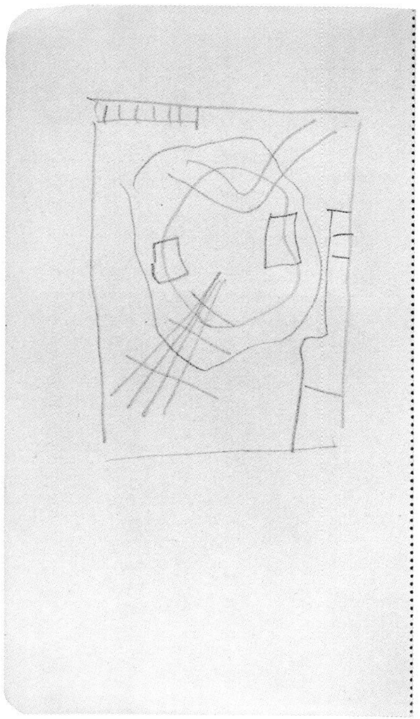

33, p.41v

**p.40** Pencil sketch for an unidentified work
Inscribed l.c.: 'b. […]ich'
On reverse: pencil sketch for an unidentified work
Inscribed l.c. on reverse: 'W Linien, helle Linien / Matt d B, d Gn, / Br.'

REFERENCES
Derouet and Boissel 1984, p.322, ill.

**p.41** Pencil sketch for an unidentified work
Inscribed l.c.: 'S. helle Formen' and with color notations: 'w / G / Gn / R / Br / Gn W / B / W'
On reverse: pencil sketch related to *Trübung* of January 1927

REFERENCES
Derouet and Boissel 1984, p.322, ill. (recto)

The sketch on the verso is reminiscent of *Trübung* of January 1927 (Roethel and Benjamin no.819).

**p.42** Pencil sketches for an unidentified work
Inscribed l.c.: 'Satt R'; l.r.: 'Linien'

REFERENCES
Derouet and Boissel 1984, p.322, ill.

**p.43** Pencil sketches of circles related to *Kreise im Braun* of December 1929
Inscribed l.c.: 'allein Schade s. undeutlich / H Br / überschei[…] durch- / sichtig.' and with color notations: 's.d. R / d. Gn / s / in's B / zin'

REFERENCES
Derouet and Boissel 1984, p.322, ill.

The sketches are probably related to *Kreise im Braun* of December 1929 (Roethel and Benjamin no.921).

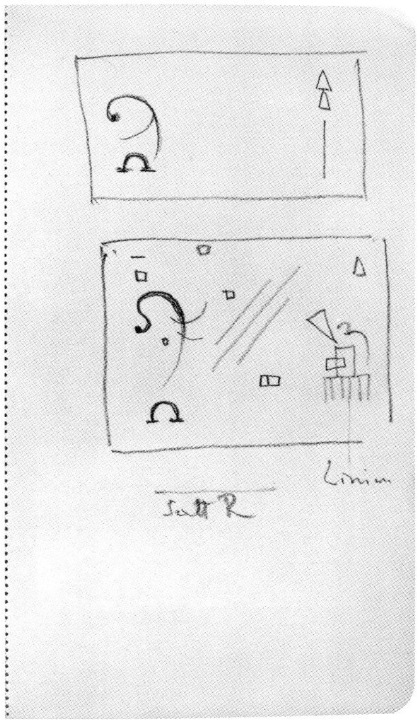

33, p.42

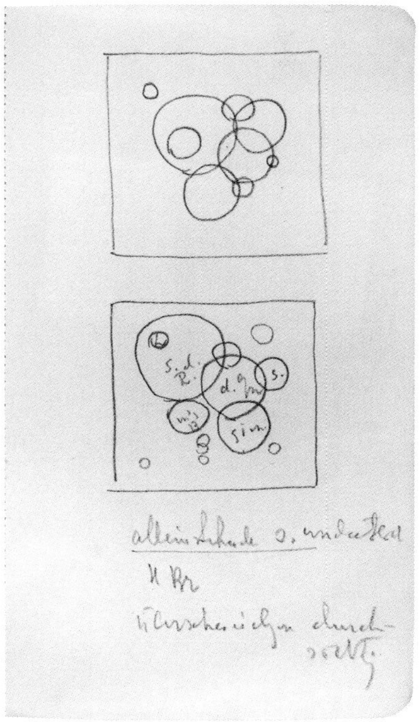

33, p.43

# Sketchbook 34

1933–1935

Brown cardboard notepad with black spine; on back cover stamp of Papierhandlung Paul Frank, Südende
Contains 22 sheets of ruled paper, each 13.6 x 9.2 cm (5¼ x 3⅝ in), of which pp.9–22 are blank. The top edge is perforated.
Pages have not been numbered

Derouet and Boissel 1984, no.502

LOCATION
Musée National d'Art Moderne, Centre Georges Pompidou, Paris (AM 1981.65.676)

HISTORY
Nina Kandinsky, Paris, until 1980

Kandinsky purchased this notepad in Berlin before he moved to Paris in late December 1933.

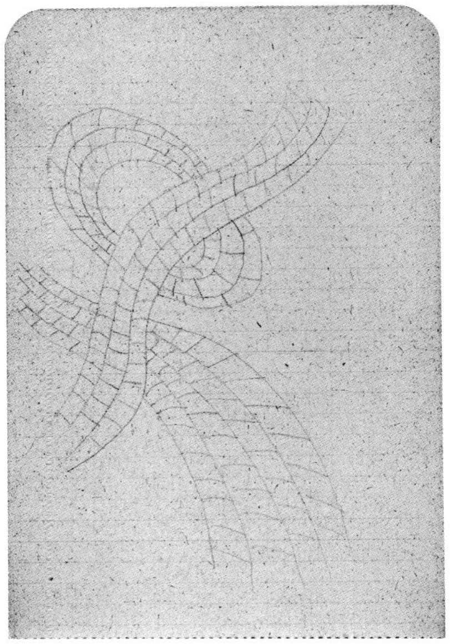

34, p.1

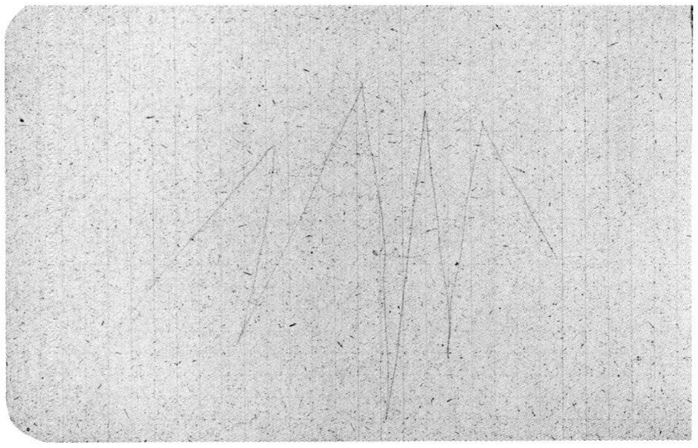

34, p.2

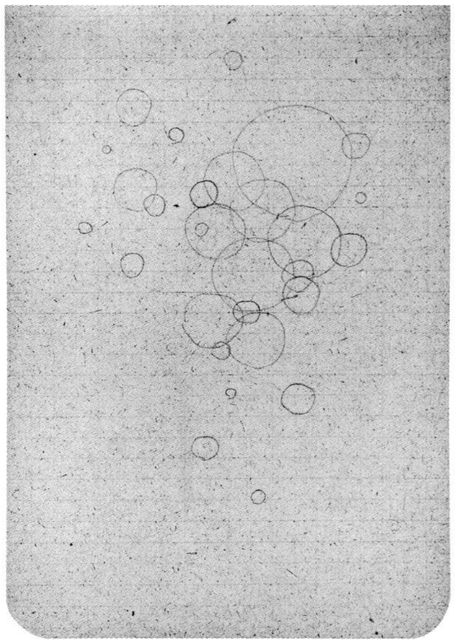

34, p.3

34, p.4

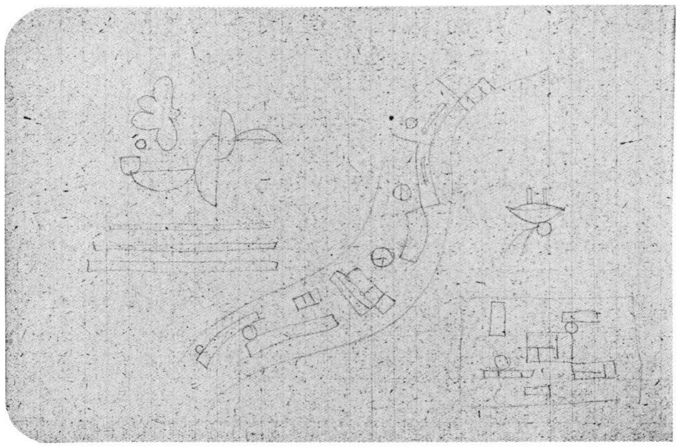

**p.1** Pencil sketch of curving forms (upside down)

REFERENCES
Derouet and Boissel 1984, p.348, ill.

The sketch can be related to *Pointillé* of May 1935, *La Ligne blanche* of June 1936 (Barnett nos.1188, 1200) and an earlier drawing (vol.I, cat. no.844).

**p.2** Pencil sketch of zigzag lines

REFERENCES
Derouet and Boissel 1984, p.348

The sketch can be related to the study for *Zickzack in Weich* on p.5 (below).

**p.3** Pencil sketch of circles

REFERENCES
Derouet and Boissel 1984, p.348, ill.

This study can be related to *Kreiskomplex* of July 1933 and *Cercles soumis* of July 1936 (Barnett nos.1139, 1201).

**p.4** Pencil sketches

REFERENCES
Derouet and Boissel 1984, p.348, ill.

The motifs are similar to those in *Rigide et courbé* of December 1935 (Roethel and Benjamin no.1063) and *Volant* of June 1936 (Barnett no.1195).

**p.5** Pencil study for *Zickzack in Weich* of July 1933

REFERENCES
Derouet and Boissel 1984, p.348

The drawing clearly resembles *Zickzack in Weich* of July 1933 (Barnett no.1138).

**p.6** Pencil study for *Zunehmen* of August 1933
Inscribed with color notations: 'Gn / R / B / Rt w / Gn'

REFERENCES
Derouet and Boissel 1984, p.348, ill.

The drawing is a study for *Zunehmen* of August 1933 (Barnett no.1140).

**p.7** Pencil sketch related to *Transmission* of May 1935

REFERENCES
Derouet and Boissel 1984, p.348, ill.

The study can be related to *Transmission* of May 1935 (Barnett no.1183).

**p.8** Pencil sketches

REFERENCES
Derouet and Boissel 1984, p.348, ill.

The motifs suggest *Kühle Entfernung* of November 1932 (Roethel and Benjamin no.1025)

**pp.9–22** Blank

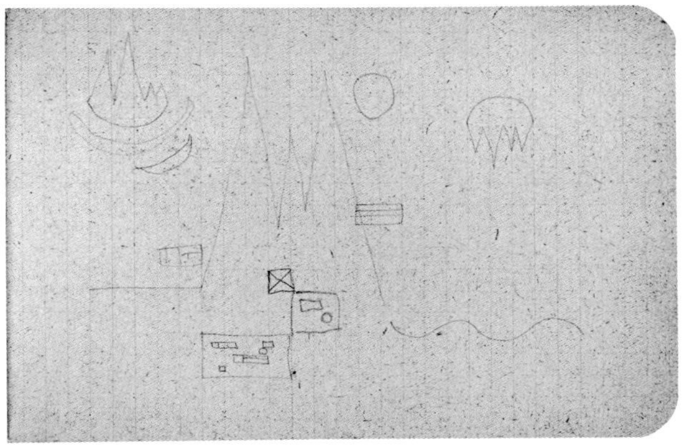

34, p.5

34, p.6

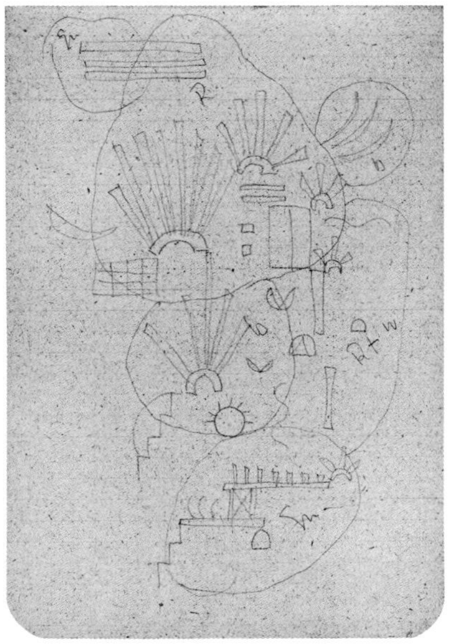

34, p.7

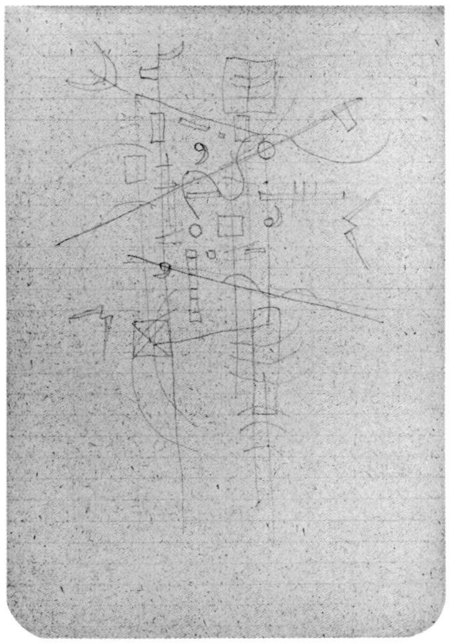

34, p.8

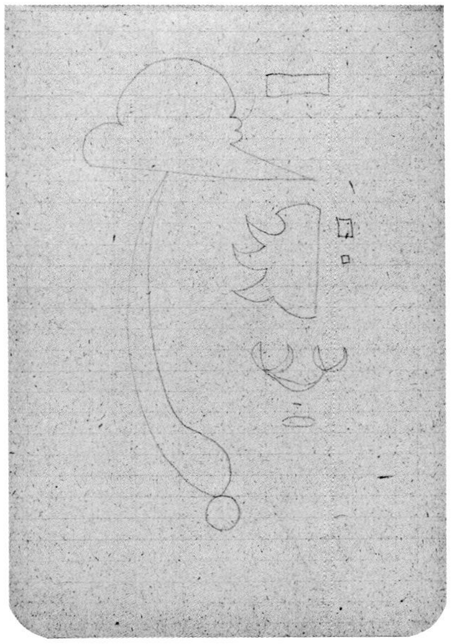

# Sketchbook 35

1935–1939

Tan cardboard with spiral-ring binding at top edge
Contains 11 sheets, each 26.8 x 21 cm (10½ x 8¼ in), and one page inserted (10.3 x 14.3 cm)
Pages have not been numbered

LOCATION
Private collection

HISTORY
Nina Kandinsky, Paris

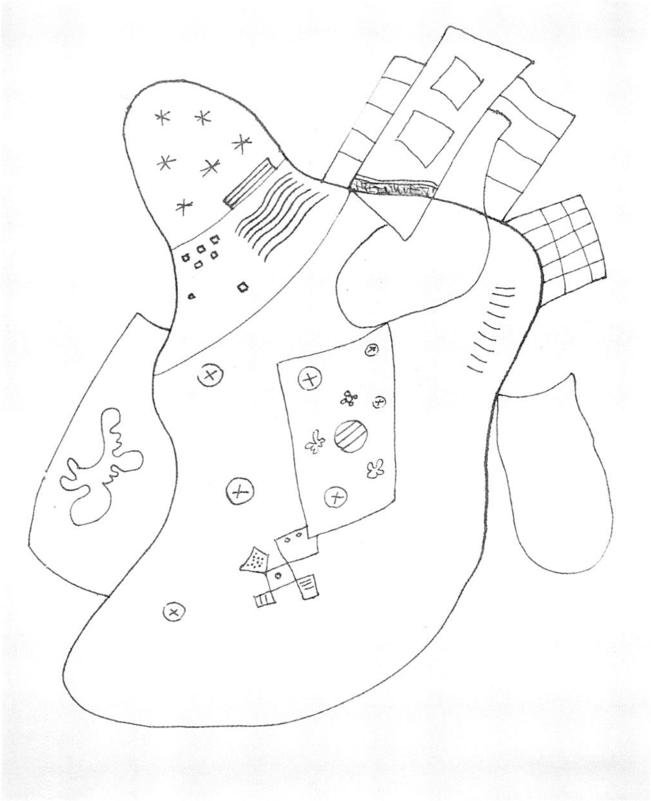

35, p.1

35, p.2

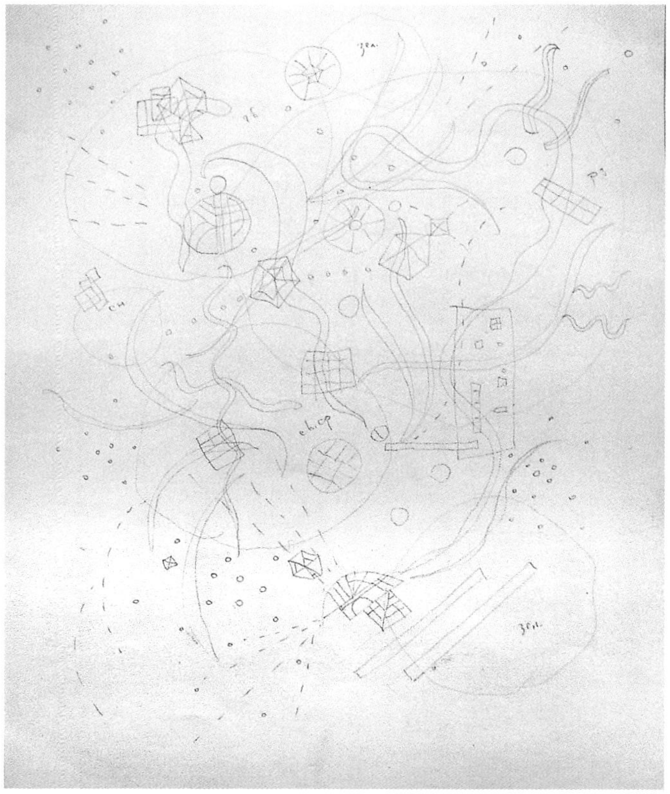

**p.1** Ink drawing

Unlike other studies in the sketchbook, this drawing was done in ink. There is a closely related pencil sketch (vol.I, cat. no.1046 verso), which can be dated c.1939.

**p.2** Pencil study for *Mouvement I* of July 1935
Inscribed with color notations in Cyrillic

Kandinsky has modified certain details and colors in the painting *Mouvement I* of July 1935 (Roethel and Benjamin no.1056).

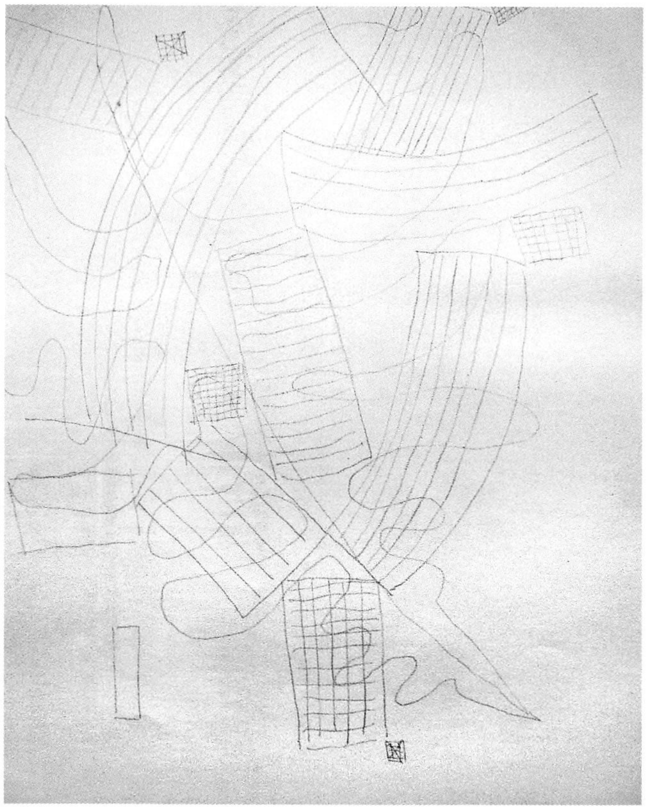

35, p.3R

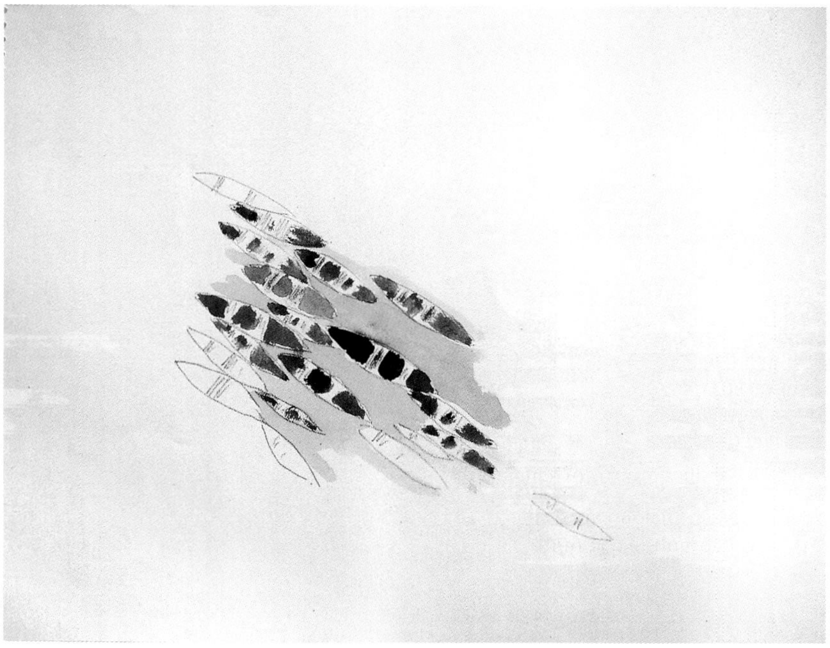

35, p.3V

35, p.4

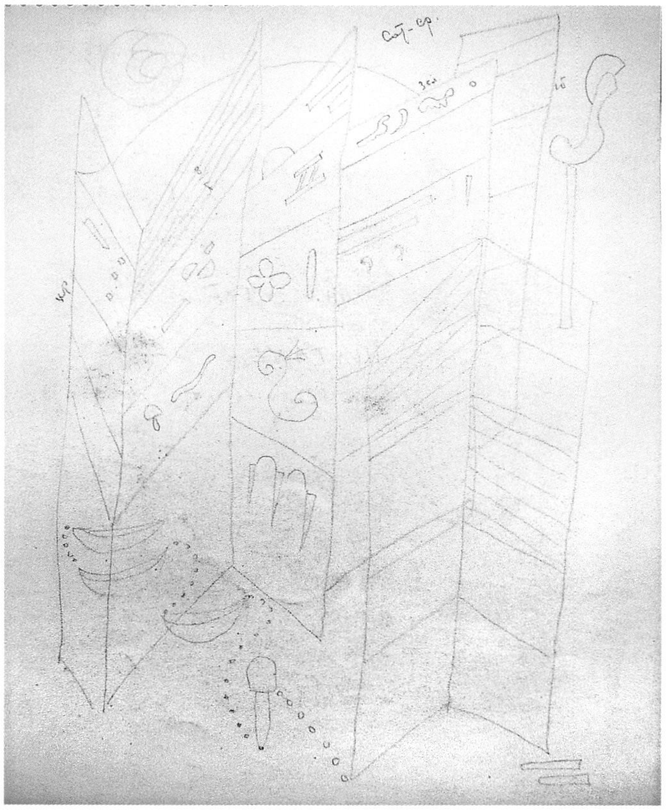

**p.3** Pencil drawing for an unidentified work
On reverse: pencil and watercolor study

The sketch on the recto bears a certain resemblance to *Tension tranquille* of July 1935 (Roethel and Benjamin no.1057) and *Montée-descente* of May 1938 (Barnett no.1230). The motif on the verso can be found in works dated 1940 (Barnett nos.1312, 1328).

**p.4** Pencil drawing for an unidentified work
Inscribed on reverse by unknown hand: 'Mr. Sert / Muntaner No 348 / Barcelona'

The reference is to the Spanish architect Josep Lluis Sert, who was preparing a series of *pochoirs* in the autumn of 1935: Sert lived at the above address in Barcelona at that time.

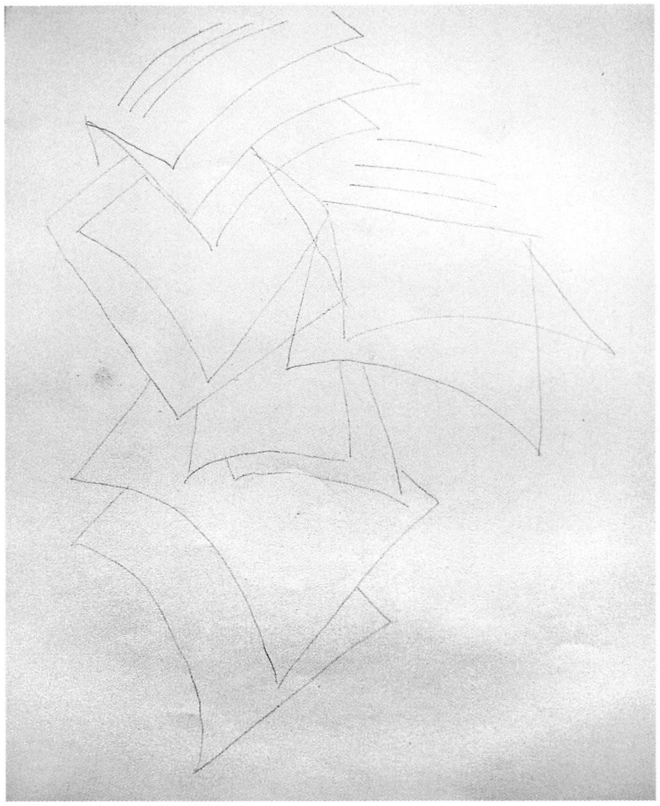

35, p.5R

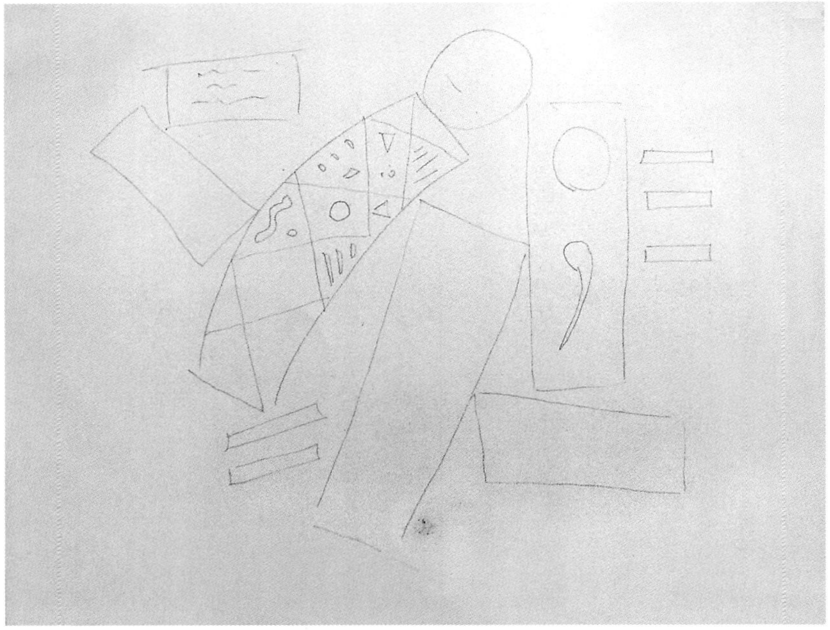

35, p.5V

**p.5** Pencil study for *Tension tranquille* of July 1935
On reverse: pencil sketch for unidentified work

Kandinsky made a study for *Tension tranquille* of July 1935 (Roethel and Benjamin no.1057) on the recto.

**p.6** Pencil sketches related to *Composition IX* and other works of 1936
Inscribed in image at l.l. in Cyrillic: 'pokryt belym / zel. les' and with color notations
On reverse: pencil study for *Composition IX* of February 1936

On the recto Kandinsky inscribed the detail sketch at the lower left: 'covered with white, the green forest' and indicated pink, violet and yellow colors. On the verso there is a study for *Composition IX* of February 1936 (Roethel and Benjamin no.1064).

35, p.6R

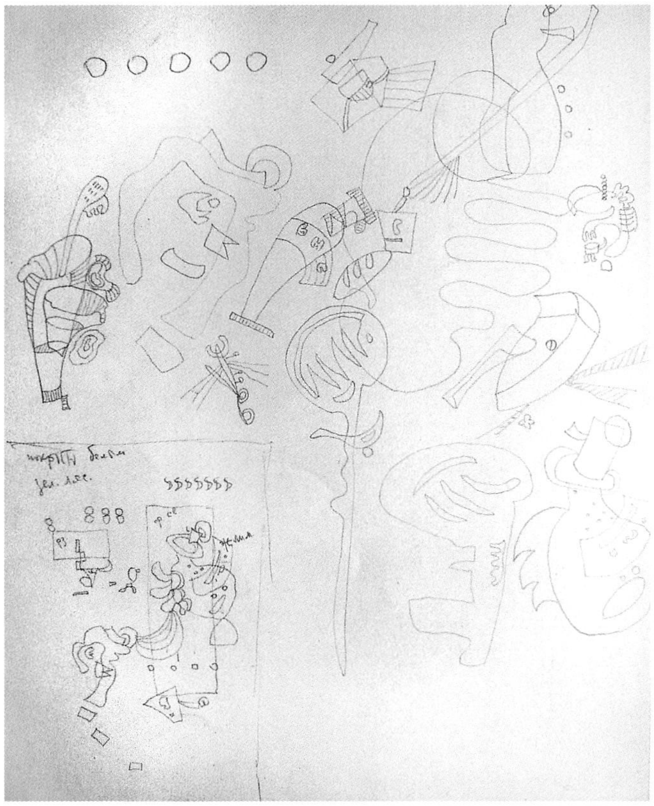

35, p.6V

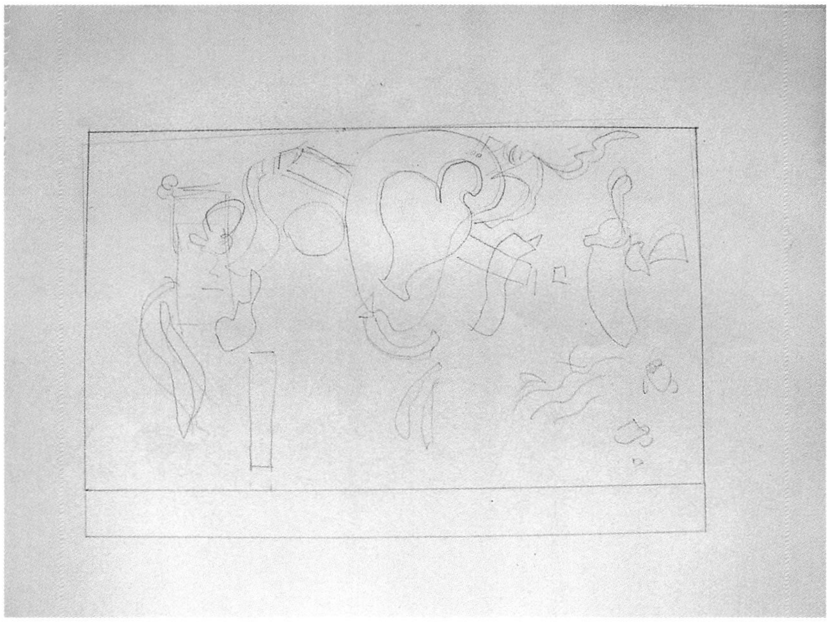

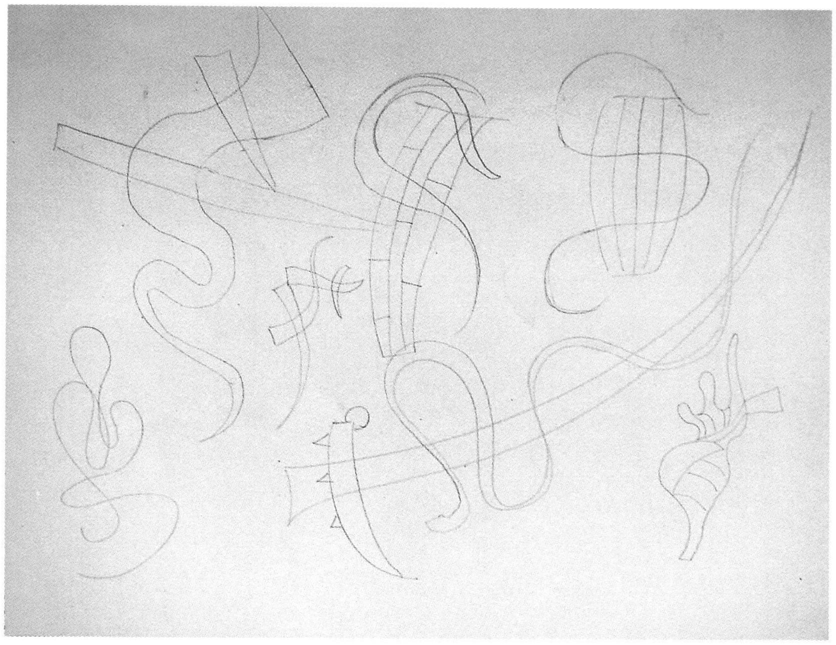

35, p.7v

**p.7** Recto blank
On reverse: pencil drawing related to *Accents délicats* of November 1935

See following page.

**p.8** Pencil drawing related to *Accents délicats* of November 1935
On reverse: pencil study for *Accents délicats* of November 1935

Kandinsky squared up the drawing for *Accents délicats* of November 1935 (Roethel and Benjamin no.1062) on the reverse: it bears a much closer resemblance to the canvas than the two preceding studies.

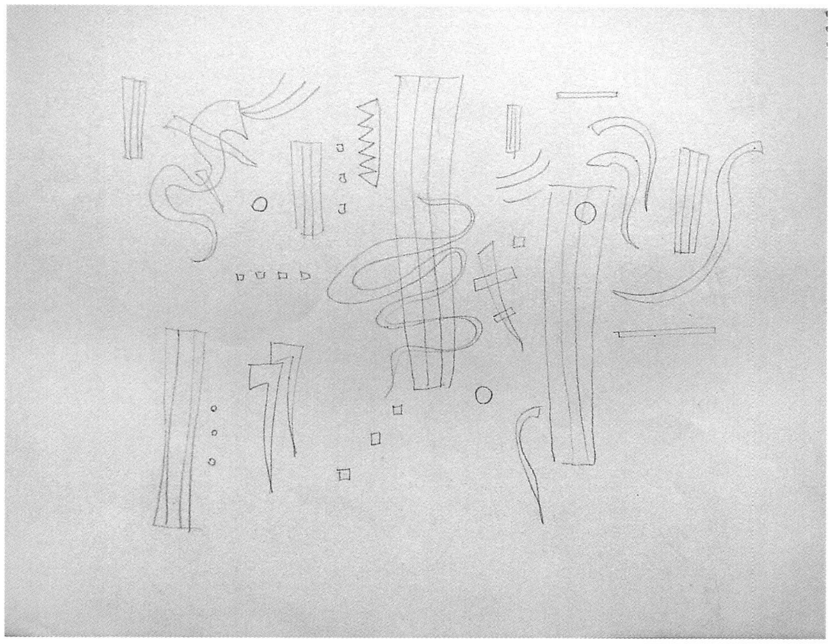

35, p.8r

35, p.8v

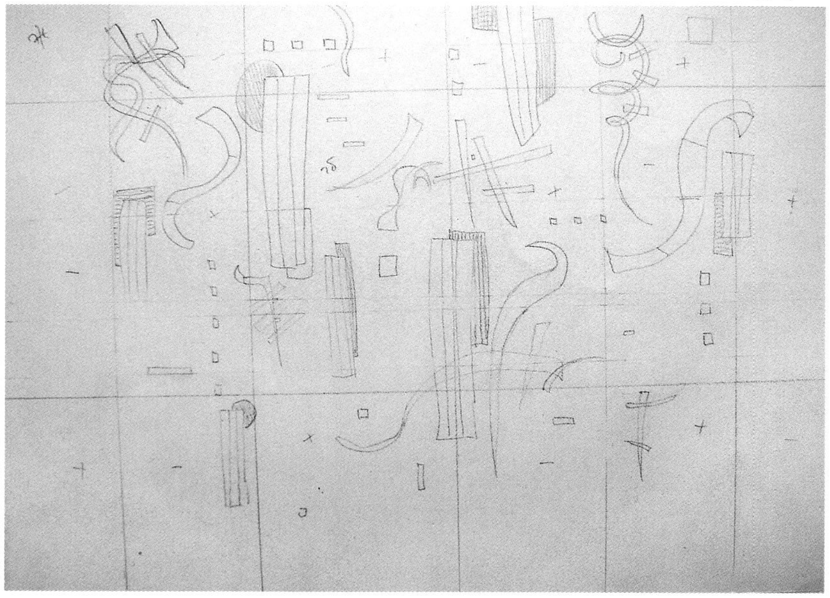

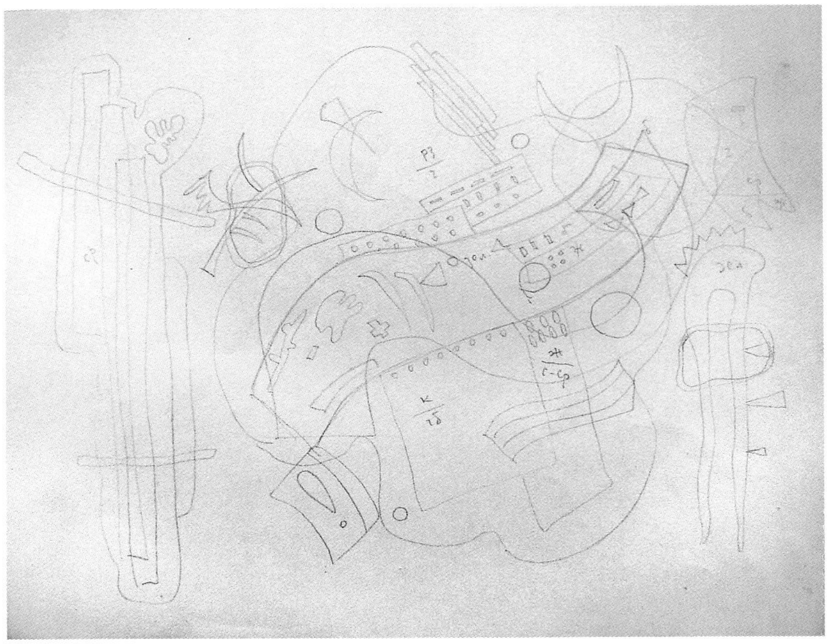

35, p.9r

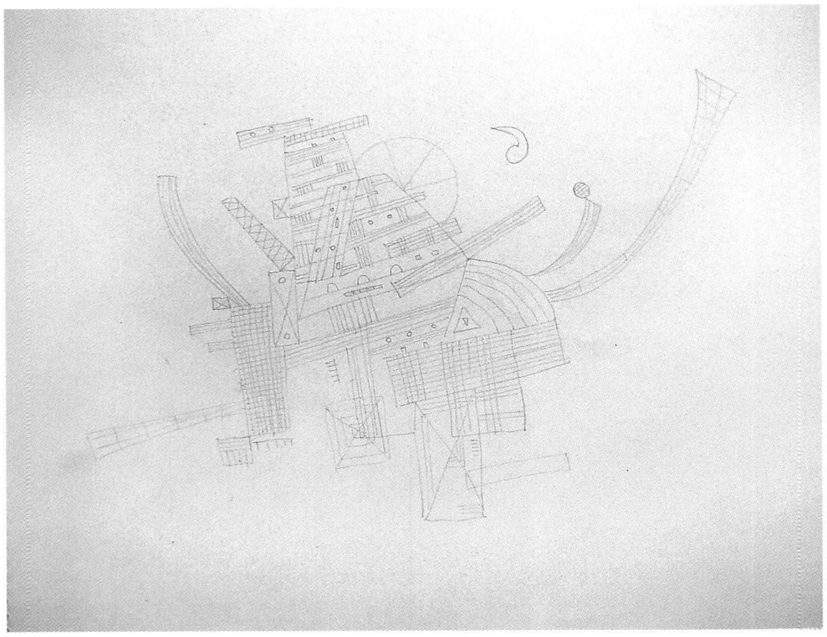

35, p.9v

**p.9** Pencil study for *Rigide et courbé* of December 1935
On reverse: pencil study for *Accent vert* of November 1935

On the recto and on p.10 verso Kandinsky made studies for *Rigide et courbé* of December 1935 (Roethel and Benjamin no.1063). See vol.I, cat. no.976 for additional studies for *Accent vert* of November 1935 (Roethel and Benjamin no.1061).

**p.10** Pencil sketches
On reverse: pencil study with ink traces

The motif at the left in the drawing on the recto can be related to the study on p.8 verso, whereas the sketch on the right resembles those from the mid-1930s (vol.I, cat. nos.916, 918, 1047). The drawing on the verso is a study for *Rigide et courbé* of December 1935 (see p.9 above).

35, p.10r

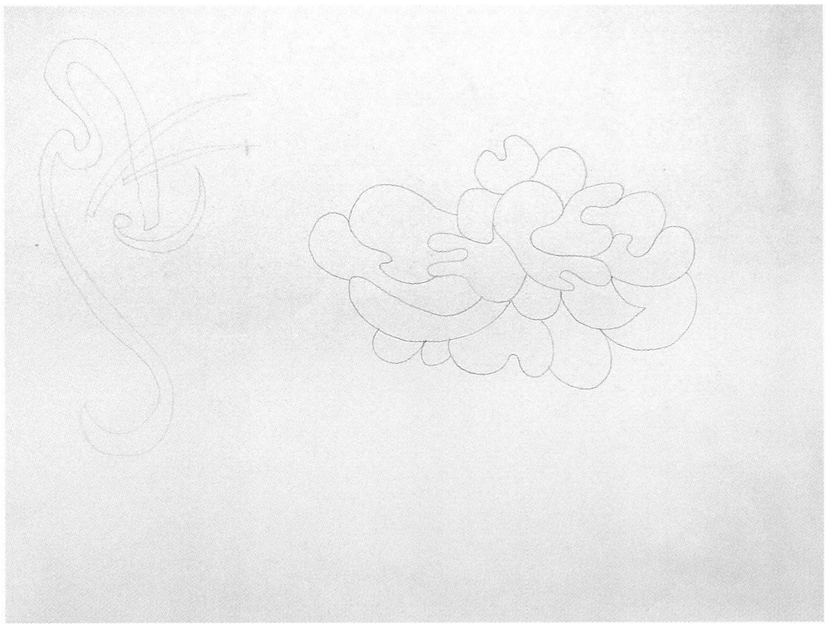

35, p.10v

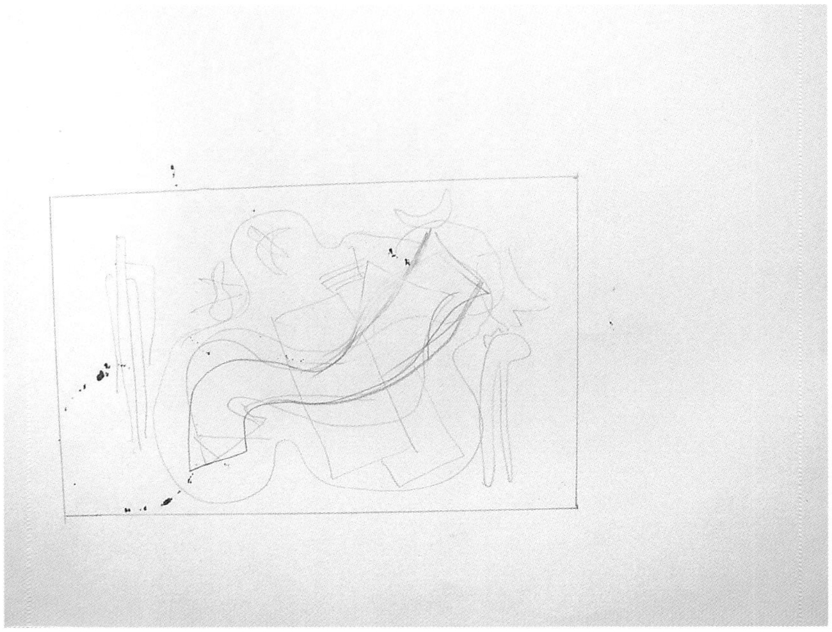

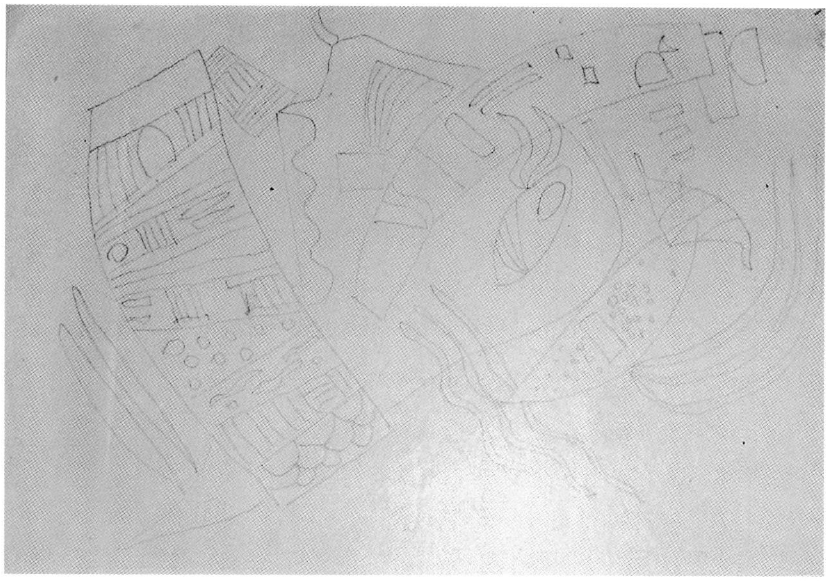

35, p.12

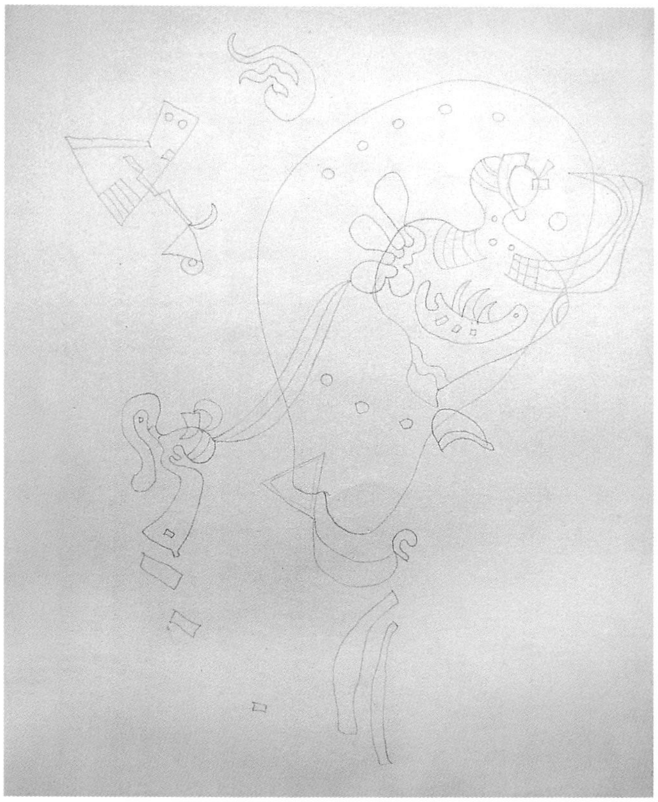

35, p.11v

**p.11** Recto blank
On reverse: Pencil sketches related to *Composition IX*

The form at the lower left of the drawing also appears in *Composition IX* of February 1936 (Roethel and Benjamin no.1064): other motifs have been modified in the final canvas. See also p.6 (above).

**[p.12]** Pencil study related to *Concentré* of 1937 on separate sheet of paper inserted in sketchbook, 10.3 x 14.3 cm
Inscribed on reverse: 'Signe avec accomp. / 2 coins rouge / coulant / Paris'

The drawing is probably a study for *Concentré* of 1937 (Barnett no.1207), although it recalls Kandinsky's related glass painting *Formes en tension* of 1936 (Roethel and Benjamin no.1072).

# Sketchbook 36

1937–1939

Blue cardboard sketchbook with grey spine; inside front cover stamp from Sennelier, Paris (3 quai Voltaire VIIe and 4 bis rue de la Grande Chaumière VIe)
Contains 35 sheets, each 27 x 33 cm (10⅝ x 13 in), with top edge perforated. One sheet detached (33 x 10.4 cm).
Page numbers inscribed by unknown hand at later date

Derouet and Boissel 1984, no.630

LOCATION
Musée National d'Art Moderne, Centre Georges Pompidou, Paris (AM 1981.65.678)

HISTORY
Nina Kandinsky, Paris, until 1980

Several drawings in Volume I – cat. nos.1000, 1002, 1019 and 1020 – probably come from this sketchbook.

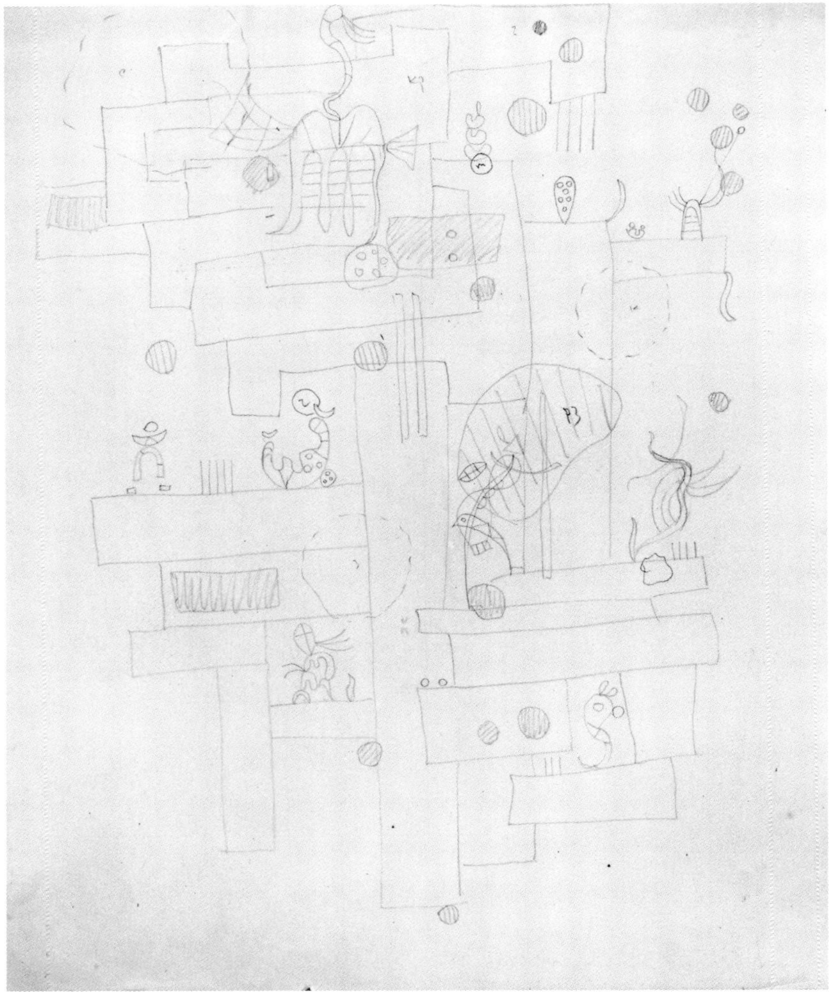

36, p.1

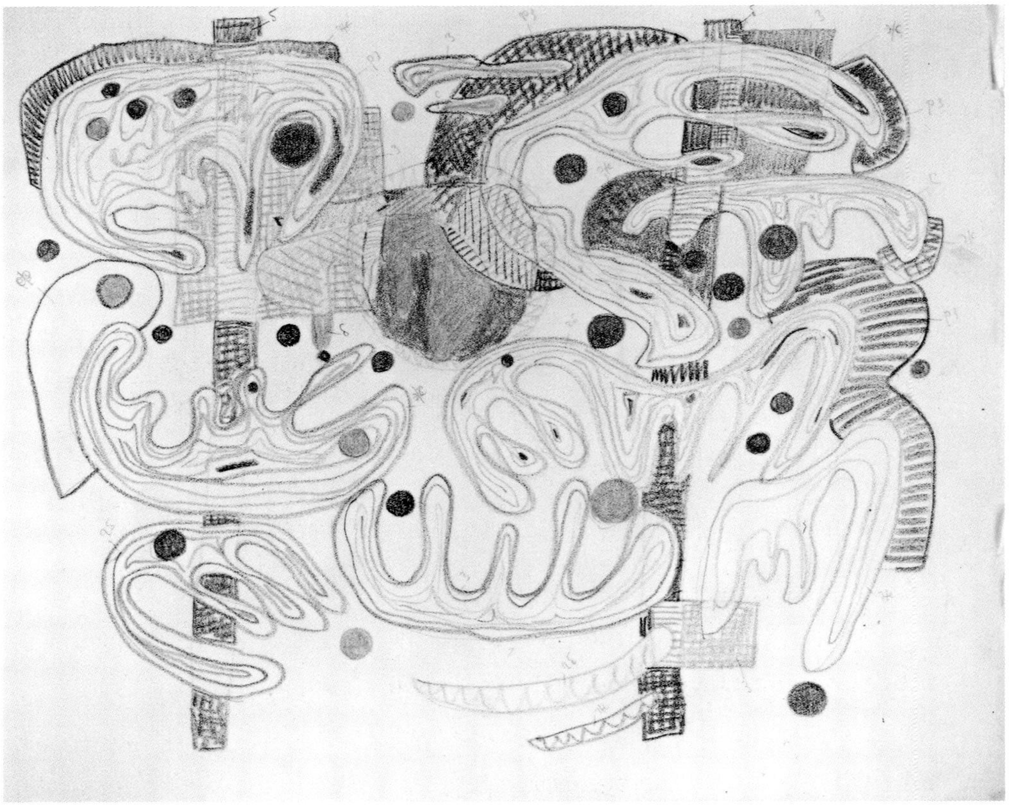

36, p.2

**p.1** Pencil study for *Contrastes* of November 1937
Inscribed with color notations in Cyrillic

REFERENCES
Derouet and Boissel 1984, pp.398, ill., 399

Kandinsky developed this drawing into the watercolor *Contrastes* of November 1937 (Barnett no.1214).

**p.2** Colored pencil and pencil study for *Formes capricieuses* of July 1937
Inscribed with color notations in Cyrillic

EXHIBITIONS
1985 New York, no.90, ill.
1998 Nantes, no.92, color ill.

REFERENCES
Barnett 1983, p.263, ill.a
Derouet and Boissel 1984, p.399, ill.

This study clearly resembles *Formes capricieuses* of July 1937 (Roethel and Benjamin no.1081), although certain colors and details have been modified.

(See color plate p.127)

**p.3** Pencil studies related to *Grilles et autres* of October 1937 (recto and verso)

REFERENCES
Derouet and Boissel 1984, p.399, ill.

The studies on both sides of this sheet can be related to *Grilles et autres* of October 1937 (Roethel and Benjamin no.1083).

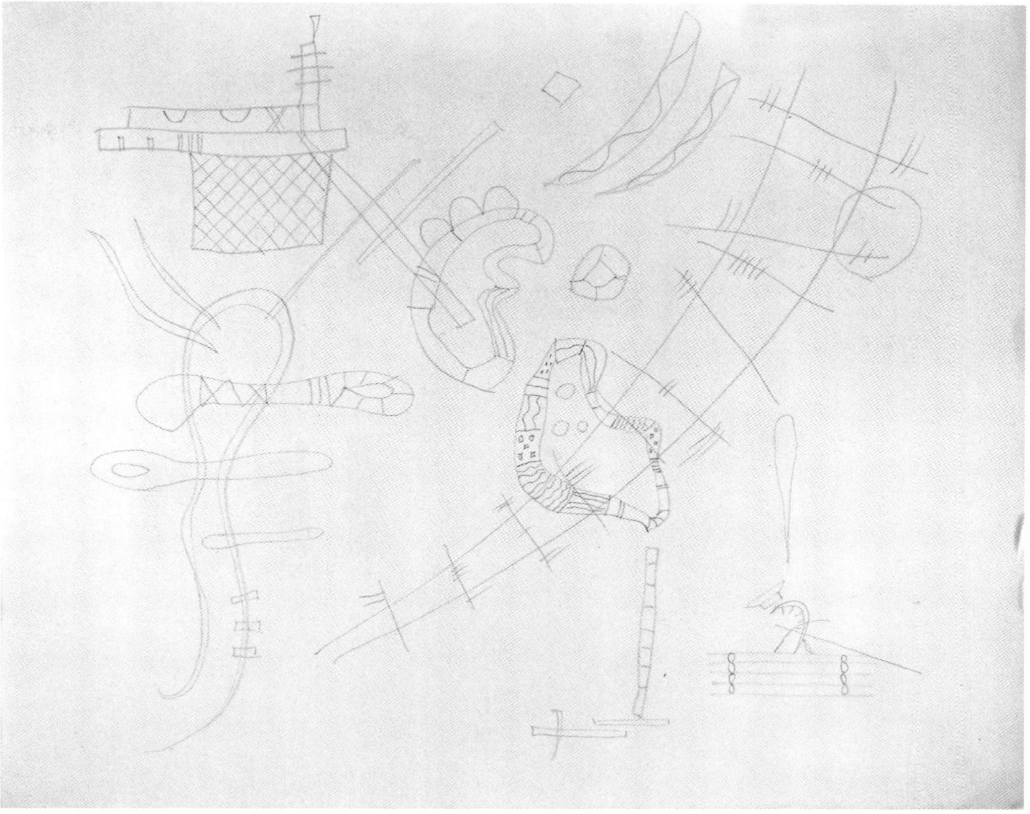

36, p.3R

36, p.3V

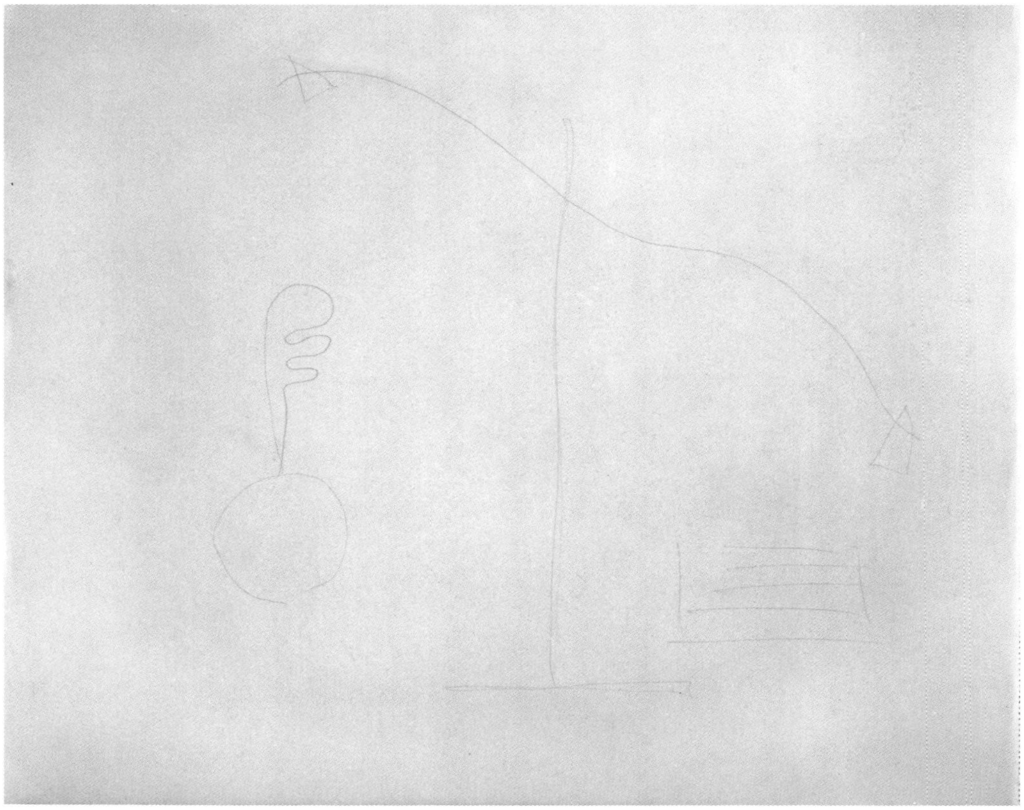

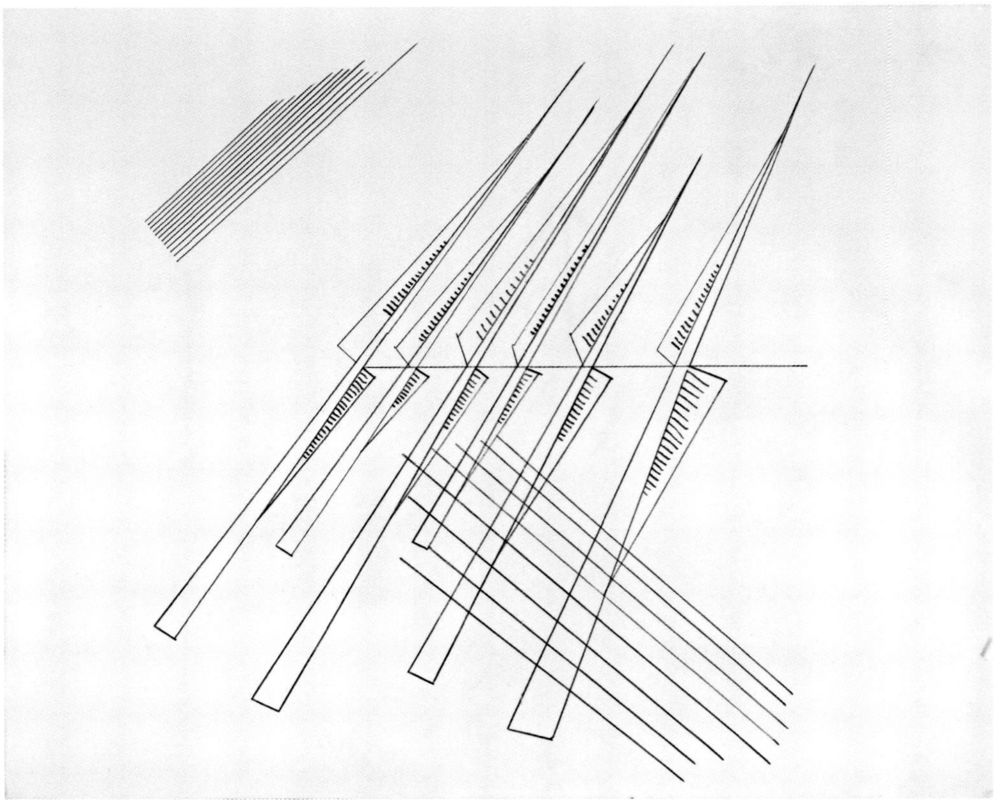

36, p.4

36, p.5

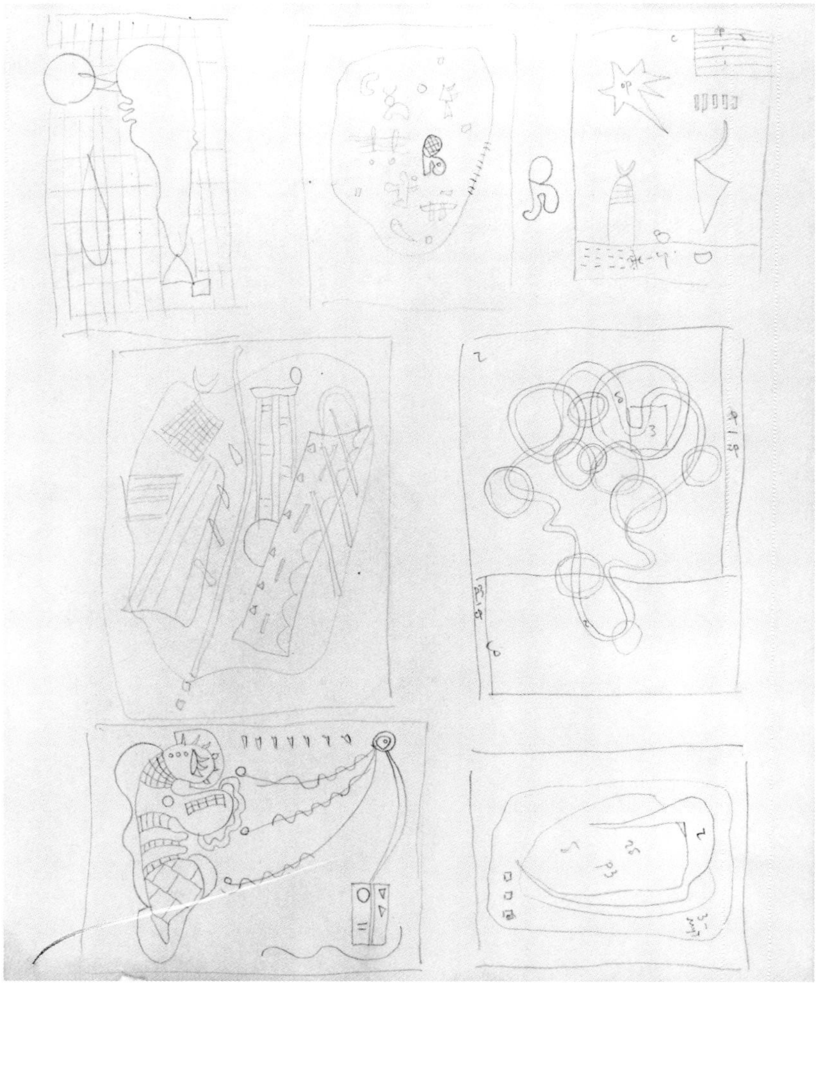

**p.4** Ink drawing

REFERENCES
Derouet and Boissel 1984, p.399, ill.

**p.5** Pencil studies for *Noir et froid*, *La Ligne accompagnée*, *Le Gros et le mince*, *De l'un à l'autre* of 1937 and *L'Ensemble* of 1939
Inscribed with color notations in Cyrillic

REFERENCES
Derouet and Boissel 1984, pp.398, ill., 399
Georgia Illetschko, 'Kandinsky en la linia divisòria: el pintor com a dibuixant' in *Vassily Kandinsky: La revolució del llenguatge pictòric* exh. cat. (Barcelona, 1996), pp.24, ill.4, 25
Illetschko 1997, p.150, ill.58

There are studies for *Noir et froid*, *La Ligne accompagnée* of 1937, *Le Gros et le mince* of October 1937, *De l'un à l'autre* of November 1937 and *L'Ensemble* of May 1939 (Barnett nos.1206, 1209, 1210, 1215, 1260) as well as two unidentified works.

36, p.6

**p.6** Pencil drawing related to *Sérénité* of 1938

REFERENCES

Derouet and Boissel 1984, p.399, ill.

This sketch can be related to *Sérénité* of 1938 and possibly *Ténèbres* of 1943 (Roethel and Benjamin nos.1092, 1158).

**p.7** Pencil drawing for *La Forme rouge* of June 1938
Inscribed l.r. in Cyrillic: 'shir. obod b / fig. [...] guash / chern.'

REFERENCES

Derouet and Boissel 1984, pp.398, ill., 399

Kandinsky's notes refer to the 'wide white border' and to 'black' found in the canvas *La Forme rouge* of June 1938 (Roethel and Benjamin no.1090).

36, p.7

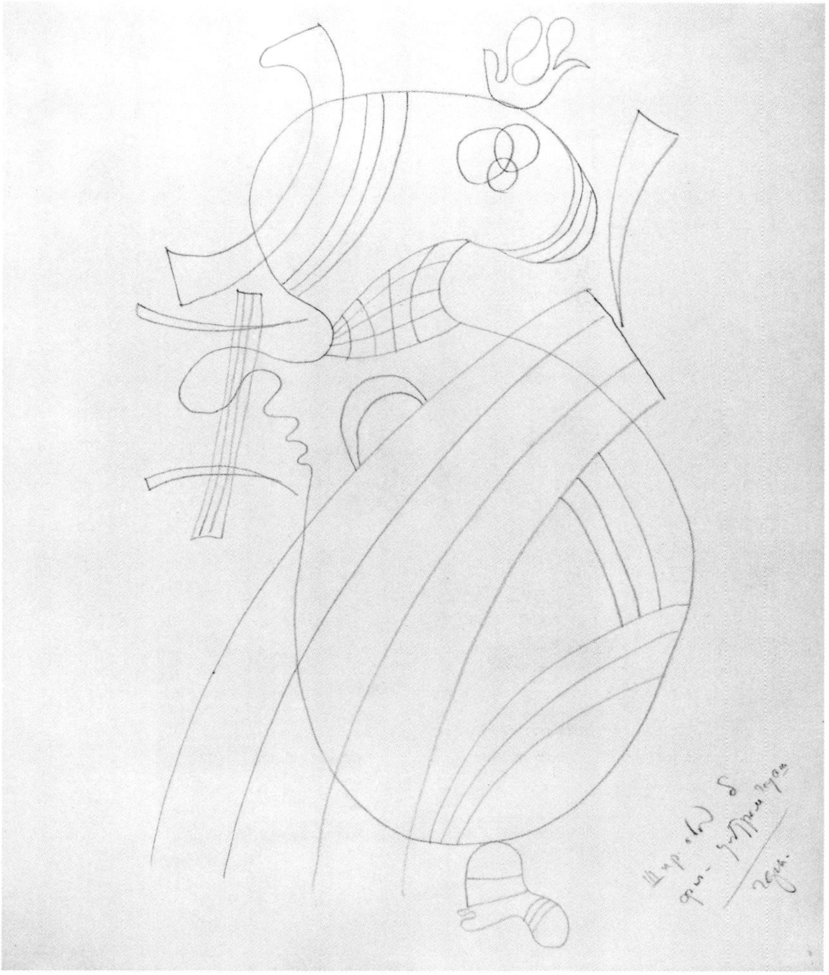

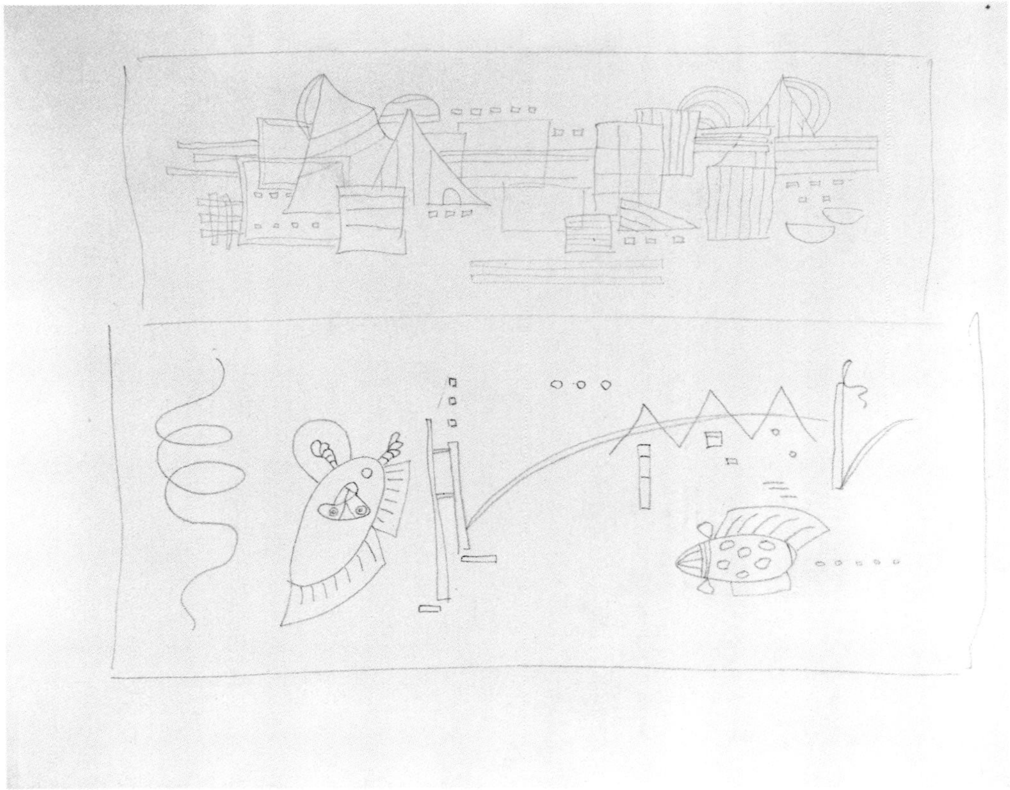

36, p.8

36, p.9

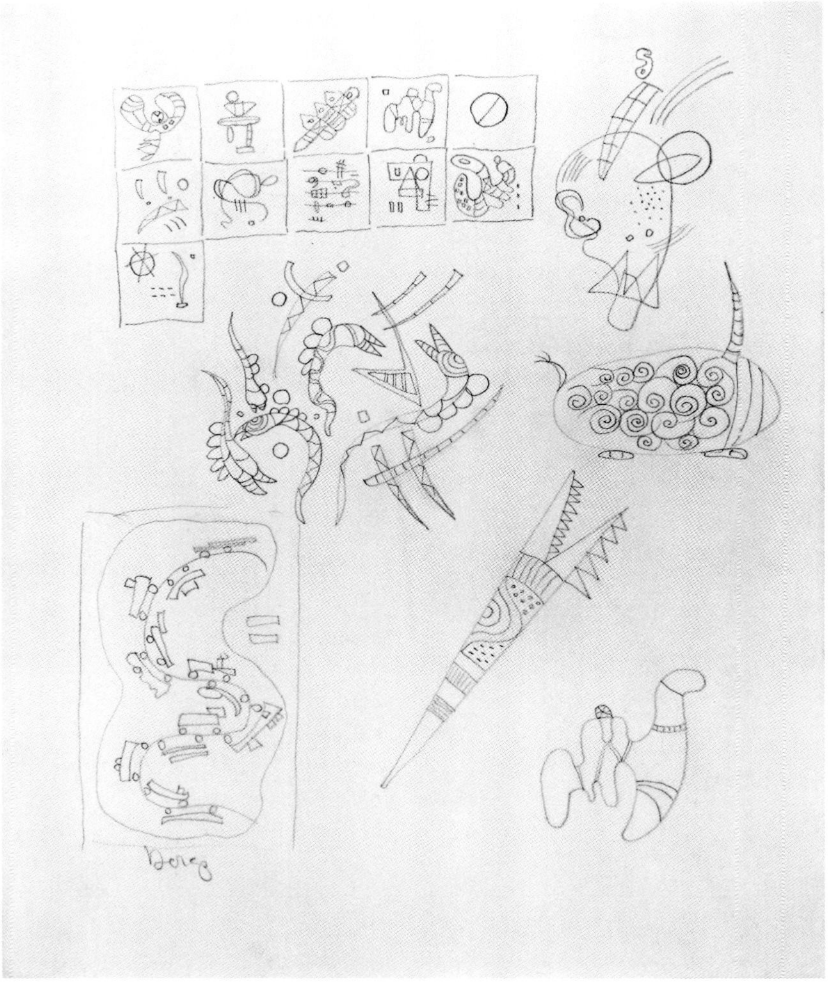

**p.8** Pencil studies for *La Petite raie* of 1937 and *Le zigzag* of April 1938

REFERENCES

Derouet and Boissel 1984, p.399, ill.

The study for *La Petite raie* of 1937 is above the drawing for *Le zigzag* of April 1938 (Barnett nos.1208, 1221).

**p.9** Pencil studies for *Quinze* and *La Figure blanche* of April 1938
Inscribed l.l. in Cyrillic: 'Vecher'

EXHIBITIONS

1985 New York, no.66, ill.

REFERENCES

Derouet and Boissel 1984, pp.398, ill., 399

These studies can be related to *Quinze* and *La Figure blanche* of April 1938 (Barnett nos.1222, 1223) as well as to a drawing of 1938 (vol.I, cat. no.1023). Below, on a drawing for an unknown (and probably unexecuted) work, Kandinsky wrote 'evening'.

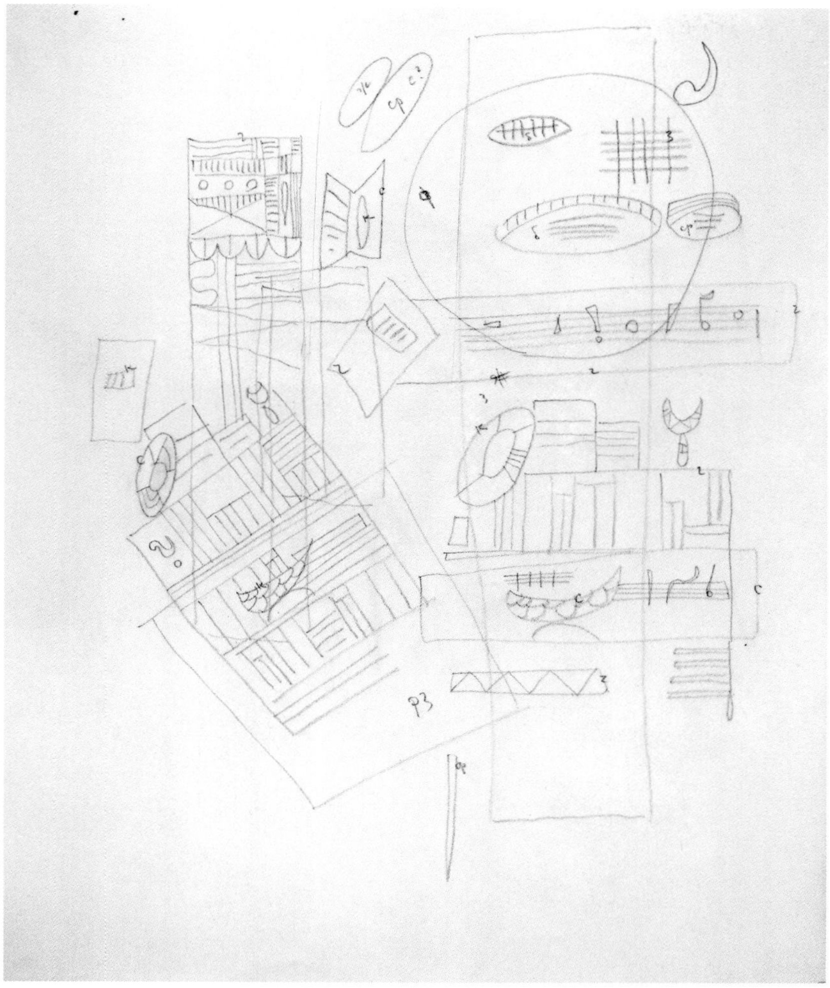

36, p.10

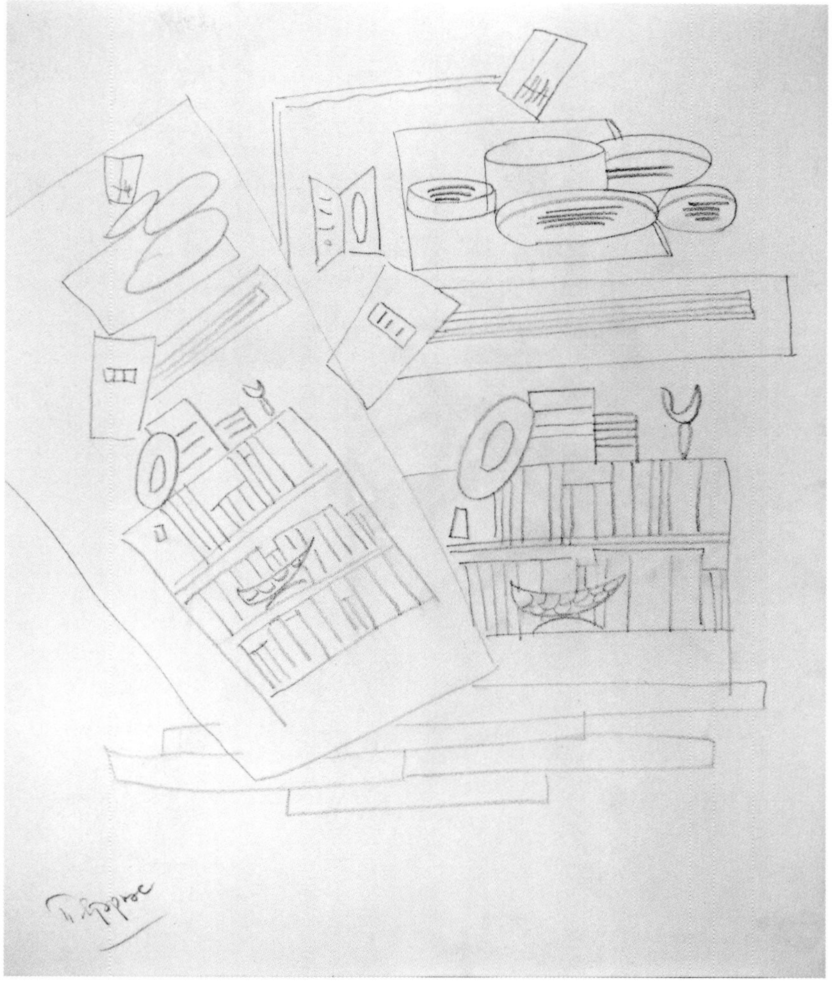

36, p.11

**p.10** Pencil study for *Stabilitée animée* of December 1937
Inscribed with color notations in Cyrillic

REFERENCES
Derouet and Boissel 1984, pp.398, ill., 399

This drawing is a study for *Stabilitée animée* of December 1937 (Roethel and Benjamin no.1084).

**p.11** Pencil study for *Stabilitée animée*
Inscribed l.l. in Cyrillic: 'Povtornoe'

REFERENCES
Derouet and Boissel 1984, pp.398, ill., 399

Kandinsky wrote 'repetition' on this study related to *Stabilitée animée* of December 1937 (see p.10 above).

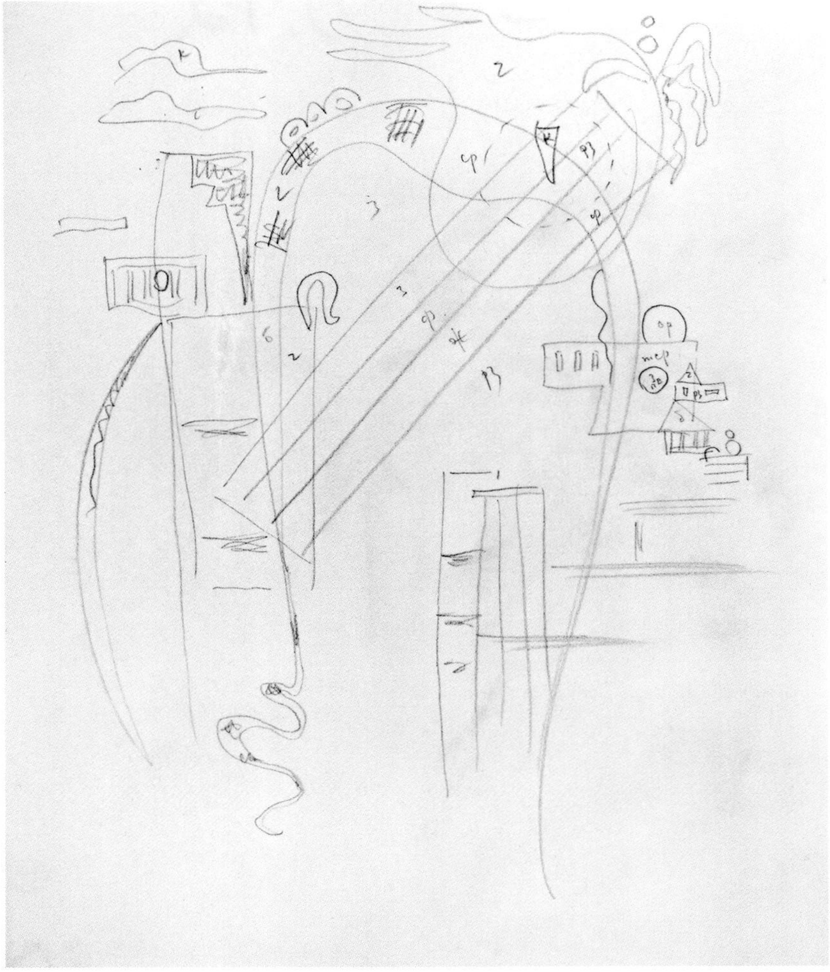

36, p.12

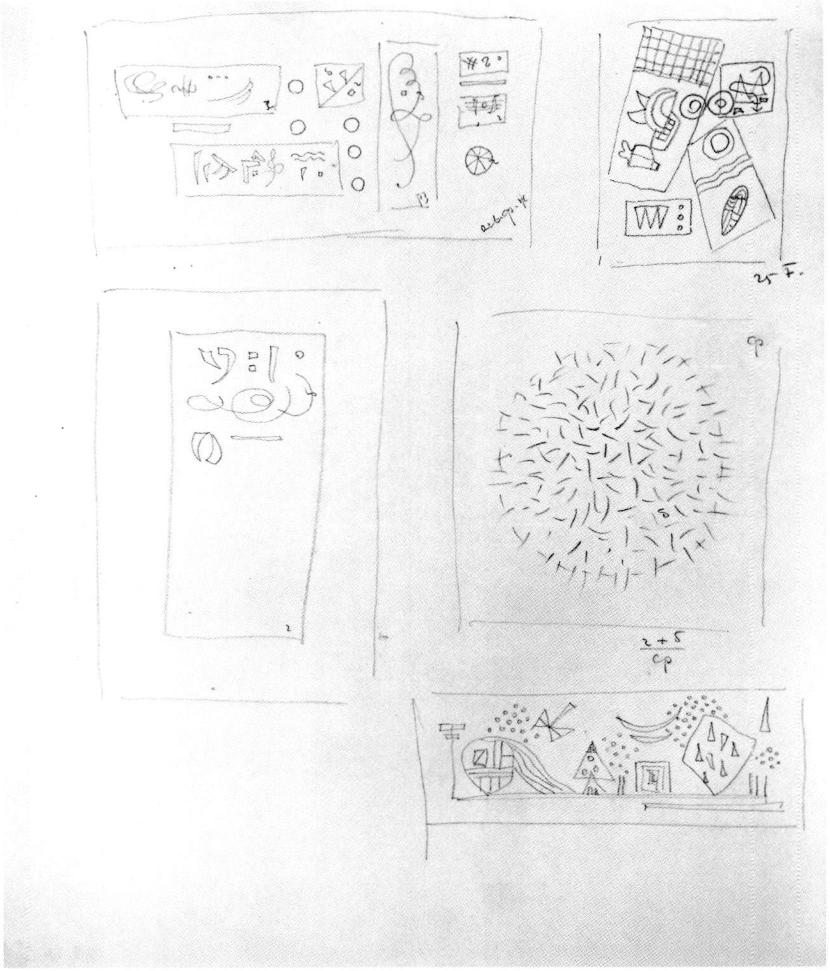

36, p.13

**p.12** Pencil drawing
Inscribed with color notations in Cyrillic

REFERENCES
Derouet and Boissel 1984, pp.398, ill., 399

**p.13** Pencil study for *Sur la ligne verte* of April 1938
Inscribed with color notations in Cyrillic

REFERENCES
Derouet and Boissel 1984, pp.398, ill., 399

The study at the lower right is for *Sur la ligne verte* of April 1938 (Barnett no.1226).

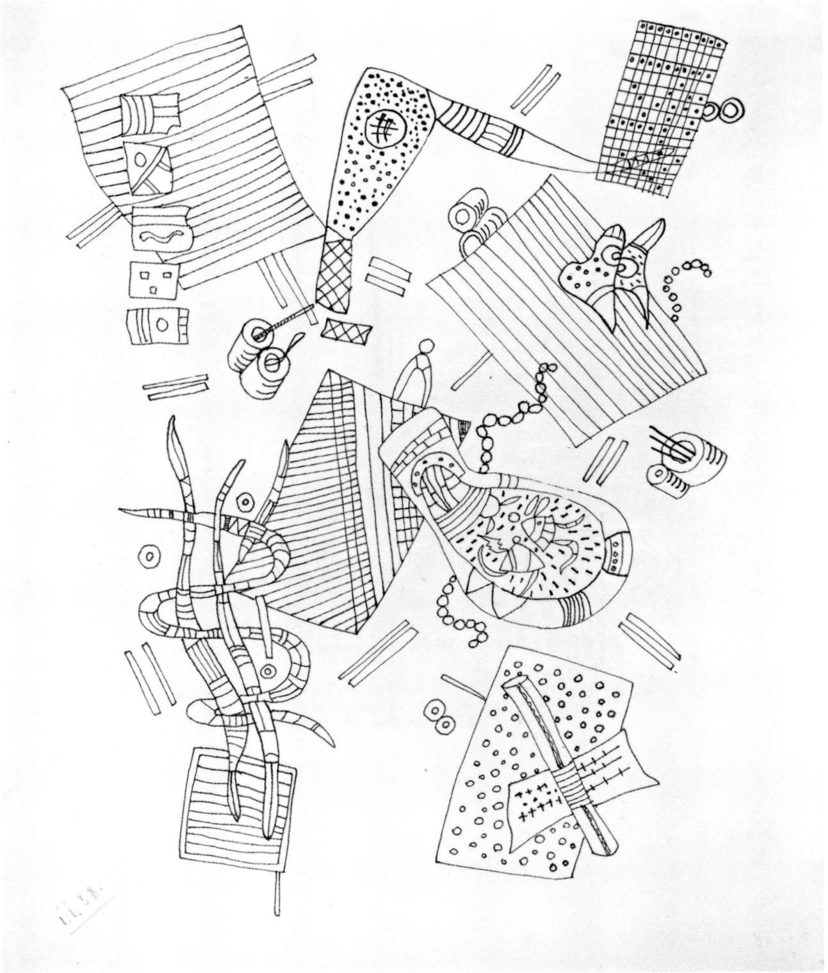

36, p.14

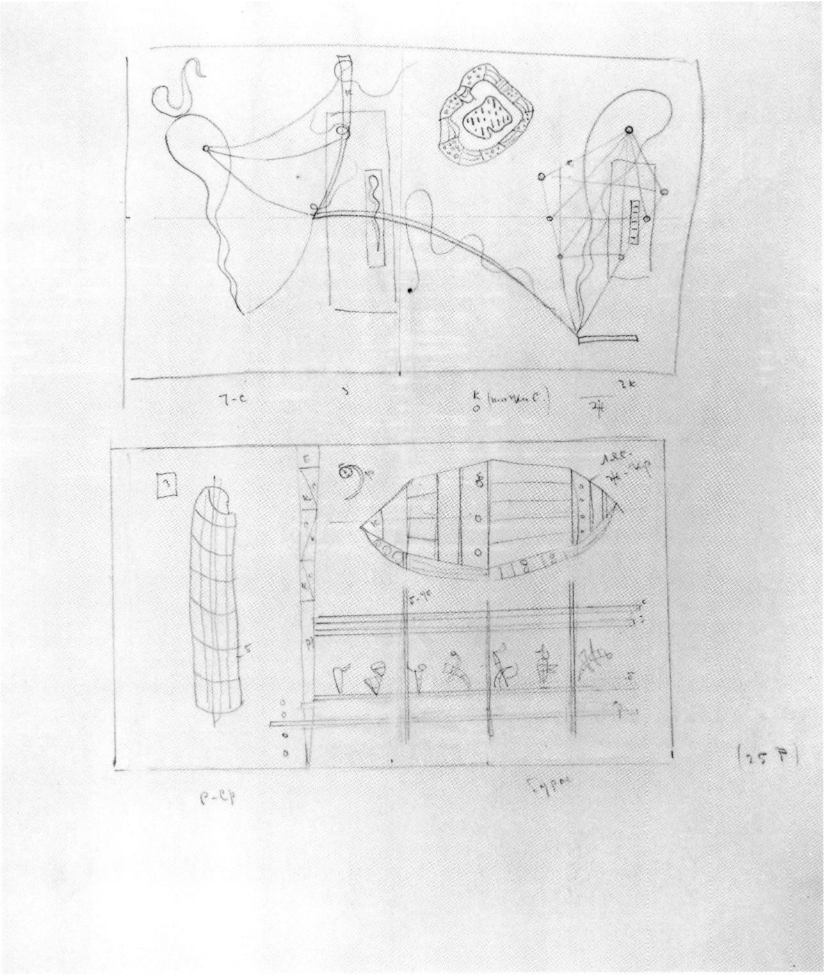

36, p.15

**p.14** India ink study for *Sérénité* of July–August 1938
Dated l.l. in pencil: '1.1.38'

EXHIBITIONS

1997 Milan, no.91, ill.

REFERENCES

Derouet and Boissel 1984, pp.398, ill., 399

Kandinsky inscribed the date 1 January 1938 on this study for *Sérénité*, which he painted in July–August 1938 (Roethel and Benjamin no.1092).

**p.15** Pencil studies for *Le Vert pénétrant* and *Au-dessus* of April 1938
Inscribed with color notations in Cyrillic

REFERENCES

Derouet and Boissel 1984, pp.399, 400, ill.

These drawings are clearly related to *Le Vert pénétrant* of April 1938 (Roethel and Benjamin no.1089) and *Au-dessus* of April 1938 (Barnett no.1220).

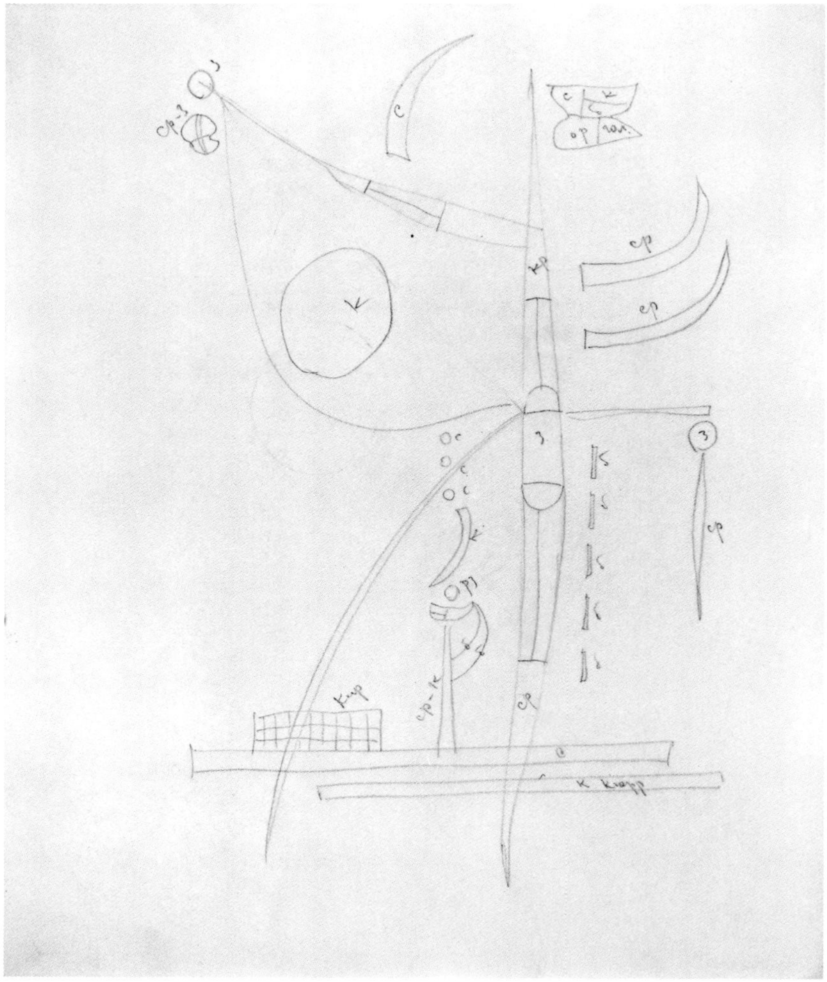

36, p.16

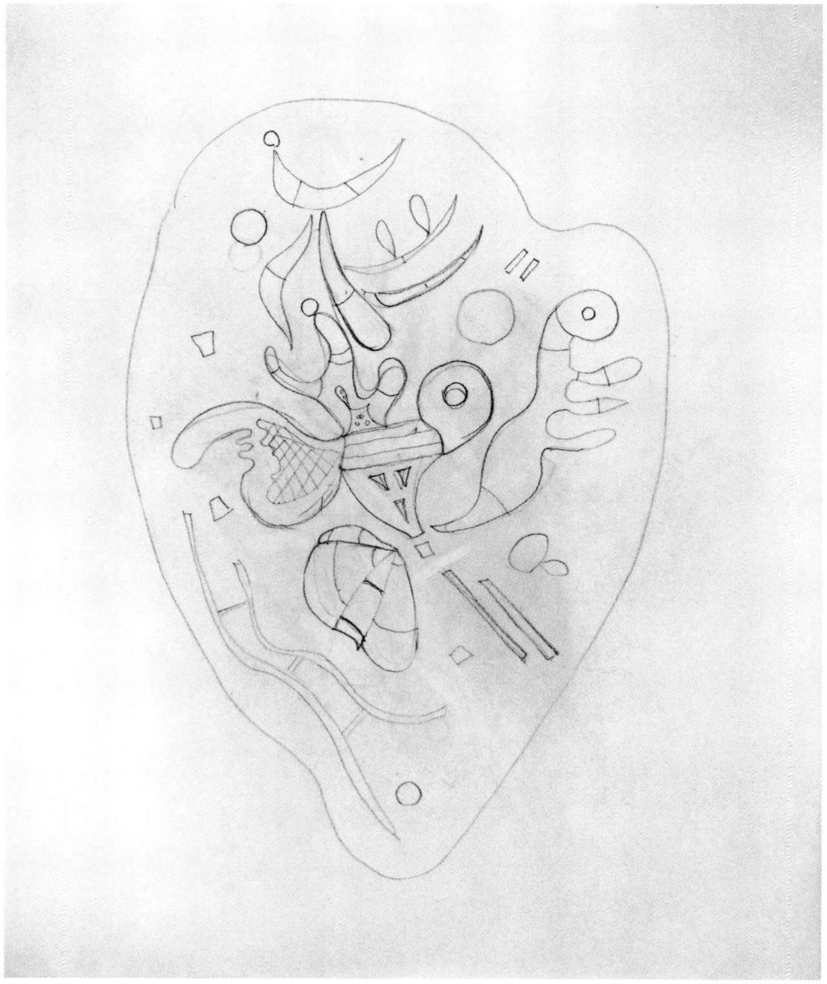

36, p.17

**p.16** Pencil study related to *L'Accent rouge* of April 1938
Inscribed with color notations in Cyrillic

REFERENCES
Derouet and Boissel 1984, pp.399, 400, ill.

The drawing bears a resemblance to *L'Accent rouge* of April 1938 (Barnett no.1224), which is known only from the sketch in the Handlist.

**p.17** Pencil study for *Ensemble multicolore* of February–April 1938

REFERENCES
Derouet and Boissel 1984, pp.399, 406, ill.
Weiss 1995, p.186 n.21
Barnett 2006, p.470

This study closely resembles a colored pencil drawing for *Ensemble multicolore* (vol.I, cat. no.1016) as well as the final canvas painted in February–April 1938 (Roethel and Benjamin no.1088).

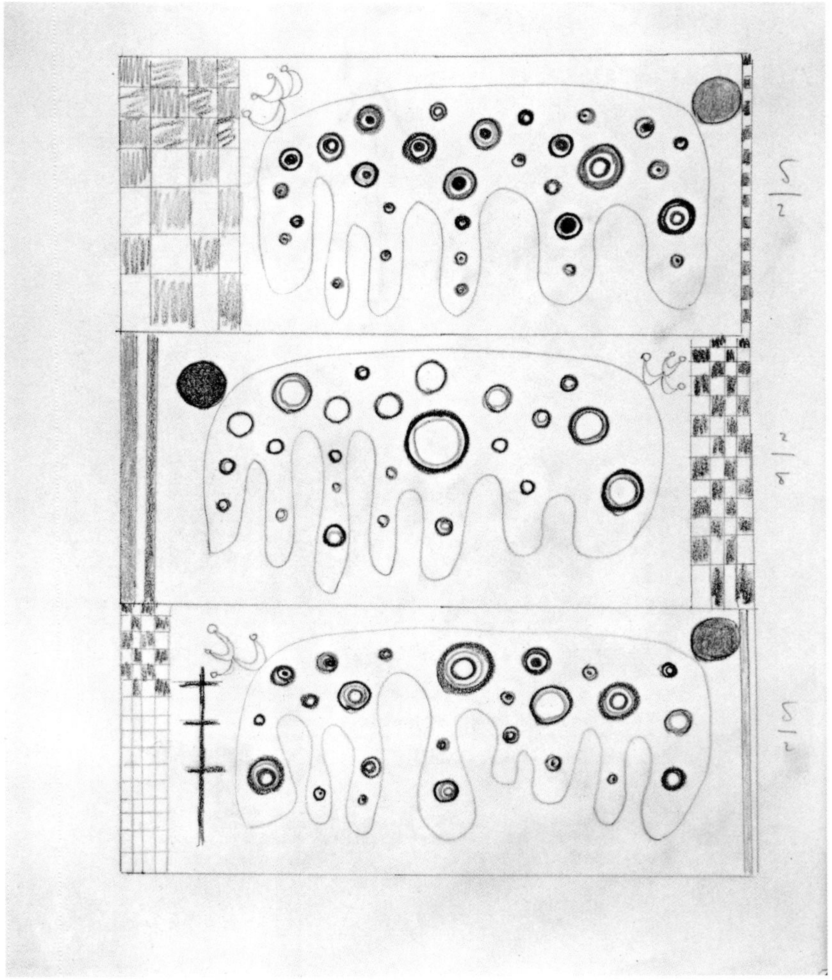

36, p.18

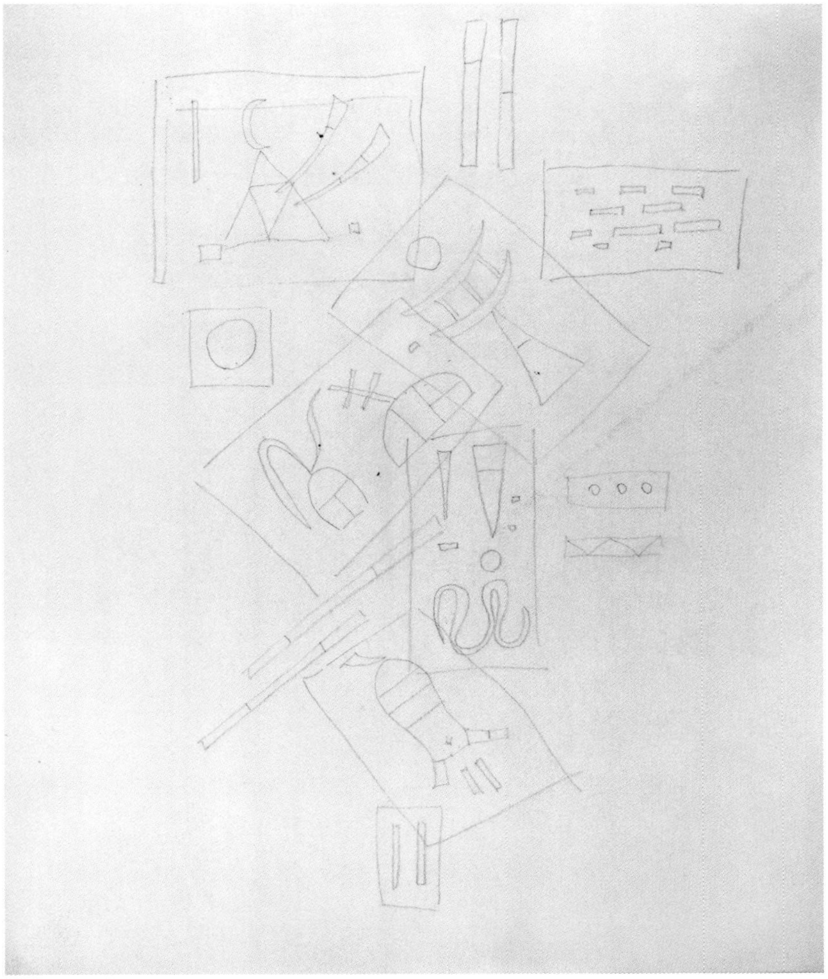

36, p.19

**p.18** Pencil and colored pencil study for *Trois* of April 1938
Inscribed with color notations in Cyrillic

REFERENCES
Derouet and Boissel 1984, pp.399, 400, ill.
Weiss 1995, p.206, ill.199

Kandinsky modified numerous details in his gouache *Trois* of April 1938 (Barnett no.1219).

(See color plate p.127)

**p.19** Pencil study for *Rectangles divers* of May 1938

REFERENCES
Derouet and Boissel 1984, pp.399, 400, ill.

This study is preparatory to *Rectangles divers* of May 1938 (Barnett no.1228).

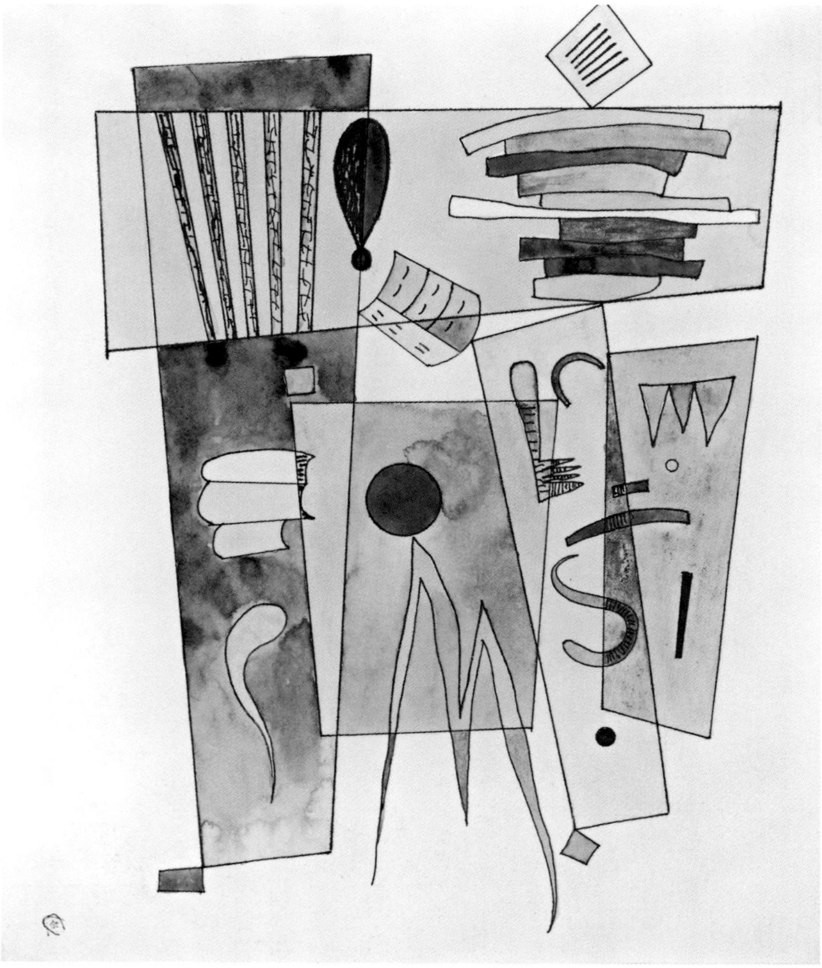

36, p.20

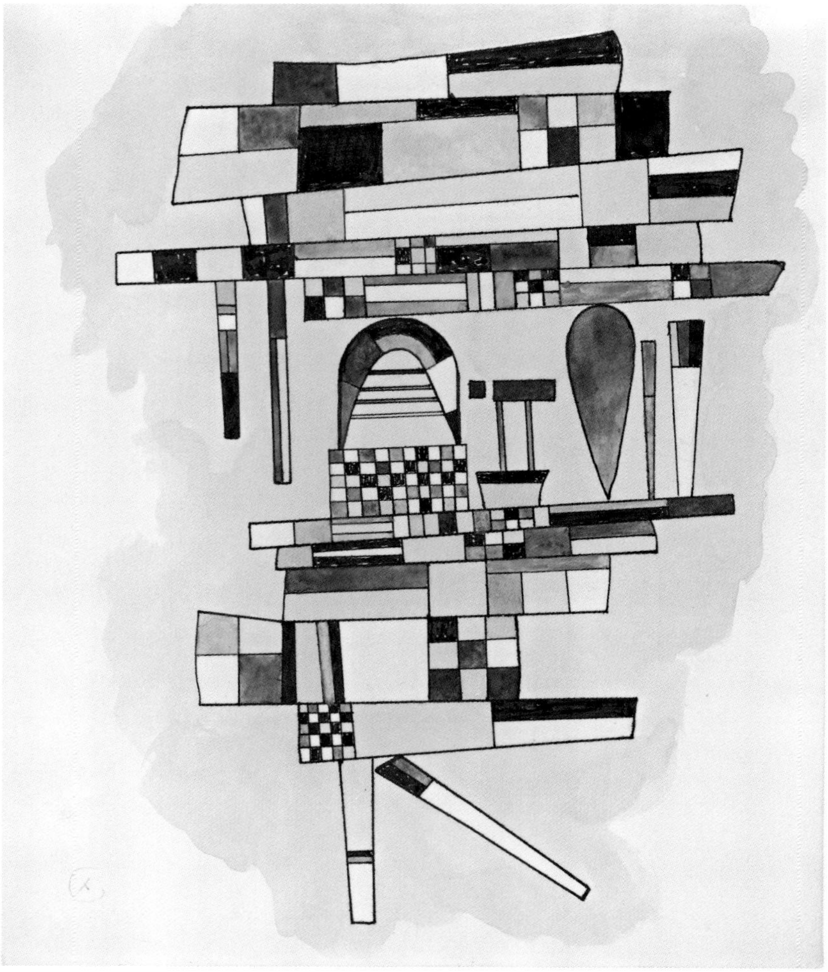

36, p.21

**p.20** Watercolor and India ink study
Signed with stamp l.l.: 'K'

REFERENCES
Derouet and Boissel 1984, pp.399, 400, ill.

The estate stamp is found on numerous watercolors and individual drawings.

**p.21** Watercolor and India ink study for *La Toile jaune* of July 1938
Inscribed l.l. by unknown hand: 'X'

EXHIBITIONS
1985 New York, no.95, ill.
1996 Barcelona, no.32, color ill.

REFERENCES
Barnett 1983, p.265, ill.a
Derouet and Boissel 1984, pp.399, 401, color ill.

This watercolor bears a strong resemblance to the painting *La Toile jaune* of July 1938 (Roethel and Benjamin no.1091).

(See color plate p.128)

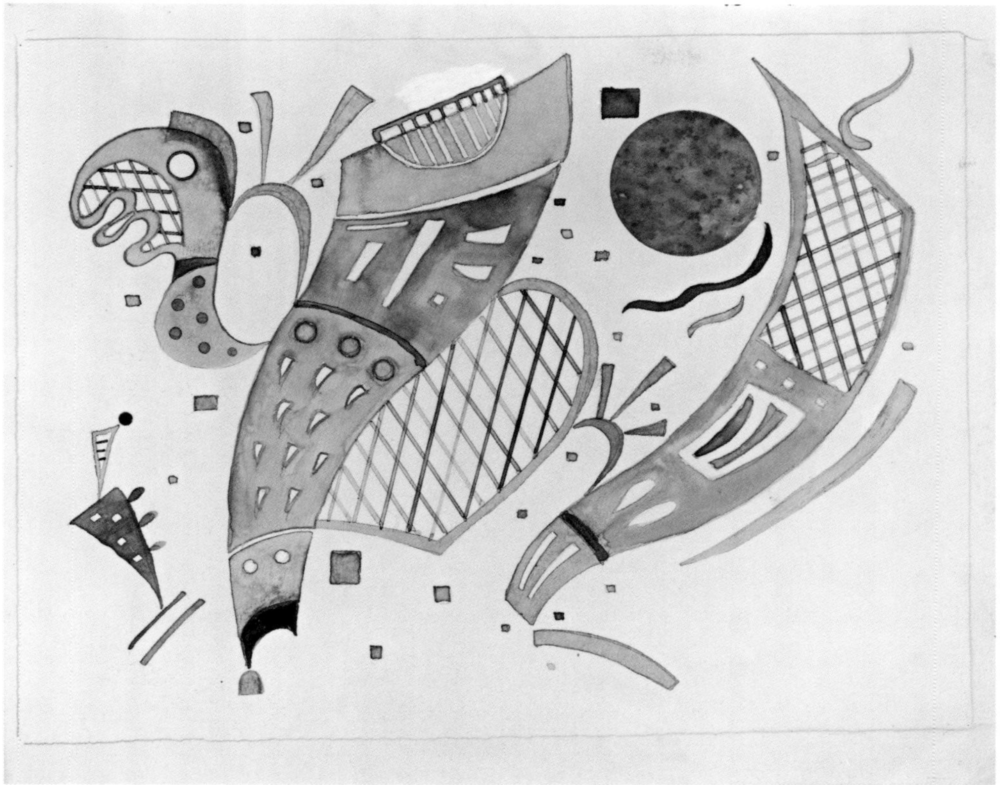

36, p.23

**p.22** India ink spilled over entire sheet

**p.23** Watercolor and pencil study

REFERENCES
Derouet and Boissel 1984, p.399, ill.
Barnett 2006, p.478

There is a closely related pencil drawing (vol.I, cat. no.1036).

**p.24** Watercolor and pencil drawing

REFERENCES
Derouet and Boissel 1984, p.399, ill.

(See color plate p.128)

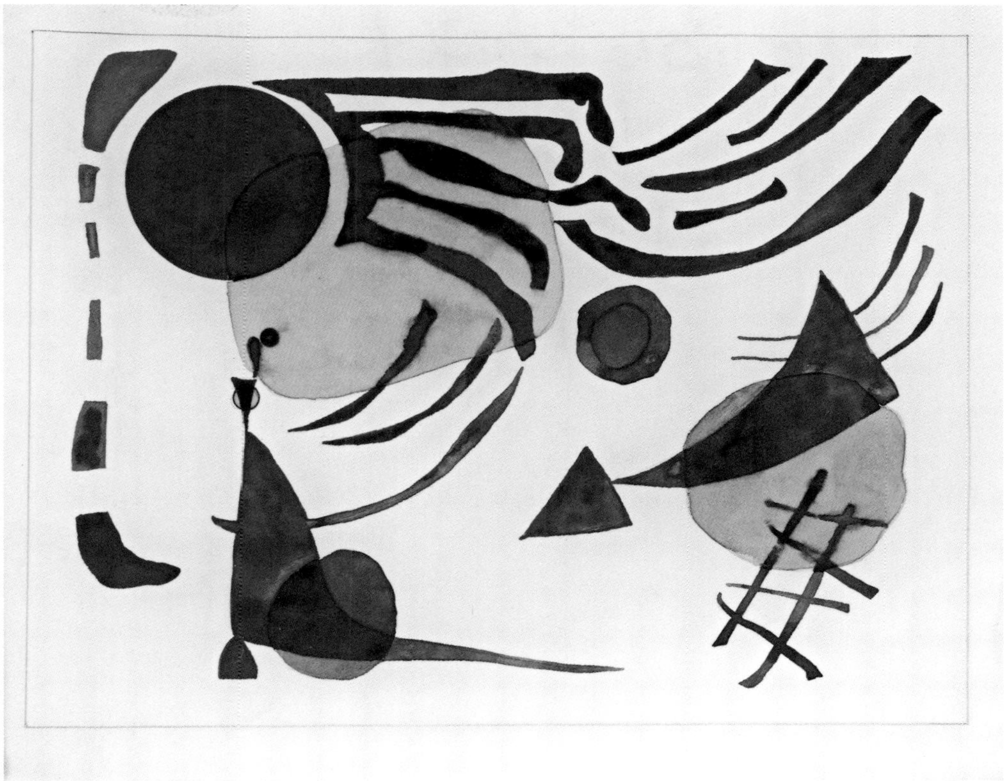

36, p.24

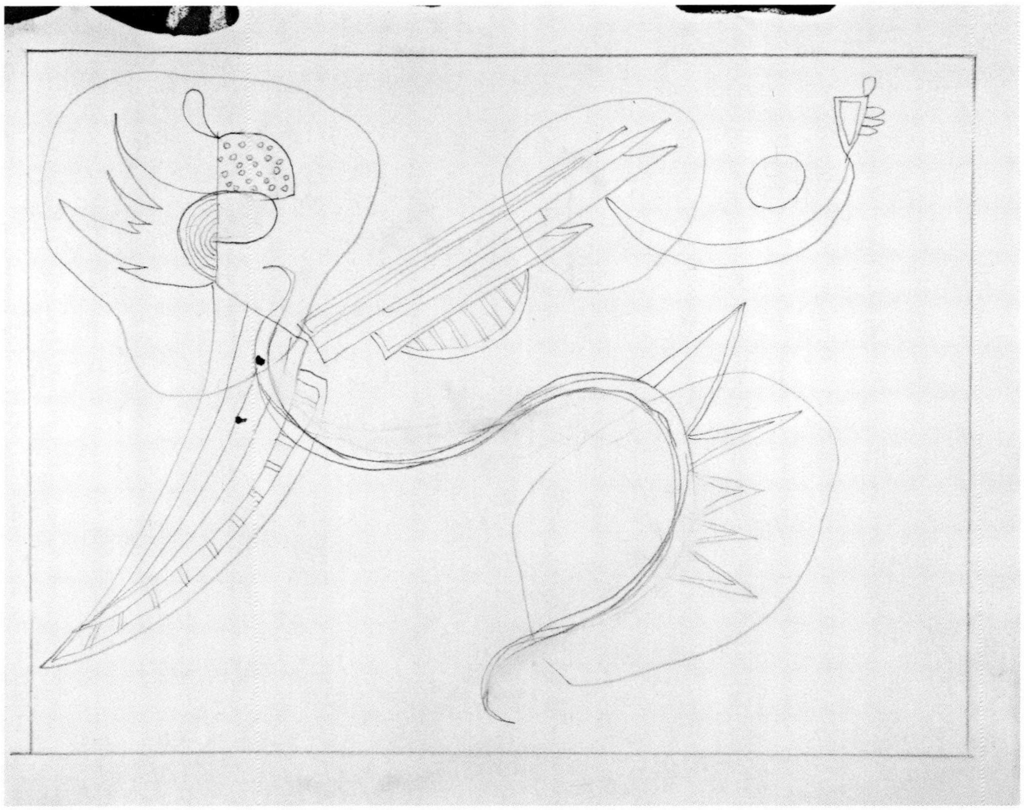

36, p.25

36, p.26

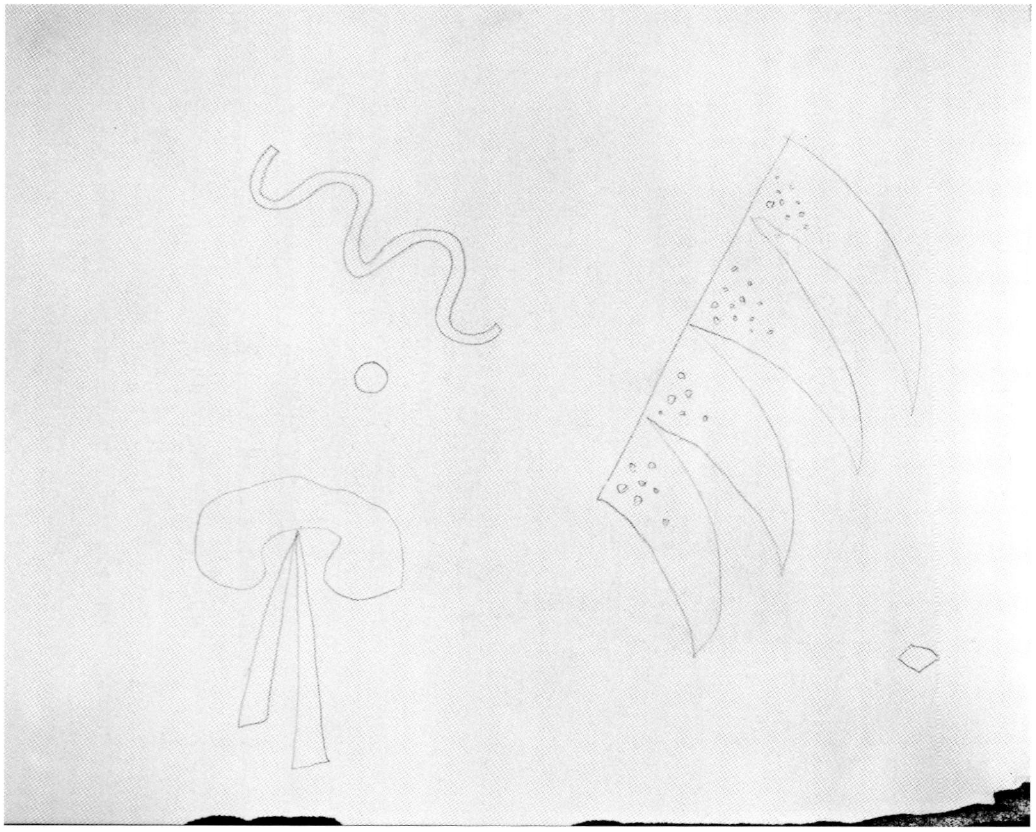

**p.25** Pencil study for *La Résolution* of November 1938

REFERENCES

Derouet and Boissel 1984, pp.399, 402, ill.

This study is for *La Résolution* of November 1938 (Barnett no.1240).

**p.26** Pencil sketches

REFERENCES

Derouet and Boissel 1984, pp.399, 402, ill.

The sketches share similarities with elements in *Le Bon contact* of January–February 1938 (Roethel and Benjamin no.1087).

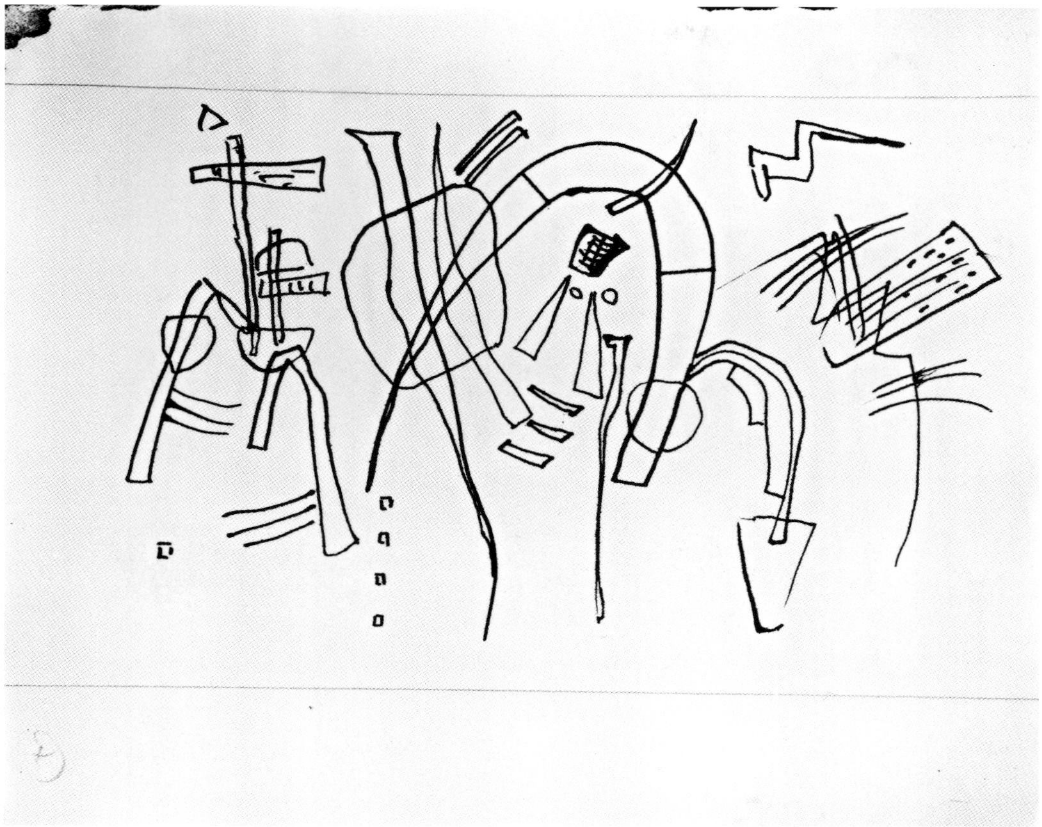

36, p.27

**p.27** India ink study for *L'Arc bleu* of December 1938
Inscribed l.l. by unknown hand: 'X'

REFERENCES
Derouet and Boissel 1984, pp.399, 402, ill.

The drawing is related to *L'Arc bleu* of December 1938 (Barnett no.1244).

**p.28** India ink study for a drawing of 1938

REFERENCES
Derouet and Boissel 1984, pp.399, 408, ill.
Barnett 2006, p.475

This study closely resembles an India ink drawing of 1938 (vol.I, cat. no.1028).

36, p.28

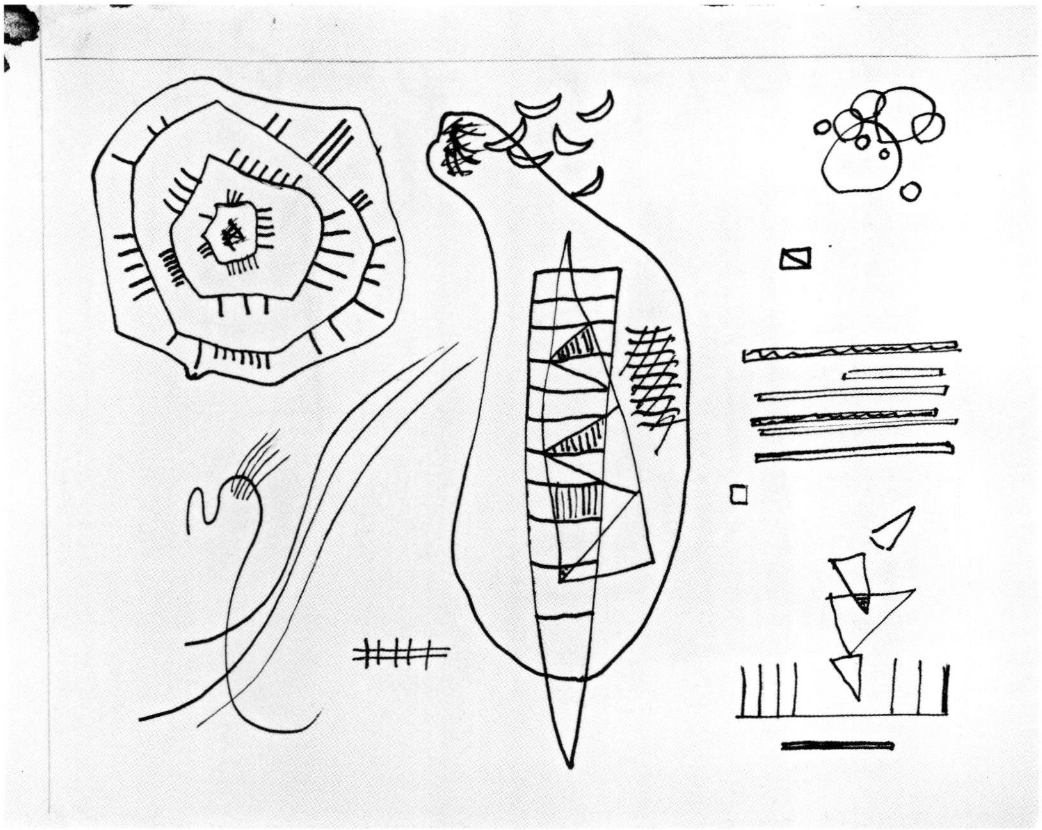

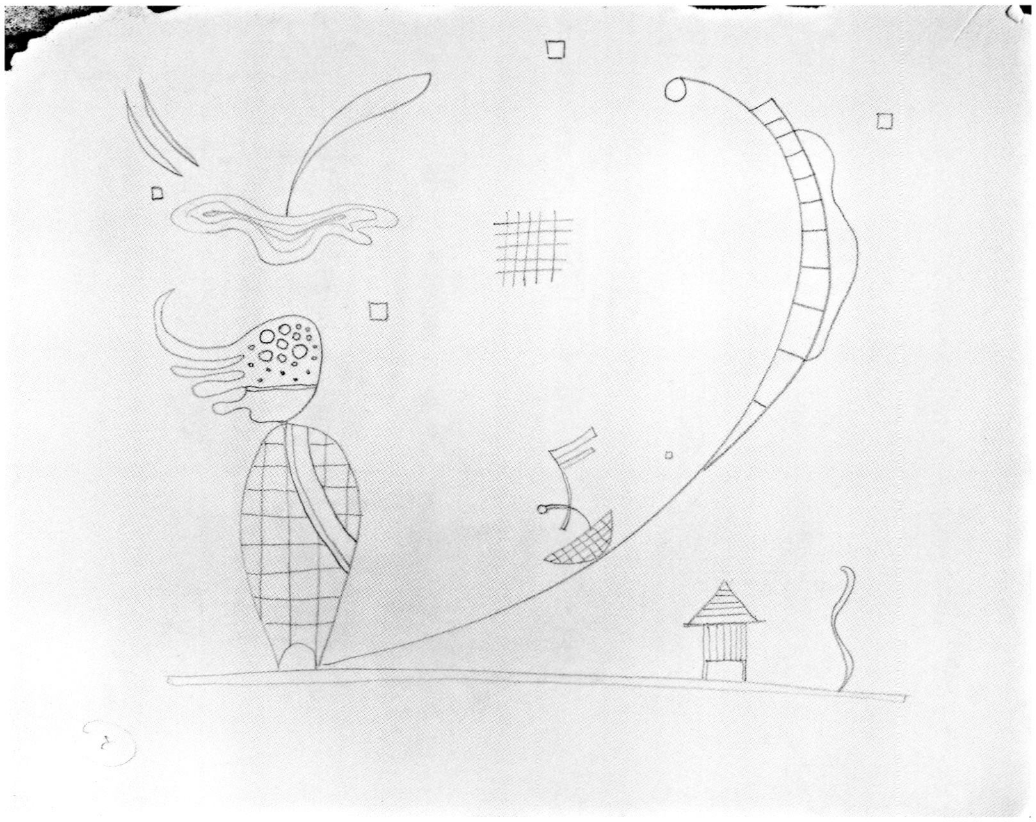

36, p.29

**p.29** Pencil study for *L'Elan* of March 1939
Inscribed l.l. by unknown hand: 'X'

REFERENCES
Derouet and Boissel 1984, pp.399, 402, ill.

Kandinsky developed this study into a painting, *L'Elan* of March 1939 (Roethel and Benjamin no.1098).

**p.30** Pencil sketch related to *Vers le bleu* of 1939

REFERENCES
Derouet and Boissel 1984, pp.399, 402, ill.

The sketch can be related to the watercolor study for *Vers le bleu* (see Barnett no.1248; Roethel and Benjamin no.1094).

36, p.30

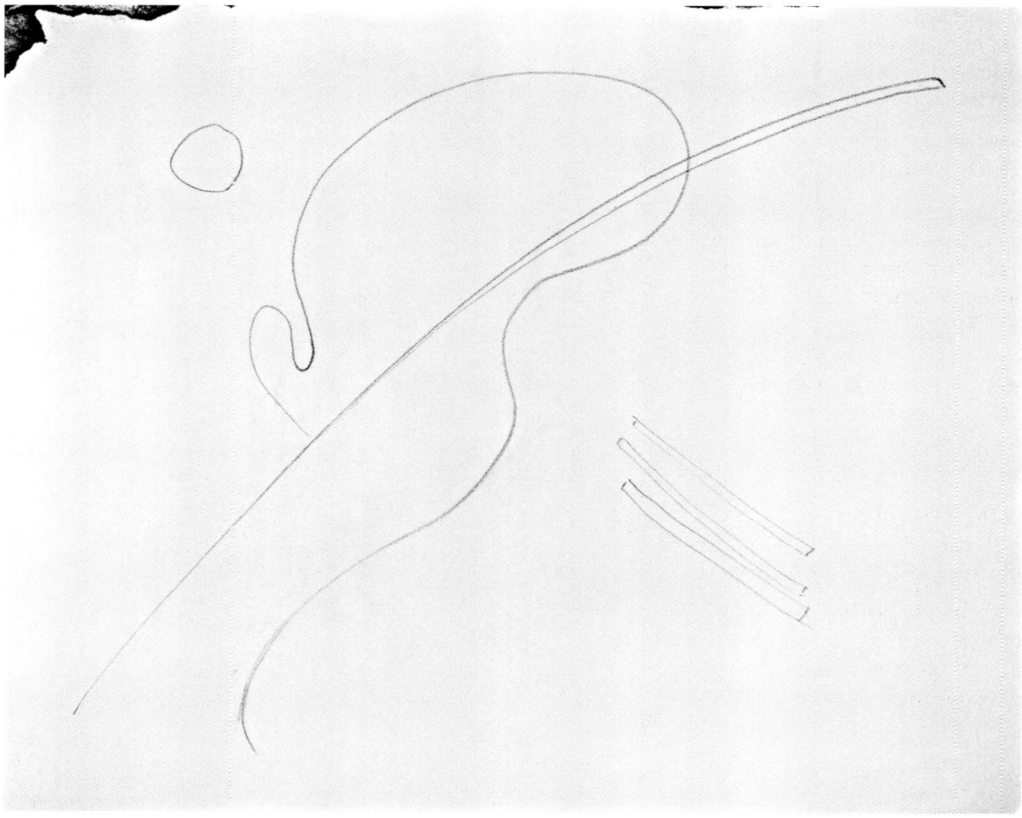

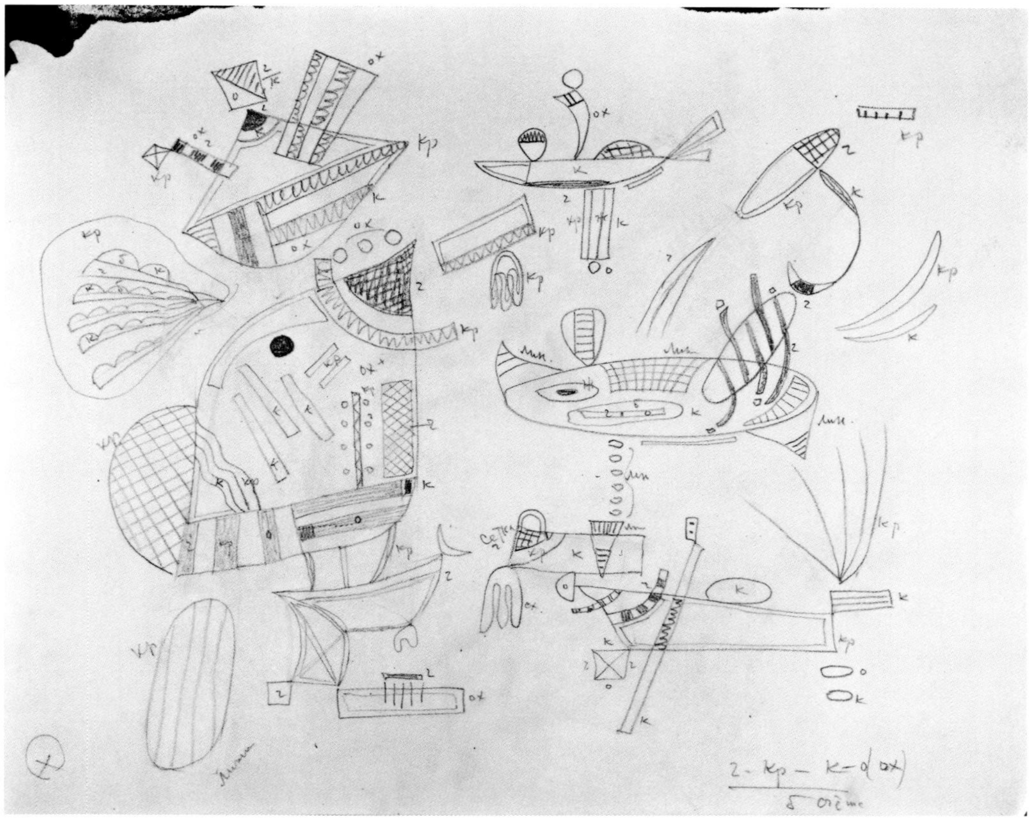

36, p.31

36, p.32

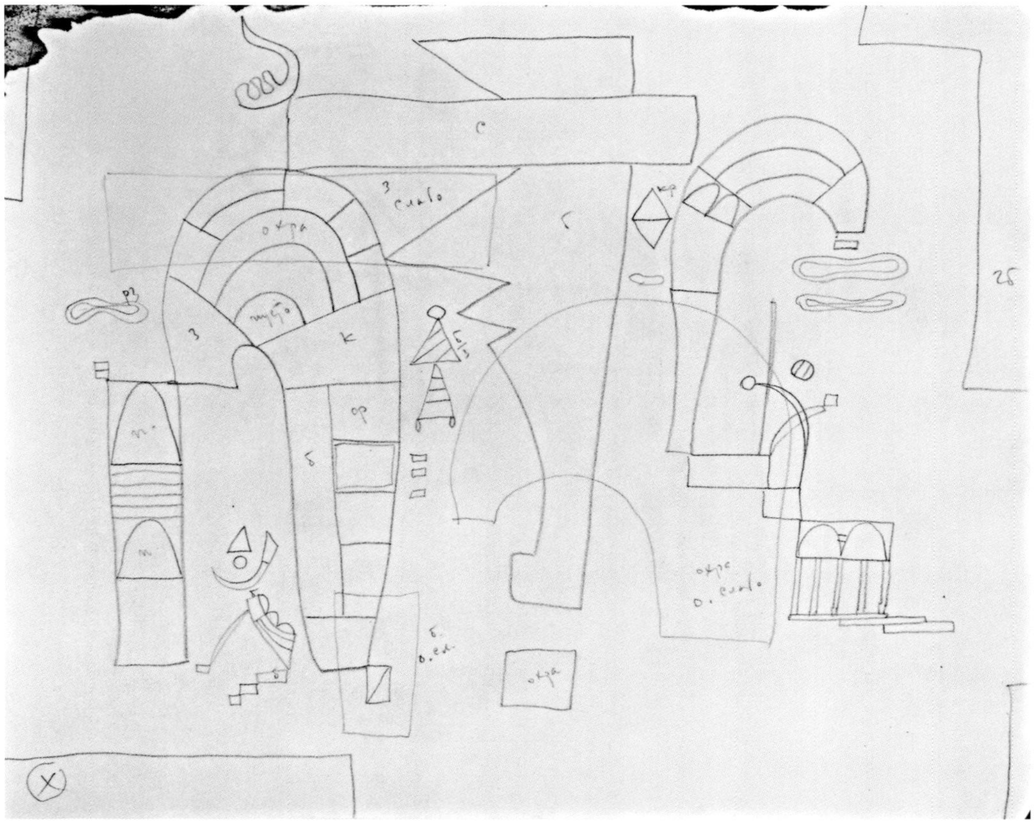

**p.31** Pencil study for *L'Ensemble chaud* of February 1939
Inscribed with color notations in Cyrillic and l.l. by unknown hand: 'X'

REFERENCES

Derouet and Boissel 1984, pp.399, 402, ill.

This drawing is a study for *L'Ensemble chaud* of February 1939 (Roethel and Benjamin no. 1095).

**p.32** Pencil study for *La Forme blanche* of February 1939
Inscribed with color notations in Cyrillic and l.l. by unknown hand: 'X'

REFERENCES

Derouet and Boissel 1984, pp.399, 402, ill.

Although the colors have been changed in the gouache, the study clearly resembles *La Forme blanche* of February 1939 (Barnett no.1255).

**p.33** Pencil study for *Le Carré rouge* of March 1939
Inscribed with color notations in Cyrillic and l.l. by unknown hand: 'X'
On reverse: pencil study of detail for *Complexité simple*

REFERENCES
Derouet and Boissel 1984, pp.399, 402, ill. (recto), 414, ill. (verso)
Georgia Illetschko, 'Kandinsky en la linia divisòria: el pintor com a dibuixant' in *Vassily Kandinsky: La revolució del llenguatge pictòric* exh. cat. (Barcelona, 1996), pp.24, ill.5, 25

There is a detailed study for *Le Carré rouge* of March 1939 and, on the reverse, a detail for *Complexité simple*, also painted in March (Roethel and Benjamin nos.1096, 1097).

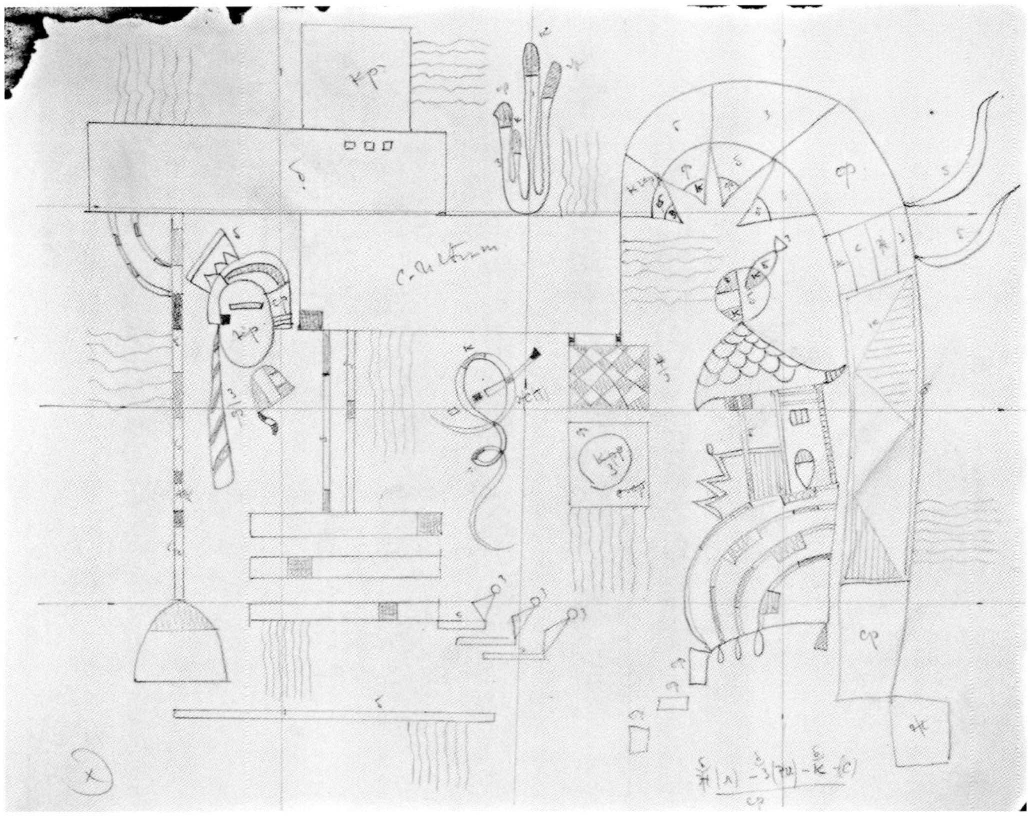

36, p.33R

36, p.33V

**p.34** Pencil study for *Complexité simple* of March 1939

REFERENCES

Derouet and Boissel 1984, pp.399, 414, ill.
Illetschko 1997, pp.162, 163, ill.85

The drawing is a study for *Complexité simple* of March 1939 (Roethel and Benjamin no.1097).

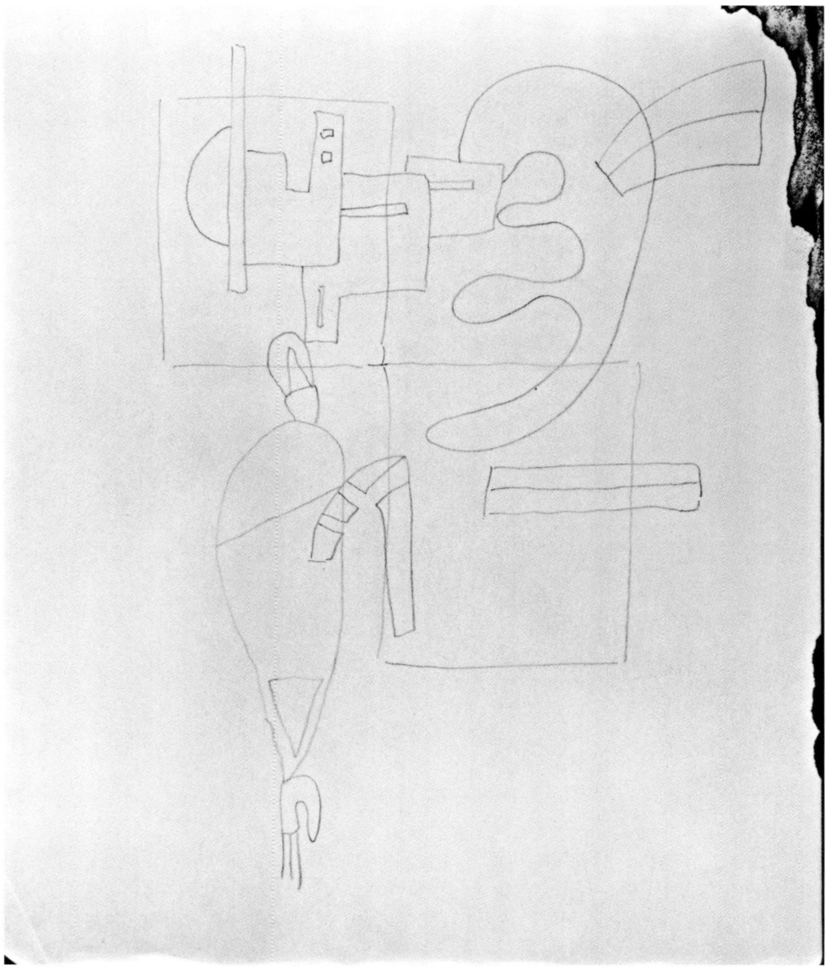

36, p.34

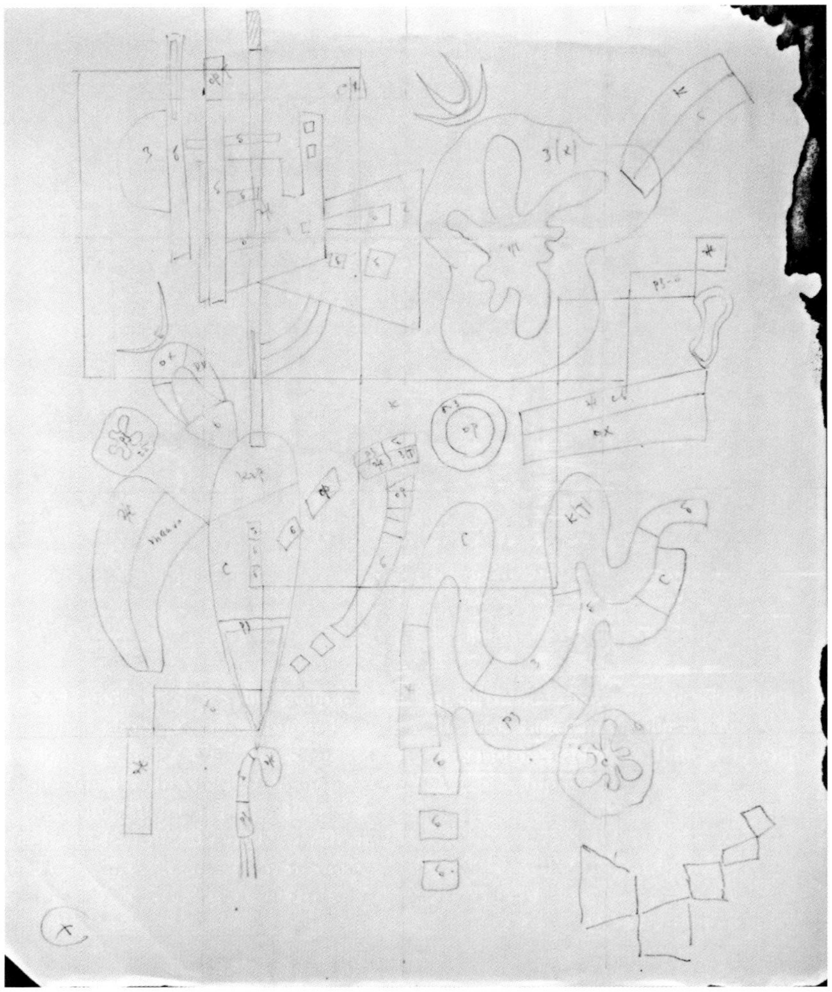

36, p.35R

**p.35** Pencil study for *Complexité simple*
Inscribed with color notations in Cyrillic and inscribed by unknown hand l.l.: 'X'
On reverse: pencil study for *Jeu des verticales* of March 1939
Inscribed with color notations in Cyrillic and inscribed by unknown hand l.l.: 'X'

REFERENCES

Derouet and Boissel 1984, pp.399, 400, ill. (verso), 414, ill. (recto)
Illetschko 1997, pp.162, 163, ill.86

Kandinsky made a detailed study for *Complexité simple* combining elements found on the preceding pages (see pp.33, 34) and, on the reverse, a sketch for *Jeu des verticales* of March 1939 (Barnett no.1256).

36, p.35V

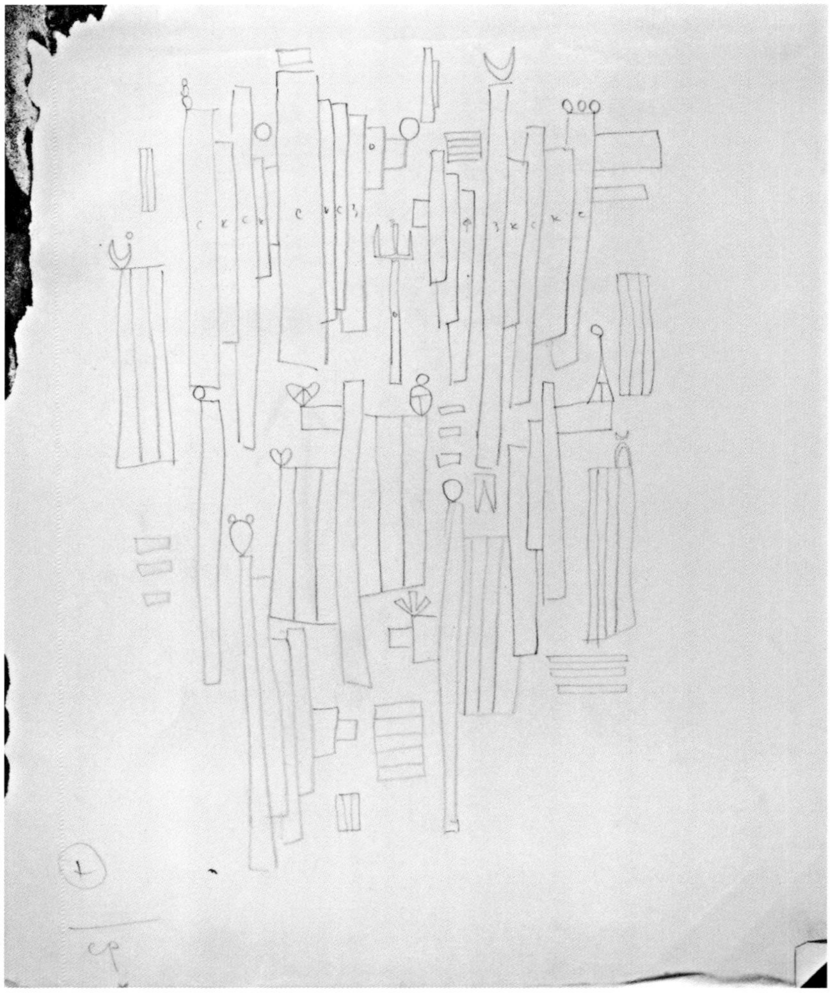

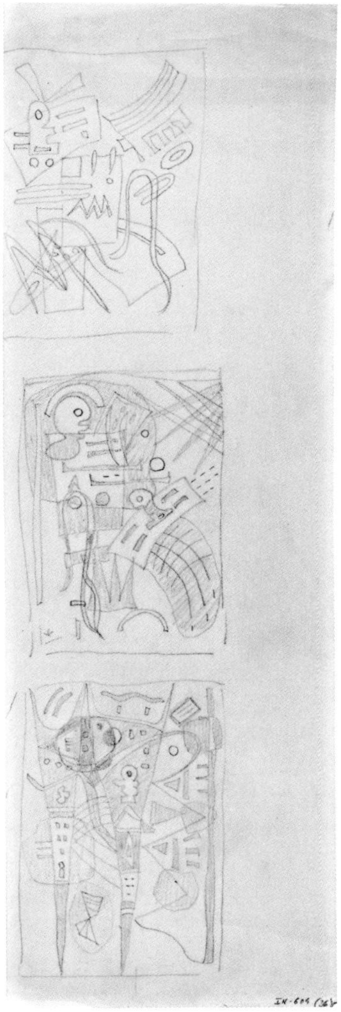

36, p.36R

36, p.36V

**p.36** Pencil studies on sheet that has been detached and cut down (33 x 10.4 cm)
Inscription on reverse erased

REFERENCES

Derouet and Boissel 1984, pp.399, 402, ill.
Barnett 2006, p.472

There are studies for *Autour de milieu* of February 1939 (Barnett no.1254), an ink drawing of c.1938 (vol.I, cat. no.1020) and *La Tension double* of June 1938 (Barnett no.1234) on the recto, and a pencil drawing for an unidentified work on the verso of this detached sheet.

# Sketchbook 37

1940–1943

Green paper-covered notebook with spiral-ring binding at left edge
Contains 12 sheets of graph paper, each 8.7 x 5.3 cm (3³/₈ x 2¹/₈ in), of which three have sketches
Page numbers inscribed by unknown hand at later date

Derouet and Boissel 1984, no.701

LOCATION
Musée National d'Art Moderne, Centre Georges Pompidou, Paris (AM 1981.65.679)

HISTORY
Nina Kandinsky, Paris, until 1980

The first seven pages of this notebook have a different orientation than pp.8–12, which are upside down. Only three of the pages have sketches.

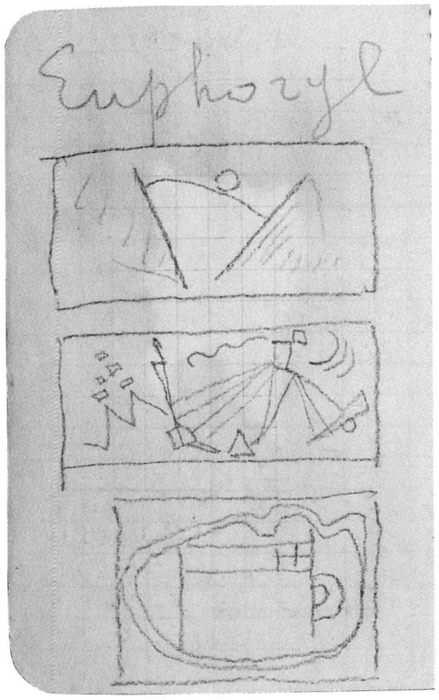


37, p.1v

**p.1** Notes on recto
On reverse: pencil sketches
Inscribed u.c.: 'Euphoryl'

REFERENCES
Derouet and Boissel 1984, p.425, ill.

Kandinsky made sketches for three untitled gouaches of 1940 (Barnett nos.1318, 1321, 1324). Eurphoryl was a homeopathic medicine.

**pp.2–6** Notes

**p.7** Pencil sketch on recto

REFERENCES
Derouet and Boissel 1984, p.425, ill.

The drawing is a study for *Trois rayons* of September–October 1943 (Roethel and Benjamin no.1164).

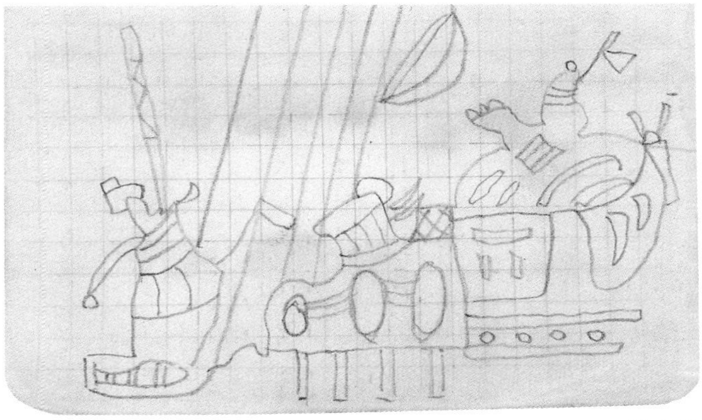

37, p.7r

**p.8** Recto blank
Inscribed on reverse (upside down): 'Cahor / Prayssac / (Lot) / Souillac / Allier'

Prayssac and Souillac are not far from Cahors in the Midi-Pyrénées region of France.

**p.9** Numerical calculations on recto
On reverse: pencil sketch (upside down) on torn sheet (approx. 2 x 4.7 cm)
Inscribed u.c.: 'Dernière toile- 680 / [Dernière] gouache- / Mai 1941'

REFERENCES
Derouet and Boissel 1984, p.425, ill.

In his Handlist Kandinsky recorded the canvas *Deux noirs* as number 680, which was painted in March 1941. This sketch shares certain similarities with the following work in the Handlist, *Contrastes réduits* of July 1941 (Roethel and Benjamin no.1119), although it cannot be considered a study for the painting.

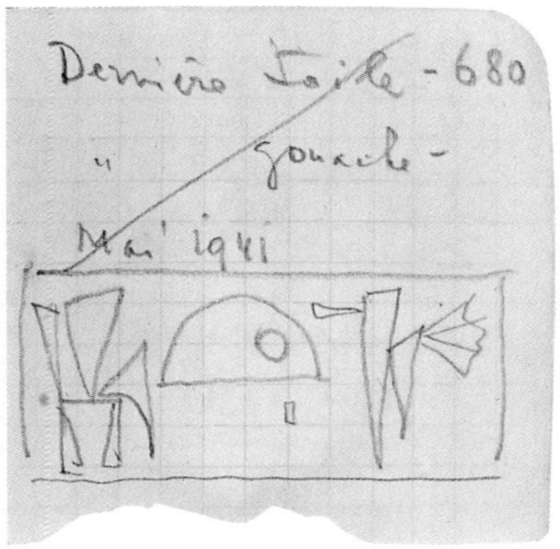


37, p.9v

**pp.10–12** Notes

# Sketchbook 38

c.1943

Green cardboard sketchbook cover with black spine; inside front cover stamp of Lucien Lefebvre-Foinet, Paris (12 rue Vavin and 2 rue Bréa)
Contains 12 sheets, each 26.9 x 20 cm (10⅝ x 7⅞ in), of which pp.9–12 are blank. The left edge is perforated. Approximately 19 sheets have been removed.
Pages have not been numbered

Derouet and Boissel 1984, no.724

LOCATION
Musée National d'Art Moderne, Centre Georges Pompidou, Paris (AM 1981.65.680)

HISTORY
Nina Kandinsky, Paris, until 1980

Numerous sheets have been detached from the sketchbook, including cat. nos.1187–1194 in Volume I.

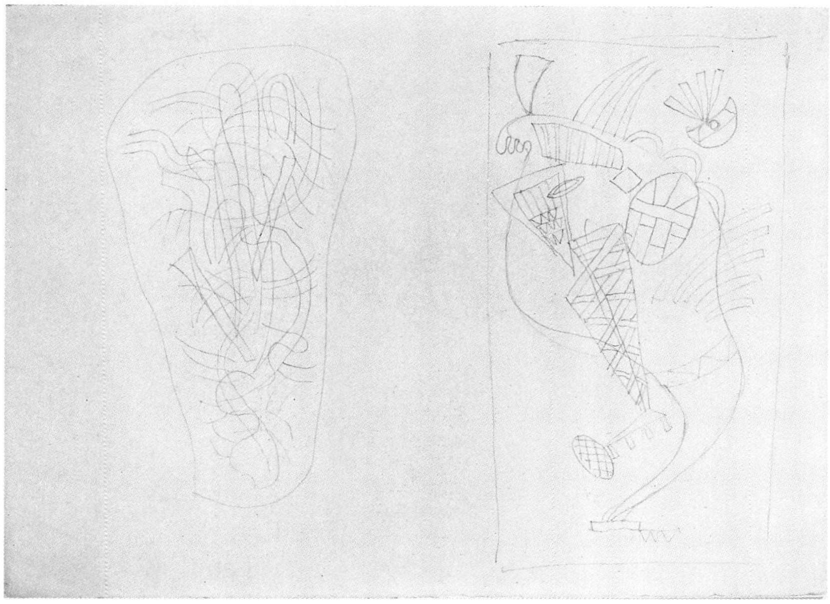

38, p.1

**p.1** Pencil study for *Figure blanche* of January 1943

REFERENCES
Barnett 1983, p.284, ill.a
Derouet and Boissel 1984, p.436, ill.

There is a study for *Figure blanche* of January 1943 (Roethel and Benjamin no.1142) on the right and a sketch for an unidentified work on the left.

**p.2** India ink drawing

EXHIBITIONS
1997 Milan, no.100, ill.

REFERENCES
Derouet and Boissel 1984, p.436, ill.

**p.3** Black crayon drawing

REFERENCES
Derouet and Boissel 1984, p.436, ill.

This study is reminiscent of *Tensions délicates* of 1942 (Roethel and Benjamin no.1128).

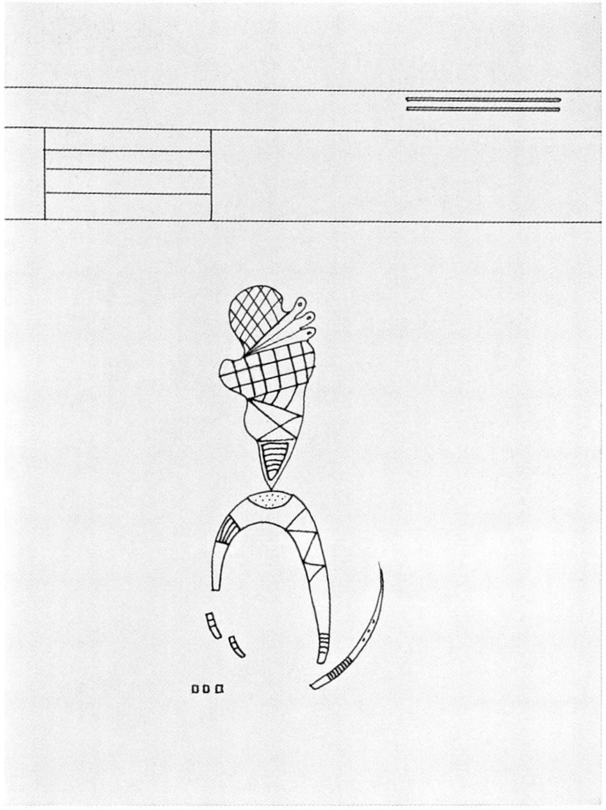

38, p.2

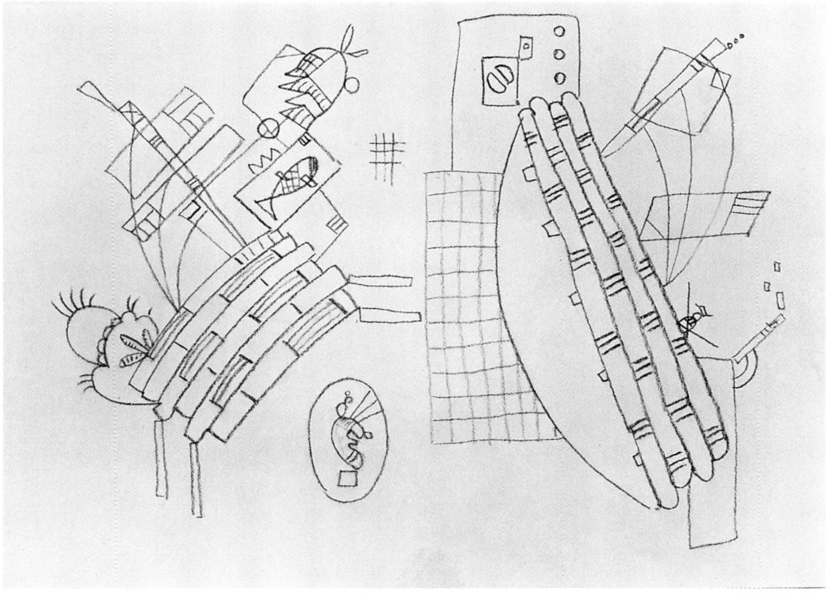

38, p.3

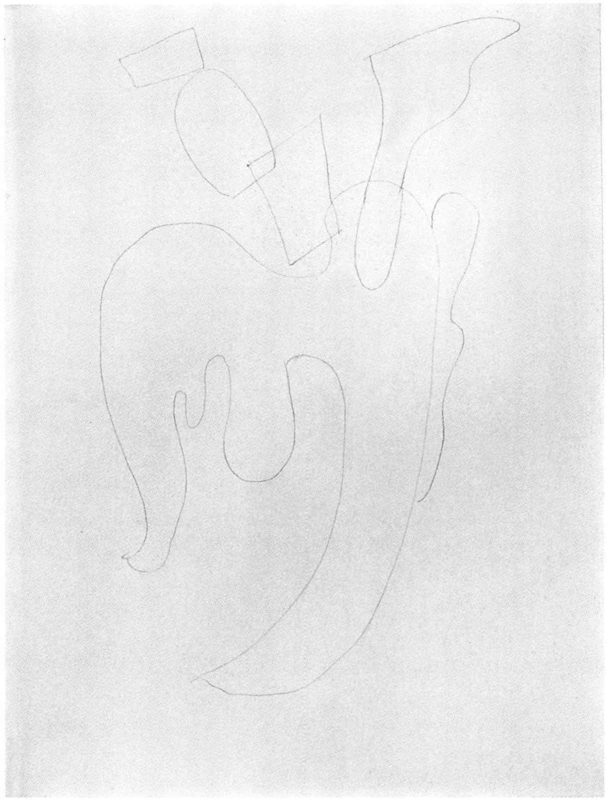

38, p.4

**p.4** Pencil study for *Une Figure flottante* of July 1942

REFERENCES

Derouet and Boissel 1984, pp.436, 437, ill.

The drawing clearly resembles *Une Figure flottante* of July 1942 (Roethel and Benjamin no.1129) and a related drawing (vol.I, cat. no.1181).

**p.5** India ink drawing

REFERENCES

Derouet and Boissel 1984, p.436, ill.

**p.6** India ink drawing

REFERENCES

Derouet and Boissel 1984, p.436, ill.
Weiss 1995, p.191 n.33

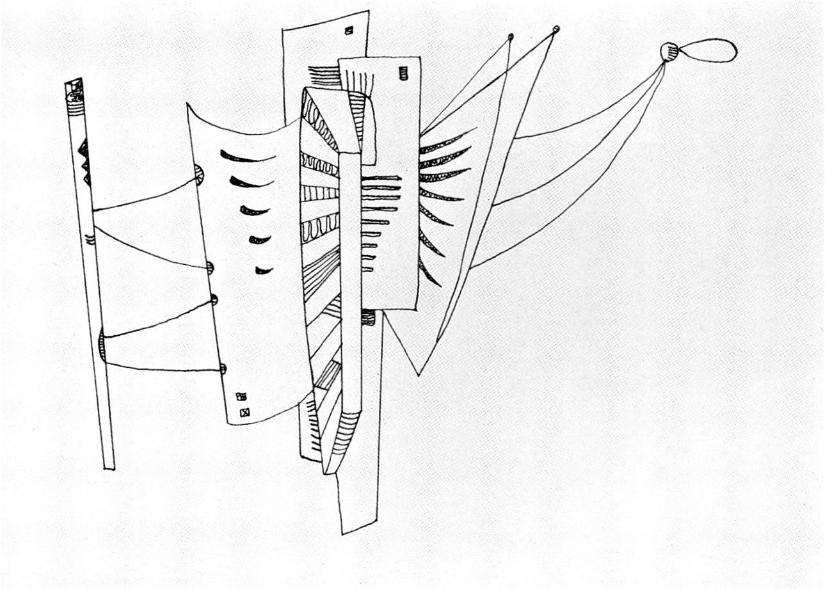

38, p.5

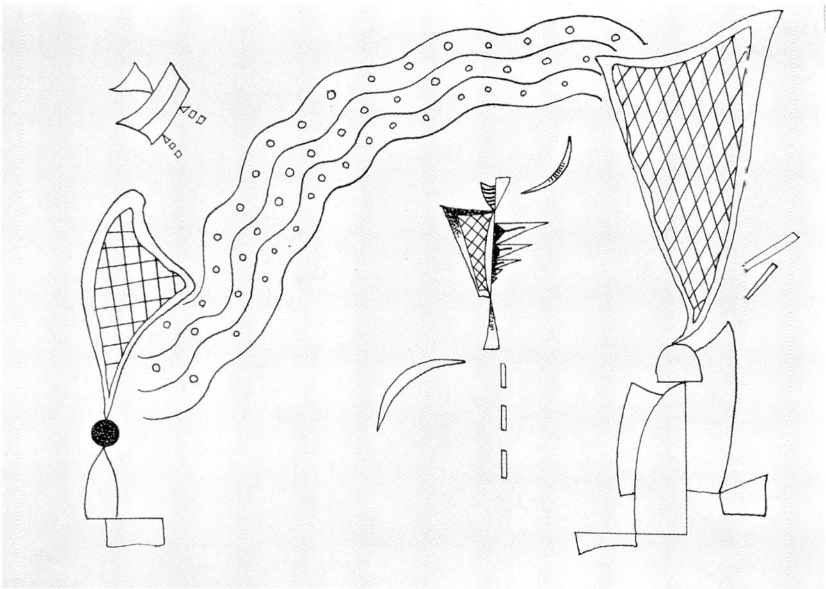

38, p.6

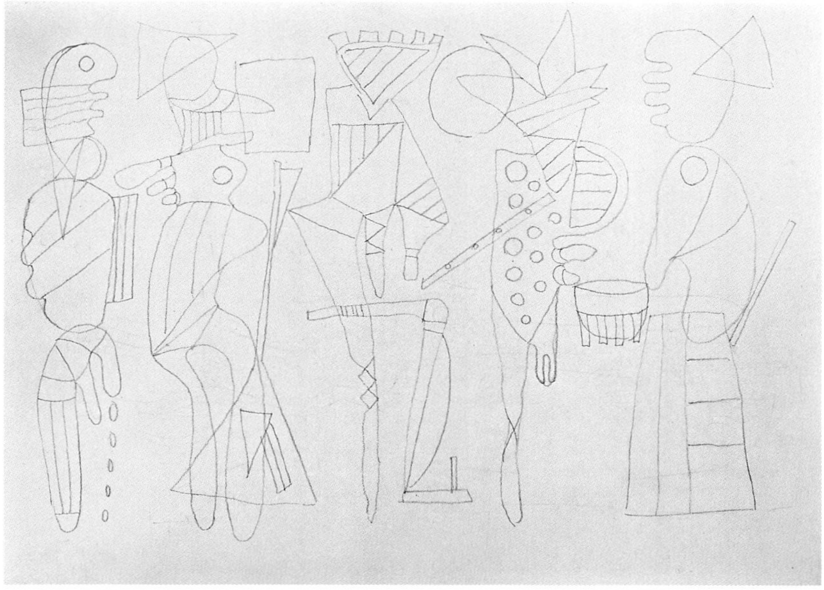

38, p.7

**p.7** Pencil study for *Cercle et carré* of April 1943

REFERENCES

Derouet and Boissel 1984, pp.434, ill., 436

Kandinsky developed this study into the painting *Cercle et carré* in April 1943 (Roethel and Benjamin no.1153).

**p.8** India ink and pencil study for *Accord* of March 1943
Signed and dated l.l.: 'K / 43'
Inscribed with color notations in Cyrillic

REFERENCES

Derouet and Boissel 1984, p.436, ill.
Georgia Illetschko, 'Kandinsky en la linia divisòria: el pintor com a dibuixant', in *Vassily Kandinsky: La revolució del llenguatge pictòric* exh. cat. (Barcelona, 1996), pp.24, ill.6, 27
Illetschko 1997, p.150, ill.59

Kandinsky signed and dated this sketchbook sheet, which is a study for *Accord* of March 1943 (Roethel and Benjamin no.1150).

**pp.9–12** Blank

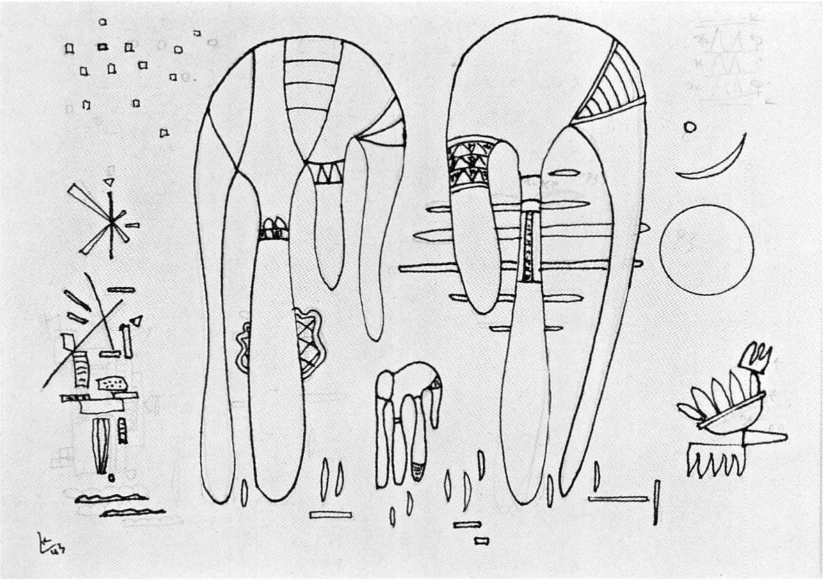

38, p.8

# *Addendum*

1237
**Rothenburg ob der Tauber**
7 November 1903

Pencil on paper, 13 x 16.8 cm (5⅛ x 6⅝ in)
Inscribed l.r. in Cyrillic: 'Rottenburg / 7 Noiabr''

LOCATION
Gabriele Münter- und Johannes Eichner-Stiftung, Munich (Kon.46/13)

HISTORY
Gabriele Münter, Murnau, until 1957

This drawing is found on p.3 of a sketchbook that Gabriele Münter used in 1903–1904. Kandinsky dated the sheet '7 November' and, on p.7, Münter wrote the date 8 November 1903. Subsequent pages were done in the Netherlands in 1904. As Isabelle Jansen noted, the same scene is depicted in a drawing by Münter in another sketchbook (37/7, p.88), which can be dated to 1903–1906, although she omitted the figure of a man and other objects in the foreground. Moreover, the present work is related to the drawing on the first page of Sketchbook 15 (GMS 331).

1238
**Landschaft**
Landscape
c.1904

Pencil on paper, 13 x 16.8 cm (5⅛ x 6⅝ in)
Inscribed c.l.: 's.d.'; l.l.: 'Schatten'; c.: 'Erde / Baume'; c.r. by Münter: 'Tisch' and u.r. by unknown hand in triangle: 'K'. Not dated

LOCATION
Gabriele Münter- und Johannes Eichner-Stiftung, Munich (Kon.46/13)

HISTORY
Gabriele Münter, Murnau, until 1957

Kandinsky made this sketch on p.62 of the same sketchbook (see cat. nos.1237, 1239) that Münter used in 1903–1904. It resembles drawings he made in Kallmünz and in the Netherlands (see Sketchbook 10, p.5 and Sketchbook 16, pp.7, 20).

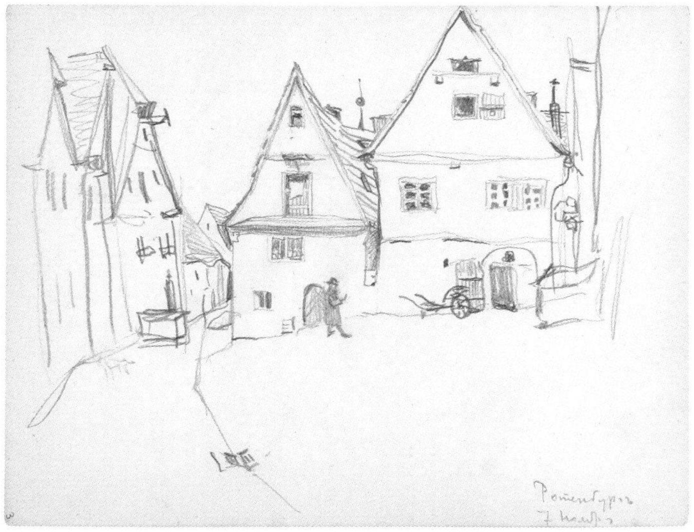

1237

1238

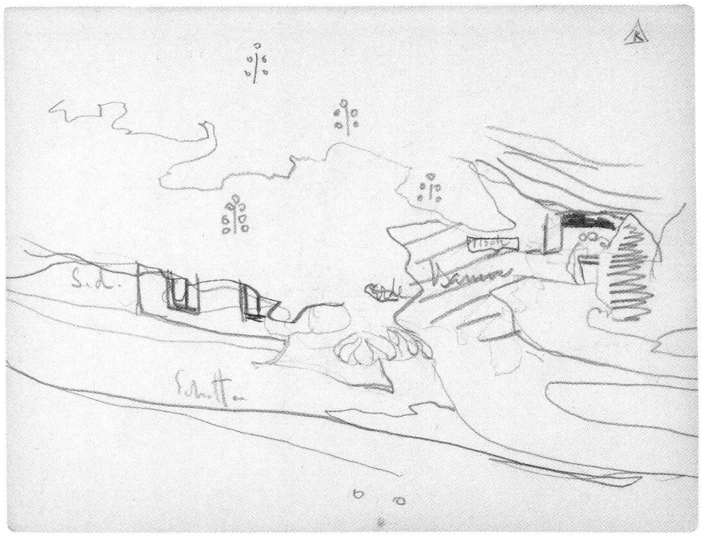

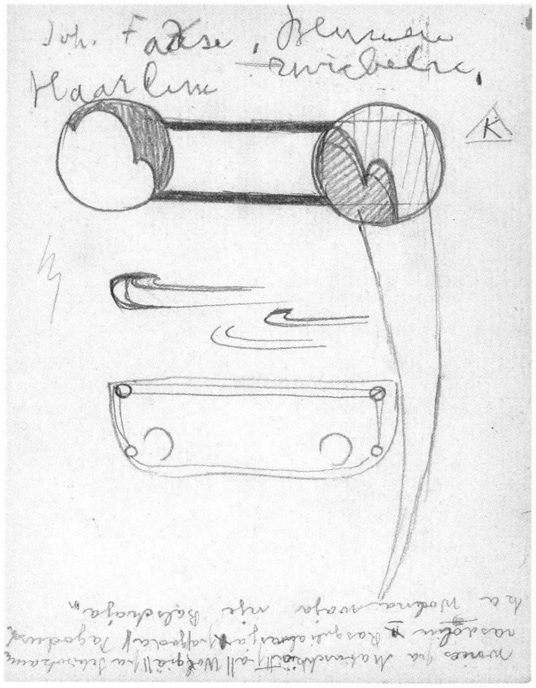

1239

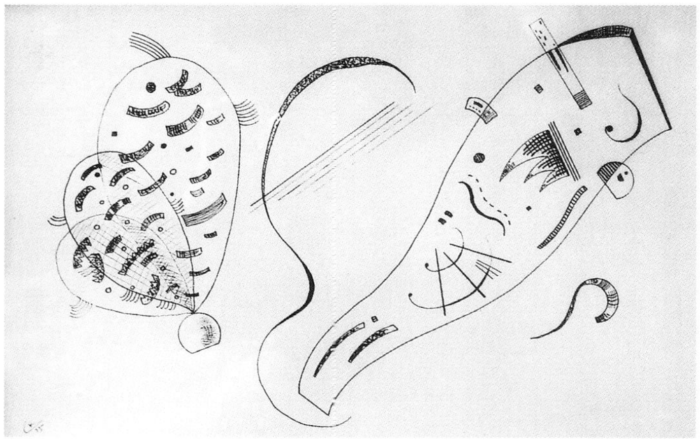

1240

1239
**Entwürfe**
Sketches
1904

Pencil on paper, 16.8 x 13 cm (6⅝ x 5⅛ in)
Signed u.r., probably by the artist: 'K'. Not dated
Inscribed above by unknown hand: 'Jos. Faase. / Haarlem / Blumen / zwiebeln.' and below by Münter: transliteration of Russian words

LOCATION
Gabriele Münter- und Johannes Eichner-Stiftung, Munich (Kon.46/13)

HISTORY
Gabriele Münter, Murnau, until 1957

Kandinsky made these decorative sketches (upside down) on the last page (p.64) opposite the back cover of a sketchbook in which he and Münter drew during their trip to the Netherlands in late May–June 1904. They can be compared to the sketches inside the back cover of Sketchbook 13.

1240
**Ohne Titel**
Untitled
1935

India ink on tan paper, 29.2 x 44.6 cm (11½ x 17½ in)
Signed and dated l.l.: 'K/35'
Information on reverse not available

LOCATION
Private collection, Belgium

HISTORY
Private collection, Switzerland
Sotheby's, London, 28 March 1984, no.347, ill.

EXHIBITIONS
1973 Geneva, Musée d'Art et d'Histoire, *Art du XXe siècle: collections genevoises*, 28 June–23 September, not in cat.

REFERENCES
Jelena Hahl-Fontaine, ed., *Kandinsky Forum I* (Fernelmont, 2006), pp.22, ill.3, 23

# *Appendix I*

## Decorative Arts

1

**Promenade gracieuse (Grosse Fassung)**
Gracious Promenade (Large Version)
c.1904

Gouache and pencil on maple, 22.8 x 59 x 2.5 cm (9 x 23¼ x 1 in)
Not signed or dated
On reverse: Incised lines related to woodcut

LOCATION
Beck & Eggeling, Düsseldorf

HISTORY
Nina Kandinsky, Paris
Private collection
Sotheby's, New York, 3–4 November 1988, no.228, color ill.
Private collection, Germany
Villa Grisebach, Berlin, 24 November 1989, no.23, ill.
Christie's, London, 7 October 1999, no.52, color ill.

EXHIBITIONS
1991 Munich, no.1, color ill.

REFERENCES
Roethel 1970, p.86
Hahl-Koch 1993, p.97, ill.115

The painted image closely resembles – in reverse – the large version of the woodcut *Promenade gracieuse* (Roethel no.43), which Hans Roethel dated 1904. A related but not identical work appears in a photograph that Münter took of Kandinsky in Dresden during the summer of 1905. In addition, Kandinsky made a lost tempera painting, *Promenade* of 1903 (Barnett no.87), for which no photograph is known.

Roethel illustrated the reverse of the present work (1970, p.469, ill.13b) and related it to *Frühling* of 1904 (1970, no.42). However, the image bears a much closer relationship to a lost tempera painting, *Stilles Wasser (Der blaue Herr und die weisse Dame)* of September 1905 (Barnett no.194), and to a photograph that Kandinsky took at Akhtyrka that belongs to the Münter-Eichner Stiftung, Munich (see Roethel 1970, p.469, ill.13a).

(See color plate p.241)

2

**Uhrenständer**
Watch Stand
c.1909

Also known as 'Vornübergeneigte'

Gouache on wood, 14.4 x 6.6 x 4.2 cm (5⅝ x 2⅝ x 1⅝ in)
Not signed or dated

LOCATION
Gabriele Münter- und Johannes Eichner-Stiftung, Munich (HP 4)

HISTORY
Gabriele Münter, Murnau, until 1957

EXHIBITIONS
1982 New York, no.37, ill.
1982 Munich, no.326, ill.

REFERENCES
Weiss 1979, p.124
Gollek 1982, no.184, ill.
Barnett and Friedel 1995, no.320, color ill.
Barnett 2006, p.70

Kandinsky made a sketch for the wood carving on a bill from the Hotel zur Post in Murnau probably in 1909 (vol.I, cat. no.115). According to Gollek, Kandinsky used this sculpture as a stand for his watch.

(See color plate p.241)

3

**Begegnung**
Encounter
c.1909

Oil on wood, 32 x 41 cm (12⅝ x 16⅛ in) image, 36.5 x 42.6 x 3.5 cm (14⅜ x 16¾ x 1⅜ in) block
Not signed or dated

LOCATION
Gabriele Münter- und Johannes Eichner-Stiftung, Munich (HP 1)

HISTORY
Gabriele Münter, Murnau, until 1957

EXHIBITIONS
1972 Munich, no.2324
1982 New York, no.35, ill.
1982 Munich, no.322, ill.

REFERENCES
Weiss 1979, pp.124, 211 n.57, fig.110b
Gollek 1982, no.182, ill.
Barnett 1992, p.218
Barnett and Friedel 1995, no.324, color ill.
Barnett 2006, p.70

There is a study on p.8 of Sketchbook 26 of 1908–1909 (GMS 328) as well as a drawing (vol.I, cat. no.116) and a watercolor (Barnett no.246) related to this sculpture. Roethel (1970, p.420) proposed that the watercolor is a study for an unexecuted color woodcut; however, it bears a clear resemblance to this painted wood relief although the colors differ. The color notations in the sketchbook (see p.225) correspond more closely but not exactly to those in the relief.

(See color plate p.241)

4
**Reiter**
Rider
c.1909

Oil on wood, 29 x 25 x 3.5 cm ($11\frac{3}{8}$ x $9\frac{7}{8}$ x $1\frac{3}{8}$ in)
Not signed or dated

LOCATION
Gabriele Münter- und Johannes Eichner-Stiftung, Munich (HP 2)

HISTORY
Gabriele Münter, Murnau, until 1957

EXHIBITIONS
1972 Munich, no.2323
1982 New York, no.36, ill.
1982 Munich, no.324, ill.

REFERENCES
Gollek 1982, no.181, ill.
Barnett and Friedel 1995, no.321, color ill.
Barnett 2006, p.70

Kandinsky made a detailed study for this relief sculpture on the same sheet of paper as figures for *Begegnung* (vol.I, cat. no.116) as well as sketches on pp.6 and 63 in Sketchbook 26 (GMS 328). Not only the color notations but also the notes regarding the depth of the carving correspond to those found in the present work: the dimensions, however, are considerably smaller than those inscribed on the drawing.

(See color plate p.242)

5
**Zwei Figuren**
Two Figures
c.1909

Oil and tempera (?) on wood, 22.3 x 15.2 x 3 cm ($8\frac{3}{4}$ x 6 x $1\frac{1}{8}$ in)
Not signed or dated

LOCATION
Gabriele Münter- und Johannes Eichner-Stiftung, Munich (HP 3)

HISTORY
Gabriele Münter, Murnau, until 1957

REFERENCES
Gollek 1982, no.183, ill.
Barnett and Friedel 1995, no.325, color ill.

The figure on the right resembles those found on p.40 of Sketchbook 27 (GMS 345) in a study for *Improvisation I* of 1909.

(See color plate p.242)

6
**Toilettenschränkchen**
Bedside Table
1909

Painted wood, 100 x 56 x 31.5 cm ($39\frac{3}{8}$ x 22 x $12\frac{3}{8}$ in)
Not signed or dated

LOCATION
Gabriele Münter- und Johannes Eichner-Stiftung, Munich (M 4)

HISTORY
Gabriele Münter, Murnau, until 1957

EXHIBITIONS
1972 Munich, no.2327
1982 New York, no.32, ill.
1982 Munich, no.317, color ill.

REFERENCES
Johannes Langner, '"Impression V": Observations sur un thème chez Kandinsky', *Revue de l'art*, no.45 (1979), pp.56, 57, ill.11
Weiss 1979, p.124
Kenneth Lindsay, 'Gabriele Münter and Wassily Kandinsky: What They Meant to Each Other', *Arts Magazine*, vol.56, no.4 (Dec. 1981), pp.61, ill.27, 62
Gollek 1982, no.186, ill.
Gollek 1984, p.12
Hahl-Koch 1993, pp.124, 125, ill.160
Barnett and Friedel 1995, no.326, color ill.
Friedel 2000, pp.46, 48, color ill., 49

In her diary Münter wrote: 'Mein Toilettenschränkchen hat K. bemalt (ebenso Spiegel drauf und Nachtkastl) zart und humoristisch. Am mittleren Fach rennen ein "blauer Reiter" und eine dunklere Reiterin. Er wendet sich um nach ihr und winkt und sie rennt was sie kann – manchmal hat mich dieser Scherz geärgert, weil er unwahr ist – denn er wandte sich nie um und sagte nie "Komm mit." (Quoted in Gollek 1982 from a Tagebuch in the Münter-Eichner Stiftung.) The bedside table is clearly visible in Münter's painting *Interieur im 'Russenhaus'* of 1909 (Friedel 2000, p.49).

(See color plate p.242)

7
**Nachtkästchen**
Night Table
c.1909

Painted wood, 84 x 40 x 32.5 cm ($33\frac{1}{8}$ x $15\frac{3}{4}$ x $12\frac{3}{4}$ in)
Not signed or dated

LOCATION
Gabriele Münter- und Johannes Eichner-Stiftung, Munich (M 12)

HISTORY
Gabriele Münter, Murnau, until 1957

REFERENCES
Gollek 1984, p.37

Münter referred to the 'Nachtkastl' and 'Toilettenschränkchen' that Kandinsky painted for her in her diary (see no.6 above). The decoration on the present work brings to mind sketches done in 1908 in Sketchbook 24 (GMS 335, p.42), Sketchbook 26 (GMS 328, p.37) and the watercolor *Abendmahl* of 1908–1909 (Barnett no.245).

(See color plate p.243)

8
**Stuhl**
Chair
c.1910

Painted wood, 85 x 41 x 37.5 cm ($33\frac{1}{2}$ x $16\frac{1}{8}$ x $14\frac{3}{4}$ in)
Not signed or dated

LOCATION
Gabriele Münter- und Johannes Eichner-Stiftung, Munich (M 7)

HISTORY
Gabriele Münter, Murnau, until 1957

EXHIBITIONS
1972 Munich, no.2326
1982 New York, no.31
1982 Munich, no.316, color ill.

REFERENCES
Eichner 1957, p.99, ill.54
Weiss 1979, p.124
Gollek 1982, no.185, ill.
Gollek 1984, pp.13, ill., 37
Barnett and Friedel 1995, no.327, color ill.
Friedel 2000, p.45, color ill.

In Sketchbook 27, which Kandinsky used in 1908–1910, he made a sketch of a chair for Münter (GMS 345, p.43) but it is not to be identified with the present work.

(See color plate p.245)

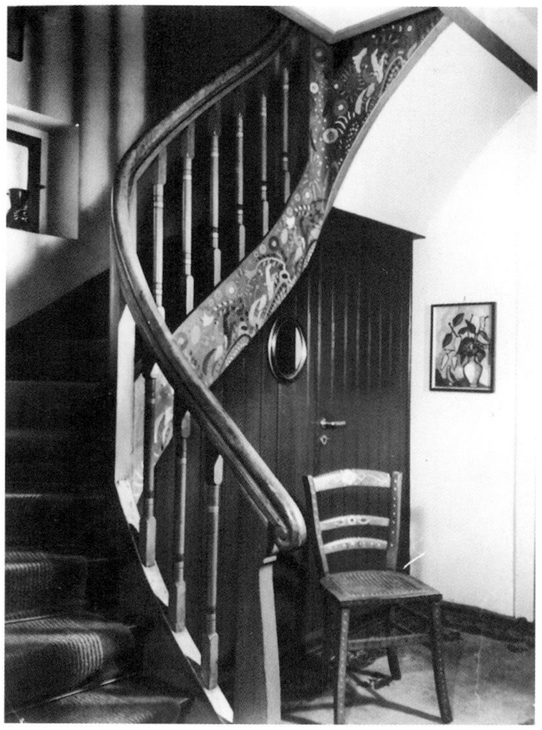

fig.a Chair and staircase decorated by Kandinsky in the "Russians' House" in Murnau, c.1910. Photograph by Sigrid Bühring, c.1930

9
**Schreibtisch**
Desk
c.1910

Painted wood, 80 x 89.2 x 60 cm (31½ x 35⅛ x 23⅝ in)
Not signed or dated

LOCATION
Gabriele Münter- und Johannes Eichner-Stiftung, Munich (M 5)

HISTORY
Gabriele Münter, Murnau, until 1957

EXHIBITIONS
1972 Munich, no.2326
1982 New York, no.30, ill.
1982 Munich, no.315, color ill.

REFERENCES
Eichner 1957, p.99, ill.54
Weiss 1979, p.124
Gollek 1982, no.185, ill.
Gollek 1984, pp.13, ill., 37
Barnett and Friedel 1995, no.328, color ill.
Friedel 2000, p.45, color ill.

In Sketchbook 27 Kandinsky made lists of furniture for the Murnau house, noting several tables, chairs and bookcases and citing 'Tische von München (als Schreib etc.)' (GMS 345, pp.26–27).

(See color plate p.244)

10
**Nachttisch**
Night Table
c.1910

Painted wood, 90 x 45 x 36.5 cm (35⅜ x 17¾ x 14⅜ in)
Not signed or dated

LOCATION
Gabriele Münter- und Johannes Eichner-Stiftung, Munich (M 3)

HISTORY
Gabriele Münter, Murnau, until 1957

EXHIBITIONS
1982 Munich, no.318, ill.

REFERENCES
Barnett and Friedel 1995, no.329, color ill.
Friedel 2000, p.20, color ill.

(See color plate p.245)

11
**Bücherregal**
Book Shelf
c.1910

Painted wood, 150 x 88.5 x 28 cm (59 x 34⅞ x 11 in)
Not signed or dated

LOCATION
Gabriele Münter- und Johannes Eichner-Stiftung, Munich (M 8)

HISTORY
Gabriele Münter, Murnau, until 1957

EXHIBITIONS
1972 Munich, no.2325
1982 Munich, no.319, ill.

REFERENCES
Eichner 1957, p.99
Weiss 1979, p.124
Gollek 1984, pp.14, ill., 37
Barnett and Friedel 1995, no.330, color ill.
Friedel 2000, pp.44, color ill., 45

The decorative figure of a woman in crinolines brings to mind Kandinsky's painting *Reifröcke* of 1909 (Roethel and Benjamin no.263).

(See color plate p.244)

12
**Küchenschrank**
Kitchen Cupboard
c.1910

Painted wood, 195 x 99.5 x 48.5 cm (76¾ x 39⅛ x 19⅛ in)
Not signed or dated

LOCATION
Gabriele Münter- und Johannes Eichner-Stiftung, Munich (M 6)

HISTORY
Gabriele Münter, Murnau, until 1957

REFERENCES
Gollek 1984, p.37
Friedel 2000, p.12, color ill.

In a notebook that Münter used in 1910 (46/34, p.51), there is a list of furniture that includes a 'Küchenschrank' as well as 'Nachttisch', 'Küchentisch' and Sofa. In addition, Kandinsky made sketches that suggest the painted decoration on the kitchen cupboard in Sketchbook 27 (GMS 345, pp.12–13).

(See color plate p.243)

# *Appendix II*

## Works included but not illustrated in the Kandinsky Catalogues Raisonnés of Oil Paintings and Watercolors

Since the publication of the two volumes on Kandinsky's oil paintings by Hans K. Roethel and Jean K. Benjamin (1982, 1984) and the two volumes on the watercolors by Vivian Endicott Barnett (1992, 1994), the following works, which were known only from the artist's Handlists, have been traced and photographs have been obtained. See also the Appendix (Barnett 1992, pp.485–488) for illustrations of works in Soviet museums. In addition, there are newly discovered paintings and watercolors not included in the four volumes of the catalogue raisonné at the beginning of *Kandinsky Drawings: Catalogue Raisonné. Volume I. Individual Drawings* (cat. nos.1–15).

Barnett no.70
**Der rote Dichter**
The Red Poet
January 1903
Oil and tempera on jute, 51 x 46.8 cm (20⅛ x 18⅜ in)
Signed l.l.: 'KANDINSKY'. Not dated
Inscribed on reverse: 'KANDINSKY- "Der Dichter" (Tempera) / No19'

LOCATION
Private collection, Germany

HISTORY
Hugo Helbing, Munich, 1904
Private collection, Germany
Neumeister, Munich, 13 November 1998, no.592, color ill.
Ahlers Pro Arte Collection
Douglas & Nash, Frankfurt am Main and New York
Galerie Sander, Darmstadt

(See color plate p.246)

Barnett no. 397
**Blaugold**
Blue Gold
1915
Watercolor and India ink on paper, 22.2 x 33.6 cm (8¾ x 13¼ in)
Signed and dated l.l.: 'K/15'

LOCATION
Albertina, Vienna: Dauerleihgabe der Österreichischen Ludwig-Stiftung für Kunst und Wissenschaft

HISTORY
Galka E. Scheyer, Los Angeles, 1925–1927
Returned to the artist, 1928
Acquired from the artist by Angermuseum, Erfurt, December 1928 (No.II III)
Confiscated 3 September 1937 as 'Entartete Kunst' (1651)
Sophie and Emanuel Fohn, Rome, 1939–1990

(See color plate p.246)

fig.a

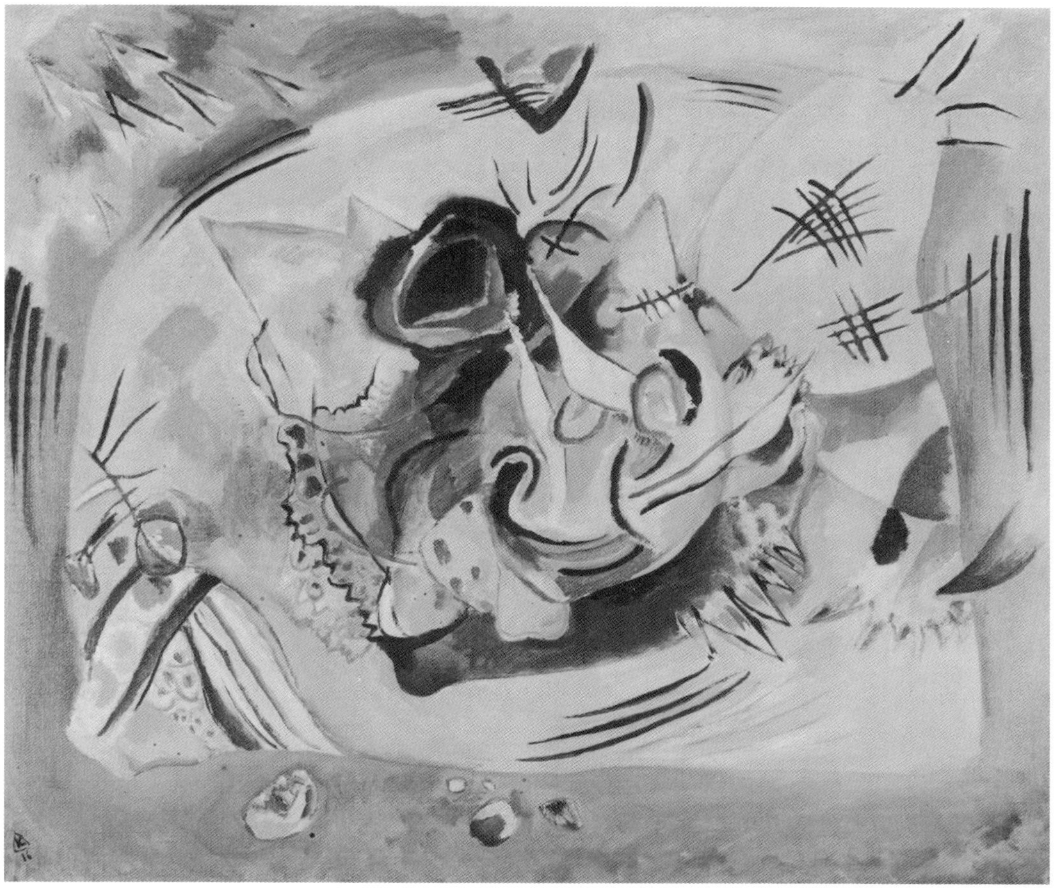

Roethel and Benjamin no.598
**Bild mit orange Rand**
Painting with Orange Border
1916
Oil on canvas, 88 x 100 cm (34⅝ x 39⅜ in) (HL)
Signed and dated l.l.: 'K/16'

HISTORY
Käte and Otto Ralfs, Braunschweig
Destroyed during World War II

(See fig.a)

Barnett no.524
**Ohne Titel**
Untitled
1920
Watercolor and India ink on paper, 34.7 x 22.5 cm (13⅝ x 8⅞ in)
Signed and dated l.l.: 'K/20'
Inscribed on reverse: 'No14b / 1920 / "Haltlos"'

LOCATION
Private collection

HISTORY
Nina Kandinsky, Paris
M. Rothenberg, Paris
Private collection, Paris, 1992–1997
Sotheby's, London, 25 June 1997, no.180, color ill.

(See color plate p.247)

Barnett no.679
**Kühlfarbig**
Cool-Colored
February 1924
Watercolor and India ink on paper, 40 x 30.5 cm (15¾ x 12 in)
Signed and dated l.l.: 'K/24'

LOCATION
Private collection, Paris

HISTORY
Nina Kandinsky, Paris
Galerie Maeght, Paris
Private collection, Paris

(See color plate p.247)

Roethel and Benjamin no.856
**Roter Kreis**
Red Circle
December 1927
Oil on canvas, 33 x 41 cm (13 x 16⅛ in) (HL)
Signed and dated l.l.: 'K/27'
Inscribed on reverse: 'K "Roter Kreis" / No413 / 1927'

LOCATION
Private collection

HISTORY
Private collection, France, 1943–1991

(See color plate p.248)

Roethel and Benjamin no.872
**Bestimmend**
Determining
1928
Oil and tempera on board, 36 x 20 cm (14⅛ x 7⅞ in)
Not signed or dated
Inscribed on reverse: 'K "Bestimmend" / No429 / 1928'

LOCATION
Private collection

HISTORY
Evelyn Mayer, San Francisco, 1928
Louise Baer, San Francisco
Private collection
Christie's, New York, 20 November 1998, no.743, color ill.

(See color plate p.248)

Roethel and Benjamin no.940
**Zentral**
Central
January 1930
Oil on cardboard, 34.2 x 24.3 cm (13½ x 9⅝ in)
Signed and dated l.l.: 'K/30'
Inscribed on reverse: '"ZENTRAL" / No495 / 1930'

LOCATION
Private collection

HISTORY
Galerie Jeanne Bucher, Paris, 1937
Dr. and Mrs. Frederick Coller, Ann Arbor MI
Private collection, Midland TX
ECN Art, Newtown PA, 2003
Max Protetch Gallery, New York, 2004

(See color plate p.249)

Barnett no.965
**Stufen**
Steps
March 1930
Gouache and watercolor on blue paper mounted on cardboard, 19.5 x 28.2 cm (7⅝ x 11⅛ in)
Signed and dated l.l.: 'K/30'
Inscribed on reverse mount: 'K / No373 / 1930 / A Madame M.Vauret / comme souvenir au Mars 1930 / à la Galerie de France / sincerement / Kandinsky'

LOCATION
Private collection, New York

HISTORY
Gift of the artist to Mme Vauret, Paris, 1930
Pierre Matisse, New York
Private collection

(See color plate p.249)

Barnett no.973
**Schimmer**
Shimmer
March 1930
Watercolor and India ink on paper, 48.3 x 31.4 cm (19 x 12⅜ in)
Signed and dated l.l.: 'K/30'
Inscribed on original mount (removed): 'No381 / 1930 / "Schimmer"'

LOCATION
Blanden Memorial Art Museum, Fort Dodge IA: Gift of Ella Wasem (1952.10)

HISTORY
Galerie Maeght, Paris
Ella Wasem, Fort Dodge IA, 1951–1952

(See color plate p.250)

Barnett no.1054
**Geschmücktes Rechteck**
Decorated Rectangle
July 1931
Watercolor on paper, 31.5 x 35 cm (12⅜ x 13¾ in)
Signed and dated l.l.: 'K/31'

LOCATION
Private collection

HISTORY
Galka E. Scheyer, Los Angeles, 1933–1945
Nina Kandinsky, Paris, late 1940s
Gift of Nina Kandinsky to Gildas Fardel, Paris, 1956
LeRoux & Morel, Paris, 1 December 1999, no.93, color ill.

(See color plate p.250)

Roethel and Benjamin no.1015
**Zu vier Ecken**
Toward Four Corners
February 1932
Oil, tempera and ink on board, 70 x 70 cm (27½ x 27½ in)
Signed and dated l.l.: 'K/32'

LOCATION
Collection of Daniel Fischel and Sylvia Neil

HISTORY
Galka E. Scheyer, Los Angeles, 1933–1940
Robert Ellsworth Gross, Los Angeles, 1940
Palmer and Charles Ducommun
Christie's, New York, 12 May 1992, no.137, color ill.
David Nahmad

(See color plate p.251)

Barnett no.1102
**Vier Teile**
Four Parts
October 1932
Gouache and India ink on paper, 39.3 x 30.5 cm (15½ x 12 in)
Signed and dated l.l.: 'K/32'

LOCATION
The Metropolitan Museum of Art, New York: Gift of William Benenson (1991.402.9)

HISTORY
Pinacotheca Gallery, New York
William Benenson, New York

(See fig.b)

fig.b

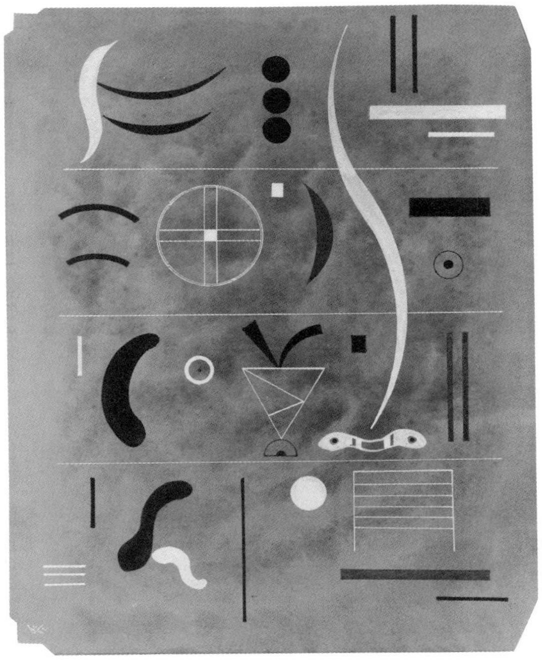

Barnett no.1211
**Oui**
Yes
October 1937
Gouache on black paper mounted on cardboard, 31.3 x 48.5 cm (12⅜ x 19⅛ in)
Signed and dated l.l.: 'K/37'
Inscribed on reverse mount: 'No580 / 1937 / "Oui" / A Madame Jeanne Bucher pour son anniversaire / le 16 Févr. 1942 / Affectueusement / Kandinsky'

LOCATION
Kunsthandel Frans Jacobs, Amsterdam

HISTORY
Gift of the artist to Jeanne Bucher, Paris, 1942
Galleria Seno, Milan
Private collection, 1970–2004
Sotheby's, London, 4 February 2004, no.490, color ill.

(See color plate p.252)

Barnett no.1242
**L'ouverture**
Opening
November 1938
Gouache on black paper mounted on cardboard, 36.4 x 49.6 cm (14⅜ x 19½ in)
Signed and dated l.l.: 'K/38'
Inscribed on reverse mount: 'No608 / 1938 / "L'ouverture"'

LOCATION
Helly Nahmad

HISTORY
Hilla von Rebay, New York and Greens Farms CT
Private collection, Germany
Christie's, London, 27 June 2002, no.358, color ill.

(See color plate p.253)

Barnett no.1285
**Sans titre**
Untitled
1940
Watercolor on paper, 50 x 33 cm (19⅝ x 13 in)
Signed and dated l.l.: 'K/40'

LOCATION
Private collection, Paris

HISTORY
Jeanne Bucher, Paris, 1942

(See color plate p.254)

Barnett no.1352
**Sans titre**
Untitled
1941
Watercolor, gouache and ink on paper, 35.2 x 25 cm (13⅞ x 9⅞ in)
Signed and dated l.l.: 'K/41'
Inscribed on reverse: 'No717 / 1941'

LOCATION
Galerie von Vertes, Pfäffikon

HISTORY
Galerie Europe, Paris
Galerie Walter Moos, Toronto
Private collection, Canada, 1966
Sotheby's, New York, 4 May 2005, no.254

(See color plate p.254)

Roethel and Benjamin no.1137
**Communauté**
Community
November 1942
Oil on cardboard, 48 x 48 cm (18⅞ x 18⅞ in)
Not signed or dated

LOCATION
Galerie Jeanne Bucher, Paris

HISTORY
Jeanne Bucher, Paris, 1943

(See color plate p.255)

Roethel and Benjamin no.1162
**4 x 5= 20**
July 1943
Oil and gouache on cardboard, 57.5 x 41.5 cm (22⅝ x 16⅜ in)
Signed and dated l.l.: 'K/43'
Inscribed on reverse: 'K No725 / 1943'

LOCATION
Private collection, Osaka, Japan

HISTORY
Private collection, Paris, 1943–1989
Guy Loudmer, Paris, 17 June 1989, no.38, color ill.
Christie's, New York, 14 May 1997, no.55, color ill.

(See color plate p.256)

# *Select Bibliography and Abbreviated References*


### Writings by Kandinsky

*Über das Geistige in der Kunst, insbesondere in der Malerei* (Munich, 1912)

*Klänge* (Munich, 1912)

*Tekst khudozhnika: Stupeni* (Moscow, 1918)

*Punkt und Linie zu Fläche: Beitrag zur Analyse der malerischen Elemente* (Munich, 1926)

*Kandinsky: Complete Writings on Art*, edited by Kenneth C. Lindsay and Peter Vergo (see below)

### Catalogues Raisonnés

vol.1, cat. no. and Barnett 2006
Barnett, Vivian Endicott, *Kandinsky Drawings: Catalogue Raisonné. Individual Drawings*, vol.1 (London and Munich, 2006)

Barnett no. (1992 and 1994)
Barnett, Vivian Endicott, *Kandinsky Watercolours: Catalogue Raisonné, 1900–1921*, vol.1 (London and Munich, 1992), *1922–1944*, vol.2 (London and Munich, 1994)

Roethel no. (1970)
Roethel, Hans Konrad, *Kandinsky: Das graphische Werk* (Cologne, 1970)

Roethel and Benjamin no. (1982 and 1994)
Roethel, Hans K. and Benjamin, Jean K., *Kandinsky: Catalogue Raisonné of the Oil-Paintings, 1900–1915*, vol.1 (London and Munich, 1982), *1916–1944*, vol.2 (London and Munich, 1984)

### Books and Essays

Ashjian 2001
Ashjian, Cristina Maria, *Representing 'Scènes et Types': Wassily Kandinsky in Tunisia 1904–1905* (PhD dissertation, Northwestern University, 2001)

Avtonomova 1998
Avtonomova, N.B., Sarabianov, D.V. and Turchin, V.S., eds., *Mnogogranniy mir Kandinskovo* (Moscow, 1998)

Barnett 1983
Barnett, Vivian Endicott, *Kandinsky at the Guggenheim* (New York, 1983)

Barnett and Friedel 1995
Barnett, Vivian Endicott and Friedel, Helmut, *Das bunte Leben: Wassily Kandinsky im Lenbachhaus* (Cologne, 1995). Published in English as *Vasily Kandinsky. A Colorful Life: The Collection of the Lenbachhaus, Munich* (1995)

Becks-Malorny 1994
Becks-Malorny, Ulrike, *Wassily Kandinsky, 1866–1944: The Journey to Abstraction* (Cologne, 1994). Originally published as *Wassily Kandinsky, 1866–1944: Aufbruch zur Abstraction* (1993)

Bill 1951
Bill, Max, ed., *Wassily Kandinsky* (Boston and Paris, 1951)

Bill 1955
_____ ed., *Kandinsky: Essays über Kunst und Künstler* (Stuttgart, 1955)

Boissel 1998
Boissel, Jessica, *Kandinsky: Du Théâtre, Über das Theater, O Teatre* (Paris and Cologne, 1998)

Bowlt and Washton Long 1980
Bowlt, John E. and Washton Long, Rose Carol, eds., *The Life of Vasilii Kandinsky in Russian Art: A Study of 'On the Spiritual in Art'* (Newtonville MA, 1980)

Cassou 1960
Cassou, Jean, *Wassily Kandinsky. Interférences: Aquarelles et dessins* (Paris and Cologne, 1960)

Dabrowski 1995
Dabrowski, Magdalena, *Kandinsky Compositions* exh. cat., The Museum of Modern Art (New York, 1995), pp.11–59

Daftari 1991
Daftari, Fereshteh, *The Influence of Persian Art on Gauguin, Matisse and Kandinsky* (New York, 1991)

Daniel 1999
Daniel, Macha, 'Kandinskys Rückkehr nach Rußland: Die Zeichnungen der Jahre 1915 bis 1921', *Kandinsky: Hauptwerke aus dem Centre Georges Pompidou Paris* exh. cat., Kunsthalle (Tübingen, 1999), pp.86–96

Derouet and Boissel 1984
Derouet, Christian and Boissel, Jessica, *Kandinsky. Oeuvres de Vassily Kandinsky (1866–1944): Collections du Musée National d'Art Moderne* (Paris, 1984)

Düchting 1990
Düchting, Hajo, *Wassily Kandinsky 1866-1944: Revolution der Malerei* (Cologne, 1990)

Eichner 1957
Eichner, Johannes, *Kandinsky und Gabriele Münter: Von Ursprüngen moderner Kunst* (Munich, 1957)

Friedel 2000
Friedel, Helmut, ed., *Das Münter-Haus in Murnau* (Munich, 2000)

Gollek 1982
Gollek, Rosel, *Der Blaue Reiter im Lenbachhaus München: Katalog der Sammlung in der Städtischen Galerie* (Munich, 1982)

Gollek 1984
_____, *Das Münter-Haus in Murnau* (Munich, 1984)

Grohmann 1930
Grohmann, Will, *Wassily Kandinsky* (Paris, 1930)

Grohmann 1958
_____, *Wassily Kandinsky: Life and Work* (Cologne and New York, 1958). Originally published as *Wassily Kandinsky: Leben und Werk* (1958)

Hahl-Koch 1993
Hahl-Koch, Jelena, *Kandinsky* (Stuttgart and New York, 1993)

Hanfstaengl 1974
Hanfstaengl, Erika, *Wassily Kandinsky: Zeichnungen und Aquarelle. Katalog der Sammlung der Städtischen Galerie im Lenbachhaus München* (Munich, 1974 and 1981)

Hoberg 1994
Hoberg, Annegret, *Wassily Kandinsky und Gabriele Münter in Murnau und Kochel 1902–1914: Briefe und Erinnerungen* (Munich, 1994)

Illetschko 1997
Illetschko, Georgia, *Kandinsky und Paris: Die Geschichte einer Beziehung* (Munich and New York, 1997)

Nina Kandinsky 1976
Kandinsky, Nina, *Kandinsky und ich* (Munich, 1976)

Langner 1977
Langner, Johannes, '"Improvisation 13": Zur Funktion des Gegenstandes in Kandinskys Abstraktion', *Jahrbuch der Staatlichen Kunstsammlungen in Baden-Württemberg*, vol.14 (1977), pp.115–146

Langner 1982
_____, 'Gegensätze und Widersprüche- das ist unsere Harmonie', *Kandinsky und München: Begegnungen und Wandlungen, 1896–1914* exh. cat., Städtische Galerie im Lenbachhaus (Munich, 1982), pp.106–132

Lindsay 1951
Lindsay, Kenneth C., *An Examination of the Fundamental Theories of Wassily Kandinsky*, (PhD dissertation, University of Wisconsin, 1951)

Lindsay and Vergo 1982
Lindsay, Kenneth C. and Vergo, Peter, eds., *Kandinsky: Complete Writings on Art* (Boston, 1982), 2 vols.

Picon 1972
Picon, Gaëton, 'Kandinsky', in *Kandinsky: Carnet de dessins 1941*, edited by Karl Flinker (Paris, 1972)

Podzemskaia 2000
Podzemskaia, Nadia, *Colore, Simbolo, Immagine: Origine della teoria di Kandinsky* (Florence, 2000)

Poling 1986
Poling, Clark V., *Kandinsky's Teaching at the Bauhaus: Color Theory and Analytical Drawing* (New York, 1986). Originally published as *Kandinsky-Unterricht am Bauhaus: Farbenseminar und analytisches Zeichnen dargestellt am Beispiel der Sammlung des Bauhaus-Archivs* (Weingarten, 1982)

Ringbom 1970
Ringbom, Sixten, *The Sounding Cosmos: A Study in the Spiritualism of Kandinsky and the Genesis of Abstract Painting* (Åbo, 1970)

Roethel and Benjamin 1979
Roethel, Hans K. and Benjamin, Jean K., *Kandinsky* (New York, 1979)

Roethel and Hahl-Koch 1980
Roethel, Hans K. and Hahl-Koch, Jelena, eds., *Kandinsky: Die Gesammelten Schriften* (Bern, 1980)

Rudenstine 1976
Rudenstine, Angelica Zander, *The Guggenheim Museum Collection: Painting 1880–1945* (New York, 1976), vol.1, pp.204–391

Sarabianov and Avtonomova 1994
Sarabianov, Dmitri V. and Avtonomova, Natalia B., *Vasily Kandinsky* (Moscow, 1994)

Schreier 1997
Schreier, Christoph, 'Wassily Kandinsky: Perspektiven seines Zeichnerischen Werks', *Wallraf-Richartz-Jahrbuch*, vol. LVIII (1997), pp 81–100

Sélection 1933
Will Grohmann, 'L'art de Kandinsky' and 'Catalogue des dessins' among other texts in *Sélection*, no.14 (July 1933)

Thürlemann 1985
Thürlemann, Felix, 'Kandinskys Analyse-Zeichnungen', *Zeitschrift für Kunstgeschichte*, 48 Jg., Nr.3 (1985), pp.363–378

Thürlemann 1986
_____, *Kandinsky über Kandinsky: Der Künstler als Interpret eigener Werke* (Bern, 1986)

Volboudt 1974
Volboudt, Pierre, *Die Zeichnungen Wassily Kandinskys* (Cologne, 1974)

Volboudt 1986
_____, *Kandinsky* (New York, 1986). Originally published in French (Paris, 1984)

Washton Long 1980
Washton Long, Rose-Carol, *Kandinsky: The Development of an Abstract Style* (Oxford, 1980)

Weiss 1979
Weiss, Peg, *Kandinsky in Munich: The Formative Jugendstil Years* (Princeton, 1979)

Weiss 1995
_____, *Kandinsky and Old Russia: The Artist as Ethnographer and Shaman* (New Haven, 1995)

Zweite 1982
Zweite, Armin, 'Kandinsky zwischen Tradition und Innovation', *Kandinsky und München: Begegnungen und Wandlungen, 1896–1914* exh. cat., Städtische Galerie im Lenbachhaus (Munich, 1982), pp.134–177

# *Kandinsky Exhibitions*

Georgia Illetschko, Katharina Katz, Sarah Johnson, Vivian Barnett

In the 1980s Georgia Illetschko initiated research on the following chronological lists of one-person and group exhibitions in which Kandinsky's work was presented. The lists were published in the two-volume *Kandinsky Watercolours: Catalogue Raisonné* (London and Munich, 1992, 1994). She studied the original exhibition catalogues, exhibition reviews and lists compiled by the artist and by his wife, Nina Kandinsky, which are preserved in the Fonds Kandinsky at the Musée National d'Art Moderne, Centre Georges Pompidou, Paris. In addition, the list in Kenneth Lindsay's unpublished dissertation (*An Examination of the Fundamental Theories of Wassily Kandinsky*, University of Wisconsin, 1951) and in Magdalena Droste's chronology (*Kandinsky Russische Zeit und Bauhausjahre, 1915–1933* exh. cat. Berlin, 1984) contained further documentation. More recently, Dr. Illetschko has published an annotated list of exhibitions from 1934–1944 (*Kandinsky und Paris*, Munich, 1997).

Basic information was provided by the artist through annotations in his Handlists (HL) and the small exhibition inventory (mss) from his early career (1901–1905). From 1922 onwards, Nina Kandinsky kept lists in which she recorded the majority of her husband's exhibitions (NK). Dr. Illetschko located and identified two of these lists (1922–1924, 1929–1939) in the Fonds Kandinsky. However, the notebooks with other two lists (1925–1928, 1939–1944) could not be consulted.

The terms 'catalogue' and 'no catalogue' are stated when this information has been determined with certainty or great probability; where no mention is made, the question remains open. 'Catalogue' has been used as a generic term with no distinctions between a brochure, leaflet or book published on the occasion of an exhibition. When a catalogue does not include a list of works exhibited, this fact is indicated as 'no checklist'.

The emphasis has been on exhibitions that took place during the artist's lifetime. One-person and group exhibitions after 1945 are selective: their historical significance, thematic context and accessible catalogue are criteria for inclusion. Due to limitations of space, it has not been possible to include all exhibitions.

Katharina Katz did further research and edited the list in 1990-1992 and Sarah Johnson continued this work in 2004–2005. Finally, I have checked many citations, corrected the order of listings as specific information became available and added information provided by Natalia Avtonomova, Vitaly Abramov, Isabel Wünsche and other colleagues. On behalf of Georgia Illetschko, I would like to thank the many scholars, archivists, librarians and colleagues who assisted with the compilation of the following lists.

Vivian Endicott Barnett
*August 2006*

**1898**
Odessa, Association of South-Russian Artists
15 October–17 November
*9th Exhibition*

**1899**
Odessa, Association of South-Russian Artists
10 October–8 November
*10th Exhibition*

**1900**
Moscow, Moscow Association of Artists
Opened 16 February
*7th Exhibition of Paintings*

Odessa, Association of South-Russian Artists
3 October–5 November
*11th Exhibition*

**1901**
Moscow
February

Munich, Finkenstrasse 2
15 August–end November
*I. Ausstellung der Münchener Künstler-Vereinigung 'Phalanx'*
Travelled in varying form to: Wiesbaden, Krefeld, Elberfeld-Barmen through 1902 (HL mss)

Odessa, Association of South-Russian Artists
29 September–28 October
*12th Exhibition*

St. Petersburg (mss)

Karlsruhe (mss)

**1902**
Munich, Finkenstrasse 2
January–March
*II. Ausstellung der Münchener Künstler-Vereinigung 'Phalanx'*
Catalogue

Berlin, Secession
Spring
*V. Kunstausstellung*
Catalogue

Odessa, Association of South-Russian Artists
26 September–28 October
*13th Exhibition*

Berlin
15 October–15 December
*Permanente Kunstausstellung Berlin*

Oldenburg
October–15 December (mss)

Berlin, Secession
November–1 January 1903
*VI. Kunstausstellung: Zeichnende Künste*
Catalogue

St. Petersburg, Imperial Academy of Fine Arts
December–January 1903 (HL, mss)
*Exhibition of Paintings of Moscow Association of Artists*

Karlsruhe (mss)

**1903**
Wiesbaden, Bangers Kunstsalon
1–15 February

Moscow (HL)
12 February

Budapest, Art Gallery
1 April–15 May
*International Spring Exhibition*
Catalogue

Prague, Künstlerhaus Rudolfinum, Kunstverein für Böhmen
1 April–31 May (mss)

Saratov
8 April

Venice
22 April–31 October
*V Esposizione Biennale Internazionale d'Arte*
Catalogue (according to mss but not in catalogue)

Munich, Theatinerstrasse 15
May–July
*VII. Ausstellung der Münchener Künstler-Vereinigung 'Phalanx'*
Catalogue

Krefeld
August (HL, mss)

Munich, Galerie Littauer
29 August–20 September (mss)

Odessa, Municipal Museum of Fine Arts, Association of South-Russian Artists
4 October–4 November
*14th Exhibition*
Catalogue

Berlin, Secession
December–early 1904
*VIII. Kunstausstellung: Zeichnende Künste*
Catalogue

Munich, Galerie Littauer
Opened 20 December (mss)

St. Petersburg (HL)

**1904**
St. Petersburg, New Association of Painters
3–24 January
Catalogue

Munich, Theatinerstrasse 15
17 January–end February
*IX. Ausstellung der Münchener Künstler-Vereinigung 'Phalanx'*
Catalogue

Rome, Palazzo dell'Esposizione, Via Nazionale, Società degli amatori e cultori di Belle Arti a Roma
Opened late January
*LXXIV Esposizione Internazionale*

Moscow, Moscow Association of Artists
7 February–March
*11th Exhibition*

Hamburg, Galerie Paul Cassirer
Opened 9 March
Travelled in modified form to: Düsseldorf, Eduard Schulte, 15 May–June; Cologne, Eduard Schulte

Munich, Galerie Helbing
27 March–20 April
*XI. Ausstellung der Münchener Künstler-Vereinigung 'Phalanx': Graphische Ausstellung*
Catalogue
Travelled to: Dresden, Emil Richter, opened April 25 (mss)

Berlin, Secession
30 April–15 September
*IX. Kunstausstellung*
Catalogue

Dresden, Hof-Kunsthändler Emil Richter
1 May–October
*Grosse Kunstausstellung* (mss)

Wiesbaden, Bangers Kunstsalon
May
Travelled to: Weimar, Museum, 6 June–September (mss)

Paris, Galerie Sagot
May (HL)

Paris, Galerie des Tendances Nouvelles, 20 rue Le Peletier
1 June
*Les Tendances Nouvelles* (Inaugural Exhibition) (mss)

Munich, Kunstverein
23 July–6 August (mss)

Munich, Piper
August (mss)

Krefeld, Kaiser-Wilhelm-Museum
September
*XII. Ausstellung der Münchener Künstler-Vereinigung 'Phalanx'*
Travelled to: Düsseldorf; Darmstadt; Frankfurt am Main; Karlsruhe; Königsberg; until June 1905

Munich, Galerie Littauer
September (HL)

Vienna, Der liebe Augustin
September (HL)

Warsaw, Salon Krywulta
September–October (HL)

Odessa, Municipal Museum of Fine Arts, Association of South-Russian Artists
1–31 October
*15th Exhibition* (HL)

Berlin, Werckmeister's Kunsthandlung
October–November (mss)

Paris, Petit Palais
November
*Salon d'Automne: 2e Exposition*
Catalogue

Paris
November
*XIIIe Exposition des Beaux-Arts* (mss)

Cracow
December (HL)

**1905**
St. Petersburg
6 January

Rome, Palazzo dell'Esposizione, Via Nazionale, Società degli amatori e cultori di Belle Arti a Roma
1 February–31 March
*LXXV Esposizione Internazionale*
Catalogue

Moscow, Moscow Association of Artists
February–April
*12th Exhibition of Paintings*
Catalogue

Paris, Salle des Fêtes, Rue Duplessis
May
*Exposition des Beaux-Arts de Paris-Province*

Berlin, Ausstellungshaus der Berliner Secession, Deutscher Künstlerbund
Summer
*Zweite Ausstellung des Deutschen Künstlerbundes*
Catalogue



**1905**
Munich, Galerie Krause, Barerstrasse 40
15 February–15 March
(oil studies, paintings, colored drawings, woodcuts)
Travelled to: Berlin, Galerie Paul Cassirer, April; Hamburg, Galerie Paul Cassirer, 19 June–17 July; Düsseldorf, Eduard Schulte, summer; Cologne, autumn

Odessa, Museum of Fine Arts, Association of South-Russian Artists
1 October–6 November
*16th Exhibition* (HL)

Paris, Grand Palais des Champs-Elysées
8 October–25 November
*Salon d'Automne: 3e Exposition*
Catalogue

Dresden
November (HL)

Paris, Société Internationale des Aquarellistes
Opened 16 November

Paris
November
*Exposition des Beaux-Arts* (HL)

Vienna, Secession
November–December
*XXIV. Ausstellung der Vereinigung der bildenden Künstler Österreichs*
Catalogue (according to HL but not catalogue)

Paris, Place Dupleix, Palais du Travail
Opened 28 November
*XIIe Exposition du Travail*

**1906**
Krefeld, Kaiser-Wilhelm-Museum
February (HL)
No catalogue

St. Petersburg
February

Vienna, Secession
March–May
*XXVI. Ausstellung*
Catalogue

Frankfurt am Main, K. Hof
April (HL)

Prague
April (HL)

Karlsruhe, Badischer Kunstverein
May
*Neue Künstler-Vereinigung* (HL)

Berlin, Secession
Spring
*XI. Ausstellung*
Catalogue

Weimar, Deutscher Künstlerbund
Summer
*Dritte Ausstellung des Deutschen Künstlerbundes*
Catalogue

Berlin, Galerie Wertheim
October–November
*Kunstausstellung Wertheim*
Catalogue

Odessa, Museum of Fine Arts, Association of South-Russian Artists
1 October–5 November
*17th Exhibition*
Catalogue

Paris, Grand Palais des Champs-Elysées
6 October–15 November
*Salon d'Automne: 4e Exposition*
Catalogue

Berlin, Secession
December–January 1907
*XII. Kunstausstellung: Zeichnende Künste*
Catalogue

Chartres
December–January 1907 (HL)

Hamburg, Louis Bock & Sohn
December (HL)

Dresden-Löbtau, Lampenfabrik Seifert, Künstler Gruppe 'Brücke'
3 December–31 January 1907
*Holzschnitt Ausstellung I.*

Munich, Secession (HL)

Moscow (HL)

**1907**
Rome
February
*International Exhibition* (HL)

Paris, Serres de l'Alma, Société des Artistes Indépendants
20 March–30 April
*23e Exposition*
Catalogue

Moscow, Moscow Association of Artists
25 March–6 May
*14th Exhibition of Paintings*
Catalogue

Paris, Grand Palais, Société Nationale des Beaux-Arts
14 April–30 June
*XVIIe Exposition*
Catalogue (according to HL but not in catalogue)

Angers, Hôtel de Chemellier, Musée du Peuple
11 May–June
*2e Salon de l'Union Internationale des Beaux-Arts, des Lettres, des Sciences et de l'Industrie*

Odessa, Association of South-Russian Artists
30 September–4 November
*18th Exhibition*

Paris, Grand Palais des Champs-Elysées
1–22 October
*Salon d'Automne: 5e Exposition*
Catalogue

Berlin, Secession
December
*XIV. Ausstellung: Zeichnende Künste*
Catalogue

**1908**
Moscow, Moscow Association of Artists
Opened 26 January
*15th Exhibition of Paintings*
Catalogue

Paris, Serres des Invalides, Société des Artistes Indépendants
20 March–2 May
*24e Exposition*
Catalogue

Dresden
1 May–15 October
*Grosse Kunstausstellung*
Catalogue

Odessa, Association of South-Russian Artists
28 September
*19th Exhibition*

Paris, Grand Palais des Champs-Elysées
1 October–8 November
*Salon d'Automne: 6e Exposition*
Catalogue

Berlin, Ausstellungshaus am Kurfürstendamm, Secession
December
*XVI. Ausstellung: Zeichnende Künste*
Catalogue

**1909**
St. Petersburg, Menchikov Museum (organized by Sergei Makovsky)
4 January
*Salon 1908–1909*
Catalogue

Paris, Serres de l'Orangerie, Société des Artistes Indépendants
25 March–2 May
*25e Exposition*
Catalogue

Berlin, Secession
Summer (HL)

London, Royal Albert Hall, Allied Artists' Association, Ltd.
July
*The London Salon, Second Year*
Catalogue

Hagen, Museum Folkwang
4 August–16 September
*Sonderausstellung: Graphische Arbeiten meist französischer Künstler. Deutsche und holländische Keramik*
Catalogue

Paris, Grand Palais des Champs-Elysées
1 October–8 November
*Salon d'Automne: 7e Exposition*
Catalogue

Odessa, Association of South-Russian Artists
1 October–15 November
*20th Exhibition*

Munich, Moderne Galerie Thannhauser
1–15 December
*Neue Künstlervereinigung München, I. Ausstellung*
Catalogue
Travelled to: Brünn, Mährischer Kunstverein, January 1910; Elberfeld, Städtisches Museum, April; Barmen, Ruhmeshalle, Kunstverein, May; Hamburg, Louis Bock & Sohn, June; Düsseldorf, Kunsthalle, late June–July; Wiesbaden, Kunstsalon Banger, late July–early August; Schwerin, Grossherzogliches Museum, late August–early September; Frankfurt am Main, Salon Goldschmidt, mid-September–early October

Odessa, Vladimir Izdebsky
4 December–24 January 1910
*Salon: International Exhibition of Paintings, Sculpture, Prints and Drawings*
Catalogue
Travelled to: Kiev, 12 February–14 March 1910; St. Petersburg, Izdebsky, 19 April–25 May; Riga, Museum of Fine Arts, 12 June–7 July

**1910**
Hamburg, Galerie Commeter, Deutscher Künstlerbund
14 May–30 June
*III. Graphische Ausstellung*
Catalogue

London, Royal Albert Hall, Allied Artists' Association, Ltd.
July
*The London Salon, Third Year*
Catalogue

Düsseldorf, Städtischer Kunstpalast
16 July–9 October
*Sonderbund westdeutscher Kunstfreunde und Künstler*
Catalogue

Munich, Moderne Galerie Thannhauser
1–14 September
*Neue Künstlervereinigung München e. V. Turnus 1910/11*
Travelled to: Karlsruhe, Badischer Kunstverein, October; Mannheim, Kunstverein, November; Hagen, Museum Folkwang, 17–26 December; Berlin, Galerie Paul Cassirer, 21 January–4 February 1911; Dresden, Galerie Arnold, April; Weimar, Museum am Karlsplatz, 29 August–30 September
Catalogue

Odessa, Association of South-Russian Artists
1 October–6 November
*21st Exhibition*

Paris, Grand Palais des Champs-Elysées
1 October–8 November
*Salon d'Automne: 8e Exposition*
Catalogue

Ekaterinoslav
December
*XI Exhibition of Paintings of the Ekaterinoslav Art and Theater Society*

Moscow, Association of Artists 'Jack of Diamonds'
10 December–16 January 1911
*Exhibition of Paintings*
Catalogue

**1911**
Berlin, Galerie Paul Cassirer
January–February
*XIII. Jahrgang, VI. Ausstellung*
Catalogue

Odessa, Vladimir Izdebsky
6 February–late April
*Salon 2: International Art Exhibition*
Catalogue
Travelled to: Nikolaev; Kherson

Paris, Quai d'Orsay, Société des Artistes Indépendants
21 April–13 June
*27e Exposition*
Catalogue

London, Royal Albert Hall, Allied Artists' Association, Ltd.
July
*The London Salon, Fourth Year*
Catalogue

Cologne, Wallraf-Richartz-Museum, Cölnischer Kunstverein
October
*Kunst unserer Zeit in Cölner Privatbesitz: Ausstellung des Cölnischen Kunstvereins aus Anlass des fünfzigjährigen Jubiläums des Wallraf-Richartz-Museums*
Catalogue

Berlin, Neue Secession e. V.
18 November–31 January 1912
*IV. Ausstellung: Gemälde*
Catalogue

Munich, Moderne Galerie Thannhauser
18 December–3 January 1912
*Die erste Ausstellung der Redaktion Der Blaue Reiter*
Catalogue, 2 editions
Travelled to: Cologne, Gereonsklub, 23–31 January 1912, catalogue; Berlin, Der Sturm, 12 March–10 April; Bremen, Vereinigte Werkstätten für Kunst im Handwerk, 27 April–end May; Hagen, Museum Folkwang, July; Frankfurt am Main, Kunstsalon Goldschmidt, 28 August–mid-September; Hamburg, Salon Louis Bock & Sohn, 14 September–end October

**1912**
Moscow, Association of Artists 'Jack of Diamonds'
25 January–26 February
*Exhibition of Paintings*
Catalogue



**1912**
Berlin, Der Sturm
2–28 October
*Kandinsky Kollektiv-Ausstellung*
Catalogue: 1st ed., 2 printings (I,Ia) published by Verlag 'Neue Kunst', Hans Goltz, Munich; 2nd ed. (II), 1913, published at Verlag Der Sturm, Berlin

Munich, Hans Goltz Kunsthandlung
12 February–April
*Die zweite Ausstellung der Redaktion Der Blaue Reiter. Schwarz-Weiss*
Catalogue

Berlin, Neue Secession e. V.
March
*V. Ausstellung*
Catalogue

Berlin, Der Sturm (Herwarth Walden)
12 March–10 May
*Erste Ausstellung: Der Blaue Reiter, Franz Flaum, Oskar Kokoschka, Expressionisten*
Catalogue ('Der Sturm', no.100, 1912)

Paris, Quai d'Orsay, Société des Artistes Indépendants
20 March–16 May
*28e Exposition*
Catalogue

Berlin, Der Sturm (Herwarth Walden)
May
*Dritte Ausstellung: Graphik*
(Kandinsky: paintings on glass)
Catalogue

Cologne, Städtische Ausstellungshalle am Aachener Tor, Sonderbund
25 May–30 September
*Internationale Kunstausstellung des Sonderbundes westdeutscher Kunstfreunde und Künstler*
Catalogue

Berlin, Der Sturm (Herwarth Walden)
June–July
*Vierte Ausstellung: Zurückgestellte Bilder des Sonderbundes Köln*

Hagen, Museum Folkwang
July
*Moderne Kunst: Plastik, Malerei, Graphik*
Catalogue

London, Royal Albert Hall, Allied Artists' Association, Ltd.
July
*The London Salon, Fifth Year*
Catalogue

Zurich, Kunsthaus Zürich, Zürcher Kunstgesellschaft
7–31 July
*Ausstellung: Moderner Bund*
Catalogue

Ekaterinodar
Autumn
*Contemporary Painting*
Catalogue

Munich, Neue Kunst Hans Goltz
October
*Erste Gesamt-Ausstellung*
Catalogue

New York, Berlin Photographic Company
December
*Contemporary German Graphic Art*

**1913**
Budapest, National Salon
January
*The Futurist and Expressionist Exhibitions*
Catalogue

Düsseldorf, Haus Leonhard Tietz
January–February
*Neue Secession Berlin*
Catalogue

Vienna, Galerie Miethke
January–February
*Die neue Kunst*



Travelled in modified form to: Rotterdam, Kunsthandel Oldenzeel, 5–18 November; Hamburg, Louis Bock & Sohn, January 1913; Groningen, May; Brussels, 25 May–June; Wiesbaden, September; Frankfurt, October; Aachen, November; Munich, Moderne Galerie Thannhauser, January 1914; Magdeburg, April; Stuttgart, April–June, and other German and European cities

Amsterdam, organized by Der Sturm (Herwarth Walden)
February
*Der Blaue Reiter*
Catalogue
Travelled in varying form to: Prague, March (?); Budapest, Museum, April–May, part of *International Postimpressionist Exhibition*, catalogue; Königsberg, September (?); Christiania, Blomquists Kunsthandel, January 1914; Helsingfors, February–March; Trondheim, Kunstforening, April–May; Gothenburg, Olséns Kunsthandel, June–July

New York, Armory of the 69th Infantry, Association of American Painters and Sculptors
17 February–15 March
*International Exhibition of Modern Art*
Catalogue
Travelled in varying form to: Chicago IL, The Art Institute of Chicago, 24 March–15 April; Boston MA, Copley Hall, Copley Society of Boston, 24 April–18 May, catalogue

London, Alpine Club Gallery
15–31 March
*Grafton Group Exhibition*
Catalogue

Moscow
24 March

London, Royal Albert Hall, Allied Artists' Association, Ltd
July
*The London Salon, Sixth Year*
Catalogue

Munich, Neue Kunst Hans Goltz
August–September
*Zweite Gesamt-Ausstellung*
Catalogue

Berlin, Lepke-Räume, Potsdamer Strasse 75, organized by Der Sturm
20 September–1 December
*Erster Deutscher Herbstsalon*
Catalogue

St. Petersburg, Artists' Bureau N.E. Dobychina
Opened 29 September
*Permanent Exhibition of Contemporary Art*
Catalogue

St. Petersburg, Artists' Bureau N.E. Dobychina
Opened 27 October
*Exhibition of Graphic Arts*
Catalogue

Amsterdam, Stedelijk Museum/Suasso Museum, Moderne Kunstkring
7 November–8 December
*Ouvrages de Peinture, Sculpture, Dessin, Gravure*
Catalogue

**1914**
Dresden, Galerie Ernst Arnold
January
*Expressionistische Ausstellung: Die neue Malerei*
Catalogue

Odessa, Museum of Fine Arts
23 March–27 April
*Spring Exhibition of Paintings*
Catalogue

Tokyo, Hibiya Art Museum, organized by Der Sturm
14 March–28 March, extended through May
(graphic works)
Catalogue

Amsterdam, Vereeniging van Beeldende Kunstenaars 'De Onafhankelijken'
May–June
*3de Internationale Jury-vrije Tentoonstelling*
Catalogue



**1914**
Cologne, Kreis für Kunst Köln im Deutschen Theater
30 January–15 February
*Kandinsky-Ausstellung*
Catalogue
Travelled to: Barmen (Wuppertal) and Aachen through March

Geneva, 6, rue de la Candolle, organized by Der Sturm
Opened 15 August

Hannover, Kestner-Gesellschaft e. V., organized by Der Sturm
September
(watercolors)

Malmö, Konsthallen
15 May–4 October
*Baltiska Utställningen*
Catalogue

London, Holland Park Hall, Allied Artists' Association, Ltd.
12 June–2 July
*The London Salon, Seventh Year*
Catalogue

**1915**
Moscow
March–April
*Exhibition of Painting: The Year 1915*
Catalogue

Petrograd, Artists' Bureau N.E. Dobychina
12 April–9 May
*Left Tendencies*
Catalogue

**1916**
The Hague, Kunstzalen d'Audretsch, organized by Der Sturm
17 March–16 April
*Zweite Ausstellung Den Haag/Holland: Expressionisten, Kubisten*
Catalogue

Christiania (Oslo), Permanent Kunstutstillung C.W. Blomquist
April–June
*Zweite Ausstellung Christiania: Kandinsky und Gabriele Münter*
Catalogue
Travelled to: Helsinki, Strindberg; Petrograd, Artist's Bureau N.E. Dobychina, 3–19 April

Berlin, Der Sturm (Herwarth Walden)
July–August
*Dreiundvierzigste Ausstellung: Expressionisten*
Catalogue

Petrograd, Artists' Bureau N.E. Dobychina
27 November–31 December
*Exhibition of Contemporary Russian Painting*
Catalogue

**1917**
Berlin, Der Sturm (Herwarth Walden)
March
*Fünfzigste Ausstellung: Sturm-Gesamtschau*
Catalogue

Zurich, Galerie Dada
17 March–7 April (1st series); 9–30 April (2nd series)
*Sturm-Ausstellung*

Berlin, Der Sturm (Herwarth Walden)
June
*Dreiundfünfzigste Ausstellung: Sturm-Gesamtschau*
Catalogue

Berlin, Der Sturm (Herwarth Walden)
August
*Vierundfünfzigste Ausstellung: Sammlung Kluxen*
Catalogue

Copenhagen, Kunstnerkabaretten 'Edderkoppen', organized by Der Sturm
September–October
*Udstilling 2: Der Sturm Kunstnere*
Catalogue

Munich, Neue Kunst Hans Goltz
*Sammel-Ausstellung*

**1918**
Berlin, Der Sturm (Herwarth Walden)
July–August
*Fünfundsechzigste Ausstellung: Marc Chagall, Kandinsky, William Wauer*



**1916**
Stockholm, Gummesons Konsthandel, organized by Der Sturm
Opened 1 February
*Kandinsky: Oljemålninger och Grafik*
Catalogue
Travelled to: Christiania 1916 (see group show)

Berlin, Der Sturm
September
*Vierundvierzigste Ausstellung, Kandinsky: Gemälde und Aquarelle*
Catalogue

**1917**
Gothenburg, Médens Bokhandel
Autumn
No catalogue

Berlin, Der Sturm (Herwarth Walden)
November
*Achtundsiebzigste Ausstellung: Russische Expressionisten*

**1919**
Moscow, Museum of Fine Arts, VZVB (Department of Visual Arts of the People's Commissariat for Enlightenment)
Opened 12 February
*Fifth State Exhibition of Paintings*
Catalogue

Dresden, Galerie Ernst Arnold
April
*Sonderausstellung Der Sturm: Expressionisten, Futuristen, Kubisten*
Catalogue

Petrograd
April–June
*First Free State Exhibition*

Zurich, Kunstsalon Rembrandt
July
(exhibition of 'Der Sturm')

Berlin, Der Sturm (Herwarth Walden)
November
*Achtzigste Ausstellung: Sturm-Gesamtschau*

Vitebsk, Club B. Borokhov
8 November–22 December
*First State Exhibition of Paintings by Local and Moscovite Artists*
Catalogue

Moscow
*New Art, Expressionism*

**1920**
Hannover, Kestner-Gesellschaft
8 January–4 February
*30. Ausstellung: Neue Kunst aus Hannoverschem Privatbesitz*

Moscow
June
*Exhibition of the Four: V. V. Kandinsky, A. M. Rodchenko, V. F. Stepanova, N. V. Sinezubov*
Catalogue

Darmstadt, Mathildenhöhe
10 June–30 September
*Deutscher Expressionismus*
Catalogue

Moscow, All-Russian Central Exhibiting Bureau of the IZO Narkompros
2 October–4 December
*Nineteenth State Exhibition*
Catalogue

Amsterdam, Stedelijk Museum, Nederlandsche Kunstkoperbond
16 October–7 November
Catalogue

New York, Galleries of the Société Anonyme
1 November–15 December
*International Exhibition of Post-Impressionists*

Kozmodemjansk (Marijskaja A.S.S.R.)
Opened 7 November
*First Kozmodemjansk Exhibition of Paintings, Studies, Sketches, Drawings: Exhibition Dedicated to the Third Anniversary of the Great October Revolution*
Catalogue

**1921**
New York, Miss Weir's School of Design
21–26 February
(exhibition of the Société Anonyme)

New York, Heterodoxy Club of New York
21 February–5 March
(exhibition of the Société Anonyme)



**1921**
Cologne, Neue Kunst (Nierendorf)

Hannover, Galerie von Garvens
March–April
*Russische Kunst: Ikone, Volkskunst, Neue Gemälde*

Hannover, Kestner-Gesellschaft
28 August–25 September
*44. Ausstellung: Aquarelle moderner Künstler. Gemälde von Felixmüller*
Catalogue

Berlin, Der Sturm (Herwarth Walden)
September
*Hundertste Ausstellung: Zehn Jahre Sturm-Gesamtschau*
Catalogue

Sovetsk (Province Kirov)
October
*Third Travelling Art Exhibition of the Soviet Regional Subdivision of the Museum Directorship*
Catalogue
Travelled to: Yaransk, November

Moscow, World of Art
October–November
*Exhibition of Work of Painting, Sculpture and Architecture*
Catalogue

Worcester MA, Worcester Art Museum
3 November–5 December
*Exhibition of Paintings by Members of the Société Anonyme*
Catalogue
Travelled to: Northampton MA, Smith College, 7 January–5 February 1922; Detroit MI, Detroit Institute of Fine Arts, 5 March–5 April; New York, MacDowell Club, 24 April–8 May

**1922**
Leipzig, Museum am Augustusplatz, Leipziger Kunstverein
April–May
*Ausstellung moderner Kunst aus Privatbesitz*
Catalogue

Düsseldorf, Haus Leonhard Tietz AG, Das Junge Rheinland
28 May–3 July
*I. Internationale Kunstausstellung*
Catalogue

Berlin, Galerie Guldendahl
1 July–1 September
(Russian artists)

Weimar, Museum
1 August–15 September
(Kandinsky and Thuringian painters)

Barmen
September

Berlin, Galerie Twardy
September

Chicago IL, The Art Institute of Chicago
19 September–22 October
*Exhibition of Paintings from the Collection of the Late Arthur Jerome Eddy*
Catalogue

Berlin, Landesausstellungsgebäude am Lehrter Bahnhof
Autumn
*Juryfreie Kunstschau*
Catalogue

Berlin, Galerie van Diemen & Co
15 October–November
*Erste russische Kunstausstellung*
Catalogue
Travelled to: Amsterdam, Stedelijk Museum, April–May 1923

Munich, Hans Goltz
November–December
*Zehn Jahre neuer Kunst in München. Der Ausstellung erster Teil: Aquarelle, Zeichnungen, Graphik*
Catalogue



**1922**
Berlin, Galerie Goldschmidt-Wallerstein
30 April–15 June
*Kandinsky*
No catalogue

Munich, Moderne Galerie Thannhauser
1–14 July
*W. Kandinsky*
Catalogue

Stockholm, Gummesons Konsthandel
1–15 October
*Kandinsky*
Catalogue

Calcutta
1 December–1 January 1923

Dresden, Galerie Neue Kunst Fides (Rudolf Probst)

**1923**
Munich, Hans Goltz
January–February
*Zehn Jahre neuer Kunst in München. Der Ausstellung zweiter Teil: Gemälde*

New York, The Brooklyn Museum
23 January–4 March
*Exhibition of Russian Painting and Sculpture*
Catalogue

New York, Galleries of the Société Anonyme
5–22 February
(graphic arts)

Darmstadt, Mathildenhöhe und Kunsthalle
18 May–1 October
*Deutsche Kunst 1923*
Catalogue

Cologne
Opened 20 May
(paintings, watercolors and drawings)

Dresden, Graphisches Kabinett Hugo Erfurth
June
*Dresdner Secession*

Jena, Theater, Kunstverein
13 June–July
(Dix, Grosz, Kandinsky)

Weimar, Staatliches Bauhaus Weimar and Landesmuseum
15 August–30 September
*Bauhausausstellung*
Catalogue

Detroit MI, State Fair Park, Detroit Institute of Fine Arts
31 August–9 November
*A Collection of Works by Modernist–Expressionist Groups*

Berlin, Landes-Ausstellungsgebäude am Lehrter Bahnhof
October
*Juryfreie Ausstellung*

**1924**
Vienna, Neue Galerie (organized by Otto Kallir and Gesellschaft zur Förderung moderner Kunst in Wien)
Opened 15 February (scheduled for one week)
*Russische Kunstausstellung*
(Kandinsky, Archipenko, Chagall, Lissitzky)

New York, Galleries of the Société Anonyme
31 March–12 April

Warsaw, Polish Artist's Club (Hotel Polonia), Kunstheim Twardy
Spring
(German art)
Travelled to: Lodz

Plauen, E. F. Schulz u. Co.
11–24 May
(contemporary watercolors, drawings, graphic works)

Berlin, Landes-Ausstellungsgebäude am Lehrter Bahnhof
31 May–1 September
*Grosse Berliner Kunstausstellung*
Catalogue

Vienna, Secession, Gesellschaft zur Förderung moderner Kunst in Wien
11 September–20 October
*Internationale Kunstausstellung*
Catalogue



**1923**
Berlin, Galerie Nierendorf
January
*Kandinsky*

Hannover, Kestner-Gesellschaft e. V.
10 February–March
No catalogue

New York, Galleries of the Société Anonyme
23 March–4 May
*Kandinsky*
Catalogue, no checklist
Travelled to: Poughkeepsie NY, Vassar College, November

**1924**
Vienna
20 February–5 March
(watercolors and drawings)

Dresden, Galerie Neue Kunst Fides (Rudolf Probst)
16 September–1 November

Berlin, Landes-Ausstellungsgebäude am Lehrter Bahnhof
October–November
*Juryfreie Kunstschau*

Zwickau, Zwickauer Kunstverein
November
*Jubiläumsausstellung*

Braunschweig, Landesmuseum, Gesellschaft der Freunde junger Kunst
November–December

Berlin, Graphisches Kabinett J. B. Neumann

**1925**
Dresden, Graphisches Kabinett Hugo Erfurth
15 February–18 March
*Sieben Bauhausmeister*
Travelled in modified form to: Erfurt, April

New York, The Daniel Gallery
20 February–10 March
*The Blue Four*
Catalogue

Leipzig, Städtisches Museum am Augustusplatz, Verein Leipziger Jahresausstellung
22 February–31 March
*Zehnte Jahresausstellung L.I.A.*
Catalogue

Wiesbaden, Neues Museum, Nassauischer Kunstverein und Wiesbadener Gesellschaft für bildende Kunst
6 March–April
*März-Ausstellung 1925*
Catalogue

Düsseldorf, Kunstpalais
30 May–4 October
*Grosse Kunstausstellung der Jubiläumsausstellung Düsseldorf*
Catalogue

Barmen (Wuppertal), Ruhmeshalle
July
*Meister des staatlichen Bauhauses in Weimar*
Travelled to: Stuttgart, Kunsthaus Schaller, January 1926; Hannover, Kestner-Gesellschaft, 10 February–7 March; Hamburg-Altona, Kunstsalon Maria Kunde, April

Zurich, Kunsthaus Zürich
8 August–30 September
*Internationale Kunstausstellung*
Catalogue

Berlin, Galerie Neumann-Nierendorf
October
*Die Maler der Gegenwart*

Dresden, Secession
October

Palo Alto CA, Stanford University
October
*The Blue Floor*
Floor plan

Berlin, Landes-Ausstellungsgebäude am Lehrter Bahnhof
October–November
*Juryfreie Kunstschau*

Berlin, Der Sturm (Herwarth Walden)
End of the year
*Hundertachtunddreissigste Ausstellung: Otto Nebel, Kurt Schwitters, Gesamtschau*

New York, Little Review Gallery

**1926**
San Francisco CA, Paul Elder Gallery
18–23 January
*The Blue Four*
Travelled to: Oakland CA, Mills College Art Gallery, February



**1925**
Erfurt, Angermuseum, Kunstverein
January
*Wassily Kandinsky*

Wiesbaden, Neues Museum, Nassauischer Kunstverein und Wiesbadener Gesellschaft für bildende Kunst
11 January–28 February
*Wassili Kandinsky*
Catalogue

Barmen (Wuppertal), Ruhmeshalle
Opened 12 March
(paintings, watercolors and graphic works)
Travelled to: Bochum, Gemäldegalerie, April; Düsseldorf, Galerie Nierendorf, October–November

Jena, Prinzessinnenschlösschen, Kunstverein Jena
15 March–12 April
(paintings, watercolors and graphic works)

**1926**
Braunschweig, Schloss, Gesellschaft der Freunde junger Kunst
9 May–6 June
*Jubiläums-Ausstellung W. Kandinsky*
Catalogue

Ulm, Städtisches Museum, Kupferstichkabinett
February
(watercolors, drawings, graphic works of the Bauhaus masters)
Travelled to: Frankfurt am Main, March

Oakland CA, The Oakland Art Gallery
2–31 May, extended to 15 June
*The Blue Four: Feininger, Jawlensky, Kandinsky, Paul Klee*
Catalogue
Travelled in varying form to: Los Angeles CA, Los Angeles Museum, October, catalogue; Los Angeles CA, University of California, So. Branch, November–December

Dresden, Städtischer Ausstellungspalast
June–September
*Internationale Kunstausstellung Dresden 1926: Jahresschau deutscher Arbeit*
Catalogue

Philadelphia PA, Sesqui-Centennial International Exposition, Department of Fine Arts
1 June–1 December
*Paintings, Sculpture and Prints*
Catalogue

Berlin, Landes-Ausstellungsgebäude am Lehrter Bahnhof
Summer
*Grosse Berliner Kunstausstellung: Die Abstrakten*
Catalogue (*Veröffentlichungen des Kunstarchivs*, no.10, 1926)

Gera, Ausstellungshalle, Geraer Kunstverein
10 October–early December
*Grosse Herbst-Ausstellung 1926: 50 Jahre Geraer Kunstverein*
Catalogue

New York, The Brooklyn Museum
19 November–1 January 1927
*International Exhibition of Modern Art Assembled by The Société Anonyme*
Catalogue
Travelled in varying form to New York, The Anderson Galleries, 25 January–5 February 1927; Buffalo NY, Albright Art Gallery, 25 February–20 March; Toronto, Toronto Art Gallery, 1–24 April

**1927**
San Diego CA, Fine Arts Gallery
January–February
*The Blue Four: Feininger, Jawlensky, Kandinsky, Paul Klee*
Catalogue, checklists
Travelled in varying form to: San Francisco CA, California School of Fine Arts, 1–20 March; Portland OR, The Museum of Art, Portland Art Association, April, catalogue; Spokane WA, Spokane Art Association, 15–31 May, catalogue; Seattle WA, Henry Art Gallery, University of Washington, October, checklist

Mannheim, Städtische Kunsthalle Mannheim
30 January–27 March
*Wege und Richtungen der abstrakten Malerei in Europa*
Catalogue

Los Angeles CA, Los Angeles Museum
April
*European Modernists*
Catalogue

Poughkeepsie NY, Vassar College
8–28 April
*Exhibition of Modern European Art*
Catalogue

Amsterdam, Stedelijk Museum
21 May–19 June
*Tentoonstelling de Onhafhankelijken 1912–1927*
Catalogue
Travelled to: The Hague, June

Zurich, Kunsthaus Zürich
30 October–27 November
*Ausstellung*
(Giacometti, Kandinsky, Soldenhoff)
Catalogue



Dresden, Galerie Arnold (Ludwig Gutbier)
16 October–10 November
*Kandinsky: Jubiläums-Ausstellung zum 60. Geburtstage*
Catalogue
Travelled to: Berlin, Galerie Neumann-Nierendorf, 14 November–15 December, catalogue; Dessau, Anhaltischer Kunstverein, opened 19 December; Munich, Neue Kunst Haus Goltz, 14 March–14 April 1927

**1927**
Plauen, Kunstverein Plauen
21 October–20 November
(recent works)

New York, New School of Social Research
12–19 December
(loans from the Société Anonyme)

**1928**
Oakland CA, The Oakland Art Gallery
4–29 January
*Thirty European Modernists*
Catalogue

Basel, Kunsthalle
8–29 January
*Januar Ausstellung*
Catalogue

Stuttgart, Kunsthaus Schaller
February
(George Grosz, Wassily Kandinsky)

Hannover, Künstlerhaus, Deutscher Künstlerbund
19 February–15 April
*96. Grosse Kunstausstellung des Kunstvereins Hannover e. V.*
Catalogue

New York, The Barbizon Arts Council Gallery
20 February–10 March
(exhibition of the Société Anonyme)

Berlin, National-Galerie
April
*Ausstellung neuerer deutscher Kunst aus Berliner Privatbesitz*
Catalogue

Nürnberg, Norishalle am Marientorgraben
12 April–2 September
*Deutsche Kunst der Gegenwart*
Catalogue

Krefeld, Kaiser-Wilhelm-Museum
1–31 May
*Farbe*
Catalogue

New York, The Worker's Center
7–21 May
(exhibition of the Société Anonyme)

Düsseldorf, Kunstpalast
May–October
*Deutsche Kunst Düsseldorf 1928*
Catalogue

Frankfurt am Main, Kunsthandlung Ludwig Schames
18 June–31 July
*Eröffnungsausstellung*
Catalogue

New York, Women's Club of New York
4 October–1 November
(exhibition of the Société Anonyme)

Essen, Museum Folkwang
9 December–early 1929
*Aquarelle zeitgenössischer deutscher Künstler*

**1929**
New York, Daniel Galleries
7–19 January
(exhibition of the Société Anonyme)

Hamburg, Kunsthalle, Kunstverein Hamburg
3 February
*Sonderausstellung: Neue Europäische Kunst* (simultaneously with *9. Ausstellung der Hamburgischen Sezession*)
Catalogue



**1928**
Frankfurt am Main, Frankfurter Kunstverein e. V.
15 January–15 February
Catalogue

Brussels, Galerie l'Epoque
24 March–April
*Kandinsky*
Catalogue

Berlin, Galerie Ferdinand Möller
October
*Oktober-Ausstellung: W. Kandinsky–Neue Aquarelle*
Simultaneously with *Erich Heckel–Zeichnungen aus den letzten Jahren, Radierungen, Holzschnitte, Lithographien*
Catalogue

Dresden, Galerie Neue Kunst Fides (Rudolf Probst)
12 October–5 November
*Kandinsky: Neue Gemälde*
Travelled to: Erfurt, Museum, 10 November–5 December
Catalogue

**1929**
Paris, Galerie Zak
15–31 January
*Exposition d'aquarelles de Wassily Kandinsky*
Catalogue
Travelled in modified form to: The Hague, Kunstzaal de Bron, 16 March–12 April, catalogue; Brussels, Galerie Le Centaure, 25 May–5 June

Oakland CA, The Oakland Art Gallery
April–10 May
*Kandinsky*
Catalogue

Dresden, Sächsischer Kunstverein, Dresdner Secession
Mid-April–June
*3. Jubiläumsausstellung: Neuere Kunstwerke aus Dresdner Privatbesitz*

Basel, Kunsthalle Basel
20 April–9 May
*Bauhaus Dessau: J. Albers, L. Feininger, W. Kandinsky, P. Klee, O. Schlemmer*
Catalogue

Antwerp
27 April–2 June
*Salon 1929: Kunst van heden/Art contemporain*
Catalogue

Chicago IL, The Art Institute of Chicago
May–June
*9th International Exhibition of Watercolors*

Kassel, Orangerie, Kunstverein
1 May–1 September
*Neue Kunst*
Catalogue
Travelled to: Hamburg-Altona, Ausstellungshalle, Altonaer Kunstverein, September–October, catalogue

Cologne, Staatenhaus
17 May–September
*Ausstellung des deutschen Künstlerbundes Köln 1929*
Catalogue

Berlin, Moderne Galerie Wertheim
July
(contemporary German prints)

Berlin, Galerie Ferdinand Möller
July
(summer exhibition)

Berlin, Landes-Ausstellungsgebäude am Lehrter Bahnhof
31 August–September
*Juryfreie Kunstschau Berlin 1929*
Catalogue

Berlin, Galerie Ferdinand Möller
October
*Die Blaue Vier: Feininger, Jawlensky, Kandinsky, Klee*
Catalogue

Zurich, Kunsthaus Zürich
6 October–3 November
*Abstrakte und surrealistische Malerei und Plastik*
Catalogue
Travelled to: Munich, Graphisches Kabinett (Günther Franke) and Künstlerbund 'Die Juryfreien', January 1930, catalogue

Berlin, Berliner Secession
November–December
*Herbst-Ausstellung: Malerei*
Catalogue

Breslau, Schlesisches Museum der bildenden Künste, Gesellschaft der Kunstfreunde
December–early 1930
*Wassily Kandinsky, Emil Nolde, Karl Schmidt-Rottluff*
Catalogue

Munich, Graphisches Kabinett (Günther Franke)
17 December–15 January 1930
*Wege abstrakter Malerei*
Catalogue

**1930**
Dessau, Bauhaus
Winter
*10 Jahre Bauhaus*
Travelled to: Essen, 16–30 February; Berlin; Mannheim, 14 May–22 June, and other German cities



Halle, Alte Garnisonskirche (oils) and Roter Turm (watercolors), Hallischer Kunstverein and Städtisches Museum Moritzburg
4–23 October
(retrospective)

**1930**
Saarbrücken, Staatliches Museum
12 January–9 February
*Kollektiv-Ausstellung Wassily Kandinsky*
Catalogue

Augsburg, Kunstverein
March
(abstract painting)

Berlin, Kronprinzenpalais, Nationalgalerie
Opened 4 April
*Neuerwerbungen der Nationalgalerie*

Wiesbaden, Neues Museum, Nassauischer Kunstverein
6 April—early June
*30 deutsche Künstler aus unserer Zeit* simultaneously with *Sammlung Kirchhoff*
Catalogue

Paris, Galerie 23
18 April–1 May
*Cercle et Carré*
Catalogue

Vienna, Künstlerhaus
April–May
*Die Kunst in unserer Zeit*
Catalogue

Venice, Biennale, German Pavilion
May–October
*XVII Esposizione Biennale Internazionale d'Arte*
Catalogue

Stuttgart, Ausstellungsgebäude auf dem Interimtheaterplatz, Deutscher Künstlerbund
31 May–21 September
*Ausstellung Stuttgart 1930*
Catalogue

Heidelberg, Heidelberger Kunstverein
July

Berlin, Galerie Ferdinand Möller
September–October
*Vision und Formgesetz*
Catalogue

Bielefeld, Städtisches Kunsthaus, Freundeskreis des Bielefelder Kunsthauses
21 September–19 October
*Ausstellung aus Bielefelder Privatbesitz*
Catalogue

Kiel, Kieler Kunsthalle, Schleswig-Holsteinischer Kunstverein
14 September–12 October
*Kandinsky-Klee-Rudolph*
No catalogue

Bordeaux, Société des Artistes Indépendants
19 October–16 November
*Salon 1930*
Catalogue

Hamburg, Kunstverein
26 October–17 November
*Kunst der letzten 30 Jahre aus Hamburger Privatbesitz*
Catalogue

New York, Rand School of Social Science
10 November–2 January 1931
*Pictures lent by the Metropolitan Museum and the Société Anonyme*
Catalogue

**1931**
New York, New School for Social Research
1 January–10 February
*Special Exhibition Arranged in Honor of the New Building of the New School*
Catalogue

New York, Rand School of Social Science
5 January–16 March
*Third Exhibition in Connection with the Rand School*
Catalogue



Hollywood CA, Braxton Gallery
1–15 March
*Kandinsky* (series of Blue Four exhibitions)
Catalogue

Paris, Galerie de France
14–31 March
*Kandinsky*
Catalogue, no checklist

Krefeld, Kaiser-Wilhelm-Museum
Opened mid-March
(watercolors)

Düsseldorf, Galerie Alfred Flechtheim
Summer
(watercolors)
Travelled to: Frankfurt am Main, August; Chemnitz, August–September; Erfurt, Kunstverein, mid-October

**1931**
Berlin, Galerie Alfred Flechtheim
February
*Kandinsky*
Catalogue

Dessau, Bauhaus
Mid-October–30 October
(drawings and graphic works)

New York, The Brooklyn Museum
23 January–24 February
*Exhibition of Water Color Paintings, Pastels and Drawings by American and Foreign Artists and Miniatures by the Brooklyn Society of Miniature Painters*
Catalogue

New York, Women's University Club
February

Belgrade
April
*Deutsche zeitgenössische bildende Kunst und Architektur*
Catalogue
Travelled to: Zagreb

San Francisco CA, California Palace of the Legion of Honor
8–22 April
*The Blue Four (1st Series: Kandinsky & Feininger)*
Catalogue

Brussels, Palais des Beaux-Arts, Société L'Art Vivant
25 April–24 May
*L'Art Vivant en Europe*

Berlin, Ausstellungsfreigelände an der Masurenallee
9 May–2 August
*Deutsche Bau-Ausstellung*

Essen, Ausstellungshallen Norbertstrasse 2, Deutscher Künstlerbund
23 May–23 August
*Ausstellung Essen 1931*
Catalogue

Frankfurt am Main, Städelsches Kunstinstitut
3 June–3 July
*Vom Abbild zum Sinnbild: Ausstellung von Meisterwerken moderner Malerei*
Catalogue

Berlin, Haus des Vereins der Berliner Künstler, November-Gruppe
3 July–3 August
Catalogue

Oakland CA, The Oakland Art Gallery
August–14 September
*The Blue Four: Feininger, Jawlensky, Kandinsky, Paul Klee*
Catalogue

Zurich, Kunsthaus Zürich
12 November–9 December
*Ausstellung*
Catalogue

Mexico City, Biblioteca Nacional de Mexico
24 November–1 December
*Cuatro Azules: Feininger, Jawlensky, Kandinsky, Paul Klee*
Catalogue, no checklist

Chicago IL, The Art Institute of Chicago
22 December–17 January 1932
*Exhibition of the Arthur Jerome Eddy Collection of Modern Paintings and Sculpture*
Catalogue

Rotterdam, Museum Boymans
Christmas–early 1932
*Kerttentoonstelling 1931/1932*
Catalogue

**1932**
Frankfurt am Main, Bund Das neue Frankfurt
February
*Abstrakte Kunst*

Vienna
February–March

Bielefeld, Kunsthalle Bielefeld
March
*Deutsche Aquarelle und Zeichnungen, 1900–1930*



Zurich, Kunsthaus Zürich
5 November–9 December
*Novemberausstellung*

**1932**
Berlin, Galerie Ferdinand Möller
February
*Sonder-Ausstellung W. Kandinsky: Zeichnungen 1910-1931/Neue Aquarelle/Grafik*
Catalogue
Travelled in reduced form to: Saarbrücken, Staatliches Museum, opened 5 June

Essen, Museum Folkwang
5 June–10 July
(recent watercolors)

Santa Barbara CA, Faulkner Memorial Art Center
3–13 March
*The Blue Four: Feininger, Jawlensky, Kandinsky, Paul Klee*
Catalogue

Amsterdam, Stedelijk Museum, De Onafhankelijken, Vereeniging van beeldende Kunstenaars
5 March–3 April
*Jubileum-Tentoonstellung*
Catalogue

Chicago IL, The Arts Club of Chicago
1–15 April
*The Blue Four: Feininger, Jawlensky, Kandinsky, Paul Klee*
Catalogue
Travelled in part to: Chicago IL, The Renaissance Society of The University of Chicago, 16–19 April

Cologne, Kölnischer Kunstverein
May
*Neue Kunst aus Rheinländischem Privatbesitz*

Königsberg, Städtische Kunsthalle, Deutscher Künstlerbund
16 June–31 July
*Aquarelle und Zeichnungen*
Travelled to: Danzig, Museum Danzig, 10 August–2 October

Weimar, Museum
Summer
(Goethe exhibition)

Mannheim, Kunsthalle Mannheim
Autumn
*Gestalt und Gestaltung*
No catalogue
(drawings)

Los Angeles CA, Isley Galleries, Inc.
12 September–1 October
*Modern Versus Academic Exhibition*
Catalogue

Stockholm, Nationalmuseum
October
*Paris 1932–10 Nationer, 24 Konstnärer: Utställning av postkubistisk och surrealistisk konst*
Catalogue

Dresden, Galerie Neue Kunst Fides (Rudolf Probst)
12 November–7 December
*Wassily Kandinsky, Karl Hofer, Gerhard Marcks*
(watercolors and drawings)

Cologne, Kölnischer Kunstverein
December
*Moderne deutsche Kunst*

Hannover, Kestner-Gesellschaft
8 December–15 January 1933
*Deutscher Künstlerbund: Aquarelle und Zeichnungen*
Catalogue, no checklist

Berlin, Galerie Alfred Flechtheim
10 December–January 1933
*Deutsche Ausstellung*

**1933**
Groningen
March
(international exhibition)

Chicago IL, The Art Institute of Chicago
1 June–1 November
*A Century of Progress: Exhibition of Paintings and Sculpture*
Catalogue

New York, The Museum of Modern Art
10 July–30 September
*Summer Exhibition: Painting and Sculpture*



Stockholm, Gummesons Konsthall
15–30 September
*Kandinsky*
Catalogue

New York, Valentine Gallery
15 November–10 December
*An Exhibition of Paintings by Kandinsky*
Catalogue

London, The Mayor Gallery, organized by Herbert Read
October
*International Exhibition: A Survey of Contemporary Art*
Catalogue

Los Angeles CA, Los Angeles Museum
4–30 October
*The Blue Four: Feininger, Jawlensky, Kandinsky, Paul Klee*
Catalogue

Paris, Association Artistique Les Surindépendants
27 October–26 November
*Salon des Surindépendants*

Los Angeles CA, University of California Los Angeles
13 November–1 December
*The Blue Four: Feininger, Jawlensky, Kandinsky, Paul Klee*
Floor plan

**1934**
Vienna, Neue Galerie (O. Kallir)
March–April
*Zehn Jahre Neue Galerie*
Catalogue (no checklist for Kandinsky)

Brussels, Palais des Beaux-Arts
12 May–3 June
*Exposition Minotaure*

New York, Julien Levy Galleries
Autumn
*Eight Modes of Modern Painting*

Hollywood CA, Hansen Music Company
Opened 17 November
*The Blue Four*
No catalogue

New York, The Museum of Modern Art
19 November–20 January 1935
*Modern Works of Art: Fifth Anniversary Exhibition*
Catalogue

**1935**
Lucerne, Kunstmuseum Luzern
24 February–31 March
*Thèse-antithèse-synthèse*
Catalogue

Paris, Grand Palais, Société des Artistes décorateurs
May–through summer
*Art et Décoration*

Paris, Galerie Castelucho-Diana
14–29 June
*Benno, Fernandez, Gonzalez, Hélion, Kandinsky, Laurens, Léger, Lipchitz, Magnelli, Picasso: Oeuvres récentes*
Catalogue, no checklist

Black Mountain NC, Black Mountain College
October–June 1936
(loan exhibition of the Société Anonyme)
Travelled in modified form to: Hartford CT, and other museums

New York, New Art Circle (J.B. Neumann)
November
*Vasily Kandinsky, Paul Klee, Max Weber: Watercolors and Paintings*

**1936**
New York, The Museum of Modern Art
14 January–16 February
*New Acquisitions: The Collection of Mrs. John D. Rockefeller, Jr.*



**1934**
Milan, Galleria del Milione
24 April–9 May
*Kandinsky*
Catalogue (*Bolletino della Galleria del Milione*, no.27, 1934)

Paris, Cahiers d'Art
23 May–3 June
*Kandinsky: peintures de toutes les époques, aquarelles et dessins*
No catalogue

Stockholm, Gummesons Konsthall
Opened 8 September
*Kandinsky 1924–1934*
Catalogue

**1935**
Oakland CA, The Oakland Art Gallery
2–30 January
*Paintings by Wassily Kandinsky, the 'Old Master' of Abstract Art*

San Francisco CA, Howard Putzel Gallery
April
(watercolors)

San Francisco CA, San Francisco Museum of Art
5 May–9 June
*Kandinsky Abstractions*

Paris, Cahiers d'Art
21 June–10 September
*W. Kandinsky: nouvelles toiles, aquarelles, dessins*
No catalogue

**1936**
New York, New Art Circle (J. B. Neumann)
1–29 February
*Vasily Kandinsky*
Catalogue

Oxford, St Giles
15–22 February
*Abstract & Concrete: An International Exhibition of Painting and Sculpture, 1934 and 1935*
Catalogue
Travelled in modified form to: Liverpool, School of Architecture, 2–14 March; London, Alex Reid & Lefevre Ltd, April, catalogue; Cambridge, Gordon Fraser's Gallery, 28 May–13 June

Charleston SC, Carolina Art Association, Gibbes Memorial Art Gallery
1 March–12 April
*Solomon R. Guggenheim Collection of Non-Objective Paintings*
Catalogue

New York, The Museum of Modern Art
1 March–19 April
*Cubism and Abstract Art*
Catalogue

Leicester, City of Leicester Museum and Art Gallery
1 May–20 June
*Contemporary Art*
Catalogue

Paris, La Galerie Pierre
2–14 May
*Oeuvres récentes de Arp, Ferren, Giacometti, Hartung, Hélion, Kandinsky, Nelson, Paalen, Taeuber-Arp*
Catalogue, no checklist

Tenerife, Circulo de bellas artes
10–15 June
*Esposición de arte contemporáneo: Collección 'Gaceta de arte'*
Catalogue
Travelled to: Barcelona and Madrid

Honolulu HI
September–July 1937
*New Forms in Art*
Travelled in western United States until July 1937

New York, New Art Circle (J.B. Neumann)
October
*Max Beckmann, Paul Klee, Vasily Kandinsky, Georges Rouault*

London, The London Gallery
15–28 November
(drawings)

New York, Delphic Studios
23 November–5 December
*A Small Collection Loaned through the Société Anonyme*

New York, The Museum of Modern Art
7 December–17 January 1937
*Fantastic Art, Dada, Surrealism*
Catalogue

**1937**
Basel, Kunsthalle Basel
16 January–14 February
*Konstruktivisten*
Catalogue

New York, New Art Circle (J.B. Neumann)
February
(oil paintings)

Philadelphia PA, Philadelphia Art Alliance
2–28 February
*Solomon R. Guggenheim Collection of Non-Objective Paintings*
Catalogue

Oakland CA, Mills College
April–May
*Modern Art: Eighty-Fifth Anniversary Exhibition*
Catalogue



Los Angeles CA, Stendahl Art Galleries
24 February–March
*Kandinsky*
Catalogue
Travelled to: San Francisco CA, San Francisco Museum of Art

Paris, Galerie Jeanne Bucher
3–19 December, extended through 29 December
*Kandinsky: toiles récentes, aquarelles, graphiques de 1910–1935*
Catalogue

**1937**
Cleveland OH, Cleveland Museum of Art, organized by the College Art Association and Karl Nierendorf
10 February–March
*Kandinsky: A Retrospective View. A College Art Association Exhibition*
Travelled to: New York, Nierendorf Gallery, 12–28 March, catalogue; Cambridge MA, Harvard University, Germanic Museum, until 24 April

Bern, Kunsthalle Bern
21 February–29 March
*Wassily Kandinsky*
Simultaneously with *Französische Meister der Gegenwart*
Catalogue

New York, Nierendorf Gallery
10–31 December
*Vasily Kandinsky: Paintings*

London, Artist's International Organization
14 April–5 May
*Unity of Artists for Peace, Democracy and Cultural Development: 1937 Exhibition*
Catalogue

Munich, Hofgarten-Arkaden
19 July–30 November
*Entartete Kunst*
Travelled in varying form to: Berlin, Haus der Kunst, 26 February–6 May 1938; Leipzig, Grassi-Museum, 13 May–6 June; Düsseldorf, Kunstpalast, 18 June–7 August; Salzburg; Hamburg; Stettin; Weimar; Vienna; Frankfurt am Main; Chemnitz and other German cities until 1941

Paris, Musée du Jeu de Paume
30 July–31 October
*Origines et développement de l'art international indépendant*
Catalogue

Copenhagen, Liniens Samenslutning
1–13 September
*Efter-Expressionisme, Abstrakt Kunst, Neoplasticisme, Surrealisme*
Catalogue

Paris, Club des Architectes, Exposition Internationale
1–30 October
*L'Art d'aujourd'hui*

New York, Nierendorf Gallery
1 December–1 March 1938
*Kandinsky, Klee, Feininger: Paintings*

**1938**
New York, Columbia University, Art Department
28 February–24 March
(loans from the Société Anonyme)

Milan, Galleria del Milione
2–17 March
*Arp, Domela, Kandinsky, Magnelli, Seligmann, Taeuber-Arp, Vézelay*
Catalogue (*Bolletino della Galleria Il Milione*, no.58, 1938), no checklist

Charleston SC, Gibbes Memorial Art Gallery
12 March–17 April
*Solomon R. Guggenheim Collection of Non-Objective Paintings*
Catalogue

Amsterdam, Stedelijk Museum
2–24 April
*Tentoonstellung abstracte kunste*
Catalogue

Paris, Galerie Jeanne Bucher
27 April–12 May
*Exposition du contenu de la Galerie, André Breton*

London, Guggenheim Jeune
21 June–2 July
*Contemporary Painting and Sculpture*
Catalogue

London, New Burlington Galleries
8 July–27 August
*Exhibition of Twentieth-Century German Art*
Catalogue

Oslo, Kunstnerforbundet
16 September–2 October
*International Nutidskunst: Konstruktivisme, Neoplasticisme, Abstrakt Kunst, Surrealisme*
Catalogue

London, Guggenheim Jeune
3–26 November
*Exhibition of Collages, Papiers-collés and Photo-montages*
Catalogue



**1938**
London, Guggenheim Jeune
17 February–12 March
*Wassily Kandinsky*
Catalogue
Travelled in part to: Bristol, New Bristol Art Club, April–May; Gloucester, Gloucester Municipal School of Arts and Crafts, May–June; Leeds

New York, The Museum of Modern Art
7 December–30 January 1939
*Bauhaus 1919–1928*
Catalogue

New York, Nierendorf Gallery
10 December–1 March 1939
*Three Masters of the Bauhaus: Kandinsky, Klee, Feininger*

**1939**
New York, Nierendorf Gallery
January
*Four Europeans: Feininger, Hofer, Kandinsky, Klee*

Baltimore MD, The Baltimore Museum of Art
6–29 January
*Solomon R. Guggenheim Collection of Non-Objective Paintings*
Catalogue

Springfield MA, Museum of Fine Arts
10–30 January
*Modern German Art*
Catalogue

New York, Nierendorf Gallery, organized by Katherine Dreier
28 March–8 April
*An Exhibition of Contrasts*
Catalogue

London, Guggenheim Jeune
10–27 May
*Abstract and Concrete Art*
Catalogue

New York, The Museum of Modern Art
May–November
*Art in Our Time: Tenth Anniversary Exhibition*
Catalogue

New York, Museum of Non-Objective Painting, Solomon R. Guggenheim Foundation
Opened 1 June
*Art of Tomorrow*
Catalogue

Paris, Galerie Charpentier
30 June–15 July
*Réalités nouvelles: 1re Exposition (2me Série)–Oeuvres des artistes étrangers*
Catalogue, no checklist

Pittsburgh PA, Carnegie Institute
19 October–10 December
*The 1939 International Exhibition of Paintings*
Catalogue

Boston, MA, The Institute of Modern Art
2 November–9 December
*Contemporary German Art*
Catalogue

Springfield MA, The George Walker Vincent Smith Art Gallery
4 November–17 December
*Anniversary Exhibition of the Société Anonyme: New Forms of Beauty, 1909–1936*
Catalogue

**1940**
Mexico City, Gallery of Mexican Art
February
*Exposición internacional de Surrealismo*

New York, New Art Circle (J. B. Neumann)
23 September–30 November
*Documents of Modern Painting from the Collection of J. B. Neumann*
Catalogue



**1939**
New York, Nierendorf Gallery
1–28 February, extended to 18 March
*Kandinsky*
No catalogue

Seattle WA, Cornish School
23 February–15 March
*Kandinsky*
Checklist

Paris, Galerie Jeanne Bucher
2–17 June
*Kandinsky: aquarelles et gouaches, 1910–1920 et 1937–1939*

San Francisco CA, San Francisco Museum of Art
6–23 July
*Paintings by Wassily Kandinsky: A survey 1923 to present*
Checklist

San Francisco CA, San Francisco Museum of Art
20 July–9 August
*Seven Additional Kandinsky Oils*

**1940**
Los Angeles CA, Stendahl Art Galleries
1–20 April
*Kandinsky*
Checklist

**1941**
New York, Nierendorf Gallery
May–7 June
*The Masters and Vanguard of Modern Art*

**1942**
New Haven CT, Yale Art Gallery
13 January–23 February
(inaugural exhibition of the Collection Société Anonyme)

Paris, Galerie Jeanne Bucher
March
*Léger, H. Laurens, Kandinsky*

New York, Nierendorf Gallery
November
*Unity in Diversity: Art as Exhibited from 1922 to 1942 by the Nierendorf Gallery*
Catalogue

**1943**
New York, Art of This Century
13 March–10 April
*Paintings: 15 Early–15 Late*

New York, Nierendorf Gallery
17 March–10 April

New York, Nierendorf Gallery
June–July
*East–West: An Exhibition of Parallels in Chinese and Western Art*
Catalogue, no checklist

Gstaad, Palace Hotel, Musiksommer Gstaad
30 July–15 August
*Moderne Malerei*
Catalogue

New York, Buchholz Gallery (Curt Valentin)
16 November–4 December
*Early Work by Contemporary Artists*
Catalogue

**1944**
Paris, Galerie Jeanne Bucher
January–1 February
*Peintures et gouaches de Kandinsky, trois tableaux-objets de Domela, peintures et dessins de Nicolas de Staël*
No catalogue

New York, Nierendorf Gallery
Until 18 March
*Gestation-Formation*
Catalogue

Basel, Kunsthalle Basel
18 March–16 April
*Konkrete Kunst*
Catalogue

Paris, Galerie l'Esquisse
Opened 7 April
*Peintures abstraites, compositions de matières: Domela, Kandinsky, Magnelli, de Staël*
No catalogue

New York, The Museum of Modern Art
24 May–15 October
*Art in Progress: Fifteenth Anniversary Exhibition*
Catalogue

Paris, Galerie Berri-Raspail
11–31 October
*Art abstrait*

New York, Buchholz Gallery (Curt Valentin)
31 October–25 November
*The Blue Four: Feininger, Jawlensky, Kandinsky, Klee*
Catalogue



**1941**
New York, Nierendorf Gallery
Until 29 March
*Kandinsky*
Catalogue

**1942**
Paris, Galerie Jeanne Bucher
21 July–4 August
*Wassily Kandinsky: peintures et gouaches récentes*
No catalogue

New York, Nierendorf Gallery
8 December–February 1943
*Works by Kandinsky: A Retrospective Show*
Catalogue

**1944**
Paris, Galerie l'Esquisse
7 November–7 December, extended through December
*Etapes de l'oeuvre de Wassily Kandinsky*
Catalogue, no checklist

New York, Nierendorf Gallery
December–January 1945
(retrospective)

Bern, Kunstmuseum
October–March 1945
*Der Sturm, Sammlung Nell Walden aus den Jahren 1912–1920*
Catalogue

New York, Nierendorf Gallery
December
*American and European Pioneers in 20th Century Art*

**1945**
Paris, Galerie René Drouin
15 June–13 July
*Art Concret*
Catalogue

Paris, Palais des Beaux-Arts de la Ville de Paris
19 July–18 August
*1er Salon des Réalités Nouvelles: art abstrait, concret, constructivisme, non figuratif*
Catalogue, no checklist

New York, Nierendorf Gallery
October
*Forbidden Art in the Third Reich*
Catalogue

Paris, Galerie Jeanne Bucher
14 December–12 January 1946
*20 ans chez Jeanne Bucher: aquarelles, dessins, gouaches, 1925–1945*

**1946**
Basel, Kunsthalle Basel
12 January–3 February
*Sammlung Nell Walden*
Catalogue

Tours, Musée de Tours
18 May–2 June
*De l'avènement du cubisme à nos jours*
Catalogue

Zurich, Kunsthaus Zürich
21 September–20 October
*Georges Braque, Wassily Kandinsky 1866–1944, Pablo Picasso*
Catalogue

**1947**
Milan, Palazzo Exreale, organized by L'altana
15 January–9 February
*Arte astratta e concreta*
Catalogue, no checklist

Brussels, Galerie Georges Giroux
2–19 June
*L'Art vivant dans les collections privées belges*
Catalogue

Avignon, Palais des Papes
27 June–30 September
*Exposition de peintures et sculptures contemporaines*
Catalogue

Krefeld, Kaiser-Wilhelm-Museum, Krefelder Museums-Verein
15 December–15 January 1948
*Expressionismus in Malerei und Plastik*

**1948**
Paris, Galerie Colette Allendy
5–26 February
*Kandinsky, Paul Klee*
No catalogue

Paris, Galerie Maeght
April–13 May
*Préliminaires à l'art abstrait*
13 May–3 June
*Epanouissement de l'art abstrait*



**1945**
Basel, Kunsthalle Basel
10 March–8 April
*Gedächtnisausstellung Wassily Kandinsky*
Simultaneously with *Vierzehn Berner Künstler*
Catalogue

New York, Museum of Non-Objective Painting, Solomon R. Guggenheim Foundation
*In Memory of Wassily Kandinsky*
15 March–29 April, extended through summer
Catalogue
Travelled in reduced form to: Chicago IL, The Arts Club of Chicago, November, catalogue; Milwaukee WI, late 1945–early 1946; Pittsburgh PA, Department of Fine Arts, Carnegie Institute, 11 April–12 May, catalogue

Zurich, Galerie des Eaux-Vives
5 May–7 June
*Zum Gedächtnis von Wassily Kandinsky*
Catalogue ('Bulletin abstrakt/konkret' no.8), no checklist
Travelled to: Paris

**1946**
Paris, Galerie René Drouin
13 March–13 April
*40 Peintures de Kandinsky*
Catalogue

Pittsburgh PA, see 1945 New York, Museum of Non-Objective Painting

**1947**
Paris, Galerie René Drouin
Opened 14 February
*Kandinsky: gouaches, aquarelles, dessins*
Catalogue

Liège, Belgium, Association pour le progrès intellectuel et artistique de la Wallonie
December
*Kandinsky: gouaches & dessins*
Catalogue

Amsterdam, Stedelijk Museum
8 December–end January 1948
*Kandinsky*
Catalogue
Travelled to: The Hague, Gemeente Museum, 13 February–14 March 1948, catalogue, and to Rotterdam, April (?)

**1948**
Basel, Kunstmuseum Basel
28 February–15 April
(retrospective)

Munich, Moderne Galerie Otto Stangl
September–October
*Kandinsky*
Catalogue

Venice, Biennale, German Pavilion
May–September
*XXIV Esposizione Biennale Internazionale d'Arte*
Catalogue

Paris, Galerie Denise René
22 October–22 November
*Tendances de l'art abstrait*
Catalogue, no checklist

**1949**
New York, Sidney Janis Gallery
14 February–12 March
*XX Century Painting*

Copenhagen
August–September

Munich, Haus der Kunst
September–October
*München und die Kunst des 20. Jahrhunderts. 1908–1914: Der Blaue Reiter*
Catalogue

São Paulo, Brazil, Museu de Arte Moderna
*Do Figurativismo ao abstracionismo*
Travelled to: other South American cities

**1950**
Basel, Kunsthalle Basel
21 January–26 February
*Der Blaue Reiter 1908–14, Wegbereiter und Zeitgenossen: Kandinsky, Marc, Macke, Klee*
Catalogue

Vienna, Akademie der bildenden Künste
18 February–10 March
*Form und Gestaltung*
Catalogue

Nice, organized by Comité des Fêtes, Arts et Sports de la Ville de Nice et Union Méditerranéenne pour l'Art Moderne
31 March–30 April
*La Belle Epoque: peintures, dessins, affiches de 1895 à 1914*
Catalogue

Munich, Haus der Kunst
May–June
*Die Maler am Bauhaus*
Catalogue

Venice, XXV Biennale di Venezia, German Pavilion
Opened 8 June
*Il Cavaliere azzurro*
General catalogue

Lille, Palais des Beaux-Arts
10 June–3 July
*Un Demi-siècle de peinture française, 1900–1950*
Catalogue

Providence RI, Museum of Art, Rhode Island School of Design
25 October–26 November
*Five Modern Old Masters: Kandinsky, Matisse, Mondrian, Picasso, Braque*
Catalogue

Paris, Galerie J & H Bernheim Jeune
16 December–12 January 1951
*Rhythmes et couleurs*
Catalogue

**1951**
Cologne, Galerie Ferdinand Möller
15 November–15 January 1952
*Eröffnungsausstellung: Die Alten Meister der modernen Kunst in Deutschland*
Catalogue (*Blätter der Galerie Ferdinand Möller*, new series, no.1/2, 1951)



New York, Sidney Janis Gallery
9–27 November
*Kandinsky*
Catalogue

**1949**
Paris, Galerie René Drouin
2 June–2 July
*Kandinsky: époque parisienne*
Catalogue

New York, Sidney Janis Gallery
21 November–24 December
*Kandinsky*
No catalogue

**1950**
Braunschweig, Galerie Otto Ralfs
19 February–19 March
*Wassily Kandinsky*

Paris, Galerie de Beaune
31 March–26 April
*Quelques tableaux de Kandinsky*

Düsseldorf, Galerie Hella Nebelung
30 April–5 May
*W. Kandinsky 1866-1944*

London, Gimpel Fils
June
*Kandinsky*
Catalogue

Venice, XXV Esposizione Biennale Internazionale d'Arte
Opened June
*Wassily Kandinsky*
General catalogue

**1951**
Rome, Galleria del Obelisco
Opened 18 January
*Wassily Kandinsky*
Catalogue

**1952**
Paris, Musée National d'Art Moderne
May–June
*L'Oeuvre du XXe siècle: peintures, sculptures*
Catalogue

Cologne, Galerie Ferdinand Möller
July
*Die alten Meister der modernen Kunst in Deutschland II*
Catalogue (*Blätter der Galerie Ferdinand Möller*, new series, no.6/7, 1952)

**1954**
Saarbrücken, Staatliche Schule für Kunst und Handwerk
19 March–9 April
*Kandinsky, Eloc, Deyrolle, Istrati, Leppien, Mortensen, Poliakoff*
Catalogue

Toronto, The Art Gallery of Toronto
2 April–9 May
*A Loan Exhibition of Paintings from the Solomon R. Guggenheim Museum*
Catalogue

Hannover, Kestner-Gesellschaft
9 May–13 June
*Zeitgenössische Kunst aus Hannoverschem Privatbesitz*
Catalogue

Munich, Moderne Galerie Otto Stangl
October–November
*Kandinsky, Marc, Münter: Unbekannte Werke*
Catalogue

New York, Curt Valentin Gallery
7 December–8 January 1955
*Der Blaue Reiter*
Catalogue



Milan, Galleria del Naviglio
22 February–9 March
*Wassily Kandinsky*
Catalogue, no checklist

Paris, Galerie Maeght
30 November–December
*Kandinsky 1900–1910*
Catalogue (*Derrière le Miroir*, no.42, November–December 1951)

**1952**
Boston MA, Institute of Contemporary Art
27 March–27 April
*Kandinsky: Retrospective Exhibition*
Catalogue
Travelled to: New York, M. Knoedler & Co. Inc., 10 May–6 June; San Francisco CA, San Francisco Museum of Art, 20 July–26 August; Minneapolis MN, Walker Art Center, 14 September–26 October, catalogue; Cleveland OH, Cleveland Museum of Art, 6 November–7 December

Venice, Galleria del Cavallino
6–19 September
*Wassily Kandinsky*
Catalogue, no checklist

**1953**
Brussels, Galerie Ex-Libris
21 March–3 April
*Oeuvres de Kandinsky*

Lucerne, Galerie Rosengart
June–September
*Kandinsky Exhibition: Paintings, Watercolours, Drawings*
Checklist

Hamburg, Kunsthalle, Kunstverein Hamburg
10 October–8 November, extended until 15 November
*Wassily Kandinsky: Arbeiten aus den Jahren 1912–1942*
No catalogue
Travelled to: Cologne, Galerie Ferdinand Möller, 21 November–16 January 1954, catalogue (*Blätter der Galerie Ferdinand Möller*, new series, no.12, 1953); Stuttgart, Württembergischer Kunstverein, 13 March–11 April; Munich, Haus der Kunst, opened 15 April; Mannheim, Städtische Kunsthalle, opened 29 May; Berlin, Charlottenburger Schloss, opened 24 July; Dortmund, Museum am Ostwall, 1–26 September; Nürnberg, Germanisches Nationalmuseum; Ulm; Wiesbaden

Paris, Galerie Maeght
Opened 13 November
*Kandinsky*
Catalogue (*Derrière le Miroir*, nos.60–61, October–November 1953)

**1954**
Paris, Berggruen & Cie
15 December–22 January 1955
*Kandinsky: oeuvre gravé*
Catalogue

**1955**
Cambridge MA, Busch-Reisinger Museum
21 January–26 February
*Artists of the Blaue Reiter*

Lakeland FL, Florida Southern College, Seventieth Founders Year Festival
Opened 27 February
*Art of Tomorrow – Bauer, Kandinsky, Rebay: Exhibition of Non-Objective Painting*
Catalogue

Pasadena CA, Pasadena Art Museum
27 May–30 August
*Feininger, Jawlensky, Kandinsky, Klee – The Blue Four: Galka E. Scheyer Collection*
Catalogue

**1956**
London, The Tate Gallery
April
*A Hundred Years of German Painting 1850–1950*
Catalogue

**1957**
Munich, Städtische Galerie im Lenbachhaus
16 February–30 April
*Kandinsky und Gabriele Münter: Werke aus fünf Jahrzehnten*
Catalogue

New York, The Museum of Modern Art
1 October–8 December
*German Art of the Twentieth Century*
Catalogue
Travelled to: St Louis MO, The City Art Museum, 8 January–24 February 1958

Saint-Etienne, Musée d'Art et d'Industrie
*Art abstrait: les premières générations (1910–1939)*
Catalogue

**1958**
Venice, Biennale, German Pavilion
Summer
*XXVIII Esposizione Biennale Internazionale d'Arte*
Catalogue

Amsterdam, Stedelijk Museum
4 July–29 September
*De renaissance der XXe eeuw*
Catalogue

Hamburg, Kunstverein
22 November–11 January 1959
*Wassily Kandinsky–Gabriele Münter*
Catalogue

**1959**
Paris, Berggruen & Cie
March
*Klee et Kandinsky: une confrontation*
Catalogue



**1955**
Bern, Kunsthalle
19 March–1 May
*Gesamtausstellung Wassily Kandinsky*
Catalogue

Paris, Galerie Maeght
24 June–August
*Kandinsky: période dramatique 1910–1920*
Catalogue (*Derrière le Miroir*, nos.77–78, July–August 1955)

**1956**
Stockholm, Galerie Samlaren (Agnes Widlund)
March
*Kandinsky: målningar, akvareller, teckningar*
Catalogue

**1957**
New York, Kleemann Galleries
January
*Wassily Kandinsky 1866–1944*
Catalogue

Copenhagen, Statens Museum for Kunst
March–April
*Wassily Kandinsky*
Catalogue

Brussels, Palais des Beaux-Arts
17 May–30 June
*45 Oeuvres de Kandinsky provenant du Solomon R. Guggenheim Museum*
Catalogue
Travelled in modified form to: Paris, Musée National d'Art Moderne, 15 November–5 January 1958, catalogue; London, Tate Gallery, 15 January–28 February, catalogue; Lyon, Palais Saint Pierre, 8 March–6 April, catalogue; Oslo, Kunstnernes Hus, 18 April–4 May, catalogue; Rome, Galleria Nazionale d'Arte Moderna, 15 May–30 June, catalogue

New York, Galerie Chalette
12 November–14 December
*Kandinsky*
Catalogue

Paris, Galerie Maeght
Opened 22 November
*Kandinsky: aquarelles et gouaches. Collection privée de Madame W. Kandinsky*
Catalogue (*Derrière le Miroir*, nos.101–103, September–November 1957)

**1958**
Cologne, Wallraf-Richartz-Museum
25 September–30 November
*Kandinsky*
Catalogue

**1959**
Nantes, Musée des Beaux-Arts
18 April–18 May
*Aquarelles et gouaches de W. Kandinsky*
Simultaneously with *Collection et Donation Gildas Fardel*
Catalogue

Basel, Galerie Beyeler
March–April
*Sélection*
Catalogue

Frankfurt am Main, Karmeliterkloster, Frankfurter Kunstkabinett (Hanna Bekker vom Rath)
4 July–28 September
*Der Beitrag der Russen zur modernen Kunst*
Catalogue

London, Marlborough Fine Art Limited
October–November
*'Art in Revolt': Germany 1905–25. Exhibition in Aid of World Refugee Year*
Catalogue

New York, The Solomon R. Guggenheim Museum
21 October–19 June 1960
*Inaugural Selection*
Catalogue

**1960**
Saint-Denis, Musée et Bibliothèque
27 March–14 April
*Peintres russes de l'Ecole de Paris, livres russes et soviétiques*
Catalogue

Edinburgh, Royal Scottish Academy, Edinburgh International Festival
Summer
*The Blue Rider Group*
Catalogue
Travelled to: London, The Tate Gallery, 30 September–30 October

Los Angeles CA, Dalzell Hatfield Galleries
20 June–30 July
*Gabriele Münter: First USA Exhibit with 7 Additional Major Paintings by Kandinsky*
Catalogue

New York, Sidney Janis Gallery
3 October–5 November
*XXth Century Artists*
Catalogue

**1961**
Paris, Galerie Europe
10 February–March
*Klee, Kandinsky, Brancusi*
Catalogue

Winterthur, Kunstmuseum Winterthur
23 April–11 June
*Der Blaue Reiter und sein Kreis*
Catalogue
Travelled to: Vienna, Österreichische Galerie, 2 August–24 September, catalogue; Linz, Neue Galerie der Stadt Linz, 30 September–29 October

**1962**
London, Grosvenor Gallery
15 March–14 April
*Two Decades of Experiment in Russian Art*
Catalogue

Rome, Galleria La Medusa
26 May–June
*Baumeister, Bissier, Kandinsky, Klee*
Catalogue, no checklist

Rome, Marlborough Galleria d'Arte
Summer
*Maestri del XIXo e XXo secolo*
Catalogue



Toronto, Art Gallery of Toronto
19 April–24 May
*Selection of Works by Wassily Kandinsky from the Solomon R. Guggenheim Museum Collection*
No catalogue

**1960**
Milan, Galleria del Naviglio
13 February–4 March
*Wassily Kandinsky*
Catalogue

Paris, Galerie Maeght
Opened 8 April
*Kandinsky: époque du Bauhaus 1921–1927*

**1961**
New York, The New Gallery
1–18 February
*Wassily Kandinsky: Paintings of 1905–1940*
Catalogue

Paris, Galerie Karl Flinker
8 February–4 March
*Kandinsky: aquarelles et dessins*
No catalogue

London, Marlborough Fine Art Limited
April–May
*Kandinsky: The Road to Abstraction*
Catalogue

**1962**
Munich, Galerie Otto Stangl
25 July–4 September
*Wassily Kandinsky: Ausstellung mit Werken von 1918 bis 1933*
Catalogue

Copenhagen, Sammenslutningen af Danske Kunstforeninger
Until 1963
*Kandinsky*
Catalogue

Paris, Galerie Maeght
October–November
*Der Blaue Reiter – Le Cavalier bleu*
Catalogue (*Derrière le Miroir*, nos. 133–134, October–November 1962)

**1963**
New York, Leonard Hutton Galleries
19 February–30 March
*Der Blaue Reiter*
Catalogue

New York, Marlborough-Gerson Gallery Inc.
November–December
*Artist and Maecenas: A Tribute to Curt Valentin*
Catalogue

Stockholm, Moderna Museet
26 December–16 February 1964
*Önskemuseet–The Museum of Our Wishes*
Catalogue

**1964**
Florence, Palazzo Strozzi
May–June
*L'Espressionismo, Pittura, Scultura, Architettura*
Catalogue

London, Hamilton Galleries
Opened 15 July
*The Blue Four: Klee, Kandinsky, Feininger, Jawlensky*
Catalogue

Bern, Kunsthalle
23 October–29 November
*Marcel Duchamp, Wassily Kandinsky, Kasimir Malewitsch, Josef Albers, Tom Doyle*
Catalogue

**1965**
Washington DC, Corcoran Gallery
19 February–28 March
*Paintings & Sculpture from the Collection of Mr. and Mrs. D.L. Kreeger: Kandinsky, Miró, Picasso and others*
Catalogue
Travelled in modified form to: Baltimore MD, Baltimore Museum of Art, 6 April–23 May

Marseilles, Musée Cantini
17 May–15 August
*Expressionisme allemand, 1900–1920*
Catalogue

**1966**
London, Marlborough Fine Art Limited
January
*Expressionism, Bauhaus, Dada: Drawings, Watercolours, Collages*
Catalogue

Columbus OH, Ohio State University, School of Art Gallery
11–30 November
*Klee, Kandinsky, Jawlensky: Works from the Bauhaus Period*
Catalogue



**1963**
Pasadena CA, Pasadena Art Museum, organized by The Solomon R. Guggenheim Museum
15 January–15 February
*Vasily Kandinsky 1866–1944: A Retrospective Exhibition*
Catalogue
Travelled to: San Francisco CA, San Francisco Museum of Art, 1 March–1 April; Portland OR, Art Museum, 15 April–15 May; San Antonio TX, Marion Koogler McNay Art Institute, 1 June–1 July; Colorado Springs CO, Fine Arts Center, 15 July–25 August; Baltimore MD, Baltimore Museum of Art; 19 September–20 October; Columbus OH, The Columbus Gallery of Fine Arts, 5 November–5 December; St Louis MO, Washington University Art Gallery, 22 December–1 January 1964; Montreal, Montreal Museum of Fine Arts, 5 February–5 March; Worcester MA, Worcester Art Museum, 20 March–20 April

New York, The Solomon R. Guggenheim Museum
25 January–7 April
*Vasily Kandinsky, 1866–1944: A Retrospective Exhibition*
Catalogue
Travelled in varying form to: Paris, Musée National d'Art Moderne, 29 April–24 June, catalogue; The Hague, Gemeente Museum, 1 July–30 August; Basel, Kunsthalle, 7 September–7 November, catalogue

Paris, Galerie Claude Bernard
March–April
*Kandinsky: dessins 1922–1944*
Catalogue

**1964**
Lindau (Bavaria), Städtisches Museum, Haus zum Cavazzen
15 April–28 June
*Kandinsky: Das druckgraphische Frühwerk aus dem Besitz der Gabriele-Münter-Stiftung der Städtischen Galerie im Lenbachhaus*
Catalogue

**1965**
Stockholm, Moderna Museet
10 April–23 May
*Kandinsky*
Catalogue

Paris, Galerie Maeght
November
*Kandinsky: Bauhaus de Dessau 1927–1933*
Catalogue (*Derrière le Miroir*, no.154, November 1965)

**1966**
Helsinki, Ateneum
10 February–6 March
*Kandinsky 1866–1944*
Catalogue

New York, Marlborough-Gerson Gallery, Inc.
April–May
*Kandinsky: The Bauhaus Years*
Catalogue

London, Marlborough Fine Art Ltd.
November–December
*Kandinsky and His Friends: Centenary Exhibition*
Catalogue

Moscow, State Tretiakov Gallery
*Exhibition of Watercolors from the End of the 18th Century to the Beginning of the 20th Century from the Collection of the State Tretiakov Gallery*

**1967**
Koblenz, Mittelrhein-Museum
4 January–5 February
*Blauer Reiter–Brücke–Bauhaus*
Catalogue

Hamburg, Kunstverein
2 September–15 October
*Meister der Zeichnung in der deutschen Kunst des 20. Jahrhunderts*
Catalogue
Travelled to: Frankfurt am Main, Frankfurter Kunstverein, 27 October–10 December

London, Grosvenor Gallery
24 October–18 November
*Aspects of Russian Experimental Art 1900–1925*
Catalogue

**1968**
New York, Leonard Hutton Galleries
18 April–12 June
*Fauves and Expressionists*
Catalogue

**1969**
New York, Hutton-Hutschnecker Gallery
16 April–28 May
*Kandinsky, Franz Marc, August Macke: Drawings and Watercolors*
Catalogue

Washington DC, National Gallery of Art
18 September–19 October
*German Expressionist Watercolors in American Collections*
Catalogue
Simultaneously with *German Expressionist Watercolors in the Collections of the Wallraf-Richartz-Museum, Cologne*
Travelled to: Syracuse NY, Everson Museum of Art; Montreal, Museé d'Art Contemporain; Kansas City KS, William Rockhill Nelson Gallery of Art; Des Moines IA, Des Moines Art Center

**1970**
Munich, Haus der Kunst
7 March–10 May
*Europäischer Expressionismus*
Catalogue
Travelled to: Paris, Musée National d'Arte Moderne, 26 May–27 July



Munich, Städtische Galerie im Lenbachhaus
2 July–16 October
*Kandinsky: Das druckgraphische Werk. Zum 100. Geburtstag*
Catalogue

Saint-Paul-de-Vence, Fondation Maeght
23 July–30 September
*Kandinsky Centenaire 1866–1944*
Catalogue

New York, The Solomon R. Guggenheim Museum
4 December–February
*Vasily Kandinsky: Painting on Glass (Hinterglasmalerei). Anniversary Exhibition*
Catalogue

**1967**
Milan, Galleria d'Arte del Naviglio
16–28 November
*Kandinsky*
Catalogue

**1968**
Paris, Galerie Dina Vierny
16 May–16 June
*Kandinsky: dessins 1886–1944*
Catalogue

**1969**
New York, The Museum of Modern Art
2 April–11 May
*Kandinsky Watercolors*
Catalogue published later by Art Gallery of Ontario
Travelled to: Fort Worth TX, Fort Worth Art Center, 13 July–17 August; Richmond VA, Virginia Museum of Fine Arts, 1 September–12 October; Ithaca NY, Cornell University, White Museum of Art, 3 November–14 December; Louisville KY, J. B. Speed Art Museum, 11 January–22 February 1970; Manchester NH, Currier Gallery of Art, 16 March–27 April; Toronto, Art Gallery of Ontario, 23 May–28 June, catalogue; Pasadena CA, Pasadena Art Museum, 20 July–31 August; San Francisco CA, San Francisco Museum of Art, 21 September–2 November; Milwaukee WI, Milwaukee Art Center, 21 January-18 February 1971; Minneapolis MN, Minneapolis Institute of Arts, 17 March–25 April; Bern, Kunstmuseum Bern, 27 May–18 July, catalogue

Paris, Galerie Maeght
June
*Kandinsky: période parisienne 1934–1944*
Catalogue (*Derrière le Miroir*, no.179, June 1969)

New York, M. Knoedler & Co., Inc.
21 October–22 November
*Kandinsky: Parisian Period 1934–1944*
Catalogue

**1970**
Baden-Baden, Staatliche Kunsthalle Baden-Baden
10 July–27 September
*Wassily Kandinsky: Gemälde 1900–1944*
Catalogue

Milan, Galleria del Naviglio
November
*Kandinsky*
Catalogue

**1971**
Turin, Galleria Civica d'Arte Moderna
18 March–9 May
*Il Cavaliere Azzurro–Der Blaue Reiter*
Catalogue

Paris, Galerie Jean Chauvelin
1–30 June
*La peinture non-objective/The Non-Objective World 1924–1939*
Catalogue
Travelled to: London, Annely Juda Fine Art, 7 July–30 September, catalogue; Milan, Galleria Milano, 15 October–15 November

Vienna, Secession, Sonderausstellung der Städtischen Galerie München anlässlich der Wochen 'München in Wien'
8–24 October
*Der Blaue Reiter*
Catalogue

New York, Leonard Hutton Galleries
16 October–18 December
*Russian Avant-Garde 1908–1922*
Catalogue

Humlebaek, Louisiana Museum
30 October–9 January 1972
*Klee–Kandinsky*
Catalogue (*Louisiana-Revy*, no.2, October 1971)

**1972**
Bridgeport CT, University of Bridgeport, Carlson Gallery
8 April–10 May
*Hommage to Hilla Rebay*
Catalogue

Munich, Stadtmuseum
9 June–15 October
*Bayern- Kunst und Kultur*
Catalogue

Hanover NH, Dartmouth College, Hopkins-Center
15 September–22 October
*Kandinsky and His Contemporaries: Selections from The Hilla Von Rebay Foundation Collection*
Catalogue

**1973**
Norwalk CT, The Lockwood-Mathews Mansion Museum
30 September–21 October
*Kandinsky and His Contemporaries: Selection from the Hilla von Rebay Foundation Collection*
Catalogue

London, Fischer Fine Art Limited
November–January 1974
*Tatlin's Dream: Russian Suprematist and Constructivist Art 1910–1923*
Catalogue



**1971**
Bern, see 1969 New York, Museum of Modern Art

Wiesbaden, Museum Wiesbaden
28 March–30 May
*Wassily Kandinsky: Druckgraphik*
Catalogue

Milan, Galleria Levi
December
*Wassily Kandinsky*
Catalogue

**1972**
Charleroi, Palais des Beaux-Arts
29 January–12 March
*Wassily Kandinsky: rétrospective*
Catalogue

Zurich, Galerie Maeght
Opened 21 April
*Kandinsky: Ölbilder, Gouachen, Zeichnungen*
Catalogue

New York, The Solomon R. Guggenheim Museum
12 May–5 September
*Kandinsky at the Guggenheim Museum*
Catalogue
Travelled to: Los Angeles CA, Los Angeles County Museum of Art, 3 October–19 November; Minneapolis MN, Walker Art Center, 5 May–15 July 1973

Basel, Galerie Beyeler
June–July
*Kandinsky: Aquarelle und Zeichnungen*
Catalogue

Paris, Musée d'Art Moderne de la Ville de Paris
7 June–30 July
*Hommage de Paris à Kandinsky: la conquête de l'abstraction, l'époque parisienne*
Catalogue

Paris, Berggruen & Cie
October
*Kandinsky: aquarelles & dessins*
Catalogue

Paris, Galerie Karl Flinker
28 October–9 December
*Kandinsky: peintures, dessins, gravures, éditions, oeuvres inédites*
Catalogue

**1973**
New York, Pace Gallery
10 March–4 April
*Kandinsky: Watercolors and Drawings 1911–1943*
Catalogue

London, Lefevre Gallery
12 April–19 May
*Oil Paintings and Watercolours by Wassily Kandinsky*
Catalogue

Cologne, Galerie Bargera
27 April–28 June
*Wassily Kandinsky, 1866–1944: Gouachen, Aquarelle, Ölbilder und Zeichnungen*
Catalogue

Bielefeld, Kunsthalle Bielefeld
9 September–4 November
*Wassily Kandinsky: Aquarelle, Gouachen, Zeichnungen*
Catalogue
Travelled to: Munich, Städtische Galerie im Lenbachhaus, 4 December–27 January 1974

São Paulo, XII Bienal de São Paulo, French section
October–November
*Hommage à Kandinsky*
Simultaneously with *Six artistes où l'expression de l'espace par le travail du support et de la couleur*

**1974**

*Group exhibitions*

Allentown PA, Allentown Art Museum
10 March–21 April
*The Blue Four and German Expressionism*
Catalogue

San Francisco CA, John Berggruen Gallery
3 April–11 May
*Berggruen chez Berggruen: European Watercolors, Drawings & Prints*
Catalogue

Pasadena CA, Pasadena Museum of Modern Art
16 April–2 June
*German Expressionist Paintings and Sculpture from California Collections*
Catalogue

Berlin, Nationalgalerie, Staatliche Museen Preussischer Kulturbesitz
11 September–4 November
*Hommage à Schönberg: Der Blaue Reiter und das Musikalische in der Malerei der Zeit*
Catalogue

*One-man exhibitions*

New York, The Solomon R. Guggenheim Museum
17 January–24 February
*The Graphic Work of Kandinsky: A Loan Exhibition*
Catalogue
Circulated by The International Exhibitions Foundation to: Cincinnati OH, Cincinnati Art Museum, 1–30 April; Little Rock AR, Arkansas Art Center, 15 May–15 June; San Antonio TX, Marion Koogler McNay Art Institute, 1–31 July; Houston TX, Museum of Fine Arts, 15 August–15 September; Fort Worth TX, Fort Worth Art Center, 1–31 October; Kansas City KS, William Rockhill Nelson Gallery and Atkins Museum of Fine Arts, 15 November–15 December; Davenport IA, Municipal Art Gallery, 4 January–2 February 1975; Detroit MI, Detroit Institute of Arts, 15 February–16 March; Worcester MA, Worcester Art Museum, 1–30 April; Washington DC, The Phillips Collection, 15 May–15 June

Madrid, Galeria Juana Mordó
16 March–20 April
*Kandinsky*
Catalogue, no checklist

Waltham MA, Brandeis University, The Rose Art Museum
1–29 May
*Kandinsky: Prints, Drawings and Watercolors from the Hilla von Rebay Foundation*
Catalogue

**1975**

*Group exhibitions*

Munich, Galerie Gunzenhauser
Opened 9 April
*Die Künstler des Blauen Reiter und ihre Freunde*
Catalogue

*One-man exhibitions*

Edinburgh, Scottish National Gallery of Modern Art, Edinburgh International Festival
15 August–15 September
*Wassily Kandinsky 1866–1944*
Catalogue

Paris, Galerie Dina Vierny
October
*Kandinsky: rétrospective des dessins de 1886 à 1944*
Catalogue

**1976**

*Group exhibitions*

Atlanta GA, The High Museum of Art
31 January–14 March
*Bauhaus Color*
Catalogue
Travelled to: Houston TX, The Museum of Fine Arts, 8 April–30 May; San Diego CA, Fine Arts Gallery of San Diego, 1 August–21 September

*One-man exhibitions*

Tokyo, The Seibu Museum of Art
2 January–11 February
*Kandinsky*
Catalogue

Bordeaux, Galerie des Beaux-Arts
7 May–1 September
*Wassily Kandinsky à Munich: Collection Städtische Galerie im Lenbachhaus*
Catalogue

Munich, Haus der Kunst
13 November–30 January 1977
*Wassily Kandinsky 1866–1944*
Catalogue

**1977**

*Group exhibitions*

Vienna, Galerie Ulysses
15 February–31 March
*Kandinsky-Klee-Kupka: Ölbilder, Aquarelle, Zeichnungen*
Catalogue

*One-man exhibitions*

Paris, Galerie Karl Flinker
25 May–2 July
*Kandinsky: 82 oeuvres sur papier de 1902 à 1933*
Catalogue

New York, Leonard Hutton Galleries
18 March–May
*Der Blaue Reiter und sein Kreis*
Catalogue

Schaffhausen, Museum zu Allerheiligen
7 May–26 June
*Zwischen Improvisation und Fuge*
Catalogue

**1979**
Stuttgart, Staatsgalerie Stuttgart
6 May–29 July
*Klee und Kandinsky: Erinnerungen an eine Künstlerfreundschaft*
Catalogue

Paris, Centre National d'Art et de Culture Georges Pompidou
31 May–5 November
*Paris–Moscou 1900–1930*
Catalogue

Milan, Palazzo Reale
18 October–18 January 1980
*Origini dell'Astrattismo*
Catalogue

**1980**
London, The Tate Gallery
6 February–13 April
*Abstraction: Towards a New Art. Painting 1910–20*
Catalogue

Los Angeles CA, Los Angeles County Museum of Art
8 July–28 September
*The Avantgarde in Russia, 1910–1930: New Perspectives*
Catalogue
Travelled to: Washington DC, Hirshhorn Museum and Sculpture Garden, Smithsonian Institution, 20 November–15 February 1981

**1981**
Long Beach CA, Long Beach Museum of Art
22 March–5 July
*The Milton Wichner Collection: Jawlensky, Kandinsky, Feininger, Moholy-Nagy, Fischinger*
Catalogue



Greenwich CT, Greenwich Library
3–30 June
*Kandinsky: A Selection from the Hilla von Rebay Collection*
Catalogue

**1978**
Tokyo, Tokoro Gallery
17–31 January
*Wassily Kandinsky: exposition de dessins*
Catalogue

London, Achim Moeller Ltd.
June–July
*Kandinsky: Fifteen Paintings by Wassily Kandinsky*
No catalogue

Madrid, Fondación Juan March
10 October–3 December
*Kandinsky 1923–1944*
Catalogue
Travelled to: Seville, Museo de Arte Contemporaneo, 13 December–31 January 1979

Zurich, Galerie Renée Ziegler
November–December
*Wassily Kandinsky: Zeichnungen 1910–1944*
Catalogue

**1979**
Paris, Musée National d'Art Moderne, Centre Georges Pompidou
1 February–26 March
*Kandinsky: trente peintures des musées soviétiques*
Catalogue

Edinburgh, The Scottish Arts Council Gallery, Edinburgh International Festival
18 August–16 September
*Kandinsky: The Munich Years 1900–14*
Catalogue
Travelled to: Oxford, Museum of Modern Art, 30 September–28 October

Tokyo, Galerie Tokoro
22 October–24 November
*Wassily Kandinsky: exposition des aquarelles de 1910 à 1944*
Catalogue

**1980**
Rome, Musei Capitolini, Palazzo dei Conservatori
12 November–4 January 1981
*Wassilij Kandinsky: 43 opere dei Musei Sovietici*
Catalogue
Travelled to: Venice, Museo Correr, 15 January–1 March 1981

Düsseldorf, Kunstsammlung Nordrhein-Westfalen
2 December–3 February 1981
*Wassily Kandinsky: Drei Hauptwerke aus drei Jahrzehnten*
Catalogue

**1981**
Baltimore MD, The Baltimore Museum of Art, organized by The Solomon R. Guggenheim Museum
6 January–1 March
*Kandinsky Watercolors: A Selection from The Solomon R. Guggenheim Museum and The Hilla von Rebay Foundation*
Catalogue
Travelled to: Atlanta GA, The High Museum of Art, 28 March–31 May; Cleveland OH, The Cleveland Museum of Art, 21 July–27 September; Chicago IL, David and Alfred Smart Art Gallery of the University of Chicago, 15 October–29 November; San Diego CA, San Diego Museum of Art, 18 December–31 January 1982; Honolulu HI, Honolulu Academy of Arts, 7 April–16 May; Portland OR, Portland Art Museum; 15 June–15 August; Chapel Hill NC, University of North Carolina, The Ackland Art Museum, 6 September–17 October; Gainesville FL, University of Florida, University Gallery, 31 October–12 December

**1982**
Rome, Galleria Giulia
December
*Lyonel Feininger, Wassily Kandinsky*
Catalogue

**1984**
New York, Leonard Hutton Galleries
30 March–24 May
*The Blue Four: Feininger, Jawlensky, Kandinsky and Paul Klee*
Catalogue

**1985**
Long Beach CA, Long Beach Museum of Art
14 April–19 May
*The Blue Four: Feininger, Jawlensky, Kandinsky and Paul Klee*
Catalogue

**1986**
Bern, Kunstmuseum Bern
21 November–15 February 1987
*Der Blaue Reiter*
Catalogue

Los Angeles CA, Los Angeles County Museum of Art
23 November–8 March 1987
*The Spiritual in Art: Abstract Painting 1890–1985*
Catalogue
Travelled to: Chicago IL, Museum of Contemporary Art, 17 April–19 July; The Hague, Gemeentemuseum, 1 September–22 November



Washington DC, National Gallery of Art
26 April–2 August, extended until 7 September
*Kandinsky: The Improvisations*
No catalogue

**1982**
New York, The Solomon R. Guggenheim Museum
22 January–21 March
*Kandinsky in Munich: 1896–1914*
Catalogue
Travelled to: San Francisco CA, San Francisco Museum of Modern Art, 22 April–20 June; in extended form to Munich, Städtische Galerie im Lenbachhaus, 17 August–17 October, catalogue

Sydney, Art Gallery of New South Wales, organized by The Solomon R. Guggenheim Museum
14 May–13 June
*Vasily Kandinsky (1866–1944): A Selection from The Solomon R. Guggenheim Museum and The Hilla von Rebay Foundation*
Catalogue
Travelled to: Brisbane, Queensland Art Gallery, 21 July–8 August; Adelaide, Art Gallery of South Australia, 26 August–26 September; Perth, Art Gallery of Western Australia, 8 October–7 November; Melbourne, National Gallery of Victoria, 12 November–12 December

Munich, see above

**1983**
New York, The Solomon R. Guggenheim Museum
9 December–12 February 1984
*Kandinsky: Russian and Bauhaus Years 1915–1933*
Catalogue
Travelled in varying form to: Atlanta GA, The High Museum of Art, 15 March–29 April; Zurich, Kunsthaus Zürich, 30 May–15 July, catalogue; Berlin, Museum für Gestaltung, Bauhaus-Archiv, 9 August–23 September, catalogue

**1984**
Zurich, see above

Berlin, see above

New York, Marisa del Re Gallery
5 January–11 February
*Kandinsky: Russia and the Bauhaus 1912–1932*
Catalogue

Paris, Musée National d'Art Moderne, Centre Georges Pompidou
30 October–28 January 1985
*Kandinsky: oeuvres de Vassily Kandinsky (1866–1944)*
Catalogue, no checklist

**1985**
New York, The Solomon R. Guggenheim Museum
15 February–14 April
*Kandinsky in Paris, 1934–1944*
Catalogue
Travelled to: Houston TX, The Museum of Fine Arts, 8 June–11 August; Milan, Palazzo Reale, 19 September–10 November, catalogue; Vienna, Museum des 20. Jahrhunderts, 6 December–26 January 1986

**1986**
Tokyo, Fuji Television Gallery
7–29 November
*Kandinsky: Bauhaus & Paris Years, 1922–1944*
Catalogue

**1987**
Budapest, Mücsarnok
5 November–11 January 1988
*Kunst und Revolution: Russische und sowjetische Kunst 1910–1932*
Catalogue
Travelled to: Vienna, Österreichisches Museum für angewandte Kunst, 11 March–15 May 1988

Munich, Staatsgalerie moderner Kunst
27 November–31 January 1988
*'Entartete Kunst': Dokumentation zum nationalsozialistischen Bildersturm am Bestand der Staatsgalerie moderner Kunst*
Catalogue

**1988**
Brussels, Musées Royaux des Beaux-Arts de Belgique
8 April–29 May
*Bauhaus 1919–1933: Le Bauhaus dans les collections de la République Démocratique Allemande*
Catalogue

**1989**
Hannover, Sprengel Museum
12 November–11 February 1990
*Der Blaue Reiter: Kandinsky, Marc und ihre Freunde*
Catalogue

**1990**
Mannheim, Städtische Kunsthalle Mannheim
17 February–22 April
*Russische und sowjetische Zeichnungen und Aquarelle von 1900 bis 1930 aus dem Puschkin-Museum Moskau*
Catalogue

**1991**
Los Angeles CA, Los Angeles County Museum of Art
17 February–12 May
*'Degenerate art': The Fate of the Avant-Garde in Nazi Germany*
Catalogue
Travelled to: Chicago IL, The Art Institute of Chicago, 22 June–8 September; Washington DC, International Gallery, Smithsonian Institution, 9 October–5 January 1992; Berlin, Altes Museum, 3 March–31 May, catalogue

**1992**
Frankfurt am Main, Schirn Kunsthalle
1 March–May 10
*Die Grosse Utopia: die russische Avantgarde 1915–1932*
Catalogue



**1987**
Tokyo, The National Museum of Modern Art Tokyo
28 May–9 August
*Kandinsky*
Catalogue
Travelled to: Kyoto, The National Museum of Modern Art, 18 August–4 October

**1988**
Nantes, Musée de Beaux-Arts de Nantes
June
*Kleine Welten–Petits Mondes: Vassily Kandinsky*
Catalogue

**1989**
Tokyo, Fuji Television Gallery
10–28 April
*Wassily Kandinsky*
Catalogue

Moscow, State Tretiakov Gallery
29 April–end May
*Vasiiy Vasilievich Kandinsky 1866–1944*
Catalogue
Travelled in modified form to: Frankfurt am Main, Schirn Kunsthalle, 18 June–20 August, catalogue; Leningrad, State Russian Museum, September–October

Frankfurt, see above

Andros, Musée d'Art Moderne, Fondation Basil et Elise Goulandris
8 July–18 September
*Wassily Kandinsky (1866–1944): aquarelles–dessins*
Catalogue

Aix-les-Bains, Musée Faure
22 September–2 November
*Kandinsky: Bauhaus*
Catalogue

Malmö, Konsthall
21 October–10 December
*Kandinsky and Sweden: Malmö 1914–Stockholm 1916*
Catalogue
Travelled to: Stockholm, Moderna Museet, 26 December–18 February 1990

**1991**
Madrid, Banco Bilbao Vizcaya
9 April–1 June
*Kandinsky Acuarelas*
Catalogue
Travelled to: Rome, Palazzo delle Esposizioni, 7 June–4 August; Vienna, Historisches Museum der Stadt Wien, 3 October–1 December

Munich, Galerie Thomas
17 May–27 July
*Wassily Kandinsky: Gemälde, Aquarelle, Graphiken*
Catalogue

**1992**
Düsseldorf, Kunstsammlung Nordrhein-Westfalen
7 March–10 May
*Kandinsky. Kleine Freuden: Aquarelle und Zeichnungen*
Catalogue
Travelled to: Stuttgart, Staatsgalerie Stuttgart, 23 May–2 August

Travelled to: Amsterdam, Stedelijk Museum, 5 June–23 August; New York, Solomon R. Guggenheim Museum, 25 September–15 December, catalogue; Moscow, State Tretiakov Gallery, March–May 1993, catalogue; St. Petersburg, State Russian Museum, July–August

Washington DC, The Phillips Collection
19 September–29 November
*Theme & Improvisation: Kandinsky & the American Avant-Garde, 1912–1950*
Catalogue
Travelled to: Dayton OH, Dayton Art Institute, 12 December–31 January 1993; Chicago IL, Terra Museum of American Art, 13 February–25 April; Fort Worth TX, Amon Carter Museum, 14 May–1 August

**1993**
Munich, Staatsgalerie moderner Kunst
2 December–13 February 1994
*Sammlung Etta und Otto Stangl: von Klee bis Poliakoff*
Catalogue
Travelled to: Münster, Westfälisches Landesmuseum, 6 March–15 May 1994

**1994**
Milan, Fondazione Antonio Mazzotta
10 April–10 July
*Il Disegno del Nostro Secolo: da Klimt a Wols*
Catalogue

Munich, Haus der Kunst
20 May–14 August
*Elan vital oder Das Auge des Eros: Kandinsky, Klee, Arp, Miró, Calder*
Catalogue

Madrid, Sala de Exposiciones de la Fundación 'la Caixa'
16 September–13 November
*Dos caminos hacia la abstracción: Kandinsky, Mondrian*
Catalogue
Travelled to: Barcelona, Centre Cultural de la Fundación 'la Caixa', 25 November–22 January 1995

Milan, Galleria Blu
5 December–25 February 1995
*K & K: Klee e Kandinskij*
Catalogue

**1995**
Munich, Städtische Galerie im Lenbachhaus
31 May–20 August
*Mit dem Auge des Kindes: Kinderzeichnung und moderne Kunst*
Catalogue
Travelled to Bern, Kunstmuseum Bern, 7 September–26 November

**1996**
Milan, Fondazione Antonio Mazzotta
19 October–9 February 1997
*Bauhaus 1919–1933: da Klee a Kandinsky, da Gropius a Mies van der Rohe*
Catalogue

Sendai, The Miyagi Museum of Art
26 October–8 December
*Wassily Kandinsky–Gabriele Münter 1901–1917*
Catalogue
Travelled to: Tokyo, Sezon Museum of Art, 14 December–2 February 1997; Nagoya, Aichi Prefectural Museum of Art, 8 February–16 March; Sapporo, Museum of Contemporary Art, 5 April–25 May



**1993**
Florence, Palazzo Strozzi
24 April–11 July
*Wassili Kandinsky tra Oriente e Occidente: Capolavori dai musei russi*
Catalogue

Verona, Galleria d'Arte Moderna e Contemporanea di Palazzo Forti
10 July–14 November
*Vasilij Kandinskij*
Catalogue

**1994**
Berlin, Brücke-Museum
1 September–27 November
*Der frühe Kandinsky, 1900–1910*
Catalogue
Travelled to: Tübingen, Kunsthalle Tübingen, 3 December–26 February 1995

**1995**
New York, The Museum of Modern Art
25 January–25 April
*Kandinsky: Compositions*
Catalogue
Travelled to: Los Angeles CA, Los Angeles County Museum of Art, 1 June–3 September

Lugano, Museo Cantonale d'Arte
4 July–8 October
*Kandinsky nelle collezioni svizzere*
Catalogue

Munich, Städtische Galerie im Lenbachhaus
29 November–10 March 1996
*Das bunte Leben: Wassily Kandinsky im Lenbachhaus*
Catalogue, no checklist

**1996**
Barcelona, Museu d'Art Contemporani
11 October–6 January 1997
*Vassily Kandinsky: la revolució del llenguatge pictòric: obres prodecents del MNAM/CCI Centre Georges Pompidou, Paris*
Catalogue

**1997**
Los Angeles CA, Los Angeles County Museum of Art
23 February–11 May
*Exiles + Emigrés: The Flight of European Artists from Hitler*
Catalogue
Travelled to: Montreal, Montreal Museum of Fine Arts, 19 June–7 September, catalogue; Berlin, Neue Nationalgalerie, 9 October–4 January 1998, catalogue

Bern, Kunstmuseum Bern
5 December–1 March 1998
*Die Blaue Vier: Feininger, Jawlensky, Kandinsky, Klee in der neuen Welt*
Catalogue
Travelled to: Düsseldorf, Kunstsammlung Nordrhein-Westfalen, 28 March–28 June

**1998**
Berlin, Brücke-Museum
3 October–3 January 1999
*Der Blaue Reiter und seine Künstler*
Catalogue
Travelled to: Tübingen, Kunsthalle Tübingen, 16 January–28 March 1999

Jerusalem, Israel Museum
October–February 1999
*The Joy of Color: the Merzbacher Collection*
Catalogue

**1999**
New York, Pierpont Morgan Library
19 May–29 August
*New York Collects: Drawings and Watercolors, 1900–1950*
Catalogue

Munich, Städtische Galerie im Lenbachhaus
2 July–3 October
*Der Blaue Reiter und Das Neue Bild: von der 'Neuen Künstlervereinigung München' zum 'Blauen Reiter'*
Catalogue

**2000**
Martigny, Fondation Pierre Gianadda
28 January–12 June
*Kandinsky et la russie*
Catalogue

Dessau, Meisterhaus Kandinsky-Klee
4 February–7 May
*Wassily Kandinsky und Paul Klee: Eine Malerfreundschaft in Dessau*
Catalogue

Vienna, Arnold Schönberg Center
9 March–28 May
*Schönberg, Kandinsky, Blauer Reiter und die Russische Avantgarde*
Catalogue

Bremen, Kunsthalle Bremen
25 March–12 June
*Der Blaue Reiter*
Catalogue

**2001**
Genoa, Palazzo Ducale
27 October–17 February 2002
*Kandinsky, Vrubel', Jawlensky e gli artisti russi a Genova e nelle riviere: Passaggio in Liguria*
Catalogue



**1997**
Milan, Fondazione Antonio Mazzotta
14 September 1997–11 January 1998
*Kandinsky: Opere dal Centre Georges Pompidou*
Catalogue

**1998**
Nantes, Musée des Beaux-Arts de Nantes
31 January–17 May
*Kandinsky: collections du Centre Georges Pompidou, Musée National d'Art Moderne*
Catalogue

**1999**
Tübingen, Kunsthalle Tübingen
2 April–27 June
*Kandinsky: Hauptwerke aus dem Centre Georges Pompidou Paris*
Catalogue

London, Royal Academy of Arts
14 April–4 July
*Kandinsky: Watercolours and other Works on Paper*
Catalogue

**2001**
Milan, Fondazione Antonio Mazzotta
17 February–10 June
*Wassily Kandinsky: tradizione e astrazione in Russia, 1896–1921*
Catalogue

Strasbourg, Musée d'Art Moderne et Contemporain
13 June–16 September
*Kandinsky: retour en Russie, 1914–1921*
Catalogue

Saint-Paul, Fondation Maeght
4 July–10 October
*Vassily Kandinsky: rétrospective*
Catalogue

**2003**
New York, Jewish Museum
24 October–12 February 2004
*Schoenberg, Kandinsky, and the Blue Rider*
Catalogue

**2004**
Verona, Galleria d'Arte Moderna e Contemporanea di Palazzo Forti
16 October–30 January 2005
*Kandinsky e l'anima russa*
Catalogue

**2006**
Zug, Kunsthaus Zug
12 August–17 December
*Harmonie und Dissonanz: Gerstl-Schönberg-Kandinsky. Malerei und Musik im Aufbruch*
Catalogue



**2002**
Tokyo: The National Museum of Modern Art
26 March–26 May
*Kandinsky*
Catalogue
Travelled to: Kyoto, The National Museum of Art, 8 June–21 July; Fukuoka, Fukuoka Art Museum, 1 August–1 September

**2003**
Barcelona, Fundació 'La Caixa'
3 June–24 September
*Kandinsky: The Dissolution of Form, 1900–1920*
Catalogue

Madrid, Fundación Juan March
8 October–25 January 2004
*Kandinsky: Origen de la abstracción: Fundación Juan March*
Catalogue

**2004**
Vienna, BA-CA Kunstforum
18 March–18 July
*Wassily Kandinsky: Der Klang der Farbe 1900–1921*
Catalogue
Travelled to: Wuppertal, Von-der-Heydt-Museum, 31 July–19 September

Murnau, Schlossmuseum
2 April–11 July
*Wassily Kandinsky: 'Klänge'. Lyrik, Bild, Klang*
Catalogue

New York, Helly Nahmad Gallery
May
*Kandinsky: Sounds of Colours*
Catalogue

Cuenca, Museo de Arte abstracto español, organized by the Städtische Galerie im Lenbachhaus
17 December–28 March 2005
Catalogue
Travelled to: Palma, Museu d'Art espanyol contemporani, 6 April–25 June

**2005**
Moscow, State Pushkin Museum, Museum of Private Collections
27 January–27 March
*Unknown Kandinsky*
Catalogue

**2006**
Strasbourg, Musée d'Art Moderne et Contemporain
Opened 16 June
*Vassily Kandinsky: Le Salon de musique de 1931 et ses trois maquettes originales*
Catalogue

London, The Tate Modern
22 June–1 October
*Kandinsky: The Path to Abstraction*
Catalogue
Travelled to: Basel, Kunstmuseum Basel, 21 October–4 February 2007, catalogue

# *Photographic Acknowledgements*

*The Städtische Galerie im Lenbachhaus and the publishers would like to thank the following institutions and photographers.*

AUSTRIA
Vienna, Graphische Sammlung Albertina

BELGIUM
Jelena Hahl-Fontaine

FRANCE
Paris, ADAGP
Atelier 53
Jacques Faujour
Jacqueline Hyde
LeRoux & Morel
Boris Lipnitski
Musée National d'Art Moderne, Centre Georges Pompidou
Réunion des Musées Nationaux: CNAC/MNAM
Studio Perrain

GERMANY
Braunschweig, Foto Rache
Düsseldorf, Beck & Eggeling
Munich, Sigrid Bühring
Gabriele Münter- und Johannes Eichner- Stiftung
Neumeister Münchener Kunstauktionshaus
Städtische Galerie im Lenbachhaus: Marianne Francke, Ernst Jank

GREAT BRITAIN
London, Christie's
Sotheby's

THE NETHERLANDS
Amsterdam, Kunsthandel Frans Jacobs

UNITED STATES
Fort Dodge, IA, Blanden Memorial Art Museum
New York, Chowaiki Mosionzhnik Gallery
Christie's
Robert Lorenzson
The Metropolitan Museum of Art
Helly Nahmad Gallery
Sotheby's

# Index

*The original titles of works of art by Kandinsky cited in the commentaries and appendices are included in the Index. Untitled works have been omitted. The numbers refer to pages in the present volume.*